Child and Adolescent Development

Kelvin L. Seifert
The University of Manitoba

Robert J. Hoffnung
University of New Haven

Houghton Mifflin Company   Boston
Dallas   Geneva, Illinois   Lawrenceville, New Jersey   Palo Alto

To three who understood children before I did—Mary Elizabeth, Mary Ellen, and Donna   K. L. S.

To Maz and my children, Aaron, David, Graham, and Heather   R. J. H

Cover and interior design by Daniel Earl Thaxton.

The cover shows a hooked rug from the 1930s; it is reproduced by permission of America Hurrah Antiques, New York City.

Printed in the U.S.A.
Library of Congress Catalog Card Number: 86–81160
ISBN: 0–395–35794–2

ABCDEFGHIJ–RM–8987

Contents in Brief

Detailed Table of Contents

Preface

The longer each of us has worked in the field of developmental psychology, the more we have wanted to share our knowledge of child and adolescent development with others. This desire became even stronger after each of us became parents and as we watched our children grow up. Both our professional and personal experiences impressed on us not only the tremendous complexity of human development, but also the practical importance of studying development to all of society. We felt in addition that acquiring a genuine understanding of how a person unfolds and develops into a unique human being was one of the most fascinating of undertakings, and we wanted to help others share in this exciting intellectual challenge.

Audience

Child and Adolescent Development is a broad-based, comprehensive, and engaging introduction to developmental psychology from birth through adolescence. The text is appropriate for all undergraduates, regardless of major, taking a first course in child development or child and adolescent development.

Purpose

This book has been designed to help students clearly understand the complex, dynamic process of development in children and adolescents. We have sought to communicate to students the freshness and vitality of real, fully dimensional children and to convey the idea that development, above all, is a *human* process.

Although our book is well-grounded in research, we have written it for the introductory student. Accordingly, we have tried to keep our writing clear, low-key, and nontechnical and to create a sense of directly engaging the reader. We have also woven countless concrete details about children throughout the text and have incorporated two very special and unique features: interviews with actual children and case-study photo essays. These serve to enliven, illuminate, and make more meaningful our discussion of developmental theory, concepts, and research. They also serve — we hope — to illustrate a key belief of ours: that developmental psychology is about real people living in a real world.

Coverage

Child and Adolescent Development provides broad and salient coverage of development from birth through adolescence. It offers a balanced and eclectic selection of topics, a firm foundation of classic and up-to-date research, and an examination of timely (and even controversial) issues such as child abuse, genetic counseling, and changing family lifestyles.

The text consists of sixteen chapters divided into six parts. Part 1, "Studying Development," introduces students to the field of developmental psychology and describes the theories and methods that guide our understanding of child and adolescent development. Part 2, "Beginnings," examines the role genetics plays in shaping whom a child becomes and traces the events of the very earliest period of development: from conception through birth. Each of the remaining four parts concentrates on a specific age-range of child development — the first two years, the preschool years, the middle years, and adolescence — and is composed of a trio of chapters on physical, cognitive, and psychosocial development. We believe that this combination of a topical organization within a generally chronological framework offers instructors a maximally flexible sequence that can be used with a variety of different course structures. In addition, it reflects one of the key themes of this book, the interrelationship of all aspects of development.

Special Content Features

Child and Adolescent Development contains a number of unique and substantive features that enhance and extend the student's understanding of developmental psychology and of children. Included among these particularly innovative features are the following:

- *Interviews* with children and adolescents of various ages, as well as with parents and professionals whose comments illuminate aspects of development, are interspersed throughout the text. These twenty-four interviews reinforce and bring to life the text's coverage of concepts and theories. The interviews consist of excerpts from an extensive collection of tape-recorded interviews conducted especially for this text by Bob Hoffnung. Follow-up questions at the end of each interview provide further reinforcement.
- *Case-Study Photo Essays* at the end of each age-level part trace the development of four different children over a period of years. There are studies of a low birthweight infant, a preschooler who must adjust to the birth of a baby brother, a school-age girl whose mother returns to work, and an adolescent son of divorced parents. Striking photos and relevant documents and facsimiles are blended with the text's sensitive narrative and explanatory comments. These original case-study photo essays can help students directly appreciate that all aspects of development are interconnected and that development is a human process that affects real people living in a real world.
- *Boxed inserts,* titled "Perspectives on Research" or "Perspectives on Issues," are incorporated throughout the text. These extend the text discussion by highlighting significant research or digging deeper into important contemporary issues.
- *Four-color inserts* with author commentary appear at various points in the text and focus on themes of special interest such as the concept of childhood in history, prenatal development, aspects of family life, and identity formation.

- *Audiotapes* — a set of four half-hour audiocassettes — are available with this textbook. The audiotapes consist of excerpts from the interviews with children and adolescents conducted by Bob Hoffnung, along with explanatory comments. Accompanying the audiotapes is a printed guide that includes all transcripts, additional commentary, exercises, and activities. The audiotapes are an ideal complement to this textbook's focus on making children and development come alive. We recommend that you contact your Houghton Mifflin regional sales office for more information about the audiotapes.

Pedagogic Features

Child and Adolescent Development incorporates a number of carefully designed pedagogic features which not only help students learn the text material but also make it easier for both instructors and students to use the book. Included are the following features:

- *A chapter outline and focusing questions* at the beginning of each chapter serve as advance organizers and help students prepare for the material to be covered in each chapter.
- *Marginal glosses* printed in color reinforce key points throughout the text.
- *Checkpoints* provide brief summaries of major topics at regular intervals in each chapter, thereby enabling students to review and absorb content.
- *An extensive photo and line art illustration program* provides further reinforcement to the text's discussion of concepts and theories.
- *End-of-chapter summaries* list the important topics covered in the chapter, grouped by heading.
- *Key terms* are highlighted in boldface type in the text and a list of key terms (with cross-references to the page numbers on which the terms are defined) appears at the end of each chapter.
- *End-of-chapter questions* — entitled "What Do You Think?" — are included to stimulate further thought about text material and call on the student to relate personal values and experiences to the issues discussed.
- *Annotated lists of selected readings* that provide further insight into the chapter's topics and may be of special interest to students appear at the end of each chapter.
- *A glossary* of approximately four hundred key terms and concepts appears at the end of the text.
- *Bibliographical references* for all in-text citations appear at the end of the text.

Student Handbook

Child and Adolescent Development is accompanied by an extensive *Student Handbook.* It provides students with many opportunities for demonstrating their understanding of course content and for actively practicing what they have learned.

Each chapter in the handbook corresponds to the text chapters and is divided into four sections. The first section presents a list of learning objectives, a chapter outline, a brief overview of material covered in the text's chapter, and a series of contextual fill-in-the-blank statements related to key concepts. The study questions included in the second section are presented in order of their coverage in the text so that students may respond as they read the text. The third section in each chapter consists of original activities that enable students to demonstrate their grasp of text content and to extend and apply their knowledge through outside research and projects, many of which involve children. The last section in each chapter is a list of key terms that students are asked to define.

The student handbook also includes six multiple-choice practice tests that correspond to coverage in each of the text's six parts. An answer key to each test is provided at the end of the handbook.

Each section in the handbook provides ample space for students to write their responses. In addition, each section has been designed so that pages may be removed and handed in to the instructor.

The student handbook is also available in a computerized version, called Microstudy.

The student handbook discussed above and the audiotapes described earlier are but two components of the extensive and well-integrated package accompanying *Child and Adolescent Development* that offers unprecedented support to both students and instructors.

Acknowledgments

This book would not have been possible without the help of many individuals. We especially wish to thank Richard Carreiro for his welcome encouragement and professional support and advice and David Hunter and Julian Ferholt whose friendship and colleagueship were invaluable. We are particularly grateful to The University of Manitoba, which provided time for this project from its beginning, and to the University of New Haven and Joseph Chepaitis, its Dean of Arts and Sciences, for their support.

We also wish to thank John Faragher, Michele Hoffnung, Susan Hollahan, Michael Morris, Allen Sack, Gary Spinner, and Ginny Woolums for their help, and the children, parents, and teachers of the New Haven cooperative daycare centers for all they taught us about development.

A number of reviewers made constructive suggestions and provided thoughtful reactions at various stages in the development of the manuscript, and we are very appreciative of the help we received from them. In particular we would like to thank:

Linda Annis, *Ball State University*
Anne Bingham-Newman, *California State University, Los Angeles*
Jim Brown, *San Diego State University*
Lillian Range, *University of Southern Mississippi*
Leonard Rappaport, *Children's Hospital, Boston*
Robert Rycek, *Kearney State College*

Duane Buhrmester, *University of California, Los Angeles*

Libby Byers, *Sonoma State University*

Dale Johnson, *University of Houston*

Charlene Melrose, *Orange Coast College*

Peter Ornstein, University of North Carolina, *Chapel Hill*

Jay Pozner, *Jackson Community College*

Samuel Securro, *West Virginia State College*

Dee L. Shepherd-Look, *California State University, Northridge*

Joseph Sparling, *Frank Porter Graham Child Development Center, University of North Carolina, Chapel Hill*

We would especially like to thank the following individuals for their assistance in developing the four case-study photo essays that appear in this book: Susan Buckler, Alan Carey, Helen Cohen, Johanna Granoff, and Sara Richlin. We are also very grateful to all of the people who participated in the interviews that appear in this book and on tape and who were so willing to share with us their thoughts and perceptions about development.

Finally, we would like to thank our families, who rearranged much of their lives so that we could have time to write this book and who provided us with numerous examples of child and adolescent development.

Kelvin L. Seifert   Robert J. Hoffnung

1 Studying Development

As infants grow into children, and children grow into teenagers, they experience a great many changes. Some of these changes are small and fleeting; many, however, are relatively permanent and long-lasting. It is these developmental changes that are the subject of this book and of the field of study known as developmental psychology.

The study of development offers much insight into human nature — why we are what we are and how we became that way. Yet describing development is a complex task, so this book begins with two chapters that orient you to what lies ahead. They explain just what development is and describe some of the most important tools of developmental psychology, namely, the theories and methods that guide our understanding of child and adolescent development. With these two chapters in mind, you will be ready to begin looking at another crucial element of developmental psychology, the children themselves.

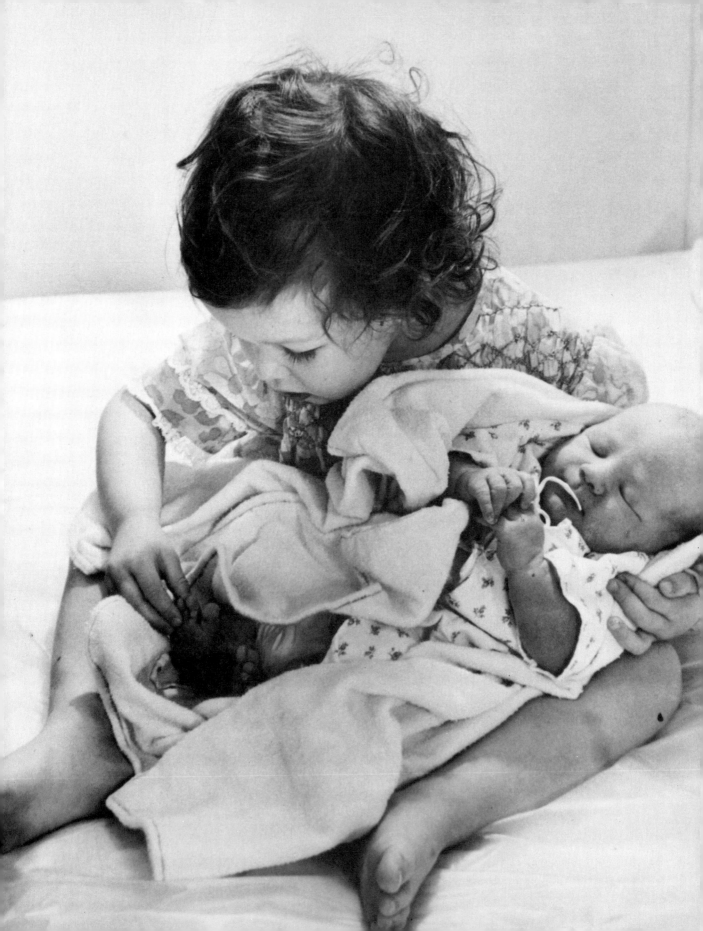

Chapter

1

Introduction: Studying Development

Focusing Questions

- What in general is human development, and why is it important to know about it?
- How did the study of children and adolescents emerge during the last several centuries?
- What general themes or issues are currently important in developmental psychology?
- How do developmental psychologists go about studying children and adolescents?
- Who in society uses knowledge of developmental psychology, and what special concerns do these people have?

YOU ARE PROBABLY A LOT DIFFERENT NOW from when you were a child. When you were two, you probably could not tie a shoelace, button your coat, or turn a doorknob reliably. When you were six, you probably struggled to read even one line of print. When you were twelve, you may have wondered whether you would ever be truly liked and respected by your friends.

Changes like these — and many others, too — mark every human life. Some are obvious, such as the transformation of a speechless infant into a talkative preschooler, or the revisions that children make in how they handle academic tasks as they get older. Other changes are subtle, and may go unnoticed: alterations in hormones circulating in the blood as children approach adolescence, for example, and gradual increases in the importance of peers from one year to the next. But obvious or subtle, changes make us human, and many of them alter our lives profoundly.

The Nature of Developmental Change

This is a book about change. In particular, it is about change that is **developmental** in nature, meaning that it contributes to a person's long-term growth, feelings, and patterns of thinking. Some developmental changes may be relatively specific, as when an infant takes her first unassisted step. Others may be rather general, as when a schoolchild becomes increasingly able to cooperate with peers in work projects or in play. But on the whole, developmental changes tend to unfold gradually, even though once they appear, they sometimes seem quite unlike any behaviors a child showed previously. A ten-year-old boy, for example, may not believe that the chances are high that he will go on a date with a girl sometime during the next five years; indeed, his own parents may find this hard to believe!

Not every change is truly developmental. Dieting may change a person's behavior and even appearance for a time, but more often than not it makes little contribution to that person's thinking, feelings, and behavior that lasts beyond the diet itself. Cold weather in the winter causes changes in behavior, such as putting on warmer clothing and selecting indoor activities and outdoor winter sports more frequently. But when the weather warms up again, these behavioral changes tend to disappear. These changes *could* result in human development (for example, when a preschooler is able to put on his winter coat and boots without any help from anyone else), but most of the time they do not.

Differences between development and other kinds of change

Three Domains of Development

As these examples suggest, human development can take many forms. For convenience, this book will distinguish among three major types, or **domains,** of development: physical, cognitive, and psychosocial. The first of these has to do with **physical development,** biological growth, or **maturation.** It includes changes in the body (in the brain, sense organs, muscles, bones, and so forth) and in the ways a person uses his or her body (motor skills and sexual development, for example). It also includes the effects of aging, such as changes in eyesight or in muscular strength. But it does not usually include physical changes when they result from accident, illness, or other special events. Like other forms of development, then, physical growth or maturation often spans very long periods.

Physical

Cognitive development has to do with changes in reasoning and thinking, with language acquisition, and with how individuals gain and store knowledge of their environments. It includes what we commonly call learning, but more as well. Learning refers to comparatively important changes in thinking, feeling, and behavior, but it tends to be limited to changes that result from relatively specific experiences or events. Often, too, learned changes occur over a short time — sometimes even just hours or minutes. These changes contribute to development; but as later chapters show, some important cognitive developments take much longer than this to occur.

Cognitive

Psychosocial development concerns changes in feelings or emotions, as well as changes in how individuals relate to other people. It includes relationships with both family and peers, for example, as well as an individual's personal identity or sense of self. Since identity and social relationships tend to evolve together, we discuss them together throughout this book. But both developments also depend on other kinds of change. How a person looks physically, for example, can affect how she feels about herself, and can affect her relationships with her friends as well. And her powers of reasoning can influence her ability to understand the needs of others, and in this way affect the quality of her relationships with others. All forms of development, it seems, affect all of the others.

Psychosocial

An Example of Development: Aaron

To understand these ideas, consider a young musical prodigy named Aaron. This boy had the good (or, some might say, bad) fortune of beginning piano lessons at

During infancy, physical maturation makes a big difference to children's development. This baby has trouble playing the piano, for example, partly because her fingers are simply not big enough for the keys. When she becomes a preschooler, holding a paint brush can also challenge her physical capacities, but practice at painting also begins making a difference at that age. (Above, Robert Maust; right, Elizabeth Crews/Stock, Boston)

the extremely early age of four. By age six, his *cognitive* and *physical development* had proceeded far enough that he could learn simple selections fairly quickly: a popular song lasting two minutes, for example, would take him "only" about four weeks to prepare. It sounded all right when he played it, but not really professional in quality — rather mechanical and "clunky," as his sister informed him.

Aaron's piano teacher said his musical talent had not yet *developed* to a professional, adult level, meaning that it had not yet evolved the numerous features and skills of a real pro. That development, the teacher said, could come only with time and much more experience with learning musical selections. And the teacher was right. By age ten, Aaron had relearned the same selection and could perform it with much more finesse and subtlety than four years before — he even played it in the school's talent show. His teacher said that part of the improvement was *cognitive:* Aaron now understood the overall organization of the musical selection much better than before. He also had developed a kind of "musical empathy," meaning that he knew increasingly well the kinds of sounds that his audiences expected from him. By age sixteen, in fact, Aaron could play the piece with near-professional ability. By that time music had become a significant part of his *psychosocial* identity; playing the piano was now a big part of what he, and everyone else, considered to be "Aaron."

Strictly speaking, each time Aaron returned to the same musical selection over the years, he was returning to the same notes. But viewed more broadly, each return also showed the effects of development. As a young beginner, among other things, Aaron's musical talent suffered from limitations in his *physical* growth, or maturation. At age four, for example, his fingers were so short that they could not reach some of the chords he sometimes had to play. In addition, because his legs could not reach the pedals, Aaron's father bought "pedal extensions," bracket-like gadgets that clamped onto the regular pedals to make them reachable by short human legs. But these extensions were awkward to use. Aaron would flail his feet in midair searching for them, and then keep his feet on them permanently, just to give them a place to rest. This, as his teacher kept telling him, made his music sound "muddied"; one of the pedals made all the notes sound all the time.

Once Aaron grew taller and larger, of course, his physical limitations decreased. By age ten, he could span large chords much better than before, and he was tall enough to use the pedals without excessive effort. By age sixteen, he had forgotten that his size had ever posed a problem. Meanwhile, though, cognitive developments had also affected Aaron's talents: as an older child, for example, he could memorize selections more easily than before, and he understood the particular purposes of musical selections more fully. These changes occurred partly because of improvements in Aaron's reasoning powers, and partly because of his increased experience with music in general. Now he could compare new selections with ones he had learned in the past, and this expertise allowed him to know better than ever how he wanted new pieces to sound.

And psychosocial developments took place as well. In both his choice and his renditions of music, Aaron increasingly took his audiences' needs into account, as if he were developing a more sensitive relationship with his listeners. Perhaps even more important to Aaron himself, though, were the feelings and motivations about music that he discovered in himself as he got older. As a young beginner, he enjoyed the attention and praise that music brought him from his parents and teachers. As he got older, though, his motivations shifted: he began wondering whether he really wanted to play the piano so much for the rest of his life, what other kids his age thought of his practicing so many hours each day, and (eventually) whether or not the opposite sex might find piano players attractive.

Interrelationship of developmental changes

Aaron's story shows the importance of each major domain of development in the lives of actual individuals. More importantly, though, it also shows how closely each domain intertwines with the others. Both for Aaron and for all the rest of us, development evolves as a pattern, rather than as discrete units or pieces. This book will identify and describe many separate threads of development. But in learning about these, return to Aaron from time to time, and perhaps pause to look at the cover of this book, to remind yourself that in real life, the threads create a tapestry.

Checkpoint   *Human development refers to long-term changes in the thinking, feeling, and behavior of individuals. It includes three major kinds of change: physical, cognitive, and psychosocial. In the lives of most individuals, these forms of development all occur simultaneously, and human development evolves as a pattern.*

Why Study Development?

Knowledge of normal development

Knowing about human development can help you in three major ways. First, it can give you appropriate expectations for children and adolescents. Developmental psychology tells you, for example, when infants usually begin talking, and it suggests when schoolchildren tend to begin reasoning abstractly. Admittedly, it tells you only averages for children, in general; it tells only when most children, or a "typical" child, acquire a particular skill, behavior, or emotion. But knowledge of these averages nonetheless can help you know what to expect from specific, individual children.

Guidance in responding to actual behavior

Second, knowledge of developmental psychology can help you to respond appropriately to children's actual behavior. If a preschool boy says that he wants to marry his mother, should she ignore his remark? Or should she make a point of correcting his misconception? If an infant child chews on every object in sight, should her parents refer her to a psychologist? Or just give her more toys to chew on? Not only parents but teachers and other professionals face choices like these daily. If a third-grade child seems more interested in his friends than in his schoolwork, should his teacher discourage contact with friends? Or try to figure out ways of using friends to support his school studies? Developmental psychology can help to answer questions like these, by indicating the sources and significance of many of the thoughts, feelings, and behavior patterns of children.

Finally, knowledge of development can help you to recognize when departures

Among other things, developmental psychology can help to give you appropriate expectations about children and adolescents. It can also help you to understand behaviors that superficially seem outrageous or inexplicable. (Paul Light/Lightwave)

from normal are truly significant. If a child does not talk very much even by age two, for example, should her parents and doctors become concerned? What if she still does not talk much by age three or four? Or take an example from adolescence: if a teenager admits to having had sexual intercourse "once or twice" by age fifteen, should his parents worry that he is becoming promiscuous? How about if he were only thirteen, or only eleven? We can answer these questions more easily if we know what *usually* happens to children and adolescents. And knowing what usually happens (being aware of the universal trends, that is) makes up a great deal of the content of developmental psychology.

Recognition of unusual development

These rather practical questions grow out of a small number of more major ones. This chapter and the next, in particular, will try to orient you to these major questions, although they will continue to crop up throughout the book:

Three major questions about development

- *What comprehensive views or theories of development does psychology offer?* Theories have guided many studies of children — though far from all of them — and not always in obvious or simple ways. Understanding theories is therefore important: important enough, in fact, to deserve special attention in Chapter 2.
- *How have psychologists actually gone about studying childhood and adolescence?* Evaluating developmental studies depends heavily on understanding where the studies got their ideas, and on what methods the studies used. Topics and methods of study in turn are both affected by the time, place, and culture in which they occur. Conflicts among results often stem from the influences of these factors. Achieving a coherent view of human development, then,

depends partly on keeping the historical and methodological context of developmental study firmly in mind.

■ *What uses can we find for developmental knowledge?* For many helping professions, understanding human development may be not only a matter of curiosity but also a professional obligation. Teachers, nurses, and recreation leaders, among others, work with children and adolescents on a daily basis. They need concrete ideas about how to do so, as well as the best general wisdom for understanding the young people they serve. In many cases, developmental psychology can help.

These questions recur throughout the book. In some ways each can be answered best in the context of the particular ages and topics discussed. But to see why the questions themselves are important, we will first look briefly at the history of the idea of childhood and of the study of children.

Checkpoint *Developmental psychology helps us understand what long-term changes to expect from normal children and guides us in responding to their actual daily behaviors and in identifying truly unusual or abnormal behaviors. This book will help with these practical concerns by focusing on three questions: (a) What major theories of development are there? (b) How have psychologists actually gone about studying children and adolescents? (c) What uses exist for developmental knowledge?*

The History of Developmental Study

For as long as people have been having children, parents and other care-givers have relied on practical or intuitive knowledge about child-rearing. But during most of human history, this knowledge remained rather informal: child-rearing advice was passed down the generations by demonstration ("Look how I feed her") and by word of mouth ("I always try strawberry tea for that illness"). Rarely, if ever, did anyone attempt to formulate existing knowledge into systematic, conscious theories about growth and development.

Childhood and Adolescence as Concepts

Until just a few hundred years ago, in fact, children in Western society were not really perceived as full members of society, or even as genuine human beings (Ariès, 1962; Hareven, 1986). During medieval times, infants tended to be regarded rather like talented pets: at best interesting, and even able to talk, but not **Early adult status** creatures worth caring about deeply. Children graduated to adult status early in

---

life — around age seven or eight — by taking on major adult-like tasks for the community. Children who today would be attending second or third grade might have major responsibilities for caring for younger siblings or working in the fields. Or they might become apprenticed to another family to learn a specialized trade, such as carpentry or tailoring. In any case they would miss out on most of what we would consider "childhood" — a time protected from the pressures and risks of adult living, and devoted to activities specially designed for children, such as school.

Because children took on adult responsibilities so soon, the period we now consider "adolescence" was absolutely unknown. Until the twentieth century, there was little awareness of the adolescent years as a unique period in a person's life, one distinct from both childhood and adulthood. Teenagers would have already assumed adult roles. Although these roles often included marriage and child-rearing, most people in their teens lived with their original families, helping with household work and with caring for others' children until well into their twenties (Laslett, 1975; Lasch, 1975–1976; Goode, 1975).

All this may seem harsh by modern standards, but it may also have been simply realistic. Relatively large proportions of children died early in life, especially in infancy. Some historians suggest that this made it unrealistic to care too deeply about children when they were first born (Ariès, 1962; Laslett and Wall, 1975). Parents were likely to be devastated by a child's death if they loved it from birth to the extent that is common today. Children instead had to "prove" their ability to survive, so to speak. Once they did so, though, their efforts were needed immediately by family and community, which more often than not were functioning at subsistence levels. Hence early recruitment to adult work became commonplace, along with early adult status.

Early mortality as a factor

These circumstances left little time for play and fun in the modern sense. But adult-style work did give children an important economic place in their communities — more important, in fact, than most modern children enjoy. In addition, most adult work was generally not difficult for medieval children to learn. They could learn their roles by observing others: they could learn to tend sheep, for example, by watching others tend sheep and by asking questions. In such conditions most children would have found modern-style classroom education strange and irrelevant, too separated from daily needs, and too reliant on reading and writing (Gardner, 1983).

Early Precursors to Developmental Study

Around the seventeenth century, certain philosophers began arguing that childhood was a special period of life with special needs that differed from the needs of adulthood. They discussed these needs in their works, even though they were a long way from agreeing about what children's special needs actually were. John Locke (1693/1699) proposed that the newborn's mind is a *tabula rasa* ("blank slate") and thus that the child must acquire all ideas from experience. His notion implied that the least experienced individuals — namely, children — differed importantly from the most experienced individuals — namely, adults. Children, it seemed, "needed" adults to teach them things — an idea that took another two hundred years to become commonplace in society as a whole.

Another philosopher, Jean Jacques Rousseau (1763), proposed methods for educating children, based largely on the assumption that young people can be "perfected" through careful observation of and respect for their emerging needs. These philosophical attitudes come close to assumptions underlying much of modern developmental study. But respect for children's special needs was still far from widespread in society as a whole.

It took changes in economic and social conditions to create awareness of childhood in the public at large. Society was becoming less rural and more industrialized. During the eighteenth century, factory towns began attracting large numbers of workers, who often brought their children with them. "Atrocity stories" became increasingly common: reports, for example, of young children in England becoming caught and disabled in factory machinery (Shaftesbury, 1868), or of children essentially abandoned to the streets during their parents' long working hours. In retrospect, it is not clear how common these situations really were (Lasch, 1975–1976) — but they were common enough to arouse considerable concern about the special needs of children and youths.

Partly because of these changes, many people became more conscious of childhood and adolescence as unique periods of life, ones that influenced later development. At the same time, they became concerned with arranging appropriate, helpful experiences for children. A French physician, Jean Itard (1806/1962), achieved considerable fame by partially rehabilitating a "wild boy" — a youngster found living alone in the woods in France in 1799. The attention given to his work reflected the new belief that children needed nurturing environments — chiefly family and schools — in order to grow up properly, or "develop." A few hundred years earlier, Itard's work might have received little, if any, notice.

The Emergence of Modern Developmental Study

During the nineteenth and twentieth centuries, the growing recognition of childhood led to new ways of studying children's behavior. Some of these methods relied on careful, detailed observation of children under natural circumstances. Others were based on scientific experiments designed to test particular ideas under carefully defined conditions. Both observation and scientific experimentation have continued to the present day as methods of studying children.

Modern observational studies of children emerged in the nineteenth century from **baby biographies,** detailed diaries of particular children, usually the authors' own. In English, one of the most famous was written and published by Charles Darwin (1877), containing lengthy accounts of his son Doddy's activities and accomplishments.

Later psychologists drew on the rich detail of this method but at the same time gave it both more focus and more generality. Arnold Gesell observed children at precise ages doing specific things, such as building with blocks, jumping, and hop-

The concept of childhood is a relatively modern invention, at least judged by the ways children have been portrayed in paintings over the centuries. Until the eighteenth century, painters generally depicted children as miniature adults, with adultlike clothing, facial expressions, and bodily proportions.

In the premodern era, childhood was not seen as a distinct period in a person's life. Children dressed like adults, mingled with adults, and took part in the same activities and pastimes as adults. By the nineteenth century, though, childhood had come to be seen—and valued—as a unique time, one that was quite different from adulthood. Children were expected to read special kinds of books; wear special types of clothing and hairstyles; and engage in their own special activities, games, and pastimes.

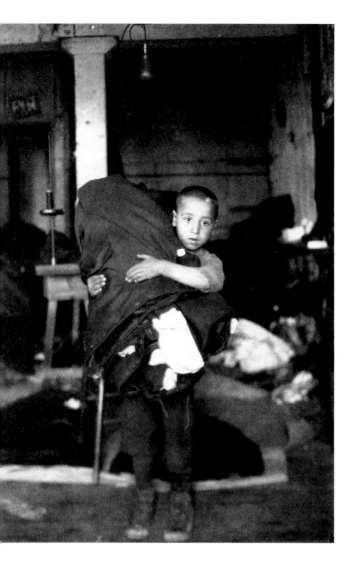

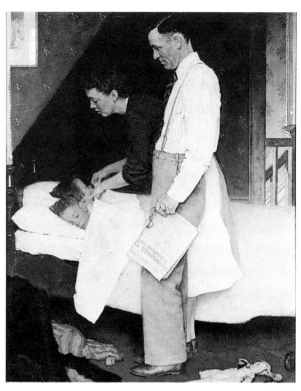

In the twentieth century, society became increasingly concerned about protecting children from the harsh world outside the family. Children were thought to need the special protection of parents and institutions dedicated to serving children, such as schools. This century also saw the emergence of the concept of adolescence; the teenage years were viewed as a period different from both childhood and adulthood.

ping (Gesell, 1926). After studying over 500 children, Gesell generalized standards of normal development, or **norms** — that is, behaviors typical of children at certain ages. Although the norms applied primarily to the white, middle-class children Gesell tested and to the specific situations and abilities he observed, they still gave a more wide-ranging picture of child development than was possible from baby biographies alone.

The method of focused observation still persists in child development research. One of the most influential observers in this century was Jean Piaget, who described many details of his own three children's behavior as infants (Piaget, 1963). He did not observe all possible behaviors of his children, however, but focused instead on behaviors that illustrated their growing cognitive skills, or ability to think. Piaget has influenced modern developmental psychology to such an extent that we discuss his work at length later in this book.

Around the turn of the century, other psychologists attempted to make observations of children more precise and systematic than written records permitted. One early attempt focused on measuring children's general intelligence. Alfred Binet developed a test that measured vocabulary and reasoning skill as an amount, called the intelligence quotient, or IQ (Binet and Simon , 1905/1916). This IQ test measured a child's skills as compared to those of other children both of the same age and of other ages. It did not reflect what the child knew, so much as whether she knew more or less than other children did. It also predicted performance situations requiring logical reasoning skills, such as school.

Unfortunately, intelligence tests soon proved to have certain limitations. For one thing, they measured only the specific kind of intelligence contained within the questions — mostly logical thinking and verbal skill (Gardner, 1983). For another thing, they really predicted the performance only of identifiable groups, rather than the performance of individual children. An intelligence test measured the average reasoning skill of an entire school of children, for example, better than the skill of particular children within the school; and it predicted average levels of school performance better than individual levels. As it turned out, racial and ethnic groups varied in their test scores, which caused considerable controversy over the meaning and appropriateness of the tests themselves. In spite of these problems, however, intelligence tests became a major component of psychology during the twentieth century, and they remain a useful tool for understanding children's development even today.

Intelligence testing

Checkpoint *Childhood and adolescence did not exist as distinct, widely recognized periods of life until sometime in the eighteenth century. At that time philosophers began arguing that children required special environments for their nurture and education. Social conditions tended to reinforce their ideas. In the nineteenth and early twentieth centuries, some writers began emphasizing the special qualities of childhood by compiling biographies of their own children. Others sought to measure and observe behaviors and abilities scientifically, through the use of standardized tests and other objective methods of observation.*

Current Themes in Developmental Study

As child development has progressed as a discipline, several themes or issues about the nature of human development have become prominent: nature and nurture, continuity and discontinuity, observation and measurement, and context. These themes pervade the entire field of developmental psychology as it currently exists; we discuss them in more detail later in this book.

Nature and Nurture

One continuing controversy has to do with the relative importance of inborn qualities of persons (their **nature**), compared to skills and qualities they acquire through their experiences and environment (their **nurture**). A few qualities may be totally inborn — eye color, for example. But psychologists agree that nearly all human qualities result from *both* nature and nuture. Your height depends on how tall your parents were (nature), but it also depends on the nutrition and exercise that you get as you grow up (nurture). Cognitive development shows the dual effects of nature and nurture, too. Infants seem biologically programmed to learn language (nature), for example, even though they learn only the language that they hear spoken to them (nurture).

Importance of heredity and environment

Continuity and Discontinuity

How much are children's characteristics preserved from one period of life to the next? Psychologists differ a great deal in their answers to this question. At one extreme are some who picture development as the gradual accumulation of "more of the same." In this view, an adolescent is like a schoolchild who knows more facts and can perform more skills; because teenagers have lived longer, they have had time to accumulate more of what they had earlier in life. This point of view makes especially good sense in studies of relatively brief periods of development: an older infant often does indeed seem to be more of a baby than when she was a few months younger.

But some psychologists argue that this view of continuity becomes rather implausible when comparing individuals of widely differing ages (Baltes, 1982). Infants and adults seem radically different in many ways; infants spend most of their time chewing and manipulating objects, for example, whereas adults use language fluently. Observations like this have led some developmental psychologists to believe that humans progress through definite *stages* of child development. Each stage is distinguished by unique patterns of behavior acquired at particular points and fundamentally different from both earlier and later patterns. Chapter 2 describes examples of both kinds of theories.

Development viewed as a series of stages

Stages create discontinuities in development. The cognitive abilities of an adolescent, for example, may seem radically different from those of either a schoolchild or a preschooler. Partly for this reason, adolescent cognition may constitute

Psychologists agree that both nature and nurture contribute to human development. Infants may be genetically predisposed to smile, for example, but experiences with parents and others help to establish and extend this behavior into a wide variety of everyday situations. (Erika Stone)

a stage distinct from the stages of younger individuals. At the same time, paradoxically, adolescent cognition develops gradually from earlier cognitive skills. Continuity in development often seems to exist side by side with discontinuous, sudden changes — as with a child who grows continuously taller, yet suddenly and discontinuously becomes able to see over the top of the kitchen table one day.

Observation and Measurement

In studying children, psychologists have definitely preferred to observe specific behaviors, that is, concrete things that children do and say. Generalizations about child and adolescent psychology have relied heavily on observations of such specifics. This strategy has made psychological research more objective than it would otherwise be, so psychologists can test each other's generalizations about development.

As we describe later in this chapter, though, psychologists vary widely in precisely how they observe children. Some researchers measure children's behavior, which means that they attach numerical values or quantities to what they see children do. As research strategy, measurement is both appropriate and easy to understand for many features of development. Consider a toddler who is just learning to talk. We can measure certain features of his language development: we can average the number of words in his early sentences (called the MLU, or mean

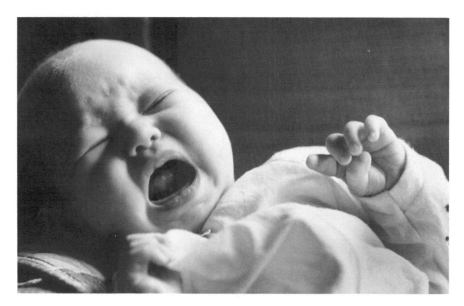

Measuring emotions has proved especially challenging to psychologists. How, for example, can we compare the anger felt by this infant with the anger felt by this school-age boy? Do they really experience the "same" emotion? (Above, David Powers; right, Paul Conklin)

length of utterance), or we can tally the size of his vocabulary, or count the number of grammatical forms that he seems to understand.

In other situations, however, measurement proves more difficult, and perhaps it is also less appropriate. How, for example, can a psychologist compare an emotion such as fear shown by an infant with the same emotion shown by a schoolchild? Since infants cry and startle more frequently than schoolchildren do, do they therefore feel more emotion, or do they just show it differently? If they express it differently, then how can a developmental psychologist compare fear in infants with fear in older children? The task may not be impossible, but it definitely requires ingenuity.

Drawbacks to measurement

In situations like these, qualitative methods prove especially helpful. Qualitative research observes or records features, aspects, or qualities of children's behavior without trying to attach amounts or quantities to them. One example of qualitative research is the baby biography, mentioned earlier. More modern examples are the works of Piaget and of Freud, who described children's cognition and emotions, respectively, primarily in qualitative terms.

Context-free and Context-specific Concepts

Wherever possible, psychologists try to explain human development in ways that are independent of specific circumstances. Most of the theories summarized in Chapter 2, for example, describe general features of children — their "intelligence," say, or their "achievement motivation" — as if children carried these qualities around with them wherever they went, and showed them in all situations. They are thus said to be context-free.

Often, however, specific circumstances make a big difference in when and how children display particular qualities. A child may seem "intelligent" about solving arithmetic problems, for example, yet not intelligent at all about understanding her friends. Or a child may display considerable achievement motivation about sports, yet only when winning, and only when important friends are watching. These variations result from the social context in which children (and all of us) constantly live, and which necessarily affects our personal development.

Influence of social context

The importance of context has caused many psychologists to focus explicitly on its impact on child development (Bronfenbrenner, 1979a). Some have studied very specific contexts, such as the child's immediate family and circle of friends: the people who most influence how children use their time, and what skills and behaviors children develop and show. Other psychologists have looked at more general social contexts, such as the school that children attend, or the neighborhoods in which they play. These settings affect whom children get to know. They also reward children for some behaviors more than others: schools reward academic excellence, for example, but neighborhood playmates may instead reward physical strength and social poise. An understanding of development is often enhanced by taking these influences into account.

The social context can have a considerable impact on children and adolescents, influencing, for example, their choice of role models—whether they be cowhands (top) or rock stars (bottom). Developmental psychology tends to emphasize processes that transcend such differences, but an understanding of development is often enhanced by taking the social context into account. (Top, Julie O'Neil; bottom, Rafael Macia/Photo Researchers)

Checkpoint   *In this century, four issues have emerged in developmental psychology: (a) the relative influence of nature and nurture on development, (b) the extent of continuity and of discontinuity in development, (c) the selection of appropriate methods of observation and measurement, and (d) the relative importance of context-free and context-specific concepts in psychology.*

Methods of Studying Children and Adolescents

The Scientific Method

Research studies of human development all follow certain general procedures called the **scientific method.** It is these procedures and not just the findings that result from the procedures that make developmental psychology a science. (Scarr, 1985). In general, being scientific in psychology means doing *all* of the following:

1. *Formulating research questions*   Research begins with questions. Sometimes they refer to previous studies, as when a developmental psychologist asks, "Do Piaget's studies of thinking work with children from third world countries?" Other times, research questions refer to issues important to society, such as "Does preschool education make children more socially skilled later in childhood?"

2. *Stating questions as hypotheses*   A **hypothesis** is a statement that expresses a research question precisely. In making a hypothesis out of the preschool education question above, a psychologist needs to be more specific about "preschool education," "socially skilled," and "later in childhood." Each term contains ambiguities that the hypothesis must clarify before it can be studied scientifically. Does "preschool education" mean a nursery emphasizing free play, or one oriented to cognitive skills? Does "socially skilled" refer to a child who initiates activities and leads other children into them? Or only to one who smiles frequently and responds to friendly overtures? Does "later in childhood" mean one year after the end of preschool, or five years?

3. *Testing the hypothesis*   Having phrased a research question as a hypothesis, researchers can conduct an actual study about it. As described further in the next section, however, they can do this in a number of ways. The choice of method usually depends on a mixture of convenience, ethics, and scientific appropriateness. Under ideal conditions, researchers might use more than one method to study a particular hypothesis. Such multiple studies usually lead to more valid and clear conclusions, but since they also take more time and effort, they are not very often done.

4. *Interpreting and publicizing the results*   After conducting the study itself, psychologists have a responsibility to report their results to others, either by presenting them at conferences or by publishing them in journal articles, or both. Their reports should include reasonable interpretations or conclusions based on the results. Ideally, the reports on research should include enough detail to allow other psychologists to repeat (or **replicate**) a study themselves, to test the conclusions. In practice, the limits of time (at a conference presentation) or space (in a journal) sometimes compromise this ideal.

Using the Scientific Method to Study Children and Adolescents

Psychologists have used a number of specific methods to study children, each of which has particular strengths and limitations. Some research questions lend

In naturalistic research, psychologists observe children's behavior as it normally occurs in a pre-existing setting or context. (Paul Conklin)

themselves better to one method than to another. Unfortunately, too, some research questions prove relatively hard to answer by *any* method.

Naturalistic Studies Studies differ in how much they control, change, or "tinker" with the events they observe. At one extreme, for example, **naturalistic research** purposely observes behavior as it normally occurs in its "natural" location. Suppose, for example, that you wondered whether young children show sex-typed preferences and behaviors more in the presence of the opposite sex than when playing in same-sex groups. How could you investigate this hypothesis?

A naturalistic study might locate pre-existing, natural groups with different combinations of the sexes. A nursery school classroom might contain such groups, so you could try observing children's daily free play in these rooms. In doing so, you could compare children's behaviors in same-sex groups with their behaviors in cross-sex groups. For this study, you would concentrate only on behaviors that seemed sex-typed — aggressive and boisterous behavior among boys, for example, and shy behavior among girls. Does playing in a mixed-sex group exaggerate these behaviors, or reduce them, or have no consistent effect? In trying to answer this question, though, you would confine your attention to situations and behaviors that normally occur.

A naturalistic study like this one can provide considerable information about children, but it also faces special complexities in interpreting results. Suppose (for the sake of argument) that the same-sex play groups turned out to show *more* stereotyped behaviors. Unfortunately, you still could not feel sure how to interpret this difference: did same-sex children reinforce each other's stereotyped behaviors? Or did children with a general tendency toward stereotyped behaviors gravitate toward same-sex groups? Or did same-sex groups tend inevitably to choose relatively stereotyped activities (like trucks for boys and dolls for girls), and did these activities in turn stimulate relatively stereotyped behaviors? You can sometimes sort out rival possibilities like these by conducting further naturalistic studies, but sometimes, too, the questions require experimental studies.

Difficulties in interpretation

Experimental Studies   Compared to naturalistic studies, **experimental studies** try to arrange circumstances so that just one or two factors or influences vary at a time. In using experimental research in your study of the effects of gender on sex-typed behaviors, for example, you would not observe naturally occurring play groups. Instead, you would set up or organize groups with very specific characteristics: only so many children in each group, perhaps, only certain specific toys available to them, and only certain amounts of time to interact. You would, in fact, hold constant any factor that might influence sex-typing in children's play, *except* for the one you are studying. In your study, the one factor you would vary would be the sex composition of the play groups: you would arrange for some groups to contain both sexes but others to contain only one sex. Sex composition would therefore be the **independent variable.** The amount of sex-typing in the children's play behavior would *depend* on your manipulation of the groups' sex composition and would thus be the **dependent variable.**

Controlling variables in this way also requires making decisions about the **population,** or group to which the study refers. The relevant population in your study might consist only of middle-class, white preschool children. Any interpretations of the results would apply only to this group and not to other ethnic groups or age groups in our society. To make sure that the experiment does indeed refer just to this population, the experimenter would have to take a **random sample** of this population, which in your case would mean selecting white, middle-class preschoolers by chance. In later studies, of course, you could sample other populations, such as other ethnic groups or other age groups. If you did so, though, you would need to generalize your results only to these other groups or populations.

Because of its logical organization, the experimental method often gives clearer results. But do preschool children normally behave as they do in the relatively artificial play groups you set up? Because people sometimes do not behave naturally in experimental situations, one criticism of the experimental method is that it runs the risk of artificiality. Naturalistic research does not face this particular problem, but it does run a greater risk of ambiguity in its results.

Clear results versus artificiality

Compromise Methods and Mixtures   Sometimes psychologists resolve these dilemmas by designing studies that have elements of both experimental and naturalistic methods. Such compromises are often called **quasi-experimental** ("partially experimental") **research.** As an example, consider again your study of sex-typing in children's play. How could you investigate this problem without either using existing nursery classrooms (the naturalistic method) or setting up contrived groups (the experimental method)? Perhaps you could find situations that include some of the real-life normality of nursery schools but also some of the systematic control of experimental groups.

Advantages of mixed designs Perhaps, for example, you could persuade an existing nursery school to modify its daily routines to create same-sex and cross-sex groupings on purpose. At certain times or on certain days teachers would encourage, or even require, same-sex play groupings; at other times they would encourage or require cross-sex groupings. Such groupings would have more naturalness to them than experimentally

---

Perspectives on Issues

Ethical Constraints on Studying Development

Sometimes ethics dictates the methods possible for studying a particular question about development. Take, for example, this possible research question: What methods of punishment by parents work best for children and adolescents of different ages? For ethical reasons we cannot study this problem experimentally. We cannot, that is, select two groups of children, one of which is systematically scolded (or spanked or deprived of dinner), and the other of which is not. We may not even be able to study the question naturalistically: observing parents actually punishing their children in their homes requires delicacy at best. At worst, it constitutes an invasion of privacy.

For ethically sensitive questions, we may instead have to satisfy ourselves with less direct but more acceptable methods of study. We can interview a variety of parents about the methods of punishment that they do in fact use, or we can ask experts who work directly with families what methods they think that parents typically use. A few courageous families might allow us to observe their daily activities, with the understanding that we are interested in observing how they punish their children. But by being volunteers these few families may not represent other families very well.

Considered in general, research about human beings must face at least three ethical issues: confidentiality, full disclosure of purposes, and respect for the individual's freedom to participate (American Psychological Association, 1981). In developmental psychology, all of these issues are complicated by the youthfulness of the subjects, and by the responsibilities their parents have for them.

1. *Confidentiality* If researchers collect information that might damage individuals' reputations or self-esteem, then they should take care to protect the identity of the participants. Observing parents' methods of punishment, for example, might require this sort of confidentiality. Mothers and fathers may not want just anyone knowing how much and how often they experience conflicts with their children. Chances are, children would not want this information made public either. In such cases investigators should not divulge the identities of participating families without their consent, either during the conduct of the study or afterward when they publish the results.

2. *Full disclosure of purposes* Parents (and their children) are entitled to know the true purposes of any research study in which they participate. Most of the time, investigators understand and follow this principle carefully. But misleading partici-

contrived groups. But their composition would also be more predictable than in most normal nursery classrooms. The procedure would therefore contain elements both of an experiment and of naturalistic observation.

Time Frames for Studying Development

Since human development by nature occurs gradually over a long period, developmental psychologists have essentially two choices: either allow a long time to observe it, or else compare people of different ages at the same point in time. The first approach is called **longitudinal study** and the second, **cross-sectional study.** Each method has its own advantages and problems.

pants can be tempting at times. In studying parents' punishment techniques, for example, researchers might suspect that stating this purpose honestly may cause certain families to avoid participation — perhaps especially the ones with the most discipline problems. Or investigators might suspect that telling families the truth about the study would make families distort their behavior — perhaps making them self-consciously hide their worst conflicts. According to this argument, therefore, purposely misleading parents would produce more complete observations of conflicts and parental punishment techniques. In this sense dishonesty might make the research more "scientific." But investigators would purchase this benefit at the cost of their long-run reputation with the participants. Purposeful deception may sometimes be permissible, but only when no other method is possible, and when participants are fully informed of the deception and its reasons after the study.

3. *Respect for freedom to participate* As much as possible, research studies should avoid pressuring parents or children to participate. This may not be so simple as it first appears. Because psychologists have a relatively high status in society, some parents may feel reluctant to decline an invitation from them to participate in "scientific research." Inves-

tigators therefore may have to bend over backward to assure parents that participation is indeed voluntary. They cannot simply assume that parents or children will automatically feel free to decline if approached. After all, what parent wants to interfere with the progress of science?

In developmental psychology, ethical principles like these are complicated further by the comparative youth of children and adolescents (Katz, 1984). In studying people of this age, investigators may sometimes wonder whether their participants can fully understand the purposes of a study, even when its purposes are explained. How well can children really understand, for example, why investigators might want to observe conflicts between them and their parents? Even if a goal like this makes sense to children, can they really feel free to participate or not? Or will children usually feel that they must cooperate with whatever adult investigators ask? If the children are very young, then perhaps parents can decide on their behalf, but when do children become mature enough to be consulted directly? Whereas none of these questions causes problems in the large majority of developmental studies, they all become difficult at times, especially in any research that places children's reputations or self-esteem at risk.

Cross-sectional Study   The cross-sectional approach compares groups of children or adolescents who are similar in every way except their age. Suppose, for example, a psychologist wonders about the ability to solve jigsaw puzzles — an important sign of small motor coordination and spatial imagination. How does this skill grow or change during childhood and adolescence? In a cross-sectional study, a psychologist would observe children of different ages attempting to solve one of these puzzles — perhaps some six-year-olds, some twelve-year-olds, and some eighteen-year-olds. If the groups came from comparable backgrounds, then comparing their performances and styles of solving the puzzle would suggest something about how this skill develops.

Cross-sectional studies have proved very popular in studying development because they can be done rather quickly and easily. The puzzle-solving study, for example, might be completed in just a few months, or even less. Unfortunately, the method can often gloss over the processes that actually contribute to long-run development. How, or by what steps, does puzzle performance improve over the years? What specific events or subskills combine to enhance performance as time goes by? By itself, a cross-sectional study often cannot answer these questions because it really compares only age groups rather than development within individuals.

Subjects of different ages at same point in time

Cross-sectional methods also obscure changes in relative abilities and performance styles. As teachers will sometimes note, a child who shows outstanding skill at one age will not necessarily remain outstanding throughout her life. Someone who excels at puzzles at age six, for example, may not still do so at age twelve or eighteen; and conversely, a child who shows only middling ability early in childhood may become more outstanding later on — not only compared to her own earlier skill, but even in her relative rank among peers. What events or processes cause shifts like these to occur? Cross-sectional studies cannot really answer this question as well as longitudinal ones can.

Longitudinal Study   The longitudinal approach observes the same subjects periodically over a relatively long period, often years. By nature, therefore, it can monitor the changes within individuals as well as between them, and it can offer more clues about what may cause the changes to occur. A longitudinal study of jigsaw puzzle ability, for example, would locate the same children at several different ages, and each time observe them attempting to solve a puzzle. Over the long run, the study could identify which children improved, and when. And it could identify which stayed the same, or even worsened in performance. Combining these observations with other information about the subjects might suggest ideas about what makes puzzle-solving ability develop, and what the "typical" developmental path for this ability is.

Same subjects at different points in time

Although longitudinal study may therefore be more truly "developmental" than cross-sectional study, it too has its problems. By definition, longitudinal study takes many months or even years to complete — and this does not even count the time a psychologist needs just to get organized. This much time can cause a researcher many headaches. For one thing, children in longitudinal studies sometimes become overly familiar with the testing and observation procedures. They

may improve their puzzle skills simply because they face the same puzzles time after time over the course of months and years.

For another thing, longitudinal studies pose certain practical problems. Some of the original children may move away; or the psychologist may become hopelessly tied up with other work and fail to complete the original study; or developmental psychologists as a group may have lost interest in the research questions. Given these obstacles, psychologists have tended to emphasize cross-sectional rather than longitudinal studies. There are prominent exceptions to this rule, however; we discuss some of them later in this book.

Mixed Designs Sometimes the dilemmas of the time frame are solved by combining elements of both cross-sectional and longitudinal studies. In the case of puzzle-solving ability, for example, children of different ages can be compared at one point in time (cross-sectional), and then followed for a few years before testing

---

again (longitudinal). Six-year-olds and nine-year-olds can be compared initially, perhaps, and then observed again three years later. Like a cross-sectional study, then, a mixed design produces relatively immediate results; and like a longitudinal one, it traces individuals' actual development. As a compromise, therefore, mixed designs have much to recommend them.

Checkpoint   *Most research in developmental psychology strives to apply the scientific method in studying children and adolescents. Studies vary, though, in how they are organized: some are relatively naturalistic, and others are experimental. Studies also vary in their time frames: cross-sectional studies compare age groups at one moment in time, but longitudinal studies follow individuals over extended periods. Some research also uses mixed designs.*

Uses of Developmental Psychology

The field of developmental psychology is alive and well in large part because quite a few occupations need it so much. The chances are good that all of us have had contact with psychology-dependent occupations, which account for a major proportion of the careers in modern society.

Occupations That Use Developmental Psychology

People in many occupations deal with children and adolescents on a daily basis and thus benefit by knowing as much as possible about how development occurs. Consider, for example, the following professions:

1. *Medicine and nursing*   Most doctors, nurses, and other medical personnel serve children and adolescents at least part of the time. And some of them (such as pediatricians) serve children all of the time. To do this well, these professionals must understand young people's psychological needs and capacities. How, for example, do children conceive of illness? As a "bug"? As a punishment for doing wrong? Their notions about sickness can influence how children care for themselves, both before and during an illness. Indeed, they may influence how soon and how well they recover.

2. *Education and teaching*   Teachers, of course, work with children and adolescents every day of the school year, and they therefore need guidance in planning appropriate learning activities. Can most sixth-graders, for example, participate meaningfully in a discussion of democracy? Can kindergartners learn to read? These questions do not have precise answers, but developmental psychology can offer important insights.

3. *Social work and human ecology*   These fields include a focus on the needs of families, and, of course, children and teenagers are a major part of families. Social workers and human ecologists are concerned with how a family influences the individuals within it. How, for example, does a parent's unemployment put stress on the whole family? How does such stress affect the children?

4. *Retail businesses*   Children (and their parents) are customers in a wide range of businesses — ranging from fairly obvious examples, such as toy stores, to somewhat less obvious ones, such as restaurants or department stores. The proprietors and staff of such businesses can serve the public better if they understand the general needs of their young clients. A book store, for example, may sell more books to *all* ages if it has designated areas where children can play freely with certain books and toys without fear of spoiling brand-new merchandise.

5. *The media*   Most of us realize that many television and radio programs are specifically aimed at children or teenagers. These programs obviously will communicate more successfully if their producers take psychological development into account. But many of us forget an equally important fact: that children and young people watch and hear a great deal of television and radio *not* specifically intended for them. Producers of these programs also need to consider these unintended viewers and listeners when planning their programs. This is especially true for programs containing a lot of violence or sex. Children and even teenagers may not be ready to witness these activities to the extent portrayed in programs intended for adults.

6. *Recreation*   Leisure programs for the community devote considerable attention to children and their families. Such programs include amateur athletic leagues for young people, summer day camps, and community clubs. They succeed best when the recreation leaders understand as much as possible about the psychological development of the participants. Many teenagers, for example, may prefer programs with relatively minimal adult involvement, so that they can spend as much time as possible socializing with their friends. But socializing may be less important to very young children, who in any case may need more assistance in planning and carrying out activities.

7. *Parenting*   Last, but definitely not least, is one of the most widespread occupations of all: parenting. Mothers and fathers feel some of the strongest emotions of all about children, and therefore need and deserve knowledge about how to handle their seven-day-a-week, twenty-four-hour-a-day job. Sometimes the occupations listed above are almost too eager to offer parents advice about how to rear their children. To help cope with this barrage of information, parents can benefit by obtaining knowledge of child development on their own.

Practical Needs Versus the Scientific Study of Development

In spite of variations among them, occupations like those just described have certain priorities in common. The priorities differ noticeably from those held by people who create developmental theories and conduct developmental research (mostly university professors). Since many of you reading this book probably are

Applied psychologists take a practical, case-by-case approach to understanding particular individuals. Compared to academic psychologists, they would be more likely to ask how each of these particular children feels about this particular cooking situation. Academics, on the other hand, would more likely wonder how each child's behavior illustrates general principles of development. (Ulrike Welsch)

practitioners, or hope to use psychology in your profession rather than conduct research on it, let us look briefly at some of these differences in priorities.

Commitment to ongoing service

Unlike academic psychologists, people who work in the helping professions must deliver a service to the public every day. Often, therefore, they face demands that require immediate solution. A teacher may face a disruptive student, a nurse may face a child afraid of an injection, or a psychotherapist may face an angry outburst from an adolescent. In these cases practitioners, unlike research psychologists, cannot wait for more studies of the problems they are encountering; they must respond at once, and do the best they can.

As a result, practitioners must somehow supplement areas of developmental research that they consider incomplete. Often they meet to discuss common, pressing problems and collective opinions within their occupation or profession. Other times, they rely on existing research even when it is sketchy — in essence, they treat preliminary findings as more definite than they really are. Still other times, they draw on personal intuition to solve a problem immediately. All of these strategies help practitioners deal with the gradual pace at which developmental research often evolves. They do not, however, really make up for the benefits of using existing research well.

Focus on problems

Ironically, the concern of the applied helping professions for improving the quality of life has often led them to emphasize human problems rather than human successes. Even though teachers want to foster learning, for example, many spend surprisingly large amounts of time with students who have learning difficulties. Even though nurses prefer to prevent illness, much of their actual work involves curing illnesses after they occur. And even though psychotherapists may wish for a society of sane and happy people, they often focus in their counseling primarily on human anxieties and frustrations. Many members of the public, incidentally, consider this emphasis quite appropriate, though not all do.

Research psychologists are well aware that all sorts of problems can interfere with development. But their research and theory making have nonetheless shown a marked emphasis on normal or typical children and adolescents. The bias is neither universal nor extreme, but it is noticeable. It makes sense, too: developmental psychologists study typical features of human nature, whereas most practitioners by definition solve human problems. As we point out later, the two groups can learn from each other in this area.

As part of their commitment to service, the applied professions often orient to *cases:* they focus heavily on particular individuals or situations. A teacher may wonder how to "get through" to one particular student; a nurse, how to improve the spirits of a young patient; or a social worker, how to involve particular teenagers in a community activity. All encounter actual persons — never the "typical" children or youths often portrayed in developmental research.

Case orientation

While this experience sometimes leads practitioners to accuse developmental theories of being too abstract, a case orientation does not really conflict with the approach of much human development research. As pointed out earlier, many research studies are purposely naturalistic — a method very similar to the way practitioners learn as well. Much developmental research, furthermore, relies on rather small numbers of children, or even just one child. In fact, Jean Piaget based much of his early research on infant development on observations of just his own three children, observed in his own home.

It is probably fortunate that academic psychologists and practitioners of the helping professions differ somewhat, since this difference makes it possible for each to offer something to the other. Theories — whether comprehensive ones, such as those discussed in the next chapter, or more specific ones, such as those discussed later in this book — can help make the practitioner practice better.

Mutual influence of theory and practice

But practice also stimulates theory. Both Sigmund Freud and Erik Erikson, for example, were psychotherapists who formulated many of their ideas from counseling particular patients. And Piaget, as already mentioned, learned much about cognitive development by being a father. The influence between theory and practice works in two directions; and wherever appropriate the chapters ahead will continue to point out this relationship.

Checkpoint *Many occupations rely on information about human development: medicine, education, business, and several others. The practitioners of these occupations have somewhat different concerns from those held by academic research psychologists, but both groups have much to learn from each other.*

The Strengths and Limitations of Developmental Knowledge

As this chapter has shown, human development has to be studied in particular ways, and with particular limitations in mind. Since time is a major dimension of development, the impact of time must be approached thoughtfully. Yet the very nature of time poses real problems for studying at least some major questions: sometimes people "take too long" to develop, compared to the time available to study them. And because developmental psychologists deal with people, they must treat their objects of study with respect, and live by the usual standards of decency and consideration for human needs. Finally, because they deal with especially young people, developmental psychologists must sometimes take extra care to determine the true best interests of their subjects, even when those subjects do not know what they are being asked to do — or do not feel free to refuse even when they do know.

Lest these limitations sound overly discouraging, however, be assured that in spite of them, developmental psychologists have in fact accumulated considerable knowledge of children and adolescents in recent decades, and that they are continuing to do so. The succeeding chapters in this book should make that point amply clear. Developmental psychology does not have definite answers for some important questions about human nature — but on the other hand, it *does* have the answers for a good many others.

Summary of Major Ideas

The Nature of Development

1. Developmental psychology concerns how thoughts, feelings, personality, social relationships, and motor skills evolve as individuals get older.

2. Development occurs in three major domains: physical, cognitive, and psychosocial.

3. The domains of development influence each other in many ways, and individuals always develop as whole persons, rather than in separate pieces.

Why Study Development?

4. Studying development can help give you appropriate expectations about the behavior of children and adolescents.

5. A knowledge of development can help you to respond appropriately to the actual behavior of children.

6. A knowledge of development can help you to recognize when behaviors are truly unusual or a cause for concern.

7. This book assists the study of development by focusing on three major questions: (a) What are the major theories of development? (b) How do psychologists actually go about studying childhood and adolescence? (c) What practical uses exist for developmental psychology?

The History of Development

8. Until just a few hundred years ago, childhood and adolescence were not regarded as distinct periods of life.

9. During the eighteenth century, philosophers began arguing that childhood was a special period of life; economic conditions lent support to their arguments.

10. In the nineteenth and early twentieth centuries, some of the studies of child development consisted of baby biographies, of structured observations of children at specific ages, and of standardized tests of ability.

11. Currently, developmental psychology focuses on at least four major themes or issues: the impact of nature and nurture, the extent of continuity and discontinuity in development, the appropriate kinds of observation and measurement, and the importance of context in developmental concepts.

Methods of Studying Children and Adolescents

12. Research about developmental psychology tries to follow the scientific method: formulating research questions, stating them as hypotheses, testing the hypotheses, and interpreting and publicizing the results.

13. Studies of children and adolescents sometimes use naturalistic methods, in which pre-existing conditions or context are preserved as much as possible.

14. Other studies use experimental methods, which try to control or hold constant most conditions while varying only one or two specified variables.

15. Still other studies combine naturalistic and experimental methods in various ways.

16. Many developmental studies use a cross-sectional organization, which compares individuals of differing ages at one point in time.

17. Others follow developmental change directly, by using a longitudinal organization.

18. Sometimes cross-sectional and longitudinal designs can be combined to get the advantages of each.

Uses of Developmental Psychology

19. Many occupations rely on information about human development: medicine, education, social work, businesses, the media, and recreation leadership. Parents, too, need information about development.

20. Compared to academic developmental psychologists, practitioners are more committed to ongoing human services, focus more on problems in development, and attend to individual needs and differences more.

21. Academic psychologists and practitioners have much to offer each other.

Key Terms

developmental *(4)*	naturalistic research *(20)*
domains *(5)*	experimental study *(21)*
physical	independent
development *(5)*	variable *(21)*
maturation *(5)*	dependent variable *(21)*
cognitive	population *(21)*
development *(5)*	random sample *(21)*
psychosocial	quasi-experimental
development *(5)*	research *(21)*
nature *(14)*	longitudinal study *(23)*
nurture *(14)*	cross-sectional
scientific method *(19)*	study *(23)*
hypothesis *(19)*	

What Do You Think?

1. How do people's experiences as children affect their interest in learning about developmental psychology? Does it make them more interested or less?

2. On balance, do you think children were happier five hundred years ago or today? Or did they feel just the same? Explain.

3. What position does your intuition tell you to take on each of the issues outlined on pages 14–18? Take note of your opinions, and see whether they remain the same after reading most of this book.

4. Can you think of an occupation that does *not* use knowledge of developmental psychology? Explain.

For Further Reading

Ariès, Phillipe. *Centuries of Childhood: A Social History of Family Life,* trans. Robert Baldick. New York: Vintage Books, 1962.

This book traces the development of family life and of the modern idea of childhood and adolescence. It has become a classic in the field of family studies, although more recent research now makes some of it seem overstated. Medieval parents, for example, probably did care about their children more than Ariès gives them credit for, and many modern families often treat their children as economic assets under certain conditions.

Bronfenbrenner, Urie. *The Ecology of Human Development: Experiments by Nature and by Design.* Cambridge, Mass.: Harvard University Press, 1979.

This book presents one of the most clear and thorough arguments for the importance of social context in human development. The author describes many psychological studies that can make sense only if the circumstances surrounding the studies are taken fully into account. He also argues that psychological research can progress only if it uses *both* naturalistic and experimental methods.

Kagan, Jerome. *The Nature of the Child.* New York: Basic Books, 1984.

The author of this volume discusses the major issues current in developmental psychology today, and challenges many of the field's most widely held assumptions. He proposes, for example, that early life experiences are not necessarily more influential on human development than later life experiences are. He also proposes that families do *not* exert as much influence on children as commonly supposed. Whether you agree with the author's ideas or not, the book is thought-provoking.

Chapter

2

Theories of Development

Focusing Questions

- What are developmental theories, and why should we spend our time learning about them?

- How have Freud's ideas about unconscious conflict and early childhood sexuality influenced thinking about development?

- What does Erik Erikson mean by a psychosocial crisis, and how does this concept help explain the stages of development?

- How do developmental theories based on learning principles contribute to our understanding of developmental change?

- What does Piaget's theory of cognitive development reveal about how our ability to think and solve problems changes from childhood through adolescence?

- What are the advantages and disadvantages of using developmental theories, and how do you decide which one is best?

WHEN ELIZABETH, AGE THREE, began nursery school, she cried and screamed every day when her mother left her. "Home!" and "Mama!" were the only words she seemed able to produce in between her sobs, which continued for much of each morning. Her teachers were concerned, and met to discuss what to do about Elizabeth.

"It's best to ignore the crying," said one teacher. "If you give her lots of special attention because of it, you will reinforce the crying, and she'll just keep going longer."

"But we can't just ignore a crying child," said another. "This is a new and strange situation, and her crying shows that she is feeling insecure and abandoned. Look at her! She needs comfort and emotional support, so that she can feel safer and more secure. At least give her a hug!"

"I think that she is unsure whether her mother really will come back for her," said a third teacher. "Perhaps we can find ways to help her understand and remember our daily routine here."

What actually happened? Whose advice did the teachers follow? They agreed to try not to make too much of a fuss over Elizabeth's tears and to give her lots of comfort and support when she wasn't crying. They also helped Elizabeth draw a picture chart of the daily schedule, and taped it to her cubbyhole. Last, they talked with her mother about what they had observed and the solutions they were trying.

How well did it work? Elizabeth did stop crying — more quickly, in fact, than any of the teachers had expected. While all three teachers agreed that Elizabeth was clearly happier and more at ease, no one was sure exactly how or why the change had come about.

The Nature of Developmental Theories

Each of the teachers' approaches reflects a different set of ideas and beliefs about children and their development. Whether they know it or not, most people — teachers, parents, students, and even children themselves — are guided by "informal theories" of human development. In reading about Elizabeth, did you find yourself agreeing with one of the teacher's comments? If so, it is probably because you share that teacher's informal theoretical orientation.

What Is a Theory?

The purpose of any theory is to help us understand the world and guide our future actions better. A good theory does four things. First, it systematically *organizes* what is already known about a subject, including facts that may be conflicting or confusing. Second, it tries to *explain* what is going on, in terms of helpful principles, mechanisms, and processes. For example, theories of social and emotional development help us to understand better how children feel and act, and how and why their feelings and actions change with age and experience. Likewise, theories of cognitive development help us to understand how children learn to think and solve problems and what we can and cannot expect of them at certain ages or stages.

How theories aid understanding

Third, a good theory is *generative,* in that it suggests and generates new ideas and research activity. For example, Piaget's theory that young children are not yet able to understand certain kinds of problems has led to research on moral development. Finally, a good theory is *testable,* allowing developmental researchers to evaluate systematically the accuracy of the theory's claims.

In this chapter we will take a closer look at the theories that have been most influential and useful in the field of developmental psychology.

What Makes a Theory Developmental?

Part of the answer to this question comes from the definition of human development that begins this book. Human development, we said, refers to long-term qualitative changes and the continuities or patterns of these changes over a person's lifetime. Developmental theories try to describe and understand these changes through principles that underlie *the process of change.* Many theories also focus on the concept of **developmental stages**, and for that reason they are known as **stage theories.**

Developmental Stages   All stage theories of development agree that stages have certain distinguishing features:

1. All intact organisms follow the same order or sequence of stages in their development. (For example, all physically normal infants go through the same three stages of sitting, walking, and running during their development.)

Many motor skills, such as throwing a ball and batting, develop in predictable sequences or stages. (Walter S. Silver)

2. Each stage is qualitatively (or structurally) unique and different from all other stages. (Sitting is qualitatively different than walking, and running is qualitatively different from walking.)
3. The stages represent a logical progression in development, with later stages achieving greater complexity and integrating the accomplishments of earlier stages. (The ability to walk will depend upon the earlier achievement of the ability to sit, and development of the complex skills involved in running will depend upon the prior accomplishment of walking.)

Children experience similar changes in other areas of their development. For example, as a child learns to write, he integrates his previously acquired skills at drawing and manipulating things with newly developing skills in using language and reading. Likewise, his development of intimacy with female friends during adolescence calls upon his earlier experiences of friendship, but also reflects a much higher level of sophistication and complexity.

How many stages?

This is a good place to note that people's informal theories take for granted the existence of developmental stages such as infancy, childhood, adolescence, and adulthood. Just as we may differ in defining how many stages there are and what happens in each, so the experts who have created more formal theories of development differ in their definitions. You may be surprised to learn that the earliest view of development recognized only two developmental stages, infancy and adulthood (Ariès, 1962). Most current theorists believe there are more; Piaget's theory, for instance, posits four main stages, Freud's five, and Erikson's eight. Nor do the theorists agree as to whether all humans must complete each stage before moving on to the next, or whether the stages necessarily coincide with various age groups. What they do agree on is that human development, like that of other living organisms, follows a logical progression that can be identified and studied.

The Process of Developmental Change Theorists also differ in how they explain the processes and mechanisms of developmental change. Some place greater emphasis on the built-in, biologically determined sources of change called maturation, whereas others emphasize experience and learning as sources of developmental change. Theories also differ in their assessment of how actively individuals participate in their own development and how aware they are of the changes that are taking place. Finally, theories differ in which aspects of developmental change they seek to explain.

To what degree are changes in an individual's development mainly dependent upon *learning* through experience, and to what degree do they depend on *maturation,* or biologically determined built-in tendencies toward physical change? Some changes, such as growth in size and muscle coordination, clearly seem maturational, while others, such as skill in playing baseball or tennis, clearly seem learned. However, for many developmental changes, the relative contributions of learning and maturation are less clear. Talking is a good example. One developmental issue is determining to what degree all children learn to talk, regardless of what they are taught, and to what extent their talking depends on particular learning experiences.

Maturation versus learning

In addition, theorists differ in their view of how active or passive individuals are in their own development. For instance, behavioral learning theorists believe that developmental change is caused by events in the environment that stimulate individuals to respond, whereas theorists such as Piaget and Erikson see change as being a more active process in which the individual tries to solve the conflicts and problems of everyday life successfully.

Activity versus passivity

There is also disagreement about how conscious or aware people are of their own thoughts and actions. At one extreme are many behavioral learning theorists, who believe that awareness is the rule; at the other extreme are psychodynamic theorists such as Freud, who believe that people are consciously aware of only a small fraction of their thoughts and feelings. Interpretations of the degree of consciousness can be very important to a parent who is trying to understand why his child has "forgotten" to do her homework, or to two friends who are trying to understand why they are fighting.

Conscious versus unconscious development

Another difference concerns what theorists try to explain. Some theories focus on broad changes in people's development, whereas others try to explain more specific issues. For example, Erikson's theory attempts to explain the development of personality over the lifespan, whereas social learning theories limit themselves to explaining specific issues such as the development of sex roles and aggression. A third type of theory limits itself to a particular developmental process. The behavioral learning theories of Skinner and Pavlov, for example, attempt to explain all developmental change in terms of stimuli and responses.

Breadth versus depth

Now that we have briefly discussed several of the ways in which theories of development differ, let us take a look at the theories themselves.

Checkpoint *Theories help us to organize our knowledge about development systematically, form and test hypotheses, and explain the underlying principles and* *processes involved. Developmental theories, which often describe developmental change in terms of stages, differ in how much they emphasize maturation versus learning, conscious versus unconscious development, and breadth versus depth of coverage.*

Psychodynamic Theories of Development

Psychodynamic theorists believe that development is an active, dynamic process which is most strongly influenced by the individual's social and emotional experiences. A child's development is thought to occur in a series of stages. At each stage, the child experiences conflicts which she must to some degree resolve in order to go on to the next stage. The psychodynamic theories that have been most influential in developmental psychology are those of Sigmund Freud and Erik Erikson.

The Freudian Approach

Sigmund Freud (1856–1939)

Sigmund Freud was the father of psychodynamic theory. Considered by many to be one of the great thinkers of all time, he produced ideas that have influenced almost all views of development, including many of the informal theories that we all hold. As you study Freud's theory, you will realize that popularly held notions about hidden or unconscious conflict, the oedipal complex, and the importance of early childhood originated with Freud.

Freud was born in 1856 and lived in Vienna, Austria, for most of his life. An intense and brilliant student, he first became a physician and then a neurological researcher. His interest in children's development grew out of the discovery that the physical symptoms of certain adult patients were not really caused by physical illness at all. Rather, these symptoms, which included paralysis of the hands, arms, and legs, loss of speech, and even blindness, seemed to be caused by emotional factors.

First through the use of hypnosis, and then by means of his own newly developed method of encouraging patients to talk freely, which he called **psychoanalysis,** Freud discovered that if his patients could remember certain hidden or unconscious emotional experiences, their symptoms would eventually disappear. Many of these forgotten experiences had occurred during early childhood; often, they involved emotionally upsetting sexual and aggressive conflicts. After discovering the power of these emotions, Freud devoted the rest of his career to developing his psychosexual theory of development and to trying to help people through psychoanalysis. As we shall see, Freud's theory strongly emphasizes developmental stages, which are biologically determined but also influenced by experience, and unconscious processes. Table 2-1 summarizes Freud's stages of development. Although Freud's theory goes into a great deal of depth and is fairly complicated

Many of Sigmund Freud's ideas about motivation, sexuality, and the unconscious have become so pervasive in contemporary society that we often do not realize that they originated with Freud. (National Library of Medicine)

(his complete works run to more than twenty volumes), the main ideas are not hard to understand.

Stages of Psychosexual Development   In Freud's view, human development is motivated by energy, or **libido.** Libido refers to all of the ways — not just the ones we think of as sexual — in which human beings seek to increase pleasure and avoid discomfort by fulfilling their physical and emotional needs. From infancy through adolescence, developmental changes are caused by the conflicts a child experiences in trying to satisfy his libido. Freud found it useful to think of each individual's personality as consisting of three parts or functions. The first of these, the **id,** contains the basic, unprocessed sexual energy — the libido. The id motivates behavior by demanding reduction of the tension that builds up around a person's physical and emotional needs. However, it is completely irrational and unrealistic, and does not manage, channel, or direct itself in any way that matches reality. The newborn infant is all id, crying for the food it desires with no idea of how to get it.

Freud called the psychosexual stage of development in which the id is dominant the **oral stage.** During the oral stage, from birth to about one year, an infant seeks physical and emotional pleasure through her mouth: through nursing a breast or bottle, and through chewing, biting, mouthing, spitting, licking, and literally tasting the world. Freud believed that infants are at first very dependent and self-centered, and very unrealistic about how to meet their needs. They live in a fan-

Sexual energy

Table 2-1 Freud's Psychosexual Stages and Developmental Processes

Psychosexual Stage	Approximate Age	Description
Oral	Birth–1 year	The mouth is the focus of stimulation and interaction; feeding and weaning are central
Anal	1–3 years	The anus is the focus of stimulation and interaction; elimination and toilet training are central
Phallic	3–6 years	The genitals (penis, clitoris, and vagina) are the focus of stimulation; resolution of the oedipal conflict, sex role, and moral development are central
Latency	6–12 years	A period of suspended sexual activity follows oedipal conflict resolution; energies shift to physical and intellectual activities
Genital	12–adulthood	The genitals are the focus of stimulation with the onset of puberty; mature sexual relationships develop

Developmental Processes

Development occurs through a series of psychosexual stages, each of which involves a different area of the body, changing investments of libido, or psychic energy in relationships with people and things, and unconscious conflicts between the three structures of psychological functioning, the id, ego, and superego. The unrealistic and impulsive efforts of the id to achieve pleasure, and the moral and ethical pressures of the superego's attempts to act realistically through delaying pleasure, create unconscious conflict that threaten the ego. The ego defends itself against these threats by means of defense mechanisms.

tasy world where the wish to be fed or comforted is no different from the reality of actually being fed or comforted.

Although an infant desires instant satisfaction of her needs and is unable to delay gratification, even the most attentive parent cannot always meet a baby's demands immediately, and sometimes the infant simply has to wait to be fed or changed. Through such delays the baby begins to learn to distinguish between fantasy and reality, and to recognize and communicate her needs, thereby becoming an increasingly competent and independent individual.

According to Freud, this is when a second personality function, the **ego,** begins to develop. Whereas the id is said to follow the **pleasure principle,** the ego follows the **reality principle.** It is the manager or executive of the personality, helping to delay immediate satisfaction so that the libido's needs can be successfully met in ways that are socially acceptable. Instead of just screaming in helpless rage when she is hungry or uncomfortable, the baby gradually learns to communicate her needs more effectively and to successfully tolerate delays in their being met.

By toddlerhood (age two to three), the infant has entered the **anal stage** of psychosexual development. According to Freud, the physical center of sexual pleasure shifts to the anus and to activities related to elimination. The toddler finds both pleasure and worry in his bowel movements. Pleasure derives both from the physical feeling of elimination and from the sense of accomplishment the child experiences after his "productive" efforts. But he may worry that in giving up his

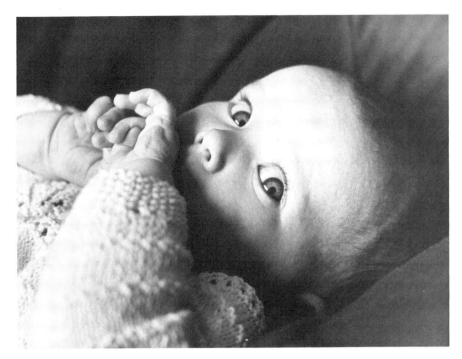

Psychodynamic theories focus on the inner life of the child. Freudian theory in particular emphasizes the importance of very early emotional experiences. Babies certainly show emotion, but since they cannot speak for themselves, critics say it is hard to assess whether early experience matters as much as Freud claimed. (David Mansell)

body product, he is losing a permanent part of himself. A second area of concern is control: who will determine when, where, and in what conditions elimination will occur. The child experiences a pressing need to go "right now," but his parents insist that he delay fulfilling this need until he finds a bathroom.

Gradually, a child's libidinal interest shifts to his genitals, and by age four or five he enters the **phallic stage** of development, when he is increasingly interested in gaining pleasure from touching or fondling his genitals, sometimes to the displeasure of his parents.

During this stage, the child also develops an intense sexual interest in the parent of the opposite sex. Thus, boys become sexually attracted to their mothers and girls to their fathers. While children are largely unaware or unconscious of these feelings, their actions often reveal their intense desire to have their parent exclusively to themselves, and they are jealous and angry when their desires are not fulfilled. For example, children of this age frequently want to sleep in their parents' bed, and the snuggling that was once so comforting can now feel a little disturbing as the children act in ways that are openly seductive. They also ask disturbing questions, such as "Daddy, do you love me as much as Mommy?" and "Mommy, will you come and sleep with me in my bed when I grow up, and marry me like Daddy?"

According to Freud, this desire for the opposite-sex parent and the tragic disappointment that follows the realization that the same-sex parent will always win the sexual competition are vividly captured in the Greek story of Oedipus. In the story, Oedipus murders his father and then marries his mother, unaware of their relationship to him. Later, on discovering what he has done, Oedipus feels so guilty that he punishes himself by putting out his eyes. Fortunately, the **oedipal**

conflict does not drive most little boys to murder, incest, or self-mutilation, but in Freud's view, it can create feelings of great intensity, as can the complementary situation for girls, which Freud called the **electra conflict.** A child's discovery of the intensity of his or her sexual feelings for one parent and jealousy of and anger toward the other leads to a conflict: the child does not want to give up the sexual desire, but fears that if he does not do so, he will be punished by the same-sex parent for his angry wish to get rid of him. Freud's view of how this works for girls will be discussed shortly.

The guilt that the child feels during the phallic stage is an indication that he is developing the part of his personality that Freud called the **superego,** which acts like an all-knowing, internalized parent. The superego punishes the child with feelings of guilt for his unacceptable sexual and aggressive thoughts and feelings, and it also sets unrealistic standards or ideals of thought and action that he must live up to. In other words, it acts as an enforcer of morality, inhibiting the irrational desires of the id with equally irrational ideals.

As the child develops a superego and contends with the conflicts of early childhood, he enters a period that Freud called **latency** — the stage between the phallic stage and the physical changes that begin adolescence. Latency is not truly a psychosexual stage, because the libido is not focused in a particular area of sexual excitation. In fact, *latent* means "hidden" and "not yet fully developed." During this stage, sexual feelings and activities are temporarily on hold, as the child struggles to resolve the oedipal conflict.

One way in which he achieves this is through **identification,** the process by which the child becomes like the parent that he fears (the father for a boy, and the mother for a girl). Over time, he unconsciously takes into his own personality, or **internalizes,** many of the important qualities of the same-sex parent. Being like his father protects a boy both from his anger and from his fear of his father's retaliation, and at the same time it allows him to continue to be close to his mother. Freud believed that identification with the same-sex parent was the basis not only for a child's development of a permanent sense of sexual identity, but also for his internalization of the moral and ethical values of his parents and society and of a personal sense of right and wrong.

Penis envy

Freud's description of how girls resolve the phallic stage is different than his theory for boys, and also more confusing and controversial. Although a girl also finds pleasure in touching her genitals — her clitoris and vagina — and is close to her mother, she envies boys because she does not have a penis. This **penis envy** leads to feelings of inferiority, and ultimately contempt for all females once she discovers that they too lack penises. Imagining that her mother is responsible for this loss, a girl shifts her desire to her father, fantasizing that it will allow her to possess a penis. In later giving up her wish to have a penis of her own, she substitutes the wish to have a baby and in so doing shifts the focus of sexual pleasure from her clitoris to her vagina and from a more active, assertive, and independent mode to a more passive, receptive, and dependent one (Freud, 1938, 1965). Because he believed that girls do not experience a traumatic resolution of the oedipal conflict, Freud theorized that they never totally give up their libidinal interest in their father and never develop as strong a superego and sense of morality and ethics as boys do.

Note that Freud's theory of how girls resolve the oedipal conflict is not supported by research observations and thus has gained little support. His prejudicial attitudes toward women have been widely criticized, as we shall see.

The resolution of the oedipal conflict leads the child into the **genital stage,** which emerges with the onset of puberty and continues throughout life. Freud believed that as boys and girls undergo the major physical changes associated with sexual maturity, their latent libidinal energy resurfaces with an intensity that can be disturbing. The center of sexual excitement is again the genitals, and the psychosexual task is to learn mature, adult patterns of heterosexual activity.

Defense Mechanisms   In Freud's view, the ego has the job of managing the conflicts that arise among the three functions of personality. It accomplishes this through the use of **defense mechanisms,** or unconscious ways of reducing anxiety by distorting reality. Because both the id and the superego are essential to life (what would life be without impulse and passion, or without conscience and ideals to strive for?), the ego cannot easily resolve the conflicts between them. The next best solution is to remove the conflict from awareness by burying it, or making it unconscious.

During the phallic stage, for example, the ego is threatened by the irrational and unrealistic desires of the id for sexual gratification and by the equally irrational and unrealistic demands of the superego for responsible behavior. One of the ego's compromise solutions is the defense mechanism of identification. ("If you can't lick them, join them.") A second is **repression,** which means that the child forces upsetting thoughts and feelings out of consciousness, for example, by forgetting a significant experience. A third is **sublimation,** in which sexual and aggressive energies are channeled into safer outlets for passion, such as schoolwork, sports, hobbies, and friendships.

Regression is among the ego's other defense mechanisms. When faced with a situation that is so frustrating that it threatens to overwhelm the ego with anxiety, a person may *regress,* or return to an earlier and less mature way of handling problems. For example, a very tense and frightened five-year-old might not be able to tolerate the upset of being left at school for the first time and might regress by wetting her pants like a two-year-old in the anal stage. Adults can also regress. A classic example is the hard-driving workaholic executive who has just suffered a heart attack and is so overwhelmed with anxiety and dread by the conflict between his helplessness and his need to be strong and invulnerable that he acts like an irrational, demanding child, throwing tantrums and refusing to cooperate with those who are caring for him.

When present in moderation, such defense mechanisms (there are others) are extremely useful for healthy development. But if a person relies on them too heavily, the resulting distortion of reality often creates psychological problems.

Strengths and Weaknesses of Freud's Theory   One limitation of Freud's theory is that it is vague in defining key concepts and does not provide rules for systematically relating concepts to each other. For example, how do we really understand the concept of libido or id?

Another weakness is that it is difficult or impossible to test many of Freud's conclusions. For one thing, Freud often did not make clear how he collected his data and on which observations he based specific conclusions. For another, the concepts of the theory are not scientifically testable, in that it is possible to predict contradictory outcomes. For example, will children who are frustrated in the anal stage develop habits of orderliness, cleanliness, and obedience, or will they be rebellious and messy? Why shouldn't a girl who fears her father seek to be like her mother?

Weaknesses

The theory is also culture-bound, meaning that it may not be true for development in other cultures. For example, the oedipus complex is not likely to be observed in societies where children are raised by aunts or uncles or by other members of their community. And how can we explain the normal development of gender identity and morality among children raised by single parents?

Freud's theory has also been criticized on the grounds that it reflects his era's prejudices against women, and that it inaccurately portrays the realities of women's social, sexual, and moral development. For example, there is no evidence to support Freud's claim that women's moral development is less adequate than men's, or that to achieve mature sexuality women must shift from clitoral to vaginal satisfaction (Gilligan, 1982; Mitchell, 1974).

A last major criticism is that Freud's conclusions are not based on direct observations of children, but rather upon the memories and fantasies of adults he treated for psychological problems. Not surprisingly, many of his findings are not supported by direct observations of children. For example, the development of the ego and basic trust seem to be more strongly related to physical closeness and responsive interaction between care-giver and infant than to the parent's fulfillment of the child's need for food, and the development of morality and sexual identity seem more closely tied to the child's desire for parental approval and to changes in his cognitive ability than to his fear of punishment.

Strengths

Among the strengths of Freud's theory are its breadth, the richness of its concepts and clinical observations, and its unwillingness to sacrifice complexity for easy understanding. Its psychosexual stages attempt to explain personality development in a very comprehensive way.

Another strength of the theory is its appreciation of conflict, both within the developing personality and between the individual and society. Rather than overlooking the irrational, hidden, and contradictory aspects of developmental change, the theory uses such concepts as unconscious conflict, defense mechanisms, and early childhood sexuality to further our understanding. For example, some critics suggest that Freud's theory does accurately describe the mental representation and beliefs of men and women who live in a society that to a large extent continues to be male-dominated and to discriminate against women in many ways. Rather than taking Freud's theory literally, they think that his theory is better viewed as a tool for understanding the myths that make it difficult for people to change unjust social realities (Mitchell, 1974).

Freud's appreciation of the importance of the inner, emotional lives of children and their parents has led developmental experts and parents to look more carefully at how the qualitative aspects of early childhood experiences, and the parent-child

Using Freud's theory as a starting point, Erik Erikson expanded it to cover the life span and modified the stages to place more emphasis on social encounters. (Historical Pictures Service, Chicago)

relationship in particular, influence development. As a result, psychoanalytic theory has been highly generative. Although difficult to scientifically test, the richness and complexity of Freud's observations and concepts have had a greater impact on our thinking about children and their development than any other theory. And whether or not we feel at home with his theory, many of Freud's ideas have become part of our cultural understanding of children and their development.

Freud's influence

In the next section, we will discuss the theory of Erik Erikson, a theory that is very much an extension of and elaboration on the work of Freud.

Erikson's Psychosocial Theory

Erik Erikson grew up in Europe. He studied psychoanalysis with Freud's daughter, Anna, and his theory of development was strongly influenced by Freud's. A fuller description of his life and work is presented in the accompanying Perspectives on Research. Stages play a central role in Erikson's theory. Social experience is more strongly emphasized than maturation and conscious versus unconscious factors. The theory is very broad and of moderate depth; it sees the child as an active participant in her own development.

Erik Erikson (1902–)

Table 2-2 *Erikson's Psychosocial Stages and Developmental Processes*

Psychosocial Stage	Approximate Age	Description
Basic trust versus mistrust	Birth–1 year	Focus on oral-sensory activity; development of trusting relationships with care-givers and self-trust
Autonomy versus shame and doubt	1–3 years	Focus on muscular-anal activity; development of control over bodily functions and activities
Initiative versus guilt	3–6 years	Focus on locomotor-genital activity; testing limits of self-assertion and purposefulness
Industry versus inferiority	6–12 years (latency period)	Mastery, competence, and productivity
Identity versus role confusion	12–19 years (adolescence)	Formation of identity and coherent self-concept
Intimacy versus isolation	19–25 years (early adulthood)	Achievement of an intimate relationship and career direction
Generativity versus stagnation	25–50 years (adulthood)	Fulfillment through creative, productive activity that contributes to future generations
Ego integrity versus despair	50 and over	Belief in integrity of life, including successes and failures

Developmental Processes

Development of the ego or sense of identity occurs through a series of stages, each building on the preceding ones and each focused on successfully resolving a new psychosocial crisis between two opposing ego qualities. No stage is fully resolved, and more favorable resolution at an earlier stage facilitates achievement of later stages.

How Erikson differs from Freud

Psychosocial Stages of Development   Erikson's developmental stages of development differ from Freud's in two major ways. The first and most obvious difference is that Erikson believed that development continued throughout a person's lifetime. Accordingly, his theory includes stages corresponding to early adulthood, adulthood, and maturity.

A second difference is that Erikson's stages are based upon a series of social, rather than sexual, conflicts that all individuals must successfully master in order to achieve adulthood. (They are summarized in Table 2-2.) For example, all school-age children in our modern society are expected to attend school in order to master certain basic academic and social skills. Doing so, as we shall see, requires that they successfully resolve the crisis of industry versus inferiority. The precise nature of the crisis may differ for different cultures and different points in history (Erikson, 1982).

Erikson's first stage corresponds to infancy and involves the psychosocial crisis of **trust versus mistrust.** Because infants are extremely helpless and dependent on their caretakers, during this period they come basically to trust their parents (and others) to care for them adequately; or, if they do not, they remain mistrustful of people, living in fear that they will be abandoned. According to Erikson, development of a belief in basic trust is fundamental to later stages of development, since failure to achieve a reasonably hopeful and trusting resolution because of inadequate parenting may seriously interfere with a child's courage and ability to meet further challenges.

Having learned to trust others, the child must go on to resolve the crisis of **autonomy versus shame and doubt,** which corresponds with Freud's anal stage. Here he must learn to what degree he can take pride in his own body and in his ability to decide how to use it, and to what degree he will experience shame and doubt about his choices. For example, it is inevitable that any child will make errors of both control and judgment during toilet training. A child who is treated respectfully for his failures as well as for his successes will eventually achieve autonomy in this area, but one who is consistently shamed and humiliated may develop an inadequate, doubting sense of autonomy.

During Erikson's third stage, the child focuses on his genitals as a source of pleasure, and on achieving greater independence of movement or locomotion and overall activity. Both contribute to the psychosocial crisis of **initiative versus guilt.** This crisis involves all conflicts that occur when a child takes on more than he can handle, including the oedipal conflict. It is easy to underestimate how strong and frightening a child's feelings and impulses can be at this age. If a child's loving and hating feelings and his conflicting impulses to be independent and dependent are ignored, belittled, or ridiculed, his resulting negative feelings can be very destructive.

Erikson interprets the next stage, which runs roughly from age six to twelve and corresponds with Freud's latency stage, as one when children must resolve feelings of **industry versus inferiority.** As children leave the protection of their family and enter the world of school, they must successfully master a new set of challenges. They must develop a belief in their ability to learn the basic intellectual and social skills required for full membership in our modern industrial society, which means that failure to be "productive" can lead to a belief in their own inferiority. The child who consistently fails in school is in danger of feeling alienated from society or of thoughtlessly conforming in order to gain a sense of belonging.

The physical changes of puberty, which include sexual maturation, occur during the next stage, when adolescents must resolve the crisis of **identity versus role confusion.** Teenagers undergo re-evaluation of who they are in many areas of development, including the physical, sexual, intellectual, and social. Frequently, conflicts from earlier stages resurface. As we shall see in Chapter 16, modern industrial society does not make it particularly easy for teenagers to establish identities that meet both their needs for independence and individuality and society's expectations for interdependence and conformity. Premature choice of identity, prolonged confusion about one's role, or choice of a permanent "negative" identity are three potentially destructive outcomes of role confusion.

Erikson's final three stages occur after adolescence. The first is **intimacy versus isolation:** the young adult must develop the capacity to develop close and committed relationships with others while tolerating the fears of fusion and loss of identity

Post-adolescent stages

that such intense intimacy raises. In adulthood and midlife, a person faces the crisis of **generativity versus stagnation.** Generativity is the feeling that one's work, family, and other activities are both personally satisfying and socially meaningful in ways that contribute to future generations; stagnation results when life no longer seems purposeful. Finally, during later adulthood and old age, people must con-

---

Perspectives on Research

Erik Erikson's Identity Crisis: An Autobiographical Perspective

How do theorists' own life experiences influence their theories of development? In one of his many books, Erik Erikson writes about his own identity crises and how they influenced his developmental theory. Later in this chapter we will consider how the personal experiences of two other theorists, B. F. Skinner and Jean Piaget, influenced their theoretical work. When you have finished reading this chapter, it might be interesting to consider how well each of their theories explains their developmental experiences.

Erik Erikson was born in 1902 and grew up in southern Germany with his mother, who was Danish, and her husband, a German pediatrician. Erikson recalls that "all through my earlier childhood, they kept secret from me the fact that my mother had been married previously; and that I was the son of a Dane who had abandoned her before my birth. . . . As children will do . . . I more or less forgot the period before the age of three, when mother and I had lived alone" (Erikson, 1975, p. 27).

As he entered adolescence, reports Erikson,

Identity problems sharpen[ed] with the turn of puberty when images of future roles [became] inescapable. My stepfather was the only professional man in an intensely Jewish small bourgeois family, while I . . . was blond and blue-eyed, and grew flagrantly tall. Before long, then, I was referred to as a "goy" [outsider] in my stepfather's temple, while to my schoolmates was a "Jew." . . . Although during World War I, I tried desperately to be a good

German chauvinist, [I] soon became a "Dane" when Denmark remained neutral (pp. 27, 28).

During this period, Erikson decided that he would be an artist and a writer — a rejection of the more middle-class values of his family. He spent most of his time traveling, painting, writing, and occasionally teaching art.

In the Europe of my youth, the choice of occupational identity of "artist" meant, for many, a way of life rather than a specific occupation — or, indeed, a way of making a living — and, as today, it could mean primarily an anti-establishment way of life. . . . At the time, like other youths with artistic or literary aspirations, I became intensely alienated from everything my bourgeois family stood for. At that point, I *set out* to be different. [After graduation from high school], I went to art school, but always again took to wandering. I now consider those years an important part of my training (pp. 25, 28).

Erikson recalls that his search for a professional identity also involved crisis. "To return briefly to the stepson theme: one might suspect that later on I had to succeed in making a professional lifestyle out of my early existence on what Paul Tillich has described as a life on boundaries, for throughout my career I worked in institutional contexts for which I did not have the usual credentials — except, of course, for my psychoanalytic training proper" (p. 30). Before he studied psychoanalysis, he was

---

front the psychosocial crisis of **ego integrity versus despair.** Ego integrity refers to the capacity to look back upon the strengths and weaknesses of one's life with a sense of dignity, optimism, and wisdom. It is in conflict with despair resulting from physical problems, economic difficulties, social isolation, and lack of meaningful work experienced by many elderly in our society.

---

an artist: "Psychology as such did not attract me [and] I must concede that the first course in psychology I ever took was also the first (and the last) I flunked" (pp. 22, 23).

It was not until Erikson was almost thirty and moved to Austria at the invitation of a close friend that his career as a psychoanalyst and developmental theorist really began. "My own training in psychoanalysis was conducted by Anna Freud, who accepted me as a fellowship candidate on the basis of the fact that she and her friends had witnessed my work with children as a private tutor and as a teacher in a small private school" (p. 24). After studying and practicing psychoanalysis in Vienna, Erikson was forced to leave Austria by the rise of Hitler. He emigrated to the United States, where he has lived and worked ever since.

Erikson's career has been exceptional, both because of the creative work he has produced and the fame he has achieved, and because he has done this without the benefit of even a college degree, much less any other professional credentials. In the 1930s, Erikson worked as a psychoanalyst with children and debated whether to return to school for a professional degree. Instead, he accepted a research appointment at Yale Medical School. He then joined the Yale Institute of Human Relations, where he worked with an interdisciplinary team of psychologists, psychiatrists, and anthropologists, and conducted field studies of the Sioux Indians in South Dakota.

In the 1940s, he moved to California to study the life histories of children living in Berkeley, and then the lives of the Yurok Indians. He joined the faculty of the University of California at Berkeley in the early 1950s, but was soon fired because he refused to sign a "loyalty oath," part of the fanatical anti-Communist crusade of Senator Joe McCarthy. Erikson says of this experience, "I was fired before the first year was up, and after being reinstated as politically dependable, I resigned because of the firing of others who were not so judged. As I think back on that controversy now, it was a test of our American identity; for when the papers told us foreign-born among the nonsigners to 'go back where we came from,' we suddenly felt quite certain that our apparent disloyalty to the soldiers in Korea was, in fact, quite in line with what they were said to be fighting for. The United States Supreme Court has since confirmed our point of view" (pp. 42–43).

It would seem almost self-evident now [says Erikson] how the concepts of "identity" and "identity crisis" emerged from my personal, clinical, and anthropological observations in the thirties and forties. I do not remember when I started to use these terms; they seemed naturally grounded in the experience of emigration, immigration, and Americanization. . . . I will not describe the pathological side of my identity confusion, which included disturbances for which psychoanalysis seemed, indeed, the treatment of choice. . . . No doubt, my best friends will insist that I needed to name this crisis and to see it in everybody else in order to really come to terms with it in myself (pp. 43, 26).

According to Erikson, the formation of identity presents a major crisis during adolescence. (Nancy Durrell McKenna/Photo Researchers)

Throughout these stages, Erikson emphasizes that a person's psychosocial development will be influenced by three interrelated developmental forces: her biological and physical strengths and limitations; her unique life circumstances and developmental history, including early family experiences and how well she has resolved the previous developmental crises; and the particular social, cultural, and historical forces at work during her lifetime—for example, racial prejudice, rapid technological change, or war.

Conflicts are never fully resolved

According to Erikson, people never fully resolve any of their psychosocial conflicts. Rather, they achieve more or less favorable ratios of trust to mistrust, industry to inferiority, ego integrity to despair, and so on. For example, if the early adulthood crisis of intimacy versus isolation is resolved strongly in favor of intimacy, the person is thought to be better equipped for future developmental challenges; a less strong leaning toward intimacy may make things more difficult. Crises are also not necessarily resolved at certain points in life: unresolved conflicts may resurface and achieve fuller resolution later in life.

Strengths and Weaknesses of Erikson's Theory   Erikson's theory shares some of

Weaknesses

the major limitations of Freud's psychodynamic theory. His concepts are difficult to define in a way that allows them to be scientifically tested, and because his evidence is based mainly on personal observations, it is hard to replicate. For example, researchers studying how adolescents resolve the crisis of identity versus role confusion (see Chapter 16) have found it difficult to determine just which of the many aspects of personal identity are most important or how their presence can be reliably measured.

Although Erikson makes it clear that development may be influenced by specific social, cultural, and historical differences, his stages are strongly biased toward Western European and North American experiences, and thus may not be valid for much of the rest of the world's population.

Two important strengths of Erikson's theory are its accessibility and its generativity. Because its concepts are simpler and more straightforward than Freud's, they help make psychodynamic theory accessible to a wider audience. Erikson's extension of developmental stages through the life cycle has significantly contributed to the growing interest in adult development during the middle and later years (Levinson, 1978, 1986); and his systematic linking of each stage to the social, cultural, and historical challenges or crises of normal development that we can readily recognize in our own lives makes it an attractive theory to both experts and newcomers to developmental psychology. Erikson's theory is also more hopeful than Freud's: by learning which social conditions help or hinder development, we may create greater possibilities for fostering development and preventing developmental difficulties.

Erikson's insights about the overall process of identity formation, and, more specifically, about identity conflicts during adolescence and young adulthood, have been very useful to parents, teachers, and developmental experts, as well as to youngsters themselves.

Strengths

Checkpoint   *The Freudian approach describes five stages of personality development, each characterized by a different mode of seeking satisfaction of emotional needs and each associated with a different sexually sensitive area of the body. Erikson's theory of development emphasizes eight stages, each defined by a unique psychosocial crisis that is never completely resolved. Although they are imprecise and difficult to test scientifically, psychodynamic theories have helped to stimulate and guide developmental research and work with children.*

Behavioral and Social Learning Theories of Development

Learning is generally defined as relatively permanent changes in observable behavior as a result of experience. Compared with psychodynamic theories, learning theories are fairly straightforward, and rely on a few basic concepts to explain development. This tendency to reduce development to simple learning, coupled with the fact that learning theorists have little to say about developmental stages or processes, leads some developmentalists to think of these theories more as approaches than as full-fledged theories of development. However, because they do share with other developmental theories the goal of creating a systematic framework for describing and understanding developmental change, we have chosen to describe them as theories rather than approaches. These theories clearly emphasize learning rather than maturation and conscious rather than unconscious developments. They also are narrow in their focus compared to Freud's and Erikson's theories.

Behavioral Approaches

Ivan Pavlov, a Russian scientist who lived from 1849–1936, and B. F. Skinner, an American born in 1904, are separated by history, geography, and culture, and their theories emphasize different models of learning. Still, most learning theorists rely on the work of both in describing and understanding development. As behaviorists, both theorists would claim that only observable behavior is useful in understanding learning and development, and that in time, all developmental activity, no matter how complex, will be explained by one basic set of laws of learning.

Pavlov: Classical Conditioning   Pavlov began developing his behavioral theory while studying digestion in dogs, work for which he won the Nobel prize. While measuring how much saliva the dogs produced in response to food, he discovered that the dogs began to salivate even before they could smell or see the food. Stimuli that were connected or associated with the food, such as the sound of the footsteps of the feeder, seemed to have the power to elicit salivation.

In his well-known experiments, Pavlov rang a bell just before feeding a dog. Eventually, the dog salivated whenever it heard the bell, even if it did not then receive any food. Pavlov called the process by which the dog learned to respond in this way **classical conditioning.**

When the experiments began, the sound of the bell was a neutral stimulus, because it really didn't affect the dog's response to food. However, once its sound had been paired with the food a number of times, it lost its neutrality; in Pavlov's terms, it became a learned or **conditioned stimulus,** since it now had the power to bring about salivation. The salivation itself was called the **conditioned response.** Pavlov named the food stimulus the **unconditioned stimulus** and the dog's responding salivation the **unconditioned response,** because the connection between the two was an inborn, **unconditioned reflex** — that is, an involuntary reaction, similar to the eyeblink.

Through the process of classical conditioning, reflexes that are present at birth may help infants to learn about and participate in the world around them. For example, classical conditioning of the sucking reflex, which allows newborn infants to suck reflexively in response to a touch to the lips, has been reported using a tone as the conditioned stimulus (Lipsitt and Kaye, 1964). Other stimuli — such as the sight of the bottle and the mother's face, smile, and voice — may also become conditioned stimuli for sucking and may elicit sucking responses even before the bottle touches the baby's lips. Because attempts to classically condition

Ivan Pavlov (1849–1936)

Early conditioning

B. F. Skinner has developed one of the most popular forms of behaviorism, operant conditioning. Its success may stem from its many practical applications. (Steven M. Stone/The Picture Cube)

a variety of other infant reflexes have met with mixed success, the developmental role of classical conditioning may be limited, at least during infancy (Sameroff and Cavanaugh, 1979).

However, numerous examples of classical conditioning, not directly tied to reflex responses, occur throughout development of classical conditioning. For example, a college student who has had a very negative experience in a particular math course may develop "math anxiety" in response to anything mathematical, even balancing his own checkbook. On a more positive note, a child who loves cuddling her mother or father may come to love bedtime stories, not necessarily because of the stories themselves, but because of their association with bedtime cuddling.

Skinner: Operant Conditioning   Like Pavlov's theory, B. F. Skinner's learning theory is based largely on research with animals, in this case rats and pigeons. Although you may protest that humans are far more complex than such laboratory animals, keep in mind that like other diehard reductionists, Skinner believes that *all* learning and developmental change, in both humans and lower-order animals, will eventually be reduced to one set of basic scientific laws of behavior.

B. F. Skinner (1904–   )

Skinner's idea of **operant conditioning** is based on a simple concept. Because children are constantly operating upon their world by responding to events that stimulate them through their senses, they learn when these operant responses are followed by a **reinforcer** — that is, by any stimulus that increases the likelihood that the response will happen again in similar circumstances. For example, consider Karen, a fourteen-month-old baby who sometimes says "doggie" when her father points to their dog, and sometimes does not. If her father says "Good girl!" every time she says "doggie" in response to the dog, and if her "doggie" responses to his question increase, then she has probably learned through **positive reinforcement.**

A **positive reinforcer** increases the frequency or rate of a correct response by rewarding the person for making it. A **negative reinforcer** has the same effect, but works by reducing a person's pain or discomfort. For instance, suppose a two-

---

Perspectives on Research

Skinner's "Dark Year"

In an article with the above title, psychologist Alan Elms (1981) proposes that a theorist's own life history and personality characteristics are likely to influence his or her choice of a theoretical model. Using information gathered from Skinner's own scientific and autobiographical writings and from what others have written about him, the article describes Skinner's "Dark Year," a period during his youth when he failed as a creative writer and seemed to experience a major identity crisis that ultimately influenced his theoretical work. Elms also reports that Skinner experienced a second developmental crisis during "mid-life" which significantly influenced his writing of the novel Walden Two. *In the discussion that follows, however, we will limit ourselves to discussing Skinner's first identity crisis and how it may have influenced his developmental theory.*

In his autobiography (1976), B. F. Skinner jokingly mentions an identity crisis, reporting that when he woke up one morning, he found part of himself — his left arm — missing. Following a frantic search, he found it "twisted sharply under his neck, with the circulation cut off" (Elms, 1981, p. 472). During his last term at college, Skinner felt that he had to choose an occupation; he decided to

become a writer. He had quite a bit of experience writing for college publications, and Robert Frost had sent him a letter encouraging him about his writing ability. Skinner decided to spend a year writing. Although his father was skeptical, he agreed to support his son at home for the year — as long as he would agree to "go to work" at the end of that year if his writing career was not well under way.

According to psychologist Alan Elms, who wrote an article about Skinner's identity crisis, Skinner was already conceding failure within three months, saying that "the results were disastrous. I frittered away my time" (Skinner, 1967, p. 394). The truth was," he wrote later, "I had no reason to write anything. I had nothing to say, and nothing about my life was making any change in that condition" (Skinner, 1976, pp. 264–265). He thought his parents were at fault for "unwittingly forcing" him into this situation; he also claimed that they ridiculed him for having "effeminate" interests (Skinner, 1976, pp. 264–265). Further, he blamed his hometown, Scranton, for being "ready to quench any ideas of my own I may have . . . I am too sensitive to my surroundings to stand it." Still, he felt bound by the agreement with his father to give writing a try for a year: "I found myself committed, with no

---

month-old named Jimmie has finished nursing and needs to be burped. If his mother responds to his little crying sounds by burping him and reducing his discomfort, and if in future Jimmie becomes more and more likely to signal his discomfort by making little crying sounds, then he has probably learned through **negative reinforcement.**

Punishment refers to any stimulus that temporarily suppresses the response that it follows. Punishment may be physical, or it may be verbal, or it may cause social and emotional pain. Another type of punishment is based on the "time-out" concept: a child is deprived of access to specific reinforcements (such as attention from friends) by removing her from the reinforcing situation. Punishment may also involve taking away reinforcing objects that a child already has, such as toys or money. Contrary to what many believe, however, punishment rarely if ever elimi-

---

hope of reprieve, to what I came to call the Dark Year" (Skinner, 1976, p. 265).

Elms believes that Skinner found the Dark Year so unhappy for several reasons. "Not only did Skinner discover that he was unable to write anything important, but he was often the object (or fancied himself to be the object) of jibes and innuendos from people who would have considered even a successful writing career as inappropriate for a healthy young man" (Elms, 1981, p. 472). "I was desperately hungry for intellectual stimulation," Skinner wrote, "but there was no one with whom I could talk or even correspond seriously. I was confined to the autistic, not to say auto-erotic, satisfactions to be found in a notebook" (Skinner, 1976, pp. 271, 279–280). Lonely and isolated, Skinner began to spend long hours sitting in the family library. He wrote,

> Cleverness lost its glamour for me. . . . Nothing is worth doing. . . . The world considers me lazy because I do not earn bread. The world expects of me that I should measure up to its standard of strength, which means that if I "got a job" for eight hours of office work . . . I should be a man. . . . I see clearly now that the only thing left for me to do

in life is to justify myself for doing nothing. (Skinner, 1976, pp. 282–283)

Skinner began to see his way out of his Dark Year when he discovered the writings of Watson and Pavlov. Their ideas about behavioral learning "gave focus to his previously scattered reading in psychology" (Elms, 1981, p. 473) — and soon, a clearer vocational purpose and sense of personal identity. Skinner soon came to think of himself as a behaviorist, and he was accepted to Harvard's graduate program in psychology. In a letter to his parents at the end of his first year at Harvard, he wrote, "I am looked upon as the leader of a certain school of psychological theories. . . . The behaviorists, whom I represent, have acquired a good deal of strength this year . . . Many of the new men, coming here this year, will come over to our 'party,' giving us moral and physical support." Convinced that his position was correct and others' theories wrong, he began to develop a group of followers. Soon his identity as a behaviorist was firmly in place. His identity crisis was resolved, at least for the moment, by his whole-hearted acceptance of the ideology of radical behaviorism.

Reinforcement takes many forms. For this child the sight and sound of pulling a tissue out of a box are positive reinforcers that encourage him to continue his tissue-pulling behavior. (Barbara Ries/Photo Researchers)

nates the unwanted behavior. (A fuller discussion of punishment is presented in Chapter 10).

Daily life provides numerous examples of operant conditioning. Kenneth, a ten-year-old, may clean his bedroom more often if he is praised for doing so; yet his parents may not have to praise him every time he cleans it. And Elaine, a teenager, will be more likely to adopt the latest fashions in dress if she is reinforced by the attention and compliments of her friends, but chances are that her friends will not notice her efforts every time. These examples, and most real-life situations, involve **partial reinforcement.**

Surprisingly, people often learn more effectively in response to partial reinforcement than to reinforcement 100 percent of the time. One classic example is gambling. The addictive quality of gambling is due to a very slim and unpredictable number of payoffs, or reinforcements, which cause the gambler to repeat his response over and over. Similarly, the negative behavior of a "problem child" in the classroom may be reinforced by the infrequent yet powerful attention from the teacher and her peers that her disruptive behavior gains her.

When removal of a reinforcer leads to the disappearance of the response it was maintaining, **extinction** is said to occur. Generally, responses that are no longer reinforced tend to be extinguished. Responses to partial reinforcement, however, are more resistant to extinction, because the pattern of reinforcement is variable and unpredictable and so the response is not completely dependent on it. Our gambler, for instance, has no way of knowing for sure whether bad luck or bad card dealing is keeping him from getting his payoff, so he keeps trying. Likewise, a child who receives occasional but unpredictable love and attention from her parents for obnoxious behavior may continue to act that way long after the reinforcements have stopped.

Strengths and Weaknesses of Behavioral Theories   The main strengths of the behavioral learning approach are the simplicity of the basic ideas and the ease with Strengths which learning techniques can be applied successfully in various situations. Teachers, psychologists, and parents find the concepts relatively easy to learn and to apply. In the classroom, teachers use behavioral learning techniques to manage difficult children and to help children control their behavior more effectively. Psychologists use these methods to help parents reduce their children's bedwetting and temper tantrums and work out better relationships with their teenagers. Behavioral learning techniques have also been used to help intellectually and emotionally retarded children increase their socially desirable behaviors and extinguish those that are undesirable.

Nonetheless, the simplicity of behavioral theories and the ease with which they can be applied can be drawbacks. Many critics believe that the behavioral learning Weaknesses approach loses sight of the humanity of children by reducing their activity to simple patterns of stimuli, responses, and reinforcers. These critics claim that a child's unwillingness to take out the garbage, achievements in school, social relationships, and feelings about herself cannot really be understood in terms of reinforcement theory.

One practical problem concerns choosing appropriate reinforcers. Although we may think that food, money, praise, and sex are effective reinforcers, all depend on both the specific conditions and the subjective judgment of the person whose behavior is to be influenced. For example, if a child feels that he is being manipulated or taken advantage of, none of the typical rewards at an adult's disposal will get him to do better at school. The problem may really boil down to whether we accept the behaviorist view that human beings are passive recipients of rather than active agents in their own development.

A second problem is the choice of the behavior to be reinforced. Even a promise of a trip to Disney World as a reward for a report card with all A's is likely to fail if the child lacks the academic background or study skills needed to make that goal a realistic possibility.

Cognitive behavioral approaches that use reinforcers to modify thoughts as well as actions have increasingly challenged the traditional view that behaviors must be Cognitive behavioral approaches directly observable to be modified (Meichenbaum, 1977). Since children's thoughts, feelings, and expectations about themselves and others often influence their actions in important ways, modification of children's thinking by means of reinforcement can be an effective way of influencing their actions. For example, impulsive children have been successfully trained to talk to themselves in ways that enhance their development of self-control (Meichenbaum, 1971).

Another important weakness of behaviorism involves the issues of power and control. The reinforcement situation is based on an inequality of power. People Risk of ignoring children's feelings who control a greater number of the reinforcers (teachers, parents, other adults) can use this power to influence those who control less of the reinforcers and who are therefore less powerful (children). Use of behavioral learning techniques to change children's behaviors may be harmful, say its critics, because behavioral theory provides little or no insight about human beings and their developmental needs.

Behaviorists respond to this criticism by claiming that because operant conditioning can be found in almost every aspect of our everyday life, it is better to use its techniques in constructive than destructive ways. But this response sidesteps the issue. A more effective response is to note that behavioral learning should be viewed *solely* as a technique and used only when guided by a clear set of understandings and values. For example, the use of the "time-out" technique for controlling the disruptive behavior of an emotionally disturbed child may be a helpful and constructive part of a broader treatment approach that seeks to understand the sources of upset. It is sensitive to what the child is thinking and feeling about things, including the "time-outs," and it is committed to discovering solutions that are developmentally best for the child.

A third learning approach may be more compatible with our general expectations of a theory of development. This is social learning theory.

Time-out technique

Social Learning Theory

Operant conditioning helps to explain why people engage in some behaviors more (or less) frequently, but it does not really explain why they develop those behaviors in the first place, or to what degree the behaviors are important to development. Why does a toddler suddenly begin combining single words into fairly complex sentences? Why does a thirteen-year-old suddenly adopt the punk look? Social learning theorists attempt to answer such questions.

Some behaviorists argue that sudden changes in behavior are not the result of either classical or operant conditioning. Rather, people seem to learn them by observing others (Bandura, 1977). The preschooler hears various sentence structures and imitates them, and the teenager sees others dressing in punk clothes and imitates what she sees. Although what the person learns may not precisely duplicate what she observes, it is close enough for us to recognize the model on which it is based.

Some theorists believe that observational learning involves more than mere imitation of the behaviors of other people. They suggest that through observing and trying out what they have seen, children actually internalize important qualities of the models they observe. Called **modeling,** this process is very similar to the psychodynamic concept of identification.

Although social learning theorists emphasize observable behavior and reinforcement, many also believe that there is more to social learning than meets the eye. To put it simply, a person who learns by observation must be able to pay *attention* to the model, must *remember* what he has learned until there is an opportunity to try it out, and must possess enough physical or *motor skill* actually to try out what he has learned. Observational learning occurs even among infants, but it becomes increasingly important as children get older and become better able to pay attention to models and to remember and later try out what they have observed.

Learning by observing models

Current formulations of social learning theory emphasize the importance of **reciprocal determinism** in learning and the development of personality. According to this view, change is a result of the mutual interaction of a person and her stimulus environment; people actively participate in changing situations and are not merely passively influenced by them. Their attitudes, expectations, and feelings about themselves and others must also be considered if their development is to be more fully understood (Bandura, 1986; Mischel, 1984).

Mutual interaction of individual and stimulus environment

Strengths and Weaknesses of Social Learning Theory In comparison with the behavioral theories, the social learning approach provides greater flexibility in defining the basic unit of what is learned, because it does not limit its scope solely to observable behaviors. As a result, teachers, parents, and other people involved with children find social learning concepts very useful for understanding complicated changes such as learning to ride a bike and the development of sexual identity and morality.

However, this approach, like the other learning theories, lacks an overall theoretical explanation for development, and underestimates the importance of children's unobservable thoughts and feelings. If we want to understand how children develop the ability to think and solve problems, and how these abilities influence other aspects of development, we need to consider Piaget's theory of cognitive development, which focuses on these issues.

Checkpoint *The behavioral learning theories of Pavlov and Skinner use the principles of classical and operant conditioning to explain developmental change. Social learning theories emphasize the role of observational learning, modeling, and, most recently, cognitive processes in a number of areas, including the development of sex roles, cooperation, competition, and aggression. Although limited in breadth and lacking developmental stages and principles of their own, learning theories have been useful in testing developmental hypotheses generated by other theories and in clarifying how certain developmental changes actually occur.*

Piaget's Theory of Cognitive Development

Jean Piaget was one of the most influential figures in psychology. Just as Freud's ideas have radically changed our thinking about human emotional development, Piaget's ideas have changed our understanding of the development of human thinking, or **cognition.**

Jean Piaget (1896–1980)

Born in 1896 in Switzerland, Piaget became interested in scientific research as a young child and published his first scientific article at the age of ten. A naturalist, philosopher, and mathematician, he devoted his early research to observing the development of his own children, and much of his later work was an effort to expand on the theories he devised as a father.

The cognitive theory of development views thinking as a conscious process and places major emphasis on developmental stages that are closely tied to maturation. Although the theory focuses on the single issue of cognitive change, it does so in great depth.

Piaget believed that children's thinking develops in a series of increasingly complex stages or periods, each of which incorporates and revises those that precede it. For example, Piaget believed that preschool children are highly egocentric in their thinking. Piaget did not mean that children are selfish; rather, they are self-centered and not yet able to observe situations from a perspective other than their own (Piaget, 1959). For example, a preschool child might say to his mother, who is in the next room, "I'm putting this here," totally unaware that she cannot possibly see where her son is pointing or to what object he is referring. A four-year-old girl who replied, "a little red wagon," when asked what her father would like for his birthday was not revealing selfishness. More likely, she was unable to distinguish her own perspective about what would make a pleasing gift from her father's per-

Egocentrism

Perspectives on Research

Piaget's *Méthode Clinique*

Piaget's unique *méthode clinique* (clinical method) for studying the growth of thought in children diverges significantly from the more systematic and controlled psychological experiments that have been the hallmark of modern developmental psychology. It combines careful naturalistic observation, individual case study, and a flexible approach to forming and testing a series of changing hypotheses that emerge from the researcher's interactions with the child being studied. (See Chapter 1 for a review of research methods in developmental psychology.)

In using the method himself, Piaget often began with careful naturalistic observation of the child's behaviors and interactions with her surroundings; he then developed hypotheses concerning the structure and rules that underlie the behaviors and interactions. Next, he tested these hypotheses by slightly changing the surroundings, either by rearranging the materials, by posing the problem in a different way, or even by suggesting to the subject a different response than the one predicted from the theory.

In the following example, Piaget reports his ob-

servations of his own infant, Laurent, who at the age of nine months is in the process of discovering object permanence (see Chapter 6):

> Laurent is placed on a sofa between a coverlet (A) on the right and a wool garment (B) on the left. I place my watch under A; he gently raises the coverlet, perceives part of the object, uncovers it, and grasps it. The same thing happens a second and a third time.... I then place the watch under B; Laurent watches this maneuver attentively, but at the moment the watch has disappeared under B, he turns back toward A and searches for the object under that screen. I again place the watch under B; he again searches for it under A.... (cited in Phillips, 1969, p. 28)

The Piagetian method of investigating children's thinking is exceptional in that it seeks to understand the reasons and rules that underlie their beliefs, opinions, and approaches to solving problems. Central to this method are conversations with each child about the responses that he or she has given; the goal is to assess the quality of think-

spective. As children enter their school years and have more and more contact with other children, they become increasingly able to see the world from another person's perspective.

What precisely makes a child develop from one stage to the next? Piaget answered this question in several ways. First, there are the methods by which a child responds to new experiences. She may use existing concepts to interpret new ideas or experiences, a process called **assimilation.** For example, a preschooler might see a truck but call it a car, because the concept "car" is already well established in his thinking. Similarly, an adolescent might joke or act tough on his first date, because these behaviors are familiar to him from past social situations with his male friends. In both cases, the boys are responding to the present in terms of the past, which is the essence of assimilation.

In **accommodation,** a person modifies existing concepts to fit new ideas or experiences better. Instead of calling a truck by the wrong name, the preschooler searches for a new name, and ends up calling it a "sort-of-car." Instead of acting

---

ing involved, regardless of whether an answer is "right" or "wrong" (Beard, 1969, p. xiv).

The following example, which Piaget designed to better understand the child's conception of number, clearly illustrates the highly interactive nature of the méthode clinique. The child was first presented with a number of coins and a large number of flowers, and then asked how many flowers could be purchased with the coins if the price of each flower were one coin. The following is a transcript of one such interaction:

> Gui *(four years, four months)* put 5 flowers opposite 6 pennies, then made a one-for-one exchange of 6 pennies for 6 flowers *(taking the extra flower from the reserve supply).* The pennies were in a row and the flowers bunched together: "What have we done? — We've exchanged them. — Then is there the same number of flowers and pennies? — No. — Are there more on one side? — Yes. — Where? — There *(pennies). (The exchange was again made, but this time the pennies were put in a pile and the flowers in a row.)* Is there the same number of flowers and pennies? — No.

— Where are there more? — Here *(flowers).* — And here *(pennies)*? — Less. (Piaget and Szeminska, 1952)

Critics have pointed out that shifting experimental procedure to fit the responses of a particular subject makes it difficult for other researchers to repeat or replicate the procedure and makes it more likely that the child may be influenced by the experimenter's expectations about how he should answer. Defenders of the procedure emphasize that efforts are made to deliberately provide the child opportunities for responses that do not fit the theory, and that Piaget believed that because the structure of knowledge is expressed through action, the investigator must continually adjust his own responses if he is to follow the child's actions and discover their underlying structure (Phillips, 1969). What both defenders and critics do agree upon is that Piaget's work has revolutionized our thinking about cognitive development and has generated an enormous amount of productive work in this area.

Jean Piaget's ideas did not become popular in North America until the 1960s—relatively late in his career. Since that time they have stimulated much research and have found wide support among educators. (Historical Pictures Service, Chicago)

like a ruffian, the boy on his first date tries to behave like a gentleman. In these cases, the individuals respond to new experiences more on their own terms, even if they do not do so perfectly.

According to Piaget, development occurs because of the interplay between assimilation and accommodation, a process he called **adaptation.** Concepts are deepened or broadened by assimilation and stretched or modified by accommodation. Often both occur at the same time. Consider this fractured version of a nursery song:

> Row, row, row your boat,
> Gently down the stream,
> Throw your teacher overboard,
> And listen to her scream.

The children who made up this song assimilated their hostile feelings to an old song, and at the same time they accommodated their concept of the song to their feelings.

Piaget's second explanation for developmental change involves the circumstances in which a child finds himself. That is, adaptations result from a combination of circumstances. Obviously, *experiences* matter; if he doesn't see a truck, a preschooler can neither assimilate that object to the concept of "car" nor accommodate his thinking to this new category of vehicle. But some experiences can only occur through **social transmission,** the process by which we are influenced by, and to some extent adopt, the information and ideas in the culture and society in which we live. This process is similar to the social learning theorists' idea of observational learning through imitation and modeling. For example, the teenager's actions on his first date involve both assimilation and accommodation, and both his roughhousing and his gentlemanly behavior are conventional, though each is learned from a different group of people. Finally, **physical maturation** influences development: a child has to reach a certain minimal level of biological development to be able to sing simple songs, much less the fractured one we just quoted.

Together, these processes create a state of cognitive equilibrium, in which an individual's thinking becomes increasingly stable, general, and harmoniously adjusted to the environment. The preschooler who is learning about trucks adapts his thinking to more varied types of vehicles. The adolescent learns how to adjust his behavior to the specific situation — when to goof around and when to behave more maturely. The singers of the fractured song learn how to use a musical framework for expressing their ideas (even if they do not learn respect for their teachers).

All individuals experience temporary cognitive disequilibrium and conflict in the process of achieving **equilibration.** If an earlier way of thinking or action does not work in a new situation cognitive change is stimulated. Inevitably, says Piaget, such changes increase the sophistication and maturity of a child's thinking, and so he moves into a new phase of development — a new cognitive stage.

Piaget's Cognitive Stages

Let us now take a closer look at Piaget's cognitive stages, which are simplified in Table 2-3.

The Sensorimotor Period (Birth to Two Years)　Piaget believed that at first, an infant's understanding of the world is based on simple, unlearned reflexes such as sucking, grasping, and looking. Piaget referred to the patterns of these reflexes as **innate schemes.** These schemes rapidly change, however, as the infant adapts them to fit new experiences. For example, a two-month-old baby has a sucking scheme. She soon learns that the nipple of a bottle requires a slightly different sucking scheme from the nipple of a breast; later, sucking her thumb involves further changes. It is through this process that cognitive development occurs.

At first the "thoughts" and "ideas" of an infant are based completely on experience of the world through her five senses (sensory experience) and through direct physical activity with objects (motor experience). For instance, an infant has no idea of a ball apart from her direct experience with actual balls. This is because she does not yet have verbal or visual symbols (words or mental pictures) for such

Table 2-3 *Piaget's Cognitive Stages and Developmental Processes*

Cognitive Stage	Approximate Age	Description
Sensorimotor	Birth–2 years	Coordination of sensory and motor activity; achievement of object permanence
Preoperational	2–7 years	Use of language and symbolic representation; egocentric view of the world
Concrete operational	7–11 years	Solution of concrete problems through logical operations
Formal operational	11–adulthood	Systematic solution of actual and hypothetical problems using abstract symbols

Developmental Processes

The earliest and most primitive patterns, or schemes, of thinking, problem solving, and constructing reality are inborn. As a result of both maturation and experience, thinking develops through a series of increasingly sophisticated stages, each incorporating the preceding ones. These changes occur through the processes of assimilation, in which new problems are solved using existing schemes; accommodation, in which existing schemes are altered or adapted to meet new challenges; and equilibrium, in which separate schemes become organized into a view of reality.

round playthings. For the baby, thinking is still limited to sensing and manipulating, and what is out of sight is literally out of mind.

While it may be hard to see how sensing and manipulating are really "thinking," Piaget in fact showed that **sensorimotor intelligence** gradually becomes organized in ways that are very similar to the more complex and abstract thinking that older children and adults are capable of. The details of this process are described in Chapter 6. Essentially, as the infant becomes more familiar with balls, she develops an idea of "ballness" that covers all of her specific experiences with such round objects. According to Piaget, the idea or mental image of "ball" also represents a **scheme.** In fact, the gradual development of schemes that represent all of the ideas and events in a child's experience is the basis for the development of thinking. The first schemes refer to specific physical actions and sensory observations, such as "the time that I pushed, licked, tasted, and drooled on the bright red ball that Daddy placed in my crib." The more sophisticated schemes of older children grow out of these earlier ones; a school-aged child's general idea (or scheme) of "roundness" might be constructed from earlier schemes like *baseball, balloon, orange,* and *beachball.*

Organizing direct experience

By the end of the sensorimotor period, around age two, the young child's schemes will have greatly increased in number and complexity. The child will also have achieved **object permanence,** the understanding that people and things continue to exist even when she can't see, hear, touch, smell, or taste them directly. This skill makes play much more interesting, but it can also make life more difficult for parents.

Continuity of existence

For example, when Linda, the babysitter, found Jill (eleven months) and her "friend" Carey (thirteen months) fighting over a stuffed dog, she easily settled their dispute by simply giving each infant a different toy. Once the original toy was out of sight, it was also "out of mind" and quickly forgotten. A year later, however, when she tried the same tactic to settle a similar dispute, both children loudly protested, indicating that they wanted the toy back and would not accept a substitute. In this case, Linda's "failure" was due to the children's "success" in achieving an understanding of object permanence.

The Preoperational Period (Two to Seven Years) During this stage, which lasts from about age two to age seven or so, there is a major shift from the action-oriented schemes of the sensorimotor period to schemes based on the use of language and other forms of symbolic representation. Something that is operational is guided by specific rules. During the **preoperational period,** a child's thinking begins to follow certain predictable rules, but the child has not fully mastered them. She also begins to develop the ability to figure things out and solve problems with words as well as actions. For example, if one of two doors into the kitchen is closed, the child can mentally "eliminate" the closed door without actually having to try it, and she will go through the other door.

Use of language and other symbols

Preoperational children experiment with using symbols to represent the world in several ways. One is **deferred imitation,** which is much like the kind of imitation social learning theorists describe. Suppose that Amanda, who is three, hears her pet dog Morris barking one morning. She may not respond to it then, but later, in the afternoon, she wrinkles her face and says, "Woof-woof, woof-woof!" This is a case of deferred imitation.

Symbolic thinking during this stage is also obvious in children's **dramatic play,** in which they try out the roles and behavior of their parents and other important people. A good example is "playing house," in which children pretend to be various family members and act out domestic scenes with which they are familiar. Although children's dramatic play is not always well organized by adult standards, it may at times confront us with performances that are all too accurate and true to life. In fact, careful observation of children's dramatic play can yield important insights into what they may be thinking and feeling.

Perhaps the most widespread sign of children's increasing symbolic skill comes from the development of language. During the preoperational years, children progress from using single words as whole sentences to mature grammatical constructions. The content of what they say changes too: early speech, such as "See dog," tends to refer mainly to current, "here and now" experiences, but later speech increasingly refers to the past or the future ("Remember when we saw that falling star?").

The Concrete Operational Period (Seven to Eleven Years) After children have become skillful at making representations, they begin learning how to coordinate them logically. As they do so, they enter the period of **concrete operations.** According to Piaget, *operations* are logical relationships among concepts or schemes. During this stage, which lasts until age eleven or so, children become able to use logical relationships for the first time, although this new ability is largely limited to objects and events that are real, tangible, and concrete.

Relating ideas logically

According to Piaget, children think in qualitatively different ways as they develop. Very young children still often think about objects and experience by doing and looking. Many adolescents, on the other hand, can plan and reason abstractly. (Above, Monika L. Anderson; right, Kent and Donna Dannen)

The changes in thinking associated with the concrete operational period are illustrated in the following Piagetian experiment. A child is shown two equal balls of clay and then watches as one of the balls is rolled into a long, thick snake. A preoperational child will think that the two balls now have different amounts of clay, but a child who has mastered concrete operations will know that despite the change in shape, both pieces still contain the same amount of clay.

Developmental psychologists have found these changes in many other similar tasks. The belief that the quantity or number of something stays constant in spite of changes in its appearance is called **conservation.** Note that conservation requires a belief in constancy, not a perception of it. A child (or an adult, for that matter) cannot really see whether the amounts of liquid are equal in two containers of different shapes; she can only know that they are. Success at this task, then, depends partly upon knowledge of the containers' past as well as on beliefs about the general behavior of liquids. Belief in constancy

Concrete operational skills help a child to explore and solve problems, but as we have noted, the child is still limited to thinking about real or concrete things rather than abstract ideas. Consider Jean-Paul, an eight-year-old who enjoys collecting bugs and butterflies and knows a great deal about their behavior. Ask him anything about how they look, their feeding patterns, or their scientific names and classifications, and he will probably be able to answer. But ask him about more abstract things, such as why different species have developed differences in size, shape, and coloring, and he will probably not know what to say. Later in the concrete operational period, of course, Jean-Paul can answer such a question increasingly well, but by then he may already be entering Piaget's fourth major cognitive stage.

The Formal Operational Period (Eleven and Up) Sometime during adolescence, children learn to think logically, abstractly, and scientifically. Here are two problems that require such **formal operational thinking** for their solution:

- *Problem 1* Suppose all *wugs* were *fets* and all *fets* were *tuts.* If you saw a *fet,* would it more likely be a *wug* or a *tut?*
- *Problem 2* What makes a pendulum swing faster or slower, its length, the amount of weight on the end, or the angle from which you release it?

The first of these problems requires logical reasoning, of course; more important, it requires reasoning in the abstract, in the absence of any real, tangible objects. Formal operational thinking allows people to solve problems by using only abstract symbols, in this case *wugs, fets,* and *tuts.* A child who has reached the concrete operational period could solve this problem if real objects were involved. Test this idea for yourself, if you like, by recasting Problem 1 in real terms: replace *wugs* with *fathers, fets* with *men,* and *tuts* with *people.* Does it make the problem easier? Yes, says Piaget — in fact, easy enough for a concrete operational child to solve. Abstract thinking

The second problem requires the person answering it to test the influence of each of the three factors or variables (length, weight, and angle) on the speed of the pendulum's swing. What is called for is an experiment in which each factor is systematically tested while the other two are held constant. The formal operational child or adult might try different lengths of cord while using only one weight and while being careful to release the pendulum from the same angle for each test. After noting the influence of the cord's length in this way, she would shift her attention to trying different weights systematically while keeping the length of the cord and angle of release constant. Finally, she would try varying the angle of release while keeping the cord length and pendulum weight constant.

A person who had not yet achieved formal operational thinking would not be able to conceive of all the hypothetical possibilities and then systematically vary each factor until the problem was solved. It is the ability to conceive of a model that exhausts all the logical possibilities and to systematically carry it to its conclusion that distinguishes both formal operational and scientific thinking from earlier stages. When a child has mastered this kind of thinking, he is an adult, at least in Piagetian terms.

Strengths and Weaknesses of Piaget's Theory

Strengths

Piaget's stages of cognitive development provide a clear and thorough framework for looking in detail at the process by which children develop, emphasizing the central role of cognition. As such, his theory has been extremely useful for educators and other professionals working with children. In fact, it has come to be the guiding force in planning curricula and in educating parents about reasonable expectations for their children.

Another strength of Piaget's theory is that it integrates a wide range of information about cognitive change and serves as an important tool for stimulating new research. In doing so, it has led researchers to become much more aware of children's intellectual capabilities and of the content of their thinking.

A third strength of the theory has been its implications for other areas of developmental psychology. It has provided a basis for stage theories of moral development, sex-role determination, play, racial awareness, and the development of identity, just to name a few.

Weaknesses

In spite of the wide implications of Piaget's theory, however, its narrow focus on intellectual change, almost to the exclusion of social and emotional influences, is problematical. If we were to depend solely on Piaget's theory, we might think that intellectual development occurs independently of the major social and emotional changes described by Freud, Erikson, and the social learning theorists. Similarly, the assumption that cognitive stages are universal — that they hold for all people in all places at all times — is a weakness that Piaget shares with all stage theorists to some degree. There are indications that some of the changes that Piaget attributes to built-in stages are due to the particular methods that he and his followers have used to study children's thinking.

Impact of Piaget's theory

In summary, Piaget's theory has had an enormous impact on our thinking about cognitive development. It has integrated a wide and diverse range of information in a systematic way and stimulated a great deal of new research. The cognitive developmental approach has also proven to be extremely useful in explaining various aspects of socialization, including sex-role development (Kohlberg, 1964), sex typing (Bem, 1981), moral judgment (Kohlberg, 1966), and the development of racial attitudes (Katz, 1976).

Developmental Theories Compared: Implications for the Student

We have now come to the end of our review of several of the most important theories in developmental psychology, having explored in some detail the suggested stages and processes involved in children's sexual, emotional, social, and cognitive development. What conclusions might we draw? And in what way are these theories useful as we investigate children's development in the rest of this book?

One conclusion is that no single theory adequately describes or explains all of development. Each theory has a somewhat different focus, a different set of assumptions, and a different set of concepts. Nevertheless, although they differ considerably, they do seem to reflect some degree of basic agreement about children. For instance, most theorists agree that children go through perceptible stages of growth (see Table 2-4). Freud, Erikson, and Piaget agree that adolescence, to take one example, is marked by achievement of adult or near-adult levels of adjustment. For Freud, that adjustment is psychosexual in nature; for Erikson, it involves identity formation and social functioning; and for Piaget, it involves the ability to think and solve problems in a formal operational way.

Agreement among the theories

The same holds true for infancy. Freud's emphasis on oral activity and the development of the ability to distinguish between what is real and what is not is consistent with Erikson's belief that this stage involves the senses and the developmental crisis of basic trust versus mistrust. Piaget's idea of a sensorimotor period defines an infant whose approach to thinking and problem solving would be recognized by Freud and Erikson, and that infant's level of cognitive development is fairly consistent with the psychosexual and psychosocial achievements that Freud and Erikson describe.

While each of the theories has contributed significantly to expanding our knowledge in its particular area of focus, none should be viewed as providing a complete explanation of development. Taken together, the theories are complementary and can be used in conjunction with one another to provide a fairly comprehensive view of child and adolescent development.

The theories complement each other

As we suggested at the beginning of this chapter, theories are useful because they help us to systematically organize and make sense out of large amounts of information about children's development. Theories also stimulate new thinking and

Advantages of using theories

| | Psychodynamic | | Cognitive | Behavioral Learning | Social Learning |
	Freud	Erikson	Piaget	Pavlov; Skinner	Bandura
Main focus	Personality (social, emotional)	Personality (social, behavior identity)	Cognitive (thinking, problem solving)	Learning specific observable responses	Learning behavior and cognitive response patterns and social roles
Key concepts	Id, ego, super-ego; psychosexual conflict; defense mechanisms	Lifespan development; psychosocial crises	Schemes, assimilation, accommodation, equilibrium	Classical and operant conditioning, extinction, reinforcement, punishment	Imitation, social learning, modeling cognitive learning
Important features					
Stages	Yes	Yes	Yes	No	No
Role of Maturation	Moderate	Weak	Strong	Weak	Weak
Role of Experience	Strong	Strong	Moderate	Strong	Strong
Role of Unconscious	Strong	Weak/moderate	None	None	None
Role of Conscious	Moderate	Strong	Strong	Strong	Strong
Breadth of focus	Wide	Wide	Moderate	Narrow	Moderate
Generativity	Strong	Moderate	Strong	Weak	Moderate
Testability	Weak/none	Weak/moderate	Moderate	Strong	Strong

Table 2-4 *Developmental Theories Compared*

research and guide parents and professionals in their day-to-day work with children. For example, knowledge of cognitive theory is helpful in providing guidelines for teachers and parents who want to design educational programs appropriate to particular children's competencies. Similarly, Erikson's psychosocial theory alerts us to the predictable developmental crises of childhood and adolescence, enabling us to be more appropriately responsive to our children's needs.

On the other hand, because they guide and direct our perceptions of and thinking about children, reliance on theories may predispose us to focus on certain aspects of development, to make certain assumptions, and to draw conclusions about development that are consistent with the theory but not necessarily accurate. For example, overreliance on the cognitive approach may lead a teacher to underestimate the contribution of social and emotional factors to a child's aca-

Disadvantages of using theories

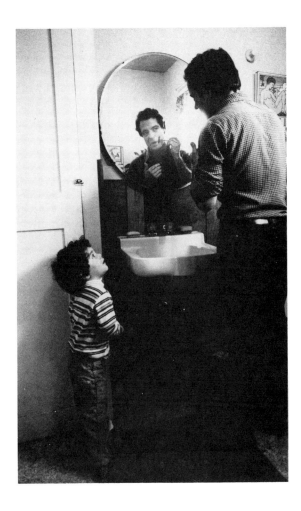

Even though developmental theories sometimes seem to contradict each other, they often are only looking at different aspects of the same behavior. If proponents of Freud, Piaget, Erikson, and Skinner looked at this scene, what would each of them see? (Robert V. Eckert, Jr./The Picture Cube)

demic difficulties. Similarly, a parent who is predisposed to interpret her child's irresponsible behavior in terms of psychological conflict may overlook the fact that this same behavior is frequently modeled and reinforced by the child's older brother.

While the usefulness of developmental theory to experts may be easy to appreciate, how do we judge its importance to students and other nonprofessionals? Clearly, we are all indirectly influenced by the work of developmental researchers and professionals, but an understanding of developmental theories can be directly useful to students and other nonprofessionals in some very important ways.

Theories help individuals to organize more easily and effectively what they already know about child and adolescent development based upon their personal experiences. They can also help people to broaden and deepen their *understanding* of the principles, processes, and stages of developmental change, and to sharpen their own informal ideas and theories about development.

Theories help deepen understanding

As you read the chapters that follow, you will notice that the theories are applied selectively, depending upon the ages and developmental issues that we are discussing. We encourage you to refer back to this chapter whenever you have questions about the material, and to make your own judgments about which theory (or theories) fit best. Last, keep an eye on how your own theory of development changes as you read the book and talk with your teacher and classmates. By the end of the course, if not sooner, you are likely to have a much clearer idea of your theoretical orientation, as well as a much clearer idea of what development is all about.

Checkpoint *Although the developmental theories differ both in their focus and in their explanatory concepts, together they provide a fairly comprehensive view of the process of developmental change. Theories are very useful in guiding the thinking of experts and nonexperts in their work with children, but at times they may limit our openness to perceiving children in ways the theories do not anticipate.*

Summary of Major Ideas

The Nature of Developmental Theories

1. Theories are useful in organizing and explaining the process of development and in stimulating and guiding developmental research, theory, and practice.

2. Developmental theories differ in the degree to which they emphasize stages, maturation versus learning, conscious versus unconscious processes, breadth versus depth of focus, and active versus passive participation of the child.

3. According to the stage theories, development proceeds in a series of stages, each of which is more complex and qualitatively different from those that precede it.

Psychodynamic Theories of Development

4. The theories of Freud and Erikson see development as a dynamic process that occurs in a series of stages, each involving psychological conflicts that the developing person must resolve.

5. According to Freud, personality development is energized by three conflicting processes: the unconscious, irrational, pleasure-seeking id; the largely conscious, rational, realistic ego; and the superego, which is the voice of conscience and morality.

6. The Freudian approach describes five stages of psychosexual development: oral, anal, phallic, latency, and genital.

7. During the oral and anal stages, the mouth and then the anus are the focus of children's social and emotional

experience — both pleasurable and unpleasurable — and of the conflicts they encounter in having their needs fulfilled.

8. During the phallic stage, the genitals are the focus of sexual and emotional activity; resolution of the oedipal conflict results in the establishment of gender identity and the development of the superego.

9. Latency, a period of little psychosexual activity, anticipates the physical changes of puberty and the genital stage, which is the final stage of psychosexual development.

10. Erikson's theory, a revision of Freud's, outlines eight developmental stages encompassing the lifespan, each defined by a unique psychological crisis that is never completely resolved.

11. Erikson's work has contributed to our understanding of the overall process of identity development, particularly the crisis of identity versus role confusion, which occurs during adolescence.

12. Although imprecise and difficult to test scientifically, psychodynamic theories have been very influential in stimulating and guiding developmental research and work with both normal and disturbed children.

Behavioral and Social Learning Theories of Development

13. Pavlov's theory of classical conditioning has helped to explain the process by which developmental changes occur.

14. Skinner's operant conditioning theory emphasizes the influence of reinforcement, punishment, and extinction in developmental change.

15. Operant conditioning approaches have been particularly helpful in helping children who have difficulty acquiring basic social skills and regulating and controlling their own behavior.

16. Social learning theories emphasize the contributions of observational learning, modeling, cognitive processes, and reciprocal determinism in developmental change.

17. Social learning theories have been successfully applied to such areas as sex role development and the development of cooperation, competition, and aggression.

18. Although limited in breadth and lacking developmental stages and principles of their own, learning theories have been useful in testing developmental hypotheses generated by other theories and in clarifying how certain developmental changes actually occur.

Piaget's Theory of Cognitive Development

19. Piaget's theory explains the underlying structures and processes involved in the development of children's thinking and problem solving.

20. According to Piaget, thinking develops in a series of increasingly complex and sophisticated stages, or periods, each of which incorporates the achievements of those preceding it.

21. New ways of thinking and problem solving are achieved through the joint processes of assimilation (fitting a new scheme of thinking or action into an existing one) and accommodation (changing an existing scheme to meet the challenges of a new situation).

22. During the first, sensorimotor period, the infant's thoughts and ideas are based completely upon his sensory experiences and direct physical activity with objects; he achieves an understanding that objects exist independent of his sensory awareness.

23. During the preoperational period, ages two to seven, the child's thinking begins to follow predictable rules and relies increasingly on his ability to use language and other symbols.

24. The concrete operational period, ages seven to eleven, witnesses an increasing ability to think logically and the achievement of conservation, the belief that the quantity of things remain constant in spite of changes in their appearance.

25. Cognitive development reaches completion during the formal operational period, when the child becomes able to rely exclusively upon abstract symbols to conceptualize and systematically solve real and hypothetical problems.

26. Piaget's cognitive theory has had an enormous impact on research, theory, and application, particularly in the field of education.

27. Cognitive theories have also been used to explain the development of sex roles, sex typing, moral judgment, and racial attitudes.

Developmental Theories Compared: Implications for the Student

28. Although the theories differ both in their focus and in their explanatory concepts, together they provide a fairly comprehensive view of the process of developmental change.

29. Theories may at times seem too complicated and abstract to be immediately useful, and may at times interfere with efforts to observe and think about children in ways that are not anticipated by the theory involved.

30. By systematically organizing what is already known about development and by proposing explanations that can be tested through our own formal and informal observations, developmental theories are so useful a tool for experts and nonexperts alike that they are well worth the effort required to understand them.

Key Terms

developmental stages *(35)*	penis envy *(42)*
stage theories *(35)*	genital stage *(43)*
psychoanalysis *(38)*	defense mechanisms *(43)*
libido *(39)*	repression *(43)*
id *(39)*	sublimation *(43)*
oral stage *(39)*	regression *(43)*
ego *(40)*	trust versus mistrust *(46)*
pleasure principle *(40)*	autonomy versus shame
reality principle *(40)*	and doubt *(47)*
anal stage *(40)*	initiative versus guilt
phallic stage *(41)*	*(47)*
oedipal conflict *(41)*	industry versus inferiority
electra conflict *(42)*	*(49)*
superego *(42)*	identity versus role
latency *(42)*	confusion *(50)*
identification *(42)*	intimacy versus isolation
internalization *(42)*	*(50)*

generativity versus stagnation *(50)*
ego integrity versus despair *(50)*
classical conditioning *(52)*
conditioned stimulus *(52)*
conditioned response *(52)*
unconditioned stimulus *(52)*
unconditioned response *(52)*
unconditioned reflex *(52)*
operant conditioning *(53)*
reinforcer *(54)*
positive reinforcer *(54)*
negative reinforcer *(54)*
punishment *(55)*
partial reinforcement *(56)*
extinction *(56)*
modeling *(58)*

cognition *(59)*
assimilation *(61)*
accommodation *(61)*
adaptation *(62)*
social transmission *(63)*
equilibration *(63)*
sensorimotor intelligence *(64)*
scheme *(64)*
object permanence *(64)*
preoperational period *(65)*
deferred imitation *(65)*
dramatic play *(65)*
concrete operations *(65)*
conservation *(67)*
formal operational thinking *(67)*

What Do You Think?

1. When you began this chapter, what negative and positive views did you have about theories? In what ways have your views changed? Why?
2. Does Freud's description of the oedipal conflict and its resolution explain what actually happens? Based upon your own observations, what evidence seems to support his ideas? What evidence contradicts them?
3. Erikson proposes that adolescence involves the crisis of identity versus role confusion, and young adulthood, the crisis of intimacy versus isolation. Based upon your own observations, how accurate is Erikson about what happens during these two stages of development?
4. Earlier in this chapter, two examples were used to illustrate the qualities of abstract thinking during Piaget's formal operational period: "wugs, fets, and tuts" and the "pendulum problem." Do you think that being able to think in this way is better than thinking more concretely? Why or why not?
5. Which of the theories do you find the most interesting? For what reasons?
6. Which of the theories do you think is most useful in understanding human development? Why?

For Further Reading

Crain, W. *Theories of Development: Concepts and Applications* (2nd ed.). Englewood Cliffs, N.J.: Prentice-Hall, 1985.

A thorough and readable review of the major developmental theories, this book's use of examples, comparisons between theories, and discussions of practical implications are helpful in understanding the theories.

Eagle, M. *Recent Developments in Psychoanalysis: A Critical Evaluation.* New York: McGraw Hill, 1984.

This book provides a high level of coverage of the most recent developments in psychoanalysis and critically examines the underlying assumptions, theoretical arguments, and conclusions of each.

Erikson, E. *Identity, Youth and Crisis.* New York: W. W. Norton, 1968.

Erikson presents his developmental theory with an emphasis on identity development during adolescence and young adulthood. Chapter 3, "The Life Cycle: Epigenesis of Identity," is most relevant for the student who wants to sample Erikson's work first hand.

Freud, S. *New Introductory Lectures on Psychoanalysis.* (J. Strachey, ed. and trans.) New York: W. W. Norton, 1965.

This basic introduction to Freud's ideas is based on his lectures to an audience that included nonexperts unfamiliar with his work. It is recommended for the student who wants to read something Freud actually wrote. While his ideas are complex, his writing style is surprisingly clear and interesting.

Hall, C., and Lindzey, G. *Theories of Personality* (3rd ed.). New York: John Wiley, 1978.

A classic, systematic, and straightforward review of the major theories of personality from the standpoint of traditional psychology. A useful reference source.

Mitchell, J. *Psychoanalysis and Feminism.* New York: Pantheon, 1974.

A high-level critique of the psychoanalytic theory of traditional and nontraditional Freudian theory from a feminist perspective. The author is willing neither to accept Freud's prejudices nor to dismiss his insights and contributions, and provides a challenging corrective to those who are willing to do so. Difficult reading, for the highly motivated student.

Phillips, J. *The Origins of Intellect: Piaget's Theory.* San Francisco: W. H. Freeman, 1969.
A clear and concise review of Piaget's cognitive theory.

Skinner, B. F. *Walden Two.* New York: Macmillan, 1948.
A novel describing a fictional utopian community that is guided by the assumptions of behavioral learning theory and the principles of operant conditioning.

2 Beginnings

Although you might think of human development as starting in infancy, it actually begins at the moment of conception. We become individuals partly because of our genetic endowments, which are determined the moment sperm meets egg, and partly also because of events that happen to us while still in our mothers' wombs.

The next two chapters look at these influences. They show some of the ways in which heredity affects whom a child becomes, not only physically but cognitively and socially as well. And they describe what actually happens during the thirty-eight weeks or so before birth, as well as the events surrounding birth itself.

By childbirth — a time of wonder, anxiety, and joy — the baby has already undergone many changes. But there is plenty of room to learn from experience — and the child will undergo many more changes throughout his or her life.

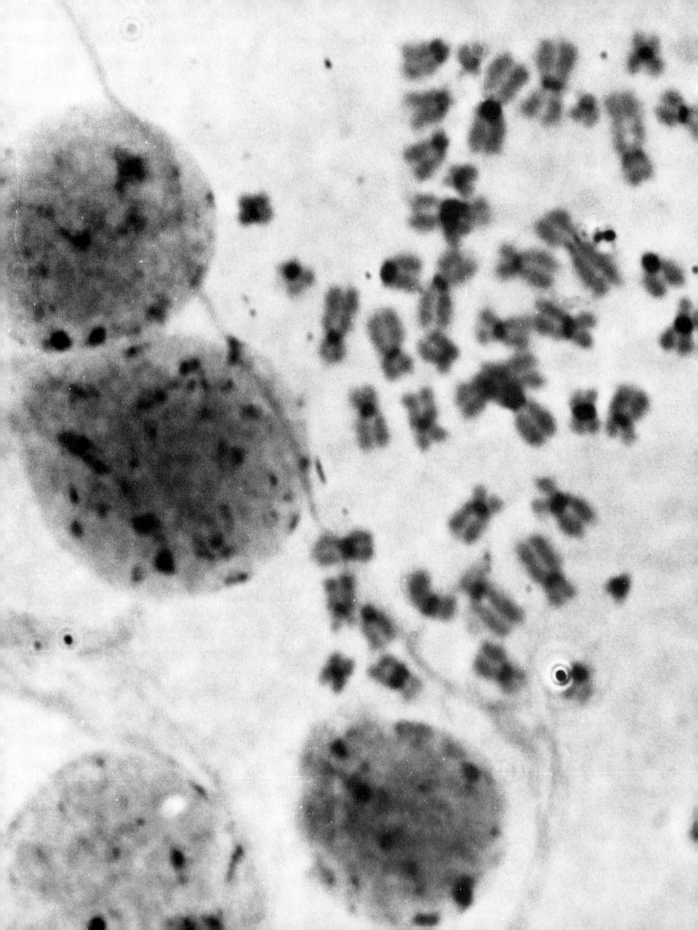

Chapter

3

Genetics

Focusing Questions

■ How are genetic differences usually transmitted from one generation to the next?

■ How do genes work to make a person a distinct individual?

■ What are the most common sorts of genetic abnormalities, and what are their causes?

■ How do heredity and environment each contribute to the development of individual children?

■ What can experts in genetics do to help parents to diagnose and respond to genetic problems?

A VAST NUMBER of human qualities are inherited, from the shape of our earlobes to the sound of our voices. Even complex personal behaviors such as how much we mull over problems may be at least partially inherited. What makes these things "run in families"? Stated more formally, how is genetic information conveyed from one generation to the next?

This chapter will explore answers to this question. To do so, we first describe the basic biological processes involved in human reproduction, then explain how genetic information from two individuals is combined and conveyed from parents to children. Genetic abnormalities receive special attention, not because these outnumber normal genetic processes, but because they shed considerable light on those processes. The chapter then addresses an issue that psychologists have found especially important: the relationships between heredity and environment. All psychologists agree that both factors influence human development, but the exact nature of these influences is often complex and ambiguous. Finally, we end by describing ways of using knowledge of these relationships to benefit parents.

Mechanisms of Genetic Transmission

Although we still lack many details about how genetic information is combined and transmitted, we do know that it begins with the reproductive cells, or **gametes,** of a child's parents. In the father, the gametes are produced in the testicles, and each is called a **sperm** cell; in the mother, they develop in the ovaries, and each is called an **ovum,** or egg cell. The sperm and egg cells contain genetic information in molecular structures called **genes,** which form threads called **chromosomes.** Any human sperm or egg cell contains only twenty-three chromosomes, but each chromosome contains literally thousands of genes.

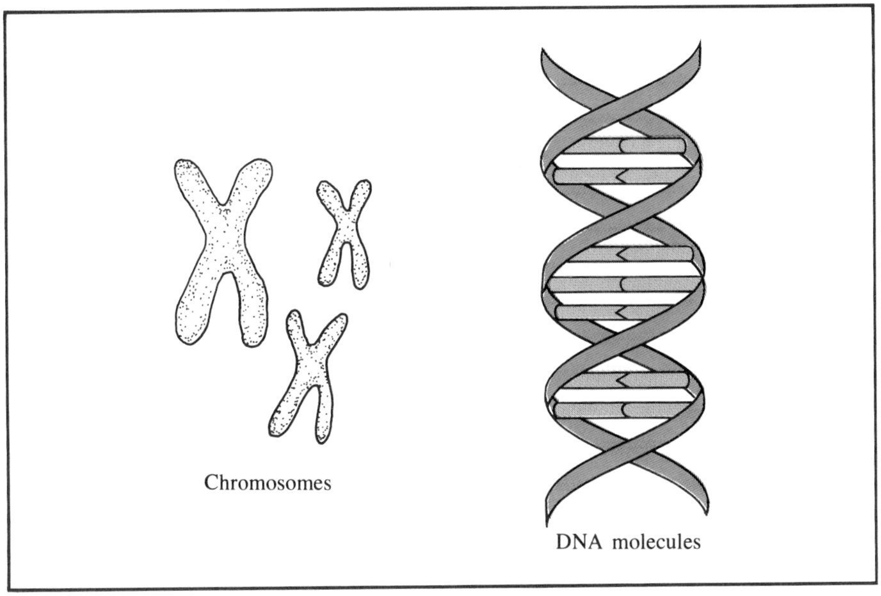

Figure 3.1   Genetic Structures

Chromosomes

DNA molecules

The Role of DNA

The genes themselves are made of **deoxyribonucleic acid,** or **DNA.** Each DNA molecule consists of a large conglomeration of just a few simpler molecules, called **amino acids,** which are arranged differently in different genes, so that the physical structure of each DNA molecule forms a sort of code that corresponds to various genetically determined features of the individual. All DNA molecules have a particular chemical structure — a double helix, or spiral — that allows them to divide easily and thus to create new, duplicate DNA molecules reliably (see Figure 3-1).

The structures of genetic transmission

Taken as a whole, then, the DNA in the genes fulfills two major requirements for genetic reproduction. First, it contains the code of genetic information that the individual needs as she develops; and second, it can share this information widely through its relatively foolproof ability to divide and reproduce. The first of these features helps account for the numerous genetic differences among individuals, and the second, for the overall consistency and regularity of many steps of individual development.

But DNA can only accomplish these things under the right conditions. In particular, the ovum and sperm cells must unite to form a single new cell, called a **zygote.** This happens when one of the father's sperm attaches itself to the surface of the egg. The attachment triggers a biochemical reaction on the surface of the ovum which prevents any further sperm from attaching and which allows the one remaining sperm to gradually penetrate into the ovum. Within a few hours, the walls of the sperm and the nucleus both begin to disintegrate, releasing the chromosomes of each former gamete into the new zygote. After a few more hours, a new wall forms around the newly combined set of chromosomes — all twenty-three pairs — and conception is complete. (See Figure 3-2.) At this point the zygote is still so small that hundreds of them could fit on the head of a pin, yet it

Fertilization

Figure 3.2   Gametes and Zygote

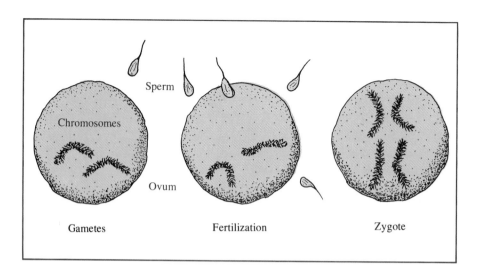

Sperm

Chromosomes

Ovum

Gametes   Fertilization   Zygote

contains sufficient genetic information in its DNA molecules to develop eventually into a human being.

Mitosis and Meiosis

Two kinds of cell division

Most cells produce living tissue by duplicating and dividing, a process called **mitosis.** The process begins with the chromosomes, which duplicate themselves and divide; then the two sets of chromosomes move to opposite sides of the cell. A wall forms between the two sets, and eventually two cells form from the one that existed before. This process goes on continually in all tissues of all human beings, from conception until death.

Gametes, however, form by a more complex process called **meiosis.** This process involves several steps: first the chromosomes duplicate, then they exchange segments with each other, then the cell divides, and then the two resulting cells divide again. The first division resembles mitosis, but the second division differs crucially: during this stage, the chromosomes do *not* duplicate but only divide evenly between the two new cells. As a result, gametes end up with only *half* the usual number of chromosomes carried by all other cells — just twenty-three chromosomes, instead of the forty-six contained everywhere else in the body. (See Figure 3-3.)

Combining genes from both parents

The single cell formed by conception contains the normal, larger number of chromosomes, since it combines the chromosomes of two gametes — one set from the sperm and one from the ovum — combine. Once the zygote forms, it and all its descendants divide by mitosis. Each cell of a developing child therefore acquires copies of the same forty-six chromosomes, and each cell thus contains the same set of genes, the same DNA molecules, and the same code or genetic instructions to guide its development. But even before birth, some cells "decide" to become legs, and others to become eyeballs, for reasons we do not completely understand. Apparently each cell uses its genetic information differently, depending on its physical and chemical relationships to other, neighboring cells.

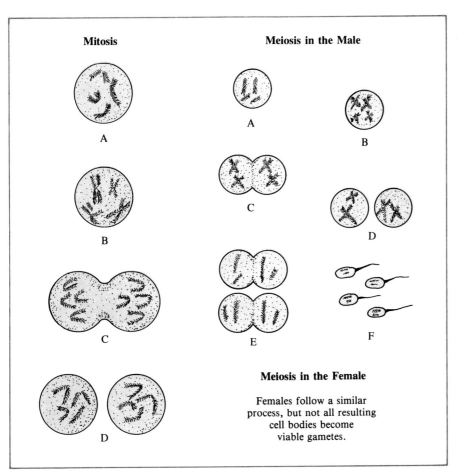

Figure 3.3   Mitosis and Meiosis

Mitosis

A

B

C

D

Meiosis in the Male

A

B

C

D

E

F

Meiosis in the Female

Females follow a similar
process, but not all resulting
cell bodies become
viable gametes.

Checkpoint   *Under normal circumstances, genetic information is transmitted through complex molecules called DNA, which are in turn organized into genes and chromosomes. Most bodily cells divide through a process called mitosis, in which the chromosomes duplicate each other. Reproductive cells, however, form cells called gametes. Gametes combine through a process called meiosis into cells that contain chromosomes from each parent.*

Individual Genetic Expression

As you may suspect, genetic information does not usually translate into a particular trait in a direct or simple way. For various reasons, genetic traits may sometimes be expressed only to a limited extent, or even not at all. This happens for a number of reasons.

Genetic transmission accounts for many of the similarities — physical and even behavioral — among relatives. But as with this family, it also accounts for some of the differences. (Alan Carey/The Image Works)

Genotype and Phenotype

Biologists distinguish between the **genotype,** which is the set of genetic traits inherited by an individual, and the **phenotype,** which is the set of traits the person actually displays during his life. The genotype therefore refers to a child's potential: to his inborn capacity to grow especially tall, to gain excess weight, or to pass blue eyes on to his children. The phenotype, however, refers to the child's actual appearance and behavior: to how tall the child actually becomes, how much weight he actually gains over the years, and whether he himself has blue eyes.

Phenotype results from the combined effects of genotypic potential and particular life experiences that modify that potential. As a result, it often does not coincide with genotype. For example, two newborn infants can have identical genotypic potential for height and weight, but one may end up heavier and the other may end up taller because one family feeds its baby more and the other family encourages more exercise. On the other hand, children may look alike — that is, have the same phenotype — even though they differ in potential, or have different genotypes. Two eight-year-olds who weigh the same may have achieved that

Influences on phenotype

weight in two different ways, one by dieting to lose weight and the other simply by eating whatever she wanted. In this case, genetic potential differs, but outward appearances are the same.

Even when phenotypic traits cannot be changed by daily activities, they may not coincide with the underlying genotype. A person who has brown eyes may or may not be able to have a blue-eyed child, because of genetic processes that do not appear in phenotypes.

Dominant and Recessive Genes

Some genes do not actually influence development unless they occur in matched pairs, one member of which originates from each parent. Eye color provides a good example. Pretend that human eyes only come in two colors, blue and brown. Most Caucasian children are born with blue eyes, but from about six months of age, a child's eyes remain blue only if he has received the appropriate blue-producing gene from both parents. If he receives it from one parent or from neither, he will end up with brown eyes. Why are blue eyes relatively uncommon? Because from a genetic standpoint, there are more ways to have brown eyes than to have blue ones. For these reasons, a trait like blue eyes is called recessive, because it recedes, or tends not to be expressed in the phenotype; and the genes governing it are **recessive genes.** The trait of brown eyes is called dominant, and its genes are **dominant genes.** Table 3-1 lists a number of common dominant and recessive traits.

Which genes influence development

Notice that dominant and recessive phenotypes convey different kinds of information about their underlying genotype. Generally, people with a recessive phenotype know more precisely what their genotype is, just by virtue of their recessiveness. In the case of eye color, a blue-eyed person (the recessive phenotype) knows that both the eye-color genes she inherited from her parents were blue-producing, or recessive, genes. A brown-eyed person (the dominant phenotype), however, only knows that his genotype is *not* fully recessive. His brown eyes can result from two dominant brown genes or from one dominant gene from either of his parents — three possible ways in all. Understandably, precise information (or its lack) about genetic makeup is important when doctors are diagnosing genetic diseases and abnormalities, many of which are recessive (Omenn, 1983).

Even for simple traits like eye color, though, the dominant-recessive distinction does not explain phenotype fully. Very few physical traits have a completely either-or quality. Not even eye color really does, for that matter — look carefully at all your friends, and you will see that a few probably have hazel or greenish eyes and some have darker brown eyes than do others. How can we account for variations like these?

Transmission of Multiple Variations

Our example of eye color assumed that the gene responsible for color can take only one of two forms, one corresponding to blue eyes and the other corresponding to

Table 3-1 Some
Common Dominant and
Recessive Traits

Dominant Trait	Recessive Trait
Brown eyes	Blue, hazel, or green eyes
Hazel or green eyes	Blue eyes
Brown or black hair	Blond hair
Blond hair	Red hair
Full head of hair	Bald-headedness
Curly or wavy hair	Straight hair
Normal color vision	Color blindness
Thick lips	Thin lips
Short fingers	Fingers of normal length
Double-jointed fingers	Normally jointed fingers
Immunity to poison ivy	Susceptibility to poison ivy
Normally pigmented skin	Albino (completely white) skin

Note: Many common traits show dominant or recessive patterns. Sometimes, too, a trait may be dominant with respect to one trait, but recessive in respect to another.

brown eyes. In reality, the gene for eye color can occasionally take a third form, which often leads to hazel eyes. These alternate forms of a gene are called **alleles.**

Since all human beings possess two sets of chromosomes, some inherit distinct forms for the same gene, whereas others inherit duplicate or identical forms. The first sort of person is called **heterozygous** and the second sort, **homozygous.** In the case of eye color, heterozygous persons tend to show the phenotype of the dominant allele and therefore have brown eyes. Only homozygous persons show the phenotype of one of the recessive alleles, and therefore have blue or hazel eyes. As discussed further below, though, not all examples of genetic transmission work this simply. Sometimes heterozygosity can lead to a unique phenotype that differs from any of those produced in purely homozygous individuals.

Matched pairs of genes versus mixed pairs

Multiple forms of genes

Many genes have more than two alleles, and when they do, the traits they govern can vary in more complex ways. The four major human blood types, for example, are based on three alleles of the same gene. Two of these are dominant forms, and one is recessive. The three alleles can combine in six possible ways to produce the four blood types. Each type has a unique chemistry that allows it to mix only with certain other blood types, so determining blood genotype matters quite a lot for medical patients who receive blood transfusions.

Not all alleles occur with equal frequency. One of the three alleles of blood type, for example, does not occur nearly so often as the other two do, and different parts of the population inherit the blood-typing alleles with different frequencies. Black people differ significantly from white people, for example, in the comparative frequencies of each of the major blood types. Because of such complexities, the phenotypes of many genetic traits sometimes seem arbitrary.

Polygenic Transmission

Unlike eye color and blood type, many traits apparently vary along a single dimension. Height shows this quality: very tall parents tend to have tall children and very short parents have short children, but a tall and a short parent most often have children of middling stature. This is because height differs from eye color in the way it is genetically transmitted. A person does not usually have "all" height or "none" of it, like she might have totally blue or brown eyes. Instead she has some amount — more or less of it.

Continuous distributions apparently result from the combined influence of many genes, each of which contributes a small part to a person's physical inheritance (Mather and Jinks, 1977). Because of their multiple sources, these traits are often called **polygenic,** meaning "coming from many genes." Many — perhaps most — physical traits are polygenic. In addition to height, skin color has this quality; so does hair color, and so does body weight. In all these cases, children show a marked tendency to have a phenotype that is intermediate between those of their parents. For example, the child of an American of German descent and an American of Chinese descent will tend to have a skin color between the shades of his parents. Notice, though, that this is only a tendency. A few children of very dark parents may look rather light-skinned, and vice versa, just as a few children of very short parents may tower above them, or vice versa. Such inconsistencies occur because parents at one extreme sometimes carry recessive genes for the other extreme. If the recessive genes combine during conception, then the child can look markedly different from his parents in that particular trait.

Combined influence of genes

Although psychologists disagree about how much genetics can determine psychological development, most agree that some genetic influence does occur, and that this influence is almost always polygenic. The potential to develop skill at taking intelligence tests, for instance, depends partly on genetic endowment. But the skill varies in amount among individuals; we each have more or less of it, not all or none of it, in spite of jokes to the contrary. And continuous variation occurs in behavioral styles, or what psychologists call temperament (Thomas and Chess, 1977). We all have greater or lesser tendencies to fidget when we are made to sit still for a long time; only a few people at one extreme can sit completely still for hours, and only a few at the other extreme are immediately climbing the walls.

Since polygenic phenotypes vary by small degrees, environment can influence them in relatively important ways. A light-skinned person can get darker by spending time in the sun; an overweight person can embark on a diet; and a fidgety person can teach herself to sit still for a longer time. Such experiences matter less to traits that are simply transmitted by a single gene; there is no way to change eye color, even though you can cover your irises with tinted contact lenses.

Effects of environment on polygenic traits

The Determination of Sex

One pair of chromosomes among the usual twenty-three pairs determines whether a child develops as a male or a female. In women this pair looks pretty much like any other pair of matched chromosomes. In men, though, one member of the pair

Chromosomes determine gender

Most physical traits result from the combined influence of many genes inherited from both parents — a fact that explains why children often have characteristics intermediate between those of their parents. (Carol Palmer)

is noticeably shorter than the other. The longer sex chromosome, in either sex, is called X, and the shorter one in men is called Y. Genetically normal men therefore always have a mixed combination, XY, whereas normal women always have an XX combination.

Whether a child becomes male or female depends on events at conception. All ova or egg cells contain a single X chromosome, whereas a sperm cell may contain either an X or a Y. If a Y-bearing sperm happens to fertilize the egg, then a male zygote develops, and if the sperm happens to be X-bearing, then a female zygote develops. Oddly enough, more Y sperm than X sperm succeed at fertilizing, even though they have no advantage in numbers. The Y advantage in success rate is considerable at conception, producing perhaps as much as 30 percent more male zygotes (Mittwoch, 1973). The advantage decreases during prenatal development; by birth, boy babies outnumber girl babies by only about 6 percent, although the ratio varies among different societies and racial groups. Later in life, the tables are turned; by about age thirty-five, women begin to outnumber men.

Genetic vulnerabilities of males

This trend suggests that males may be more vulnerable than females, at least genetically. Much of this vulnerability probably stems from the nature of the Y chromosome carried by all males. The Y chromosome is much shorter than its matching X chromosome and therefore may lack many of the gene locations of its matching X chromosome. In males, therefore, any genetic abnormalities on the single complete X chromosome may translate relatively often into phenotypic abnormalities. Most of these abnormalities are either fatal or else put the male

Table 3-2 *Sex-linked Recessive Traits*

Condition	Description
Color blindness	Inability to distinguish certain colors —usually reds and greens
Hemophilia	Deficiency in substances that allow the blood to clot; also known as "bleeder's disease"
Muscular dystrophy (Duchenne's form)	Weakening and wasting away of muscles, beginning in childhood
Diabetes (two forms)	Inability to make use of sugars digested by the body
Anhidrotic ectodermal dysplasia	Lack of sweat glands and teeth
Night blindness (certain forms)	Inability to see in dark or very dim conditions
Deafness (certain forms)	Impaired hearing or total hearing loss
Atrophy of optic nerve	Gradual deterioration of vision and eventual blindness

All of the above traits are carried by the X chromosome, and all are recessive. As a result, they occur only rarely in females.

fetus at serious medical risk. Female fetuses and infants possess a second X chromosome, and since it tends usually to be both normal and genetically dominant, women are protected from many of the genetic abnormalities common among men.

Note, however, that beyond childhood men may also die sooner than women for environmental reasons: they more often hold stressful or physically dangerous jobs, for example, and gender roles more often discourage them from attending to their medical needs when illnesses first develop. In recent decades, as more women have taken on traditionally male habits (like smoking) and entered traditionally male jobs, they have begun narrowing the gender gap in health and longevity.

Even so, the sex difference in longevity is probably partly genetic. This conclusion is supported by the rather large number of genetic abnormalities linked to genes on the X chromosome (Tobach and Rosoff, 1978). Table 3-2 lists a few of these, which are often called **sex-linked recessive traits.** One of these is **hemophilia,** an inability of the blood to clot and therefore to stop itself from bleeding. Hemophilia occurred widely in various royal families of Europe, where princes and kings frequently died because of it. Why were men more affected than women? Because hemophilia apparently derives from particular defective recessive genes on the X chromosome. Since women by definition always have two X chromosomes, they had to inherit two of the recessive, problem-causing genes before they actually suffered from hemophilia. Men, though, only needed to inherit one of the recessive genes, so they were more vulnerable.

Living with Hemophilia

Hemophilia is a genetic disorder that prevents blood from clotting properly. Children with the disease usually suffer from repeated episodes of internal bleeding, which are brought on by ordinary active play or occur for no apparent reason at all (Omenn, 1978). The episodes can be quite painful and long-lasting, and in severe cases the child must be hospitalized in order to receive transfusions of substances that help his blood to clot properly and therefore helps end the bleeding.

The disease is contracted almost entirely by males, since it is carried on the X chromosome that determines a child's gender. Since it is also recessive, women can carry the hemophilia genotype without getting the disease. They are "protected" by their extra X chromosome, which not only makes them genetically female but overrides the effects of the defective X chromosome. Women can guess that they are carriers only by noticing whether some of their male relatives have actually suffered from hemophilia.

That, in fact, is what one woman — call her Karen — deduced (Mattsson, 1983). Her father had lived with hemophilia all of his life, and both of Karen's sisters had given birth to hemophiliac boys. She suspected she was a carrier. Yet she wanted children, and she knew that as long as spouses are genetically normal, half of all offspring of carriers are neither hemophiliacs nor carriers themselves. When she was about to get married, therefore, she told her future husband of the genetic risk, so that all would be out in the open and honest. Her father, she emphasized, had lived to be sixty-four and had never complained openly about his condition; so she felt that her children could cope with it, too, if necessary. In any case, they might turn out perfectly normal. So Karen and her husband went ahead and conceived two children. As it turned out, both children were boys, Andy and Bill. And both were hemophiliacs.

By the time that Bill was ten and Andy was eight, Bill had been to the hospital about thirty times for transfusions, and Andy had gone about twenty times. The last of these twenty visits proved fatal for Andy; his bleeding was severe, and transfusions failed to save him. Naturally, this experience proved difficult for Andy's parents, but after a period of turmoil and grieving, family life seemed to return to normal. Three months after Andy's death, Bill moved back into the bedroom he had shared with Andy.

But Bill began doing poorly in school, and eventually his mother sought counseling for him. His worst subject was science. Why? "I don't much like hearing about the human body," he told the counselor. With a bit of further diplomatic probing, it became clear that he actually had considerable interest in the human body, and especially in the workings of hemophilia, which he understood poorly. Bill was convinced that he too would die young.

In this case, as in many others, talking with a counselor did help (Lewis and Lewis, 1983). After a year or so, Bill's schoolwork improved again, and he began talking of becoming a baker ("You can make good money and don't have to be afraid of getting hurt."). The counseling helped Bill's mother, too; she found herself more able to talk about Andy's life because Bill was talking about it more. Eventually, discussing Andy did not make her upset, as it had for so long. Looking back, she suspected that her own strong feelings about Andy's death had partially caused the topic to be suppressed and therefore had interfered with Bill's coming to terms with it. In the counselor's view, though, this was probably only part of the story. To some extent, Bill may have brought silence about Andy upon himself; after all, Bill had developed a strong, and in this case overlooked, attachment to Andy.

An individual's physical qualities (the phenotype) result from that person's particular combination of chromosomes (the genotype). The genotype in turn results from the relationships between dominant and recessive genes, both singly and in combinations. Sex is determined by one particular pair of chromosomes, the X and Y chromosomes, which also account for the greater incidence of certain genetic abnormalities in men than in women.

Genetic Abnormalities

Once in a while, genetic reproduction goes wrong. Sometimes too many or too few chromosomes transfer to a newly forming zygote. At other times, the chromosomes transfer properly but carry particular defective genes that affect a child physically, mentally, or both. The changes almost always create significant handicaps for the child, if indeed they do not prove fatal.

Variations in the Number of Chromosomes

Most of the time, inheriting one too many or one too few chromosomes proves fatal. One extra, after all, forces several thousand "wrong" genes on the developing fetus, and it would be surprising indeed if the fetus could cope easily with so much genetic misinformation. In a few cases, though, children with an extra or a missing chromosome survive past birth, and even live fairly normal lives. Three such cases are mentioned here; as it happens, each is named after the doctor who first published a description of it.

Down Syndrome   People with **Down syndrome** have an extra twenty-first chromosome, which causes them to have characteristic physical features: almond-shaped eyes, round heads, and stubby hands and feet, among others. More important, they show some degree of mental retardation, although usually not enough to keep them from learning to manage a good deal of their own lives or from holding routine jobs; nor does it prevent them from having agreeable dispositions. Unfortunately, people with Down syndrome also show greater-than-usual vulnerability to a number of serious diseases; for instance, they have twenty times the usual chances of contracting leukemia, a type of cancer of the bone marrow tissue.

An extra twenty-first chromosome

Down syndrome occurs in about one baby in every six or seven hundred in the human population as a whole. Probably it happens much more frequently than this at the time of conception, but significant numbers of affected fetuses do not survive until birth. The condition occurs much more often in babies of older mothers (over forty years) and very young ones (under eighteen). Recent genetic studies show that the age of the father may matter as well — older fathers have

Children with Down syndrome, like these two girls, learn academic material only very slowly. But with special educational help and proper social support, they can lead very satisfying lives. (Meri Houtchens-Kitchens/The Picture Cube)

more risk — but the effect is not as obvious as in the case of mothers (Arehart-Treichel, 1981). Older fathers may produce larger numbers of defective sperm because they have had longer exposure to environmental hazards. Older mothers experience longer exposure to hazards as well and in addition face another problem: their ova were all formed before birth. By the time mothers reach their forties, therefore, their ova have been waiting several decades to be released by their ovaries, and many may have begun to deteriorate during this period.

A single X chromosome

Turner's Syndrome   A person with **Turner's syndrome,** which affects only women, has a single X in the sex chromosome instead of the normal XX. The single X results in a female who is short — around four or five feet tall. Her neck tends to be short as well, and extra folds of skin give it a webbed appearance. A woman with Turner's syndrome has ears that are set lower than usual. When she reaches puberty, she tends not to develop secondary sexual characteristics such as breasts and pubic hair. She does show basically normal intelligence as defined by conventional IQ tests, with one proviso: she may have serious difficulties at solving problems that require spatial visualization, such as finding her way through a maze.

In the population as a whole, this condition is much less frequent than Down syndrome; only about one in 3,500 adult women have Turner's syndrome. As with other genetic abnormalities, though, the numbers are higher if we measure from conception instead of from birth or among adults; abnormal pregnancies account for much more than their share of spontaneous abortions.

An extra X chromosome

Klinefelter's Syndrome   Instead of missing a sex chromosome, a person with **Klinefelter's syndrome** has at least one extra one, most commonly an extra X, to create an XXY pattern. Such a person is phenotypically male, but he tends to have small testes even after puberty and to remain sterile throughout life. In contrast to the short, squat build of a Turner's syndrome woman, the Klinefelter's syndrome man tends to be long-legged, and he often develops small breasts. Overall, Klinefelter's syndrome affects about one in 500 newborn males.

Abnormal Genes

Even when a zygote has the proper number of chromosomes, it may inherit specific genes that can create serious medical problems for the child after birth. In many cases these prove lethal. But not always; here are three that are at least manageable, if not fully curable.

Rh Disease   **Rh disease** (or *erythroblastosis*) is a condition in which the mother's blood develops antibodies which attack the red corpuscles of a fetus' blood, thereby weakening or even killing the fetus before it is born. The problem is caused by a substance in the blood called the **Rh factor** (named after *rh*esus monkeys, in whom it was first discovered). The dominant form of this factor is called *Rh positive,* which is the form that most individuals inherit. The recessive (and less common) form is called *Rh negative.*

Rh disease occurs when a man who is Rh positive conceives with a woman who is Rh negative. In most of these conceptions, the child inherits the dominant, positive form of the Rh factor, and a small amount of the children's blood crosses the placenta into the mother's own bloodstream. This causes no problem for the first baby, but this pregnancy stimulates the mother to form antibodies to Rh positive blood, as if the positive blood were actually a harmful foreign substance. This process resembles what happens when a person's blood forms antibodies to fight off viral illnesses, but in this case the mother's immune system has mistakenly identified the fetus' blood as harmful.

How Rh disease occurs

Later pregnancies suffer from the antibodies formed during the first pregnancy: the mother's antibodies attack the red blood cells of later fetuses. The severity of the attack varies, depending on the amount of Rh positive blood which crosses the placenta in both the first and second pregnancies, and on the general health of the mother. Until the early 1960s, Rh disease used to kill about 10,000 infants each year and caused various birth defects in at least twice this number (Butnarescu and Tillotson, 1983).

Since the 1960s, however, new medical techniques have made Rh disease very rare. Infants at risk can now be given blood transfusions before they are born, even through the walls of the mother's uterus. And the mothers themselves can be inoculated shortly after the birth of their first infant with Rh negative blood that already contains antibodies (called **Rhogam blood**). This treatment seems to prevent Rh negative mothers from forming any further antibodies which might jeopardize future pregnancies. When Rhogam blood is given to the mother, any antibodies that she has already formed usually disappear within a month or two after birth.

Managing Rh disease

PKU   **Phenylketonuria (PKU)** is a disorder that severely diminishes a child's ability to utilize a particular amino acid, called phenylalanine, which is found in milk and milk products and is essential to normal nutrition and growth. The disorder is caused by a single recessive allele carried by a relatively small fraction of people; but since it is recessive, many people are carriers without realizing it. Left untreated, PKU causes phenylalanine to build up to dangerous levels in the child's blood and spinal fluid, which can eventually lead to brain damage and mental retardation.

Prevention of PKU through diet

A carefully planned diet during infancy and childhood, though, can prevent these problems if PKU is diagnosed early in infancy (Ambrus et al., 1978). In recent years, therefore, many hospitals and states have routinely tested all newborns for this condition, and they have had dramatic success at preventing the effects of it. This strategy has helped individual children and their families, but of course it has not removed the gene that causes the problem in the first place.

PKU shows clearly the difference between genotypes and phenotypes. Infants with one particular genotype — the PKU deficiency — can grow either into a healthy phenotype or get sick enough to die, depending on the nutrition they receive. On the other hand, infants who differ in PKU sensitivity can end up with similar phenotypes: both normal and sensitive babies can be healthy genetically when conditions are right.

Sickle-Cell Anemia   By now you may be wondering why nature tolerates so many harmful genetic abnormalities. Don't they disappear as the generations go by, simply because people with abnormalities have such serious health problems? Even in societies with modern medical services, genetically different people have a harder time than most in simply surviving.

Sickle-cell anemia suggests one possible answer to this question: sometimes a genetic condition may benefit people in general even though it hurts individuals in particular. **Sickle-cell anemia** is a condition in which a person's red blood cells intermittently acquire a curved, sickle shape instead of having the usual circular shape. The condition is not harmful if only a small proportion of blood cells become sickle-shaped, but a large proportion can clog circulation in the small blood vessels, because the cells literally cannot squeeze through the tiny channels.

Explanations for sickle-cell anemia

Sickle-cell anemia is caused by a single recessive allele of a gene that is especially common in people living in tropical climates, such as Africa and the Middle East. But therein lies a clue to its real "purpose." The gene that causes the anemia also confers increased resistance to malaria, an especially troublesome disease in tropical areas. It does so, though, only among people with a particular genotype: those who carry just one unmatched sickle-cell allele, along with one dominant, non-sickle-cell allele.

In the case of this condition, heterozygous individuals have a few signs of sickle-cell anemia but strong immunity to malaria, which is probably a large benefit to their health at a relatively small physical cost. Homozygous people either avoid anemia completely, by having two dominant genes, or suffer badly from it, because they have two recessive genes. Either way, they contract malaria at very high rates. As it turns out, very large proportions of individuals in tropical areas are heterozygous. The troublesome allele seems to have been "invented" for their benefit — and at the expense of people who contract anemia. This is not very democratic, perhaps, but it is functional for the population as a whole.

Huntington's Chorea A **chorea** is a gradual deterioration of the nervous system which leads to increasingly jerky, involuntary movements. **Huntington's chorea** appears only after about thirty-five years of age, and it always proves fatal. Before that age, a person usually has no way of knowing whether he will get the disease.

Unlike most genetic diseases, Huntington's chorea is carried by a dominant gene rather than a recessive one. By their nature, diseases carried by dominant genes usually disappear after a number of generations, since they usually cause the carriers to die before reaching child-bearing age. Since Huntington's chorea appears late in life, however, individuals have been able to confer the unwelcome gene on their offspring before they know that they have the disease, so this particular dominant genetic disorder has persisted.

Tay-Sachs Disease **Tay-Sachs disease** is a disorder of the nervous system that occurs mainly among infants of Jewish people of Eastern European descent. In the United States, about one Jewish person in thirty carries the gene for this disorder, but since the gene is recessive, only about one Jewish infant in nine hundred develops the disease, or even less. Nevertheless, this still constitutes a serious genetic concern (Muir, 1983).

Tay-Sachs disease disturbs the chemical balance in an infant's nerve cells. At birth the baby may seem fairly normal, but by about six months of age she may show poor tolerance for sudden loud noises and seem weak and slow to develop. Motor skills that she initially acquires may later be "forgotten" or lost, and the baby becomes progressively more apathetic and irritable. Eventually, deterioration of the nervous system may cause convulsive seizures and lead to deafness and blindness. Most Tay-Sachs babies die by their third birthday. Ironically, though, they may actually die from a much more common illness, such as pneumonia, simply because their condition has robbed them of their bodily resistance to illness.

Checkpoint *Down syndrome, Turner's syndrome, and Klinefelter's syndrome are genetic abnormalities caused by the presence of too many or too few chromosomes. Other abnormalities — the Rh blood allergy, PKU syndrome, sickle-cell anemia, and Huntington's chorea, among others — result from abnormal genes within otherwise normal chromosomes. In some cases, genetic abnormalities can be predicted and treated; in others, they can only be predicted; and in still others, they can be neither predicted nor treated.*

Relationships Between Heredity and Environment

Most psychological traits and behaviors result from both genetic and environmental influences. As we have seen, genetic processes themselves can be rather complex. They probably set limits on development, but the limits vary in subtle ways among individuals and are sometimes hard to determine precisely. Environment,

How much of the resemblance between this mother and daughter is due to heredity, and how much due to environment? Note the similarities in their body postures, and even in their smiles. (Melissa Shook/The Picture Cube)

on the other hand, may affect how closely an individual reaches his genetic limits. Since environment includes everything external to a person — food, family life, school, political events, and the like — it can influence a person with the same degree of subtlety and complexity that genetics can.

Untangling the precise, relative effects of heredity and environment has become the special focus of **behavior genetics,** the scientific study of the relationship between genotype and phenotype, especially with regard to complex human behaviors such as intelligence, personality, and mental health. For both ethical and practical reasons, behavior geneticists can manipulate human environments in only limited ways, and they cannot reliably manipulate human genetics directly. They have therefore devised other ways to study the relative influence of heredity and environment on development, including observations of species-wide behaviors, studies of animal breeding, and studies of genetics within families.

Observations of Species-wide Behavior

Many behaviors seem to come naturally — without learning — to every member of a species. Young goslings, for example, will follow almost any moving object as soon as they are able to move, a behavior that biologists have called **imprinting**

(Lorenz, 1960). The moving object does not have to be an adult goose; a mother chicken will attract them just as well, or even a motorized robot. For several reasons, imprinting seems to be hereditary. First, all goslings can be imprinted as newborns, before they have had any experiences to teach them the behavior. Second, imprinting occurs only during a rather short, well-defined period after birth — what biologists and psychologists call a **critical period.** And third, once imprinting occurs, it is irreversible; goslings get stuck, so to speak, on the first large moving object that they happen to see.

Significance of species-wide behavior

A broad range of animals, including humans, exhibit species-wide behaviors. Some psychologists believe, for example, that smiling may be genetically programmed, since even deaf and blind infants smile. And some think that a capacity to acquire language may be genetically programmed, since nearly all children learn their first language easily without any explicit effort by their parents.

Genetic predispositions

Note, though, that the animal or human must have certain experiences for even the most universal behaviors to develop properly. Goslings may be genetically ready to imprint on any moving object, but only experience can provide them with that object. If by chance their environment contains nothing moving during the first few days of their lives, the goslings will never learn to follow anything. All children may be predisposed to smile, but some eventually learn to smile much more broadly and more often than others do. And all infants may be genetically ready to acquire language, as shown by the universal tendency to babble. But a few infants — notably those who are deaf — never actually hear spoken language, so their speech becomes impaired.

Lessons from Animal Breeding

Studies of animal breeding consistently suggest the combined effects of heredity and environment. In one classic study, for example, psychologists produced a strain of "maze-bright" rats and another of "maze-dull" rats by selective breeding, similar to the methods used by professional animal breeders (Tryon, 1940; Lindzey and Thiessen, 1970). They began with a group of fairly average laboratory rats, which they tested for their skill at learning a maze; that is, the psychologists counted the errors each rat made as it repeatedly navigated the runways of the maze. Eventually every rat learned the maze perfectly, but some took much longer than others to do so. Over several generations, the "bright," fast-learning rats were allowed to breed only with one another, and the "dull" rats were allowed to breed only with other slow ones. Eventually, the two groups diverged widely in the maze-learning skill: even the dullest of the bright rats outperformed the brightest of the dull ones.

Breeding for specific traits

All hope was not lost, though, for the dull rats. Later research showed that the rats differed only in the way that they had been bred to differ — that is, in their ability to learn a particular sort of maze (Searle, 1949). If the rats had to press a lever to get food, both groups learned at about the same rate. The breeding experiments, then, apparently did not show that a generalized skill — a sort of animal IQ — follows the same genetic rules as physical characteristics or simple inherited behaviors. Current research shows similar patterns for a whole barnyard of animal species, including ducks, chickens, mice, cats, and cattle (Simmel and Bagwell, 1983).

Adjusting environments

Related experiments on animals have suggested that the proper environment can make animals more "competent." Laboratory rats and mice, for example, seem to benefit from being kept in a cage enriched with extra objects to handle and chew, interesting nooks and crannies to explore, and the like (Krech et al., 1962, 1966). Such animals learn mazes more quickly as a result of their "better upbringing," regardless of their original level of skill. As with humans, though, the animals show wide individual differences in spite of their equally improved environments.

Pros and cons of animal studies

For psychologists, studies of the genetics of animal behavior have both advantages and problems. They have the obvious advantage of speed: animals, especially rats and mice, can create new generations in weeks instead of years. And psychologists do not need to concern themselves deeply with the ethics of their matchmaking; presumably rats do not really care which rat they mate with. But studying animals carries the risk of **anthropomorphism,** the tendency to imagine that animals think, feel, and behave in the same ways that humans do. Fast-learning rats may at first seem to show "intelligence" in the human sense of the term, but closer observation suggests other interpretations. Perhaps the "maze-bright" rats were just more impulsive physically, and therefore less apt to sniff their way around a maze in a way that an observer might interpret as "taking wrong turns."

Nevertheless, the essential conclusions of these studies have been supported widely by current research on several species of animals (Simmel and Bagwell, 1983). For animals, learning a particular skill depends on both inheritance and the proper opportunities. As the following section shows, this idea applies to people, too.

Genetics Within Families: Twins and Adopted Children

Identical twins (those that develop from one fertilized egg) provide one sort of natural experiment for comparing the effects of heredity and environment. By developing from one egg, they offer two individuals with the same genetic endowment. Any differences between them therefore probably reflect the influence of environment. The catch is to find twins who grow up in different environments that are

"Natural" experiments on heredity and environment

different for one twin than for the other; usually parents and society offer twins similar experiences, thus compounding their pre-existing genetic similarity. Still, twins sometimes do grow up with very different life experiences, particularly if they grow up in separate families because of the death of their parents.

Unrelated children adopted into a family provide another sort of natural experiment for comparing the effects of heredity and environment. These children share environments with their adopted siblings and parents, even though they have completely unrelated genotypes. Differences between adopted children and their adopted relatives therefore should tell something about the influence of their genetic differences. Such comparisons are far from precise, though, because fam-

Because the twins in the photo above are identical, they share entirely the same genotype, and differences between them reflect differences in their environments. The twins shown at left, however, are fraternal and therefore are no more genetically alike than ordinary siblings. (above, Muffy Friend; left, Susan Lapides)

ily members never live in exactly the same environment; one sibling may be encouraged to wash dishes whereas another may be urged to study especially hard.

In spite of these limitations, studies of twins reared apart and of adopted children have shed considerable light on the relative contributions of heredity and environment to human development. General intelligence as measured by standardized IQ tests, for example, shows both hereditary and environmental components. Close relatives tend to have more similar IQ scores than distant relatives do, and relatives of any type have more similar scores if they live together than if they live apart (Nichols, 1978; Bouchard and McGue, 1981). Adopted children score more closely to their biological parents than to their adopted parents (Skodak and Skeels, 1949; Honzik, 1957).

Influence on intelligence

Taken together, these facts suggest that heredity plays a significant role in determining general intelligence. The relative amount of influence, though, has caused a good deal of debate. Some psychologists argue that intelligence is mostly inherited (Jensen, 1969, 1978), but most argue that relative influence cannot, in principle, be decided. No one seriously doubts that heredity plays some significant role (Scarr and Carter-Saltzman, 1983).

Perspectives on Research

Being Twins

Tom was a twin in his thirties. He described his relationship with his brother, Tim, this way: "In social activities . . . I'm more willing to talk and do things when we're together than when I'm alone, because Tim and I, thinking alike and doing things alike, at least I've got Tim that's there to back me up, to do the same thing, join in the conversation" (Ainslie, 1985, p. 23).

Twins do tend to share more activities, attitudes, and values than ordinary siblings. As infants, they spend more time together than other siblings do, and perhaps as a result, infant twins often seem well tuned in to each other's needs and activities. If they discover an interesting new toy, for example, they quickly learn to share it comfortably, and show relatively little of the possessive tug-of-war common among other infant peers. As schoolchildren, they continue to see more of each other than siblings generally do, partly because they are the same age and therefore share similar interests and partly because society expects them to share experiences and spend time together. Schools may place twins

in the same class, on the assumption that they need each other in order to function well academically.

As Tom's comments indicate, twins sometimes do need each other for emotional support, but perhaps they don't need each other as much as is commonly believed. One study investigated this possibility by asking twins to complete a standardized personality test in two ways, first by describing themselves and then by describing the way they expected their twin to answer it (Vandenberg, 1979). In this case, twins described themselves as more similar than they really were. The effect occurred in both fraternal and identical twins, but it was especially strong among identical twins.

The widespread belief in their similarity can cause twins problems as they mature. Take Vicki and Valerie, who were attractive identical twins (Ainslie, 1985, p. 137ff). In high school, only Vicki was nominated for their school's beauty-queen competition ("They *choose* you," said Vicki, "you don't really volunteer to enter"). The nomination precipitated awkwardness between the two

Comparisons of twins reared apart, in fact, suggest that a wide variety of personal behaviors and traits are at least partially hereditary. Many twins who grew up separately report liking the same sorts of foods, for example, and the same sorts of clothing. Often they independently adopt similar hair styles, use their free time for similar recreations, and laugh at the same sorts of jokes. What makes these similarities surprising is that twins do not need to live together to acquire them (Bouchard, 1981).

But experience also creates differences between such twins. Each twin may dislike strange dogs, for example, but one of them will show the dislike much more openly than the other will. Or each twin may enjoy reading and school learning, but only one of them may have the money or encouragement from family to attend college. A difference in education may in turn create long-term differences in occupations and careers.

Nonetheless, the similarities between twins reared together are often striking. Some of the resemblance may result from similarities in environments: separated twins often are adopted by different branches of their family, and as a result they may experience similar lifestyles. But environments probably do not account for

---

girls. Why had only one been chosen, when everyone agreed that they looked virtually alike, and even had similar personalities? For months the girls discussed this question unsuccessfully. "If my figure was like yours," Valerie said on one occasion, "I could have run in the contest." But both knew that such explanations made little sense, since the difference in their figures was so small that even close friends and relatives often could not see it.

Perhaps as a result of experiences like this, some twins gradually become rather different in personal values, behaviors, and activities. The process might be called "niche-picking," since each twin finds a special psychological niche, or place, to call his own. As adults, for example, Tom and Tim became noticeably different in sociability; Tom became progressively quieter ("I guess most people would call me shy now"), and Tim became progressively more outgoing. This development helped to reduce the constant comparisons that the twins had had to endure when they were younger.

In general, twins remain strikingly similar throughout life, but not all of these similarities stem from the force of common experiences and social expectations, as implied by the examples above (Juel-Nielson, 1980; Farber, 1981). This conclusion follows from studies that compare twins who have been wrongly classified — many parents, it turns out, are mistaken about whether their twins are identical or fraternal. These parents sometimes go for years believing that their children are identical when they are really fraternal, or vice versa.

What happens when parents rate these children for similarity of personality? Not surprisingly, they rate true identical twins as more similar than true fraternal twins. What is surprising, though, is that they also rate false fraternals as more similar than false identicals; that is, parents' ratings depend on their twins' *real* status and not on the status that their parents attribute to them (Vandenberg, 1979). This implies that similarity between twins develops independently of parents' expectations, at least to some extent.

all similarities that have been found, since **fraternal twins** (those that develop from two separately fertilized eggs) do not show the same degree of resemblance when they are reared separately (Cassill, 1982).

Genetics Within Families: Infant Temperament

Temperament refers to the styles of behavior shown by individuals in a variety of situations: whether they like to race around getting things done, or whether they act emotional in response to others' comments. A variety of studies clearly show genetic influence on temperament in young infants, well before the babies have had much time to learn unique behavioral styles.

Consider, for example, the tendency to smile. Some infants smile more quickly and frequently than do others, or for longer periods of time. Young identical twins, it seems, are rather similar in their smiling styles: they tend to smile at the same sorts of stimulation and at similar frequencies, even within the first few months of life. Compared to fraternal twins, in fact, identical twins are significantly more alike in smiling behavior (Freedman, 1976). And identical twins show similar responses to strangers: they both become about equally anxious, or equally curious (Plomin and Rowe, 1979). Again, the fraternals differ more markedly from each other than do genetically identical twins.

Some aspects of temperament are inborn

Parents certainly report differences in their infants' temperaments even when the babies are newborn. One major study of parents' reports, for example, identified nine dimensions along which parents said that their babies differed (Thomas and Chess, 1977, 1981):

1. *Activity level*   How much does the baby move around?
2. *Rhythmicity*   How much does the baby's need for food, sleep, and elimination follow a regular, clockwork schedule?
3. *Approach-withdrawal*   How much does the baby seem drawn by novel stimuli and new situations, instead of withdrawn from them?
4. *Adaptability*   How easily does the baby adjust to new situations and new people in her life?
5. *Intensity of reaction*   How expressive or strong are the baby's emotional reactions — does she laugh instead of smile, or whimper instead of howl?
6. *Threshold of responsiveness*   How sensitive is the baby to stimulation — does she require a lot before she responds?
7. *Quality of mood*   How much of the time does the baby seem happy versus fussy?
8. *Distractibility*   How well does the baby pay attention to an ongoing activity in spite of other stimulation going on around her?
9. *Attention span*   How much does the baby stay with one activity of her own accord, instead of shifting repeatedly from one to another?

By studying these dimensions, Thomas and Chess found three general patterns of temperament. They called the first of these "easy" babies, because they showed mostly positive moods, regular body functions, and good adaptation to new situa-

Although infants vary widely in temperament, most adopt a relatively "easy" style of responding, which allows parents to meet their needs more reliably and completely. (Cathy Cheney/EKM-Nepenthe)

tions. The second group, the "difficult" babies, showed the opposite: negative moods, irregularity, and high stress in new situations. A third group, the "slow to warm up" babies, resembled the difficult ones but were less extreme: they were negative and relatively unadaptable, but did not react violently to new stimuli. As we might expect, many babies did not fall neatly into any of these groups.

Since these differences emerge immediately after birth, some psychologists believe they result at least partly from genotypes. The original classification of temperaments, though, depended partly on a biased source of information: parents' reports about their newborn children. Later research has tried to guard against parental bias by phrasing interview questions as precisely as possible (Rothbart et al., 1981) — by asking how often an infant smiles, for example, instead of how cheerful he is. But the parental bias persists. One study found that fathers with insecure, anxious temperaments tended to describe their babies in relatively favorable terms (Goldsmith and Campos, 1982), as easy and happy children. There is no way to know what to make of this. Were their babies indeed happy, or just happier than the fathers? Or were these fathers just unusually pleased to have children?

Parental bias

Given these uncertainties, it is not surprising to find that infant temperament often changes in infancy and childhood (Thomas and Chess, 1981; Feiring et al., 1980). That is, difficult newborns may become easy toddlers, and (unfortunately)

Changes in temperament

easy newborns may become difficult toddlers. Such changeability may not mean that temperament has no genetic basis, but that it has a strong environmental basis as well. As common sense might suggest, some changes in temperament may result from the child-rearing efforts of parents. But other characteristics may persist, whether the parents like them or not, and indirectly shape the relationships between children and their parents (Kagan, 1983).

Sociobiology

Research on breeding and on species-wide behaviors has helped to create the relatively new field of **sociobiology,** which studies the biological and genetic basis of social behavior, including human social behavior (Wilson, 1975). Sociobiologists have proposed that many familiar human behaviors may really constitute **genetically transmitted response strategies,** inborn tendencies or styles for responding to important social situations. These response strategies, they argue, may govern such diverse things as forming attachments between parents and children, handling personal conflicts, selecting a sexual partner, forming and maintaining work groups, and deciding whether to perform acts of kindness. The inborn strategies, however, are not specific behaviors, since cultures and societies around the world obviously differ in how they carry out each of these activities. Rather, it is general tendencies or types of behavior that are inborn; that is why sociobiologists call them strategies.

The Genetics of Altruism   To help understand these ideas, consider how sociobiologists might explain why parents are so often altruistic, that is, willing to make sacrifices for their children. Why, for example, do parents cuddle their babies affectionately, even after they have fussed and cried for impossibly long times? Why do parents literally give up sleep if their children are sick or distressed? Why do parents spend hard-earned (and often scarce) money on their children, and often give up their favorite adult recreations to care for them?

The general public — and many psychologists — regard these behaviors as learned: society (supposedly) encourages and rewards parents for being generous with their time and energy, and as a result parents learn to act this way. When they become parents, adults learn to give up certain personal satisfactions. They do so because society (supposedly) rewards them with an even greater satisfaction, the knowledge that they have "done right" for their children. In this popular view, parents are made, not born.

Sociobiologists agree that people do indeed learn to be parents. But they also argue that parental altruism may constitute a genetically transmitted response strategy (Mellen, 1981). Parents, that is, may have an inborn tendency to help their children, even though they probably learn specific methods for helping from their culture. If the disposition is biologically based, it may have evolved because it helps to maintain the parents' genetic heritage: even in prehistoric times, helpful, self-sacrificing parents may have produced children who were healthier and more skilled, and therefore more likely to reproduce themselves successfully. Because of their genetic advantage, then, a line of relatively self-sacrificing parents became

Margin notes:

Genetically transmitted response strategies

Are parents born or made?

established. Over the very long run of evolution, in fact, people with a "self-sacrificing" genotype may have come to outnumber those with other sorts of genotypes. The whole process probably happened without any parents (or children) realizing it; today, according to sociobiologists, parents cannot help but be helpful.

Inclusive Fitness In this and other examples, sociobiologists argue that biological evolution does not promote any one genotype, but instead promotes **inclusive fitness,** or an entire lineage of genotypes (Wenegrat, 1984). Some individuals can therefore inherit specialized roles that actually may not improve their own welfare as long as the roles further the survival of the species as a whole. Inclusive fitness, then, explains why parents give up so much for their children: it promotes the long-run continuation of the human race even after the parents themselves age and die.

Inclusive fitness also accounts for other features of family relationships, such as sibling rivalry and the demands children place on their parents (Ortner, 1983). From the parents' standpoint, if they divide care equally among all their offspring, they will optimize the chance that their children will collectively survive and reproduce the parental genotype successfully. From the standpoint of any one child, however, the genetic lineage stands the best chance of being transmitted if she receives as much parental attention and care as possible; in that way, that child (and her genes) stands the best chance of developing successfully and of eventually reproducing. Parents and children therefore have a natural conflict of interest: children always want more care and attention than their parents are prepared to give. And in the child's view, her siblings always seem to be the reason she does not get the attention she feels she deserves.

Criticisms of Sociobiology The idea of genetically transmitted response strategies has been criticized in at least two major ways. First, critics argue that the viewpoint leaves little room for human variation. If parental altruism is inherited, why are some parents *more* altruistic than others? Why do some show so little altruism, in fact, that they even abuse their children? In response to this criticism, sociobiologists note that genetic lineages evolve and not individuals. This means that variety among individuals remains possible throughout evolutionary history: even though a lineage of people may be rather altruistic as a whole, some individuals may be rather selfishly inclined, and some may be excessively altruistic. Such variations occur by means of the genetic mechanisms described earlier in this chapter.

Second, critics sometimes fear that sociobiology leaves little room for ethical behavior or other expressions of human free will. If altruism is inborn, then it does not seem to count, ethically speaking, as a good deed. In response to this idea, sociobiologists argue that the concept of genetically transmitted response strategies is neither good nor bad, but a bit of both. Inborn strategies exist, they say, both for negative behaviors (such as waging conflicts with a sibling) and for positive ones (such as acts of kindness). Given the wide genetic variation among individual human beings, and given the broad range of experiences from which human beings can learn, free will does seem to have a place in the sociobiological framework.

The question of free will

Sociobiologists argue that they have not done away with freedom of choice; rather, they have merely pointed out some of its limits.

Personality and Heredity

Not only infant temperament, but also certain features of personality show genetic influence. Judged by written personality tests, for example, identical twins resemble each other more closely than fraternal twins do. Identicals are more closely matched in their levels of **extroversion,** which is the tendency to be outgoing and interested in things and people other than yourself (Eaves and Eysenck, 1976). And identicals are more closely matched in levels of anxiety and fearfulness.

Heredity may create these similarities directly, as it seems to do with infant temperament. Or it can contribute indirectly, by creating unique environments for children with unique genotypes. Consider two pairs of twins. Claire and Yvette are fraternal twins, and perhaps because of this they score more differently on standardized tests of school achievement than Carl and Nicholas, who are identical twins. Over a period of time, these children's differences in school performance lead their parents and teachers to offer them different educational opportunities. Claire, who seems brighter, gets more special attention during class than her twin, Yvette. In first grade, Claire is placed in the top reading group in her class, while Yvette ends up in the bottom group. Because Carl and Nicholas seem more similar to begin with, however, they are put in the same reading group — the middle one. By the end of the year, Claire has not only learned to read significantly better than Yvette has, but she seems more confident as well. Carl and Nicholas, in contrast, continue to seem rather similar both in achievement and in self-confidence.

Genetic differences may have affected the original levels of academic performance of these children. But as time went on, experiences increased these differences through a **self-fulfilling prophecy:** teachers and parents responded to beliefs about each child's capacities and arranged experiences for each in response to these beliefs. In this indirect way, genotype influenced phenotype, even over a rather long period.

Mental Illnesses and Disturbances Serious mental illnesses reveal genetic influences. One such illness is **manic-depression.** A manic-depressive person experiences extreme alternations of mood, sometimes feeling very elated and excited, then shifting suddenly to a period of deep depression or despair. Manic-depressive conditions run in families in ways that are somewhat independent of the personal relationships among family members (Claridge and Margan, 1983). Family members do not share the condition just because they share the same conglomeration of family conflicts and tensions. This does not mean that family conflicts and tensions play no role in mental illness; it only means that they are not the only cause.

How do we know? One reason is a phenomenon called **concordance,** or the tendency for pairs of close relatives to become mentally ill. Identical twins show much stronger concordance than fraternal twins do. If one twin becomes manic-depressive, the chances of his sibling also becoming manic-depressive are substantially higher if that sibling is an identical twin rather than a fraternal one. This fact

Indirect influences on personality

Relatives' tendencies toward similar illnesses

suggests that genetic endowment may somehow affect an individual's tendency to become manic-depressive. But it does not prove that the influence is direct. As we have seen, at least some genetic influences are rather indirect.

Hereditary patterns also occur in **schizophrenia,** a common, severe mental disorder with a number of symptoms (American Psychiatric Association, 1980; Dierden, 1983). The thinking of schizophrenics often seems fragmented or incoherent; in conversation, they may shift topics suddenly and unaccountably, and with no apparent awareness that a shift has occurred. Schizophrenics may suffer from delusions of persecutions ("Everyone is out to get me!"), and they may experience hallucinations, such as voices that seem to be speaking to them. When the disorder is at its worst, it may also involve a blunting or flattening of feelings. The person's face and voice may convey little expression of any kind, although sometimes inappropriate feelings burst out at unexpected moments. For example, a schizophrenic person may laugh loudly about a painful early memory.

Concordance among schizophrenic relatives is strong, and it is particularly strong among especially close relatives. If one member of a pair of identical twins becomes schizophrenic, her twin sibling has thirty times the usual chances of becoming schizophrenic herself (Gottesman, 1978). The condition traces through biological families more consistently than through adopted families; children placed for adoption show high concordances with their biological siblings and parents, not with their adopted families. In other words, a healthy child adopted into a schizophrenic family shows no special likelihood of becoming ill herself. Unfortunately, the converse is also true; a child from a schizophrenic family acquires no special protection through adoption into a normal family.

Accounting for such trends has stimulated much research but led to few definite answers (Erlenmeyer-Kimling, 1978). Current professional opinion tends to favor a predisposition hypothesis. According to this viewpoint, future schizophrenics may differ metabolically — and therefore genetically — in ways that make them more likely to become ill. But the illness itself may only occur under unusual, rather stressful circumstances. No single gene or chromosome has been found to mark schizophrenics or their metabolism clearly, but certain differences in bodily chemistry have been found and are suspected to play a role in predisposing individuals toward schizophrenia. In this way mental illness differs from Down syndrome, which is clearly associated with a particular, observable chromosomal error. With schizophrenia, instead, analysis of genes remains ambiguous, and we cannot know for sure who will become ill.

Cautions about the Genetics of Human Behavior   The genetics of personality suggests the power and influence of hereditary mechanisms in human development. Unfortunately, the role of heredity does not show it in ways that are precise enough for professionals who are providing services to people in need. All the concordances and mechanisms described above occur very indirectly indeed, if judged from the perspective of a single, developing individual. Often they refer only to small parts of the population, and even then, they deal only in probabilities. For both ethical and practical reasons, professionals in the human services cannot afford to rely on such imprecise information about individuals. Even if a profes-

Ambiguous multiple causes

sional knows that schizophrenia runs in a client's family, for example, he does not know whether a particular sibling of a schizophrenic child will eventually become mentally ill.

Checkpoint *Research both on animals and on children closely related to each other (such as twins) suggests that heredity and environment cause development jointly rather than independently. Some of the clearest examples of joint influence exist for the development of human intelligence, but evidence also exists for personal temperament and other individual traits.*

Genetic Counseling

Some genetic problems can be reduced or avoided by sensitive counseling for couples who may carry genetic disorders. Couples in need of such counseling may know of relatives who have suffered from genetic diseases, or they may belong to an ethnic group at risk for a particular disorder, as black Americans are at risk for sickle-cell anemia. More immediate signs of genetic risk include the birth of an infant with some genetic disorder or the spontaneous abortion of earlier pregnancies.

Genetic counselors should be thoroughly trained both in genetics and in working with other professionals, since the counselor must have complete access to a

Difficulties in estimating risk

couple's medical and genetic history in order to help them estimate their chances of having a healthy baby. Making such estimates may be harder than it first appears, because couples (and their doctors) do not always know all the genetically relevant information, such as what diseases various relatives experienced in past generations. Of course, estimates of risk may be even harder for couples to live with than for counselors to make, since the parents must face considerable uncertainty about the fate of their future child. Nonetheless, it is probably better to decide whether to risk conception on a basis of knowledge, rather than ignorance.

Once the actual genetic risk is clarified, counselors can recommend alternatives from which a couple can choose. The two most obvious alternatives, of course, are to avoid conception completely or to take the chance of conceiving a healthy baby. Modern medical techniques sometimes offer two further options: prenatal diagnosis and possible abortion, and medical treatments early in infancy. The usefulness of these techniques, however, depends on the specific genetic problem, and all four alternatives have certain drawbacks.

Prenatal Diagnosis

Sometimes genetic disorders can be detected after conception but before birth. Blood tests of a couple, for example, can determine their infant's risk for Rh disease or Tay-Sachs disease. Blood samples can even be drawn from the fetus itself, through the mother's womb, to aid in this diagnosis.

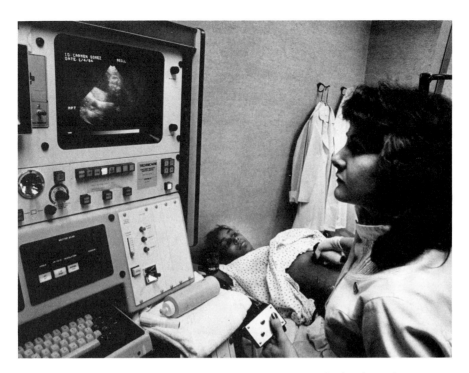

In the photo above, ultrasound helps a mother to "see" her unborn child on a television screen. In the photo at left, amniocentesis is under way; it will indicate whether the fetus's chromosomes are normal. (above, David Whitbeck/The Picture Cube; left, Andrew Brillant/The Picture Cube)

Amniocentesis is another diagnostic method, which can detect abnormalities in the fetus's chromosomes well before birth. The method involves drawing and analyzing a tiny amount of the amniotic fluid in which the infant floats during pregnancy. This fluid contains cells that have the fetus's genetic makeup rather than the mother's, so it can be used to determine whether the fetus has abnormal chromosomes, as children with Down syndrome or neurological disorders do.

Ultrasound allows medical personnel and parents actually to view the fetus by projecting high-frequency sound waves through the mother's womb. The sound waves apparently cause no harm to either mother or fetus. When they bounce off the fetus, medical equipment uses the echoes to create a television image of the child, in much the way that sonar works. The resulting image often helps to determine whether the fetus is oriented properly for birth with its head down; but it can also help determine whether the child has approximately normal limbs and external and internal organs.

Perspectives on Issues

Genetic Screening and Counseling for All Couples?

The risks of genetic disorders, and the advantages that sometimes result from knowledge about them, make some professionals propose that all couples should receive screening and counseling, regardless of their personal history or particular situation. In fact, mass screening has occasionally been tried for selected genetic problems in the United States. In 1976, for example, Congress passed a law requiring all citizens to be tested for vulnerability to sickle-cell anemia, and several states even began to implement this law (Nyhan, 1976).

But this screening program and others like it have created considerable ethical debate. Critics argue that mass screening constitutes an invasion of privacy, since it requires disclosing personal medical information to public agencies. According to this viewpoint, individuals and couples should be free to choose whether or not to participate in any particular screening program. If a couple is at risk for sickle-cell anemia, Tay-Sachs disease, or any other genetic disorder, then no one but that couple should decide whether to make the fact public.

But advocates of mass screening also have ethical reasons for their position. The suffering caused by genetic disorders, they point out, affects many people besides the child. Parents and relatives also suffer, both psychologically and often economically as well, in their efforts to care for a permanently disabled child. And the medical profession uses up valuable resources in managing and treating a disabled child — resources that are scarce and could be used in other ways for the greater good of society. Since genetic disorders affect so many people for such long periods, some argue that society has a right to demand mass screening.

Those favoring mass screening also argue that an effective screening program pays for itself by reducing human misery and increasing health and overall productivity. They also point to widespread ignorance about genetic risks. Surprisingly large numbers of couples apparently do not know of or understand even the most common genetic problems, such as Rh disease and the risk of Down syndrome for older mothers (Massarik and Kaback, 1981). Since many couples are at risk without knowing it, a universal screening program might

Medical personnel can combine these techniques with information about a couple's genetic background to make more precise predictions about whether a particular pregnancy will end with a normal, healthy baby. Note, though, that prenatal diagnosis may not detect certain kinds of problems. Huntington's chorea is carried by a single gene and therefore escapes all current methods of prenatal diagnosis, and fetuses destined to get this disease look quite normal not only before birth but for a long time thereafter. Note too that even a clear diagnosis of a genetic disorder presents couples with an agonizing decision about abortion (Schowalter et al., 1983). If they continue the pregnancy, they know they will encounter a lifetime of special responsibilities as parents; if they abort, they may regret losing the baby or feel that they have abandoned their responsibilities. On the other hand, they may believe that they have acted responsibly in protecting their child from a painful or abnormal life and in protecting society from the burden of special care.

---

help these individuals and produce a healthier society in the process.

Unfortunately, given the number of known genetic disorders, truly universal screening may not be practical, even if it were ethical. Many couples would be tested unnecessarily; those who missed a particular test would have to be tracked down; and taxpayers would have to pay for all this activity. A more practical approach might be to screen only specific groups known to be at high risk. Amniocentesis, for example, currently tends to be used only for the very oldest mothers. Only blacks might be tested for sickle-cell anemia, and only Jews might be tested for Tay-Sachs disease.

This strategy might work for some genetic disorders, but focused screening can create unnecessary, negative stereotypes about the groups targeted for screening (Falek, 1975). Testing Jews for Tay-Sachs disease could create the impression that most Jewish people have this disease, when in fact only a small minority do. Routine testing for sickle-cell anemia in fact eventually ended for a similar reason. Black leaders argued that the program made black people seem more universally afflicted by sickle-cell anemia than they really are; in doing so, the program amounted to a subtle form of genocide, because black couples were indirectly being discouraged from conceiving children, even when they were free to do so.

Genetic counseling also has its share of ethical problems. Rightly or wrongly, some couples feel that their medical and genetic backgrounds are their own business, and no assurances of confidentiality by counselors can make them feel otherwise (Money, 1975). Other couples oppose counseling for religious reasons; even if they know that they are genetically at risk, they are unwilling in principle to abort a pregnancy. At best, counseling simply wastes their time; at worst, it coerces them. Counselors can avoid these problems, of course, by working only with volunteers. But then they fail to reach some couples who might actually welcome counseling, if only they knew how and where to get it. Apparently, no strategy of screening and counseling, whether universal or voluntary, works perfectly.

Early Medical Treatments

If a couple does decide to continue an abnormal pregnancy to term, medical treatments can sometimes alleviate or even eliminate certain genetic disorders. As we have already discussed, the effects of PKU can be avoided by careful planning of an infant's diet, so as to avoid the particular amino acids that PKU babies cannot utilize. And Rh disease can be treated even after it affects a pregnancy, by giving

---

A Talk with a Genetic Counselor

The Role of Genetic Counseling

Gail Farmer is a genetic counselor at a university medical center. She was interviewed in her office, which is located next to the cytogenetics laboratories.

INTERVIEWER: What does a genetic counselor do?

GAIL: Genetic counselors work with three main groups of people: families who don't have any children at all yet and are not pregnant; people who are currently pregnant and who want to know what their risk is of having a child with a genetic condition; and families with either a child or adult member who has already been immediately affected by a genetic condition.

Based on their family medical history and life circumstances, genetic counselors help assess what their risks are of having children with genetically related problems. We explain the condition and recommend prenatal tests, where appropriate. We help the family reach the best decision for them given their particular religious, cultural, and emotional situation. We help them cope with the decision they do make and remain available to help them live with those decisions. In addition, we provide training and education for professional and non-professional groups, including support groups of families with genetic difficulties.

INTERVIEWER: Can you give an example?

GAIL: Yes. Jewish people of ... Eastern European, background have a one-out-of-thirty chance of carrying a gene for Tay-Sachs disease, as compared with only one in three hundred in the general population.

INTERVIEWER: What effects does Tay-Sachs have?

GAIL: Tay-Sachs is a very severe neurological condition that is lethal by the age of four for a child. The child is born looking normal and develops normally during the first few months, but then begins progressive deterioration until [he or she dies]. It involves a deficiency in an enzyme that is necessary for neurological development. There is as yet no cure and no way to give enzyme therapy for this. It happens to be inherited in a recessive fashion, which means that both parents must carry the information for their children to get it. A simple blood test will identify whether parents are carriers or not.

INTERVIEWER: How does a family deal with the knowledge that they have a Tay-Sachs gene? What decisions do they face?

GAIL: Well, if a couple comes in and they are both found to be carriers, we discuss with them all of their reproductive options. The first is to go ahead and take their chances and have their own children.

INTERVIEWER: A calculated risk.

GAIL: Right. They have a 25 percent, or one-in-four, chance of having a child who inherits double recessive genes for Tay-Sachs and is therefore affected. Two out of four times a child will inherit only one recessive gene for the disease and become a carrier, and one out of four times no Tay-Sachs gene will be inherited.

INTERVIEWER: What if a pregnancy has already occurred?

GAIL: In this case prenatal diagnosis is possible by means of amniocentesis during the fifteenth or sixteenth week of pregnancy. An enzyme test then determines if Tay-Sachs is actually present. A newer test called a chorionic villi biopsy has recently become available at specific medical centers. It samples the chorionic membrane that is

the fetus blood transfusions through the wall of the mother's womb. If necessary, transfusions can also be given to the newborn infant.

More often than not, however, genetic disorders cannot be cured or controlled this well. Couples at genetic risk need to face this fact and decide what they want to do about it (Lebel, 1978). Genetic counselors cannot make these choices for couples. Instead, they must lay out the facts and alternatives, and offer support for whatever choices the couples end up making.

Treat or not?

---

produced between the eighth and tenth week of pregnancy.

INTERVIEWER: What is the advantage of this earlier test?

GAIL: If a couple decides to terminate the pregnancy, it is much easier during the first rather than second trimester. There has been no fetal movement for the mother to feel at this point, and not as much emotional bonding with the infant. The father is also generally less involved with the infant.

INTERVIEWER: What other reproductive options are available?

GAIL: Another option is artificial insemination, which takes away the risk of the father's gene for the Tay-Sachs, presuming that it is known that the donor's sperm does not carry the gene for the disease. Sperm donors are screened quite well at this point in time, but there is no 100 percent guarantee that there might not be some other condition present.

INTERVIEWER: Are there additional options?

GAIL: Yes. You can offer such a family a surrogate mother, that is, contract with another woman to carry their child. In this case, although the father's sperm which

would have the Tay-Sachs gene would be used, it would be with a surrogate mother who is known not to be a Tay-Sachs carrier. Another option is in vitro fertilization. Here you can use the father's own sperm and the egg of a female donor. The fertilization would occur in a test tube, but the mother would physically carry the child—a baby who would be certain not to have Tay-Sachs. There are, of course, psychological issues associated with each option.

INTERVIEWER: If a couple decides to go ahead and have a baby which ends up being affected by a genetic problem, what difficulties do they face?

GAIL: Well, for Tay-Sachs, although there are not immediate problems, the baby will die at a very young age. In the case of Down syndrome, 50 percent of Down babies have heart problems, and one out of eight such babies has gastrointestinal problems. That means surgery, so if a couple has prenatal tests and finds out they are carrying a Down syndrome child and decide to have it, it might be advisable to prepare for it.

INTERVIEWER: What are the long-range problems with managing a

child that has a genetic problem such as Down syndrome or phenylketonuria [PKU]?

GAIL: Well, because Down children are born with a whole extra piece of chromosome number 21, virtually all of them have subnormal intelligence quotients, or IQs. Since the top range of intellectual ability for Down children overlaps a little bit with the bottom range of normal intellectual functioning, there are in some cases Down syndrome individuals who are able to live and work in a sheltered workshop environment and earn their own keep and ride a bus and handle their own money. But it takes a lot of effort to help even this higher-functioning group to achieve that.

Follow-up Questions

1. How does the inheritance pattern for Tay-Sachs illustrate the concept of phenotype and genotype in genetic expression?

2. Why is an understanding of dominant and recessive genes important in genetic counseling?

3. What are some of the psychological issues associated with each of the various options discussed by Gail Farmer? What are some of the ethical issues?

Genetics and Developmental Psychology

In spite of its limitations, knowledge of human genetics contributes to human welfare in two ways. First, it clarifies the origins of many behaviors (Kaplan, 1976). According to conventional wisdom, behaviors are either simply "learned" or simply "inborn"; human genetics suggests instead that many of them are actually both. Second, knowledge of genetics can suggest realistic limits to how much to expect from many ordinary life experiences. How much can education really make people "more intelligent"? How much can parents expect a child with an active temperament to learn to be quieter? After learning the complex answers that genetics usually gives to questions like these, professionals can, and should, shift attention to individuals: How can we know whether *this* child will develop normally, or whether *that* one will experience a chronic disorder? For these more personal questions, we need more knowledge of individual development, such as that offered by genetic counseling. Such an orientation is also provided by other branches of developmental psychology, which we describe in the following chapters.

Summary of Major Ideas

Mechanisms of Genetic Transmission

1. Genetic information is contained in a complex molecule called deoxyribonucleic acid (DNA).

2. Most bodily cells produce tissue by simple division of their genes, chromosomes, and other cellular parts by means of a process called mitosis.

3. Reproductive cells, or gametes, divide by a process called meiosis, and recombine into a zygote at conception.

4. The process of meiosis gives each gamete half of its normal number of chromosomes; conception brings the number of chromosomes up to normal again, and gives the new zygote equal numbers of chromosomes from each parent.

Individual Genetic Expression

5. A person's phenotype is the pattern of traits that the person actually shows during his or her life.

6. A person's genotype is the set of genetic traits inherited by the person; it depends on the pattern of chromosomes and genes inherited at conception.

7. Although most genes exist in duplicate, some — called dominant genes — may actually influence the phenotype if only one member of the pair occurs.

8. Recessive genes do not influence the phenotype unless both members of the pair occur in a particular form.

9. Many genetic traits are transmitted by the combined action of many genes.

10. Sex is determined by one particular pair of chromosomes, called the X and Y chromosomes.

Genetic Abnormalities

11. Some genetic abnormalities occur when an individual inherits too many or too few chromosomes.

12. The most common abnormalities of this type are Down syndrome, Turner's syndrome, and Klinefelter's syndrome.

13. Other genetic abnormalities occur because particular genes are defective or not normal, even though their chromosomes are normal; examples are the Rh blood allergy, PKU syndrome, sickle-cell anemia, and Huntington's chorea.

Relationships Between Heredity and Environment

14. Studies of animal breeding show that heredity and environment operate jointly to affect problem-solving skills in animals.

15. Studies of identical twins and of adopted children suggest the joint operation of heredity and environment.

16. Observations of infant temperament suggest that babies may be born with somewhat individual temperaments or styles of emotional reaction.

17. Certain personality traits, such as extroversion, and certain mental illnesses, such as schizophrenia, may be inherited to a certain extent but they also are substantially influenced by environmental experiences.

Genetic Counseling

18. Experts on genetics can provide parents with information about how genetics influences the development of children, and about the risks of transmitting genetic abnormalities from one generation to the next.

19. Several methods now exist for diagnosing genetic problems before a baby is born, such as amniocentesis, ultrasound, and various blood tests.

20. After a child is born, some genetic abnormalities are treatable with current medical techniques.

21. Given the permanence and importance of genetic problems when they occur, genetic counselors should help couples to reach informed decisions about their pregnancies that take personal circumstances into account, as well as scientific information.

Key Terms

gametes *(80)*	homozygous *(86)*
sperm *(80)*	polygenic traits *(87)*
ovum *(80)*	sex-linked recessive
genes *(80)*	traits *(89)*
chromosomes *(80)*	hemophilia *(89)*
deoxyribonucleic acid	Down syndrome *(91)*
(DNA) *(81)*	Turner's syndrome *(92)*
amino acids *(81)*	Klinefelter's
zygote *(81)*	syndrome *(92)*
mitosis *(82)*	Rh disease *(93)*
meiosis *(82)*	phenylketonuria
genotype *(84)*	(PKU) *(93)*
phenotype *(84)*	sickle-cell anemia *(94)*
recessive genes *(85)*	Huntington's
dominant genes *(85)*	chorea *(95)*
alleles *(86)*	Tay-Sachs disease *(95)*
heterozygous *(86)*	behavior genetics *(96)*

anthropomorphism *(98)*	schizophrenia *(107)*
sociobiology *(104)*	amniocentesis *(110)*
manic-depression *(106)*	ultrasound *(110)*
concordance *(106)*	inclusive fitness *(105)*

What Do You Think?

1. Does our society overrate or underrate the impact of genetics on human development? Does genetics affect our lives more than we care to admit, or less than most of us realize? Explain your opinion.

2. How would you feel if you had a child with Down syndrome? What do you think would be your first reactions? (If possible, you might also discuss this question with some parents who really did give birth to such a child.)

3. Are modern medical techniques unwittingly maintaining many hereditary disorders, by keeping many abnormal children alive now who in the past might have died? If so, does this pose an ethical problem?

For Further Reading

Anderson, J. Kerby. *Genetic Engineering.* Grand Rapids, Mich.: Zondervan, 1982.

Walters, William, and Singer, Peter. *Test-Tube Babies.* New York: Oxford University Press, 1982.

Both books discuss current and future methods of artificial reproduction, and the many practical and ethical issues surrounding them. The first book concludes that artificial methods of genetic control should be used only sparingly, if at all; the second conveys more hopeful optimism.

Massarik, Fred, and Kaback, Michael. *Genetic Disease Control: A Social Psychological Approach.* Beverly Hills, Calif.: Sage Publications, 1981.

This book discusses ways of using current knowledge about genetics in order to reduce the frequency and severity of genetic diseases. It evaluates programs in general public education, as well as programs in individual genetic counseling. Overall, it finds that such programs are worthwhile although not always ideally effective.

Wenegrat, Brant. *Sociobiology and Mental Disorder.* Reading, Mass.: Addison-Wesley, 1984.

The author describes the sociobiological viewpoint: how principles of evolution can be used to explain various important human behaviors. He then suggests how many mental disorders can be understood as specific deviations from biological and evolutionary norms.

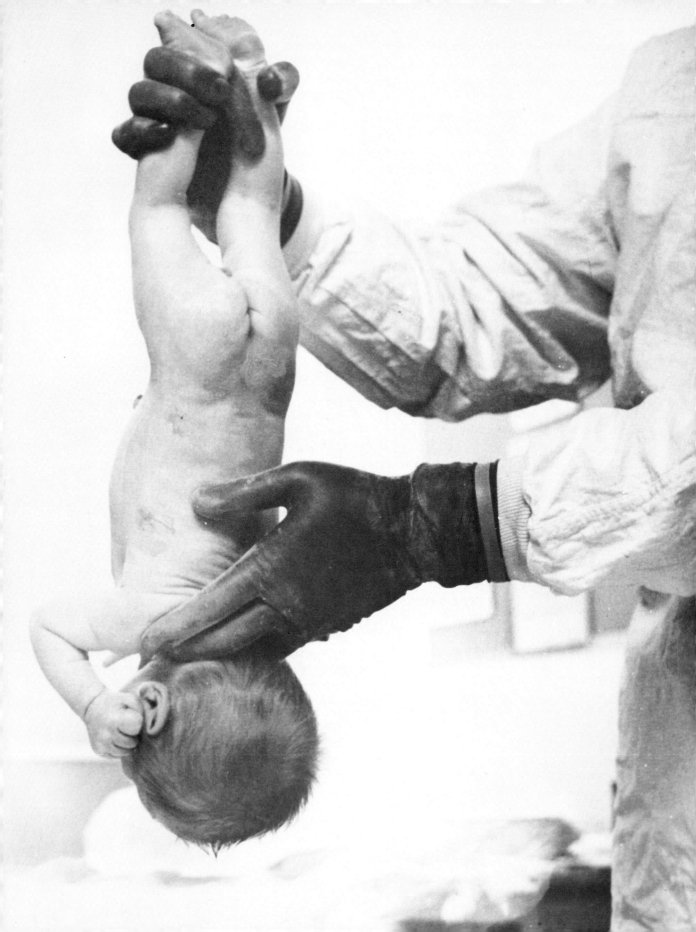

Chapter

4

Prenatal Development and Birth

Focusing Questions

- Sometimes it seems very easy to get pregnant, and other times it seems very difficult. Exactly what conditions must be met for conception to occur?
- What are the three stages of development that occur between conception and birth, and what important changes occur during each?
- What prenatal risks may the developing baby be exposed to during a typical pregnancy?
- In what ways, if any, is it necessary for an expectant mother to change her life-style?
- How long do each of the three stages of the birth process take, and what happens during each?

FROM THE MOMENT of conception, a child becomes a biological possibility, even if the one-celled zygote's status as a human being is ambiguous. Early during its nine months inside the womb, a fetus acquires all the essential human physical features, and some rudimentary human behaviors as well. It is influenced by changes in its environment, by its own rapid physical growth, and by the well-being of its mother and the stresses and supports that affect her. Altogether, these internal and external influences create a truly unique person.

How do microscopic cells become people? In this chapter we describe the events and processes of development before birth, pointing out how these developments affect the child after birth. We also look at some of the risks and problems of prenatal development and of birth, and at their long-term impact on the child.

Early Stages of Development

In the section that follows, we shall see that prenatal development begins with conception and then, just like later development, divides into discrete periods or stages. The first is the **germinal stage,** or period of the ovum, which occurs during the first two weeks of pregnancy; the **embryonic stage** lasts from week 3 through week 7; and the **fetal stage** lasts from the eighth week until birth.

Conception

Let us look first at the microscopic actors of prenatal development, the gametes that we described in Chapter 3. One of them is the **ovum,** or egg cell. The egg cells develop in two small, almond-shaped organs, the ovaries, which normally release one egg cell during each menstrual cycle. The egg travels down one of the fallopian

Egg cells develop in the ovaries

tubes toward the uterus, where the baby will develop. The opening of the uterus, the cervix, connects to the woman's vagina, which receives the male's penis during intercourse and, upon ejaculation, the male's reproductive cells.

Egg cells begin to develop well before a girl begins having menstrual cycles or is otherwise ready for intercourse. At birth, in fact, a girl's ovaries contain several hundred thousand ova, which are already partially developed. Many of these degenerate or die, though, during the dozen or so years before the girl begins menstruating, and many more fail to mature fully after that. So a woman ends up with a relatively small, fixed supply of potential ova (Butnarescu and Tillotson, 1983). In this respect she differs markedly from a man. (See Figure 4–1.)

Male reproductive cells are called **spermatozoa,** or sperm cells. They develop in the testes, which are located in the bag of skin called the scrotum, underneath and behind the penis. The sperm get a late start compared to ova; the testes do not begin producing sperm in quantity until puberty, or about twelve to fourteen years after birth. They soon make up for lost time, though, by producing literally millions of sperm, and production continues relatively undiminished well into a man's old age. Each sperm cell has a head and a long tail, rather like a tadpole, that helps it swim through the female reproductive organ. (See Figure 4–1.)

Sperm cells develop in the testes

To create a **zygote** — a fertilized egg cell — at least one sperm cell from the man has to find and penetrate one egg cell from the woman. That moment marks **conception.** Even though potential parents may consider conception all too easy to accomplish, from the gametes' point of view the job is extremely challenging. For a couple to conceive successfully, every one of the following conditions must be met:

1. The ovaries must release one healthy egg cell.
2. The egg cell must migrate most of the way down the fallopian tube.
3. A large supply of sperm cells must be deposited as far as possible up the vagina, preferably at or near the cervix.
4. At least some of the sperm must swim the right way instead of the wrong way — that is, up through the uterus to the fallopian tubes.
5. At least some of these sperm must survive the journey, even though the woman's uterus is slightly acidic and therefore toxic to sperm.
6. A few sperm must reach the ovum.
7. One sperm must penetrate the ovum to form a zygote.

Conditions necessary for conception

Timing is crucial in this process. The ovum normally lives only about twenty-four hours after it is released, and the sperm only about forty-eight (Harris, 1983). These limits give a couple about three days, or seventy-two hours, each month when intercourse is likely to result in conception and pregnancy. The period lasts from about two days before the egg is released (the sperm can survive that long) until about one day afterward (when the egg dies). This fertile period usually occurs about halfway through a woman's menstrual cycle, but it may happen at some other time.

Timing is critical

Other, less direct factors also affect whether conception occurs. For example, some men produce much denser concentrations of sperm than others do, although

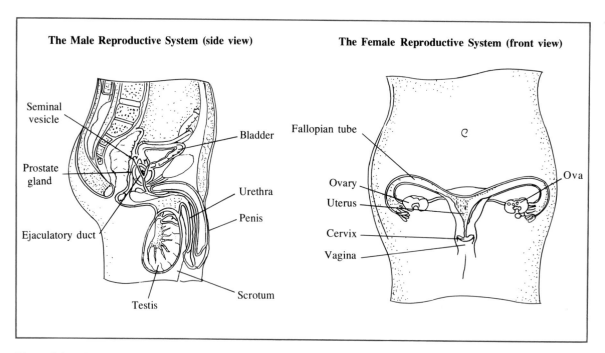

The Male Reproductive System (side view)

Seminal vesicle

Prostate gland

Ejaculatory duct

Testis

Bladder

Urethra

Penis

Scrotum

The Female Reproductive System (front view)

Fallopian tube

Ovary

Uterus

Cervix

Vagina

Ova

Figure 4.1   Male and Female Reproductive Systems

even a relatively low concentration usually contains more than enough gametes to insure conception if the sperm can just get to the ovum (Silber, 1980). The numbers of sperm are also reduced considerably if intercourse has already occurred recently — say, within the previous twenty-four hours. And conception becomes less likely if either partner is relatively old, meaning over about forty years (Silber, 1980). Age apparently diminishes the man's concentration of sperm somewhat; more important, it may lead to an increased number of defective gametes in either the man or the woman. Stress can also reduce the chances of conception. This can happen in the obvious way, by discouraging lovemaking in the first place, or more mysteriously and indirectly, by somehow preventing ovulation or implantation of the zygote.

All these influences can amount to either obstacles or protections, of course, depending on whether a woman wants to become pregnant. Either way, they can be frustrating because of the indirectness with which they operate. And either way, getting pregnant can prove as difficult for some couples as it is easy for others.

The Germinal Stage

Once a sperm and ovum join successfully, the resulting zygote begins to divide and redivide. The original cells form a tiny sphere called a **blastocyst,** which looks something like a miniature mulberry or raspberry. After about three days, the blastocyst contains about sixty cells; but these become smaller at the same time as they become more numerous, so the blastocyst is still scarcely larger than the original zygote. While these divisions occur, the blastocyst floats down the remainder

Cell division and changes

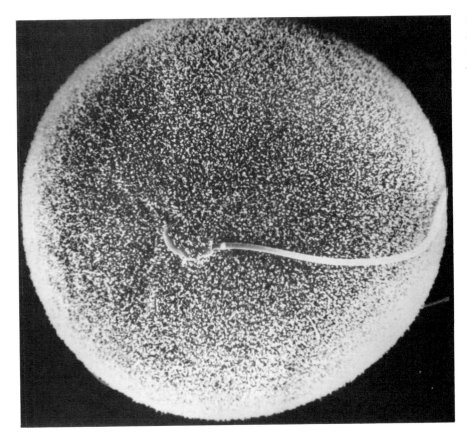

Conception occurs when a sperm cell penetrates an ovum, or egg cell. Almost immediately the wall of the new zygote changes so that no other sperm can enter. (Fawcett/Phillips/Photo Researchers)

of the fallopian tube, helped in part by gentle squeezing motions similar to the digestive motions of the intestines.

The blastocyst, which is filled with fluid, rapidly undergoes a number of important changes. The cells along one of its sides thicken to form the **embryonic disk,** out of which the baby will eventually develop. The blastocyst also differentiates into three different layers: an upper layer, or **ectoderm,** which later develops into the epidermis (outer layer of skin), nails, teeth, and hair, as well as sensory organs and nervous system; the **endoderm,** or lower layer, which becomes the digestive system, liver, pancreas, salivary glands, and respiratory system; and, somewhat later, the **mesoderm,** which becomes the dermis (inner layer of skin), muscles, skeleton, and circulatory and excretory systems. In a short time, the placenta, the umbilical cord, and the amniotic sac (to be discussed shortly) will also form from blastocyst cells.

After a few more days — about one week after conception — the blastocyst adheres to the wall of the uterus. The attachment is called **implantation,** since the blastocyst literally buries itself like a seed in the wall of the uterus. (See Figure 4–2.) Implantation is made possible by threadlike **villi,** which are produced by the outer layer of blastocyst cells, called the **trophoblast.** The fully implanted blastocyst is now referred to as the **embryo.** Implantation takes about another week to occur fully, so it is complete at about the time that the woman might expect

*Figure 4.2 The
Germinal Stage of
Prenatal Development*

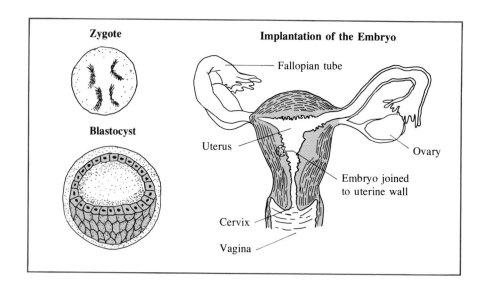

another menstrual period. It also signifies the end of the germinal stage and the beginning of the next phase of prenatal growth, during which the developing child begins to grow differentiated cells.

The Embryonic Stage

Growth during the embryonic stage (and the fetal stage that follows) exhibits a **cephalocaudal** (head to tail) as well as a **proximodistal** (near to far) pattern of development. Thus the head, blood vessels, and heart — the most vital body parts and organs — begin to develop earlier than the arms, legs, hands, and feet. Figure 4–3 illustrates some of these changes in slightly simplified form. Already the heart is beating; inside, the embryo already has a small digestive system and a nervous system. Since it measures only about one inch long, its parts do not have fully adult shape, but they are nonetheless unmistakable (Harris, 1983).

Structures supporting the embryo While these developments occur, a **placenta** forms between the mother and embryo. This is an area on the uterine wall through which the mother can supply oxygen and nutrients to the child and the child can return waste products from her bloodstream. In the placenta, thousands of tiny blood vessels from the two circulatory systems intermingle; although only minute quantities of blood can cross the separating membranes, nutrients pass easily from one bloodstream to the other, some of them pushed actively from one to the other as if by a sort of pump, and others floating freely through the vessel walls by a process called **osmosis.** Fortunately for the baby, many toxic chemicals and drugs in the mother do not spread easily by osmosis. Contrary to a common belief, though, many others do spread in this way; at most the placenta simply slows the passage of such chemicals to the embryo. Often the man-made chemicals seem harmless, but as we discuss later, they can sometimes also prove devastating to the child.

The embryo is connected to the placenta by the **umbilical cord,** which consists of three large blood vessels, one to provide nutrients and two to carry waste products

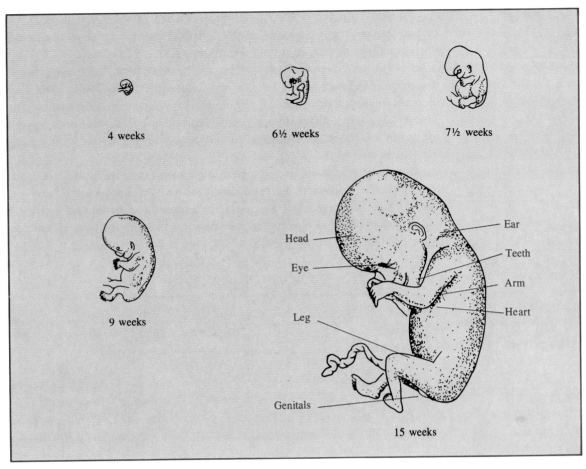

4 weeks

6½ weeks

7½ weeks

9 weeks

Head

Eye

Ear

Teeth

Arm

Heart

Leg

Genitals

15 weeks

Figure 4.3 Development During the Embryonic and Fetal Stages

into the mother's body. The cord enters the embryo at a place that becomes its belly button, or navel, after the cord is cut following birth. The cord contains no nerves, so cutting it hurts neither the mother nor the child. For the same reason, no neural signals or messages can pass through the cord between mother and child before birth, even though they certainly communicate in other ways.

By the end of the eighth week, an **amniotic sac** has developed. The sac is a tough, spongy bag filled with salty fluid that completely surrounds the embryo and serves to protect the future baby from sudden jolts and to maintain a fairly stable temperature. The baby floats gently in this environment for nine months, protected even if its mother goes jogging, sits down suddenly, or takes a walk in a snowstorm.

The Fetal Stage

After about eight weeks of gestation, the embryo develops its first bone cells, which mark the end of structural differentiation. At this point the embryo acquires a new name, **fetus,** and begins the long process of developing relatively small features, such as fingers and fingernails and eyelids and eyebrows. Their smallness, however, does not make them unimportant; for example, the eyes experience their major growth during this stage of development. The fetus's newly developing eyelids fuse shut at about ten weeks, and do not reopen again until the eyes themselves are essentially complete, at around twenty-six weeks.

Landmarks of fetal development

Not only the eyes, but most physical features become more adult-looking during this period, and more truly human in proportion (Harris, 1983). The head becomes smaller compared to the rest of the fetus's body (even though it remains large by adult standards) partly because the fetus's long bones — the ones supporting its limbs — begin growing significantly, so its arms and legs look increasingly substantial.

By the third month the fetus is able to spontaneously move its head, legs, and feet. If its palm is touched, it exhibits a grasp reflex by closing its fist; if the sole of its foot is touched, its toes will spread (Babinski reflex); and if its lips are touched, it will respond with a sucking reflex (see Chapter 5). In addition, the fetal heartbeat

---

Perspectives on Issues

Alternatives to Normal Conception

Approximately 10 percent of all couples cannot get pregnant, either because of medical problems or because they are simply unlucky. Earlier in this century, the only alternative for such couples was to adopt a child. Now, though, medical techniques offer at least three additional options (Staurovsky, 1983). These vary in practicality and popularity, but from a strictly medical standpoint, they all work fairly reliably.

The most common alternative is **artificial insemination.** This method involves inserting sperm into the woman's vagina, either on or near the cervix, and holding the sperm in place for a few hours. The male donor is usually *not* the husband of the woman, because studies have shown that inserting the husband's sperm in this way is in most cases no more effective than normal intercourse (Silber, 1980). Instead, the donor remains anonymous. In practice, donors are often male medical students or interns who are easily accessible to doctors and who are physically and mentally fit. Usually they are paid for providing their sperm, but they never learn who receives it.

Artificial insemination is safe and easy to carry out. Most important, it induces pregnancy just as effectively as normal intercourse among fertile couples does; about 20 percent of couples get pregnant in any one month, whichever method of insemination they use. But artificial insemination has one major limitation: it requires a fertile, healthy female. Stated differently, it can help couples only when the male alone lacks fertility. It can do nothing for women whose ova are not healthy, or whose reproductive tracts (the fallopian tubes) have been damaged, or who lack a normal, healthy uterus.

For some of these women, **in vitro fertilization** can help. In this technique, one or more ova are removed from the mother surgically and are mixed in a test tube with sperm from the father (hence the popular name "test tube baby"). If conception takes place, the zygote is allowed to grow in the test tube briefly and then is reinserted surgically into the mother's womb. If all goes well, the embryo implants itself in the wall of the womb and proceeds to develop normally. The surgery uses small, needle-like instruments inserted through the mother's abdomen; since she is anesthetized, she feels no pain.

Even so, the procedure demands a lot, both of

---

can now be heard through the wall of the uterus. As muscles develop more fully, the reflexes which first appeared during the third month become stronger.

By the fourth or fifth month, the mother may feel **quickening** of the fetus, or movement inside her womb. These are generally simple and reflexive actions — hiccups, a wave of an arm, or a kick. These movements have in reality been going on for many weeks by the time most mothers notice them, but as the womb becomes more crowded, the fetus inevitably hits its walls more often.

Feeling the fetus move

Although weight increases throughout pregnancy, large gains do not occur until nearly the end of pregnancy. By twenty weeks, or about halfway to birth, the fetus typically measures about half its final prenatal length but only about 10 percent of its final weight (Hamilton, 1984). That makes the fetus about twelve inches long and only about ten ounces in weight; it is still a very tiny baby. But this slow weight gain only seems slow in comparison with the development lying ahead; compared

medical technology and of the embryo itself. And it can only help certain women, such as those with defective fallopian tubes; a woman still must have a usable, healthy womb, and produce usable, healthy ova. As a result, in vitro fertilization does not occur very often. In 1985, for example, only four hundred babies were conceived by this method in the entire United States, compared with over 10,000 that were conceived by artificial insemination (Harper's Index, 1986). Most of these test-tube babies, however, developed normally after they were reimplanted in their mothers' wombs.

Perhaps a better parallel to artificial insemination is a controversial variation called **surrogate mothering.** This alternative uses artificial insemination, but instead of inserting sperm from a substitute father into the real mother, it inserts sperm from the real father into a substitute mother. Like any other case of artificial insemination, the procedure works well at creating a new baby. Some parents and medical staff therefore argue that surrogate mothering offers an important service to couples who learn that their infertility results from the woman instead of from the man.

But many potential parents feel less comfortable with a substitute mother than with a substitute father (Menning, 1980). Probably this feeling stems at least partly from the prolonged biological connection between mother and fetus; the two of them live with each other, so to speak, for nine months. Whether this biological attachment always translates into psychological intimacy is unclear. But many parents worry that it might, and their worry makes them mistrust surrogate mothering as an alternative to normal conception.

In any case, surrogate mothers usually expect to be paid several thousand dollars for their services — quite a bit more than sperm donors — in order to compensate for the months of time and effort in gestating a baby. The cost naturally restricts their services to relatively well-to-do couples. It probably also contributes to negative opinions about surrogate mothering, since cultural stereotypes dictate that women should love babies for their own sake and not deal with them as economic commodities.

In about the fourth or fifth month of pregnancy, a woman begins feeling the fetus move. The timing varies: some babies are more "gymnastic" than others, and many women notice movement more in later pregnancies. (Nancy Durrell McKenna/Photo Researchers)

with what has already happened, it has gained impressively. At four weeks, for example, it measured only about one eighth of an inch long, and weighed only about one one-hundredth of an ounce!

Fetal weight gain

By the beginning of the seventh month, or start of the third trimester, the fetus is about sixteen inches long and weighs approximately three to five pounds. It is able to cry, breathe, swallow, digest, excrete, move about, and suck its thumb. The reflexes mentioned earlier are fully developed. By the eighth month it weighs five to seven pounds and has begun to develop a layer of body fat, which will help it to regulate its body temperature after its birth.

Checkpoint *A considerable number of conditions must be met for sperm and egg to meet successfully. The zygote that they form soon forms a blastocyst, which implants itself into the uterine wall. During the embryonic stage, most of the major organs and physiological systems are established; they become more fully developed during the fetal stage.*

Prenatal Influences on the Child

In spite of the individuality sometimes attributed to unborn children, biologically they develop in ways that are far more alike than different. As we have noted, physical structures develop in a particular sequence and at fairly precise times. Psychologists and biologists sometimes call such regularity **canalization,** which refers to the complex, seemingly inevitable unfolding of growth or developmental processes (Scarr-Salapatek, 1976; McCall, 1981). In normal conditions, specific events or influences have little long-term effect on highly canalized maturation, even if they affect development temporarily. Whether a pregnant mother drinks four glasses of milk every day or never drinks milk may not change the course of her pregnancy noticeably, as long as she does include calcium in her diet and her fetus does get enough nutrients. By nature, ordinary differences like this make no difference to maturation, as long as they *are* "ordinary."

Typically, prenatal development is a highly reliable process so that prospective parents generally worry much more than they should about whether their baby will be all right. In fact, 97.5 percent of human infants are perfect at birth, and of the 2.5 percent that are not, half have only minor defects such as hammer toes, extra fingers or toes, and birthmarks (Guttmacher and Kaiser, 1984).

But certain conditions can interfere with even the highly canalized processes of fetal development. These conditions are sometimes called **risk factors,** since they increase the chance that the future baby will have medical problems but do not guarantee that these problems will actually appear. Risk factors vary widely in nature and scope, but all have in common the capacity to influence embryonic and fetal development negatively (Stechler and Halton, 1983). Some of them are related to the mother's biological characteristics, including characteristics that are influenced by psychological and social stress. A second set of risks involves exposure to disease, especially to viruses; exposure to drugs and other chemicals constitutes a third set of risk factors.

As the complex sequence of prenatal development proceeds, the timing of the development of each new organ or part of the body is particularly important. There is a limited, "one-time-only" time period during which each particular change can occur. This **critical period** is strictly determined by the complex genetic codes in each cell and by the particular set of prenatal conditions that must be in place for each change to occur. If the critical period is impeded or blocked, the changes that were scheduled to occur may be disrupted or prevented from occurring at all.

Importance of timing

The nine months of pregnancy are generally divided into three **trimesters,** each lasting three months. Development is most vulnerable during the first trimester, so disruption during this period may lead to spontaneous abortion or to serious birth defects. For example, disruption during the third week, when the basic structures of the heart and central nervous system are just beginning to form, is likely to threaten further development. Similarly, interference in the fourth and fifth weeks, which are within the critical period for the first stage of arm and leg development, may lead to underdeveloped and malformed limbs. Most of the critical periods for embryonic and fetal development are in the first trimester, so disruptions in the second and third trimesters are in general likely to have less severe consequences.

Biological Risks

Certain circumstances and physical characteristics of mothers are related to problems in pregnancy, although these may not actually cause the problems directly. All of the following, for example, lead to increased chances of spontaneous abortion, or miscarriage (McKenzie, 1983):

Perspectives on Research

The Death of Hope: Coping with Loss in Pregnancy

Modern medicine has made labor and delivery much more successful than they were in the past. At the beginning of the twentieth century, more than one baby in ten died on or soon after the day it was born, but by the 1970s, that percentage was down to only one baby in a hundred (Antenatal Diagnosis, 1979). This has made pregnancy a much more hopeful time than it used to be.

Yet losing a baby is just as much of a tragedy today as it always has been. Parents often respond to the news of miscarriage or stillbirth with shock and disbelief. "This isn't really happening," they say, or "I can't believe this; at any moment I'll wake up." As the impact sinks in, they are likely to have a variety of feelings, including sadness at their loss, of course, and anger that this should have happened to *them.* Many grieving parents also report physical ailments — headaches, poor digestion, and the like — as well as sleeplessness. Periods of anger about the death alternate with powerful feelings of guilt ("I keep wondering what *I* did to cause my baby's death"). How strong these feelings are has little relation to how carefully the parents took care of themselves during pregnancy. Nor does it have much to do with how long the baby actually managed to gestate or live (Borg and Lasker, 1981); a three-month pregnancy ending in miscarriage or spontaneous abortion can hurt parents just as much as a full-term pregnancy in which the baby dies two days after delivery.

Fetal and infant death can put serious stress on many marriages, in part because mothers' reactions often differ from fathers'. Many mothers report feeling empty in the aftermath of a failed pregnancy. One bereaved mother put it this way: "Nothing seemed to matter anymore. People talked to me, and sometimes I looked at them; but I didn't listen." Another said, "It's like my womb was supposed to be a shelter for my baby, but it didn't really give shelter. Now I keep telling my baby how sorry I am for failing her." These reactions are very personal and physical, as if mothers lose part of themselves when they lose their babies (Berezin, 1982).

Fathers care too, of course, but they do not actually experience the physical changes of pregnancy. This fact can sometimes make men seem uncaring about a miscarriage or stillbirth, especially if they conform to society's expectation that men should not show their feelings openly in public (Schiff, 1977). In addition to feeling sorrow and guilt, therefore, fathers may often feel left out of the process of grieving that they witness in their wives. They may feel ignored by their wives, and believe

1. Being relatively old (over forty) or relatively young (under twenty)
2. Having had several previous pregnancies (at least four or five), especially if some of these involved medical problems
3. Being very overweight or underweight — that is, more than about 25 percent different from the average weight for the mother's height and frame (being only a little overweight does not create risk)
4. Being very short in stature (under five feet tall, to be specific) and small in size of frame

We should note several cautions in understanding the relationships among these factors. First, many of these characteristics do not operate independently of one another. Older mothers, for instance, are likely to have had several previous preg-

---

that their honest efforts to help are rejected. One father commented, "My wife had been moping all week, so I asked her to talk about it. But all she said was, 'I don't want to cheer up! You wouldn't understand.'" As unfriendly as these words sound, this wife was right: her husband could never experience a failed pregnancy directly, and in this sense would never "understand."

Too often, modern living conditions interfere with giving bereaved parents much real help in coping. Relatives such as grandparents or the parents' siblings may live too far away to be available when needed. The mobility of modern life means that neighbors are often casual acquaintances rather than friends on whom the parents can really rely for support. "My next-door neighbor sent me a gift, rather than coming to see me," said one grieving mother. "I was puzzled by it, because it wasn't my birthday."

Professional helpers are usually around, in the form of religious leaders and medical personnel. But although a majority of parents profess a religious affiliation, many do not actually participate in church or a religious community, and if they do, they still may not want to trust their clergy with news as important as their baby's death. Sometimes they find their clergy's comments simplistic

or wrong-headed ("He told me to pray; but I never believed in God much anyway").

Medical staff can seem even less sensitive, perhaps because they are used to the high success rate among pregnancies. "The nurse told me to forget about this baby," said one mother, "and get pregnant again as soon as possible." But parents do not want to forget a lost baby; they want to remember it. Only by remembering can they get on with life without feeling like they have betrayed their original commitment to their dead child.

No wonder, then, that some psychologists argue that the strongest taboo in modern society is not sex, but death (Becker, 1973). These days, we are not supposed to die. More accurately, we are not supposed to *know* that we — or our children — will inevitably die. Modern medicine emphasizes its life-preserving powers, not acceptance of death; dying individuals, both young and old, spend their final moments in hospitals, safely out of everyday view; and by moving frequently from one community to another, friends and families weaken their memories of the past, including memories of their deceased children.

---

nancies, just by virtue of their age. Many older mothers are also likely to have gained weight over the years.

Second, even though the list refers to biological circumstances, the relationships of those circumstances with pregnancy actually may be caused by other, psychological or social processes. For example, very young mothers may experience more stress than older ones when they are pregnant; they may well be short of money, or lack the emotional and economic support of a husband. These circumstances may cause them to worry, which directly contributes to miscarriage. Lack of money and support can also mean that the future baby is unprotected if she needs unusual medical attention, because intensive care at a hospital costs thousands of dollars, only some of which is covered by insurance. This fact may prevent a relatively poor mother from giving her baby the care that she needs, and thus aggravate the baby's problems indirectly.

Third, keep in mind that many women who live with risks like these have no problems at all with their pregnancies. This qualification is especially true of women who have only one risk factor, but it is even true of women with more than one. To be "at risk" means only that there is a higher than usual chance of problems; it does *not* mean a certainty. The distinction is important for all risks to pregnancy, including the ones we discuss in the next sections.

Illnesses

Until recently, the disease that most commonly created problems during pregnancy was German measles, or **rubella,** which is caused by a virus that apparently can infect the embryo or fetus by passing through the placenta into the fetal bloodstream if the mother contracts the illness. If the virus invades during the first two months of pregnancy, it is likely to cause blindness, deafness, heart defects, damage to the central nervous system, and mental and emotional retardation. Should it

Effects of rubella   occur during the second trimester, after the fetus is fully formed, its effects are less severe but may include hearing, vision, and language problems.

The chances of abnormalities in an infant born to a mother who has been exposed to rubella depend largely on the timing of the exposure. Approximately 47 percent of babies born to mothers who had rubella during the first month of pregnancy displayed abnormalities, while 22 percent of newborns whose mothers had the disease during the second month and 7 percent of those who contracted it in the third month were seriously affected (Michaels and Mellin, 1960). Because of the successful public health efforts during the past decade to inoculate schoolchildren and women at risk, the current incidence of rubella in the United States is now extremely low, perhaps affecting only one out of every one thousand deliveries.

Certain other viruses are also able to infect the fetus, in spite of the protection offered by the placenta: typhoid, diphtheria, syphilis, and gonorrhea.

If a pregnant woman is in the first years of a syphilis infection, the fetus is likely to die if the mother is untreated. Later in the course of the infection, syphilitic

Effects of syphilis and   women may give birth to healthy children. The newborn's symptoms include
gonorrhea   lesions, rashes, and anemia; if the syphilis is untreated, the child may develop den-

tal deformities, hearing problems, and many of the problems associated with adult syphilis discussed in Chapter 14 (Beeson & McDermott, 1971). Fetuses that contract gonorrhea in the birth canal may later develop eye infections or become blind. It is now standard practice to put drops of silver nitrate or penicillin in newborns' eyes to protect against this, since gonorrhea may be present in the mother without obvious symptoms.

About 25 percent of the U.S. population contracts **toxoplasmosis,** a disease caused by a parasite that is present in uncooked meat and the feces of infected cats. Although the mother may show no signs of illness, this disease can lead to fetal brain damage, blindness, or even death.

All of these diseases are risky partly because the extent of illness in the mother does not reliably match the extent of its effect on the fetus; a mother with a mild case of rubella can carry what turns out to be a badly deformed child. The uncertainty makes prevention of illnesses the best strategy, and curative treatments only a distant second best.

Uncertainty of risk

Teratogens

During the early weeks, the embryo is especially vulnerable to various unusual or unnatural substances taken by the mother. Since many of these substances can permanently damage an embryo's growth, they are sometimes called **teratogens,** after ancient Greek words meaning "monster-creating." Teratogens include substances that most people consider obviously harmful, such as alcohol and cigarette smoke, but they also include medications — substances intended simply to help.

Early vulnerability of embryo

Drugs A drug called thalidomide illustrates dramatically how this can happen. Thalidomide is a seemingly harmless sedative, prescribed for calming the nerves, promoting sleep, and reducing morning sickness and other forms of nausea. But if a woman uses it during the first two months of pregnancy, the embryo's arms and legs become badly deformed.

Effects of thalidomide

Thalidomide was prescribed widely in the early 1960s, and soon after the affected children began to be born, medical researchers began to suspect that a drug was responsible.

Unfortunately, the damage done by toxic drugs or chemicals does not always show itself as obviously or as soon as thalidomide did. Another drug, diethylstilbestrol (DES), was prescribed frequently to pregnant women for about twenty-five years following World War II, because of its ability to prevent miscarriages. The drug was especially useful during the early months, when such abortions happen most often. At birth the babies of women who took DES seemed perfectly normal, and they remained so throughout childhood. As they became young adults, however, many of the daughters of DES mothers developed cancers in the vagina or cervix. The sons of these mothers did not develop cancer, but they did have abnormalities in the structure of their reproductive organs (Johnson et al., 1979; Bibbo et al., 1977). Even the daughters who did not get cancer had significantly more problems than usual with their own pregnancies; they had more spontaneous abortions

Effects of DES

and stillbirths as well as more minor problems, and they had these whether or not their families had had histories of difficult births (Barnes et al., 1980).

All of these effects only emerged years after DES had achieved wide use. While the unfortunate first generation of DES children was growing up, doctors continued to prescribe the drug and thereby created still more children with problems.

Effects of narcotics Not surprisingly, heavy narcotics such as heroin also affect the fetus. At birth, the child of a woman who uses heroin immediately begins to have withdrawal symptoms, vomiting, trembling, and acting irritable (Zelson, 1973). Unfortunately for the baby, the symptoms may not become serious until several days after birth, when it has left the hospital. Even when the infant has recovered from withdrawal, he often develops slowly during the first year (Strauss et al., 1976), and he is at risk for dying suddenly and unaccountably during this time as well (Chavez et al., 1979).

Almost all drugs may potentially affect the developing embryo or fetus, depending upon their particular characteristics, dosage, frequency, timing of use, and so on. This has led many doctors to stress the dangers to pregnant women and to prescribe medication in only extreme cases. **General precautions** Yet single drugs rarely act as dramatically as thalidomide or DES (Heinonen et al., 1977), and many commonly used drugs — even aspirin — seem to have no observable effects at all, as long as they are used only occasionally and cautiously.

More often, drugs have their bad effects by overuse, or by acting jointly with other drugs and problems (Fein et al., 1983). A woman, for example, who takes the usual dose of aspirin — one or two tablets every four hours — usually creates no harm for her child. But a woman who doubles this dose, and in addition smokes two packs of cigarettes per day, puts her baby at serious risk (Benawra et al., 1980). In between extremes like these lie gray areas where drugs and behaviors that may hurt one fetus may not hurt another; or where drugs and behaviors may risk moderate, but not serious physical harm.

Alcohol Even in biblical times, people suspected that alcohol harms an unborn child:

> Behold, thou shalt conceive and bear a son; and now drink no wine nor strong drink, neither eat any unclean thing . . .
>
> *Judges 13:7*

Both then and now, babies born to mothers who consume too much alcohol have **fetal alcohol syndrome,** which means that they do not arouse easily and tend to behave sluggishly in general (Clarren and Smith, 1978). In addition, babies of heavy drinkers have more than twice the usual chances of showing minor physical abnormalities, such as a thin upper lip or a short nose. Particularly if drinking occurs during the last trimester, they may also suffer from heart defects, small heads, and distortions of the joints, and may show mental retardation and slowed motor development (Palmer et al., 1974; Streissguth et al., 1978).

Even moderate drinking can be dangerous Even moderate drinking and occasional binges can put the fetus at risk. In one study, pregnant women drank gingerale mixed with one ounce of vodka — about

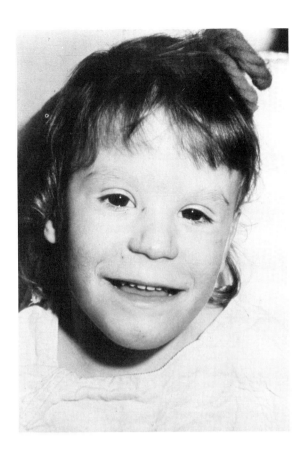

This child has the short nose and thin upper lip characteristic of fetal alcohol syndrome. She, like other children with the syndrome, is at risk for a variety of motor and neurological impairments. ("Fetal alcohol syndrome experience with 41 patients," Journal of the American Medical Association, 235, N. 14)

as much alcohol as a typical mixed drink at a restaurant or bar contains. The researchers observed the fetuses in the second trimester both before and during the drinking, and found that their breathing became seriously disturbed within a few minutes of the mothers' beginning to drink (Fox et al., 1978). Most fetuses slowed down or even stopped breathing for many minutes at a time. They did not die, of course, because they did not yet really need their lungs to obtain oxygen, but their behavior suggested serious physical depression caused by a modest amount of alcohol.

Apparently alcohol depresses not only brain functioning but the very growth of the brain. Several pieces of evidence support this idea. Brain nerve cells of "alcoholic" fetuses may fail to develop properly, that is, to connect widely with numerous other brain cells, as the cells in normally developing infants do (Clarren and Smith, 1978). This effect occurs most strongly during the time when the fetal brain is growing the fastest, namely during the last three months of pregnancy. Brain cells seem almost unaffected by drinking during the first few months of pregnancy (Matsunaga and Shiota, 1980). However, there are indications that *any* degree of drinking during pregnancy may increase the risk of miscarriage, and that there may be fairly wide individual variations regarding what frequency and quantity will cause problems (Harlap and Shiono, 1980). And programs to help pregnant mothers curb their drinking have had best results for the children when they

Mothers who smoke during pregnancy tend to have babies who are smaller than usual. If the baby experiences any other medical problems before or around the time of birth, low birth weight can put it at risk. (Erika Stone/Peter Arnold)

emphasize the importance of abstention during the last few months of gestation; mothers who cut back throughout pregnancy give birth more often to healthy, alert babies, compared with mothers who only cut back early and resume drinking later in their pregnancy (Rosett et al., 1980).

Cigarettes Smoking too can harm the fetus, but the effects are more general than is true for alcohol. Observations of mothers suggest that two key elements of cigarette smoke, nicotine and carbon monoxide, interfere with the supply of oxygen to the fetus. Because of the reduced amount of oxygen entering the fetus's bloodstream, the baby's heart must beat much faster than usual, so that by the time the mother has finished a five-minute cigarette, the fetus's heart is beating 20 percent faster than it normally does, and it will continue doing so for ten or fifteen minutes (Quigley et al., 1979). By reducing the supply of oxygen, smoking slows the baby's metabolism and growth generally.

Smoking interferes with the fetal oxygen supply

Not surprisingly, the babies of heavy smokers are smaller than usual at birth. A wide range of studies, using literally thousands of mothers and children, consistently point to this conclusion (Greenwood, 1979). Smoking may not harm babies who are otherwise healthy and well cared for, but it can put babies who already have other medical problems at risk, since low birth weight (under about five pounds) can jeopardize survival and contribute to slow development in childhood.

Some studies suggest that infants of smoking mothers have other problems as well. They have more chance of being born with minor physical deformities such as cleft lip or palate, and more chance of becoming jittery or excessively active during early childhood (Evans et al., 1979). These effects, though, are less pronounced than the effect on birth weight, and as always we must consider the effects of family experiences commonly connected with smoking. For example, parents with highly strung, nervous dispositions may tend to pass this disposition on to their children, and such parents may smoke a lot just to calm their nerves.

Diet and Nutrition

Studies of animals show clearly that undernourishment during pregnancy hurts the offspring in various ways (Hurley, 1977, 1980). As a rule, deprivation early in the gestation leads to specific physical deformities, and later deprivation leads to overall low birth weight. These and other facts imply that most nutrition for the fetus comes from the mother's current diet and not from her reserves of fat. At least among animals, a poor diet for the mother therefore harms both the mother and the offspring; the fetus is not isolated nutritionally by virtue of living in the uterus.

Although the principle seems to apply to human mothers and children as well, ethical considerations prevent testing it, because of course we cannot starve pregnant mothers on purpose, just to clarify our knowledge about diet during pregnancy. A number of indirect trends, though, do suggest that undernutrition can hurt unborn children seriously.

First, children born during World War II in combat areas tended to be smaller than usual, and there were more than the usual number of stillbirths (Stein et al., 1975). The families of these children generally experienced severe famine during the war, but of course they also experienced other serious stresses that probably also contributed to problems during pregnancy.

Second, children who die in the womb or immediately after birth sometimes show features that resemble malnutrition in animals: they lack normal amounts of fat tissue, and certain internal organs are sometimes relatively underdeveloped (Naeye et al., 1973; Naeye, 1979). However, not all stillborn and aborted children show such signs, even when their mothers seem undernourished.

Third, very slender or underweight mothers experience birth complications more often than other women, including more premature births and more babies who are quite small (Edwards et al., 1979). Not all small babies develop in underweight mothers, though, and sometimes mothers are naturally slender rather than malnourished.

Taken together, these trends suggest that poor nutrition may affect human fetal development just as it affects animals. But the evidence applies primarily to very severe restrictions of diet — those that are severe enough to endanger the mother's health as well as her child's. In more moderate cases, the evidence remains unclear. Human mothers are not as nutritionally vulnerable as small laboratory animals: human beings are comparatively large as animals go, and therefore may only be harmed by sustained and serious deprivation of food. Also, pregnancy takes a proportionally smaller diversion of a human mother's nutrition than of a small animal's nutrition; a rat almost doubles its weight during pregnancy, but if a human mother did the same, she would gain more than one hundred pounds in nine months!

Because of these factors, moderate failures of nutrition may make comparatively little difference to humans — as long as they are only moderate. To a certain extent, human mothers can get away with eating too many candy bars during pregnancy, as long as that is their only nutritional mistake. Even so, no medical expert would ever condone such mistakes, because even moderately poor nutrition can cut down on a mother's reserves of health and energy.

For the majority of well-nourished mothers, nutrition specialists make surprisingly few precise recommendations about foods and nutrients that help fetal devel-

---

A Talk with an Ob-Gyn Nurse Practitioner

Preparation for Childbirth

Chris Czemanski was interviewed in her office at a primary health care clinic.

INTERVIEWER: What is your work like?

CHRIS: Well, I work with two obstetrics-gynecology [Ob-Gyn] doctors and share responsibility for prenatal care and preparation for birth.

INTERVIEWER: What advice do you give women about their nutrition?

CHRIS: We provide information about what is a good, healthy diet for a pregnant woman and her baby. The kinds of food that are good to eat and those that are not.

INTERVIEWER: What are the general guidelines?

CHRIS: Three to four glasses of milk a day. Increased consumption of fruits and vegetables, which many people don't eat very regularly. Bottom line, we recommend a balanced adult diet, with a few extra calories and with vitamin supplements. We also recommend a twenty-five- to thirty-pound gain over the course of a pregnancy, depending upon the size of the woman and her build and weight.

INTERVIEWER: Why do you recommend weight gain?

CHRIS: The reasons are truly physiological. At the time of delivery, if you figure in the average weight of the baby being approximately six and a half to seven and a half pounds and the weight of an average placenta at maybe three to five pounds, as well as the extra fluid that a woman gains and extra subcutaneous fat that she stores in her body just as extra protection, they all add up to approximately twenty to twenty-five pounds.

INTERVIEWER: How do weight gain and other changes of pregnancy affect women?

CHRIS: Body image changes, certainly. How people feel about that is directly dependent upon how they feel about being pregnant.

INTERVIEWER: Could you say more about that?

CHRIS: Well, for someone who is thrilled about being pregnant, she's going to be thrilled — or at least more happy — to see her belly getting bigger. Someone who resents her pregnancy from the moment she knows about it is likely to have a harder time with the changes that occur. It's not just that her breasts are getting larger or that her stomach is getting bigger. She can't run

up and down the stairs as easily and she can't find a comfortable position to sleep in. Pregnancy gets in the way of her life. You have to alter how you move and how you eat and how many times a day you go to the bathroom and how many times a night you get up to go. And when you get up to go to the bathroom five times a night, 'round about time three or four, you start wondering if it is all worth it, when all you really want to do is have a good eight hours of sleep.

INTERVIEWER: Pregnancy can be stressful.

CHRIS: Yes. In a way, pregnancy is a crisis. How a person copes with the stresses of pregnancy has a lot to do with how she feels about being pregnant as well as what her social and emotional support system is like. If her partner or parents or friends provide good solid support and appreciation for what she is experiencing, pregnancy is likely to be a more positive experience than if such support is lacking.

INTERVIEWER: Can you say more about pregnancy as a crisis?

CHRIS: Yes. I believe that a crisis tends to enhance and strengthen what is already there and bring to

opment, and some of their suggestions are hedged with qualifications (Vermeersch, 1981). Nutritionists do agree, though, on one major modification of diet: pregnant women should eat more than usual, though not necessarily "for two," as the saying goes. How much more? Estimates range from 200 to 1,000 calories per day more than the woman ate before pregnancy, as long as the extra calories consist mainly of carbohydrates and protein. The extra calories help to promote weight gain, which in turn helps to insure a healthy baby at birth (Naeye, 1979b; Cater, 1980). Contrary to the advice given just a generation ago, nutritionists and doctors now

Pregnant women should eat more than usual

---

light and intensify whatever weaknesses are present.

INTERVIEWER: Intensify them?

CHRIS: Exactly. Or at least bring them to the surface. Issues which may not have been obvious to begin with or may have been present but very easy to ignore or not address, for whatever reasons, will come out. Self-esteem issues, how to communicate, how to share responsibilities, how to accept responsibilities for parenting. You're not just having a baby, but you're becoming a parent, which is a lifetime job.

INTERVIEWER: What preparation for childbirth do you offer your patients?

CHRIS: Most medical practices encourage some kind of childbirth classes. Classes typically cover, in some depth, the various stages of pregnancy, the physiological changes in a woman, the psychological changes, changes in the relationships of couples. They describe in detail what to expect from the minute you think you're in labor, what the hospital will be like, what to bring to the hospital, and what not to bring. You learn about the different kinds of pain medications that might be offered, what their

effects are, what their benefits are, and what their risks are. Most of them also teach basic relaxation and breathing techniques, which are very important. Knowing what to expect and how to deal with the anxiety and pain can contribute significantly to making labor a more positive experience.

INTERVIEWER: What are your feelings about birthing clinics and home deliveries?

CHRIS: For many people who want an experience that is not a hospital, then a birth center is ideal, whether it is free-standing or directly attached to a hospital. It offers you a little more freedom of movement, a little more comfort, a little bit different atmosphere, and yet there is reassurance that there is medical backup available should it be needed, including . . . quick transfer to a fully equipped hospital if needed. Of course, the population that comes to a birth center should be carefully screened beforehand for any potential medical complications.

INTERVIEWER: What about home birth?

CHRIS: I think that home birth is a good option as well for the very

small percentage of the population that are truly candidates for it.

INTERVIEWER: Why is that?

CHRIS: It takes a very high level of commitment to arrange a home birth. If it's not something that both partners agree on and have a very deep commitment to and belief in, then there can be real problems. In a situation where the partners are very present for each other and where the home situation is a nice, clean place to be and where there is a pediatrician as well as an obstetrician or a midwife who is well trained and experienced and good medical backup is available in the case of an emergency, then go for it.

Follow-up Questions

1. What are Chris's views about the stresses associated with pregnancy?

2. If you were asked to teach a session of a childbirth class similar to the ones described by Chris, which topic(s) would you be able to discuss knowledgeably and what would you say?

3. To what extent are Chris's comments about alternatives to hospital births consistent with the discussion in this chapter?

---

encourage women to gain about twenty-five or thirty pounds during pregnancy. Contrary to common belief, most of this gain does not go to making the baby bigger, it simply contributes to the health of both mother and baby. In addition, nutritionists recommend that pregnant women get extra calcium (usually by drinking milk), since they must provide for the growing bones of the fetus, and sometimes for breast feeding.

Stress

Stress refers to chronic feelings of worry and anxiety. Most mothers and fathers feel significant stress just about having a baby, which is something of a crisis even in the most positive families. Parents often feel surprised and shocked at the news of pregnancy, even if they have planned to have a child. Later they might worry about whether the baby will be all right, about whether they can really afford to have it, and about whether they are really ready psychologically to be parents. These feelings are all stressful, but when they are kept within reasonable bounds, they are quite inevitable and normal. They cause no long-run damage to the baby.

Very high and persistent stress, however, can put the fetus at risk. Parents who know that they carry genetic abnormalities may worry excessively about whether their baby will develop normally, just as a mother in the midst of a failing marriage **Stress-induced** may worry about whether she will be able to give her child the care it needs after it **hypertension** is born. Such serious worries can persist through most of a pregnancy, or even all of it, and may contribute to hypertension, or high blood pressure.

Hypertension is more likely to occur in the third trimester and is frequently associated with **eclampsia,** a disease that in its early ("pre-eclampsia") stages involves a buildup in the mother's bloodstream of waste materials from the fetus that are normally eliminated by the kidneys. Due to the resultant water retention, the mother gains weight and her hands, feet, and ankles swell. Generally the fetus is not at risk and these pre-eclampsia symptoms can be treated with a restricted salt diet, diuretics (which help to eliminate excess body fluids), and bed rest. If the condition persists, the mother's health may be endangered and the fetus may be delivered prematurely (Beeson and McDermott, 1971).

Environmental Hazards

A broad range of environmental hazards can also be destructive to prenatal devel-**Radiation** opment. These include exposure to radiation from nuclear explosions, nuclear plant accidents, industrial materials, and medical x-rays; to industrial chemical pollutants such as carbon monoxide, lead, mercury, and PCBs in the air or water; to fertilizers, herbicides, and pesticides in the food chain; to food additives; and even to excessive heat and humidity. Although the careful parent may take steps to avoid some of these hazards, many are beyond the range of individual control and require efforts on a national or even international scale.

Poor and minority mothers experience higher rates of miscarriage and other prenatal difficulties than do mothers from more favorable circumstances because their living conditions involve greater exposure to prenatal risks, including less adequate prenatal nutrition and health care.

Checkpoint *If mothers are exposed to certain conditions during pregnancy, their developing embryo and fetus may be at risk, particularly during certain "critical periods" when specific fetal developments take place. The age, physical size, health, and nutritional habits of the mother are all factors in the health of the fetus. If the mother contracts certain illnesses, such as rubella or syphilis, if she ingests drugs such as alcohol, heroin, or thalidomide, or if she is exposed to chemical or radioactive pollutants, she may miscarry or give birth to a child exhibiting physical malformations or developmental retardation, or both.*

Parental Reactions to Pregnancy

Expectant parents have a number of reactions to pregnancy. Most do worry about the process to some extent (Blum, 1980). All parents want their babies to be born healthy and physically normal. They say so to each other from time to time, and think it even more frequently than they say it. Both parents take precautions to insure the baby's health: mothers try to "eat right" and cut down on or eliminate activities that they consider harmful to the baby, and fathers often support, or at least tolerate, these efforts.

Effects of Pregnancy on the Mother

Naturally, the developmental changes in the fetus have a profound effect on its mother. During the germinal stage (the first two weeks of the first trimester), the mother may not detect any signs of pregnancy; in fact, she may lose the microscopic "baby" at any time without ever knowing that it existed. After implantation, though, the future infant makes its presence felt rather quickly by its impact on the mother's metabolism, or body chemistry. Implantation initiates changes in about thirty different bodily chemicals, or **hormones,** that regulate the pregnancy (Vermeersch, 1981). Some of these changes cause the nausea or morning sickness that often marks early pregnancy; it is one of the earliest signs, in fact, that the woman can actually experience. And of course the hormones suppress further menstrual cycles, another obvious sign that a baby is on the way.

Morning sickness

The mother can deal with some nausea by eating smaller meals more frequently. Many women also experience increased fatigue during this period, perhaps because their bodies have not yet adjusted to the new demands of pregnancy. A woman's breasts may feel uncomfortable and become somewhat enlarged, with the nipples increasing in size and becoming darker in color.

By the start of the second trimester, or fourth month of pregnancy, most women have recovered from morning sickness and fatigue, but the hormonal changes continue to cause various physical reactions. Estrogen and progesterone, for example, have mixed effects. Estrogen, among other things, promotes water retention during pregnancy, which increases the volume of the mother's blood substantially. It also causes edema, or generally swollen tissues, giving some mothers puffy skin and swollen ankles. Progesterone promotes new fat deposits all over the woman's body. These may have served as nutritional insurance in prehistoric days, when food was scarce, but now they can be frustrating to a woman who wants to be slender.

A more serious effect of progesterone is that it causes muscles to relax. This apparently helps the uterus to stretch, which is essential during pregnancy. By the same token, though, the muscles of the intestines can become lazy, or too relaxed to digest properly. Constipation often results, especially in later pregnancy, when the uterus squeezes the intestines into a smaller-than-usual space.

The quickening that the mother usually first experiences during the fourth or fifth month, is often good news for the mother: feeling the fetus's movements is proof that the baby exists and is alive. But quickening can constitute a nuisance, too. An especially active fetus can feel like an internal boxing match or gymnastics tournament. Ironically, mothers often find the movements more noticeable when they rest or lie still, so quickening can sometimes interfere with sleep.

As the pregnancy progresses, the mother may find that she needs to urinate more frequently because as the baby grows it exerts pressure on her bladder. It also grows upward and presses on the diaphragm, making it hard for the mother to breathe. By the middle and latter part of the third trimester, she may find it uncomfortable to sit for long periods of time or walk with the usual ease. This is because her pelvic joints have become more flexible in preparation for the baby's passage through the birth canal and because of the increased weight that she is carrying — usually between twenty and thirty pounds, depending upon her size.

Women also experience psychological changes with pregnancy. By the third trimester, the various discomforts and the many months of waiting can begin to seem endless. Even though they know the changes in their bodies are not permanent, many women feel that they are becoming less and less attractive and have concerns that they will not be able to get back into shape once the baby is born. First-time parents in particular have many concerns about the responsibilities of caring for a new baby and about the changes it will make in their lives, and the complex metabolic and physiological changes the mother undergoes can contribute to mood swings and feelings of upset and anxiety.

At times, these experiences can preoccupy women enough to make them withdraw attention and energy from other activities. Their husbands may get less attention, both sexually and socially, than before. Older children require just as much care as always, but some pregnant mothers may give it grudgingly, and less thoroughly, than usual. Women who work outside the home may find themselves using up a lot of their sick leave during pregnancy, in response to their discomfort, but even sick leave may not help fully.

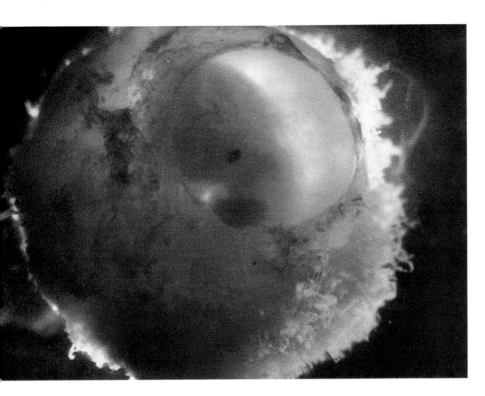

Prenatal Development and the Neonate

The environment and anatomy of an embryo change dramatically during the first three months of pregnancy. By the end of the third week, the embryo is surrounded by a thin sac of fluid, which cushions it from bumps and provides a more uniform temperature. A group of cells form villi, tiny threadlike structures that intermingle with the mother's uterus and eventually form the placenta, the organ that transmits nutrients to the embryo and carries away its waste products.

While all these support systems for the embryo are developing, the embryo itself is acquiring most of its major organs and physical structures. By the beginning of the third month, arms, hands, and fingers are clearly visible. So are the eyes and, under proper lighting conditions, the mouth and nose. But the embryo is still only about two inches long.

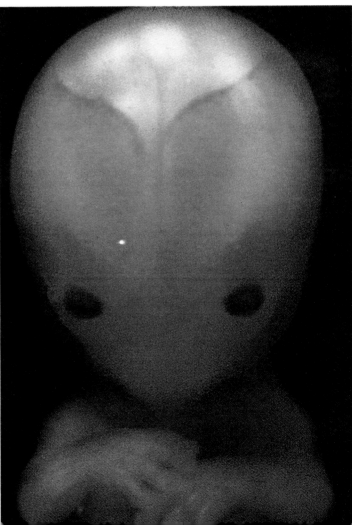

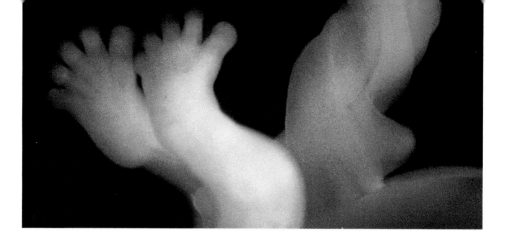

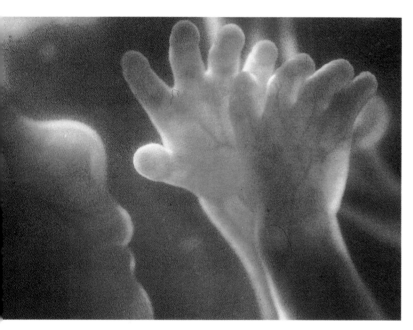

During the middle trimester of pregnancy, the fetus grows rapidly. The umbilical cord connecting it to the placenta remains taut—and therefore untangled—because it is constantly filled with blood. Vessels and arteries proliferate throughout the fetus's body and are easily visible because the skin is still rather transparent. The fetus begins exercising its limbs almost as soon as they develop, but it is not until sometime around the fourth or fifth month that the mother begins feeling these movements.

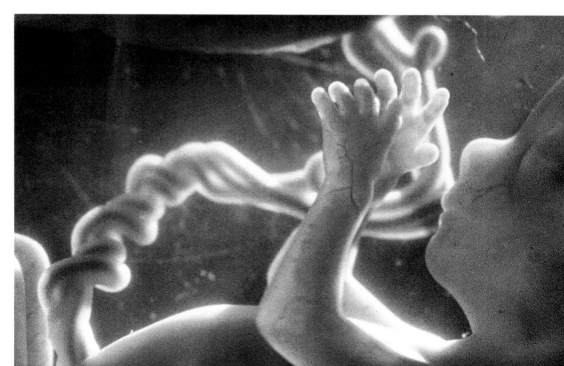

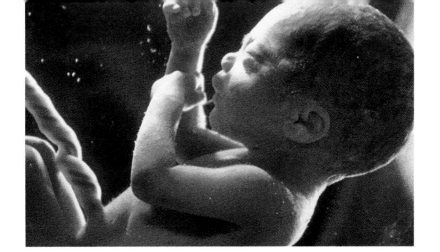

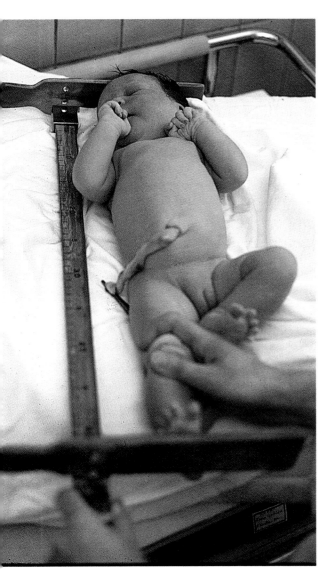

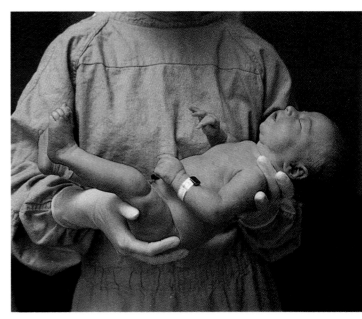

Not surprisingly, a fetus just short of full term looks and acts very much like a newborn baby. It has hair, it will startle at sudden noises, it sometimes sucks its fist, and it shows cycles of sleep and wakefulness. But there are some crucial differences: the newborn must immediately begin breathing and regulating his or her body temperature, and almost immediately begin digesting food.

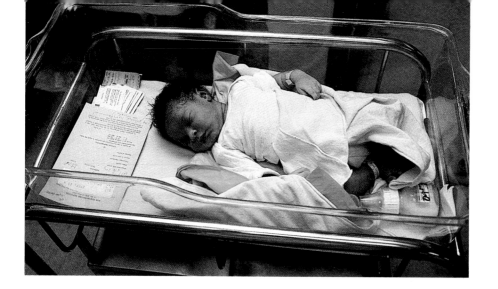

For the first day or two especially, newborns spend most of their time sleeping, but they also have periodic fussy times, especially when they are hungry. By the time they go home from the hospital, they will have been through a lot during the past nine months, and they will be ready to begin the life-long process of development and change that lies ahead.

Parents often develop attachments to their baby even before it is born. But hopeful times like this one often alternate with worries, especially for first-time parents. (Andrew Brillant)

Effects of Pregnancy on the Father and Other Family Members

Pregnancy challenges a father's sense of responsibility in several ways. He may find himself resenting his wife's emotional withdrawal, or competing for attention and concern with a baby that has not even been born yet. After a bad day at work, an expectant father may find that his wife just does not feel like listening to his problems the way she used to, because her worries about the baby take precedence. Sexual activity between a couple may come to a halt for weeks or even months at a time, if the woman is feeling too sick or too bloated to make love. These events can make fathers question how welcome and needed they really are. Ironically, they are probably needed more than ever.

Fathers' reactions

Of course, various circumstances do not apply to all pregnancies, and all expectant parents experience various kinds and degrees of stress. Some mothers can draw on a relatively extended network of family members during their pregnancy, so that grandparents and aunts and uncles can help care for the future baby's older siblings. This extended family can offer reassurance and concrete assistance to worried parents, although of course it can also undermine parents' confidence by hinting that various people are too busy to help out. This is especially likely during later pregnancies, which often seem to generate less enthusiasm among relatives than the first one does. In any case, some parents do not want help from relatives, even when it is available. If grandparents do not approve of a marriage or a pregnancy, or if they offer advice that the parents consider inappropriate, family "support" can be more trouble than it is worth.

Support from other relatives

Brothers and sisters are usually keenly interested in the "new arrival," although they may not show it directly because of the mixed feelings often involved. Whereas on the one hand they want to be part of the family excitement and preparations, on the other hand the energy and excitement that is already being focused

Siblings' reactions

Multiple Pregnancies

In about one out of ninety cases, the mother conceives more than one child in her womb — usually twins. This sometimes happens because the woman releases two ova during one menstrual period, leading to so-called **dizygotic twins**. Or twins can result from a single fertilized ovum that unaccountably divides into two zygotes before developing further; these are **monozygotic twins**. Because dizygotic twins resemble ordinary siblings genetically, they are sometimes also called *fraternal* twins, even if they are sisters, and since monozygotic twins by definition share all their genes, they are sometimes called *identical* twins.

Noticing the presence of an extra fetus would seem to be a task that modern medicine can perform, but in fact it can still only do so with about 75 percent accuracy. One pair of twins out of four, in other words, is a surprise when it arrives (Harris, 1983). The other three quarters can usually be predicted by a combination of signs. Mothers carrying multiple fetuses often weigh more than usual, considering how far along they are in the pregnancy. Later in the pregnancy, doctors and nurses can sometimes hear more than one fetal heartbeat or feel extra arms and legs when the babies move. And family histories of multiple births can make doctors suspicious. None of these signs is foolproof, however; a history of twins in the family only suggests the possibility of fraternal twins, not identical twins.

Twins and their parents are often envied or admired by the public and the local press. In fact, though, they may deserve sympathy more than anything else. Mothers of multiple fetuses experience no special risk because of carrying an extra baby, but the fetuses do. Infants involved in multiple births die five times as often as single infants, and as newborns they get sick ten times as often. These problems may occur in part because twins and other multiple infants tend to be premature or smaller than usual at birth (Korner, 1981); small-

Caring for twin infants (whether dizygotic or monozygotic) is a lot of work, but it can be done. (David S. Strickler/The Picture Cube)

ness in general is risky for a young infant. Once the babies are home from the hospital, the immediate physical dangers tend to subside, but the stresses for the parents begin; coordinating two irregular eating schedules at once, for example, means either making twice as many bottles of formula or keeping the mother available for breast feeding twice as much of the time. Such arrangements can be made, but they demand a lot of the parents' time, energy, and finances, and relatives may have to be called for help. If any of these are in short supply, the families of multiple newborns may be genuinely at risk.

on the new baby does not bode well for the future. What will this new focus of their parents' interest mean for them? Will they have to share their special place with another child? Understanding where babies come from and what their coming will mean is particularly confusing for young children whose fantasies about it all may far outstrip their ability to understand. As a consequence, it is important for parents to talk with their children about these things, to be aware of their children's feelings, and to be responsive to their need for attention, emotional closeness, and reassurance.

By and large, families, friends, neighbors, and medical professionals offer most expectant parents enough support to help them weather the normal stresses of this period and to become relatively well prepared for what is to come. And despite all the potential problems, most people are delighted to find that they are going to have a new baby. As pregnancy nears its end, parents tend to shift their attention from wondering whether their baby will be all right to anticipating the birth process itself. Expectant parents — particularly those who are having their first baby — wonder what the experience of labor will be like and what life will be like with a new baby.

Checkpoint *The hormonal and other physical changes of pregnancy profoundly affect expectant mothers. Expectant mothers and fathers may share feelings of impatience, discomfort, and uncertainty during the course of pregnancy, as well as great feelings of closeness, excitement, and wonder as they near the anticipated birth date. Having friends, family, and neighbors to talk to and rely on for support can help to reduce stress and anxiety and to make pregnancy a positive experience.*

Birth

After thirty-eight weeks in the womb, the fetus is considered "full term," or ready for birth. By this point it will weigh around seven and one half pounds, but it can weigh as little as five or as much as ten pounds and still be physically normal. The fetus measures about twenty inches or so at this stage — almost a third of its final height as an adult.

During the last weeks, the womb becomes so crowded that the fetus assumes one position more or less permanently. This orientation is sometimes called the fetus's presentation, and it refers to the body part closest to the mother's cervix. The most common orientation, and the most desirable medically, is a **cephalic presentation,** which means that the head is pointing downward. But two other presentations also occur: feet and rump first **(breech presentation),** and shoulders first **(transverse presentation).** These orientations used to jeopardize an infant's survival, but modern obstetric techniques have reduced their risk greatly.

When the baby is ready

Although parents and doctors often dearly wish that they could predict the exact moment of the onset of labor, so far no one has been able to do so. Several theories

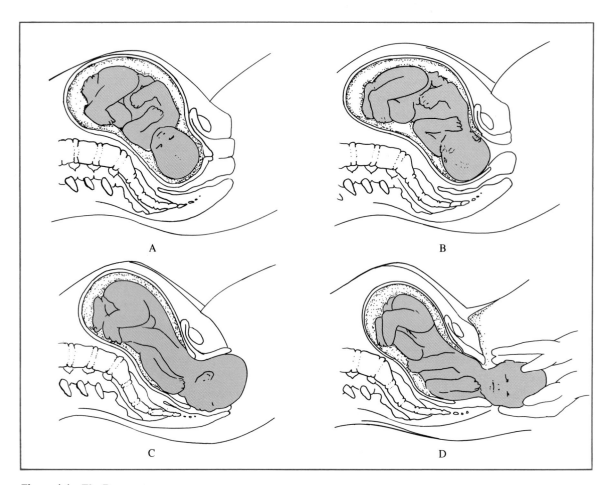

Figure 4.4 The Process of Delivery
(A) before labor begins; (B) labor; (C) crowning; (D) emergence of the head

have been suggested, though, to explain why labor begins when it does. It may be that the uterus becomes stretched beyond some natural limit, and as a result it evacuates itself, rather like an over-full intestine does. Or perhaps certain hormones in the fetus combine with hormones in the mother to initiate the process; the combination may reach some crucial concentration or balance. If so, then to some extent the fetus tells the mother when it is ready.

Most fetuses develop normally for the usual thirty-eight to forty weeks and face their birth relatively well prepared. When the labor process begins, it too usually proceeds normally. The uterus contracts rhythmically and automatically so as to force the baby downward through the vaginal canal. The contractions occur in a relatively predictable sequence of stages, and as long as the baby and mother are healthy and the mother's pelvis is large enough, the baby is usually out within a matter of hours.

Stages of Labor

It is not uncommon for the mother to experience "false labor," or Braxton-Hicks, contractions in the last weeks of pregnancy, as the uterus "practices" contracting

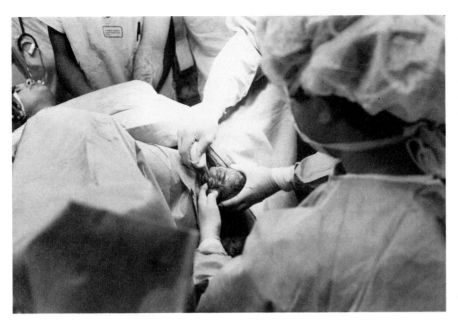

Crowning — when the baby's head can first be seen at the opening of the vagina — marks the beginning of the second stage of labor. (Eric Kroll/Taurus Photos)

and relaxing in preparation for actual labor. She may also have a vaginal discharge of mucus mixed with blood, called "show," one or two days before true labor begins.

The **first stage of labor** usually begins with relatively mild and irregular contractions of the uterus. As contractions become stronger and more regular, the cervix (opening of the uterus) widens, or dilates, enough for the baby's head to fit through. Toward the end of this stage, which may take from eight to twenty-four hours for a first-time mother, a period of **transition** begins. The cervix nears full dilatation, contractions become more rapid, and the baby's head begins to move into the birth canal. Although this period generally lasts for only a few minutes, it can be extremely painful because of the amount of stretching involved and the increasing pressure of the contractions.

Dilatation

The **second stage of labor** starts with "crowning" — the first moment that the baby's head can be seen at the opening of the vagina — and ends when the baby is born. It usually lasts between one and one and a half hours. During the **third stage of labor,** which lasts only a few minutes, the afterbirth (consisting of placenta and umbilical cord) is expelled.

Crowning

Pain in Childbirth

Women vary widely in how much pain and discomfort they experience during labor. For one thing, some babies fit the birth canal more easily than others do, and therefore are easier to expel. In addition, women vary in their tolerance for pain, partly because of basic physiological differences — perhaps even genetic differences — and partly because of the stresses of modern childbirth techniques. A typical hospital birth calls for a sterilized, clinical delivery room, full of bright lights

Women vary in tolerance for pain

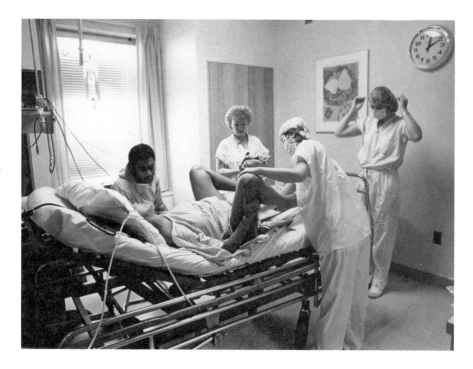

Many hospitals have tried to create a more natural atmosphere for labor and delivery. This mother, for example, is giving birth in the same room where she labored, and the room has been decorated to seem homelike. (Harriet Gans/The Image Works)

and imposing equipment, and is attended mostly by comparative strangers — the doctors and nurses. The surroundings may make some women anxious, and therefore more vulnerable to pain.

To counteract this possibility, various methods of **prepared childbirth** have been devised to help parents rehearse or simulate the actual sensations of labor well before the actual delivery date. Typically, such programs encourage the mother to find a coach (often her spouse or a relative) to give her personal support during labor (Lamaze, 1976). Some hospitals have experimented with more homelike settings for uncomplicated labors and deliveries (Leboyer, 1975; Kliot and Silverstein, 1980; Parker, 1980); they have turned the lights down, kept involvement of medical personnel to a minimum, and encouraged the involvement of spouses or close friends. Though they do not prevent serious birth problems from occurring, these methods, for the majority of uncomplicated births, help to reduce the discomfort of childbirth and may shorten somewhat the labor and recovery period of both mother and newborn.

In spite of good psychological preparation, however, most mothers do feel some pain during labor contractions. In good conditions, many mothers can endure this pain until the baby is delivered. But conditions are not always good: sometimes labor takes unusually long, and sometimes a mother finds herself less well prepared than she thought she was. In such cases, pain-reducing drugs such as narcotics or other sedatives can make the experience bearable. But they must be used cautiously. Most pain relievers cross the placenta and can therefore depress the fetus seriously if they are given at the wrong time or in improper amounts.

During the final stages of delivery, two other forms of pain relief are available.

Rehearsing for labor

Pain relief

Doctors may inject a sedative into the base of the woman's spine; the two most common of these sedatives are called an "epidural" and a "saddle block." They allow the mother to remain awake and alert during the final stages of labor. But they also prevent her from controlling her contractions, which can be quite helpful when the baby is finally expelled. Nitrous oxide, which is commonly used by dentists, has also been used to take the edge off the pain of the peak contractions of labor while allowing the mother to remain conscious.

A more drastic approach is to give the mother a general anesthetic and remove the baby surgically, a procedure called **caesarean section** (from the Latin meaning "to cut"). Techniques for this surgery have improved substantially over the past decades; the operation now takes only about half an hour, most of which is devoted to sewing the mother up again after getting the baby out. The incision is also smaller than it used to be (just a few inches), generally oriented horizontally, and located rather low on the mother's abdomen. Partly because of these improvements, hospitals now deliver increasing numbers of babies by C-section — up to 25 percent of all the births in some hospitals.

This last fact has worried some medical experts and parent advocates, in spite of the safety of the practice (Hausknecht and Heilman, 1978; Kliot and Silverstein, 1980). They agree that caesareans save lives, but they wonder whether surgical delivery of babies has actually become too easy to choose. If it has, then some doctors may actually turn the natural process of childbirth into an unnecessarily complex medical emergency. Not only does such surgery cost money, but it also robs parents of participation in an event that they may consider extremely meaningful.

Giving a mother a general anesthetic before surgery removes all pain, of course, but both mother and child may take a long time to recover from it. Mothers who receive general anesthetics for delivery stay in the hospital for more days after delivery, on the average, than mothers who receive other kinds of medication, at least partly because it takes several days for them to recover from the medication (Hamilton, 1984).

Problems During Labor and Delivery

What can interfere with labor and delivery? Problems can develop in three ways: through faulty power in the uterus, through a faulty passageway (the birth canal), or through a faulty passenger (the baby itself). These problems actually interconnect in various ways, but it is convenient to distinguish among them (Buckley and Kulb, 1983).

Faulty Power   Sometimes the uterus does not contract strongly enough to make labor progress to an actual delivery. The problem can occur immediately, at the beginning of labor, or it can develop midway through a labor that begins quite normally, especially if the mother becomes worn out and discouraged after hours of powerful contractions. In many cases, doctors can make the contractions stronger by giving the mother an injection of the hormone oxytocin. But the resulting artificial contractions have to be watched carefully, since they often do

Too many caesareans?

Oxytocin-induced contractions

not match the needs of the baby or the mother as well as natural contractions do. Such **induced labor** can damage the baby and mother by forcing the baby through the canal before the canal is ready, or by wasting the mother's scarce energy just when she needs it the most.

In about one delivery in two thousand, the uterus itself may rupture because of the power of its contractions (Hamilton, 1984). The condition is quite serious: the mother may bleed to death in just a few moments if she is unattended, and in the process the baby almost always dies. Because uterine rupture happens somewhat more often among mothers who have previously delivered babies surgically, hospitals used to require such mothers to plan on delivering all babies by caesarean section. Recent improvements in surgical techniques, however, have left these mothers with stronger uterine walls, and as a result, many doctors now permit them to attempt natural labor, as long as hospital staff watch carefully for any signs of rupture. If problems do develop, then a caesarean section can still be organized and performed quickly and safely.

Perspectives on Issues

Alternatives to Hospital Labor and Delivery

These days, both hospitals and parents often treat labor and delivery as a medical crisis, even when it is not. Parents frequently come to the hospital too soon after labor contractions begin, so they find themselves spending many hours in the relatively forbidding atmosphere of the labor ward, surrounded by strangers and by the sounds of other women's cries of pain. During these first hours, hospital staff can do little for a mother except keep her comfortable; she might as well be at home, among friends and family. When she nears delivery, she is usually moved to the even more impersonal atmosphere of a delivery room that is full of bright lights, medical equipment, and a narrow, high table for her to lie on. Unfortunately, this transition occurs at the worst possible moment, just when the mother feels an overwhelming urge to expel the baby.

All these inconveniences may be justified for medically risky labors and deliveries. But the large majority of pregnancies simply are not risky: labor proceeds more or less predictably and ends in a gratifying delivery of a healthy baby. These deliveries are not medical crises but personal and intimate celebrations of a new person's very first birthday. Parents and medical experts have sometimes criticized hospitals for interfering with this aspect of labor and delivery; they make the process seem like either a disease or a catastrophe, even when it is not (Leboyer, 1975).

In recent years, several alternative methods of delivery have developed in response to these criticisms. The least drastic are alternative birthing centers within existing hospitals, sometimes nicknamed ABC rooms (Butnarescu and Tillotson, 1983). ABC rooms consist of ordinary hospital rooms that have been decorated to look more homelike; they may have a carpet and nice curtains, and other amenities usually associated with a bedroom. ABC rooms also have ready access to medical staff and hospital equipment, in case of emergencies. Mothers spend their early labor in the ABC room, in more comfort, it is hoped, than in a standard hospital room. As long as no complications occur, they stay in the ABC room for the delivery itself, and are spared the awkward transition to a separate delivery room. But hospitals usually allow only low-risk mothers who have had a

Faulty Passageway Problems can also occur with the placenta. Sometimes it develops too close to the cervix, so that it blocks the baby from moving down the birth canal during labor. This condition is called *placenta previa,* from Latin words meaning "placenta in front of the passageway." Placenta previa usually makes itself known by causing bleeding from the vagina late in pregnancy, but because this bleeding is painless, mothers (and doctors) have a tendency to underestimate its significance. If left untreated, placenta previa can leave the fetus somewhat undernourished, since it prevents enough blood from reaching the fetus, and it sometimes blocks a normal delivery entirely so that the baby must be delivered by caesarean section.

Even if the placenta implants far enough away from the cervix, it may occasionally partly separate from its base against the wall of the womb, a condition called *abruptio placenta.* This condition also causes vaginal bleeding, but unlike placenta previa, the bleeding can be quite painful. Partly as a result, doctors are more likely to detect the problem relatively soon after it occurs. No sure remedy exists,

Placenta blocking the baby

---

healthy and normal pregnancy and who volunteer to use ABC rooms.

ABC rooms have proved so popular that many cities now have entire alternative birthing clinics devoted to this style of labor and delivery. Usually they contain a number of comfortable rooms, and usually they are affiliated closely enough with a hospital so emergencies can be handled smoothly. Often the staff of an alternative birthing clinic includes trained midwives or nurse-midwives (Diers, 1981), who have medical training in assisting labor and delivery for low-risk couples. Their training is either in nursing or in the newly emerging profession of midwifery; either way, it enables the midwife to deliver a low-risk baby without having to call in a physician. For relatively routine labors and deliveries, many families prefer a midwife, since she can often spend more time with the mother than most doctors can.

Perhaps the most drastic alternative to hospital delivery is home birth. Even though a century ago most children were born at home, the rise of modern medicine has made home birth seem like a sign of poverty or ignorance rather than a good idea.

Recently, however, a small number of couples (around 2 to 5 percent) have begun choosing to deliver their babies at home (Lubic, 1981). Usually these parents consider themselves at low risk by medical standards, and often they call in a midwife to assist in labor and delivery.

Even in good conditions, though, home birth leaves most medical experts uneasy. Many parents underestimate the risk of bearing a child. For instance, a baby born prematurely at home needs immediate medical attention to survive, and would get that help faster at a hospital or in a birthing clinic than it will if its father or the midwife must drive it to the nearest hospital. And some labor complications, such as a ruptured uterus, virtually assure the death of the mother and child unless they are attended within a few precious minutes.

For reasons like these, most parents still prefer to put up with the inconveniences of hospital labor and delivery. But the new alternatives have attracted significant numbers of parents, and for the right kind of pregnancy and the right kind of parents, they may be preferable.

A Talk with New Parents

The Childbirth Experience

Paul and Alice Ascari were interviewed in the dining room of their home. Robert, aged six months, rested contentedly in Paul's lap for most of the interview.

INTERVIEWER: What was the experience of having a baby like?

PAUL: Well, I'm sure it was different for each of us, but it was thrilling for me. We had some misconceptions about what it would be like. We'd taken our cassette recorder . . . and sort of thought that it was going to be kind of a home birth setting [at a birthing center]. Unfortunately, Alice's water broke, and they ended up using drugs and fetal monitors so that we were a little bit disheartened at the outset.

Anyway, after we got all hooked up and we changed our mindset about what it was going to be like, we really got into the routine of pushing and counting and breathing and my being the coach and massaging. I was really right there and it really felt spectacular. When the little guy finally came out, it seemed like the ultimate triumph. Like reproduction itself.

INTERVIEWER: How did you decide to use a birthing center?

PAUL: I don't like hospital settings and white stuff. And I tend to think of birth as a natural process, not as an illness. And, you know, for

thousands of years, billions of people have been born in places other than hospitals, so that it is clearly possible to do so. So we wanted, as much as possible, to have a natural birthing experience. We were extremely fortunate in having a birthing center near us with really top-notch medical facilities — while it is still a fairly relaxed environment — and very professional, competent midwives. As it ended up, we had the midwives, but not the birthing center.

INTERVIEWER: What reservations did you have about using a birthing center?

ALICE: People gave us examples of situations where there really had been emergencies, and where not being in a hospital really made a difference. And I would say that I don't share Paul's aversion to medical facilities. I thought being in a hospital was fine. So I wasn't crushed when we couldn't do it in the birthing center. I was, in fact, relieved to learn that we couldn't have gone there anyway, because of my water breaking so early.

INTERVIEWER: What kind of preparation did the two of you have for the birth?

PAUL: We took a standard four-week birthing class at our health plan and practiced the breathing patterns. We also did some reading.

ALICE: We spent a lot of time wishing that we were preparing more, but our lives were so busy that we just didn't have a chance to do it and I went in feeling very unprepared and afraid.

INTERVIEWER: What fears did you have?

ALICE: I had fears about what the pain would be like and just not knowing what it took to give birth and how hard it would be. While it was happening I remember saying, "Oh, now I know why people don't do this very often; it's painful." And I was fine. And the experience was not horrible. Afterwards, I kept on repeating to people who asked me how it was, "If I knew this person was coming out, I would have been rushing to the hospital hours early because it was such a wonderful thing to have this baby."

INTERVIEWER: How did you know that labor had begun?

ALICE: It was around six in the evening. We had had a big potluck supper here and I was coming down the stairs just after people had left when my water broke. So I had a flood on the staircase. I called and checked with the midwives and they said that if I hadn't gone into heavy labor by the morning they would check me into the hospital, which is what happened. So we went to the hospital to be checked but then were sent home. My contractions had started during the night, so that I had begun, officially, having my birth in the early hours of the morning. At eleven o'clock the next morning we checked into the hospital.

INTERVIEWER: How did you first know that labor was beginning?

ALICE: Everyone had said this and it's true — it's unmistakable. Once you're really having contractions, you can't confuse them with anything else. But they are impossible to describe; at least I found that other people's attempts to describe them to me in advance were not helpful.

INTERVIEWER: Paul, what did she say to you?

PAUL: Well, I was supposedly timing them and yet we were asleep, so she would wake me up and say, "I'm having another one." I had my little stopwatch and the contractions seemed about twenty minutes apart and she said they were too painful to sleep but not intolerable. It was kind of deceptive because they never advanced beyond what was first-phase contractions, so they were painful but she wasn't dying.

INTERVIEWER: About how long did it take from the time your contractions started until the baby's head showed?

PAUL: About four or five hours.

ALICE: The other thing that I think surprised us was that I didn't physically go through the stage of birthing that all the books and all the classes tell you about. I used one slow breathing pattern through all of it. The contractions didn't change, but I didn't feel physically different so that everybody, including myself, was really shocked when we did finally check and learn that the baby was almost there. But I kept saying, "But I didn't experience much change and what happened to transition? And all the phases. . . .

INTERVIEWER: What was it like to first see your baby?

ALICE: We were pushing and pushing and they had a mirror, which I wasn't really looking at because I was intensely concentrating on pushing, and everyone went, "Oh!" And I didn't know what was wrong, and they could see his dark hair coming out so I knew that he was on his way. So that was just such a wonderful, exciting moment. And then I barely felt like I was part of the process. And, in a way, you don't know when you're having contractions because you know that if you're doing everything successfully, you're just letting your body do its own work. So, pushing was really an exciting thing and each time I felt Paul and the midwives

were really being helpful in letting me know how far the baby's head was coming out. It was just so wonderful!

INTERVIEWER: You both have big smiles on your faces!

ALICE: It was just really super. And he's so wonderful. There is something so unique and wonderful about having an infant that I think if women who are frightened the way I was before the delivery only *knew* in a concrete sense that they would be guaranteed this wonderful, exhilarating, challenging experience rather than just hearing someone else say it, that fear would really disappear.

Follow-up Questions

1. What were the Ascari's reasons for choosing a birthing center? In your opinion, how appropriate were their concerns?

2. Based on Alice's description of her labor and delivery and your reading of this chapter, in what ways did her childbirth experience follow a typical pattern and in what ways was it atypical?

3. Did the Ascari's classes and other preparation for childbirth prove helpful?

4. In what ways did the attitudes of Alice and Paul toward childbirth change as a result of their own experiences with it?

except for the mother to live sensibly and relatively quietly. Sometimes doctors advise absolute bed rest if they believe that substantial portions of the placenta have separated, but this much enforced inactivity can make mothers worry almost as much as the condition itself (Hamilton, 1984).

Problems with the baby's position or size

Faulty Passenger Usually a baby enters the birth canal head first, but occasionally one may turn in the wrong direction during contractions. A breech presentation, with the bottom leading, is risky for the baby, whose spine can be broken if a contraction presses it too hard against the mother's pelvis. Or the baby may not get enough oxygen, since it cannot begin its own breathing until after its nose comes out. In many cases, a skilled midwife or doctor can deliver a breech baby with no problem, but if the baby gets stuck part way out of the vagina, medical staff may use **forceps** to pull it the rest of the way out of the birth canal. Used with care, forceps, which resemble scissors with long, blunt ends, need not hurt the baby.

A small but significant proportion of babies are simply too big to pass through their mother's pelvis and vaginal canal, a problem sometimes called cephalopelvic disproportion (literally, a disproportion of the head and pelvis). Extra hours of labor do not help to push such babies through; their heads are simply too big to fit, though often by only a fraction of an inch. Unfortunately, the problem does not usually reveal itself until well into labor. Such a mismatch of size can result from genetic influence, but, ironically, it also results from an especially healthy, well-nourished pregnancy, which creates an especially large baby. In any case, if the mismatch is too severe, it can threaten the life of the mother or the child, so doctors may interrupt the labor and deliver the baby surgically.

Premature Birth

Occasionally, of course, a baby is born prematurely: approximately 6 to 8 percent of the live births in the United States occur before the full term of pregnancy is reached. An infant is generally considered **premature** (or **preterm**) if it has a prenatal age of less than thirty-seven weeks. The bigger and more mature the infant at birth, the greater its chances for survival. With the best medical care, approximately 85 percent of infants weighing 2.2 to 3.2 pounds and approximately 55 percent of those weighing 1.6 to 2.2 pounds survive (Paneth et al., 1982). Intensive-care nurseries use computerized equipment to continuously monitor the vital signs of the newborn, including blood pressure, heart rate, temperature, and blood chemistry so that immediate steps can be taken if problems arise.

Respiratory distress syndrome (RSD) is a leading cause of death among preterm infants. One cause of RSD is a lack of surfactant, a substance which develops in the amniotic fluid at about the thirty-fifth week and which helps lubricate the air sacs and prevent the lungs from sticking together. This problem may be reduced by providing surfactant to babies who lack it. It should be noted that even full-term babies with normal surfactant development are more likely to have trouble with breathing than with any other single physical process (Root, 1983).

Breathing problems of preterm infants

Compared with full-term babies, preterm infants experience a higher incidence of abnormalities in physical growth, motor behavior, neurological functioning, and intellectual development (Taub et al., 1977; Kopp and Parmelle, 1979). Paradoxically, the high-level equipment and intensive medical care that have helped to save the lives of preterm infants may also contribute to the developmental difficulties they are more likely to experience. It has been discovered that the incubators and banks of monitoring equipment and intensive treatment may restrict the important physical and emotional contact and interaction between infant and parent that is essential to the formation of early emotional bonds (Cornell and Gottfried, 1976; Gottfried et al., 1981).

Interference with bonding

It has also been discovered that preterm babies account for between 23 and 40 percent of all battered children even though they make up less than 10 percent of all babies, suggesting that this may be due to the prolonged separation imposed by intensive care units (Kennell et al., 1979). As a result, parents with infants in intensive-care units are now encouraged to spend as much time as they want with their infants and to assume as much of their routine care as is possible in order to facilitate physical and emotional contact and more normal development of early parent-infant relationships. This is discussed at greater length in Chapter 5.

Checkpoint   *The birth process occurs in three overlapping stages. During the first stage of labor, contractions of the uterus increase and the cervix dilates to accommodate the baby's head. The second stage of labor lasts from first sight of the baby's head until birth. During the third stage, the afterbirth is expelled. Prepared childbirth, delivery in more homelike settings, and the judicious use of drugs can contribute to reducing the pain and discomfort of childbirth. Insufficient contractions, blockage of the birth canal, and a baby with a large head or in the wrong position can cause complications during the delivery. The birth of a preterm baby also poses additional risks.*

From Biological to Psychological Development

The process of prenatal development presents a contradictory picture. On the one hand, it seems highly predictable and insensitive to the influences that might change its course. Starting from a single cell, it rapidly unfolds and develops in an increasingly complex sequence of interrelated patterns of change, all of which have become highly canalized over the thousands of years of human evolution. It is as if from the moment of conception, the emergence of the newborn baby nine months later is never in doubt. Although deviations from these normal developmental pathways do occur, they are not really genuine alternatives to normal prenatal development; rather, they seem to emphasize further the predictability of most embryos and fetuses.

On the other hand, while birth marks the end of prenatal development, it is only

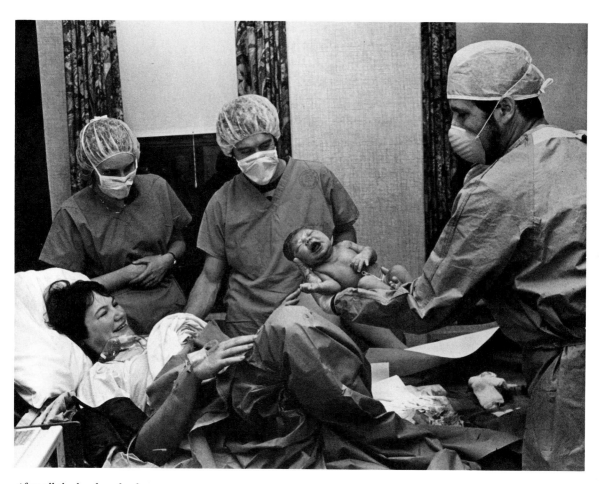

After all the hard work of labor, a baby! No matter how exhausted she may feel, a mother usually is glad to see her new child, especially once reassured that it is healthy. (Milton Feinberg/The Picture Cube)

the beginning of the incredible range of developmental changes that are to follow: changes that are much less canalized or predictable. The knowledge that biology seems to lose its hold on the child once it emerges from the womb and that the environment and experience take over may be overwhelming to a new parent. Indeed, the range of problems that might occur between conception and birth are quite limited when compared to what a child will experience between birth and adulthood. Nevertheless, as we shall discover in the chapters that follow, biology and experience will continue to stay too closely intertwined to be sharply distinguished from one another. The path a child's development takes will be only partially determined by her experiences, including the efforts of her parents.

Summary of Major Ideas

Early Stages of Development

1. Prenatal development begins with conception, in which a zygote is created by the union of a sperm cell from the father and an egg cell, or ovum, from the mother.

2. Prenatal development divides into discrete periods or stages, just as later development does.

3. The germinal stage occurs during the first weeks following conception; the zygote forms a blastocyst, which differentiates into three different cell layers and then implants itself in the uterus wall to form the embryo.

4. During the embryonic stage, which lasts from the third through the seventh week of pregnancy, the placenta and umbilical cord form and the basic organs and biological systems begin to develop.

5. During the fetal stage, which spans from the eighth week until the end of pregnancy, all physical features complete their development.

6. Embryonic and fetal development follow a cephalo-caudal (head to tail) and a proximo-distal (near to far) pattern of development.

Prenatal Influences on the Child

7. Pregnancy is generally divided into three trimesters, each lasting three months.

8. Particularly during the early part of the first trimester, there are critical periods when embryonic development is highly vulnerable or at risk to disruption.

9. Certain biological risks to prenatal development are associated with the physical and biological characteristics of the mother, including her age, physical size, and state of health.

10. Illnesses such as rubella and syphilis can irreversibly harm the embryo or fetus, particularly during its critical period of development.

11. Teratogens, which include alcohol, smoking, and drugs such as thalidomide, DES, and heroin, can cause physical malformations, developmental retardation, or death.

12. Inadequate diet and nutrition and stress can adversely influence prenatal development.

Parental Reactions to Pregnancy

13. Pregnancy causes many complex hormonal and biological changes in the mother that can be physically and psychologically uncomfortable, particularly at the beginning of the first and end of the last trimester.

14. An expectant mother may not only feel physically uncomfortable but also feel impatient, and concerned about her baby's well-being; in addition, she may experience excitement, wonder, and elation about the special experiences of pregnancy, childbirth, and motherhood.

15. Whereas an expectant father shares many of the mother's concerns and upsets and may even feel threatened by the loss of his wife's attention and support, he also experiences great pleasure and excitement about the events.

16. The presence of adequate social and emotional support from friends, family, and neighbors can contribute significantly to reducing the stress of pregnancy and to making it a positive experience.

Birth

17. Toward the end of the third trimester, the mother may experience "false labor," including contractions of the uterus; she also may have a bloody vaginal discharge shortly before true labor begins.

18. Labor occurs in three distinct but overlapping stages.

19. During the first stage of labor, which may last from eight to twenty-four hours for a first-time mother, uterine contractions increase in strength and regularity, and the cervix dilates sufficiently to accommodate the baby's head.

20. The second stage of labor lasts from the "crowning" of the baby's head until birth and takes one or one and a half hours.

21. During the third stage of labor, which lasts only a few minutes, the afterbirth is expelled.

22. Prepared childbirth and pain-reducing drugs such as narcotics, sedatives, and nitrous oxide can make the experience of childbirth more comfortable.

23. In recent years drugs have been used more cautiously in childbirth because of their potential to have adverse effects on the recovery of both infant and mother.

24. One of the problems that may arise during labor and delivery is insufficient uterine contractions, or faulty power.

25. A faulty passageway caused by blockage of the birth canal by the placenta (placenta previa) is another problem that may occur.

26. A third type of problem — faulty passenger — may occur if the baby's physical position or large head size prevent it from completing its journey through the birth canal.

27. Preterm babies may experience significant complications after birth; however, the bigger and more mature they are at birth, the greater are their chances for survival.

Key Terms

germinal stage *(118)*
embryonic stage *(118)*
fetal stage *(118)*
ovum *(118)*
spermatozoa *(119)*
zygote *(119)*
conception *(119)*
blastocyst *(120)*
embryonic disk *(121)*
ectoderm *(121)*
endoderm *(121)*
mesoderm *(121)*
implantation *(121)*
villi *(121)*
trophoblast *(121)*
embryo *(121)*
cephalocaudal
  development *(122)*
proximodistal
  development *(122)*
placenta *(122)*
osmosis *(122)*
umbilical cord *(122)*
amniotic sac *(123)*
fetus *(123)*
artificial
  insemination *(124)*
in vitro
  fertilization *(124)*
surrogate
  mothering *(125)*
quickening *(125)*
canalization *(127)*

risk factors *(127)*
critical period *(127)*
trimesters *(127)*
rubella *(130)*
toxoplasmosis *(131)*
teratogens *(131)*
fetal alcohol
  syndrome *(132)*
eclampsia *(138)*
hormones *(139)*
dizygotic twins *(142)*
monozygotic twins *(142)*
cephalic
  presentation *(143)*
breech
  presentation *(143)*
transverse
  presentation *(143)*
first stage of labor *(145)*
transition *(145)*
second stage of
  labor *(145)*
third stage of labor *(145)*
prepared
  childbirth *(146)*
caesarean section *(147)*
induced labor *(148)*
forceps *(152)*
premature *(152)*
preterm *(152)*
respiratory distress
  syndrome (RSD) *(152)*

What Do You Think?

1. How has reading this chapter influenced your views about pregnancy?

2. Based on your reading, what advice might you give to prospective parents concerning changes in their lifestyle to minimize prenatal risks?

3. How might you reassure expectant parents about their concerns regarding whether their baby will be all right?

4. What do you know about your own parents' reactions to their pregnancy with you?

5. What was the process of your own birth like? What problems or complications may have been involved in it?

For Further Reading

The Boston Women's Health Collective. *The New Our Bodies, Ourselves: A Book by and for Women.* New York: Simon and Schuster, 1984.

This revised and updated version discusses many aspects of women's bodies, health care, and well-being from the personal perspectives of women themselves. Its section on pregnancy is an excellent source of information about what the events and experiences are really like.

Caplan, F. *The First Twelve Months of Life.* New York: Bantam Books, 1981.

A very readable presentation of research and the everyday experiences of parents during pregnancy, childbirth, and the early days of new parenthood.

Falkner, F., and Macy, C. *Pregnancy and Birth.* New York: Harper and Row, 1980.

A book focusing on the experiences of mothers during pregnancy and childbirth.

Feldman, S. *Choices in Childbirth.* New York: Grosset and Dunlap, 1978.

A guide to decision making during pregnancy that discusses the options for method of childbirth, hospital versus home deliveries, the use of medication, and so on.

Hees-Stauthamer, J. *The First Pregnancy: An Integrated Principle in Female Psychology.* Ann Arbor, Mich.: UMI Research Press, 1985.

This book presents an in-depth study of the subjective, emotional experiences of four women, each over thirty and pregnant for the first time.

Nilsson, L. *A Child Is Born.* New York: Dell, 1977.

A book that clearly and thoughtfully describes prenatal development and problems that may occur; it includes many beautiful color photographs of the developing embryo and fetus.

3 The First Two Years

As parents and other proud relatives keep discovering, infants grow and change more rapidly than the rest of us. Parents who take snapshots of their children find that they must do so every few months — or even weeks — in order to keep up with these changes. In a matter of months, infants become able to smile, sit, and babble. In just a few more months, they acquire language and the first symbolic skills, and take their first tentative steps. And throughout all these events, they acquire definite attachments to particular care-givers.

These changes are crucial in many ways: they make infants seem much more "human" than they were as newborns. And they lay important foundations for all future development. The next three chapters describe these critical changes.

Chapter

5

The First Two Years: Physical Development

Focusing Questions

- What do newborn infants look like, and how do they act?
- How do infants' sleep patterns change as they get older?
- How much are infants — especially young ones — aware of their surroundings?
- How do motor skills evolve during infancy? What influences the course of their development?
- What are the effects of low birth weight on infant development?
- What do infants need nutritionally during the first two years?
- What are the relative advantages of breast feeding and bottle feeding?
- What dietary deficiencies occur commonly in infants' diets, both in North America and around the world?

As THE LAST CHAPTER showed, birth continues rather than begins physical development. Most organs have already been working for several weeks, or even months, prior to this event. The baby's heart has been beating regularly; his muscles have been contracting sporadically; and his liver has been making its major product, bile, which is necessary for normal digestion after birth. Two physical functions, though, do begin at birth: breathing and ingestion (the taking in of foods). Even some behaviors, such as sucking and arm-stretching, have already developed, though generally these have not advanced as far as the baby's physical functions. During the first months of life, the baby's behaviors evolve rapidly. By his second birthday — considered the end of infancy — he seems much more mature or human — more able to think for himself and to express interest in people, and more able to choose how to use his energies and attentions — than he did at birth. He is still "just a baby," of course, but at twenty-four months he is a very competent one.

This chapter will trace some of these physical developments through the first two years of life. It begins by discussing very young infants: what they look like and how they act immediately after birth. It then investigates babies' nervous systems, including the growth of their brains and how they are affected by sleep patterns, before going on to discuss the development of the senses. Then the chapter shifts attention to how infants develop motor skills, beginning with their early, inborn reflexes and ending with the first major voluntary skills, such as walking and grasping at objects. For normal infants these skills develop at much the same time and in much the same sequence. But the skills also vary significantly according to the circumstances that individual children encounter, and the chapter describes several circumstances that can cause variation. Finally, the chapter discusses infants' nutritional needs: what food they need immediately at birth, how these needs change as they get older, and how a poor or inappropriate diet can affect infants' physical development as they move into childhood.

Appearance of the Young Infant

The First Few Hours

When first delivered, the newborn baby, or **neonate,** definitely does *not* resemble most people's stereotypes of a beautiful baby. No matter what her race, her skin may look rather red — redder than parents usually expect, especially if they have never paid close attention to newborn babies before. She may be covered with various substances, such as fluid from the amniotic sac, blood from the placenta, and bits of brownish fluid from her own bowels. Many babies, especially if born a bit early, also have a white waxy substance called **vernix** on their skin, and their bodies may be covered with fine, downy hair called **lanugo.** If an infant is delivered vaginally rather than by surgery, her head may be somewhat elongated or have a noticeable point on it; the shape comes from the pressure of the birth canal, which squeezes the bones of her skull together for several hours during labor. Within a few days or weeks the baby's head fills out again to a more normal shape, leaving gaps in the bones. These are sometimes called **fontanelles,** or "soft spots," although they are actually covered by a tough membrane that can withstand normal contact and pressure. The gaps do not all grow over with bone until about eighteen months.

Typically, newborns react vigorously to their surroundings during the first fifteen or thirty minutes of life. They may cry, look around, or suck, generally using their inborn reflexes (described later in this chapter). Before long, though, they fall asleep (labor can wear them out, too!), and usually they do not revive again for a few hours. Some psychologists therefore consider the earliest minutes and hours **Early bonding** of life especially important for getting parents and children interested in each other — for "parent-infant bonding," as it is sometimes called (Klaus and Kennell, 1976).

Unfortunately, not every delivery goes smoothly enough to allow immediate or leisurely contact following birth. Some babies and mothers will only survive the aftermath of a difficult labor and delivery if they receive instant medical attention that requires their separation. Are such parents and babies jeopardized in their relationships with each other? Are they less able to become attached to each other over the long run? Not necessarily, as long as other forces exist to encourage a good relationship as the baby gets a little older (Lamb and Hwang, 1982).

Is the Baby All Right?

The Apgar Scale Since hospitals cannot always afford to have a pediatrician attend every birth, doctors and nurses need a way of deciding quickly which newborns need immediate attention from a pediatrician and which are healthy enough to wait a bit longer. The Apgar Scale (named after its originator, Dr. Virginia Apgar) helps to meet this need (Apgar, 1953). The Apgar Scale does not give a lot of detail about a baby's condition, but it does help identify those infants who may need special medical help right away.

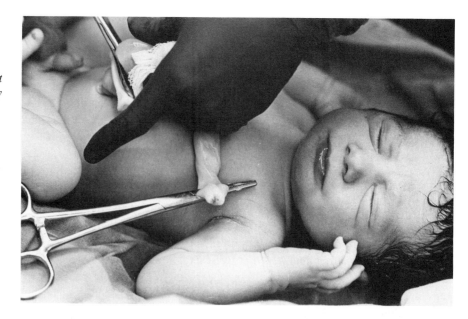

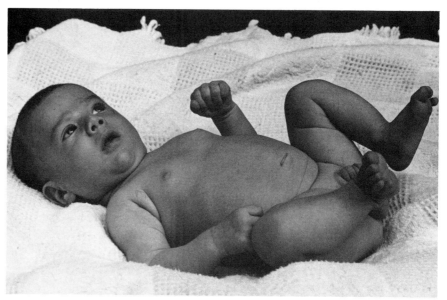

The **Apgar Scale** consists of ratings that are simple enough for nonspecialists to make, even during the distractions surrounding the moment of delivery. To use it, someone at the delivery calculates the baby's heart rate, breathing, muscle tone, color, and reflex irritability and assigns a score from 0 to 2 to each of these five characteristics. Babies are rated one minute after they emerge from the womb, again at five minutes, and occasionally also at fifteen minutes. Each time they can earn a maximum score of 10, as shown in Table 5-1. Most babies in fact earn nine or ten points, at least by five minutes after delivery. If a baby scores between four and seven points at one minute, she is given immediate special medical attention

Characteristic	Score		
	0	1	2
Heart rate	Absent	Less than 100 beats per minute	More than 100 beats per minute
Efforts to breathe	Absent	Slow, irregular	Good; baby is crying
Muscle tone	Flaccid, limp	Weak, inactive	Strong, active motion
Skin color	Body pale or blue	Body pink, extremities blue	Body and extremities pink
Reflex irritability	No response	Frown, grimace	Vigorous crying, coughing, sneezing

Table 5-1   *The Apgar Scale*

Source: Apgar, 1953.

(Apgar and Beck, 1973), which almost always includes examination by a pediatrician, and is then carefully observed during the next few hours and days for problems that may develop.

Babies who score below 4 on the Apgar Scale face serious medical risk. Their heart rate is slow, their breathing is irregular and difficult, and their muscle tone is rather weak. Instead of the healthy pink color that results from an ample supply of oxygen in their blood, babies with low Apgar ratings may look blue in their extremities, or even all over their bodies. And they do not respond strongly when stimulated; a sudden noise, for example, produces no startle reaction. Such babies need intensive care immediately if they are to survive. Their most immediate problem usually concerns breathing: often they require oxygen and special apparatus to make breathing less difficult. With intensive medical care, however, most of these babies do survive.

Signs of risk

The Brazelton Neonatal Behavioral Assessment Scale   Although Apgar scores reflect a baby's condition in the moments after birth, other observations are needed to assess health and behavior later in infancy. One such method is the **Brazelton Neonatal Behavioral Assessment Scale** (Brazelton, 1973, 1979), a neurological and behavioral test that is usually given on the third day of life and often repeated again a few days later. It is intended to determine how well infants can regulate their responses to various stimuli.

To give the test, a skilled observer purposely arouses the infant from deep sleep and moves it through alert wakefulness to distressed crying, then back through the quieter states and eventually to sleep again. To accomplish all these changes, the observer presents the baby with various rattles, pictures, and other stimuli, including the examiner's face and voice. Altogether, he or she notes twenty different neurological reflexes during the test, as well as responses to twenty-six different stimuli. At each step the observer notices not only how well and how quickly the infant responds but also how quickly she quiets herself afterward. Having the abil-

Assessing responsiveness

ity both to respond and to quiet shows good neurological health. As babies develop further during infancy, they continually need both abilities; they cannot afford to ignore the interesting sights and sounds around them, but they also cannot afford to let those sights and sounds overwhelm them (Sameroff, 1979).

Newborn Weight

As adults we are used to having a fairly fixed bodily size, with only minor changes in our waistlines, perhaps, as the years go by. Not so for young infants: changes in size, weight, and bodily proportions are a constant occurrence in their lives. Viewed by casual adult observers, a young infant seems first to be small and second to be growing rapidly. Viewed by adults who know the infant well, though, the baby seems primarily to grow and change weight and only secondarily to be small (Eichorn, 1979).

At birth a typical baby weighs about seven and one-half pounds, or 3,400 grams — about as much as a large cat or a small dog. Because they are so small, neonates have a rather large surface area compared to their weight. As a result they lose heat more easily than adults do, and they have to eat proportionately more calories just to keep warm. But neonates also need to gain weight during the earliest months; by four months of age they have typically doubled their birth weight (see Figure 5-1). How, then, can they keep themselves warm and gain quite a lot of weight at the same time?

Need for calories

Figure 5-1 *Height and Weight Growth During the First Two Years*

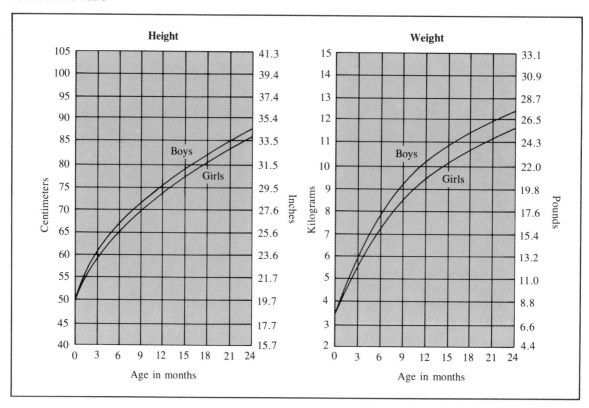

The answer is, they eat. Because the baby still has no teeth, he has to drink all his calories. A newborn will usually consume about one quart of breast milk or infant formula in twenty-four hours. Considered as a proportion of his body weight, this is the same as if an adult drank ten to twenty quarts per day. And of course the baby must excrete after capturing the valuable nutrients from these huge amounts. No wonder, then, that diapers and feedings form the center of a new-born's life.

Size and Bodily Proportions

Lying down, a new baby measures about twenty inches, or fifty centimeters. His length matches his adult size more closely than his weight does: his twenty inches represent more than a quarter of his final height, whereas his seven and one half pounds represent only a small percentage of his adult weight.

Even though this fact suggests that newborns should look skinny, they usually look chubby or overweight instead. Babies' heads take up almost a quarter of their length, and their limbs are disproportionately short (see Figure 5-2). Their chests seem small compared to their stomachs, which often stick out like a middle-aged person's pot belly. Bones contribute much less to overall weight than they do for adults: they are small and thin in proportion to the baby's size. For all these reasons, babies tend to look rather fat and cute.

Babies' proportions and general physical appearance may have psychological consequences by fostering **attachments** or bonds between infants and the people who care for them, which promotes feelings of security. The cuteness of infants' faces in particular seems to help; most babies have an unusually large forehead, features that are concentrated in the lower part of the face, eyes that are large and round, and cheeks that are high and prominent. Dolls and cartoon characters have

Effects of cuteness

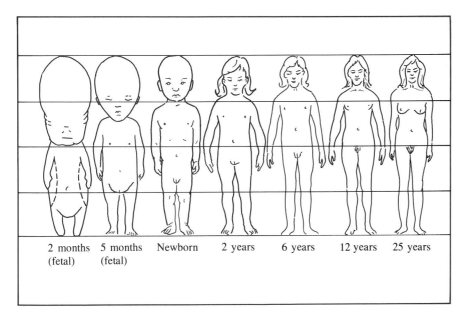

2 months (fetal)   5 months (fetal)   Newborn   2 years   6 years   12 years   25 years

Figure 5-2 Body Proportions, Fetal Period Through Adulthood

these facial features too, though often in exaggerated form, and so do a variety of animal species. The pattern of babyish features occurs so widely among animals, in fact, that biologists who study animal behavior suspect that it has universal and genetically based power to attract parental or nurturing responses among adult animals (Lorenz, 1970). Mothers in some species of ducks, for example, take care of baby ducks even when the babies are not their own.

Cuteness apparently affects humans in comparable ways, though not as automatically as among other animals. The mere sight of a babyish face creates interest in a wide variety of human beings, and in a wide variety of situations. Interest occurs both consciously and unconsciously. Not only do people say that they find babies attractive, but their pupils enlarge and their hearts actually beat faster as well. Unlike many other animal species, humans are interested even if they are not mothers or adults; babies, for example, seem at least as interested in fellow babies as many adults are (McCall and Kennedy, 1980; Berman, 1980).

Checkpoint *A newly delivered infant, or neonate, has a number of distinctive physical features, such as lanugo and several fontanelles. The first hours are especially important for initiating positive relationships between parents and their new child and for assessing the infant's overall health. The bodily proportions of a newborn infant differ distinctively from those of adults, and these differences may actually encourage care-givers to become attached to the infant.*

Development of the Nervous System

The **central nervous system** consists of the brain and nerve cells of the spinal cord. Together, they coordinate and control the perception of stimuli, as well as motor responses of all kinds. The more complex parts of this work are accomplished by the brain, which develops rapidly from just before birth until well beyond a child's second birthday. At seven months past conception the brain weighs about 10 percent of its final adult weight, but by birth it has more than doubled, to about 25 percent of final adult weight. By the child's second birthday it has more than doubled again, to about 75 percent of final adult weight (Tanner, 1978b).

Brain growth   Most of the increase results not from increasing numbers of nerve cells, or **neurons,** but from the development of a denser or more fully packed brain. This happens in two ways. First, the neurons put out many new fibers that connect them with one another, and second, certain brain cells called **glia** put out special sheathing, or **myelin,** which gradually encases the neurons and their fibers and which helps the fibers to transmit impulses faster and more reliably. Myelinization may account for some of the improvements in motor and perceptual skills during infancy (though certainly not all of them). The first neurons to be fully myelinated, for example, are the ones associated with the sense organs; and partly for this reason, infants' senses work nearly as well as adults' within just a few months of birth (Brierley, 1976).

Growth of the Brain

Growth of cerebrum

At birth neural activity is dominated by the relatively primitive or lower areas of the brain, called the **brain stem** and the **midbrain,** which regulate relatively automatic functions such as breathing and digestion and general alertness or consciousness. During the first year, however, growth occurs most rapidly in the higher parts of the brain, called the **cerebrum** and the **cerebral cortex,** and is especially noticeable in two areas: those that control simple sensations such as vision, hearing, and touch, and those that control simple motor actions such as lifting an arm or wiggling the fingers. These parts of the brain are sometimes also named the primary sensory cortex and the primary motor cortex, after their major functions.

By the end of infancy the overall anatomical features of the brain are reasonably well established, but various parts of the cerebrum continue to develop specialized functions. The left hemisphere, for example, appears to specialize in language. As a result, most three-year-olds understand language more accurately and easily if it is fed into the left hemisphere (or half) of their brain with special earphones (Hiscock and Kinsbourne, 1980). In spite of such specialization, though, other facts suggest that children's brains retain flexibility for many years. Children whose normal brain language centers are damaged, for example, can usually recover most of their language ability as long as the damage occurs before adolescence. Apparently they recover because the brain finds new areas of the cerebrum to devote to language processing.

Effects of sensory stimulation

To a large extent, brain specialization appears to be driven or stimulated by sensory experiences. For instance, animals who are blindfolded or physically restrained become handicapped for life in ways related to their deprivation (Parmalee and Sigman, 1983). Dogs who are prevented from experiencing pain can burn themselves badly simply by sniffing at an ordinary candle flame too closely. Such dogs apparently do not develop normal sensitivity to pain. Partly as a result of this neural deficit, they have trouble learning to protect themselves from ordinarily painful stimuli such as heat from a candle. The nerve fibers that register pain, either in their nose or in their brain, simply do not grow properly.

States of Sleep and Wakefulness

One important function of the brain is to control infants' states of sleep and wakefulness. It thus regulates how much stimulation infants experience, both externally and internally. Periodic sleep helps infants to shut out external stimulation, and thereby allows them to obtain general physical rest. But as pointed out below, certain kinds of sleep may also increase internal stimulation, and thereby encourage healthy brain development.

Sleep Very young infants vary from deep sleep to wakefulness, with much more of the former than of the latter. In the days immediately after birth newborns sleep an average of sixteen hours per day, although some may sleep as little as eleven hours a day and others as much as twenty-one (Berg and Berg, 1979). For most infants the amount of sleep decreases steadily with each passing month. By the age of six months, babies average just thirteen or fourteen hours per day, and by twenty-four months, just eleven or twelve. But these hours still represent considerably more sleeping time than is typical for adults.

REM sleep

Newborns divide their sleeping time about equally between relatively active and quiet periods of sleep. The more active kind is named **REM sleep,** after the "*r*apid *e*ye *m*ovements" or twitchings that usually accompany it. REM sleep generally seems restless: sometimes infants' limbs or facial muscles twitch, and their breathing seems faster and more irregular. In the quieter kind of sleep **(non-REM sleep),** infants breathe regularly and more slowly, and their muscles become much limper.

During the night infants experience cycles of REM and non-REM sleep; for young infants, these begin with REM sleep, and each cycle lasts about one hour. Adults experience similar cycles of sleep, but they usually begin with non-REM sleep, and each cycle lasts at least two hours. Furthermore, adults usually report dreaming during REM sleep. Although infants may also dream during REM sleep, the unique cycles of their sleep suggest that REM sleep may serve other purposes. One possibility is that periods of REM sleep stimulate babies' brains in gen-

---

Perspectives on Research

Sudden Infant Death Syndrome

Every year about two out of every thousand young infants die in their sleep for no apparent reason. Doctors call this **sudden infant death syndrome,** or SIDS. The problem is most frequent among infants between the ages of two months and four months, although SIDS, also called crib death, can happen to babies as young as one month and as old as one year. It is the leading cause of death among infants who survive the first few weeks after delivery.

SIDS is disturbing because it is so mysterious. Typically, parents put a seemingly healthy baby down to sleep as usual, but when they come in to get him up again, they discover that he is dead. A few cases have even occurred when parents are actually holding their sleeping infant (Franciosi, 1983). Sadly, because of the absence of obvious health problems, parents often blame themselves for the death, suspecting that somehow they have

neglected their child or hurt him in some way (Halpern, 1983). Even more unfortunately, friends and relatives often concur in blaming the parents, simply because they can think of no other way to explain SIDS. Other obvious causes simply do not occur; the baby does not choke or vomit or suffocate. He seems just to stop breathing.

One proposed theory about SIDS emphasizes abnormal breathing patterns among infants who may be at risk. Most infants (and children too) experience occasional **sleep apnea,** or temporary stoppages of breathing during sleep. But some experts argue that SIDS infants experience apnea more frequently than usual, or that they experience it for longer periods at a time (Shannon, 1980). Another theory suggests that SIDS happens primarily at a special developmental transition: just when inborn reflex control of breathing begins to fade in importance but before infants have firmly established

eral, and in doing so foster healthy growth of nerve fibers and glial cells. This possibility is supported by studies that show that neonates engage in shorter and fewer REM sleep periods if they receive a lot of sensory stimulation when they are awake (Boismier, 1977).

Unfortunately for parents, a baby's extra sleep does not usually include long, uninterrupted rest periods, even at night. It is more common in the first few months for the baby to wake frequently — often every two or three hours — but sometimes unpredictably. Studies of brain development suggest that much of the unpredictability may result from the physical immaturity of the baby's nervous system: his brain may have frequent, accidental "storms" of impulses because it is not yet fully formed (Parmelee and Stern, 1972; Emde and Robinson, 1979).

States of Arousal By the age of about six months or so, the infant typically shows various states of arousal that resemble those of older children and adults (Berg and Berg, 1979). Table 5-2 summarizes these. The largest share of time, though, even for older infants, goes to the most completely relaxed and deepest form of sleep.

Variations in arousal matter considerably to parents and other caretakers of infants. Only during the alert times can a baby look at her surroundings and begin forming initial impressions of them. She begins seeing human faces, particularly

Effects of arousal

breathing under voluntary control (Lipsitt, 1979, 1982). For most infants this transition happens at about two to four months of age — just when SIDS happens most often. Perhaps at this time infants cannot respond effectively to *any* blockage of their nasal passages.

Medical research has identified several factors that make a particular family or infant more likely to experience SIDS. Very young mothers and fathers (under twenty years) stand more chance of having a SIDS infant; so do mothers who smoke cigarettes or who have serious illnesses during pregnancy. Mothers who are poorly nourished during pregnancy also carry more risk than mothers who keep reasonably well nourished. But certain babies also have more risk of SIDS, independent of their parents' qualities; boys die of SIDS more often than girls, for example, and infants born small (less than seven pounds) die more often than bigger infants.

Even taken together, though, factors like these do not predict SIDS very accurately. The vast majority of high-risk infants never die, whereas some infants with few risk factors do die of SIDS anyway (Standfast et al., 1983). This fact creates problems in translating the studies of risk factors into concrete recommendations for medical personnel and parents, because following the risk indications too literally can arouse fears among many parents unnecessarily. The most useful recommendations are ones that are good for all families, whether or not they are at risk for SIDS. For example, it is a good idea to recommend that parents should not smoke, and that an infant's room should be humidified if possible whenever she catches a cold. This is sound medical advice for everyone, but unfortunately it is not a guarantee against SIDS.

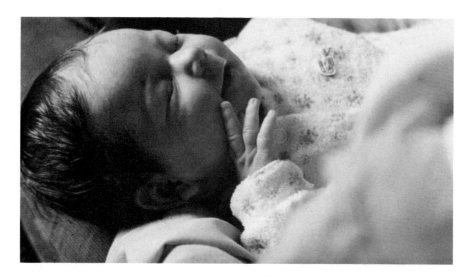

Newborn infants exhibit three basic types of behavior: deep sleep, vigorous distress, and periods of alertness, but most of their time is spent sleeping. (above, Julie O'Neil; right, Linda Benedict Jones/ Lightwave

the faces that care for her the most, and she begins noticing that various sounds and sights usually occur together — that a mouth opening and shutting, for example, usually occurs when a human voice comes her way. These experiences constitute the earliest perceptions, and may stimulate the earliest attachments.

On the other hand, a fully alert state may not be the only condition in which young babies learn. Infants fail to **habituate,** or get used to, sounds and other stimulation that occur during more active REM sleep. Heart rates speed up in reaction to such stimulation, suggesting the possibility that infants do some sort of mental processing of the stimulation even while asleep (Johnson et al., 1975; Weinberger et al., 1984). The processing may constitute a sign of learning about the environment, but at present this is not certain.

State	Behavior of Infant
Non-REM sleep	Complete rest; muscles relaxed; eyes closed and still; breathing regular and relatively slow
REM sleep	Occasional twitches, jerks, facial grimaces; irregular and intermittent eye movements; breathing irregular and relatively rapid
Drowsiness	Occasional movements, but less than in REM sleep; eyes open and close; glazed look; breathing regular, but faster than in non-REM sleep
Alert inactivity	Eyes open and scanning; body relatively still; rate of breathing similar to drowsiness, but more irregular
Alert activity	Eyes open, but not attending or scanning; frequent, diffuse bodily movements; vocalizations; irregular breathing; skin flushed
Distress	Whimpering or crying; vigorous or agitated movements; facial grimaces pronounced; skin very flushed

***Table* 5-2** *States of Arousal in Infants*

Source: Wolff, 1966.

Checkpoint *During infancy a child's brain — especially the cerebrum — grows rapidly and it achieves most of its final size by the end of infancy. At the same time certain parts of the brain begin to acquire specialized functions, but the specialization is not really complete until adolescence. Newborns spend most of their time sleeping; but sleep decreases substantially during the first two years, and more alert states begin to dominate.*

Sensory Development

All of the human senses operate at birth. This conclusion follows from a variety of observations and experiments with neonates. Sometimes, for example, newborn infants prefer slight changes in brightness, as shown by their staring longer at a light that changes slightly in intensity than at one that does not. And sometimes newborns' heart rates change when a sensation changes; a slightly louder or higher sound can have this effect. Under certain conditions, too, newborn babies respond overtly to a sensation; they sometimes turn toward a sound, for example, or away from a bad odor. Behaviors and responses like these show that newborns have a full complement of senses. But observations also reveal that they have certain sensory limitations as well.

Visual Acuity

Infants can see at birth, but without the clarity of focus or acuity characteristic of adults with good vision. They can track a bright light even before they leave the hospital delivery room, as long as the light lies near their line of vision and moves fairly slowly. When looking at single lines, though, newborns reveal their poor acuity. To be noticed by newborns, such lines must be about ten times as wide as necessary for adults, and if the lines lie off to one side of the infants' line of vision, they must be even wider (Cohen et al., 1979). These facts imply that infants have distance vision of about 20/200 or worse, which means that they can see at twenty feet what an adult with good vision can see at two hundred feet. Newborns see more clearly at short distances, and especially at about eight to ten inches, but even their near vision may not become well established until about one month of age (Banks, 1983).

Limitations of early vision (margin note)

Sometime during infancy visual acuity approaches adult levels, but precisely when remains unclear. Early studies suggested that infants achieved 20/20 vision by about six months of age (Fantz, 1963). But these studies offered infants complicated stimuli such as faces and patterns, which may have proved easier to detect than the single lines used in the newer research. By offering added visual cues, the complex stimuli allow infants to combine sensations into meaningful patterns, an activity called **perception,** discussed in the next chapter.

Auditory Acuity

Auditory acuity refers to sensitivity to sounds. Infants can hear at birth, but not as well as adults. Any sudden loud noise, such as the sound caused by dropping a large book on the floor, demonstrates that they can hear. The sound produces a dramatic startle reaction, called a Moro reflex: the neonate withdraws her limbs suddenly, sometimes shakes all over, and sometimes also cries (Bench, 1978). But not all noises produce this reaction. Pure tones, like the sound of a flute, cause relatively little response. Complex noises containing many different sounds usually produce more; a bag of nails spilling on the floor, for example, tends to startle infants reliably (Bench et al., 1976).

Limitations of early hearing (margin note)

Even when they do not startle overtly, though, newborn infants do respond internally to sounds. Electrodes attached to their heads register small electrical responses to most ordinary noises that are moderately loud (Schulman-Galambos and Galambos, 1979). Soft sounds or noises, however, do not produce electrical responses, even when they are loud enough to do so in adults. Judged in this way, infants seem just a bit hard of hearing compared to adults, though of course they are far from deaf. These differences persist through much of the second year of infancy. Children begin sensing very soft sounds sometime toward the end of infancy, judging both by the electrical brain waves described above and by their increasingly overt responses to sounds, language, and music, as observed by parents.

Taste and Smell

Even at birth infants clearly prefer sweet tastes; they suck faster when an artificial nipple delivers sugar water than when it delivers plain water. Other taste preferences, however, seem much less clear-cut than they are among children and

Preference for sweet tastes (margin note)

adults. Newborn infants will suck *less* for saltwater, for example, but only if the saltwater is delivered automatically between bursts of sucking. If saltwater comes as a result of each suck, they show no significant decrease from their normal rates of sucking (Crook, 1978). Other tastes (bitterness and sourness) have even less effect on newborns' sucking behavior. This fact does not prove that neonates do not experience these tastes; it only shows that they do not respond to the tastes by modifying one of their most powerful reflexes, sucking.

Newborns react to a variety of smells, both good and bad. A faint odor of ammonia or vinegar, for example, makes one-week-old infants grimace and avert or turn away their heads (Rieser et al., 1976). They can even locate the general direction of the bad odor. If it is presented repeatedly, but from different directions each time, newborns usually turn away from the odor, and rarely toward it. Presumably they respond to differences in the amount of stimulation to each nostril; the one closer to the odor probably receives a stronger dose, and perhaps also receives it sooner. This difference apparently gives infants the information they need to turn in the most effective direction, which is away.

Discrimination among odors

Breast-feeding newborns can also recognize the odor of their mothers' breasts. One study demonstrated this sensory ability by hanging two breast pads in front of one-month-old infants, one pad on each side of their head (MacFarlane, 1977). One breast pad had previously been worn by the infant's mother, but the other had not. The used pad therefore carried the mother's aroma, unlike the alternate pad. When confronted with this choice, infants spent more time facing or looking at their mothers' breast pads. They did so even when the experimenters substituted a pad from another breast-feeding mother for the clean pad. Apparently the newborns discriminated among various mothers' odors and preferred the aroma of their own mother.

Touch

Newborn infants have many reflexes that show sensitivity to touch. A light stroke on the cheek, for example, normally causes a baby to turn her head in the direction of the stroke; placing a finger on the baby's lips normally causes her to begin sucking motions; and touching the bottoms of her feet normally causes her to fan her toes outward. Parents in many cultures have discovered that wrapping a newborn infant in a cloth or blanket, or even just holding her firmly, tends to reduce crying and fussing; in part such quieting implies sensitivity to touch, although it may also result from the interesting sights and sounds involved in being swaddled or held (Hirschman et al., 1982).

At birth one particular kind of touch — pain — seems less well developed than among slightly older infants or children. It is possible to evoke a painful or negative response to a pinprick, such as a baby might receive for a blood test, in one-day-old infants. But most infants this young seem somewhat less sensitive to painful stimulation than they do even a few days later (Lipsitt and Levy, 1959; Anders and Chalemian, 1974). Unfortunately (or perhaps fortunately), sensitivity to pain cannot be studied systematically, because it would be unethical to inflict pain purposely just to study infants' reactions.

Changes in sensitivity to pain

Checkpoint   *At birth infants can use all of their senses to some extent. At first each sense has certain limitations, but these are overcome sometime during infancy. By age two children normally have about as much sensory acuity as normal adults do, although they still do not use sensory information as efficiently as they will later on in life.*

Motor Development

The very first movements or motions appear to be inborn and automatic; they are called **reflexes.** During the first months of life, most reflexes disappear or become incorporated into relatively purposeful or voluntary movements. When they have these qualities, they are called **skills.** Both reflexes and skills are also called **motor abilities;** the term *motor* refers to movement or motion.

Early Reflexes

Pediatricians have identified over two dozen inborn *reflexes,* or behaviors that occur automatically in response to the proper stimulus. A few of these, such as sucking, clearly help the baby to adapt to his new post-uterine environment. Others look more like evolutionary vestiges of behaviors that may have helped earlier versions of *Homo sapiens* to cope — by clinging to their mothers, for example, at the sound of danger. Although a few reflexes, such as blinking, breathing, and swallowing, persist throughout a person's life, most reflexes disappear from the infant's repertoire of skills during the first few months. Their disappearance, in fact, helps doctors to judge whether a baby is developing normally. Persistent newborn reflexes may suggest damage to the nervous system or generally retarded development.

Nature of reflexes

Rooting and Sucking   If you gently stroke the cheek of a newborn, she will turn her head to the side that is being stroked. Her searching behavior is called **rooting.** Under normal circumstances it helps the baby to locate her mother's breast, since she will nose around for it if it happens to brush the side of her face just prior to nursing.

If the baby then finds the nipple, she will begin **sucking** powerfully and rhythmically — and without being taught. Actually, any object will cause sucking if it intrudes far enough into her mouth; a finger, for example, makes a good pacifier. Later in the infant's first year, the sucking reflex comes under more voluntary control and broadens to become **mouthing,** a mixture of gnawing and chewing. The infant begins using her mouth as a major way to learn about new objects; for a time, it seems, she puts practically everything into her mouth. Her preference for mouthing and chewing is not surprising given her earlier reflexes of rooting and sucking.

Sucking is a behavior that changes purpose during the course of development. As a survival reflex, sucking helps newborns to meet their nutritional needs; but with time, sucking comes to serve other, more psychological purposes. (above left, Erika Stone; above right, Frank Siteman/The Picture Cube; right, Ulrike Welsch)

Moro Reflex A newborn will startle dramatically in response to sudden loss of support, even if the loss does not really threaten to hurt him. The startle response is called the **Moro reflex**. A common way of testing for it begins with the baby lying flat on his back. The tester first lifts the baby's arms gently so that his shoulders no longer touch the table, although the rest of his body still safely contacts it, then releases his arms. Normally the infant will spread his arms, shake, make horrible faces, and possibly cry. Gradually he will then bring his arms together again, as if to grab at something. The response looks much like the startle of children and adults, and may in fact be a precursor to it. At some time earlier in human evolution, the Moro reflex may have helped infants who were being carried to grab more tightly when they experienced sudden loss of support. At present, however, it is significant mostly because it helps doctors to diagnose normal development of the nervous system. Healthy infants show the response when they are born but lose much of it as they approach their sixth month.

Some sudden, loud sounds also cause infants to startle, although not all. This inconsistency may make some parents wonder whether their newborn can actually hear, but careful observation shows that the nature of the stimulation matters to young babies. Their state of alertness affects whether or not they startle to a particular sound; sometimes the same noise will simply produce attention rather than startle behaviors (Leavitt et al., 1976). Well before their second birthday, though, their reactions resemble those of normal adults: they startle less and less often, and their response no longer shows the reflex pattern described above.

Stepping Hold a newborn upright, so that her feet touch the floor lightly, and she will tend to lift one of her feet as if she were stepping. Tilting her slightly from side to side, in fact, will make her "walk" — each foot will lift in turn. Since young babies spend so much time lying down or bundled up, the reflex often goes unnoticed, and it may disappear in a few months, apparently from lack of use. The behavior does seem related, though, to later, genuine walking; as shown in an experiment done many years ago, practice in early reflex walking seems to make an infant develop later walking sooner and more skillfully (Andre-Thomas and Autgaurden, 1953).

Grasping Place something — say a finger — into a newborn's palm firmly, and he will grasp it. Like the stepping reflex, his early grasping may facilitate later, more intentional grasping behaviors like the ones that a child needs to explore toys and to balance himself. But unlike the case with the stepping reflex, opportunities for grasping normally continue throughout infancy. Once past the first few weeks of life, infants are generally left free to use their hands for large parts of the day, or even all the time. The opportunity gives extra practice, and may explain why most babies become skillful with their hands sooner than they become skillful with their feet.

Table 5-3 summarizes the significant reflexes that babies have immediately after birth. Like the stepping and grasping reflexes, some may set the stage for development of more refined versions of the same skills later on; but many serve no obvious purpose. To a certain extent, then, babies begin life already prepared to

Table 5-3 *Major Reflexes in Newborn Infants*

Reflex	Description	Development	Significance
Survival Reflexes			
Breathing reflex	Alternating inhaling and exhaling	Permanent, but becomes partially voluntary	Brings in oxygen and expels carbon dioxide
Rooting reflex	Turning of cheek in direction of touch	Weakens and disappears by six months	Orients child to breast or bottle
Sucking reflex	Strong sucking motions with throat, mouth, and tongue	Gradually comes under voluntary control	Allows child to drink
Primitive Reflexes			
Moro reflex	In response to loud noise, child throws arms outward, arches back, then brings arms together as if to hold something	Arm movements and arching disappear by six months, but startle reaction persists for life	Indicates normal development of nervous system
Grasping reflex	Curling of fingers around any small object put in the child's palm	Disappears by three months; voluntary grasping appears by about six months	Indicates normal development of nervous system
Stepping reflex	If held upright, infant will step as if to walk	Disappears by eight weeks unless infant practices the response	Indicates normal development of nervous system

Source: Butnarescu and Tillotson, 1983.

acquire certain skills more easily than others. At the same time, though, they must have particular experiences, such as the chance to walk or to grasp, for these skills to develop properly.

The First Motor Skills

Motor skills are voluntary movements of the body or of parts of the body. They can be grouped conveniently according to the size of the muscles and body parts involved. **Gross motor skills** involve the large muscles of the arms, legs, and torso. **Fine motor skills** involve the small muscles located throughout the body. Walking and jumping are examples of gross motor skills, and reaching and grasping are examples of fine motor skills.

On the whole, the sequence in which skills develop follows two trends or principles that guide development in general. The so-called **cephalocaudal principle** (literally, "head to tail") refers to the fact that upper parts of the body become usable and skillful before the lower part. Babies learn to turn their heads before learning to move their feet intentionally, and they learn to move their arms before they learn to move their legs. The **proximodistal principle** (literally, "near to far") refers

Principles of motor-skill development

to the fact that central parts of the body become skillful before peripheral or outlying parts. Babies learn to wave their whole arms before wiggling their wrists and fingers. The former movement occurs at the shoulder joint, near the center of the body, but the latter occurs at the periphery. Stated differently, the shoulder movement is relatively proximal, whereas the finger movement is relatively distal.

Large Motor Development in the First Year Almost from birth, and before reflex behaviors disappear, babies begin doing some things on purpose. By the age of four weeks or so, most babies can lift their heads up when they are lying on their stomachs. What makes this achievement remarkable is its purposefulness: babies seem to practice the action repeatedly when they get the chance and are not preoccupied with hunger or other discomfort (Ames et al., 1979). Unlike, say, the sucking reflex, head lifting is not inevitably provoked by any particular stimulus or event. Babies are apparently rewarded simply by getting a new view of the world and a better feel for how their muscles work.

Early voluntary movements   After a few months voluntary movements become much more common than the reflexes with which babies are born. By two or three months, half of all babies can roll over in bed; but it takes until the age of five or six months for half of all babies to sit without props or supports (Frankenburg and Dodds, 1967). At six or seven months, many babies have become quite adept at using their limbs; they can stick their feet up in the air and "bicycle" with them while a parent tries valiantly to fit a diaper on this moving target. At ten months the average baby can stand erect, but only if an adult helps. By their first birthday (twelve months), half of all babies can dispense with this assistance and stand by themselves without toppling over immediately.

By the age of about seven months, on the average, babies become able to locomote, or move around, on their own. At first their methods are crude and slow; a baby might simply pivot on her stomach, for example, in order to get a better view of something interesting. Consistent movement in one direction develops soon after this time — although the movement does not always occur in the direction that the baby intends!

Locomotion   Techniques for getting around vary a lot among infants. The most common first method is *crawling,* in which the infant uses his arms to drag himself across the floor. Many babies also figure out the more efficient method of *creeping,* or walking on hands and knees with the body suspended above the ground. Still others learn to *hitch* themselves, alternately folding and unfolding themselves like a caterpillar. And by the age of nine or ten months, most babies learn to *cruise,* or move about the room upright by holding onto furniture for support. But these techniques do not develop in a reliable sequence. Most infants do not learn them all, and a few never learn any of them but go straight from sitting to walking.

Crawling, creeping, and cruising offer new opportunities to children and make new demands on parents. On the one hand, locomotion means that babies can entertain themselves better than before. They can relieve their own boredom simply by traveling to new locations and getting new toys for themselves. By the same token, though, babies that move can get into everything, including poisons under the kitchen sink or heavy tools stacked in the basement. As locomotion develops,

parents find that they must continually scrutinize their living quarters for safety, a process some parents call child-proofing.

Reaching and Grasping   As pointed out earlier in this chapter, even newborn infants will reach for and grasp objects that they can see immediately in front of themselves. As you might expect, they often fail to grasp objects successfully; they often make contact with the object but fail to enclose it in their fingers. This early, crude reaching disappears fairly soon after birth, only to reappear at about four or five months of age as two separate skills, reaching and grasping. These soon serve infants in many ways. By their second birthday, for example, most babies can turn the pages in large picture books one at a time, at least if the paper is relatively indestructible.

How do early and later reaching differ from each other? Careful, filmed observations of both kinds have given some answers to this question. The earlier reaching and grasping seem fused in a single act: the baby's hand closes on the object at the same instant that it arrives at the object. Older babies separate the two actions: first they reach, and then they grasp at the object a split second later. The delay makes them much more successful at actually grabbing things.

Changes in reaching and grasping

In addition, early reaching and grasping seems to be guided by sight rather than by touch. A very young baby will try to grasp an optical illusion — an object projected by mirrors, for example, or by a camera (Bower, 1981). Older babies, around five months of age, will not close their hands around an optical illusion; they must first touch the object before trying to grab it. Moving their hands *to* an object, though, now seems under skillful visual control.

These changes in reaching and grasping probably constitute refinements from constant practice, but how so? The earliest reach-and-grasp action may change simply because it succeeds so rarely. The reaching part of the action may remain, however, since it often rewards the baby with interesting results. Grasping, meanwhile, is generally not reinforced unless an object is actually touched. Over the long run, then, grasping comes under tactual (that is, touching-related) as well as

With time and practice, infants improve and modify their early grasping reflex to fit a variety of objects and circumstances. (H. Armstrong Roberts)

visual control. The different ways in which reaching and grasping are rewarded may therefore account for their evolution. The early, fused reflex gives way to two independently rewarded and more precise skills. The differentiation occurs with little or no conscious encouragement by adults.

Walking A reasonably predictable series of events leads up to true walking in most children; Table 5-4 describes some of these. By the age of about twelve to thirteen months, most children take their first independent steps. Well before two years, they can often walk not only forward but backward or even sideways. Some two-year-olds can walk upstairs on two feet instead of on all fours (Bayley, 1969). Usually they use the wall or a railing to do so. Usually, too, coming downstairs proves more difficult than going up; one solution is to creep down backward, using all four limbs.

Learning to walk
How do these changes develop? To some extent, the earlier skills may stimulate and give practice for the later ones. Sitting, for example, may give practice in balance, which helps in standing next to furniture; standing by furniture in turn improves balance and muscle development so that standing alone becomes possible; and so on. Each step in such a sequence rewards the child simply by giving her new opportunities to explore her body and to see her world from new perspectives. Her parents may motivate her by praising her occasionally, but their comments may actually matter relatively little. The practice itself may be its own reward.

Motor Skill	When 25% of All Infants Can Do This	When 50% of All Infants Can Do This	When 75% of All Infants Can Do This
Lift head up 45 degrees	Birth	1.2	2.0
Roll from stomach to back	2.0	2.8	3.7
Push chest up with arms	2.0	3.0	3.1
Pull up with assistance	3.2	4.0	5.0
Sit without assistance once up	4.8	5.5	6.5
Stand holding onto furniture	4.9	5.8	8.6
Pull self up to stand	5.9	7.1	9.0
Sit self up without assistance	6.1	7.1	9.2
Walk holding onto furniture	7.2	9.2	10.2
Stand well alone	9.7	11.5	13.1
Walk well alone	11.1	12.1	13.4
Walk backward	12.2	14.2	15.5

Table 5-4 Milestones of Motor Development (in months)

Source: *Denver Developmental Screening Test* (Frankenburg and Dodds, 1967).

As reasonable as this explanation sounds, it has certain flaws. Not all children do learn movement skills according to a predictable sequence; some, for example, creep only after they have mastered walking. And individual children, normal in all respects, learn motor skills at rather different ages: full-fledged walking, for example, may happen as early as nine months or as late as eighteen months. Yet these children presumably all have access to the crucial learning tool, namely their own legs and feet. Do some infants therefore practice harder, or just have an inborn ability to learn faster?

Nature and Nurture in Skill Development These questions about walking illustrate an important issue that pervades developmental psychology: the relative contributions of genetic endowment (nature) and of experience (nurture) to children's overall growth. Most developmental trends obviously depend on both genetics and experience, but the *way* in which each factor contributes is often unclear. Consider the ambiguities of the following examples:

■ Heavier children (and adults) are significantly less active than lighter-weight ones (Rodin, 1977). If this difference exists for infants as well, it might cause heavier infants to practice motor skills less. Here genetics might be guiding the original weight differences, but learning would account for the later differences in physical skills. At the same time, though, experience may contribute to differences in weight; in particular, some children gradually become heavier because their family diet is unusually high in calories.

Accidents in Infancy and Early Childhood

Although crawling, creeping, and walking allow children to learn more about the world, these skills also allow them to hurt themselves while doing so. They can fall down a flight of stairs, trip on the sidewalk, or plunge into a nearby swimming pool or river. Their newfound ability to get around also enables infants and toddlers to find and play with things that they really should not have, such as medicines, toxic cleaning fluids, and matches. Parents and caretakers are justified in worrying about these possibilities, because accidents, rather than illnesses, account for the large majority of deaths and serious disabilities among infants and children. Recent statistics show that about eight to ten thousand children between ages one and four die each year, mostly as the result of accidents *(Vital Statistics of the United States, 1985)*. If this number seems small, keep in mind that it refers to accidents only in any *one* year. Children repeat this risk each year of early childhood, and experience comparable risks as they get older; thus, during childhood as a whole, the risk of a fatal accident is many times higher.

Adding to parents' concerns are mishaps that are not fatal but are nonetheless serious, disfiguring, or disabling: every year, there are several hundred of these for every one fatal accident. Many children may need stitches at some point, for example; or break an arm or a leg; or need treatment for poison. All things considered, then, any one child stands a rather significant risk of experiencing at least one minor disaster sometime during childhood.

Most of these accidents can be prevented. Parents and others who care for infants and small children can reduce accident rates by taking precautions like the following:

1. Blocking the ends of stairs with a gate or similar device

2. Covering electrical outlets with plastic guards
3. Storing medicine and poisons out of the reach of children, and in child-resistant containers
4. Supervising closely when children are playing in or near large tubs or pools of water
5. Keeping young children away from hot stoves and from pots, pans, and other vessels containing hot liquids and foods
6. Using car safety seats appropriate to the child's age

By far the largest number of deaths and injuries occur during motor vehicle accidents (National Safety Council, 1985). During a collision, infants or young children who are not restrained by proper car safety devices essentially can become flying missiles within the car, crashing hard into the windows or metal frame. They are not protected by being held in parents' arms, no matter how strong and secure those arms might feel. And they are usually not protected well by the standard seat and shoulder belts used by adults: ordinary shoulder belts are usually mounted too high to span young children's shoulders, and ordinary lap belts are usually mounted too low for their center of gravity. (Infants and toddlers are rather top-heavy compared to adults.) Until they weigh about forty or fifty pounds and measure at least forty inches tall, children definitely need specially designed child restraint systems. Several states now legally require infants and young children to be secured in appropriate child restraint systems whenever they ride in a car.

At first, walking takes concentration, and it often seems to be its own reward. Note the wide stance that characterizes this beginning walker. (George Bellerose/Stock, Boston)

■ Identical twins are especially likely to acquire motor skills, including walking, at very nearly the same age (Wilson, 1972). This fact suggests that genetics influences how fast infants learn to walk. But it does not really prove it, because identical twins also tend to have environments that are similar. Twins therefore end up with unusually similar learning opportunities as well as identical physiology. In principle, studying identical twins reared apart might solve this particular ambiguity; but in practice, separated twins are often not very representative of children as a whole since only highly unusual circumstances can cause twins to be separated.

Confusion between nature and nurture seems inevitable, even in experiments that try explicitly to vary only one of these factors without varying the other. The problem is illustrated by two studies — one a classic and the other more recent — that tried to "teach" older infants specific motor skills. In the classic study (Gesell and Thompson, 1929), one member of a pair of identical twins was taught to climb stairs, beginning at the age of forty-six weeks. Her training began with assistance from an adult at moving from one step to the next, often at first simply by being lifted. Her twin received no training, and in fact was prohibited from all encounters with stairs until she was fifty-three weeks old. At this point the trained twin could climb stairs much better than her inexperienced sister. Yet even on her very first attempt, at fifty-three weeks, the untrained sister managed to climb the stairs. After just three weeks more, both girls performed equally well, in spite of the prior differences in training.

Maturation versus learning

Although this study seems to suggest that **maturation** (or effects due to the aging process) matters more than **learning** (acquired knowledge and skill), it may really show only how many different ways there are that a child may learn a motor skill. In this case the untrained twin indeed encountered no stairs during her waiting period, but she was free to crawl every day, and free to practice any motor techniques that she might choose. Such crawling may have given her as much preparation for stair climbing as her sister got. If so, then learning or experience in addition to maturation may account for the results.

A second, more recent study also suggests that maturation and learning both play a role in learning to walk (Zelazo et al., 1972). In this study newborn infants

---

A Talk with Elizabeth and Her Father

Physical Development at Eight Months

The following interview took place in the Fuller family's kitchen, where Mark Fuller was feeding his eight-month-old daughter, Elizabeth.

INTERVIEWER: What are Elizabeth's eating patterns?

MARK: She pretty much eats whatever we feed her. She's not very picky. She doesn't have any teeth yet, but at this point, even if she had teeth, it would be, you know, two or four, not really useful for much of eating. So she's still at the soft food stage.

INTERVIEWER: How often does she eat?

MARK: Oh, she has her three meals a day and we give her bottles in between. She's still shifting over from a complete liquid diet to pretty much a solid diet, so there'll be some days when she won't have three solid meals. I think we began giving her solid foods when she was six months old, but usually only once a day. Over the last month or

so, more and more of her food is solid, so she's almost made the changeover.

INTERVIEWER: Does she like to help feed herself?

MARK: Definitely. The big thing is that a lot of times she seems to prefer to feed herself even though she can't do it with anything that's the typical baby mush-type stuff because she can only do it with her hands. She can hold a spoon, but she can't really use it yet to get food into her mouth very well.

INTERVIEWER: I see she has a cup on her high chair feeding table. Can she hold it, or does she spill that?

MARK: No, she spills the cup but she's really interested in a cup, which we think is very positive because her brother, Paul — who is three — never was interested in a cup and has only been completely without a bottle for the past three or four months. Elizabeth . . . want to drink from this cup? That's the way. Good girl!

INTERVIEWER: What is she doing now? What do you think she wants?

MARK: She wants the cup. She's having trouble reaching it. At eight months I don't think she really has the coordination to hold cups, but she's very interested in this idea. She sees us drinking and she tries, too. She slurps rather than really drinks, but she has the idea.

MARK: Elizabeth, we have some delicious carrots.

INTERVIEWER: Do you think she knows what is coming?

MARK: Yes, she does know what's coming. It's very clear to her what feeding is. Here. I know, carrots are probably not your favorite food in the world, but . . . Okay. Now this is harder.

INTERVIEWER: She's spitting it out. What are you giving her now?

MARK: This is rice. She responds to texture a lot. She likes things that are smooth. But, you see, she'll pick up the rice . . . she's trying to pick it

were encouraged to practice the stepping reflex described earlier in this chapter; someone held the babies upright so that their feet lightly touched a table, stimulating them to "walk." These infants did learn true walking earlier than the average, even though their reflex walking had long since disappeared. Evidently the experience of early practice did somehow influence their walking, although the precise connection between their early, inborn reflex and their later walking remains unclear. In this case learning built upon a genetically given base, and the final product, walking, was a mixture of the two influences.

Checkpoint *Infants are born with a variety of reflexes. Some of these have obvious survival value, but others seem simply to indicate whether the child's nervous system is developing normally. As infants grow older they acquire many motor*

up now. She doesn't want it fed to her, but she'll try to pick it up herself.

INTERVIEWER: It looks like she is almost managing. Were those Cheerios that she was picking up a little earlier?

MARK: Yes, she can pick up things like that with her fingers. She can pick up a spoon, too, but she can't manage to get any of the food into her mouth with a spoon yet. . . . She's probably only a month or two away from being able to do it.

INTERVIEWER: What other things have you noticed abut Elizabeth's physical development?

MARK: She's grown so big so fast. She's almost twenty-five pounds now. And she's also long for her age, above average in length. Her head size is also very big for her age.

INTERVIEWER: Has her size made a difference?

MARK: Well, one thing her mom has noticed is that because she is so heavy she finds herself wanting to

lift her up less. It's physically difficult to lift her. In fact, I sprained my hand the other day lifting her.

In a way, it's actually easier to carry her older brother because it's sort of live weight versus dead weight. She's not holding on or supporting herself with her arms or anything. You are both carrying her weight and keeping control of her.

INTERVIEWER: Are there any other ways in which Elizabeth's size has made a difference?

MARK: Well, we know she is well fed and healthy. But it also helps her when she plays with her brother. Even though he is really strong for his age, he has trouble moving her and we're not as concerned that when he sometimes falls on her — you know, sort of accidentally on purpose. We are less concerned that she will be hurt. She isn't fragile. I also think that because she is a chub, it may take her a little longer to crawl and walk than it did for her brother.

INTERVIEWER: What is Elizabeth able to do physically?

MARK: She sits up, and she is about to crawl. She can go from a sitting to a crawling position and back again, but she can't really crawl forward. She can crawl backwards, which she doesn't like to do because it never accomplishes what she wants. It's very frustrating. She can also slither on the ground without being up; she can move forward by herself this way.

Follow-up Questions

1. Based on your reading of this chapter, how typical is Elizabeth's development for infants her age?

2. How comfortable do Elizabeth's parents seem to be about her physical development?

3. How does the interview illustrate the interdependence of physical, cognitive, and social development?

4. How might Elizabeth's size influence her future development?

skills, such as reaching, grasping, and walking. Assessing the relative contributions of learning and maturation to these skills often proves difficult, even for this young age.

Variations in Growth and Motor Development

Infants vary, of course, in how they grow and develop. Some grow faster than others, and not all acquire motor skills in the same order. Two otherwise similar children may learn to walk at different times: one when she is only ten months old, and the other when she is nearly sixteen months old. Yet both may fall within the normal range of motor development. Several factors contribute to differences like these. The most important is the weight of the infant at birth, but gender and ethnic or cultural background seem to make some difference as well. Consider, for example, these three children:

- Jeffrey was born two months before his due date and is now almost two years old. He has begun speaking in two-word sentences only recently, saying, "Daddy home," for example, and "Truck loud." His slow language development is not a serious problem, at least so far. But his parents feel sure that he is taking longer to acquire language than other children of his age.
- Susan and William are fraternal twins. Like a lot of twins, they have spent considerable time playing together. Now that they are eighteen months old, both of them can walk without assistance. But William practices this skill much more than Susan. Often he runs (or stumbles) down the hall, apparently just for the fun of it. Sometimes Susan will do this too, but not as often. More typically she sits in one place, using her hands for some purpose, like pulling clothes out of her parents' dresser drawers.
- Kate has been cruising (walking by holding onto furniture) since she was only seven months old — some sort of record, her parents feel sure. Perhaps as a result she has developed an early taste for exploring the entire house where she lives and for investigating the cupboards, boxes, and wastebaskets that it contains. Her parents worry about accidents that may result from her curiosity, but they also feel proud of her motor ability, and enjoy encouraging her in order to see what she will do next. Now, at two years, she can walk to the grocery store faster than her two older sisters did at the same age. Her mother finds that she no longer needs the baby stroller for this errand.

Each of these children raises important questions about what makes growth and motor development vary. Is Jeffrey's somewhat slow language development somehow the result of the stresses of his unusually early birth? Have the twins, Susan and William, acquired different activity levels by subtle learning processes, or was some of this conferred on them genetically? And how much can Kate's parents really influence Kate's precocious motor development? The next sections discuss such questions as these.

Low-Birth-Weight Infants

Small-for-date and preterm infants

For medical purposes, newborns are considered **low-birth-weight** infants if they weigh less than 2,500 grams, which is about five and one-half pounds. Such low weight can happen for either of two reasons. First, some babies do not develop as fast as normal, even though they are carried for about the usual term of forty weeks. They are called **small-for-date** infants. Second, some babies develop at about normal rates but end their gestation significantly earlier than usual. If they are born sooner than about thirty-seven weeks from conception, they are called **preterm** or short-gestation infants. Until recently, medical research did not distinguish clearly between small-for-date and preterm infants; both were simply regarded as "premature infants" (Kopp and Parmalee, 1979).

Appearance of physically immature infants

Preterm infants face many more medical risks than do small-for-date infants. The extent of the risks depends on the infant's physical maturity. Physically immature infants look different from normal full-term infants: they tend to be redder and darker than normal, whatever their race, and their skin is often transparent enough to see blood vessels through it (Nelms and Mullins, 1982). Often they are covered with lanugo and have a thicker coating than usual of the white, waxy vernix. And of course, immature newborns are smaller than usual; a normally developing infant will weigh only about two pounds, for example, if born two months early, compared to the average of seven and one-half pounds for normally developed full-term infants.

Causes of Low Birth Weight   Low birth weight, either preterm or small-for-date, can result from several factors. As pointed out in Chapter 4, one of the most common is malnourishment of the mother during pregnancy; mothers who do not eat well during pregnancy tend to have small-for-date babies. But other harmful practices — smoking cigarettes, drinking alcohol, or taking drugs — can also depress birth weight. Mothers from certain segments of the population, such as teenagers and the very poor, are especially likely to give birth to preterm babies, most likely because of their own poor nourishment or because of their lack of access to good prenatal care. Even among mothers who are well nourished and well cared for, however, some infants are born smaller than is medically desirable. Multiple births (twins, triplets) usually result in small-for-date babies; so can some illnesses or mishaps, such as a serious traffic accident that causes damage to the placenta.

Consequences of Preterm Birth   The neurological abilities of infants, which are especially important for psychological development, are affected by preterm birth (Dubnowitz et al., 1970). In general, the reflexes of preterm infants tend to be sluggish, weak, and poorly organized. Preterm infants do not startle reliably or grasp automatically and strongly at objects (Parmalee, 1975). Muscles often seem flabby or overly relaxed, which is a sign not only of immature muscle development but also of insufficient nerve impulses to stimulate good muscle tone. Preterm infants tend to lie fully extended instead of with their arms and legs slightly flexed or bent, and if someone pulls gently on their arms to extend them, their arms do not recoil as completely or smoothly as those of a full-term infant. Jerky, random movements dominate instead, and sometimes there is no recoiling movement at all. At comparable points in their gestation, full-term infants presumably have these limitations too; but they are still inside their mothers' wombs at the time.

Outside that protected environment, preterm infants must cope with many tasks for which they are not well prepared. These include the obvious vital processes, such as breathing and digesting food. But they also include some less obvious ones. Once outside the womb, preterm infants must suddenly regulate the amount of sensory stimulation they receive. Just like full-term babies, they need to see things and hear things in order to stimulate the development of their senses. But they also need to avoid overloading their senses with too many sights and sounds. One way to avoid overstimulation is to sleep periodically and deeply; yet even though preterm infants sleep more than full-term infants do, they have more trouble keeping their sleep peaceful and smooth. For example, they have more sleep apnea — or times when breathing stops for perhaps fifteen or twenty seconds.

In the long run, some preterm infants experience difficulties in forming stable attachments to their parents, and sometimes they have learning disabilities in school as well. But these effects may depend largely on the economic and social environment in which they grow up (Rode et al., 1981). Children from stable and relatively well-off homes tend to develop better; by the time they begin school, they show good relationships with their family and no or few signs of learning impairment. Children from families under economic or social stress, though, are more likely to continue to show social and cognitive deficiencies (Cohen and Parmalee, 1983).

Helping Low-Birth-Weight Infants Since conventional hospital routines often do not help preterm infants to regulate their sensory needs, health care providers have begun experimenting with ways to do so. Some doctors and nurses have provided such babies with miniature waterbeds, for example, which rock gently and slowly at about the same speed as a mother's normal breathing (Korner, 1981; Barnard, 1981). In theory, at least, the arrangement simulates a normal experience in the womb. Studies of preterm infants raised with such waterbeds have shown very encouraging results. After several months the infants are healthier and physically larger than preterm infants raised in conventional stationary hospital cribs. In addition, their sleep shows fewer disturbances, and their reflexes are stronger. All in all, they seem more like full-term infants.

Low-birth-weight infants and their parents face special challenges in becoming attached to each other. Hospitals have recently tried to facilitate these attachments by encouraging parents to handle their low-birth-weight infants even during the first days after birth, when the babies are still receiving intensive care in the hospital. Whether or not this practice really has much effect on the infant, it at least encourages parents' confidence and increases their faith in their child's capacity to develop normally eventually.

After low-birth-weight babies go home, however, their parents may continue to worry about their health and face challenges in forming good relationships with them. Low-birth-weight infants tend to respond to their parents less than normal babies do, at least at first, and perhaps to compensate, parents of these babies sometimes initiate more contacts — poking, talking, offering a pacifier, and the like — than parents of full-term babies do (Crnic et al., 1983). From the perspective of a preterm infant, therefore, parents may sometimes "try too hard" to interact; and from the perspective of the parents, the infant may sometimes seem unresponsive.

Parents and their tiny babies also smile at each other less than usual (Field, 1980). Under good conditions these initial differences need not become lasting problems, and the parents and children eventually develop relationships that are healthy and gratifying. But if the parents face other stresses (such as poverty), they may lack the time or energy to overcome the initial difficulties in making contact with their baby. To avoid forming a permanently poor relationship, such parents may need help from a social worker or a nurse in understanding their infant's development, so that they can enjoy that development as it unfolds.

Gender Differences

During the first two years the genders do not differ in competence and only sometimes in performance. That is, what babies *can* do under good conditions has relatively little to do with their gender, at least during the first year or so of infancy. Boys and girls sit upright at about the same age and stand and walk at about the same time. All the major milestones, in fact, develop at about the same rate.

How infants in fact use their time, however, is another matter. Almost as soon as they can move, for example, boys show more activity. Even before birth, late in pregnancy, they move about in their mothers' wombs more than girls do. The trend continues after birth: by the age of one year, boys engage in more gross motor activity than girls do (Teitelbaum, 1976). Boys move around more, using whatever locomotor skills they have developed thus far, whereas girls spend more time quietly using fine motor skills to investigate the contents of the kitchen wastebasket, for instance. Presumably these gender differences stem at least partly from different encouragement by parents, and perhaps also from the children's own desires to model "correct" sex-role behavior. But given the very young age of the children, some of the difference may be genetically based.

By age two, however — and onward throughout early childhood — boys and girls tend to show different motor abilities, even in optimal testlike situations. In general, girls excel more often at fine motor skills; for example, they usually can build a tower of blocks sooner, taller, and with fewer mistakes than boys can (Ames et al., 1979). Girls also excel more often at skills involving balance and rhythm, such as the dancing sometimes done in nursery school classrooms. Boys excel more often wherever speed or strength are required: they usually run faster outdoors and pound the play dough harder at nursery school (Malina, 1982).

The underlying reasons for such differences, though, remain ambiguous. The differences could stem partly from differences in practice during infancy, partly from children's self-consciousness about excelling at the "wrong" skills, and partly

Early difference in level and kind of activity

from slight but undeniable biological differences between the sexes. In spite of these trends, though, boys and girls are more alike than different during their early years. Many boys have good balance, and many girls pound the play dough very hard indeed.

Cultural and Racial Differences

Physical growth and motor development also vary among racial and cultural groups around the world. At birth, for example, Swedish infants weigh about 3.8

Perspectives on Research

Cultural Differences in Motor Stimulation

Around the world, societies vary greatly in how they stimulate infants and toddlers physically. In some societies babies go through the day swaddled tightly in cloth slings carried by their mothers. Babies in these cultures get little chance for the kind of sensorimotor exploration described by Piaget. In other societies, including our own, babies spend a lot of the day in cribs or on the floor or ground. The physical openness of this arrangement gives them comparatively more chances to explore the world.

These differences in stimulation often have effects on both motor and social development. Certain African cultures give their infants unusually frequent chances to sit upright and to practice "walking" when held at a standing position by adults and older children (Munroe et al., 1981). These opportunities appear to stimulate toddlers in these societies to learn to walk early and well, compared to North American toddlers. Early walking in turn may prove especially valuable in these societies, which do not yet rely heavily on cars, bicycles, and the other vehicles so commonplace in North American society.

Tight swaddling of infants also affects both motor and social development. Consider Navaho Indian infants, who spend nearly all of their first year of life bound and swaddled to a flat board, so that their arms and legs extend straight down along their bodies (Whiting, 1981). Apparently as a re-

sult, Navaho toddlers acquire certain motor skills, such as walking, a little more slowly than Anglo-American children do. But the delays do not apply to many other skills, such as reaching and grasping, and the deficit disappears entirely by the end of early childhood; six-year-old Navahos do not differ significantly from cradle- or crib-raised children in overall motor ability (Kagan, 1973, 1984).

The Navahos' swaddling may have social effects that are more lasting, however. In particular, Navahos may develop different feelings about their mothers from those of cradle-raised children. In a sling, a baby communicates with her mother through **kinesthetics,** or subtle movements and changes of balance. With a small wiggle, for example, a baby can inform her mother that she is uncomfortable or that she wants to nurse. Crying and vocalizing are seldom needed, and mothers can satisfy most discomforts almost immediately. Infants therefore lead a comparatively contented life, but only until they must leave the sling; then they experience an unusually abrupt reduction in their contact with their mother.

The cradles and cribs of Anglo-Saxon infants offer a rather different experience. Such babies must summon their mothers by crying or fussing, and very often mothers are too far away to come immediately. Vocalizing and capturing adults' attention therefore take on special importance for such babies (Whiting, 1978). Unlike the sling-

kilograms, 40 percent more than Hindu infants born in India (2.3 kilograms). Black American children weigh about 10 percent less at birth (3.0 kg) than white American children (3.3 kg). These differences apparently do not result from simple malnutrition or from other obvious health problems among the smaller children. The differences, and others like them, exist even among well-off groups in all countries (Meredith, 1981).

As infants grow, they show further differences according to the culture or society in which they live. In general, infants in a number of African societies develop motor skills sooner than North American infants, even when the families live in

Swaddling infants, a practice in many cultures, tends to slow children's motor development temporarily, but not permanently. (Lionel Delevingne/Stock, Boston)

raised infants, cradle babies experience no sudden reduction in contact with their mothers; in this sense, their weaning is more gradual and gentle.

These circumstances may help explain a number of observations by anthropologists about the social development of children (Munroe et al., 1981). Children from sling cultures, it seems, tend to express more mixed feelings about their mothers as they grow older. Such children, and especially boys, find relations with the opposite sex especially problem-filled, since their first intimate relationship was both extremely gratifying and unaccountably betrayed. Sling cultures help deal with these feelings by encouraging strong separation of the sexes during childhood and youth.

Children from cradle cultures, on the other hand, may express more worries about dependency, since their first intimate relationship took real effort to maintain. For cradle children, independence is therefore both valuable and difficult to achieve. Such children are supposed to get along with a constantly changing set of classmates, baby sitters, and neighbors, for example, even though these people are comparative strangers and may have alien interests and temperaments. Cradle societies try to deal with this challenge by giving young children extra training in human relations, through nursery schools and books that help parents raise happier children.

similar economic circumstances (Super, 1981). The difference is especially marked in sitting and walking: African infants can do both actions almost two months earlier than white American infants. The reasons for this precocity in motor development remain unclear, but at least some of the difference may result from cultural practices. Anthropologists have reported efforts in several African societies to actively teach children both to walk and to sit. Sitting is taught by placing infants in a small depression and propping them up with blankets or clothes (Super, 1982); walking is taught by holding infants upright when they are still rather young and encouraging them to exercise their inborn stepping reflex. As discussed earlier in this chapter, this method does indeed promote earlier and more skillful walking (Zelazo et al., 1972). In underdeveloped Third World communities, acquiring sitting and walking skills may in fact assist children and their families; life in an African village may indeed require more walking than life in a North American town. Over time, therefore, early motor development may become a general cultural value, even among well-off members of underdeveloped societies.

Precocious walking *(margin note)*

Checkpoint *Several factors can affect physical and motor development in infants. One of the most important is low birth weight: small-for-date and preterm infants face both physical and social risks immediately after birth. But as long as the infants' families are not under other stresses as well, most low-birth-weight infants eventually develop normally. In addition to birth weight, gender influences motor behavior, even early in infancy; and infants from different cultural or racial groups generally vary in both their growth and their early motor behavior. Once again, sorting out the relative contributions of learning and maturation proves difficult.*

Nutrition During the First Two Years

The physical developments described in this chapter depend, of course, on good nutrition during the first two years. Like older people, babies need diets with appropriate amounts of protein, calories, and specific vitamins and minerals. For various reasons, though, infants do not always get all the nutrients that they need. Often poverty accounts for malnutrition: parents may not be able to afford the right foods, in spite of good intentions. In other cases conventional eating practices interfere: in spite of relatively expensive eating habits — like going to fast-food restaurants — some families may not provide their children with a balanced diet.

Special Nutritional Needs of Infants

Compared with other children, infants eat less in overall or absolute amount. A well-nourished young baby in North America might drink somewhat less than one

liter (or about .95 quart) of liquid nourishment per day. This amount definitely would not keep an older child or young adult well nourished, although it might prevent starving.

In proportion to their body weight, however, infants need to consume much more than children or adults. Every day, for example, a three-month-old baby should ideally take in more than two ounces of liquid per pound (or about 150 ml of liquid per kilogram) of body weight. An eighteen-year-old only needs about one-third of this amount (NAS/NRC, 1980). Similar differences occur in the need for calories (or energy), for protein (or chemical building blocks), and for most vitamins and minerals. The changes are due to more efficient nutritional processing and less vigorous growth.

In recent decades, increasing numbers of mothers have chosen to breast-feed their babies, as recommended by most pediatricians. But bottle-feeding does have some advantages, however, such as allowing other family members to participate in feeding. (left, Carol Palmer; right, Yan Lukas/Photo Researchers)

The Breast Versus the Bottle

Someone (usually parents) must somehow provide for an infant's comparatively large appetite. Whenever breast feeding is possible, health experts generally recommend human milk as the sole source of nutrition for the first six months or so of most infants' lives, and as a major source for at least the next six months. In some cases, of course, this recommendation proves difficult or impractical to follow. Babies who need intensive medical care immediately after birth cannot be breast fed without special arrangements; and for one reason or another, some women may choose not to breast feed and certain babies and mothers may not succeed well in this activity, even after trying it. For these infants, formulas can be prepared and fed in bottles.

Why do pediatricians recommend breast feeding? Studies of infants suggest three major reasons. First, human milk seems to give young infants more protection from disease: breast-fed infants catch fewer colds and viruses of all types, and experience fewer serious illnesses as well. For instance, one of the proteins of human milk, called **secretory IgA,** binds or attaches to viruses and bacteria in the infant's intestine. By acting like a sort of intestinal paint, this protein prevents the viruses and bacteria from creating gastrointestinal disorders (Goldman and Goldblum, 1982). This sort of benefit is important enough that many hospitals now try to offer human milk in bottles to infants needing intensive care.

Immunity from disease

The second reason for preferring human milk concerns its chemical composition. Overall, such milk matches the nutritional needs of human infants more closely than formula preparations. Commercial preparations try, of course, to

---

A Talk with a Pediatrician
Eating and Sleeping Schedules in Infancy

Dr. Ellen Ross is a pediatrician who treats newborn infants through adolescents. She also is on the faculty of the medical school in her city, where she teaches nurses and pediatricians in training. At the start of the interview, which was conducted at her office, Dr. Ross mentioned that her own experiences as the mother of two children have helped her better appreciate the feelings and needs of her patients and their families.

INTERVIEWER: What are the typical questions and problems that a family faces in caring for their newborn infant?

DR. ROSS: For really young babies, under a month old, the fact that nobody gets a decent night's sleep drives everybody crazy. That's the big one. The schedule, the schedule! How can I get my baby on schedule? I know when I was being brought up, they were very rigid

about feeding. You had to feed a baby every four hours, and if you varied from that schedule, you were going to spoil and ruin [the baby] for life. Now we have a very strong feeling that demand feeding — that is, feeding the baby when he or she is hungry — is right. However, it's often hard to know when a baby is hungry.

INTERVIEWER: How do babies and their parents get their sleep schedules straight?

DR. ROSS: In the beginning, they don't have them straight, and sleep schedules can be a big source of frustration. Then gradually, by the end of the second to fourth week, the baby will usually sleep a longer stretch at night, perhaps four to five hours, and that's a great relief. Being awakened night after night by a baby can be a great source of stress

to a family who are already exhausted by the responsibilities of adjusting to the care of a new baby. Some babies need more help in trying to stretch that out, and I sometimes say don't let the baby sleep for more than four hours in the day so that the baby will sleep longer at night.

Very often the best medicine is for somebody else to put the baby to sleep, rock the baby, and change the baby after the mother has breast-fed, so that the mother has only actually been up for fifteen minutes or so and can let somebody else do the rest. During the day the mother should get some rest and if possible have help from somebody else in caring for other children, housework, and chores so that she can concentrate on nursing the baby.

INTERVIEWER: A little earlier, you said that it is often hard to know

duplicate the components of human milk. But inevitably they do not do so completely; certain proteins, carbohydrates, and other nutrients usually differ slightly in composition from their natural versions, and these differences sometimes have a surprisingly negative impact on certain infants. Formulas made with cow's milk, for example, contain much more of a protein called **casein,** which some infants have trouble digesting (Pipes, 1981). Human milk has similar amounts of overall protein but much lower levels of casein, so it tends to be more digestible.

A third reason for preferring human milk has to do with its effects on mother-infant relationships. Infants who breast feed spend more time snuggling close to their mothers (and vice versa). A breast-feeding pair seem to spend more time gazing into each other's eyes, like two people in love, and the mother appears to offer feeding sessions in closer response to the infant's true hunger. Apparently these behaviors may promote strong, secure attachments between mother and child, which help infants' social and cognitive development later in childhood (Cunningham, 1979).

Why should breast feeders engage in more attachment behaviors? The answer

Digestibility

Attachment formation

---

when a baby is hungry. How do parents learn to tell?

DR. ROSS: As a baby gets older you get to know the different cries. In the beginning, though, you don't really know. And so a baby who is asleep, wakes up and may need to be changed or held, and may not calm down may be rooting around and sucking on his fist and everything he can get his hands on. He is relieved when he gets either the breast or the bottle, so you say, aha, hungry. However, babies will suck on anything. They have a sucking reflex. So that sucking is not necessarily connected to hunger.

INTERVIEWER: So he could be sucking just because he enjoys it rather than for food?

DR. ROSS: Exactly. So some people will pop a bottle in the baby's mouth every time he cranks or cries. Or the breast. So the bottle or

breast becomes a human pacifier and the mother is resentful and tied to the baby and it feels horrible. I tell people that although I do believe in demand feeding, if the baby has had a decent feeding and it's under two hours, it's very, very unlikely that your baby is truly hungry. And you should try other alternatives. Maybe a pacifier. Maybe holding the baby and letting him suck on your finger. If you have to, you can feed the baby, but as a regular pattern it should not be less than two hours between feedings.

INTERVIEWER: What other concerns do parents have about feeding?

DR. ROSS: Is my baby getting enough? Sometimes parents are upset about breast feeding because you can't measure the quantity of milk. They say, how will I know the baby's had enough? So I say if the

baby is urinating well, and having regular bowel movements, and is comforted and falls asleep and at least is calm and satisfied after feeding, and is showing some weight gain between visits to the pediatrician, you know the baby has had enough.

Follow-up Questions

1. If you were a new parent, how might you feel about Dr. Ross's way of talking with parents?

2. What are some of the advantages and disadvantages of breast-feeding mentioned in this interview? What do you think are Dr. Ross's views concerning the issue of breast-feeding versus bottle-feeding?

3. The infant's rooting and sucking behaviors that Dr. Ross describes are discussed in this chapter. Where do they come from? What functions do they serve?

remains unclear. Perhaps the benefit stems from the kind of mothers who choose breast feeding; maybe they are people who already have extra time to spend with their infants, no matter what feeding practice they happen to adopt (Pollitt et al., 1984). Or maybe, as Freud suggested, breast feeding is satisfying sensually, if not sexually, to mother and child. If so, they may become more attached to each other than if they shared only a bottle.

These considerations have probably contributed to a rise in the popularity of breast feeding during the past two decades. In 1971, for example, the proportion of North American mothers who breast fed immediately after the birth of their child was about one in four, but by 1981 this proportion had risen to one in two. Even more dramatic increases have occurred in women's persistence at breast feeding. In 1971 only one woman in twenty was still breast feeding when her infant was six months old, but by 1981 this proportion had risen to one woman in four (Martinez and Nalezienski, 1981). Increases occurred in all parts of society, but they were largest among women who were relatively well educated and well informed about experts' advice on child-rearing.

Benefits of the bottle
Nonetheless, bottle feeding produces healthy, thriving babies for most parents who use it. Breast feeding does have definite medical and practical drawbacks. As already pointed out, not all babies are able to breast feed, especially those who need so much medical attention that they must live in the hospital instead of at home. And not all mothers are able to breast feed either; some work situations (like a noisy factory) make breast feeding so difficult that infants are better off receiving a bottle somewhere else. The bottle makes feeding by friends and relatives, such as fathers and grandparents, possible. As many new mothers discover, the trouble with breasts is that only one person, the mother herself, can supply them.

Whether they feed by breast or by bottle, parents must decide when and how often to offer their infant milk. At one extreme, babies can be fed at regular intervals, such as every three or four hours, whether they become fussy in the meanwhile or not. At the other extreme, babies can be fed *on demand,* no matter how recently they may have had a previous meal. A fixed schedule creates a certain predictability in the lives of new parents, since they can know relatively precisely when to take time out for feedings. Whether it also creates predictability in the minds of young infants, though, is more questionable, since many infants can protest long and hard if they do not get to eat when they feel hungry. Demand feeding relieves the stress of waiting out such protests until the designated meal time. It creates more interruptions, however, which can be especially bothersome for parents of bottle-fed infants, who must keep preparing formula. Sometimes parents worry that feeding on demand will make their infant overweight or obese. If formula is prepared properly, though, infants cannot become overweight on it; and breast milk is inherently incapable of giving an infant excessive calories (Spock, 1976).

Nutrition after Weaning

After about six months infants can graduate from the breast or bottle to solid foods, such as strained cereals and strained fruits. As babies become tolerant of

Parents should introduce solid foods slowly, to insure that their infants have developed enough to digest the food comfortably. (Sam C. Pierson/Photo Researchers)

these new foods, parents can introduce others, which sometimes require a more mature digestive system: strained meats and cooked eggs, for example. Overall, the shift to solid foods often takes many months to complete. As it occurs, parents must begin paying more attention to their baby's nutritional needs. Many solid foods do not contain the broad range of nutrients that breast milk and formula so conveniently do.

In order to thrive after weaning, infants should consume about fifty calories per day for each pound of body weight. By about their first birthday, their diet should include all the major food groups and nutrients: cereals, milk products (including cheese), meats, and fruits and vegetables. Somewhere in this mixture there should be about twenty-three grams of protein per day (Eichorn, 1979). In relatively well-nourished parts of the world, such as North America, families usually have no trouble in providing these dietary requirements for their infants.

Malnutrition in North America   Often North American diets do fail, though, to provide enough of three specific nutrients: vitamin A, vitamin C, and iron. Prolonged deficiencies of these nutrients may contribute to deficits in motor ability and cognitive performance when children enter school (Pollitt et al., 1984). But these effects are far from strong ones; some very deficient infants show surprisingly good motor ability during their first two years of life, and surprisingly good (if hardly outstanding) cognitive performance during early childhood and beyond. Severe undernutrition does occur in North America, but not nearly as often as in other parts of the world. More commonly in our society, undernutrition is "only" moderate.

Specific nutritional deficiencies

The Effects of Serious Malnutrition

In certain developing nations, large numbers of infants grow up seriously undernourished. Their nutritional deficiencies do not concern specific vitamins or minerals, as is more often true of malnourished infants in North America. Instead they consist of basic insufficiencies of either or both of the major nutritional building blocks, protein and calories. When both of these are deficient for prolonged periods, an infant or child develops a disease called **marasmus** (from a Latin word meaning "to waste away"). Babies with marasmus become increasingly emaciated, weak, and listless as their condition worsens. They also suffer significant delays in motor development and perform significantly lower than healthy children on standardized tests of intelligence (Cravioto and Delicardie, 1982). If marasmus has gone far enough, the motor and cognitive delays persist even if the child's nutrition eventually improves.

Serious malnutrition can also take the form of **kwashiorkor,** if the child receives enough calories but little or no protein. Children suffering from kwashiorkor are noticeable because they develop enlarged or bloated abdomens; but they also tend to lose their hair and to develop lesions (cuts or breaks) in their skin, which do not heal. Children with either kwashiorkor or marasmus have lowered resistance to disease, and often die from a virus or infection from which a well-nourished child might recover.

Although both forms of malnutrition can affect infants or children at any age, each form has a "preferred" age group. Marasmus tends to afflict infants relatively often. This happens because the mother may also be severely undernourished, so that she cannot produce enough breast milk, or enough milk of sufficient nutritional quality. It also happens because many Third World mothers have attempted to feed their infants from bottles under conditions that can actually harm their babies rather than nourish them. Many such mothers cannot read the instructions on the containers of formula; and in any case, conditions of poverty make sterilizing bottles and water difficult, if not impossible. Probably for these reasons, bottle-fed infants suffer from marasmus much more often in impoverished areas of the Third World than they do in well-off areas of those same countries or of North America (Grant, 1982). In essence, the infants reject the wrongly prepared formula or become too sick to digest it.

Kwashiorkor tends to affect toddlers and young children rather than infants. This happens because in many Third World societies, mother's milk is the only high-quality source of nutrition. Infants who are breast feeding therefore remain relatively healthy. When they are weaned, though, they must start eating other foods, and if these lack enough protein, they may develop kwashiorkor.

These ideas suggest three ways of responding to severe malnutrition. First, mothers in Third World countries should usually be encouraged to breast feed rather than bottle feed. Persuading them to make this change may be possible, although it is not simple: many mothers (in North America as well) regard bottle feeding as better because it is more "modern." Second, the prevalence of kwashiorkor among toddlers suggests that nutritional programs should pay special attention to children's transition from breast or bottle feeding to solid foods. Are mothers finding easily digestible foods for children, to initiate this phase of nutrition? Do local conditions even provide easily digested alternatives to mother's milk?

Third, and perhaps most important for developmental psychologists, the facts about severe malnutrition suggest that even poorly nourished parents need more than food (McKay et al., 1978): they need information about health — about the significance of sterilization, for example — and they need basic general education, too, so that they can read the labels on jars when they are trying to feed their children.

This fact creates ambiguities in assessing the effects of undernutrition in North America. Infants from poorly nourished families typically also experience other serious deprivations, such as poor sanitation, poor health care, and lack of educational opportunity. Since their parents may also suffer from poor health and a general lack of resources, the parents may not offer much stimulation for their babies' development, nor a very secure base from which to explore and learn about life. These conditions may contribute to the retarded motor and cognitive development mentioned above.

Obesity and Overnutrition In calorie-rich societies such as our own, eating too much can pose a serious problem for some individuals. The most obvious result of eating too much is to become extremely overweight, or **obese.** The nature and extent of this effect depends partly on just how much an infant overeats and on when during development the overeating occurs.

In the short run, what infants eat affects how much they weigh. Big, heavy infants tend to have diets that are high in calories. They tend to drink more milk than usual, and they tend to be started early on solid foods, which are often relatively high in calories (Dubois et al., 1979). Contrary to what some parents fear, however, weight in infancy correlates little with weight in childhood, and even less with weight in adulthood (Poskitt and Cole, 1977). Heavy babies stand only a slightly greater chance than lighter ones of becoming heavy children, and then only if they are very heavy indeed to begin with.

Effects of moderate excess

This fact stems from the way in which fat cells store energy during most of infancy. For most children, extra calories are indeed stored as extra fat. Under normal circumstances most of this fat is deposited within existing fat cells, a process called **hypertrophy.** As a baby grows and becomes more active, much of this fat is burned off; the fat cells shrink in size, and the child looks more slender or less chubby as she approaches her second birthday (Knittle et al., 1979). The shrunken fat cells remain ready, however, to enlarge later in life, whenever the child eats more calories than she really needs.

Infants seem to develop somewhat differently, however, if they are extremely overweight (say, more than 30 percent above average). In addition to developing enlarged fat cells, these infants also grow completely new fat cells, a process called **hyperplasia.** Once formed, these new fat cells do not disappear; they remain as extra storage places for any extra calories in the future. Extremely overweight infants therefore may live with some added risk of remaining overweight throughout childhood and adulthood. However, the risk does not guarantee obesity later on. As long as such children follow a moderately healthy diet and get reasonable amounts of exercise, they tend to develop quite normally.

Effects of extreme excess

Checkpoint *Infants require a high-quality diet: one with high proportions of protein and calories and with highly digestible foods. These requirements can be met either by breast feeding or by bottle feeding, at least in North American society. Breast feeding and bottle feeding each have certain advantages, although pediatricians and increasing numbers of mothers favor breast feeding. After weaning,* *infants and toddlers continue to need a diet high in protein and calories, as well as increasing amounts of solid foods. In our society parents and care-givers can generally meet these nutritional needs, although they sometimes fail to include certain specific nutrients in children's diets. Sometimes, too, infants become overweight by eating too much, but this poses a permanent problem only in extreme cases.*

Infancy: The Real End of Birth

In some ways babies are not really "born" until they complete infancy. During the first two years several changes make infants seem much more like individuals or real people than they did on the day they were born. As children approach their second birthday, for example, many of their basic physical needs and skills have stabilized. Now they can swallow and even chew a variety of foods, even if they still lack a lot of teeth and make a mess out of eating. And now too they can (sometimes!) sleep through the night.

Complementing the new forms of stability are new forms of variety in behavior. Two-year-olds can move around, even if they are sometimes still clumsy. And most important, a lot of their movement is voluntary; a toddler may wander away in a department store, for example, because *he wants to.* Such movements are facilitated by infants' physical growth during the first two years. By their second birthday, they can use their hands and feet to help them implement choices, however crudely at first. As the next chapters show, the first two years also make infants seem more human in two other major ways: by preparing them to think in symbols, and by helping them to form definite attachments to parents and peers.

Summary of Major Ideas

Appearance of the Young Infant

1. The newborn infant has several distinctive physical characteristics: it is covered with lanugo and vernix, and it has several "soft spots," or fontanelles, on its head, which will eventually grow over with bone.

2. For most mothers, the first few hours are an important time for establishing a positive relationship with their new baby.

3. The health of most newborns is assessed quickly after delivery with the Apgar Scale. For infants who may need it, a more complete assessment can be done a few days later with the Brazelton Neonatal Behavioral Assessment Scale.

4. The average newborn infant born at full term weighs about seven and one-half pounds. Its bodily proportions, such as having a large head, make it look cute. These proportions may foster the formation of attachments with adult care-givers.

Development of the Nervous System

5. A child's brain grows rapidly during infancy, especially in the cerebrum, and at the same time parts of it begin to develop special functions.

6. Infants sleep almost twice as much as adults do, but the amount gradually decreases as they get older. They also experience various states of arousal.

Sensory Development

7. At birth infants can already see and hear, but without as much accuracy or acuity as adults.

8. Newborn infants show a definite preference for sweet liquids, a definite aversion to foul odors, and less sensitivity to pain than older infants.

9. All of the senses develop rapidly and reach adult levels of acuity and sensitivity by the end of infancy.

Motor Development

10. Infants are born with a number of physically useful reflexes, such as rooting and sucking.

11. Infants also are born with several reflexes, such as the Moro reflex, whose primary significance is to indicate normal development of the nervous system.

12. Motor skills appear during the first year of infancy and include reaching, crawling and its variations, and walking.

13. Learning opportunities contribute to the development of motor skills, but so do infants' inborn reflexes and growth processes.

Variations in Growth and Motor Development

14. One of the most important influences on early motor development is low birth weight, caused by either slow prenatal development or short gestation.

15. Preterm infants often show many abnormalities: they may have trouble breathing and digesting, and their reflexes may not be well developed.

16. Gender differences in motor behavior appear even during infancy, when boys are generally more active than girls.

17. Infants from different cultural and racial groups vary significantly in size and in the time when they develop certain motor skills, such as walking.

Nutrition During the First Two Years

18. Infants need more protein and calories per pound of body weight than children do.

19. Compared with bottle feeding, breast feeding has several advantages: it conveys immunity to illnesses; breast milk is often easier for infants to digest; and breast feeding may promote positive relationships between mother and child.

20. Bottle feeding also has several advantages: it provides a way to feed children who are medically at risk; it allows family members other than the mother to participate in feeding; and it may be more practical in some circumstances.

21. After weaning from breast or bottle, infants need a diet rich in protein and calories. Most North American families can provide these requirements, although many fail to provide specific nutrients that children need.

22. A common problem with North American diets is overnutrition, which can make infants seriously overweight or obese. Mild amounts of extra fat in an infant, however, do not usually influence how much the infant weighs as a child or adult.

Key Terms

neonate *(163)*
vernix *(163)*
lanugo *(163)*
fontanelles *(163)*
Apgar Scale *(164)*
Brazelton Neonatal
  Behavioral
  Assessment
  Scale *(165)*
central nervous
  system *(168)*
neurons *(168)*
glia *(168)*
myelin *(168)*
brain stem *(169)*
midbrain *(169)*
cerebrum *(169)*
cerebral cortex *(169)*
REM sleep *(170)*
sudden infant death
  syndrome *(170)*
sleep apnea *(170)*
reflexes *(176)*

skills *(176)*
motor abilities *(176)*
rooting reflex *(176)*
sucking reflex *(176)*
mouthing reflex *(176)*
Moro reflex *(178)*
stepping reflex *(178)*
grasping reflex *(178)*
motor skills *(179)*
gross motor
  skills *(179)*
fine motor skills *(179)*
cephalocaudal
  principle *(179)*
proximodistal
  principle *(179)*
low birth weight *(189)*
small-for-date *(189)*
preterm *(189)*
marasmus *(200)*
kwashiorkor *(200)*
hypertrophy *(201)*
hyperplasia *(201)*

What Do You Think?

1. Do you think you are attracted to babies because they look cute? How do you think you would feel about cuddling an infant who did not look cute but who was physically deformed with, say, a cleft palate?

2. If walking develops at least partly through learning, then why not simply teach infants to walk as soon as possible? What do you think would be the short- and long-term effects of doing so, both on the infant and on you?

3. If you were to become a parent, would you breast feed or bottle feed? If you are a parent, which did you choose? Explain why.

4. How, specifically, can you keep an older infant from becoming seriously overweight? What keeps some parents (and infants) from implementing these suggestions?

For Further Reading

Ames, L., Gillespie, C., Haines, J., and Ilg, F. *The Gesell Institute's Child from One to Six.* New York: Harper and Row, 1979.

This book describes recent detailed observations of children's skills, arranged by age of the child and beginning at about age one. It emphasizes motor development and compares observations made in the 1920s and in the 1940s by the Gesell Institute.

Brazelton, T. B. *Infants and Mothers: the First Twelve Months* (revised ed.). New York: Delacorte Books, 1983.

The author gives very colorful and readable descriptions of the behaviors of three infants during their first year of life. He intersperses these descriptions with commentary that helps put the babies' behaviors into perspective. Since the three babies constitute case studies, Brazelton deals with all aspects of their development: physical, cognitive, and social.

Harth, E. *Windows on the Mind.* New York: Quill Press, 1983.

Here is a very readable presentation of the physical development and functioning of the brain. The author describes what we currently know about the relationships between the brain and psychological activity.

Klaus, M., and Kennell, J. *Maternal-Infant Bonding.* St. Louis: Mosby, 1976.

The authors describe experiments to promote stronger attachments between mothers and infants by encouraging the mothers to handle their babies immediately after delivery. They also comment upon the obstacles to good maternal-infant bonding that hospital routines sometimes create.

La Leche League International. *The Womanly Art of Breast Feeding* (3rd ed.). New York: Plume Books, 1983.

This is one of the more widely read books about the advantages to breast feeding. Note that it is published by an organization devoted to encouraging more mothers to breast feed, so it has relatively little to say in favor of bottle feeding.

Leboyer, F. *Birth without Violence.* New York: Alfred Knopf, 1978.

This book discusses not only the birth process but also infants' experiences during their first few minutes and hours of life. It describes methods (some of them controversial) for making those first few hours pleasant, both for infants and for parents.

Tanner, J. *Fetus into Man: Physical Growth from Birth to Maturity.* Cambridge, Mass.: Harvard University Press, 1978.

This book gives a very complete description of human physical growth, including one chapter on brain growth and another on assessing the significance of abnormal growth in children.

Chapter

6

The First Two Years:
Cognitive Development

Focusing Questions

- What clues do infants give about their cognitive processes? How can we learn about infants' thinking?
- Do infants see and hear in the same way that adults do?
- What does "thinking" or cognition consist of at different periods of infancy?
- How do sensory and motor experiences contribute to infants' cognitive development?
- What steps do infants and toddlers go through in acquiring language?
- How do adults affect language acquisition in infants and toddlers?

FROM BIRTH, INFANTS begin acquiring knowledge about their environment. Consider, for example, William and Elaine:

- William, nine months old, laughs when his father puts on a Halloween mask. But two days later, when a family friend tries on the same mask, William cries in distress. Six months later he laughs when the friend tries on the mask again, but he shies away from trying it on himself. The same mask seems to have changed meaning more than once.
- Elaine, eighteen months old, discovers her mother's box of postage stamps. For a time she forgets all else in favor of staring at the stamps and making little piles of them according to color. She is so engrossed that she cannot hear her mother calling her for dinner while she is doing this.

Underlying these examples are two psychological processes, perception and cognition. The first of these, **perception,** refers to the brain's immediate or direct organization and interpretation of sensations. Perceptual processes occur, for example, when an infant notices that a toy car is the same car no matter which way she orients it. As the infant girl turns the car upside down in her hands, her visual image of it changes, yet she still perceives the changing patterns as one unchanging car. She is not fooled into thinking that the car has acquired a different identity when she turns it upside down. Perception has an automatic, involuntary quality as well: Elaine cannot help staring at the postage stamps and comparing one with another, and William cannot help noticing that different people wearing the same mask look similar but also just a bit different.

Cognition is a more general term, referring to all the processes by which humans acquire knowledge. It includes the combination and interaction of perception, reasoning, and language skills which make up thinking and learning. Elaine, for example, uses cognitive skills: she goes beyond merely perceiving the stamps and groups them by color as well. William, on the other hand, is so young that we cannot be sure whether he really reacts cognitively to the mask he sees. But older children or adults would almost surely do more than perceive the mask if faced with the same situations that William experiences; they might consciously wonder who is behind the mask each time, why the person has put it on, and the like. As these examples show, cognition not only draws on perception but influences it as well. Elaine thinks about what she sees (or perceives), but her thoughts also keep her from perceiving her mother's voice or her own hunger pangs just before dinner.

Most activities include both perception and cognition, and distinguishing between them is sometimes rather hard to do. When you read a road map, for example, you perceive patterns of lines and colors. But you also know something about the region to which the map refers, and you apply this knowledge in reading the map. Likewise, when you hear a university professor lecture, you may perceive the sounds that he or she makes as language, but you probably also apply cognitive skills to making sense of them. Otherwise (heaven forbid), the lecture is only so much linguistic noise.

This chapter looks at how infants develop cognitive and perceptual activities like these. To do so, it first explains how thinking in infancy can be studied. How can we learn anything psychological about a person who cannot talk, and who may not even be able to gesture or move very well? The answer to this question makes possible many other answers about infant perception and cognition. A number of these are presented throughout the middle of the chapter. Finally, discussion of the most human of all cognitive qualities — language — completes the chapter, and incidentally suggests how children behave and think when they are on the verge of leaving infancy and entering childhood.

Ways of Studying Perception and Cognition in Infants

How can we know whether a very young infant, who mostly just sleeps, is actually noticing an interesting sight or sound, much less thinking about it? Consider Elizabeth, for example, who was only two months old:

> For two hours Elizabeth had slept. Now she lay in her mother's arms with eyes barely open, while her mother talked affectionately to her. The mother nodded her head while she talked, exaggerated her voice to sound singsong, and even dangled a key chain in front of Elizabeth's eyes for a moment. Elizabeth stared more or less in the direction of all these events; she did not respond in an obvious way, although she did not avert her eyes from it all or go back to sleep.

Maybe Elizabeth noticed her mother's efforts, and then again, maybe she did not. Either way, understanding Elizabeth requires more than simple observation. Infant psychologists have developed several interrelated techniques for inferring the perceptions and "thoughts" of babies. One of these focuses on changes in infants' states of arousal; another, on how they respond to especially familiar sights and sounds; and still another, on their readiness to perform more often those behaviors that they find rewarding.

Arousal and Infants' Heart Rates

One way to understand an infant's cognition is to measure his heart rate (**HR** for short) with a small electronic stethoscope attached to his chest. The changes in HR are taken to signify variations in the baby's arousal, alertness, and general contentment.

Heart rate studies   Why do infant psychologists make this assumption? Among adults, HR varies reliably with attention and arousal (Lacey and Lacey, 1978). Typically HR slows down, or decelerates, when adults notice or attend to something interesting but not overly exciting: when they read the newspaper, for example. If adults attend to something *very* stimulating, though, their HRs speed up (or accelerate) rather than slow down. Watching a lab technician draw blood from your own arm, for example, often causes a faster HR. On the whole, novel or attractive stimulations produce curiosity and a slower HR; potentially dangerous or aversive stimulations produce defensiveness, discomfort, and a faster HR — at least among adults.

Very young infants — from one day to a few months old — show similar changes, but we need to take several precautions about how we study their HRs. For one thing, young infants need to be observed when they are truly alert, and as we have already pointed out, newborn babies often spend a lot of time drowsy or asleep. For another thing, newborn or very young infants require relatively gentle and persistent stimuli, such as a quiet, continuous sound or a soft light that moves slowly or blinks repeatedly (Berg and Berg, 1979; Hirschman et al., 1982). Many stimuli that seem harmless to adults or to older children apparently overstimulate very young infants, and consequently accelerate their HRs instead of decelerating them. Many one-month-olds show a faster HR at the mere sight of their mothers, for example, even though the infants may look like they are just studying their mothers' faces calmly (Field, 1979). In spite of these problems, however, studies of HR have provided a useful way of measuring infants' attention, perception, and memory.

Recognition and Infant Habituation

Even though infants cannot describe what they remember, they often do indicate recognition of particular objects, people, and events. Familiar people, such as mothers, bring forth a special response in one-year-olds, who may coo suddenly at the sight of them, stretch out their arms to them, and even crawl or walk to them, if they know how. Less familiar people, such as neighbors or the family doctor, tend not to produce responses like these, and in fact may even produce active distress.

Habituation studies   Babies' responses to the familiar and the unfamiliar provide infant psychologists with a second way of understanding infant perception and cognition. The technique relies on **habituation:** infants' tendency to get used to and therefore to ignore stimuli as they experience them repeatedly (Fagan, 1977). One habituation strategy, for example, offers a baby a standard or "study" stimulus — a simple picture

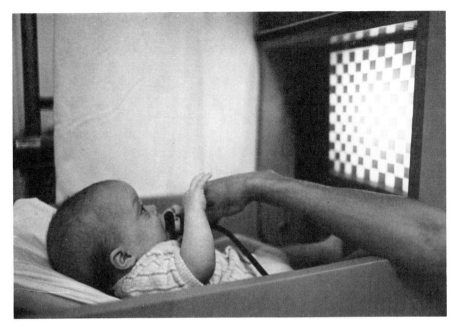

Babies often show preferences for novel stimuli. By sucking on a special nipple, the baby in the experiment pictured here brings a visual pattern into or out of focus. Typically, a new pattern prompts intense and rapid sucking at first, but as the baby habituates or gets used to the pattern, he sucks less frequently and strongly. (Jason Laure/Woodfin Camp and Assoc.)

to look at, or a simple melody to hear. Like most adults, the baby will attend to the study stimulus carefully at first, but gradually pay less attention to it. In other words, she will habituate. After the baby has studied the stimulus for a suitable period of time, the investigators present the original study stimulus along with a few other stimuli. If the baby really recognizes the original, she probably will respond to the others as comparatively novel. She will look longer and harder at the new stimuli, and her HR will slow down as well.

This method has shown that young babies recognize quite a lot of past experiences. One classic habituation study, for example, found that four-month-old girls recognized a familiar visual pattern among three others that differed from the original (McCall and Kagan, 1967). Another showed that HR slowed down when five-month-olds heard a familiar melody replayed in a different rhythmic pattern (Chang and Trehub, 1977). Still another found habituation even in newborns: they "noticed" when a light brush on their cheek changed location, as revealed by changes in their HR (Kisilevsky and Muir, 1984). Sometimes, too, recognition persists for very long periods. Six-month-olds, it seems, can still recognize an original study picture two weeks after they first encounter it — a performance that matches adults' recognition memory in some situations (Fagan, 1973).

Results of habituation studies may help explain why parents rapidly become convinced that their babies know them as special people. Elizabeth, described above, may already have been recognizing her mother or responding to her differently from other interesting sights and sounds, and her mother may have sensed this. Overall, monitoring infants' HR has given psychologists a useful method for learning something about what infants attend to and perceive in their environment, especially when the infants are too young to respond in other ways.

Infant Perception

As mentioned earlier, *perception* refers to how the brain organizes and interprets sensations. Perception operates relatively automatically; when your best friend walks up to you, for example, your brain almost instantly converts an oval-shaped pattern of colors and lines from an unorganized batch of sensations into an organized whole called your friend's face. This automatic quality has made some psychologists wonder whether children are born already possessing perceptual skills. Others believe that many such skills originate during infancy, through some sort of learning that happens naturally to most normal infants. As it turns out, research on these possibilities suggests a bit of truth in both of them.

Children acquire a number of perceptual skills during infancy. Each corresponds to one or another of the five human senses: vision, hearing, touch, taste, and smell. The first of these, vision, has been studied more than any of the others; and the first two, vision and hearing, account for the large majority of research about infants' perception. This emphasis reflects society's widespread (but probably unjustified) belief that touch, taste, and smell are "minor" senses, ones that we can live without more easily than vision and hearing.

Visual Perception

Given that children can see at least to some extent during infancy, what do they perceive? Some of the earliest research on this question excited a lot of interest because it seemed to show that infants — even newborns just two days old — could discriminate between human faces and abstract patterns, and that they looked at faces longer than at either patterned disks or plain, unpatterned disks

Early visual preference (Fantz, 1963). The researchers presented infants with various combinations of these stimuli side by side and carefully observed which of them the babies spent the most time looking at. At all ages studied (birth to six months), infants showed a clear preference: they stared at a picture of a human face almost twice as long as at any other stimulus picture. Young infants, it seemed, were inherently interested in people.

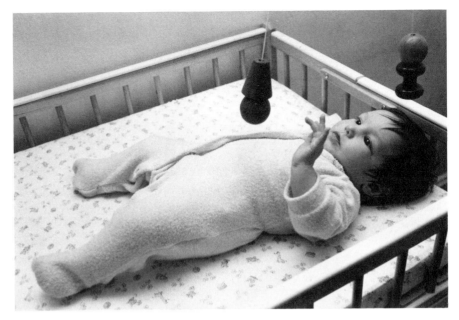

Young infants concentrate longer on certain shapes and contours, even when these are not part of a human face. Newborns are especially attracted to contours and to patches of light and dark. A few months later, they prefer complex patterns over simpler ones, and curved lines over straight ones. Such changes may sometimes explain why a baby's interest in a mobile like this one waxes and wanes. (J. Berndt/Stock, Boston)

More recent studies of visual preferences, however, have qualified this conclusion substantially (Haith, 1979; Banks, 1983). It is not the humanness of faces that infants enjoy looking at, but their interesting contours, complexity, and curvature. Newborns are particularly attracted to contours, or the edges of areas of light and dark. But such edges can be provided either by the hairline of a parent's head or by a properly constructed abstract drawing. When infants get to the age of two or three months, their perceptual interest shifts to complexity and curvature. At this age an infant will prefer looking at a pattern of many small squares rather than at one of just a few large squares. And he will prefer looking at curved lines to looking at straight ones. These qualities, too, are provided by human faces, but not by faces alone.

Changes in preferences

Object Constancy **Object constancy** refers to the perception that an object remains the same in size or shape in spite of constant changes in the sensations that it sends to the eye. A baby's favorite toy duck, for example, never casts exactly the same image on her retina from one second to the next. The image continually varies depending on its distance and on its orientation or angle of viewing. Somehow the baby must learn that this kaleidoscope of images really refers to only one constant duck — that the duck always *is* the same but keeps *looking* different. Several studies have begun to show that infants acquire this knowledge very early indeed.

For example, very young infants do perceive constancy of size. In one early study, newborn babies were conditioned to suck at the sight of a cube that measured precisely twelve centimeters across and was placed exactly one meter away (Bower, 1966). Later the babies were shown several cubes of different sizes and at different distances. These included one that cast an image exactly the size of the

Size constancy

original but that was in fact larger and farther away. The babies were not fooled by this apparent identity of retinal images. They preferred to look at the original cube regardless of its distance — that is, they sucked on their pacifiers more while looking at the original cube than at any substitute one. Apparently they knew when an object really was the same size and when it only looked the same size.

This conclusion is clouded, however, by infants' preference for objects at certain distances (Day and McKenzie, 1977). In particular, they prefer near objects — things at about one meter or less — to objects that are farther away. Anything that babies see at this relatively close distance promotes attentiveness, whether or not they have seen it before. Visual life occurs literally within an arm's reach for infants, especially when they are young; and it is hard to know for sure what they think about sights that are beyond this range.

Do babies perceive an object as being the same even when its shape changes because of different angles of viewing it? This particular perception is sometimes called **shape constancy.** The perception depends on allowing for apparent but unreal changes of shape. A rubber doll held upright, for example, casts a different image on the eye from the same doll lying down. Its changes in shape are only apparent; compare them with the real changes caused by squeezing the rubber doll hard with both hands.

Shape constancy

In general, research on this skill suggests that infants acquire shape constancy gradually, beginning at around three months of age. Typically they demonstrate this skill, like many others, by habituating — in this case, to shapes viewed at various angles or orientations. In one study, for example, young infants looked at a two-dimensional square presented at various sidelong or oblique angles (Caron et al., 1979). When the square was later presented "flat on," along with another, novel shape, the infants paid more attention to the novel shape and tended to ignore the familiar one. Since the infants had never seen the familiar square at a flat-on angle before, they must have somehow made mental allowances for its various changes in orientation during the experiment. Somehow, that is, the infants abstracted its true squareness from several not-so-square viewings of the shape.

Generally, young infants (about three months) show constancy only for simple shapes. Older infants — around eight months — can also recognize complex forms such as faces or abstract drawings, even when they are presented at sidelong or tilted angles (Cohen and Strauss, 1979; Ruff, 1980). For the most difficult figures, gentle movement or rotation seems to help infants to identify shapes. In these cases the older infants react somewhat like adults who are viewing a piece of sculpture: they must see all sides of it in order to take it in or perceive its full identity.

Depth and Space Perception Even if the infant perceives the size and shape of objects fairly accurately, he must still navigate successfully from one place to another. Consider a baby named Joel, who has recently learned to crawl around his house. Joel must realize that the rooms in his house stay put when he crawls or walks, even though they look like they move. And he must notice that stairs are different from floors: one of them makes him fall, if he is not careful, but the other feels secure. Realizations like these require Joel to orient his actions to the world

or space outside his own body and to understand its layout accurately. In other words, he must perceive depth and spatial orientation accurately. Each of these perceptions appears and then changes during the course of infancy.

Depth perception refers to a sense of how far away objects are or appear to be. Infants begin having this kind of perceptual skill about as soon as they can focus on objects at different distances, at around two or three months of age. This conclusion is demonstrated by the now classic experiment with the **visual cliff** (Gibson and Walk, 1960). In its basic form, this consists of a table covered with strong glass, under which is a surface textured with colored squares, such as shown in the photograph on this page. Part of the textured surface contacts the glass directly, but another part is separated from it by several feet. Visually, then, the set-up resembles the edge of a table, but the glass provides ample support for an infant even in the dropped-off area. A baby who crawls onto it will seem to float in midair.

The visual cliff

On this apparatus, even very young babies, just two months old, discriminate between the two sides of the visual cliff. They find the deep side more interesting, as suggested by the extra time they take to study it. Young babies show little fear of the deep side, judging either by their overt behavior or by their heart rates, which tend to decrease during their investigations of the cliff. This finding implies that they are primarily curious about the cliff rather than fearful of it.

Babies old enough to crawl, though, show significant fear of the visual cliff; their heart rates increase markedly, and they will not crawl onto the deep side in spite of coaxing from a parent and in spite of the solid support they feel from the glass (Rader et al., 1981; Campos et al., 1978). Why the change? Perhaps infants' crawling skills allow them to perceive distances more accurately than before, or perhaps once they can crawl, they know from experience that falling can be painful, so they become more cautious about heights.

Infants also show depth perception in their responses to looming motions, in what is sometimes called a "loom-zoom" procedure. Here the infant watches a screen on which a shape seems to approach rapidly (loom) and then retreats again (zoom). Children and adolescents typically respond by wincing or by raising their arms to protect themselves from what looks like a sure collision. If infants perceive depth in the way adults do, then presumably they too should respond defensively.

Sensitivity to looming

Do they? Some experiments have reported defensive reactions in infants as young as three months (Bower et al., 1970b, 1977); in these, the babies raise their arms, widen their eyes, and act distressed. In similar studies of looming, though, the babies do not react defensively at all (Yonas, 1979; Yonas and Pettersen, 1979). Skeptics therefore suggest that the occasional defensive reactions may really show something else — perhaps poor muscle coordination when the baby is tracking a looming shape. Often the contour of such a shape rises substantially as it looms; the baby must therefore look up to keep watching it, even if she is not actually afraid of it. If she looks too high, a young baby will have trouble keeping her arms and face from suddenly flipping backward: hence her "fearful" response.

This possibility, though, does not mean that genuine depth perception is impossible in younger babies. A baby may know that something is looming at her but not be afraid of it. Or she may simply be too poorly coordinated to show fear, even if she feels it. As with the visual cliff studies, fear and perception may be two different developments.

Later on in infancy, children use their perceptions of depth to orient themselves in three-dimensional space. Eighteen-month-olds come to believe that their spatial environment remains still or fixed even when they themselves move. As adults we take this orientation for granted. Walking from one room to another, for example, does not make the rooms move; it only makes them look like they do.

Spatial orientation

One psychologist studied the development of spatial orientation by placing infants in a room with two windows, one to their left and the other to their right (Acredolo and Evans, 1980). The babies were taught to expect the experimenter to appear at one of the windows whenever a buzzer sounded. They easily learned to do so, and before long turned to the proper window whenever the buzzer sounded but before the face appeared. At this point the babies were moved to the other side of the room, so that finding the face now meant turning in the opposite direction from before. As it turned out, only relatively old infants — nearly eighteen months old — corrected the direction in which they turned to see the face.

Younger infants responded much more egocentrically — that is, with reference only to their own bodies. If they originally learned to turn right, they apparently assumed that turning right remained correct even though they had moved.

But even young babies did not ignore their surroundings completely. Some six-month-olds switched their directions appropriately, and many more did so when the two windows in the experiment were distinguished clearly with unique and obvious star decorations. In another, related experiment, younger infants proved less self-centered if tested in their own homes rather than in a comparatively barren laboratory room (Acredolo, 1979). Perhaps knowing the layout of their homes made them more aware of the reality and permanence of space outside their own bodies. Or perhaps the younger babies felt more relaxed at home, and therefore performed better. Or perhaps both.

Auditory Perception

Infants respond to sounds even as newborns; but what do they perceive from sounds? What kind of sense do they make from the sounds that they hear? Consider Cheryl and Daniel:

- At about five o'clock each day Cheryl, two months old, cries unaccountably. Her father finds that running the vacuum cleaner quiets her down immediately. He also finds that it keeps her quiet more or less indefinitely, or at least until he cannot stand the sound of the vacuum anymore.
- Daniel, fourteen months old, sometimes gets fussy. His mother finds that playing a record quiets him down rapidly. Popular vocal singing seems to keep him quiet the longest, though every kind of music works for at least a little while.

Most adults would guess that Daniel is perceiving some sort of meaning from what he is hearing, such as the melodic structure of the songs or possibly some of the words being sung. It seems as though Cheryl, on the other hand, cannot be getting meaning from what she hears; more likely she is quiet because she is tuning out or "averting her ears" from the noise.

Research confirms these informal impressions. Under certain conditions infants can indeed organize the sounds they hear, and in this sense they can not only hear but also perceive what they hear. For example, infants just two days old can locate sounds, as shown by the way they orient their heads toward the noise of a rattle (Clifton et al., 1981a). But they often take much longer than children or adults before responding. Instead of needing just a fraction of a second, as adults do, full-term infants require an average of two to three seconds before orienting (or looking at) a sound that occurs off to one side. Infants born one month preterm require even more time — an average of twelve seconds — to respond (Field et al., 1980). These delays may explain why pediatricians and others used to believe that newborn infants could not hear: the sounds that they offered to the babies, such as a single hand clap, may not have lasted long enough for the infants to respond.

Although infants can locate sounds, their skill at doing so has certain limita-

Locating the direction of sound

tions. They localize better with relatively high-pitched sounds, such as those made by a flute or a small bird, than with low-pitched sounds, such as that made by a foghorn (Morrongiello et al., 1982). This fact has sometimes led ethologically minded experts to suggest that infants have a "natural" preference for female — that is, high-pitched — human voices. Studies of voice preferences, though, have not confirmed this possibility (Aslin et al., 1983), probably because newborns' range of special sensitivity lies well above the pitch of even female voices, and because male and female voices are usually more similar in overall quality than gender stereotypes would suggest.

For the first few months of life, infants localize sounds only by the differences in loudness of the sounds when they reach each ear (Clifton et al., 1981b). This allows only fairly crude judgments about the direction of a sound (during the newborn period, of course, a baby may not need very precise judgments). By about the fourth month of life, however, infants begin using an additional source of information that increases their accuracy considerably, namely the slight differences in

Refinements in sound localization

Perspectives on Issues

What to Look for in Toys for Infants

Some toys are better for infants than others. Several factors make the difference, including the following:

1. *Sturdiness* In general, toys with solid construction last longer, regardless of whether they are made from wood, plastic, or metal. Up to a point, too, most parents and care-givers (and children) prefer long-lasting toys. But there is a limit; sturdiness can sometimes interfere with other desirable qualities, such as fine detail. A car made from a single chunk of wood, for example, may hold up well to rough use, but it also may not appeal to older infants or toddlers, who are beginning to look for realistic representations in their dramatic play.

2. *Color* Bright colors catch the eye, but they can sometimes also interfere with appropriate use of a toy. Rings that stack on a peg, for example, may be made to stack according to size, from largest at the bottom to smallest at the top. But if each ring also has its own color, an infant does not need to pay attention to the dimensions; instead he can solve the problem more easily by learning the sequence of colors provided by the toy manufacturer.

3. *Implied Social Values* Among commercially manufactured toys, two simplifications of values are especially common: too much aggression and too much sentimentality. Among infant toys, aggression is implied by the many varieties of superhero- and war-related materials, ranging from rubber squeeze toys shaped like guns to superhero bats. Excessive sentimentality is implied by the many dolls and stuffed animals that suggest an overly happy view of the world — one in which children (or stuffed animals) never cry or get angry. Themes of assertiveness and of nurturance can be expressed in toys without going to stereotyped extremes.

4. *Safety* Toys do cause accidents, especially when they involve large-motor activity. The most dangerous toys currently in wide use are outdoor climbing bars and their indoor variants; they account for twice as many accidents as any other common toy or piece of children's equipment (Aronson, 1984). The next most dangerous toy is the outdoor slide; together with climbing bars, slides account for the majority of accidents. Indoor toys are comparatively safe, but they can still cause

when a sound arrives at each ear. A sound originating off to the left, for example, will arrive at the left ear a few thousandths of a second sooner than it will arrive at the right ear. The exact difference in timing in fact reflects the exact direction of the sound fairly precisely. Toward the middle of their first year, infants show signs of noticing these split-second differences when they are created artificially through stereophonic loudspeakers. Much more often than would occur by chance, they turn toward the direction of these artificial sounds.

Checkpoint   *Early studies suggested that infants look more at human faces than at other images, but recent work shows that many other visual patterns can hold just as much interest. From the age of about three months, infants visually perceive constancies of size and shape. They also perceive depth at this age, although they do not become fearful of heights until they are old enough to creep or crawl. During their second year, infants acquire an accurate spatial orientation.*

---

problems. Watch out for plastics that can shatter suddenly and get into infants' eyes, for sharp points and wooden splinters, and for tiny pieces that can break off and be swallowed.

Many toys may serve certain children well but not satisfy others (Fowler, 1985). An infant just learning to manipulate stacking rings, for example, may not much care whether the rings are color-coded, but an older child who is trying to learn about size would profit more without the distraction of color. Likewise, toddlers and children who especially like caring for dolls and stuffed animals should probably be helped to do so, even if some of their dolls or animals seem a bit stereotyped. Toys cannot be all things to all children.

In spite of these individual differences, certain toys do hold special appeal for children of specific ages. For instance, toys that require moving about cannot be used properly until children learn to walk. Keeping developmental milestones in mind, here are a few examples:

- *For Infants under One Year*   A mobile to hang over the crib; plastic rings or other objects for teething and feeling; a homemade chain of spools; seashells (but avoid sharp edges); a soft crocheted ball; a small latex ball with a bull's-eye design on it; latex squeaky toys; rattles of various sizes and designs.

- *For Infants over One Year*   Plastic refrigerator containers for nesting and stacking; pots and pans from a kitchen cupboard; a ring-stacking toy; a form board of simple geometric shapes; pull toys, such as a wooden duck or car; a toy lawn mower or "popper."

- *For Infants of Any Age*   A small mirror (preferably not glass); soft, cuddly animal toys; lightweight balls of various sizes; a phonograph or tape recorder for listening to music.

There are many variations on these examples. As long as toys meet high standards of safety and durability, they are all equally good. But perhaps one more "toy" should be mentioned explicitly, because it may be the best one of all: an interested, friendly parent or other care-giver who will get involved in what an infant is doing.

Auditory perception also develops rapidly during infancy. Newborns can localize (or locate) sounds if given many seconds to do so. By about four months, they can locate sounds rapidly and accurately, using minute differences in when a sound arrives at each ear.

Infant Cognition

As perceptual skills develop, children begin to put them to cognitive uses. A one-month-old infant may notice the dark eyes painted on the face of a doll, for example, and stare a long time at them out of interest. But an eighteen-month-old can do more than that: she can talk to the doll in babbles that resemble language, or cuddle her briefly, as if the doll were a real person. All in all, the older infant combines perception with other skills she is developing. In doing so, she shows the first signs of *cognition*, or methods for thinking or gaining knowledge about the world.

At first infant cognition has little to do with the symbolic forms that develop in most children and adults. Instead it emphasizes active experimentation with and manipulation of materials. Only by the end of infancy does truly symbolic thought emerge. Even then it is still scattered among large amounts of concrete doing, seeing, and hearing; but its mere existence marks a significant new development for the child.

Piaget's Theory of Sensorimotor Intelligence

Piaget's theory of cognitive development, described in Chapter 2, provides one of the most complete outlines of infant intelligence (Piaget, 1936). According to this viewpoint, infants think by way of *sensory* perceptions and *motor* actions: by doing things to and with the objects that they see. Piaget called this activity **sensorimotor intelligence.** He identified six stages during infancy that mark significant developments in sensorimotor intelligence; these are summarized in Table 6-1.

In general, these stages show three trends as infants grow older. First, infants' thinking becomes less **egocentric,** which means that they become increasingly able to take others' viewpoints into account. Being less egocentric in this sense does not necessarily make infants less selfish in everyday behavior — less apt to grab others' toys, for example — but it does make them more aware of any differences between their own needs or opinions and those of others.

Second, Piaget's stages of infant development show a trend toward abstract or symbolic thinking. Instead of needing to handle a toy car in order to understand it, infants become increasingly able to form an idea of a car without touching and seeing one tangibly. This ability becomes very strong by the end of the first two years of life; for Piaget, it helps to mark the end of infancy.

Third, as infants' motor skills become more complex, the infants tend to group them according to the objects or activities to which they refer. Piaget called these

Less egocentrism

More symbolic thinking

More organized skills

Stage	Age in Months	Characteristics
1: Early reflexes	Prenatal–1	Reliance on inborn reflexes to "know" the environment; assimilation of all experiences to reflexes
2: Primary circular reactions	1–4	Accommodation (or modification) of reflexes to fit new objects and experiences; repeated actions focusing on infant's own body
3: Secondary circular reactions	4–8	Repeated actions focusing on objects; actions used as means toward ends, but haphazardly; early signs of object permanence
4: Combining secondary circular reactions	8–12	Deliberate combinations of previously acquired actions (or schemes); AnotB error; early signs of sense of time
5: Tertiary circular reactions	12–18	Systematic application of previously acquired actions (or schemes); well-organized investigations of novel objects, but always overt
6: The first symbols	18–24	First symbolic representations of objects; true object permanence; deferred imitation

Table 6-1 Some Features of Infant Cognition According to Piaget

Source: Piaget, 1936.

groupings **schemes.** They are the precursors to simple concepts, ideas, and other symbolic representations, which eventually become important during early childhood.

As we discuss more fully in Chapter 2, Piaget argues that sensorimotor intelligence develops by means of two complementary processes, assimilation and accommodation. **Assimilation** consists of interpreting new experiences in terms of ideas or action-skills that the infant already has. A baby who is already used to sucking on a breast or bottle, for example, might use this same action on whatever new, unfamiliar objects she encounters, such as rubber balls or even her own fist. **Accommodation,** on the other hand, consists of modifying existing ideas or action-skills to fit new experiences. After sucking on a number of new objects, an infant might modify this action to fit the nature of each new object; she might chew on some new objects (her sweater) but not on others (a plastic cup).

The interplay of assimilation and accommodation leads to new motor skills, and eventually to the infant's ability to symbolize objects and activities. Let us look at how Piaget believes this occurs.

Stage 1 — Early Reflexes: Using What You're Born with (birth to one month)

According to Piaget, cognitive development begins with *reflexes,* those simple, inborn behaviors that all normal babies can produce at birth. As it happens, a majority of such reflexes remain just that — reflexes — for the child's entire life;

sneezing patterns and blinking responses, for example, look nearly the same in adults as in infants. But a few reflexes are notable for their flexibility — chiefly sucking, grasping, and looking. These behaviors resemble reflexes at birth, but they quickly begin to be modified in response to the experiences that the newborn encounters. They give infants a repertoire from which to develop more complex skills, and their susceptibility to influence makes them especially important to cognitive development during infancy.

Modifications of reflexes

Take sucking, for example. Mothers who have breast fed know that the first feeding or two can be awkward: the infant noses around inefficiently for the nipple, and may fail to connect with it even when the nipple is right under his nose, so to speak. But within just a week or two he is noticeably faster at finding it, usually to the relief of his mother. In that same period, too, he has probably begun sucking on other objects as well: his own fist, the corners of his blanket, or his daddy's little finger. Sometimes he simply sucks on thin air. All these sucking motions differ slightly from one another in style or form, and each evolves into a *scheme,* in the Piagetian sense: an organized pattern of thoughts or actions that helps the baby to make sense out of his environment, as well as to adapt to its requirements.

Stage 2 — Primary Circular Reactions: Modifying What You're Born with (one to four months)

Soon after the baby begins modifying his early reflexes, he begins building and differentiating action schemes quite rapidly. Within a month or so, in fact, he sometimes repeats them endlessly for no apparent reason. Because of its repetitive quality, Piaget calls this behavior a **circular reaction.** The baby seems to be stimulated by the outcome of his own behavior, so he responds for the mere joy of feeling himself act. At this point the circular reactions are called **primary circular reactions** because they still focus on the baby's own body and movements. Waving an arm repeatedly, for example, would constitute a primary circular reaction; so would kicking his legs over and over again.

Repeated actions involving the body

During this period, the young infant practices his developing schemes widely. He grasps everything in sight, or sucks on it, or looks at it, or listens to it. These behaviors rapidly become less reflexive. By now the baby may literally shape his mouth differently for sucking his fist and for sucking his blanket. In this sense he can begin to recognize the objects all around him, and he implicitly also begins to remember previous experiences with each type of object. But this memory has an automatic or compulsive quality, unlike the relatively conscious memories that children have later in life.

During this stage babies begin to vary in their preferred schemes. Some emphasize looking; others, grasping; still others, vocalizing. The variations may foreshadow later differences in temperament and personality, at least if "later" means simply later in infancy or early childhood. Nearly all babies, though, develop and exercise certain schemes in common. For example, nearly all suck their thumbs at least occasionally — a scheme that evolves from early grasping and sucking reflexes. Nearly all do a good deal of active looking around; doing so helps give them the wide eyes that can make infants so appealing. And nearly all begin to vocalize (just openmouthed cooing at first) during this period, apparently for the sheer joy of hearing their own voices. The schemes for visual inspection may help

Commonly occurring schemes

make possible the perceptual developments that were described earlier in this chapter, and the vocalizations may contribute to early sensitivity to language, as described at the end of this chapter (Molfese et al., 1982).

Stage 3 — Secondary Circular Reactions: Making Interesting Sights Last (four to eight months)

As they practice their first schemes, young infants broaden their interests substantially. Before long, in fact, they move their attention beyond their own bodily actions to include objects and events immediately around them. Shaking her arm, for example, no longer captivates a baby's attention for its own sake; she has become too skilled at arm shaking for it to do so. Now a behavior like this becomes useful rather than interesting. A baby at this stage may accidentally discover that shaking her arm will make a mobile spin over her head in a crib, or create an interesting noise in a toy she happens to be holding, or make parents smile with joy. In all these cases, shaking an arm becomes a primitive means to other ends. At best it is primitive, though, because the usefulness of the behavior originally occurs to the baby by chance.

Once primitive means are discovered, a baby at this stage will repeat a useful procedure endlessly in order to maintain and study the interesting results. The repetition is a circular reaction like the ones in the previous stage, but with an important difference: now the circular reactions orient to external objects and events rather than to the baby's own body and actions. Now results matter. If arm shaking fails to keep the mobile spinning, the baby will soon stop her effort; if she finally figures out the nature of the mobile, she will also stop. Either way, the repetition is not governed by her earlier motivation simply to move — her squirming scheme, so to speak. To differentiate this new orientation from the earlier one, Piaget calls such repetitions **secondary circular reactions:** repetitions motivated by external objects and events.

New focus on objects

Secondary circular reactions create two parallel changes in the child's motor schemes. On the one hand, she uses existing schemes ever more widely than before. For example, she tries to suck on more and more of the toys that come her way. On the other hand, she begins to coordinate schemes that previously existed only separately for her. She may carefully reach for an object (one scheme) in order to grasp it (another scheme). Such coordination of course implies that the earlier, more reflexive schemes do in fact exist separately and only later become coordinated. As discussed below, though, some schemes may also develop in precisely the opposite direction: from early integration toward later separation.

Secondary circular reactions also implicitly show that the infant is now acquiring at least a hazy notion of **object permanence,** a belief that objects have existence separate from her own actions and continue to exist even when she cannot see them. In the first two stages of infant cognition, objects often seem to disappear from the baby's mind as soon as she loses sight of them, or as soon as she no longer touches them. She may stare at or grasp a toy duck, for example, but a parent or an older sibling can sometimes take it from her without causing distress; at most the baby will simply keep staring blankly where the duck used to be, and then turn to other activities. In a phrase that Piaget might have invented (but did not), out of sight is out of mind in early infancy.

Early signs of object permanence

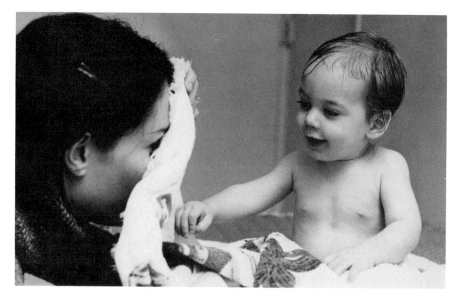

Playing peek-a-boo becomes popular with babies when they acquire the secondary circular reactions that Piaget described for Stage 3 of infant cognition. Even though the mother disappears temporarily, an infant at this stage knows *that she must still exist behind that blanket. The baby is delighted to have this belief confirmed when she reappears. (Suzanne Szasz/Photo Researchers)*

This is not so, though, as babies enter the second half of their first year. By Stage 3 they will look for an object briefly if they have been watching it carefully or manipulating it just beforehand. Naturally their first searching skills leave something to be desired, so it helps if the hidden object is actually partially visible and within easy reach — the toy duck's tail should stick out from under a blanket, if that is where it is hidden, for example. But the first signs of symbolic thought are there, since infants must have some sort of idea of the toy duck if they are going to bother searching for it.

Stage 4 — Combining Secondary Circular Reactions: Applying Means to New Ends (eight to twelve months) At this stage, instead of just happening upon connections between actions and objects, the infant creates them deliberately. When he first finds a new toy, for example, he now runs through his repertoire of schemes suitable for toys: he may suck on it, then bang it, then scratch, then look, and so on. Eventually, after enough occasions like this, the repertoire itself can become a new, more abstract scheme, one that helps the infant explore objects more systematically. For now, though, the baby's efforts are confined to familiar behaviors or schemes. This limitation can make his behavior seem stereotyped at times. "He chews on everything," his mother may say. By this she means that he performs this particular scheme in a way that is not only predictable but somewhat insensitive to variations in objects and circumstances.

The relatively fixed, stereotyped quality of schemes at this stage may derive from the infant's heavy reliance on motor action as a method for understanding objects. **The AnotB error** One of the most dramatic illustrations of this possibility is the so-called **AnotB error** (read "A, not B, error"), illustrated by the following sequence. Hide a toy under a blanket while the infant carefully watches. Normally he can retrieve the toy easily at this stage. But then make the problem more complicated: hide the toy under blanket A, and then transfer it to blanket B. Do this in full view of the infant. Where does the child first look for it? Not under the correct blanket, B, but under blanket A, where he previously retrieved the toy successfully.

The infant makes this mistake, Piaget argues, because his knowledge of the toy really amounts to memory of the actions he has taken with it — especially of successful actions. Other studies of the AnotB error support this interpretation. In one study, for example, babies were moved from one side of a table to the other after watching the toy be moved from blanket A to blanket B (Bremner and Bryant, 1977). Under these conditions the babies tended to reach for blanket B, which now required the same motor action that blanket A had required originally. The babies' relatively fixed motor response therefore still governed their actions, even after they had been moved. The behavior resembled the egocentric head-turning experiments described earlier in this chapter.

Despite the repetitive quality of the baby's actions, he is now developing an intentional quality that allows him for the first time to anticipate events in the near future. For parents, the new sense of time can be both good news and bad. The baby may open his mouth wide for bananas, but clamp it shut for medicine. He may wave his arms in delight at the sound of his bathwater being drawn, but he may fuss and protest at being carried anywhere in the vicinity of his diaper-changing table. In each case he anticipates the results of actions or schemes. More precisely, he anticipates accurately as long as the consequences are fairly immediate; "far time" — just a few hours or even several minutes away — still has little meaning to him.

Early awareness of time

Stage 5 — Tertiary Circular Reactions: Active Experimentation with Objects (twelve to eighteen months)

At Stage 5 the infant deliberately varies the means of producing interesting events, apparently simply in order to see what happens. Piaget calls the variations **tertiary circular reactions** (meaning third-level circular reactions), to distinguish them from the simpler forms of repetition that dominate earlier stages.

Consider bathtime again. Now, at Stage 5, the infant purposely varies how he splashes: first gently with one hand, then harder, then gently again but with two hands, and so on. These actions resemble secondary circular reactions in focusing on the results of actions rather than on the actions themselves. But they go beyond earlier forms of repetition by their deliberate variation. The baby now acts as if he is comparing the variations among themselves, and the comparisons in fact seem to occupy more attention than the individual results as such. In the bath, the baby does not care so much about the individual splashes as about their differences and similarities.

Systematic application of schemes

The purposeful variations in behavior, though, are still organized largely by trial and error, and not by systematic plans. Given a rubber ball, for example, some babies may try dropping it from different heights and onto different objects. But no matter how delighted these infants are with the results of these variations, they will not think to vary the dropping conditions carefully or experimentally. They will not try slight changes in altitude each time, or assemble objects with slightly differing bounciness for landing platforms. These more systematic efforts require mental representations of the ball and of the bouncing activity, and must therefore wait until the next and final stage of sensorimotor development.

Meanwhile, babies still cannot solve problems by insight — that is, by mentally forming or running through solutions prior to overt action. Their belief in object permanence at Stage 5 shows this limitation. They no longer make the AnotB error, but they can still be fooled, if the search problem is made a little harder. A ball shifted from blanket A to blanket B can still baffle infants if they do not actually get to see it moved; they may not think to look under blanket B if they did not actually see the ball put there. Instead they will simply stare at the situation, looking surprised, perhaps, and confused. Babies respond this way even though a moment earlier they may have successfully solved a classic AnotB problem in which they did in fact see the ball get moved. Taken together, these behaviors suggest two things: first, that infants are not tied as much as before to particular successful actions for help in solving problems; and second, that they still fail to imagine the solutions to problems.

Stage 6 — The First Symbols: Representing Objects and Actions (eighteen to twenty-four months)   At this stage, the motor schemes that the child previously explored and practiced overtly begin to occur symbolically. The resulting mental schemes constitute the first symbolic representations for the child. For the first time she can begin to imagine or envision actions and their results without actually having to try them out beforehand.

Consider, for example, a Stage 6 child who wants a favorite toy that is just barely out of reach on a high shelf. Near the shelf, as it happens, sits a small stool that she has played with numerous times. How to get the toy? Earlier in infancy the baby might simply have stared and fussed, and eventually either given up or cried. At this late stage, though, things are different. The baby surveys the situation; observes the stool; pauses briefly. Then, with a purposeful air, she places the stool under the toy, climbs up, and retrieves the toy. What is important here is the lack of false starts, or, conversely, the presence of only a single, correct attempt. The infant may succeed even though she may never before have used the stool to reach high objects. According to Piaget, trial and error is no longer the method of choice; now the infant tries out solutions mentally to envision their results. Only when she determines a workable action in her mind does she carry it out.

True object permanence   Skill with mental representations makes true object permanence possible. A child at the end of infancy will search for a toy even after it has been hidden in the fully adult sense. If a ball disappears behind some shelves, she will go around to the other side to look for it. She will search appropriately, even though she cannot know in advance exactly where behind the shelves the ball will turn up. In the ball-and-blanket situation described above, too, the child can now play more complex games of hide-and-seek. She usually looks first under the blanket where the toy disappeared; but if she fails to find it there, she will search under any and all other blankets, and sometimes even under the table and in the experimenter's pockets. Relatively extensive search is made possible in part by the child's new conviction that toys and other objects do in fact have a permanent existence in-

dependent of her own activities with them. They do not, in other words, just disappear.

Mental representations also make possible **deferred imitation,** a behavior that will figure importantly in play and learning later in childhood. In deferred imitation, the child copies or duplicates a behavior, or at least aspects of a behavior, at a significantly later time than when she first experiences it — sometimes days or even weeks later. Having seen her father brush his teeth, for example, the Stage 6 child does so too; but she may do so twelve hours later, when her father is not even around. Or having heard her older sibling exclaim "Yum! Good!" at one night's dinner menu, the child may do so as well. But she makes her exclamation at din-

Deferred imitation

ner two days later, even if none of the other family members happens to feel quite so ecstatic about the food.

These behaviors all depend on the child's ability to form and maintain representations (thoughts or memories) of the relevant experiences, which later become available for expression again. As we shall see, representational skill proves crucial in early childhood. It contributes to children's play, for example, because much play involves re-enactment of previous experiences and roles. It makes possible much language development, since the child must learn to use words and expressions when they are appropriate and not just at the time she hears them uttered. And it makes possible the first real self-concept, since sooner or later the child realizes that she too has a (relatively) permanent existence akin to the permanence of all the things and people in her life, whether toys, pet dogs, or parents.

Baby Jill's Intelligence: An Example

The relationships among the six stages of sensorimotor intelligence become clearer if we look at how an infant might use the same object differently at different ages. Baby Jill acquired a ball when she was born, and used it for the next several years. During that time, of course, her ways of using the ball changed dramatically, as shown in the following descriptions (comments are in italics). The ball was about four inches in diameter and was made out of rubber, but had a cloth covering. Mostly it was red, but it had a large black spot on each side, so that it looked rather like an eyeball when viewed from the proper angle.

1. *Stage 1: Early Reflexes* When Jill first came home from the hospital, her mother suspended the ball over Jill's diaper-changing table, so that the black spot looked down at Jill directly. Day after day Jill stared hard at the ball and its black spot, and followed it whenever her mother made it swing gently.

Here Jill used one of her earliest reflexes, in this case visual tracking of objects.

2. *Stage 2: Primary Circular Reactions* At two months, Jill sucked on the ball a lot, and grabbed at it whenever one of her parents put it directly into her hands. The ball was just soft enough for Jill to do these things. She still liked to look at the ball swinging above her changing table, but she was starting to find her parents' faces more interesting.

Jill was modifying or accommodating her reflexes — sucking, grasping, tracking — to fit new experiences that were occurring to her. Her interest still lay primarily with her own actions, rather than with the objects she was encountering.

3. *Stage 3: Secondary Circular Reactions* At six months, Jill discovered that *she could make the ball swing above her*

By now her attention had shifted away from her own body (primary circular reactions) to an object out-

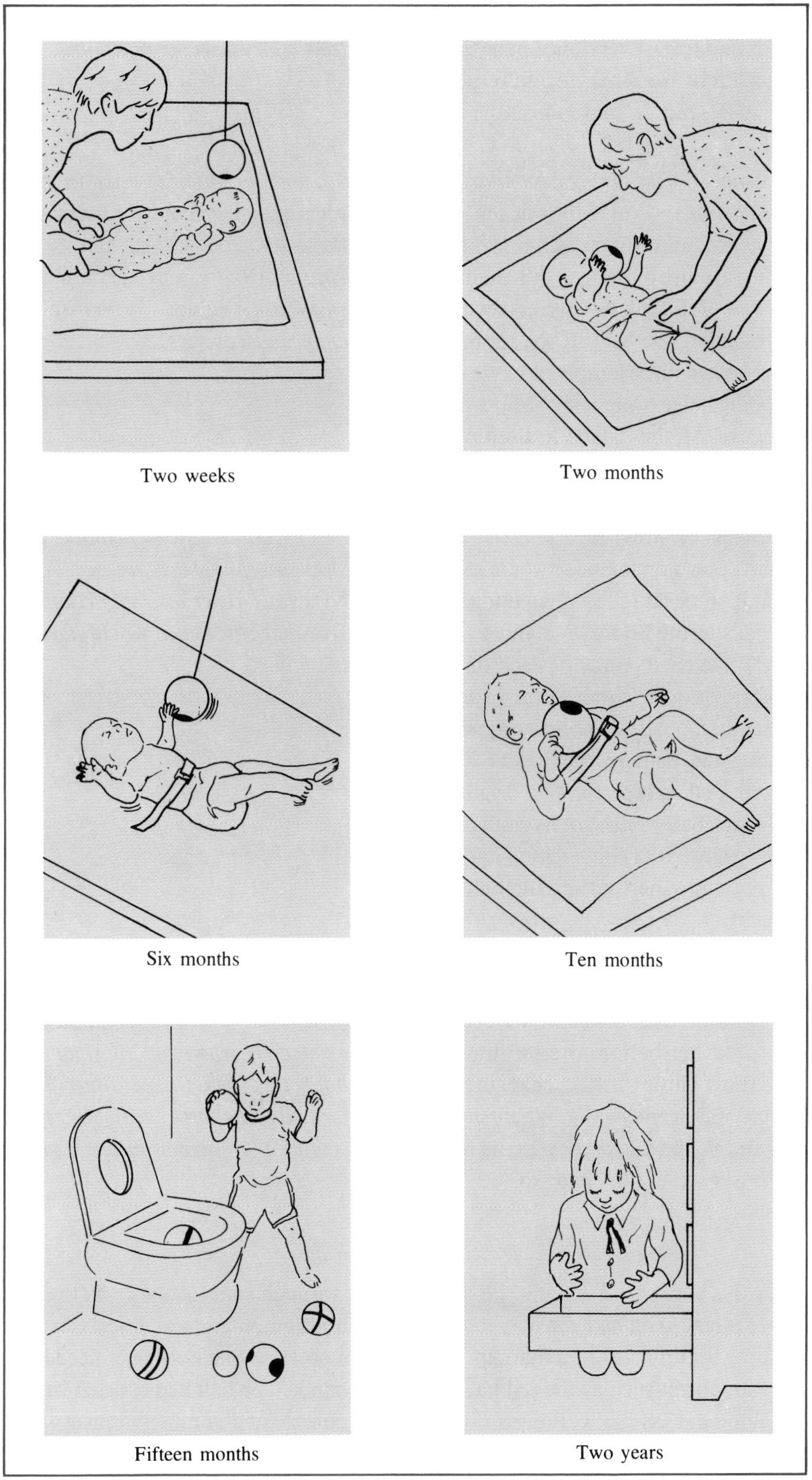

Figure 6-1 *Six Stages of Baby Jill's Intelligence*

Two weeks

Two months

Six months

Ten months

Fifteen months

Two years

changing table, simply by waving her hands and feet. Every once in a while one of her limbs would accidentally catch the ball and send it spinning and swinging wildly.

4. *Stage 4: Combining Secondary Circular Reactions* When Jill was ten months old, her father took the ball down one day during a diaper change. Jill managed to get hold of it. She discovered several new things about the ball. If she rapped it on her stomach, for example, it made a funny plopping noise. And if she dropped it over the edge of the table, it thumped and disappeared!

5. *Stage 5: Tertiary Circular Reactions* At fifteen months, Jill preferred to have the ball down on the floor where she could get at it. One day she gathered together all the balls in the house — about five, to be exact. She tried bouncing each one down the stairs in turn; some seemed to bounce higher than others. Another time she tried floating the balls in the toilet. They all floated well except for her original red-and-black ball, which got its cloth covering waterlogged. (For some reason her parents did not enjoy her putting the balls in the toilet.)

6. *Stage 6: Symbolic Representation* Just before her second birthday, Jill lost her red ball. She looked in her usual storage spots: her bottom dresser drawer and her (now little used) changing table. Where was it, anyway? When she could not find it, she asked her parents for help, since she knew it had to be around somewhere.

side herself and to what it could do (secondary circular reactions).

Jill had become interested in using a variety of schemes or actions on the ball. Her exploration of the effects of these schemes, however, was still guided primarily by chance discoveries.

Her investigations of the ball now had become rather systematic, as if she were purposely trying out a conscious repertoire of actions to see what effect each would have on the ball.

In searching for the lost ball, Jill showed object permanence — a belief that the ball continued to exist even when out of sight. To hold this belief, she must have formed some sort of symbolic representation of the ball in her mind.

By this point, both Jill and the ball had gone through a lot together. At the end of her infancy, Jill had considerable skill at motor manipulation of objects, as well as some beginnings of mental representation of objects. She no longer needed to have an object such as the red ball literally in hand. The ball had assisted in this development, as had countless other toys, of course, and countless sensory and manipulative experiences with them.

Assessment of Piaget's Theory of Infant Cognition

Piaget's theory has stimulated considerable study of infant cognition. A lot of this research has confirmed the main features of the theory (Harris, 1983), whereas other parts have called attention to additional aspects of infancy that at least complicate Piaget's original presentation, even if they do not contradict it outright. Here is a sampling of both the confirmations and the complications.

The Integration of Schemes   Do infants begin life with fundamentally separate sensorimotor schemes, as Piaget argues, and only gradually learn to combine or integrate them? Some such combining must surely happen, but there is also evidence for the opposite trend: some important schemes may begin as integrated wholes and only later become differentiated into parts. As pointed out in Chapter 5, for example, newborn infants will reach for and grasp a small object placed in front of them at the proper distance. They will do so even if the object is created only by a projected image (Bower et al., 1970b; Bower, 1981). Such behavior implies that young babies tend to regard sight and touch as connected rather than separate, or, in Piagetian terms, that they have a single early scheme for seeing-and-reaching, not one scheme for seeing and another, separate one for reaching.

Connections among early schemes

Vision and hearing may also have inborn integrated schemes. Infants just a few days old will turn to look at the source of a sound, as long as the direction lies within their physical capacity to turn (Muir and Field, 1979). In addition, they show signs of connecting their parents' face and voice within two or three weeks: they will look more at a photograph of their mother, for example, if a recording of her voice is playing (Spelke and Owsley, 1979). And infants just a few months old prefer looking at a film that matches a soundtrack to one that does not match (Spelke, 1979). This conclusion was suggested by a study in which young infants looked at two films side by side, one with a kangaroo bouncing up and down and the other with a toy donkey doing the same thing but at a different speed. When a soundtrack of bouncing rhythms was made to coincide with one film but not the other, the infants spent more time watching the coordinated picture.

"Looking" at sounds

Such evidence complicates Piaget's assertion that schemes primarily begin as separate, discrete reflexes and do not start integrating until midway through infancy. At the same time, though, the evidence does not really contradict Piaget. Given the complexity of human organisms, it is perfectly possible for both trends to occur at once. Some schemes may begin as integrated wholes and develop that way in at least certain situations, and others may begin as relatively specific reflexes and later combine.

Motor Limitations Versus Cognitive Limitations   Some infant psychologists question Piaget's six stages because they feel that the stages confuse the child's motor abilities with his cognitive or thinking abilities (Bower, 1981). Object permanence, for example, implicitly depends on a child's capacity to conduct a search: to walk around the room, to lift and inspect objects, and the like. Perhaps younger infants "lack" classic object permanence, this argument goes, simply because they lack motor skills, or at best use them only clumsily.

To test this possibility, psychologists have redesigned the usual object permanence test so that it requires very little motor coordination from the infant. In one variation (Bower and Paterson, 1973) the baby simply watches an object disappear behind a screen. A moment later the object either does or does not reappear at the other edge of the screen. Under these conditions, even twenty-week-old infants show what looks like surprise if the object does not reappear: they stare more intently and widen their eyes. The behavior suggests a belief in object permanence; after all, why else would they show surprise? Unfortunately, their behavior can also be interpreted in other ways; it resembles attention to an interesting and changing visual display — a scheme that Piaget predicts to be well within the abilities of even young infants (Gratch, 1977).

The Effects of Memory Piaget explains most infant thinking in terms of motor schemes: repeated, familiar actions that allow infants to know their environment.

The AnotB error in particular supposedly reflects the child's dependence on overt actions or motor schemes of this type. But does it really? Maybe the error really

---

Perspectives on Issues

Support and Education for Parents of Infants

Given the unremitting demands of caring for an infant, it is not surprising that programs have emerged to help parents with this job. The programs take several forms, such as actual care for infants in child-care centers and discussion groups organized by parents. Most often, however, programs to enrich infants' development consist of home visits to individual parents by trained educators.

A good example is the Florida Parent Education Infant and Toddler Program (or PEP, for Parent Education Program). This program consists of a series of intervention projects for infants between the ages of three months and three years; it began in 1966 and continues into the present (Gordon et al., 1977; Jester and Guinagh, 1983). Altogether the projects have involved more than five hundred parents and infants, as well as about fifty parent educators. The parents all come from poverty-level communities, as do the educators, who receive five weeks of special training by the PEP project before beginning their work. By using members of the parents' own communities, the project leaders hope to create

better rapport between the parents and the parent educators.

After their training, the parent educators visit each family once a week, for about thirty to sixty minutes per visit. During each visit they demonstrate at least one new activity that is appropriate for that infant's level of development. At the same time they discuss the activity with the parent (usually the mother), and often discuss any other concerns that she may have about her child as well. Project leaders devise activities from a variety of sources, ranging from Piaget's cognitive tasks to standardized observations of infant development (Bayley, 1969; Gesell, 1943) and to informal opinions and personal experiences of the staff with infants. With a three-month-old, for example, one activity is simply to reach repeatedly for a toy animal. With a twelve-month-old, one activity is hiding a toy under a blanket (the AnotB problem).

The visits have created considerable warmth and support between the educators and many of the parents. But problems have occurred. For one thing, the adults are sometimes tempted to "test"

---

shows the infant's poor memory, which has not yet developed very far. In the AnotB task, after all, the baby does at least have to remember, first, that the toy has been moved recently, and second, that it began by lying under the first blanket. As obvious as these ideas may seem to adults, a young infant may have trouble remembering them.

Considerable evidence suggests that memory does in fact affect infants' performance in the AnotB task. One study, for example, found that imposing slight delays on the infant's search interfered with performance much more for younger infants than for older ones (Kagan, 1979). Seven-month-olds who correctly solved the problem without any delay could generally also tolerate a three-second delay before searching for the toy, but they failed if they had to wait seven seconds. Ten-month-olds, on the other hand, could manage even seven seconds without difficulty.

Effects of delays on performance

These trends imply that the infants find it demanding simply to remember the relevant facts in the task: where things are and are not located, and when and whether they were in fact moved. Their memory problems, though, do not so

the babies rather than simply encourage them to play and practice the new activities; once a child has succeeded at an activity, both the parent and the educator tend to move on rapidly to the next activity in the sequence. Another problem has been balancing the educator's attention between the parent and the infant: some educators prefer to interact with the child, and leave the parent feeling ignored. Still another problem concerns older siblings in the family: often they want special attention from the visitor, to the point where some mothers feel obliged to arrange baby sitting for the siblings, just to achieve enough quiet for a successful home visit.

In many ways the PEP project is typical of home-based programs to assist parents of infants. How successful are such programs, all things considered? In the short run, home visits produce important gains in infants' cognitive skills, as measured by standardized tests of infant IQ (Bayley, 1969). Home visits also make parents' interactions with their infants more positive and improve their self-esteem as parents (Slaughter, 1983). The long-run effects are not nearly as obvious, but longitu-

dinal studies of parent education programs nonetheless suggest that there are several positive ones. Children from the PEP project, for example, have been much less likely than children from similar socioeconomic backgrounds to require special education classes or services when they enter elementary school.

In general, the exact curriculum selected for home-visit activities does not affect the success of the programs as much as the warmth and enthusiasm of the parent educators who implement the activities (Powell, 1986). This finding does not mean, however, that curriculum is not important, or that any curriculum will work with any child or parent. Instead it means that curriculum activities are probably construed or interpreted very differently by individual parents and children, depending on their individual needs and levels of development. In general, therefore, the curriculum may simply act to encourage parents to observe their infants more closely, to enjoy what they see in their infants, and to share their concerns and questions with another interested adult, the parent educator.

much contradict Piaget's emphasis on motor development as supplement it. The most complete explanation of the AnotB error therefore seems to use both ideas: infants probably use memory when they can, but supplement it with Piagetian motor schemes whenever necessary. If an infant cannot recall where the toy is hidden, at least she can re-enact the actions she used for finding it in the past (Butterworth, 1977). This multiple strategy actually resembles the way adults sometimes search for a lost object: if you cannot recall where you left it, you may retrace your steps up to the time you remember seeing it last — using, in essence, an action scheme.

The Effects of Motivation   Piaget's account of infancy implies that motivating infants to perform presents no large problem; it assumes that they will carry out cognitive tasks without much coaxing and within a reasonable time period. If a baby has partially developed an action scheme, then practicing that scheme will be its own reward, and almost inevitably adults will be able to see the child perform it.

Unmotivated infants

This may have been true for Piaget, who observed his own infant children in natural play in his own home. In many situations, though, motivation cannot be taken for granted, as research on infants frequently suggests. There are times, as every parent knows, when a baby is just too tired to look, or too indifferent to bother shaking a rattle, or too hungry to search for a hidden object. And there are times when he is just too content to do much of anything active. Often these conditions impair an infant's performance and make him seem more immature than he really is.

Ambiguous lack of performance

Often, too, such conditions simply create confusion about an infant's preferences. If a baby looks equally at two pictures, for example, is it because he sees no differences between them, or because he just likes the pictures equally well, or because he is patiently waiting for the experiment to finish? This kind of ambiguity seems to be inherent in any study that identifies human preferences simply by overt behavior.

Even adults sometimes lack object permanence: they may give up the search for a missing object without ever finding it, and literally forget that they ever even tried to search for it. Such behavior strongly resembles Stage 3 infant behavior. It happens particularly when adults do not really care whether they find the object or not. By the same token, babies asked to search for toys under blankets may not care whether they find the toys; from their point of view, the search may amount to just an arbitrary task. If so, and if they fail to pursue the search, do they lack object permanence, or merely lack interest in the task?

Performance Versus Competence   These questions about motivation illustrate a more general problem with Piagetian theory, as applied to both children and infants: by emphasizing the nature of competence, it tends to neglect the immediate causes of performance. An infant — or anyone, for that matter — may be *able*
 to do something without necessarily *choosing* to do it. Even if an infant does show her highest competence in one situation, she may fail, for various reasons, to do so in a situation that differs from the first one only slightly. As mentioned above,

Immediate causes of performance

even a few seconds' delay can change some infants' success rates on the AnotB task, creating very different impressions about their abilities in the two conditions. Problems with distinguishing competence from performance crop up throughout psychology, and throughout developmental psychology in particular. As it turns out, identifying the immediate causes of performance may be done more easily outside the Piagetian framework than inside it.

Checkpoint *Piaget's theory of cognitive development proposes six stages of infant cognition, which are increasingly less egocentric, more symbolically oriented, and more organized or integrated. The most important result of the six stages is the achievement of symbolic thinking, as shown by the infant's increasingly firm belief in object permanence. The stages have stimulated much study and observation of infant cognition. On the whole this research has confirmed Piaget's original observations, but it also calls attention to the effects of motor skills, memory, and motivation on cognitive performance in infancy.*

Behavioral Learning in Infancy

One framework for studying the specific performance of infants has come from **behaviorism,** or what psychologists sometimes also call **learning theory.** As described in Chapter 2, learning theory focuses on changes in specific behaviors (sometimes called responses), and on the specific, observable causes and consequences (stimuli and reinforcements) of these behaviors. Typically, learning theorists identify three kinds of behavioral learning: classical conditioning, operant conditioning, and imitation.

Three kinds of learned behavior

Infants show signs of all three types of learning, at least by the age of about three months. Infant psychologists have not concentrated equally on each type of learning, however. Instead the large majority of studies of infant learning concern operant conditioning (Olson and Sherman, 1983). This fact makes conclusions about operant conditioning in infants more definite than those about the other types.

Classical Conditioning

As described in Chapter 2, this form of conditioning consists of transferring control of a reflex response by pairing two stimuli together. One of the stimuli (the "unconditional stimulus," or UCS) is chosen from among ones that automatically produce a particular response, and the other (the "conditional stimulus," or CS), from those that do not. Here, for example, is how classical conditioning might occur for an infant:

Nature of UCS and CS

$$\text{puff of air (UCS)} \quad \rightarrow \quad \textit{(produces reflex)} \quad \rightarrow \quad \text{eye blink}$$

$$\uparrow$$

(paired with)

$$|$$

musical tone (CS)

Classical conditioning occurs when the puff of air and the musical tone are paired repeatedly. Eventually the tone establishes a connection with the eye-blink response, where none existed before, and the tone causes the infant to blink even without a puff of air. That, at least, is the theory.

When tried on infants under about six months of age, classical conditioning has produced conflicting results. Some infant reflexes prove conditionable to some neutral stimuli, but not all combinations of stimuli and responses can be conditioned. The musical tone, for example, can in fact be conditioned to an eye-blink response even in three-month-old infants (Sameroff and Cavanaugh, 1979), but it cannot be conditioned successfully to a reflex change in infants' pupil size. A change in the lighting can reliably make infants' pupils get smaller, but pairing a tone with the change in lighting does not condition this reflex, no matter how many pairings occur.

These irregularities imply that young infants may be genetically prepared to learn certain sorts of connections from their environment and are genetically constrained from or limited in learning others. It is as if they notice some connections in their world, such as a tone and a puff of air, but not others, such as a tone and a change in brightness. Since such constraints have long been recognized in studies of conditioning among animals, it seems reasonable to expect analogous limitations among human beings (Hinde and Stevenson-Hinde, 1973). As infants become toddlers, presumably, they overcome some of these limitations in classical conditioning, thanks in large part to their growing abilities to think and reason about connections among stimuli. Unfortunately, developmental psychologists have done little research to test this possibility among older infants and toddlers. Instead they have given the bulk of their attention to another form of behavioral learning: operant conditioning.

Mixed results with infants

Genetic predispositions to some associations

Operant Conditioning

In this form of learning, infants get a reward or reinforcement if they perform some simple action or set of actions. By turning their heads, for example, they may get to see an interesting toy or picture; in this case the reinforcement is viewing the interesting toy, and head turning becomes the learned or conditioned behavior. Such actions tend to be performed more often than actions that are not reinforced.

Many studies have found infants quite capable of learning through operant conditioning. Newborns will learn to suck on a pacifier more rapidly if doing so yields a tiny amount of sugar water; or they will learn to blink their eyes more often if doing so causes a pleasant voice to speak or a melody to play (Olson and Sherman, 1983). One reason that infants seem to learn to breast feed so easily is the strong

Nature of operant conditioning

Imitation provides a rich source of learning for most infants and toddlers — as it apparently has done for this young "driver." To occur, though, imitation depends both on symbolic thought and on motor skills, both of which improve rapidly as children move into the preschool years. (Walter S. Silver)

reinforcement which that behavior brings, in the form of mother's milk and motherly comfort.

As with classical conditioning, though, infants are predisposed to learn these particular behaviors. All examples of operant conditioning in infants rely on those few behaviors that young babies can already do, which are mainly their inborn reflexes. By nature, reflexes occur easily — in fact, almost *too* easily. As parents often discover, for example, any slight provocation — such as a touch on the baby's cheek — can stimulate sucking movements in young babies. Such readiness to respond creates confusion about when infant responses really constitute learning rather than general excitement. For example, when do sucking movements show true operant learning: a specific behavior performed more often because a specific reinforcement results from it? And when do sucking movements simply amount to a reflex that is itching to occur, so to speak, and that would happen in response to almost any stimulus?

The confusion between learning and excitement diminishes as babies grow older, because they acquire behaviors that are more truly voluntary. Early in infancy, though, the ambiguity is widespread and probably cannot be avoided.

Operant learning versus reflex responses

Imitation

Types of imitation

As make-believe play demonstrates, children obviously learn to imitate at some point in development; but exactly how early, and by what processes? Early research on these questions generally found that infants could engage in different kinds of imitation at different points during infancy. In general, they imitated actions that they could see themselves perform sooner than they imitated actions that they could observe only in a model. Imitating a hand gesture such as waving, for example, proved easier than imitating an unusual face made by an adult (Uzgiris and Hunt, 1975). And deferred imitation proved hardest of all: only children nearing their second birthday could save their imitations until the day after they saw a model perform them (McCall et al., 1977). All of these findings are consistent with Piaget's theory of infant cognition.

Perspectives on Research

Assessing Infant Intelligence

Do some infants learn more rapidly than others? And if they do, does that make them more intelligent, in some sense, than other infants? The problem with answering this question is that infants do not "think" in the language-oriented way that we usually associate with intelligence in adults. Instead infants think with their hands, feet, and senses: they manipulate objects, move around the house, and look at and listen to whatever they find.

Tests for measuring infant intelligence therefore have to focus on motor actions. In one widely used infant test (Bayley, 1969), for example, an examiner sits (patiently) with a baby and tries various simple things:

- She offers the baby a cube to hold. Does the baby pick it up skillfully?
- She shows the baby a mirror. Does the baby look at his reflection with curiosity?
- She says one or two simple words like *mama* and *baby.* Does the infant imitate them?
- She encourages the baby to build a small tower of cubes. Can he do it?

In general, performance on tasks like these shows how quickly an infant is developing motor skills. The overall score that results is sometimes called a **developmental quotient,** or **DQ** for short.

Since the activities mostly emphasize motor activities, it is not surprising that infants' performance correlates rather poorly with their later performance on intelligence tests intended for children and adults (Lewis, 1976). The skills being tested are just too different. Intelligence tests emphasize language and logical skills, as in the problem "How much is one-third of one-third of nine?" Being able to answer this question is a far cry from the problems that infants face, such as learning to vocalize pleasure or learning how to pat the family dog gently. Indeed, motor skills and verbal skills correlate poorly at any age, even for adults (Sternberg and Powell, 1983).

Infant intelligence tests do serve important purposes, though, in identifying babies with serious physical or intellectual handicaps. Infants who are extremely slow at motor development do run more chance than other infants of intellectual and other handicaps as they grow up into childhood (Smeriglio, 1981). For this reason, infant tests are often used to assess the progress of children born at risk, such as preterm infants and babies born with particular physical handicaps. The rest of us, though, are better off not worrying about the exact speed of a particular infant's development; in a few years it does not matter anymore.

But not all psychologists agree with this account of the development of imitation. Some carefully done studies have found what seems to be imitation performed even by newborn infants (Meltzoff and Moore, 1977): purposeful efforts by newborns to stick out their tongues in imitation of adults, for example, and efforts to wiggle fingers after seeing adults model this behavior. Later studies have confirmed that newborns respond to visual stimuli with motor behaviors like these. But the stimuli do not need to consist of actual human behaviors performed by human beings. A ball moving toward a young infant's mouth, for example, stimulates the infant to stick his tongue out almost as well as a real tongue on a real human face does (Harris, 1983). At present, therefore, we still have more to learn about the origins of imitation during the newborn period.

Possible imitation of facial expressions

Checkpoint *Infants can acquire behaviors through at least two of the three processes that learning theorists emphasize for adults: operant conditioning and imitation. In assessing these processes with infants under the age of about three months, however, developmental psychologists face serious ambiguities about whether infants' responses really constitute learning or instead show other processes, such as simple reflexes and general excitement.*

Language Acquisition

When Michael, the son of one of the authors, was an infant, he went through several phases in using language.

- At twelve weeks of age, Michael made openmouthed cooing noises when he was feeling content. Sometimes these sounds were vaguely similar to ordinary vowel sounds, but they seemed to vary unpredictably. Michael cooed a lot in the morning when he first woke up, which pleased his father and mother. His sister said that his cooing sounded rather like the heavy breathing of an obscene telephone call, but his parents disagreed (and wondered how on earth his sister knew what obscene calls sounded like).
- By six months of age, Michael had added consonant sounds to his vocalizations, to produce complicated babbling noises. His most productive time for this activity continued to be the morning, although he "said" quite a lot whenever he was feeling generally content. Certain sounds seemed to be favorites: "da" and "gn." Sometimes Michael repeated these and other sounds — "da, da, da, da . . . ." His father thought Michael repeated sounds when he was feeling especially happy.
- At fifteen months, Michael could produce about six words, but he did not pronounce them as adults would. The family cat was "dat"; his favorite food, yogurt, sounded like "yugun"; and airplanes were simply "der!" (as in "Look

there"?). He seemed to understand dozens of words and sentences, although it was hard to be sure, because he probably picked up clues about meaning from the behavior of his parents. When Michael was tired one day, for example, he came immediately when his mother said, "Come sit here" in a sympathetic tone of voice. But when she said the same thing in a cross tone of voice the next day, he looked at her with an impish smile and went the other way.

- At about his second birthday, Michael sat "reading" a children's book to himself. Occasionally real phrases could be heard (". . . bug ate leaf . . ."), but mostly Michael sounded like he was mumbling, or like someone talking in the next room. When he finished, he walked to the kitchen and phrased a three-word question: "What's for lunch?"

As these examples show, a great deal of language develops during infancy; indeed, language is one of the most clearly human of all developments of this age period, and perhaps of the entire lifespan.

Language has several aspects, and infants must acquire them all to become verbally competent. First of all, they must learn the sounds of the language — its so-called **phonology.** Second, they must begin learning something of its purposes and meanings — its **semantics.** And third, they must piece together its organization, or **syntax.** Infants must learn to use all three aspects of language in two ways: both to talk meaningfully and to listen with comprehension.

Phonology and semantics develop rapidly during infancy, and will therefore be the focus of this chapter. Syntax, however, begins developing late in infancy, when children begin combining words together into phrases and sentences. Since syntactic development finishes well after infancy — around age four or even later — it will be discussed with other aspects of early childhood cognition in Chapter 9.

Theories of Language Acquisition

How can infants make such major cognitive strides in a matter of just months? Linguists and psychologists have proposed several theories to answer this question. Learning theories of language propose several processes that may affect language acquisition. Originally one of these processes was thought to be reinforcement: parents praise or respond to their babies' vocalizations, and in so doing stimulate more mature forms of language (Skinner, 1957). This idea makes some sense for parents of infants who have not yet learned to speak; just looking at babies often makes them coo and babble more (Harris, 1983). It is not true, though, for parents of toddlers and preschoolers. Research shows conclusively that parents of these children respond just as positively to ungrammatical utterances as to grammatical ones (DeVilliers and DeVilliers, 1978), so reinforcement cannot be shaping or modifying children's language toward more mature forms.

More likely learning processes are mutual imitation and accommodation. Infants and parents engage in games of mutual imitation even before the infants can speak (Stern, 1977). One of them utters a noise or a coo; then the delighted partner responds with the same noise or coo, which is followed by another imitation, and so on. In games like these, infants not only practice the phonology or

Three aspects of language

Learning theories of language

Limits of reinforcement

Imitation of language

sounds of their native language, but also practice taking conversational turns. As a child begins to acquire a usable vocabulary and syntax, her parents may also simplify and rephrase their utterances to make them more accessible to her. These efforts seem to model language more effectively for toddlers, by giving them samples of language to study as they converse.

For some linguists, even imitation and accommodation do not go far enough in explaining the ease and speed with which infants acquire language. They propose a nativist theory instead; all human beings, they argue, are genetically predisposed to acquire language (Chomsky, 1976). The inborn skills that accomplish this task are sometimes called the **language acquisition device** (**LAD,** for short). Evidence for LAD comes from three facts: (a) that all healthy infants acquire language without explicit training, (b) that no other species of animal acquires language to nearly the same extent as the human species, and (c) that certain areas of the brain become clearly specialized for language functions during childhood.

LAD and inborn language predisposition

The debate between learning theories of language and nativist theories of language is far from over — if indeed it ever will be. Because of its importance and complexity, we return to these issues in more detail in Chapter 9, which discusses language development in preschool children. First, though, let us look at the steps that infants actually experience as they acquire their native language.

Phonology

Every language uses a finite number of sounds, or **phonemes,** which combine to make the words of the language. English, for example, has about forty-one of these, which are illustrated in Table 6-2. Particular phonemes result from particular physical arrangements of the vocal apparatus: the tongue, mouth, nose, throat, and vocal cords. Often very small physical changes in the apparatus can create distinctively different phonemes. The sounds /th/ and /t/, for example, differ primarily in how tightly the tongue is held against the upper teeth. Holding it loosely causes air to leak out and creates the sound /th/, as in *there;* holding it tightly leads to an explosion of air and creates the sound /t/, as in *tear.* In typical speech we often produce sounds partway between /th/ and /t/, but these inaccurate phonemes are almost always perceived as if they belong squarely to one category or the other. We hear the badly spoken examples as either a true /th/ or a true /t/.

Nature of phonemes

Perceiving Phonemes In acquiring language, infants must learn to notice phonemes and to ignore any meaningless variations. Although the task might seem demanding, it actually proves surprisingly easy, even for a baby. It proves so easy, in fact, that some language specialists suspect that human beings are genetically and physiologically disposed toward noticing phonemic differences (Eimas and Miller, 1980).

Sensitivity to phonemes

A variety of evidence supports this possibility. As mentioned earlier in this chapter, infants just one month old can distinguish between vocalizations and nonhuman sounds. They tend to turn toward the source of the vocalizing and to show other physical signs of attending to human voices even in the midst of non-

Table 6-2 *The Phonemes of English*

Vowel	As in:	Consonant	As in:
a	can, carrot	b	bet, nib
ā	late, day	d	dog, bid
ä	father, mama	f	fog, cuff
		g	gas, big
e	men, ferry	h	hot, ahead
ē	be, honey	j	job, fudge
		k	kiss, sack
i	bit, mist	l	list, mellow
ī	pie, nice	m	mother, slim
		n	nut, can
ō	open, hoe	p	pod, cup
ô	claw, for	r	rug, sort, clear
o̅o̅	cool, flew	s	sit, hiss
oo	cook, bull	t	tar, bit
yo̅o̅	use, dew	v	vast, cave
yoo	union, sure	w	wish, sweet
oi	foil, boy	y	yes, opinion
ou	out, loud	z	zoo, ooze
u	but, color	ch	check, catch
ʉr	curse, infer	sh	shoe, fashion
		th	thin, bath
ə	around, item, circus	th	this, bathe
		zh	measure, seizure
ər	larder, persuade	ng	sing, ringer

Note: The examples given for each phoneme often sound slightly different from each other but are grouped together because they are commonly *perceived* as the "same" sound.

human noise (Eisenberg, 1976). At the very least, such attention should make learning phonemic distinctions possible, although not inevitable.

Infants also seem disposed to hear certain phonemes *categorically*, which means that they perceive sounds as belonging completely to one phoneme or another, and never as partway in between (Eimas and Miller, 1980, 1981). Such categorical perception should make language acquisition inherently easier. It is not, however, a uniquely human ability. Similar perceptual abilities exist in rhesus monkeys (Morse and Snowdon, 1975) and even in chinchillas (Kuhl, 1976); yet monkeys and chinchillas do not learn to talk! Presumably they lack other crucial skills, anatomy, and experiences that human infants normally have. So perception of phonemes must be necessary to language acquisition, but not sufficient for it.

Babbling Although skill at producing phonemes takes longer to develop, it too seems biologically influenced. Sometime around four to eight months of age, infants begin babbling in increasingly complex and random ways. They apparently do so for the sole reward of hearing themselves vocalize — an example of a Piagetian primary circular reaction.

What suggests that babbling is motivated intrinsically? For one thing, the sounds made during babbling go far beyond the phonemes uttered by a child's parents, so babies apparently do not learn to babble by directly imitating the language they hear. For another thing, even deaf children babble in normal ways, except that they stop somewhat abruptly around their first birthday, presumably because they lack the reward of hearing themselves speak (Lenneberg, 1967).

Intrinsic motivation to babble

Babbling persists well into the second year, and overlaps with the appearance of the child's first meaningful words. Unlike the development of words and verbal utterances, though, it never proves susceptible to teaching. Parents can increase a baby's overall amount of babbling by reinforcing it with smiles and praise, but they cannot influence the selection of particular babbling sounds (Dodd, 1972). When infants finally do begin using the sounds of their own language, they apparently do so by their own choice, and in the context of producing their first real words.

Immunity to teaching

Late in infancy, some babbling may sound rather like true language, because it becomes quite complex and because it acquires the normal **intonation,** or rise and fall in vocal pitch, of the child's native language (Elbers, 1982). Mostly, though, babbling seems simply to reflect the baby's pleasure at hearing himself speak. Given its playful quality, adults usually enjoy hearing him "speak" as well.

Learning the melody of language

Semantics and First Words

The semantics (or meanings) of a language are never mastered fully, even by adults. To test this idea on yourself, scan any page of a large unabridged dictionary and see how far you must go before you encounter an unfamiliar word. Most people, it seems, never learn even a majority of the words or terms in their native language. This happens partly because words get much of their meaning from the real world rather than from each other. Most of us simply do not live long enough to learn all of these relationships with the real world.

Learning semantics, therefore, is something that children begin in infancy but do not nearly complete. Somewhere around their first birthday, most infants will use their first words — or at least make sounds that parents take to be words. By their second birthday, they may be using as many as fifty words appropriately. At this age, though, some children may still be acquiring their first words, and most still have only a shaky, limited command of many words. From age two to three, vocabulary increases rapidly, thanks partly to the child's newly emerging skill with longer sentences. An average three-year-old may know several hundred words, and an average five- or six-year-old can use a few thousand, or about half the vocabulary she will ever command, even as an adult (Smith, 1926). Note this, though: the averages hide large differences among individual children, both in the overall size of their vocabularies and, as explained below, in the types of words that they select to learn.

These figures refer only to children's **expressive language,** which is their ability actually to use a word appropriately in conversation. Expressive language is complemented by **receptive language,** which is the ability to understand or comprehend language used by others. At all ages, children's receptive language exceeds their expressive language significantly; put in plainer terms, they can understand more than they can say. The difference in receptive and expressive capacities shows up in many exchanges between parents and their infants. For example, if a father asks his ten-month-old, "Can I have a bite of your cookie?" the baby may offer him one. The same infant may not use any of those words herself, though, for several more months, or combine them into a sentence for another year or more.

Functions of First Words   The first words of a child are sometimes called **holophrases** — literally, "whole phrases" — since the child often uses one word to express a complete thought. Like the longer utterances of adults, holophrases serve a variety of purposes, depending on the situation or context. Sometimes

infants utter a word in order to get or deal with an object, saying "Hankie!" to mean "I'm now going to reach for the handkerchief." Or they may use a word to guide or regulate the actions of people; the same "Hankie!" may then mean "Please play peek-a-boo with me, using the handkerchief." Or they may simply use a word to comment on a situation, as a sort of infant version of idle conversation; in that case, "Hankie!" may just mean "Look at that interesting handkerchief right there with the pretty colors on it."

Knowing which function the child intends depends on knowing the situation in which he is speaking as well as something about his growing interests and previous experiences. Responding to one-word utterances therefore involves guesswork,

even for the best of parents. Interpreting them is made easier, though, by the fact that children learn to communicate even before they acquire verbal holophrases to attach to their nonverbal messages (Halliday, 1979; Ziajka, 1981). Gestures, facial

Table 6-3 Milestones in
Language Acquisition
During Infancy

Approximate Age	Vocal Accomplishment
4 weeks	Cries of displeasure
12 weeks	Contented cooing, squealing, gurgling; occasional vowel sounds.
20 weeks	First signs of babbling; most vowel sounds, but only occasional consonants
6 months	Babbling well established: full range of vowel sounds and many consonants
12 months	Babbling includes the melody or intonation of the language; utterances signal emotions; first words are produced; the child understands several words and simple commands
18 months	Expressive vocabulary between three and fifty words; intricate babbling interspersed with real words; occasional two- and three-word sentences
24 months	Expressive vocabulary between fifty and three hundred words, though not all used accurately; babbling gone; many two-word sentences or even longer; nonadult grammar; the child understands most simple language intended for him/her

Source: DeVilliers and DeVilliers, 1978.

expressions, and the like can and do accomplish all the functions described in Table 6-3. Since these continue and accompany a child's first words, they sometimes provide a method for "translating" first words into adult language.

Individual Differences in First Words What words do children use first? On the whole, they seem to prefer objects that stand out from their surroundings in some way: ones that move, or make noise, or go away and come back (Greenfield, 1982). The child's own mother or father may fulfill these criteria, but often not as well as some other people and things around the house. One study found that *dog* appeared as an early word more than *sun* or *diaper,* even though the latter two objects are probably experienced more frequently and universally by children than dogs are (Nelson, 1973). Proud parents notwithstanding, words for family members — including *mama* and *daddy* — may appear early, but not necessarily at the very beginning.

In spite of some overlap, children continue to differ as they expand their vocabularies. Researchers found that one- and two-year-olds learned nonsense words more easily if those words were constructed from the phonemes already in their very first words. They learned *bex,* for example, faster if its sounds — /b/, /e/, and /x/ — were already occurring in words of their existing vocabularies (Schwartz and Leonard, 1982). This trend suggests that infants may pick and choose new vocabulary, at least at first; perhaps they bias their selection in favor of words that they already find easy to pronounce.

Other research finds that children vary in how much they emphasize different language functions in their first utterances (Nelson, 1981). Some use their first

Choices of first words

Impact of phonemes

language to refer to objects and objective events — *car* and *book* and so on — whereas others use it more to express feelings and relationships — *hello,* for instance, and *goody!* Presumably these differences are encouraged partly by differing family environments. Some families, after all, may speak of objects more than of feelings, or vice versa. But to some extent word preferences may also represent a learning strategy adopted by the child; just as she may find a word easier if she already knows the phonemes in it, so she may also find an utterance easier if she has already used similar ones on previous occasions.

Parental Influences on Language Acquisition   Even though many of these comments may make language acquisition seem beyond human influence, parents do in fact affect this process. When infants are very young, parents will often talk with them as if they were full-fledged adult partners in a conversation. Consider this mother speaking to her three-month-old child:

A Talk with Melissa and Her Parents

Early Infant-Parent Communication

The interview and observations that follow are based on a visit with eight-month-old Melissa Diaz and her parents, Maria and Andrew, in their home.

INTERVIEWER: How does Melissa let you know what she wants?

MARIA: She makes little clicking sounds that are something like this. *(She demonstrates.)* And she also shakes her head. I think that she learned that from her older brother. He taught her that.

INTERVIEWER: What is she trying to communicate with her head shaking?

MARIA: I'm not sure. In the last couple of days she stopped doing that. A week ago she spent large portions of the day shaking her head "no."

INTERVIEWER: Was it at times that she didn't want to do something, or was she just practicing?

MARIA: No, no, I think that she just

wanted to do something. To show us something.

ANDREW: She's an understandable child.

INTERVIEWER: How else does she communicate?

MARIA: Of course, she cries when she is unhappy. And she is a very good smiler.

INTERVIEWER: She seems to have noticed me again. She stopped for a minute to look at me and give a big smile.

ANDREW: She is a wonderful smiler. She does use it to get attention. She also makes various baby-type sounds. She usually doesn't get upset, but when she does she has a good, loud cry.

MARIA: She was always an easy baby to read. She whimpered or cried when she was unhappy and cooed and smiled when she was content, which was most of the time. If she was gassy after a feed-

ing, she scrunched up her face in a funny way and you knew that you had to burp her.

INTERVIEWER: She's looking at us. What do you think she is thinking? When you have a young baby, do you make guesses about what is going on inside her head?

MARIA: We did that a lot with our first baby. We used to make up all this stuff about what he was doing. We were always trying to guess what he was thinking.

ANDREW: The reason we would try to figure out what he was thinking and doing is that there was no doubt that you were dealing with another human being who had thoughts and clear motives and stuff, even when he was very young.

INTERVIEWER: Even when he was two or three months old?

ANDREW: Even that early. Certainly by the time he was Melissa's age. I mean, he almost demanded

MOTHER: How is Kristi today? *(pause)* How are you? *(pause)* Good, you say? *(pause)* Are you feeling good? *(pause)* I'm glad for that. *(pause)* Yes, I am. *(pause)* What would you like now? *(pause)* Your soother? *(pause)* Um? *(pause)* Is that what you want? *(pause)* Okay, here it is.

By asking questions in this "conversation," the mother implies that Kristi is capable of responding, even though her infant is really much too young to do so. Furthermore, the mother leaves pauses for her baby's hypothetical responses. Observations of these kinds of pauses shows that they last just about as long as in conversations between adults (Stern, 1977); it is as if the mother is giving her baby a turn to speak before taking another turn herself. When her child remains silent, she even replies on her behalf. In all these behaviors, the mother teaches something of turn-taking in conversations, and she expresses her faith that the infant will eventually learn these conventions herself.

Turn-taking exchanges

---

that style and level of interaction. You know, he wouldn't be happy until he had that level. Which is still true now.

MARIA: Melissa is less outwardly directed. She will be happy by herself . . . finding things for herself to do for longer periods of time. As you can see, she's just going to play with her foot for awhile. Check out her fingers. Hold her hand up in the air, looking at it just to see it.

ANDREW: In a way, she is just as easy to communicate with, but just doesn't demand as much communication as her brother did when he was an infant.

INTERVIEWER: What changes have you observed in Melissa's way of thinking and solving the problems she encounters?

MARIA: Well, for the first month or so she probably didn't do too much thinking. She certainly was alert. She spent most of her time looking around at things and listening. She had a strong grip and would grab onto your finger so tightly that you could pick her up that way. And, of course, she was a good eater and spent a lot of time sucking.

INTERVIEWER: How about when she was two or three months old?

MARIA: Well, she was very quick to learn how to suck the nipple of a bottle and her pacifier, and by the time she was three months old she was able to grab her bottle and sort of hold it while she sucked, if you propped it up a little.

ANDREW: I also noticed that she learned to look for you when you came into the room and turn her head when you talked to her. She also became very interested in playing with her fingers and seemed to be much better coordinated in general.

INTERVIEWER: What about more recent developments, say, in the last two or three months?

MARIA: Well, she certainly has learned to make noise. When she was six months old her grandmother gave her one of those little rubber froggies that squeak when you squeeze it. At first she was only able to make a sound with it by accident, but soon she learned to squeeze it again and again. She also has learned to make sounds in response to your talking to her, almost like carrying on a conversation.

Follow-up Questions

1. How closely does Melissa's development follow the stages described by Piaget?

2. Which of Piaget's cognitive stages do you think Melissa is currently beginning? Why?

3. Do you think that Melissa will be an early, average, or late talker? Why?

You do not have to be a mother to speak "motherese," a simplified form of talking that helps infants and toddlers acquire language. (right, Elizabeth Crews/Stock, Boston; below, James Holland/Stock, Boston)

Parents' response to early language

When infants finally do begin speaking, parents continue these strategies. At the same time, however, they also simplify their language significantly. Sentences become shorter, though not as short as the child's, and vocabulary becomes simpler, though not as restricted as the child's (Garvey, 1984). These extra strategies help teach a new lesson, namely that words and sentences do in fact communicate, and that language is more than interesting noises and babbling. By keeping just ahead of the infant's own linguistic skills, parents can stimulate the further development of language.

This style is sometimes called **motherese,** meaning a dialect or version of language characteristic of mothers talking with young children (Gelman and Shatz, 1977). In addition to shorter sentences and simpler vocabulary, speech in motherese has several unique features. It tends to unfold more slowly than speech between adults, and to use a higher and more variable or singsong pitch; it generally contains unusually strong emphasis on key words ("Give me your *cup*"). Parents speaking motherese also tend to repeat or paraphrase themselves more than usual ("Give me the cup. The cup. Find the cup, and give it."). Presumably the

Perspectives on Research

The Effects of Hearing Loss on Language Development

The sense of hearing contributes a great deal to the normal development of language. Infants with significant hearing loss cannot distinguish the usual phonemes or sounds of their language, and words and phrases seem indistinct. As a result, cracking the code of language does not come as easily to such children as it does to most others. And they cannot be sure that their own speech reproduces their native language accurately.

Because of these difficulties, hearing-impaired children tend to lag behind most children in verbal skills. Children with hearing loss tend to test relatively poorly on standardized intelligence tests (Furth, 1973), which rely heavily on language in all of its forms. In taking such a test, children must listen to spoken instructions, read problems or statements, and state things clearly to an examiner. All of these activities pose more of a challenge to the hearing-impaired, especially if their hearing loss is very great.

Part of the problem lies with their lack of opportunity for verbal give-and-take. Infants (and children) profit from chances to engage in conversation actively: to respond to others' comments, using whatever language skills they command at the moment. This fact was illustrated dramatically by one hearing child whose parents were profoundly deaf (Bard and Sachs, 1977). The parents were anxious that their child's language should not be impaired by their own linguistic limitations, so they encouraged their child to watch as much television as possible, in order to give him lots of "good" language models to imitate.

Unfortunately, however, simply listening to others talk on television did not help the child's language at all. By the time he was three and a half, he still could not speak normally. He could lip-read somewhat, however, and communicate with his deaf parents by using standard sign language. He could also use a few words (like *Kool-Aid*) that he had picked up from watching television, but he could not combine them into strings that made meaningful phrases or sentences. Fortunately, speech therapy helped this boy to acquire oral skills relatively quickly. In his case, therapy consisted of lots of chances to converse.

As it happens, this case also shows the ease with which infants and children learn languagelike systems of communication, even if the system happens not to rely on the usual verbal skills. The lip-reading that this boy apparently learned naturally derived its structure and sense from the same grammar and semantics that hearing children learn, and so did the sign language that the boy learned. Making signs and lip-reading were just as complicated as oral speaking and listening, yet just as easy for him to learn. These facts give strong support to the idea that human infants are predisposed to learn language in one or another of its many forms, and to use it conversationally (Garvey, 1984; Geschwind, 1985).

repeated attempts are needed just for parents to make themselves understood, though they probably also give the infant practice in comprehending the relationships among sentences, and in responding appropriately.

Language exposure and competence

Research shows clearly that parents' conversations with infants are extremely important to the infants' development. The Harvard Preschool Project, a longitudinal study conducted at Harvard University, for example, observed the contacts (both social and nonsocial) between parents and their infants that occurred naturally in the families' own homes (White et al., 1979). At various intervals the infants were assessed both for their intelligence and for their social skills. When the assessments were correlated with the results of the home observations, one result stood out clearly: the most competent infants, intellectually and socially, had parents who directed large amounts of language at them. The most competent received about twice as much language, in fact, as the least competent infants in this study. But the most competent infants also stimulated interactions with their parents, primarily by procuring various simple kinds of help, for instance, in pouring a glass of juice or placing the final block on a tower. These "services" probably benefited the infants by offering many opportunities for parents to talk with them ("Shall I put the block on top?").

Checkpoint *From the age of three months onward, infants show considerable sensitivity to the phonemes of their native language. Around their first birthday, they start using their first words. To begin with they use single-word utterances, but by age two they are linking several words together into simple sentences. Infants' selection of words shows important individual differences, and parents have significant influence on their children's language development.*

The End of Infancy

The word *infant* comes from a Latin term meaning "not speaking." By this standard, a child approaching his second birthday is no longer an infant. He is talking now, and often using more than one word at a time.

Almost from birth he communicates nonverbally: he smiles and frowns, gestures and babbles. He uses these skills to both develop and demonstrate his cognitive abilities, but he also uses them to develop social relationships, as described in the next chapter. Both by thinking and by communicating, the two-year-old learns who he is, as well as who his parents and siblings are. At the same time, when all goes well, he becomes attached to these people as individuals, and his early, vague emotions turn into feelings with more focus. Pleasure becomes love, for example; rage becomes anger; and anxiety becomes fearfulness. As the next chapter shows, these are not mere changes in labels, but signify real emotional and social growth.

Summary of Major Ideas

1. Perception is the immediate organization and interpretation of sensation, whereas cognition refers to all the processes (including perception) by which humans acquire knowledge.

Ways of Studying Perception and Cognition in Infants

2. Infants' arousal is reflected by changes in their heart rates (HRs), as long as the stimuli that caused arousal are relatively gentle and persistent.

3. Infants' recognition of the familiar is reflected by their habituation to stimuli — the tendency to attend to novel stimuli and to ignore familiar ones.

Infant Perception

4. Studies of visual perception show that infants under six months of age perceive, or at least respond to, a variety of lines and patterns, such as those usually found on a human face.

5. Young infants, including newborns, show size and shape constancy in visual perception, which means that they respond to objects somewhat independently of their distance and orientation.

6. Infants also show sensitivity to depth, as in the visual cliff experiments, as well as to objects that loom at them.

7. Infants do not orient themselves in space reliably and accurately until they are nearly eighteen months old.

8. Newborns can already localize sounds to some extent, but babies do not do this accurately until about six months of age.

Infant Cognition

9. Piaget has proposed six stages of cognitive development during infancy, during which infants' schemes become less egocentric and increasingly symbolic and organized.

10. The most important achievement of these six stages is the use of symbolic representation, as shown by infants' increasingly firm belief in object permanence.

11. Research on Piaget's six stages generally confirms his original observations, but it also raises questions about the integration of early schemes and about the effects of motor skills, memory, and motivation on infants' cognitive performance.

Behavioral Learning in Infancy

12. Learning theory offers a framework for understanding immediate, specific changes in infant behavior.

13. Like children and adults, infants can experience at least two kinds of behavioral learning: operant conditioning and imitation.

14. Behavioral learning tends to be ambiguous among infants less than three months old.

Language Acquisition

15. Infants as young as three months show special sensitivity to human language.

16. Babbling begins around six months of age, and becomes increasingly complex until it disappears from use sometime before the infant's second birthday.

17. Around their first birthday, infants begin using single words or holophrases to serve a variety of language functions.

18. Infants show important individual differences in their selection of first words.

19. Parents probably influence language acquisition mainly through modeling simplified utterances, recasting their infant's own utterances, and directing considerable language at the infant as she grows.

Key Terms

perception *(208)*
cognition *(208)*
habituation *(210)*
object constancy *(213)*
shape constancy *(214)*
depth perception *(215)*
visual cliff *(215)*
sensorimotor
  intelligence *(220)*
egocentric *(220)*
schemes *(221)*
assimilation *(221)*
accommodation *(221)*
circular reaction *(222)*
primary circular
  reaction *(222)*
secondary circular
  reaction *(223)*
object permanence *(223)*
AnotB error *(224)*
tertiary circular
  reaction *(225)*

deferred imitation *(227)*
behaviorism *(235)*
learning theory *(235)*
classical
  conditioning *(235)*
operant
  conditioning *(236)*
developmental quotient
  (DQ) *(238)*
phonology *(240)*
semantics *(240)*
syntax *(240)*
language acquisition
  device (LAD) *(241)*
phoneme *(241)*
intonation *(243)*
expressive
  language *(244)*
receptive language *(244)*
holophrase *(244)*
motherese *(249)*

What Do You Think?

1. Given the research described at the beginning of this chapter, what would you tell an enthusiastic new mother who is convinced that her four-week-old infant recognizes and responds to her more than to any other person?

2. If infants perceive constancies of size and depth even during the first few months of life, does this fact imply that they really acquire object permanence well before Piaget's theory says that they do?

3. Between about eight and twelve months of age, some babies show distress at separations from their primary caregiver (usually the mother). How might Piaget's theory of infant cognition explain why this distress occurs?

4. Think about how you might get through a day using only one-word utterances, or at most two-word utterances. How would you keep from being misunderstood, and how would you satisfy your various needs?

For Further Reading

Bower, T. G. R. *Development in Infancy.* (2nd ed.). San Francisco: Freeman, 1982.

Lamb, M., and Campos, J. *Development in Infancy: An Introduction.* New York: Random House, 1982.

Many textbooks about infant development are available, but these two are especially good at conveying a feel for *how* research is done on infants: how one study evolves out of another, for example, and why certain controls or constraints are needed in order to get useful results. In addition, Bower describes many intriguing studies of infant perception, his specialty.

Carew, J., Chan, I., and Halfar, C. *Observing Intelligence in Young Children.* Englewood Cliffs, N.J.: Prentice-Hall, 1976.

This book describes observations of infants' and toddlers' competence, carried out in naturalistic settings (mostly their own homes). It identifies characteristics of the infants and their families that seemed to make the infants especially competent (for example, their parents were good observers and also good models of behavior).

DeVilliers, P., and DeVilliers, J. *Early Language.* Cambridge, Mass.: Harvard University Press, 1979.

Here is a very readable account of language acquisition, beginning at birth and extending through the preschool years. The book is intended to stimulate interest but not to be especially thorough. For a more complete discussion of language development, see another book by the same authors called *Language Acquisition* (Harvard University Press, 1978).

Dunn, J. *Distress and Comfort.* Cambridge, Mass.: Harvard University Press, 1977.

This book takes infants' distress as its starting point. Why do babies cry so much? It shows that this behavior has several causes — physical, cognitive, and social — and that parents learn to distinguish among these by their infants' behavior and the sounds they make. The book has practical value for anyone who is responsible for giving care to infants.

Greenfield, P., and Tronick, E. *Infant Curriculum.* Santa Monica, Calif.: Goodyear Publishers, 1983.

Dittman, L. (Ed.) *The Infants We Care For.* Washington: National Association for the Education of Young Children, 1985.

These books describe what a person needs to know in order to set up and run a child-care center for infants. They cover the same topics as curriculum guides for preschool programs: daily organization, parent relationships, selection of activities, and developmental sequences. But they focus on the unique challenges and satisfactions of infants rather than older children.

Lewis, D. *The Secret Language of Your Child: How Children Talk Before They Can Speak.* London: Pan Books, 1978.

This book offers interesting insights into nonverbal communication in infants, toddlers, and young children. It shows how facial expressions and gestures convey meaning — often more than parents or other adults realize. There are (nonverbal) illustrations to supplement the (verbal) descriptions.

White, B. *The First Three Years of Life* (rev. ed.). Englewood Cliffs, N.J.: Prentice-Hall, 1985.

This book discusses the cognitive development of infants and toddlers primarily from the point of view of parents. It offers suggestions for how to foster optimal cognitive development of children, based partly on the results of the Harvard Preschool Project, discussed at the end of this chapter.

Chapter
7

The First Two Years: Psychosocial Development

Focusing Questions

- What are the social capabilities of a newborn infant?
- What is parent-infant synchrony, and why is it so important to the social development of infants?
- How do an infant's interactions with fathers, siblings, and peers differ from those with her mother?
- What are an infant's emotional capabilities, and how do differences in infants' temperament affect social development?
- What major personality changes take place during infancy?
- What experiences enable an infant to develop secure attachments, and what are the consequences if such attachments fail to develop?
- What are the causes of child abuse and neglect?
- What are the sources of a toddler's increasing self-awareness?
- Why is autonomy so central to development during toddlerhood?

As we described in the preceding chapters, infancy is the time when children learn to walk and think and talk and, in a very broad sense, to become more fully "human." Although infants are highly dependent upon their care-givers for meeting their needs, they are anything but passive. Almost from the moment of birth, infants become increasingly active and sophisticated participants in their social worlds, observing and interacting with the people around them.

As an infant grows older, he comes to form close and enduring emotional attachments with the important people in his life, and sometimes shows his concerns about them very dramatically. He wails when a strange nurse approaches him in the doctor's office, and he greets his mother or father warmly when one of them "rescues" him from the nurse. At other times the baby may participate in relationships in more subtle ways, such as attending closely to older brothers and sisters while they play — more closely, in fact, than his siblings ever attend to him. At still other times he may express his needs or feelings in ways that are downright confusing to the people around him; for example, he may refuse particular foods when a parent offers them, but take them happily from a baby sitter.

These behaviors convey two of the major themes of psychosocial development in infancy: trust and autonomy. On the one hand, infants are learning who they can count on, and to what extent. If, thinks the baby, my mother and father leave me with a stranger, can I count on them to return? What if they leave me with a new baby sitter for the whole evening? Infants are also learning when and how to make choices for themselves. When, thinks the baby, can *I* decide what strangers to investigate? And when can *I* decide which foods I will eat? Infants' concerns for autonomy and for intimate trust intertwine closely during their first two years, although many observers of children consider trust to develop earlier than autonomy (Maccoby, 1984).

In this chapter we explore the essential role that early social interactions and attachments play in the development of trust and in the achievement of autonomy. We also briefly look at theories of personality development during infancy, the ways in which attachments are formed, and the problem of child abuse, before concluding with a discussion of the emergence of self-knowledge and self-awareness during later infancy.

Early Social Relationships

Infants seem to have a natural tendency to be social participants. Immediately after birth, they are capable of many social responses. For example, a newborn will turn her head toward the sound of a human voice and actively search for its source; attend to, and show preference for, a voice with a female pitch; pause regularly in her sucking pattern for human voices but not for similar nonhuman tones; and look at and visually follow a complete picture of a complete human face but not a picture of a scrambled one. She will even prefer the smell and taste of human milk over formula, water, or sugar water (Brazelton, 1976).

Parent-Infant Synchrony

Frequently the social interactions between parent and infant involve a pattern of close coordination and teamwork in which each waits for the other to finish before beginning to respond. This pattern of closely coordinated interaction is called **parent-infant synchrony.** For example, infants only a few weeks old are able to maintain and break eye contact with their mothers at regular intervals, and to take turns in making sounds and body movements (Stern, 1977). Studies using videotapes reveal that a mother and her baby actually have "conversations" that resemble adult dialogues in many ways, except for the child's lack of words.

Early "conversations"

How do such exchanges occur? A mother may gaze steadily at her baby, waiting patiently for him to vocalize, move, or at least look at her. When the action eventually happens, the mother may respond by imitating the infant's gesture or by smiling or saying something to him. She will time her responses to allow the baby a turn in this game, just as if the child were a fully competent person in a social exchange (Stern, 1977). As the interaction continues, the baby typically shows increasing tensions: his movements and sounds become not only more frequent but more sudden and jerky as well. At some point the infant releases or breaks the tension by looking away from his mother, and spends the next few moments looking at or touching objects, instead of people. This provides a break from sociability, although social exchanges may of course serve equally well as rest periods from nonsocial interactions. In any case, after a suitable interval the mother and infant catch each other's attention again, and the cycle of turn-taking begins all over.

Parents and their infants often show a striking synchrony in their movements and gestures. In these exchanges, it is often hard to tell who is leading whom. (Carol Palmer)

The infant's contribution

Until an infant is several months old, responsibility for coordinating this activity rests with the parent. But after a few months the baby becomes capable of initiating social interchanges and of influencing the content and style of his parent's behavior. Not surprisingly, babies who are especially sociable early in infancy are likely to have mothers who form especially strong emotional attachments or connectedness with them later in infancy (Clarke-Stewart, 1973). Some of this continuity is caused by the baby, not the mother. The smiles, gazes, and vocalizing of a friendly baby prove hard for his mother to resist, and after several months of experience with such a baby, the mother becomes especially responsive to his communications. Presumably the mother's increased responsiveness in turn reinforces her infant's social nature.

Of course babies who are older influence their mothers in other ways. For example, in a study of mothers' efforts to teach infants under a year old to reach for a hidden object, researchers found that a mother's teaching style depended a lot on how her baby acted during the orientation period that preceded the experiment. Mothers adjusted their teaching approach to the skill level of the child: if the baby already showed some skill at reaching for objects, the mother tended simply to demonstrate or model the task; if not, she was more likely to work up to the task through many steps, first placing the object visibly within easy reach, then hiding it partially, and then hiding it still more (Kaye, 1976).

Changes in mothers' responses

Although this was a cross-sectional study, investigating children of several different ages at a single point in time, similar results have been found in longitudinal studies. One such study followed a group of infants from eight months to twelve months of age (Hubley and Trevarthen, 1979). Mothers were asked to teach their infants to put three toy people into a toy truck. As the infants got older, the mothers increasingly relied on gestures and verbal comments, saying things like

"How about this one?" At the same time they used actual demonstrations less and less, suggesting that they no longer needed to show the task but could simply describe it to their babies. This shift toward verbal comments parallels infants' developing language and thinking abilities, and suggests that mothers make efforts to keep pace with or match the changing abilities of their children.

Social Interactions with Fathers, Siblings, and Peers

Even though infants may interact more with their mothers than with anyone else, they actually live in a network of social relationships, in which a number of other people make at least minor contributions to their social life — and sometimes major ones (Hodapp and Mueller, 1982). Fathers often belong to this network and so do siblings and peers. How do contacts with these people compare with a baby's contacts with her mother?

Father-Infant Interactions For a long time developmental psychologists largely ignored the fathers of infants, in part because of a belief that fathers had little direct contact with young babies. For example, one early study suggested that fathers talked with their three-month-old infants only about one minute per day (Rebelsky and Hanks, 1971). Later studies have reported much higher rates of involvement — in the neighborhood of two or three hours per day for fathers, as compared with nine hours for mothers (Pleck, 1983). Even with this much involvement fathers are not generally the primary care-givers, but they definitely play a significant role in their infants' experiences.

Infants' social episodes with fathers follow the same cycle of build-up and withdrawal that characterizes their interactions with their mothers (Yogman et al., 1977). Nevertheless, although mothers and fathers play many of the same games, their styles differ. Play episodes with fathers tend to have sharper peaks and valleys — higher states of excitement, and more sudden and complete withdrawals by the baby. Compared to mothers, fathers tend to jostle more and talk less, and they roughhouse more and play ritual games like peek-a-boo less. Fathers also devote a higher proportion of their time with the baby to play than mothers do (40 percent versus 25 percent) (Kotelchuck, 1976).

More active interchanges

How do we explain these differences? Past experience with infants, the amount of time routinely spent with them, and the usual ratio of care-giving to play that parents assume may influence parents' style regardless of their sex. For example, when fathers who served as primary, full-time caretakers were compared with fathers who took the more traditional secondary caretaker role, researchers found differences in how the two groups played with their infants. Primary-caretaker fathers acted very much like mothers, smiling more and imitating their babies' facial expressions and vocalizations more than secondary-caretaker fathers. However, primary-caretaker fathers were just as physical as secondary-caretaker fathers (Field, 1978).

Do stylistic differences mean that fathers are less competent than mothers with their infants? Most studies suggest not. In one, fathers played with their newborn

Paternal competence

infants in virtually the same ways that mothers did (Parke and O'Leary, 1976), cooing and smiling at them and talking to them. In another, fathers were found to feed their babies just as successfully as mothers; they intervened appropriately when the baby spit up, and fed comparable amounts of formula (Parke and Sawin, 1976).

In conclusion, it appears that although their styles may be somewhat different, both mothers and fathers are capable of interacting with their young infants in responsive and appropriate ways; this is particularly true of whichever one is the primary or full-time care-giver. However, whether or not a particular father or mother will be a responsive care-giver depends on his or her personal qualities, past experiences, and motivation, as well as on the care-giving situation and the particular infant.

A Talk with Benjamin and His Family

The Impact of a New Baby on His Family

Having a new baby generally means big changes for the whole family. In the following interview, George and Kathy Simon and their thirteen-year-old daughter, Lisa, discuss how four-month-old Benjamin has influenced their lives.

INTERVIEWER: How has having a new baby affected your family socially? *(Pause)* Lisa, you're raising your eyebrows. How does it affect an older sister?

LISA: Well, it's an extra responsibility because your parents are always asking you to do little things like, will you get the bottle, or can you watch him for five minutes while I go get dressed? You know, just little things. Can you pick him up, he's crying. But it adds up, I think.

INTERVIEWER: Do you keep track?

LISA: I do.

INTERVIEWER: How many hours do you spend doing these things? On second thought, don't answer that question. It's entrapment. *(They laugh.)* Do you make them pay?

LISA: No, of course not. Not with money. Well, if it's for more than an hour, that's different. But if it's just one little thing, I don't get paid. It's also like when I'm trying to watch TV and Mom will walk out of the room for a few minutes and then Ben will start crying. And I just have to pick him up and it kind of annoys me.

INTERVIEWER: So, for an older sister, having a new baby on the scene can be frustrating sometimes. How about for the two parents?

KATHY: Oh, I hardly notice the difference. Just kidding. *(She laughs.)*

INTERVIEWER: Both of you work and both of you are very much involved in parenting. As a dual-career family, how do you manage to balance those things?

KATHY: Poorly. I don't think we do manage to balance them. There's just not enough time to do things. Like we just finished doing our income tax for last year. Now we are going to do this year's. And

there are little things — like our mail gets stacked up for a week or more sometimes.

GEORGE: It's just that there are so many things that if everything ran perfectly, you could almost get through. But that never happens. So almost all the time you're like two things behind at home and you're caught up at work or two things behind at work and caught up at home. I still think that there's time to do both, but it's hard.

INTERVIEWER: How do you manage child care for a typical week? You mentioned that Lisa had been in day care when she was a baby.

KATHY: We have a woman take care of him whom we like very much. A problem we are having now is that the work I'm doing is writing, and it seems that before you can write you need to calm down and relax. You can't just switch over immediately, as soon as the baby walks out of the door. It's hard for me to switch over, so I don't get much work done.

Interactions with Siblings Approximately 80 percent of children in the United States and Europe grow up with siblings, and the time they spend together in their early years is frequently greater than the time they spend with their mothers or fathers. In many cultures children are cared for by siblings; from the age of one or two they are nursed, fed, disciplined, and played with by a sister or brother who may be only three or four years older (Dunn, 1985). First-born children are likely to monitor very closely the interactions of their mother with a new baby and try to become directly involved themselves. In one observational study, children as young as eighteen months old tried to join in bathing, feeding, and dressing their sibling; of course, they also tried to tip over the baby's bath, tune the television, spill things, and reorganize the kitchen when their mothers cuddled and cared for the new baby (Dunn, 1985).

INTERVIEWER: *(Turning to George)* Do you also find that switching between work and caring for Benjamin is hard?

GEORGE: Yes, but I think it's hardest to switch over if your work is at home. It's a little easier for me to concentrate when I am away at work. But if my work day has been tense, it's sometimes hard to relax when I am with the baby.

INTERVIEWER: In what other ways has the new baby affected your family?

KATHY: Before baby Benjamin was born, Lisa was furious that we were having a baby. We figured that she didn't want to have siblings. She made our life miserable all through the pregnancy. It got to the point where I told her to keep her feelings to herself, we didn't want to hear them any more.

INTERVIEWER: Lisa, if you want, when I get to the section on teenagers, I will interview you and give you equal time.

LISA: I'll prepare myself.

INTERVIEWER: How about sharing the baby? Is there sometimes a feeling of competition about who he likes best?

GEORGE: Conveniently, our babies have pretty regularly switched back and forth. Right now Benjamin has switched back to liking his Mommy better.

INTERVIEWER: Have you noticed that too, Kathy?

KATHY: Yes, he'll go through different stages. Up until this week, he'd be kind of dull around me but when he saw George, he would light up like a different baby.

INTERVIEWER: Do you sort of hold onto the fact that it's going to switch back?

KATHY: You sort of know it's going to switch back and forth. It doesn't bother us too much. The first time around it feels harder. But you realize that it's going to come back again. It's not a permanent state.

Lisa used to go back and forth every three or four months.

GEORGE: At least for now, his favorite parent is the one who is not about to put him to sleep or to say no to him.

Follow-up Questions

1. How typical are Lisa's responsibilities for the new baby? How typical are her reactions?

2. What special stresses and conflicts are the Simons experiencing as a dual-career family? Do you have any suggestions about how they might lessen them?

3. What are your feelings about the family rivalries that baby Benjamin has stimulated in his sister and parents? How well are they dealing with this issue?

Each member of a family has a unique style of interacting with a new infant. (Linda Benedict Jones/Lightwave)

In talking to their younger siblings, children make many of the same adjustments as their mothers do, using much shorter sentences, repeating comments, and using lots of action-getting features (baby talk, or motherese). In turn, infants tend to respond to their siblings in much the same way as they do to their parents. However, they also quickly learn the ways in which siblings are different from parents, particularly if the sibling is young. Because younger children lack their parents' maturity and experience, they are less able to focus consistently on meeting the baby's needs rather than their own. For example, a four-year-old who is enjoying playing with his eight-month-old sister may not notice that she is becoming overstimulated and tired and needs to stop; or on another occasion, he may become jealous of the attention that she is getting and "accidentally" fall on her while giving her a hug. If parents keep in mind the needs and capabilities of each of their children and provide appropriate supervision, interactions with siblings are likely to make an important positive contribution to an infant's development.

Interactions with Peers   Until very recently there were few studies of infant-infant interactions, perhaps because in most families, infants do not have regular, long-term relationships with peers (Mueller and Vandell, 1978). It was generally believed that interactions with peers do not develop as quickly as those with parents (Bridges, 1933). According to this view, infants do not get along very well:

In their first contacts with peers, infants often treat each other like interesting objects and show little awareness of each other's thoughts and feelings. (Carol Palmer)

they grab each other's toys and hair and treat each other as mere objects or toys, especially if no real toys are available. True cooperation, it was thought, does not emerge until well beyond age two, after such skills have been learned through earlier interactions with parents.

Recent observations of infants, however, have found that even young babies show considerable interest in other babies, and in much the same ways that they show interest in their parents — by gazing, smiling, and cooing. Sociability of this kind develops with peers at the same time and at the same rate as it does with parents (Field and Roopnarine, 1982; Vandell, 1980).

Interest in other infants

As might be expected, babies become more social with experience. In one study, for example, eleven infants and eleven toddlers were observed over time in a nursery-school class. All of the children became friendlier with each other over the four-month semester of the nursery, vocalizing, smiling, and exchanging toys more frequently. Interestingly, although the infants were fifteen months younger, they came close to equaling the toddlers in both types and amounts of social behavior (Roopnarine and Field, 1982).

When given the choice, infants often prefer playing with their peers to playing with their mothers. In one study, infants aged ten to twenty-four months were each placed in a room with both their mother and another infant. The ten-month-olds looked at and followed their peers more often than their mothers; toddlers (aged twelve to twenty-four months) talked with, imitated, and exchanged

Playmates of choice

toys with their peers more frequently than with their mothers (Rubenstein and Howes, 1976).

In conclusion, while an infant's social interactions with his mother and father are generally the most important of his early social experiences, interactions with siblings and peers also contribute to his social development. The quality and developmental impact of experiences with siblings and peers will reflect, to some extent, the degree to which parental supervision of such contacts is responsive to the needs of their baby and of the other children as well. Both under- and over-protectiveness may have negative consequences. For example, a parent who does not allow an older brother or sister to play with the baby is depriving both siblings of an important social experience. On the other hand, allowing siblings to play without adequate supervision or delegating too much child-care responsibility to an older brother or sister is likely to have negative effects.

Taken together, these early social interactions provide the basis for the emotional and personality development that follow.

Checkpoint   *Soon after birth, infants are able actively to initiate and respond to interactions with their care-givers. These interactions show a high degree of coordination, or synchrony. Although interactions with mothers, fathers, siblings, and peers do differ to some degree, they all contribute to the infant's rapidly developing emotional relationships, communication skills, and knowledge of the social world.*

Emotions, Temperament, and Personality Development in Infancy

As in adult relationships, emotions play an important role in the social relationships of infancy. In the following sections we discuss the role of emotions and **temperament** — the infant's typical or characteristic way of feeling and responding. Following that we discuss theories of personality development during the first two years.

Emotions in Infancy

Changes in infant crying, smiling, frustrations, and fear of strangers and of novel or unusual stimuli, have long been recognized, but only recently have researchers appreciated the range and complexity of infant emotion (Yarrow, 1979). One reason for the delay is the difficulty in studying the feelings of infants, who are not fully aware of or able to communicate the subtleties of what they are feeling. Take the case of an infant's fear responses: whereas earlier it was thought that an infant's fear could be fully explained in terms of fear-producing stimuli such as noise or loss of support, current research has taught us that the baby's expectations and understandings play an important role. Loud sounds or incongruous stimuli such as a mother's face covered with a mask will in some situations lead to fear responses but in other circumstances to smiling and laughter (Scarr and Salapatek, 1970; Sroufe and Wunsch, 1972).

Physiological correlates of emotion such as changes in heart rate can be reliably measured, but their relationship to specific emotional responses still remains unclear. Specific emotions such as happiness, sadness, fear, and anger can be reliably identified from facial expressions, but more subtle variations in emotion are more difficult to pinpoint (Yarrow, 1979). In the long run, reports and ratings of children's behavior by their parents and others who know them well probably hold the most potential for learning about what they are feeling; in fact, parents' reliable judgments about their infants' feelings play an essential role in parent-infant synchrony.

It is generally recognized that infants show joy and laughter by three to four months, fear by five to eight months, and other more complex emotions like shame sometime in the second year of life. Some researchers believe that even younger infants are sensitive to the positive and negative feelings of their caregivers, and are quite capable of responding to adult fears and anxieties. It is likely that they respond to cues similar to those used by adults, such as slight variations in voice quality, smell, and touch, as well as variations in facial expression and body language (Yarrow, 1979).

Infant sensitivity to parents' feelings

Despite the problems in studying infant emotions, it is clear that they play an important role in social development. One area where emotions are important is in an infant's temperament.

Temperament

Even at birth, infants differ in their patterns of physical and emotional activity and responsiveness. These characteristic patterns are called temperament. In the now classic New York Longitudinal Study, more than 130 infants were studied from birth through their elementary school years (Thomas and Chess, 1977) and rated on nine aspects of temperament. Three main combinations or patterns of these emerged, and each was found to have a different effect upon the individual child's social interactions.

The New York Longitudinal Study

- *Average or easy children* tended to be very regular and adaptable. They were happy babies who generally responded positively to new experiences, were easy to comfort, and developed secure relationships readily. They also were less likely to have behavioral problems.
- *Slow-to-warm-up children* were relatively inactive and slow to adapt to new experiences. They rarely showed strongly negative (or positive) moods, and reacted moderately to new situations. Somewhat shy and standoffish at first, these babies tended to do fine once they warmed up.
- *Difficult children* were irregular in their patterns of eating, sleeping, and general activity. They were moody, reacted intensely to new or stressful situations, and were more likely than other children to stimulate criticism and negative reac-

tions from their care-givers. As you may guess, formation of secure relationships was most difficult for these children and their parents.

This approach has been helpful in predicting problems for the minority of children who are difficult or slow to warm up. For example, newborn infants whose biological rhythms are irregular, who experience discomfort during feeding and elimination, and who do not communicate their needs very clearly are often difficult for their parents and are more likely to experience problems in developing good relationships with them. This is particularly true when mothers have little or no help and emotional support from relatives and friends in caring for their diffi-

---

Perspectives on Research

The Development of Smiles

Parents are not imagining things when they see their newborn infants smile from time to time. The first smiles happen mostly when infants are asleep, rather than awake. "She is dreaming," some parents might suggest; others might say, "She has tummy gas." Most likely, though, neither of these ideas is correct. Infant psychologists suspect that the first smiles show responses to moderate but sudden stimulation during sleep. Early smiles, they point out, only occur during REM sleep, when bursts of mental impulses often occur in young babies (Emde et al., 1976; Sroufe and Waters, 1976).

After a few weeks, external stimulation will also make an infant smile, but only if it is presented carefully. Rousing an infant gently from a deep sleep to a lighter, drowsy sleep often works; ringing a bell, for example, or making some other soft noise usually elicits a smile. Moderate jostling or jiggling can produce a smile even when the baby is awake and alert. Still later, around three months of age, the stimulation no longer has to involve her body at all. Now even an interesting picture will make an infant smile if it is presented repeatedly. So will a game of peek-a-boo, at least if someone familiar is playing it. These more mature pleasures apparently draw on infants' developing ability to remember or recognize earlier experiences; in peek-a-boo, for example, babies recognize earlier encounters with the familiar face (Emde et al., 1976; Sroufe and Waters, 1976).

At all of these stages, smiles actually *follow* the stimulation rather than accompany it. Even the sleep smiles of newborn babies happen only after bursts of nerve impulses, as electrodes attached to infants' skulls demonstrate (Sroufe, 1979). The consistent, notable delay suggests what adults often report about their own smiles of pleasure, namely that they signify relaxation from mild excitement and not the excitement itself. You smile *after* the punch line to a joke, not during it.

In both infants and adults, the key to pleasurable smiling consists of temporary tension or excitement. Other patterns of stimulation create other emotions. Too much excitement, for example, or sustained and unending excitement, creates distress and prolonged tension and prevents smiling; certain feature films may emphasize excitement so much that some adults feel upset rather than satisfied by them. Likewise, some infants may feel distressed by a peek-a-boo game that goes on too long or that is managed too aggressively. On the other hand, too little stimulation creates boredom. Then infants (and adults) tend to go looking for interesting sights and activities; perhaps this is one origin of mischief-making among babies (and some adults).

Infants vary in temperament, from easy-going to difficult; these variations may affect their long-run development significantly. (left, Jean Claude Lejeune/Stock, Boston; right, Andrew Brillant)

cult babies (Waters et al., 1980; Crockenberg, 1981). On the other hand, few predictions have been successfully made regarding the "easy" group, which includes most children. Finally, although predictions of infant emotions and personality based on temperament may be of limited use when globally applied, a more interactive approach which also considers the characteristics of their parents and their family situations can be useful.

Brazelton, for example, who has categorized babies as *quiet, average,* and *active,* has found that the developmental outcomes for each group depend largely on the expectations and temperaments of the particular care-givers involved (1983). Thus, an active baby may be a pleasure for one parent and a serious problem for another.

Because a newborn infant's temperament can strongly influence his parents' earliest feelings and responses to him, it can have a significant impact on the infant-child relationship. For example, babies who are described as "cuddlers" appear to receive more warmth and affection from their parents than "non-cuddlers" do (Schaffer and Emerson, 1964). Similarly, if parents early on find their baby difficult (or easy), they may then label and consistently treat him as such. Over the long run, this may influence the development of his **personality,** the unique pattern of physical, emotional, social, and intellectual characteristics that will distinguish him from all other individuals. Whereas babies are thought to be born with certain temperaments, differences in personality are largely determined by the child's experiences — and particularly by his interactions with others.

Influences of temperament

Personality Development During the First Two Years

Even in the first weeks and months of life, an infant's temperament and the reactions she elicits from her care-givers may provide the initial basis for her personality development. At the same time, changes because of physical and cognitive maturation and the increasingly complex social and emotional interactions that emerge between the infant and her care-givers come to play an increasingly important role.

In this section we briefly discuss three main views of personality development during infancy: Freud's oral and anal stages of psychosexual development, Erikson's psychosocial crises of basic trust versus mistrust and of autonomy versus shame and doubt, and Mahler's mother-child symbiosis and individuation.

The Freudian View   According to Freud's psychosexual theory, which is discussed in Chapter 2, the **oral stage** of development occurs during the first year of infancy. Feeding and other oral-incorporative activities provide the infant with his earliest

---

A Talk with Jennifer and Her Parents
Infant Temperament

The following is part of an interview that was conducted with the Granoff family in the living room of their apartment. Members of the family are Jennifer, age eight months; her brother, Thomas, age three; her sister, Loretta, age fifteen; and her parents, Joyce and Michael.

INTERVIEWER: You mentioned earlier that Jennifer has been an easy baby from the time she was born. Please tell me more about that.

MICHAEL: She has always had a very even disposition. The only time she is ever cranky is when she needs to sleep or when she's hungry, but we usually feed her often enough so that doesn't happen too much.

JOYCE: She is an extremely regular baby. She goes to bed every night at about the same time and sleeps all night long. When she wakes up she is cheerful and waits patiently in her crib until we get there. Sometimes we don't even know that she's awake. Some babies are grumpy. They wake up screaming and crying. Her brother is sometimes that way. People I used to work with have a little girl who's a little younger than Jennifer, and a completely different baby — wiry, squirmy, and difficult to hold and to comfort.

INTERVIEWER: Is it harder or easier to have that kind of baby?

JOYCE: I don't know. I think that her parents find her more difficult. She seems to need to interact with her parents all of the time and constantly demands attention. Jennifer is remarkably independent. And although she'll fuss a little if she realizes that you have left her by herself in her room for more than a couple of minutes, once you come back, then she'll be all right. Her brother, Thomas, was very different. It was always a struggle to put him to sleep and he was much more difficult to comfort.

INTERVIEWER: What calms Jennifer when she's unhappy?

MICHAEL: Singing, food, walking with her, rocking her, sitting with her on the couch.

INTERVIEWER: Is it different for different children?

MICHAEL: I think that many of the same things work, but there are also differences. One of the things that works for her brother is patting him on the back, which she doesn't like. It has never worked for her. She could care less. I keep trying to do it and it's never worked.

JOYCE: The astonishing thing about having more than one kid is how unique they are.

INTERVIEWER: How early can you tell that?

encounters with the outside world, and with his first basis for distinguishing between fantasy and reality. Conflicts between the infant's desire for immediate gratification and the care-giver's ability and willingness to be responsive contribute to the beginnings of a separate and differentiated sense of self (Freud, 1983).

An infant who fails to receive good enough care during this stage may become overly dependent as an adult, or unable to depend upon others at all. More serious disturbances in this early infant-caretaker relationship may lead to basic insecurity and serious disturbances in the individual's ability to form interpersonal relationships and a coherent and integrated sense of self.

At approximately age one, infants enter the **anal stage** of psychosexual development. The focus of personality development shifts to the pleasurable (and unpleasurable) experiences related to elimination and the control of the bodily functions. Again, the quality of parental responses to the child's successful and unsuccessful attempts at self-control will affect personality development. If parents are overly harsh and negative in their responses, or if they provide too little support and guidance, the child may later experience problems in controlling her

---

JOYCE: From the first day.

MICHAEL: I probably can't say the first day, though I'm sure that Joyce can. I would say I definitely noticed it in the first week, though.

INTERVIEWER: Your husband mentioned earlier that Thomas was much more active and communicative from the start.

JOYCE: Oh, he was. It was clear very early that he was tuned into exactly what we were doing. His doctor called him a very visual kid. He was always looking, looking, looking at everything. You could always see that he was intensely interested in things around him. Jennifer is also interested and curious. Her brother was more focused. She'll get interested and curious, but without that intensity. She'll get interested in things that come her way, or play by herself. He reaches out. He'll look out at

things, for example, when he is riding in a car.

INTERVIEWER: You seem to have a strong feeling that temperamental differences are important.

JOYCE: Yes, I do. Often I feel that kids turn out to be the way they are. You really can't do much about it. Their temperaments seem to come with them. You can mold and shape other things, but temperament seems to be pretty much set.

INTERVIEWER: Is that something that you discovered early on?

JOYCE: No. It took me fifteen years to learn. *(She laughs.)* I think I was surprised at the level at which this temperament is almost, if anything, innate. Their activity level, their cheerfulness, curiosity, and all that stuff. I think that in the first week you can tell what your baby's going to be like on those levels. It doesn't mean that you can tell how your

baby is going to turn out. Environment also plays an important part.

But the temperament sets them up for everything else. If you've got an easy-to-get-along-with baby, a baby that sleeps a lot, you don't get angry at the baby, you don't get frustrated, you're not uptight all the time, you're more relaxed. So you're easier on the baby.

Follow-up Questions

1. Can you explain Jennifer's qualities that her parents describe without referring to the concept of temperament?

2. How closely does Joyce and Michael's understanding of temperament fit with what is presented in this chapter? In what ways is it different?

3. If you could talk with them, what additional questions would you like to ask the Granoff family?

---

impulses. Anal-compulsive personality styles and obsessive-compulsive neuroses later in life are thought to be related to earlier disturbances during the anal stage (Freud, 1983). Although these predictions have not received much empirical support, Freud's theoretical views have helped focus the attention of researchers on the importance of early parent-child interactions.

Erikson's Crises   As you probably recall from Chapter 2, Erikson believed that infants explore and experience not only with their sense of taste but with their other senses as well. During an infant's first year, which Erikson (1963) called the oral-sensory period of development, she must successfully resolve the psychosocial **crisis of basic trust versus mistrust** that she will be adequately cared for by her parents. Care-giving that is consistently and sensitively responsive to the infant's needs forms the basis of trust and provides a foundation upon which she develops her social and emotional relationships with others and her personality. Inconsistent, inappropriate, or neglectful care-giving is likely to interfere with or undermine the development of such trust.

Between the ages of one and three, children encounter the muscular-anal period and must successfully resolve the psychosocial **crisis of autonomy versus shame and doubt** (Erikson, 1963). Much as in Freud's anal stage, the conflicts here involve the child's struggles to control his own thoughts, feelings, and actions. According to Erikson's theory, insensitive, unresponsive parenting which is overly controlling or which fails to provide the supervision and guidance that ensure the child's physical and emotional safety may contribute to a child having problems with autonomy in the future (Erikson, 1963).

Mahler's Theory of Symbiosis and Individuation   Margaret Mahler and her colleagues have proposed that following the first few weeks of infancy, during which an infant is autistic and largely unaware of the world around her, the first year of infancy is characterized by a **symbiotic mother-child relationship.** In this symbiosis, the mother psychologically experiences the child as an extension of herself rather than as an independent person, and the infant experiences herself as part of her mother (Mahler, 1974; Mahler et al., 1975). During this period the infant must develop a secure basis from which to explore the world later. Clinical observations of mothers and their infants indicate that there are differences in the degree to which such symbiosis occurs, depending in part on the extent to which a particular parent derives pleasure and enjoyment from such intense closeness and upon how receptive the infant is to her mother.

Beginning about halfway through the infant's first year and continuing through her second, the process of **separation-individuation** occurs. Separation means that the infant achieves increasingly greater autonomy and independence from the care-giver to whom she has been so closely connected. Individuation reflects the child's development of a unique and individual identity, distinct and separate from that of her parent.

Similarities in the three theories   These three theories of personality development during infancy are remarkably similar. To a large extent, this is due to their common roots in Freud's psychoanalytic theory. Each emphasizes the importance of an intense, responsive, and secure

---

relationship between infant and care-giver during the early months of infancy, and each suggests that the security of such a relationship naturally leads to the next development: the infant's individuation as a distinct and separate person through the assertion of autonomy, independence, and self-control. Finally, each theorist believed that a relatively successful resolution of the conflicts or crises involved in this process prepares the infant to take on the new challenges of childhood.

In the following section, we discuss more fully how a secure and responsive bond, or attachment, develops between an infant and his care-giver.

Checkpoint *Only recently have we become aware of the degree to which infants are able to express emotions and respond to the positive and negative feelings of their care-givers. The infant's temperament — the physical and emotional responsiveness that the infant shows from birth onward — appears to influence her interactions with her care-givers. Personality development during infancy is organized around several closely related tasks. By the end of the first year, an infant has generally achieved a basic sense of trust in his relationship with his care-givers. He has also begun the process of individuation from the earlier symbiosis with his mother. As a toddler, he must achieve greater autonomy, learning to regulate his own thoughts, feelings, and actions successfully without feeling undue shame and doubt or loss of self-esteem about his failures and limitations.*

Attachment Formation

Attachment refers to the intimate and enduring emotional relationship between infant and care-giver during the infant's first year of life — a relationship that is characterized by reciprocal affection and a shared desire to maintain physical closeness (Ainsworth, 1973). Because attachment cannot be observed directly, it must be inferred or deduced from a number of commonly observed infant behaviors that serve to establish and maintain physical closeness with care-givers (Bowlby, 1969, 1973, 1980). Three of these — crying, cooing, and babbling — are **signaling behaviors;** four others — smiling, clinging, non-nutritional sucking, and following — are **approach behaviors.** Although researchers do not agree as to whether these *specific* attachment behaviors are biologically inherited, the tendency to seek proximity is thought to be biologically determined and essential to infant survival, in much the same way that food is.

The concept of attachment

One important source of support for these ideas has come from a well-known series of studies of attachment in infant rhesus monkeys (Harlow 1959; Harlow and Harlow, 1962). Infant monkeys who were taken away from their mothers at birth and raised with artificial wire and terry-cloth substitute mothers displayed many of the attachment behaviors mentioned above.

Harlow's studies of monkeys

Of particular interest was the finding that if these infant monkeys were forced to

Attachment — the tendency of young infants and their care-givers to seek physical and emotional closeness — provides an important basis for achieving secure and trusting relationships during early childhood. (Hella Hammid/Photo Researchers)

make a choice, they preferred physical contact with a warm, soft, terry-cloth substitute mother that did not provide food to contact with a cold, hard, wire mother that provided milk from a bottle but that was not soft and huggable. Harlow also found that infant monkeys who were deprived of physical closeness but who were otherwise well cared for exhibited extreme fear and withdrawal, an inability to establish social and sexual relations with peers, and much higher rates of illness and death.

Although we must be cautious about drawing conclusions about human infants from studies of monkeys, these findings suggest that **contact comfort,** a key attachment behavior, may be a primary need during infancy, much like the need for food. They also suggest that severe deprivation of physical closeness with a caregiver may have major negative consequences for subsequent development.

Current views Currently, most developmental psychologists believe that attachment relationships develop over time. They also believe that attachment involves a highly mutual and interactive partnership between parent and child, who both have strong, though unequal, needs to achieve physical and emotional closeness with each other. This view is influenced by recent discoveries about the interactive nature of social relations between infants and their caretakers.

Phases of Attachment Formation

When baby Alberto was five weeks old his parents and older brother and sisters remember that he just loved attention. His smiles and excitement were irresistible, and he would respond to anyone who gave him attention — even Louisa, the family dog — and when he was hungry or unhappy, almost anyone could feed or comfort him. By the time Alberto was four months old, this began to change somewhat. While he still happily responded to his family and even friends, he began to show a distinct preference for his mother and his oldest sister, Lydia, who helped her care for him. When he saw or heard either of them, he became especially happy, active, and noisy. As you might expect, this caused some jealousy among the rest of the family.

Somewhere between the age of nine and eleven months, Alberto's preferences for specific people became much stronger and clearer. He clearly preferred his mother to any other adult and responded to his sister Lydia more than to any of the other children. Now able to crawl, he would try to follow his mother wherever she went and cry when she left the room. During this period he also began to do something he had never done before: he sometimes became upset when unfamiliar people visited, even if they were friendly.

By the time he was two, Alberto was walking and talking well. Although he still demanded a good deal of attention from his mother and still preferred to play with Lydia, he rarely got upset when other family members cared for him, and he seemed quite happy to socialize with almost all friendly visitors, even those he had never met before.

These changes in Alberto are typical of the changes in attachment during infancy. Attachments are thought to develop in a series of phases, which are partly determined by the cognitive changes described in the previous chapter and partly by the interactions that appear to develop quite naturally between infants and their caretakers (Bowlby, 1969).

Phase I: Indiscriminate Sociability (birth through two months)   As we mentioned earlier, infants just a few weeks old are able to respond actively to and promote contact and attraction with other people. Their cries, smiles, coos, and gazes are hard to resist or ignore — just try listening to the prolonged crying of a baby or looking into an infant's smiling face, and see if you can resist responding!

In this phase an infant uses her limited attachment behaviors less selectively than she will as she grows older. If she is crying, for example, a variety of people will probably be able to comfort her, and she will not be too particular about which faces she smiles at and who receives her coos and gazes. Not all adults will be equally effective at comforting an infant, but the point is that most very young babies are not highly choosy.

Phase II: Attachments in the Making (two through seven months)   Almost as soon as an infant begins smiling and socializing with everyone, he begins to show an increasing preference for the individuals with whom he is most familiar and who are most responsive to his needs. A baby's preferences in turn reinforce his parents' affection. During this phase, most babies still generally accept certain forms of attention and care from comparative strangers as well, and also tolerate temporary separations from their parents with little upset.

Phase III: Specific, Clear-cut Attachments (seven to twenty-four months)   In this phase the infant's preferences for specific people become much stronger. In part

Beginning around the third month of age, infants begin showing an increasing preference for the company of a familiar parent to that of other adults. (Julie O'Neil)

this is due to the ability to represent persons mentally, achieved in Piaget's fourth stage of sensorimotor development (see Chapter 6). In addition, the greater mobility that comes with crawling and walking contributes to the development of specific, clear-cut attachments, enabling toddlers to seek proximity to their caregivers and to use their mother or father as a safe base from which to explore the world. Toward the end of the second year, most toddlers are developing significant verbal skills, which allow them to increase their involvement with their parents and others.

Both **separation anxiety** — an infant's upset at being separated from his caregiver — and **stranger anxiety** — a wariness and avoidance of strangers — appear near the beginning of this phase. The achievement of object permanence — the understanding that objects, including people, continue to exist even when they cannot be directly seen, heard, touched, tasted, or smelled — is thought to be an important basis for separation anxiety and attachment development. The source of stranger anxiety is still unclear, since it sometimes occurs even when the caretaker is present.

Phase IV: Goal-Coordinated Partnerships (twenty-four months onward) By the age of two the infant is becoming skilled at mentally representing and remembering both objects and events; she is moving beyond the sensorimotor thinking described by Piaget. She also is better able to understand the feelings and points of view of her parents and to adjust her own accordingly. For example, she is now better able to tolerate delays and interruptions in her desire for her parents' undivided attention, whether it is the competing need for attention of an older brother or sister, a telephone call, or a household chore that intervenes. The baby can also increasingly tolerate short parental absences, safe in the belief that her parents will

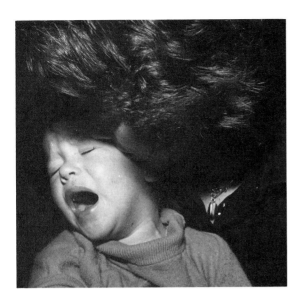

By sometime after their first birthday, many infants have formed clear-cut attachments to particular adults; this positive development is sometimes shown by the difficulties many infants have separating from their parents, however briefly. (Tony Mendoza/ The Picture Cube)

in fact return. This ability is related not only to past experience but, more important, to attachment relationships grounded in a sense of basic trust.

Assessing Attachment: The "Strange Situation"

The most widely used method for evaluating attachment is called the **"strange situation."** Originally developed by Mary Ainsworth for infants who are old enough to crawl or walk, the procedure consists of eight brief social episodes with different combinations of the infant, his mother, and a strange adult (Ainsworth et al., 1978). It confronts the infant with a cumulative series of stressful experiences: being in an unfamiliar place, meeting a stranger, and being separated from his parent.

The first episode lasts for half a minute and the remaining seven for three minutes each. First the parent and infant enter the room; then the baby is allowed to explore the room while his mother is present. Then a stranger enters the room, talks to the mother, and moves toward the baby; the parent leaves the infant alone with the stranger. After a while the mother returns to her baby and the stranger leaves; then the baby is left alone in the room. The stranger again enters the room and is alone with the infant, and at last the mother again returns to the room and the stranger leaves.

Episodes in the situation

Based upon the infants' patterns of behavior in the strange situation, three main groups were identified: Types A, B, and C. Type B infants, consisting of about 70 percent of all infants studied, show the following **secure attachment** pattern of responses to the "strange situation." When first alone with their mother, they typically play happily. When the stranger enters, they are somewhat wary, but continue to play without becoming upset. However, when they are left alone with the stranger, they typically stop playing and search for or crawl after their mother; in some cases they cry. When the mother returns, they are clearly pleased to see her

Characteristic response patterns

and are likely to stay closer to her and to cuddle more than before. When left alone with the stranger again, the infants are easily comforted, although signs of distress may be stronger, and they quickly recover from the upset by actively seeking contact comfort with the mother on her return. Type A infants (20 percent) display an **anxious-avoidant attachment** pattern. They rarely cry when separated from their mother and when reunited, show a pattern of mixing proximity-seeking and avoidant behaviors or a pattern of ignoring their mother altogether. Finally, Type C infants (10 percent) display an **anxious-resistant attachment** pattern. They show some signs of anxiety even in the periods preceding separation. They are intensely upset by separation, and when reunited with their mother actively seek close contact with her while resisting her efforts to comfort them (Ainsworth, 1979).

As we shall see, these three patterns appear to be related to parental child-rearing styles as well as to children's future personalities.

Consequences of Different Attachment Patterns

Benefits of secure attachment

Secure attachment early in infancy benefits babies in several ways during their second year of life. For one thing, Type B toddlers tend to cooperate better with their parents at twenty-two months than other babies do (Londerville and Main, 1981). They comply better with rules like "Don't run in the living room!" and they are also more willing to learn new skills and try new activities that their parents show them (as when a parent says, "Sit with me for a minute and see how I do this"). In the face of problems that are too difficult for them to solve, toddlers who are securely attached are more likely than others to seek and accept help from their parents. At age five, these children are found to be better able than other children to adapt to changes in preschool situations (Matas et al., 1978; Arend et al., 1979).

Learning problems of Types A and C

Less securely attached infants may not learn as well from their parents. Anxious-resistant (Type C) infants often respond with anger and resistance to their parents' attempts to help or teach them. Such babies may at times invest so much time and energy in conflicts that they are unable to benefit from their parents' experience and to explore their environment. Given a roomful of toys and a mother who has recently returned from an absence, for example, a Type C child may use up a lot of time alternating between being angry at and snuggling with her mother, instead of getting on with her play. Anxious-avoidant (Type A) infants do not have this particular problem, but because of their passivity, they also miss out on parental efforts to teach or help them and ultimately may discourage parents from even trying to be helpful.

Such differences persist even into the preschool years. One study found that children rated as securely attached at age one seemed more likely to seek attention in positive ways in nursery school at age four (Sroufe et al., 1983). When they needed help because of sickness or a hurt, or just wanted to be friendly, they found it easy to secure attention by approaching their teachers fairly directly, and they

Cross-Cultural Variations in Attachment

Even though almost all infants become attached to their parents somehow, the patterns by which they do so vary around the world. Results from the "strange situation" suggest this clearly. Among infants from northern Germany, for example, Type A responses occur nearly twice as frequently as among infants from North America (Bretherton and Waters, 1985). Among infants from Japan, on the other hand, Type C responses occur much more frequently than among infants from North America.

These differences result partly from differences in cultural values around the world, and from the child-rearing practices that these values foster. In northern Germany, for example, people value personal independence especially strongly (Grossman et al., 1985), and children ideally should obey parents more consistently than is usually expected in North America. As a result, infants need to learn not to make excessive demands on parents; they must minimize crying and fussing, for example, and do without extra bodily contact. During early infancy, mothers encourage these qualities by remaining relatively unresponsive to their infants' moment-by-moment behavior, so in northern Germany, unresponsiveness may signify not personal rejection of the child so much as an ordinary desire to raise a good citizen. The results show up in the "strange situation" as Type A attachment: a larger than usual number of young children seem not to care when reunited with their mothers.

Child-rearing practices probably also influence the responses of Japanese children to the "strange situation." Separations between Japanese infants and their mothers are quite rare by North American standards. One study of attachment patterns reported that one-year-old Japanese infants were left alone or with another adult only two or three times per month, on the average (Mikaye et al., 1985), and when they were left with another adult, that adult was usually someone already intimate with the child, such as the father or a grandparent. In Japan, therefore, babies frequently develop almost no experience with strangers. Probably as a result, the "strange situation" proves especially traumatic for them. Their extreme protests resemble Type C resistance: crying, anger, fear, and clinging when the mother returns. As with the German infants, these behaviors do not necessarily represent failures in child-rearing; they more likely represent the fulfillment of typical cultural practices.

But cultural values and practices cannot explain all the differences. Even in northern Germany, many babies become securely attached, Type B individuals. In fact, many do so, even though observations show that their mothers follow culturally approved practices of aloofness. In Japan, on the other hand, some infants become Type C infants even though they have had considerable experience with strangers as baby sitters and even though their mothers follow essentially Western child-rearing styles. Observations of these babies in their homes suggest that they were born with somewhat irritable or fussy temperaments, which may predispose them to becoming Type C in spite of their mothers' practices.

On balance, then, attachment seems to result from the combination of several influences: cultural values, inborn temperament, and the child-rearing practices of a particular family. The meaning of these attachment relationships, however, may not always be revealed by the "strange situation"; what looks like an attachment failure for one child may in fact be a success, given that child's circumstances.

Greater dependency of Types A and C

seemed to enjoy the attention when they received it. Less securely attached infants, whether Type A or Type C, tended to grow into relatively dependent preschool children. They sought more help more frequently, but seemed less satisfied with what they got. Their methods of seeking attention differed too: anxious-resistant children showed signs of chronic complaining or whining, while anxious-avoidant children tended to approach the teacher very indirectly, literally taking a zigzagging path to reach her. Having done so, they then tended to wait passively for the teacher to notice them.

Note, however, that these findings do not necessarily imply that secure attachments are set early in infancy once and for all. Instead, attachment is likely to be an extended process, one that in fact takes years to unfold fully (Main et al., 1985). The parental factors that contribute to a baby's insecure relationships at age one are still likely to be operating at age four, and the child's attachment style will continue to reflect the quality of his experiences with his parents. On the other hand, changes in family circumstances and in parent-child relationships can to some degree alter the quality of earlier attachments, for better or worse.

Before concluding this section, one additional point should be noted. Although we have emphasized the major role of the parents in parent-child interactions and in the development of the attachment relationship, it is by no means a one-sided process. From birth onward, the infant plays an active role in initiating and responding to interactions with her care-givers. How strongly her temperamental predispositions influence this process depends to a large degree upon how well they fit and interact with the temperaments, expectations, and capabilities of her parents. Therefore, it would be incorrect to give parents too much credit for raising a happy and well-adjusted child and unfair to place too much blame on parents whose child has encountered developmental problems.

Influences on Attachment Formation

Although children are most likely to form strong attachment relationships with their mothers — who most often are their primary care-givers — they may form equally strong attachments with their fathers as well. And because a growing proportion of families with young children have two working parents or are headed by a single mother who works, maternal employment and day care have come to play an increasing role in the development of attachment. The following section explores the roles of mothers and fathers as well as the contribution of maternal employment and nonmaternal child care to the development of attachments in infancy.

The Role of the Mother A major determinant of individual differences in attachment is the quality of the infant-mother relationship during the first year of life. A mother's capacity to respond sensitively and appropriately to her infant and to feel positively about her baby and the baby's strengths and limitations appears to be more important than the sheer amount of contact or care-giving. Mothers of securely attached infants are more responsive to crying, more careful and tender in holding their baby, and more responsive to their infant's particular needs and feel-

Quality vs. quantity of care

ings during both feeding and nonfeeding interactions than are mothers of less securely attached infants (Crockenberg, 1981; Ainsworth et al., 1978).

How much maternal stimulation an infant receives also makes a difference. In a study of mother-infant interactions at home when the babies were one, three, and nine months old, babies who were judged to be securely attached at one year received a moderate degree of maternal stimulation at each of the three ages. Anxious-avoidant children received overly high levels of stimulation, and anxious-resistant children received the lowest level of reciprocal interaction (Belsky et al., 1984).

Appropriate stimulation

The Role of the Father   Most studies have found no differences in most babies' preferred attachment figure during their first two years. Infants appear to be equally attached to both mother and father, even though the mother is typically the primary care-giver (Lamb, 1977a,c). As we pointed out earlier in the chapter, however, there are differences in how fathers and mothers interact with their infants; fathers are generally more vigorous and physical, and mothers are quieter and more verbal in their interactions.

The Effects of Maternal Employment   As with other important aspects of a caretaker's life, a mother's work activities may affect her infant's development. Women who have positive and relatively unconflicting feelings about both child-rearing and work, and who are satisfied with themselves and their lives, are likely to be most successful with their children (Etaugh, 1974; Hoffman, 1974; Lamb, 1982). The availability of sufficient time, money, and social and emotional support are important as well. Not surprisingly, positive feelings about parenting and the presence of adequate support are also associated with secure attachment for infants whose mothers are not employed.

Importance of parents' feelings

On the other hand, feelings of unhappiness and conflict between work and family roles are likely to influence the quality of parent-child relationships adversely. One study found that in families where mothers worked but wished they didn't or where mothers did not work but wished they did, both mother-child and father-child relationships were more likely to be disrupted; parents were also more likely to express negative feelings toward their children (Stuckey et al., 1982).

For many families, including those headed by a single parent, maternal employment is an economic necessity; for others it is more of a personal choice. In either case, a woman's feelings about being both a mother and a worker or a mother and a full-time homemaker are likely to affect the quality of the parents' relationships with their child.

The Effects of Day Care   The growing number of dual-career and single-parent families and changing views about child-rearing and family life have led to increased interest in nonmaternal child care to supplement the care given within families. It is estimated that as of 1978, 11 million children under age fourteen, including 2.5 million infants and toddlers, spent a considerable portion of their waking day being cared for by someone other than their parents (Belsky et al., 1984). Approximately 2.6 million families used in-home care (relatives, baby sitters) for more than ten hours per week; 3.4 million used family day care, in which groups of more than six children are cared for in a private home. In addition, approximately 1.3 million families used professionally staffed day care centers, each typically serving twelve or more children, although only a very small number of these involved children under two.

In general, participation in out-of-home care that is stable, well staffed, and responsive to each child's needs does not appear to interfere with the emotional

---

Perspectives on Research

The Family and Work

Conventional gender role expectations often stimulate concern that two kinds of employment situations will create stress for families: mothers who work, and fathers who do not. From the perspective of traditional stereotypical roles, each situation is a problem; theoretically, working mothers may be neglecting their child-rearing duties and nonworking fathers may be failing to support the mothers' child-rearing duties adequately. Both situations should therefore create stress for families that encounter them.

Studies of work patterns, however, support only half of this conclusion — the male half. Unemployed fathers, that is, do indeed put strains on their entire families (Cobb and Kasl, 1977), primarily because of their own feelings of depression and anxiety, and because of their resulting tendency to isolate themselves from others. These strains are stronger among families whose fathers lose a job than among those living at a consistently low economic level or those who experience chronic unemployment (Hoffman, 1983). A father laid off from a factory job after years of continuous service, for example, suffers more than a father who has experienced only partial or sporadic employment.

On the other hand, mothers who work create relatively little stress among intact two-parent families. On the contrary, their jobs have three beneficial effects in addition to the income that they bring. First, families with working mothers have less traditional divisions of household work; husbands do a larger portion of chores such as cooking, that society conventionally regards as female jobs

(Hoffman, 1983). Second, working mothers provide a model of independence for their daughters, who can more easily contemplate nontraditional careers for themselves as a result (Gold and Andres, 1979). And third, children in families with working mothers tend to take more responsibility for household work; they do more simple cleaning chores and minor preparation of meals, even at relatively young ages. These responsibilities seem to build the children's self-confidence (Medrich, 1981).

These descriptions oversimplify the effects of parental unemployment and maternal employment, of course. Fathers do not all react severely to losing their jobs; during an economic recession, for example, men are especially likely not to blame themselves for such a loss, and to draw emotional support from their families and relatives. Family relationships often benefit as a result, and children often grow up with more rather than less respect for themselves and for their parents (Elder, 1978). And mothers who do work outside the home can sometimes put serious strains on their families. Fathers may resent the extra child-rearing duties that mothers' employment causes for them, particularly when the children are very young (Zaslow et al., 1985). And the sons of working mothers do not necessarily benefit by seeing a model of female independence; sometimes, in fact, their relationship with their mother deteriorates (Cowan and Cowan, 1985). This drawback does not mean that mothers should not work, but it does mean that employment may have a psychological price, even in the best of circumstances.

Day care, even for infants and toddlers, has few negative effects on children, as long as the care is of high quality and parents feel satisfied with it. (Martha Stewart/The Picture Cube)

attachments between an infant and her parents. Day-care experiences during infancy appear to promote greater peer orientation and peer-related social skills, but they also appear to promote lower levels of cooperation with adults and conformity to adult expectations, although these findings may be more a function of the particular educational and child-rearing philosophies of the adults rather than of day care in general (Schwartz et al., 1974).

Effects on social skills

However, infants who are disadvantaged or otherwise at risk are more likely to develop anxious-avoidant infant-mother attachments in day-care situations that lack stability and are inadequately responsive to children's needs (Belsky and Steinberg, 1978; Vaughn et al., 1980).

In concluding our discussion of attachment, several points should be noted. First, the great majority of infants exhibit a strong and persistent tendency to form intense attachment relationships with their important care-givers, who are usually (but not necessarily) their mother and father. Second, the secureness of an infant's attachments are closely related to the overall responsiveness and consistency of the relationship between infant and care-giver. Third, the development of secure attachments is closely tied to successful resolutions of the crisis of trust versus mistrust in early infancy and the crisis of autonomy versus shame and doubt during toddlerhood (Erikson, 1963).

Checkpoint Attachment *refers to the pattern of behaviors that are associated with the infant's needs and efforts to establish and maintain close physical and emotional contact with her care-givers. Over the course of infancy, attachments become increasingly selective and coordinated. The quality of the infant's interactions with her care-givers as well as the emotional climate of the family influence the degree to which a secure pattern of attachment is established. Research using the "strange situation" indicates that early difficulties in attachment may adversely influence later development.*

The Emergence of Autonomy

By the second year of life, the relatively secure base of attachment that most infants have achieved with their parents and other family members allows them to begin to shift their attention outward to exploring the physical and social world. In spite of remaining anxieties about separations, the achievement of a sense of basic trust in their relationships with their care-givers enables toddlers to show increasing interest in new people, places, and experiences. For example, an eighteen-month-old may no longer bother to smile at his mother while he plays near her, and he does not need to return to her for reassurance as often as he used to.

Parents may welcome this behavior as a move toward greater independence and at the same time experience a loss of intimacy for which they may not be quite ready. But for various reasons this shift is both inevitable and developmentally important. For one thing, an older infant can move about rather easily and therefore find much to explore without help from others, and these newfound abilities to crawl, climb, and walk make her more interesting as a playmate for other children and thus less dependent upon her parents for her social life. For another, her rapidly developing thinking and communication skills contribute to her increasing autonomy.

Effects of mobility and communication

These competencies create new challenges for both the toddler and her family as they reach a new developmental crisis: autonomy versus shame and doubt. **Autonomy** is the ability to govern and regulate one's own thoughts, feelings, and actions freely and responsibly, while at the same time overcoming feelings of shame and doubt. Toddlers must somehow practice making choices — an essential feature of autonomy — in ways that cause no serious harm to themselves or others.

Parents must learn to support their child's efforts to be autonomous but must do so without overestimating or underestimating her capabilities or the external dangers and internal fears that she faces. If they are unable to provide such support, and show their disapproval of failures by shaming their child, a pattern of self-blame and self-doubt may develop. In such cases a child is more likely to be painfully shy and unsure of herself, or overly demanding and self-critical, and relatively unable to undertake new activities and experiences freely.

Effects of parental support

No matter with whom they are formed, secure attachments give infants a safe base from which to explore the world as they grow and develop. (Susan Woog Wagner/ Photo Researchers)

Parents must help their infants to master this crisis by continually devising situations in which their relatively mature baby can play independently and without undue fear of interference — by putting the pots and pans where they can be reached, for instance, but hiding the knives. And children need social as well as physical safety. Chewing on a sister's drawing, say, or dumping the dirt out of the flowerpots can have negative social consequences even when it does not have dangerous physical ones, so parents must help their infants learn how to avoid social perils by being selective about their activities.

Sources of Autonomy

Why should infants and toddlers voluntarily begin to exert self-control over their own behavior? Developmental psychologists have suggested several possible answers to this question, based on the various theories outlined in Chapter 2. Each has some plausibility, although none may be complete in itself.

Identification According to psychoanalytic theory, **identification** is the process by which children wish to become like their parents and other important attachment figures in their lives. The intensity of a young child's emotional dependence upon his parents creates an intense desire to be like them, so as to please them and guarantee their love; it also creates anger, because of the helplessness and fear of abandonment that the infant inevitably experiences during even brief periods of separation. Because it is so upsetting to be angry at the very person upon whom one is so dependent for love and care, identification can also be motivated, as is the later oedipal situation, by the unconscious desire to protect oneself from the upset

After their first birthday, infants begin to show increasing autonomy in their play and other activities. This autonomy is fostered by their improving motor skills and cognitive development. (Carol Palmer)

by being like the person who is the object of that anger. Both mechanisms, of course, may operate at once; and either may occur without the child's knowledge.

Operant Conditioning **Operant conditioning** stresses the importance of reinforcement for desirable behaviors, including behaviors that reflect self-control. If a two-year-old gives her infant brother a gentle hug, for example, her parents are more likely to praise her than if she squeezes him so hard that he cries. According to the principles of operant conditioning, the reinforced behavior should eventually occur more frequently and the unreinforced ones should happen less often. Over time, reinforcement should therefore lead to an increasingly responsible child — or, more accurately, to a child who behaves in increasingly responsible ways.

According to this view, adults will tend to reinforce a child for more grown-up behaviors — sometimes for independent exploration ("What did you find?"), for instance, and at other times for self-restraint ("I'm glad you didn't wet your pants"). Operant conditioning resembles identification in assuming that parents can motivate children, but it also assumes their influence occurs in piecemeal ways; that is, the child acquires specific behaviors rather than whole personality patterns, and the behaviors eventually add up to autonomy and self-restraint.

Observational Learning According to the theory of **observational learning,** the key to acquiring autonomy and self-control lies in the child's inherent tendency to observe and imitate parents and other nurturant individuals. If parents act gently with the child's sister, for example, then the child will too. For that matter, if the parents use the toilet regularly, so will the child (in theory, at least!). The process of observational learning implies that autonomy and self-control are acquired in units or behavioral chunks that are bigger than those described by operant conditioning but smaller than those of psychoanalytic identification.

Social-referencing: A Common Denominator　All three explanations of developing autonomy have something in common: they involve **social-referencing,** the child's sensitive awareness of how his parents and other adults are feeling and his ability to use these emotional cues as a basis for guiding his own emotional responses and actions (Campos and Stenberg, 1981). For example, infants and toddlers reveal social-referencing when they visit a strange place. Should they be afraid of the new objects and people or not? How safe is it to be friendly and to explore? In the absence of past experiences of their own, they evaluate such situations on the basis of their parents' responses: if their parents are relaxed and happy, they are likely to feel that way too; if their parents are made tense or anxious by the situation, the children will be more likely to feel that way also.

Referring his feelings to important adults requires skills that only an older infant possesses. He must know, for example, how to interpret his parents' bodily gestures and facial expressions, as well as understand their verbal comments. And he must do so while at the same time monitoring or paying attention to the people and events around him. Because younger infants cannot divide their attention in these ways, their reactions tend to be less sensitive to subtle changes in parents' moods.

Development of Self-knowledge and Self-awareness

The sense of self that develops late in infancy shows up in everyday situations as well as in situations involving self-restraint. One very interesting series of studies explored the development of self-knowledge in infants who were nine to twenty-four months old by testing their ability to recognize images of themselves in mirrors and on television (Lewis and Brooks-Gunn, 1979a).

Since most of the infants could not verbally indicate whether or not they recognized themselves, the researchers devised an ingenious method for assessing self-recognition: they secretly marked each infant's nose with red rouge while pretending to wipe it. Then they observed the infants as they examined the mirrors. Infant responses included smiling at the mirror, touching the mirror, touching their bodies, pointing at the mirror, acting silly, and touching the red mark on their noses.

Mirror recognition

Nose touching was interpreted as a clear-cut sign of self-recognition. Infants of all the ages studied directed more behavior toward themselves when their noses were marked than when they were not. However, only infants fifteen months old and older were able to focus specifically on what was different — their red noses — an ability that increased with age.

In the TV experiments, infants were tested under three conditions: in the live condition, they watched images of themselves live on TV; in the prerecorded condition, they watched videos of themselves that had been recorded a week earlier; and in the other-baby condition, they watched TV recordings of another baby. In each of the three conditions a stranger was shown sneaking up on the infant at the

TV recognition

As infants approach their second birthday, they begin showing signs of awareness of themselves as individuals. (Erika Stone)

end of the experiment. The researchers recorded the infants' attempts to imitate and to play with the TV images, their facial and vocal expressions, their movements toward and away from the screen, and their reactions to the stranger. A key question was whether the infants would turn toward the stranger they had seen in the live condition, and whether they would do so in the prerecorded and other-baby conditions as well.

The researchers found that infants as young as nine months old responded to the live images of themselves by playing more, by acting more positively, and by turning more often to the approaching stranger than in the other two conditions. This early self-recognition appeared to be based on **contingency** — that is, on the connection between their own movements and the movements of the image they were viewing. By the time infants had moved into their second year of life (approximately fifteen months), they had become increasingly able to distinguish themselves from other infants by using noncontingent cues such as facial and other physical features.

Aspects of Self-awareness   Recent studies have outlined several dimensions or themes in the development of self-awareness late in infancy (Kagan, 1981). As shown below, often a child expresses self-awareness in very ordinary situations, but this fact does not diminish the importance of the expression to the child. In fact, the very commonness of such situations means that they are influential in the lives of infants and toddlers.

Knowledge of standards   By the end of their second year, most children show an increasing appreciation of the standards and expectations of others regarding how they should behave toward both people and things. For example, a broken toy can be troubling, even if the child did not break it; she may show it to an adult and verbally express concern and a need for help (like "Broken!" or "Daddy fix?"). A crack in the kitchen linoleum may now receive close scrutiny, even though several months earlier it went unnoticed and several months later it may go unnoticed again. Language that implies knowledge of standards — evaluative vocabulary like *bad, good, dirty, nice,* and the like — appears as well (Bretherton et al., 1981). Such knowledge combines with other behaviors to suggest that the child is beginning to sense an identity for herself.

The modeling or performance of simple behaviors by an unfamiliar adult can prove distressing for older infants and toddlers. One study showed this by having an adult perform some simple act, like making a doll talk on the telephone, which was well within the children's current abilities. Even though each child's mother was present, and even though the children had previously seemed happy and content, seeing the action carried out by a strange adult made many two-year-olds fret, cry, or cling tightly to their mothers (Kagan, 1981). Most children at least looked worried, and most interrupted their play for significant periods of time to watch — reactions that went beyond ordinary "stranger reactions" to the adult.

Distress at modeled behaviors

Why should such overtly modeled behavior upset a child? For one thing, seeing a stranger perform an activity usually reserved for family members may be disturbing. But more important, the child probably senses that his own performance may differ from the adult's, and in particular may fall short of it. The child's reactions imply that he now considers himself a separate entity or person; why else might his performance differ from someone else's? This interpretation seems especially plausible in light of the child's growing awareness of standards in general.

Comparisons of performance

By the age of two, children show satisfaction in purposely initiating challenging activities or behaviors for themselves, and they often literally smile at the results. A girl may build a tower of blocks higher than usual and smile broadly the moment she completes it; another may make a strange noise — like, say, a cat meowing — and then smile; still another may put her teddy bear carefully to bed under a blanket and then giggle. In each case the child confronts a task that is somewhat difficult by her current standards, but she purposely attempts it anyway. Her behavior suggests an awareness of what competent performance amounts to and of her own ability to be successful. This knowledge reflects part of her sense of self, and contributes to its further development. (We discuss the development of competence more fully later in this chapter.)

Smiles at accomplishment

Whether or not he can talk much yet, a two-year-old sometimes directs adults' behavior. He may invite an adult to play, handing a pretend teacup to the adult, or he may request help, looking imploringly at a nearby adult after struggling unsuccessfully to open a small box. These behaviors may include language, but they do not need to; a gesture or well-timed glance can often accomplish the same result. Whether verbal or not, though, the child apparently believes that he can in fact influence adult behavior. In essence, he implies that he is now a person living among other people, even if he still lacks many of the skills he may see in older children and adults.

Giving directions to adults

By their second birthday, most children have made a good start at using language (see Chapter 6). They have gone beyond using single words and are combining two or three words into rudimentary sentences: "Me go," "Big cat," "See

Self-descriptive utterances

truck!" and the like. Frequently they express personal needs and wants, implying an awareness of themselves as individuals. Also scattered among their utterances are indications of knowledge about their social roles; saying "my sister" or "That's Daddy," for example, implies a knowledge of who plays which roles within the child's family. At this point, of course, the knowledge may be far from accurate or complete, but evidence for it has at least begun to emerge.

Development of Competence and Self-esteem

From the beginning of infancy through the end of toddlerhood, children achieve a growing sense of basic trust, autonomy, competence, and ultimately self-esteem. In fact these developments go hand in hand. **Autonomy,** as we have discussed, is made possible by secure and basically trustworthy relationships with a child's primary care-givers. **Competence** develops as a result of the child's natural curiosity and desire to explore the world and the pleasure that she experiences in successfully mastering and controlling that world (White, 1959; 1975a,b). Much like the infant's need for proximity and attachment to her care-givers, her motivation to explore and master the world is thought to be relatively autonomous and independent of basic physiological needs for food, water, sleep, and freedom from pain.

Importance of high-quality interactions

In a series of studies of toddlers and their mothers, researchers found that although mothers of highly competent children did not spend more time interacting with them than mothers of children who were not as competent, there were important differences in the *quality* of their interactions and the stimulation that they provided. These mothers supported and encouraged their infants' curiosity and their desire to explore the world around them by providing a rich variety of interesting toys and experiences which were both safe and appropriate to the children's level of competence. They played with their toddlers in ways that were responsive to the children's interests and needs and used language that their infants could clearly understand.

These parents were also more likely than others to encourage their children to accomplish the tasks they had initiated themselves by actively guiding them and praising them for accomplishments, rather than actually performing the tasks for them (White, 1975a). As you might have guessed, this approach requires considerable patience, the ability to tolerate the child's frustration when things don't work out the first few times, and a firm belief in the child's need and potential to be an autonomous and competent person. Perhaps the most important quality of these parents was their ability to interact sensitively and appropriately with their children and to experience pleasure and delight (at least most of the time) in these interactions. This same quality appears to be most important in the development of secure attachment relationships and continues to be important throughout childhood.

A natural outcome of such parenting is the early emergence of a strong sense of **self-esteem:** a child's feeling that she is an important, competent, powerful, and worthwhile person who is valued and appreciated by those around her. As we shall see, the childhood experiences that follow infancy continue to make major contributions to this important aspect of identity.

Checkpoint *During toddlerhood, parents must learn to appreciate and support the efforts of their infant to gain greater autonomy and control his own activities, and in a way that neither overestimates nor underestimates the potential dangers. Self-knowledge and self-awareness also expand at this time. Children become increasingly aware of adult standards and more competent at successfully taking on new challenges. An important outcome of this period is an increased sense of self-esteem.*

Child Abuse and Neglect

In a small but significant number of cases, infants and children experience serious maltreatment at the hands of their parents or other caretakers. Most often, maltreatment results from a complex set of factors, which we will discuss shortly. Maltreatment can take several forms. Sometimes the child may be injured physically: he may turn up at a doctor's office with an odd or disturbing combination of cuts, burns, bruises, or broken bones. His parents or guardians may report that he "had an accident," even though no typical accident could cause the injuries that the child actually has. In other cases, maltreatment may consist of emotional **neglect:** the mother may simply ignore her child, feel indifferent to him, and chronically fail to respond to his bids for attention or to his other needs. The most tangible evidence of neglect is the so-called **failure-to-thrive syndrome,** in which the infant seems seriously delayed in his physical growth, and is noticeably apathetic in his behavior. In still other cases of maltreatment, the child may not be neglected so much as abused emotionally: one or both parents may continually ridicule or belittle him, for example. Physical problems in such cases may be minor or even absent, though the child's self-confidence, of course, may be seriously undermined.

The abuse and neglect of children has historical roots in biblical, ancient Greek, and Roman times, when parents' absolute power and authority over their young children was justified by the philosophy "spare the rod and spoil the child." During much of European history, infanticide (the killing of infants) was widely used to limit population growth and rid society of infants with birth defects and diseases; and until child labor and compulsory education laws were passed to protect very young children, they were exploited and abused in factories, farms, and other workplaces (Langer, 1972).

Not until 1960 was the concept of child abuse brought to public attention. Henry Kempe, a pediatrician, observed a very high rate of nonaccidental injuries which pediatricians were reluctant to diagnose or report. He called this abuse the **battered-child syndrome:** "a clinical condition in young children who have received serious physical abuse, generally from a parent or foster parent" (Kempe et al., 1962, p. 4). In 1974 Congress passed the Child Abuse Prevention and Treat-

Historical roots

The scars left by child abuse are psychological as well as physical. Abused children can develop pervasive mistrust of adults and stand more risk of becoming abusive parents themselves. (Frank Siteman/The Picture Cube)

Legislation to protect children

ment Act, and by then all fifty states had passed legislation requiring those in the helping professions to report cases of abuse and neglect (Bybee, 1979).

These changes resulted from shifts in attitudes about the rights and developmental needs of children and about the responsibilities of parents. They were also influenced by advances in medical care and diagnoses. In particular, regular medical care, the routine use of x-rays, and more systematic record-keeping have made the identification of suspicious injuries in young children much more likely.

Defining Abuse

The definition of any problem significantly influences any attempts to solve it. Kempe's original battered-child syndrome defined abuse exclusively in terms of its physical effects on the child. David Gil proposed a somewhat broader, social definition of abuse as a product of parent-child interaction: "Physical abuse of children is the intentional, nonaccidental use of physical force, or intentional, nonaccidental acts of omission, on the part of a parent or other caretaker interacting with a child in his care, aimed at hurting, injuring, or destroying that child" (Gil, 1973). The Child Abuse Prevention and Treatment Act includes emotional abuse, legally defining abuse as "the physical or mental injury, sexual abuse, negligent treatment or maltreatment of a child under the age of eighteen by a person who is responsible for the child's welfare under circumstances which indicate that the child's health or welfare is harmed or threatened thereby" (Bybee, 1979).

Incidence of Abuse

Differences in how abuse is defined, in methods used to study it, and in the proportion of cases that are actually reported make it difficult to estimate accurately how much abuse there is. A national survey of family violence against children in 1975 estimated that fourteen out of every hundred parents of children aged three through seventeen treated their children violently enough to be abusive (Gelles, 1978). This adds up to approximately 46 million children per year. Violent acts included kicking, biting, punching, hitting with an object, beating up, and threatening or hurting with a knife or gun (Belsky et al., 1984). Because infants are even more vulnerable to physical and emotional abuse and neglect, the rate of abuse among them is likely to be even higher.

Causes of Abuse

Abuse is caused by a variety of factors, which vary in how directly or indirectly they affect the individuals involved. Together, they form a multilevel **causal environment** or context. Each level of influence is embedded or "nested" in a broader level, and each has the potential to affect, more or less directly, all others. As Belsky (1980) points out, each of the four levels (described below) is significant to some degree in families where abuse occurs.

Ontogenic Level: Developmental History of the Individual Parent A parent's own childhood history can contribute to child abuse. Parents who were abused, neglected, or rejected as children are more likely than others to neglect and abuse their own children. Parents who were not directly abused themselves but who observed family aggression and violence are also at greater risk of abusing. Ignorance about children's development because of lack of knowledge about and experience with the parenting role also may contribute to maltreatment, as might a parent's untreated emotional or drug-related problems.

The Microsystem: Family Interactions **Microsystem** refers to a person's everyday life situations and environment and it is the microsystem that is most directly responsible for child abuse. For young children, the microsystem is the family. The family can be viewed as an interactive system in which every member, including each child, is a potential contributor to the quality of life and to abuse. Infants who are premature, passive, and socially unresponsive and children who are hyperactive, colicky, and difficult to comfort are more likely than others to be abused.

Role of the infant

Whether or not such "difficult" infants elicit abuse depends on how their parents respond and on the patterns of parent-child interactions that develop. For example, studies comparing abusive and neglectful families with those that were not abusive found that mothers from maltreating families had 40 percent less positive interactions (affection, support) and 60 percent more negative interactions (threat, punishment) with their children than mothers from nonabusive families did. In addition, children from abusive families displayed almost 50 percent more negative behavior than children from normal families did (Burgess and Conger, 1978). In a study of thirteen- to thirty-five-month-old toddlers in day care, children who had been abused were found to display more physical aggression toward peers and care-givers than those who had not been abused did (George and Main, 1979).

Violence between parents

Families in which physical and verbal violence occurs between parents suffer from a higher than usual likelihood of parent-child abuse (Steinmetz, 1977). Parents who are having problems in their own relationship and who may have unhappy childhood histories may unconsciously participate in a **role reversal,** expecting their children to act like parents and to fulfill the emotional needs that neither their own parents nor their spouses can adequately meet (Belsky, 1980).

The Ecosystem: Work and Neighborhood   Ecosystem refers to the somewhat broader influences outside of the family that indirectly contribute to the quality of life and patterns of abuse within it. Two very important ecosystem influences are work and neighborhood. One major way in which the world of work influences the family is by its absence: unemployment has been found to be highly related to family violence, against both women and children. Financial stress, personal powerlessness, and lack of self-esteem, as well as the conflicts that are created by the increased presence of an unemployed father in the home, all serve to trigger abuse (Belsky, 1980). As we noted earlier in this chapter, the quality of parents' work experiences, their level of satisfaction (or dissatisfaction) with work, and the level of conflict between work and family life are all likely to influence patterns of child-rearing.

Stress of unemployment

The neighborhood in which a family lives and the quality of community life that it offers also contribute to abuse. For example, in a study of high-risk and low-risk neighborhoods, families' ratings of the quality of life were predictive of the likelihood of abuse, even when neighborhoods were comparable in terms of the incomes and backgrounds of the families that lived there. Thus two neighborhoods could be economically and culturally very similar but very different in their risk of abuse. Life in high-risk neighborhoods involved greater social isolation and "social impoverishment" — a pervasive lack of informal and formal social support for child-rearing from neighbors, schools, and community services. Socially isolated and without support, abusive families were unlikely to be observed by anyone else, and they were often unable to turn to others for advice or help. Families in high-risk neighborhoods were also found to make little or no use of preventive services and to seek help primarily in times of crisis, as compared with families in low-risk neighborhoods, who sought help as a part of everyday life (Garbarino and Sherman, 1980).

Social isolation in poor neighborhoods

The Macrosystem: Culture and Society   A society's **macrosystem** — its social and economic conditions, its social and political policies, and its values and beliefs (especially with regard to children, families, and violence) — also plays a very significant role in the existence of child abuse. The willingness of contemporary U.S. society to accept violence on an international scale (war and the arms race) and on the domestic scale (violence on TV) creates a context in which family violence is acceptable. Observation of violent models outside the family is likely to increase violence within it.

In addition, the widely held belief that physical punishment is an acceptable means of controlling children provides a context in which physical abuse is more likely. In one survey, two out of three educators, police officers, and clerics who were questioned condoned physical discipline (e.g., spanking with the hand), and more than 10 percent believed that hitting children with belts, straps, and brushes was acceptable for maintaining control (Belsky, 1980). Less than ten years ago the Supreme Court ruled that schools have the right to use corporal (physical) punishment for disobedient children — a decision based on the assumption that, unlike adults who have been convicted of criminal behavior, children who have been disobedient do not have the right of protection under the Eighth Amendment from cruel and unusual punishment (Belsky, 1980). The difficulty in eliminating child abuse as long as such microsystem influences exist is emphasized by research findings that child abuse is rare in countries where physical punishment is infrequently used (e.g., Sidell, 1972).

Pervasive acceptance of physical discipline

Treatment and Prevention

There are two major approaches to solving the problem of child abuse: treatment and prevention. Treatment involves working directly with the parents and child after abuse (or the danger of abuse) has been discovered, and its goals are to reduce or eliminate instances of further abuse and to provide rehabilitative treatment for the physical and psychological injuries suffered by the child, for the abusing parent or parents, and for other family members.

Casework and intensive individual and family counseling and psychotherapy are often used to help the parents and their child to understand the causes, consequences, and personal meanings of their destructive feelings and behaviors and to make changes that will allow them to live together in less destructive ways. Self-help groups such as Parents Anonymous, parent aides who assist abusive and neglectful families in their homes, crisis nurseries, foster care for the abused child, and short-term residential treatment for family members or for the entire family unit are among the treatment alternatives that have been employed with some success (Starr, 1979). A fairly recent study that evaluated the effectiveness of eleven different model treatment programs involving more than 1,200 families found a reduction in abuse and neglect in 42 percent of the treated families, but a recurrence of abuse or neglect in 30 percent. Parent aides and/or Parents Anonymous in conjunction with casework proved to be most effective, with a 53 percent reduction in abuse or neglect, but researchers also found a greater likelihood that abuse would recur among these cases (Starr, 1979).

Types of treatment

While treatment is an important aspect of dealing with abuse, it has several important limitations. It is very costly, and the number of families in need far exceed the helping resources available. It is a reactive approach, offering help only after considerable damage has often already occurred. And it holds little promise of successfully challenging the factors that contribute to maltreatment or of preventing new cases from occurring.

Whereas treatment of abuse focuses on limiting the negative consequences to abusive families through rehabilitation, prevention attempts to protect families from factors that cause abuse and to reduce or eliminate those factors when possible. There are two levels of prevention, secondary and primary. Secondary prevention attempts to reduce the likelihood of abuse by (a) strengthening and supporting families who are at risk for abuse; (b) helping high-risk families to avoid situations that might make abuse likely; and (c) taking steps to help families when the first warning signs occur.

Goals of secondary prevention

The major strength of secondary prevention is obvious: families can be helped *before* rather than after most of the damage occurs. It also has major weaknesses, however. First, because it is extremely difficult to identify high-risk families reliably, many families are wrongly labeled, resulting in unnecessary upset, misuse of helping resources, and potential violation of individual rights. High short-term cost is a second weakness of secondary prevention, although if this strategy actually prevents abuse among high-risk families, its long-term costs may in fact be very small.

Primary prevention has the goal of reducing or eliminating the factors that contribute to or cause abuse on a population-wide basis. Rather than helping particular families that are abusing or are at risk of doing so, primary prevention attempts to alter the general conditions that affect *all* children and families. Primary preventative approaches include education for parenthood, elimination of corporal punishment, the development of a bill of rights for children, and various social policy supports for parents and their children, including more and better jobs, funding for preschools and day-care centers, inexpensive health care, and so forth.

Primary prevention: eliminating the causes

For example, education-for-parenthood programs exist in quite a number of junior and senior high schools, and allow adolescents to learn firsthand about children and parenthood. Day-care centers and preschool programs that involve parents also appear to contribute to the prevention of abuse (Hoffnung, 1983). The limitations of primary prevention include its high initial cost and the difficulties involved in evaluating its effectiveness.

Checkpoint   *Child abuse and neglect are a growing social problem. Major causal factors include the background and personal problems of the parent, disturbances in family functioning, unemployment and stressful jobs, and neighborhood conditions, cultural values, and social policies that condone violence. Treatment focuses on helping individuals already in trouble; prevention identifies and helps families at risk and tries to eliminate the basic causes of abuse through education and changes in social policy.*

The Competent Infant

In just a matter of months a baby has often tripled in weight and doubled in height; she has learned to move about freely and independently; she has formed important relationships with particular people and places. The mature toddler is starting to know that she is a unique and separate individual, like everyone else. As we saw in Chapter 6, she has also made a good start in developing her capacities to think, listen, and talk. It generally becomes clear somewhere around her second birthday that she is definitely not a baby anymore.

But what, then, has she become? For convenience, the next several chapters simply call her a preschooler — a child who is too young to begin elementary school. It should be noted, however, that a considerable number of children who are not yet school age attend day-care centers, family day care, or nursery school on a regular basis. Although a preschool child may be too young for elementary school, she is definitely ready and eager to learn more about the physical and social worlds outside her immediate family. If all has gone reasonably well up to now, she can use her family as a secure base to explore these larger worlds, which include such things as the children next door, the department store downtown, and the children and teachers at a nursery school or day-care setting.

From the two-year-old's point of view, home is still a very important place, but it is no longer the world in its entirety. From her parents' point of view, the daily burden of child care has declined markedly, although it certainly has not disappeared yet. A toddler may not need to have her diapers changed for much longer, but she will still need prepared meals for years to come. She may no longer seek attention several times per hour, but she still will seek it many times a day. The child still has a lot of growing and learning to do in the preschool years.

Summary of Major Ideas

Early Social Relationships

1. A newborn infant has the capacity to react in different ways to stimulation and to protect himself from overstimulation by closing his eyes or going to sleep.

2. As early as the first day of life, an infant's body movements are closely coordinated or synchronized with the rhythms of her mother's speech.

3. The similarities in the type and quality of an infant's interactions with both his mother and his father are much greater than the differences.

4. Recent studies indicate that, when given the opportunity to do so, infants engage in active social interactions with their siblings and peers, and often prefer them to their parents as playmates.

Emotions, Temperament, and Personality Development in Infancy

5. Infants appear to be capable of a complex range of emotional responses and are quite sensitive to the feelings of their care-givers. It is likely that they use cues similar to those used by adults, such as variations in voice quality, smell, touch, facial expression, and body language.

6. Even at birth, infants exhibit differences in their patterns of physical and emotional responsiveness and activity level, called *temperament;* these differences both influence and are influenced by the feelings and responses of their care-givers.

7. Freud, Erikson, and Mahler each emphasize the importance of developing an intense infant-parent relationship which is emotionally responsive to the baby's oral-dependent needs and which allows a basic sense of trust in others to develop.

8. Freud, Erikson, and Mahler emphasize the infant's need to individuate from her parent during the second year of life, and to become a separate, autonomous person who can successfully regulate her own feelings, thoughts, and actions without undue anxiety.

9. Failures to achieve a reasonably intense and trusting relationship during early infancy or to gain autonomy and self-control during toddlerhood may interfere with a child's future development.

Attachment Formation

10. Attachment — the tendency of young infants and their care-givers to seek physical and emotional closeness with each other — is thought to provide an important basis for achieving secure and trusting relationships during early infancy.

11. The "strange situation," which confronts the infant with the stress of being in an unfamiliar place, meeting a stranger, and being separated from his parent, has been used to study the development of attachment.

12. Secure attachment is most likely when the care-giver is able to respond sensitively and appropriately to the infant.

13. Infants are equally capable of forming secure attachments to their mother and their father, even though the mother is typically the primary care-giver.

14. The effects of both maternal employment and day care on attachment depend largely on how the mother feels about herself and her role as a parent and on the ways in which the situation helps or hinders her ability to care for and enjoy her baby. The quality of her experience and the quality and consistency of the day care are also important.

15. Insecurely attached infants tend to be less able than securely attached infants to get help from parents and teachers when they need it or to accept it when it is offered.

The Emergence of Autonomy

16. Sources of the growing autonomy that characterizes the second year of infancy include identification, operant and observational learning, and social referencing.

17. During toddlerhood there are also significant increases in self-knowledge and self-awareness. These changes are reflected in the growth in the toddler's aware-ness of adult standards, distress at behaviors modeled by adults, and the tendencies to smile following an accomplishment, to give directions to adults, and to describe his own activities.

18. Toddlers are strongly motivated to achieve greater competence through successfully mastering and controlling the physical and social worlds around them. Competence is fostered by parents who encourage their infant's curiosity by providing opportunities that are challenging, safe, and appropriate to the child's capabilities.

19. As the toddler enters the preschool years, she is ready to use her family as a secure base from which to take on the challenge of exploring the physical and social worlds beyond the home.

Child Abuse and Neglect

20. Child abuse or neglect is thought to affect almost 46 million children per year; causes occur at the level of the individual parent, the family, work and neighborhood life, and society.

21. Responses to abuse most frequently focus on treating the victims and their families. Although of greater long-run potential, attempts to prevent abuse by identifying and helping families at risk or by eliminating the social causes of abuse have been less common because their initial costs are high.

Key Terms

parent-infant synchrony *(257)*

temperament *(264)*

personality *(267)*

oral stage *(268)*

anal stage *(269)*

basic trust versus mistrust *(270)*

autonomy versus shame and doubt *(270)*

symbiotic mother-child relationship *(270)*

separation-individuation *(270)*

attachment *(271)*

signaling behaviors *(271)*

approach behaviors *(271)*

contact comfort *(272)*

separation anxiety *(274)*

stranger anxiety *(274)*

"strange situation" *(275)*

secure attachment *(275)*

anxious-avoidant attachment *(276)*

anxious-resistant attachment *(276)*

autonomy *(282)*

identification *(283)*

social-referencing *(285)*

contingency *(286)*

self-esteem *(288)*

failure-to-thrive syndrome *(289)*

battered-child syndrome *(289)*

causal environment *(291)*   ecosystem *(292)*
microsystem *(291)*   macrosystem *(292)*

What Do You Think?

1. What advice would you give new parents about establishing social relationships with young infants? In what ways would your advice to fathers differ from your advice to mothers? What would you advise them about their baby's interactions with siblings and peers?
2. When you were an infant, did you have a quiet, average, or active temperament? How did your temperament suit your parents and other family members? To what degree do you think your current temperament is consistent with your temperament as an infant?
3. What have been your own family experiences with maternal employment and child-care alternatives? What are your reactions to the discussions of these topics in the chapter? How do you think you will deal with these issues should you become a parent?
4. In your opinion, what needs and behaviors of young infants and toddlers cause the most difficulties for the typical parent? Which of these might be hardest for you?
5. If you were asked your opinions about how state and federal funds should be used to deal with the problem of child abuse, what would you recommend?

For Further Reading

Belsky, J., Lerner, R., and Spanier, G. *The Child in the Family.* Reading, Mass. Addison-Wesley, 1984.

This book explores how the contexts of family, work, neighborhood, culture, and society jointly and interactively influence the social and emotional development of children and their care-givers. Its discussions of such complex and timely issues as divorce, maltreatment, and the dual-worker family are particularly interesting.

Brazelton, T. B. *Infants and Mothers: Differences in Development* (Rev. ed.). New York: Delacorte, 1983.

The author provides a very lively and readable description of infants and their families during their first year together. Using many delightful examples of everyday activities, he helps the reader to compare the developmental changes in Louis, an "average" baby, Laura, a "quiet" baby, and Daniel, an "active" baby, on a month-by-month basis. His clear, nontechnical writing style conveys an appreciation of what life is really like for infants and their families.

Brazelton, T. B. *Toddlers and Parents: A Declaration of Independence.* New York: Delta, 1974.

The author describes and explains the developmental changes in toddlers and their families from twelve to thirty months. He is particularly appreciative of the satisfactions and frustrations experienced by both children and the members of their families. As with Brazelton's book on younger infants, this is an invaluable source of down-to-earth information about what children are really like.

Parke, R. *Fathers.* Cambridge, Mass.: Harvard University Press, 1981.

This book thoughtfully discusses the important role of fathers as care-givers and parents during infancy and childhood. It includes coverage of divorce, father absence, and stepfatherhood, issues that present difficult challenges to fathers and their families.

Rapoport, R., Rapoport, R., and Strelitz, Z. *Fathers, Mothers, and Society: Perspectives on Parenting.* New York: Vintage, 1980.

This clearly written but fairly high-level book provides a comprehensive review of what is known about the nature and experience of parenthood in a rapidly changing society. While it covers development from before birth through the adult years, many of the issues are directly relevant to this chapter.

White, B. *The First Three Years of Life.* New York: Avon, 1978.

This book, which is based on a TV series by the same name, is written as a guide for parents (and future parents) during the first three years of their baby's life. A particularly useful feature is its specific recommendations for how parents can actively support the physical, emotional, and intellectual development of their child.

David's Case

David was born nine weeks preterm. Before his birth, his mother had looked forward to seeing her baby in the delivery room. Instead, her first contact came in the intensive care unit of the hospital, where nurses had already attached David to a respirator to help him breathe. Like many preterm infants, David's biggest problem was his lungs; he had respiratory distress syndrome and experienced many episodes of apnea. He was fragile for many weeks after he was born, and this fact affected his parents deeply for a long time. They worried about whether David would survive and about whether he would develop normally.

This hospital report shows just how immature David was. He was born weighing less than 4 lbs. — enough to have good chances of survival but only given intensive hospital care. His Apgar scores were lower than normal primarily because of his breathing problems and his general lack of responsiveness.

Patient's Name: Baby boy Bernhard

AMCH #: 819290

DOB: 6-25-84

Adm: 6-25-84   **Disch:** 7-21-84

HISTORY AND PHYSICAL:

Baby boy Bernhard was born in our DR and admitted to the NICU with RDS and prematurity. He was born to a 29 year old 0+ G3P0020 female. EDC and dates by temperature chart suggested approximately 31 weeks, and the ultrasound indicated a 1300 gram baby. The delivery was by low oulet forceps and the child weighed 1650 grams with apgars of 4/8. The baby needed bagging in the DR and GFR began immediately. Subsequent chest x-rays were consistent with RDS.

DISCHARGE SUMMARY:

In summary, this is a baby who was born 31 weeks of gestation, mildly SGA for size, who had moderate respiratory distress syndrome and needed the respirator for 3 days. The lungs resolved and the remainder of the hospital course was uncomplicated. During the hospitalization, the parents were greatly involved in the child's therapy and showed a very sophisticated level of parenting. At the time of discharge, the physical exam was quite normal and the followup routine was set up with the baby and the private pediatrician.

JEFFREY GREENE, M.D.
NEONATOLOGIST

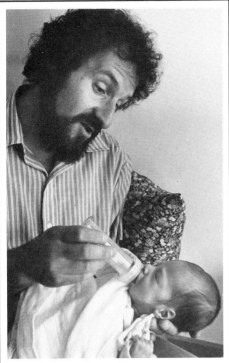

During David's hospital stay, the medical staff encouraged his parents to visit with him often. These visits seemed to help ease their worries. Because his sucking reflex was not well developed, David was fed his mother's milk from bottles. Before long, his reflexes strengthened and he was able to drink well.

David went home from the hospital after one month. During his early months his mother worried about him a lot. At first he seemed limp and floppy and often not very alert. She read avidly in books about infant care, looking to see whether David was developing "on schedule."

In time David's parents became less concerned about their baby's sheer physical survival. But they still worried. David seemed a bit quieter than they thought a baby should be and by five months of age he still had not rolled over. But David did seem to hear sounds — like the family cat whenever it meowed — so his pediatrician urged them to be patient.

By the time David was six months old, his doctor said that he was indeed developing well, although he was definitely behind full-term infants in most motor skills. By now, for example, he still could not sit up reliably without a pillow or hand behind his back. But he watched his parents avidly whenever they came in the room, and often smiled at them when they talked to him.

A real change occurred in David's mother one day when David was ten months old. A neighbor who was visiting commented, "He's so observant, and so interested and careful in the things he handles!" That was the first time that David's mother began thinking that her son might be truly talented in some ways, rather than simply slow to develop in general. The doctor had already stated this idea to her, but it had not sunk in until now.

When David was about thirteen months old, sometimes he even became too active. Now he could stand up in his crib during nap times, pound on the wall, and talk loudly in a mixture of babbling and occasional real, single words. Both his parents enjoyed his new accomplishments, and only now and then thought about the fact that some of them were still "behind schedule" compared to other babies.

As David neared his second birthday, his parents' concerns were generally typical of parents of toddlers. They tried to support his efforts to gain greater autonomy and self-control. David became interested in using the toilet, for example, though not often at the right time. His mother was patient with his erratic bladder and bowels, believing that time would eventually cure this particular problem.

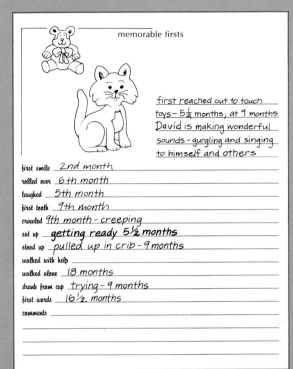

memorable firsts

first reached out to touch toys— 5½ months; at 9 months David is making wonderful sounds — gurgling and singing to himself and others

first smile   2nd month
rolled over   6th month
laughed   5th month
first tooth   9th month
crawled   9th month - creeping
sat up   **getting ready 5½ months**
stood up   pulled up in crib - 9 months
walked with help
walked alone   18 months
drank from cup   trying - 9 months
first words   16½ months
comments

By the time he was two, friends and neighbors could not guess that David had been preterm unless his parents told them. He was just as big and tall as other children his age. And even though he had a somewhat quiet temperament, he loved playing outdoors just like other children. He even adopted a favorite tree stump, which he turned into a "horse" that he rode often. David's mother found herself willing (and even relieved) to let him play on his own for brief periods — a far cry from her attitude when David had been younger.

4 The Preschool Years

Although most of us remember relatively little of our preschool
years, parents often believe they are among the most gratifying for
their children. Perhaps this is because children begin participating
more fully in their families during this time. Now they talk and
play with parents and siblings much more — and of course, they
sometimes infuriate everyone more, too. In all these senses they
"belong" more fully than ever.

Preschoolers become more social during this period partly because
of the more complex motor skills they acquire — riding a trike or
climbing a jungle gym can impress parents as well as friends. In
addition, with their new cognitive skills, preschool children can
engage in extended conversations and try out new social roles in
play. The preschooler's world is a rapidly expanding one, and for
parents as well as children, the preschool years are both exhausting
and exhilarating.

Chapter
8

The Preschool Years: Physical Development

Focusing Questions

- What influences how fast preschool children grow, and why do they develop different bodily proportions?
- How does the brain become organized during early childhood?
- How often do young children get sick?
- When and why do children first gain control of their bladders and bowels?
- What motor skills do children acquire during the preschool years, and what refinements do they make in them?
- How do drawing skills evolve during early childhood?
- What differences in physical development exist between the sexes during early childhood?
- How does children's physical and motor development affect their relationships with their parents?

CHILDREN GROW MORE SLOWLY during the preschool years — from two to six — than they do during infancy, but nonetheless growth has a major impact on their lives as a whole. Not only does physical growth make new motor skills possible, but it also affects children's social, emotional, and cognitive development. To understand something of these relationships, consider two children learning to swim. They may enroll in the same swimming class, but before long one is likely to be swimming better than the other. Why does this happen?

Most of the time such a difference stems from a mixture of physical, social, emotional, and cognitive factors. One child may be larger or physically more mature, even at the beginning of the swimming class; she may be able to hold her breath longer or paddle more powerfully. Or she may get more social support from home for learning to swim; perhaps her parents are devoted swimmers and take her to the pool in between lessons. Because of differences like these, one child may develop a concept of herself as a good swimmer, one who is strong, holds her breath well, and can count on help at swimming when she needs it.

This chapter will look closely at such factors, investigating how physical growth and motor skills influence not only each other but also psychological processes during early childhood. To do so, it will first describe the overall nature and extent of physical growth. Then we will look at some motor skills typically acquired during early childhood. Some of these, such as learning to walk, are relatively universal among children around the world. Other skills, such as ice-skating, are rather specialized to particular groups of children. Woven into our descriptions are implicit notions of what constitutes typical or normal physical development. As we point out repeatedly, however, such norms do not in and of themselves constitute prescriptions for how children *should* develop physically. Evaluating growth is also important, but it is different from describing growth. The chapter tries to respect this separation.

Normal Physical Development

Physical growth in the preschool years is relatively easy to measure and gives a clear idea of how children normally develop during this period. Table 8-1 shows the two most familiar measurements of growth, standing height and weight. At age two, an imaginary average child in North America measures about thirty-three or thirty-four inches tall, or about two feet and ten inches. Three years later, at age five, he measures around forty-four inches, or about one-third more than before. The typical child weighs about twenty-seven pounds on his second birthday, but about forty-one pounds by his fifth. (See also Figure 8-1.) Meanwhile, other measurements change in less obvious ways. His head grows about one inch in circumference during these years, for example, and his body fat decreases as a proportion of his total bodily tissue.

Changes in dimensions

Rate of Growth in Early Childhood

However, it is more informative to measure how rapidly children are growing at any one point in time — the so-called **velocity** of growth — than how much they have grown over a period. Table 8-2 shows velocities for height and weight during

Figure 8-1 Growth in Height and Weight from Two to Eighteen Years

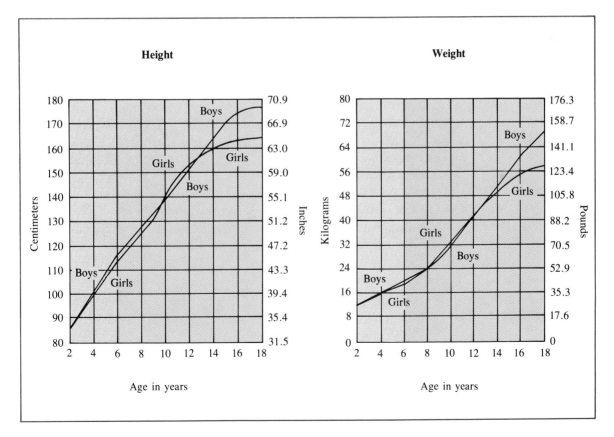

Table 8-1 *Average Height and Weight, Early Childhood*	Age (Years)	Height (Inches)	Weight (Pounds)
	2	34.5	27.0
	3	37.8	31.5
	4	40.9	36.0
	5	43.6	40.5

Source: Hamill et al., 1979.

Slower rate of growth

early childhood. As the chart shows, increases in height slow down during this period, even though height itself, of course, continues to increase. In other words, a young child puts on inches most quickly during the early part of the preschool period. Weight, in contrast, increases by fairly equal increments each year: by about four or five pounds, to be exact. Sitting height — measured from the buttocks upward — grows more slowly than standing height during early childhood, and it slows in proportion to overall standing height throughout the period (Johnson, 1979).

Perspectives on Research

Irregularities in Physical Growth

Even though growth is normally very smooth, most children experience slight irregularities, and a few experience large irregularities. In proportion to the individual's total size, these variations matter more in small children than they would in full-grown adults. Height and weight vacillate slightly throughout a single day, for example, because of normal activities; eating can make a child weigh one or two pounds more, and posture usually deteriorates toward the end of the day, which means that height tends to be shorter when measured in the evening than when measured in the morning, sometimes by more than half an inch. Even though these changes reflect measurement error rather than real growth, they do affect parents' impressions by making children seem bigger or smaller, and fatter or thinner, than they really are.

Another irregularity, though, does involve real growth. Like flowers and trees, children grow almost three times faster in the spring (April through June) than in the fall (October through December) (Marshall and Swan, 1971). The difference is large

enough to be perceptible, making a child seem much faster-growing in one season than in another. The reasons for the cycle are not clear. Obviously it does *not* depend on photosynthesis (as tree growth does), but the growth spurt does seem to depend somehow on how much light the child experiences. Blind children do not show seasonal cycles of growth; nor do children living near the equator, where sunlight remains relatively constant throughout the year.

A few children experience irregularities of growth that go beyond these universal variations. Sometimes too much stress in a family can keep children from growing normally, a condition called psychosocial dwarfism or **reactive attachment disorder** (RAD) (American Psychiatric Association, 1980). Children with this condition seem apathetic and weak, and they simply fail to grow at normal rates (fail to thrive).

The condition apparently results from any situations that interfere with normal positive relationships between parent and child, especially during

Age (Years)	Height Increase per Year (Inches), from Previous Year	Weight Increase per Year (Pounds), from Previous Year
2	5.0	5.2
3	3.3	4.5
4	3.1	4.5
5	2.7	4.5

Table 8-2 *Velocities of Growth for Height and Weight, Early Childhood*

Source: Hamill et al., 1979.

These velocities and their relationships lead to steady changes in bodily proportions, which cause preschool children to look less and less like babies. Children's
legs become longer as a proportion of their total length. Their build becomes less
chunky, because each addition of weight represents a smaller proportion of their
previous weight, and because skinfolds of fat become relatively thinner over time.
As they get older, preschool children look increasingly like school-age children.

Changing proportions

infancy or the early preschool period. For example,
parents may make a child a scapegoat because of
stresses resulting from unemployment, chronic
conflicts, or other painful circumstances. Sometimes parents somehow decide that one particular
child "causes" these problems, perhaps by needing
more care and attention than the other children in
the family. Bad relationships then lead indirectly to
physical stunting, through poorly provided food,
poor appetite, or constant anxiety, which may interfere with sleep and perhaps suppress production
of growth hormones.

Before blaming the parents of such children too
much, however, note that the causes of failure to
thrive are speculative rather than well-established
fact. Mothers of children who fail to thrive usually
show no dramatic qualities that might account for
the children's growth problems. One study observed such mothers with their preschool-age children once a week for many months, and interviewed the mothers about their children as well
(Pollitt et al., 1975). As a group, the mothers ex-

pressed reasonably normal beliefs about and goals
for their children. In practice they did impose fairly
strict discipline, spank their children more than
usual, and seem a bit less affectionate than mothers
of normal children. The observers could not tell,
though, whether the mothers caused these problems, or whether the children had temperaments
that created barriers between them and other members of the family.

If reactive attachment disorder has not persisted
for too long, it can usually be reversed in the short
run through special nutritional and medical intervention to help the child regain his strength and
begin growing normally again. This strategy does
not solve any long-term problems in the relationships between parents and RAD children, of
course. Such problems require relief from stress for
the parents, and perhaps also psychological help for
the child in learning new, less passive responses to
people. These long-run strategies are difficult to
implement, and in some cases they may never work
fully.

Velocities of growth vary both among children and among the major parts of children's bodies, and these differences help to accentuate the unique appearance of each child as she gets older. During the preschool years some children become relatively long-legged, although not necessarily tall; others develop relatively big shoulders, or especially small feet. And facial dimensions, of course, change in ways unique to each child. Often these specific changes reshuffle somewhat during the growth spurt of adolescence, and to a certain extent the child looks like a new person at that time. But the essential proportions and patterns remain afterward. Like it or not, a child's looks begin taking shape (literally) during early childhood.

Influences on Growth

For any preschool child who is reasonably healthy and happy, physical growth is remarkably smooth and predictable, especially compared with many cognitive and social developments. All in all, physical growth contains no discrete stages, plateaus, or qualitative changes like the ones described by Piaget for cognitive development. At the same time, though, large differences do develop both between individual children and between groups of children. Sometimes these differences affect the psychological development of young children; at other times they simply create interesting physical variety among human beings.

Growth is usually smooth

Genetic Background Most dimensions of growth are influenced substantially by heredity. Tall parents tend to have tall children and short parents have short children. Weight shows similar patterns, even though it can be influenced strongly by habits of exercise and diet; a tendency to be heavy or thin is inherited to a significant extent. Contrary to popular belief, both parents contribute equally to these tendencies. Sons do not necessarily resemble their fathers' growth patterns more than their mothers', nor do daughters resemble their mothers' more than their fathers'.

The most obvious evidence for genetic influence on growth comes from comparing identical and fraternal twins. Identical twins develop from a single fertilized egg or zygote, and they are therefore completely alike in genetic makeup. Fraternal twins develop from two eggs which the mother's ovaries happen to release at the same time, and which become fertilized and develop at nearly the same time. In genetic makeup fraternal twins are no more similar than ordinary siblings. Comparing identical and fraternal twins should therefore give clues about the relative importance of genetics and environmental experience.

Comparisons of twins

At birth the two types of twins are about equally different in length — generally just under two centimeters. By about age three, though, identical twins are noticeably more similar to each other in height than fraternal twins are. At that age identicals differ in height by only one centimeter, but the fraternals by almost three. The difference between fraternals approximates the differences found between ordinary siblings — not surprisingly, given the twins' genetic differences. Over time, then, identical twins remain very similar to each other and fraternals become less similar. The same trends occur with other major dimensions or measurements of growth, particularly weight (Wilson, 1976).

Races and ethnic groups around the world also differ in growth patterns (Eveleth, 1979). The differences often, though not always, reflect physical stereotypes about such groups. Children from Asiatic groups, such as Chinese and Japanese, tend to be shorter than European and North American children. The latter in turn are shorter than children from African societies. Shape differs among these groups as well, though the differences do not always become obvious until adolescence. Asiatic children develop comparatively short legs and arms, relative to their torsos, and relatively broad hips. African children do just the opposite: they develop relatively long limbs and narrow hips. Olympic athletes reflect these differences; records consistently show Asiatics performing better in events requiring upper-body strength, such as wrestling, gymnastics, and weight-lifting, whereas Africans tend to excel in events requiring a long stride, such as running (Tanner, 1978b; Eveleth and Tanner, 1976).

Ethnic differences in growth

Such trends do not result from differences in nutrition or health care. Well-off children from these societies show the same relative differences, even though their diets are comparable in overall quality. And with a minor exception noted below, the same differences exist whether children are living in their native country or have emigrated to another, more affluent one, where medical care might tend to be better. Apparently nutrition and health care do affect growth, but they affect all racial groups equally.

Nutrition and the Secular Trend   During the last one hundred years or so, children in industrialized countries have been getting larger and heavier (Van Wieringen, 1978). The tendency is often called the **secular trend.** Each decade since 1900, five-year-olds have been taller than in the previous decade by about one or two centimeters, or about half an inch. Recently the trend has extended to certain non-Western countries; in Japan, for example, five-year-olds have been getting taller by as much as three centimeters per decade since 1950.

Historical changes in size

Although all ages have been getting larger, the secular trend has been more pronounced among children than among adults. British seven-year-olds, for example, averaged twenty centimeters taller in 1980 than in 1840; but in the same time period, eighteen-year-olds "grew" only fifteen centimeters, and older adults "grew" somewhat less than this. These facts suggest that the trend reflects how quickly children grow more than how tall they eventually grow. Children these days do eventually grow taller than children in the past, but even more important, they reach maturity more rapidly. This possibility is further supported by the secular trend for girls' first menstruation: on the whole, girls have their first period about thirty or forty months (or three years) earlier now than they did one hundred years ago (Tanner, 1973).

Faster maturity

The facts also suggest that the trend may reflect general improvements in nutrition during infancy and early childhood, as well as decreases in serious or "classic" childhood diseases. Growth changes in Japanese children illustrate this possibility. In 1950 young children growing up in Japan were significantly shorter than children of Japanese ancestry growing up in the United States, and the Japanese-

As a result of improvements in nutrition and health care, children in industrialized nations have grown larger over the last century. Nevertheless, certain specific nutritional problems remain—in particular, the consumption of excess sugar and fat. (Dennis Mansell)

Americans were in turn shorter than Anglo-American children. These children had all been born near the end of World War II, when food and medical services in Japan did not match those found in the United States. By the 1970s, however, Japanese children in Japan had become just as tall and heavy as children of Japanese descent growing up in the United States, though they were still not as tall as Anglo-American children. During the intervening decades, diet and medical service had come to resemble or even surpass those found in the United States.

Some of the secular trend may also result from so-called **hybrid vigor**: the tendency of genetically dissimilar individuals to produce comparatively larger and more vigorous offspring (Van Wieringen, 1979). The notion of hybrid vigor is borrowed from the study of plants; fruit trees, for example, produce larger and healthier fruit if they cross-pollinate with differing strains of trees rather than with highly similar or identical strains. In like manner, according to this view, human beings may bear stronger and healthier children if they come from genetically dissimilar lineages. Some population specialists have argued that over time people tend to marry and reproduce with dissimilar individuals, so that over time they also tend to produce children who are more vigorous and generally larger. The process may have accelerated in recent decades, because modernization of society has encouraged emigration. Now more than ever, people move from the country to the city to the suburbs, or from one city to another, or even from one nation to another, which enables them to meet and marry people from dissimilar genetic backgrounds.

In spite of these facts, new evidence shows that the secular trend may be coming

Physical benefits of hybridization

to a conclusion. The most recent surveys of growth show smaller increases among children than earlier ones did (Greulich, 1976; Ljung et al., 1974). Apparently the benefits of diet and medicine may have reached their natural limit. If so, then future differences in growth patterns among individuals and groups may reflect genetic differences to a comparatively greater extent than in the past.

The end of the secular trend

Disease Although serious illnesses do interfere with growth, it can often be hard to judge exactly how much. The trouble is that children with serious illnesses often have other conditions that retard growth; they may have been small-for-date, or they may have suffered from chronically poor nutrition during infancy. These conditions can lead not only to slow growth but also to various sicknesses, which in turn may contribute to the problem.

To hold back growth, an illness must be fairly major. Preschool-age children in certain impoverished rural parts of Central America, for example, tend to be shorter and lighter in weight if they have suffered continually from diarrhea during infancy (Condon-Paolini et al., 1977), but similar children are not shorter and lighter if their illnesses have mainly consisted of upper-respiratory-tract infections (colds). Children from affluent parts of these same societies do not usually get sick enough to impair their growth. Nor do children from societies that are generally well-off; a middle-class American child, for example, is just as likely to grow large (or small) if she catches colds frequently as if she does not (Johnston, 1978).

Differential effects of diseases

Certain specific diseases and conditions do retard growth, in many cases by reducing the normal absorption of nutrients over a long period of time. Childhood diabetes can retard growth, at least partly by interfering with the normal use of sugars in the body. So can any chronic infection of the intestine, such as amoebic dysentery or worms, by preventing the normal digestions of foods. Nutritional deficits can also develop because of chronic intolerance to certain foods, such as to the gluten in wheat products or to the lactose in milk products. Children with these conditions suffer in various ways, but to a large extent they simply become malnourished, and like other malnourished children, they do not grow as rapidly as usual (Merck Laboratories, 1985).

Effects of disease on nutrition

Not all diseases that influence growth do so by affecting nutrition. About one preschool child in ten thousand develops a deficiency in his **endocrine glands**, which produce growth hormones (Tanner, 1978b). As a result, growth simply slows down considerably; by age five, for example, an afflicted child might measure only about two and one half feet tall (or eighty-five centimeters), which is about nine inches (or fifteen centimeters) shorter than average. Occasionally doctors can trace such growth deficiencies to an anatomical disorder (such as a tumor) of the glands that control growth. More often, though, they can find no obvious cause. In either case, the condition can usually be treated by injections of whatever hormones the child appears to be missing.

Effects of hormone deficiencies

Once the causes of slow growth are diagnosed correctly and treated, children can often recover by growing much faster than usual until they have reached the normal range of size for their age. At that point growth slows down again to relatively normal rates, and becomes relatively immune to short-term and minor changes in the children's health and nutrition. This process is often called **catch-up growth,**

Catch-up growth

and it suggests that genetics may influence the rate of physical growth significantly, as long as children receive basically good nutrition and physical care.

Understanding Physical Growth

In some ways physical growth has proved relatively easy to study in large populations or societies. Growth lends itself to numerical measurements — a child weighs so many pounds, or stands so many inches high — and we can take these measurements relatively quickly on large numbers of people.

Individual differences
But for several reasons, trends in growth among populations can be misleading. First, as you may already suspect, group trends hide important individual differences. Even though Asiatics may average a shorter height than Africans, certain

---

Perspectives on Issues

Good Nutrition for Preschool Children

Insuring good nutrition can become a challenge during the preschool years, as children begin eating more varied foods and consequently begin preferring some foods and avoiding others. Unfortunately, children do not always want to eat what they should eat; they may like candy bars better than vegetables. When this happens, how can parents foster good nutrition and eating habits?

Meal planning   The answer starts with planning meals that contain a healthful variety of calories, protein, and vitamins and minerals. Fortunately, parents do not have to plan these different nutrients with precision for each meal; children's own appetites will do any fine-tuning, as long as the children are generally healthy and happy (Cohen, 1982). Nonetheless, parents should try to provide the following foods in about these amounts every day:

1. One or two pints of milk, or the equivalent in cheese
2. Two or three servings of another protein source, such as meat, fish, or eggs
3. Three or four servings of fruits and vegetables — at least one of which is high in vitamin C (like an orange) and one high in vitamin A (like a carrot)

4. Three or four servings of grains (such as bread) and starchy vegetables (for example, potatoes)

Meals built around these servings should also include roughage or fiber, to help children's intestines pass food along at a healthy rate. Fiber is available in lettuce, as well as in whole wheat bread and in most fresh fruits and vegetables.

Just as certain foods promote good health, others discourage it. For young children in North America, the most common culprits are sweet or sugary food and fatty food. Sweets include the familiar cookies, candy, and soft drinks but they also come in somewhat less obvious forms, such as canned fruit and ketchup, both of which often contain 30 percent or more refined sugar. Excess sugar causes tooth decay, provides a diet with too many calories in it, and kills a child's appetite for other, more necessary foods.

Food high in fat includes most red meat, such as hamburgers, and anything deep-fried, such as potato chips. Certain foods that are otherwise nutritious, such as whole milk (versus skim) and eggs, also contain large amounts of unnecessary and unhealthful fat. Limited amounts of fat will not hurt the growth of a child, and in fact some fat is needed for normal nutrition. But parents should discour-

---

Asian children nonetheless are taller than certain African ones. Facts like these become especially important to remember whenever physical stereotypes may influence a child's opportunities in life. It is not fair to assume that a child will have health or learning problems just because he happened to have a very low birth weight; the success of such children depends on too many other factors to support that conclusion (Meisels, 1984; Brazelton, 1980). Low birth weight may create risk, but it does not imply certainty of failure. Likewise, we cannot assume that every tall preschooler will make a good basketball player, nor that every overweight child will turn out to be clumsy.

Second, population differences in growth can create the impression that heredity and environment affect all aspects of growth to the same extent, when in fact they do not. Some features of growth change noticeably because of experiences; a

---

age unnecessary or excessive consumption of fat. For most children, this means limiting their fat to the nutritionally good sources like eggs and meat and avoiding junk-food sources entirely. Like sugar, fatty foods provide a diet too high in calories. They may also contribute to heart problems later in life.

Mealtimes Young children will more likely enjoy healthful foods if parents try to make mealtimes relaxed and cheerful occasions. While this sounds like reasonable advice, it often requires patience and flexibility. For example, parents should try not to worry if children do not eat everything on their plates on every occasion. As long as the children do not feel pressured to eat and have a healthy selection of food to choose from, their appetites will insure a balanced diet over the long run (Wanamaker et al., 1979).

Keeping meals relaxed also means introducing new foods slowly, without insisting that preschool children necessarily enjoy them. Sometimes it helps to serve a new food alongside tried-and-true foods that the child is sure to enjoy. Sometimes, too, it helps to serve new food several times without actually expecting the child to eat it, just expecting him to notice that others already are eating it and enjoying it.

Snacks Between-meal snacks need not be harmful to children's health, and in fact they can provide important energy supplements to regular meals. But they do so only if they follow the nutritional guidelines on the preceding page. Parents can offer a small serving taken from any of the major food groups: milk products, other protein sources, fruits and vegetables, and grains and starches. That means that snacks can vary; a piece of cheese, for example, makes a good snack, as does a small piece of fruit. It also means that snacks should not contain too much sugar, as presweetened cereals do, or excess fat, as ice cream does.

In theory, preschoolers should have snacks about midway between meals, so as not to spoil their appetite for the next meal. In practice, though, timing requires a lot of judgment from parents or caregivers. While some children do lose their appetites because of premeal snacks, others do not, as long as the snack is not too large or overloaded with appetite-killing sugar. A few parents, in fact, serve snacks just before meals on purpose, for the same reason that restaurants serve appetizers: as a way of keeping hungry customers (or children) patient until the real meal arrives.

child may become more overweight or underweight depending on what he eats and on how much exercise he gets. Other features seem to depend almost completely on genetic endowment; at what age a child acquires permanent teeth, for example, seems to depend entirely on genetics and not at all on nutrition or illness (Demirjian, 1978). And as we have already discussed, some features of growth, such as the secular trend, may be guided by both genetics and experience.

Variations in relative importance of heredity

The third caution about growth trends concerns the value of physical size. Since low-birth-weight children experience more risks, are bigger children therefore likely to be healthier? In North American society, for the vast middle range of sizes, the answer to this question seems to be no; normal variations make little difference to children's later health. But sheer size has a different significance in less affluent societies. In non-Western rural communities, for example, being large actually reduces a child's chances for good health and long life (Stini, 1972), and small mothers in such societies actually give birth successfully more often than large mothers do (Frisancho et al., 1977). The reasons are not clear. Perhaps being small reduces the amount of food a person needs, and in a society where food may be scarce, needing less may be an advantage.

Relationship of size and health

Checkpoint *During the preschool years, growth slows down and children take on more adult proportions. For most children, growth proceeds very smoothly at this time, although differences in size and proportions among individuals do occur as the result of genetic and ethnic background. During the past century, too, children from industrialized societies have gradually been growing up faster and taller. In general, diseases can affect all of these trends, but only if they are serious and long-lasting.*

Brain Development and Other Bodily Changes

Taken as a whole, the brain does most of its growing quite early in life. By the age of two, it averages about 75 percent of its final adult weight, and by the age of five, about 90 percent of final adult weight. Only a few other organs (for example, the eyes) are so well developed at such an early age (Tanner, 1978b).

Brain growth during early childhood happens in two ways. First, as we note in Chapter 5, a lot of growth comes from the development of *myelin sheaths*, the insulating covers that surround mature nerve fibers and allow the fibers to conduct impulses reliably and efficiently. Myelinization among fibers that connect the "higher" cerebral cortex with the somewhat "lower" cerebellum does not finish until about the age of four. These particular fibers assist children in achieving fine motor skills, such as writing and drawing. To some extent, therefore, such school-related skills depend partly on brain development, as well as on muscular development, social encouragement, and opportunities to practice.

Increasing brain complexity

In addition to myelinization, some nerve cells continue to extend fibers between and among themselves, and capillaries continue to grow near these fibers to provide them with the nutrients that they need. As a result, a young child's brain looks increasingly dense and complex when viewed under a microscope (Lynch and Gall, 1979). Viewed without a microscope, though, the brain continues to look amazingly uniform, and offers no obvious clues about how it might be organized internally.

Organization of the Brain

How, then, does the uniform gray mass of the brain sort out and perform the diverse functions of being human? Contrary to a widespread belief, it does *not* work like a telephone switchboard; individual stimuli or thoughts do not confine themselves to select nerve fibers, as if the fibers acted like wires. Instead a stimulus generates neural activity over wide areas of the brain, and sometimes even in the entire brain. Some of this response shows itself when electrodes are placed on an individual's head. But the locations of brain activity can be mapped even more accurately by injecting tiny, harmless amounts of radioactive substances into the blood and measuring which parts of the brain then accumulate especially large amounts of the substances (Lassen et al., 1978). Active brain cells and fibers require larger amounts of blood, and therefore can be "photographed" by this technique.

Generalized brain activity

In spite of responding widely to most stimuli, the brain also shows relationships between the kind of stimulation it receives and the area that responds most strongly. A visual image, like the sight of a cat, produces the strongest activity in an area called the **visual cortex,** located near the back of the head in the cerebral cortex. The sounds of speech, on the other hand, produce their primary response in the **auditory cortex,** and specifically in a place called **Wernicke's area,** located near the left side of the cerebral cortex.

Specialized brain areas

By the end of the preschool years, similar relationships between brain activity and many overt behaviors exist. Simple voluntary movements, such as lifting an arm, produce their largest neural activity in the **motor cortex,** located just forward of the top of the head, and the child's own speech usually produces its primary activity in a place called **Broca's area,** located on the left side of the cerebral cortex and somewhat to the front. These and other areas of specialized activity are illustrated in Figure 8-2.

Hemispheric Lateralization

During the preschool years, children begin showing definite **hemispheric lateralization,** which is a tendency for the left and right halves of the brain to perform separate functions. In general, the left hemisphere deals increasingly with information on an item-by-item or linear basis, and the right hemisphere identifies relationships or patterns among the items (Kinsbourne, 1982).

The difference in function is quite noticeable, for example, in a task called **dichotic listening.** In this task, a child wears headphones that feed sounds or infor-

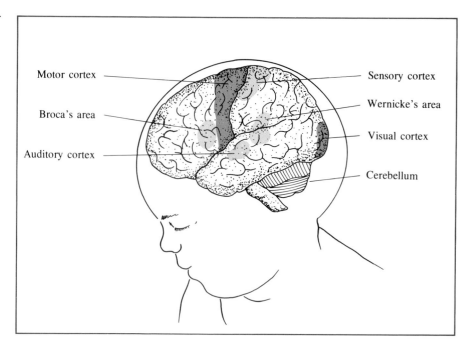

Figure 8-2 *Regions of the Brain*

Motor cortex

Broca's area

Auditory cortex

Sensory cortex

Wernicke's area

Visual cortex

Cerebellum

mation to each ear separately. Because of the layout of the nerve cells in the brain, the experimental sounds are conducted to particular hemispheres for processing. As it happens, the sounds initially go to the hemisphere *opposite* the ear that receives each sound. Under these conditions, if the information given to each ear is relatively linear or sequential, such as a string of digits, then the ear connected to the left hemisphere tends to hear its sounds relatively earlier and with fewer errors. But if the information emphasizes patterns, such as melodies, then the right hemisphere will function better.

Examples of brain lateralization

Similar trends happen with the other senses, including touch and vision (Gazzaniga and LeDoux, 1978). Consider, for example, these two tasks:

- *Touch* Give preschool children a simple three-dimensional shape, such as a wooden cube, inside a bag or box. Ask them to feel it without seeing it. On the average, children figure out its overall shape more easily by feeling with their left hands, but they can count the corners of the shape more easily with their right hands.
- *Vision* Show a drawing of a simple shape to preschoolers. If you ask them to copy it line by line (a linear task), they will tend to do this faster and more accurately if they view the drawing in their right visual field. But if you ask them to match the drawing with other identical ones (a patterning task), they will perform better if both shapes lie to the left side of their visual field.

Experiments like these imply that the hemispheres specialize in function even among young children. Note, though, that most everyday tasks probably obscure hemispheric specialization, simply because they usually require the activity of both

halves of the brain. A child in nursery school, for example, might discover that a shape is a cube, but most likely she will handle it with both hands, look at its over-all shape, and count the corners — all at once.

Lateralized Behaviors

In contrast to hemispheric lateralization, lateralized behaviors are quite evident in everyday life, even among preschool-age children. **Lateralized behaviors** are actions that individuals prefer to perform with one side of their body more than with the other. The best example is handedness: offer a toy to a five-year-old, and most likely he will take it with his right hand rather than his left. But persons of all ages show lateral preferences (usually right-sided) for a variety of behaviors. Most of us have a favorite eye for looking through a telescope or keyhole, for example, and a preferred ear for listening on the telephone, and a preferred foot for squash-ing a bug on the floor (Coren et al., 1981).

Lateral preferences emerge during the preschool years and become stable at adult levels by about the time children begin school. In general they correlate among themselves a little, but not strongly; right-handed children, for example, stand slightly greater chances than left-handed children of being right-eyed, but very often they turn out left-eyed instead. A few children (and adults) become truly equal in their lateral preferences, or at any rate become very selective about their preferences. They may learn to write equally well with both hands, or they may learn to write with one hand but throw a ball with the other.

Lateralized behavior must have at least partly biological or genetic origins. It is hard to see what experiences might cause a majority of three-year-olds to choose to

Causes of lateralization

use their right ears for listening to a seashell. And efforts by generations of teachers and parents to make left-handed preschoolers become right-handed have had remarkably little effect; for about the last century, left-handers still number about one child in ten (Segalowitz, 1983).

But learning probably does affect lateral preferences somewhat. A right bias is strongest among preschool children for behaviors that are taught explicitly, such as eating with a spoon; the bias is weakest for behaviors that children usually learn spontaneously, such as digging in a sandbox. And right-hand bias increases during the lifespan. About 85 percent of children during the preschool years favor their right hand, but well over 95 percent of adults during old age do so. This shift may not seem large, but it evolves steadily, suggesting that society influences left-handers to switch hand preference if they can (Fincher, 1977). Subtle influences may begin early, as in nursery-school classrooms that do not contain enough left-handed scissors.

Childhood Diseases

Colds and Other Minor Viruses During the preschool years, children catch numerous viral illnesses, but the number declines as they get older. Two-year-olds generally get more than eight respiratory ailments (mostly colds) each year, whereas five-year-olds catch only about six or seven (Denny and Clyde, 1983), although the number sometimes rises temporarily when children first enter nursery school or kindergarten. Since these illnesses tend to occur mostly during the winter months, some preschool children may seem sick almost continuously at that season and families with more than one young child may have someone sick with a viral illness virtually constantly.

These illnesses definitely cause inconvenience to parents and create crankiness in young children. But they do have cognitive and social benefits (Parmalee, 1986). Minor illnesses teach young children about the nature of disease — that it originates both with germs and with unhealthful behaviors, and that it can sometimes be contagious. Minor illnesses may also develop children's sensitivity to their own and others' feelings. For example, they learn that physical discomfort differs from personal unhappiness: one requires comfort and love, and the other requires rest, and perhaps medicine as well. Making this distinction probably helps preschool children to understand the nature of feelings more clearly.

Psychological benefits of minor illness

Serious Illnesses During Early Childhood Serious illnesses are ones that incapacitate children for may days or weeks, that require close medical supervision, and that can even end in death if left untreated. Until recent decades, such illnesses included most of the classic childhood diseases such as measles, mumps, and diphtheria.

Improved living conditions, better medical care, and immunization programs have decreased the incidence of these diseases and have made fatalities from them much less common. In 1930 five or six preschool children (ages two to four) out of every thousand died of one of the major infectious childhood diseases, or from

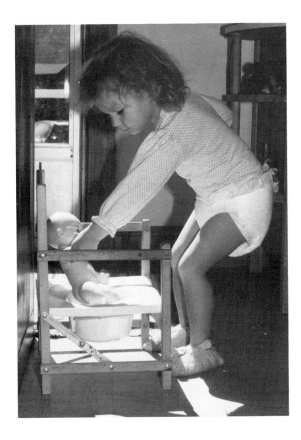

In the long run, successful bladder control depends on both physical growth and the child's own motivation. (Nancy Sheehan)

complications of the disease. By 1980, in contrast, less than one child in every thousand died in this way (Select Panel for the Promotion of Child Health, 1981a).

Decreases in major illness

Ironically, the very infrequency of serious illness creates medical dangers. Parents may become too casual about immunizing their children, in the belief that the major diseases have been eliminated and that "children don't get really sick anymore." This idea is indeed true, but only because of the thoroughness of immunization programs and because of the continued vigilance of medical personnel in identifying cases of serious illness, however rare.

The apparent good health of preschool children also hides wide differences in health among individuals and groups of children. Rural and low-income children in particular are about twice as likely to die of an infectious disease as urban and middle-income children are, probably because of their lack of access to medical care. And throughout society, boys are about twice as likely to die from a disease as girls are, probably because of poorly understood genetic differences between the sexes (Butler et al., 1984).

Variations in incidence of fatalities

Bladder and Bowel Control

Sometime during the preschool years, most children acquire control of their bladder and bowels. As parents will testify, the process includes many false starts and accidents. Most commonly, daytime control comes before nighttime control —

sometime before a child's third birthday, although individuals vary widely and somewhat unpredictably. Typically, too, daytime control of the bladder and of the bowels occurs at very nearly the same time. Some pediatricians believe that this fact implies that children decide when they wish to begin exercising control, perhaps in order to begin feeling more grown-up (Brazelton, 1980). If so, then reminders and enforced visits to the toilet may make rather little difference to most toddlers. Too many reminders, in fact, may actually slow their progress down, by making them anxious or defiant about bladder or bowel control.

Daytime control

Nighttime bladder control often takes much longer to achieve than daytime control. Somewhere around half of all three-year-olds still wet their beds at least some of the time, and as many as one in five six-year-olds do the same (Spock, 1976). The timing of nighttime control depends on several factors, such as how deeply children sleep and how large their bladders happen to be. It also depends on anxiety; worried children do tend to wet their beds more often than relaxed children. Unfortunately, parents may sometimes contribute to young children's anxieties by becoming overly frustrated about changing wet sheets night after night.

Nighttime control

Achieving control over bladder and bowels reflects the large advances children make during these years in controlling their bodies in general. As infants, they could not always be sure of reaching successfully even for an object that was nearby, and their first efforts to crawl and to walk often ended in falls or in moving in the wrong direction. During the preschool years, those problems no longer occur. Instead of concentrating on whether they can simply get their bodies to move, children of this age can begin concentrating on what they actually want to do with their bodies.

Checkpoint *The bodies and behavior of preschool children change in several important ways. Not only does the brain complete its general growth, but it develops various areas associated with specialized mental functions. Many of these become lateralized, as do a number of behaviors, such as handedness. Preschool children experience many more viral infections than older children or adults do, but in our society they tend to remain free of serious illnesses. Early in the preschool period, usually, they acquire daytime bladder and bowel control, and by the end of the period a majority have also acquired nighttime bladder control.*

Motor Skill Development

As a young child grows, she becomes more skilled at basic physical actions. Often a two-year-old can walk only with considerable effort — hence the name *toddler*. But a five-year-old can walk comfortably in a variety of ways: forward and backward, quickly and slowly, skipping and galloping. A five-year-old can do other vigorous things, too, which were impossible a few years earlier. She can run and jump and climb, all with increasing smoothness and variety. She can carry out certain actions that require accuracy, like balancing on one foot, or catching a ball reliably, or drawing a picture.

This section describes in more detail how milestones like these are reached under naturally occurring conditions. Since so-called natural conditions vary a great deal in real life, we actually must take for granted a certain range of conditions. In particular, we assume that children have no significant fears of being active; that they have a reasonably daring attitude, but not an excessively daring one, toward trying out new motor skills; that they are in good health; and that their physical growth has evolved more or less normally. For some children, unfortunately, these conditions are not at all natural (Malina, 1982). For them, therefore, the following descriptions may need to be modified.

Influences on motor development

After describing motor development, we look at the effects of altering such conditions. Can very young children be taught motor skills? Can they become skillful sooner or more fully by receiving training from adults? Will such training affect physical skill development later on in childhood and adolescence? As you will see, the answers to these questions are not definite, but they do have interesting implications for people who care for young children.

Fundamental Motor Skills

Preschool children have obviously moved well beyond the confines of reflex action, which constituted the first motor skills of infancy. From age two to about age five, they experiment with the simple voluntary actions that adults use extensively for their normal activities — actions like walking, running, and jumping. For older individuals, these actions are usually the means to other ends. For very young children, though, they lie very much in the foreground and are frequently goals in themselves. As a result, children often vary their methods for doing such actions; sometimes they walk from the hip, at other times in a sort of marching gait, and at still other times in a sort of shuffle. Such variations make describing a child's skills complicated, but they probably help the child to learn and develop.

In any case, close observation suggests two somewhat contradictory trends. First, given a long enough time, children do eventually improve their basic gross motor skills. As they do so, the skills become much smoother, more predictable, and efficient (Ames et al., 1979). Whereas a very young preschooler may throw a ball by lurching his whole body straight forward, a school-age child will twist his torso just enough to compensate for the forward movement of his throwing arm.

Long-term improvement

Second, over the short or medium term, children's skills do *not* usually improve smoothly or continuously, and frequently they even deteriorate temporarily. Among five-year-olds, for example, about 80 percent can hop up or down a few stairs, and about 90 percent can walk along a balance beam. For the next two or three years, however, these figures do not change significantly: seven- and eight-year-olds do not perform these tasks much better than five-year-olds, and sometimes actually perform worse (DeOreo, 1974). Any preschooler, it seems, actually has these skills on some occasions but not on others. Vacillations apparently

Short-term variation

Even early in the preschool period, some motor skills are acquired through purposeful teaching. But most—such as running—develop through children's own informal activities. (Bohdan Hrynewych/Stock, Boston)

reflect changes in children's motivations to perform from one occasion to the next, and they also result from distractions and explorations. A familiar skill may deteriorate temporarily while a child concentrates on learning a new one or while he searches for a way of combining the new skill with the old one.

Walking and Its Variations From a child's point of view, walking may seem absurd at first: it requires purposely losing balance, then regaining balance fast enough to keep from falling. As older infants, children must still pay attention to these facts, even after a full year or so of practice. Each step is an effort unto itself. Children watch each foot in turn as it launches (or lurches) forward; they may pause after each step before attempting the next. Typically, too, infants are top-heavy, and this requires them to keep their feet far apart, as if straddling a horse, to keep from falling down. In spite of these precautions, though, spills are plentiful in infancy, and walking is often rather slow.

After a year or so of experience, though, children can usually walk without looking at their feet. Around their second or third birthday, their gait becomes more regular and their feet get closer together. Stride — the distance between feet in a typical step — still remains considerably shorter than that of a normal adult, which makes short distances easy to walk but long distances hard for a few more years. A child must take many more steps to reach even nearby destinations, such as the house across the street or the grocery store in the next block.

Running appears early in the preschool years, shortly after walking begins to smooth out. At first it looks more like a hurried walk than a true run, and the child may have trouble stopping herself once she has begun. At first, too, the run may not really involve one of its defining features, namely a brief instant of complete separation from the ground (Wickstrom, 1977). Not until the end of the preschool

Approximate Age	Gross Motor Skill	Fine Motor Skill
2½–3½ years	Walks well; runs in straight line; jumps in air with both feet	Copies a circle; scribbles; can use eating utensils; stacks a few small blocks
3½–4½ years	Skips; hops on one foot; catches large ball	Buttons with large buttons; copies simple shapes; makes simple representational drawings
4½–5½ years	Balances on one foot; runs far without falling; can "swim" in water	Uses scissors; draws people; copies simple letters and numbers; builds complex structures with blocks

Table 8-3 Milestones in Preschool Motor Development

Note: The ages given above are very approximate, and skills vary with the life experiences available to individual children and with the situations in which the skills are displayed.

Source: Ilg et al., 1981; Gesell et al., 1977.

period, around age five, are these problems corrected. By then the child will probably have begun swinging her arms as she strides in order to counterbalance the large twisting motions of her legs. These arm motions also help the child to stop. Without their counterbalancing effect, children go into a sort of uncontrolled spin at the end of the run.

Jumping and Its Variations   At first a jump is more like a fast stretch: the child reaches for the sky rapidly, but his feet fail to leave the ground. Sometime around his second birthday, one foot may finally leave the ground — or even both feet may. Such early successes may be delayed, though, because the child may put his arms backward to help himself take off, as if he were trying to push himself off the floor. Later, perhaps around age three, he shifts to a more efficient arm movement — reaching forward and up as he jumps — which creates a useful upward momentum.

Early jumping

Success in these actions depends partly on what type of jump the child is attempting. Jumping down a step is easier than jumping across a flat distance, and a flat or broad jump is easier than jumping up a step. By age five or so, most children can broad jump across a few feet, although variations among individuals are substantial (Espenschade and Eckert, 1980).

A more complex variation of jumping is hopping. Since hopping uses one foot instead of two, children must have more strength in their jumping leg, and especially good balance in it as well. Not surprisingly, hopping appears later than jumping — usually sometime between children's third and fourth birthdays. Even then they may only succeed at a few hops at a time, and only if they do not need to propel themselves to any particular place. As children's strength and balance improve, they can of course hop longer and begin going places while hopping; a five-year-old, for example, can cover a distance of fifty feet or so in a matter of just seconds. As they perfect skills like these, many five-year-olds also become able to jump rope, a skill that requires precise timing of hops sustained over a period of

Hopping

Riding a tricycle requires a combination of leg coordination and balance. Because not all children have access to tricycles, this skill varies more among individuals than running or walking, for which nearly all children possess the required "equipment." (Leonard Speier)

time. Most children do not become truly accomplished at jumping rope until well into the school years, and many boys never do, since this skill often becomes stereotyped as "girls' play."

Climbing As parents often note, a child may learn to climb stairs even before she learns to walk. At first she simply uses her crawling skills to go up the steps. Soon after she does learn to walk, she applies her new form of locomotion to steps. She walks up in a lock-step or mark-time style, placing one foot up, then bringing the other foot up to the same level before attempting the next level with the original foot. A railing or adult hand to hold helps in trying these actions; not until well into the school years can children manage stairs completely without holding onto anything. By age three or four, with these qualifications, most children can go up stairs fairly smoothly. By then, in fact, many can use their feet alternately, just as adults do.

Going down stairs presents a more difficult challenge than going up, since the child has to look at the large depth into which she is descending, and since she must also lean into the chasm a little each time she takes a step. These facts may account for delays in learning this particular kind of climbing. Often children revert to earlier, more infantile methods when they begin trying to descend stairs, such as sitting down, moving in the mark-time style, or crawling down backward. Even by about age five, some children still dislike descending stairs and will do so only with encouragement from adults. This fact illustrates a common feature of most fun-

Difficulties of descending

The development of some motor skills, such as ballet dancing, require the special efforts of teachers, of parents, and of the children themselves. (Carol Palmer)

damental motor skills: they often depend on children's motivation, courage, and confidence, and not simply on physical maturation.

Throwing and Catching   For infants or toddlers, first throws may happen by accident. The child may just be waving an object and happen to release it suddenly: away it goes. Once intentional throwing begins, though, children actually adopt more stereotyped methods at first than they do later in childhood (Roberton, 1977). At first, for example, they launch all balls in much the same way — usually with a general forward lurch — regardless of the balls' size or weight. As skill develops, however, children vary their movements according to the balls' characteristics; they give more wrist movement to small balls and more arm movement to large ones. At the same time, children begin to vary among themselves even in throwing the same type of ball; some develop a persistent wrist twist over and above the needs of particular balls, whereas others develop a special torso turn all their own (Roberton, 1978).

Early throwing

Catching proceeds through similar phases. Early in the preschool period, children may extend their arms passively to receive an oncoming ball. This method naturally works only if the thrower aims the ball perfectly. By around age four, though, children introduce flexibility to their methods, by moving their hands in last-minute response to the oncoming ball and so forth. By school age, some children have become very skillful at catching: their arms and hands remain flexible until the ball actually arrives, and therefore, can compensate for unexpected angles and speeds as the ball approaches. Not surprisingly, this technique puts far less demand on a thrower to be accurate.

Styles of early catching

Can Fundamental Motor Skills Be Taught?

Fundamental versus specialized skills

Such skills as jumping, throwing, and catching seem to improve as children practice them, which implies that motor skills can be taught just as other skills are. To find out whether this is true, we must distinguish between *fundamental* motor skills and relatively *specialized* motor skills. Fundamental skills are ones that nearly every child learns eventually, simply by participating in human society. Walking, for example, is a fundamental motor skill; so are reaching and grasping. Specialized motor skills are ones that not everyone learns and that require special training, such as ballet dancing, swimming, and ice-skating. Among physically normal children, specialized skills are much more teachable than fundamental skills (Espenschade and Eckert, 1980). The reverse may sometimes be true among children with particular physical handicaps; for them, a normally fundamental skill such as walking may amount to a specially learned achievement.

Perspectives on Research

The Suzuki Method of Learning the Violin

During the last several decades, many preschool children have learned to play the violin according to a method originated by a Japanese violinist, Shinichi Suzuki (1969). The Suzuki method shows that under the right conditions, even very young children can acquire perceptual and motor skills that North Americans ordinarily do not expect from children until the middle years, or even later.

In its classic version, the Suzuki method relies heavily on the child's mother to motivate the child. Even when the child is still an infant, the mother begins playing recordings of great performances for him — mostly of classical works from the eighteenth and nineteenth centuries. These recordings also include repeated playings of twenty particular selections that the child will eventually learn to play on the violin. Sometime after his second birthday, the child begins attending group lessons with other Suzuki students, many of whom are two or three years older and correspondingly more experienced. At first the child mostly observes these other children perform, but he is always encouraged to participate as much as possible.

During this period, the mother is expected to play the violin on a daily basis for her young pre-

school child (and even to get lessons for herself if she needs them). As soon as possible, the two of them begin practicing the violin each day together. After reaching a certain level of proficiency, the child begins individual lessons, but daily practice with his mother continues for many more months, and group sessions continue indefinitely along with the individual lessons.

All of the practice sessions and lessons emphasize "correct" modeling of musical sounds and techniques. Children therefore refine their auditory perception to an unusual degree; they must hear whether their own notes match the approved recordings as well as the sounds made by other students and by their teachers. They also refine the fine motor skills needed to make these sounds: holding a violin bow exactly right, and for precisely the right length of time. The results of such practice often surprise Western musicians: by age six, many Suzuki students can perform simple violin masterpieces by Vivaldi or Mozart. Such great progress is possible partly because the Suzuki method bypasses one standard requirement of Western musical training — namely, learning to read musical notation. Instead of taking time with this rather cogni-

The relationship between fundamental and specialized skills is illustrated well by a classic study of two twins, Jimmy and Johnny. These boys were given different amounts of motor training during infancy and early childhood (McGraw, 1935, 1939). One twin, Jimmy, got systematic, supervised practice in a number of motor skills that varied in complexity all the way from simple rolling over to walking, jumping, and riding a tricycle. Meanwhile, brother Johnny received no special training, although he was allowed to play actively in normal conditions.

How much did Jimmy's training help? For the simpler skills, his special training and practice made no difference. After two years, for example, the brothers walked equally well and jumped equally well. But certain complex skills did respond to training; Jimmy learned to swim better and sooner than Johnny did. Perhaps even more important, Jimmy displayed a more daring, confident attitude in trying new motor skills, even when he showed no particular advantage in actual ability. Presumably the extra confidence helped him later in childhood, but unfortunately the research did not follow these twins that far in life.

---

tive skill, teachers focus fully on auditory perception (developing a "good ear") and fine motor skills.

In spite of its obvious successes, the Suzuki method has its critics (Gardner, 1983, pp. 376–378). Some musicians point out that the official Suzuki curriculum draws on only a narrow range of the world's music, the baroque and romantic styles often popularly associated with classical music. It ignores older, newer, and non-Western styles.

The narrow selection of music might not limit the children's long-run development if it were not also for Suzuki's heavy emphasis on modeling and imitation. By training children only to copy others, argue the critics, the program prevents children from developing personal styles of playing and from acquiring personal preferences for musical selections not in the approved curriculum. This lack of musical independence is aggravated by children's inability to read music. Just as verbal illiteracy forces a child to learn only knowledge that others can tell in person, so musical illiteracy may force a child to perform only music that others can demonstrate or model in person.

For Westerners, though, probably the most difficult part of the Suzuki method to accept is the many demands it places on mothers. Their involvement may seem excessive and unreasonable even though there is no doubt that it can be an extremely effective motivation. As you might suspect, in fact, programs using the Suzuki method in North America often do not aim for as high a level of maternal involvement as has been typical in Japan.

Nonetheless, mothers and children who follow the program usually report enjoying it immensely, and apparently they do not mind the costs in time and energy (Holland, 1982). Presumably Suzuki musicians can eventually learn to read music anyway when they reach school age, in spite of their earlier experience playing by ear — or perhaps they can even learn better *because* of earlier ear training. All in all, the Suzuki method contradicts an impression popular in the West, that early motor and perceptual skills are "too fundamental" to be trained. On the contrary, it seems: auditory perception and fine motor skills can indeed be trained, even in the preschool years. And the results can be a pleasure for everyone.

Since most activities during early childhood emphasize fundamental motor skills rather than specialized ones, some researchers have concluded that it is harder to train young children in motor development than it is to train somewhat older ones (Cratty, 1979; Zaichowsky et al., 1980). According to this viewpoint, children pick up most of their training from naturally occurring, universal events in life. Every child, for example, must get from here to there during infancy and toddlerhood, and this need may not only motivate normal children to learn to walk but give ample practice at this skill as well.

Training in fundamental skills

Nonetheless, even preschool children acquire some skills that are specialized. Certain children learn to swim, and others learn to skate. Neither of these skills happens without special efforts by the children and their teachers. Children respond to training in part because such skills take advantage of their growing abilities to plan and coordinate specific actions. To this extent, therefore, specialized skills are really perceptual and cognitive as well as physical or motor in nature.

Training in specialized skills

As children leave the preschool period and enter the school years, specialized skills may also acquire social qualities, since mastering a unique skill usually confers status and respect on a child and helps to win friends. A good baseball player is usually in demand, for example, and children who know how to swim are more likely to be invited to swimming parties.

Fine Motor Coordination: The Case of Drawing Skills

Not all motor activities of young children involve the strength, agility, and balance of their whole bodies. Many require the coordination of small movements but not strength. Tying shoelaces calls for this **fine motor coordination;** so do washing hands, buttoning and zipping clothing, eating with a spoon, and turning a doorknob.

Importance of drawing skills

One especially widespread fine motor skill among young children is drawing; in North American culture, at least, virtually every young child tries using pens or pencils at some time, and often tries other artistic media as well. The scribbles or drawings that result probably serve a number of purposes. At times they may be used mainly for sensory exploration: a child may want to get the feel of paintbrushes or felt-tip pens. At other times, though, they may express thoughts or feelings; a child may suggest this possibility by commenting, "It's a horse, and it's angry," for example. Children's drawings also probably reflect their knowledge of the world, even though they may not yet have the fine motor skills necessary to convey their knowledge fully. In other words, children's drawings reveal not only fine motor coordination but their self-concept, emotional and social attitudes, and cognitive development.

Representational and nonrepresentational drawings

Drawing shows two overlapping phases of development during the preschool period. From the ages of about two and a half to four, children focus on developing nonrepresentational skills, such as scribbling and the purposeful drawing of simple shapes and designs. Sometime around age four, however, they begin to attempt to represent objects (Kellogg, 1969). Yet even though representational drawings usually follow nonrepresentational ones, the two types also stimulate each other simultaneously. Children often describe their early scribbles as if they

referred to real things, and their practice at portraying real objects helps to develop their nonrepresentational skills further.

Prerepresentational Drawing Around the end of infancy, children begin to scribble. A two-year-old experiments with whatever pen or pencil is available to him, almost no matter what its color or type. In doing so, he behaves both like an infant and like a child. As with an infant, his efforts primarily focus on the activity itself — on the motions and sensations of handling a paintbrush, for example. But like an older child, a two-year-old often cares about the outcome of these activities: "That's a Mommy," he says, whether it looks much like one or not. Contrary to a popular view of children's art, even very young children are concerned not only with the process of drawing but with the product as well (Gibson and Yonas, 1968).

The child's interest in the results of his drawing show up in the patterns he imposes on even his earliest scribbles. Sometimes he will fill up particular parts of the page quite intentionally — the whole left side, say, or the complete middle third. And he often emphasizes particular categories of strokes — lots of straight diagonals, or lots of counterclockwise loops (Golomb, 1981). Different children select different types of motions for emphasis, so the motions are less like universal stages than like elements of a personal style. Even after a child learns to combine simpler strokes and motions, his combinations remain unique. Some children

Patterns in early drawings

Figure 8-3 *Samples of Preschool Children's Drawings*

make many mandalas, or circles with a cross through them, as shown in Figure 8-3 (Goodnow, 1977; Kellogg, 1969). Others make shapes that they call letters, even though they may not actually look like letters.

In general, then, the scribbling of very young children resembles their early babbling. All infants vocalize, and most infants produce the same overall range of sounds. But the particular phonemes selected by one child escape prediction; at any point in time, the choices often seem to come out of nowhere. Likewise, given the opportunity, all children scribble, at least in North American society; and most children produce a similar range of lines and curves. But any one child selects a unique set. Predicting her selection proves almost impossible (Gardner, 1980; Goodnow, 1977), but the very uncertainty constitutes one of the delights of working with young children.

Representational Drawing   While preschool children improve their scribbling skills, they also develop an interest in representing people, objects, and events in their drawings. This interest often far precedes their ability to do so. A three-year-old may assign meanings to scribbles or blobs in his drawing: one blob may be "Mama," and another may be "our house." Events may happen to these blobs, too: Mama may be "going to the store" or "looking for me."

Attributing the "real" to drawings

During the preschool years, and for a long time thereafter, the child's visual representations are limited by her comparatively rudimentary fine motor skills. Apparently she knows more, visually speaking, than her hands can portray with pens or brushes. Prefabricated materials suggest this possibility. Given an outline of a person and some cutouts of body parts (nose, mouth, eyes, and so on), a young preschooler can assemble a human being quite skillfully, putting most of the parts where they ought to go. Given a pencil and paper, though, she may still produce a person that looks like a tadpole with two legs: a circle with dots for eyes, perhaps, and sticks for legs (Fucigna and Wolf, 1981).

Effects of motor skill level

Early representations, then, do not show poor observation by children of the visual realities around them. More likely they show good but approximate representations that are possible with the graphic skills available to the child. If a child has practiced a particular set of loops and curves a lot, then he uses these to portray objects and events; he cannot in fact do otherwise. He may furthermore assign meanings to his loops and curves that often go well beyond their visual content. The tadpole person, for example, may represent both a head and a torso, even though it looks like only a head (Freeman, 1980). Often, too, a child will describe his tadpole drawing by mentioning many more body parts than actually can be seen in the picture. And sometimes he can draw a much more sophisticated human being if simply asked to do so; the tadpole, in other words, functions as a visual shorthand in the child's spontaneous drawings.

Cross-cultural Differences in Picture Perception   Of course, the tadpole may also be a culturally conventional shorthand. From society, perhaps, children learn particular ways of depicting human beings and other objects, in much the way they learn particular children's games or particular linguistic expressions. If so, then children around the world should vary a lot in the content and style of what they

Variations in picture content

draw, as well as in what they see in others' drawings. Do children from Africa and Asia make their first human beings look like tadpoles? And whether they do or not, would they recognize North American tadpole drawings as representations of people?

The answers are mixed. What children draw does depend, not surprisingly, on what they see in the world around them. If their world contains cars and tall buildings, then these objects are relatively likely to turn up in their drawings. If their world contains oxen and grass houses, then they will more often draw oxen and grass houses (Winner, 1982). Children who are encouraged to draw flowers in school tend to draw more flowers, and those who are encouraged to draw airplanes draw airplanes. To this extent, culture makes a difference in learning to draw.

But not all aspects of children's drawings show variation among cultures. One *Constancy in depth* example is the perception of depth in pictures. Bantu children and adults from *perception* South Africa, for example, have no exposure to drawings of any kind in their normal lives. Yet when shown ordinary line drawings of outdoor scenes, they have no

---

A Talk with Jimmy's Mother

Physical Development in the Preschool Years

This interview was conducted over coffee in Carol Levin's kitchen. Her three-year-old son, Jimmy, was taking a nap in his room.

INTERVIEWER: What types of active play does Jimmy do?

CAROL: He likes building. He's in a building phase. He builds with big blocks a lot. He also loves to play with [plastic blocks that snap together]. He builds all kinds of great structures with those.... We have also been doing some hammering and nailing in the garage with scrap lumber.

INTERVIEWER: Can Jimmy hammer a nail if you start it for him?

CAROL: Yes. He hammers and saws.... He also loves digging dirt.

INTERVIEWER: When he digs, is it for the joy of digging? Or is he planning on making something with it?

CAROL: He seems to have some-

thing going on. He digs with earth-moving equipment and shovels and pails. He likes the sandbox, but likes to dig just in the dirt out in the yard if we let him.

INTERVIEWER: What else does he do?

CAROL: There is a little bike that he rides. It's a two-wheeler with training wheels, but he has trouble with it because it doesn't work very well. He climbs more than he ever did. At the playground he'll climb up "climbs." He climbs trees at home.

INTERVIEWER: Does he sometimes get so high that he can't get down?

CAROL: No, he always gets down. He brings ladders over to the apple tree and he puts that against the tree and climbs up and hangs out there and swings off the lower branches.

INTERVIEWER: Does he run a lot?

CAROL: Yes. In the house especially. He runs everywhere. He runs more than he walks.

INTERVIEWER: What about things like throwing a ball?

CAROL: He has a good arm. He always has. Even when he was younger he could throw. He throws straight. He plays once in a while when we play baseball and he'll bat the ball.

INTERVIEWER: Can he hit it?

CAROL: Yes, he has hit it. He doesn't hit it consistently, but he tries. His new interest is croquet. I have no idea where he picked this up, but he takes a rock and a stick and says he is playing croquet.

INTERVIEWER: How about his play with smaller things like puzzles or drawing?

CAROL: He's never been a puzzle kid. He never likes to do puzzles. He draws more now. He makes his letter *J* and he scribbles on paper and comes up with fantastic stories about what they are. He doesn't draw things yet, but after he scrib-

trouble discerning the depth intended by such pictures; they know, that is, which objects are supposed to be near the front of the picture and which ones are in the background (Hagan and Jones, 1978).

Neither do the fine motor skills for drawing show much cultural variation. Tibetan children easily learn to make complex drawings with Western-style crayons. Like the Bantus, they lack exposure to pictorial drawings, yet one study found that they needed only a few hours to catch up to the skill levels of North American children of equivalent ages (Gardner, 1980). After this much practice, the school-age children made rather realistic drawings of trees and houses, though of course these objects looked like the ones that Tibetan children knew rather than like the North American versions.

Checkpoint *Preschool children mostly acquire fundamental motor skills rather than specialized motor skills. Walking and running become more efficient and*

---

bles he'll look at it and tell you something about it. What's on his mind.

INTERVIEWER: I would like to move to a different topic now. What was Jimmy's toilet training like?

CAROL: A nightmare. We started him too young. He fought us all the way. Plus he's had a physical problem with his colon that we only found out about recently. For the past two years, he has either been constipated or had diarrhea for long periods of time. He's getting medication now to soften his stool and the doctor says his colon will eventually be back to normal. This problem, coupled with his reluctance to be toilet trained, has not made it easy.

INTERVIEWER: When did he become toilet trained?

CAROL: As soon as he turned three — almost the day after he turned three — he decided to give up diapers and he toilet trained himself. Which I guess is what many kids do.

INTERVIEWER: So you had a sense that he actually made a decision?

CAROL: Yes. Because he stopped fighting. He just didn't want to fight us any more. And not only did he stop using diapers in the daytime, he immediately stopped using them at night, too. . . . He never wakes up in the night, and he never wets the bed. Something just clicked in him. Once in a while we have an accident, but that is because he has the diarrhea problem and he can't always hold it in.

INTERVIEWER: How has he responded to that situation?

CAROL: It often occurs in public places because he tells us too late that he has to go to the toilet and it takes too long to get there. We were at a fair and we were riding on a ride and we were having a wonderful time and all of a sudden he jumped off and he said, "I pooped in my pants." It's been really hard on him. He's very self-conscious and embarrassed about it. And he gets negative attention for it because we're so tired of having accidents. But this was a couple of months ago and things seem to be going better now.

Follow-up Questions

1. What *fundamental* and *fine* motor skills does Jimmy display? How typical are they of a child his age?

2. Based on your reading of the chapter, how typical has Jimmy's development of bladder and bowel control been of preschoolers in general? Explain.

3. What challenges might Jimmy's physical development create for his parents?

graceful; jumping and hopping become more like older children's attempts; climbing stairs becomes possible, and later so does descending; throwing and catching become more accurate. Some aspects of these skills can be fostered explicitly by adults, but others cannot. Among the fine motor skills that develop rapidly during the preschool years are drawing skills. At first children make scribbles, but they soon begin using drawings to represent various objects, including people. The content of representational drawings depends somewhat on what children have experienced seeing. Depth perception of pictures shows constancy across cultures, however, as does motor skill at using drawing implements.

Sex Differences in Physical Development

In spite of wide individual differences, preschool boys and girls develop at almost exactly the same average rates (Pissanos et al., 1983). This applies to practically any motor skill of which young children are capable, and it applies to both gross motor skills and fine motor skills. Any nursery classroom is therefore likely to contain children of both sexes who can run very well, and children of both sexes who can paint well or tie their shoelaces without help. This is especially true among younger preschool children, those of three or four.

Slight average difference between the sexes

By the time children begin kindergarten at age five, slight differences in physical development and motor skills appear, but only if the size and performance of very large numbers of children are averaged (Tanner, 1978b). Across an entire city or state, for example, about 5 percent of five-year-old boys are slightly larger than *any* girls in that city or state. About the same proportion (though not necessarily the same actual boys) may develop stronger arms and shoulders than *any* girls in the region, and as a result may be able to throw or hit a ball farther. The other 95 percent, however, will find themselves better than some members of both sexes and worse than other members of both sexes.

Likewise, a small percentage of girls in a large region will outperform *any* boys in the same geographic region at motor tasks that require balance and coordination, such as skipping and standing on one foot for a long time. But most will not excel the other sex in this way; instead they will find themselves somewhere in the middle of a distribution of children of both sexes.

Significance of gender differences

Of course, even these small numbers of excellent performers may contribute to the reputations of their genders. Simply by their unusual appearance and performance, for example, the few very large, muscular boys may create the (mistaken) impression that boys in general are larger and more muscular than girls. And likewise for the unusually coordinated girls: their uniqueness may contribute to the stereotype that girls tend to be better coordinated than boys.

Much of the impression of gender differences in children's growth and motor development probably also comes from differences in how preschool children

On the average, boys and girls develop motor skills at almost the same rate during the preschool years. (left, Robert Kalman/The Image Works; right, Rodney Van Gogh/The Picture Cube)

spend their time. Compared with girls, preschool boys do spend more time in active and rough-and-tumble play for example; and girls spend more time doing quiet activities such as drawing or playing with stuffed animals (Fagot and Kronsberg, 1982). These differences may give the impression that boys are incapable, or at least less capable, of fine motor skills and that girls are physically weaker.

Perhaps such differences do develop for some children by the end of the school years, simply as a result of differences in practice that accumulate over a period of years. Perhaps, too, boys choose active play partly for genetic or hormonal reasons. But in any event, five-year-olds have only begun to accumulate these differences in motor experience and to make appropriately gender-typed choices in their play. Taken as groups, preschool boys and girls do not really differ very much.

Checkpoint *Boys and girls differ slightly in rates of physical growth during the preschool years, but the differences are far smaller than those among children as individuals. Even slight differences in motor abilities, as well as differences in daily behavior, may create reputations that contribute to gender stereotypes.*

Effects of Children's Physical Growth on Adults

The physical and motor developments that affect a child during the preschool years also affect the adults in the child's life — most notably, his parents or other care-givers. The changes in the child create, or at least encourage, major changes in how these people deal with him (Maccoby, 1984).

Consider, for example, the changes in size that preschool children experience. A two-year-old is often still small enough to be literally handled. When necessary, his parents can pick him up and move him from one place to another, physically remove him from danger, and carry him (at least partway!) if a distance is too far for him to walk. Showing feelings at this age is a relatively physical activity as well: a two-year-old is usually still small enough to cuddle or to spank. In these ways, he still has the properties of a physical object, though obviously he has truly human qualities as well.

By age five, a child has often outgrown these physical interactions, not only figuratively but literally. His parents or other adults may still lift and cuddle him sometimes in play or in an emergency, but they probably are beginning to avoid doing so on a regular basis. It is not just that such handling may be undignified for the parents or humiliating for the child; to a significant extent, the child may now simply be too bulky and tall. More and more rarely can parents save a child from danger by picking him up suddenly, or speed him along a long hallway by carrying him piggy-back. They must somehow get the child to do these things for himself.

Usually, of course, parents succeed at this task. By age five, the child can think and talk about his own actions much more than before, and his improvements help him guide his own actions. The handling that used to be literal now becomes mostly figurative; now *handling* means negotiating and discussing with the child, not lifting him up or carting him around.

Increasing physical competence

More than sheer physical growth brings about these changes. By age five or so, the child has also improved various motor skills quite a lot. Walking, for example, poses much less of a problem than it did just a few years before, which is fortunate for the child's parents, since they find themselves expecting much more walking from the child anyway. It is fortunate for the child, too, since she now finds it easier to comply with these raised expectations.

Improvements in motor skills also change the agenda for the child's daily activities. A two-year-old may spend a good part of her day experimenting with fundamental skills: walking from one room to another, for example, or tearing toilet paper to shreds, or taking pots and pans out of a cupboard. These activities are often embedded in an active social and cognitive life: the child may smile (or frown) at her parents while she works, and she may "talk" about what she is doing as well. But the motor aspects of her activities absorb a significant part of her attention throughout the day. The child may return repeatedly to a staircase, for instance, as if compelled to get the hang of climbing it; no reward needs to lie at the top step, except the satisfaction of a job well done.

A two-year-old's parents must therefore spend significant time making sure that the child comes to no physical grief in her motor explorations. They must make

The new motor skills that preschoolers develop bring with them new risks, and create new safety concerns for their parents and other caretakers. What hazards may be waiting for these three-year-olds? (Susan Woog Wagner/Photo Researchers)

sure that the child does not fall down the stairs, or splash into the toilet bowl, or discover a sharp knife among the pots. Their role as safety experts can dominate their contacts with the child, particularly if the child is active.

By the end of the preschool period, though, minute-to-minute physical surveillance recedes in importance. A concern with safety remains, of course, but it is more abstract than before; rules about dangers make their appearance ("Don't climb on that fence; it's rickety"), along with the hope that a five-year-old can remember and follow the rules at least some of the time. The shift toward rules also results from increasing confidence in the child's motor skills. Now parents are apt to believe that their child can go up and down stairs, for example, without stumbling very often. Less parental surveillance

The child's motor development has contributed to this belief, and to the increasingly indirect methods of surveillance that go with it. Overworked parents may sometimes think to themselves, "She's five now and ought to be able to handle the stairs by herself." But to a large extent they also think, "I have seen her handle the stairs pretty well, so now I do not have to watch her every time." To this extent the child herself has created a new, more mature child-rearing practice in her parents.

During the preschool period, many parents discover a special need for patience in their dealings with their children. Simple actions like tying shoelaces or putting on socks may take longer than before, simply because children now insist on doing many of these things themselves. For similar reasons, walking to the store may now take longer; a three- or four-year-old may prefer to push the stroller rather than ride in it, thus slowing everyone down. And preschoolers may have their own agenda on a walk, such as noticing little rocks on the sidewalk or airplanes in the Increased parental patience

Table 8-4 *Common Accidents, Remedies, and Preventions Among Preschoolers*

Accidents	What to Do	How to Prevent
Drowning	Unless you are trained in water safety, extend a stick or other device. Use heart massage and mouth-to-mouth breathing when and as long as needed.	Teach children to swim as early in life as possible; supervise children's swim sessions closely; stay in shallow water.
Choking on small objects	If child is still breathing, do not attempt to remove object; see a doctor instead. If breathing stops, firmly strike child twice on small of back. If this does not help, grab child from behind, put your fist just under her ribs, and pull upward sharply several times.	Do not allow children to put small objects in mouth; teach them to eat slowly, taking small bites; forbid vigorous play with objects or food in mouth.
Cuts with serious bleeding	Raise cut above level of heart; apply pressure with cloth or bandage; if necessary, apply pressure to main arteries of limbs.	Remove sharp objects from play areas; insist on shoes wherever ground or floor may contain sharp objects; supervise children's use of knives.
Fractures	Keep injured limb immobile; see a doctor.	Discourage climbing and exploring in dangerous places, such as trees and construction sites; allow bicycles only in safe areas.
Burns	Pour cold water over burned area; keep it clean; then cover with *sterile* bandage. See a doctor if burn is extensive.	Keep matches out of reach of children; keep children well away from fires and hot stoves.
Poisons	On skin or eye, flush with plenty of water; if in stomach, phone poison control center doctor for instructions; induce vomiting only for selected substances.	Keep dangerous substances out of reach of children; throw away poisons when no longer needed. Keep syrup of ipecac in home to induce vomiting, but use *only* if advised by doctor.
Animal bites	Clean and cover with bandage; see a doctor.	Train children when and how to approach family pets; teach them caution in approaching unfamiliar animals.

(Continued)

Accidents	What to Do	How to Prevent
Insect bites	Remove stinger, if possible; cover with paste of bicarbonate of soda (for bees) or a few drops of vinegar (for wasps and hornets).	Encourage children to recognize and avoid insects that sting, as well as their nests; encourage children to keep calm in presence of stinging insects.
Poisonous plants (e.g., poison ivy)	Remove affected clothing; wash affected skin with strong alkali soap as soon as possible.	Teach children to recognize toxic plants; avoid areas where poisonous plants are growing.

Source: Brody, 1982.

sky, which differs from parents' goals. On good days these behaviors offer some of the joys of raising children, but on bad days even well-meaning parents often lose their tempers over them.

Physical development changes recreation and play, too. At age two, the child probably cannot play baseball — in spite of parental hopes and occasional jokes. By age five, though, he may make something of a start at it. At age two, he may enjoy looking at pictures in a book and drawing a few lines of his own; by age five, he may spend long periods making elaborate pictures himself. At age two, he may listen and bounce to music in a general way; by age five, he may swing to it with more refined, rhythmical movements.

New recreations

These new skills often have teachable elements to them, and that fact creates a new sort of contact with parents and with others who care for the child. Now the adults can begin showing and encouraging the practice of new skills in a more active, sustained, and focused way than before; depending on their personal interests and values, in fact, they may even feel obliged to do so. Both adult and child may find such teaching and learning easier, since they no longer have to monitor every fundamental physical action of the child. A few years before, one false step might literally have made a young child fall. But now these terms have shifted to metaphorical meanings. False steps for a five-year-old usually mean mistakes, not actual physical stumbling; and while a fall may still mean a physical tumble, it is also beginning to refer to a failure.

Checkpoint *The increasing physical competence of preschool children causes their parents to encourage them to be more self-reliant. At the same time, children's increasing mobility causes parents to monitor their children's safety closely, and to make and revise rules for children to follow to insure their safety. These new demands can sometimes try parents' patience, but they also reflect the increasing maturity of family relationships during this period.*

Summary of Major Ideas

Normal Physical Development

1. Between ages two and five, growth slows down and children take on more adult bodily proportions.

2. Usually growth is rather smooth during the preschool period. Genetic and ethnic background affect its overall rate, as does the quality of nutrition and children's experiences of illness.

3. During the past hundred years, children in industrialized countries have tended to grow larger and faster, although the trend may now be slowing.

4. If children fall behind in growth because of poor nutrition or hormonal deficiencies, they can often achieve catch-up growth, if slow growth has not been too severe or prolonged.

Brain Development and Other Bodily Changes

5. Between ages two and five, the brain completes its overall growth by developing new fibers and myelin sheaths.

6. Although the brain continues to function as a whole, certain areas develop special importance for particular mental and motor functions.

7. During the preschool period, children first begin showing hemispheric lateralization in certain mental and motor functions.

8. Minor viral illnesses occur repeatedly during these years, although young children rarely get seriously ill.

9. Children tend to achieve daytime bladder and bowel control early in the preschool period, and nighttime bladder control late in this period.

Motor Skill Development

10. Preschoolers acquire and refine many fundamental motor skills, including walking, running, jumping, hopping, climbing, throwing, and catching.

11. Adults can teach some motor skills, but many seem to develop simply through natural daily experiences of young children.

12. Fine motor skills such as drawing also emerge during the preschool years.

13. Children's drawings begin with scribbles or prerepresentational drawings, and later include representational drawings as well.

14. The content of drawings varies widely with children's cultural and personal experiences, but their per-

ception of depth and motor skills may develop fairly universally around the world.

Sex Differences in Physical Development

15. Boys and girls differ only slightly in growth and motor performance during the preschool period; individual differences are far greater than gender differences.

16. The slight differences in performance, and somewhat larger differences in daily motor behavior, may contribute to gender stereotypes about motor ability.

Effects of Children's Physical Growth on Adults

17. Between ages two and five, children's increasing physical competence causes parents to monitor their safety in new ways and to make up and revise rules for their children to follow.

18. Preschoolers' increasing physical independence can challenge parents' patience in a variety of situations.

19. In general, children's growth and motor development help them to learn about their world, and help parents to teach their children as well.

Key Terms

velocity *(307)*	motor cortex *(317)*
reactive attachment	Broca's area *(317)*
disorder *(308)*	hemispheric
secular trend *(311)*	lateralization *(317)*
hybrid vigor *(312)*	dichotic listening *(317)*
endocrine glands *(313)*	lateralized
catch-up growth *(313)*	behaviors *(319)*
visual cortex *(317)*	fine motor
auditory cortex *(317)*	coordination *(330)*
Wernicke's area *(317)*	

What Do You Think?

1. If a child is relatively tall at age four or five, do you think that she will still be relatively tall later in childhood? What about in adulthood? Explain.

2. Why do you suppose that human beings tend to have a preferred hand? Speculate about why this quality may have evolved.

3. How (if at all) should parents and care-givers try to train toddlers to use the toilet? Give some reasons for your recommendations.

4. What ways do you think would work best in fostering the development of motor skills in preschool children? Do you consider these methods to be genuine teaching or not?

5. As stated in the chapter, young children clearly affect the behavior of parents. Do you think that these effects cause permanent psychological changes in parents? Or do they disappear when the children get older?

For Further Reading

Frost, J. *Children's Play and Playgrounds.* Boston: Allyn and Bacon, 1979.

This book relates current knowledge about children's play and motor development to the design of children's playgrounds. It describes the value of active motor play, the best ways of encouraging such play outdoors, and various safety precautions one must take in providing effective playgrounds.

Gazzaniga, M. *The Social Brain.* New York: Basic Books, 1985.

This book describes most of what we know about brain lateralization and its effects on behavior. The author proposes an interesting (but still controversial) theory about the effects of lateralization on personality development: that we each develop two "selves," one for each half of our brain, and that coordinating the experiences of these two "selves" poses a constant challenge to us as whole human beings.

Paley, V. *Superheroes in the Doll Corner.* Chicago: University of Chicago Press, 1984.

The author describes her experiences as a kindergarten teacher, focusing on how her students used their free active play periods. As she points out, the children did not differ much in inherent physical abilities, but boys and girls displayed wide differences in their choice of large-motor activities and dramatic play. Their choice of activities, not physical differences, created different impressions or stereotypes about each sex.

Winner, E. *Invented Worlds: The Psychology of the Arts.* Cambridge, Mass.: Harvard University Press, 1983.

The author describes the development of artistic performance in three major realms: literature, music, and visual art. The latter topic relates especially well to the discussion of children's drawings in this chapter. It explains competing theories of how children acquire artistic sensitivity and the motor skills needed for drawing; it evaluates the evidence for stage theories of the development of drawing skills; and it discusses cross-cultural comparisons of the development of children's art.

Chapter

9

The Preschool Years: Cognitive Development

Focusing Questions

- What are the special strengths and limitations of preschoolers' thinking?
- How does the syntax used by preschool children differ from that used by older children and adults?
- What processes probably account for language acquisition, and how can adults assist those processes?
- How well do preschool children perceive their environments, compared both to infants and to older children?

WHILE A CHILD GROWS physically, another miracle begins: when he is just about three years old, he begins representing the world to himself and others. For one thing, he can talk, and understand much of others' speech as well. "Kitty run!" the boy says, pointing to the local cat. "Yes," replies his father. "She's chasing a bird." The young boy nods and says, "Bird gone now. Bad kitty?" and he looks to his father for confirmation. "It's okay this time," the father says. "The bird flew away soon enough." Unlike an infant, this child does not really need to handle or manipulate the objects he is thinking about. He can comment on the cat even after it disappears.

For another thing, a young preschool child can re-enact experiences in new and creative ways, through **make-believe**, a form of pretend play in which he simulates people, objects, animals, and activities in his efforts to understand them. This child, for example, may "become" the cat — crouching down, ready to pounce — the next day. If asked about what he is doing, he probably will know that it is "just pretend." He is not likely to think that he has actually become a cat, no matter how convincing his performance. In make-believe, he is beginning both to create symbols and to understand them.

Even though his symbolic or representational skills still leave much to be desired, they mark a major achievement. This chapter and the next will look at several kinds of these skills, and at how young children make use of them. Chapter 9 concentrates on thinking, or problem solving, and on early language acquisition. Chapter 10 concentrates on more social activities, such as play, family relationships, and early relationships outside the family. As we shall see, these topics do not divide as easily in real life as they do in textbooks.

Thinking in Preschoolers

Preschoolers' thinking has a mixed, in-between quality: in some ways it is still like that of an infant, but in others it is like a schoolchild's thinking. This quality occurs in nearly every aspect of cognition, but here we will look at just a few, especially egocentrism, animism, classification skills, and reversibility. Other major aspects of cognitive development (for example, memory and attention) change importantly during the preschool years, too, but for convenience we will save major discussion of them for Chapter 12. The aspects of cognition considered here stem from the observations and theorizing of Jean Piaget. As pointed out below, though, recent studies of children's thinking have significantly modified his ideas about these aspects.

Piaget's Preoperational Stage

At about the age of two, according to Piaget, children enter a new stage in their cognitive development (Piaget, 1963). Infancy has left them with several important accomplishments, such as the belief that objects have permanent existence. It has also left them with the capacity to set and follow simple goals, as when they purposely remove all the clothes from every drawer in their house or apartment, and with the knowledge that their senses are integrated or all deal with the same world — now children know that hearing their mother in the next room means that they probably can see her soon, and that seeing her probably also means that they will hear from her.

The preoperational stage — roughly ages two through seven — extends and transforms these skills. During this stage, children become increasingly proficient at using **symbols,** which are words or actions that stand for something else. During this stage, too, children extend their belief in object permanence to include **identities,** or constancies, of many types: a serving of milk remains the same milk even if a parent transfers it from one glass to another, and a flower growing out of the sidewalk remains the same flower even though its growth changes its appearance from day to day.

Preoperational children also sense many **functional relationships,** or variations in their environments that normally occur together. Preschool children usually know, for example, that the hungrier they are, the more they will want to eat; and that the bigger they are, the stronger they tend to be; and that the faster they walk, the sooner they will arrive somewhere. Of course they still do not know the precise functions or relationships in these examples — exactly how *much* faster they will arrive if they walk a particular amount faster. But they do know that a relationship exists.

These are all cognitive strengths of preschool children, and they mark cognitive advances over infancy. But as the *pre-* in the term *preoperational* implies, Piaget's original theorizing actually focused on the limitations of children's thinking during early childhood. He pointed out that from age two to seven, children often confuse their own points of view with those of other people, that they cannot classify objects and events logically, and that they often are misled by single features of their experiences. Taken together, these limitations distinguish preschool children from school-age children. They are important enough to deserve discussion, but before we get to them, let us look in more detail at the most achievement of the preoperational period: the child's use of symbols.

Achievements of the preoperational stage

Limitations of the preoperational stage

Preschoolers' play often relies on their growing abilities to represent objects and events symbolically. A groove in the sand may become a canal and a sand ridge may become a dock or a castle. (Dennis Mansell)

Symbolic Thought

As we just noted, *symbols* are words, objects, or behaviors that stand for something else. They take this role not because of their intrinsic properties, but because of the intentions of the people who use them. A drinking straw is just a hollow tube, and does not become a symbol until a preschooler places it in the middle of a mound of sand and declares it a birthday candle. Likewise, the sound /bahks/ lacks symbolic meaning unless we all agree that it refers to a hollow object with corners: *box*. Some words, objects, and behaviors (such as the sound /bahks/) are usually intended symbolically, but others (such as sneezing) often are not.

Nature of symbols

Probably the most significant cognitive achievement of the preoperational period is the emergence of **symbolic thought,** the ability to think by making one object or action stand for another. Throughout their day, two-year-olds use language symbolically, as when they say "Milk!" to procure a white, drinkable substance from the refrigerator. They also use symbolic thought in make-believe play, by pretending to be people or creatures other than themselves. By about the age of four, children often include not only actions (getting down on all fours) but objects (a table napkin for a saddle) and words (saying "Neigh!" in a loud voice) as symbolism in such play.

Significance of symbolic thought

Symbolic thinking helps preschool children in three ways. First, it gives them convenient ways of remembering objects and experiences. If a young child can recall the word *swing,* she can more easily recall the pleasant experience she had sitting on a board suspended from two chains. Second, symbols help young children to think and solve problems about their experiences. Suppose, for example, that a child sees two four-footed, furry pets outdoors, and wonders how they are different. She can probably solve this problem easily if she knows a few relevant symbols, such as the words *dog, cat, large,* and *small.*

Third, symbols help children to communicate what they know, even after they have had an experience. Having gone to the store, they can convey this experience to others either in words ("I went shopping") or through pretend play ("Let's play store, and I'll be the clerk."). By its nature, communication fosters social relationships among children; but it also fosters cognitive development, by allowing individual children to learn from the experiences of others. More precisely, communication allows individuals to learn from the symbolic representations of others' experiences.

Not surprisingly, these benefits do not occur all at once. Preschool children need time and practice to develop symbolic skills to high levels of proficiency. Piaget recognized this fact by dividing the preoperational period into two substages, the preconceptual phase and the intuitive phase. In the **preconceptual phase** — which corresponds to ages two to four — children begin using symbolic thinking widely, but they are still limited in its use; they confuse their own thoughts with those of other people, and think that objects and events are constructed primarily for their own benefit. When they enter the **intuitive phase,** between the ages of four and seven, they begin to overcome these limitations — but not completely; and in any case, their thinking in the intuitive phase remains overly reliant on single features or cues in their experiences. In the lives of most children, the two phases actually overlap a lot, and the distinction between them is therefore helpful mostly in sorting out the features of the larger preoperational stage.

Preoperational substages

Egocentrism in Young Children

Egocentrism refers to the inability of a person to distinguish between his or her own point of view and that of another person. It is literally a centering on the self in thinking. As used here, the term does *not* mean a motivation to be selfish at the expense of others; such an attitude presupposes a knowledge of differences among individuals that young children usually do not have. Instead, egocentrism stems more from **perceptual dominance** or **centration** — the tendency (common among preschoolers) to focus on only one aspect of an object or situation and to ignore other aspects. Perceptual dominance or centration occurs, for example, when a child thinks that the volume of a glass of milk depends entirely on how tall the glass is and forgets to notice how wide it is.

Young children think egocentrically sometimes, but not always, as illustrated by one classic problem posed by Piaget, in which children sat at a table on which models of three mountains had been constructed (see Figure 9-1). Piaget asked each child how a doll would see the three mountains if the doll sat at various positions around the table. A three-year-old — one of Piaget's preoperational children — commonly believed that the doll saw the layout no differently from the way he did himself; given several drawings of mountains from which to pick the doll's

Preschoolers' perspective

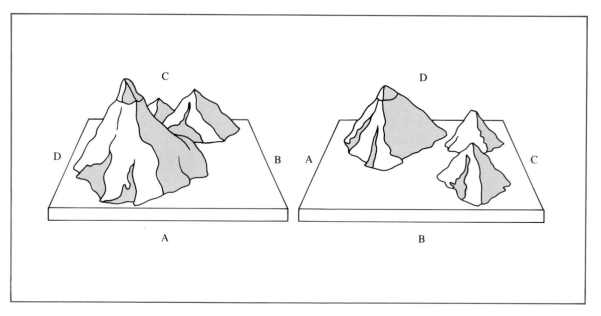

Figure 9–1 *Piaget's*
Three Mountains
Experiment

view, the child tended to choose the one that simply reproduced his own view-point, rather than some other perspective (Piaget and Inhelder, 1967).

With some modifications, though, even young children adopt others' perspectives on a task like this (Donaldson, 1978). In one variation, four-year-olds were shown a table with two partitions that formed a cross, as shown in Figure 9-2 (Donaldson, 1978). At the table, too, were two dolls, one dressed as a policeman and the other dressed as a boy. The policeman was put in various positions around the table, and the child was asked to place the boy doll behind the partitions where

**Modifications that
improve perspective**

the policeman could not see it. According to the experimenter, the policeman was trying to chase and catch the boy. The preschool child thus had to imagine the perspective of the policeman — much the same challenge as in Piaget's mountain experiment.

Preschool children in this experiment proved quite skillful at taking the policeman's perspective, even when the task was made more complicated by having two police dolls search for the boy doll at the same time — requiring the children in effect to coordinate *three* perspectives at once. Why the difference in performance on this task and on Piaget's? The policeman situation may have seemed more familiar, perhaps, and therefore easier to solve. Few children literally have been chased by a policeman, but most have been chased by their friends in play. To this extent, then, the children may have practiced the policeman task in their own lives. At the same time, they may have felt more motivated to solve the police-chase version, since it may have seemed less arbitrary than Piaget's version.

In situations requiring communication, too, young children show definite, but incomplete, signs of egocentrism. A variety of studies — along with much common observation — show that preschoolers often explain tasks and events rather

**Poor communication
skills**

poorly (Flavell et al., 1981). In describing a drawing to someone, they may leave out crucial terms or relationships. They may leave out so much, in fact, that copy-

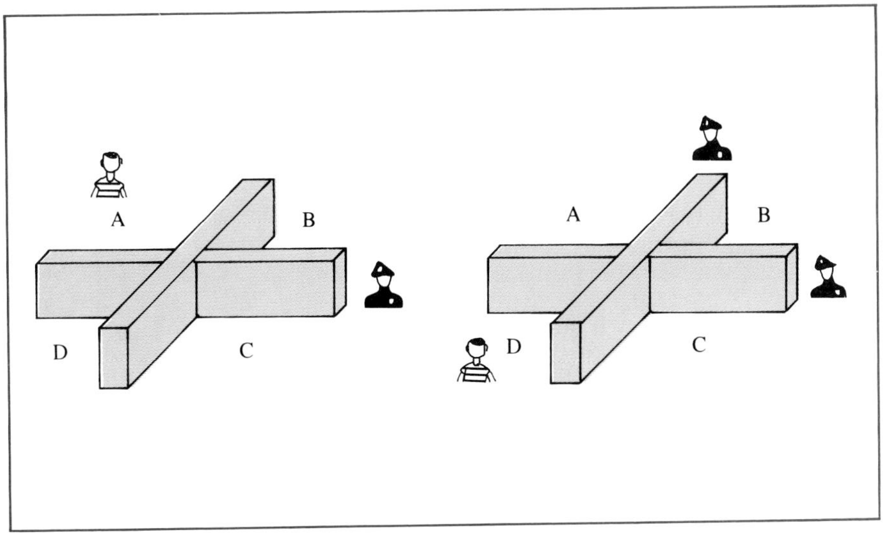

Figure 9-2 *Variation on Three Mountains Experiment*

ing a simple diagram according to their instructions is virtually impossible, no matter how sensitive the listener may be.

On the other hand, preschool children do sometimes show awareness of confusion and ignorance when it is expressed by others. One study found that preschool children explained a drawing better to a person who was blindfolded than to someone who was actually looking at the drawing while the child was explaining it (Maratsos, 1973). The blindfold apparently signaled or emphasized the gap in perspective between the child's knowledge and the listener's, and encouraged the child to consider the other's needs more carefully when talking.

But there are limits to such sensitivity. In another communication study, young children heard some good and some poor explanations of a task, and these were accompanied by expressions of understanding or confusion from the listener (Beal and Flavell, 1983). The listener's responses were counterfeit, however: they were purposely manipulated so as *not* to correspond to the actual quality of the explanations that he had heard. Later the preschool children were asked to evaluate the adequacy of the explanations. In these circumstances, they evaluated the explanations more according to how well the listener thought he understood than by the quality of the explanations. If the listener claimed to have understood, then the child was likely to believe him or her, even when the actual explanation could not possibly have been adequate, and even when the child could not understand the explanation.

Limits of sensitivity to others

Taken together, these studies suggest that egocentrism exists in early childhood, but is not always in evidence. Preschool children do recognize the existence of different perspectives and sometimes make allowances for that fact. They judge other people's comprehension separately from their own comprehension, and separately from the intrinsic qualities of utterances. On the other hand, they often fail to realize just how badly people can misunderstand each other even in simple, ordinary communication — as when one of these four-year-olds tries to teach a friend how to tie shoelaces:

JILL: You want to learn to tie laces?

KATE: Okay. *(She stares in another direction.)*

JILL: First you make a . . . make a . . . Do this. *(She makes a loop.)* Do you see?

KATE *(still staring elsewhere):* Uh-huh.

JILL: Okay, so then you stick it through, I think that's called a knot. *(She fumbles a bit.)* Actually I'm not so good at this part. Oh, now it'll work. *(She succeeds.)*

KATE: Yep.

JILL: You ready to try it now? *(She unties the laces again.)*

KATE: Sure, now I know what to do. *(There is a long pause; then she walks off to play, leaving her laces untied.)*

Like a lot of preschool conversations, this one fails for a mixture of reasons. In the first place, the children do not agree on how to gain each other's attention reliably; Kate is looking away and possibly daydreaming when Jill thinks she is paying attention. In the second place, Jill (and probably also Kate) lacks facility and accuracy in calling attention to and labeling her actions; is she making a knot, a bow, or something else? And in the third place, Kate does not understand how to signal real understanding to Jill; apparently she thinks that simply being agreeable is enough.

Animism and Artificialism

Examples of animism

In the preschool years, a child often expresses **animism,** a belief that nonliving objects are in fact alive and human. One child, for example, showed animism by discussing his shoe like this: "Hey! This shoe won't fit. Get on there, shoe! There; that's more like it . . . Shoe, are you tired of squeezing my foot?" Here the shoe is treated like a person, or at least as something human enough to take on the role of listener in this conversation.

Even without being actual participants in a conversation, though, objects and events can take on living qualities:

PARENT: Why do the clouds move?

CHILD: Because the wind blows them. It goes *poof!* at them.

PARENT: Is that the only reason?

CHILD: Well . . . um . . . sometimes the wind gets tired, so it stops to rest for a while.

As these examples suggest, animism generates a lot of the cute remarks that adults enjoy in young children.

Artificialism refers to a belief that all objects, whether living or not, are made in the same way, usually by human beings. A child may believe that cats and dogs are made from play dough, since she has made many other familiar objects from this substance. Or she might overgeneralize about how certain foods are made, as in this example:

CHILD TO PARENT: You know where milk comes from?

PARENT *(playing dumb)*: Where?

CHILD: From the store! And orange juice comes from a factory.

To a certain extent, animism and artificialism are both special forms of egocentrism. In animism, children assume that various objects and events have the same qualities that they themselves have, namely human and living ones. In artificialism, they assume that their immature, incomplete knowledge of the world is in fact complete, and they therefore overgeneralize from it.

Causes of animism and artificialism

But egocentrism may not be the whole cause for these errors; imitation of adults may also contribute. An adult might easily say, "My car doesn't like me today," because the car will not start; in so doing, he implies that the car has feelings like a person, or at least like some sort of intelligent being. Even though the adult may excuse his comment as "just a figure of speech," a young child who happens to be listening may not dismiss the expression so lightly: for her, it may model animistic thinking.

As with egocentrism, children express animism more in some situations than in others. As a rule of thumb, they are more likely to attribute human qualities to objects with which they are relatively unfamiliar (Laurendeau and Pinard, 1972). They may persist with animism longer, for example, in describing an airplane than in describing a toy truck that they play with every day. By about school age, though, children usually figure out which objects are genuinely alive, even by adult standards, and which are not.

Classification Skills

Classification refers to putting objects in groups or categories according to some sort of standards or criteria. Young children can reliably classify objects that differ in just one dimension or feature, especially if that dimension presents fairly obvious contrasts. Given a collection of pennies and nickels, for example, a preschooler can usually sort them by color, which is their most obvious dimension of difference. Given a boxful of silverware, a young child might sort it by type: knives, forks, and spoons. Or he might group dishes by how they are used in real life, putting each cup with one saucer rather than separating all cups from all saucers (Sigel and Cocking, 1977). These simple groupings represent cognitive advances over infancy.

Groupings made by preschoolers

Preschoolers can sometimes also manage more complex classification tasks, but not as reliably. One prime example of their mixed success is **class inclusion**: the ability to compare a subset of objects with some larger, more inclusive set of objects to which it belongs. Red flowers and white flowers, for example, both belong to the larger, more inclusive (or general) class of flowers, and white cows and black cows both belong to the larger class cows.

The class-inclusion task

Most preschool children can classify objects according to simple, obvious dimensions such as color and size. They have trouble, though, in classifying according to more than one dimension at the same time, or when categories are based on abstract properties. (Peter Southwick/Stock, Boston)

How well can preschool children handle inclusive relationships? Piaget found that young children can easily compare subsets with each other, but cannot easily compare one subset with the group as a whole (Piaget and Inhelder, 1969). Suppose, for example, a preschooler is asked, "Are there more red flowers or more white flowers?" and then "Are there more red flowers or more flowers?" She typically can answer the first question correctly, but often fails at the second, which she tends to answer as if she is comparing the red and white groups, in spite of being asked to compare the red group with the whole group. She will say, for example, that a collection of four red flowers and two whites has more red flowers than flowers (incorrect); but she will also say that the collection has more red flowers than white flowers (correct).

Reasons for inclusion errors

So sometimes the child seems to answer a different question from the one asked. Why? Piaget suggests that the preschooler cannot **decenter** her thinking, meaning that she cannot broaden her focus to take account of more than one dimension at the same time. In class-inclusion tasks, the child must pay attention to the dimensions of color (is it white or red?) *and* of "flowerness" (is it a flower or something else?). In practice, though, a preschooler can sustain attention to only one of these at a time, so any question that refers to both dimensions may cause her trouble. In the second question, for example, the child must remember to count certain flowers twice — once as representatives of color, and again as representatives of "flowerness." The first question, however, demands attention only once.

Successful class-inclusion tasks

Piaget believed that young children's problems with class inclusion happen rather generally, in various situations and types of problems. More recent studies, though, have shown convincingly what many observers of children have sensed all along: that in some conditions, young children can solve surprisingly complex problems, including class-inclusion problems. One study modified the inclusion task by changing the wording and materials slightly. It used white and black cows, but laid them all on their sides — "because they are sleeping," as the experimenter explained. Then children were asked one of two questions: "Are there more black cows than cows?" (Piaget's version of the question), and "Are there more black cows than sleeping cows?" (new version). The addition of the word *sleeping* to the question caused twice as many young children to succeed at this task (McGarrigle et al., 1978). In another variation in the same study, even the first question produced more success if the last word — *cows* — was spoken with heavy emphasis.

These changes suggest that communication problems may influence children's success as much as their thinking abilities do (Grieve, 1981). Evidently children can in fact compare a subset (black cows) with its inclusive set (sleeping cows) if the question and the materials make clear the need for that kind of comparison. Piaget's form of the problem, some argue, does not do so. As a result, a young child may simply answer questions that he considers likely to be asked. In effect, when faced with an unusual or unexpected question, he does what many older children and adults do: he gives the interviewer the benefit of the doubt and responds to what he thinks the interviewer must have meant to ask (Donaldson, 1978). In the inclusion task in particular, this means giving simple, one-dimensional comparisons, not comparisons between specific classes and general ones.

Thus a preschool child may understand more than Piaget originally gave him credit for. Note, however, that this still does not make him the cognitive equal of an older child. As we will see in Chapter 12, a school-age child handles cognitive problems in ways distinctively different from those of a preschool child. The older child is less apt to find Piagetian questions as ambiguous as the younger child does and she knows more ways to clarify surprising or vaguely phrased questions when they do occur. The preschooler can seem relatively skillful when someone else arranges the conditions properly, but the school-age child can take a larger role in arranging the proper conditions herself.

Developmental differences in problem solving

Reversibility and Conservation

Many problems require **reversibility** in thinking, which is the ability to undo a problem mentally and go back to its beginning. If you lose a pair of glasses, reversible thinking can help to find them: you retrace your recent actions in your mind until you encounter or visualize the glasses again. Reversibility, it turns out, contributes to a major cognitive achievement of middle childhood, **conservation,** which is the ability to perceive that certain properties of an object remain the same or constant in spite of changes in the object's appearance. Usually, though, children do not achieve conservation until after early childhood.

Often preschool children either cannot or do not use reversible thinking, even when the situation calls for it; and this fact can sometimes make their thinking disjointed or fragmented, and in turn make them solve some problems incorrectly. As with other symbolic skills in this age period, however, a lot depends on how the task is presented. Typically, Piaget's classic tests for reversibility in thinking make children seem less capable or mature than more recent revisions do.

Limitations of preschoolers' reversibility

Consider, for example, the following Piagetian test of reversibility. First you show a preschool child two tall glasses of water with exactly the same amount in each. Then the child watches you pour the water from one of the tall glasses into a third, wide glass. Naturally, the water line in the wide one will not be as high as it was in the tall one. Finally, you ask the child, "Is there more water in the wide glass than in the [remaining] tall glass, or less, or just as much?"

How will a young child respond to this problem? According to Piaget, his nonreversible thinking may make him forget the identity of water levels that he saw only a moment earlier; after all, as a nonreversible thinker, he cannot easily imagine pouring the water back again in order to convince himself of the tall glasses' equality. Instead he is forced to solve the problem on the basis of the current appearance of the water — by comparing the looks of the tall and the wide glass. More often than not, the big difference in their appearance leads him to say **Conservation of liquid** that the amount of water has changed as a result of its being poured. In Piagetian terms, he fails to conserve, or believe in the constancy of the amount of liquid in spite of its visible changes (Inhelder and Piaget, 1958).

Note that the preschool child's lack of reversibility does not handicap him in all

---

A Talk with Audrey's Mother

Cognitive Development in the Preschool Years

Audrey's mother, Elaine, was interviewed in her living room. Audrey, a four-year-old, was still at her day-care center; her eight-year-old brother, Kyle, was not yet home from school.

INTERVIEWER: What was verbal development like for Audrey?

ELAINE: Well, her first word was "doll," and then, after that, she didn't say much else. She didn't develop sentences very fast. She used kind of a telegraph-type speech for a long time.

INTERVIEWER: What would she do?

ELAINE: There were signs, there were a lot of sounds and grunts and things. And then, after that, she would say one or two words like "go" or "me go," "red truck," or "Kyle play." What she meant wasn't always very clear, but she was very expressive.

INTERVIEWER: And what happened next?

ELAINE: She was one-ish when she started communicating, but it was a long time before it became English. Really a very uneventful, slow kind of development. She took her time.

INTERVIEWER: And what is it like now?

ELAINE: She never shuts up. Audrey is very concrete and she's very detail oriented. She's not interested in concepts as much as she's interested in what is there. So a lot of her language centers around figuring out what is going on rather than figuring out what is behind it.

INTERVIEWER: Can you give an example of this?

ELAINE: Sure. When I was pregnant with Audrey, Kyle, who wasn't four yet, started saying, "Well, when I'm four, Audrey will be zero. And when I'm twelve, Audrey will be eight." And he was going up through the years: "When I'm sev-

enty, and an old man, Audrey will be sixty-whatever." Audrey, at the same age, was also very interested in the number four. But she wanted to know why sometimes it is made like a triangle and sometimes it is made like a chair, and she would count four things. Her dad used to say that Audrey was interested in fours and Kyle was interested in fourness.

INTERVIEWER: And the concept of four.

ELAINE: And the *concept* of four — not *counting* four. I mean, Audrey will count four things: "I'm going to be four," and "We have four of this," and "This is a four even though it looks like this," and "This is a four, even though it doesn't." So in a lot of her language she will nitpick, but she will nitpick on concrete, seeable things, while Kyle will nitpick on values.

INTERVIEWER: For example?

types of problem solving. Questions involving nonreversible phenomena do not prove as difficult as those involving reversible phenomena (Piaget et al., 1968). Consider, for example, these questions:

Identity problems

- *(After a candle burns to a short stub)*: "Is it still the same candle as before?"
- *(After a seedling grows taller)*: "Is it still the same plant as before?"
- "Could you ever be a boy/girl?" *(whichever the child is not)*

All three questions prove confusing for a very young preschooler (age three or so), but are answered confidently and correctly by most children by about age five — about two years earlier than children typically can answer conservation-related questions (Seifert, 1973). The difference may stem from several factors, among which is the nonreversible nature of the truth in these cases; since the crucial object or feature in fact remains visibly fixed over time, reference to the past proves unnecessary, or even distracting. In other words, even if the candle becomes short,

---

ELAINE: For example, with Kyle the classic argument is, "You go right up those thirteen steps and go take your bath," and he will say, "The last time I took a shower, so I should have a shower tonight." And with Audrey you say, "Go right up those thirteen steps and take your bath," and she'll say, "There are twelve steps, not thirteen."

INTERVIEWER: Do you notice differences in how Audrey and Kyle, at age four, figure things out?

ELAINE: Yes. You could convince Kyle to do something by arguing with him, and he would accept your explanation of why it should be, and you cannot do that with Audrey. With Audrey you can only pray that it fits into her scheme of things. And if it does, she'll do it. She seems to have a set pattern for how the world should be. Audrey is like a whole package. She's already there and it just comes out, and any-

thing that happens in her life has to fit her preconceived notion of how life should be. Kyle, you feel, is really like a clean slate when he approaches something new. And it doesn't have to fit into anything because he is more willing to accept what it is for itself. He very rarely compares something new to something old.

INTERVIEWER: Has this difference always been there?

ELAINE: Always. And Audrey, when she sees something new, it's just like something that is old. The word "similar" is a word in Audrey's vocabulary, and I don't think it's a word in Kyle's vocabulary yet. When he learns something new, it's the first time it has ever been invented in the world. And that affects their reasoning. A good example is when Andrea, our dog, died.

INTERVIEWER: How did she understand that?

ELAINE: In a very concrete way. According to Audrey, "Andrea went to the doctor and had a shot and the shot made her die. And she died because she was very old and she was very sick, and we're very sad." But . . . I don't think Audrey suffered for it.

Follow-up Questions

1. In what ways does Audrey's thinking illustrate the preoperational stage of cognitive development?

2. Are there any examples of duos and telegraphic speech in Audrey's language development as described by Elaine?

it still looks like a candle, and even if the seedling becomes tall, it still looks like a plant. Because of these constancies, even preoperational children can be relatively skillful in problems involving nonreversible phenomena.

But problems that do require reversibility are affected a great deal by how they are presented or described to the child. Consider the water conservation task. One study found that asking children the question not only after but also before pouring the water causes them to conserve *less often* than asking them only afterward (Rose and Blank, 1974). Why the difference? Perhaps repeating the question makes some children believe that the experimenter wants them to change their response; after all, why else would she repeat herself? Since most children begin the conservation task by agreeing that the glasses hold equal amounts, obliging children may feel compelled to give nonconserving responses against their own better judgment.

Procedures that increase conservation responses

Another study further confirmed the importance of the experimenter's intentions by arranging for reversibility experiments to occur "by accident" (McGarrigle and Donaldson, 1974). The study used "Naughty Teddy," a teddy bear who occasionally swooped over the interview table and disarranged everything on it. The bear might "accidentally" cause the tall glass of water to spill into a wide tray; in these conditions, young children conserved far more frequently than when an experimenter poured the water on purpose. The result suggests that the classic version of the experiment may underestimate young children's ability to reason. Rather than being handicapped by nonreversible thinking, some children may do what adults often do: respond to the expectations of the situation and of the people in it. Apparently children, like everyone else, edit their responses.

How Skillful Is Preschool Symbolic Thinking?

As the studies described so far suggest, preschool symbolic thinking often has a "now you see it, now you don't" quality. In many ways — through language and dramatic play — young children can represent experiences reliably. In other ways, though, they cannot give adultlike responses to many tasks that require symbolic thought; the classic Piagetian experiments illustrate this limitation. And in still other ways, young children prove more capable of symbolic thought than Piaget gave them credit for, at least in his original theorizing (Murray, 1981).

Variability

Such variations make sense in children who are just beginning to represent experiences symbolically. After all, they still have a lot of developing to do before they can consolidate their thinking skills fully. The experiments that qualify or limit Piaget's findings do not, however, really disprove the basic usefulness of Piaget's stage theory of development. Instead they suggest a number of complexities about cognitive development in early childhood.

Impact of social developments

In particular, research on early cognition suggests that children often combine their social motivations and intuitions with their cognitive ones; perhaps only adults try to separate them for convenience in studying children. And the research suggests that language affects cognitive performance significantly, and possibly affects cognitive capacity as well. Somehow words and sentences guide a child in solving problems, and they do so more significantly than Piaget believed, at least originally. This idea is important enough to deserve further attention and explanation in the next part of this chapter.

Checkpoint *During the preschool years, children begin using symbolic thinking in a wide variety of activities and for solving a wide variety of problems. In some, but not all, situations, their thinking is limited by egocentrism, animism, and artificialism. Preschoolers also gain new skills in classifying objects, as long as the criteria for classification are relatively simple or basic. In certain situations they show reversible thinking, as well as conservation. In all of these areas, recent research has found preschool children more skillful than Piaget originally predicted.*

Language Acquisition in the Preschool Years

For most children, language expands rapidly after infancy. Dramatic development occurs in *syntax,* or the way the child organizes utterances. But significant changes also happen in semantics and in communicative competence. As we mentioned in Chapter 6, *semantics* refers to what the child means by his utterances; **communicative competence** is how the child adjusts his utterances to the needs and expectations of different situations and speakers.

Aspects of language development

Because of the comparative importance of syntactic development during the preschool years, we emphasize this particular topic here, leaving major discussion of semantics and communication for Chapter 12. Making this division, though, does not imply that these three aspects of language develop in isolation from one another. Quite the contrary: as the discussion of syntax emphasizes, how a child organizes an utterance (his syntax) depends in part on what he wants to say and the meaning of his words (his semantics) and in part on when he wants to say it and to whom (communicative competence). Conversely, his meanings and intentions sometimes stimulate him to learn new ways of organizing utterances — and stimulate the adults in his life to model them as well (Whitehurst, 1982). Some of these relationships are illustrated in the examples that follow.

The Nature of Syntax

The *syntax* of a language is a group of rules for ordering and relating its elements. Linguists call the elements of language morphemes. **Morphemes** are the smallest meaningful units of language; they include words as well as a number of prefixes and suffixes that carry meaning (for example, the /s/ in *houses* or the /re/ in *redo*) and verb-tense modifiers (for example, the /ing/ in *going*).

Syntactic rules operate on morphemes in several ways. Sometimes they mark important relationships between large classes or groups of words. Consider, for example, these two pairs of sentences:

> **1a.** John kissed Barbara.
> **1b.** Barbara kissed John.
>
> *and*
>
> **2a.** Frank kisses Joan.
> **2b.** Frank kissed Joan.

Significance of syntax for language

These sentences differ in meaning because of syntactic rules. In the first pair, a rule about the order or sequence of words tells us who is giving the kiss and who is receiving it: the name occurring before the verb is the agent (the kisser), and the name after the verb is the recipient (the kissee?). In the second pair of sentences, the morphemes /es/ and /ed/ tell something about when the event occurred: adding /es/ to the end of the word signifies that it is happening now, but adding /ed/ means that it happened in the past. These rules, and many others like them, are understood and used by all competent speakers of the language. Unlike textbook

---

Perspectives on Research

Dealing with Gaps and Silences

Among adults, an ideal conversation is supposed to flow continuously, with each partner speaking immediately after the preceding person finishes. In fact, however, listeners often are not sure when the previous person has finished speaking. As a result, unintentional gaps and silences are actually quite common in normal conversation. The gaps vary in actual time from a split second to many seconds, but whatever their actual length, they feel "too long" to the participants in a conversation.

Conventionally, "good" conversation usually requires people to fill gaps and silences somehow. When one conversational partner senses a gap, therefore, he may fill it with **prestarts,** which are words or phrases that have little substance but that indicate to listeners that the speaker is about to take a conversational turn (Umiker-Sebeok, 1980). Prestarts take several forms. Some affirm or acknowledge what the other person has said just prior to a silence, as with the italicized words below:

PERSON 1: I feel like eating a ham sandwich. *(pause)*

PERSON 2: *Yeah.* Let's go to the cafeteria. *(pause)*
PERSON 1: *Okay.*

Prestarts may be connectives; that is, they may help move the conversation past a silence by linking the previous turn with the upcoming turn, as in this example:

PERSON 1: The boss seems to like everything that Joe does, but he never seems to notice work of mine. *(pause)*

PERSON 2: *But* you don't assert yourself enough about it. *(pause)*

PERSON 1: *Because* he's such a dumbbell.

Prestarts can also help to hold the floor during a single speaking turn, by expressing hesitation:

PERSON 1: Giving birth to a baby is like . . . *uh* . . . diving into cold water. Sometimes I am . . . *um* . . . amazed . . . *well* . . . that I ever got through it.

authors, though, the speakers may never state them and may only barely be aware of them.

Syntactic rules vary in how regular or general they are. Some apply to large, open-ended groupings or classes of words; this quality makes them **generative** — that is, speakers can create or generate brand-new sentences almost infinitely by applying the rule to brand-new morphemes. The examples above are generative in this sense. Replacing *John* with *fish,* for example, and *Barbara* with *water* creates the strange sentence "Fish kissed water." This sentence may sound odd, but it nevertheless conveys some idea of who was doing the kissing and who was receiving it. Even nonsense words can fit into the same syntactic framework: "Gokems kissed splibs." We may have no idea of what (or who) *gokems* and *splibs* are, but the syntax of the sentence still tells us which one was the kisser and which was the receiver of the kiss. To this extent, the syntax conveys meaning independent of the words slotted into the sentence form.

Kinds of syntactic rules

Unfortunately for a child learning to talk, some syntactic rules have only a small range of application, and still others are completely irregular. Most words, for

Young children understand and use these conventions for handling conversational gaps and silences, but they do so more egocentrically and less consistently than adults. Consider the following dialogue between a preschool child and an adult. The prestarts have all been italicized:

ADULT: I'm drawing a picture of my dog. How do you like it? *(pause)* My dog is big and black — he's a Labrador.

CHILD: *But* MY picture is about Batman. See it?

ADULT: *Uh-huh.*

CHILD: *Yes, and* Batman can catch you — can catch anyone, actually.

ADULT: *I know.* Who does he catch the most?

CHILD: *Well,* mostly he catches ... *oh* ... bad guys.

This conversation shows not only the child's ability to fill gaps but also her unreliability and self-centeredness in doing so. After the pause, the child does not take a turn speaking, even though the adult invites her to do so by asking for a comment on the adult's picture. Although her silence may seem rude by adult standards, it may just reflect the child's lack of skill at filling in conversational gaps. The child's remaining prestarts all help her to hold her turn at talking; they show little concern for the adult's drawing. The adult, on the other hand, uses prestarts essentially to pass the turn back to the child; they assist in focusing attention on the child's comments.

During the preschool years, children gradually use prestarts more commonly, but still not as commonly as adults do (Umiker-Sebeok, 1980). The word *well,* for example, occurred twice as often in the conversations of five-year-olds as in the conversations of three-year-olds. But even the five-year-olds used *well* only about one-tenth as often as did adults (Gelman and Shatz, 1977). Connective words (*and, but, because*) show similar increases in frequency — up from 1 percent of turns at age three to 3.5 percent at age five. Children also begin using more varied connectives as prestarts; instead of chronically answering questions with *because,* for example, they will try other prestarts as well.

example, signal pluralization (the existence of more than one) by adding /s/ or /es/ at the end; *book* means one volume, and *books* means many. But a few words use other methods to signal the plural. *Foot* means one, for example, and *feet,* not "foots," means many; *child* means one and *children* means many; and *deer* can mean either one animal or many of them.

Impact of syntax on language acquisition

In acquiring syntax, then, a young child confronts a mixed system of rules. Some apply widely and regularly, and others narrowly and exceptionally. Whatever skills the child brings to learning language, she must take these differences into account. Relying too much on the regularity of syntax will make her often sound ungrammatical, yet treating language rules too often as irregular will limit the child's ability to generalize and to generate truly new sentences. As shown below, most children require several years to balance these features of learning language — and some may never really achieve such a balance completely.

Beyond First Words: Duos and Telegraphic Speech

Before the age of two, the child begins linking two words together when he speaks; these utterances are sometimes called **duos** (meaning "twos"). Typically, morphemes of duos express relationships to each other that resemble the syntactic relationships in adult language. For example, a two-word utterance can express nonexistence ("Hat gone") or possession ("My hat"), just as adult utterances can. The difference lies, of course, in the subtlety and explicitness of the relationships expressed. Adult utterances are apt to convey several syntactic relationships in one sentence ("That blue hat of mine is gone now"); two-word utterances must state multiple relationships through multiple utterances ("Hat gone. My hat. Blue hat. Now gone. That hat . . .").

Two-word sentences

By nature, early speech also leaves out most small connecting words: articles (like *the* and *a*), prepositions (like *of* and *in*), and conjunctions (like *and* and *but*). These clarify relationships among morphemes and generally make complex grammar possible. Without them, syntactic relationships are still possible, but the child's speech sounds stilted. Early utterances are therefore also called **telegraphic speech,** presumably because they sound like a telegram ("Send money. No money? Send chocolates."). The telegraphic quality persists even after the child begins linking more than two words at a time, but it disappears by about age four or so, at least in simple conversations on familiar topics (Brown, 1973).

Function words omitted

Individual Differences and Undergeneralizations Even though all children express syntactic relationships in their first utterances, they differ significantly in the particular relationships they express and in the rate at which relationships emerge. A number of universal "first grammars" have been suggested, but none has stood up to close scrutiny by psychologists and linguists. One system, for example, proposed that children begin by expressing eleven kinds of relationships, similar to those listed in Table 9-1 (Brown, 1973). Unfortunately, there is little evidence that the relationships actually reflect the child's own first methods of organizing morphemes; in other words, the child's grammar and the linguist's grammar may not coincide (Whitehurst, 1982).

Relationship	Meaning of Relationship	Form	Example
1. Nomination	Naming, identifying	that + NOUN	"That dog"
2. Notice	Greeting, pointing out	hi + NOUN	"Hi cat"
3. Recurrence	Noting repetition, procuring more	more + NOUN, 'nother + NOUN	"More juice"
4. Nonexistence	Noting departure	allgone + NOUN, no more + NOUN	"Allgone Daddy"
5. Attributive	Describing object	ADJECTIVE + NOUN	"Loud truck"
6. Possessive	Indicating ownership	NOUN + NOUN	"Billy shoe"
7. Locative	Indicating location of object	NOUN + NOUN	"Milk fridge"
8. Locative	Indicating destination or location of action	VERB + NOUN	"Walk home"
9. Agent-action	Indicating who is doing what	NOUN + VERB	"Billy play"
10. Agent-object	Indicating two objects connected by an action	NOUN + NOUN	"Billy cupboard"
11. Action-object	Indicating connection between action and object	VERB + NOUN	"Open door"

Source: Brown (1973).

Table 9-1 *Relationships Expressed by Two-Word Sentences*

To understand this problem, consider these two early duos: "My truck" and "Red truck." In the child's mind, do these express two types of relations, the first of possession and the second of physical attribution? Or does the child regard them as two examples of one relationship, simply a general one of attribution? Given the limited language of very young preschoolers, there is no way to be sure. First utterances are not numerous enough to allow linguists to group them reliably and thereby to infer the child's "true" grammar, and the children are still too young to comment usefully on their own utterances, as adults sometimes can do.

Early grammars

Some syntactic relationships apparently have a narrower meaning for some children than for adults. One study found that one child expressed recurrence with the form "More X," where X was the name of any object; but he would not say "Again X," or even "X again," even though he freely used *again* as a single word. That is, he would freely say "More drink" and "Again" both to mean "I would like another drink." But he would not say "Again drink" or "Drink again," even though these duos would seem to express recurrence just as well, and even though the child had the necessary vocabulary and syntactic capacity to combine all the terms. Eventually the child did begin using *again* with other morphemes, but not until significantly later in his language development (Braine, 1976; Bowerman, 1976).

Narrower syntactic rules

A wide range of such **undergeneralizations** occur in early sentences (Nelson, 1981). A child's first sentences may draw on both nouns and verbs, for example, but not combine every available noun with every available verb. As holophrases (or one-word sentences), the child may be using *kitty, daddy,* and *sister* (all nouns), as well as *run, stand,* and *walk* (all verbs). But she may never use some of the nine sentences possible with these words; she may say "Daddy stand," but never "Daddy walk." When the situation calls for it, she will instead use *daddy* and *walk* as single words. Eventually, of course, she does combine them; but throughout the preschool years she continues to define grammatical categories more narrowly than adults do (DeVilliers, 1980).

Regularities and Overgeneralizations After highly individual beginnings, certain aspects of syntax do develop in universal and predictable patterns. The present progressive form *-ing,* for example, occurs quite early in most children's language, the regular plural morphemes *-s* and *-es* somewhat later, and articles such as *the* and *a* still later (Brown, 1973).

Wider syntactic rules

At a slightly older age, most children will begin using auxiliary verbs to form questions, but they do so without inverting word order, as adults normally do. At first, for example, a child will say, "Why you are cooking?" and only later "Why are you cooking?" This suggests that language acquisition involves more than just copying adult language; after all, adults rarely model incorrect forms. To a certain extent children's language seems to compromise between the new forms that children hear and old forms that they can already produce easily.

Sometimes, in fact, early syntax becomes too regular, and children make **overgeneralizations.** Around age three, for example, preschool children often make errors like these:

- "I runned to the store."
- "Unpour this water, please."
- "All the childs came!"

In each case, the child used the correct but irregular forms at an earlier age, but later shifted to the wrong but more regular forms (Brown, 1973). Usually by early school age he shifts back again, though not necessarily because anyone teaches him or forces him to do so. Apparently his overgeneralizations represent efforts to try out new rules of syntax that he has finally noticed (Bowerman, 1982).

The Predisposition to Infer Grammar As these examples suggest, young children seem to infer grammatical relationships rather than simply copy others' speech. Few parents try purposely to teach talking, and those who do usually discover that direct efforts tend to fail. Consider this example (Bellugi, 1970):

Significance of early grammars

CHILD: My teacher holded the rabbits and we patted them.

MOTHER: Did you say your teacher held the baby rabbits?

CHILD: Yes.

MOTHER: What did you say she did?

CHILD: She holded the rabbits and we patted them.

MOTHER: Did you say she held them tightly?

CHILD: No, she holded them loosely.

In spite of his mother's apparently unsuccessful attempt to encourage adult grammar in this situation, the child will almost certainly switch from *holded* to *held* eventually. The child, not the adults around her, seems to control the timing of this change; she, not her mother, must solve the grammatical puzzles posed by language.

A classic study of early syntax shows the importance of the child's own inferences about grammatical rules. Instead of asking children about real words, the experimenter showed them pictures of imaginary creatures and actions that had nonsense words as names (Berko, 1958). With one picture, a child was told, "Here is a wug." Then he was shown two pictures and told, "Here are two of them. Here are two——." Most children, even as young as age two and one half, completed the sentence with the grammatically correct word, *wugs.* Since they could not possibly have heard the term before, they must have applied a general rule for forming plurals, one that did not depend on copying any language experiences specifically but came from inferring the underlying structure of many experiences taken together. The rule most likely operated unconsciously, since these children were very young indeed.

The Limits of Learning Rules   Such skill at acquiring syntactic rules, however, obscures a seemingly contradictory fact about the acquisition of syntax: much of it apparently must be learned by rote. As we have pointed out, most children use irregular forms (like *foot/feet*) correctly before they shift to incorrect but more regular forms. The most reasonable explanation for the change is that they pick up the very first sentence forms simply by copying, word for word, the sentences that they hear spoken (MacWhinney, 1978). Presumably they copy many regular forms by rote too; but the very regularity of these hides the haphazard, unthinking way in which they are acquired.

Even though children eventually do rely on rule-governed syntax, they probably still learn a lot of language by rote. Many expressions in a language are **idiomatic,** which means that they bear no logical relation to normal meanings or syntax. The sentence "How do you do?" for example, is not usually a literal inquiry as to how a person performs a certain action; and the sentence "How goes it?" meaning "How is it going?" does not even follow the usual rules of grammar. Since words and phrases like these violate the rules of syntax and meaning, children must learn them one at a time.

Mechanisms of Language Acquisition

Exactly how, or by what means, do children learn to speak? For most children, several factors may be operating at once. In general, current evidence can best be summarized like this: language seems to grow by the interaction of an active, thinking child with certain key people and linguistic experiences. The preceding

Rote learning of language

A Talk with Audrey Herself

Cognitive Development in the Preschool Years

Audrey was interviewed shortly after she returned from her day-care center. She asked me to come with her to the porch, where her toys were.

INTERVIEWER: Audrey, you were saying that you like to eat chicken. What is chicken?

AUDREY: Chicken is animal. And when it's dead it turns into food chicken.

INTERVIEWER: When it's dead it turns into food?

AUDREY: Yes.

INTERVIEWER: And then you eat it up?

AUDREY: Yes.

INTERVIEWER: Where does the food go after you put it in your mouth?

AUDREY: First we put it in the oven.

INTERVIEWER: And then what?

AUDREY: And then we eat it all up.

INTERVIEWER: Audrey, you seem to be very big. Are you growing?

AUDREY: Yes, I'm four. First, I was one, then I was three, and then four. And now I'm almost five.

INTERVIEWER: And what happens when you get to be four? do you get bigger?

AUDREY: Yes. And I get five. You get 1, 2, 3, 4, 5, 6, 7, 8, 9, 10, 11, 12, 13, 14, 15, 16, 17, 18, 19, 20, 21, 22, 23, 24, 25, 26, 27, 28. We die when we get to be thirty.

INTERVIEWER: We die when we get to be thirty? Why?

AUDREY: 'Cause we're old. We're too much. We're too much numbers.

INTERVIEWER: Audrey, do you know any stories you can tell me?

AUDREY: No. I can't read stories. I'm going to sing "Somewhere over the Rainbow."

INTERVIEWER: Okay.

AUDREY *(singing)*: Somewhere, over rainbow, clouds are blue, and the land that I love, the one thing I love about . . . it's happy little blue bird fly beyond the rainbow, fly away . . . goodbye!

INTERVIEWER: That was a lovely song.

AUDREY: When am I going to come on the tape recorder?

INTERVIEWER: You are on the tape recorder. You can see, when the little red light went on, it shows you are on the tape recorder.

AUDREY: When is my voice going to come on it?

INTERVIEWER: You want to hear your voice?

AUDREY: Yes.

INTERVIEWER: Okay, I'll turn it off and I'll let you hear yourself and then we can talk some more. Okay?

AUDREY: Okay. When we turn it off we can hear my voice gonna come on the tape recorder.

INTERVIEWER: Now, I'm going to play it back so you can hear your voice. . . . Now I have turned the recorder on again.

AUDREY: I curled my hair today.

INTERVIEWER: You did? Why did you do that?

AUDREY: Because I wanted a haircut. I got hair in my eye.

INTERVIEWER: Why are you holding your hair up now?

AUDREY: So it can't get inside my ear.

INTERVIEWER: Oh, when you put the earphones on to hear yourself on the tape recorder.

AUDREY: So I can hear myself sing "Somewhere over the Rainbow."

INTERVIEWER: Okay, I'm going to stop the tape recorder now. . . . Now the tape recorder is back on again.

AUDREY: Hickory, dickory dock. The mouse ran up the clock. The clock struck one and the mouse went down. Hickory, dickory dock.

INTERVIEWER: That's a nice one.

AUDREY: Yes. But I can do it in Spanish. Do you want to see me do letters in Spanish?

INTERVIEWER: You can do letters in Spanish?

AUDREY: Yes. Uno, dos, tres, quatros, cinquo . . .

INTERVIEWER: How did you learn to do that?

AUDREY: I didn't. Sammy told me because Sammy can do that.

INTERVIEWER: And Sammy is your friend?

AUDREY: Yes.

Follow-up Questions

1. What specific comments of Audrey are good examples of the characteristics of preschool thinking discussed in this chapter?

2. In what ways are Audrey's comments examples of typical preschooler speech?

3. After reviewing the interview with Audrey's mother, how accurate (in your opinion) was her mother's assessment of Audrey's cognitive development?

sections describe in part this active, thinking child; the sections below describe some possible key interaction experiences.

Reinforcement   One common-sense view, which was held formerly by some psychologists, is that children learn to speak through reinforcement. According to this idea, a child's parents reinforce vocal noises whenever they approximate a genuine word or utterance, and this reinforcement causes children to vocalize in more and more correct (or at any rate adultlike) ways (Mowrer, 1960; Skinner, 1957). In the course of babbling, for example, an infant may happen to say "Mmmm," to which her proud parent smiles and replies cheerfully, "How nice! You said 'Mama'!" The praise reinforces the behavior, so the infant says "Mmmm" more often after that. After many such experiences, her parents begin to reinforce only closer approximations to *mama,* leading finally to a true version of this word.

Reinforcement of babbling

Among preschool children, the same process could occur if parents reinforced correct grammatical forms and ignored or criticized errors or relatively immature utterances. Parents might respond more positively to a sentence like "I have three feet" than to one like "I have two foots." According to the principles of reinforcement (see Chapter 2), the child would tend not only to use the correct version more often but also to generalize the correct elements of this sentence to other, similar utterances.

Analysis of conversations between parents and children, though, shows convincingly that these kinds of reinforcements do not occur. Under normal circumstances, parents correct children's language for factual errors and ignore faulty grammar (DeVilliers and DeVilliers, 1977). They are more likely to criticize or correct "I have three feet" than "I have two foots." Furthermore, as we have pointed out, reinforcing infant babbling does not effectively shape early vocalizing in particular directions; it only creates more vocalizing overall (Dodd, 1972).

Reinforcement of truth value

Imitation and Practice   In some sense, children must obviously imitate their native language in order to acquire it. But the process of imitation is subtle and often indirect. Children do not imitate everything they hear, but most copy certain selected utterances — often immediately after hearing them (Bloom et al., 1974). Sometimes the utterances chosen for imitation involve familiar sentence forms that contain new, untried terms, and sometimes they contain familiar terms cast into new, untried forms. The imitated terms and forms return later in the child's spontaneous speech. At first, though, they resemble the rote learning mentioned above, and they seem to help the child by emphasizing or calling attention to new morphemes and syntax (Clark, 1977).

Importance of language models

The following four-year-old child, for example, had never before heard the form *-ish,* meaning "something similar to":

FATHER: We need to paint the fence soon. Maybe a kind of brownish-red.

CHILD *(pauses, listening)*:   Brownish-red. What's brownish-red?

FATHER: It's what you get when you mix brown and red. Brownish-red, or reddish-brown, or brownish-reddish.

CHILD *(smiles, and pauses again)*:   Brownish-red. Brownish-red.

Children learn a great deal of language by imitating other, more experienced language models. Sometimes this learning happens intentionally, as with the mother and child at right. Other times, as in the situation below, adults may not realize just how much of what he hears a child is absorbing. (right, Andrew Brillant; below, Victoria Arlak)

Imitation may also help children acquire language by initiating playful practice with new expressions. The child in essence plays around with the new forms he learns, and in doing so he consolidates his recently acquired knowledge (see Chapter 10 on play). Since quite a bit of language play remains unobserved by adults, its extent is hard to judge, but a lot obviously does go on (Garvey, 1977). For example, the four-year-old mentioned above was talking to herself a few days later, just before falling asleep at night:

Language play

CHILD: You know what you get when you mix blue and red? Bluish-red. Bluish-reddish. Bluish-radish. Reddish, radish. You know what you get when you mix white and red? Whitish-red. Reddish-white. What do you get when you mix white and white? Whitish-white. Whitish-white?!

The earlier discussion of colors evidently set the stage for this monologue. At the least, the earlier, imitative encounter helped call the form *-ish* to her attention; and at the most, it precipitated practice of it.

Innate Predisposition to Acquire Language: LAD

As we pointed out in Chapter 6, the ease and speed that children show in acquiring language have made some linguists and psychologists conclude that children have an innate predisposition, or built-in tendency, to learn language (Chomsky, 1976; Slobin, 1973). For convenience, the tendency is sometimes called the *language acquisition device,* or *LAD* for short. According to this viewpoint, LAD functions like a kind of inborn road map to language. It guides the child to choose appropriate syntactic categories as he tries to figure out the comparatively confusing examples of real speech that he ordinarily hears, and it helps him find his way through the mazelike structure of language with relatively few major errors, instead of having to explore and construct his own language map, as the Piagetian viewpoint implies.

Nature of LAD

Several pieces of evidence support this view. First, when exposed to appropriate models, all healthy infants acquire language without explicit training. Children learn languages almost universally, both in our own society and around the world. Contrary to a popular impression, the languages and dialects that children acquire are all about equally complex, at least in their syntax. Children from any one language community show surprisingly small individual differences in syntax by the time they reach age five or six.

Universality of language acquisition

Second, as described earlier in this chapter, certain specific features of syntax appear in the same sequence in a wide variety of children, and even in a variety of languages. Prepositions referring to location (*in, on, between,* and so on), for instance, develop in the same sequence in several widely differing languages (Johnston and Slobin, 1979).

Common features of syntax

Third, children have trouble learning to speak if circumstances discourage them from learning normally during the first few years of their lives. Children isolated from language through parental neglect, for example, have learned some language later in life, but usually not normal amounts or the complexities of it. In a less

Critical periods for language acquisition

LANGUAGE ACQUISITION IN THE PRESCHOOL YEARS

369

tragic example, identical twins often create a private language which they speak only with each other. In many cases their private language seems to delay normal language development, and occasionally it has caused serious language handicaps in later childhood (Savic, 1980).

Early grammars

Fourth, also as pointed earlier in this chapter, preschool children do not simply copy their parents' language directly; yet they seem to figure out and use many of its basic syntactical relationships remarkably well. For instance, most seem to know (Chomsky would not say "learn") intuitively what a verb is, as shown by the

---

Perspectives on Research

Bilingualism as a First Language

When children grow up bilingual, do they keep their two languages separate from the outset, or do they really acquire a single language system which they differentiate only gradually into two fully separate languages? Evidence for both possibilities exists, although the majority of linguists favor the idea of a single bilingual language that gradually differentiates (Grosjean, 1982). To help you make up your own mind, look briefly at the evidence.

In two ways, children raised bilingually seem to keep their two languages separate. First, bilingual preschoolers will rarely, if ever, confuse or mix the phonemes or sounds of their two languages. Thus a three-year-old who speaks both French and English will say "J'ai du papier" (I have some paper) with a relatively perfect French accent; the word *du,* for example, will sound something like an English /u/ pronounced with the lips nearly closed. This uniquely French sound, however, will never occur in the child's English words, such as *during* or *cure.*

Second, bilingual preschoolers almost always select words from just one language or the other, rather than from both, for any one sentence. A Spanish-English child will say "It's raining," but not "Esta raining," and "Comma esta usted?" but not "How are usted?" (Bergman, 1976). This bias in word selection suggests that bilingual preschoolers organize their languages separately.

But two other pieces of evidence suggest that bilingual children begin with a single language system and differentiate it gradually into two separate languages. First, the overall vocabulary, or **lexicon,** of bilingual preschoolers seems to begin with a single "dictionary" of words which intermingles the two languages and which contains few, if any, equivalent words in both languages. If a French-English three-year-old knows and uses the French word *rue,* for example, he is unlikely to know and use its English equivalent, *street.* Conversely, if the child understands and uses the English word *water,* he will probably not understand or use its French equivalent, *eau.* Early in the preschool years, vocabularies from the two languages complement each other rather than duplicate each other (Imedadze and Uznadze, 1978). By the end of the preschool period, bilingual children learn translations of most common words, but the process of acquiring duplicate vocabularies continues for many years after — well into adulthood, in fact.

Second, bilingual preschoolers begin by applying a single set of syntactic rules to their utterances, derived primarily from whatever rules are common to both languages. The three-year-old French-English bilingual child begins forming questions by using a rising intonation ("Daddy is coming home?") or by tagging a statement with the word *eh?* ("Silly cat, eh?"). These methods are grammatically permissible in both languages. As the child develops, he eventually adds questioning methods that are unique to one language or the other, such as the inversion of the auxiliary verb *is* in "Is Daddy coming home?" (Volterra and Teaschner, 1978).

way they use verbs more or less correctly almost as soon as they begin linking words into duos. Yet a concept like "verb" is extremely abstract — far more so than other concepts mastered by three-year-olds.

The Limits of LAD Although this evidence does suggest that children have a built-in talent for acquiring language, it does not show that experience plays no role in the process at all. The evidence from twins and neglected children emphasizes just the opposite: that certain experiences with language may be crucial, especially early in life. Ordinarily, these experiences happen to practically every preschooler. They may consist of hearing others talk and of being invited to respond to others verbally. But the fact that they happen to everyone does not mean that children do not learn from them; it only means that what children learn is universal.

Experiences that may create LAD

Furthermore, experiences affect the version of language that children acquire, even when they grow up supposedly in the same language community. As pointed out earlier, children vary in the vocabulary they learn, and they vary in the grammar they use: even by age three or four, children often do not define grammatical categories as abstractly as adults do, or necessarily in the same way that other children do. Most preschoolers eventually do revise their grammatical categories to coincide with conventional adult grammar, thus obscuring their individuality. But as Chapter 12 shows, large differences persist in older children's styles of communicating, even after children have mastered the basic structure of language.

All things considered, then, the fairest summary is a moderate one: that children are both predisposed to acquire language and in need of particular experiences with it. Skill with language is neither given at birth nor divorced entirely from other cognitive development. A special talent for language may be given to all normal children, though, and many crucial experiences for developing that talent may just happen to occur rather frequently to infants as they grow up.

Parent-Child Interactions

Certain kinds of verbal interactions apparently help children to acquire language sooner and better. Parents are comparatively helpful when they speak in relatively short sentences to their preschool-age children, and when they use relatively more concrete nouns than pronouns (Furrow et al., 1979). In this pair of comments, for example, the first one helps a child to learn language more than the second does:

Short sentences, concrete terms

PARENT 1: Take your shoes off. Then put your shoes in the closet. Then come kiss Mama goodnight.

PARENT 2: After you take off your shoes and put them in the closet, come kiss me goodnight.

As we noted in Chapter 6, this simplified style is one aspect of a version of language sometimes called *motherese.* Another aspect of this version of language is the use of a high-pitched voice. Motherese is spoken intuitively by adults with young children, and even by older children with younger children (Snow and Ferguson, 1977).

One of the most helpful kinds of verbal interactions is **recasting** a child's utterances: repeating or reflecting back what the child says, but in slightly altered form. For instance:

CHILD: More milk.
FATHER: You want more milk, do you?

or

CHILD: Raining! Mama. Raining!
MOTHER: It sure is raining.
CHILD: Yeah. It sure raining.

Benefits of recasting   Recasting helps because it highlights slight differences among ways of expressing an idea. In doing so, it may make the child more aware of how he expresses his idea — its form or organization — as well as call attention to the idea itself (Nelson, 1981).

These findings, and others like them, have been translated into language development programs for young children, and even for infants (Tough, 1977; Fowler and Swenson, 1979). Fortunately, the methods of interaction that help are often ones that parents and teachers do intuitively anyway; training for them therefore really consists of emphasizing and refining their use.

Language Variations

Not surprisingly, parents vary in how they talk to their children, and these differences may influence the version of language that children acquire as they grow up. It is unclear, though, how language variations affect other aspects of children's development, such as their thinking ability.

Gender Differences in Language   Within any one community, girls learn nearly the same syntax as boys, but they acquire very different ways of using language. **Conversational styles**   On the whole, the differences in language reflect society's gender stereotypes. For example, girls phrase requests indirectly more often than boys; girls more often say "Could you give that to me?" instead of "Give me that." And they more often expand on comments made by others rather than initiating their own. These differences appear especially in mixed-gender groups, and are noticeable not only in adults but in children as soon as they are old enough to engage in conversation (Lakoff, 1975).

The sexes reinforce their differences in language by certain nonverbal gestures **Nonverbal communications**   and mannerisms. Girls and women tend to maintain better eye contact than boys and men; they blink their eyelids at more irregular intervals, and tend to nod their heads as they listen (Maltz and Borker, 1982). Boys and men, on the other hand,

Signing and the Development of Language

Children with hearing impairments often do not develop verbal skills as well as other children, but they are quite capable of acquiring a language of gestures called **American Sign Language** (ASL for short). The language development of ASL children in fact provides much of the reason for considering ASL a true language, just as useful for communication as any verbal language, such as English.

To understand why this is so, consider the nature of ASL. Signing consists of subtle gestures of the fingers and hands, made near the face. In general, each gesture functions like a morpheme. For example, holding the fingers together gently (which signers call a tapered O) can mean either *home* or *flower,* depending on whether it is placed near the cheek or under the nose. There are also sign-morphemes that affect the syntax of expressions — gestural equivalents of *-ing,* for example, and of *-ed.* Individual signs are linked together according to syntactic rules, just as in English. After some practice, signers can "speak" (or gesture) just as fast and effortlessly as people who use English.

What happens to infants and young children who are hearing-impaired and who grow up learning ASL from their parents as their first language? Studies show that they experience the same steps in signing development as speaking children do in language development. At about the age when infants babble, signing children begin babbling with their hands, making gestures that strongly resemble genuine ASL signs but that signers recognize as gestural nonsense (Dale, 1976). As with verbal babbling, signing infants apparently engage in gestural babbles playfully, when they are waking up in the morning or going to sleep at night.

When the signing infants become two- and three-year-olds, they experience a phase of one-word signing similar to the holophrases often observed among speaking children. And they experience two-word, telegraphic signing as well. As with speech, their signs at this point often omit important syntactic gestures and do not follow the usual conventions of word order (or in this case, signing order). Signing vocabulary increases rapidly during the early preschool period, in amounts comparable to the increases experienced by speaking children. Even the kinds of words acquired parallel those acquired by speaking children (Bonvillian et al., 1983); signing preschoolers tend to learn signs for dynamic, moving objects first, just as other children do.

Still more reason for considering ASL a true language comes from observations of hearing preschoolers whose parents purposely used both English and ASL during the time when the children normally acquired language (Prinz and Prinz, 1979). During their preschool years, these children became thoroughly bilingual, using ASL and English interchangeably. Especially significant, though, were their patterns of language development, which essentially paralleled those shown by conventionally bilingual children. A clear example concerned vocabulary. As with verbal bilinguals, these children first acquired a single vocabulary that mixed or intermingled elements from both ASL and English but that included few direct translations. If a child understood and used the sign for "tree," for example, she would not be likely to understand and use the spoken word *tree.* The children did eventually acquire translations, so that they finally possessed duplicate vocabularies. But acquiring duplicate terms took several years, just as it does with verbally bilingual children (Prinz and Prinz, 1979).

use eye contact a good deal less in ordinary conversation, blink at regular intervals, and rarely nod their heads when listening. When these actions accompany the verbal differences, boys and girls (and men and women) run a distinct risk of misunderstanding each other. A boy talking to a girl may find the girl overly agreeable, since she nods her head so much and never changes the subject, whereas a girl talking to a boy may find him self-centered, since he seems not to acknowledge her comments when he listens and tends to change the subject.

Socioeconomic Differences in Language Most research finds low-income children less verbal than middle- or high-income children (Guthrie and Hall, 1983). What this means, though, is that low-income children perform less well in verbal test situations; outside of these situations, language differences are less clear-cut. These facts have created controversy about the importance of socioeconomic differences in language development.

Low-income children less verbal on tests

Some psychologists point out that most tests of language skills favor middle-class versions of English, both in vocabulary and in style of discourse (or conversational patterns). This bias happens because of the content selected for individual test questions and because of the ways in which tests are normally conducted. A question on one of these tests might ask children to describe a dishwasher, yet low-income families rarely own this machine. Other questions might draw on experiences that usually only occur to middle-income children, such as trips on airplanes or attendance at symphony concerts.

Biases in test contents

Other psychologists point out that normal methods of testing are inherently more threatening to low-income children. For one thing, the people who give such tests (teachers, graduate students) usually have more power and status. The greater inherent threat of test taking makes low-income children more cautious in their responses, and hence less verbal (Kagan, 1978). Middle-class children may worry about getting answers right, too, but not as much, on the average.

Threatening testing situation

Perhaps most important of all, middle-class families use styles of discourse (or conversational patterns) that include many "test" questions, or questions to which parents already and obviously know the answer. At the dinner table, parents may ask their preschooler, "What letter does your name begin with?" even though they already know the answer, and even though their child knows that they know. Exchanges like these probably prepare young children for similar exchanges on genuine tests, by making testing situations seem more natural and homelike.

Practice with test questions

In contrast, low-income children tend to lack prior experience with "test" question exchanges. Observations of their conversational and test behavior show that they can give relatively elaborate answers to true questions, such as "What did you do yesterday morning?" when the adult really does not know the answer (Steffenson and Guthrie, 1980). But they tend to fall silent when they suspect that the adult already can answer the question (for example, "What are the names of the days of the week?").

Checkpoint *Preschool children begin combining single words into longer utterances according to increasingly sophisticated rules of syntax. Their first utterances* *include both syntactic undergeneralizations and overgeneralizations, but suggest that children try actively to teach themselves adult grammar. This probably does not involve direct reinforcement by adults; however, it may include imitation and practice by the children, as well as efforts by parents to simplify and recast their own speech for children. Some linguists argue that language acquisition may be a largely innate human quality, whereas others argue for a larger role for experience, pointing to variations in language because of differences in social, economic, and gender experiences.*

Relationships Between Language and Thought

How do language and thought relate? Is language just another sort of thought, or a skill unto itself? The close connection between these two activities makes this question important but at the same time hard to answer. If you are talking, chances are that you are also thinking (except for occasional mindless blathering); and if you are thinking, you are probably either talking to others or verbalizing inwardly at least a little.

In spite of the potential confusion between these activities, language specialists and psychologists have attempted to explain their relationship (Rice, 1982). One explanation, often associated with Piaget, emphasizes the importance and priority of action in creating both language and thought. Another, often associated with the psychologists Jerome Bruner and Lev Vygotsky, proposes more equal roles for language and thought, in which they develop independently but eventually become interdependent. Let us look briefly at each of these viewpoints.

Fusion of language and thought

Piaget: Action as the Basis for Both Language and Thought

Piaget and his supporters argue that action or activity promotes initial language development. Children, they argue, need to manipulate objects and to have a rich variety of concrete experiences (Piaget and Inhelder, 1971). This idea makes considerable sense to anyone who works with preschool children; such children often learn the concepts of *heavier* and *lighter,* for example, more easily if they can have lots of actual experiences with hefting and observing objects of different weights. If young children are taught the definitions of these words without having such experiences, they often just learn the words by rote (Kamii and DeVries, 1977) — presumably an inferior way to learn them.

Sensorimotor experiences precede language

According to the Piagetian viewpoint, children's language can achieve no more sophistication or complexity than their general level of cognitive development (Inhelder, 1976; Sinclair, 1976). Cognitive ability consists of several interrelated symbolic skills, such as those described earlier in this chapter. All symbolic skills supposedly develop together, and their mutual dependence results in the general

In addition to learning how language is structured, preschoolers begin acquiring skill with communication, or how language is used. By nature, competent communication requires practice at talking and listening with others. (Betsy Fuchs)

cognitive stages of development described by Piaget. But their mutual dependence also means that language cannot, in principle, become more complex than a child's other symbolic skills.

Much evidence supports the idea that activity governs initial language acquisition. Two-year-olds tend to show more advanced language if they have achieved object permanence — the belief, described in Chapter 7, that objects exist even when they are not directly experienced (Smolak, 1982). Older children, too, show a close correlation between certain language habits and conservation tasks, like the water-glass task described earlier in this chapter. Children who are able to conserve use coordinated expressions relatively often; they say the glass is "shorter but wider" or "taller but thinner" (Sinclair, 1969). The nonconservers more often express such ideas in two separate statements: "This one is wider. That one is taller."

Language development reflects cognitive performance

Piagetians point out that language has no priority in the normal timetable of development; for twelve to eighteen months, in fact, an infant obviously thinks without much help from language. And when language does appear, it develops in conjunction with other symbolic activities, most notably make-believe and dramatic play. Even children's dreams follow a timetable that parallels other symbolic activity (Foulkes, 1982); as a child gets older, it seems, dreams become less egocentric and tend to include more abstract themes or "thoughts."

Vygotsky: The Gradual Integration of Language and Thought

As plausible as these facts and arguments sound, though, they ignore important evidence that language also can sometimes guide other cognitive developments, including both early sensorimotor development and later symbolic thinking (Bruner et al., 1966; Berk, 1985). Three-year-old Carolyn, for example, seems to talk to herself in order to improve her sensorimotor skill at making a sandcastle:

CAROLYN: Now pour this *here.* Now little more. Oops! Too much. No spill.
First I clean this up, then start again. Like *this. (pouring)*

Events such as this led the Soviet psychologist Lev Vygotsky (1962) to propose that language and thought develop independently at first but gradually become integrated with each other sometime during childhood. In his view, early speech is learned without much understanding; toddlers imitate words and grammatical constructions, but with only superficial comprehension of what they hear. At this point in development, toddlers' thinking occurs without much help from language; it resembles a sort of mental shorthand, which Vygotsky called **inner speech.**

> Early language and thought are independent

As two- and three-year-old children acquire more verbal skill, they begin using speech to guide their actions. But this self-guiding speech does not show egocentrism, as Piaget argued, so much as preschool children's need for help in solving problems — as Carolyn, in the example, perhaps does. When problem solving is

---

not a priority, even very young children can sound very socially aware in their communications. Carolyn had this conversation with her mother at about the same time that she built the sandcastle:

CAROLYN: What's an eggplant?
MOTHER: A purple thing that people eat.
CAROLYN: Does it have eggs on it?
MOTHER: No, but it's long like an egg.
CAROLYN *(pausing)*: When can I see one?
MOTHER: Tomorrow at the store. I'll show you.

Later language and thought are integrated In this conversation, Carolyn's language and thought worked together closely, one guiding the other. Adults, too, often use verbal knowledge to guide further learn-

---

Perspectives on Issues

Options in Early Childhood Education

In recent years early education has evolved a good deal, and several approaches that especially emphasize the cognitive development of children have been formulated. All the programs are designed to serve about ten to fifteen preschool children at a time and to operate for several half-days per week. Generally they have beneficial effects, although not necessarily the ones promised by the program developers.

At one extreme are highly structured language training programs, like the one called **DISTAR,** which stands for "directed instruction in arithmetic and reading" (Engelmann, 1980). In programs like DISTAR, teachers drill small groups of children in basic academic skills — primarily language arts and mathematics. The lessons have been sequenced clearly and logically by the authors of the curriculum, and teachers are expected to follow the sequence carefully in order to promote maximum learning in the children. Most of the time, DISTAR is used with children who are educationally at risk, perhaps because they speak Standard English poorly. The drill and practice of the program in fact resembles techniques used in programs for teaching English as a second language.

Some early education programs use special materials, such as these measured rods, to assist young children's reasoning abilities. Such props may help preschoolers to relate their well-developed sensorimotor skills to their newly emerging symbolic skills. (Victoria Arlak)

ing, even before they quite know what they are talking about; for example, scientific theories predict or state relationships that no person has ever actually experienced (or observed) before (Manicas and Secord, 1983). In this sense, the verbal content of such theories stimulates new thought and experiences about the world, and it does so precisely *because* it goes well beyond prior experiences.

Whatever their actual relationship, language and thought remain only partly coordinated during the preschool years, and especially during the early part of this period. This partial coordination resembles children's development in many cognitive areas, ranging from their symbolic representations (described at the beginning of this chapter) to their syntax and vocabulary (described later). Partial development also characterizes children's perceptual skills during the preschool years. In seeing, hearing, and touching objects, young children show definite improvements over infants, but they still lack some of the sensitivities of older children and adults.

Other programs have attempted to construct a curriculum out of Piaget's theory of cognitive development (Kamii and DeVries, 1977). Consistent with the developmental stages expected of preschool children, Piagetian programs emphasize a mixture of sensorimotor and preoperational activities. For example, children spend a lot of time manipulating materials such as sand and water. But they also are encouraged to represent activities and objects symbolically; they may use the sand-table to build make-believe roads. Language activities are incorporated, but do not become as much of a focus of attention as they are in the DISTAR program.

Still another approach organizes activities around highly structured materials developed by Maria Montessori (Montessori, 1964). The materials are made to illustrate particular geometrical and mathematical relationships: a set of cylinders, for example, may be graded by size, and each designed to fit snugly into a set of size-graded holes in a board. A child choosing this toy experiments with the cylinders and holes in order to discover the best way to fit them. Language is de-emphasized in a Montessori program even more than in a Piage-

tian program; the program's chief purpose is to guide children in their use of materials rather than to stimulate a lot of verbal interaction.

In spite of their differences in style, all of these programs emphasize features of cognitive development in early childhood. The DISTAR program focuses on language skills, the Piagetian ones on general stages of logical thinking, and the Montessori ones on perceptual skills. Evaluations of all the approaches suggest that they are about equally effective in promoting overall cognitive development (Consortium for Longitudinal Studies, 1983). Differences in style do create differences in the cognitive skills developed by young children, but only minor ones. More important, it seems, is teachers' careful attention to the cognitive development of children, a feature that all cognitively oriented programs foster. When children receive such attention, they seem to stand better chances of succeeding during grade school and beyond (Berreuta-Clement et al., 1984).

Psychologists have proposed two major theories about how language and thought may be related as young children develop. One of these, associated with Piaget, argues that language is only one of several expressions of symbolic thinking and therefore develops only as rapidly and as far as other kinds of symbolic skills. The other viewpoint, associated with Vygotsky, argues that language and thought begin independently but gradually become integrated during the preschool years, so that one skill can assist the other.

Perceptual Development in Preschool Children

During the preschool years, a subtle change occurs in children's perceptual priorities: vision becomes increasingly important, compared to the other senses. Teachers can see this development when they watch children skip rope. Four-year-olds have much more trouble with this task than eight-year-olds do. Their problems do not center on the jumping part of the task, though; many four-year-olds can jump quite reliably and regularly. What they cannot do is inspect a moving rope visually and then use these visual perceptions to dictate precisely when and how they should begin jumping. Instead of carefully watching the rope, like eight-year-olds often do, preschoolers leap before they look.

Increasing visual dominance

By the end of the preschool years, however, this has changed, and vision provides most children with much, if not a majority, of their most important information. When combined with improvements in hearing and touch, visual perception makes possible many new cognitive skills, ranging from longer, more sustained conversations to silent reading.

Visual Perception

Preschool children can see better than infants but still not as well as adults. They are usually far-sighted; that is, they can see distant objects almost perfectly but have trouble focusing on nearby objects, such as a line of ordinary print in a book (Cratty, 1973). For some children, far-sightedness probably causes certain practical problems, such as discomfort in drawing for long periods or in doing other work that takes close visual concentration. As preschoolers get older, however, their near vision tends to improve, a fact that helps children cope with the major tasks of elementary school, such as reading and writing.

Far-sightedness

Not only does visual acuity improve during early childhood, but visual perception also improves in several ways. First, children learn to *discriminate*, or notice visual differences among objects, better. Second, they *integrate* what they see increasingly well, which means that they coordinate one sight better with another sight, as well as with specific motor actions. And third, children improve their *visual memory*, or ability to recognize and recall specific visual stimuli. The three processes overlap a lot in daily life, but it is helpful to consider examples of each process separately.

Visual Discrimination   **Visual discrimination** refers to distinguishing or discerning differences in what is seen. Preschool children can make visual discriminations as long as they involve relatively simple or obvious distinctions. A four-year-old can usually tell you which of two stuffed animals looks brighter, or whether two pencils look exactly the same in length, or whether two toy cars have exactly the same shape (Frostig et al., 1966). *Simple distinctions possible*

But when visual discriminations require noticing underlying dimensions of objects, preschool children do not perform as well. Researchers demonstrated this limitation by showing preschool children slides of objects in groups of three (Farnham-Diggory and Gregg, 1975), then asking them to match two of the objects in some way. One slide, for example, showed a red truck, a red apple, and a brown book; for this slide, children were asked, "Which objects are most alike in color?" On this test, even older preschoolers (five-year-olds) did not perform very well: only about 12 percent could match the objects reliably by color. In fairness to the children, however, note that adult subjects in this study did not perform well either: only about 50 percent of adults matched the pictures by color reliably. In spite of the simplicity of the task, both adults and children made numerous discrimination errors. *Abstract groupings more difficult*

The difficulty of discriminations like these depends a great deal on the particular dimension or distraction in question. In general, children find so-called identity discriminations the easiest; these are ones in which the child must simply decide whether or not two objects are exactly alike. Harder than these are discriminations about color, and still harder are ones about shape. Most of the time, adults' discriminations reflect this same sequence — identity, color, and shape — although at more sophisticated levels (Williams et al., 1977). The sequence has implications for the design of educational toys: if a puzzle is supposed to teach differences in shape, for example, then painting each piece a different color can distract from this goal, because the colors constitute easier clues in sorting the pieces. *Variations in difficulty of discriminations*

Visual Integration   **Visual integration** refers to the ability to coordinate particular sights with each other as well as with appropriate physical actions. Throwing and catching a ball requires visual integration: a child must watch the ball carefully from one instant to the next and move his hands appropriately to make the catch. The fact that children generally improve at catching balls shows that they are acquiring visual integration during the preschool years. A variety of other motor skills from drawing pictures and tying shoelaces to jumping rope and playing tag with another child suggest the same idea. All of these activities require children to coordinate what they see, and to coordinate these sights with what they do. And children improve at all such tasks between the ages of two and five. *Coordinating sights and actions*

But there are limits to these improvements. Preschool children often have particular trouble in coordinating actions and sights in the presence of distracting stimuli. Many four-year-olds are quite capable of dressing themselves, for example, but fail badly at this task if they are listening to a favorite record at the same *Problems with distractions*

Coordinating touch and smell with the sight of these strawberries is one form of visual integration, a skill that children achieve early in the preschool period. (Andrew Brillant)

time. Others can draw skillful pictures, but only as long as they do not talk; to comment on their drawings, they must temporarily interrupt their work.

Some problems in visual integration occur because children try to take account of increasingly large numbers of stimuli. In some ways, therefore, older preschoolers set themselves harder perceptual problems than younger preschoolers do. Suppose, for example, that children must sort a stack of cards by shape; but suppose also that the cards differ not only by shape but sometimes also by color. How well do the children do? When the cards are all the same color and differ only in shape, older children sort the cards better than younger children do (Williams et al., 1979). Eight-year-olds make fewer errors than five-year-olds; they demonstrate a better discrimination of basic shapes, such as triangles, squares, rectangles, and circles. But when the cards differ in both dimensions at once — in both shape and color, that is — then older children perform no better than younger children. Apparently the older children cannot purposely disregard color, even though they know it is irrelevant to this particular task; in everyday terms, they get mixed up. Younger children, however, do just as well in the presence of the distracting dimension. Apparently, therefore, they are not so much confused by the irrelevant dimension as oblivious to it.

Coordinating visual perception with physical actions can also prove challenging. When very young children track a moving object, such as a ball suspended from a string, they often have trouble separating their eye movements from their head movements. Three-year-olds cannot separate them at all; they inevitably move their heads to follow an object (Bizzi et al., 1974). Four- and five-year-olds can separate these actions a bit, but more for vertical movements (a falling or rising ball) than for horizontal ones (a moving train). Not until school age can children track objects consistently in all directions, including even diagonal ones (Williams et al., 1979).

Visual Memory **Visual memory** refers to an ability to recall or recognize simple sights, such as a familiar face or the color of a friend's clothes. During the preschool years, children become better at this sort of task, at least when they only have to remember for fairly short periods of time (Williams, 1983). Flashing shapes onto a screen for a few seconds demonstrates the nature of these changes. When the number of shapes is fairly small — say, just three or four — then even rather young children can remember what they have seen quite well. In this case, in fact, they remember almost as well as adults do. Preschool children reach their limits when remembering larger numbers of shapes (say, six or eight).

Whether this difference results completely from perceptual skills, though, is not clear. Older children and adults have many cognitive or thinking skills that help them to perceive more clearly (Gibson, 1969). For example, they can draw on a larger vocabulary of accurate descriptive labels; they are more likely to know terms like *ellipse, diamond,* and *parallelogram* in addition to *circle, square,* and *triangle.* They also tend to use labels for parts of shapes, such as *corner, angle,* and *curve.* These labels may relieve older individuals from actually having to visualize certain shapes in order to remember them. Some of the time, instead, they may simply recall the labels and their meanings, and thus piece together a mental picture of the shape.

Auditory Perception

In some ways, hearing develops more quickly than vision. By the age of two or three, for example, most children have very good **auditory acuity,** meaning that they can notice small or soft sounds as well as young adults can. They can in addition usually discriminate speech sounds quite well. These sounds are the so-called *phonemes* of language, like the /b/ and /d/ sounds in the word *bad.*

But producing these sounds still poses problems for many children (DiSimoni, 1975). Their errors are the source of many endearing remarks heard by parents and nursery-school teachers. "See that fuwwy teddy beah," says a three-year-old, meaning "See that furry teddy bear." Another says, "I'm shaning my cothes; then I'll have some zhuice," meaning "I'm changing my clothes; then I'll have some juice." Most of the time, preschool children can perceive (or hear) phonemic differences long before they can produce them (Birch, 1976), as in this conversation at the dinner table:

Margin notes:

Visual tracking

Improvement in visual recognition and recall

Language as an aid to visual memory

Good acuity of hearing

Common errors in producing phonemes

CHILD: Daddy, please give me a pomato.

DADDY: Do you mean a tomato or a potato?

CHILD: A POMATO!

DADDY: A tomato?

CHILD: No.

DADDY: A potato?

CHILD: Yes!

Most children (though not all) eventually grow out of such mistakes, but the process by which they do so is unclear. Perhaps they eventually listen more carefully to themselves speaking, and finally hear the difference between their own speech and adults'; or perhaps their vocal apparatus grows in ways that facilitate making adult phonemes; or perhaps it's a bit of both.

Tactile Perception

Beginning of recognition by touch

The term *tactile* refers to touch, and **tactile perception** refers to the ability to recognize and discriminate among objects by touching them. If a child feels a spoon, for example, will she recognize it as a spoon, just as she might if she sees it? With familiar objects, at least, the answer seems to be yes; young children often do recognize them by touch. But there are serious limitations to this ability for most preschool-age children.

Vision and touch still separated

One limitation is that tactile perception does not yet connect or integrate fully with other perceptual abilities (Van Duyne, 1973). A popular nursery activity shows the problem. Give three-year-olds a grocery bag full of familiar objects, such as toy animals, trucks, simple kitchen utensils, and the like. Ask them to feel each object until they think they know what it is. Then ask them not to feel but to look at a similar array of objects and to point to the ones they have just felt. Preschool-age children can usually recognize visually a majority of objects that they have previously recognized tactually. Reversing the procedure, however, usually spoils their performance; young children, that is, have a lot of trouble in recognizing by touch objects that they previously have only seen.

Touch sensations not fully localized

Another limitation of early tactile perception concerns its **localization**, or how easily a person can discriminate between sensations at separate points on the body. If someone touches two places on your back, for example, how far apart must the places be for you to feel two touches rather than one? Younger preschoolers, aged three or four, have significant difficulties with this sort of task, and are much less accurate than school-age children (Ayers, 1978). Partly, of course, their limitations may stem from relatively unskilled language: they may sense differences in touch better than they are able to tell about them. Whatever the reason, their poor discrimination limits their ability to integrate visual perceptions (the sight of a toy) with tactile ones (the feel of the toy).

Checkpoint   *During the preschool years, children become increasingly skillful at making visual discriminations, at integrating visual and motor stimulation, and at* *recalling and recognizing what they have seen before. Their auditory and tactile perception also improves significantly. In spite of these improvements, though, many perceptual skills continue to be limited, compared with the same skills in adults.*

Cognition and Social Development

As this chapter shows, children make impressive gains in their cognitive skills during the preschool years. They begin using symbols widely; they acquire considerable language skill; and they sharpen their perceptual powers. They are not yet fully adult in any of these respects, of course, but by about the age of five, they have moved far beyond the cognitive limitations that helped to define them as infants.

Given the importance of these cognitive developments, it is not surprising that they affect young children's social development as well. Children's increasingly sophisticated thinking, for example, helps them to form increasingly astute concepts of morality or ethics, as well as increasingly subtle concepts about friendship. Their growing language ability allows social interactions to become more complex and probably also more gratifying and meaningful. Their growing perceptual skills allow them to attend to what they experience more precisely. Such new sensitivity in turn helps children to respond more appropriately to their experiences, including social experiences in particular.

Cognitive effects on social development

The next chapter describes these social gains and others. For convenience it places the cognitive developments described in this chapter somewhat in the background, but in real preschool children, social and cognitive developments depend on each other intimately.

Summary of Major Ideas

Thinking in Preschoolers

1. The preoperational stage of thinking, defined by Piaget, is characterized by increased symbolic thinking and by new knowledge of identities and of functional relationships.

2. Children's new reliance on symbolic thought helps them to recall experiences, to solve problems more effectively, and to communicate with others about their experiences.

3. In spite of advances in thinking, preschoolers also reveal egocentrism, or an inability to distinguish between their own viewpoint and those of others.

4. Egocentrism seems to result partly from perceptual dominance (or centration), which is a tendency to focus attention exclusively on a single obvious feature of a problem or situation.

5. In spite of frequent egocentrism, preschoolers can take the perspective of others in certain conditions.

6. In certain conditions, preschoolers can also communicate relatively effectively with others in solving problems.

7. Two other limitations of preschoolers' thinking are animism (believing that everything is alive) and artificialism (believing that objects are all made by human beings).

8. Preschool children can classify objects accurately, as long as the system or criteria for classifying are relatively simple.

9. Preschoolers often cannot perform a class-inclusion

task unless special efforts are made to clarify the nature of this task.

10. Preschoolers often cannot solve problems that require reversible thinking, such as the classic Piagetian tasks of conservation.

11. As with other classic Piagetian tasks, changes in the procedures often improve children's performances.

Language Acquisition in the Preschool Years

12. During the preschool years, children make major strides in acquiring the syntax or grammar of their native language.

13. Young children's first efforts to combine words often omit function words and ignore other rules of syntax common in adult speech.

14. Syntactic errors of preschool children include both undergeneralizations and overgeneralizations.

15. Both undergeneralizations and overgeneralizations suggest that children actively try to deduce adults' syntactic rules.

16. Infants and preschoolers probably do not learn syntax by being actively reinforced for correct grammatical usage.

17. Children probably do acquire some syntax by imitation and practice of language models.

18. The ease of language acquisition has made some linguists argue that all children possess an innate language acquisition device, or LAD.

19. Parents probably assist children's language acquisition by directing at their children short sentences and recastings of the children's own utterances.

20. Language varies among children according to their gender and their socioeconomic class, and these differences have a variety of causes.

Relationships Between Language and Thought

21. Two major theories have been proposed for the relationship of language and thought.

22. According to Piaget, language develops only as rapidly and as far as other symbolic functions, such as dramatic play.

23. According to Vygotsky, language and thought begin as independent functions and gradually become integrated during the preschool years.

24. Piaget's viewpoint implies that language primarily reflects general cognitive development, whereas Vygotsky's implies that language and thought eventually come to assist each other's development equally.

Perceptual Development in Preschool Children

25. During the preschool years, children come to rely increasingly on vision for sensing their environment.

26. Preschoolers show improvements in visual discrimination as well as in integration of visual perceptions among themselves and with motor skills.

27. Young children also show improvements in visual recall and recognition.

28. Auditory and tactile perception improve significantly during the preschool years.

29. In spite of improvements in perception, many perceptual skills remain less complete and less well controlled than the comparable skills in adults.

Key Terms

make-believe *(346)*
symbols *(347)*
identities *(347)*
functional
   relationships *(347)*
symbolic thought *(348)*
preconceptual
   phase *(349)*
intuitive phase *(349)*
egocentrism *(349)*
perceptual
   dominance *(349)*
centration *(349)*
animism *(352)*
artificialism *(352)*
classification *(353)*
class inclusion *(353)*
decenter *(354)*
reversibility *(355)*
conservation *(355)*
communicative
   competence *(359)*

morphemes *(359)*
prestarts *(360)*
generative *(361)*
duos *(362)*
telegraphic speech *(362)*
undergeneralizations *(363)*
overgeneralizations *(364)*
idiomatic *(365)*
lexicon *(370)*
recasting *(372)*
American Sign
   Language *(373)*
inner speech *(377)*
DISTAR *(378)*
visual
   discrimination *(381)*
visual integration *(381)*
visual memory *(383)*
auditory acuity *(383)*
tactile perception *(384)*
localization *(384)*

What Do You Think?

1. As this chapter has shown, Piaget may have underestimated the cognitive skills of preschool children. How about the rest of society: do people generally underrate what preschoolers can do? Explain your opinion.

2. Given that nearly all preschoolers learn language without instruction, how do you account for the differences in verbal skill that seem to exist among older children and adults?

3. Do you ever think without talking, or talk without thinking? Describe these incidents, and why you believe that they show a separation of language and thought.

4. How might perceptual limitations affect preschoolers' abilities to engage in academic or school-like tasks? Describe some perceptual problems that four-year-olds might face on these tasks.

For Further Reading

Bissex, G. *Gnys at Wrk: A Child Learns to Read and Write.* Cambridge, Mass.: Harvard University Press, 1980.

Schickedanz, J. *More than the ABC's: The early stages of reading and writing.* Washington, D.C.: National Association for the Education of Young Children, 1986.

The author of the first book describes how just one child, her own son, taught himself to read and write, beginning when he was about five years old. Her comments are thorough and insightful about the nature of reading and about how adults might foster reading and writing in the late preschool and early school years. The second book discusses the issues raised by Bissex in more general terms. Both books highlight the wide range of cognitive processes and motivations that usually surround early reading and writing.

Bower, T. G. R. *The Perceptual World of the Child.* Cambridge, Mass.: Harvard University Press, 1977.

Here is a short (100-page) guide to many of the major findings about perceptual development during infancy and the preschool years. Bower emphasizes vision, but he also deals with the other senses as well as with how the senses may become integrated.

Donaldson, M. *Children's Minds.* London: Croom Helm, 1978.

As the result of her observations of and experiments with preschool children, the author of this book developed serious reservations about how widely applicable Piaget's theories of cognitive development really are. She describes numerous experiments that show preschoolers to be more competent at problem solving than Piaget originally claimed them to be. Her observations do not really disprove Piaget's claims, but they do specify the range of conditions in which they are true.

Garvey, C. *Children's Talk.* Cambridge, Mass.: Harvard University Press, 1984.

This book focuses on how children use language during normal conversations with each other. It is therefore *not* a book about syntax or the structure of language as such. Instead, it looks at how children learn to organize their comments so as to communicate as effectively as possible. Often they do so quite competently, but as the book shows, they also experience various problems in learning how to communicate.

Chapter

10

The Preschool Years: Psychosocial Development

Focusing Questions

- What is the main developmental task or crisis that a preschool child must master?
- What distinguishes play from other activities, and why is it so important in preschoolers' development?
- How does children's play change during the preschool years?
- How do different styles of raising children influence young children?
- What are a preschooler's relationships with other children like?
- How does a young child learn the differences between boys and girls and how each should behave?

The thinking and use of language described in the last chapter usually occur in *social* situations: in spite of a preschooler's egocentrism, she usually talks *with* someone else and often thinks *about* some other person. Even behaviors that at first do not appear to be social often have social elements. For example, an adult usually helps a child to solve a Piagetian conservation problem by guiding her and questioning her about her understanding. The child's success at such a task will therefore be influenced by her relationship with that adult and by her beliefs about who deserves a reply to which sorts of questions, as well as by her social skill in communicating her answers. Viewed from this perspective, even a child's thinking and problem solving are to some degree social activities.

Many other activities and events, of course, are more obviously social. Children make friends, and sometimes lose them; they play with peers and adults and not just with inanimate objects. The social skills and the unique personality that a preschool child develops are largely a result of experiences within and outside of her family as well as a function of her gender and social circumstances.

In this chapter we first describe what theorists have to say about social development during the preschool years. Then we look at evidence for these theories in three areas of social activity: play, relationships with others, and gender roles. As you will discover, each of these topics offers at least partial support for one or another of the developmental theories.

Theories of Early Social Development

Erik Erikson's psychosocial theory of development, and to a lesser extent Freud's psychosexual theory, out of which it grew, have proven to be particularly helpful in understanding the changes that occur during the preschool years. As you recall from the chapters on infancy, a child has achieved both a basic sense of trust in others and a sense of autonomy by the end of his second year. He is by now firmly convinced that he is a person on his own, separate and distinct from his parents. At the same time, he is still "deeply and exclusively *identified* with his parents, who most of the time appear to him to be powerful and even dangerous" (Erikson, 1968, p. 115).

According to the psychoanalytic view, this intense identification is largely a product of the oedipal conflict and its resolution, which Freud believed occurs during the phallic stage of psychosexual development (see Chapter 2). It allows the child to protect himself unconsciously from fears that his father will punish him for being sexually attracted to his mother and for the angry and competitive feelings he has toward his father. According to Freud, the superego and the sense of conscience and ego ideal that develop during this stage help a child to regulate his feelings and actions in socially acceptable ways. **The Freudian viewpoint**

According to Erikson (1968), three important changes during the preschool years contribute to a crisis of identity: greater mobility, improved communication skills, and greatly expanded imagination. The child is now able to move about more freely and aggressively and to establish a wider range of goals for himself; by the age of three, he has mastered walking and running and takes them for granted. **Erikson: improving skills** He can forget about the walking itself and shift to actively exploring what he can do now and what he may possibly do in the future. As he enters the preschool years, the child's sense of language and communication skills are good enough for him to understand and ask questions about almost everything (though often he hears just enough to misunderstand thoroughly). And the child's ability to use language and to move around on his own lead to a dramatic expansion of his imagination; in fact, he is now able to imagine so many different roles that he cannot avoid sometimes frightening himself with the very things he has dreamed or thought up.

In Erikson's view, the child, faced with secret fantasies of very large and at times frightening proportions, must master the developmental crisis of **initiative versus guilt.** As we mentioned above, one of the most powerful of these fantasies is that of winning the competition with his same-sex parent for the parent of the opposite sex. Guilt and conscience, according to Erikson, grow out of a sense that such fantasies are wrong and punishable. They come to serve as an inner voice of right and wrong, and serve to limit, sometimes rigidly and cruelly, the child's sense of initiative. Consequently, it is important for parents and society to support the child's sense of initiative and action in his fantasy play, in his physical activities, and in his social interactions, and to appreciate the ways in which a preschooler is frequently his own worst critic.

Harry Stack Sullivan (1953) proposed several other concepts that are useful for understanding the developments during this period. He believes that preschoolers use **egocentric escape** to distance themselves from unpleasant and overwhelming experiences by acting as if they are unaffected by such experiences or by quickly **Sullivan: protective behaviors** forgetting them. For example, a child who has somehow become separated from her parents and been lost while at an amusement park may act like she has been totally unaffected by the experience shortly after she is reunited with her parents, and she may not even remember the incident later on.

Another development during this period takes the form of **dramatizations,** which are "as if" performances in which the child tries out the role of or plays at being someone else, typically her mother or father. As described by Sullivan, dramatizations allow a child to explore new psychological and social roles and to gain greater control over disturbing feelings and experiences. In acting as if she were an angry mother scolding her young daughter, for example, a four-year-old both learns about the mother's role and is able to become more comfortable with the feelings of fear, anger, and guilt that may be involved. A final concept of Sullivan's is the **malevolent transformation,** which may occur if a child's attempts to initiate contact and to obtain closeness with others are ridiculed and rejected. The feelings of anxiety and mistrust that result may lead to the development of a sense that the world is a harmful and evil place in which it is difficult to achieve closeness with others. If children successfully negotiate the psychological obstacles to their continuing development, however, they are ready to begin "social life" in more adult terms. One of the ways preschoolers do this is through play, which takes up a major part of their time.

Checkpoint   *During the preschool years, children's increasing mobility, rapidly improving language and communication skills, and greatly expanded powers of imagination contribute to the psychosocial crisis of initiative versus guilt. At times preschoolers may feel frightened or guilty as a result of their own vivid imaginations and need support and reassurance from their care-givers. Dramatizations allow children to gain greater control over disturbing feelings and experiences by safely exploring new psychological and social roles.*

Play in Early Childhood

In our society and many others, play dominates the preschool years. Every child plays, it seems, and virtually all observers of young children agree that they have seen lots of examples of it. What are the play activities of a preschooler like, and what important contributions does play make to a child's development? Before we tackle these questions, we must first agree on what we mean by the term *play.*

The Nature of Play

One useful approach to defining play focuses on the attitudes and dispositions of children themselves (Rubin et al., 1983). First of all, children at play generally show **intrinsic motivation,** which means that they engage in the play because the activity is enjoyable and rewarding for its own sake rather than because it is useful in achieving something else. Think about ring-around-the-rosy or farmer-in-the-dell. It's hard to imagine a reason for playing these games other than the sheer sat-

Rewards of playing

In early childhood, the process of doing things often matters more than the outcome: Even washing a car can seem like play. (Ulrike Welsch)

isfaction gained from the activity. As a result, to a large extent no one can command children to play. Although the mother who tells her children to go outside and play may succeed in getting them out of the house, the play part is up to them and really remains beyond her control.

A second characteristic of play is that children are generally more interested and involved in the *process* of doing things than in the *product* of what they do (Vandenberg, 1978; Schwartzman, 1978). At the local playground, for instance, children may care very little about the goal of using the slide, which is to get from top to bottom. But they are likely to care a lot about their style of sliding — whether they go head first or feet first, or up the slide instead of down.

Process-oriented activity

A third important aspect of play is that it *differs from exploration* of objects and materials, and in fact usually happens after a lot of exploration has already occurred (Fein, 1981a). Consider a young child with a typewriter. At first, when he is still unfamiliar with it, he is likely to focus cautiously on exploring what the machine can do, carefully trying out particular keys and noting the results. Later, though, after he has become more familiar with the machine, he is likely to focus on what is enjoyable about the experience: he may type combinations of favorite letters, even if he cannot yet read, or he may play with the automatic carriage return or the repeat keys or with pleasing patterns of type. Compared to exploration, play in the sense we describe has no goal other than its own enjoyment.

Goal of enjoyment

Different from reality

A fourth aspect of play is **pretense,** meaning that it both resembles real-life activities and differs from them in that it is not bound by reality. For example, a child who is playing at fighting looks different from one who is truly fighting (Aldis, 1975), and a child playing mommy will typically act differently from a child who is actually caring for a baby brother or sister. However, the features that reveal that an activity is play rather than the real thing vary with the particular type of play and situation; a play fight may contain smiles and laughter, whereas a make-believe mother may be overly bossy. Whatever the signs, they communicate the message that "this behavior is *not* what it first may appear to be." Even so, it is not uncommon for a preschooler to become so caught up in a round of dramatic play that she forgets for a moment that it is not real and truly becomes frightened when her make-believe mother tells her she has been bad and must sit in the corner.

A fifth aspect of play is that it tends to be governed by *implicit rules,* that is, rules that can be discovered by observing the activity rather than rules that are formally stated and exist independently of the particular play activity. For example, although there is no rule book for playing house, it is implicitly understood that there can be only one mother and one father, and that these actors must live up to certain expectations. If one player deviates too widely from the expected role, the other children are likely to correct her for it ("Hey, mommies don't suck on baby bottles; only babies do!")

Flexible rules and roles

Of course, the rules and roles can change to accommodate the needs of the participants; the mommy can become a baby too, so that she gets her quota of nursing, or what begins as a family scene may end up with mommies or teachers having tea together. The particular roles can also be enacted in various ways: "Mommy" can be either bossy or loving, and still be a perfectly acceptable mommy. Such flexibility, which is a hallmark of pretend play, distinguishes it from the more formal games, such as hopscotch and hide-and-seek, that are common among somewhat older children. Games, as distinguished from pretend play, involve relatively fixed, explicit rules which are unlikely to be changed once a game has begun (Sutton-Smith, 1984).

Active participation

A sixth and final characteristic of play is that it requires *active involvement* of the participants. The involvement may be obvious, as when a child carefully constructs a "house" out of kitchen chairs, or it may be subtle and unnoticed, as when a child slowly undoes his shoelaces instead of listening to a story that his mother is reading to him. But either way, the involvement is active; loafing and goofing off do not count as play. Neither does being a spectator, as many parents have discovered when they have taken their preschoolers to athletic events and had trouble keeping them out of the action.

Theories of Play

There are three main theoretical approaches to play: psychoanalytic, learning, and cognitive. Although each theory emphasizes a somewhat different aspect of play, all hold that play activities make a major contribution to developing important social and emotional skills and understandings during the preschool years.

Psychoanalytic Theory   The psychoanalytic theories of both Freud and Erikson emphasize the social and emotional importance of play in early childhood. For one thing, play provides an opportunity for a child to *gain mastery over problems* by rearranging objects and social situations in ways that allow her to imagine that she is in control. Especially in the case of a painful and upsetting experience, a child may display **repetition compulsion,** again and again repeating the experience   Ways of gaining control
in symbolic play and thereby gaining greater control or resolution of it. For example, a young boy who felt abandoned by his hospitalized mother invented a game in which he tied a long string to a wooden doll and then repeatedly made the doll (his mother) leave by throwing her away, only to make her then come back by pulling the string (Erikson, 1963).

Play also allows a child to use fantasy *to gain satisfaction for wishes* and desires that are not possible to fulfill in reality because of limitations in the child's abilities and life situation. A third function of play is to provide an opportunity for **catharsis,** the release of upsetting feelings that cannot otherwise be expressed. Last, play allows a child *to gain increased power* over the environment by rearranging it to suit her own needs and abilities, or to allow her to explore various tasks and activities that in reality might be beyond her current reach (Peller, 1954).

A major strength of the psychoanalytic approach to play is its focus on the importance of fantasy and inner life in children's play. On the other hand, it is vague about precisely how the changes result from play.

Learning Theory   Learning theorists view play as an opportunity for children to try out new behaviors and social roles safely. In their view, play is a major way in which children progressively learn adult social skills, either through successive   Learning adult skills
reinforcement of behaviors which come closer and closer to correct adult behavior or through the processes of observational learning and imitation described in Chapter 2.

What, for example, might a toddler who is playing with wooden blocks be learning about the adult world? For one thing, building with blocks provides an opportunity to learn about the nature and design of physical structures and space; about how hard blocks are, how high they can be piled, and how many small ones equal a larger one. He might also learn about his own capabilities and limitations as a builder: about how high he can reach, how many blocks he can carry at once, and so forth.

More important, perhaps, playing with blocks exposes him to adult expectations and practices, such as when and where blocks can be used, picked up, and stored; and about how to share blocks, how to take turns, and how to cooperate with others. According to learning theory, a child learns both through observation of adults and other children being reinforced for their activities and through his own experience of being directly praised, encouraged, or otherwise reinforced for his own behaviors.

A major strength of the learning theory approach is that it describes the specific processes by which play influences development. A limitation is that it focuses almost exclusively upon the external or extrinsic functions and consequences of play rather than on its intrinsic qualities.

Cognitive Theory Cognitive theorists have identified four major kinds of play, which they believe develop sequentially in parallel with the major stages of cognitive development (Piaget, 1962; Smilansky, 1968). According to their theories, *functional play* occurs during the sensorimotor period; *constructive play* and *dramatic play* during the preoperational period; and *games with rules* during the concrete operational period. The basic idea is that a child's play abilities depend upon her abilities to think and solve problems.

Because the cognitive theory of play is more systematic and specific than the other two theories and has generated a considerable body of literature, we will discuss the cognitive approach to play in somewhat greater depth. Following that, we will describe a systematic approach to thinking about the social levels of play (Parten, 1932).

Cognitive Levels of Play

Because most children do seem to develop certain styles of play in a standard sequence, the four cognitive levels of play are thought to reflect a developmental pattern or trend. (We should point out, however, that not every child engages in all four types of play, or follows the developmental sequence described below.)

Functional Play Functional play involves simple, repeated movements and a focus on one's own body. Sometimes the movements also involve objects, and sometimes not; in any case, they tend not to have a purpose other than movement itself. An infant exhibits functional play when she shakes a rattle joyfully or splashes the water in her bath just to see the effects. A preschool child shows functional play when he runs around the playground for no apparent reason other than the pleasure of running, when he digs in a sandbox with no visible purpose in mind, or when he pounds on some clay without forming anything. Despite its apparent purposelessness, functional play is important to a child because it teaches him about the physical world and the effects of his actions.

Since functional play by definition requires no symbolic activity, it makes up an especially large part of the play activity of older infants and toddlers — more than half, in fact (Sponseller and Jaworski, 1979). By the time a child reaches kindergarten or first grade, though, functional play has decreased to less than one quarter of her total play, or even less (Hetherington et al., 1979). The shift happens partly because many symbolic activities incorporate some of the physical activity characteristic of functional play; a make-believe superhero story, for example, necessarily involves a good deal of moving around, while at the same time it requires symbolic skills like role taking ("I'll be Batman!") and language. Functional play does not disappear in later childhood, then, so much as it becomes combined with other playful ends.

Some purely functional play continues throughout life. Any new activity or object tends to re-create it. A child, or an adult, may ride a new bicycle just to get the feel of it; only later will riding the bicycle become a means to other ends, a part of some larger playful or recreational purpose.

> Functional play decreases with age

*A great deal of the time that families spend
together centers around food—not only do
parents and children usually eat together, but
often they share grocery shopping, meal
preparation, and cleanup. These activities
provide more than physical nourishment:
they also offer opportunities for family
members to tell each other about their
separate activities and special interests and
concerns. These conversations can provide
much of the emotional support that both
parents and children depend on from day
to day.*

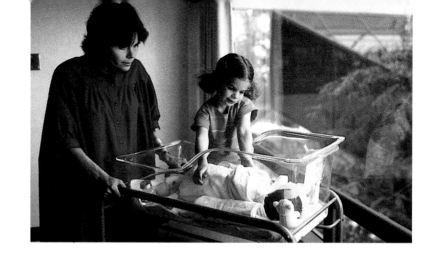

Caretaking—in all its many dimensions—is another important focus of family life. Families provide its members with many forms of physical care: shelter, food, clothing, hygiene, and, when necessary, medical attention. But they also provide intellectual stimulation as well as emotional support—literally a hand to hold, an ear to listen, or a shoulder to cry on. And, of course, families offer love.

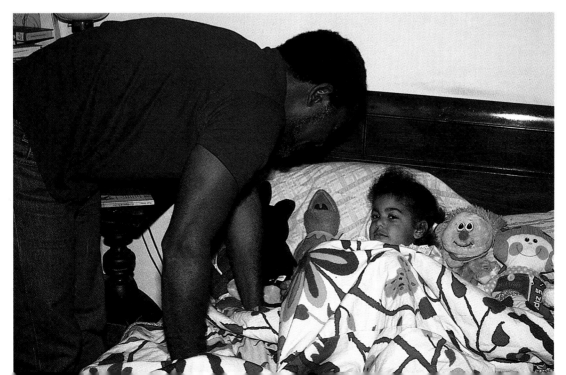

Over and over, family life mixes good feelings with bad ones, genuine caring and love with conflicts, jealousies, and resentments. Siblings may often hug each other one minute but argue the next. The range and intensity of feelings among family members probably reflect the large amount of time they spend together as well as the great emotional importance that family members have for each other.

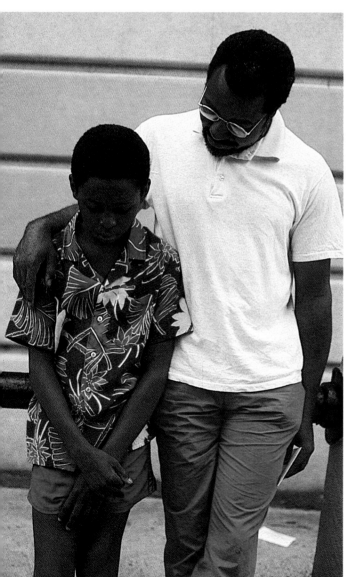

Riding a go-cart involves functional play — a focus on simple, repeated body movements. Although this kind of play is especially prevalent among infants and toddlers, older children often engage in it, too. (Ulrike Welsch)

Constructive Play   In contrast, **constructive play** involves manipulation of physical objects in order to build or construct something. It is not always clear where functional play ends and constructive play begins, especially in older infants and younger preschoolers. For example, a child who at first appears to be building a mountain out of sand may forget about his goal and end up just shoveling the sand for the fun of it. As a child becomes older, however, the constructive elements of play become quite clear. Not only does he build a mountain, but there is a road leading to it and perhaps a car or two that make the trip regularly.

Building things

Dramatic or Make-Believe Play   For several years after infancy, the most significant new form of play involves pretense — **dramatic** or **make-believe play.** Whether for only an instant or for minutes at a time, a preschool child will "be" something else: a bird with arms as wings, perhaps, or a teacher with a stern face and a bossy manner, or a monster with bared teeth. Sometimes objects are transformed as well: a block of wood becomes a telephone, a miniature toy car a real car, or a doll a live baby.

Pretending to be someone or something else

Such pretense occurs even among toddlers, and probably begins as soon as a child can symbolize or mentally represent objects. For example, one of the authors observed a little girl become a cat when she was just two years old:

Building a tower is a form of constructive play. It is probably the most common form of play in early childhood, though not the most cognitively advanced. (Carol Palmer)

Elizabeth would crouch down on the floor with her rear end sticking out in imitation of the prominent haunches of Tigger, the family's cat. From time to time, she would make a noise sort of like a cat's meow. Keeping her head low, she would look around carefully for acknowledgment from her parents. Occasionally she would walk like a cat, although her walk looked more like a rabbit's hopping. Tigger herself was not impressed by all of this.

Such pretense grows in frequency and complexity during the preschool years, and eventually begins to decrease again later in childhood (Rubin and Krasnor, 1980; Rubin et al., 1978).

Make-believe play serves a number of important purposes for the child. For one thing, it helps her to practice or consolidate previously acquired knowledge or **Practicing motor and social skills** skills (Piaget, 1962; Vygotsky, 1967). Building a make-believe house out of blocks, for example, gives practice in the motor skills of building as well as in rehearsing knowledge about typical arrangements and functions of rooms and furniture. At the same time, make-believe play may promote creativity by encouraging diverse uses for objects; a block of wood, the child learns, can represent a chair or a bed (Hutt, 1979). Pretense can also foster social skills by allowing young children to practice a variety of social roles: in play, a child can become a parent or a teacher, a

In dramatic play, children take on pretend roles, like the "doctors," "nurses," and "patient" here. Realistic props, such as the stethoscope in this photograph, encourage dramatic play, but they are not always necessary. (Carol Palmer)

hero or a monster (Saltz and Brodie, 1982).

Overall, make-believe play can help a child maintain optimal levels of arousal, in which she is neither too bored nor too excited (Fein, 1981b). As we mentioned earlier, when certain aspects of life become too taxing or anxiety-provoking, the child can sometimes master such experiences through play and thereby make peace with them. Moving to a new house, for instance, may lead to make-believe re-enactments of the move until the child feels more at ease with the experience. On the other hand, make-believe can add excitement and interest to otherwise dull times; being Cinderella or Superman may be more interesting and cognitively challenging than doing everyday activities like brushing one's teeth.

Games with Rules As children move into their school years, play becomes dominated increasingly by **games with rules.** Compared to make-believe play, these are relatively formal activities, like jump-rope or hide-and-seek. The rules governing them remain fixed during any one occasion of play, although they may generate heated debate and negotiation. In fact, on many occasions a group of children use all their playtime to focus on making, changing, and agreeing on the rules; at times this process seems more important than the game itself. Such play first appears in

Developing a conscious formality

By early elementary school, most children can play games with rules. Not only do these games cultivate motor skills, but they also teach social skills, such as learning to take turns and knowing how to be a good loser. (Raymond Depardon/ Magnum Photos)

the late preschool years — especially when it is supervised or led by an older child or adult — and it reaches a peak late in elementary school (Eifermann, 1971; Rubin and Krasnor, 1980).

The rules for many such games apparently develop out of the more flexible, *ad hoc* rules of make-believe play. Instead of continuing to negotiate roles and behaviors as they go along, young children gradually learn to agree on them beforehand, and learn as well to stand by their agreements throughout a play episode. Given their relatively conscious formality, games with rules can become traditions handed down from one sibling to another and from older playmates to younger ones (Opie and Opie, 1969). Hopscotch, for example, has been around in some form for decades.

The relative formality of games with rules also can help comparative newcomers to fit into play episodes more easily than they can join the more improvised make-believe play, which tends to be unique to particular times and particular groups of children. Gaining access to an episode of make-believe play may therefore actually take relatively more social sensitivity (Corsaro, 1981). The very formality of games with rules, though, also separates participation in them from true social acceptance. Being allowed to play on a team may happen simply because the team needs one more player, and not necessarily because the team likes the newcomer personally.

Whereas older children have been observed engaging in all of the levels of play just discussed, to a significant degree the particular level of play depends upon whether other children are present, who they are, and where and under what circumstances the older children are playing.

Social Levels of Play

Play also varies according to how social it is — according to how much and in what ways children involve others in their play activities. Several decades ago, Mildred Parten studied social participation among preschool children (aged two to five) and proposed that children's play developed according to a series of six stages or levels of sociability (Parten, 1932). Although subsequent researchers have questioned whether her categories actually form a developmental sequence (in much the same way they have questioned Piaget's stages), her distinctions continue to be useful to people who are studying young children (Rubin et al., 1976, 1978). The six types of play identified by Parten are the following:

Parten's six levels

1. *Unoccupied play* This category describes a child who is wandering about, watching whatever is going on, and who does not become involved in any activity for more than a moment or two. He may pick up a ball, then walk over to a table and sit down, then quickly get up and wander over to watch what another person is doing.

2. *Solitary play* Here a child plays alone with toys or other objects, without any direct or indirect awareness of or involvement with other children, even if they are nearby. A preschooler might work a puzzle when she is alone at a table or while other children play with different toys, and another might climb on the jungle gym when no one else is using it.

3. *Onlooker play* In this kind of play, a child watches others at play without actually entering into the activities himself. A two-year-old might simply watch two older children build with blocks without contributing to the building, and a five-year-old might watch classmates make paintings without making one himself. The difference between this and unoccupied behavior is that the child is clearly involved with what is happening and is usually within speaking distance of the actual participants.

4. *Parallel play* Parallel play involves two or more children playing with the same toys in much the same way, in close proximity and with an awareness of each other's presence. However, they do not share their toys, talk, or interact except in very minimal ways. For example, two or three children may work at the sandtable in a preschool or day-care center; they might occasionally glance at each other and at each other's work, but they don't talk with one another or cooperate in the activity. If one child leaves, the others may notice, watch her go, or even quit the activity as a result.

5. *Associative play* Here children become more explicitly sociable. They engage in a common activity and talk with one another about it, but they do not assign tasks or roles to particular individuals in the group, nor are they very

These children are involved in parallel play. They are aware of each other's presence, but they are using separate toys and are preoccupied primarily with their own activities. (David E. Kennedy/TexaStock)

clear about exactly what they are trying to accomplish in the first place. For example, a group of preschoolers may play house together, but the roles and purposes of the episode never become clear: four children cook the meal, then two cooks lie down to be babies who need feeding, then three suddenly start cleaning the place up, and so on. Lots of friendly conversation and interchanges occur, but the activity lacks coordination.

6. *Cooperative play*   In cooperative play, children consciously form into groups to accomplish some activity. Often the activity is dramatic or make-believe play, like playing house; now, however, the children assign themselves roles and stick to them ("You be the mama, and I'll be the sister"). At other times the activity may be a game with rules, in Piaget's sense; tic-tac-toe, for example, is a favorite among kindergartners. Since each person in this sort of play makes a definite contribution to a common goal, cooperative play has a less hectic and competitive air than associative play does.

Often a preschooler's play includes several of the types Parten described. In one recent study of free play among three-year-olds, it was found that parallel play was frequently followed by associative or cooperative group play, and that parallel play served as a transitional or warm-up strategy that enabled a child to move into play involving others (Bakeman and Brownlee, 1980). These findings suggest that the emergence of the ability to cooperate develops sequentially, and also that this sequence of play styles probably continues to help individuals successfully cooperate with others in new situations. The ability to cooperate with others in achieving common goals is an important aspect of successful social relationships throughout life.

Other Influences on Play

Setting While the cognitive and social levels of play are important, the composition of a particular child's play is also likely to be influenced by the range of play opportunities that his caretakers provide and by the types of play they encourage.

A Talk with Larry

Friendship and Play in Early Childhood

Larry, age four, was interviewed in his bedroom after he returned from his day-care center.

INTERVIEWER: Tell me about your friends, Larry. Do you have a best friend?

LARRY: No.

INTERVIEWER: Who are some of the friends that you play with?

LARRY: Kimmy, Judy. Nobody else.

INTERVIEWER: And what do you do with your friends? What do you play?

LARRY: Play Dough. . . . You make it into things.

INTERVIEWER: Why is someone your friend?

LARRY: We play together. With baseball cards.

INTERVIEWER: How?

LARRY: We put doubles together.

INTERVIEWER: What do you do with your doubles?

LARRY: You pile them together.

INTERVIEWER: What do you do during the day?

LARRY: I like to play games and Mousetrap and Safely Home and Wheel of Fortune and go to that store across the street.

INTERVIEWER: What do you do when you get up in the morning?

LARRY: Get dressed. Sometimes I watch T.V.

INTERVIEWER: And then what do you do?

LARRY: I eat breakfast. I have all kind of food. What you want. Bubble gum!

INTERVIEWER: I mean for regular breakfast, not silly breakfast. What would you have?

LARRY: Cereal.

INTERVIEWER: And then what happens, after you have your breakfast?

LARRY: I go to day care.

INTERVIEWER: Tell me about day care. What is day care?

LARRY: You play and there's a lot of toys and there's bikes and balls. A lot of bikes. And Big Wheels. Tricycles. A train. And drinks.

INTERVIEWER: And drinks?

LARRY: Right. And food. And there's a couch there. And there's a closet.

INTERVIEWER: What about people. Who else is there?

LARRY: Kimmy and Judy.

INTERVIEWER: How many other kids are there at day care?

LARRY: Ten people. And two new kids. Eric and Jason. And Aaron.

INTERVIEWER: And are there grown-ups at day care, too?

LARRY: Yes. Lots and lots and lots.

INTERVIEWER: What do the grown-ups do at day care?

LARRY: They tell us what to do.

INTERVIEWER: What do they tell you?

LARRY: Don't do bad things. Like hit or bite.

INTERVIEWER: No hitting, no biting.

LARRY: No throwing pillows, but you can make a hideout.

INTERVIEWER: Do you make a hideout?

LARRY: No. But you can if you want to. If you ask them if it's okay, you can make a hideout. And if they say no, we can't. And if they say yes, we can. And we play and go outside.

Follow-up Questions

1. In Larry's view, what is the basis of friendship? How does this fit with the discussion of preschool friendships in this chapter?

2. Which of social and cognitive levels of play described in this chapter characterize Larry's play?

3. How typical are the types of aggression that Larry reports of children his age?

For example, in a recent study of the effects of day-care quality on children's free play activities, researchers found that children in centers with qualified staffs, child-oriented programs, and appropriate facilities and equipment engaged in much less unoccupied and solitary play than children in centers of lower quality. In addition, preschoolers in the better centers interacted more positively with adults (Vandell and Powers, 1983).

Siblings The presence of siblings also influences play. A series of studies of two-year-olds revealed that their older siblings often (and with some success) tried to engage them in dramatic role playing well before they were two. In some of these families the children played together constantly, and many of the two-year-olds were able to collaborate in the play at levels that were surprisingly sophisticated (Dunn, 1985).

Changes with Age Social participation in various types of play also varies with age. Parallel play, which appears to be the most frequent type of preschool play activity, declines with age, as does solitary play. On the other hand, associative and cooperative play, which involve greater social participation, increase with age (Parten, 1932). While play involving high degrees of social participation increases through childhood and adolescence and tends to be dominant throughout the rest of life, all forms continue to be important, though sometimes more limited. For example, the random, nondirected activity of a shy teenager at a party has much in common with the unoccupied play of a preschooler; devotees of jigsaw or crossword puzzles are clearly involved in forms of solitary play; television viewing and involvement in spectator sports are basically onlooker play activities; and aerobics, weightlifting, and jogging sometimes have strong parallel play aspects.

What is important here is that although developmental shifts appear to be associated with increasing age and social competence, social play takes a variety of
forms throughout childhood and later life. Of course, heavy reliance on onlooker, solitary, and parallel play in a young preschooler is more likely to be seen as age-appropriate than similar reliance on these less social forms among older children and adults. On a broader scale, the increasing reliance on spectator activities in our culture may reflect an increase in social isolation and alienation. Because of this, the development of social relationships, which we discuss in the next section, is more important for preschoolers than ever.

Checkpoint *Play is an activity that is rewarding in itself and that involves active engagement with the social and emotional world through fantasy, and the manipulation of rules and roles. Play occupies much of preschool children's time and is thought to allow children to master problems symbolically, to express upsetting feelings safely, and to practice new social skills.*

Relationships with Others

As our discussion of play shows, young children spend a good deal of time relating to others. Most of the time, these contacts are positive: children share and cooperate, converse with and smile at each other, and in general show at least rudimentary evidence of empathy or mutual understanding. Such **prosocial behavior** sometimes leads to genuine friendships, even among preschool children. But social contacts can be negative, too. Conflict and aggression happen at least as often among young children as among older children and adults, and certain forms happen more often. The sections below describe both prosocial and aggressive social interactions during the preschool years.

Relationships with Parents

As we have noted already in this chapter, the preschool child's expanding powers to initiate verbal and physical activity and the explosive expansion of her powers of imagination lead to a crisis of initiative versus guilt. Successful resolution of this crisis requires parents to support a child's efforts to take on the world and at the same time to appreciate her need for restraints that respect her limitations and self-esteem. Preschoolers often test the limits that parents impose on their behavior and are often very uneven in their ability to understand and consistently conform to parental wishes.

Encouragements and limits

Patterns of Parental Authority One of the most important aspects of a parent-child relationship is the parent's style of authority. Observations of families of preschoolers suggest that styles of child-rearing can be classified into three groups: *authoritarian, permissive,* and *authoritative* (Baumrind, 1967, 1973). Each of these groups reflects a unique combination of four dimensions of child-rearing behavior that Baumrind observed: parental control (strictness of discipline); clarity of parent-child communication (parents' willingness to listen to their child's views and feelings and to give reasons for disciplinary actions); maturity demands (parental pressure and encouragement toward high achievement); and nurturance (warmth and concern for the child's feelings and well-being).

Styles of child-rearing behavior

Authoritarian parents score high on control, low on clarity of communication, high on maturity demands, and low on nurturance. In these families, parents impose their wills by asserting their own power and authority. They tend to remain aloof or reserved from their children, except when they feel that their authority is needed or challenged.

Permissive parents, in contrast, are just the opposite. They score low on control, high on clarity of communication, low on maturity demands, and high on nurturance. Some of these parents tend to be **permissive-indulgent,** making relatively few demands on their children but clearly communicating their warmth and interest and providing considerable care and nurturance. A second subgroup can be thought of as **permissive-indifferent;** for these parents, permissiveness tends to

Two types of permissive parents

All parents discipline their children sometimes. Their methods make a difference: calling attention to the consequences of misbehavior is more effective than spanking, at least in the long run. (Top, Jim Cronk/ Photographic Illustrations; right, Edward Lettau/ Photo Researchers)

reflect a "cop-out" or avoidance of their child-rearing responsibilities, sometimes with very detrimental results.

Authoritative parents score high on control, clarity of communication, maturity demands, *and* nurturance. Thus they differ from both authoritarian and permissive parents in important ways. They do set rules and impose limits, as authoritarian parents do, but they do not justify these in terms of their own power. Instead, they rely on more democratic techniques. For example, in most situations they foster family decisions and resolve differences between themselves and their children through fairly open discussion of each person's feelings, needs, and overall perspective. When their children misbehave, they are interested in understanding the reasons why and in explaining the reasons for the restrictions or punishments that may follow.

Not surprisingly, these three parenting styles have different consequences for children. Children who grow up with authoritarian parents tend to be relatively distrustful and unhappy with themselves; they also tend to achieve less well in school than other children. Children who grow up with permissive parents, on the other hand, tend to lack self-reliance and self-control. As preschoolers, for example, such children might ask for special help in completing an arts-and-crafts project.

Children of authoritative parents show the most desirable personal qualities, judged by the standards of our society: they are the most self-reliant and self-controlled, yet also the friendliest and highest-achieving. Interviews with families of young children found that parental use of reasoning was related to warmth toward their children; parental restrictiveness was related to power-assertion techniques, including physical punishment (Becker et al., 1962).

In addition, researchers have found that mothers who are more accepting, supportive, and loving, who are consistent in enforcing limits, and who are willing to listen to their children's views have sons with better self-esteem than mothers who are less warm and accepting, less consistent, and less willing to listen (Coopersmith, 1967). Similarly, discipline based on a combination of reasoning and a warm and caring relationship with the child appears to be related to positive moral development (Hoffman, 1970). Finally, the ability of parents to act as consultants in response to child-initiated requests for help appears to be related to the development of competence and self-esteem among preschoolers (White, 1975).

One should interpret these findings with caution. For one thing, most ordinary parents do not fall neatly into one or another of these categories, but instead show mixtures of all three types of behaviors. At one time or another, even the best parents justify themselves on the basis of sheer power — perhaps when they, or their child, are too tired to bother discussing for the fourth time why it's time to go to bed. And even the best parents ignore their children from time to time — for example, when they are preoccupied with some pressing matter — and at least for a moment let their children get away with murder.

Furthermore, parents, children, and their patterns of interacting tend to change over time. When their children grow older, for instance, authoritarian parents often ease up and shift to a more permissive or authoritative style. Changes in family situation, including the addition of more children, can also influence pat-

Consequences of parenting styles

Advantages of the authoritative style

Variations in parenting styles

terns of child-rearing. Because of the experience gained from rearing a first child, parents frequently are more comfortable and flexible in rearing subsequent children. In addition, older brothers and sisters often help parents in child-rearing, which in most cases lessens the stresses of parenting. Since additional children also increase the family's overall child-care and economic burdens, however, more relaxed parenting is not always the outcome. Other changes within a family — such as improvement or deterioration in work, income, neighborhood, and health

---

Perspectives on Research

Why Punishment Doesn't Work

Many parents rely on punishment as a means of disciplining their children or penalizing them for misbehavior. Punishment can take many forms: some parents slap, spank, or physically punish their child in other ways. Other parents verbally punish their child, for example, by threatening or yelling at her. Still others inflict various penalties, such as withholding a child's allowance, or "grounding" her, or making her sit in a corner. Research consistently shows that punishing children may work in the short run, but it does not work in the long run. In the short run, it stops or suppresses unwanted behavior. Children will generally stop using curse words, for example, if they are scolded harshly, punished with a slap on the behind, or deprived of dessert. The dramatic success that often follows punishment can immediately reinforce an exasperated adult, and this success can tempt a parent to use the punishment repeatedly.

The catch comes later, however, often well after the punishing incident is over. In the long run, punishment is likely to cause several problems. One is that to be effective, punishment must be rather harsh (Radin, 1982). A mother's shaking her head in mild disapproval is unlikely to stop two children from fighting; for some, only loud words and physical restraint will work. But harsh punishment is destructive to a young child — a thorough spanking risks physical harm and abuse and can be a humiliating experience.

Even punishment that is not physical, such as

very strong criticism, can have negative effects. In part this is because preschoolers are easily confused about the reasons for punishment, and very sensitive to attacks on their feelings of competence and self-esteem: "Was I spanked because I was fighting? Or because I said nasty things? Or because I am a bad person?" This confusion may also have the unintended effects of inhibiting a child's sense of initiative and increasing his feelings of self-blame and guilt.

Another unintended result of punishment is that it often undermines the child's desire to conform to adult standards of behavior. This problem occurs whether the punishment is verbal or physical. A barrage of criticism may simply make a child ignore or "tune out" his parents, because it is too painful to do otherwise, rather than stimulate him to think about his actions and their consequences (Parke, 1977). And the irrational nature of such punishment may lead a child to believe that more reasonable evaluations of his own actions are not really desired.

Punishment has two other important negative consequences. The first is that a parent who uses physical or verbal punishment in responding to a child is likely to discover the child imitating that way of relating to others at some future time, through the processes of modeling and observational learning (see Chapter 2). A good example of this is the parent who yells at and spanks a child to punish him for hitting and teasing his sister. The

— may also influence child-rearing. Families under stress tend to be more rigid, arbitrary, and authoritarian in rearing their children than families that are not.

Last, the child-rearing and disciplinary techniques that a parent chooses may be influenced to some degree by the particular actions of the child. One study, which interviewed mothers of children aged four through eight years old about how they responded to different types of misbehavior, found that the disciplinary responses these parents chose appeared to be determined more by what the child did than by

Children's influence on parenting styles

"do as I say, not as I do" philosophy generally backfires, because an adult's actions often speak much louder than words, especially for preschool-age children. A second undesirable consequence is the negative feelings that a punitive parent often has following the incident. At times these guilt feelings may make the parent behave more affectionately toward the child, confusing him about his parent's true feelings.

If the goal of punishment is to eliminate unwanted or undesirable behavior, it probably rarely works. Rather, punishment serves to suppress the behavior for a given interval of time. Unless an alternative behavior is substituted, however, the suppressed behavior is likely to recover spontaneously.

With these conclusions in mind, parents might use the following guidelines to help make punishment relatively effective in situations where it is used as a temporary means of suppressing certain behaviors — say, stopping a three-year-old from running into the street (O'Leary and O'Leary, 1977):

1. *Explain why you are punishing,* focusing on the specific undesirable behavior. Even if the child does not seem to be listening to the explanation, give it anyway.
2. *Give a positive alternative to the unwanted behavior.* For example, say "Instead of running into the street to get your ball, you must come tell me and I will get it for you."

3. *Emphasize verbal rather than physical punishment.* Since punishment often comes at an emotional time for adults, they are in danger of running out of control. Physical punishment in this situation can be dangerous to the child and potentially abusive.
4. *Punish the beginning of unwanted behavior,* not the end. In this way the child will need to suppress less behavior and will need less punishment overall (Walters and Grusec, 1977).

While punishment may be a useful technique for stopping destructive or dangerous behavior in the short term, because of its undesirable side effects it should be used only when absolutely necessary. Parents can minimize their need to use punishment by carefully arranging their children's play environments and in teaching their children to understand rules and limits and to seek adult assistance when needed. They can emphasize *positive reinforcement* of desirable behaviors instead ("What a good boy you are for coming to get mommy to help get your ball and for not going into the street yourself!"). Also, many undesirable behaviors contain positive elements that deserve recognition and praise. A child who climbs dangerously high in a backyard tree, for example, may deserve criticism for her poor judgment but may also deserve praise for her courage and her climbing ability.

a general child-rearing style. Threats of punishment were widely used for most misdeeds, but reasoning and discussion were frequently used when the child's actions caused psychological harm to others (Grusec and Kuczynski, 1980).

Ultimately, it is the parents' responsibility to establish the sort of parent-child relationship that fosters the child's confidence and self-esteem and that sets the stage for his future social interactions. The authoritative parenting style seems to be most in tune with the goals just mentioned. Simply stated, for most children, the parent-child relationship establishes the central model for a child's relationship to himself and others. Authoritative parenting is probably successful over the long term because it models and promotes qualities that all children need. Although it is doubtful that many parents display these desirable qualities 100 percent of the time, it is very likely that given adequate motivation and support, the great majority of parents can more fully develop these qualities in their relationships with their children.

Relationships with Siblings

As we have noted in our discussion of play, brothers and sisters are major participants in the social activities of many preschoolers. Studies of children's behavior toward their siblings have shown that most young children are very interested in babies, and that their repetitions, explanations, and "language practice" speech are very similar to those of adult care-givers (Dunn, 1985). Older siblings provide important role models for their preschool brothers and sisters, facilitating the learning of social skills and parental expectations. Further, observations of both friendly and aggressive interactions of siblings suggest that such interactions provide an important basis for the development of social understandings and the beginnings of children's grasp of the particular feelings, intentions, and needs of people other than themselves (Dunn, 1985).

Older siblings as role models

The sophisticated understandings that young children have of their siblings may be due to several factors. First, they are very familiar with each other, since they spend so much time together; second, they share very similar sources of excitement, pleasure, joy, and fear; third, the family setting in which brothers and sisters work, play, and fight is emotionally intense, involving feelings of conflict, jealousy, and affection. It is therefore very important for young children to understand what their siblings are feeling or intending to do (Dunn, 1985).

Given the social opportunities that siblings make available, one might guess that children growing up with brothers and sisters will develop social skills earlier and more rapidly, and also, perhaps, end up with better skills than children who have not had this opportunity. However, although an older sister (or brother) can be an excellent teacher and role model, her competence and need to outshine her younger brother might also discourage him from developing certain social skills as easily as he might if he weren't in his older sister's shadow. Similarly, while experience with a younger sibling is likely to enhance social competence with younger children, being burdened with the care of a younger brother or sister might limit an older child's opportunities to spend time with children her own age. Just how siblings will affect a particular child's social development is likely to depend upon the degree to which parents recognize and respond appropriately to the social needs of all of their children.

Friendships in Early Childhood

Preschool children are simultaneously pulled in two different directions. On one hand, they seek the security and intimacy that comes from playing continuously with a familiar friend; on the other hand, they want to participate in the variety of activities that are possible with many different children.

Although preschool friendships often involve shared activity and recognition of similarities, sometimes solidarity between two children involves exclusion of a third. In the following example, which takes place at a sink in a preschool classroom, Yolanda's alliance with Deanne involves exclusion of Shawn:

Importance of shared activity and similarities

YOLANDA: I have some gum and candy — not for Shawn.

SHAWN: Why not?

YOLANDA: 'Cause you won't help.

SHAWN: I'm rinsing.

DEANNE: These are hardly even clean. I have a whole bunch of suckers.

YOLANDA: Me too. I'm not giving Shawn any gum.

SHAWN: Yes, you are.

YOLANDA: No, I ain't. I'm going to give Deanne gum 'cause —

DEANNE: 'Cause I don't fight with you?

YOLANDA: Yes.

DEANNE: I'll give Shawn a little teeny piece.

YOLANDA: Yes, give him a little teeny piece. . . . See, you're not helping.

SHAWN: I'm rinsing.

DEANNE: I already rinsed it twice.

The Evolution of Friendship Even infants and toddlers show preferences for particular other children of their own age. Given a choice among several peers in a playroom, a one- or two-year-old is likely to smile at and approach his particular friend more often than a nonfriend (Furman, 1982). He will also be more skillful at taking turns with a friend than with a nonfriend; if two friends are playfully making noises or movements, for example, they will wait longer for each other to finish and generally coordinate their activity better than two children who are not friends might (Vandell, 1980; Howes and Mueller, 1984). Although these early friendships are somewhat unstable and often change on a daily or weekly basis, they do suggest that young children begin discriminating among their peers at an early age. These preferences are an important step toward forming more lasting friendships later in childhood.

Early sensitivity to friends

By age four, friendships become more involved and durable. Certain pairs of children develop a liking for each other and purposely try to spend time together. Typically, the pairings develop in situations that encourage physical proximity,

During early childhood, friendships depend heavily on shared activities that children enjoy. Only later do more abstract qualities, such as intimacy and mutual loyalty, become important. (Carol Palmer)

like the children's neighborhood play group, day care, or preschool classroom. Typically, too, the friendships that develop emphasize shared activities more than shared feelings, thoughts, and dispositions (Chandler and Boyes, 1982). In part this is because preschoolers still lack the language skills needed to communicate effectively what they are thinking and feeling.

Emphasis on shared activities

But preschoolers do have enough symbolic skills to know — and to say — who their friends are. For example, if a child names Jose as a friend, then observations of the child and Jose show that the two really do have many more positive interactions than most pairs of children do, and fewer negative ones (Masters and Furman, 1981). Home observations of children between the ages of three and six at play with best friends and new acquaintances indicate that self-declared friends are more willing to answer their friend's questions, to explain the reasons for their actions, and to discuss the reasons for disagreements that might arise (Gottman and Parkhurst, 1980). Interestingly, this is more true of three- and four-year-olds than of five- and six-year-olds, probably because younger children feel less able to manage disagreements and therefore attempt to avoid them.

Instability of early friendships

Such management problems and the concrete emphasis on overt, shared activities tend to make early friendships unstable. A preschool child will drop a friend relatively easily — but then make up to her later just as easily. Sometimes she will even exchange goods for friendship; one child will say to another, "If you give me a piece of candy, I'll be your best friend!"

By the end of the preschool period, stable friendships do emerge, but they are not necessarily as reciprocal or intimate as adult friendships are. A child may choose a friend because the friendship enhances his status among his peers. Having an especially popular friend, for example, may help a child feel more popular himself. Or a child may choose a friend because the friend has a desired possession or skill — perhaps an especially attractive train set at home, or the ability to protect herself from unwanted playmates. Because these relationships are somewhat more permanent than earlier ones, they are in a sense more mature or adultlike, but they still tend to focus mainly on fulfilling one-way or self-centered needs. Truly mutual and reciprocal relationships do not become common until the school years.

Conceptions of Friendship During their preschool years, children also develop ideas about the nature of friendship — ideas that parallel, to a large degree, the actual friendship behaviors they reveal. In the minds of younger preschoolers, a friend is someone who does certain things with you; he is someone (*anyone,* in fact) that you like to play with, share toys with, or talk with a lot. "A friend," as one preschooler put it, "lets you hold his doll or truck or something."

Disagreements and fights between preschool friends are upsetting to them. When friends fight, the fights generally have to do with objects and activities — whether to build a sandcastle, say, or how to draw pictures or cook a pretend dinner. However, because the children usually are not yet able to think in terms of lasting feelings and dispositions, they do not usually hold grudges, and making up is relatively easy (Selman, 1981a).

As children near school age, though, more permanent, personal qualities enter into their conceptions (Furman, 1982). Now the crucial features of a friend are more often **dispositional** — that is, related to how the friend is likely to behave in the future. A friend is still very much "someone you like," but she is also someone whom you trust, whom you can depend upon, and who may like and admire you. To be friends in this sense, two children must know each other's likes and preferences better than before, and they must also be increasingly aware of thoughts and feelings that the friend may keep hidden and unstated. However, each child is still likely to focus primarily on her own needs, to the exclusion of her friend's. As one child said, "A friend is someone who does what you want"; and as another said, "A friend doesn't get you in trouble." Neither of these children happens to think that sometimes they should return these favors; later, during the school years, this is likely to occur to them.

Empathy and Prosocial Behavior

Empathy is a sensitive awareness of the thoughts and feelings of another person, and **prosocial behavior** refers to actions that benefit others. The development of both is related to good parent-child relationships and secure attachment during infancy and toddlerhood (see Chapter 7).

The Extent of Empathy and Helpfulness   In a variety of situations, preschool children will respond helpfully to another person's distress. For example, slides or films depicting people with various feelings elicit similar emotions in young children who watch them, as judged by the expressions on the children's faces (Eisenberg-Berg and Neal, 1979). In naturalistic situations as well, young children show an ample tendency to empathize. A study of children at a day-care center playground found that a crying child almost always (more than 90 percent of the time) generated concerned responses from the other children, almost all of whom were helpful (Sawin, 1979). About half of the children who were near the distressed child showed similar facial expressions, looking as though they might cry them-

Empathy with distressed children

Perspectives on Research

Shyness: What Are Its Causes?

Although shyness is a difficult concept to define clearly, it is something that is experienced very widely. In fact, in one study, more than 80 percent of people surveyed reported that they had been shy at some point in their lives — presently, in the past, or always — and of these, more than 40 percent considered themselves presently shy (Zimbardo, 1977). Phillip Zimbardo has written extensively about shyness, and the discussion that follows is based largely on his work.

Shyness is a particularly painful experience for young children who are struggling to achieve strong-enough senses of autonomy, initiative, competence, and self-esteem, and to achieve these without being overcome by feelings of shame, doubt, guilt, and loss of esteem. Observations of nursery-school and school-aged children at home and at school, as well as interviews with children and their caretakers, reveal that patterns of shyness appear to relate to five major areas: the self-image of the shy child, the child's birth order, parents' and children's sensitivity to shyness, experiences with parents, and experiences at school.

1. *Self-image of the shy child*   Shy boys feel that they are too tall, too fat, too weak, too ugly, and generally less attractive than their classmates who are not shy. Shy girls are more likely to describe themselves as thin, unattractive, and less intelli-

gent. Shy children view themselves as being less popular, and more than three fourths of the boys surveyed by Zimbardo felt downright unpopular.

Is the lower sense of self-esteem reported by shy children a result of their really being less attractive, or is it because they hold unrealistically high standards for themselves? In general, it appears that even when shy children are seen by others as attractive, intelligent, and competent, they remain convinced that this is not the case, and reinterpret evidence to confirm their view. For example, even though a shy child may get grades that are as good as those of children who are not shy, he believes that because he is quiet and doesn't have as much to say in class, he is not as intelligent as the others.

2. *Birth order*   First-born girls are somewhat more likely to be shy than later-born girls, a difference that appears to continue into adolescence. For boys, first-borns are shyer through the preschool and very early school years, but by early adolescence birth-order differences disappear.

These findings are thought to reflect the greater concern and anxiety that new parents have about their first-born child as compared with their later-born children. They may set higher standards for their first child and place greater demands on her. First-born children appear to have greater need for approval and lower self-esteem than later-borns (Forer, 1976).

---

selves. Almost one fifth of the nearby children tried to console the child directly — and their actions did in fact usually reduce the crying. Other children sought out an adult on the playground; still others threatened revenge on the child who caused the upset.

Not surprisingly, however, there are limits to how empathic and helpful young children can be. In part this is because of their limited sensitivity to the feelings of others, and in part because of their limited capacity to distance themselves from the emotion and protect themselves from the feelings it creates. In the playground study just mentioned, for example, not all the children responded in a truly helpful way; about 12 percent withdrew from the scene of the distress, and occasionally

Limits to empathy

---

3. *Sensitivity to shyness* Although young children do not appear to be sensitive to their parents' shyness, parents are sensitive to shyness in their children. Both shy mothers and shy fathers are quite accurate in knowing whether or not a child is shy, with mothers being the most accurate. Mothers who are not shy are fairly accurate, while fathers who are not shy have little sensitivity to such feelings in their children.

4. *Parents' role* Shy children are very likely to have at least one shy parent in the family. In one study, this association occurred about 70 percent of the time (Zimbardo, 1977). Often only one child in the family is cast in the shy role, and more often than not that child is the first-born rather than later-born.

5. *Shyness and schools* Teachers in general are not very good at perceiving shyness in their students, although teachers who are shy themselves are more aware of shyness than those who are not (Ziller, 1973). Children who are shy in the classroom are afraid to try activities that expose them to public scrutiny, such as dancing, leading a game, or being first to do something. They tend to talk too softly to be heard, and are afraid to sing out, speak out, or make mistakes. When asked a question, they frequently answer, "I don't know."

There are several reasons why the problem of shyness persists in the classroom. For one thing,

shy children are rarely seen as troublemakers and are very easy for a teacher to overlook, particularly if there are many children in a preschool or kindergarten. The shy child's inability to ask for help is another contributing factor. Because shy children find it hard to engage their teacher on a personal level and to accept his help and advice, the teacher may find them less rewarding and at times feel rejected by them.

Whether it is at home, in the day-care center, or at a preschool, children of this age need to feel confidence in their environment and security in their relationships with others. A reasonable degree of order and predictability as well as enough flexibility and freedom to allow exploration and experimentation are needed to achieve this. Parents and teachers are most helpful to shy (and to not-so-shy) young children when they respond to what a preschooler is feeling in a warm and sensitive way, are reasonable in their expectations, and respect the child's self-esteem by not humiliating him or being unduly critical of his mistakes. Last, it is important for parents and teachers to resist the temptation to label a child as shy, for acceptance of a shy identity creates much of the problem for the shy child.

children were overtly aggressive or teasing toward the child who was upset. Nearby children were also much more likely to empathize with positive feelings than with unhappy ones. Looking happy in particular proved more contagious than looking sad, angry, or hurt. A second, and perhaps more important, limitation in the ability of young children to be empathic and helpful is that they do not yet have the cognitive maturity to see things from another person's perspective (see Chapter 9).

Developmental Changes   Helpfulness or prosocial behavior is well established by the time a child reaches the preschool years. An early, classic study found that all of the following helping behaviors occurred with significant frequency among four-year-olds (Murphy, 1937): assisting another child; comforting another child; protecting another child; warning another child of danger; giving things to another child; and inquiring of a child in trouble. Fifty years later, these and similar helping behaviors are still quite evident, not only among preschool children but even among children under two (Radke-Yarrow and Zahn-Waxler, in press; Zahn-Waxler and Radke-Yarrow, 1982). For instance, when a toddler sees her brother cry, she may give him her bottle, or when a four-year-old at nursery school worries because his parents are late in picking him up, another child may put her arm around him and say, "It's okay — they'll be here soon."

Reasons for helping change with age

Between ages two and six, children give increasingly complex reasons for helping, and are more strongly influenced by nonaltruistic as well as altruistic motives and concerns (Yarrow and Waxler, 1978). An older child may justify his helpfulness in terms of gaining approval from peers in general, rather than in terms of his concern for the well-being of the particular child in distress. Or he may justify withholding help because of fear of disapproval from adults — if he has been instructed, perhaps, to let the day-care or nursery-school teachers handle children in trouble. In fairness to older preschoolers, though, younger children may also have reasons like these and simply not yet be able to verbalize them clearly.

Fostering Empathy and Prosocial Behavior   Preschool children are more willing to help if adults call attention to other children's distress. In one experiment, young children played a game in which they won plastic tokens which could later be turned in for prizes (Howard and Barnett, 1981). Some children were told that certain other children who played the game would not be winning any tokens, and that they could share their tokens with the less fortunate children later if they wished. In these conditions, a number of children voluntarily donated tokens after the experiment, and also reported feeling sad for their unfortunate peers. But they were particularly likely to do so if the experimenters had called attention not only to their peers' lack of winnings but also to the nonwinners' distressed feelings.

Influence of adult encouragement

Does this sort of encouragement result in a permanent tendency to empathize? Authoritative answers to this question are scarce. It seems plausible, though, that parents who emphasize the expression and discussion of feelings should have children who tend to be relatively empathic and helpful. A study of young adults confirmed this possibility: college students who showed especially empathic attitudes also reported having had parents who valued and fostered attention to feelings (Barnett et al., 1980). How accurate such self-reports are, though, remains open to question; to some extent, the empathic adults may have reconstructed memories of their childhoods to fit their current personalities, rather than the other way around.

Some additional help in answering the question of how significant parental encouragement is comes from cross-cultural studies. One study, now a classic, compared child-rearing experiences in the United States and five other, non-Western cultures (Whiting and Whiting, 1975). The researchers found that in mainly rural societies where mothers work in the fields and children assume major child-care and household responsibilities, children have a greater opportunity to experience prosocial roles and to behave prosocially. First-born children, who have the most helping experience, tend to be more prosocial than last-born or only children. Another study, which used a cooperative game to compare the performance of children from urban and rural cultures, found that children from small, closely knit urban communities were more cooperative than children from rural or big-city areas (Madsen, 1971). These findings suggest that exposure to empathic and prosocial role models and direct participation in community life rather than merely living in a rural or urban area are likely to increase empathy and prosocial behavior in children.

Conflict and Aggression

So far our discussion of social relationships has focused on the ability of preschoolers to get along reasonably well with one another, but of course preschoolers have also been known to get very angry and to express their feelings in aggressive ways: grabbing each other's toys, pushing, hitting, scratching, and calling names. It is possible that research on friendship and altruistic behavior underestimates the role of conflict and aggression among preschoolers, because the observations on which it is based are often conducted in adult-supervised settings (Sutton-Smith, 1981; Sutton-Smith and Kelly-Byrne, 1984a, 1984b).

The Nature of Aggression No one agrees about how to define aggression. Some people define it strictly in terms of its consequences: as an action that results in harmful consequences to a person or object. Others point out that since harmful consequences can result from unintended or accidental actions, and actions that *are* intended to harm another sometimes fail to do so, harmful motivations or intentions are the key to defining an act as aggressive. Thus, **aggression** is an action that is intended to hurt another person or object and that in most circumstances succeeds in its objective. Quite frequently, aggressive behavior is associated with a child's frustration at not being able to solve a conflict; for example, one child may hit another because her attempts to get a turn with a favorite toy have all failed.

Aggressiveness differs from assertiveness. **Assertiveness** is the more general tendency to communicate clearly and effectively and thus fulfill one's needs, but not necessarily with the intention of or in a way that succeeds in hurting another person. Judgments about the extent to which a person is aware of his motivations and, more important, of the consequences of his actions are critical in deciding

Early in the preschool years, aggression focuses on getting access to desirable toys and activities; physical and emotional harm are often unintentional by-products of these instrumental goals. (Andrew Brillant)

whether a hurtful incident is the result of aggressive behavior or the accidental by-product of assertiveness.

For instance, a preschooler may accidentally knock over another child's sky-scraper, or she may knock it down on purpose; she might run over another child with her tricycle because she is intent on winning a race and doesn't see the other child standing there, or she may do it because she is angry at him. Frequently preschoolers (and at times their adult caretakers as well) find it difficult to distinguish between their own aggressive and assertive motivations; similarly, they become upset when hurtful acts occur, which makes it more difficult to figure out what has really happened. The context in which an action occurs can also be important; for example, a teacher's good-natured teasing may cause considerable anguish if it is aimed at his students, but the same teasing among fellow teachers after school may have little in the way of negative results.

Distinguishing between aggression and assertion

Generally, judgments about a child's aggressiveness are based on her motivations, on her level of knowledge of the effects of her actions, and on whether or not there have been destructive consequences. Knowledge of the child's previous patterns of response in similar situations is also helpful in making reliable judgments.

Changes in Aggression During Early Childhood Young preschoolers show aggression more physically than older preschoolers do. As children get older, they shift to more verbal methods, and insults and demands replace pushing and grabbing — though aggression as a whole declines in frequency with age. These changes can be observed directly in nursery-school classrooms (Hartup, 1974), and are also confirmed by parents' diaries about their children (Goodenough, 1931).

When a younger child behaves aggressively, he often has a more assertive, practical goal in mind, like retrieving a toy from a child who has walked off with it. Grabbing the toy back is not necessarily aggressive, and usually does not result in the other child's feeling wronged. The action ends when the little boy gets his toy back, rather than when the other child shows pain or humiliation. This type of assertive behavior is referred to as **instrumental aggression.** Having a practical goal

Sometimes, of course, a child who feels that she has been hurt or mistreated may retaliate by trying to hurt the child who wronged her. Such behavior, which is aggressive in the sense of our earlier definition, is sometimes referred to as **hostile aggression,** because harm is an important intent. A key change, then, among five- and six-year-olds is that aggression often involves a motivation to hurt the other person and his feelings. Wanting to hurt

Consistent with these changes are shifts in what stimulates or brings about aggression. Preschool children of all ages respond to assertiveness and instrumental aggression with about the same frequency. In the case of **blocking behaviors** — actions that interfere with a child's current activities or keep her from the toys she is using — preschool children of all ages will respond with hostile aggression around one quarter of the time (Hartup, 1974). Personal insults, however, are another story. As preschool children get older, they insult each other more and respond to insults with increasing frequency — nearly four fifths of the time by age five (Krasner and Rubin, 1983). And they respond in kind; insulting remarks and ridicule generate insults and ridicule in retaliation. In part this occurs because children perceive each other's intentions more accurately as they get older, and they are also more vulnerable to these kinds of attacks. Insults increase with age

Influences on the Development of Aggression   When it is expressed in acceptable ways, aggression may be not only tolerable but even desirable. Assertive or instrumental aggressive actions allow a child to communicate and fulfill legitimate needs, as when the child takes back a toy that is rightfully his or stands up for his integrity against unfair insults. Quite often, though, hostile motivations complicate matters and create additional upset. This is particularly true for preschool children who are working hard to master the aggressive impulses associated with the oedipal conflict and to assert their initiative successfully without experiencing undue guilt. The anger and rage that children sometimes experience can be quite upsetting to them as well as to their parents and others. For example, a mother who observes her four-year-old attack a playmate, perhaps biting him or pulling his hair, is likely to be upset for multiple reasons, including her child's unhappiness, the pain and upset of the other child, her feeling that biting is "dirty fighting," and concerns about how this all reflects upon her as a parent.

Several factors strongly influence the overall development of aggression. Important among them is willingness of parents and others both to accept their children's "hostile-aggressive" impulses and actions and to help them to discover nonhostile or "instrumentally aggressive" alternatives for resolving conflicts and asserting their needs.

Biological influences

While biology does not typically cause aggressive behavior, it can contribute to it indirectly. As we explain in Chapter 7, temperamental differences in children at birth may make aggressive behavior more likely during early childhood. Babies with especially "difficult" temperaments at six months of age, for example, have been found to have more conflict with their mothers at age three than other babies do (Bates, 1979).

"Difficult" babies experience greater conflict

As six-month-olds, these difficult babies tended to have irregular levels of activity, including sudden bursts of arm waving and general restlessness. When they were three years old, their mothers used a very wide variety of methods to attempt to control them, including forbidding certain activities, threatening punishment, and using physical restraint. These children responded less cooperatively than did children who had had "easier" temperaments as infants. They were also more likely to get into trouble a second time, to ignore their parents' disciplinary efforts, and to respond in insulting and unpleasant ways. Thus, the ongoing interactions between these difficult children and their parents seemed likely to promote rather than reduce further aggression. (Of course, many active or difficult babies do not become aggressive three-year-olds, perhaps because the expression of tempera-

---

Perspectives on Research

Preschoolers' Judgments of Aggressive Intent

As children move through the preschool years, they become increasingly skillful at accurately judging the intentions of others and distinguishing between situations that involve hostile aggression and those that do not. To demonstrate this, researchers in one study asked preschoolers to evaluate various stories about children who were naughty (Rule et al., 1974). Some of the stories illustrated hostile aggression — actions that are motivated by the desire to hurt. Others showed instrumental aggression — assertive behavior that is not hostile in its intentions but that might accidentally cause harm. A third group of stories showed aggression that was altruistically motivated — for example, grabbing a toy back from a bully who had just taken it from a weaker child. Both younger and older preschoolers judged the third, or "Robin Hood," themes more positively than they did the other two types.

In a similar study, children heard two different versions of a story about one person hurting another (Rotenberg, 1980). In one version the harm happened by accident; in the other it was inten-

tional. Kindergartners evaluated the situations in both stories in much the same ways as older children did, judging the intentional aggression as worse than the accidental aggression. Interestingly, however, the younger children did not make negative judgments about the future behavior of intentional aggressors, whereas the older children did.

In part this result may reflect a greater readiness among younger children to avoid conflict and to forgive and forget. It also reflects their ignorance of personality as an enduring, stable feature of human beings. In fact, actions rather than people provide the main play themes for younger preschoolers, who are more likely to re-enact "everything you can do in the kitchen" than "everything that Mama ever does" (Forbes and Yablick, 1984). Thus, whereas younger and older preschoolers alike can usually determine whether an aggressor is a Robin Hood or a common thief or bully, they can safely predict how peers are likely to behave in the future only when they reach school age.

---

ment is, to a significant degree, a product of child-caretaker interactions [Bates, 1979]).

Physical looks may also make a difference. Preschool children seem just as able to judge physical attractiveness as adults are, and are just as apt to attribute stereotyped behaviors to good and bad looks. Attractive children are thought to possess various positive traits like friendliness, whereas unattractive children are thought to possess negative ones, including meanness and aggressiveness (Langlois and Stephan, 1981).

To some extent these stereotypes can actually be observed in young children (Langlois and Downs, 1980). Attractive and less attractive children, it seems, tend to be equally sociable or outgoing, but the less attractive ones hit their peers more often, and generally exhibit more boisterous play. A probable explanation for these differences is a self-fulfilling prophecy: adults, peers, and the unattractive child himself learn to expect undesirable behavior from someone who is judged to be unattractive, and eventually the child learns to live up to those expectations.

Aggressiveness of less attractive children

Throughout the preschool years, boys exhibit more aggressive behavior than girls do (Maccoby and Jacklin, 1980). This difference holds true across a broad range of social classes, ethnic groups, and cultures. It is also true across a wide range of aggressive behaviors; contrary to popular belief, for example, girls do not specialize in verbal aggression (such as name calling) or boys in physical aggression (such as pushing and hitting).

Gender differences

Overall levels of aggressive behavior and gender differences in aggressiveness depend on a number of circumstances. Preschool boys initiate aggressive actions a little more often than girls do, but they retaliate against aggression a lot more (Darvill and Chenye, 1981). When two children play together in nursery classrooms, they are more aggressive when the pairs include boys, and particularly when they consist of two boys.

Child-rearing and educational philosophies and practices of parents and teachers also influence both overall levels of aggression and gender differences. For example, day-care centers that tolerate aggression and disobedience are likely to experience more of it than those that are less tolerant (Belsky and Steinberg, 1978). The same is probably true of families and informal play groups. And child-rearing environments that actively work to minimize sex-role stereotyping of young children are likely to minimize gender differences in aggression. If girls are encouraged to be as assertive as boys in their play and other social interactions and if their hostile aggressive actions are not unduly criticized, gender differences will probably be smaller than they are in situations where girls are expected to be less assertive and aggressive (Hoffnung, 1983).

Influence of child-rearing practices

Parents' overall style or pattern of child-rearing is likely to influence both the desirable and undesirable behaviors of their children significantly. All of the following child-rearing characteristics have been found to contribute to aggressiveness in preschoolers, especially when they are part of an ongoing pattern (Baumrind, 1971; Martin, 1975):

1. Lack of acceptance of the child, dislike of the child, and criticism of the child for being the sort of person she currently is or is becoming

2. Excessive permissiveness, particularly if it involves indifference to the true needs of the child for reasonable but consistent limits and emotional support
3. Discipline that does not respect the child's ability and need to understand the reasons for the punishment and its meaning to the parent
4. Inconsistent discipline, which does not provide the child with a reasonable and predictable basis for learning to regulate her behavior
5. A "spare the rod and spoil the child" attitude, which often results in impulsive and overly harsh use of discipline
6. Unclear rules and expectations for the child, particularly regarding her interactions with other family members.

Provocation by peers

As we pointed out earlier, peers can also contribute to aggression, by acting in ways that provoke aggressive retaliation. Presumably a child surrounded by provocative peers will eventually acquire a similar style himself, and in doing so will stimulate further aggressive behavior in his peers. At the beginning of a nursery-school year, for example, Bill may argue with Fred over who should use a favorite truck. Fred may hit Bill to get his own way; Bill may discover that unless he hits back, he will rarely get a turn with the truck. After several conflicts involving shoves and punches, Bill may begin hitting too, even though he never intended to do so. Of course, Bill may instead become passive and withdraw to avoid being punched.

Hierarchical relationships

A series of aggressive exchanges among pairs of preschool children sometimes results in a **dominance hierarchy** — a pattern of status and authority which is influenced by who wins and who loses, but which is also related to leadership and popularity within a group (Abramovitch and Strayer, 1978). These hierarchies are temporary and are generally maintained more by bluffing and threats than by overt acts of aggression. Although they do serve to reduce overt aggression in the short run, the climate they create can be destructive to the social development of both winners and losers; relationships based upon dominance and submission are not the best basis for the development of friendship and self-esteem.

Some preschool children find themselves involved in frequent conflicts anyway; they continually either lose battles and arguments or lose potential friends by depending too much on hostile aggressive actions to get what they need. Why do some children have such troubles? Possibly because they lack skill in resolving conflicts peacefully; they may resort to violence too soon (Asher and Renshaw, 1982). Or their conception of social relationships might be poorly developed; they may think, for example, that a friend is simply someone who gives you what you want, and that someone who does not is an enemy (Shantz and Shantz, 1985). Finally, a preschooler who is overly aggressive toward her peers may be upset and angry about other things, such as her family situation. Because she is unable to express her anger directly, she behaves aggressively at her day-care center.

Influence of media

As many concerned parents realize, television, films, and other media exert strong influences on children, and much of the influence centers on physical violence. According to a wide variety of well-documented studies, watching violence **disinhibits** or releases violent behavior in children who are already prone to be angry and aggressive. Most children, however, react by becoming desensitized to the pain and hurt that result from aggression.

Preschool children have a special problem in coping with violence in the media: their lack of skill in figuring out the motives of actors and the subtleties of plots. A completely villainous murder on television, for example, may look the same to a preschooler as one committed in self-defense or to protect innocent people (Collins et al., 1981). Adult supervision and help in understanding television programs therefore seem especially important for very young children. Unfortunately, one of television's main attractions for some parents is that it makes adult supervision "unnecessary" by keeping children passively occupied.

Although aggressive responses to conflict are fairly common among preschoolers, then, physical differences, gender, child-rearing styles, peers, and the media may influence the frequency and type of aggressive behavior. Aggression is much less likely to cause problems when caretakers provide adequate guidance for preschool children and have realistic expectations of young children's ability to resolve conflicts and to regulate their aggressive impulses.

Checkpoint   *The child-rearing style of their parents and the nature of their interactions with siblings and other children strongly influence preschool children's social development. Preschool friendships are based largely upon shared activities and recognition of similarities. Empathic, prosocial, and aggressive behaviors are influenced by the nature of the situation and the behavior of others, as well as by limitations in the preschooler's ability to assume another person's social perspective.*

Gender Development

Gender influences important aspects of social development in early childhood. As used here, the term **gender** refers to the behaviors and attitudes associated with being male or female. Most children experience it in at least three ways (Shepherd-Look, 1982). First, they acquire **gender constancy,** a belief that the sex of a person is biologically determined, permanent, and unchanging, no matter what else about them may change. Second, they develop beliefs about **gender identity,** that is, which sex *they* are and will always be. And third, they develop **gender preferences,** attitudes about which sex they wish to be. Gender preference does not always coincide with gender identity.

All three aspects of gender contribute to a child's general knowledge of society's expectations about sex roles. This particular knowledge is sometimes referred to as **sex-role stereotypes.** Even very young preschoolers have some awareness of these stereotypes and often act in ways that reflect them.

Developmental Trends During Early Childhood

Usually even two-year-olds can label themselves correctly as boys or girls; for that matter, they can correctly label other children and adults. At this age, though, a child may not believe in gender constancy, the idea that sex is biologically determined and permanent. A young preschool child may say that he can switch gender just by wanting to, or he may say that even though he is a boy now, he was a girl as an infant or may grow up to become a woman as an adult. And a two-year-old may have only a hazy notion of what defines gender, believing, perhaps, that certain hair styles, clothing, and toys make the crucial difference. Most children achieve gender constancy by age eight or nine (Emmerich and Sheppard, 1982). Meanwhile, though, they undergo several significant developments.

Toys and Activities   Somewhere between ages two and three, children learn the conventional gender stereotypes associated with a variety of common objects and activities (Ruble and Ruble, 1980). They connect gender with many toys: they learn that trucks are "for boys," for instance, and that dolls are "for girls." They learn similar associations for most items of clothing ("Who wears a dress/pants?"), for many common tools ("Who uses a saw/eggbeater?"), and for common games ("Who plays hockey/hopscotch?"). By early school age they begin to connect certain family and occupational roles with the male or female gender: females stay home and take care of children and the house, males go to work; nurses are female and pilots are male.

Gender stereotypes are learned early

In a variety of situations, children this young implement gender stereotypes by choosing toys and activities associated with their own sex (Maccoby and Jacklin, 1974). To a significant extent, in fact, many children simply will not play with toys that they strongly associate with the other gender. Boys especially show a tendency to disown anything female in their lives; for example, they may reject playing with dolls because it is "yucky girl stuff!" Girls seem somewhat less extreme in avoiding male interests and are more likely to play with trucks and blocks than boys are to play with dress-up clothes (Greenberg, 1984). A nursery-school teacher who works to overcome such stereotyping by encouraging children to choose activities freely may discover that additional efforts are needed to achieve that end. Parents and teachers who feel it is important enough, however, can have a significant effect on sex-role stereotyping in preschool-age children.

Personal Qualities   In contrast to toys and activities, preschool children develop gender stereotypes about personal qualities relatively slowly (Huston, 1983). Only by age five or so do children begin to know which sex is supposed to be aggressive, loud, and strong and which is supposed to be gentle, quiet, and weak. This kind of knowledge continues to develop throughout childhood and adolescence, but during the preschool years it has just begun.

Difficulty in grasping concept of gender

This fact should not surprise us, since an individual's understanding of personal qualities is based on abstractions from many experiences. The judgment that someone is a "loud" person, for example, is generally based on the observation that that person has behaved loudly on many occasions. Understanding such qualities requires cognitive skills that are beyond many preschool children. Even

Sexism in Preschool and Day-Care Settings: Can It Be Reduced?

Do preschool and day-care teachers contribute to male-female or gender differences in young children? Several studies suggest that they do, especially through their moment-to-moment interactions with children.

Consider, for example, how teachers label objects in preschool classrooms. One study purposely varied how teachers label new materials and activities (Serbin, 1979). Sometimes the teachers introduced activities in gender-linked ways, and sometimes they didn't. In the gender-linked condition, they described a particular activity in gender-related terms, saying, for example, "This is a sewing card like mommies often use"; they related the activity to the child's own experiences with gender ("Can *you* remember when your mommy used one?"), and they chose a child of the "appropriate" sex to demonstrate the activity ("Sally, can you show us how to use the sewing card?"). Later, when the children had a chance to choose among several new activities, their choices were affected by the gender-linked introductions. Boys tended to choose male-typed activities and girls to choose female-typed ones, and there was almost no overlap between the sexes.

When teachers described the activities in gender-neutral ways, the effects were very different. For example, teachers described an activity in neutral terms ("This is a lacing card. Shoes have laces."). They related the activity to the children's personal experiences ("Who is wearing laces today?"), and they chose children of *both* sexes to demonstrate the activity ("Sally and Steven, can you show us how to use these lacing cards?"). Gender-neutral introductions like these prompted children of both sexes to try the activity.

Teachers also influence the sex composition of children's play groupings in nursery school. In one preschool program, teachers purposely reinforced children whenever they happened to form groups that included both sexes. If several boys and girls happened to be playing together with the blocks, the teachers made sure to comment on and praise their activity and to encourage further effort (Serbin et al., 1977). If only boys or only girls were playing with the blocks, however, the teachers refrained from any comment. In these conditions, the proportion of cross-sex groupings in the class jumped dramatically; within a two-week period, mixed groups rose from 25 percent of all groups to 75 percent. Equally dramatically, though, the proportion fell back to its original level almost immediately after the teachers stopped reinforcing cross-sex groupings and returned to praising any group activities, regardless of their sex composition. Apparently two weeks of reinforcement was not long enough to make a more lasting difference in these children's sex-role habits.

These findings suggest not only that teachers can build gender biases deliberately but also that they can do so accidentally, simply by tolerating any biases that they and the children already have. In making introductions, for example, teachers probably do gender-link many toys and activities, though often without dwelling on these connections. Many mommies do sew, but not many daddies do; avoiding mention of this fact may take less effort than simply stating it. But children deserve to know this bit of information about our culture. Likewise, groups composed only of one sex often do very good work and therefore deserve praise. Would it be fair to confine praise to groups that happen to include both sexes? The answer is not as simple as it first appears; it depends on how important gender equity is to children's development and on how hard educators are willing to work to find ways of achieving it that are compatible with the other important goals of preschool education.

the concept of gender may require a level of abstract thinking that is difficult for a young child, so that it does not become a clear, stable idea for most children until the school years. Before this occurs, children apparently must sort through numerous ever-changing behaviors related to gender and somehow figure out which ones, if any, are essential to being a male (or female) and which ones are not.

A Talk with Cindy

Preschool Social Development

Cindy, age four, was interviewed in the porch-playroom of her house. Her mother and father were in the living room, and her eight-year-old brother played upstairs while we talked.

INTERVIEWER: What room is this, Cindy?

CINDY: My playroom.

INTERVIEWER: What do you play?

CINDY: Croquet. This is my croquet set.

INTERVIEWER: When you play, who do you play with?

CINDY: Kenny. Kenny my friend, my boyfriend.

INTERVIEWER: He's your boyfriend?

CINDY: Yeah.

INTERVIEWER: And you play croquet with him. What else do you do with him?

CINDY: I . . . I forget.

INTERVIEWER: Do you talk to him?

CINDY: Yes.

INTERVIEWER: And do you go to his house?

CINDY: Yes.

INTERVIEWER: And does he come to your house sometimes?

CINDY: Yes.

INTERVIEWER: Do you sometimes tell jokes to each other?

CINDY: Yes.

INTERVIEWER: What kind of jokes do you tell?

CINDY: Knock! Knock! Who's there? Mickey Mouse's underwear!

INTERVIEWER: That was a funny one. Do you have another one?

CINDY: Yes. Why didn't Mickey Mouse let Minnie Mouse sing?

INTERVIEWER: Why?

CINDY: Because he was in his underwear!

INTERVIEWER: Do you have other friends?

CINDY: Yes. Annie.

INTERVIEWER: Annie is your friend? Why is Annie your friend?

CINDY: Because she plays with me.

INTERVIEWER: Because she plays with you?

CINDY: Kenny always says, "I'm not your boyfriend." Because he *is* my boyfriend. He thinks he's not.

INTERVIEWER: But Annie's not your boyfriend?

CINDY: No. she's my girlfriend.

INTERVIEWER: And what do you play with Annie?

CINDY: I always come to her house.

INTERVIEWER: You go to her house. And when you walk into her house, what do you do?

CINDY: I eat animal cookies. . . . See my pony? I got to put on her hat and her blanket.

INTERVIEWER: Oh, and is that your pony's blanket?

CINDY: No, that my pony's foot. Now, I'm going to go get her hat.

INTERVIEWER: Okay.

CINDY: Oh, I see it. You got to tie it on.

INTERVIEWER: What is that pony's name?

CINDY: My Little Pony.

INTERVIEWER: Can you ride it?

CINDY: No. I can ride this pony.

INTERVIEWER: This is a bigger toy pony — a rocking horse. Can you really ride it?

CINDY: I'll show you. *[Gets on rocking horse]*

INTERVIEWER: Let me see. Does this pony have a name — this big pony that you are climbing on?

CINDY: Billy.

INTERVIEWER: Billy? Wow! You are a good rider.

Follow-up Questions

1. Which of the social and cognitive levels of play discussed in this chapter characterize Cindy's play?

2. According to Cindy, what is the basis of friendship? How does it compare with Larry's understanding of friendship and with the discussion in the chapter?

3. What indications are there of gender and sex typing in Cindy's play activities? In Larry's?

Theories of Gender-Role Development

Gender-role differences affect so much of life that every major theory of child development has proposed explanations of how they develop in children.

The Psychodynamic Approach   According to the Freudian or psychodynamic point of view, boys and girls develop similarly during infancy and toddlerhood. But as they approach the end of early childhood and confront competition with their same-sex parent for the attention and affection of their opposite-sex parent, the genders diverge. According to the theory, boys identify with their father and reject the earlier intimate bond they felt with their mother. Girls become disappointed with their biological status as females; they feel disappointed with their mother and envious of their father's power and status. They therefore adopt the female gender role as a strategy to gain their father's interest.

The oedipal conflict

The Social Learning Approach   Gender development may result from the combined effects of imitation and reinforcement: this is the **social learning theory.** In this view, children frequently observe adults and other children behaving in gender-typed ways (Bandura, 1977). They see girls playing with dolls and women caring for babies, and they see boys pretending to be superheroes and men fixing cars. Moreover, they see that all of these people are positively reinforced with praise and support — and even money — for behaving in the ways that boys and girls are supposed to behave, whereas rewards may be withheld or punishments applied for behaviors that do not conform to what is expected. For example, a boy may be criticized for "crying like a girl," and a girl may be warned that "girls are not supposed to be so pushy." As a result of such observations and direct experiences, children tend to learn the gender roles and stereotypes that are held by the people around them.

Imitation and reinforcement

The social learning theory helps to explain variations in sex typing among children. Presumably children observe sex-typed behaviors to differing degrees, and are differently reinforced for conforming to them. In contrast to the psychodynamic viewpoint, the social learning theory places less emphasis on the family's overall influence on gender development by pointing out how people outside of the family provide models for children's gender development. Dress-up dolls and superheroes are not created by parents but by other members of society.

The Cognitive Approach   In the tradition of Jean Piaget, cognitive explanations of gender development emphasize changes in children's active construction of knowledge, in this case about gender. According to this viewpoint, gender identity is a concept that takes time to develop and that depends on children's general cognitive maturity (Kohlberg, 1966). Young children must figure out the essential elements of gender identity, and they do so in several distinct phases. As toddlers, for example, boys and girls do not understand that gender actually stays constant; they think that they can change sex if they want to. Over the next several years, though, they gradually realize that gender doesn't change, although they need several more years to discover the true basis for classifying individuals into one sex or the other.

Phases of cognitive maturity

Does clothing determine whether a person is a boy or girl? Hairdo? Genitals? Eventually, most children conclude that gender depends on genitals; but they do not necessarily give up other, irrelevant criteria immediately. During the elementary school years, children often still believe that gender stereotypes represent essentials of gender — that girls *must* have long hair, or that boys *must* play more roughly. As a result, many children put considerable effort into acquiring these "essentials," even though doing so sometimes makes them seem more gender-stereotyped than adults.

Which Theory? These explanations call attention to different features of social life in early childhood, but they do not necessarily conflict with one another. The Freudians are probably right in emphasizing the importance of family experiences. Social learning theorists are correct in pointing out that gender modeling probably extends well beyond the confines of family life, and cognitive theorists are right to emphasize that gender is a complex concept, one that preschool children probably cannot grasp overnight. A real comparison of all three theories, however, must go beyond their plausibility to look at evidence from the lives of actual developing children.

Influences on Gender Development

Much theorizing holds parents responsible for the development of gender differences, either blaming or congratulating them, depending on the theorist's point of view. A close look suggests that parents do deserve some credit, but perhaps not as much as commonly thought. Other influences also matter.

Parents When asked about their child-rearing philosophies, parents tend to express belief in gender equality, but their actions often differ from their statements (Fagot, 1982). Observations of parents playing with their preschool children show that parents support their children for sex-stereotyped activities more than for cross-sex activities; a boy gets praised more for playing with blocks, for instance, than for playing with dolls. Parents generally support physical activity in boys more than in girls, both by praising it and by participating in it. Possibly as a by-product of these differences, boys get punished more often, and more physically, than girls do. And as children approach school age, parents begin assigning household chores according to gender; boys more often have to take out the trash, for example, and girls more often have to fold the laundry (Huston, 1983). By the nature of things, many of these differences lead to greater freedom and independence for boys. Playing relatively actively leads to wider exploration and movement, whether around the house or around an entire neighborhood. Boys' larger territories remove them from adult surveillance more of the time, and make peers relatively more important in their social lives.

> **Different treatment of boys and girls**

Nevertheless, there are similarities in parents' treatment of the sexes. Observation shows that parents give similar amounts of warmth and affection to both boys and girls in the preschool period; they set similar limits on children's behavior, and they encourage similar levels of achievement (Maccoby and Jacklin, 1974).

Usually parents do not teach gender roles intentionally. Instead, they provide models that their children frequently imitate. (Top, Alan Carey/The Image Works; left, Ulrike Welsch)

How can we reconcile these two pictures of family influences on gender? One view is that in spite of considerable gender overlap, parents do indeed treat the sexes differently, although the difference becomes larger later in childhood, when parents may become more concerned about preparing children for adulthood (Block, 1978). Even the differences in treatment that do begin in early childhood may not have their full impact until well into middle childhood or even beyond. Learning gender stereotypes about jobs, for example, begins around kindergarten age; but this knowledge may not seem important to a child until she actually begins looking for work herself, in adolescence. Before that time, the knowledge may not affect her behavior very much; she may willingly play at being a doctor (traditionally a male job) and at being a nurse (traditionally a female one).

Greater sex typing with age

Parents' influence also depends somewhat on which parent is involved. Usually the younger a child is, the more likely it is that he will be cared for by his mother. Women tend to express less stereotyped attitudes and practices about gender in dealing with their children than men do. Compared with fathers, they better tolerate boys' playing with dolls or boys' crying. From the child's perspective, then, the family may seem to expect less sex typing when he is very young. As he gets older, his father may enter his life more, and may bring with him more sharply defined sex-role expectations. But this is the "typical" case. Real children, real mothers, and real fathers vary widely and therefore call for a variety of modifications to this picture (Lamb and Sagi, 1983).

Peers In some ways, peers may shape gender differences more effectively than parents. Early in the preschool years — even before age three — children respond differently to partners of the opposite sex than to ones of the same sex (Jacklin and Maccoby, 1978). In play situations, girls tend to withdraw more from a boy partner than from a girl, and boys heed prohibitions more often if they come from another boy than if they come from a girl. Even when preschoolers are not playing actively, they will watch peers of the same sex more often than peers of the opposite sex.

Peer reinforcement of gender typing

Children of this age respond to a reinforcement more reliably if it comes from a child of their own sex. If a boy compliments another boy's block building, for example, the second boy is much more likely to continue building than he is if a girl compliments it. And conversely, if a boy criticizes the building, the boy will more likely stop than he will if a girl criticizes it. Parallel patterns occur for girls, who tend to persist in whatever other girls compliment or praise and stop whatever is criticized or ignored. For both sexes, teachers' reinforcements have less influence than peers in determining children's persistence at activities (Fagot, 1982).

What makes these patterns important is one additional fact, namely that children tend to reinforce play activities appropriate for their own sex. Boys praise and support large-motor activity more than quiet art activities, for instance, and girls do the reverse. Over the long run, therefore, children probably shape each other's play preferences along sex-typed lines. Children who deviate from conventional preferences find themselves largely ignored (Lamb and Roopnarine, 1979) — even after finally returning to conventional activities. So peer pressures to practice conventional gender roles are both strong and continuous, and they occur even if teachers and other adults do not fully approve of them.

The Media   To some extent, peer expectations like these may result from the wider impact of the media. Television in particular shows heavy gender biases. Most programs, even the daytime soaps, are dominated by men (Lemon, 1977), as judged both by numbers of characters and by the importance assigned to them. In spite of recent efforts to broaden the portrayals of gender roles, the women who do appear on television are in strongly sex-typed roles: they are teachers, secretaries, nurses, or (most commonly) housewives. On television, women solve problems less often, need help more often, listen better, and talk less than men, and otherwise behave in stereotypical ways (U.S. Commission on Civil Rights, 1977). The patterns also prevail for children's television despite efforts to present roles more equally (Shepherd-Look, 1982). One reason for this may be the large number of reruns of situation comedies and cartoons produced in the 1950s and 1960s, in which sex-role stereotyping was extremely common.

Media role models are strongly sex-typed

Advertising on television shows similar biases, but adds to them the style of presentation. Commercials aimed at boys and men tend to show more activity and to use rapid cuts and loud music. Those aimed at girls and women rely more on visual fades and dissolves and use gentle background music (Welch et al., 1979). Given the subtlety of these techniques, commercials may well influence children more strongly than the obvious, conscious biases of television shows themselves.

Androgyny

Androgyny refers to a state of affairs where sex roles are flexible, allowing all individuals, male and female, to behave in ways that freely integrate behaviors traditionally thought to belong exclusively to one sex or the other. In this view, both girls and boys can be *both* assertive and yielding; independent and dependent; instrumental (task-oriented) and expressive (feeling-oriented) (Kaplan and Bean, 1976).

In research using the Bem Sex-Role Inventory, Sandra Bem (1974, 1976) has found that both males and females used both masculine and feminine characteristics to describe their own personalities. In a sample of over two thousand undergraduates from both a university and a community college, approximately one third of both populations could be classified as androgynous based on having masculinity and femininity scores that were approximately equal. One third of the respondents were significantly sex-typed as either masculine or feminine; fewer than 10 percent were classified as "sex-reversed," based on the fact that they relied most heavily on characteristics of the opposite sex to describe their personalities.

What are the implications of androgyny? It has been suggested that the possibilities for the more flexible, integrated, and less stereotyped sex roles implied by androgyny will depend upon the sex stereotypes and child-rearing orientations of parents, families, schools, and the media and of the broader culture in which they exist (Block, 1973). For preschoolers, television programs with little sex stereotyping, such as "Sesame Street," are likely to help, as are increased awareness and efforts on the part of parents and day-care and preschool teachers in supporting and encouraging more androgynous roles.

Checkpoint   *A child's awareness and understanding of gender constancy, identity, and preference develop over the preschool years and significantly influence choices of playmates and play activities. Theories of gender development emphasize resolution of the oedipal conflict via identification, imitation and reinforcement, and cognitive maturation. Sex-role expectations and behavior of parents and peers, as well as media role models, strongly affect children's gender-linked attitudes.*

The End of the Preschool Years

Although the preschool period, considered as a whole, may not bring about physical changes as dramatic as those of infancy, the cognitive, social, and emotional changes that occur may be even more striking. By age five or six, a child has both worked and played with symbolic skills quite a lot, and sometimes she is beginning to do so according to prearranged rules. She can form friendships that last at least a little beyond the here-and-now, and that both foster and draw upon genuine understanding of others. Her new social skills do not eliminate hurting others, and in fact they may allow her to hurt others in more sophisticated ways — by using personal qualities for example, rather than just immediate activities. Increasing social sophistication may also allow the child to use less aggressive means of asserting her needs and of dealing with conflict. All these new skills, both positive and negative, are guided significantly by the child's gender role — a concept to which the child herself (or himself) makes important contributions during the preschool years.

But human development is far from over at this point. The child's social world broadens widely in the years ahead, most obviously through her entry into school and the development of important social relationships independent of her family. Major changes also occur in the child's cognitive abilities and in her physical growth and ability to use her body. The following chapters will explore these and other important features of the child's development as she progresses through middle childhood.

Summary of Major Ideas

1. Even the physical and cognitive activities of preschool children are highly social.

Theories of Early Social Development

2. Freud's theory emphasizes the importance of identification and superego development during the phallic stage, whereas Erikson sees resolution of the psychosocial crisis of initiative versus guilt as the central task of the preschool years.

3. According to Sullivan, preschoolers use egocentric escape to avoid unpleasant or overwhelming situations and dramatizations to act out new relationships safely. If their anxiety and mistrust become too great, a "malevolent transformation" may occur.

Play in Early Childhood

4. Play is the major waking activity of preschoolers.

5. Play involves intrinsic motivation, process rather than product, pretense, implicit and flexible rules, and active involvement on the part of the child. Play differs from exploration and occurs even with familiar objects.

6. Psychoanalytic theory emphasizes the mastery and wish-fulfillment functions of play, whereas learning theory stresses the acquisition of social skills through imitation and observation.

7. Cognitive theory emphasizes that play develops in a sequence that generally parallels the major stages of cognitive development.

8. Functional play involves simple, repeated movements or manipulation of the body or inanimate objects; in constructive play, a child manipulates objects in order to build or construct something.

9. Dramatic or make-believe play allows the child to practice motor skills and rehearse social roles, and play involving games with rules focuses more on the rules themselves.

10. Parten has identified six social levels of play: unoccupied, solitary, onlooker, parallel, associative, and cooperative play.

11. Unoccupied and solitary play are fairly unsocial. Onlooker and parallel play indicate increasing social awareness but minimal social interaction.

12. Associative play involves mutual interaction in a common activity, and in cooperative play children develop common goals.

13. The type of setting and the presence of siblings and other playmates facilitate the development of social play.

14. Although the preferred forms of social play change with age, all forms are observable throughout life.

Relationships with Others

15. Authoritarian parents exhibit a high degree of control and demands for maturity, but low clarity of communication and a low degree of nurturance. Their children tend to be more distrustful, to be less happy with themselves, and to show lower school achievement than other children.

16. Permissive parents communicate clearly and are nurturant, but they exert little control and make few maturity demands. Their children tend to lack self-reliance and self-control.

17. Authoritative parents show high levels of control, strong demands for maturity, clarity of communication, and nurturance. Their children are likely to be better adjusted than children reared by authoritarian or permissive parents, showing greater self-reliance, self-control, and achievement.

18. Parents often use mixtures of more than one parenting style, and may change in their preferred style as their children grow older.

19. Both siblings and friends also contribute to social development during the preschool years; ultimately, however, it is the parents' responsibility to establish the sort of parent-child interactions that foster positive social relationships.

20. Whereas early friendships are unstable and depend on specific shared activities, friendships among older preschoolers involve expectations about future behavior and popularity considerations.

21. Preschoolers' friendships become more durable and involve a greater degree of shared activity with age. As they near school age, the more permanent and personal qualities of a friend become increasingly important.

22. As children grow older, the support and judgments of parents and other adults contribute more and more to their feelings of empathy and prosocial activities.

23. Preschoolers commonly exhibit both hostile aggression and instrumental (nonhostile) aggression to assert their needs and resolve conflicts. As they grow older, verbal methods replace physical ones and overall aggression declines.

24. Biological differences, gender, family child-rearing tactics, peers, and the media influence the form and frequency of aggressive behavior.

Gender Development

25. During early childhood, an understanding of gender-typed behaviors and of gender identity are acquired. A sense of gender constancy — the belief that being male or female is permanent — typically is not achieved until age eight or nine.

26. Because the development of stereotypes about personal qualities appears to depend on the ability to think abstractly, children do not gain a clear and stable concept of gender until the school years.

27. Each major child development theory proposes explanations for gender development: resolution of oedipal conflict; modeling and other forms of social learning; and the growth of a child's cognitive abilities.

28. Influences on gender development include differential expectations and treatment of boys and girls by parents, peers, and the media.

Key Terms

initiative versus guilt *(391)*
egocentric escape *(391)*
dramatization *(392)*
malevolent transformation *(392)*
intrinsic motivation *(392)*
pretense *(394)*
repetition compulsion *(395)*
catharsis *(395)*
functional play *(396)*
constructive play *(397)*
dramatic or make-believe play *(397)*
games with rules *(399)*
prosocial behavior *(405)*
authoritarian *(405)*
permissive *(405)*
permissive-indulgent *(405)*
permissive-indifferent *(405)*

authoritative *(407)*
dispositional *(413)*
empathy *(413)*
aggression *(417)*
assertiveness *(417)*
instrumental aggression *(419)*
hostile aggression *(419)*
blocking behaviors *(419)*
dominance hierarchy *(422)*
disinhibit *(422)*
gender *(423)*
gender constancy *(423)*
gender identity *(423)*
gender preference *(423)*
sex-role stereotypes *(423)*
social learning theory *(427)*
androgyny *(431)*

What Do You Think?

1. Why is play so important to preschool children? If someone criticized a four-year-old for "just playing," what might you tell the critic?

2. In what ways is play during the preschool years similar to play during the college years? In what ways is it different?

3. Which style of parental authority best describes what you experienced as a child? What changes did you notice as you grew older?

4. What pattern of parenting do you plan to provide for your children? Why?

5. How would you help your child to be sensitive and helpful to others and be able to deal with conflict and aggression?

6. How should the problem of sex-role stereotyping in young children be handled? Why is it difficult for many parents and teachers to do anything about it?

For Further Reading

Adcock, D., and Segal, M. *Making Friends: Ways of Encouraging Social Development in Young Children.* Englewood Cliffs, N.J.: Prentice-Hall, 1983.

The authors of this book describe the development of friendships among preschool children in preschool and day-care settings. They provide many examples, illustrations, and useful suggestions for parents, teachers, and other care-giving adults.

Bernstein, A. *The Flight of the Stork.* New York: Dell, 1980.

Based on interviews with a large number of children aged three to twelve, this book describes and analyzes the development of children's knowledge about sex.

Comer, J., and Poussaint, A. *Black Child Care: A Guide to Emotional and Psychological Development.* New York: Pocket Books, 1976.

Written by the two most eminent black child psychiatrists in the country, one from Harvard and the other from Yale, this book for parents provides important insights into the special concerns and issues faced by black families, as well as those faced by all families with young children.

Dunn, J. *Sisters and Brothers.* Cambridge, Mass.: Harvard University Press, 1985.

Based largely on careful observations of families with two or more children, this book comprehensively explores the importance of siblings in the preschool and early school years. It does so in an interesting and easy-to-read style and includes many vivid descriptions of what actually happens between brothers and sisters.

Erikson, E. *Childhood and Society.* New York: W. W. Norton, 1950.

A classic. Of particular interest are Erikson's cross-cultural observations of childhood among the Sioux Indians, who were hunters, and among the Yuroks, who were fishers. Also interesting are his discussion of play and his presentation of the psychosocial theory of development.

Parke, R. *Fathers.* Cambridge, Mass.: Harvard University Press, 1981.

Interesting and informative coverage of father-child relationships and the special role of the father in child development.

Robinson, N., Robinson, H., and Darling, M. *A World of Children: Daycare and Preschool Institutions.* Monterey, Calif.: Brooks/Cole, 1979.

This book offers in-depth coverage of the challenges, history, goals, and domestic and international models of child care, as well as discussion of the organizational nuts and bolts of running day-care and preschool programs.

Zimbardo, P., and Radl, S. *The Shy Child.* Garden City, N.Y.: Doubleday, 1982.

This book, based on the authors' research on shyness, discusses the definition, causes, treatment, and prevention of this problem.

Jennifer's Case

Jennifer was a relatively easy-going first child. She did her share of fussing, of course, but overall her moods were mostly happy — and her bad moments were at least predictable. Jennifer's frequent smiles and affectionate nature seemed to make all her parents' efforts worthwhile.

By the time she was three, Jennifer was no baby any more. She had conversations with her parents on all sorts of topics; went eagerly on walks outdoors even on the coldest days; dressed herself (mostly); and used the toilet when she needed to. For the time being, things seemed comfortable around the house.

One month after Jennifer's third birthday, her mother became pregnant. Her parents told Jennifer about the expected baby almost as soon as the pregnancy was confirmed. "You'll have a brother or sister," her parents said, "but we don't know which it will be. Someone to play with." Jennifer seemed to like the idea and was curious about how the baby was growing inside her mother. But she also started to waken in the middle of the night and began to suck her thumb more, and her parents wondered if these changes were related to the new baby.

"It" eventually turned out to be a baby boy, Joey. But Joey himself was something of a disappointment, in spite of all the talk and preparation for him beforehand. "He doesn't do much, does he?" commented Jennifer one day. Joey just slept, and sometimes Jennifer liked to cuddle with him then.

Disappointment soon turned to frustration. To her dismay, Jennifer found that you had to touch and hold Joey in the "right" ways and be really gentle. It seemed, too, as if her parents were always fussing over Joey more than he deserved. Jennifer tried to fuss over him, too, but it didn't seem to work for her.

But having Joey around was not all bad. After a few months he began smiling at his mom and dad, and sometimes even at Jennifer! Gradually Jennifer figured out how to hold Joey's attention for several minutes, by showing him toys at just the right distance, and by doing it very quietly. Her parents encouraged these times by praising Jennifer's successes with Joey. They also encouraged her to "help" with Joey's baths — mainly by looking on. And her mother made a baby carrier for her so that Jennifer could carry her own "baby" on errands, "just like mama."

Dear Mom,

I think things are going OK these days with Jennifer. I feel bad because lately I just haven't had the kind of time for her that I used to have — I realized yesterday that I had not sat down with her alone for 3 days. Maybe it would help if I got a babysitter sometimes so Jennifer and I could do special things together.

She really does have some good times with Joey, especially now that he's begun babbling. You should see them! She tries to imitate his sounds; then they have a "conversation"; and then they both giggle.

Hope that one of these days you can come visit us. I know that Jennifer would love to see you — and so would I!

Love, as always,
Diane

Even so, life was not the same after Joey arrived. Jennifer spent more time by herself, partly because her parents were often busy with Joey, but partly also because she was sorting out what had happened to her life since becoming a big sister. Sometimes she wondered how anyone as incompetent as Joey could ever deserve so much attention!

As Joey developed new skills, Jennifer began finding him more interesting. Often, when Joey woke up early in the morning, he would wake Jennifer and she would climb into his crib — much to his delight — and the two of them would "talk" and play together. Jennifer's mother was glad to see the two children getting on so.

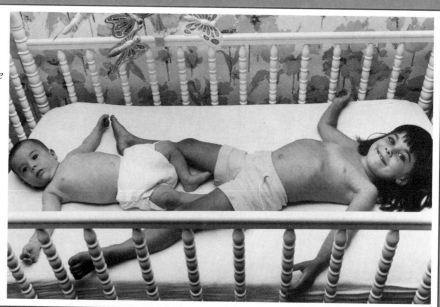

Me

Mommy

Joey

Daddy

After Jennifer entered kindergarten, she had less time for feeling jealous of Joey. She made several new friends at school and found herself relying less on Joey for companionship. "He's not as smart as my friends," she told her parents. But when a friend came, she always introduced Joey. "That's my brother," she said with pride and emphasis.

By the time Jennifer was six and Joey was two, she had stopped thinking of him as a baby. Joey still infuriated her sometimes, like the time he stuck clay inside her shoes. But other times it was nice to have him around. With two children to suggest buying ice cream, for example, her parents found it harder to resist than before. And Jennifer had to admit that with Joey for a brother, she felt a bit more like she belonged to a whole "family," and not just to a pair of parents.

5 The Middle Years

Because growth slows after the preschool years, children in the middle years have more time and energy to develop skills of all sorts — from riding a skateboard to writing in script to making friends. And all their years of language practice and symbolic play finally pay off: school-age children can often think rather logically, even if only about concrete matters. Partly because of these new competencies, and partly because of school life, peers take on more importance than ever before.

  Maybe because children are now old enough to be aware of these changes, they often later remember the middle years as the best ones of their childhood. For most children, the world seems secure, their health is excellent, and their abilities improve visibly and steadily year by year.

Chapter 11

The Middle Years:
Physical Development

Focusing Questions

- How do differences in growth affect children's feelings about one another and about themselves?

- What improvements in motor skills do children usually experience during the school years?

- What are some of the physical and psychological effects of athletic activity during childhood?

- What kinds of illnesses and accidents tend to occur among school-children? How are they affected by children's family and community circumstances?

- What causes some children to become excessively active, and how can adults help children with this tendency?

- What are learning disabilities, and how can adults help children who develop them?

IN GENERAL, CHILDREN'S PHYSICAL GROWTH slows down in the middle years (ages six to twelve) even more than it does in early childhood. But the results of growth begin to show more than ever before. Specific physical skills are easier to teach than they were, because children now find them easier to learn. For a school-age child, instruction and practice in baseball makes a more obvious difference to skill than it did when he was still a preschooler. This means that the child can now acquire physical and athletic skills that may give him a lifetime of satisfaction. But children *can* get hurt during physical activity, and athletic games can emphasize competition that is unrealistic or unpleasant.

Children are relatively healthy during the school years, but of course they sometimes have accidents or get sick. A few children also develop problems because of ambiguous physical causes, and show excessive motor activity even in quiet situations or difficulties in learning specific academic skills. Such problems may originate from subtle differences in how the nervous system operates in these children, though this is far from certain.

This chapter reviews these ideas in more detail. We begin by looking at normal trends and variations in overall growth during the middle years. Then we look at specific motor-skill and athletic development, including in particular the psychological effects of these on children. The chapter ends with a discussion of health in the school years, with special reference to children who are overly active and children who experience specific learning problems.

Trends and Variations in Height and Weight

Typical six-year-olds are about forty-six inches tall, but individual children vary two or three inches in each direction from this figure (Tanner, 1978a). This means

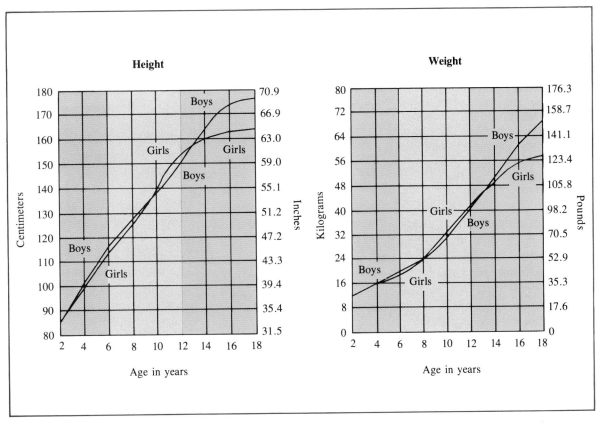

Figure 11.1 Growth in Height and Weight from Two to Eighteen Years

that two first-graders can differ by as much as five or six inches and still be physically normal. Over the next several years, children usually grow just over two inches per year, so that by age ten, they typically measure about fifty-four inches tall, and by age twelve, more like fifty-nine or sixty inches tall (see Figure 11-1).

During later childhood, variation around these averages becomes even more extreme than before. A small number of twelve-year-old girls may be sixty-six inches tall, for example — essentially adult in stature. And a small number of boys of this age may measure only about fifty-four inches, a full foot shorter. Such extremes result partly from the growth spurt that most children experience at the beginning of adolescence. Since girls tend to undergo this spurt a year or two earlier than boys, they are especially likely to pull ahead of boys in size near the end of elementary school or at the beginning of junior high.

Variations in height

Similar patterns occur for weight. Six-year-olds average about forty-five pounds, but may weigh as little as thirty-five or as much as fifty-five (Tanner, 1978a). By age ten, children average about sixty-six pounds; by twelve, more than eighty pounds. As with height, variations in weight increase along with the averages. A perfectly normal twelve-year-old may weigh well over one hundred pounds or as little as seventy. Among the heavier children of this age — and especially among girls — are some who have achieved the weight of young adults.

Variations in weight

A Talk with Ruth Ellen

Growing Older

Ruth Ellen is almost eight. She has long brown hair, a big smile, and eyes that sparkle. She was looking forward to being interviewed, and she wanted to know who was going to read this book.

INTERVIEWER: Do you like to be called Ruth or Ruth Ellen?

RUTH: I like to be called Ruth, except in my class, where sometimes I have to be called Ruth Ellen because there are two Ruths.

INTERVIEWER: How do you like that?

RUTH: It's all right. One of my friends in my class this year — who is the other Ruth — she always asks when we write our names that I be sure to put Ellen on it so the teacher won't mix us up.

INTERVIEWER: Ruth, what is it like to be almost eight years old?

RUTH: It's hard because your parents give you a lot of work to do.

INTERVIEWER: Because you are getting bigger?

RUTH: Yes.

INTERVIEWER: What kinds of work does someone your age have to do?

RUTH: Sponging off the table, which I'm not that good at, and emptying the dishwasher. And when the dishwasher is all full of clean dishes when we're not emptying it yet, washing our own dishes. Can I tell you one thing I like about being my age?

INTERVIEWER: Yes.

RUTH: One thing I like is that when you're grown up you wouldn't be able to get an allowance, but I can get one now because I am still a child.

INTERVIEWER: Have you noticed any changes in your size?

RUTH: Sort of. I sort of feel like I was always the same size, but then when I look at some of the things like the apron that my grandma gave me when I was really little — it's getting much smaller now.

INTERVIEWER: Have you noticed anything else?

RUTH: It seems that whenever I get bigger I grow faster because I just got these shoes a little while ago and now they're pretty small on me.

INTERVIEWER: Are there things that you are able to do now that you couldn't do when you were younger?

RUTH: Well, I can put my own things on my food, like salad dressing on my lettuce. And get my own food. Dish out my own portion. So if I don't like the food, I could sneak and put less on my plate.

INTERVIEWER: Are you getting stronger?

RUTH: Yes. When my brother gets mad at me sometimes by accident maybe I might accidentally hurt him. And I used to not even be able to hurt him by accident. I can ride my bike. I could do that since I was four, but I've learned that training wheels make bikes very hard to ride now because they are too small for me.

INTERVIEWER: What else have you noticed?

RUTH: Well, I like it when my friend — the other Ruth — tries to punch me because then I can just catch both of her fists and hold them. Right when she does it, I quickly grab on and I hold her really tight. Sometimes even to her pinkies.

Now I can go to the garden myself and check to see if there are any vegetables. Then I make my parents a surprise — maybe a salad.

INTERVIEWER: Oh, so you help them make it?

RUTH: I don't let them help me. I don't let them see what I am doing so it will be a surprise.

INTERVIEWER: And all of a sudden, there's the salad and you've done it all by yourself!

RUTH: One time — do you want to hear a funny story of what happened?

INTERVIEWER: I certainly do.

RUTH: This really happened. One time when I made the salad there was this pepper I picked from the garden. It was a hot pepper but the end was pretty sweet, so I had my Dad taste it and he said it was sweet. So I cut it all up and put it in the salad. The pepper was really hot and the night that we ate the salad my mother and father found out it was hot. Then I began to eat my carrots and the first thing I ate was very hot. It had the spice taste on it. So I didn't have to eat my salad that night! And I got dessert anyways!

Follow-up Questions

1. How clear is Ruth's awareness of her physical development?

2. What are the main changes that make Ruth aware that she is getting older?

3. In what ways has Ruth's physical development affected her psychosocial development?

Late in childhood, girls often grow taller and faster than boys of the same age. This disparity can create awkward moments for members of both sexes. (Donald Dietz/Stock, Boston)

But these trends and variations do not express the experience of growth as individual children know it over time. Any one child is blessed (or perhaps cursed) not only with particular dimensions at any one moment but also with unique patterns of growth rate over the months and years.

Problems Related to Growth and Body Build

Growth gives children the potential to participate in many new activities. But it can also create problems for them, and the problems typically have both physical aspects and psychological ones. Stereotypes about size and shape exist among school-age children as well as among adults. Wearing glasses may type-cast some children as eggheads, and big ears may type-cast others as clowns. The most important physical stereotypes, however, concern overall size and weight. Very small children may seem younger than they really are, and as a result their teachers and friends may treat them with less respect than they deserve. An overweight child may be regarded as unattractive, so friends and teachers may not respond as warmly to her as they otherwise would. Such reactions may happen unconsciously. And even though physical appearance may really stem largely from biological influences, children with the "wrong" looks may blame themselves.

Stereotypes about body build

Height Variations Because of Puberty As we have noted, toward the end of the elementary school years, girls tend to become significantly taller than boys of the same age. The difference results partly from girls' earlier puberty and partly from the timing of the growth spurt associated with puberty for each sex. For boys, a spurt in height tends to follow the other physical changes of adolescence, such as the growth of pubic hair and the deepening of the voice. For girls, though, a spurt in height usually happens almost first, preceding the growth of breasts and pubic hair.

Inevitably, these changes create temporary embarrassments for at least some girls and boys. Late in childhood, most children become aware of social expectations or stereotypes about attractiveness, such as the idea that men "should" be taller than women. But this awareness dawns precisely when many boys and girls embody the opposite pattern. The discrepancy is undoubtedly felt more acutely by some individuals than by others; presumably it feels worse for children who

---

Perspectives on Issues

The Effect of Children's Puberty on Parents

For most girls and many boys, puberty begins well before the end of the school years. The experience creates many worries for children. Some girls worry that they will grow too tall. Others worry that their breasts will get too large, or have the wrong shape, or fail to develop at all. Still others worry about when they will menstruate for the first time; socially, it is better to start early, or at least not to be last. Boys worry about their changing appearance too, though in different ways: instead of worrying about getting too tall, a boy is more likely to worry that he will not grow tall enough. Another boy worries about whether his penis is big enough or whether he has enough pubic hair.

Puberty also creates new challenges for the parents of older children and young adolescents. Among other things, most children need reassurance about their physical acceptability, both in the short run and in the long run (Winship, 1983). They need to know that at least at home they are not too tall or too short, or cursed with too much pubic hair or not enough. In essence, parents should say to their children, "You and your body are unique, and I like you the way you are." Such reassurances will not save children from their peers,

who may make embarrassing comments about each other's looks anyway. But reassurances will give a growing, changing child a secure base for learning to cope with social stresses about physical appearance.

Of course, children may not talk about some of their concerns about puberty, either because their concerns are too private or because they detect special anxieties within their parents (Norman and Harris, 1981). A ten-year-old boy may not feel like discussing the relative size of his penis with his parents, and a girl of the same age may not feel like sharing her concern about being overweight if she suspects that her parents have had worries about their own weight over the years. For matters like these, parents can be helpful by encouraging or arranging for other confidants and sources of information. One simple way of doing this is to buy or borrow books for children about the physical and emotional stresses of growing up; good ones are usually available in public libraries. Another way is to encourage school courses and other programs in family living, sexuality, and other aspects of adolescent growth. When taught well by trusted adults, such programs can encourage older children and

seek the attentions of the opposite sex most strongly, yet find that they are the "wrong" height. The exact amount by which a child violates height standards may matter little, except at the extremes. Very tall girls and very short boys probably have the most trouble forgetting about their unusual heights.

On logical grounds, then, boys who mature early and girls who mature later should have the easiest time socially regarding their body builds and heights. Research, though, suggests that this idea is only partly true (Livson and Peskin, 1981). The timing of puberty may have unique effects for each sex; "looks" matter more for girls than for boys. And the onset of adolescence has different effects in the short run from those in the long run.

Excess Weight and Obesity   At least one American child in ten suffers from **obesity,** meaning that he weighs more than 130 percent of the normal weight for his

young adolescents to discuss their true concerns about their bodies. At their best, too, such courses can help children get past the bluffing and critical evaluations that often characterize such discussions among peers.

In spite of emphasizing reassurance, though, parents need to identify any truly significant medical or physical problems that may disturb children during a growth spurt. These are usually less common and less serious than children themselves believe, but they do occur. For example, many children — perhaps a majority — worry that they are gaining too much weight (Elkind, 1984). A few of these children — perhaps one in ten — do end up seriously overweight or obese, and parents should get medical advice and help for them. Likewise, most children worry if they get even a few pimples or patches of acne on their face. This problem usually does not last forever or pose any serious health hazard, but children with severe acne deserve help from medical specialists immediately; urging children to wait out the problem is not good enough (Gross, 1981).

While responding in these ways, parents may experience new feelings about their children. Among other things, witnessing a growth spurt in their child can create regret and sadness, since it shows that the child is literally growing up and soon will not be a child anymore. For parents, a growth spurt can also create a new sense of protectiveness; they may find themselves worrying about their child's selection of friends and dates, especially when puberty arrives early. Other parents grow jealous as they are reminded of the advantages of youth — children seem to have their whole lives ahead of them, and they may seem to have more physical vigor as well.

All these feelings are legitimate and acceptable, as long as they do not interfere with giving pubescent children the help and support they need. But they suggest just how challenging being a parent of an older child can be. Caring for older children may take less constant physical care than caring for younger ones, but it takes substantial emotional commitment and intelligent long-range planning.

height and bone size (Bray, 1976). This means that instead of weighing about sixty-five pounds when he is fifty-four inches tall, for example, he weighs well over eighty-five pounds. How does such a child feel about his size? In most cases, probably not very good. If he accepts social stereotypes about weight, then he must regard himself as unattractive; but if he rejects those standards, he may find himself in subtle but chronic disagreement with his peers about what makes people good-looking — not to mention disagreement about his own looks. No matter what attitude he adopts, obesity causes psychological problems (Winick, 1975).

Over the long run, it causes physical problems as well. Children who continue

---

Perspectives on Issues

Treating Obesity Successfully

A number of factors cause children to become seriously overweight or obese (that is, at least 30 percent over normal weight). Children and parents can control some of these, but not others. Two factors beyond human control, for example, are *heredity* and *age*. Like it or not, thinness and fatness do run in families. Overweight children tend to have overweight parents, and underweight children tend to have underweight parents (LeBow, 1984). And most people inevitably put on fat more during some periods of life than others. Late childhood and early puberty form one of these periods; at this time, most children gain fat tissue out of proportion to increases in other tissues, such as muscle and bone. The change is especially noticeable in girls, who often look more shapely or sexually attractive as a result. Too much additional fat at this time, though, can create a definite weight problem for some children, male or female.

But not all influences on weight are beyond control. At least three depend on people's activities and choices, and therefore make good areas in which to make efforts to lose weight (White, 1986):

1. *Amount and type of foods eaten*   Children often get started toward obesity by eating foods that are overly rich in energy value. The chief culprits are foods full of sugar (like cakes and pastries) and fat-filled foods (like deep-fried chicken and potato chips). While in theory a child might be able to

burn off these foods with enough exercise, in practice very few children (or adults) lead lives that are active enough to do so.

2. *Amount and type of exercise*   If a child is relatively inactive, any excess energy provided by her daily food is gradually converted into fat. Relatively high levels of sustained activity raise the rate at which the body processes food, and therefore prevent fat from forming. Exercise has this effect, though, only if it emphasizes the development of endurance rather than of strength. Walking a mile every day, for example, helps more than lifting weights, unless the weight-lifting sessions are organized to focus on persistence or endurance.

3. *Attitudes and habits about eating*   Most of us attach important meanings to certain foods and eating times. A particular family may prefer children who are hearty eaters, to the point of unconsciously making children with small appetites feel antisocial. Another family may have an informal custom of serving a rich snack like ice cream late in the evening, and turning the snack down may seem both unnecessary and unfriendly.

By focusing on these three factors, children *can* control excess weight, if they get proper support from family and friends (Pringle and Ramsey, 1982) as well as from a doctor or trained nutritionist. Such support can be given by following four

---

to be obese into adulthood run more risk of a variety of minor illnesses as well as of a few major ones such as heart attacks and diabetes (LeBow, 1986). Partly as a result, they also tend to live shorter lives. Overweight people tend to be significantly less active than people of normal weight, even by the standards of our relatively sedentary society, and their lack of exercise can further aggravate their weight problem and the risks connected with it. For all these reasons, children who are obese deserve help, even if their problem cannot be cured easily.

Unfortunately, as anyone who has tried it knows, losing weight permanently is difficult to do. It is even more difficult for children than for adults, for both physi-

---

steps. First, make sure that the child really needs to lose weight. Weighing only a little more than average poses no medical risk, and may cause few social problems in the long run. Children certainly dislike being teased about their appearance, but if a child really has relatively small amounts of fat, then the teasing may be caused by problems with social stereotypes and peer relations, and losing weight may prove to be a rather inefficient way of avoiding it.

Second, if the child does have a serious weight problem, start her on a diet under the care of a doctor or trained nutritionist. For most children, a diet should simply aim at stabilizing weight or at most at causing a loss of only about one pound a week. At all costs, avoid crash diets or other faddish "miracle" diets: these can jeopardize the child's health, and almost never result in permanent weight loss. A truly effective diet should include three meals a day, draw on all the major groups of food, and include healthful, low-calorie snacks. Determining the appropriate amounts of food, however, can prove difficult if parents have not been trained in nutrition or weight control, so professional advice is useful (Cahill and Rossini, 1978).

Third, develop a program of exercise appropriate for the child. Doing so can sometimes prove challenging at first, since overweight children tend to be less active than others. But with some thought and persistence, it can be done. A sustained exercise program should always begin slowly, so as to avoid overtaxing undeveloped muscles and help insure feelings of success. In general, too, overweight children should avoid activities that inherently handicap them (like jogging), or call attention to their appearance (like ballet dancing). Wherever possible, they should try to incorporate more activity into their daily lives, by walking to and from school, for example. A few activities, such as swimming, actually give overweight children a physical advantage, because their extra fat tissue helps such children stay afloat.

Fourth, seek support from the child's whole family, as well as from teachers and other adults who may work with the child regularly. It helps to have these people express respect for the child's efforts — even if their own diets and exercise are not perfect! Since there are no short cuts to controlling weight, a child is bound to get discouraged at times about keeping to a diet or exercise program. At these times, encouragement from others can make the difference between success and failure. For most children (and adults), controlling weight permanently usually depends on thousands of everyday decisions about eating and physical activity. The decisions may seem minor in the short run, but in the long run they add up to a major, and crucial, change in life-style.

Being overweight can interfere significantly with a child's social relationships. Sometimes overweight children are teased, both openly and behind their backs; and over time this may affect their own opinions of themselves. (Leonard Speier)

cal and psychological reasons. Unlike people who become overweight as adults, children may sometimes gain weight by growing more fat cells; and once these cells have formed, they prove very difficult to lose or destroy (Cahill and Rossini, 1978). With dieting and exercise, they can become smaller, but not less numer- **Obstacles of weight** ous. Any return to overeating therefore creates pounds relatively easily: the ready- **control** made fat cells simply fill up again. In contrast, adults who begin gaining weight later in life do not grow new fat cells but expand the volume or size of existing ones. Compared to childhood obesity, therefore, "middle-aged spread" is a rela- tively correctable problem — though still far from an easy one to cope with.

Losing weight can be difficult for a child for other reasons as well. Any dieting or exercise scheme must have the full support of the child's parents and siblings, since they usually have a substantial influence on meal preparations and on the child's daily life-style. Yet family members may find that support is difficult to sustain over the long periods of time that most weight-control programs require. The collective will power may just not be there, especially since overweight chil- dren tend to have siblings and parents who are overweight themselves.

In spite of the weight problems they sometimes experience, though, growth for most children is slow and predictable enough that they can afford to ignore it a lot of the time. For large parts of the middle years, children can therefore shift their attention away from their bodies as such, toward what in particular they can do with their bodies. The development of new motor skills becomes possible during middle childhood in part because of this shift in focus.

Motor Development in the Middle Years

Fundamental motor skills continue to improve during the school years, and gradually become specialized in response to each child's particular interests and physical aptitudes as well as to the expectations of the people and experiences in his life. Unlike a preschooler, an older child no longer feels content simply to run, jump, and throw things; now he puts these skills to use in complex active play. Sometimes this consists of informal, child-organized games like hide-and-seek in which the child uses motor skills. At other times, as described below, active play involves formal sports — gymnastics, for example, or swimming or hockey.

Refinements of Fundamental Skills

During the elementary school years, all basic motor skills improve, but how much each does so depends on whether it relies primarily on strength and size or on coordination and timing. Skills relying on strength and size improve more or less in proportion to overall bodily growth: around 25 to 35 percent over the middle years as a whole. Running and jumping illustrates this difference clearly. As six-year-olds, children on the average can run faster than twelve feet per second, or about thirty-two yards in just under eight seconds. By age ten, though, they can often run faster than fifteen feet per second, or about thirty yards in about five and a half seconds (Roche and Malina, 1983). Likewise for jumping: as six-year-olds, children can broad jump about three feet; but by age ten, they can jump more than four and one-half feet. By age twelve, a child typically can do even better at both of these tasks. How much better, though, depends partly on when puberty begins for that particular child. An early growth spurt can create long legs and stronger muscles and therefore allow relatively large improvements in performance by the end of the elementary school years.

Smaller improvements for strength and size

Much more dramatic improvements — 100 percent or more — happen with skills that depend mostly on coordination and timing. Basic ball skills (throwing and catching) show this pattern. A typical child can throw a ball only about fifteen feet at age six, but can throw the same ball more than thirty feet at age ten or twelve. Similarly, most six-year-olds can catch an eight-inch rubber ball most of the time if it is bounced to them from a distance of fifteen feet; many ten- or twelve-year-olds, though, can catch a ball from two or three times this distance, and sometimes even if it isn't bounced (Cratty, 1979).

Larger improvements for coordination and timing

Climbing on playground bars requires a great deal of strength. Strength improves slowly during childhood, and partly as a result it is easy for older children to "dominate" the climbing bars when playing with younger children. (Alan Carey/ The Image Works)

Such changes probably do not reflect increases in power or size so much as better use of existing muscles and better timing of reflexes. Although this idea may seem obvious for catching a ball, it also holds true for throwing. A preschool child barely senses at what instant or at which angle to release a ball during the act of throwing, and this fact often spoils her distance and accuracy. As she overcomes these timing problems, her throwing improves, even though she doesn't develop new muscles or longer bones.

Individual differences in motor development

As with other physical developments, children vary widely around these averages. Schoolteachers see this variation especially clearly whenever they plan group athletic activities. A baseball team from a class of eight-year-olds, for example, may contain both children who can catch a baseball well and children who fail about half the time. It may also contain children who take twice as long to run the bases as some of their teammates do. And batting shows extreme differences. When good batters come up to bat, the outfielders become noticeably more alert and move twenty feet back. When a bad batter comes up, though, outfielders may come close in to home plate, or even sit down and daydream. Obviously, such differences can prove embarrassing to less skilled players, and are a challenge to teachers who are trying to foster every child's best development.

Influences of Early Athletics

As we have noted, children in the school years develop the ability to play games with rules. Some of these are informal, as in afterschool hopscotch, and some are

Walking on a balance beam does not take special stength as much as coordination and agility. Improvements in this kind of skill are especially dramatic during the middle years. (Dennis Mansell)

formal and adult-sponsored, as in Little League softball. In any case, traditional team sports now begin to have meaning for children; soccer, for example, makes sense to school-age children, since they can understand and abide by its rules. At the same time, children's improvements in coordination and timing make performance better in all kinds of sports, whether individual or group. Swimming, for instance, reveals the benefits of increasing coordination: some preschoolers can swim quite well, but usually only school-age children achieve adultlike coordination, speed, and grace in their strokes and breathing. The same can be said for other informal, individual activities, such as riding bicycles, roller skating, and jumping rope.

What lasting physical and psychological effects do early athletics have on children? This question has not been studied as carefully for children as for adolescents and adults, but even so, a few tentative answers are possible. On balance, athletic activity probably helps children much more than it hurts them. But it does carry a few significant risks.

Physical Effects of Early Athletics   The most obvious risks are sports-related injuries: bruises of various kinds and severity, damage to muscles (sprains), and broken or dislocated bones (DiStefano, 1982). Do such injuries actually constitute a problem for child development? Pessimists point out that injuries happen to a substantial number of athletes, even in childhood. For example:

Physical risks of sports

1. Child baseball pitchers (age eight and up) universally develop enlarged bones in their pitching arm (Bailey et al., 1978), and frequently develop pain in their pitching shoulder as well.

2. About two thirds of child gymnasts report chronic stiffness in their lower back, and about 20 to 30 percent report recurrent back pain (Cratty, 1979).

3. Virtually all children who play football become injured sooner or later, even when they play touch football rather than the tackle version of the game (Cratty, 1979).

Such injuries usually receive medical attention, but the attention is almost always short-term; once bones or muscles seem cured, they are promptly ignored, and the athlete is sent back to play. Given the special stresses of athletic activity, this relatively short-run approach may allow minor disabilities to develop (Larson, 1973). Children who play a lot of football throughout childhood, for example, may have vulnerable knees before they even begin more serious, competitive football playing, in adolescence.

Optimists point out that most children who are injured during sports have relatively minor injuries, and that the benefits of participation therefore considerably outweigh the risks. They cite the physical benefits of athletics. Children involved in regular athletics may be more in shape physically than other children; this means that their hearts and large muscles may function more efficiently (Bailey et al., 1978; Bailey, 1982). As a result, they may feel more able to undertake ordinary daily activities with less effort. They also develop coordination and strength earlier.

Physical benefits of sports

Psychological Effects of Early Athletics The immense popularity of early athletics probably stems at least in part from the psychological benefits attributed to participation; sports, it is hoped, develop achievement motivation, teamwork, and a tolerance for or even enjoyment of competition. How well do early athletics in fact realize these goals?

1. *Training in achievement motivation* Most sports provide standards against which children can assess their performances. Goals can be scored, distances can be measured, and times can be clocked. Children's performances can then be compared with their own previous scores, with those of their peers, or with those of top-scoring individuals or teams.

Whether this information really encourages higher athletic achievement depends on how a child uses it. A young child — say, five or six years old — tends to process the facts of his sports history poorly. He often ignores the significance of his wins and losses and of his long-term improvements and declines (Thomas et al., 1982). He therefore approaches each performance in much the same way. He may find each swim meet enjoyable in its own right, but he will not think much about bettering his previous performance or about correcting previous mistakes.

During the school years, though, comparing oneself to standards becomes a prominent concern (Smith and Smoll, 1982). Often this concern can motivate some children to better performance. But it can also undermine motivation, if a

Influences on motivation

In addition to their obvious physical benefits, team sports may also encourage achievement motivation and cooperation. Critics worry, though, that sports sometimes also cause injuries and destructive competition. (Paul Conklin)

child begins feeling that the standards are arbitrary, externally imposed, or too difficult to meet.

2. *Teamwork and competition* Many sports promote teamwork — meaning cooperation with a selected group of individuals. This goal is certainly a positive one, but research on children's teams suggests a problem: children practice teamwork better if their team tends to win than if it tends to lose. In other words, cooperation within a team is sometimes purchased at some cost — a cost to the losers.

What happens to the losers? Among schoolchildren, even the most gracious loser shows noticeable stress because of losing (Passer, 1982). Losers become less sociable, refuse to talk about the game, and miss game practices more often than winners. Teams of losers also show a marked tendency to search for blame by scapegoating individual members or individual events during a sporting season (Gelfand and Hartmann, 1982). If one "big play," for example, seemingly lost a crucial game of basketball, the players may dwell upon that event more than it deserves, and they may stew about one or two players who seemed most responsible for that play. Such blame is made worse if coaches and parents emphasize winning a lot; but all losing teams suffer from the problem to some extent. And team sports, of course, guarantee many losers.

Psychological effects of competition

For some children, the path away from being a loser consists of training harder to win. For substantial numbers of others, though, it consists of learning not to take sports too seriously — to treat them as "just a game." This often requires a child to adopt new interests or goals in life, and perhaps a more sedentary life-style in the bargain. In surveys of athletic dropouts, most children and adolescents cite too much competition as their major reason for leaving organized sports, and about one third to one half do not pursue their sport even recreationally after they drop out (Orlick and Botterill, 1975).

Gender and Early Athletics In North American society, girls seem especially likely to drop out of athletic activity late in their middle years. Apparently they do so for cultural reasons rather than physiological ones. Throughout childhood, they compare well to boys in strength, endurance, and motor skill, and late in childhood girls tend to be physically more mature than boys, and presumably therefore potentially more rather than less athletic. But at about age twelve, they begin to test poorly: they run slower, jump less far, and lift less weight. Since physical training at this age can virtually eliminate these differences (Wilmore, 1982), their poor performance must result from social expectations about gender. Instead of continuing to play ball as they reach puberty, some girls begin to emphasize nonathletic interests such as listening to rock music or playing a musical instrument. Some boys, of course, do the same. In the process, these children lose the

---

Perspectives on Research

The Making of an Olympic Swimmer

The public recognizes swimming in Olympic competition as a physical achievement, but this view ignores how other, social developments underlie the physical accomplishment. Studies of Olympic swimmers' development show these relationships especially clearly. Becoming a world-class swimmer, it seems, requires the sustained efforts of many people over long periods of time.

Olympic swimmers generally do not begin their swimming careers in very remarkable ways (Kalinowski, 1985a; 1985b). In one study, most began swimming lessons at a local summer recreation program around age four. The first programs and teachers were chosen for convenience — because they were only a few minutes away by car. In retrospect, however, swimmers and parents remember these teachers as warm, pleasant people who were "good with children" and who made swimming enjoyable. Since many of the first lessons were conducted in groups, the future Olympic swimmers had many chances to learn bad swimming habits, just like everybody else. In these years, little was expected of the children beyond attendance at classes once a week or so.

Sometime during the early school years, many future Olympic swimmers joined local community or swimming clubs. Again, convenience and enjoyment governed this choice: "If we had lived ten more minutes away," said one swimmer in retrospect, "I bet my parents would never have bothered." The clubs mainly gave the swimmers more pool time, as well as new friends at the club who especially enjoyed swimming. The clubs usually did sponsor competitive meets, but these were relaxed, local affairs compared with what would come later. By the third or fourth grade in school, the future Olympic swimmers were still practicing only about one hour per day on only three or four days per week. This is somewhat more than necessary for an average adult to maintain good fitness, but not much more.

The children's physical skill, however, was noticed by coaches and parents, and by the children themselves. Everything they learned in the water seemed to go well. The coaches and parents began to suspect that the children were "good," though not necessarily of Olympic potential. Partly as a result, parents became willing to invest more time and money in their children's swimming (Sloane, 1985). Most switched their children to local swimming chapters of the Amateur Athletic Union (AAU), which offers demanding training in swim-

benefits of physical activity. Fortunately, though, sex-role standards may be shifting, and as one indirect result, athletic activity has become more attractive for *both* sexes.

Checkpoint *During the middle years, children refine their motor skills, especially those that emphasize coordination and timing. Many children also become involved in organized athletics of some kind, and in doing so they experience a variety of physical and social risks as well as benefits. These activities tend to appeal more widely to boys than to girls, although the sexes may be more equally involved in athletics than they used to be.*

---

ming for local and regional competitive tournaments. Parents now found themselves willing to make unusual sacrifices for their school-age children: driving them long distances for practices and swim meets, cooking separate meals for them before or after long practices, selling tickets to meets, and paying expensive club membership fees.

By the late school years, the future Olympic swimmers found themselves increasingly absorbed in swimming. Friendships faded if they had no connection with swimming; real leisure disappeared as swim practices and schoolwork came to use up most waking hours. Siblings of the swimmers noted that they received less attention from their parents because of the demands of swimming; even family vacation sites began to be chosen according to how much swimming practice they offered. Parents paid somewhere between $1000 and $2000 per year for the prodigy's special expenses, which primarily consisted of fees for lessons and memberships and travel costs.

Through these years, no one really resented the time and cost of these developments (Sosniak, 1985). Partly, the escalating demands of the children's swimming careers made assessing the cost difficult: parents simply lacked the time to stop and

think about the investments they were making from one month to the next. Partly, too, the swimmers' performance seemed to justify the money and efforts. The children did indeed perform well in the water, even if only on a local scale; and in the early phase at least they definitely seemed to enjoy themselves.

What made these children successful was apparently a mixture of physical talent and psychological qualities. Once the future Olympic swimmers began practicing regularly, their coaches commented that they had a "feel for the water." But parents emphasized psychological qualities: they said that their children showed unusual determination to succeed, strong immunity to failure, discipline in organizing their busy schedules, and a growing competitive spirit that made winning especially gratifying to them (Bloom, 1985). The swimmers concurred with their parents' emphasis on psychological motives rather than physical talent. But there was one significant difference of opinion: the swimmers played down their passion for competition, and emphasized their enjoyment of the sport instead.

Health and Illness in Middle Childhood

In the middle years, children are usually rather healthy, in the sense that they rarely experience serious illnesses or accidents with medical consequences. They also have colds and minor viral illnesses less often than preschool children and infants do. But illnesses and accidents still occur among this age group, which partly accounts for why medical professionals and parents sometimes disagree about whether or not schoolchildren are really healthy. From a doctor's perspective, schoolchildren do not need advanced medical services as much as most other age groups. From a parent's perspective, though, the illnesses that schoolchildren do get can still be very disruptive.

Death Rates among Schoolchildren

One sign of the good health of schoolchildren is their very low **mortality,** or the proportion who die at a given age. In 1980, only about three or four children in every 10,000 between the ages of six and thirteen died, compared to about ten times this number in the population as a whole (Select Panel for the Promotion of Child Health, 1981b). The low rate for children is part of a long decline dating back several decades. In 1940, for example, more than ten school-age children out of every 10,000 died every year, and earlier in this century the figures were even higher (Preston, 1976).

The decline in mortality has changed the relative importance of different causes of death. Infectious diseases, such as pneumonia and chronic diarrhea, have become very infrequent among children from well-off families in North America. As a result, accidents have become relatively more important as a cause of death among children. Almost half of all childhood deaths in recent years have occurred because of motor vehicle accidents (Zill, 1982; Canada Safety Council, 1983). A majority of these deaths were children who were *not* wearing seatbelts while riding with their parents or other relatives.

Comparative importance of accidents

But school-age children do sometimes die from other kinds of accidents. For every two children who die in traffic accidents, for example, a third dies from drowning and a fourth dies in a fire of some sort (see Table 11-1). However, stating the figures in this way makes it sound as if accidents are evenly distributed throughout society, when in fact they are not. Some children face much more risk for certain accidents than others do, either because their environments contain more risks or because their parents and other adults responsible for them do not recognize the risks and therefore fail to teach the children proper safety precautions.

Accidents

For most school-age children, physical safety poses a serious health problem (Pringle and Ramsey, 1982). During these years, children begin playing in and exploring larger territories. They investigate the neighborhood around their home and

	Frequency per 100,000 Children	
Cause of Death	Ages 5–14	Ages 15–19
Accidents		
Motor vehicle accidents	9	43
Drownings, fires, and poisons	4	17
Other accidents	5	17
Disease		
Cancer (all kinds)	5	6
Heart disease	1	2
Other illnesses and congenital abnormalities	11	16
Violence		
Homicides	<1	9
Suicides	<1	9

Table 11-1 *Causes of Death in Childhood and Adolescence*

Source: U.S. Department of Health, Education, and Welfare (1985). *Vital statistics of the United States.* Washington: U.S. Government Printing Office. Also U.S. Department of Commerce (1984). *Statistical abstract of the United States.* Washington: U.S. Government Printing Office.

school in particular, in spite of its unknown dangers. Since improvised sports need more room than the play of preschoolers does, children in urban and some suburban areas often play ballgames in the street; they do their best to avoid traffic, but home runs may require sudden sprints and allow no time to check for cars.

When not playing at sports, school-age children have a curiosity about the wider world that has increased since their preschool years. Poking around neighbors' back yards, they may find old equipment or machinery that looks too interesting *not* to investigate. Or they may find flammable or toxic substances, such as gasoline or paint thinner, which supposedly have been stored away safely. Construction sites are especially inviting: they contain old pieces of wood and partially completed nooks and crannies that make good hiding places. Unfortunately, these interesting spaces often lack structural strength; children can slip and fall in them, and pieces of steel or wood can land on their heads.

Increase in environmental dangers

Most of the time, accidents from such sources are relatively minor. But a significant number cause fractures, poisoning, or open wounds that require medical attention. Somewhere between 5 and 10 percent of all visits to doctors by schoolchildren, in fact, are because of accidents like these (Roghmann and Pless, 1975).

Illnesses

On the average, schoolchildren get sick only about half as often as preschoolers. From their parents' point of view, however, illnesses probably still seem rather fre-

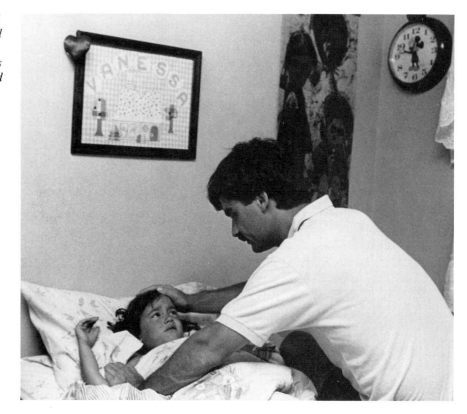

How often has this child stayed home from school because of a flu or a cold? And how often has one of her parents stayed home to care for her? Sick days become so frequent that most parents lose count of them. (Victoria Arlak)

quent; nearly one quarter of the parents in one survey reported that during the preceding two weeks their children had been "too sick to carry on as normal" (Roghmann and Pless, 1975), meaning that the children stayed home from school for at least one day. As parents often point out, a sick child has a substantial impact on the work and leisure schedules of the rest of the family, and especially of parents.

Nature of acute illnesses

Acute Illness Most of these childhood diseases are **acute illnesses,** which means they have a definite beginning, middle, and end. Acute illnesses include colds and gastrointestinal flu and slightly more serious childhood diseases such as chicken pox and measles. Modern medicine cannot really cure these illnesses, because they develop from **viruses,** which are complex protein molecules that only come alive when they infect a host tissue (like a child's nose). In spite of popular belief, no drugs can combat this type of infection, unlike the antibiotic drugs that can effectively fight off bacteria that invade the body. Viral illnesses must instead run their course, and the child's natural immunities must work the real cure.

For such diseases, doctors usually prescribe simple bed rest. Sometimes they also prescribe medications, but these are not to cure the illness so much as to prevent complications. Many ear infections, for example, arise from viral infections, but doctors sometimes prescribe antibiotic drugs to prevent a more serious bacterial ear infection from developing.

Chronic Illness By the school years, about 5 to 10 percent of children develop **chronic illnesses,** or conditions that persist for many months without significant improvement. The most common chronic conditions occur in the lungs and affect breathing (Pless and Satterwhite, 1975). Some children develop **asthma,** or persistent congestion in their lungs; others develop chronic coughs or allergies. Still other chronic complaints concern specific sensory organs. About one child in one hundred, for example, reports problems in hearing or seeing — or, technically speaking, parents report these problems to doctors.

Nature of lasting illnesses

Social Influences on Illness The seriousness and frequency of illnesses vary a lot according to children's social and economic circumstances. Consider income differences among families. In general, parents from higher-income families report that their school-age children get sick just about as often as parents from lower-income families do. But the higher-income parents also report keeping their children at home for *shorter* periods of time. In the highest 25 percent of families, children stay at home for an average of only one and one half days per illness, whereas in the lowest 25 percent, they stay at home for nearly five days per illness (Roghmann and Pless, 1975).

Effects of income level

What is the reason for this difference? Low-income families probably lack money for doctors' visits and time for tending to sick children. To merit staying home from school, therefore, or to merit visiting a doctor, a child must have a relatively major illness, such as a seriously high fever or severe diarrhea. The result of these circumstances shows in the longer average stay at home when illness finally receives special attention.

Race and gender matter, too. Black families report fewer illnesses per child than do white families of similar income. And all families, black or white, report more illnesses for girls than for boys of the same age (Butler et al., 1984). School-age girls in fact appear to get sick almost as often as preschool children of both sexes; only boys decrease in frequency as they get older.

Note, however, that these trends result partly from families' beliefs about illness, as well as from real differences. Girls may not necessarily get sick more often than boys; instead, training in gender roles may lead them to talk about their ailments more and to request medical treatment more often (Roghmann, 1975). For similar reasons, parents may be more apt to consider girls physically delicate, and therefore to keep them home for minor illnesses that they would not consider serious in boys. These facts may mean that girls exaggerate the extent of their illnesses or that boys hide the extent of theirs, or both.

Beliefs about illness

Dental Health

Tooth decay presents the most widespread health problem of middle childhood. When children enter school at about age six, they already average more than two dental caries (or cavities) per child. Throughout the school years, more than half of all children have one or more teeth that are decayed, filled, or missing; and a third have two or more such teeth (Kovar and Meny, 1981). Cavities result from improper diet and faulty habits in brushing and flossing teeth. Snacks containing a

Dental problems are widespread

lot of sticky sugar, such as candy bars, are especially bad for teeth, since the sugar creates a breeding ground for bacteria that lasts for many hours.

Since schoolchildren are beginning to acquire their permanent teeth, their cavities can pose a significant health problem over the long run. Left untreated, they can create enough discomfort ("toothache") to interfere with learning in school and to ruin their dispositions quite thoroughly. Left untreated still longer, cavities can result in serious infections of the gums and jaw as well as the loss of any infected teeth. Missing teeth mean that neighboring teeth lose their natural vertical alignment and become less effective as food processors.

Children do vary considerably in the numbers of cavities they develop during

---

Perspectives on Research

Children's Conceptions of Illness and Health

Many psychologists believe that children often understand illness differently from adults and that their concepts tend to evolve through stages that parallel Piaget's cognitive stages of development (Bibace and Walsh, 1979). Children of any age, though, show a lot of variation in their concepts of illness and health, and the variations suggest problems that families face in helping their children to take responsibility for their own health care.

A majority of younger children (aged five or six) are likely to explain minor illness in terms of single, obvious symptoms which are acquired by contact with some external contagion, though not necessarily "germs" or viruses (Bibace and Walsh, 1981). In this view, illness is not really in a child's body so much as in certain behaviors of the child. Amy shows this kind of thinking:

Q: What is a cold?

AMY: It's coughing a lot.

Q: Why do you catch a cold?

AMY: From going outside.

Q: How can you make yourself well again?

AMY: Don't know. Later I go to school again.

Amy's ideas resemble the preoperational thinking described by Piaget. She centers or focuses on a

single, observable symptom (coughing) and cause (going outside), and does not take account of the multiple features that in fact constitute the illness.

Later in childhood (around ages eight and nine), most children do begin taking account of multiple symptoms and causes:

KEITH, age eight: A cold is coughing, and you feel tired a lot, and at night you can't breathe.

MARIA, age nine: Measles are bumps on your skin; they itch for a long time. At first you're tired; then you're bored about staying home.

Attending to multiple features of illnesses makes these two children more concrete-operational in their thinking, as defined by Piaget. These children also show more awareness of the reversibility of many illnesses:

KEITH: You get well from a cold by taking pills — usually vitamin C.

MARIA: I think measles go away by rubbing a cream on the bumps. You're supposed to rest, too.

These children, however, still make little reference to processes actually inside the body that might

the school years, but contrary to a widespread impression, numbers of cavities do not depend on the economic level of the child. Children from poverty-level families acquire about as many cavities, on the average, as children from affluent families do (Kovar, 1982). What does vary by income is a family's ability to find dental treatment. Not surprisingly, low-income families are more likely to leave their children's cavities untreated, presumably because they cannot afford the cost of a dentist or because they live in areas where dental care is scarce or even nonexistent. Sometimes school health programs can fill these gaps in service, but even they cannot meet all the dental needs of school-age children (Anderson and Creswell, 1980).

Variations in dental treatment

---

constitute particular illnesses, or that might eventually lead to a cure. To this extent, they show a type of egocentrism, or failure to distinguish between self and nonself. In this case, children fail to distinguish between the causes of illness (often external) and the illness itself (usually internal). Instead, they regard both illness and cause as external.

By later childhood (around age eleven), some children — but not a majority — do begin referring to physiological processes. But as with many adults, their information about inner processes often relies on fairly crude analogies (Perrin and Gerrity, 1981):

Q: What is a cold?

PETER, age eleven: Little germs get into you from the air. They get into your blood, but after a while your blood kills them off again.

Q: Why do you get stomach flu?

PETER: Your stomach is a bag of food. When it doesn't like the food, it turns inside out!

These explanations of illness are a far cry from the complex, abstract accounts given in medical textbooks. But they do attribute at least some features of disease to internal workings, so such explanations may help children to begin taking more re-

sponsibility for their own illnesses. From the perspective of older children, illness belongs to the self more than it did at earlier ages.

From the perspective of a young child, in contrast, illness often seems like a role that parents assign: the parents, and not the child himself, decide when the child is sick (Parmalee, 1986). More often than not, parents find themselves teaching their young children how to "act sick." They must often encourage or even require quiet behavior, for example, even when the child wants to play outside actively. And parents must encourage children to comply with medical advice without questioning it ("You *have* to take this medicine; the doctors said so!").

Assigning children to the sick role may help cure some childhood illnesses, but it also risks teaching children too much passivity about illness. Without realizing it, children may conclude that they can do little either to ward off illness or to get well from it once it does arrive (Lewis and Lewis, 1983). In the long run, this attitude can actually make children indifferent to ways of keeping healthy, such as eating the right foods and getting enough sleep. Parents (and doctors) therefore have a difficult task: knowing how much to prescribe to and doctor young patients while encouraging children to care for and evaluate their health for themselves.

Hyperactivity and Attention Deficit Disorders

A small number of school-age children seem extremely active and have considerable trouble concentrating on any one activity for long (Douglas and Peters, 1979). Their problem is called **hyperactivity,** or **attention deficit disorder (ADD).** A second-grade teacher described one student with ADD like this:

> Joey was friendly when you greeted him; "Hi!" he would say brightly, and smile. But he would never settle down. First he dumped the class's main supply of pencils out on a table; he sort of lunged at one of the pencils, but before he began writing, he left the table, looking for something new. During a reading lesson, I asked Joey to read silently until I finished helping another child; but Joey found this hard to do. He glanced in my direction; tapped a neighboring child on the shoulder; giggled; and kept scanning the room for "more." A child happened to drop a book; Joey laughed at this harder than the others, and jumped up quickly to pick the book up. He was probably trying to help, but in doing so he knocked his own papers all over the floor. Instead of picking up the papers, he only picked up his pencil, and headed off to sharpen it. And the morning was still only half over!

In the long run, behavior like this contributes to emotional problems, to conflicts with teachers and other adults, and to poor relationships with peers. Such social

---

A Talk with John

Growing Older

John was interviewed after school in his bedroom, which contained three fish tanks, plants, a cat, and a number of models and other construction projects that he had worked on.

INTERVIEWER: John, how old are you now?

JOHN: I was eleven in August.

INTERVIEWER: What is it like to be eleven? Have you noticed yourself getting bigger?

JOHN: I don't know. You do grow more.

INTERVIEWER: How do you know?

JOHN: I just have. My parents tell me, too. They say I've grown a lot.

INTERVIEWER: Can you notice some things about your body compared with the way you were at nine or ten?

JOHN: I don't know. I can reach things better. And I can run better, faster, and for a longer time if I go for a jog with my mom and dad.

INTERVIEWER: What other things can you do better?

JOHN: It's easier to play my guitar with bigger hands. It used to be harder to reach my fingers around the neck to make chords and now it's getting easier. It's still not that easy, though.

INTERVIEWER: What about sports?

JOHN: I like to play baseball, soccer, and basketball. Getting bigger and stronger helps there. You can hit the ball farther and throw better. In soccer being able to run and kick hard are important, and I can play much better than I did a couple of years ago. Of course, I also have more experience at playing.

INTERVIEWER: What other things can you do that you couldn't do a couple of years ago?

JOHN: I'm a better bike rider than I used to be. It's easier for me to ride. My legs are longer, and my seat is as high as it can go. Some of my clothing is also too small for me.

INTERVIEWER: How is your size compared with other kids your age?

JOHN: I think about the same size. Some kids are smaller and some are bigger . . . taller and heavier.

INTERVIEWER: What does an

problems eventually aggravate the child's troubles in concentrating. Joey, for example, may become wrought up over conflicts with teachers and self-conscious about what peers think of his behavior. He may become so upset, in fact, that he gets even more fidgety than before.

Reactions to Children with ADD   Overly active children cause parents and teachers a lot of worry, and excessive activity is one of the most common reasons for referring children to psychiatrists and other health professionals (Rutter and Garmezy, 1983). How many children really have ADD, though, depends some- **Prevalence of ADD** what on who is doing the estimating. Professional school psychologists usually estimate that around 5 to 10 percent of school-age children are seriously overactive; teachers give a somewhat higher figure. Parents give the highest figure of all; in one survey, fully half of all parents of preschool and school-age boys considered their child's activity level a major source of concern (Lord, 1982). All the estimates agree that the large majority of highly active children — about 85 percent — are boys. Whatever else these figures may show, they certainly reveal that adults find dealing with highly active children very difficult.

Excessive activity presents more problems in some situations than in others. During outdoor play, for example, very active children hardly stand out at all, and seem to make and be friends about as well as any other children (Schleifer et al.,

---

eleven-year-old do to stay healthy and strong?

JOHN: They don' want to get too fat.

INTERVIEWER: Do you think about that?

JOHN: Yes.

INTERVIEWER: What would make you too fat?

JOHN: Not getting any exercise and maybe eating too much candy and things like that. I don't think that will happen to me, but some kids are overweight and that's not healthy.

INTERVIEWER: What other changes have you noticed in yourself?

JOHN: My parents used to have to tell me to clean up my room, but I just keep it clean now. And I do my work and my parents don't have to tell me to do it.

INTERVIEWER: Do you think differently about your work now? Does it feel different?

JOHN: I still don't like it — I never have and I probably never will. I just do it before my parents tell me and then I'm done. And that way I don't get nagged.

INTERVIEWER: Do people treat you differently now that you're older?

JOHN: Yes. They treat me more like an adult than a little kid. Instead of just telling me to do something, now they sometimes talk about it. They discuss it with me. I also have more responsibilities. I have to take care of my sister when I get home from school and sometimes till five o'clock when my parents get home.

INTERVIEWER: Any other changes?

JOHN: I can go to my friend's house by myself. And I can stay home alone. And I can have my own room, too.

Follow-up Questions

1. What physical changes seem most important to John?

2. What effects have athletics had on John's development?

3. In what ways has John's physical development affected his psychosocial development?

1975). The structured atmosphere of most school classrooms poses more problems. During class, children with ADD often get out of their seats, respond aggressively to teachers and peers, and run the risk of losing not only opportunities to learn but also the affection and respect of friends.

Note, though, that *most* children show excessive activity *some* of the time. This fact may not make dealing with ADD any easier, but it does make the disorder seem more understandable and manageable. Only a few children really exhibit extremely high activity consistently enough to deserve professional attention. Experts suggest four criteria for deciding when activity poses a truly serious problem (Ross and Ross, 1982):

When is ADD serious?

1. The overactivity happens even when it is clearly inappropriate, such as when riding in a car or sitting at a meal.
2. Seriously overactive children consistently fail to respond to pressures to inhibit their activity.
3. Seriously overactive children seem always to respond at the same fast speed, even when they are trying to respond more slowly, as in drawing a picture.
4. Seriously overactive children show other, related problems, such as high distractibility and problems with making friends.

Only children who meet all four criteria deserve the often misused label *hyperactive;* all others should probably just be called "very active" or "overactive."

Causes of Hyperactivity and ADD No one can say why some children become extremely active or have trouble concentrating. But three major possibilities exist. The first of these is genetic. Some children may inherit stronger tendencies toward activity than other children do. And some children may inherit a temperament or disposition to shift attention frequently. Since infants show differences like these almost as soon as they can move and respond, it seems reasonable that children may show similar differences.

Physical causes of ADD The second explanation for ADD concerns hidden physical differences because of events during gestation or delivery. ADD resembles the problems that occur when children are known to experience damage to or disease of the brain or central nervous system; a noticeable number of such children become excessively active afterward (Shaffer et al., 1975). This fact suggests, but does not prove, that ADD or hyperactivity may reflect unidentified brain differences, or other physiological problems. The trouble with this line of reasoning, though, is that doctors have no practical way to test it. Most of the time, the only evidence for physiological or neurological problems is the behavior problems.

Social causes of ADD A third explanation concerns children's family and other social environments. Some parents or teachers may accidentally create hyperactive children by setting rules for behavior that are too precise or rigid (Lambert and Hartsough, 1984). In class, for example, forbidding children to wiggle in their seats actually makes many children more restless rather than less so. At home, watching television for too long can have the same effect. And on the way to school, very long bus rides, such as those experienced by children in many rural areas or large cities, can also create overactivity. When circumstances like these operate over a long period of time on children with a naturally active temperament, they may help to create the extremes of ADD, or hyperactivity.

Helping Children with ADD and Their Families Since no one is quite sure what makes some children overactive, no single strategy exists for treating or dealing with the condition. Amid much controversy, doctors have sometimes prescribed medication. Ironically, the most effective medications for calming overactive children are the same drugs that stimulate normal adults. If not used properly, though, these drugs can have serious side effects — impairment of speech, eating problems, and decreased alertness — especially on young children (Sprague and Ullman, 1981).

Effects of drugs

Other experts have proposed feeding highly active children a diet that is completely free of artificial substances such as food colorings, preservatives, and flavorings. The best-known of these is the Feingold diet, named after its originator (Feingold, 1974). Although many parents are convinced that such a diet has helped their children, scientific evaluations of dietary changes have not found much support for this strategy. Many children on the diet do quiet down eventually, but their improvement could just as easily come from the passage of time, which seems to "cure" many cases of ADD. A strict diet may also work by encouraging parents to give more care and attention to their children, which may actually cause the cure. In any case, parents and professionals may sometimes mistakenly give credit to the diet when other factors are equally important.

Effects of diet

Classical psychotherapy also does not work well, probably because active children do not sit still long enough for all the talking involved. But two variations on traditional therapy both show promise. With younger children, therapists can engage in **play therapy,** a technique in which child and therapist communicate through make-believe play, using dolls and other props. Together the adult and child might make up a story about "a child who could never stop running," constructing an ending to the story that helps the child finally to slow down. While play therapy continues with the child, more traditional, verbally oriented therapy with family members can help relatives to cope with the frustrations of living with such an active child.

Psychological techniques

With overactive children of all ages, **behavior modification** often helps. This approach identifies specific behaviors that need changing, as well as straightforward techniques for eliminating or reducing them. In classrooms, one behavior modification technique consists of using high-status peers to model or demonstrate appropriate behaviors. The active child simply watches a classmate complete an assignment slowly instead of at lightning speed; then the child tries to copy the same slow style in doing the assignment herself. The teacher of course reinforces (usually with praise) the slower behavior when it occurs. He may also make reinforcement more likely by limiting the active child's choices to help prevent unwanted distractions. Instead of offering a choice of three activities, he might offer only two. As the child begins concentrating on activities better, the teacher can begin offering more options again (Ross and Ross, 1984).

One effective way of helping overly active children is for teachers to set very specific learning goals. Another is to encourage an active child to watch and imitate a slower-paced child complete the same assignment. (Meri Houtchens-Kitchens/The Picture Cube)

Learning Disabilities

During the middle years, somewhere around 5 percent of children develop **learning disabilities,** or difficulties in learning specific academic skills such as reading and arithmetic (Grant and Snyder, 1984). Learning disabilities have no obvious physical cause, such as blindness or hearing impairment; however, as we point out below, they may result from subtle differences in the ways in which children's brains organize and process information.

Features of reading problems

Learning disabilities take many forms, but the most common is called **dyslexia** — literally, an inability to read. For some children, dyslexia consists of "word blindness": they find that they can read letters singly (like *c* or *a* or *t*) but not in combinations that make words like *cat* (Farnham-Diggory, 1977). In other forms of dyslexia, children can read words but fail to comprehend them. They can copy words accurately or take them from oral dictation, but they cannot explain what they have written afterward, no matter how simple the vocabulary. Sometimes children with dyslexia can read combinations of digits that make large numbers; they can read *123,* for example, as "one hundred and twenty-three," but not as "one, two, three," even when they try. Most children with dyslexia have these problems in combination. Yet they seem normal in every other respect; their everyday conversations seem perfectly intelligent, and their motor skills seem just as skillful as other children's.

Causes of Learning Disabilities   What causes some children to have learning disabilities? Their symptoms resemble what happens to individuals who suffer injuries to certain parts of their brains (Rutter and Garmezy, 1983). For this reason, some professionals have suggested that many learning disabilities, including dyslexia, may reflect undetected **minimal brain damage** which occurred during the birth process or even before birth. By nature, though, this hypothesis is extremely hard to prove. It also discourages some parents and professionals from helping learning-disabled children, on the grounds (probably mistaken) that organically based problems are beyond their control.

Physical causes of learning disabilities

A more helpful explanation for learning disabilities focuses on brain functions rather than brain anatomy. In this view, disabilities may result from subtle differences in how the brain normally organizes and processes information (Farnham-Diggory, 1977). To see what this idea means, consider what children must do to read an ordinary page of print. First they must perceive the letters and words as visual patterns. Then they must combine these patterns into larger strings that constitute phrases and sentences. Finally they must connect these strings with meanings to form ideas. While all of these steps are going on, they must also scan ahead to recognize the next visual patterns on the page. If any of these steps fails, or occurs in the wrong sequence or at the wrong speed, a child may appear dyslexic (Siegler, 1983).

These mistakes in cognitive processing may indeed lie at the heart of many learning disabilities. Some children with dyslexia, for example, may find visual recognition especially difficult or time-consuming. Several researchers have reached this conclusion by studying a phenomenon called **perceptual masking,** in which some letters are hard to read because of the presence of other letters nearby. To understand this problem, consider the letters below:

Causes related to cognitive processing

wek

qwekl

aqweklm

asqweklmn

dsaqweklmnp

gfdsaqweklmnpyb

cvghdsaqweklmnpybht

If you look at the *e* in the top line, you will probably still be able to see the letter *w* and *k* clearly, using your peripheral vision (the corner of your eye). If you look at the *e* in a line further down, you can still see the end letters relatively clearly, but the middle letters become almost impossible to pick out clearly. Trying to notice the middle letters does help in perceiving them, but when you make this effort, the end letters become hard to discern. Perceiving one set of features in this display, then, masks others; hence the name *perceptual masking.* Without a lot of practice, few people — adults or children — can see very many letters at once.

Some children with dyslexia, it seems, show especially strong perceptual masking (Wilkinson, 1980). Compared to normal readers, they must stare at words for rather long periods, consciously shifting attention from one subset of letters to another, in a way similar to the staring required to "see" the letters displayed on the preceding page. Once they figure out the letters in a word, though, they can connect meanings with them fairly quickly and accurately. For these children, verbal association may happen much faster than visual perception.

The gap in speed between perceiving and associating may account for many errors made by children with dyslexia. A ten-year-old may look at the word *conceal,* for example, and say something like "concol," or look at *alternate* and say "alfoonite." In making these mistakes, children may literally be reading what they see and guessing about the rest. Unfortunately, they may see fewer letters than normal readers usually discern. To put it differently, trying to see all letters clearly may simply take too much time and effort, and overall reading comprehension bogs down as a result.

Helping Children with Learning Disabilities Since learning disabilities only really constitute a problem in school settings, school professionals have taken increasing responsibility in recent years for helping children who develop these disabilities. Most commonly, help consists of careful diagnosis of which steps of **Individual diagnosis and** thinking cause a child's problem, followed by individual instructional plans to **tutoring** strengthen those particular steps. Children with problems in perceptual masking, for example, can be given exercises in which they purposely work to improve this skill. Often such special work can be done in a regular class during a normal school day, but at least some of it requires individual tutoring, so that the professional can monitor and give precise assistance to the child's thinking as it actually occurs. Depending on the child's needs and the school's circumstances, regular classroom teachers, parents, or trained special educators can act as tutors.

Note that children with learning disabilities are usually old enough to have feelings and opinions about their problems. Eventually, in fact, the major part of some learning disabilities may become *self-consciousness* about not learning, in **Social support** addition to any cognitive or perceptual problems as such. A child who cannot read well usually becomes painfully aware of this fact sooner or later, and worries about what teachers, parents, and peers may think of her as a result. Adults can help this problem by being optimistic about the child's eventual capacity to learn academic skills, and by encouraging tolerance of differences among classmates and other peers.

Checkpoint *School-age children are usually rather healthy, as reflected in their low mortality and low rates of accidents and illness. Nonetheless, they are subject to a wide range of illnesses and injuries. Their most widespread medical problem is tooth decay. A few children also show excessive levels of activity, and a few others develop specific learning disabilities which interfere with academic work. These problems may have physical or neurological origins, but we do not really know how many children may be affected, or to what extent.*

Effects of Growth on Thinking and Feeling

This chapter has shown some ways in which physical growth can influence the other aspects of a child's development during the elementary school years. Growth may seem slower or less eventful than either before or after these years, but this is true only in a strictly physical sense. Psychologically, a child's growth makes new social opportunities possible, as in children's sports. When growth problems such as childhood obesity do develop, they often cause serious psychological side effects during the school years. And some abnormal physical developments, such as brain damage, have effects that closely resemble purely psychological developments — so closely, in fact, that distinguishing between the physical and mental aspects may confuse our understanding of the child as much as help it. Real children consist of minds, bodies, and feelings combined; only textbooks separate these three. Keeping this idea in mind may help to clarify the next two chapters, which concern children's thinking and social relationships.

Summary of Major Ideas

Trends and Variations in Height and Weight

1. Although growth slows down during the middle years, children of any single age still show significant differences in height and weight.

2. Differences in size and body build contribute to the stereotypes and impressions that children form about one another.

3. Toward the end of the elementary school years, girls tend to grow taller than boys, and this difference can create embarrassment for some children.

4. A few children weigh significantly more than average, and these children sometimes experience social rejection and risk medical problems if their condition persists.

Motor Development in the Middle Years

5. During the middle years, children refine a wide range of motor skills which first appeared during the preschool years.

6. Improvements are especially marked for skills that emphasize coordination and timing rather than strength and size.

7. Many children become involved in athletics, whether they are formal and organized or informal and spontaneous.

8. Certain popular sports carry definite physical risks, but these may be outweighed by the physical benefits of regular activity.

9. Athletics may encourage achievement motivation in children, and (in some sports) teamwork as well.

10. Team sports encourage both cooperation and competition; the latter can have harmful social effects on some children.

11. Even though gender roles are now less distinct than they used to be, boys still tend to become involved in athletics more than girls do, especially toward the end of the school years.

Health and Illness in Middle Childhood

12. Overall, schoolchildren are among the healthiest people in society, as shown by their low mortality.

13. Because children now die much less often from infectious illnesses, accidental injuries (especially traffic accidents) have become comparatively more serious problems.

14. Compared to preschoolers, schoolchildren catch fewer minor acute illnesses, but a small percent do suffer from significant chronic medical problems.

15. Parents' income levels and beliefs about illness affect how much children actually stay at home as a result of getting sick.

16. The most widespread medical problem in childhood is tooth decay, which can lead to serious complications if left untreated.

17. Attention deficit disorder, or hyperactivity, affects a small percentage of school-age children.

18. Because parents and teachers find ADD very difficult to deal with, they may be inclined to overestimate its prevalence.

19. ADD may result from a combination of genetic, physical, and social causes.

20. Treatment of ADD sometimes includes special drugs, special diet, play therapy for younger children, and behavior modification techniques.

21. A few children have specific learning disabilities during the school years.

22. The most common learning disabilities are reading disabilities, or dyslexia, and probably involve subtle differences in how affected children process or organize information.

23. Children with learning disabilities need detailed diagnosis of their individual learning styles, followed by individual instructional plans to meet their diagnosed needs and social support for their continuing efforts to learn.

Key Terms

obesity *(449)*
mortality *(460)*
acute illnesses *(462)*
viruses *(462)*
chronic illness *(462)*
asthma *(462)*
hyperactivity *(466)*
attention deficit disorder
  (ADD) *(468)*

play therapy *(469)*
behavior modification *(469)*
learning disabilities *(470)*
dyslexia *(470)*
minimal brain damage *(471)*
perceptual masking *(471)*

What Do You Think?

1. How well do you like your particular height and weight? Do you remember when you began to feel this way about your build?

2. Are competitive athletics inevitably hard on some children? Explain what you think about this issue.

3. Some experts argue that excessively active children are not so much "disturbed" as "disturbing." What do you suppose they mean by this comment?

4. If you were a teacher, how would you feel about having a hyperactive child in your class? What about a learning-disabled child? Explain your reasons for your feelings.

For Further Reading

Buscaglia, L. (Ed.). *The disabled and their parents: A counseling challenge.* Rev. Ed. New York: Holt, Rinehart, and Winston, 1983.

This book discusses the impact of handicaps on individuals, their families, and counselors or others responsible for offering help. It conveys the personal points of view of these different people especially well, conveying the feel of living with a handicap or of living close to someone with a handicap.

Magill, R., Ash, M., and Smoll, F. (Eds.). *Children in sport* (2nd Ed.). Champaign, Ill.: Human Kinetics Press, 1982.

In this book, various authors look at the physical and social effects of athletic activity in childhood. They consider both positive and negative effects, exploring injuries and conditioning benefits, for example, and cooperation and competitive stress.

Marshall, H. *How to save your teeth.* New York: Penguin, 1980.

Silverstein, A., and Silverstein, V. *So you're going to get braces: A guide to orthodontics.* Philadelphia: Lippincott, 1978.

The most widely occurring medical problems in childhood concern teeth. The first of these books explains why this tends to be so, and also explains ways of maintaining better dental health. The second book describes both the mechanics of orthodontic work and children's (and parents') reactions to it. As children who have done it will confirm, getting braces can be a very frustrating experience.

Turecki, S., and Tonner, L. *The difficult child.* New York: Bantam Books, 1985.

The authors have talked with parents and other adults who are responsible for excessively active children. They mix support and encouragement with advice for specific techniques, and their discussion distinguishes among settings (home vs. school) and ages of children (infants, preschoolers, school-age).

Saunders, A., and Remsberg, B. *The stress-proof child.* New York: Pocket Books, 1984.

This book purposely tries to build a bridge between the mind and the body: between children's physical growth and health and their mental and emotional development. It therefore discusses how one realm can help the other. For example, the authors explain how illness can actually assist children's long-term sense of well-being, and how touching and hugging can do the same. They also point out how anxiety and worries can contribute to poor physical health in children, just as they sometimes do in adults.

Chapter

12

The Middle Years: Cognitive Development

Focusing Questions

- What new cognitive skills do children acquire during the school years? What psychological and practical effects do these new skills have?
- How do information-processing skills affect memory capacity?
- What learning strategies do children acquire during the middle years, and how do these strategies affect their overall cognitive development?
- What unique cognitive styles do children begin to show during the school years?
- What limitations do school-age children still have in their use of language?
- How does bilingualism affect children's language development?
- What is general intelligence, and how can it be measured?
- What are the limitations of standardized tests of ability and achievement?
- What changes in moral reasoning do children undergo during the school years?

ONE DAY, TWO BROTHERS, aged seven and nine, constructed a "science museum" in their living room. They systematically selected all the best chairs and blankets as building materials. Then they found all their stuffed animals and put them on display in this museum, grouping them both by color and by size. They finished the museum by hanging a sign on it: "ANIMAL MUSEUM. TIKETS $1." Not many people bought tickets, but this did not stop these boys from having a lively conversation about their project.

The activity drew on the kind of cognitive skills that school-age children have in more abundance than preschool children. It required the boys to make the building and to remember where to find particular stuffed animals. It took a rudimentary knowledge of reading and writing, so that they could make the sign. And it took the knowledge that museums store interesting objects in systematic ways and that they often cost money to visit.

This chapter describes the development of cognitive skills like these, as well as others that characterize school-age children. It begins by looking at Piaget's findings about thinking during children's middle years, because as always, his theory offers one of the most comprehensive overviews of cognitive development. Then we discuss how children organize and process information, paying special attention to the ways in which children use memory and learning strategies during the school years. After that, the chapter shifts focus to some practical implications of cognitive development. We look at how children differ in their thinking and learning styles and how these variations affect success in school, and we look at how children differ in their styles of speaking and how language variations can affect children's educational and social success. We then discuss the nature of intelligence and why the measurement of intelligence has been not only one of psychology's major success stories but also one of its biggest sources of criticism over the years. Finally, the chapter includes a look at various theories about schoolchildren's moral development.

Concrete Operational Skills

During the middle years, children become skilled at **concrete operations,** which are particular kinds of mental activities focused on real, tangible objects and events. Concrete operations have three interrelated qualities: decentration, sensitivity to transformations, and reversibility (Piaget, 1965). None of these is reliably present among preschool children. **Decentration** means attending to more than one feature of a problem at a time. In estimating the number of pennies spread out on a table, for example, a school-age child will probably take into account not only how large the array is but also how far apart individual pennies seem to be. **Sensitivity to transformations** means noticing and remembering significant changes in objects. When judging whether the amount of liquid in a glass stays the same after it is poured into a new container, a school-age child concentrates on the actual process of change in appearance — the transformation — rather than on how the liquid looks either before or after pouring. **Reversibility** of thought means solving problems by mentally going back to the beginning of them. In judging the amount of liquid in a container, the child can imagine pouring the liquid back into its original glass without actually doing so.

Qualities of concrete operations

To understand these features of concrete operations, we should compare how preschool and concrete operational children solve the same problem. Consider how Ken and Murray each got started making a batch of muffins:

- Ken, age four, needed guidance from his day-care teacher in order to cook, but even so he kept coming dangerously close to ruining the recipe. The teacher set out the ingredients Ken needed: flour, sugar, salt, baking powder, and the like. Ken liked the look of the bag of flour (it was bright red), so he picked the bag up and happily began pouring flour into a large bowl. His teacher stopped him from overdoing it: "We only need two cups," she said. "But there is not as much in the bowl," said Ken, meaning that the bowl made the flour spread out and therefore look like less. "Okay," said Ken's teacher, "but we still need to measure two cups. How can we do that?" Ken took the measuring cup, filled it, and added one *more* cup of flour. Now there was far too much flour; apparently Ken did not think it was necessary to pour the first flour out of the bowl.

- Murray, age ten, worked much more independently than Ken, and when he made mistakes, they were less serious blunders. After setting out all the ingredients that he needed, Murray poured some flour into the bowl. "Oops," he said, "I forgot to measure it." So he poured the flour carefully back into the bag and checked the instructions in the recipe. Then he began again, first pouring exactly one cup into the measuring cup. "How am I going to get two cups into this small measuring cup?" he thought. He solved his problem by pouring the first cup of flour into the bowl and then carefully measuring out a second cup.

There are many reasons why these two boys differed in their cooking performance, including variations in their prior experiences with cooking, measuring, and even reading. But part of the difference reflects the appearance of concrete operations in Murray. He was less distracted by immediate sensory cues, like the color of the flour bag and the attractive feel of pouring out large amounts of flour. Murray was also more able to reverse his first mistake by returning the flour to its bag. And Murray seemed aware that the amount of flour did not depend on where the flour happened to be — that one cup of flour is one cup whether it is in the bowl or in the measuring cup.

Refinements of Preoperational Thinking

In some ways, concrete operations amount to refinements of the skills that children form in the preoperational period, including skills in classification and belief in animism and artificialism. **Classification** involves putting objects into groups or categories according to some sort of standards or criteria. By about age seven, children have improved their classifying or grouping ability substantially over what they could do as preschoolers. In particular they are less confused than they used to be by **class inclusion** — groupings in which one type of object is compared with some larger, more inclusive type of object. Boys and girls, for example, both belong to a larger category, children. School-age children not only realize this fact, but usually can handle the logical relations among these three categories quite accurately. No matter what the particular mix of boys and girls in a classroom, they can usually answer correctly the question "Are there more boys in this class, or more children?" Preschool children, in contrast, often fail to answer this question correctly without further clarifying questions.

Improved classification skills

Likewise, animism and artificialism are both refined in comparison with earlier periods of development. **Animism** is the belief that nonliving objects are alive and human; **artificialism** is the belief that all objects (whether living or not) are human-made creations. As children grow into the middle years, both of these beliefs become more restricted in scope. A three-year-old may talk to a bar of soap while she washes her hands, whereas an eight-year-old talks to the family dog instead. Or a three-year-old may say, "People invented carrots for us to eat," whereas an eight-year-old may say, "People discovered carrots growing someplace, and then began growing some to eat." Neither animism nor artificialism really disappears from children's thinking, but children begin to apply them in more adult ways. *Why* this change occurs is an important question, which we discuss later in this chapter.

Other improvements in preoperational thinking

Conservation in the Middle Years

Some cognitive skills make their first real appearance during the middle years. Probably the best-known of these is **conservation,** which is a belief that certain

In one of the most widely known Piagetian tasks, children evaluate whether the amount of liquid stays the same when poured into a beaker of a different shape. Most children over six believe that it does stay the same. (The New York Times)

properties of an object remain the same or constant in spite of changes in the object's appearance. An example of conservation of quantity is the one described in Chapter 9 involving two tall, narrow glasses with exactly the same amount of water in them. If you empty one glass into a wide, low tray, you create a substantial perceptual change in the water; it looks quite different from before, and quite different from the water in the remaining tall glass. Will a child believe that the wide tray has the same amount of water as the tall glass does? If he does, then he conserves, meaning that he shows a belief in the water's underlying constancy in spite of a perceptual change.

Piaget found that after the age of about seven, most children did indeed conserve quantity in the water-glass experiment (1965). He found, in fact, that by a year or two later, children conserve on a lot of other tasks as well, including the following (which are illustrated in Figure 12–1):

1. *Clay balls* Start with two identical clay balls. Flatten one so that it looks like a pancake. Ask, "Do these two balls weigh the same, or does one weigh more than the other?"

   Conservation of mass

2. *Pennies and nickels* Lay out two matching rows of coins, one of pennies and the other of nickels. The rows should have the same number of coins in them, and each penny should be set next to one of the nickels. Then bunch up the

   Conservation of number

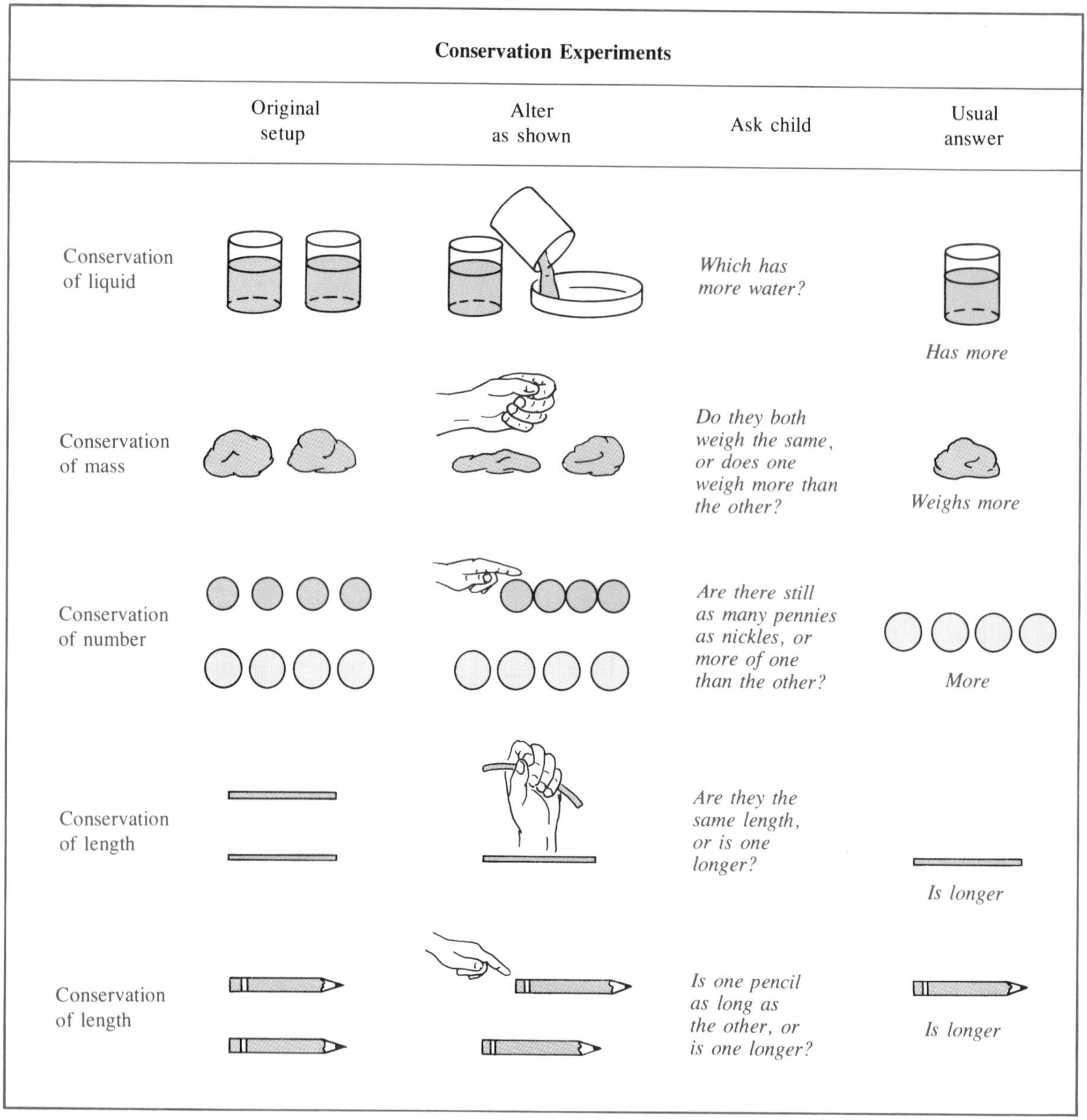

Conservation Experiments

	Original setup	Alter as shown	Ask child	Usual answer
Conservation of liquid			*Which has more water?*	*Has more*
Conservation of mass			*Do they both weigh the same, or does one weigh more than the other?*	*Weighs more*
Conservation of number			*Are there still as many pennies as nickles, or more of one than the other?*	*More*
Conservation of length			*Are they the same length, or is one longer?*	*Is longer*
Conservation of length			*Is one pencil as long as the other, or is one longer?*	*Is longer*

Figure 12–1
Conservation Experiments

Conservation of length

coins in one row but not those in the other. Ask, "Are there still as many pennies as nickles, or are there more of one than the other?"

3. *Bent wires* Start with two identical wires or pipe cleaners. Then bend one of them in an arc or circle. Ask, "Is one wire just as long as the other, or is one of them longer?"

4. *Overlapping pencils* Set two identical pencils parallel to each other. Then shift one pencil up or down by an inch or so. Ask, "Is one pencil just as long as the other, or is one of them longer?"

Each of these tasks requires a belief in some sort of conservation. The clay balls, like the water glasses, require conservation of mass; the bent wires and the pencils, conservation of distance or length; and the coins, conservation of number. Children in the middle years tend to conserve on all of them.

Typically, a child does not acquire all of these conservations at exactly the same time, a phenomenon that Piaget calls **décallage,** which is a French term for "gap." Piaget believes that such gaps occur because children's thinking is still concrete. Perhaps, he argues, they do not grasp the general principles underlying conservation, and therefore do not apply them to tasks that are logically similar. However, critics have argued that *décallage* may prove that concrete operational skills do not really form a coherent, universal stage, in the sense proposed by Piaget (Brainerd, 1978). This skepticism in fact has led some psychologists to investigate whether skills such as conservation can be learned through explicit teaching.

Gaps in times of acquisition

Conservation Training

Everyone agrees that children do not begin life conserving but instead acquire this skill somehow. How do they do it? Piaget argues that they mentally construct or build conservation for themselves, because of biological maturation and because of countless experiences with physical objects that show conservation properties. These experiences are too numerous and too diverse ever to be taught explicitly, Piaget believes, so parents and teachers cannot expect to train children in conservation or to force it to appear any earlier in children's lives.

But many psychologists have tried anyway. In general, they have had moderate but not complete success. One classic set of studies, for example, varied the usual water-glass experiment by putting a screen between the child and the glasses during the actual pouring of liquid (Bruner et al., 1966). In these conditions, children could rely only on their visual memories of the glasses and on their verbal reasoning abilities. As it turned out, the barrier caused many more children to conserve than had done so in Piaget's experiment. Apparently, therefore, some children found *not* seeing the glasses helpful, perhaps because it kept them from being distracted by the dramatic visual changes. With nothing to see, the children had to reason more carefully, and relied less on their perceptions.

Conservation without viewing objects

More recent studies have tried to help children avoid being distracted by coaching them to talk about what is happening ("Nothing is being added or taken away") or to compare the important dimensions closely ("Watch the height *and* width") (Gelman, 1969, 1978). More often than not, these efforts do produce larger numbers of conserving children, especially among children who are uncertain how to respond. To this extent, conservation can be taught.

But trained children often do not stay loyal to conservation in the way that "natural" conservers tend to do; they are more likely to give up their belief at even a slight provocation. One study documented this tendency by using the clay-balls task described above (Robert and Charbonneau, 1978). Following Piaget's procedures closely, experimenters flattened one ball while keeping the other one round, and then asked children to predict whether one would be heavier than the other or

Limitations of trained conservation

whether the two would still weigh the same. Then they actually weighed the balls on a balance scale. But here the experimenters changed the usual procedure. Without letting the children know, they removed some clay from one of the pieces before they weighed it. Of course this made it weigh less, and therefore made it seem to violate the principle of conservation.

When recently trained conservers confronted this violation, most accepted it easily and reverted to their pretraining predictions. When "natural" conservers confronted it, however, about half persisted in their conservation beliefs. Some even suggested that a mistake had been made — that some clay had dropped on the floor accidentally, perhaps. All together, the results suggest that natural learning of conservation works better than training, but that neither works perfectly. In this experiment, even some "naturals" changed their beliefs when they confronted a violation of conservation.

Other studies have found similar results among university students (Shultz et al., 1979). Even though these individuals all conserve when asked about any of the classic Piagetian tasks, less than half of them continue to conserve when confronted with a violation that the experimenter has covertly arranged. The majority make up spur-of-the-moment explanations, like "Maybe the weight is distributed differently in a clay pancake from in a ball." Conservation, it seems, may not be as inevitable and universal as Piaget led us to believe.

Other Concrete Operational Skills

Piaget has described many other forms of knowledge that appear during the middle years (Piaget, 1983). Among other things, school-age children can seriate, or arrange objects in sequence, better; they understand time more fully and accurately; and they can understand spatial relations better. Let us look briefly at each of these accomplishments.

Seriation   **Seriation** refers to the ability to put items into a series or sequence. Given a dozen or so sticks of different lengths, for example, an eight-year-old can usually arrange them easily in order of length. Four-year-olds, however, often have trouble with this task; they may sequence a few of them correctly, but not others. Or they may fudge their measurements, making one end of the sticks appear sequenced but allowing the other ends to extend at random.

A Sense of Time   School-age children understand the nature of time much better than younger children. Eight-year-olds generally know that time refers to a single, constant flow of incidents, marked off by calendars, clocks, and landmark events. This understanding helps them to realize that parents are indeed older than children, that "tomorrow" is usually sooner than "next week," and that a half-hour television show is shorter than a two-hour show.

Spatial Relations   Although preschool children usually can find their way around their own home, only concrete operational children can reliably navigate in complex and unfamiliar spaces, such as a neighborhood shopping mall. Even so,

Improved sequencing ability

Grasp of temporal relations

schoolchildren experience severe limitations to their spatial knowledge. For exam- <authorimage id="a" /> New spatial abilities
ple, one study found that eight-year-olds can usually create a small-scale model of
a set of rooms if they first have a chance to explore the full-scale rooms themselves
(Siegel et al., 1979). By the end of elementary school, furthermore, children can
often create simple maps of places familiar to them, such as their classroom at
school (Presson, 1981). But going the other way — from representations to the
real thing — remains much more difficult throughout this period. After first seeing a small-scale model of an unfamiliar set of rooms, for example, seven-year-olds
have trouble finding their way through the real rooms; and even ten-year-olds have
trouble with this task if they must work from a map (Hays and Siegel, 1981).

Piaget's Influence on Education

The cognitive theory of Piaget, described here and elsewhere in this book, has had
an important influence on schools and education. Educators have evolved numerous programs that reflect Piagetian principles and findings, or at least that try not
to be inconsistent with them. Often these programs draw on other psychological
approaches as well; but in one way or another, they all show Piaget's influence
(Consortium for Longitudinal Studies, 1983). This influence is revealed in three
areas: the overall style and sequencing of teaching, the content of particular curricula, and methods for assessing student progress.

Style and Sequencing of Teaching   Educators have borrowed Piaget's idea that
true knowledge originates from active manipulation of materials. Children learn | Emphasis on active
about weights, for instance, by actually weighing various objects on a scale rather | manipulation
than by reading about weights in a book or by hearing their teacher talk about such
activities. A commitment to active learning in turn leads teachers and curriculum
planners to put more tangible activities into educational programs wherever possible, as well as to sequence activities from the tangible to the abstract. Reading
about bugs still has a place in learning about these creatures, but collecting (and
handling) some real bugs should probably come first.

Curriculum Content   Piagetian theory has influenced particular curriculum content by providing many specific ideas about what cognitive competencies to expect
from children of particular ages or levels of development. The conservation skills
described in this chapter imply that elementary schoolchildren should be developing relative immunity to *how* problems are presented to them. Compared with
preschoolers, older children should be less distracted by seemingly small changes
in drawings in their books or by seemingly insignificant changes in how a teacher
phrases assignments. In Piagetian terms, the children have become more
decentered.

   Likewise, acquisition of concrete operations should help school-age children in
a number of other ways. For instance, many academic tasks require multiple clas- | Use of multiple
sification, which preschoolers often cannot understand reliably. A written assign- | classification
ment may ask children to "list all the machines you can think of that begin with
c." This task requires classifying objects in two ways at once, first by whether or

not something is in fact a machine, and second by whether or not it begins with the letter *c*.

Piaget's cognitive theory has helped many curriculum planners and teachers to select and evaluate academic tasks such as these. It does not, of course, lead to accurate selections for all children, since not all children move through Piagetian stages at the same rate. Some preschoolers, it seems, can already conserve, and some school-age children still cannot (Lewis et al., 1986). But Piagetian ideas do give valuable guidance.

Assessment of Students' Progress   Throughout his work, Piaget has emphasized the importance of children's actual thought processes and of what these processes actually allow children to accomplish. This approach is shown graphically in Piaget's emphasis throughout his research on semistructured, informal interviews.

Focus on content of progress

Many educators feel that interviews offer a much better way of assessing students' progress than traditional classroom testing, which tends to promote comparisons among students and to obscure what they have actually learned (Elkind, 1976). The same criticism applies — perhaps even more strongly — to standardized achievement tests. Instead of helping teachers to know *what* their students have learned, the scores on such tests tend to focus on how much *better* one student performs than another. At best, such comparisons do not help teachers (or students) to diagnose students' learning needs; and at worst, they can hurt the self-esteem of students who do not rank high when tested.

Checkpoint   *As suggested by Piaget, school-age children acquire many concrete operational skills, which are relatively decentered, sensitive to transformations, and reversible. The best-known of these skills is conservation, but important changes also occur in classification, seriation, temporal relations, and spatial relations. Efforts to train children in these skills have been moderately successful, but not fully so. These facts, and Piaget's theory, which supports them, have influenced education in several important ways.*

Information-Processing Skills

Information-processing theories of development focus on the precise, detailed features of or steps involved in mental activities (Newell and Simon, 1972). The steps are modeled on the workings of a computer, and often such machines are used to test specific hypotheses about how human thinking occurs.

Initial sensing of information

Figure 12–2 shows one information-processing model of human thinking. According to the model, when a person tries to solve a problem, she first takes in information about features of her environment through her senses. In more everyday terms, she looks at a page of print or listens to the words spoken by another

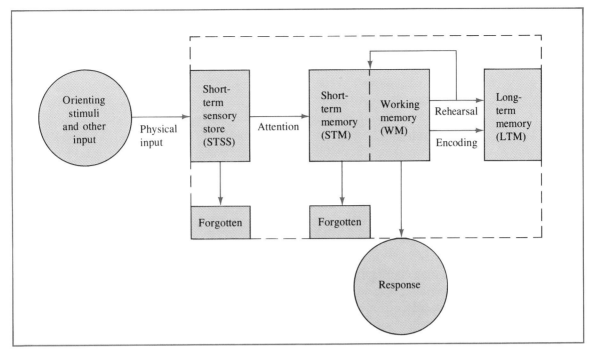

Figure 12–2   An Information-Processing Model of Memory

person. The information gained in this way is kept briefly in a **short-term sensory store** (or **STSS**) in the brain. The STSS saves information exactly as it originally receives it, in much the way that a camera might take a snapshot of a scene. Unlike a photograph, though, information in the STSS fades or disappears within a fraction of a second unless the person processes it further.

By attending to the STSS, the person sends the information on to **short-term memory (STM)**. STM corresponds roughly to "momentary awareness," or whatever the person is thinking about at a particular instant. It also combines and reorganizes the contents of the STSS for more efficient handling. For example, the senses may provide the STSS with a warm, soft tactile sensation, a purring sound, and the sight of brown fur. The STM might combine these into a single perception: a contented cat. But compared to the STSS, the STM can handle only limited amounts of information — in fact, only about seven pieces of it at any one time. After a few seconds, information in the STM is either forgotten or moves into working memory for further processing.

Initial organizing of information

Working memory (WM) is much like STM, except that it focuses attention on information already in the mind rather than information as it arrives from outside the person. WM is like a mental scratch pad or chalkboard: a place for figuring things out on the spur of the moment, when the person does not need to save the results. You need WM when you do an addition problem mentally, or when you purposely try to remember a phone number that you looked up just a moment ago. To function, WM requires conscious activity, and its contents last only as long as that activity continues.

Mental work space

The contents of WM can be saved permanently in **long-term memory (LTM)**.

Doing so requires various cognitive strategies, such as rehearsing information repeatedly or organizing it into familiar categories. You can remember the main ideas of a textbook chapter longer, for example, if you go over the chapter more than once and group its ideas logically while you do so. Ironically, the organizing process also works better if you already have a lot of knowledge about the information you are trying to remember. Prior knowledge probably helps by giving you a richer network of categories and ideas for organizing your new knowledge.

Permanent storage

Unlike STM and WM, LTM probably has unlimited capacity for storage of new information. The problem comes in retrieving information. As odd as it sounds, a person cannot always remember how to recall something. Most of us experience this problem when an old acquaintance's name is on the tip of our tongue, or when we remember only that the friend's name "begins with the letter *w*, I think." But most of us can remember certain events that happened long ago better than many events that happened much more recently.

The information-processing model provides a useful way of understanding human thinking, including children's thinking. As the following discussion shows, certain processing functions are already well developed in school-age children, whereas others are not yet complete. The model helps to clarify these differences.

Memory Capacity

According to popular wisdom, children remember better as they get older. Yet how true is this idea, really? In everyday life, children obviously do not perform as well as adults on some tasks, such as remembering to put away their clothes at the end of the day. But in other ways they do perform as well; they will remember their grandparents, for instance, when they see them again after months or even years of absence.

Short-Term Memory Some of these differences in memory may depend on which parts of the information-processing model the children happen to be using. On tasks that rely on STM in particular, school-age children — and even preschoolers — perform just about as well as adults do. Experimenters demonstrated this trend by showing subjects a set of numbers briefly and then immediately asking them whether a particular number had been included in the set (Baumeister and Maisto, 1977). This procedure did not allow time for organizing and storing the number sets in LTM; the subjects simply had to use their STM.

STM is constant across ages

In these conditions, individuals from age five through adulthood performed about equally well. Not surprisingly, the time people took to recognize a test digit did depend on how many digits were shown in the original set. Showing six digits made the task take longer than showing just three, no doubt because the person evaluated the test digit against a larger number of alternatives. What is striking, though, is how *little* performance depended on the age of the child or adult. Whether the subject was young or old, this particular problem took a certain amount of time and effort to solve.

This study assessed a variation of **recognition memory,** in which a person merely compares an external stimulus or cue with pre-existing experiences or knowledge.

School plays are often full of mistakes and awkward pauses, partly because children tend to store their exact lines, rather than the essence of the lines, in long-term memory. When they forget a cue, they have more trouble "ad libbing" back to the script. (James H. Karales/Peter Arnold)

Recognition memory is involved when children look at snapshots of a holiday celebration months in the past: their faces light up, and they may describe aspects of the celebration that they had apparently forgotten. In general, recognition memory develops early in life; even toddlers will respond to, or "recognize," a picture of a familiar face more than they will one of a stranger.

Long-Term Memory Capacity for long-term memory develops more slowly than short-term memory, probably because it relies more often on complex methods of storage and retrieval. This is the more difficult process of **recall memory,** in which we bring information back into awareness using relatively few external cues. In tasks of this type, schoolchildren generally perform better than preschoolers but not as well as adolescents or adults.

LTM develops more slowly

Consider, for example, how individuals — both children and adults — recall short stories that they have heard (Liben, 1982). At the beginning of the school years, children already show many similarities to adults at this task. Like adults, they recall important features of a story ("Goldilocks was not supposed to enter the bears' house") and ignore or forget trivial features ("Goldilocks was wearing brown shoes"). They also recall the essence of sentences rather than their exact wording.

But compared with adults, school-age children include fewer inferences based on the sentences they actually hear. If adults hear the two sentences "Red Riding Hood's grandmother was baking" and "Grandmother set the cookies out on the table," they automatically infer that (a) Grandmother had an oven, and (b) she was the one who took the cookies out of the oven. Because of these inferences, adults

Recall of stories

are relatively likely to think they actually heard this information and to offer a sentence such as "Grandmother finished her baking in the oven before she put the cookies out" (Paris et al., 1977). Schoolchildren are significantly less likely to include such inferences, although they are more likely to do so than preschool children. As children get older, they seem to read between the lines more, at least in recalling stories. This tendency lends color and detail to their retellings as they get older, even though they sometimes risk misstating the "facts" of the story.

Effects of Information Processing on Memory Development

As the example of recalling stories shows, long-term memory develops partly because other, related cognitive changes occur during childhood. One of these is an improvement in logical reasoning, such as described by Piaget. Another is an increase in specific knowledge or facts. Still another is an improvement in learning strategies used in solving problems — including problems that depend on long-term memory.

The Effects of Logical Reasoning on Memory   Reasoning skills affect children's memory, and since reasoning often improves with age, memories of specific experiences sometimes actually improve gradually rather than deteriorate. In one study that illustrates this fact, experimenters showed children a series of sticks of various lengths (see Figure 12–3); then they asked the children to reproduce the series from memory by drawing pictures of it (Piaget and Inhelder, 1973). Six or eight months later, they asked the children to draw the series from memory again.

On both occasions, not surprisingly, preschool children reproduced the series worse than older, school-aged children did; the younger ones would simply draw a random group of sticks, or perhaps correctly sequence only part of the series. The *Possible spontaneous* later drawings, though, showed a surprising result: nearly three quarters of the *improvement of memory* children's drawings actually improved in accuracy compared to the first time. While some of the change probably reflected improvements in motor skills, the drawings were too simple to depend on motor development entirely. Some improvement probably also reflected the children's increasing understanding of the underlying concept of sequencing or seriation, discussed earlier in this chapter. Development of this concept apparently aided their later drawings, at least in part (Maurer et al., 1979).

Other research suggests that children's ability to make inferences affects what they remember. Consider, for example, this task, which calls for recognition of *False recognition of* sentences: Ask children to listen to a set of sentences that express simple relation- *sentences* ships, such as "Joe is older than Bill," "Bill is older than Nicole," and so on. Later, ask them to recognize whether certain sentences were in fact part of the original list. Some of the test sentences should indeed be identical to originals (like "Bill is older than Nicole"); some should be logically true but worded differently (like "Bill is younger than Joe"); and some should be logically false but worded similarly (like "Nicole is older than Joe").

On a task like this, people of all ages will falsely "recognize" some sentences that

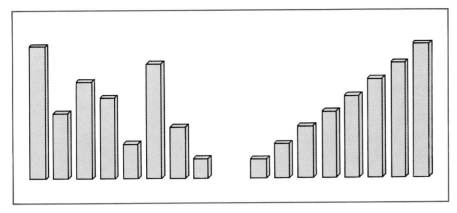

Figure 12-3 Seriation Task

never really occur in the first list. Their mistakes, as it turns out, suggest how memory and reasoning may affect each other.

What determines which sentences they falsely recognize? The sophistication of their reasoning skills is responsible, in part. Among young children (around age five), the similarity of wording seems to matter the most; in the examples above, a kindergartner is comparatively likely to think he heard "Bill is older than Joe." By the middle elementary school years, though, logical consistency matters more; a third- or fourth-grade child will think, for instance, that he heard "Joe is older than Nicole." Apparently his more developed reasoning skills color his memory. In reality he may have heard only the sentences "Joe is older than Bill" and "Bill is older than Nicole." From these he reasons immediately that Joe must be older than Nicole, but he apparently forgets that a sentence about Joe and Nicole was never actually spoken (Liben and Posnansky, 1977).

Studies of both false recognition and spontaneous improvements in recall suggest that memory is active rather than passive. Memory, it seems, is more than just a sort of mental filing cabinet for experiences. It also involves reorganizing those experiences, using the best cognitive skills that children have at their command. For schoolchildren, these "best cognitive skills" may resemble those that Piaget described for the concrete operational period; but as we point out below, they may differ in some ways too.

Memory as active reorganization

Familiarity and Richness of Knowledge   Common sense suggests that what a child already knows influences both what he can learn and what he can remember. A child who knows a lot about cars, for example, will have an easier time learning the meaning of the term *vehicle* than a child who knows little about cars; and both will learn *vehicle* more easily than a child who has never seen a car in his life.

Familiarity matters not only during learning but during recall as well. One study showed this to be true by observing a young child who had expert knowledge about dinosaurs (Chi and Koeske, 1983). The child could name and describe forty-six different dinosaurs, telling about their size, appearance, eating habits, and behavior. He could do so, though, only if given ample time (literally hours) and encouragement from adults. In a short, straightforward test of his recall, he named familiar dinosaurs far more often than he named less familiar ones. Being "familiar" in this case meant that the child had had more prior experience with reading about a particular species in books, playing with toy models of it, and viewing its skeleton in a museum (though *not,* presumably, more experience with seeing it on the hoof).

Benefits of familiarity More often than not, older children will show greater familiarity with or richness of knowledge about a variety of topics, simply because they have lived longer and therefore have accumulated more facts. But this is not always true; like the dinosaur expert, many young children have special areas of knowledge or experience that outstrip those of older people and that therefore promote unusually good memory. There are child experts in baseball and chess, for example, and among music lovers and performers.

Metacognition and Learning Strategies

As children grow older, they pick up more knowledge about thinking itself — about how learning and memory operate in everyday situations, and about how a person can improve her cognitive performance. Psychologists sometimes call this sort of knowledge **metacognition,** meaning "knowledge about cognition" (Flavell and Wellman, 1977).

Compared with older children, young children are notably oblivious of factors that can affect their problem-solving performance. For example, ask two children of different ages which set of numbers will be harder to remember:

8 1 5 or 3 9 2 6 8 1 4 7

A preschool child is more likely to judge the two sets of digits as equally hard (or easy) to memorize. If she admits to any difference in difficulty, she is likely to be rather vague about how to cope with the special challenges. She may suggest that "thinking hard" will suffice to learn the more difficult set.

Knowledge about knowledge By age ten or so, though, a child's approach to learning the two sets of digits will be quite different — or at any rate, her statements about learning them will be different. By that age she will more likely say that the longer series is harder to memorize than the shorter one; that she might learn the longer series temporarily but fail to recall it later; and that learning the longer series would be easier if she used cognitive strategies such as writing the numbers down. All these ideas are metacognitive, and all are less likely to come from a very young child who evaluates the same task.

Types of Learning Strategies Such tasks are made easier by the use of broad **learning strategies,** or general methods or techniques that help in solving a variety of problems. Typically they draw not only on pre-existing skills, such as the language skills developed during early childhood, but on brand-new ones, such as the conservation ability described by Piaget. Learning strategies give school-age children major advantages over younger children in solving certain sorts of problems, as explained below.

1. *Attention to detail*   During the school years, children become much better at noticing details. For example, try showing children several similar pictures, only two of which are exactly the same. On the whole, younger children make relatively more errors in finding the identical pictures. Observing their eye movements carefully shows that they get sidetracked more often by the most noticeable aspects of the drawings. As a result, they sometimes forget to check all the details systematically, even when the details are crucial to solving the problem (Hale, 1979).

Focusing on small details

2. *Rehearsal*   This term literally means "hearing again"; it refers to a purposeful repetition of information, either silently or out loud. Older children engage in rehearsal more often and with less prompting than younger children do (Ornstein and Naus, 1978). To see this difference, just ask children of different ages to remember a set of numbers (1, 2, 3, 5, 8, 13, . . .), and take note of how they do so. Older children are more likely to review the digits to themselves somehow, perhaps by whispering them, or looking at them, or pointing to each of them repeatedly. If younger children use any of these strategies at all, they are likely to apply them haphazardly.

Repeating information

3. *Organizing tactics*   Older children more often notice the structure or organization of new information, and exploit that structure more effectively. For example, older children are more likely to notice that each number in the list above is the sum of the two numbers preceding it, and they may simply use this relationship to remember the entire series.

Finding structure

Strategies like these explain a lot of the advantage that older children have over younger ones in learning new material. Not only do older children know more strategies, but they use them more widely, spontaneously, and appropriately. The developmental difference is especially obvious when they are learning arbitrary information — the kind that takes deliberate effort to remember.

Note, though, that young children do not completely lack learning strategies; often they simply fail to use them (Brown et al., 1983). A three- or four-year-old will often point at and label the objects and words in a book, for example, but he will not do so consistently. And preschool children can be trained to use strategies such as rehearsal, even if they never do so as effectively as older children do. Simply reminding them to say each name on a list makes a big difference to later recall. So does recasting a problem in more familiar terms; preschoolers can learn a list of "things to buy at the store," for example, much more effectively than if the very same list is presented as an arbitrary memory task (Istomina, 1975).

Preschoolers' use of learning strategies

Much of the difference between younger and older children, then, concerns how reliably and automatically they invoke learning strategies. Older children are less likely to need special coaching or specially designed problems in order to remember successfully. They can extract organization from material that is not already well organized, and they do so more often even when not explicitly asked for such behavior. In this sense, they make more able learners than younger children do.

Chess players improve through a variety of mechanisms. Sometimes they discover winning strategies through trial and error; sometimes through logical deduction; and sometimes by observing and imitating other, more skilled players. (David Phillips)

Mechanisms for Acquiring Learning Strategies How do children acquire these strategies? Probably in at least three ways, or **mechanisms**: trial and error, logical construction, and observational learning (Shatz, 1983; Brown et al., 1983). Each mechanism is proposed by one or another of the major theorists of child development. Each can be seen in children's own naturally occurring activities, but it can also be assisted by parents and teachers.

1. *Trial and error* Sometimes children happen upon effective strategies more or less by accident, or trial and error. Often this process occurs in the midst of pre-existing, more logical learning strategies. Some schoolchildren write many essays and follow all the advice of their teachers before they discover, by accident, the methods that work best for them. Even though their teachers advise them to make an outline first, and even though they do so repeatedly, they may eventually discover that simply writing a first draft produces better results. The crucial part of this discovery is its accidental quality.

Accidental discovery of strategies

2. *Logical construction* A lot of so-called random learning of strategies may really reflect **logical construction** of knowledge instead. Logically constructed knowledge refers to children's active efforts to understand the world — the sort of learning emphasized by Piaget's theory of development. Such thinking may especially help children to extend learning strategies to brand-new situations.

Inference and deduction

For example, children sometimes demonstrate knowledge of certain social relationships even though they rarely see people actually acting out the relationships. They can dramatize the behavior of firefighters even though they have not seen actual fires to observe the details of these people's conduct. Even what they see of fires in the media tends to lack the detail that children put into their re-enactments (Anderson, 1978). Instead, they seem to follow mental scripts or inferences constructed from knowledge of what fighting a fire *must* be like.

3. *Observational learning* These examples may also involve observational learning, as described in Chapter 2. In many situations, children watch others talking and acting, and witness the consequences of these activities as well. The observations provide models for children's learning strategies at other times and places, even far from the original demonstrations.

Modeling and imitation

Siblings often learn by observation. A younger sister may watch her older sibling plead with her parents for an extra cookie. If the pleading proves successful, then she is likely to use the same method herself later; but if the pleading does not work, she is relatively unlikely to imitate this particular behavior. And important sex-role behaviors can develop through observational learning. Children may notice that men more often say "Damn!" and that women more often say "Oh, dear!" By the end of their elementary school years, they will have adopted the expression associated with their own sex (Edelsky, 1977).

Helping Children to Acquire Learning Strategies The processes described above can all be assisted by adults, and often are. Parents may purposely demonstrate effective ways of remembering the time of an appointment by writing it down as soon as they hear it and by pointing out the fact that they have done so to their child. Or teachers may help children to solve a problem in long division by encouraging them to whisper each step in the process to themselves as they do it.

When interventions like these are carried out systematically, they constitute various sorts of **strategy training,** or coaching in when and how to apply learning strategies to new and difficult problems. Studies of strategy training show that it improves learning substantially (Campione, in press), although the amount of improvement depends on exactly how the training is done. The simplest forms — what might be called **blind training** — lead children to use particular learning strategies but do not give them any reasons for doing so, or even explain that they are actually using strategies. More complex forms not only lead children to use strategies but also emphasize the advantages of using them. Sometimes, too, they may teach children ways to monitor the progress of their own learning. These more complex forms might be called **informed training** (Brown et al., 1981).

To understand the distinction between blind and informed training, imagine how teachers might help sixth-grade children to learn a lot of new biological terms. Suppose that the current biology unit requires students to learn the names of a large number of animal species. Suppose, too, that the species are rather diverse; they include a number of birds, fish, and mammals. This task is one that usually reveals large differences among children. Some learn material like this much more easily and quickly than others do, so the task is a good one for teachers to help with.

Blind training methods

Blind training simply gets children to apply learning strategies to the task. Teachers might encourage children to say each species' name to themselves whenever they see it in a book. Or teachers might covertly organize all their questions on the material: "First tell me all the birds you know," they might say, "and then tell me all the fish." Techniques like these do improve children's learning substantially, even when teachers make no real effort to justify the techniques. And they help *all* children, whether they are slow learners or fast ones. Ironically, though, such methods sometimes help faster learners more than slower ones, thereby increasing differences among children rather than decreasing them (Corno and Snow, 1986; Siegler, 1978).

Informed training methods

Informed training goes beyond techniques like these and advises students about the value of using learning strategies as well as about techniques for checking on progress. In teaching the biology unit, teachers might suggest that "saying the name whenever you see it will help you remember it better." Or they might say, "Remembering the species in groups helps most people remember them better." In addition, teachers might give clues that help students to monitor their performance: "You might note that there are twenty-five species to remember altogether. And notice that there are the same number of birds and mammals, but fewer fish, to remember." Comments like these lead to even better learning than simple blind training does. Apparently they do so by motivating students and by helping them to take charge of their own learning (Paris et al., 1984).

Perspectives on Research

Learning to Read

In modern society, one particularly useful cognitive skill is reading. Even though it may be quiet, reading is far from passive. It requires active effort and a broad range of cognitive strategies (Calfee and Drum, 1986). In particular, it requires skills at decoding written symbols, strategies for checking immediate comprehension, and techniques for recalling the content at some later time. Each of these processes both reflects and stimulates cognitive development.

No matter what else it may require, reading involves decoding words and parts of words: translating written symbols into their verbal equivalents (Perfetti, 1986). Beginning readers demonstrate this skill in relatively pure form. Even when a book contains pictures or other clues about the meaning of the text, beginners often focus haltingly on words and parts of words.

By focusing hard on literal decoding, beginning readers may have little attention left over for comprehending what they read. Listening to an unskillful reader often reveals this problem; the child

pronounces words and phrases carefully and separately, as if just saying them is a challenge. The effort to translate the words from print to speech prevents thinking about the words as organized sentences or ideas.

Skillful reading therefore also requires comprehension of the overall meaning of sentences and other sections of text. Compared to beginning readers, skilled ones tend to correct or check on their reading errors as they go along, and in the process they make their reading sound more sensible (Kavale and Schreiner, 1979). Take this girl, for example:

TEXT: "Help!" cried the rancher. To his horse, he whistled softly . . .

JUDITH, age eleven: "Help!" cried the rancher to his horse. He whistled softly . . . er . . . I mean, "Help!" cried the *rancher.* To his *horse,* he whistled softly . . .

Which strategies for checking are most helpful

In any case, learning strategies do seem to help children to organize and process information, at least for problems similar to the ones for which they first learn the strategies. In and of themselves, though, they do not guarantee metacognition, or conscious knowledge about thought processes. Metacognition first appears early in the school years, but children do not show it in a wide variety of situations until adolescence or even adulthood, and it does not assist children's problem-solving performance reliably until then either (Flavell, 1978). Given the rather abstract quality of knowledge *about* thinking, we should not be too surprised at this. After all, a child cannot judge a math problem's difficulty or select strategies for solving it — metacognitive skills — before he has accumulated some basic experience with math problems, and accumulating that experience may simply take more time than most children have had by age ten or twelve.

Checkpoint *Information-processing theories provide a model for understanding both the short-term and long-term memory capacities of children. Memory is helped by gradual improvements in children's logical reasoning, as well as by their*

depends on the child's general purposes for reading. Speed reading and skimming, for example, benefit from attention to topic sentences and key terms, whereas studying for a test may require unusual attention to details. Effective readers sense variations in the purposes of reading and adjust their strategies accordingly (Forrest and Waller, 1979).

In addition to mastering decoding and comprehension skills, truly developed or skilled readers need to remember written material, whether textbooks, stories, or any other form of writing. Whereas literal decoding translates printed words into spoken ones, and whereas comprehension skills help insure immediate understanding, study skills help to make the essential message available later on.

Here, one necessary cognitive skill is to identify the main theme or idea and distinguish it from details or less important ideas within a text. Doing so proves very difficult for readers who are especially young or unskillful. Children younger than about

ten, for example, have trouble devising topic sentences for short passages of simple prose (Baker and Brown, 1983), and they even have trouble identifying topic sentences when passages already provide them prominently and explicitly.

Because of problems like these in organizing what they read, beginning readers lack a basis for allocating or dividing up their study time. As a result, they tend not to give extra effort to more important material; details receive as much attention as main ideas, and in the end, such readers study inefficiently. As with other cognitive strategies, children can often use reading strategies if encouraged; telling them to pay special attention to topic sentences, for example, can prompt them to use this strategy temporarily (Owings et al., 1980). But they still do not find and use such strategies reliably on their own. Therein lies an important difference between the skillful reading of older children and the less skillful reading of younger children.

increasingly rich knowledge in many areas. During the school years, children also become aware of their own thought processes and begin using certain learning strategies for acquiring and remembering information. They learn to use these strategies in several ways, some of which can be taught to them.

Styles of Thinking

By the middle years, children begin thinking in definite **cognitive styles** — the forms or manner of thinking — rather than in terms of performance skill as such. For example, some children habitually reflect about a problem before responding to it, whereas others respond fairly quickly; and some children separate a problem into many independent elements, whereas others tend to treat it as a single unit. Such differences are important to students of child development in two ways. First, they indirectly affect children's cognitive performance, and second, they may reflect differences in children's personalities. Here are examples of some major differences in cognitive styles, which are summarized in Table 12-1.

Convergent and Divergent Thinking

Focused problem solving

One way in which schoolchildren differ is in their use of convergent and divergent thinking. **Convergent thinking** refers to focused, deductive reasoning that leads to a particular solution to a problem. Solving an arithmetic problem requires convergent thinking; so does working a jigsaw puzzle. A lot of school learning requires convergent thinking, since there is often just one right answer, which students are supposed to figure out. The prevalence of convergent thinking in school in fact may partly explain why nearly all children can use this style of thinking at least some of the time. Over the years, they simply receive a lot of training in it.

But some children seem especially disposed to using convergent thinking widely. Such children seek out and prefer structured learning tasks, such as those offered by books of puzzles or by complex building toys. They may even engage in structured activities at the expense of freer, more open-ended recreation, such as hanging around with friends. When they carry this tendency to an extreme, such children are often labeled as "gifted" by parents and teachers (Lewis et al., 1986). At less of an extreme, they may simply impress others as being rather logical in temperament and motivations.

Wide-ranging thinking

Divergent thinking refers to the production of a wide variety of ideas, regardless of how unusual or disconnected they may be. It closely resembles the notion of "creativity," but lacks its emphasis on quality; divergent thinking simply diverges, and in doing so it can end up as either bizarre or uniquely valuable. Divergent thinkers tend to produce ideas fluently and elaborately, and they tend to form associations among ideas relatively flexibly. Most of us use this style of thinking from time to time; it is illustrated by our answers to open-ended questions like "How many uses can you think of for a brick?" (Guilford, 1967).

Style of Thinking	Characteristics
Convergent thinking	Focused, deductive thinking; seeks single right answer to problems
Divergent thinking	Produces a wide range of unusual associations; elaborates on ideas; seeks many possible answers to problems
Metaphoric thinking	Recognizes associations between seemingly unrelated ideas or objects; related to divergent thinking
Field dependence	Perceives visual displays as whole patterns; socially, a willingness to rely on others' opinions and modify one's own
Field independence	Perceives visual displays as many discrete parts; socially, a relative autonomy in responding to others' opinions
Reflectivity	Responds slowly to cognitive problems; a slow conceptual tempo
Impulsivity	Responds quickly to cognitive problems; a fast conceptual tempo

Table 12-1 *Cognitive Styles in School-Age Children*

Some children seem predisposed to think divergently. They are not necessarily better than average at focused, logical reasoning (Kogan, 1973). And they do not necessarily use their divergent thinking only in situations that explicitly encourage it. Throughout the elementary school years, some children produce ideas fluently even on timed tests of creativity, in spite of the stress that such tests can create. For them, divergent thinking is just as likely then as in situations that are untimed, relaxed, and fun (Hattie, 1980).

On the whole, children who engage in a lot of make-believe play tend also to engage in divergent thinking, although it is often not clear which behavior is causing which. Both skills require departing from the conventional meanings or uses of objects. In make-believe play, a child must imagine and use an object as something new; he may transform a block of wood into a truck, for example. In divergent thinking, the child thinks about that same block of wood in some unusual way; he may name it as "something to make a truck with." Both play and divergent thinking foster associations between diverse ideas. The activities differ, though, in that play calls for acting out an association and divergent thinking calls for stating it (Lieberman, 1977).

Divergent thinking and play

The connection between play and divergent thinking has provided a method for professionals to encourage divergent thinking in children. In one experiment, some children were given open-ended play materials (a variety of shapes and vehicles and toy animals); other children received more convergent or focused materials (puzzles that assembled into formboards). Children who received the more open-ended materials later proved to be more fluent at verbal tasks involving divergent thinking, such as thinking up alternate uses for a common object (Pepler and Ross, 1981). After their open-ended play, incidentally, these children also did better at focused, convergent tasks like putting puzzles together.

Metaphor and Figurative Language

Children also use **figurative language,** which is language that either states or implies an unusual comparison among objects or events. In developmental psychology, the most well-studied form of figurative language is **metaphor,** an expression that implies resemblances but does not state them. "Your eyes are stars" is a metaphor, because it suggests an association between a physical organ and certain heavenly objects. In the study of literature, metaphors are often distinguished carefully from **similes,** which are expressions that make explicit comparisons, using words such as *like* and *as.* The distinction may not matter a lot, however, in studying thinking styles of school-age children. Both figures of speech probably involve similar thinking processes — although this idea has not actually been proved with research (Honeck and Hoffman, 1980).

Kinds of figurative language

Metaphoric thinking stands divergent thinking on its head: instead of calling for the production of many associations among ideas, it calls for the comprehension of associations among just a few diverse ideas or objects. One well-known test of metaphoric thinking shows children pairs or groups of pictures and asks them to explain any connections or associations among them (Kogan et al., 1980). One item shows a toddler, a bag of potatoes, and a rosebud. The child demonstrates metaphoric thinking by pointing out relationships among these: that a toddler is young like a rosebud, perhaps, or that a toddler can be picked up like a bag of potatoes. Another item shows a flock of geese flying, an army marching in forma-

A Talk with Shawn

School and Cognitive Development

Shawn is a tall, curly-haired, freckle-faced eleven-year-old who is in fifth grade. He was interviewed in his bedroom after school and before his music lesson.

INTERVIEWER: You are a fifth grader now. How has the way in which you think and solve problems changed since you first started school?

SHAWN: When you first started school you learned about some things that you really didn't know — like the world is round — all of the simple stuff that you know as a human fact when you get older. You don't really know what's going on and you just sort of listen and it sticks in your head as an interesting fact. Like, for example, the world looks like an orange when you're out there in space. Like wow, I could eat my world!

INTERVIEWER: What did you think about all of this?

SHAWN: You don't really think about it scientifically. You think about it like a fairy tale. There's story time and these little periods that are about ten minutes and the teacher says all right, now it's time to do such and such and they sort of get you ready for having a little more common sense. You know, for knowing that the world is shaped like an orange but isn't edible, or for knowing how to put on your socks by yourself. I mean just little common-sense things. You just learn them.

INTERVIEWER: How does your thinking change when you are in second and third grade?

SHAWN: Now that you have learned all of that common-sense stuff about the world, you start to learn more advanced things in spelling and a little harder math. Like two-digit numbers. You also learn to figure things out about people. Sometimes kids get excluded or left out of things and it can happen to you. So you learn to figure it out. Mostly by the process of elimination.

INTERVIEWER: How does that work?

SHAWN: Well, it's like saying you have two choices on almost every rule. You have to figure out what the rule is.... You say I might as well try this, and if it's wrong I'll learn my lesson and I'll do it the other way now. And you try it and if it's wrong, you just have to take the consequences, like missing a party or having to stay after school.

INTERVIEWER: What is it like once you have reached fifth grade?

SHAWN: By now you have learned the basics. At the end of third and beginning of fourth grade, you were still playing Monopoly and easy card games and little electronic games. But once you're ten or eleven and in fifth grade you are able to learn almost anything you want to if you put in the effort.

INTERVIEWER: What changes?

SHAWN: Well, first of all by now you know so much more about English and history and math and science and you have read a lot of books. When you are faced with a math or science problem to solve, by now you have the confidence that "I can really do this." Like figuring out the missing number in a series. Once you notice that each new number is twice the last number minus seven, or something like that, then you can figure out the missing number.

INTERVIEWER: How about in science?

SHAWN: Well, our teacher sometimes gives problems where we have to set up an experiment to figure them out. You know, to see whether the chemical you have is really what you think it might be. At the moment I forget what it's called.

INTERVIEWER: Solving for an unknown?

SHAWN: Yeah, an unknown. So what you have to do is take this unknown, which the teacher gives you, and mix it with other chemicals that you know react in certain ways. If you make a list of all of the possible combinations and then check off each one as you try it, you can cross them out one by one until you are left with the answer. I really discovered how to do this this year, but sometimes it's hard to figure out all of the possibilities and you need to ask the teacher for help.

Follow-up Questions

1. Based upon what Shawn has said, which of Piaget's cognitive stages best describes his stage of thinking? Why?

2. What learning strategies do you think Shawn has acquired?

3. How would you characterize Shawn's cognitive style?

Figure 12-4 A Test of Field Dependence

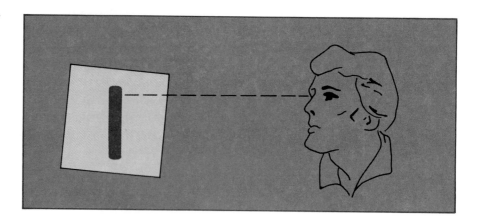

tion, and a rifle. In responding metaphorically to these, the child might note that these objects all point in a straight line, or that all show rigid movement in some way.

Divergent thinking and metaphor

Since metaphors require fairly far-fetched or remote associations, they share some of the style of divergent thinking. In the latter, a child tries to think of as many unexpected or distant connections as possible among objects or ideas. The more distant of these are essentially metaphorical in nature. As the terms are used here, though, divergent thinking involves production of ideas, and metaphoric thinking involves comprehension of them.

Field Dependence and Field Independence

Noticing patterns vs. noticing parts

Field dependence and **field independence** refer to how people analyze the world. By definition, individuals who are field dependent see things in relatively large, connected patterns. Looking at a picture of a mountain, for example, such a person would primarily notice its overall shape, and perhaps also the larger patches of color that make it up. Field independent individuals, on the other hand, tend to see things more as discrete, independent parts. Such a person might notice the individual trees on the mountainside, or many individual rocks. Children as well as adults vary along this dimension, and most people show a mixture of the two viewpoints.

Tests for FD and FI

Features of Field Dependence and Field Independence One aspect of these styles refers to relatively simple behaviors about visual judgment. In one widely used test, an individual looks at a vertical rod surrounded by a tilted frame in a darkened room, such as shown in Figure 12-4. The person has to judge whether the rod is truly vertical. In these conditions, the tilt in the frame tends to affect the judgments of highly field dependent (FD) people more than those of field independent (FI) people. The latter group in general is much more accurate in judging verticality.

Another test of field dependence and independence asks individuals to find familiar figures that are embedded in larger, more complex drawings. People who are very field independent can do this task relatively successfully, whereas very field dependent people have more trouble with it. Both tasks — the embedded figures and the rod and frame — share an emphasis on visual analysis: for each, the person must identify or isolate parts of what she sees from the whole, and deal with them as independent units (Witkin and Goodenough, 1977).

The notions of field dependence and field independence have also been extended to personal relations (Witkin, 1978). FI individuals supposedly deal with others in relatively autonomous ways — by forming and relying on their own opinions, for example, and by expecting others to do the same. FD people, on the other hand, rely on others more often, by modifying their own opinions to be consistent with others' and by more often asking for help in solving problems. These differences imply only that the two styles are different, not that one is necessarily better than the other. After all, there are times when working alone or autonomously gets a job done best (like reading a book), and other times when concern for others matters more (like deciding what to give someone for a present).

Personality and FD/FI

Field Dependence or Independence and Child-Rearing Practices Styles of field dependence in parents do affect their child-rearing practices, although not always in simple ways, nor in ways that cause their children to develop the same cognitive style. One study observed mothers while they taught their children to build something with Tinkertoys (Laosa, 1980). Mothers who tested high on field independence tended to ask more questions as a teaching technique, and they tended also to give more praise for their children's efforts. In contrast, mothers who tested high on field dependence tended to rely on modeling the task (showing or demonstrating what to do) for their children. But these differences referred to the *mothers;* the children's cognitive styles did not depend consistently on the kind of coaching they received.

Family relations and FD/FI

Other studies, though, have sometimes found style differences in the children. For instance, one group of researchers observed mothers and children when they disagreed about everyday matters, such as which television program to watch when the mother preferred one and the child preferred another (Hoppe et al., 1977). In situations like these, boys (but not girls) who tested high on field independence tended to assert themselves relatively more against their mothers. Researchers conducting another study interviewed mothers about their child-rearing practices, and found that mothers who fostered competition and independence in their children tended to have children who performed well on tests of field independence (Claeys and DeBoeck, 1976).

Taken together, these results suggest two things. First, parents do not teach their children to be field dependent or field independent directly; the children pick up a style in rather complex, subtle ways, and may even teach their parents field dependence or field independence some of the time. Second, field dependence or independence is not a pervasive trait that a person displays in all possible situations, like having blue eyes or big earlobes. Instead, it depends a lot on specific situations. There are times and places in which one or the other style is preferable. Apparently both children and parents learn that fact, whether consciously or not, and they express it in changeable styles of behavior.

Reflectivity and Impulsivity

Still another style of thinking varies along the dimension of **reflectivity** and **impulsivity** (**R-I** for short). These terms refer to cognitive tempo, or speed of thinking. At the reflective extreme, a person takes a relatively long time to respond to a problem — perhaps many seconds — and then finally does so rather carefully and accurately. At the impulsive extreme, a person responds almost instantly, and often makes relatively more errors as a result. Psychologists often measure R-I in children by asking them to match a simple figure (say, a drawing of a face) to several other figures that resemble it. Only one resembles it exactly, and the child must discover this perfectly matching one (Kagan et al., 1964; Messer, 1976). Highly reflective children are defined as the ones who take a relatively long time at a task like this, or who make fewer errors at it, or both.

This description makes the reflective style seem more desirable than the impulsive style. Naturalistic observations of reflective and impulsive children, though,

---

Cognitive Effects of Television, Radio, and Books

Television has become a major competitor for the attention of children. In recent years, surveys show, children have spent about as much time watching TV shows as they have spent in school (Re:act, 1984). Many parents worry about all this watching, and for good reasons: some programs portray considerable violence, significant sexuality, and various other behavior that makes undesirable viewing for children.

In addition to these social concerns, parents and experts worry about the cognitive effects of television, compared with those of strictly verbal media such as radio and books. Do children really learn and retain information as well from a well-made television show as they do from radio or printed presentations of the same topic? Does television stimulate the imagination, or stifle it? And does television encourage reflective thought, or interfere with it? These are questions about cognitive development. Given the importance of television in children's lives, it is not surprising that psychologists have conducted research to find answers to all of them.

Television is indeed a powerful learning device, in large part because it does make use of people's sense of vision. In one study, for example, school-age children watched a movie that had no dialogue, called *The Red Balloon*. Some children saw only the silent film of this story, but others heard a tape-recorded narration that had been carefully matched with the film, scene for scene (Pedzek and Stevens, 1985). Afterward, the children who had seen the silent film recalled the story better than those who had heard the soundtrack. The effect was strongest for the youngest children (age five) and weakest for the oldest (age twelve). A related experiment found that adults showed about equal immediate recall for *The Red Balloon,* whether they heard it or saw it, but over the long run, even adults remembered better when they had seen the silent film (Baggett, 1979). To this extent, vision seems to dominate human information processing throughout life.

Another frequent criticism of television is that it leaves nothing to the imagination, and therefore stifles creativity. In some ways, research seems to confirm this popular impression. One group of researchers asked children to provide endings to incomplete stories, some of which were presented on videotapes and others through sound recordings (Greenfield et al., 1981). On the average, school-

---

show a more complex picture. For example, one group of experimenters observed young children who tested at the extremes; they were either very reflective or very impulsive (Susman et al., 1980). The highly impulsive ones, by definition, responded quickly to simple cognitive tasks, but they did *not* tend to respond quickly during free play periods at school. On the contrary, their behavior appeared less aggressive than that of highly reflective children, their teachers rated them as more responsible, and they waited more patiently during classroom delays than their more reflective peers did. Reflectivity and impulsivity did not correlate very well with tempo of behavior; if anything, the two tended toward opposite extremes.

Cognitive tempo vs. tempo of behavior

Up to about age ten, children generally become more reflective, in the sense used here (Salkind and Nelson, 1980). On the test of matching familiar figures, for example, children take longer to respond as the years go by, and also make fewer errors. After about age ten, though, they begin to respond more quickly again —

Changes in tempo with age

---

children gave more imaginative endings to the soundtrack stories, by introducing more novel elements into the stories. Another research group obtained comparable results when they asked children to draw pictures about stories that they had either seen on video or heard on recordings (Meringoff et al., 1981). Drawings based on audio stories incorporated more diverse elements, and children also introduced more novel elements that had not actually occurred in the stories at all.

Does television discourage reflective thinking? To some extent it does; but the effects may not matter much to most children's long-term cognitive development. The act of watching a program must interfere with reflection almost by the nature of the activity: television stories unfold in real time, leaving almost no chance for children to stop and think about what they are seeing. In this way, television viewing contrasts sharply with reading, in which print remains constantly available for backtracking and review.

Whether these facts permanently impair children's reflective tendencies, though, is another question. School-age children who watch extremely large amounts of television do seem less re-

flective, as measured by standardized tests of this cognitive style (Greenfield, 1984). But the amount of television these children view is large — much more than the twenty-seven hours or so per week that constitutes the national average of the United States. And there is no guarantee that television really causes this trend. Perhaps nonreflective children seek out television more, simply because the medium, by presenting material at a fixed pace, makes fewer demands for reflection.

Compared with radio and printed materials, then, television seems especially good for some purposes but less good for others. It encourages better memory, at least if children make a special point of trying to remember what they are viewing. It may not really discourage imagination, as critics fear; but some evidence does suggest that it may not stimulate imaginative thinking as well as nonvisual presentations do. And its effects on reflective thinking remain unclear; large amounts of television viewing and less reflective children do go together, but we still do not really know why.

Children with an impulsive cognitive style respond quickly on cognitive tasks, at the risk of making more errors. But this style does not necessarily carry over to noncognitive tasks. (Rick Friedman/The Picture Cube)

but they continue to make few errors. Should this final shift be regarded as a return to more impulsivity, or as a shift toward some higher level of competency? At present, developmental psychologists do not agree; but the question does raise the possibility that the R-I dimension needs to be redefined for older individuals and adults (Kogan, 1982). Matching familiar figures quite possibly may mean one thing when a person is young and lacks experience with the task, but something rather different when she is old enough to have done a lot of that sort of thing before.

As differences in cognitive styles emerge, they begin accounting for much of the individuality among children, both in cognitive skills as such and in personalities. General stages of development, such as described by Piaget or Erikson, still occur and explain many important changes in the middle years. But development gradually becomes less channeled by stages, and more dependent on the unique experiences of individuals. This new mixture of influences is also reflected in children's language development during the middle years. Some aspects of language retain the predictable, universal quality of the earlier steps in language acquisition, but others clearly result from events and circumstances that happen only to some children, and not to others.

Checkpoint *In addition to increasing their cognitive capacity, children during the middle years begin showing differences in their style of thinking. They vary in how convergent or divergent they tend to be in solving problems and in their use of metaphor and figurative language. They also vary in field dependence and field independence, as well as in reflectivity and impulsivity.*

Language Development in the Middle Years

Language continues to develop during middle childhood. Vocabulary keeps growing, of course; but even more important, word meanings become more subtle and complex and more like adults'. And contrary to the impressions that young school-age children sometimes give, they have not necessarily mastered syntax. They often become confused by a number of common sentence forms until well into the elementary school years — confused enough, in fact, to cause misunderstandings from time to time.

Word Meanings

Do children go through predictable levels or stages in giving meanings to words? According to one commonly held view, children first define words by the concrete actions associated with them, or by using them in appropriate sentences (Wood, 1981). Only later do they begin categorizing words, as a dictionary does. In defining the word *dog,* for instance, children might give the following responses:

Levels in defining words

- Level 1: "You pat it on the head." *(action)*
- Level 2: "A dog plays with you. A dog chases cats." *(appropriate sentences)*
- Level 3: "An animal with fur and four legs." *(dictionary classification)*

Research using word-association tests implies at least some universality to these levels of definition-making. In word-association tests, a child is given a series of familiar words and asked to respond with the first word that comes into her head — with whatever occurs to her before she has time to mull over the stimulus word. The procedure assumes that response words reflect the network of meanings within the child's vocabulary, and it tries to reveal which words are connected with which others in the child's mind (Brown, 1973).

On this kind of test, young children tend to respond differently than older children do to a wide variety of words. The younger ones — around kindergarten age — more often respond with words that naturally occur in sentences with the stimulus words. A prompt of *cup,* for example, leads to a response of *drink,* just as *sit* leads to *down,* because these pairings occur together in sentences. By about age eight, however, children respond more according to the syntactic class of the prompts, and their responses often share certain elements of meaning as well. Now *cup* may lead to *bowl,* and *sit* may lead to *rest* (DeVilliers and DeVilliers, 1978). These shifts in associations parallel the shifts in levels of definition-making. At the earlier level, the child associates (or defines) words in context, and at the later level, she tends more to classify or categorize them.

Often, though, children do not seem to go through stages in building word meanings; on the contrary, all three levels sometimes seem equally available at any point. Very common words are frequently easier to demonstrate in a sentence (Level 2) than to analyze in any formal or abstract way (Level 3). For example, how should the word *the* be defined? Or the word *I?* Furthermore, unfamiliar

Exceptions to levels

words are sometimes used unconsciously at first. An older child may correctly use the word *trepidation,* for instance, without realizing he has done so, and without being able to give definitions for it at any level at all. Evidently, then, meanings can consist of more than definitions, and one may not necessarily develop in the same way as the other.

Grammatical Usage

As we discuss in Chapter 9, most five-year-olds use a grammar that closely resembles that of adults, except that it often is more regular. A young child may say, "I runned to the store" instead of "I ran to the store." When he does, he applies a common adult rule of syntax more widely than adults do. At first glance, mistakes like these may seem like children's only noticeable deficits in grammar; and even they disappear during the school years.

More careful observations, though, often reveal a number of other grammatical limitations. Each of the following sentences can confuse most kindergartners, and do not become completely clear until after about age ten (Chomsky, 1969).

Confusing the subject with the observer

1. *The baby is easy to see.* Older children and adults take this sentence to mean that the baby is clearly visible, and that observers are looking at it. But children under age nine or ten seem to think that the sentence means that the baby can see well. How do we know? If we suggest blindfolding the baby, a younger child will say that the baby is no longer "easy to see" but has become "hard to see." Apparently the child models the syntax of this sentence on other adjective-infinitive expressions, like "eager to see" and "willing to see." In these latter expressions, the baby (rather than observers) does indeed do the seeing.

Confusing opinion and fact

2. *I don't think it will rain tomorrow.* Instead of understanding this sentence as a statement of opinion, as adults and older children usually do, young children tend to take it as a statement of fact. For them, the sentence means about the same as "I know that it will not rain tomorrow." This interpretation rids the sentence of its sense of uncertainty, which older children usually recognize reliably (Hopmann and Maratsos, 1978).

Confusing words that emphasize

3. *Even the rabbit is in the garage.* Many young children apparently confuse the words *even* and *only* in sentences like this one, because the sentence often produces a comment that the rabbit is alone (Shatz, 1983). In other words, the children take the sentence to mean *only* the rabbit is in the garage.

Since these sentences all involve rather simple vocabulary, children's confusions stem largely from their grammatical organization. Note, though, that some confusion may also come from their immature cognitive abilities. "The baby is easy to see," for example, may reflect children's egocentrism, as described by Piaget; perhaps children assume that their own ability to see does not differ from anyone else's, including the baby's. For similar reasons, they cannot yet properly understand statements like "I don't think . . . ," because they still lack firm awareness of how often viewpoints can vary among individuals.

Bilingual children have cognitive advantages over monolinguals, but only as long as both languages are treated with respect by their teachers and by society. (Paul Conklin)

Bilingualism and Its Effects

In the United States and around the world, substantial numbers of children learn two languages, and thus develop **bilingualism** (Grosjean, 1982). Does this skill benefit their cognitive development? Research suggests that it does, but only when they acquire both languages equally well (Diaz, 1983). For convenience, such children are sometimes called balanced bilinguals.

Cognitive Effects of Bilingualism For one thing, balanced bilingual children show more **cognitive flexibility** — skill at detecting multiple meanings of words and alternative orientations of objects — than monolingual children. In one study, children were asked to substitute arbitrary words for normal words without changing any other features of the sentence (Ben-Zeev, 1977). For instance, they were asked to substitute *spaghetti* for *I* in the sentence "I am cold." Compared to monolinguals, bilingual children found this task relatively easy; they more often produced the exact substitution "Spaghetti am cold" and resisted the temptation to correct the grammar ("Spaghetti is cold"), thereby violating the instructions for the task. Presumably such a skill stems from bilinguals' early experience with the arbitrary, conventional nature of words and language.

Ease with substituted syntax

Growing up with two languages also fosters **metalinguistic awareness** — the ability to attend to language as an object of thought rather than attending only to the content or ideas of the language. One study found that Gaelic-English bilinguals were quite comfortable with and skilled at renaming objects arbitrarily (Cummins, 1978). A question like "What if a dog were called a cat?" posed no conceptual problem for these children; nor did the questions "Would this 'cat' meow? Would it purr?"

Ease with substituted vocabulary

Knowing two languages may also affect cognitive style (see pages 498–506). One study, for example, found that Spanish-English bilinguals showed more field independence than either Spanish or English monolinguals (Duncan and DeAvila,

More field independence

Perspectives on Research

Black English

In the United States, black people often speak a dialect or version of English called **black English,** which differs from "educated" speech, which linguists sometimes call **Standard English.** The two versions differ in various ways; in considering the examples below, keep in mind that people vary widely in how much they use these features, and that blacks often switch between Standard and black English (Labov et al., 1977).

1. *Sounds*   Certain sounds or phonemes are used differently in black English. The sound /th/, for example, often becomes /d/; so the word *this* sounds like *dis.* Many middle and ending consonants are dropped, so the word *help* sounds like *hep* and the word *more* sounds like *mow.* In general, black English often stresses the first syllables of words, as in *DE-troit* (Detroit) and *PO-lice* (police). So the sentence "Da PO-lice no hep," means "The police did not help."

2. *Syntax*   One of the most noticeable features of black English grammar is its use of the verb *to be.* This verb often indicates a continuing situation or condition. The sentence "The coffee be cold," for example, means something like "Every day, the coffee is always cold." But the sentence "The coffee cold" simply means "This time, the coffee is cold."

Black English is spoken by some black Americans, but not by all. And some blacks use the dialect only in selected situations. (Joel Gordon)

1979). In this case, "field independence" referred to performance on a child's version of the embedded-figures test, described on pages 502–503. Bilingual children more easily identified figures hidden within larger, more complex drawings.

But note that all of these cognitive advantages apply primarily to balanced bilingual children — the ones with equal skill in both languages. What of the unbalanced bilinguals — the ones with more skill in one language than in the other? Does knowledge of a second language help, even if it is poor knowledge? Evidence is scarce, but what there is suggests that unbalanced bilingualism has mixed effects on children's thinking skills (Cummins, 1977). These effects seem to result from broad social attitudes surrounding the child's primary and secondary languages.

Balanced vs. unbalanced bilinguals

---

3. *Semantics* Black English is filled with expressions rarely found in Standard English, and with meanings rather different from their literal translation. Take the word *bad.* Both dialects use this word to mean something undesirable, as in "I have a bad cold." In black English, however, it can also mean something very good; "She look bad" usually means something like, "She looks very attractive indeed."

Many black English terms have been adopted by speakers of Standard English. The word *cool,* as in "Be cool," is used all over the United States; it means "maintaining a calm manner all the time." "I'm hip" is also used in both dialects, and means "I am well informed and aware of what I should be noticing." Even the word *okay,* according to some linguists, originated in black English, which in turn borrowed it from certain African languages (Smitherman, 1977).

4. *Modes of conversation* One popular form of black conversation is **signifying** (or "siggin"), which consists of teasing, humorous exchanges of insults. These are usually done in fun, although they often make points that cannot be stated directly or bluntly. When the insults are directed toward close relatives (especially against "yo momma"), and when they become more aggressive, this pattern is sometimes called *doin' the dozens* instead. People

who can "dish it out" with subtlety and humor are greatly respected, but only if they can take it as well.

As these examples show, black English is full of rich meanings. Thorough studies of the dialect find it just as complex as any other language, including Standard English, and just as capable of expressing the full range of human thought and emotion (Smitherman, 1977).

Unfortunately, attitudes toward black English remain rather negative throughout North America (Lambert and Tucker, 1977). This fact has created a dilemma for teachers of black students. Should such students be taught in black English, because they know that dialect best? Or should they be expected always to use Standard English, in order to prepare them to function better in mainstream, white society? Most likely, some sort of compromise may serve black students best. Teachers should respect black English, understand its richness, and allow students to use it in class (Guthrie and Hall, 1983; Brooks, 1985). But they should also encourage students to practice Standard English, since that dialect will probably help them better to "make it" in adult life.

Social Effects of Bilingualism When children acquire two languages, one of them usually has more prestige than the other. In the United States, the "best" or most important language almost always is English. Its prestige results not only from its widespread use but also from its association with success and power: all the important people in American society, it seems, speak English fluently. These circumstances cast a stigma or negative attitude on other languages.

Self-consciousness about primary language

The lower prestige of non-English languages has three important effects on bilingual people. For one thing, they may sometimes feel unwilling to use their primary or "home" language in public, even when it is appropriate to do so. One study documented this tendency among bilingual Mexican-Americans by observing their conversations with white Americans (Barker, 1975). Even when the whites spoke perfect Spanish, and even when the Mexican-Americans knew that they did, the Mexican-Americans preferred to use English.

Lack of confidence

Second, social biases against a child's primary language can contribute to lack of confidence about linguistic skill in general. Studies of a number of bilingual groups, in both Europe and the United States, have found that bilinguals often underrate their language skills in both languages (Gal, 1979). Lack of confidence is felt most strongly when the bilingual is speaking to a monolingual, such as when a Polish-American child is talking to a teacher who speaks only English.

In-group loyalty

On the other hand, the lower prestige of one language can also stimulate loyalty among the group that speaks it. Observations of bilinguals in eastern Canada, for example, suggest that even though many of them speak both French and English perfectly, they often refuse to use English in public places such as restaurants and department stores, even with English-speaking customers (Giles et al., 1977). This may help to give the lower-status language (in this case, French) more prestige, at least in the minds of individuals who use that language. But its effect on the rest of society seems less clear.

In general, language contributes importantly to children's cognitive functioning, as well as to their confidence in their abilities. It contributes so much, in fact, that psychologists have emphasized language in many tests of ability and achievement. The emphasis on language can pose problems for some children (such as bilinguals), as described in the next section. But given the nature of our society and of North American culture, it is hard to know how *not* to give language high priority in assessing many abilities.

Checkpoint *Although school-age children have already acquired many aspects of language, they continue to develop new levels of meaning in their vocabularies and to have difficulty with the more subtle features of syntax. Bilingual children sometimes show cognitive and linguistic advantages at this age, at least if their use of the two languages is fairly balanced. Often, though, they experience social prejudices against one of their languages.*

Defining and Measuring Intelligence

Intelligence refers to adaptability, or, put differently, to a general ability to learn from experience. Usually intelligence also refers to the ability to reason abstractly, sometimes using language to do so; and it includes the ability to integrate old and new knowledge. Because these skills have proved especially helpful in school, measuring or assessing intelligence has become very important to those who plan educational programs, such as school administrators and school psychologists. Many tests of general ability or intelligence have therefore been developed, both for adults and for children.

Definitions of intelligence

Concepts of Intelligence

Partly as a result of devising and using ability tests, educators and psychologists have continually debated the precise nature of intelligence. Disagreement surrounds all of the following questions, among others.

One Ability or Several? Both common sense and research suggest that abilities come in many forms. But do these forms add up to one truly general "intelligence"? Some psychologists (and their tests) emphasize relatively specific skills; others emphasize one rather general ability, sometimes named *g* (Sternberg and Davidson, 1985). Most tests (and their psychologists) acknowledge the presence of both general and specific factors, even though they differ in emphasis.

Specific vs. general abilities

Conglomeration or Compound? Granted that specific skills contribute to intelligence in some way, how do they do it? Some psychologists argue that general ability consists of a loose conglomeration or grouping of many diverse skills, and that these do not necessarily relate to one another in any logical way (Humphreys, 1979). This viewpoint also seems implicit in many ability tests that give only one general score of intelligence; questions on such a test are not grouped in any particular way, and simply add up to general intelligence.

Others argue, however, that the specific elements of intelligence bear logical relationships to one another, and that general intelligence cannot develop unless all these elements exist and develop together. Probably the most widely known advocate of this idea is Piaget. In his view, specific cognitive skills, such as conservation, inevitably affect other specific skills, such as classification. Only together can these skills create the truly general ability of children — concrete operations.

Relations among abilities

Qualitative Development or Quantitative? As children grow, how does their intelligence change? Does it become different in nature, as Piaget argues in his stage theory? Or does it simply become "more of everything"? Some ability tests imply the latter view by the way they are constructed. On these tests, children of all ages answer more or less the same questions, and the older, better-developed

Changes during development

These boys' skill at repairing a bicycle would not be well assessed on most tests of general ability. But specialized tests of mechanical aptitude might give a valid indication of what they can do. (David Strickler/The Picture Cube)

children simply answer more of them correctly. But not all ability tests work this way; some purposely give different sorts of questions to children of different ages, and score the results differently.

As these comments imply, ability tests have not only resulted from widespread concepts of intelligence but also helped to create them. The tests have also affected the educational careers of numerous children during the twentieth century. For these reasons, among others, some psychologists point to intelligence testing as one of the major success stories of psychology. At the same time, others have expressed serious misgivings about and criticisms of such tests.

Nature and Purposes of Standardized Tests

Tests of general ability or intelligence are one type of **standardized test.** All standardized tests (including intelligence tests) have several well-defined features. First, they always contain clearly stated questions that have relatively specific answers. The questions usually draw on logical reasoning and verbal skill, which are what schools typically require. Second, standardized tests always include clear, standard procedures for administration and scoring. Often they provide a script for the person giving the test, as well as specific printed advice about when and how to credit particular answers. Third, such tests present information about how large groups of comparable individuals perform, in order to allow evaluation of the performance of particular groups or of individual children (Scarr, 1984).

Features of standardized tests

Kinds of Standardized Tests Standardized tests serve many purposes, but for convenience we can classify them into two major groups, achievement tests and aptitude or ability tests. **Achievement tests** measure skills or knowledge that individuals have already learned; they try to indicate current attainment in a particular realm of human behavior. Children often encounter such tests in the form of scholastic achievement tests: tests of reading achievement, for example, or of arithmetic achievement. By nature, such tests usually draw heavily on the typical curriculum content of the subject area being tested.

Aptitude tests measure ability, or try to estimate future performance in some realm of behavior. A test of scholastic aptitude, for instance, tries to estimate a child's potential for success in school. Because of their goal, aptitude tests contain a broader range of questions than achievement tests do; a scholastic aptitude test would probably include questions from several major school subjects and draw on basic academic skills such as reading and mathematical reasoning.

In practice, aptitude and achievement tests are not as distinct as these definitions make them sound. Often achievement tests work very well as predictors of future performance; children's current skills in arithmetic, for instance, predict their future mathematical performance about as well as any aptitude tests can do (Anastasi, 1985). And aptitude tests can succeed at predicting future progress only by sampling skills and knowledge that children have already attained. Nonetheless, the distinction remains useful for those who develop and use tests. In general, measuring aptitude means looking to the future, and measuring achievement means assessing the past.

Interpreting Standardized Test Scores To accomplish these purposes, standardized tests require **norms,** or information about how large groups of individuals typically perform on the test and how they vary or differ among themselves. In developing norms for a test, psychologists usually give the test to a particular group called the **standardization sample.** A standardization sample for a school achievement test might include hundreds, or even thousands, of schoolchildren taking the particular school subject related to the test.

Having collected the scores of the standardization sample, psychologists do two things with them. First, they calculate a measure of **central tendency,** which is usually a single, "typical" score for the standardization sample. Second, they calculate or devise some indicator of **variability,** which is how widely individuals are arrayed around the typical score. Most commonly, the typical score consists simply of the **mean** or arithmetic average: the sum of all the scores divided by the number of scores. In some circumstances, other indicators of central tendency are also used, such as the **median** (the score that ranks in the middle of the group) or the **mode** (the most frequent score).

Variability is usually indicated in less straightforward ways than is central tendency. The most common measure on standardized tests is the **standard deviation,** which is found by averaging the squares of each person's deviation from the average test score, and then taking the square root of this figure. This measure requires considerable calculation if large groups are involved, but for various statistical reasons it has proved very popular with psychologists and others involved in testing.

Once norms have been calculated, standardized tests — and especially achieve-

Margin notes:

Achievement vs. aptitude tests

Indicators of central tendency

Indicators of variability

Standardized tests, such as the one this child is taking, usually either measure past achievement or predict future performance. Either way, they often strongly resemble typical academic tasks. (Elizabeth Crews)

Comparing groups of children

ment tests — can serve two purposes. On one hand, they can help educators to know how well particular schools or classrooms are functioning in general. Norms from particular groups of children are calculated and then compared with norms from other groups, or from the larger standardization sample. For example, all classrooms using a particular curriculum can be compared with classrooms using another curriculum, or all classrooms in one school can be compared with all classrooms in the city, or even with a national cross section.

Assessing individual children

On the other hand, standardized tests can sometimes aid individual children. The most common way involves screening students for special educational help. If teachers find a certain student learning the curriculum very slowly, they may ask a school psychologist to test her general scholastic ability, in the hope of diagnosing or clarifying her learning problems. Although the results of such a test cannot stand alone, they often do contribute to the complex process of assessing the learning needs of a particular child.

Limitations of standardized tests

As you may suspect, standardized tests do not serve either of these purposes perfectly. Reasons other than ability, such as a child's health or motivation to succeed, affect performance. In psychological terms, therefore, the tests always lack full **reliability** and **validity.** In this context, being highly reliable means that an individual's test scores vary relatively little from one test taking to the next, or even from one half of a test to the other half. Being highly valid means, among other things, that test scores predict the important outcomes they claim to measure as accurately as possible. For intelligence tests, the important outcome is often academic success.

Examples of Intelligence Tests

Some intelligence tests are given to groups, and others are given individually. Group tests need less time and effort to administer, and this convenience makes them especially attractive wherever large numbers of children must be tested, as in public schools. They have generally proved to be less reliable and valid, however, than tests given to children individually, so individual tests are usually preferable in assessing individual children's learning needs. Both kinds, however, contain similar items.

Tests for Individuals   One important individual test of intelligence is called the **Stanford-Binet Intelligence Scale** (Terman and Merrill, 1974). Its questions vary widely in difficulty, but they all emphasize verbal skill and abstract reasoning. To be tested, a child sits alone in a quiet room with an adult, who asks questions like these:

The Stanford-Binet

- "Repeat these numbers backwards after me: 5 9 2" *(for a typical six-year-old)*
- "What day comes before Tuesday? Thursday? Friday?" *(for a typical eight-year-old)*
- "Why is this foolish? A man had the flu twice. The first time it killed him, but the second time he got well quickly." *(for a typical eight-year-old)*

The adult has been trained to score the child's responses, which are not always as straightforward as you might expect. In the second question, for example, a child may only get two of the three day-sequence questions correct. Or the adult may have to state the question more than once before getting a reply; and even then the reply may be partially mumbled. Trained test administrators have to be ready for these possibilities.

On the Stanford-Binet, questions are roughly matched to an individual child's age and ability. Usually it takes somewhat more than one hour to give the test, so the Stanford-Binet is impractical for large-scale testing programs. The results give one score that supposedly reflects overall intelligence; this score is sometimes called an **intelligence quotient,** or **IQ.** It is based not only on how many questions the child answers correctly but also on how the child's performance compares to that of other children of the same age.

Another well-known individual intelligence test is called the **Wechsler Intelligence Scale for Children, Revised Form,** or **WISC-R** for short (Wechsler, 1974). Its items and procedures generally resemble those of the Stanford-Binet, but with one important exception. Instead of yielding just one score reflecting general ability, the WISC-R also gives twelve separate subscores. Each of these represents performance on some particular cognitive skill, such as vocabulary or arithmetic reasoning. Some of the skills are nonverbal, such as the ability to solve mazes or to assemble puzzles. These features make the WISC-R attractive in diagnosing the specific learning needs of individual children. Because the subtests are necessarily shorter than the whole WISC-R, though, they prove less reliable than the test considered as a whole.

The WISC-R

Tests for Special Purposes Since some children seem to think better than they talk, intelligence tests that bypass language, which dominates the usual tests, have also been designed. Here are a few examples of tests of this kind.

Pattern completions

1. *Raven's Progressive Matrices Test* (Raven, 1962) contains incomplete patterns or figures. The child completes each pattern by choosing from several alternatives printed next to the test item. With this format, the test avoids using very much language, so it can help to assess children who may not speak or hear well, such as those with speech or hearing impairments. It is not specifically intended for non-English-speaking children, even though they too may not always be able to speak to a test examiner. Verbally oriented tests exist in many languages, such as Spanish and Japanese.

Drawing tests

2. *The Draw-a-Man Test* (Harris, 1963) is another nonverbal test. For it, children simply make a pencil drawing of a human being. The result is scored in particular ways described in the test administrator's manual; higher scores usually, though not always, go to more complex features in the drawings. This test relies on the fact that children with experience in drawing normally improve steadily from preschool through late elementary school. Like Raven's test, it avoids language;

Perspectives on Research

One Intelligence or Many?

If intelligence really consists of just one unified factor, then different human talents should share common features — the ones that underlie basic intelligence. How much do they do so? To help answer this question, imagine children with each of the following talents.

1. *Language skill* A child with this talent can speak comfortably and fluently, and can learn new words and expressions easily. He can also memorize verbal materials, such as poems, much more easily than other children can.

2. *Musical skill* This child not only plays one or more musical instruments, but can also sing and notice subtle musical effects. Usually musical talent includes a good sense of timing or rhythm, too.

3. *Logical skill* A child with this skill can organize objects and concepts well. Using a microcomputer comes easily, for example; so do mathematics lessons at school.

4. *Spatial skill* This is a child who can literally find her way around. She knows the streets of the neighborhood better than most children her age, or if she lives in the country, she can find the way across rather large stretches of terrain without getting lost.

5. *Kinesthetic or body skill* This child is sensitive to the internal sensations created by body movement. As a result, he finds dancing, gymnastics, and other activities requiring balance easy to learn.

6. *Interpersonal and intrapersonal skills* A child with interpersonal skill shows excellent understanding of others' feelings, thoughts, and motives. A child with intrapersonal skill has good understanding of her own. For children with either or both of these skills, handling social encounters comes relatively easily.

Described in this way, these talents do not look like they have much in common. In fact only two

---

but it obviously cannot work well with children handicapped in the use of their arms or hands. Nor can it work with adolescents and adults, whose drawings often do not improve as they get older, even though their intelligence (we hope) does.

3. *The Peabody Picture Vocabulary Test* (Dunn and Dunn, 1981) requires children to understand words but not to produce them. In this test, the administrator shows sets of four pictures to the child and asks her simply to point to the one that goes with a certain word. The child does not need to say anything in this process. Studies have found that this test reflects general intelligence to a large extent. But as its name implies, it really measures only one part of intelligence, knowledge of vocabulary. As a result, it lacks some of the reliability and validity of broader ability tests; children's scores vary more from one testing session to the next, and scores do not predict school success as well.

Vocabulary comprehension

Biases of Intelligence and General Ability Tests

In spite of trying to measure general qualities, tests of ability and intelligence contain various biases. For example, many intelligence tests rely heavily on language in all its forms — listening, speaking, and reading. Many also emphasize problems

---

of them, language skill and logical skill, relate very closely to the content of most intelligence tests, even though the tests supposedly measure general ability (Wallach, 1985).

Some psychologists therefore urge that we give up the idea that one general intelligence exists, and instead focus attention on the diversity of abilities possible among human beings. For a starting point in this change of focus, one psychologist, Howard Gardner, has proposed that each of the talents listed above may actually constitute a distinct form of intelligence (Gardner, 1983). (Interpersonal and intrapersonal skills may really amount to two distinct forms of intelligence; but the research evidence makes him unsure about this.)

These intelligences are separate, he argues, for several reasons. First, some of the six can be physically located within the brain. Certain language functions occur within particular, identifiable parts of the brain, as do kinesthetic or balance functions. Second, the intelligences sometimes occur in pure

form; some retarded individuals play a musical instrument extremely well, for example, even though they cannot talk well or reason abstractly. Third, the intelligences each have particular, core skills that clearly set them off from the others. Being musical requires a good sense of pitch, but this skill does not contribute to any of the other intelligences very much.

These comments may sound like criticisms of conventional intelligence testing. Strictly speaking, though, they really criticize extensions in the use of conventional tests beyond their intended purposes. As we point out in the text, such tests are designed to predict academic skills, and therefore they heavily emphasize verbal and logical activities. But school is not everything in life, in spite of its prominence in children's lives. Perhaps the fact that school attendance is compulsory has actually interfered with understanding intelligence, because it may have made us all value verbal and mathematical skills more than we should.

that have specific answers and that play down divergent or creative thinking. And although they do not focus on speed, intelligence tests tend to favor children who answer fairly rapidly and who do not take much time to mull over their solutions.

Since all of these features are also emphasized by schools, intelligence tests measure academic ability better than any other skill. Some psychologists in fact have suggested calling them measures of *academic intelligence* or of *school ability,* in order to make this limitation clear (Anastasi, 1985).

Cultural Assumptions   The biggest problem with intelligence tests, though, comes from their cultural assumptions, which have originated entirely from white, middle-class experiences in Western Europe and North America. The tests show their assumptions or biases in at least two ways. First, individual questions often

Selection of content demand knowledge that children can gain only by thorough immersion in white, middle-class society. One question might ask children to describe the purpose of a garden hose, thereby assuming previous contact with running water. Another question might ask children to define the word *drama* or *concerto,* thereby assuming the sort of education that provides this information (Eysenck, 1979).

Even when tests avoid this sort of bias, they suffer from other, more subtle cul-

Biases of testing situations tural assumptions. Many ethnic groups and cultures do not value conversations based on logic; speaking in abstractions may seem rude, or at least boring (Neisser, 1979). Children from these groups therefore cannot be expected to take tests that rely heavily on this sort of dialogue. In some cultural groups, too, contact with strange adults is extremely rare, so children from such groups may find sitting alone in a room with an unfamiliar test administrator rather perplexing or even frightening. For such children, any questions the administrator asks may seem much less important than figuring out this adult's real motives (Laboratory of Comparative Human Cognition, 1982).

Common Misinterpretations of Intelligence Tests

Because of these problems, intelligence tests have sometimes been criticized strongly. Some school districts and states have even banned the less reliable group tests altogether. Individual intelligence tests have usually remained in use, however, because they are especially helpful in diagnosing children with special learning needs, and because they are always administered by relatively well-trained psychologists.

A lot of criticism has stemmed from misinterpretations of the results of intelligence tests. In one way or another, all of the following mistakes have turned out to be all too easy to make.

Intelligence test scores vs. intelligence **1.** *Equating test scores with true intelligence*   As we have already pointed out, intelligence tests primarily measure academic talent. Yet life is full of many other kinds of talent, from cooking or playing the piano to always saying the tactful thing. The further removed these talents are from academics, the less well intelligence tests can measure them or predict them.

2. *Confusing intellectual differences with intelligence* Most intelligence test scores reflect how much a child differs from other, comparable children. They usually do *not* report how much a child actually knows at any given point in time. Yet actual knowledge may matter more than differences in knowledge in many situations, such as when a child is trying to fix his bicycle or trying to find his way home along an unfamiliar street.

Individual differences vs. actual skills

3. *Assuming too much precision* Because intelligence tests give numerical scores, adults are tempted to think that they are more precise than they really are. In reality, however, small differences in scores between children often reflect random variation rather than true differences in intelligence. Test manuals usually point out this fact, but unfortunately, the information sometimes does not reach parents, and even teachers or school psychologists may forget it.

Overestimating precision

Implications for Teachers and Parents Properly used, tests of intelligence and general ability can help parents and teachers to understand children. However, the tests cannot substitute for the many other ways of gaining such understanding, such as through extended, informal observation in class or at home or just plain conversation. Most commonly, intelligence tests simply add to information already known or suspected about a particular child; they do not replace that information. Also, intelligence tests play a role with children who are academically at an extreme, whether extremely gifted or extremely slow. For the vast majority of children — the "middling" ones — the tests usually contribute little information that is really useful in planning their personal educational futures. For such children, teachers can usually learn more by devising or selecting achievement tests focused more precisely on the class's current curriculum. Parents can usually learn more by observing their children informally at home, and by talking with teachers and other adults who know their children. This still leaves important work for ability tests, but the work has specific purposes and limitations.

Checkpoint *Although psychologists agree that intelligence refers to an ability to learn from experience, they disagree about the precise implications of this definition. Nonetheless, they have developed and used many standardized tests of ability and achievement and have devised relatively objective ways of interpreting the results. Many of these tests have been highly reliable and valid. But they have also suffered from cultural biases and from other common misinterpretations.*

Moral Development

During the school years, cognitive development also affects the social and emotional lives of children. One of the most important ways in which it does so is by influencing the development of morality. **Morality** refers to a sense of ethics, or of

---

right and wrong. Questions of morality come up whenever one child can help or hurt another child. Since children nearly all have contact with their peers, questions of helping and hurting arise rather often: in deciding whether to share a lunch with a classmate, for example, or whether to take a sibling's favorite book without permission.

As these examples suggest, morality has several aspects, and to varying degrees all require cognitive skills. First of all, children must learn to identify how various situations actually affect other children's welfare. For instance, what would be the consequences of "borrowing" a neighbor's bicycle without asking? Second, children must learn good moral judgment — how to select actions that truly help others and do not hurt them. Children must learn that forcing a candy bar on a friend who does not want it does not really constitute a good deed. And third, children must acquire skills for implementing moral judgments and actions. When someone cries because of an injury, a child may sympathize deeply yet not know how to respond. Should she say something, and if so, what? Or just offer a handkerchief?

These complexities may help explain an important quality of moral development during childhood, namely its lack of consistency. As has been documented now for decades, very few children do the "right thing" all the time, or even a majority of the time (Hartshorne and May, 1928). At some time or other, virtually every child cheats at schoolwork, and virtually every child tattles or betrays a friend at least occasionally. These lapses may result from difficulties with some aspect of morality, ranging from lack of sensitivity to others' welfare, to poor judgment about appropriate actions, to lack of skill in implementing good intentions.

In an effort to make sense out of such complexities, theorists of cognitive development such as Piaget have focused on how children make moral judgments or form beliefs about right and wrong. They have given less attention to how children translate these judgments and beliefs into moral actions. Two major stage theories of moral development have come out of this effort, a relatively simple one originated by Piaget himself, and another, more complex one developed by one of his followers, Lawrence Kohlberg.

Piagetian Stages of Moral Thinking

In observing children at play, Piaget noted differences in how younger and older children conceived of the rules for simple games such as marbles (Piaget, 1964). Younger children, aged about six to nine, tended to use what Piaget called **heteronomous morality,** or a "morality of constraint." In this way of thinking, children regarded the rules of a game as sacred and unchangeable, yet they were very lax about actually following the rules. Infractions were judged according to the amount of objective damage that a child did, regardless of whether the damage was accidental or purposeful. Knocking all the other children's marbles out of the playing circle was worse than knocking only one marble out, for example, whether or not the child had meant to do so. Yet children at this age would often commit precisely such a "sin" whenever they could get away with it, in spite of judging it rather harshly.

By the later years of elementary school (around ages nine to twelve), however, children shifted toward what Piaget called **autonomous morality,** or a "morality of cooperation." In this more mature philosophy, children began to take their peers' desires and intentions into account in evaluating their actions. Now, spoiling the entire circle of marbles might be judged less harshly if it happened accidentally, and moving just one marble illegally might be judged more harshly if the child moved it on purpose. At the same time, the children Piaget observed felt that they could change the rules if they wanted to, through group discussion and decision; the rules were no longer fixed or sacred. Perhaps as a result, children at the later stage adhered to the rules more carefully, because they felt more responsible for creating them. The very awesomeness of rules may have prevented younger children from taking responsibility for following them.

Piaget argued that children in the middle years shifted from heteronomous to autonomous morality because of repeated encounters in playing with peers. Inevitably, disagreements would arise, and the conflicts would stimulate children to take other viewpoints into account in playing games with rules. Over the long run, according to Piaget, children therefore become more democratic — more willing to cooperate in changing rules, on the one hand, and more willing to follow the rules, on the other. Unfortunately, as plausible as this process sounds, very little research evidence actually supports it (Lickona, 1976). Children who must deal repeatedly with peers, that is, do not necessarily become more democratic over the long run. But Piaget is right about the sequencing of the two types of morality: heteronomous morality does appear more often in younger children, and autonomous morality does appear more in older ones (Karniol, 1978, 1980).

> The morality of cooperation

> Influence of experience

Kohlberg's Six Stages of Moral Judgment

Lawrence Kohlberg extended Piaget's ideas by proposing six stages of moral judgment rather than just two, and by proposing that these span almost the entire first half of life (Kohlberg, 1976). The stages were derived from interviews conducted in much the same style as Piaget's classic interviews about cognitive development: children and adults of various ages responded individually to hypothetical or imaginary stories that contained moral dilemmas.

The six proposed stages are summarized in Table 12-2. In two ways, the stages form a progression. First, earlier stages represent more egocentric thinking than later stages do; and second, earlier stages by their nature require more specific or concrete thinking than later stages do. For instance, in Stage 1 (called "heteronomous morality," just as Piaget's concept is), a child makes no distinction between what he believes is right and what the world tells him is right; he simply accepts the perspective of the authorities as his own. By Stage 4 (social system orientation), he realizes that individuals vary in their points of view, but he still takes for granted the existing overall conventions of society as a whole. He cannot yet imagine a society in which those conventions might be purposely modified. Only by Stages 5 and 6 (ethics) can he do so fully.

> Progression away from egocentric and concrete thinking

In the middle years, children most commonly show ethical reasoning at Stage 2, but a minority may begin showing Stage 3 or 4 reasoning toward the end of this

Table 12-2 Kohlberg's Stages of Moral Judgment	Stage	Nature of stage
	Preconventional Level *(emphasis on avoiding punishments and getting rewards)*	
	Stage 1: Heteronomous morality; ethics of punishment and obedience	Good is what follows externally imposed rules and rewards, and whatever avoids punishment
	Stage 2: Instrumental purpose; ethics of market exchange	Good is whatever is agreeable to the individual and to anyone who gives or receives favors; no long-term loyalty
	Conventional Level *(emphasis on social rules)*	
	Stage 3: Interpersonal conformity; ethics of peer opinion	Good is whatever brings approval from friends as a peer group
	Stage 4: Conformity to social system; ethics of law and order	Good is whatever conforms to existing laws, customs, and authorities
	Postconventional Level *(emphasis on moral principles)*	
	Stage 5: Ethics of social contract and individual rights	Good is whatever conforms to existing procedures for settling disagreements in society; the actual outcome is neither good nor bad
	Stage 6: Ethics of self-chosen universal principles	Good is whatever is consistent with personal, general moral principles

Moral stages in the middle years

period (Colby et al., 1983). In Stage 3 (interpersonal orientation), a child's chief concern is with the opinions of her peers: an action is right if her immediate circle of friends says that it is right. Often this way of thinking leads to helpful actions, like taking turns and sharing toys or materials. But often it does not, as when a group of friends decides to let the air out of the tires of someone's car. In Stage 4 (social system orientation), children shift from concern with peers to concern with the opinions of their broader community, or of society as a whole: now something is right if these wider groups approve. This broader source of moral judgment spares Stage 4 children from the occasional tyranny of friends' opinions; they will now no longer steal hub caps just because their friends urge them to do so. But they still cannot imagine the wider public holding unethical opinions or taking unjust actions; the notion of racial bigotry, for example, or of an unjust war, still seems like an impossibility. Such ideas become very real possibilities to some individuals in adolescence and beyond.

Evaluation of Cognitive Theories of Moral Development

Support for the six stages

Although research has tended to find Piaget's two-stage theory too simplistic, Kohlberg's six-stage theory has held up well when tested on a wide variety of children, adolescents, and adults (Colby et al., 1983). The stages of moral thinking in Table 12-2, that is, do seem to describe changes in moral judgment as children

For this youngster, stealing may be wrong only to the extent that her friends say it is. As with the rest of us, too, her actions may not always coincide with her moral beliefs. (Robert Hauser/ Photo Researchers)

grow up, at least when children express their judgments about hypothetical dilemmas posed in stories.

Note, though, that Kohlberg's stages describe only the *form* of thinking, not its content. According to Kohlberg's theory, a child's specific moral opinions are relatively independent of his moral development. Three children may all believe that telling a fib is wrong. Yet the first child may hold this opinion out of fear of being caught lying (Stage 1); the second may want to agree with friends (Stage 3); and the third may feel a commitment to following existing rules (Stage 4). In Kohlberg's theory, the form of ethics develops, but the content does not.

In spite of the theory's plausibility, a number of developmental psychologists have questioned important aspects of it. Can the form of ethical thinking really be separated from content as much as Kohlberg proposes? Perhaps not. Some studies have found that when children reason about familiar situations, they tend to give more mature (that is, higher-stage) ethical responses (Damon, 1977). For instance, children have a better sense of fairness about playing four-square on the playground than about whether to steal a drug for a spouse who is dying (one of Kohlberg's fictional dilemmas). A similar bias for the familiar occurs among adults as well; women think in more mature or developed ways about ethical problems of special concern and familiarity to women, like whether to procure an abortion (Gilligan, 1982). To some extent, therefore, what someone thinks about affects the ethics she or he applies.

These variations challenge Kohlberg's theory. According to some psychologists,

Effects of familiarity on moral reasoning

the problem may arise because the theory does not fully distinguish the concepts of social convention and morality (Nucci, 1982; Turiel, 1978). **Social conventions** refer to the arbitrary customs and agreements about behavior that members of society use — things like table manners and forms of greeting. Morality, as we have already pointed out, refers to the more weighty matters of justice and right and wrong. By nature, social conventions inevitably generate widespread agreement throughout society, whereas morality does not necessarily do so. Yet Kohlberg's six-stage theory glosses over these differences by defining some of its stages in terms of social conventions and others in terms of morality. Stage 4 ("social system orientation"), for example, seems to refer to social conventions as well as to moral matters, but Stage 5 ("social contract orientation") refers only to moral judgment.

Studies that have in fact distinguished between convention and morality have produced a less stagelike picture of moral development. In one such study (Nucci, 1978), children between the ages of six and seventeen were asked questions like

- Is it wrong to steal? *(morality-related)*
- Is it wrong to hit another person? *(morality-related)*
- Is it wrong for a group to change the rules of a game? *(convention-related)*
- Is it okay for a country to make the traffic lights blue and purple instead of red and green? *(convention-related)*

At every age, most children felt that hitting and stealing were wrong but that changing the rules of a game or changing the color of traffic lights was acceptable. If morality had developed at all, then, this study suggested that it had already done so before the school years began. By the youngest age tested, six, children already clearly distinguished between moral behavior and conventional behavior.

Checkpoint *Cognitive development contributes to changes in children's moral reasoning. According to Piaget, children move from a heteronomous morality early in the school years to an autonomous morality later on. Kohlberg has extended and modified Piaget's ideas to include six stages of moral judgment. According to research, these stages do seem to occur; but they are influenced by children's familiarity with a particular moral issue and by whether the issue includes conventional as well as moral elements.*

Cognition and Social Development

Among the varieties of cognition discussed in this chapter, one idea predominates: that cognition does not usually occur in isolation from social and emotional experiences. In order to use learning and memory strategies successfully, children must want to use them, must feel that using them is valued by others, and must enjoy the efforts they put into solving problems. Certain styles of thinking, such as divergent thinking, may depend heavily on social play, an activity that is certainly only partially cognitive. And language development involves more than acquiring a system of grammatical rules; it also involves some highly social communication.

Evidently, then, the social surroundings of children make a big difference to their development. The next chapter looks at these surroundings more closely. Instead of taking social and emotional development somewhat for granted, it will highlight these areas while temporarily placing cognitive development in the background.

Summary of Major Ideas

Concrete Operational Skills

1. School-age children develop concrete operational thinking, or reasoning that focuses on real, tangible objects. Compared to preoperational thinking, it is more decentered, sensitive to transformations, and reversible.

2. Some cognitive developments during the school years resemble refinements of earlier preoperational skills and beliefs, such as classification, animism, and artificialism.

3. A very important new skill is conservation, which is a belief that an object's properties remain constant in spite of perceptual changes in the object.

4. Efforts to train children in conservation have had moderate success, although when applied in a variety of circumstances training does not persist as well as naturally developed conservation.

5. Concrete operational children also acquire new skills in seriation, temporal relations, and spatial relations.

6. Considered as a whole, Piagetian ideas about cognitive development have influenced many educators' styles of teaching, the content of their curricula, and their methods of assessing students' progress.

Information-Processing Skills

7. Information-processing models divide thinking into several parts, such as short-term sensory storage, short-term memory, working memory, and long-term memory.

8. Short-term memory capacity does not change much during the school years, and in fact approximates adult capacity.

9. Long-term memory does improve with age, partly as a result of other cognitive developments.

10. Improvements in logical reasoning sometimes assist the development of long-term memory, as does increasing richness or familiarity of knowledge as schoolchildren grow older.

11. During the school years, children also begin being aware of how they think, and begin using various learning strategies for improving their memory and reasoning.

12. Learning strategies are acquired in a variety of ways, and sometimes they can be taught to children purposely.

Styles of Thinking

13. In addition to increasing their cognitive capacities, school-age children acquire unique styles of thinking.

14. One way in which children vary is in their preference for convergent or divergent styles of solving problems.

15. Many children also become sensitive to metaphor and other forms of figurative language during the school years.

16. Field dependent children tend to perceive things in relatively large, connected patterns, whereas field independent children tend to perceive things as discrete parts.

17. In some circumstances, field dependence and independence are associated with differences in social relations.

18. Children begin to vary in how reflective or impulsive they are in solving problems.

Language Development in the Middle Years

19. Although school-age children are already quite skillful with language, they continue to develop new, more mature ways of defining words.

20. Schoolchildren continue to have difficulties with certain subtle features of syntax.

21. Bilingual children develop certain cognitive advantages over monolinguals, at least if their bilingualism is relatively balanced.

22. Often, though, bilinguals must cope with prejudices against one of their languages and against the culture which that language represents.

Defining and Measuring Intelligence

23. Intelligence is a general ability to learn from experience, although psychologists do not agree about many of the specific implications of this definition.

24. To measure both abilities and achievement, psychologists have developed standardized tests, as well as norms and procedures for interpreting the scores on these tests.

25. Two major individual ability tests are the Stanford-Binet and the WISC-R; examples of other standardized tests are Raven's Progressive Matrices, the Draw-a-Man, and the Peabody Picture Vocabulary Test.

26. Standardized tests often contain cultural biases, both in their content and in the method by which they are administered.

27. Standardized tests are sometimes misinterpreted in various ways: by equating scores with true intelligence, by confusing individual differences in scores with actual intelligence, and by overestimating tests' precision.

Moral Development

28. Moral development refers to the development of a sense of ethics, or right and wrong.

29. In ordinary circumstances, most children's moral behavior is rather inconsistent.

30. Piaget proposed two stages of moral development during the school years: an earlier stage of heteronomous morality, and a later stage of autonomous morality.

31. Lawrence Kohlberg proposed six stages of moral judgment: two at the preconventional level, two at the conventional level, and two at the postconventional level.

32. School-age children tend to exhibit the middle two of Kohlberg's stages, called the ethics of peer opinion and the ethics of law and order.

33. Research supports Kohlberg's six-stage model, but it also shows that moral reasoning depends partly on children's familiarity with particular moral issues as well as on the distinction between social convention and true morality.

Key Terms

concrete
  operations *(479)*
decentration *(479)*
sensitivity to
  transformations *(479)*
reversibility *(479)*
classification *(480)*
class inclusion *(480)*
animism *(480)*
artificialism *(480)*
conservation *(480)*
décallage *(483)*
seriation *(484)*
information-processing
  theories *(486)*
short-term sensory store
  (STSS) *(487)*
short-term memory
  (STM) *(487)*
working memory
  (WM) *(487)*
long-term memory
  (LTM) *(487)*
recognition
  memory *(488)*
recall memory *(489)*
metacognition *(492)*
learning strategies *(492)*
logical
  construction *(494)*
cognitive styles *(498)*
convergent
  thinking *(498)*

divergent thinking *(498)*
figurative language *(500)*
field dependence *(502)*
field independence *(502)*
reflectivity *(504)*
impulsivity *(504)*
bilingualism *(509)*
cognitive flexibility *(509)*
metalinguistic
  awareness *(510)*
black English *(510)*
Standard English *(510)*
intelligence *(513)*
standardized test *(514)*
achievement test *(515)*
aptitude test *(515)*
intelligence quotient
  (IQ) *(517)*
morality *(521)*
heteronomous
  morality *(522)*
autonomous
  morality *(523)*
preconventional level of
  moral judgment *(524)*
conventional level of
  moral judgment *(524)*
postconventional level of
  moral judgment *(524)*
social conventions *(526)*

What Do You Think?

1. Is concrete operational thinking "better" than preoperational thinking, or just different? Explain your opinion and what it implies for training conservation and for educating children in general.

2. Do you believe that a computer makes a good model for human thinking? How does real human thinking differ from the operations of a computer?

3. Consider all the cognitive styles described in this chapter. Are they equally valuable to children, or are some somehow more useful or advantageous to the individuals who possess them? Explain your opinion.

4. Think about a language that you wish you could speak. Why would you like to be able to use this language? In forming your opinion, what assumptions are you making about the culture or people who use the language?

5. Should standardized tests be used in schools? If so, what limitations should be placed on the kinds of tests used, on who gets to see the results, and on how the results are used?

6. In daily life, moral principles seem like a matter of personal opinion; yet Kohlberg's model of moral development seems to imply that we all develop toward some final common morality. How can these two impressions be reconciled?

For Further Reading

Gardner, H. *Art, Mind, and Brain: A Cognitive Approach to Creativity.* New York: Basic Books, 1982.

The author has published quite a lot about individual differences in styles of thinking, and in particular about how children acquire styles that encourage creativity in general and visual sensitivity and artistic talent in particular. This book collects many of these essays, which were written with the general public in mind.

Gilligan, C. *In a Different Voice: Psychological Theory and Women's Development.* Cambridge, Mass.: Harvard University Press, 1982.

The author argues, among other things, that girls and women develop a uniquely female perspective on morality, which is based on learning to care within a network of social relationships and on learning to include oneself in that network. She proposes that the major psychological stage theories, including Piaget's and Kohlberg's, do not take this feminine perspective into account; as a result, they may really only describe male development.

Greenfield, P. *Mind and Media: The Effects of Television, Video Games, and Computers.* Cambridge, Mass.: Harvard University Press, 1984.

This book explores the effects of visual media — especially television and video games — on children's cognitive development. It finds these media beneficial in many ways, and more effective than printed books for certain purposes. The author favors a balanced use of visual and printed media, and she urges keeping an open mind about visual media until we acquire more reliable information about their effects.

Gould, S. J. *The Mismeasure of Man.* New York: Norton, 1981.

The author describes the history of efforts to measure human intelligence. Much of this history, it seems, has been influenced by a pre-existing desire to "prove" that some kinds of people (such as blacks and American Indians) are genetically inferior to others (chiefly whites of northern European stock).

Neisser, U. (Ed.) *Memory Observed: Remembering in Natural Contexts.* San Francisco: Freeman, 1982.

This book presents research and observational studies of memory as it occurs in everyday life. As a result of this focus, it makes fascinating reading. You can learn about memory for traffic accidents, about how individuals memorize very long poems and pieces of prose, and about how exceptional children and adults acquire photographic memories for objects and events. The book shows convincingly that memory is not necessarily a dry topic constructed by psychologists for artificial study.

Chapter

13

The Middle Years: Psychosocial Development

Focusing Questions

- What are the major changes in children's achievement motivation during the middle years?
- What special contributions do peers make to children's development?
- What affects the structure of peer groups, and what affects children's popularity within those groups?
- How do parents influence children, and how do parents and children view their relationship?
- What effects does divorce have on children and their families?
- How do maternal employment and paternal unemployment affect family relationships?
- What progress toward a sense of self do children make during the middle years?
- How does a handicap influence the psychological and social development of a child?

Middle childhood is a time when the developmental changes of infancy and the preschool years are rapidly consolidated and children ready themselves for adolescence and the movement to full adulthood. By the time they start school, most children have learned something about human nature and are beginning to pick up various practical skills. During the middle years, society fosters these developments further, by "inviting" children to attend school, where they learn socially valued skills such as reading and writing.

School also provides them with more contacts with other children of similar age and maturity, or **peers.** In doing so, it complicates their psychological and social lives, as compared with those of preschool children (Youniss, 1980). Peers offer certain benefits, such as freedom from the watchful eyes of parents and teachers. But they also demand loyalty and conformity. "Be nice to everyone except Rachel" was a rule in one circle of friends; "Do the assignment, but don't work too hard on it" was a rule in another. Middle years children must learn to coordinate these expectations with those of parents, who sometimes disagree with peers.

To meet all of these demands simultaneously requires children to learn to regulate their behavior from within. Somehow they must find ways to control their expressions of aggression, impatience, grief, and other strong impulses and emotions. Doing so becomes easier as they develop concepts of themselves as individuals and knowledge of their own needs and values and of how these compare with the needs and values of other people.

Psychosocial Challenges of the Middle Years

This chapter discusses these developments as they occur during the years from approximately age six to about age twelve, considering in particular four major challenges to children's psychosocial lives: the challenge to achieve, the challenge of peers, the challenge of family relationships, and the challenge of knowing who you are. Lastly, the chapter looks at how these challenges are met by children with special needs.

The Challenge to Achieve　Some psychologists consider the major crisis of this age period to be the development of competence and of willingness to achieve to the best of one's ability. Of course, children do care about their competence even in infancy. But during the middle years, this motive is complicated by children's growing awareness of others' opinions about their efforts.

Awareness of standards of excellence

The older of two siblings showed this awareness one afternoon when talking with his sister about their paintings. Michael, age seven, said, "That's a nice painting, Elizabeth, but not as nice as usual." Elizabeth, age three, seemed unaware of possible insult; she simply smiled, and continued to show her picture to Michael. Then she tried to be friendly by reciprocating: "That's a nice picture, too, Michael, but not as nice as yesterday's." Michael looked pained and replied, "It is *so* a good one!"

Both Elizabeth and Michael revealed some understanding of achievement in this interchange: they seem to know that paintings vary in quality, and that painters need encouragement for their work. But Michael seemed more concerned about meeting certain standards of achievement. He worried about Elizabeth's implication that he might have fallen below these standards, and he also worried about whether Elizabeth had noticed this fact.

The Challenge of Peers　After discussing the motive to achieve, we look at the second major challenge of the middle years, namely other children, or peers. As we point out, peers serve even more important purposes for schoolchildren than they do for preschoolers. The influence of peers is not always good, but peers do help each other a lot, and in any case, most children usually prefer peers to social isolation.

Relating to other children

The Challenge of Family Relationships　In spite of peers, family relationships have far from disappeared from the lives of schoolchildren. This chapter discusses several important aspects of family life, including recent changes in family roles and family membership, which have become much more varied than in the past. Who is supposed to do what within a family? What even constitutes a family in the first place? The chapter provides several answers currently given by parents and psychologists, and examines in detail how changing family patterns affect school-age children.

Impact of family

The Challenge of Knowing Who You Are Ironically, peer and family pressures may actually help schoolchildren to evolve better ideas of the kind of people they are. These notions do not yet constitute a final, stable identity, such as that developed during adolescence and adulthood, but they do lay the groundwork for later development. During the middle years, a child can at least ask, "Am I a popular sort of person?" or "Am I athletic?" The answers may still be rather simplistic, but they are nonetheless beginning to take on meaning.

Identity formation

The Challenge of Being Different Some school-age children have special physical, emotional, or cognitive needs. These vary widely in nature, and include such difficulties as a missing limb, a learning disability, and general retardation. To a large extent, children with these handicaps face the same challenges as other children: they need to achieve, to get along with peers, and to develop lasting, positive relationships with their families. But they also must learn how their differences affect what they can do with their lives and their relationships with others.

Adapting to special needs

Checkpoint *During the middle years, children face several psychological and social challenges: (a) the challenge to achieve in some area of activity; (b) the challenge to get along with peers and to benefit from relations with them; (c) the challenge to get along with family members and to cope with any stresses felt by the family as a whole; and (d) the challenge to develop some sense of identity or self. Children with a disability or handicap also face a fifth challenge, that of being different from their peers.*

The Age of Industry and Achievement

When looked at as part of the entire lifespan, the years from six to twelve seem especially important to achieving competence. Children spend countless hours in school, of course, acquiring skills in reading, writing, and mathematics. And many of those hours also contribute to learning the unofficial curriculum of school: how to get along with teachers and with other children. Outside of school, children often devote themselves to the long, slow mastery of particular skills. One child may spend literally years learning to play baseball, and another may devote just as much time to learning to care for a zoo of pet hamsters, dogs, and birds.

Latency and the Crisis of Industry

Psychodynamic theories such as those proposed by Freud and Erikson explain such behavior in terms of the emotional relationships that precede it in early childhood. As we described in Chapter 10, preschool children feel envy, awe, and competitiveness about their parents. At first these feelings have a magical quality;

children simply want to be like their parents. Inevitably, they are disappointed to learn that merely wanting such things does not make them come true.

Freud here emphasized the emotional hardship of preschoolers' disappointment, and their consequent repression of their magical wishes toward their parents (Freud, 1983). A five-year-old, he argued, cannot continue indefinitely to wish for intimacy with one parent and for success in competition with the other. These feelings disrupt life if they continue too long. So the child eventually represses the feelings, which means that he pushes them completely out of awareness. As it happens, this **repression** occurs at about the time that most children begin school — around age six or seven — and continues until adolescence. Because the child's earlier feelings have gone underground, Freud called this a period of **latency.** During this period, the schoolchild focuses on building competencies and skills as a **defense** — an unconscious, self-protective behavior — against his earlier romantic feelings about his parent. Developing talents, whether in sports, art, academics, or whatever, also helps to keep the child's mind off his earlier disappointment, which lingers on unconsciously.

Freud's theory of middle childhood

Erikson agreed with Freud's account as far as this, but he went beyond it to stress not only the defensive, negative functions of skill building but its positive functions as well (Erikson, 1963, 1968). According to Erikson, children do indeed experience magical feelings toward their parents, and the feelings do remain unsatisfied. Children respond, however, not only by repressing their romantic feelings but also by trying consciously to become more like their parents, and more like adults in general. Becoming competent helps children to reach this goal in two ways. First, it helps them to see themselves as people capable of becoming genuine adults; and second, it helps them to gain this recognition from others.

Erikson called this process the crisis of **industry versus inferiority,** meaning that children of this age concern themselves with their **industriousness,** or the capacity to do good work. Children who convince themselves and others of this capacity develop relatively confident, positive concepts of themselves. Those who do not, tend to suffer from feelings of poor self-esteem and **inferiority,** which is a sense of inadequacy or general lack of competence. According to Erikson, most children end up with a mixture of self-confidence and fears of inferiority, but self-confidence predominates in most cases (we hope).

Erikson: The crisis of industry versus inferiority

In addition, the crisis of industry gives healthy school-age children a more or less permanent motivation to achieve particular, definable standards of excellence. No longer are they happy just to draw pictures, for example; now they must draw *well.* With persistence and support, children often do reach higher standards of excellence in many activities than they did as preschoolers, and most of the time they are happy about doing so.

Industry and achievement motivation

Partly because of the connection between industry and increasing competence, psychologists have devoted a lot of attention to the development of the achievement motivation in middle years children. The next section of this chapter describes some of this work. In reading it, though, note that Freud and Erikson have not explained the development of all middle years children equally well. Some children seem relatively indifferent to developing their competencies, at least in the sense of focused, disciplined skill improvement. Instead, they care rela-

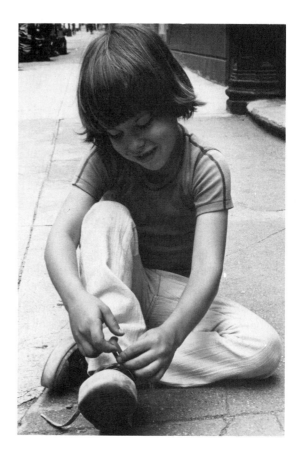

During the middle years, children focus considerable energy on acquiring specific skills. Tying a shoelace can be a major achievement. (Erika Stone)

tively more about participating in a network of friendly (or at least social) relationships (Gilligan, 1982). More often than not, these children are girls, but some boys also develop in this way.

To understand such individual differences, consider what happens on a school playground during recess. Some children conscientiously match athletic skills with one another, repeatedly jumping off the swings to see who can jump the farthest. But others seem content simply to pass the time sociably; they stand against the school building, chatting in small groups. Much of this activity, of course, perfects social skills, no matter how casual it may look. In this way it may simply constitute a particular form of industry, one that leads to increased social skills with time and practice. But this possibility is hard to evaluate because children often try purposely to look casual, and to conceal or play down their eagerness to be socially skillful and their worries about social failure.

Achievement Motivation

Achievement motivation refers to behavior that enhances competence, or that enhances judgments of competence (Beck, 1978; Atkinson and Feather, 1966). It often refers to a desire or tendency to strive for some high but reasonable standard

Achievement motivation becomes more complex in the middle years as children begin paying more attention to how others evaluate their work. These violinists may be concerned about each other's opinions and that of the audience, as well as about their own. (Marion Bernstein)

of excellence in a skill or area of knowledge. What matters is the approach to a task, not the importance of the task itself. An individual can reveal achievement motivation as either a student or a college professor, for example, and as either an amateur checkers player or a world-class chess grand master. As long as the individual strives toward a standard of excellence that is reasonable for her, she possesses achievement motivation. Usually, too, her motivation leads to increased competence, compared with her previous level.

The nature of achievement motivation

To understand these ideas, think about a big, blond nine-year-old named Jason. For weeks after a computer appeared in his home, Jason lost himself in the magic of the keyboard and video display. His parents had not bought any ready-made games or software for the computer, so Jason had to content himself with messing around, as he put it, and with typing out the simple programs in the owner's manual. This was often tedious work, but Jason did not seem to care. Every day after school he spent time at the keyboard, trying to get his programs to work properly. And he did become skilled at it; after several months, he could make up simple games to play with his parents, and he began to enjoy computer magazines for children.

Throughout this period, Jason showed a lot of achievement motivation: he devoted considerable energy to the particular goal of learning to write programs. In the process, he became more competent; and in this case, his behavior made his parents judge him as more competent. If he had worked on the computer at school, some of his peers might have come to a similar conclusion, but since he did not, relatively few of his classmates knew that Jason had acquired so much of this skill. We cannot know how their opinions might have affected him, but as we note below, peer opinions often do make quite a difference.

Two Kinds of Achievement Motivation Notice that the definition we have given implies two distinct kinds of achievement motivation: one that is focused on competence as such, and another that is focused on the judgments that people make about competence (Dweck and Elliott, 1983). The first of these leads children to concentrate on learning as such; they will practice jumping rope, for example, just to see if they can do it. The second kind of motivation, though, orients children much more to performance; in this case, they will practice jumping rope so as to impress others at a later time. For convenience, let us call these two attitudes **learning orientation** and **performance orientation**. In a learning orientation, motivation is intrinsic; it comes from within the learner and the task. In a performance

Intrinsic and external motivation

Perspectives on Issues

Cultural Variations in How to Display Achievement

Over the years, certain ethnic groups have persistently achieved less well in school, on the average, than other ethnic groups. Some experts have regarded this as the result of some sort of deficit in the low-achieving groups; families in these groups, they argue, lack the economic or intellectual resources to help their children to succeed properly in school. This explanation became prominent during the 1960s, and it still guides many educational programs to improve the academic performance of these children (Erikson, 1986).

But whatever its merits, the deficit explanation suffers from a major problem: it ignores important cultural differences in how ethnic groups define the right or best ways for children to display their accomplishments. Normal school practices, it seems, have grown out of certain assumptions about how and when children like to learn and work. Unfortunately for some minority children, these sometimes contradict the expectations and practices of other ethnic cultures. Consider, for example, each of these common teaching practices:

1. *Spotlighting a child* During class discussion, teachers often ask one child to answer a particular question in front of the rest of the class. The other children are supposed to learn by watching this child display knowledge (or ignorance!); the named child is supposed to feel proud of having been selected, at least if he gets the answer right.

2. *Rhetorical questioning* During a discussion, teachers often ask questions to which they already know the answers ("How many states are in the United States?"). Children are supposed to answer these questions even if they realize that the teacher already knows the answer. Rhetorical questioning in fact helps to establish "who's boss" in the class; children acknowledge the teacher's authority by answering rhetorical questions willingly.

3. *Working individually* On the whole, children are supposed to complete assignments alone. Assisting other children significantly without the explicit permission of the teacher is forbidden; it is cheating, rather than a laudable concern for others. Working individually tends to be considered the best expression of achievement, even if it means ignoring the learning needs of classmates some of the time.

But many ethnic groups (and individuals, for that matter) interpret these teaching practices in rather different ways. Spotlighting a child, for example, can seem overly brash and direct, rather too much like interrogating or putting pressure on the child for no good reason. Rhetorical questioning can seem either pointless or arrogant; why should

orientation, the opposite is true: motivation comes not from the learner but from other individuals who may see and evaluate the learner.

The differences between these two orientations show in children who are learning to swim. To the extent that they adopt a learning orientation, they will enjoy the actual activity — practicing new strokes, working up to faster speeds, and so on. They will also feel relatively free to invite criticisms from coaches or fellow swimmers, since these comments can often help them to improve.

But for children who adopt a performance orientation, swimming will be less enjoyable in itself and more a means of winning approval from others. The children will be concerned more with receiving compliments from coaches and swim-

---

an adult ask a child something if the adult already knows the answer to it? And the individualistic emphasis can seem like a callous disregard of cooperation and concern for others. In this view, children not only should help each other to learn but should do so at every opportunity, not just when teachers allow it.

In departing from conventional practices, teachers of several Native American groups have sometimes stimulated higher levels of achievement than usual for such children (Phillips, 1982; Barnhardt, 1982; Erikson and Mohatt, 1982). Observational studies of these classrooms showed a paradox: the Native American children worked harder and talked more if their teachers did *not* demand participation directly, and if the teachers encouraged the children to work in groups as much as possible, rather than individually.

Observational studies of Hawaiian children had much the same results. In these studies, teachers found that achievement improved if they allowed children to interrupt each other during discussions instead of requesting them to speak one at a time (Au and Mason, 1981). Overlapping speech seemed to be customary among Hawaiians; it signified not bad manners, but lively interest in the current topic of conversation. But overlapping speech among Hawaiian children did make "classroom control" in the usual sense difficult to achieve.

Often there were simply too many children talking at once for anyone to be sure where a particular discussion was heading or who was in charge of it. Overlapping speech discouraged the use of the conventional teaching techniques described above; the teachers could not call on one child at a time very conveniently, nor ask rhetorical questions, nor insist on a lot of individual displays of effort.

These findings raise a dilemma for educators: how much should they teach ethnic groups in their preferred cultural styles, and how much should they emphasize the more widespread but alien academic style of most classrooms? Opting for the first strategy may encourage higher achievement, at least in the short term. But it may also prevent children from learning how to function in the mainstream of public education. Opting for conventional academic methods, however, may convey lack of respect for students and their culture, and in this way it may create poor relations between teacher and students and interfere with academic achievement. The best strategy probably therefore mixes both ethnic and mainstream classroom styles. Educators continue to debate what this mixture should consist of in the daily practice of teaching.

ming friends or with performing well in competitive swimming meets. If others do happen to criticize aspects of their swimming, the comments will not be welcome. Ironically, this fact may indirectly limit the children's ability to learn.

This description may make a learning motivation sound more desirable than a performance one, but keep in mind that most of us usually experience a mixture of the two throughout our lives. Like it or not, we all encounter situations in which judgments about achievement compete with achievement itself, such as taking an examination or serving a complicated gourmet dinner to friends. Ignoring these judgments does not really make our lives any happier, although worrying about them unduly can certainly make our lives more miserable.

Achievement Motivation in the Middle Years During the middle years, children become more performance oriented than they were at earlier ages. This change is either a blessing or a curse, depending on how we view it.

Increases in performance orientation

At the beginning of this period, children express considerable optimism about their abilities. Kindergartners tend to rank themselves at the top of their class in scholastic ability, even though they rank other children relatively accurately (Stipek and Hoffman, 1980). This implies a learning orientation; for young children, achievement is something that they do without either the involvement or the evaluations of others (Frieze et al., 1981).

During the next several years, however, children begin believing that whether they have ability depends partly on whether other people give them credit for having it (Ruhland and Feld, 1977). This belief lies at the core of the performance orientation. It does not replace a learning orientation but takes its place alongside it. Being "smart," for example, now partly means that a child's teachers, parents, and friends *say* that she is smart, but it also partly means that she possesses certain skills in reading, mathematics, and the like, regardless of what others say (Feld et al., 1979).

Effects of performance orientation

Achieving successfully, then, becomes more complicated in the middle years. Consider swimming again. Late in infancy and during the preschool years, a child may be motivated to learn to swim simply if she is given chances to experiment in the water. In the middle years, however, she may ask herself what other people, especially parents and friends, will think about learning to swim: will they consider this skill a true achievement? Most people will value swimming to some extent, of course. But whether they do so quite a lot or only a little will depend partly on what values and standards they hold. Even very respectable progress in swimming may not look like much of an achievement if the child's family and friends hold very high athletic standards or if they do not value athletics much in the first place.

In good conditions, though, a performance orientation can help children by motivating them to acquire skills that prove especially valuable later in life. An obvious example is the academic basics, reading and arithmetic. Although some children pick up these skills on their own, many others require a bit of performance motivation in the form of periodic judgments such as grades on tests, teacher comments, and the like. With good teaching, such judgments do not prevent pupils from setting learning-oriented goals as well. As a result, if the academic basics are well taught, large numbers of schoolchildren later acquire other competencies that they might not have picked up spontaneously. After all, a wide range of life skills depend on prior literacy and skill with numbers (Donaldson, 1979).

The shift toward a performance orientation makes children more similar to adults in their achievement motivation. The shift reflects another major social development of childhood, namely the increasing importance of peers, or children of roughly the same age and status. As children grow older, they take others' opinions more and more seriously, and often even seek out those opinions on a variety of matters. Achievement motivation, it turns out, is just one peer-related concern among many.

Checkpoint *Psychodynamic theorists hold that middle years children focus much of their energies on achievement. Research supports this general idea. Children begin the middle years with a learning orientation to achievement, but as they get older, they add a performance orientation, or concern with others' opinions about their achievements.*

Peer Relationships

Throughout childhood, some of the most important relationships involve *peers,* or people of roughly equal age and maturity. As early as age two, children enjoy playing with or next to each other, and by age three or four they often prefer the company of peers, even when adults are available. Time spent with peers increases steadily during the middle years. By late elementary school, children devote about half of their social interactions to peers (Ellis et al., 1981; Barker and Wright, 1955).

What Theorists Say about Peer Relationships

Piaget Many psychological theories emphasize the importance of peers in children's development, especially during the middle years. For example, Piaget argued that peers help children to overcome their egocentrism — their tendency to assume that everyone views the world in the same way as they do (Piaget, 1963). In the course of playing together, children inevitably run into conflicts over toys and priorities, arguing over who should use a new set of felt pens or over what and where they should draw. In settling disagreements like these, they gradually acquire understanding of others' points of view. They also come to understand and value the democratic process, at least in the down-to-earth form of minor haggling and compromise.

Peers help overcome egocentrism

According to Piaget, parents and other authority figures cannot foster these cognitive developments, because they cannot behave like true equals with children.

Often adults give outright orders to children, and although they may give them pleasantly ("Please clean up your room before supper"), they expect compliance, not discussion and negotiation. And even when parents are not acting as managers, they cannot really function as equals with children. For one thing, they often do not have the same leisure interests or tastes; a father may like to play cards after dinner, but his son may prefer to ride bikes with his friends. For another thing, parents' skill levels often do not match those of their children; a mother and daughter may both enjoy cooking, but the child cannot really do it as well as her mother can. The mother can become "equal" with her child only by pretending to be less experienced than she really is.

Peers stimulate cooperation and competition

Harry Stack Sullivan   The most well-developed theory about peers has been proposed by the psychiatrist Harry Stack Sullivan (1953). Like Piaget, Sullivan argues that relationships with peers have fundamentally different qualities from those with adults; in particular, peers stimulate skills in compromise, cooperation, and competition. But unlike Piaget, Sullivan emphasizes the value of peers in promoting emotional health. Peers create a life for children outside their families, and in doing so, they help correct the emotional biases that families inevitably give their children — biases that Sullivan calls emotional **warps.** An eight-year-old with shy, reserved parents, for instance, may learn from peers that not all people are shy and reserved, or a ten-year-old whose parents care little about competitive athletics may discover from peers that athletic competition matters quite a lot to some people.

The first intimate friends

According to Sullivan, this sort of learning occurs during the **juvenile period,** which begins around age five and continues until nine or ten. In this period, children show increasing interest in playmates of similar age and status. As they near the end of the elementary school years, they supposedly focus this interest on just a few select friends of the same sex, whom Sullivan calls *chums.* These relationships provide children with models for later intimate relationships. They also mark the end of the juvenile period and the beginning of what Sullivan calls **preadolescence,** roughly ages ten through twelve. This period, and its "chumships," finishes when puberty begins; at that point, most children become more interested in relationships with the opposite sex, and begin giving less energy to relationships with the same sex.

Limitations of peer relations

Support for Theories about Peer Relationships   Research into peer relationships supports Piaget's and Sullivan's ideas in broad outline, but not in certain specifics. Conflict with peers does stimulate children's progress at solving cognitive problems, as Piaget proposed. Two seven-year-olds do learn from a discussion with each other about whether "the oldest people are always the tallest," for example, but they learn only if they are already thinking at about the same level of maturity (Bell et al., 1985). Otherwise, such discussions easily turn into confrontation and brow-beating, as the more advanced child forces the other to comply with her point of view.

Research also supports Sullivan's claim that playmates and peers matter a lot to schoolchildren. But children's relationships usually do not evolve into intimate chumships toward the end of this period. On the contrary, friendships and peer groups become more complex and diverse during preadolescence (Chapman and Chapman, 1980). Some relationships become closer and more important than others, of course, but rather few actually become intimate in the sense proposed by Sullivan; that is, very few friendships involve sharing children's most private or personal thoughts and feelings. Peer relationships do acquire special intensity just before adolescence, and sometimes even rival family relationships in emotional impact at this time. This fact may account for some of parents' worries about their children "growing up too soon." An eleven-year-old may seem excessively concerned about attending parties, for instance, or a twelve-year-old might taste a can of beer without consulting the traditional authority, his parents.

Functions of Peers

All things considered, peers probably serve a variety of purposes, including some that duplicate the functions of parents. Like parents, peers can give a child a secure emotional base during anxiety-provoking experiences. Sometimes the mere presence of a friend increases a child's confidence in such situations; observing another child being examined by the dentist, for example, tends to calm the observing child when her turn comes (Melamed et al., 1975). Like parents, peers help to define ethical norms for a child. Peers also help to define friendship in particular, although contrary to widespread belief, standards of likability parallel those of adults more often than not (Hartup, 1983). And like parents, peers do a lot of teaching: they show a child how to paint or how to throw a ball. Sometimes schools take advantage of this process by arranging for children to tutor each other in academic skills (Allen, 1976).

In addition to these similarities, though, are several features unique to peer relationships. They are by nature voluntary and involve comparative equals. These facts mean that a child must act in a way that explicitly supports the relationship — be friendly, that is — if he expects the relationship to survive. And he must do so with another individual whose social skills may not be much better, or may sometimes even be a bit worse, than his own. Children apparently understand these differences intuitively, because they typically attribute an obedience orientation to relationships between adults and children, but attribute play and recreation orientations to relationships among children (Youniss, 1980). In acting out a family scene with dolls, for instance, children tend to make adult dolls blame child dolls, or deprive child dolls of privileges, and they tend to make the child dolls demand something of or submissively obey the adult. When acting out a scene between two child dolls, however, children tend to make the dolls play together as equals, and bossiness disappears (Edwards and Lewis, 1979).

Differences between parent and peer relationships

Influences on Peer Group Membership

As implied by the fact that peers are comparatively equal, children's peer groups are not simply random assortments of individuals but are influenced by many fac-

During the middle years, children tend to associate with peers of the same sex. Girls' friendships tend to be more intimate, whereas boys' friendships often reflect male stereotypes. (right, Ulrike Welsch; far right, Andrew Brillant/The Picture Cube)

tors. Three of the most important of these are age, gender, and race or ethnic background of the children. Let us look briefly at each of these in turn.

Age Children do play mostly with others of approximately their own age. But contrary to a common impression, children spend considerable amounts of time with peers who are *not* their own age. One study found that schoolchildren spend anywhere from one quarter to one half of their time with companions who are more than two years older or younger (Ellis et al., 1981). School imposes an upper limit on these cross-age contacts, however, because classrooms usually group children according to age.

Qualities of mixed-age groups

Groups with mixed ages have certain special qualities. Older children show more nurturant behavior, such as tying the shoelaces of a younger child or buttoning her sweater. And younger children show more dependence, by asking for help with schoolwork or agreeing to older peers' preferences as to play activities. In spite of these qualities, however, mixed-age groups tend to be less "sociable" than single-age groups; they chat less or have friendly conversation less often. Furthermore, when group members differ in age, they are less aggressive than children in same-age groups; they get in fewer fights and have fewer arguments (Whiting and Whiting, 1975). All in all, same-age groups encourage the opposites of all these qualities: children give and receive less practical help, show more friendliness to each other, and get into conflicts more often.

Gender segregation

Gender Although mixed-sex play does occur during the elementary school years, first graders generally name children of their own gender as best friends. Observations of younger schoolchildren during free play show that they interact during cooperative play periods about four times as often with children of their own gender as with those of the opposite gender (Serbin et al., 1977). This ratio actually increases as children approach adolescence; by third grade, most peer groups contain only one sex, and by fifth grade, virtually all do.

How do groups of boys differ from groups of girls? In general, boys' play parallels gender stereotypes about maleness: it is louder, more boisterous or active, and more competitive. It includes more rough-and-tumble play or mock fighting. Boys more often play in large groups of at least half a dozen children, and perhaps as a result, they more often play outdoors or in other large, expansive areas such as a gymnasium or a long hallway (DiPietro, 1981; Lever, 1976). Girls, in contrast, more often play in pairs or small groups, and they initiate interactions with members of the opposite sex more often than boys do (Foot et al., 1980).

Structure of boys' and girls' groups

Given these differences, it is not surprising that girls' long-term friendships tend more often toward exclusive intimacy. One study tested this idea by using a **sociometric questionnaire,** which is a written ballot that invited children to name their best friends (Hallinan, 1981; Eder and Hallinan, 1978). Tabulations of the friendship patterns showed differences between the boys and the girls, as illustrated in Figure 13-1. Compared to the boys, the girls more often made mutual exclusive choices (**dyads,** as in Figure 13-1), and all-girl triads, in which a third girl's choice was not reciprocated, occurred more often too. Boys more often formed patterns in which no choice was reciprocated. Several boys might pick each other as friends, for example, as illustrated in Figure 13-1, even though not one was picked in return. Judging by these choices, therefore, boys spread their social attention widely, and girls tend to focus it on just a few individuals. Stated differently, boys' friendships tend to be extensive, and girls' tend to be intensive.

Friendship patterns of boys and girls

To a large extent, children acquire preferences for their own gender even before they begin school. Even toddlers tend to play longer and more happily with other toddlers of the same sex (Jacklin and Maccoby, 1978). Later, when children begin

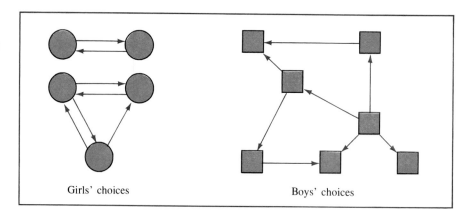

Figure 13–1 Typical Patterns of Peer Friendships in Girls and Boys

Girls' choices   Boys' choices

A Talk with a Teacher

Boy-Girl Differences in Peer Groups and Play

Linda Maleska is a fourth-grade teacher at a "follow-through" elementary school that serves students from Head Start preschool and kindergarten programs from all over the city, as well as children from the neighborhood in which the school is located. She was interviewed in her classroom toward the end of the school year.

INTERVIEWER: How would you describe peer relations among fourth graders?

LINDA: Often children's academic ability sets the tone and pace for their friendships. Children who do well academically tend to be friends with other kids who are bright.

INTERVIEWER: Why do you think this is so?

LINDA: In part because of parent pressure. Parents are interested in their children having good friends. Another reason may be that much of the teaching here occurs in small skill groups, which enable children with the same academic needs to work together. When we go outside

for recess, the children do tend to stay in those same groups.

INTERVIEWER: What other factors seem to influence peer groups?

LINDA: Boy-girl differences are very important. As much as I've tried to encourage girls to play football or soccer and boys to do other things like four-square and jump-rope, it really does break down sexually as to how they play outside. Girls tend to play jump-rope and boys tend to play soccer on the field — that is almost automatic. Girls also tend to go to the swings and slide much more than the boys.

INTERVIEWER: Why do you think this happens?

LINDA: Girls are getting, at this age, more social, much less reliant on an adult for any kind of ideas or suggestions about what to do outside. They are much more self-reliant. Their play is also more directly social and interactive. Often I see girls walking slowly and talking. Or they'll make up clapping games. There are a lot of hand-clapping

games. Even their jump-rope is more consistently interactive and coordinated — with turn taking and things like that — than the boys' play.... They like to use the swings and to play ... four-square. And that involves a lot of verbal interaction and social coordination.

INTERVIEWER: Can you describe four-square?

LINDA: There are four people standing in a 10-foot-by-10-foot square drawn in chalk and divided into four squares. And the person in the fourth square is in control of whatever the category will be. So, that person will say "colors." She will bounce the ball into any of the other players' squares and they will have to name a color and catch the ball, or they are out.

INTERVIEWER: There's a rhythm to it?

LINDA: You have to keep the rhythm and you can't name the same color twice (if color is the category), or animal, country, movie star, or whatever the category is.

school, teachers do more than simply tolerate these pre-existing gender preferences; they reinforce same-sex groupings of children when they occur (Fagot, 1977, 1982). Teachers are especially likely to do so if the group is doing something that is traditionally gender-specific. If several girls are playing with dolls, for example, a teacher is more likely to compliment them than several boys, or even a mixed boy-girl group, who are doing so. To some extent, such experiences may help create conscious gender stereotypes in the minds of children.

Race and Ethnic Background   Racial preference and prejudice are a fact of life in much of our society, and middle years children are not immune from it (Asher et al., 1982). One study found racial preference suggested in who sat with whom at an elementary school cafeteria (Schofield and Sugar, 1977). The cafeteria served

Racial preferences among peers

They get more complex as the year goes on. They almost always start the year with colors and by the end of the year it will be something much more specific, for example, Madonna's songs or rock stars. This group of girls also made up a real great hand-clapping game about music groups, and the way they thought it all through and the rules that were made up were fascinating.

INTERVIEWER: What are the boys doing?

LINDA: They are playing soccer and kickball, building forts, or surfboards, if they can. They may also be collecting things and investigating the environment. For example, at the beginning of the year we studied insects and their natural habitats in science. And once the boys got outside, they tried to find every single little bug they could, and they would come and show it.

INTERVIEWER: It seems that fourth-grade boys are less interested in made-up games than girls.

LINDA: Yes, that is true. Girls are much more likely to create their own games and rules which involve social interaction. Boys tend to play games which emphasize physical rather than social interaction and where they follow rules that are already made up for them.

INTERVIEWER: How permanent are these peer group patterns?

LINDA: They seem to be long-lasting. The group I described was made up of five girls who are very, very close. They're all good students and all white. They're into fads. They're into Madonna, the singer, and even come to school dressed up like her, although I think that is somewhat going by the wayside now. I've been trying to encourage them to interact with other people more because they are sort of the clique of the class.

INTERVIEWER: Are there other things that teachers do to encourage greater interaction?

LINDA: Yes. One of the things our school works to achieve is to have

children interact in a way that does not break down along sex-role or racial lines. What I do in school is to try and compensate for that. I talk to them about it, very up-front, and I say that I think there should be more interaction between boys and girls and blacks and whites. So when we have social studies activities, the rule is that groups will be mixed. The children understand this and help make it work.

Follow-up Questions

1. How closely do the girl-boy differences described parallel those described in the chapter?

2. According to Linda, what are the main ways in which girls' play and boys' play differ?

3. Do you agree with Linda's approach to reducing cliques based on gender and race? What suggestions do you have?

4. How do the perceptions of Linda, a teacher, compare with those of Rebecca, a student (whose interview appears elsewhere in this chapter)?

about 250 students, about half of whom were black and half of whom were white. With these numbers, about one hundred cross-race seatings — blacks and whites sitting next to or across from one another — would have occurred if race had made no difference to the students. In fact, though, only about a quarter of this number actually occurred. In this situation, racial preference was clearly visible.

This kind of preference is also revealed when children name best friends, as in the sociometric procedure described earlier in this section. Children nominate people of their own race more often than people of another race, particularly if their own race is the majority one and the other race is a minority (in the United States, usually black or Hispanic). The trend begins in the preschool years and becomes stronger throughout the middle years and adolescence (Singleton and Asher, 1979; Asher et al., 1982). The pattern may reflect not a general dislike, however, but only cautiousness about having a best friend of another race. When children instead nominate their "best playmate" or "best working partner," they choose someone of another race more frequently.

Difference between gender and racial prejudice

Note that even though children segregate themselves both by race and by gender, the two prejudices differ significantly in nature and origin. Much gender prejudice in childhood appears to cover up children's implicit belief that eventually they will have to reconcile themselves to living with the opposite sex. This expectation is betrayed by the way in which children avoid the opposite sex; their behavior contains large amounts of good-natured teasing, as well as poorly disguised interest in actual sexual activity. Children seem intuitively to sense that gender segregation will not last forever (Schofield, 1981).

This is not the case for racial prejudice. Unlike the sexes, different races do not usually grow up in the same families, nor often in the same neighborhoods. And more often than not, they do not expect to live in the same families or neighborhoods when they become adults. Unlike gender segregation, therefore, racial segregation can easily persist across the lifespan and is often strongly supported by social circumstances. For this reason, some professionals who work with children consider it the more serious social problem of the two.

Popularity, Social Acceptance, and Rejection

Early in the middle years, children begin to evaluate one another in various ways. By second and third grade, children already hold cultural stereotypes about body build; for example, they judge boys who are muscular more favorably than boys who are fat or thin (Staffieri, 1972). Easily noticed characteristics are quite important to acceptance in the early grades, when having the "right" kind of hair can help, as can having a name that sounds attractive. As children get older, they choose their friends increasingly on the basis of personal qualities such as honesty, kindness, humor, and creativity (Furman and Bierman, 1983; Reaves and Roberts, 1983). They still evaluate one another, however, and confer more popularity on some children than on others.

The Popular Child Well-liked children are good at initiating and maintaining social interactions, and at understanding social situations (Asher et al., 1982).

They recognize that group acceptance is not automatic but a slow process which takes work and patience. As one eight-year-old said, "You can't go up to kids who are playing and say, 'That's no good; let's do something different.' You have to do it their way for a while — and sometimes a long while."

Popular children are viewed by their peers as being confident, good-natured, and energetic (Hartup, 1983). Highly visible abilities and achievements help — especially in athletics, but also in academics or social activities. Nice clothing and special material possessions, such as an expensive digital watch, also influence status with peers. Some of these assets (like athletic ability) remain valuable to children as they move into adolescence, and others (like the digital watch) may not. But during childhood, such advantages create prestige for individual children within particular peer groups and also make membership in the "best" or highest-status groups possible.

The Unpopular Child Peers describe unpopular children as unpleasant, disruptive, selfish, and aggressive (Coie et al., 1982). Such children tend to be actively disliked and excluded from activities. All schoolchildren, it seems, struggle to control aggressive and selfish impulses, in order to make themselves more likable. Unpopular children, by their nature, make this struggle more difficult. One child described the problem this way: "When Ginny doesn't get to play, she grabs things — like the checker pieces we were using today. Then the other kids feel like they have to grab things too, just to get them back. And then no one feels good any-

Social abilities of popular children

Social deficits of unpopular children

more." In contrast, well-liked children are more likely to use indirect approaches to get what they want: "When Sonia sees you playing checkers, she just stands there, waiting for you to finish. She doesn't say anything until it's time for the next game."

Friends During the early middle years, children base friendships on shared interests and activities, on exchanges of possessions, and on concrete supportive behaviors (Selman, 1981a). "A friend," according to one six-year-old, "is someone who plays what *you* want to play." And another says, "A friend lets you use his painting set." These comments emphasize the child's own needs rather than the friend's. But even when both parties are considered, friendships among younger school-age

---

A Talk with Rebecca

Peer Relationships During the Middle Years

Rebecca is a fifth grader. She is a good student and is involved in a variety of activities, including music, soccer, and writing.

INTERVIEWER: What can you remember about friendships and social relationships when you first started school?

REBECCA: Well, in kindergarten and first grade, everything is sort of loose. It's your first year with a big group of kids in a real class in a "real school." Everybody feels really proud of themselves. You don't worry about boy-girl stuff or about cliques or anything. You're just friendly and no one is smart enough to figure things out like that. I mean you don't have the brains to think that this kid is weird. Nobody teases you, even if you do something stupid like knock over a can of paint. Outside of school it's about the same.

INTERVIEWER: How do you decide whom to play with?

REBECCA: You don't have to. You just hang around and play with whoever is available. You don't have many cliques.

INTERVIEWER: What about popularity?

REBECCA: There's popular and unpopular, but you don't know it. ... You don't know the words. Popular would be like someone who doesn't have to worry about getting a turn at the paint easel. Unpopular would be someone who sort of has to cut in and be a little obnoxious to have their chance. If you're obnoxious or mean, the kids can sense it. Some kids will say so, because they're not uptight. Other kids will just sort of ignore you.

INTERVIEWER: Do things change in second grade?

REBECCA: In second grade, you start realizing that it's not just who is nice and who isn't. You start to notice how kids dress and who combs their hair or not and who is smarter or not and who comes in to school wearing sneakers and who comes in wearing fashionable boots and things like that. You start thinking, well, I'm still wearing mit-

tens, not gloves, and you start being a little bit more conscious of the way you look and the way you feel.

You become more conscious about what you say. You don't say, "Joanne isn't good at this. She just can't do it!" Instead you say, "Sometimes she does it right and sometimes she doesn't," you know. ... You are real careful about what you say and how you say it because you start learning that kids are going to turn it right back at you. You begin to know that there are kids who are popular and kids who are in the "bottom" or least popular group.

INTERVIEWER: And what happens next?

REBECCA: When you're in third grade, there really are groups.

INTERVIEWER: How did they work?

REBECCA: There were fads and if you didn't go along with them you weren't right. You were out of the group for a couple of weeks. Then when it started slowing down, they took you back in and sort of regained their senses and started to

children tend to focus on practical behaviors rather than on psychological qualities:

TONY, age eight: Benjy, if you share your galactica rocket with me, I'll be your friend.

BENJY, also age eight: Give me another piece of candy, will you? Then we'll see.

TONY: But I already gave you three pieces. It's time that I got to play with your rocket.

BENJY: It's really *my* rocket.

---

give you another chance. And the next time a fad came in, you stayed with it. You're not gonna get kicked out again. You learned your lesson.

INTERVIEWER: And in fourth grade?

REBECCA: By fourth grade you have already formed solid groups and those groups are kept. They are not changed at all. You aren't going to be friends with somebody that's really obnoxious or who is in the *lowest* group forever! You don't do that. That's too much of a risk, no matter how well respected you are.

INTERVIEWER: Do boys and girls play together?

REBECCA: Starting in third grade, boys and girls hardly ever play together, but in fourth and fifth grade you just don't do it.

INTERVIEWER: How come?

REBECCA: Because if you do, you will get teased by the other kids. In fourth and fifth grades you also begin trying to find "friend-friends" — real friends that you can really trust and be really good friends with

like grown-ups can. Also you can really tell the popular kids from the other kids now. They come in with all the fancy clothes and all the confidence and they're always good at sports and singing or unbelievably good at something that's not academic. You can't be good at spelling or reading to be popular. You can be great at drawing, but you can't get popular with it because it's not noticeable enough.

INTERVIEWER: What if you like a kid who is not popular?

REBECCA: You have to even out how you divide your time between the popular and unpopular kids if you want to avoid getting permanently in one group. The kids are just beginning to be really cruel to the unpopular kids. It's awfully hard to speak up for someone who is getting teased because you don't know whether you will get somebody to back you up or whether you will be all alone. If they're popular and you're not all that popular, they can get the whole fifth grade down on you.

INTERVIEWER: Not a very good situation.

REBECCA: It's funny. We're all friends, but underneath there's a lot of tension. It's like when two friends start teasing each other a little bit. One says something good-naturedly, but it hurts. Then the other teases back, and pretty soon it gets to be too much and it's a big fight. Of course, they eventually do make up.

Follow-up Questions

1.   How closely do Rebecca's observations parallel the discussion of peers and friendship in this chapter?

2.   According to Rebecca, what are the sources of popularity during the middle years? In what ways have they changed since you were her age?

3.   In what ways might a boy describe peer relations differently than Rebecca? Which of Rebecca's observations might hold true for both boys and girls?

4.   Would you consider Rebecca a "typical" fifth grader? Why or why not?

TONY: I *am* your friend, you know. So you should give me a turn.

BENJY: Not now. Maybe later. Where's the candy?

Exchanging favors and sharing activities continues to matter as children get older, but by the time they enter the fifth and sixth grades, children place more emphasis on psychological qualities such as intimacy, trust, mutual support, and loyalty (Youniss and Volpe, 1978). Actually doing the same things or sharing the same objects becomes correspondingly less important.

Concepts of friendship

To some extent this change reflects children's increasing ability to coordinate social perspectives, which means that they can increasingly see themselves as others view them. Younger children realize that in many situations, two people see things differently, but they nonetheless have trouble coordinating their own perspective with that of a friend. As a result, they often alternate between trying to change their friend's viewpoint to fit their own and trying to make themselves feel the same way as their friends.

By second or third grade, children become more able to live with differing perspectives within their friendships, and feel less forced to choose between one or the other. By fifth or sixth grade, children can even adopt an independent or third-party perspective, comparing their own point of view with their friends' (Selman, 1980). As one eleven-year-old put it about a good friend, "He thinks that I don't study enough, and that he studies just about the right amount for schoolwork. But you know what *I* think? I think that I'm just trying to keep schoolwork from bothering me too much, and that *he* works too hard. I wonder what the teachers think." Judging by statements like this one, friendship at this stage appears to be an intimate collaboration of two people who are mutually committed to building the relationship, which has acquired an importance beyond the particular needs of either friend.

Conformity to Peers

Because peer groups involve social equals, they give children unique opportunities to develop their own beliefs without having parents or older siblings dominate or dismiss them. But in doing so, peer groups also present challenges. Acceptance and support by the group matter intensely to children, who are still learning what kind of people they are and who are still acquiring the skills needed to deal with others. As a result, peer groups often influence their members very strongly indeed: they demand conformity to group expectations in return for continued acceptance and prestige.

Negative effects of peer pressure

Pressures to conform sometimes leads children to violate personal values or needs, or those of parents and other adult authorities (Fine, 1982). A child might feel pressured into paying dues that she cannot afford, or into joining fights that she does not want to participate in, or into shunning children who do not belong to her own group. Another might feel pressured to wear clothes that his parents consider outrageous, or to perform poorly at school. In return for these behaviors and attitudes, the children remain in good standing with their peers.

Note, however, that peer groups can exert positive pressures as well. For example, they can encourage athletic achievement above and beyond what physical education teachers can produce in their students, and they can create commitments to fairness and reciprocity, at least within an immediate circle of peers: "When someone buys a candy bar at the drugstore, she shares it with the rest of us. Then we do the same thing the next time, if *we* get something nice." Whether the pressures are positive or negative, however, peer groups offer a key setting for acquiring social skills, for evaluating and managing personal relationships, and for handling competition and cooperation.

Positive effects of peer pressure

Checkpoint *Peers play a unique role during the middle years in fostering cooperation and competition and in laying the basis for more intimate relations later on in life. The structure and behavior of peer groups vary according to the age and gender of the children in them, and groups tend to segregate by gender and race. Children are generally popular with their peers if they are confident and socially skillful, and unpopular if they are aggressive, bossy, or selfish. Groups can and do exert pressure on children to conform, but the pressure can have either positive or negative effects on individual children.*

Family Relationships

In spite of the growing importance of peers, families continue to influence children's development strongly during the middle years. Their influence differs in nature from peers', however, because of parents' much greater material power and psychological maturity. To some extent, the material and psychological gaps between parent and child dominate all families. At the same time, though, the circumstances and organization of particular families creates variations in family relationships.

How Parents Influence Children

Even though children probably do influence their parents to some extent, most of the influence goes the other way, from parent to child, even in the middle years (Radin, 1982). Parents influence children in at least six different ways:

1. *Modeling of behaviors* Whether they intend to or not, parents often demonstrate or model a variety of behaviors that children later imitate. Some parents curse when they are angry; they should not be surprised if they hear the very same words from their children when their children get angry. But desirable behaviors are also modeled; if parents give lots of affectionate hugs when they feel happy, they may see pleasingly similar behavior developing in their children.

---

2. *Giving rewards and punishments* Parents influence their children by praising some of their behaviors and disapproving of others. A boy who is playing football with his friends may earn an approving comment from one of his parents, whereas a boy who is learning to draw may elicit indifference, or even a look of disgust and a comment like "What are you doing *that* for?" (Maccoby, 1980). To some extent, children learn sex-appropriate behaviors in this way.

3. *Direct instruction* Sometimes parents simply tell their children how to act: "Don't pinch your brother"; "Come straight home from school without talking to any strangers." Much of the time, children seem to learn from such instruction (Radin, 1982).

4. *Stating rules* Over and over, parents state general rules such as "In this family, everyone washes his or her own dishes." Children are supposed to deduce correct behavior by comparing the rule with the situation at hand ("Did I forget to wash my dishes this time?").

5. *Reasoning* In exasperated moments, parents may question their children's capacity to reason, but in fact parents often use reasoning to influence children anyway. For example, they might remind their children of gaps between their behavior and their values ("Is yelling at her a good way to make friends?"). Or they might define and label activities in ways calculated to influence behavior ("You did badly on the test because you didn't study hard enough, not because you're dumb.")

6. *Providing materials and settings* Parents can affect children's behavior by controlling materials and settings. They can buy certain things, like a computer instead of new clothing, or they can offer situations, like a place to do homework but not a place to keep pets. These influences make some behaviors more likely to occur than others.

Notice, however, that in spite of their importance, these six methods are not really unique to parents. Peers also use them. How, then, do relationships with parents differ from those with peers? The answer lies not in the methods of influence but in how parents and children view their relationship.

The Separate Perspectives of Parent and Child

In getting along together, children and parents approach their relationship in very different ways. For the most part, parents already know how social relationships work, whereas their child is trying to discover this for the first time. This gap makes misunderstandings almost certain (Sullivan, 1953). Because of their maturity, parents cannot help but regard social relationships as multifaceted and as unfolding over long periods of time. As a result, every action of their child, however simple, seems full of potential meanings. If the child resists going to school for two days in a row, parents are likely to wonder why. *Is he developing a permanent dislike of school? Is he socially clumsy, and therefore unable to find friends? Did I say something wrong before breakfast this morning?* Like it or not, layers of meaning present themselves for parents' consideration.

How parents view social relationships

Children bring much less understanding to their social relationships, and in fact look to their parents to gain more of that understanding. Unfortunately, developing social sensitivity and skill can prove very confusing. On one occasion, parents may say that getting angry is acceptable, but on another occasion, they may say that it is not. Many social skills do not seem to be open for discussion or modification; if a child interrupts her father when he is talking to a friend, he is likely to insist that his daughter follow his rule of etiquette (namely, "Don't interrupt"). If the parent discusses this rule at all, he is likely to do so only to persuade the child to comply, not because he is really open to applying a different rule of etiquette.

How children view social relationships

From a child's viewpoint, therefore, getting along with parents — and with most other adults, for that matter — can seem like the old game of blind man's bluff, in which a blindfolded child searches clumsily for some person or object. In this case, the child searches for the "right" way to conduct his social relationships. If he blunders socially, he may simply have to keep hunting for better, more socially acceptable actions, and pass up any hope of understanding his mistakes in the short run (Youniss, 1980). This happens because many social rules and conventions are based on subtleties that escape children's understanding. Parents may urge a child always to tell the truth, but the rule actually has many exceptions, such as when a person needs to be tactful. Or parents may repeat the rule "If you can't say something nice, don't say anything at all." But there are many exceptions to this one, too; sometimes people do need to tell someone that his or her behavior is very unacceptable.

The Quality of Parent-Child Relationships in the Middle Years

As middle-years children gradually learn more about their parents' attitudes and motivations and the reasons for family rules, they become more able to control their behavior. This change has a major impact on the quality of relations between school-age children and their parents. Parents find themselves monitoring the moment-to-moment behavior of their children less than in earlier years. They don't always have to watch carefully as their kids pour themselves a glass of milk, and they don't always have to remind them to use the toilet before they go out.

Less close surveillance

Nevertheless, parents do continue to monitor children's efforts to take care of themselves but in more indirect ways (Maccoby, 1984). Instead of simply arranging for a child's friend to visit, parents increasingly use comments like "If you want to have Lin over next week, you'd better call by tomorrow." And instead of helping their child to put on each item of clothing in the morning, they will more likely confine themselves to some simple reminder ("It's time to get dressed"), on the assumption that the child can take care of the details of dressing.

More distant monitoring

These changes contribute to one of the stereotypes of parenting during the middle years: that it just consists of fixing meals, providing taxi service, and enforcing a few rules. In reality, this stereotype does not take into account the activities that parents and children often still do together, ranging from grocery shopping to holiday celebrations. And it also does not take into account the emotional ties that underlie these activities. If children have become securely attached during the preschool years, they and their parents often enjoy each other's company more than ever during the middle years.

By this period, parents and children have accumulated a backlog or history of experiences together, and this shared history makes family relations increasingly unique and meaningful. One study documented this idea by analyzing letters that school-age children wrote to a local newspaper about "What Makes Mom Great." Many of the children said that they valued their mother's enduring presence in their lives (Weisz, 1980); "She is always there to listen," said one child. And they also valued the empathy or sensitivity that their mother provided; "She always seems to know how I feel." Judging by comments like these, the bonds between parents and children are normally very strong during the middle years.

Special feelings between parents and children

The Changing Nature of Modern Families

Until recently, the popular stereotype of a typical family contained four people: a father who worked, a mother who cared full-time for the family, and two children. Whether or not this norm ever really existed in the past, it certainly does not exist anymore. Only about 15 percent of today's North American families consist of these particular individuals playing these particular roles (Masnick and Bane, 1980). Significant changes have occurred in recent decades, both in the composition of families and in how families earn the money that they need.

More mothers working

During this period, mothers have begun working outside the home in large numbers (U.S. Department of Labor, Bureau of Labor Statistics, 1981). In 1940, less than 10 percent of mothers with children younger than eighteen did so. The numbers have increased steadily since then; by 1980, almost 60 percent of mothers worked outside their homes. The figure is lower among mothers with very young children, but even in their case the proportions have become substantial; in 1980, about one quarter of all mothers of preschool-age children were employed outside their homes, at least part-time. Figure 13-2 summarizes this trend. If current increases continue, then by the year 2000, an even larger majority of mothers of children under eighteen will work.

More parents divorcing

Divorce has also become much more common (see Figure 13-3). Recent figures show about one third of all marriages in the United States end in divorce (Emery et al., 1984). Something over half of these divorces involve children under the age of eighteen. If this trend continues, by the end of this century about one third of all children born in North America will experience their parents' divorce sometime during their childhood (Select Committee on Children, Youth, and Families, 1983). And a significant percentage of children will experience a remarriage, which often creates a **blended family:** a combination of stepchildren, stepparents, and stepsiblings.

These changes have raised new questions about children's development. How does divorce affect children in the family? And how (if at all) do the increased demands of employment affect children's relationships with their parents?

Divorce and Its Effects on Children   Most parents who divorce must make major adjustments in their lives, and these adjustments often affect their children deeply.

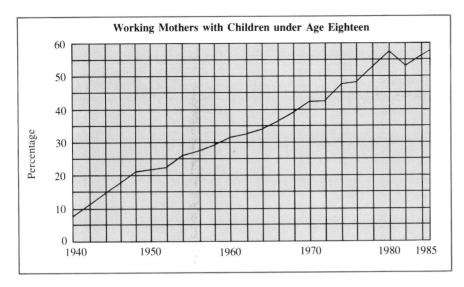

Figure 13-2 Working Mothers with Children under Age Eighteen, 1940-1985

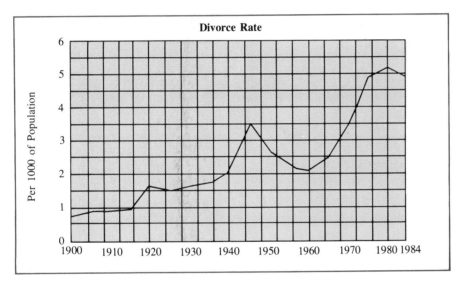

Figure 13-3 Percentage of U.S. Marriages Ending in Divorce, 1900-1982

First, many divorcing parents face sudden economic pressures. Some find themselves financially responsible for two households, that of their former spouse and children and that of a new spouse and children. Others (especially some mothers) find themselves responsible for only one household, but for the first time in their lives or in many years, they bear sole responsibility. Many divorcing parents have to take on new or additional employment to meet these responsibilities, and even so, their standard of living frequently declines, often severely.

Second, the parent who takes major custody of the children must learn to manage a household alone, which is a major physical and psychological burden. Now there is no one with whom to share household chores, particularly if the children are very young. And there is no one to confide in about problems in child-rearing or household management. To a recently divorced parent, it may seem like scant

Economic pressures on parents

Housework pressures on parents

When a marriage breaks down, it can be especially hard on children. What is this girl thinking and feeling about her parents' argument? (Erika Stone/Photo Researchers)

comfort that the former spouse didn't share much of the housework in the months leading up to the divorce anyway.

Isolation of parents

Third, some parents may feel deeply isolated from relatives or friends to whom they used to feel close. If relatives do live nearby, divorcing parents must often rely on them for the first time, simply to procure help with child care and household work. Yet these helpers may not approve of the divorce.

For most families, these pressures create considerable stress for at least two or three years following separation (Hetherington et al., 1982). Even before actual separation and divorce, such families go through long periods of distress, tension, and discord. Nearly half of divorced parents, in fact, separate and reconcile at least once before they finally separate permanently (Kitson and Raschke, 1981).

Divided loyalties for children

During all this time, children must endure several problems not of their own making. For one thing, they face problems of divided loyalty: loving, helping, or spending time with one parent often seems to alienate the other parent. In the months preceding a separation, this problem often arises because of inconsistent discipline. A mother may forbid her children to watch a certain television show, for example, "because it is too violent," but her husband may permit or even encourage them to watch it "because it is just a show." Opposing expectations like this can persist for long periods, because the parents communicate very little, or because one parent may want to prove himself (or herself) more likable or authoritative than the other parent. No matter which parent "wins" in this situation, the children lose; they necessarily must displease at least one parent.

For another thing, marital breakups can make children feel deeply lonely and isolated from their parents. Parents are preoccupied with their distress about the marriage; as a result, they may withdraw from their children emotionally or otherwise be unable to exercise their parental responsibilities effectively. Even when they are not withdrawn, they might have bitter and hurtful outbursts in front of the children. These scenes encourage children to be emotionally cautious, and thus leave them lonelier than ever. Unfortunately, such behavior also provides undesirable models of how to handle social conflicts, by demonstrating aggressive confrontation rather than compromise and respect for the people with whom you disagree (Emery, 1982).

Isolation of children from parents

On the whole, boys and girls tend to respond differently to divorce. Boys often become more aggressive and willful during the period surrounding a separation and divorce, possibly because they accept male sex roles in their response to stress. But they also often lose access to the parent with whom they identify most strongly, their father; the majority of divorced children live with their mothers (Santrock and Warshak, 1979). Even in intact families, boys tend to be disciplined relatively more by both parents jointly; so during a divorce, boys tend to become victims of power struggles and inconsistencies in matters of discipline.

Special effects on boys

Girls' responses are less obvious than boys'. Some studies suggest that girls become *less* aggressive as a result of divorce, that they tend to worry more about schoolwork, and that they often take on more household responsibilities (Block et al., 1981). These changes could mean that they are **internalizing,** or holding inside, any stress they feel about their parents' divorce, by trying to act more helpful and responsible than usual. Other research suggests that daughters of divorced parents develop a continuing preoccupation with their relationships with males; for example, such girls tend to become involved earlier — sometimes before the end of elementary school — in dating, and they engage in more sexual activities at earlier ages, than other girls do (Wallerstein and Kelly, 1980).

Special effects on girls

Who Has Custody? In these conditions, it is not surprising that relationships between parents and children deteriorate during and immediately after a divorce. The parent with chief custody of the children (usually the mother) finds herself dealing not only with her children but also with major new responsibilities for earning a living and making peace, at least in her mind, with the fact of divorce. The children may need more reassurance than usual, even though the mother feels less able to give it. These circumstances can create willfulness and aggression in some children, and withdrawal or anxiety in others.

Impact of custody

Parents without custody of the children (usually fathers) do not face these daily hassles, but they do report feeling rootless and dissatisfied and as though they have been unfairly cut off from their children. Seeing his children once a week may not really allow a father to know them intimately. Over the long run, therefore, noncustodial parents may feel increasingly awkward about something as simple as dinner-table conversation, and increasingly reliant on special events, like going to Disneyland, for whatever contacts do occur. Over the long run, too, noncustodial parents report feeling that their financial and emotional support for their children goes unappreciated. Perhaps for these reasons, fathers often actually increase the

Impact of not having custody

amount of time they spend with their children immediately after divorce; yet they soon decrease such time well below what it was before the divorce (Furstenberg et al., 1982).

Sometimes these problems can be alleviated by **joint custody** of children, in which the parents divide their child-rearing responsibilities relatively equally. The exact mechanics of the division vary with the circumstances of the family. The children may live with each parent during alternate weeks, parts of weeks, or even parts of the year. In other cases, especially when the children are relatively old, one or more children may live with one parent, and the other or others with the other

Methods for sharing custody

Perspectives on Research

The Psychological Tasks Facing Children of Divorce

Since 1971, Judith Wallerstein and her colleagues have been studying divorce and its consequences in sixty divorcing families and their 131 children, aged three to eighteen. The families were first interviewed at the time of the decision to separate and again at one year after separation. Fifty-eight of the families were seen again five years after separation, and fifty-one families and ninety-eight children were interviewed again after ten years (Wallerstein and Kelly, 1980).

According to Wallerstein, the typical child's experience of divorce is similar to the experience of a child who loses a parent through death or whose community is destroyed by a natural disaster. Such children have strong feelings of anger, vulnerability, sorrow, abandonment, and a fear of being unloved. Each divorce disrupts close family relationships and threatens the security of the family structure, and each results in an acute, time-limited crisis followed by an extended period of disequilibrium. Each also has a long-lasting impact on multiple areas of family life. Therefore, the child of divorce must master an additional set of challenges as well as the common tasks of childhood. Although the emotional climate in the family and the degree to which the parents have resolved their problems are important, the child must carry the major burden of mastering and resolving these tasks and issues on the way to successfully achieving adulthood.

Wallerstein and her colleagues propose six psychological tasks that all children of divorce must master.

Task 1. *Acknowledging the reality of the marital rupture* This requires the child successfully to overcome the powerful denial that she subconsciously uses to defend herself against vivid and terrifying fantasies of parental abandonment and disaster. The child accomplishes this by learning to separate fantasy and reality, thereby achieving a greater degree of safety and freedom from anxiety.

Task 2. *Disengaging from parental conflict and distress and resuming customary pursuits* This poses a dual challenge to the child, who must actively and painfully remove herself emotionally from parental distress and conflict to safeguard her individual identity and separate life course. The pervasive sense of desolation that children experience before they do so is vividly expressed by the children themselves. Arthur, a nine-year-old, soberly told interviewers, "I'm at a dead end in the middle of nowhere." Roberta, age seven, volunteered sadly, "No one likes me because I don't have a house."

Task 3. *Resolution of loss* This often takes many years. Children must learn to live with the loss of a parent, which leads them to feel that "my father left because I was not lovable." The voluntary nature of both the divorce and the parent's departure

parent (though perhaps this should really be called divided custody). In still other cases, the children may reside in a house or apartment and the parents take turns living with them.

But none of these arrangements is ideal. Most of them assume that divorced parents still live close enough geographically to make frequent exchanges possible. Most also assume that the parents still trust each other enough after the divorce to support equal sharing of the children. And joint custody does not always please the children; often they must shuffle between two schools and two sets of friends, even when they are only moving between different parts of the same city.

---

makes divorce more difficult to deal with than the death of a parent, which is involuntary. For many children of divorce, the secret feeling of rejection makes it difficult to overcome their sense of unlovableness and unworthiness. The task of mourning their loss is greatly helped by regular and reliable contacts with the absent parent, which allow parent and child to restore a sense of psychological wholeness and rightness in their new part-time relationship.

Task 4. *Resolving anger and self-blame* This task reflects the discovery that children and adolescents do not believe in no-fault divorce. They may blame one or both parents or themselves, and the anger they experience is likely to be intense and long-lasting. It keeps them alienated from their parents and is frequently associated with delinquency, difficulty in school, and failure to achieve, particularly when children reach adolescence. The cooling of anger and the child's growing capacity to forgive herself and one or both parents are central to achievement of this task.

Task 5. *Accepting the permanence of the divorce* This requires the child to give up his deeply felt fantasy of parental reunion. The task is made more difficult if both parents are available and if one or both parents harbor similar fantasies. The child's fantasies yield to reality, however, as he makes and consolidates a clear psychological sepa-

ration between self and parent during the adolescent years.

Task 6. *Achieving realistic, hope-regarding relationships* Successful completion of this task may be most important both for the child and society. Here the young person must reach and sustain a realistic vision of her own capacity to love and be loved. She must bring together and integrate the results of her earlier coping efforts, so the task can stimulate many of the conflicts and feelings of previous stages.

Even though these tasks are listed in a particular order here, they actually tend to occur together. Acknowledging the reality of marital rupture, for example, often recurs long after the actual separation, when a child is also working to achieve realistic new relationships with her separated parents. From a child's perspective, in fact, getting fully over a divorce may seem to be an endless task. Fortunately, though, the hardest of the adjustments do not take forever; a relatively normal life can (and does) continue for a majority of the children of divorce.

Blended Families Most parents who get divorced remarry within a few years, creating what some call reconstituted or **blended families.** The new relationships in these families pose challenges for the children of both parents. The most common type of blended family occurs when a mother marries a man who does not have custody of his children by a previous marriage. In these situations, the stepfather and stepchildren must somehow acknowledge the previous attachments that they bring to the new family. Children must recognize and accept that their new stepfather has other children, about whom he cares a great deal, living somewhere else. And the new husband must recognize and accept that his stepchildren have another, "real" father somewhere, and strong attachments to their mother.

Relationships with stepparents

Perhaps because of these complications, stepfathers initially tend toward extremes in their involvement with their stepchildren: either they remain aloof, or they get so involved as to seem restrictive to the children (Zill, 1983). Eventually, many stepfathers find an appropriate middle ground for involvement, especially if the mother helps them to do so, but it may take them as long as two years. Love and sensitivity do not occur automatically or immediately in blended families.

Relationships among stepsiblings

More difficult challenges arise when both parents bring children from previous marriages to live in the same household. The children must learn to get along not only with the parents, but also with each other, in spite of the prolonged distress of previous divorces. Parents in this sort of blended family report especially high rates of stress and daily conflict, at least during the first year or two of the new marriage (Hetherington et al., 1982). This fact is not surprising, given the complexities of the new relationships. The two families almost surely use somewhat different standards of discipline, for example, and they were probably inconsistent about these standards during the period surrounding their divorces. When the parents begin a new family together, then, their children may at first feel betrayed by the presence of stepsiblings and of the stepparent. At the same time, the new stepparents may find it hard not to treat their biological children differently from their stepchildren.

Long-Term Effects of Divorce These comments have focused on the difficulties associated with divorce, but divorce can have positive outcomes as well. After all, it does remove spouses and their children from an extremely difficult relationship. As a result, the unpleasantness surrounding many divorces usually diminishes greatly after two or three years (Hetherington et al., 1982). After that time, many children and parents report feeling reasonably happy with their new family situations, whatever they may be; and they report a general acceptance of the events surrounding the divorce (Hetherington et al., 1982). These long-term improvements do not erase the pain that everyone experienced in the process, but they do suggest that most divorced parents and their children lead fairly normal and satisfying lives as they get older.

The Effects of Work on Families

Work affects family life profoundly, although not always in ways that are simple or straightforward. Jobs determine daily schedules, of course, which in turn affect

When both parents work, children often take on added responsibilities around the house. This boy, for example, has learned how to prepare his own meals. (Erika Stone)

how much time parents have for their children. Job schedules also influence which parent or child does particular household chores. At a more subtle level, work affects parents' self-esteem and thus their happiness as human beings and as parents. And jobs determine income and therefore affect many aspects of family life.

Effects of Maternal Employment   In spite of the once popular view that mothers should stay at home for the sake of their children, research suggests that maternal employment as such usually does children no developmental harm (Hoffman, 1984). What does matter is a woman's choice about employment. Mothers who choose to work or who choose not to work and who live in relatively supportive families apparently do no harm to their children by their employment situation. Mothers who feel forced either to work or not to work are less fortunate; they report more stressful relations with their children.

Importance of mother's choice

Maternal employment often does influence children's development in some ways, though. Most of these are positive, or at least not negative. Families with working mothers, for example, divide housework and child care more evenly than families without employed mothers (Hoffman, 1983). In two-job families, fathers wash dishes relatively more often, and they spend more time alone with their children (though mothers still do the large majority of housework and child care).

Effects on daily life

At the same time, mothers who work gain influence over financial matters in the household, as compared with mothers who are not employed. And their children tend to be responsible for more household chores, such as walking the dog every afternoon, preparing part of dinner, or taking out the trash. These tasks are often set up according to regular rules and schedules which do not require immediate supervision from parents.

The blend of housework and breadwinning seems to create less stereotyped attitudes about the proper roles of mothers and fathers in the children of working mothers (Gold and Andres, 1978). Both sons and daughters witness nurturant behavior in their fathers, and occupational competence in their mothers. As the children approach adolescence, they are especially likely to support women's employment generally (Scarr, 1984), and the daughters are likely to expect to work outside the home when they get older.

In considering these trends, keep in mind two facts. First, mothers who work outside the home usually differ from mothers who do not both in circumstances and in personality. Surveys show that working mothers tend to have fewer children than nonworking mothers do (Hoffman, 1984). Presumably this difference

Qualities and circumstances of working mothers

Perspectives on Research

What Children Know and Feel about Death

In modern society, death has become rare in childhood and common in old age. This seemingly natural state of affairs is actually quite unusual; throughout history and around the world, the majority of deaths have happened to infants and children. The modern reversal of this trend has had many benefits, of course, but it also may be leaving children unprepared to understand and cope with death when they do experience it at close hand. Instead of seeming natural, inevitable, and universal, death now seems to be a rare event, an unusual catastrophe happening to only a few people. In these circumstances, confusion about the nature and meaning of death may set in.

Studies confirm that children have only hazy understandings of death, even well into the middle years. Early in this period, around age six, they describe death with analogies that are often reversible (Wass and Corr, 1984): "Death is when you go to sleep," said one six-year-old; "It's like a flower wilting," said another; "Death is going on a trip," said a third. These analogies can be "undone": real sleep, for example, ends with waking up. In addition, many of the analogies refer not to universal events but to special ones; not everyone goes on trips. Perhaps for these reasons, young children do not

seem to fear death as much as older children and adults do. They reveal concern and distress about the general idea of death, but unless they experience the death of a close relative (like a parent) directly, their concerns tend to be comparatively limited (Swain, 1979).

Somewhere between the ages of eight and ten, most children realize that death is irreversible, permanent, and universal. "Dying is when you never, ever come back again," according to one child, and "Your heart stops beating forever," said another. But they still focus on very concrete aspects of death, and show relatively little understanding of its spiritual or psychological aspects (White et al., 1978). Many children of this age are easily persuaded that dead people can send and receive messages, as described in ghost stories. This fact may account for increases in fear which children have about death later in childhood, when they sometimes ask their parents questions about death and occasionally have nightmares related to death and dying.

All of these developments happen more rapidly and vividly for children who do in fact lose a close relative, especially a parent, during early or middle childhood (Kane, 1977). These children face the

helps to reduce the amount of child care and housework in the working mothers' families. On the other hand, working mothers have more often experienced a marital breakup recently, and they often lack money as a result. These circumstances explain not only why some mothers go to work in the first place, but also why employment can prove difficult for many women and their families — their work as such may not be a problem, but the hard times that surround their need to work are.

A second fact also helps us to understand the effects of maternal employment: it is extremely common. As we have pointed out already, working mothers were a rarity a few decades ago but are in the majority today. This trend has resulted partly from changing sex roles, but perhaps more importantly, from a changing economy during recent decades. Technological advances such as microwave ovens and home freezers make housework less time-consuming than it used to be

---

same two challenges as adults who lose a close relative. First, they must *understand* the death as realistically as possible: it has indeed happened, cannot be ignored, and will never be undone. Unfortunately, younger children may have trouble understanding this reality, because their general cognitive understanding is limited. Second, children must have chances to *mourn* the death, or experience and work through the feelings that they still have about the person who died. For adults, mourning usually includes periodic rushes of sadness, pain, anguish, and guilt about how they treated the dead person (Kubler-Ross, 1983). Children may also experience these emotions. In the short run, though, the extent and mix of their feelings will depend on how emotionally attached they were to the deceased person, and on their overall cognitive maturity. As one nine-year-old girl put it, "What bothered me most about my brother's death was that I did not seem to care about it as much as my parents did." The brother had died suddenly one year before, when he was five and she was eight. She did care about her brother, and did mourn him. But she may not have understood the full importance of his death, either to her parents or to her own future development as a member of her family.

In spite of limitations like this, most children react strongly to the death of the most important people in their lives, their parents. Research shows that the effects can be quite long-lasting. Even five or ten years after losing a parent, bereaved children tend to be more submissive and introverted and less aggressive than other children, including children who lose a parent through divorce (Berlinsky and Biller, 1982). The difference shows both in interviews of these children and in observations of their behavior with peers, and it happens to both sexes.

Losing a parent affects children most strongly, too, when they are younger. A parent's death tends to be harder for a six-year-old than for a ten-year-old, but it is even harder for a three-year-old. Age may matter partly because younger children experience the most confusion about the nature of their parent's death, so they tend more easily, and erroneously, to blame themselves for their parent's "leaving." At the same time, younger children probably need their parents more, both for affection and for practical care, so death deprives them more severely than it deprives older children. And the loss lasts longer for younger children; they have more years of growing to do before they can reach the relative independence of adulthood.

(Robinson, 1980). At the same time, general prosperity and its higher wages have made it relatively less economical to trade time at home for time at work; for example, it may be cheaper to buy bread for a family than to bake it on a regular basis.

Because of these conditions, employment has become an increasingly sensible choice for women, compared to full-time homemaking. Ironically, these same conditions may also create guilt in women who prefer *not* to work. Now, for the first time, some women may feel that they have to justify homemaking rather than employment to relatives and friends.

Effects of Paternal Unemployment Whereas some segments of society regard maternal employment as worrisome, society in general regards paternal unemployment as a serious problem. Presumably this double standard occurs because of society's traditional emphasis on breadwinning for males (Bronfenbrenner and Crouter, 1982). Men, according to the popular impression, should be relatively hard hit by lack of work.

Fathers' reactions to unemployment

In this case, the popular impression contains a lot of truth. Studies of unemployed fathers find that they feel a great deal of stress and disruption, which seem likely to hurt their families (Cobb and Kasl, 1977). Unemployed fathers are depressed and anxious, and report chronic lack of sleep. Such reactions are even more noticeable among fathers who have lost jobs than among fathers with steady work at near poverty-level wages (Moen et al., 1981).

Stresses of unemployment

These stresses may explain the high frequency of violence in families with unemployed fathers. Wife beating is much more frequent among such families than among families generally. So is child abuse, although it is not necessarily committed by the father alone (Justice and Duncan, 1977). Presumably these problems develop because the fathers feel self-conscious, anxious, and ashamed about losing their status as the family breadwinner. At the same time, their wives and even their school-age children may worry about the family's economic future, so all members may get on one another's nerves.

Note, however, that the stress of unemployment is not unique to men. Since women, too, often work because of economic necessity, their loss of employment sometimes proves just as devastating as that of many men. Sometimes, in fact, maternal unemployment can prove even more difficult, especially if a woman must suddenly care for children by herself after losing her job, without significant help from a spouse, relatives, or friends. The idea that men experience hard times because of unemployment is definitely true; but it does not mean that women have an easy time.

Other Sources of Social Support for Schoolchildren

The network of supports

This chapter has emphasized two major sources of social experience for children, peers and parents. In reality, though, most children in their middle years establish other sources of social support as well. One study documented this fact by interviewing schoolchildren about people, places, and activities that they found satisfy-

Pets offer a surprisingly important source of emotional support for many children. So do special or "secret" places to go, as well as informal hobbies. (Dennis Mansell)

ing and helpful in conducting their lives (Bryant, 1985). To help the children think of these, the interviewers took them on long walks around their neighborhoods. From time to time, the interviewers asked questions about what they saw ("Do you know who lives there?" or "Is this where you go to relax?").

This method revealed a tremendous number of social supports for children in their middle years, many of which are summarized in Table 13-1. Large numbers of children reported seeking out adults other than their parents — especially grandparents — to talk with and confide in. Family pets, and sometimes even the pets of neighbors, also served as confidants. Children reported using hobbies to unwind and feel better about themselves, although some of the hobbies were relatively nonsocial, such as stamp collecting or playing a musical instrument. Other children reported having special hideaways where they went to be alone for a while, which they said helped them to feel better. Many children sought out peers

Table 13-1 *Sources of Support Reported by School-Age Children*

Support	Average Number Mentioned in Interviews
Peers and siblings named among ten most important individuals	4.5
Adults (including parents) named among ten most important individuals	3.0
Grandparents and others of grandparents' generation named among ten most important individuals	1.3
Pets (including neighbors') considered as a special friend	1.7
Make-believe friends and make-believe identities	1.6
Hobbies that child attributes to self	2.3
Special places to go to be alone	2.1
Formally sponsored activities (public library, community pool, and church or temple)	4.5
Homes and informal meeting places where child feels free to visit	5.5

Source: Bryant, 1985.

for activities when they needed an emotional lift or when they felt confused, but not on every occasion and not all children did so.

In general, as children moved through the middle years, their sources of support became increasingly broad. This made them better able to manage particular stresses, whether inside or outside their families, when they arose. At all ages during the elementary school years, children seemed happiest when they reported the widest range of social supports, and when that range emphasized informal supports rather than formal ones. For example, friends on the block to play games with offered more support than an adult-sponsored hockey league, and fooling around with a guitar offered more emotional release than regular formal music lessons. The most important trend, however, was the developmental one: the older children got, the more they lived in an expanding social world.

Qualities of effective supports

Checkpoint *Parents influence children's development in a number of ways, but parents and children differ significantly in how they view their relationship. Divorce creates a number of problems for parents and children, both in the short run and in the long run. Employment for mothers has little harmful effect on children, but it does affect children's attitudes about gender. Unemployment for fathers creates stress for both parents and children. In addition to family relationships, a number of sources of emotional and social support are available to children during the middle years.*

The Sense of Self

Throughout infancy, childhood, and adolescence, a child develops a **sense of self,** which is experience and knowledge about her uniqueness as a human being. This sense evolves over the middle years, becoming more organized and generally more complex. In fact, even though a sense of self is often called a **self-concept,** it functions more like a theory than a single concept, since it is a set of related ideas that the child continually tests and revises, based on his experiences, as he gets older (Wylie, 1974/1979).

At age six, for example, a girl named Leila loved playing with dolls, and loved holding and caring for babies. She noticed that her parents and others commented on this, so nurturance became part of Leila's idea of herself; "I'm someone who likes babies," she sometimes thought. But later experience modified this idea. Toward the end of elementary school, Leila discovered that she often preferred playing softball to playing house. Somehow, at age ten or eleven, she had to incorporate this reality into her sense of self; "I'm a good ballplayer," she realized. By the start of adolescence, she still was not sure how to reconcile these two concepts of herself — her interest in child care and her interest in sports. Someday she might succeed in doing so, but at age twelve she was not yet able to.

To a large extent, a child's notion of self grows out of social experiences with other selves — or put more plainly, out of contacts with other children and adults. Learning what it means to be female, for example, happens as girls meet other individuals who are also female. And learning what it means to be happy occurs as children see happiness expressed by other people. As personal and individual as a sense of self is, then, it reflects generalizations about others, and it cannot develop without considerable social contact (Lewis and Brooks-Gunn, 1979b).

Social influences

The Development of Self in Childhood

How do children acquire a sense of self? The first step involves basic social labels or categories. By the end of the second year of life, for example, most children can correctly label their gender ("I'm a boy" or "I'm a girl"), their age ("I'm two"), and their species ("I'm a person"). Labels like these pave the way for later, more complete knowledge of self.

Self-Constancy   At first, though, most such labels lack permanence. At age two or three, a boy may claim that he can become a girl under certain circumstances — "when I grow up," or "if I grew my hair long" (Marcus and Overton, 1978). Or a very young child may say that she can become a different individual "if I change my name" (Guardo and Bohan, 1971). **Self-constancy,** a belief that identity remains permanently fixed, does not become firm until the early school years, sometime after age six. At this time a child becomes convinced that he will stay the same person indefinitely into the future, that he will remain human in all circumstances, and that he will keep his gender forever. Beliefs like these are what people mean by a sense of self.

Belief in a stable identity

At the same time that the child is developing a sense of personal constancy, his reasons for believing in constancy are shifting. Younger children, up to age five or six, tend to define themselves in terms of observable features and behaviors such as hairdos or how fast they can run (Rosenberg, 1979; Bannister and Agnew, 1971). These qualities have the advantage of being easily seen and comprehended, but as features of self-identity they have certain disadvantages. For one thing, they are often not really very stable; a child's running speed usually improves as the weeks and months go by. And observable features are often relative to particular people or situations; being big, for example, defines a child in one way among his nursery-school peers but in another way among members of his family.

Basis for self-constancy

The First Beliefs in Psychological Traits   Older children, around age eight, form a more stable sense of self by including psychological traits as part of their self-descriptions. At first the traits are feelings and qualities that have no apparent reference to other human beings; "I am brave," says the child, or "I am cheerful." By implication these traits describe her as an entire personality and in all possible situations, with little recognition of people's usual variations in moods. At first, too, the child describes the traits in bold, global terms — terms that ignore the possibility that opposing feelings or qualities can sometimes exist within the same person. The child may vacillate in describing her own qualities without realizing it. Sometimes she will say, "I am dumb," meaning *completely* dumb, and other times she will say, "I am smart," meaning *completely* smart (Harter, 1977). Neither statement suggests the recognition that both descriptions contain an element of truth.

Traits as general dispositions

How does a child eventually coordinate contradictions like these? A first step is often to assign one trait to a particular person or situation and its opposite to another person or situation (Harter, 1982a). The belief that "I am cheerful," for example, may become attached to the school playground and to the children who play there, whereas "I am grumpy" may attach itself to the classroom and to its usual leader, the teacher. The child will then describe herself in the two situations in very different ways: on the playground, as cheerful, but in class, as grumpy. Both traits are permitted to exist, so to speak, but for the time being they lead isolated lives, at least in the child's mind.

Resolving contradictions in traits

By the end of the middle years, true integration of contradictory traits does occur. Around age ten or twelve, children begin to recognize that they can feel more than one way about any particular situation or person — they can both like their teachers and hate them, or enjoy school and dislike it, more or less at the same time (Selman, 1980). As they do so, they also begin using trait labels in less global ways, and more to express qualities in particular situations. When an older child says, "I am smart," she no longer means "I am always smart in every possible way and in every activity." Now she more likely means "I am smart in a number of significant situations, but not in all."

These changes make possible a more stable sense of self. The situation-bound qualities expressed by older children do in fact usually describe them more accurately than the global traits and observable features that younger children rely on. But a middle-years child's consciousness of inner traits still lacks the subtlety found in adolescents and adults. A child may know that she is smart, but she may

not know clearly how this quality differs from being intelligent, say, or creative, or wise.

Processes in Constructing a Self

Middle-years children construct their identities or self-theories by distinguishing their thoughts and feelings from those expressed by others. This idea is supported by studies of children's thinking and emotions. One group of researchers asked children of various ages how they would feel if their parents expressed certain emotions, such as sadness, anger, and happiness. Compared with school-age children, preschoolers more often said that they would feel the same emotion, and be angry if their parents were angry, sad if they were sad, and so on (Harter and Barnes, 1983). Older children more often named complementary emotions rather than identical ones. If their parents felt angry, for example, they would feel fearful.

Another study showed how children gradually acquire a full understanding of the words *ashamed* and *proud* (Harter, 1982b). Among adults, these two feelings often depend on others' responses and opinions as well as on one's own; it can be hard to feel ashamed or proud unless someone is thinking about you and evaluating your behavior at least some of the time. As the study revealed, though, young children are only dimly aware of the importance of others in creating these emotions. When asked to define *ashamed* or *proud,* they simply said that *ashamed* was a bad feeling and *proud* was a good one; they did not mention how other people's opinions might help create these feelings.

Distinguishing self from others

By the early middle years (age six or seven), children began explicitly mentioning others in defining these two terms. For example, one seven-year-old's definition was "My teacher was proud when I earned 100 percent on the test"; another's was "My mother was ashamed when I lost my temper at the neighbor." Such attention to others implies awareness that others sometimes observe the child's self. Even more important, though, it suggests that school-age children distinguish between their own emotions and those of others — something they must do in order to develop a mature sense of self.

Checkpoint *During the middle years, children begin to acquire a stable identity or sense of self. The first sign is a sense of self-constancy. Somewhat later in this period, children also acquire their first beliefs in psychological traits. These developments set the stage for the more profound crises about identity that sometimes occur during adolescence.*

Psychosocial Challenges Facing Children with Handicaps

Children who have special needs or handicaps face much the same challenges as any other children. They need to achieve in some area of activity; they need to feel accepted by other children; they need to get along comfortably with their families, and especially with their parents. By meeting all of these challenges, they develop some understanding of who they are. In these ways, such children are exactly like other children.

Effects of the handicap

But for children with special needs, solutions to these challenges are often complex, and at times may require extra encouragement or support from others. The nature of the complexities depends partly on the nature of the handicap: a child with Down syndrome lives a very different life from a child who is missing a leg or an arm. Some handicaps by their very nature affect peer relations strongly; a child with a hearing impairment, for example, may have daily difficulties in speaking and hearing, and may therefore have trouble keeping up with everyday conversations among his classmates. Other handicaps may be relatively invisible to the general public but have a strong impact on the child's family. For instance, a child's elementary school classmates may not know that she has leukemia, since acute phases of this illness simply cause her to stay home. But parents and siblings feel the impact of this health problem profoundly, in the form of frequent trips to the hospital, disrupted family schedules, and general worry about the child's health.

In spite of variations like these, children with special needs have something in common: they are substantially different from "normal" or usual children, whether the difference is physical, emotional, or cognitive. This section looks at how the fact of being different affects the psychological and social development of these children during the school years.

The Challenge to Achieve

For children with disabilities, achievement may not be tied to conventional standards of success. Striving for conventional or "normal" standards of excellence can be frustrating and self-defeating. A child who learns academic material very slowly, for example, eventually discovers that no amount of extra study will put her at the top of her class, or even anywhere near the top. A child with poor vision eventually discovers that he probably cannot become a star baseball player, or even an average one.

These realities do not mean, however, that children with disabilities cannot achieve at all. On the contrary, many handicapped children find activities in which their disabilities make relatively little difference to their performance (French, 1983); impaired vision may interfere with learning to draw, but it does not interfere with listening to and playing music. Some activities can be carried out in unconventional ways or with special physical aids that reduce the importance of a particular disability; poor motor control may make it difficult to write assignments in school, for instance, but special typewriter keyboards can often eliminate this problem altogether.

Part of learning to achieve, then, consists of selecting appropriate realms of activity and helpful (if unconventional) ways of achieving. Parents and teachers can assist in this selection, and probably should, but in the end, children themselves must recognize how they can hope to achieve the most and then commit themselves more fully to those activities. The process really does not differ from the way in which we all arrange our lives: we all tend to find and emphasize activities in which we do especially well and in which our limitations interfere as little as possible.

Selecting activities for achievement

However, these strategies do not solve all the achievement problems experienced by children with handicaps. Some "normal" standards of behavior and skill are hard to avoid. Society may not expect everyone to be a good athlete, but it does expect everyone to be able to walk gracefully for reasonable distances. Yet children with physical disabilities such as cerebral palsy may be incapable of meeting this everyday expectation; because of their condition, they walk clumsily and fitfully.

Problems with pursuing conventional standards

Situations like these put children with handicaps in a bind. Striving to meet society's usual standards can be frustrating and self-defeating; yet ignoring those standards exposes them to continual reactions of surprise and discomfort whenever they appear in public or meet new people. Sometime during the school years, children with disabilities gradually become aware of this dilemma and of the continual pain it promises to bring them.

Even when a child does achieve normal standards, the success often proves problematic (Buscaglia, 1983). Others may not view the success as a heroic triumph. "Look at how well she walks this year," they say, meaning something like "She is approximating our standard of graceful walking better than ever." But the child herself, and anyone close to her, realizes that the achievement cost an

For children with handicaps, achievement still matters, but tasks have to be selected carefully. These two Down syndrome children, for example, are experiencing both challenge and a sense of accomplishment in this cooking activity. (Meri Houtchens-Kitchens/The Picture Cube)

extraordinary amount of effort, worry, and time. For this reason, when an achievement like walking well actually occurs, it sometimes feels more like a defeat than a victory. Children with handicaps cannot escape this sort of reaction, and they need constant encouragement to set their own standards of success rather than relying on those used by the rest of society.

The Challenge of Peers

Though children with disabilities want and need the acceptance and affection of other children, their disabilities often interfere with gaining acceptance (Gottlieb et al., 1978). The problem is more complicated than the rejection that "ugly ducklings," or children who have jug ears or an oversized nose, sometimes experience.

Limitations to peer relations

Genuine handicaps make other children anxious and defensive. Eventually children with handicaps begin to sense this fact and begin to expect less from their contacts with peers. Some handicaps, such as a speech problem or mild retardation, also limit a child's ability to interact skillfully. Over the long run, these circumstances can combine to limit social life severely.

Studies of peer preferences have found that children often do not merely ignore but actively reject peers with handicaps (Hartup, 1983). The rejection applies to a variety of handicapping conditions, from learning disabilities and mild (or "educable") retardation to emotional disturbance. The extent of isolation and rejec-

Mainstreaming Children with Cerebral Palsy

Cerebral palsy (or CP) is a disorder of the nervous system that children usually acquire before or during birth; it causes certain muscles to tighten uncontrollably. As a result, children with CP have trouble moving gracefully. Ordinary movements like walking and reaching often look jerky or clumsy. Sometimes muscular tightness affects the fine motor movements of the mouth as well, impairing speech. Except in severe cases, however, children with cerebral palsy can function very well in ordinary classrooms, as long as teachers follow certain principles in assisting them (Spodek et al., 1984). The most important of these concern two areas of classroom life, language and self-management skills.

In the area of language, teachers of children with cerebral palsy should generally assume that speech impairment does not indicate low intelligence. Most of the time, poorly articulated utterances simply result from tight, hard-to-control muscles in the mouth and larynx, not from lack of knowledge or lack of motivation. CP children usually perform better if teachers give them ample time to speak or to answer questions — usually much more time than normally speaking children need. Whenever it is appropriate, too, teachers should not feel shy about asking CP children to repeat utterances that cannot be understood. More often than not, such children are aware of the gap between their own speech and normal speech, and feel responsible for making themselves understood, provided that teachers and classmates make reasonable efforts to understand them.

Since CP children cannot move as quickly or predictably as other children, they need special arrangements to encourage independence in their work. Schoolwork that requires them to sit in ordinary classroom chairs may not be possible; they may find themselves lurching uncomfortably forward to reach for objects on a table, or even accidentally falling out of the chair. But sitting is possible with the right equipment. A wheelchair or other chair with sides on it helps a lot, as does a table that is high enough to accommodate such a chair, and a pillow or a soft pad between the child and the edge of the table.

Given their clumsiness, children with CP may find conventional reading difficult, and writing may be virtually impossible. Again, though, substitutes exist. Books can be held in book racks or by classmates, and special typewriters with large keys that do not require precise movements help in writing. For more severe cases of cerebral palsy, such typewriters can be activated by a plastic "finger" on a rod attached to the child's head; the child can then write by poking the "finger" at the right place on the keyboard.

But procedures like these deal only with the mechanics of learning. To be effective, teachers must care about such children and about their special needs. Children with CP have feelings just like other children, and they can usually sense whether teachers welcome their presence or feel uncomfortable about dealing with their handicap. Integrating or mainstreaming CP children works best with teachers and classmates who value all children as individuals, who can see the handicapped children's talents in spite of their superficial differences from "normal" children, and who encourage other children in the class to think in the same ways. Such teachers and classmates can benefit everyone, in fact, handicapped or not (Buscaglia, 1983).

tion depends a lot on the severity of the handicap; usually, the more severe it is, the more the child is rejected (Guralnick, 1981). Peers seem to dislike handicaps primarily because of the strange or unfamiliar behavior sometimes connected with them, and not because children with handicaps often perform poorly at schoolwork.

Benefits of integrating special-needs children

In an effort to reduce this isolation and rejection, many educators have worked in recent years toward integrating or **mainstreaming** children with handicaps into regular classrooms (Turnbull and Turnbull, 1986). Obviously, such children often also require special, separate educational services along with their ordinary daily experiences in classrooms. For example, children with learning disabilities may need individual tutoring to help them keep up with their class. But with appropriate support and with encouragement and training for teachers, mainstreaming may help at least some children to feel more accepted by their peers.

The Challenge of Family Relationships

Disabilities of course affect children's relations with their parents and other family members (Gallagher and Gallagher, 1985). For one thing, parents often cannot influence and teach their disabled children in the ways described earlier in this chapter. A physically handicapped child may not learn easily from his parents' demonstrations of how to tie shoelaces and how to button a shirt or blouse. He may still learn such simple behaviors, but his parents may have to modify their demonstrations to fit the child's capacities, and they may have to persist longer than usual.

Modified methods of influencing children

On the other hand, children who are retarded or emotionally disturbed may not learn easily from parents' direct teaching or statements of family rules. Simply telling a retarded child not to pull other children's hair may not get the message through very fast, and parents must expect to repeat themselves often before the child successfully understands.

Practical demands on parents

Parents often experience a lot of stress as a result of having a child with a disability. Such children have special practical needs: they may have to be lifted, bathed, fed, and toileted. They may also require frequent trips to the doctor or hospital for physical therapy or medications. All of these needs can disrupt parents' and siblings' lives substantially, and meeting them sometimes costs money; not all insurance policies cover such needs adequately, and not all families can afford sufficient insurance coverage in any case.

Regardless of the kind of disability involved, families vary in how well they cope with these challenges. Among families with two parents, for example, larger ones seem to fare better than smaller ones (Powell and Ogle, 1985). Possibly a larger number of siblings means more help for the parents, or possibly the siblings help to create an atmosphere of normality, or possibly parents with more children have accumulated extra skill in raising children and therefore feel less pressured by the special demands of a child with a handicap. Some mixture of these factors may operate; at present we do not really know.

One-parent families must cope with the pressures intrinsic to single parenthood in addition to the child's disability. Since most of these families are headed by women, they tend to have substantially less income than two-breadwinner families; yet they may need more money than usual to care for the child. Educational and therapeutic programs for the disabled child may demand significant parental involvement, yet because single parents must work, they may have less time than others tc attend meetings or get to special appointments.

Siblings react in various ways to a disability in the family. On one hand, many siblings report feeling emotionally neglected because parents give so much attention to the disabled child (Vadasy et al., 1984). On the other hand, they also report developing greater tolerance than usual for differences among people, and more commitment to altruistic values and life goals as a result of having a disabled sibling (Cleveland and Miller, 1977). As one girl put it, "My parents always expected me to do more things for my retarded brother; so I did them, and they seemed to appreciate my help." As long as parents do not overemphasize this helpfulness ethic, siblings apparently benefit from their experience, and do not lose their own identities in the process.

Effects of disability on siblings

The Challenge of Knowing Who You Are

As these comments imply, children with handicaps face the same task as other children in developing a unique identity or sense of self, but their disabilities may complicate this task in special ways. Of course, by accentuating uniqueness and difference, a disability should facilitate the development of self-identity, because a child with a handicap learns in many social encounters that she cannot do everything that other children can do. Some disabled children therefore may learn sooner than "normal" children to distinguish between their own thoughts and feelings and those of others (Buscaglia, 1983). Making this distinction is crucial to forming an identity.

Early knowledge of human differences

But there are two problems with this idea. First, how quickly and thoroughly children learn about the significance of their handicap depends on their cognitive and emotional capacities. By nature, some disabilities limit or delay the child's understanding of the significance of her disability; mental retardation is the most obvious example. Such children often take longer than usual to develop self-constancy.

Second, even when children experience no cognitive limitations, they must learn to accept their disability as only one part of themselves. Whether they like it or not, their identity or sense of self must include their handicap. Yet they must also realize that as individuals, they consist of *more* than their handicap. Like everyone else, they can express happiness, have good ideas, and pursue special hobbies.

Creating an identity beyond the handicap

Because this dual realization is complex, children need time — perhaps even a lifetime — to develop it. Parents can help this process along by showing pride and pleasure in their children and by not giving undue attention to the disability (Rousso, 1984). For example, they can keep the disability in perspective by cultivating personal and family activities that purposely have nothing to do with the limitations of their child. This strategy is good advice for all parents, whether their children have handicaps or not.

Checkpoint *Children with handicaps face many of the same psychological and social challenges as other children do, but they also encounter some differences. They must more often define achievement by personal standards rather than by conventional standards of performance. Peer relations can prove awkward unless the child or adults make special efforts to facilitate them. Family members can experience stress because of helping a child with a disability, but they may also gain certain psychological benefits from the experience. The effect of a disability on a child's sense of self depends on the nature of the disability and on how the child and others evaluate it.*

On Beyond Childhood

In a variety of ways, then, the middle years are the time when a child becomes a person in a more adult sense than ever before. This happens in part because the child has begun accumulating considerable experience with other people of roughly his own age and maturity, and in part because of cognitive developments. Children begin setting goals and working toward them in more adult ways, by taking into account others' opinions about their achievements as well as their own interest in learning.

As we have pointed out several times in this chapter, the developments of the middle years do not always result in happy feelings and experiences. With their newly developed maturity, children are able to hurt and snub some of their peers as well as to make new friends, and they are now able to worry about peer evaluations as well as to become commendably openminded. Life has not gotten happier just because the child has gotten older; but it is not necessarily unhappier either.

Taken together, these experiences create a new, more mature sense of self within children of this age, one that has more inward or psychological properties than that of early childhood. In the years ahead — during adolescence — this psychological self becomes still more elaborate. Contrary to widespread belief, the adolescent years do not necessarily prove any more or less difficult than the middle years or early childhood, though some individuals, for special reasons, encounter special challenges.

Summary of Major Ideas

Psychosocial Challenges of the Middle Years

1. During the middle years, children face challenges concerning achievement, peer relationships, family relationships, and the development of identity or sense of self.

2. During this period, children with disabilities face the same challenges as other children, but solve them in somewhat different ways.

The Age of Industry and Achievement

3. According to some psychodynamic theorists, schoolchildren repress their earlier romantic attachments to their parents and focus instead on developing a sense of industry and achievement.

4. During the middle years, children shift their achievement orientation from an exclusive focus on learning or task mastery to one that is also concerned with others' responses to their achievements.

Peer Relationships

5. According to Piaget, peers help children to overcome egocentrism by challenging them to deal with differing perspectives.

6. Harry Stack Sullivan argued that peers help children to develop democratic ways of interacting, and also offer the first opportunities to form close or intimate relationships with others.

7. In general, peers seem to serve unique functions by creating relationships of equality among children.

8. Groups of peers vary in membership and behavior according to the age mixture and gender of their members.

9. Peer groups tend to segregate themselves by both gender and race.

10. Popular children possess a number of socially desirable qualities, such as social skill and confidence in themselves.

11. Unpopular children possess less desirable qualities, such as aggression, selfishness, and bossiness.

12. Early in the middle years, a friend is someone with whom a child shares activities and toys, but later in this period, a friend becomes someone who the child can count on and with whom she can share intimacies.

13. Peers do exert pressure to conform on individual children, and this pressure can have either good or bad effects.

Family Relationships

14. Compared with parents, children must engage in more hypothesizing and guesswork in order to understand family relationships.

15. In recent years, divorce has become more common in North American families, and it usually creates stress for all members of the family.

16. Many mothers now work at least part-time; their employment does not seem to have any negative effects on children.

17. Maternal employment does influence the division of household labor and children's attitudes about gender roles.

18. When fathers are unemployed, both they and their families experience significant stress.

19. Schoolchildren often find emotional support from adults other than parents, friends, pets, and from hobbies.

The Sense of Self

20. During the middle years, children acquire a belief in self-constancy and a belief in permanent psychological traits.

21. Belief in self-constancy and permanent psychological traits lays the groundwork for the more complex personal identities that are developed during the adolescent years.

Psychosocial Challenges Facing Children with Handicaps

22. Children with handicaps can and should achieve, but they often must define achievement by more personal and less conventional standards than those used by others.

23. Handicapped children sometimes experience awkward relations with peers, but intervention by parents and teachers can alleviate this problem.

24. Families with disabled children often must cope with unusual amounts of practical care, special financial burdens, and emotional stress.

25. Children with handicaps need an identity just like other children; their identity should recognize their disability but not be limited by it.

Key Terms

peers *(532)*

repression *(535)*

latency *(535)*

defense *(535)*

industry versus inferiority *(535)*

industriousness *(535)*

inferiority *(535)*

achievement motivation *(536)*

learning orientation *(536)*

performance orientation *(536)*

warps *(542)*

juvenile period *(542)*

preadolescence *(542)*

sociometric questionnaire *(545)*

dyads *(545)*

blended family *(556)*

internalizing *(559)*

joint custody *(560)*

sense of self *(569)*

self-concept *(569)*

self-constancy *(569)*

mainstreaming *(576)*

What Do You Think?

1. What do you consider an appropriate balance between a learning and a performance orientation toward achievement? Explain whether you think this balance should apply to all children or should vary with individuals.

2. Do you feel that peer groups have the same structure as they used to? Are children still segregating themselves by gender and age as much as they did in the past? Are they still segregating themselves as much by race? Explain.

3. Given that mothers' employment generally does no harm to children, why do you think many parents (and some segments of society) continue to worry about the impact of employment on child development?

4. Do children in the middle years really know who they are? Explain.

5. What are the most important things that children and adults can learn or do to assist children with handicaps?

For Further Reading

André, R. *Homemakers: The Forgotten Workers.* Chicago: University of Chicago Press, 1981.

This book examines homemaking as work: how the tasks of homemaking compare to the tasks of other, paid workers, and what their approximate economic value may be to families. The author especially considers whether women who work outside the home essentially hold two jobs, one inside and the other outside the home. She also describes and evaluates several strategies that couples and families have tried for distributing homemaking work more equitably.

Axline, V. *Dibs: In Search of Self.* New York: Ballantine, 1964.

This classic tells the true story of an emotionally disturbed boy and how he eventually overcame his condition with the help of therapists and others. The story reveals several of the ways in which a disability — in this case, emotional disturbance — can interfere with the usual challenges of childhood, and especially the challenges of identity development.

Dunn, J. *Brothers and Sisters.* Cambridge, Mass.: Harvard University Press, 1985.

The author describes how siblings' relationships evolve during childhood, especially during the middle years. She cites many vivid examples of brothers and sisters getting along — and failing to get along. The examples challenge many common assumptions about siblings, such as the impression that siblings show that they do not care about each other by fighting. On the contrary, siblings seem to understand each other better in some situations than their parents do.

Klagsbrun, F. *Married People: Staying Together in the Age of Divorce.* New York: Bantam Books, 1985.

This book explores the reasons why some marriages improve and flourish the longer they last, whereas others dissolve quickly, and still others persist under considerable tension. The author describes interviews with numerous couples and uses the couples' comments to suggest why some marriages survive better than others.

Saunders, A., and Remsberg, B. *The Stress-Proof Child.* New York: Signet Books, 1984.

This book is intended for the general public, and describes how and why some children experience debilitating stress. In general, it suggests ways for parents to relieve stress in children. The advice is often quite concrete, and ranges from giving children more hugs and phrasing comments in positive terms to encouraging a healthy diet.

Johanna's Case

In many ways, the years from six to twelve were among the best of Johanna's childhood. During this period, she developed many new skills and interests, and she felt mostly happy and secure at school. Although she was somewhat shy, she always seemed to have at least two or three "best" friends to play with and confide in.

Johanna was an only child who was used to spending a lot of time with her parents. As a six-year-old, she especially enjoyed doing things with her mother. She liked to help her mother cook, and they often preferred similar foods. She even adopted many of her mother's mannerisms and vocabulary. But life changed for Johanna during this time, and she was not the same girl at twelve that she was at six.

During the early years of school, her teachers often commented on Johanna's physical energy: she tried hard at anything active and enjoyed physical education classes a lot. During second and third grades, she often took a long time to get home after school because she liked to stop and play at a park along the way.

But things did not stay the same at home during these years. When Johanna was ten, her mother took a full-time job. The effects on Johanna were immediate. Suddenly she had to get herself ready in the morning, including even packing her own lunch. She grumbled about this at first, but all those previous cooking experiences with her mother actually proved helpful.

Student Progress Report

Name **Johanna Wallace**   Grade: 1   2   3   4   ⑤   6

Student's Teacher **Mrs. Eleanor Leitner**

ATTENDANCE DATA:
QUARTER AND NO. OF DAYS: 1(43) 2(40) 3(38) 4(50)   Total ( )

	1	2	3	4
Absences	2	3	3	3
Late	5	3	0	2

ENGLISH LANGUAGE ARTS

Qrtr.	1st	2nd	3rd	4th	Final
Grade	A-	A	A-	A-	A-

Comment *Good progress in composition skills. Johanna often brings humor and originality to her treatment of topics. Work in spelling, grammar and vocabulary has been variable but good overall. Very good work in literature. Very good L.A. skills.*

MATHEMATICS

Qrtr.	1st	2nd	3rd	4th	Final
Grade	A-	B-/B	B	B+	B+

Comment *Tests and quizzes - very good. Daily assignments range 60's - 80's. Strong problem solving skills.*

SCIENCE

Qrtr.	1st	2nd	3rd	4th	Final
Grade	B	B	C	B+	B

Comment *Johanna continues to hold back during class discussions. She is usually prepared with homework and does well on tests.*

SOCIAL STUDIES

Qrtr.	1st	2nd	3rd	4th	Final
Grade	A	B+	B-	A-	A-

Comment *Johanna has done nicely on tests and her report. Her quizzes were very good, but she had several homework assignments missing.*

PARENT'S SIGNATURE _____

PARENT'S COMMENTS: _____
Please return this form immediately except after final quarter.

By the end of the year in which her mother began working, Johanna was doing just as well in school as she ever had. Her teacher, in fact, was not even aware that Johanna's mother had gone back to work.

Actually, what bothered Johanna more than getting ready in the morning was entertaining herself alone after school. Some days none of her friends were available for visiting, and now and then this made her feel lonely. But the time alone did have its rewards: she could ponder and sort out how she felt about things, and she could work on her guitar playing without feeling self-conscious about it.

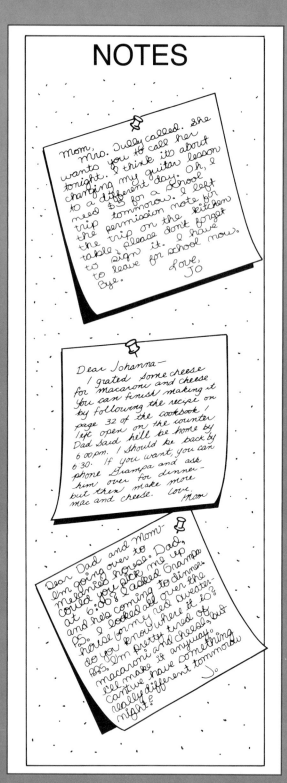

NOTES

Mom,
Mrs. Tully called. She wants you to call her tonight. I think it's about changing my guitar lesson to a different day. Oh, I need $5 for a school trip tomorrow. I left the permission note for the trip on the kitchen table. Please don't forget to sign it. I have to leave for school now. Bye.
Love,
Jo

Dear Johanna —
I grated some cheese for macaroni and cheese. You can finish making it by following the recipe on page 32 of the cookbook I left open on the counter. Dad said he'll be home by 6:00pm. I should be back by 6:30. If you want, you can phone Grampa and ask him over for dinner — but then make more mac and cheese. Love, Mom

Dear Dad and Mom —
I'm going over to Melanie's house. Dad, could you pick me up at 6:00? I asked Grampa and he's coming to dinner. P.S. I looked all over the house for my red sweater. Do you know where it is? P.P.S. I'm pretty tired of macaroni and cheese, but I'll make it anyway. Can't we have something really different tomorrow night?
Jo.

With her mother gone in the afternoons, Johanna found herself having more household responsibilities, such as cooking dinner on certain days each week. Sometimes her grandfather came over to help her and (she suspected) to keep her company. All he said, though, was that he liked having company, too.

By the time that Johanna was eleven, she had become pretty responsible about planning her own time. Her parents now let her go by herself to the public library — one of her favorite spots — as long as she let them know ahead of time.

By age eleven, too, Johanna's friendships had become really important to her. On weekday afternoons, she was sometimes privately glad that both her parents were out of the house; then she and her closest friend, Melanie, could talk or play games without fear of parental intrusion.

One indirect result of her mother's working was that Johanna began feeling closer to her father. She found that they talked a lot more than they used to about things that happened at school, or about her friends, or about what she wanted to do when she grew up. Her father seemed interested in all these things, and especially in her ideas about careers.

By the time she was twelve, Johanna was well on her way to becoming a young woman. After pestering her parents, she got them to pay for contact lenses, although she still wondered privately whether boys would ever find her attractive. On balance she felt better than ever. "I like being older," she said, "because older kids can do more."

6 Adolescence

The adolescent years present new and unique challenges for children. They must come to terms with their bodies as they suddenly grow taller and become sexually mature; they must establish more equal relationships with their parents; and they must come to grips with the need to leave home eventually and to become independent individuals.

How stressful these challenges prove, however, depends on a variety of circumstances. For some teens, the timing of puberty can make these years especially hard — or easy. For others, their newly forming ability to reason abstractly can make life seem suddenly confusing, at the same time that it also reveals exciting new possibilities for the future. For most young people, dating — or even just talking to — the opposite sex proves both intriguing and frustrating, as they slowly overcome childhood habits of relating only to members of their own sex. All in all, the changes of adolescence can be difficult, but on average, they are neither more nor less challenging than those faced during other periods of life.

Chapter

14

Adolescence: Physical Development

Focusing Questions

- What is meant by adolescence, and how did it come to be created as a period of development?
- What changes in height and weight occur during adolescence?
- What is puberty, and what are its important effects on physical development during adolescence?
- How does the timing of puberty — early, average, or late — affect the psychological experience of adolescence for boys and girls?
- What are the major health problems encountered by adolescents?

DAVID IS FOURTEEN. Ever since the beginning of last summer, there have been some very noticeable changes in the way he looks and acts. He has grown nearly two inches in the last six months, and his dad jokes that his pants and sleeves will have to be reintroduced to his ankles and wrists before it is too late. But this rapid growth is no joking matter to David. Although he was well coordinated and athletic in junior high school, he is now awkward and klutzy, tripping over himself and bumping into things. His increased height, rather than being an advantage, seems to be limiting his ability to play basketball, his favorite sport.

David's voice is changing, too. Sometimes it sounds the way it always has; at other times it is deeper, like his father's; and often it seems to bounce around out of control, cracking and breaking as it fluctuates between the two. David has definite signs of a mustache on his upper lip and the fuzzy beginnings of a beard on his cheeks, and although he has become very shy and modest about his body lately, his dad has noticed that he has hair under his arms and around his pubic area.

David's personality has also changed. Usually a pretty easy-going and responsible person who is a pleasure to be around, he now seems very moody and self-centered. He blows up or sulks at unpredictable times, and often fails to do what is expected of him around the house or at school.

David's sister, Debbie, is twelve. Over the past year she too has been undergoing some striking physical changes. Not only has she gained three inches and thirteen pounds, but it is obvious to everyone that her body is rapidly changing from that of a girl to that of a woman. Her bust and hips have filled out, and she has considerable curves where just a year ago she had none at all. Debbie has begun to menstruate, and she too has grown hair under her arms and in her pubic area. Like David, she has become much shier and more uncomfortable about her body. Although she seems proud of becoming a woman, she easily blushes when someone mentions how grown-up she has become, and she worries that she is too fat.

Except for her increased shyness and embarrassment about the changes in her body, Debbie has not shown any striking changes in personality. She is much less willing to wrestle with her brother than she was just a few months ago, but she continues to be quietly responsible around the house and to do well at school. She lives up to her childhood reputation of being "emotionally steady as a rock."

As you have certainly guessed, both David and Debbie are undergoing many of the changes of adolescence. In this chapter and the two that follow, we will explore the major physical, cognitive, social, and emotional developments that occur during adolescence. But first, let us take a brief look at the concept of adolescence itself.

The Concept of Adolescence

Adolescence is defined as the stage of development that leads a person from childhood to adulthood. Marked by the major physical changes of puberty and important cognitive and social changes, it is generally considered to begin around age twelve and to end with the completion of physical growth, sometime around age twenty.

In every society, ceremonies and rituals such as baptism, circumcision, confirmation, bar mitzvah, marriage, retirement, and even college graduation are used to signify important changes in a person's development and social standing, and the transition to adulthood is perhaps the most important and widely recognized change that all people experience. In societies that still have relatively simple, agricultural economies and traditional cultural and social arrangements, this transition is fairly smooth and predictable, and grows out of a long period of preparation. For example, when a teenaged Australian aborigine goes on his year-long walkabout through the desert, with only a few simple weapons to protect him, his chances of returning safely are high, because much of his childhood has been spent in learning skills that help him to meet this challenge. Similarly, a girl's initiation into womanhood in many tribal cultures is preceded by years of instruction in and imitation of the adult roles and activities she is now expected to perform.

Rites of passage

In modern industrial societies such as ours, however, the roles and responsibilities that a person is to assume when he or she reaches sexual maturity are much less predictable, largely because technology and values are changing so rapidly. Our rites of passage tend to be more symbolic than real, and the transition from childhood to adulthood can be rather difficult and prolonged. For example, whereas a girl in a hunting-and-gathering society has a good idea of what her adult work will be — bearing and caring for children, gathering and preparing food, etc. — how can a girl in computer-age America know what kind of work she will do, what kind of family she will have, or even where she will live? Much of this confusion results from our concept of adolescence.

Adolescence: From Idea to Social Fact

Although most of us take the idea of adolescence for granted, it is a relatively modern concept. Its invention, or discovery, in America was largely a response to the

There is no doubt that some teenagers experience periods of turmoil connected with growing up. But for most, adolescence is neither more nor less difficult than earlier periods of life. (Bernard Pierre Wolff)

Emergence of the idea of adolescence

social changes that accompanied this country's industrial development in the nineteenth century (see Chapter 1).

In fact, some researchers have proposed that adolescence was defined as a separate stage of development principally to prolong the years of childhood, so that the aims of the new urban-industrial society that rapidly developed after the Civil War could be fulfilled (Bakan, 1975). According to this view, the spread of railroads and the telegraph, accompanied by a general shift in population from the country to the industrial cities and the addition of a huge number of immigrants, threatened Americans' way of life. Because so much was changing so fast, people felt a growing fear that society would get out of control — that the country would be overrun by foreigners and that the dirty, unpleasant cities would breed crime and immorality. There were three major legal responses to this national "identity crisis" — compulsory education, child labor laws, and special legal procedures for juveniles — and together they played a major role in making adolescence a social reality (Bakan, 1975).

State-controlled education was believed to be so essential to insuring law, order, morality, and obedience in the workplace that school attendance was made compulsory for children between the ages of six and eighteen. Children and adolescents had made up a significant part of the labor force until this point, but an increasing awareness of the harmful effects of factory work spurred the movement toward child labor laws. Perhaps more important, the rapid introduction of modern machinery that was both expensive and complex required workers who were mature and responsible enough to run it. The introduction of laws to restrict child labor came to define the end of adolescence.

As early as 1899, when the first Juvenile Court Act was passed by the Illinois State Legislature, special legal procedures for juveniles were established as a way of dealing with the newly invented idea of "juvenile delinquency." Such developments served to solidify the social reality of adolescence further. Once this was accomplished, adolescence became an important focus of study for the newly emerging field of developmental psychology.

Adolescence as a psychological concept was popularized by psychologist G. Stanley Hall, one of the first developmentalists to study adolescence. He believed that each stage of a child's physical and biological growth and personality development was in a sense predetermined, in that it repeated or recapitulated the same stages of development that occurred in the evolution of the human species. Thus a child's selfish, self-centered, and aggressive nature was thought to reflect the more primitive stages of human history. Adolescence, according to Hall, represented a second birth, in which evolutionary instinct was replaced by social and cultural influences in the form of parents and other adults, who now replaced nature in protecting the child from unfavorable social conditions and in guiding his transformation into an altruistic, self-sacrificing, and moral human being. Hall believed that adolescence was a stressful period, due both to the repetition of evolutionary conflicts and to teenagers' increased vulnerability to social pressures. Although there is virtually no support for Hall's theoretical explanations, his view of adolescence as a time of "storm and stress" (sometimes called *Sturm und Drang*) remains popular today.

Hall's theory

Theoretical Views of Adolescence

Since the "creation" of adolescence in the United States, there have been two somewhat conflicting views about its basic nature. One view concurs with Hall's — that adolescence is a time of "storm and stress," a time when major physical, intellectual, and emotional changes create tremendous upset and crisis within the individual and conflict between the individual and society. As you may recall, both Freud and Erikson believed that development, especially in adolescence, is full of conflict.

The other view, which has grown out of observation and research with adolescents, suggests that for the most part, adolescence contains no more conflict than any other period. Most youngsters seem to adapt to the changes in themselves quite well, and adjust to the changing demands and expectations of parents and society in a relatively smooth and peaceful way.

As with so many differences in point of view, there is truth to both these views of adolescence. For the minority of adolescents at the two extremes, the transition to adulthood can be either smooth and effortless or a period of ongoing conflict. But for the vast majority, it is much more likely to fluctuate, with long periods of relative calm and shorter periods of surprisingly intense upheaval, which usually occur when they are least expected.

We discuss these and other social aspects of adolescence in greater detail in the next two chapters. Here, however, we must look more closely at the physical changes of adolescence and at their effects on development.

Checkpoint *Adolescence involves important physical changes that have psychological consequences. Adjustment to adolescence is stormy for some and calm for others, but mixed for most children and their families.*

Growth in Height and Weight

Compared to childhood, the years of adolescence — roughly twelve to twenty — include less overall growth in height and weight but significantly greater irregularity and unevenness in the pattern and pace of growth. This is clearly illustrated by Figure 14-1. As it shows, the average height for both boys and girls at twelve years is about fifty-nine or sixty inches. By age eighteen, however, the average height for boys is sixty-nine inches, while the average for girls is only sixty-four.

Much of this rapid change in height and weight is due to a dramatic **growth spurt,** which is preceded and followed by years of comparatively little increase. The change in height is particularly striking, as Figure 14-2 shows. The maximum rate of growth happens around age eleven or twelve for girls, and about two years later for boys. In those years, many girls grow three inches in a single year, and many boys grow more than four inches (Marshall, 1978).

Contrary to popular belief, though, it is not the growth spurt that accounts for males' greater average height. Instead, the difference results because boys start their growth spurt two years later than girls and so have two more years of childhood growing than girls do. Thus, the average girl is around fifty-four or fifty-five inches tall when she begins her growth spurt, whereas the average boy is fifty-nine or sixty inches tall when he begins his. Since both boys and girls add around nine or ten inches during adolescence, and grow relatively little afterward, women end up being shorter than men, on average (Thissen et al., 1976).

Interestingly, growth patterns and height during childhood are better predictors of adult height than growth patterns and height during adolescence are. That is, a tall ten-year-old is more likely to become a tall adult than is a tall thirteen-year-old who was short as a ten-year-old (Faust, 1977).

Because being the "right" height is important to many children (and their parents), there is an increasing interest in making early predictions about the final adult heights of children who are much shorter or taller than average. Measure-

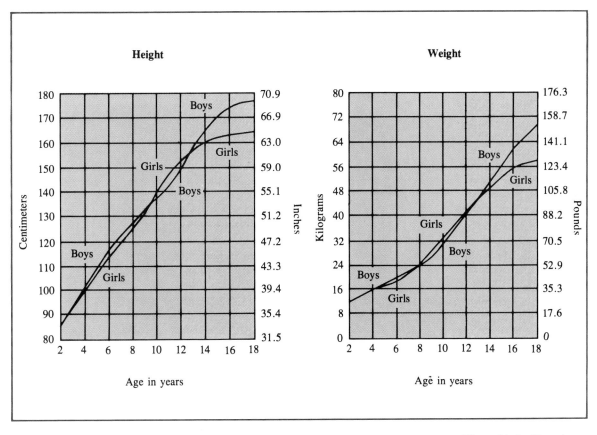

Figure 14–1 Growth
in Height and Weight
from Two to Eighteen
Years

ment of bone size and density in late childhood has proven to be an accurate pre-
dictor of how much more a child will probably grow. For example, Joan, a very tall
and "gangly" eleven-year-old, has been "growing like a weed"; she already measures five-nine in her bare feet and was relieved to learn that she would probably not
grow much more.

Should tests reveal that a child will be unusually tall (or short), doctors may prescribe hormone therapy, but they are extremely cautious about doing so, particularly during the growth spurt. One reason is that the hormones may have
unintended negative side effects. A second reason is that many doctors — and parents — believe that it is the meanings and values that individuals, their families,
and society attach to tallness and shortness, rather than the height itself, that is
often most important. Decisions to alter physical growth patterns may be irreversible, but meanings and values may change. For example, tallness, which has long
been valued for males, is gradually becoming more desirable for females, too, in
part because of society's changing attitudes about the female body and the roles
women play, and possibly because some female role models — for example, fashion models and female athletes — are tall.

Although weight also increases during adolescence (see Figure 14-1), it is more
easily influenced than height by diet, exercise, and general life-style, and therefore
changes in weight are less predictable. Girls begin puberty with slightly more total

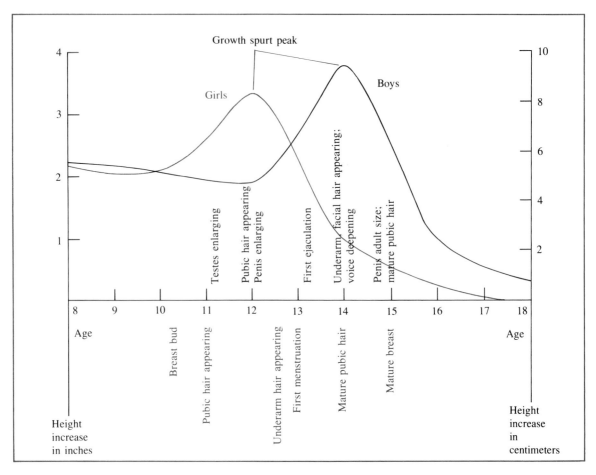

Growth spurt peak

Girls

Boys

Testes enlarging

Pubic hair appearing; Penis enlarging

First ejaculation

Underarm, facial hair appearing; voice deepening

Penis adult size; mature pubic hair

Age

Breast bud

Pubic hair appearing

Underarm hair appearing

First menstruation

Mature pubic hair

Mature breast

Age

Height increase in inches

Height increase in centimeters

Figure 14–2 Physical Development During Adolescence

Sex differences in weight and body fat

body fat than boys. During puberty, total body fat declines for boys from an average of 18 or 19 percent to 11 percent of body weight, whereas for girls it increases from about 21 percent to about 26 or 27 percent (Sinclair, 1978). The average weight gain during the growth spurt is about thirty-eight pounds for girls and forty-two pounds for boys, although there is considerable individual variation in how it is distributed.

Of course, adolescents differ greatly in their rates and patterns of growth; the growth spurt in some may be barely noticeable and may have little impact on their day-to-day existence, whereas for others it may be very striking and may radically alter their lives and feelings. These differences are further complicated by the fact that different parts of the body, including hands, feet, legs, arms, and torsos, often grow at different rates.

David, the fourteen-year-old we described at the beginning of the chapter, is a good example. Although he is somewhat below average in height and weight for his age group, he currently wears a size 12½ shoe — five shoe sizes larger than he wore two years ago. Although his family teases him about this, David secretly fears that he will always have very oversized feet, since his arms, legs, and other assorted body parts haven't yet caught up.

On the other hand, Debbie is concerned that she is too fat, that her chest is too big, and that her legs are too short for the rest of her body — or for boys to find attractive. Since Debbie's parents and friends, both male and female, think that she is very attractive and not fat at all, we might ask why Debbie has such different perceptions of herself. One answer might be **adolescent egocentrism,** the tendency of adolescents to find it difficult to perceive the world (and themselves) through anyone's eyes but their own. This is particularly true of their perceptions of how they look and how others perceive them. An adolescent's view of her own irregularities and regularities, her personal ideals regarding how she should look, and current social ideals of attractiveness all contribute to a very complicated and confusing state of affairs. Many adults cannot remember their own adolescent confusion and thus cannot understand teenagers' dissatisfaction with themselves. As a result, the physical changes that accompany puberty are a common source of emotional upset for both teenagers and their parents.

Much of the unevenness in growth that is typical of this period becomes better coordinated with time. Of course, though, not everyone ends up with the height, weight, and other physical characteristics that match society's ideals, or for that matter the individual's own.

The Secular Trend

During the past century children have gradually begun the physical changes of adolescence earlier and ended up taller and heavier than their parents, tendencies that are referred to as the **secular trend.** (In this context, *secular* means not tied to any specific economic or ethnic group in a society.) For example, the average age at which girls have their first menstrual period has dropped from between fifteen and seventeen a hundred years ago to between twelve and fourteen today, in both the United States and Western Europe. And while today's boys generally reach their full height between eighteen and twenty and girls between thirteen and fourteen, in 1880 the average male did not reach full height until between twenty-three and twenty-five, and the average female between nineteen and twenty (Tanner, 1971).

How can the secular trend be explained? Improvements in health care, diet, and overall living conditions are thought to be the major reasons for these changes. In particular, early childhood diseases that limit growth have been largely eliminated, and nutrition and medical care are greatly improved for children in developed countries. We can predict that a similar trend will occur wherever adequate nutrition and living conditions are available to all children and their families.

Checkpoint *A rapid increase in height and weight — the "growth spurt" — is the first step in a series of changes that lead to full physical and sexual maturity, or puberty. Because of improved living conditions, during the last century, children have tended to begin puberty earlier and to grow taller and heavier than their parents. Primary sexual maturation for boys and girls allows them to reproduce. For*

Puberty

Rapid increases in height and weight are only one part of a larger pattern of changes, called **puberty,** that leads to full physical and sexual maturity. Puberty is marked by striking changes in both primary and secondary sex characteristics. **Primary sex characteristics** make sexual reproduction possible. For girls, these include complex changes in the vagina, uterus, fallopian tubes, and ovaries; the most obvious sign of these is the beginning of menstrual periods. For boys, changes in primary sex characteristics include development of the penis, scrotum, testes, prostate gland, and seminal vesicles, which lead to the production of enough sperm for successful reproduction. Changes in **secondary sex characteristics** include enlargement of breasts, growth of body hair, and deepening of the voice. Associated with these developments are important changes in the levels of hormones present in the bloodstream; these powerful chemicals play a major part in initiating and regulating all of the changes associated with puberty.

Readiness for sexual reproduction

Primary Sexual Maturation

For boys, the most significant sign of sexual maturation is rapid growth of the penis and scrotum (the sack of skin underneath the penis which contains the testicles), which begins at around age twelve and continues for about five years for the penis and seven years for the scrotum — although individuals may vary by a year or two in either direction (Meredith, 1967). The penis typically increases in length by two or three times, so locker-room comparisons are almost inevitable as boys become increasingly aware of obvious changes in themselves and their friends. Ironically, penis size has almost nothing to do with eventual success at overall sexual functioning (Marshall and Tanner, 1974), but for adolescent boys it can sometimes seem all-important as a sign of their new status as men.

Production of sperm

During adolescence, enough live sperm are produced in the testes to make reproduction a real possibility for the first time. Sometime around age twelve, boys are likely to experience their first ejaculation of **semen,** a sticky fluid produced by the prostate gland, which is located near the penis just inside the body cavity. Semen carries the sperm to the penis and provides it with a medium in which to live after ejaculation. Most boys have their first ejaculation during masturbation or as **nocturnal emissions,** or wet dreams, during sleep, or, less frequently, as waking emissions that occur spontaneously. Most males report experiencing nocturnal emissions about one or two years before puberty; the accompanying dreams are frequently but not always erotic in nature. The sexual changes just discussed and the unexpected erections and uncomfortable sexual fantasies and sensations that boys sometimes experience are common sources of embarrassment. Less frequently they are a source of more serious discomfort and conflict.

For girls, the appearance of the first menstrual period, which is called **menarche,** signals sexual maturity. In most societies, menarche also symbolizes the shift from girlhood to womanhood (Logan, 1980). However, menarche occurs rather late in a girl's sexual maturation and is preceded by a number of other changes, including enlargement of the breasts, appearance of pubic hair, and broadening of the hips and shoulders. Next, as the growth spurt peaks, the uterus, vagina, labia, and clitoris develop, as do the ovaries.

The menstrual cycle is a fascinating and complex biological process that repeats itself approximately every twenty-eight days. Menstrual bleeding, which typically lasts between three and seven days, can be thought of both as the end of one cycle and as the beginning of the next. At this point, the hormone that regulates women's sexual functioning, estrogen, is at its lowest concentration in the blood, and the uterus sheds its lining, which is carried away in the menstrual flow. The cycle that follows is controlled by a system involving the hypothalamus, the pituitary gland, the ovaries, and the hormones produced by each. (See Figure 14-3.) **The menstrual cycle**

The hypothalamus, the part of the brain that monitors the level of ovarian hormones in the bloodstream, "senses" the low level of estrogen and causes the pituitary gland to release a hormone which in turn stimulates one of the egg-containing ovarian follicles to mature and the ovaries to produce more estrogen. As the level of estrogen increases, the mucous membrane that lines the uterus, the endometrium, develops in preparation for the zygote, if fertilization occurs. (As you will recall from Chapter 3, a zygote is formed when an egg is fertilized by sperm. It is from this single-celled zygote that the fetus eventually grows.)

When the fully matured egg tears away from its resting place in the follicle — a process called **ovulation,** which occurs about halfway through the cycle — the high level of estrogen in the blood triggers the pituitary gland, which releases a new hormone into the bloodstream. This is carried to the ruptured follicle, causing it to develop into the corpus luteum, a gland that produces both estrogen and progesterone, the pregnancy hormone, which together stimulate the glands of the endometrium to prepare it for the zygote. If fertilization does not occur, the pituitary stops production of its hormones and the corpus luteum dies. The level of estrogen drops, causing the endometrium to disintegrate into the mixture of blood, mucus, and tissues which make up the menstrual discharge. The low estrogen level now signals the hypothalamus to stimulate the pituitary, starting the entire cycle all over again (Williams, 1976).

For most girls, menstruation involves a certain degree of inconvenience and discomfort, but also feelings of happiness about the specialness of their reproductive capacity and womanhood. Adequate information about menstruation — including practical details about the purchase and use of sanitary napkins and tampons, about personal hygiene, and about birth control — is important. In addition, contact with women who have positive feelings about their monthly cycles will help to make menarche a positive experience and to allay fears and negative attitudes. As we shall see, the same informative and supportive climate is also helpful in dealing with the other physical changes of puberty. **Mixed feelings about menstruation**

Figure 14–3 The Menstrual Cycle This figure illustrates a typical 28-day cycle, showing (A) day 5, (B) day 14, ovulation, (C) day 19, and (D) day 1 of new cycle, which is the first day of menstrual period

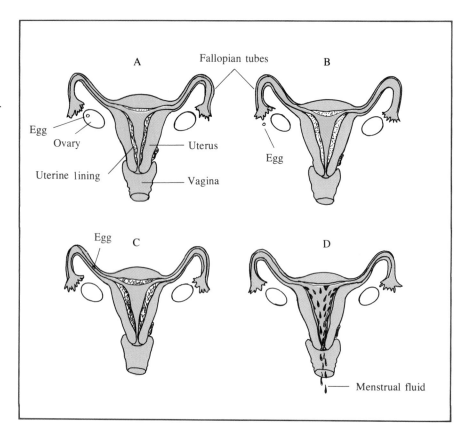

Maturation of Secondary Sex Characteristics

Breast development

Breasts Girls first develop breast "buds," or slightly raised nipples, with the beginning of puberty. During the following several years, the nipples grow darker, the areolas around the nipples increase in size, and the breasts continue to grow until they reach their full size.

Given the attention that our culture focuses on breasts, it is not surprising that breast development is a potential source of concern for many adolescent girls. Breasts that are too big, too small, or the "wrong" shape may cause embarrassment, and in rare cases girls experience outright harassment because of these physical developments.

Boys also have a small amount of breast development, especially in the areolas, which become larger and darker much as girls' areolas do. A few boys may experience enough tissue growth to cause them some embarrassment, but these "breasts" usually return to typically male levels in a year or two.

Hair When their genital development is relatively advanced, boys and girls both acquire more body hair, although boys generally grow more of it than girls do. The first growth is simply a fine fuzz around the genitals; later this **pubic hair** darkens and becomes coarser. At the same time underarm or **axillary hair** begins to appear; this eventually becomes dark and coarse as well.

For girls, breast development is one of the major occurrences of puberty, and getting a first bra can be an important event. Likewise, the growth of facial hair — and thus the need to shave — is a significant milestone for adolescent boys. (Top, David Witbeck/The Picture Cube; left, Jean B. Hollyman/Photo Researchers)

Pubic and axillary hair Although there are considerable differences among individuals, in girls pubic and axillary hair begins to appear around age eleven and is fully grown by around age fourteen. In boys it begins around twelve and continues until about eighteen. At age fifteen or so, many boys begin growing facial hair, which usually appears first as just a suggestion of a mustache that begins on the outer corners of the lips and gradually grows in toward the nose. It should be noted, however, that there are inherited ethnic and individual differences in the amount of facial hair and body hair that develops for both boys and girls. For example, some boys have little or no facial hair at all, or growth that is limited to their upper lips or chins.

Eventually boys may grow real whiskers on the chin and cheeks, as well as hair on the chest and back, though these later developments do not usually become obvious or significant until around age seventeen, or even beyond (Neyzi et al., 1975).

Social stereotypes to the contrary, girls typically grow facial and body hair as well. As with boys, a wide range of ethnic and individual differences exist. Differences in the lightness and darkness and coarseness and fineness of body hair will influence how noticeable it is. Cultural attitudes and expectations influence women's feelings about axillary hair during puberty. For example, while many women in our culture spend considerable time and money to rid themselves of "unsightly" underarm, leg, and facial hair, women in a number of European countries feel that this hair is attractive and do not attempt to remove it.

Voice In both sexes the voice deepens near the end of puberty and becomes richer in overtones, so that it sounds less like a flute or whistle and more like a violin or clarinet. These changes make the adolescent's voice sound more truly adult and less childlike, but they can lead to some difficult situations. It is not uncommon for a mother to be startled by the deep voice of a strange man in the house, only to discover that the voice belongs to her adolescent son. As mentioned earlier in this chapter, the fluctuations in voice qualities that some adolescents experience can be a cause of considerable — though usually temporary — embarrassment. Adolescent voice changes can also complicate the work of music teachers who direct junior and senior high school choruses.

Voice deepening Like many of the other changes of puberty, the deepening of the voice is not limited to one sex. Boys' voices do deepen somewhat more than girls', but social expectations encourage many girls to talk in voices that are higher than is comfortable, necessary, or really natural for them (Sachs et al., 1973; Henley, 1977). Similarly, boys who end up with voices that are higher than the deep male stereotype may face problems in asserting their masculinity.

Hormonal Changes and Their Consequences

As we have noted, at puberty boys and girls begin producing substantially more of several sex-related hormones. **Hormones** are chemicals produced by the endocrine glands and released or secreted directly into the bloodstream, by which they are carried to various organs of the body. Both the female sex glands, or **ovaries,** and the male sex glands, or **testes,** contain low levels of hormones that play a major role in sexual maturation. The pituitary gland, which is located at the base of the brain, can stimulate the testes or ovaries to produce more of the needed hormone. This overall process is in turn regulated by the hypothalamus, which is located in the upper brain stem.

Endocrine glands

Puberty increases the levels of all sex hormones in the blood of both sexes, but the pattern by which it does so differs for each sex. Consider **testosterone** and **estrogen,** two of the most important sex hormones. Testosterone is sometimes called the male sex hormone, because its high concentration in boys stimulates the growth of the penis and related male reproductive organs. For similar reasons, estrogen is sometimes called the female sex hormone, because its high concentration in girls stimulates the growth of the ovaries and vagina.

Sex hormones

Hormones affect more than just sexual characteristics — for example, they are responsible for the typical differences between boys' and girls' overall body builds. In general, the sex that has shorter bones and more rounded curves — namely, female — also has higher estrogen levels; and the sex that has longer bones and larger muscles — namely, male — also has higher levels of testosterone (Villee, 1975; Cheek, 1974).

Testosterone stimulates muscle and bone growth in both sexes. Throughout childhood, boys and girls are about equally muscular. They have roughly the same number and sizes of muscle fibers, and they can exert about the same amount of strength with their muscles. Although individual children vary around the averages, as groups the two sexes differ very little (Malina, 1978a).

Puberty significantly changes this equality. During puberty, boys typically become more muscular-looking than girls, even though girls, too, become more muscular as they grow. Boys experience close to a fourteen-fold increase in the size of the largest muscle fibers between early childhood and adolescence, with most of the increase occurring during adolescence. Girls, in contrast, experience only a tenfold increase (Malina, 1978b; Brasel and Gruen, 1978).

Sex differences in muscle growth

Some of this difference may result from life experiences more specific to teenage boys than to girls. For example, teenage boys receive greater encouragement and opportunity to participate in sports, and more responsibilities that involve work and other heavy muscular activity (Frisch, 1983; Warren, 1983). Differences in hormone levels may also be influenced by differences in behavior and life experiences. Sustained exercise, for example, tends to increase a person's level of testosterone (Rogers and Walsh, 1982).

Estrogen stimulates increased deposits of subcutaneous fat, that is, fat under the skin. It also stimulates the final maturation of bones, a process in which the growing areas within individual bones finally become hard and fixed in size.

Throughout childhood, boys and girls tend to possess almost identical amounts of fat (or adipose) tissue (Johnston et al., 1974). In the years just prior to the growth spurt, the body of a typical child might consist of about one fifth fat; boys tend to have just a little less than this amount, and girls just a little more.

Sex differences in fat

During adolescence, however, the two sexes begin to differ noticeably in their proportions of fat tissue. Boys tend to keep most of their deposits of fat and simply stretch them over an increasingly larger body. Because their muscles and bones tend to grow particularly rapidly during puberty, boys' fat tissue decreases as a proportion of their total body weight. The overall result? A relatively muscular, bony-looking person, at least compared to a typical girl (Chumlea et al., 1983).

Girls, on the other hand, develop significant new deposits of subcutaneous fat during adolescence while maintaining their previous ones from childhood. The new fat develops in all the locations that make girls look typically female: in their breasts, hips and buttocks, thighs, and upper arms (Sinclair, 1978). The new fat tissues combine with girls' smaller muscles and bones to make young females significantly more rounded than young males. By the end of adolescence, fat accounts for more than one fourth of their body weight, but among males, it accounts for only about one eighth.

Note, however, that this difference does not mean that girls tend to be overweight — only that their bodies are composed of different proportions of tissues, and that these tissues are distributed differently. Adolescent boys and girls of the same height tend to weigh almost the same, yet in most cases the girls do not look fat, but simply female. Cultural standards of female beauty make some perfectly normal adolescent girls want to lose weight even though they do not need to or should not do so for their own health; this sort of weight "problem" is cultural and not physiological.

Cultural influences

These relationships make it tempting to conclude that testosterone and estrogen "cause" physical sex differences in adolescence. To some extent, they may in fact do so, but the relationship is probably also more complicated. A large number of hormones act together at puberty, so that no one hormone can claim unique credit for "producing" physical sex differences. To some extent, too, hormone levels may also result from sex differences in behavior and life experiences. As already noted, for example, sustained exercise tends to result in a higher level of testosterone. So if one sex is consistently encouraged to exercise a lot and the other is not, then cultural practices may account for some of the difference in hormone levels and body build — and not the other way around.

The Extent of Physical Sex Differences

As the preceding information reveals, the sex differences that develop during puberty are matters of emphasis or degree. Except for eggs, sperm and form of genitals, every physical structure and characteristic exists in both sexes, sometimes in surprisingly similar amounts or levels. Both sexes grow new hair as a result of puberty, and both sexes develop substantially larger muscles and bones. The physical differences between males and females, which are referred to as **sexual dimorphism,** are triggered by the same set of hormones, which are produced in much the same ways in both.

Even differences in the timing of puberty are less significant than they first appear to be: the two-year gap between the sexes occurs mainly in the most visible of the physical changes of puberty, the growth spurt. As it happens, the spurt in growth is one of the first changes to happen to girls and one of the last to happen to boys. Changes that are less visible, such as the development of adult genitalia and

Where Do Adolescents First Learn about Sex?

Many pre-adolescents are confronted with pressure to become sexually involved prior to the onset of puberty and thus before they are physiologically and emotionally prepared for such experiences. This "social puberty" is to a large extent a product of exposure to sexual behaviors through television, motion pictures, literature, music, and advertising; children are also subjected to peer pressure to become sexually active. The naturalness of sex and its consequences are rarely understood or realistically presented to the preadolescent (Thornburg, 1975).

To better understand what types of early sex information teenagers have and from whom they generally obtain such information, Hershel Thornburg asked 451 students enrolled in major universities in California, Illinois, Louisiana, and Pennsylvania to state how old they were when they learned about sex, how accurate the information was, and where they first learned about it. Thornburg specifically asked them about twelve topics: abortion, contraception, ejaculation, homosexuality, intercourse, masturbation, menstruation, origin of babies, petting, prostitution, seminal emissions, and venereal disease.

According to the results of this survey, adolescents appear to get approximately comparable amounts of information from schools and literature. With the exception of information gained from mothers about menstruation (43.2 percent) and the origin of babies (44.6 percent), parents' contributions are quite low. The importance of peers is clear: they provide 60 percent of the information on petting and 56 percent on intercourse, the two most prevalent areas of adolescent sexual expression. More reliable sources of information such as parents and schools contributed little here, perhaps because they are hesitant to discuss sexual behavior, despite their interest and concern.

When the data were analyzed to determine if boys and girls are likely to seek out different sources of information to learn about sex, two major differences were found. Girls depended more on their mothers for information than boys did (19.3 percent versus 5.4 percent), and boys depended more on peers for information than girls did (45.2 percent versus 35.3 percent).

Subjects rated each of the sources of information as highly accurate, accurate, distorted, or highly distorted. The overall average accuracy rating (highly accurate, accurate) for the twelve sexual concepts was 73.75 percent. The highest accuracy ratings were reported for abortion, menstruation, and venereal disease. (Interestingly, the subjects obtained most information about abortion from literature, about venereal disease from school, and — as already noted — about menstruation from their mothers.) Accuracy of information about homosexuality, intercourse, and masturbation, which was most likely to come from peers, fell within the 60 percent range. Thornburg notes that the accuracy ratings found here are higher than those of previous studies of populations that were not as well educated.

Information from this and similar studies may be useful in guiding parents, teachers, and adolescents in increasing the range and reliability of their information about sexual behavior and its consequences.

shifts in hormonal balances, occur at almost the same average ages. On the whole, puberty begins and ends at nearly the same age for both sexes (Tanner, 1978).

From the biological standpoint, then, the sexes do not represent physical opposites so much as related but distinct patterns of similar physical elements and processes. The physical similarity between the sexes has not, of course, prevented society from constructing different roles and expectations for males and females. Indeed, society tends to focus a great deal of attention on gender differences and to exaggerate their significance.

Nor has the physical similarity between males and females kept individual adolescents from developing rigid standards for and preferences about their own physical development. Sometimes very slight physical differences either in amount of development or in its timing can have very significant psychological effects on a teenager. For example, the size of breasts or of the penis can be a source of pride or embarrassment, depending on personal expectations as well as the responses of others. So can being too tall, too short, too fat, or too thin, or having physical characteristics that do not closely approximate cultural "ideals." The tyranny of fashion, emphasized by the media, plays a significant role in this, causing discomfort to boys and girls whose bodies do not fit the current ideals of physical attractiveness.

Checkpoint *Male and female hormones stimulate muscle, fat, and bone growth and the development of secondary sex characteristics — enlarged breasts and the growth of pubic and axillary hair, for example. But they do so in differing degrees for boys and girls, which helps account for the different physical appearances of male and female adolescents.*

Psychological Effects of Physical Growth in Adolescence

Considering how rapid the physical changes of puberty are, it is not surprising that young people are often preoccupied and dissatisfied with the way they look (Hamburg, 1974). Dissatisfaction is most noticeable during the early adolescent years, when most teenagers are attending junior high school. During this time, every young adolescent must somehow continue to live with himself and manage relationships with others as well. He cannot ignore how tall he has grown within just a few months, or how suddenly he has "developed." Even if he does try to ignore such changes, his peers will probably notice them and form their own opinions, either positive or negative, about them. At this age, adolescents find comparisons among their peers very important, for these comparisons provide an important basis for self-evaluation.

Because of the many rapid changes their bodies are undergoing, and because of the emphasis our society places on physical attractiveness, teens are apt to worry about how they look. These high school students are all developing normally, but privately they may worry about being too tall or too short, too heavy or too thin. (Paul Conklin)

Body Image and Self-Esteem

Almost all adolescents are concerned about their changing bodies and their attractiveness. Even the most attractive teenager worries about her hair, her nose, or a pimple on her chin. What determines just how much discomfort a particular adolescent feels about her own body?

For one thing, conventional standards of attractiveness have considerable influence. In our culture, people of all ages find certain body builds more attractive than others. One researcher documented these preferences by showing children and adolescents pictures of people with various builds and asking them for their opinions about the comparative attractiveness of the pictured people (Lerner, 1969). Some of the pictures showed people with muscular or **mesomorphic** builds; the second group showed rounder, more padded, **endomorphic** people; and the third group of pictures showed people with slender, **ectomorphic** builds. (See Figure 14–4.) Children and adolescents clearly considered the mesomorphic bodies to be the most attractive, especially if they were male. To some degree mesomorphic qualities were preferred even for females, although standards for females also allowed for bodies that were fuller, with more padding and curves. In general, too much or too little fat was judged to be less attractive, though not necessarily "ugly."

Adolescents evaluate themselves and their peers according to such stereotypes. Teenagers with mesomorphic body builds tend to be judged relatively more attrac-

Standards of attractiveness

Figure 14–4   Three Body Types

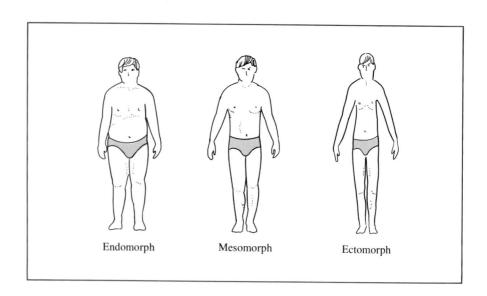

Endomorph   Mesomorph   Ectomorph

tive than those with endomorphic and ectomorphic builds; they also tend to have more friends, and to be rated relatively high in status or prestige among their peers (Clausen, 1975). To a certain extent, positive judgments from others become a fact of life for many mesomorphic teenagers. Of course, such a fact of life does not guarantee happiness. In the right conditions, conventionally attractive youngsters may indeed develop greater self-esteem than others because of the appreciation they receive. In the wrong conditions, though, such appreciation can have negative effects. By receiving approval for something that is a matter of genetic chance, the person may come to believe that he is not appreciated for other important qualities, and that he cannot influence the opinions of his friends by his conduct (Livson and Peskin, 1980). Teenagers who are physically "unattractive" may compensate by developing other kinds of attractive qualities including being energetic and outgoing, having a good sense of humor, and being a good listener.

Peers' and parents' influence   In any case, whether or not an adolescent considers himself truly attractive depends on more than what he thinks his peers think. The impressions conveyed by parents and other close family members undoubtedly influence an adolescent's attitudes toward his body, no matter how conventionally attractive he is. Parents who value qualities other than physical attractiveness can help their teenager to cope better with the awkwardness of puberty (Schonfield, 1966). An adolescent's feeling of attractiveness also depends on how he feels about himself in general. If he suffers from low self-esteem — if he feels badly about himself as a human being, regardless of his physical characteristics — he is more likely to worry about and feel negative toward his body (Schonfield, 1971).

Perceptions about attractiveness are strongly influenced by the existing cultural stereotypes for feminine and masculine beauty. Role models such as fashion models and actors help create and gain widespread acceptance for these stereotypes. Although there may be more than one "ideal" type for men and women — which may reflect to some extent changing views of physical fitness and body

Body build probably does not affect these boys directly. But it may affect their self-confidence indirectly, because peers tend to prefer muscular, or mesomorphic, builds over other sorts. (Janice Fullman/The Picture Cube)

building, for example — still only a very small percentage of teenagers happen to have bodies that come even reasonably close.

One consequence is that successive generations of teenagers have attempted to modify their bodies to fit the prevailing stereotypes, sometimes with tragic results. For example, compulsive efforts to increase muscle mass may combine body building, unsafe dieting, and using steroids and other drugs. Such a regimen poses serious health hazards to an increasing number of male and (more recently) female athletes. Steroids have been banned in most athletic programs because they have been shown to cause liver damage.

Influence of stereotypes

Obsessive concern about being slender has led many teenage girls to adopt diets that are seriously deficient in nutrition. Anorexia nervosa and bulimia are eating disorders that involve distorted relationships between eating and body image; they appear to be connected, at least in part, to cultural stereotypes. We discuss them more fully later in the chapter.

Adolescents who have atypical physical characteristics because of inherited or acquired abnormalities sometimes face more serious psychological problems regarding their bodies. For example, children who are badly scarred or whose movements are spasmodic must learn to cope with these added burdens. As suggested by the film *Mask,* which is about an adolescent whose face and head are

Atypical adolescents

grossly disfigured, strong, loving, and honest support from parents and friends can make it possible for a handicapped child to feel good about himself and his body. While physical appearance is certainly important, beauty and positive self-concept really are more than skin deep.

Early- Versus Late-Maturing Adolescents

The timing of puberty can make a lasting difference to the psychological development of an adolescent, particularly if physical maturation is very early or very late. The effects of early and late maturation depend partly on the sex of the teenagers, and they tend to change over the long term.

Support for these ideas comes from several old but valuable longitudinal studies of adolescents in Oakland and Berkeley, California (Livson and Peskin, 1980).

Perspectives on Research

Body Satisfaction in Adolescence

As part of a series of studies investigating body image and self-concept among adolescents, 146 males and 194 females completed a survey of body satisfaction (Clifford, 1971). The subjects were between the ages of eleven and nineteen, with an average age of about fourteen; they were from a wide range of social backgrounds.

The adolescents rated forty-five items on a five-point scale: 1 = I don't like it at all and wish it could be changed; 2 = I don't like it; 3 = I have no special feelings about it one way or the other; 4 = I am satisfied; 5 = I am completely satisfied and I would not change it if I could.

Total body-satisfaction scores were obtained for each adolescent by summing their ratings for each item. The mean score for males (3.71) was significantly greater than for females (3.39), indicating that females are less satisfied or more critical of their bodies than males are. Body satisfaction did not correlate with age. Higher intelligence test scores were significantly associated with a greater degree of body satisfaction for males, though not for females.

The mean satisfaction rating for each item was calculated separately for males and for females. The items were then ranked in order of these values, with the rank of 1 assigned to the item with the most positive mean rating. Some differences do occur in how males and females rank particular items. For example, while females give eyes the highest rank of 1 and "myself" a rank of 20, males reverse this ranking, giving "myself" a rank of 1 and eyes a rank of 20. Overall, however, there is a great deal of similarity in how the sexes rank the forty-five items.

The significantly lower mean satisfaction scores for females support the widely held idea that females are more critical of their bodies because of the greater cultural emphasis placed on standards of beauty and appearance for women. However, a number of similarities in body satisfaction were also found, which suggests that cultural pressures concerning physical appearance operate for males as well. For example, both sexes indicated relative dissatisfaction with their heights, weights, chests, waists, and hips, as well as with their noses, hair, and overall looks.

Finally, Clifford notes that the levels of body satisfaction are high for both sexes, and that neither the satisfaction nor the dissatisfaction that adolescents express about their bodies should be overemphasized.

Because girls tend to have their growth spurt earlier than boys, relationships between the sexes can be especially awkward early in adolescence. Differences in height between early-maturing girls and late-maturing boys are particularly evident at school dances like this one. (Elizabeth Crews)

These children were all born in the 1920s and 1930s and reached their teens during the 1940s. At that time, they were given a variety of psychological tests and were interviewed to learn more about their personalities. Records of these observations were preserved carefully, and the individuals were retested and interviewed at regular intervals throughout their lives to provide fairly direct comparisons with earlier observations. The results have indicated a number of ways in which the timing of puberty can affect individuals' psychological and social development.

For example, boys who mature early seem to experience certain advantages. As we have described, puberty tends to make all boys more muscular and mesomorphic in appearance. Those boys who acquire this appearance earlier than usual — by age twelve, say, instead of fourteen — gain favorable responses from peers, teachers, and other important people sooner and for longer than their agemates do. Some observers suggest that early-maturing boys seem to respond to these changes and the positive attitudes they elicit in very advantageous ways: they seem relatively more self-confident in their behavior and generally strike others as being more grownup or mature (Livson and Peskin, 1980; Mussen and Jones, 1957). They are also more likely to be chosen as leaders in high school.

Early-maturing boys have social advantages

However, a careful look suggests that there may also be some disadvantages in early maturation for boys. Though they are perceived as more mature, self-confident, and competent than others, they are also more somber, less creative, and less spontaneous, perhaps because of their need to live up to the expectations that accompany their adult, masculine body image.

Late-maturing boys are a different story. These boys still resemble children, at least physically, as late as age sixteen. Teachers, parents, and other observers tend to judge them unfavorably, viewing them as being impulsive, immature, and lacking in self-confidence. In school, late-maturing boys tend to be regarded as socially inferior to earlier-maturing peers; they often regard themselves this way as well.

Late-maturing boys are viewed less favorably

So, although early-maturing boys seem to have happier lives than late maturers do, the two groups may differ only in that one group receives more social approval. Long-term follow-ups of these youths strongly suggest that this explanation is correct. At age thirty-eight, for example, early-maturing boys who were still participants in these studies continued to be relatively responsible, sociable, and self-controlled; they also continued to be more rigid, moralistic, and conforming than their peers (Jones, 1965). Late-maturing boys interviewed at age thirty-eight

---

A Talk with Kenny

Physical Development During Adolescence

Kenny is eighteen years old; he was interviewed toward the end of his senior year in high school.

INTERVIEWER: What have you noticed about the physical changes in yourself over the last few years?

KENNY: Well, first off I always wanted to be taller. I'm five-eight and my father's six-three and I always thought I would be at least six-three. Didn't quite make it, but . . .

INTERVIEWER: When did you notice that you weren't going to make it?

KENNY: Probably in the beginning of my junior year. I said, "Gee, I'm only five-six and a half. I don't think I'm going to make it."

INTERVIEWER: Are you still growing?

KENNY: Yes, a little bit, but that's when my growing tapered off.

INTERVIEWER: When did you notice that you were starting to grow?

KENNY: Probably around my freshman year . . . end of eighth grade and going into high school. I noticed that I just started shooting up a little bit. I kept saying to my father, "See how tall I am? I'm going to catch you, I'm going to catch you." But I don't think so. Other physical changes that I noticed were obviously with the basic parts of your body, your penis, testicles, pubic hair.

INTERVIEWER: Did that come as a shocker, or was it easy?

KENNY: It was easy. I always thought I was going to have hair on my face before I grew it anywhere else.

INTERVIEWER: I see you have a mustache, which looks great.

KENNY: I've had the mustache for a long time. It started as dirt on my upper lip.

INTERVIEWER: That was how you thought of it?

KENNY: That was one thing I thought I had an edge over the other

kids with. A-ha! I have a mustache and you don't! I pretty much had the beginnings of a mustache for a long time, but other kids said, "Shave it off and let it grow back and it will grow back thicker." I haven't done that. I've just let it grow and that's all I've basically done. Now I'm starting to shave more regularly now. I have a fear of getting razor bumps, so I let my facial hair grow and cut it off and you just get used to it. You sort of ease into it instead of trying to rush it.

INTERVIEWER: Do most teenagers like to have a mustache or some other sign of maturing physically?

KENNY: Yes, I think so. It makes you feel older, wiser, more in control of the situation. They can't wait until they grow a mustache and a beard, because it tends to make them look a lot older and it's harder for people to tell how old they really are.

INTERVIEWER: Are there other

appeared to have developed certain positive qualities not strongly evident during adolescence. Although they still conveyed the impression of being impulsive and inappropriately assertive, they also seemed more insightful and perceptive, and more creative in solving problems. All in all, over the long run, a mixed picture emerges for both kinds of boys.

A mixed picture over the long term

Achieving puberty and sexual maturity may involve considerably more potential conflict for girls than for boys, in large part because of widely held stereotypes that associate puberty with increased willingness to engage in sexual activity as well as with a desire to become wives and mothers. Although a youngster who has achieved puberty may have the physical characteristics of a mature woman, there is no reason to assume that she is emotionally ready to make decisions about birth control or about sexual relationships; neither should it be assumed that she is

---

physical changes that are important?

KENNY: I think that physical build was kind of important to me and some other people. It was like we were freshmen and you wanted to do anything and everything so that you fit in. When you were a sophomore, you thought that you owned the place, and you started to change more physically and you said, "Hey, now that I'm a big sophomore, I've been in the school and I know the juniors who are now the seniors, and the sophomores who are now the juniors. Everything is different." Many kids shot up over the summer. And a lot of kids got into physical training. Weightlifting, gymnastics, martial arts, whatever. I got into bodybuilding for a while, but I said no, this isn't really what I want to do. But there are a lot of phases. You want to play sports, get a letter, girlfriend, jackets. . . .

INTERVIEWER: How do you think girls feel about these things?

KENNY: I think most guys got into bodybuilding and working out because girls look more for a big, strong, macho football player type of person than really anything else at this point . . . like in my sophomore and junior year. They weren't really looking for how intelligent a person was, how caring they were. They were mostly attracted to you physically . . . what does his face look like, how his hair is, what his build is, what his butt looks like, how nice are his legs, and so on. But I think one thing that was kind of funny was in my junior year, I got voted the best legs in the school. I thought that was pretty funny. I got a kick out of it. Later, during my junior year and into my senior year, a lot of people started seeing me for what I really was.

INTERVIEWER: What do you think this period is like for girls?

KENNY: I think that some girls are smart enough to realize that boys are interested mostly during your

sophomore-junior year in their physical development. Period. How big their breasts get, their hair, their eyes, how large their butt is, how nice their legs look, and so on and so forth . . . if they're not overweight; if they're dressed right.

Follow-up Questions

1. In what ways do conventional standards of physical attractiveness appear to influence Kenny's feelings of self-esteem?

2. What role does sexual dimorphism play in the types of body build that are most highly valued in Kenny's peer group?

3. How does Kenny feel about the effects of early physical maturation? How consistent are his views with those presented in the chapter?

developmentally ready to assume a greater degree of responsibility for adult work, in or outside the home.

Keep in mind, too, that early maturation for a girl means that she enters puberty at around nine or ten, an age that most adults would definitely consider to be a child. Early maturation also puts a girl out of step with common standards for female beauty. Because of the hormonal changes of puberty, she becomes relatively tall, muscular, and sometimes heavy-set for a ten-year-old; her later-developing agemates remain relatively slender and short. And since she also becomes more shapely and sexually mature, she may find herself in dating and sexual encounters for which she is not psychologically ready. Remember, a ten-year-old is still in the fifth grade.

The Oakland and Berkeley studies found that very early-maturing girls seemed relatively awkward and ill at ease in social situations, and that they seemed chronically under stress and preoccupied with their looks (Peskin, 1973). However, once physically precocious fifth-graders had successfully lived through the next several years, they were likely to have increased status and popularity and to be better able to cope with the challenges of adolescence than their peers. This may partly be a result of the skills they learned in dealing with adversity, or life may have become easier for these early maturers as their later-blooming peers caught up.

In contrast, girls who matured comparatively late — around age fourteen — experienced social advantages throughout adolescence. Teachers and other observers rated these late-maturing girls as more attractive and as better leaders, and they did in fact become school leaders relatively often.

As with boys, though, the long-term effects differed from the immediate or short-term effects. When the Oakland and Berkeley girls were studied at age thirty, the anxiety-filled, early-maturing individuals seemed more poised and self-directed than the late-maturing girls did. The difference was especially visible in those women who had encountered difficult circumstances, such as divorce or serious illness, as adults. In such circumstances, late-maturing adolescents appeared to cope noticeably better than did early maturers.

Two explanations may account for how timing of puberty affects later development (Peterson and Taylor, 1980). First, peers and adults are likely to think of and treat a very early or late maturer in ways that deviate from attitudes expressed toward the individual's more average peers. The results may either be positive or negative, depending on the nature of this treatment. Among boys, very early maturation creates positive responses in others, although the longer-run effects for the children themselves are not necessarily all positive. This may be partly because the muscular, mesomorphic physiques of many of these boys often enable them to excel early in athletics and to physically resemble culturally desirable stereotypes. On the negative side, boys who become overdependent upon these early advantages may experience a loss of self-esteem and self-worth when their normal and later-developing peers eventually catch up.

Deviation toward late maturity tends to create more negative responses, though here again the longer-range effects may not be all negative. Boys who are very late developers may be perceived as being childish and socially immature, in part because their self-consciousness about their delayed physical development limits

Early maturation can be stressful for girls

Late-maturing girls have social advantages

Long-term changes

their opportunities to become involved in sports and social activities. On the other hand, their physical immaturity may to some degree protect them from the increasing pressures to become sexually and socially active — which are harder for their normal and early-developing peers to resist — and allow them greater freedom to develop their own unique identities.

Among girls, the effects are somewhat the opposite. Early maturation for a girl initially creates negative responses, but in the longer run, it often has positive results. As discussed earlier, the task of dealing with stereotyped and inappropriate sexual and social expectations is likely to be stressful for a physically mature fifth- or sixth-grader, although why this may be helpful in the longer run is still unclear. Later-maturing girls have an easier time during adolescence — perhaps for cultural reasons similar to those that benefit early-maturing boys — but it is not clear that they experience significant longer-range benefits.

How timing of puberty affects development

A second possible explanation is that the timing of puberty influences how much freedom and opportunity a child has to develop a strong sense of self and to prepare for the eventual challenges of adolescence. If puberty comes when society prefers it to come — early for boys and late for girls — then the adolescent may have little reason to develop a strong inner sense of himself, because he may be too busy living up to social expectations: that he be sexually active and involved in structured extracurricular activities, for example, rather than spending more time on informal activities and on his own. On the other hand, if puberty comes when society does not approve, then the adolescent may feel much more pressed to understand himself. Indeed, he may feel forced to do a lot of reflecting in order to understand and overcome the feelings of anger and social inferiority that arise from failing to fulfill society's timetable for physical maturation. As with all developmental conflict, the experience of mastering the challenge may actually be beneficial rather than detrimental to future personality development.

Most adolescents, of course, mature at more or less the average age, rather than at the extremely early or late ones discussed here. Thus the typical adolescent experiences a mixture of both pressure to conform to social standards and the need to reflect on his true identity.

Checkpoint *Many adolescents experience considerable concern and stress about their rapidly changing bodies. Cultural ideals of physical attractiveness, judgments by peers and parents, and self-evaluations influence how comfortable an adolescent feels about how he or she looks. There are both advantages and disadvantages for boys and girls who are early or late in achieving puberty.*

Health in Adolescence

In some ways, adolescents are among the healthiest of all people. They are past most childhood diseases such as chicken pox, mumps, and measles, and tend to have fewer colds and ear infections than young children or adults (Fry, 1974). And compared with adults, they suffer fewer of the illnesses and physical damage that are associated with prolonged exposure to physical and emotional stress and with aging.

High health risks However, adolescents actually experience *greater* health risks than either younger children or adults do. Compared with either age group, they are much more likely to be injured in motor vehicle accidents, to misuse alcohol and other drugs (Bachman et al., 1981), to find themselves unexpectedly pregnant, and to have poor eating and health care habits.

Continuity with Health in Childhood

The health and health-care patterns of most individuals show considerable consistency and continuity from early childhood through adolescence (Starfield and Pless, 1980). This is true of common, recurring illnesses, of patterns of utilization of medical services, and of individuals' overall levels of health as judged by doctors and other health-care professionals.

Recurrences of Specific Illnesses Even though children tend to get sick less often as they grow into adolescence, individuals tend to show consistent patterns of illness over time. For example, a five-year-old who catches more colds than most children her age is likely to catch more colds than her agemates when she is fifteen, **Similar but less frequent problems** even though neither she nor her peers will be sick as often as they were when they were five-year-olds. The same pattern holds true for ear infections, though in this case frequent infections in childhood may contribute to chronic ear problems in adolescence and adulthood (Starfield, 1977). Children with chronic coughs during their preschool years have twice the risk that others have of persistently coughing as adolescents and young adults, even if they never take up smoking (Kiernan et al., 1976).

Use of Medical Services These trends are based on analyses of patients' medical records, and therefore represent doctors' opinions about the state of people's health. What do we know about how adolescents use health-care services? First, as you might expect, individuals differ in how often they visit the doctor, for what reasons, and in what circumstances. Second, individuals appear to remain relatively consistent in how often they make visits, no matter what their age. People who visit the doctor frequently as young children continue to do so as adolescents, while those who visit less frequently early in life tend to maintain this pattern later on (Densen et al., 1959; Starfield and Pless, 1980).

Three different but related explanations are useful in accounting for these patterns. The first focuses on an individual's attitudes and expectations about health **Reasons behind health-care patterns** and the treatment and prevention of illness. Obviously, a person who believes that visits to doctors and other health-care professionals are an essential part of solving health problems is likely to make greater use of such resources than someone who does not believe that doctors are necessary or helpful.

Health care is extremely expensive and not available to all; many families are too poor to afford to pay for care that adequately meets their needs. Thus, an individual's economic situation is apt to influence his use of medical resources. If poor families receive inferior medical care and are treated in humiliating ways, as is often the case, their children will probably develop negative attitudes toward doctors and hospitals. In contrast, children from families whose financial resources allow them more regular and positive contacts with the health-care system are likely to have more positive attitudes and better health habits.

Regardless of their family situation, however, adolescents in general are less likely than other age groups to have consistently positive attitudes toward health care, or to use health-care resources in a consistent and appropriate manner. Why is this the case? For one thing, adolescents tend to believe that they are invulnerable; that is, they have an unrealistic sense that they are safe from illness and other physical harm. For another, adolescents' struggles for independence and autonomy frequently include at least temporary rejection of their parents' positive attitudes and practices.

Concepts of Illness and Health in Adolescence

As we mentioned in Chapter 11, children's understanding of the relationship between their behavior and their health plays a key role in how much responsibility they can assume for their own health.

It is not until adolescence that children are able to understand health in terms of multiple causes and cures and to realize that interrelationships among thoughts, feelings, and changes in physical health are significant.

In spite of this new capability, however, many adolescents (and adults) understand illness in terms of single events or causes rather than multiple ones. A teenager may say, "I caught a cold because I went out in the rain last night," when in reality she was tired to begin with and the friends she went out with were already sick. Only a minority of adolescents include psychological factors as a partial reason for getting sick or as contributing to feeling ill. The teenager who went out in the rain may fail to mention that she has felt depressed and anxious lately, and that these feelings have been interfering with her sleep and making her generally rundown. She may also fail to point out that her cold feels worse because of her poor spirits; if she felt better psychologically, the illness might be hardly worth mentioning.

Misunderstanding of multiple causes of illness

Such incomplete understandings of illness and its causes contribute to adolescents' seemingly irresponsible health habits. If a teenager happens to believe (wrongly) that she will catch a cold only if she doesn't wear enough warm clothes, then presumably she should remain healthy if she bundles up. If she also believes (wrongly) that curing an illness is just as desirable as preventing it in the first place, then she may not work particularly hard at preventing it. Breaking a leg while doing gymnastics may not seem like much of a risk, as long as appropriate medical services can repair the leg; contracting an infection in her ears may not seem like much of a risk either, as long as she believes that a doctor can always give her a drug to cure it.

Automobiles give teenagers a great deal of independence. But they also have drawbacks: auto collisions are the leading cause of death in adolescence. (Ulrike Welsch)

Such beliefs reduce an individual's sense of personal responsibility for taking care of herself. From the point of view of young people, health, like schools and families, is managed by the adult world (Lewis and Lewis, 1983). This fact does not necessarily create hostility to health care, but it probably does encourage passivity or indifference to personal health.

But it need not do so. In certain circumstances, adolescents and even children can become very careful managers of their own health. Programs to encourage **Learning self-care skills** self-care have had significant success in elementary schools and high schools. In one program, for instance, students were given special passes to visit the school nurse whenever they needed to, and they were encouraged to use the passes freely (Lewis and Lewis, 1977). Contrary to the fears of the teachers, students rarely overused the passes or used them as excuses to get out of academic work. Instead, they nearly always used them for what the nurses judged to be genuine, health-related reasons. In the opinions of the nurses, in fact, the effectiveness of school health care improved because of the free-pass policy: students visited the nurses more often when they really were sick and less often when they were not. The former policy, in which teachers decided whether to refer students to the nurse, led to more visits when students were not really ill.

Causes of Death among Adolescents

Although adolescents appear to be relatively unaffected by the health problems **High death rate** that cause death in younger children and adults, the death rate during adolescence is one of the highest of all age groups. The major causes of death for adolescents and young adults (ages fifteen to twenty-four) are accidents, murder, and suicide.

Motor vehicle accidents — a high proportion of which involve the use of alcohol — kill more than 14,000 adolescents and young adults each year, more than all other accidents combined. Approximately 2,100 teenagers die from homicide and 1,800 from suicide, the second and third major causes of adolescent death, followed by drownings, accidental shootings, and poisonings (Smith, Bierman, and Robinson, 1978). It should be noted that a very high proportion of these accidental and induced deaths occur among males, who as a group have much riskier lifestyles than females do. Middle- and working-class males are likely to believe that risk taking and experimentation with cars and motorcycles, alcohol, and other drugs are signs of masculinity. Poor and minority males are at still greater risk for accidental death. The inner-city environments in which they generally live and the lifestyles they lead are even more likely to involve the use and sale of drugs, participation in gangs, and exposure to various forms of physical violence, including the use of lethal weapons.

Among the additional causes, war accounts for more deaths among adolescent males than any other. Cancer, cardiovascular, respiratory, and congenital disorders, kidney disorders, and infectious diseases kill both male and female teenagers (Smith, Bierman, and Robinson, 1978).

Adolescent Health Problems

Although adolescents are not prone to the infectious diseases of childhood, they often adopt habits that are damaging to their health. Poor diet, lack of sleep, use of drugs, and casual sexual relationships can all lead to a number of serious diseases.

Infectious mononucleosis Also known as mono, infectious mononucleosis is caused by a virus and results in sore throat, irregular fever, swollen glands, extreme fatigue, and an enlarged spleen. It frequently occurs among adolescents whose resistance to illness has been lowered by lack of sleep and poor diet. Although mono generally lasts for two weeks or less and is easily treated with rest and good nutrition, it can cause injury to the spleen and lead to hepatitis.

Hepatitis Hepatitis is an acute infection of the liver which most frequently occurs in adolescents and young adults and can cause permanent damage. One type of hepatitis is spread through poor sanitation, while another type is transmitted through blood transfusions or other injections which means that drug users are at especially high risk. Hepatitis may also be transmitted sexually.

Sexually Transmitted Diseases Syphilis and gonorrhea appear frequently among adolescents, who are often experimenting sexually without much experience, knowledge, or good judgment about sexual partners. Of the more than one million cases of gonorrhea reported each year, the greatest recent increase has been among children between the ages of ten and fourteen. Current estimates indicate that one in five high school students will contract either syphilis or gonorrhea.

Syphilis is highly contagious and is almost always transmitted by direct sexual contact with a person who already is infected. Signs of the infection — which appear two to six weeks after contact — are sores or lesions on various parts of the genitals and mucous membranes. Without treatment, other areas of the body are

Syphilis

likely to become infected as well; ultimately, syphilis can lead to slow chronic inflammation and destruction of the skin, mucous membranes, skeletal system, heart, and central nervous system. The disease can be prevented by avoiding sexual contact with carriers. Treatment with penicillin and related antibiotics is highly effective and should begin immediately after contact or in the early stages of the disease.

Gonorrhea

Gonorrhea, an infection of the mucous membrane of the urethra and genital tract, is highly contagious and is almost always caused by sexual contact with an infected person. If untreated, it may cause infections of other areas of the body, including the liver, the joints, and the heart. Symptoms, which occur from two to eight days after exposure, include inflammation of the urethra, discharge of mucus from the penis or vagina, and difficulty and discomfort in urinating. Use of a prophylactic during sex is an effective prevention, and penicillin is an effective treatment.

Genital herpes

Recently there has also been an increase in the incidence of genital herpes, a sexually transmitted viral disease that causes chronic and painful inflammation and lesions on the genitals and in other areas of sexual contact and for which there is not yet a cure. (Common cold sores, a different kind of herpes, are caused by a different virus.) While the physical pain of genital herpes is a burden, for many adolescents, the stigma of having this highly infectious, sexually transmitted disease for the rest of their lives can be extremely upsetting. In fact, some high schools and universities have set up special counseling programs and support groups for youngsters who have contracted this illness.

AIDS

AIDS (Acquired Immune Deficiency Syndrome) is perhaps the best-known and most feared sexually transmitted disease in the 1980s. To date, no one who has been positively diagnosed as having AIDS has survived for more than a few years. First diagnosed in the United States in the early 1980s, the disease destroys the body's ability to maintain its normal immunity to diseases, and death often is caused by pneumonia or related complications. Although a full picture of the causes, symptoms, and treatment of AIDS is not yet available, the disease seems to be transmitted mainly through introduction of body fluids from an infected person. It is associated with blood transfusions and anal sexual intercourse, so adolescent males who have multiple sexual contacts with other males or who are drug users are at great risk. The AIDS virus can also be transmitted between men and women, and between women and their unborn babies.

Sexually transmitted diseases have become a major problem among adolescents largely because of the increased acceptability of sexual activity throughout our culture. The pill has also contributed by replacing condoms — which provide significant protection against venereal diseases — as the favored method of birth control among teenagers. Inadequate health and sex education at home and in the schools must also be held accountable.

Drug and Alcohol Abuse High rates of experimenting with drugs and of drug abuse are typical of adolescence, although individuals' choices of drugs and patterns of use may change over time. In the late sixties and early seventies, for example, there was considerable concern about the widespread use of drugs in junior

Alcohol makes some teenagers feel more grown-up and more sociable and accepted by their friends, so it is very tempting for them to drink it. As a result, alcohol abuse is increasing among adolescents. (Susan Lapides)

and senior high schools. In a study that sampled more than 7,000 tenth-, eleventh-, and twelfth-graders about their drug usage, 85 percent reported using alcohol, 27 percent marijuana, 8.6 percent LSD, and 2.6 percent heroin (Yancy, Nader, and Burnham, 1972). These findings were supported by other researchers (Barnes, 1977; Johnston, 1974). More recently, a national survey of more than 2,000 teenagers and 2,000 young adults was conducted by the National Institute on Drug Abuse (1979). Seventy percent of the teenagers (ages twelve to seventeen) reported using alcohol, 30.9 percent marijuana and hashish, and 5.9 percent cocaine.

Alcohol and drug abuse are increasing

What the drug of experimental or long-term choice is depends in part on educational and economic background and life circumstances as well as on prevailing social and cultural conditions, and on what drugs are currently available and at what price. While marijuana and psychedelics such as mescaline, LSD, and psilocybin were popular during the sixties and seventies, "crack," a highly potent form of cocaine, is currently popular, and alcohol use has increased dramatically.

Whatever drugs adolescents are using, though, they are using drugs more frequently than they were twenty years ago. Some teenagers are searching for altered states of consciousness and new forms of excitement; others just want to feel high, or to escape from boredom, anxiety, poor self-esteem, or peer pressure. Easier access to drugs and parental and other adult drug use also contribute to this trend (Huba and Bentler, 1980, 1982). While the popular myth that using "soft" drugs like alcohol and marijuana will automatically lead to harder drugs is not supported by research, many adolescents do follow a fairly consistent pattern of use: in Stage I, they drink beer or wine; in Stage II, they use hard liquor or cigarettes; in Stage III, marijuana; and in Stage IV, cocaine, crack, and heroin. (Kendler and Faust, 1975; Huba and Bentler, 1982).

For several reasons, the effects of drug abuse on development are extremely destructive, particularly if the use is prolonged or chronic. For one thing, even short-term use of illegal drugs such as heroin, cocaine, crack, and Quaaludes exposes the user to considerable physical risk of injury or death due to overdose, contamination of the drug, or both. Second, even moderate use of certain drugs

Destructive effects of drugs

may have destructive physical and psychological effects, in that they disrupt normal patterns of eating, sleeping, and physical activity and mask psychological problems that require solution. Third, a number of these drugs cause physical addiction and psychological dependence. Physical addiction involves a biological

---

A Talk with Jason

Physical Development at Age Fourteen

Jason agreed to be interviewed if I would give him a ride to soccer practice afterward. The interview was conducted in the kitchen of his home over an after-school snack.

INTERVIEWER: What physical changes have you noticed in kids your age?

JASON: When we were in fifth grade, all the guys were taller than the girls or at least the same height. And then in sixth grade the girls shot up and all got much taller than us.

INTERVIEWER: How did that feel?

JASON: We didn't grow in seventh grade. We had sex education so we started to understand it. So in sixth grade, seventh, and part of eighth grade, all the guys were much less developed than the girls and much less tall and less heavy and everything. And then the later part of eighth grade we all shot up.

INTERVIEWER: I noticed. How tall are you now?

JASON: Five-eleven.

INTERVIEWER: Almost as tall as me.

JASON: We all shot up. I'm as tall as my older brother.

INTERVIEWER: Are there other differences besides height that you've noticed in kids your age?

JASON: Weight, for example, because some people were heavy before. The weight was not really part of them. It was excess. Now people have become heavier but more solid. I'm gaining weight, not a lot of weight. I've gained weight and it's in my bones, in my muscle, and in my skin and just a little bit of fat. I'm gaining it all over as opposed to gaining it in just fat. I'm gaining it in muscle.

I think that as you get older guys become less ashamed of their bodies and more likely to expose them. Not necessarily all the way, but just to take off your shirt. It's easier for them to do that because now they're bigger . . . now they feel that they can expose their chest and they don't have to be embarrassed about it.

INTERVIEWER: Have you noticed differences in how rapidly people develop?

JASON: Different parts of people develop at different times. Some people stay shorter but get a full

beard sooner. But they're not gonna shoot up as far. And some people shoot up and grow a beard at about the same time, but people in all four years of high school are getting interested in shaving and stuff like that. And usually it would seem ridiculous to an outsider to shave the little hair that you grow on your mustache, but it's a big thing to someone to have to shave or at this age it's important to look the best you can even if it's just a few hairs to get off.

INTERVIEWER: How do kids your age deal with staying healthy?

JASON: They know what is healthy, but they don't necessarily follow what is always healthy.

INTERVIEWER: Why do you think that is?

JASON: 'Cause, you know, there's the simple fact that junk food tastes good. And the other thing is that it is overemphasized that kids shouldn't eat that much junk food. I don't eat that much junk food. I eat a little bit, but I also eat really good food, too. I eat plenty of it to survive. So anything above that really doesn't matter.

---

dependence upon the drug; withdrawal can be painful and sometimes life-threatening. In most cases, tolerance to the drug increases with prolonged use, requiring higher doses to maintain the same level of effect and thus increasing the user's exposure to the drug's negative effects.

Finally, even if a proper medicinal dose of the drug itself is not physically dangerous — as is true with heroin — the physical, social, and psychological risks involved in supporting a habit are enormous. Teenagers addicted to heroin are, with few exceptions, forced to sell drugs and steal to support their habit. They are at great risk for contracting hepatitis or AIDS from dirty and infected needles.

INTERVIEWER: Do you think that most kids basically eat a good diet and that junk food is on top of it?

JASON: A lot of girls don't need to eat as much, because they have stopped growing. But they still need to eat more than they do eat. They starve themselves to a certain extent when they are hungry because they think, "Oh, God, I have to lose weight!" I think it's just a fad just to be able to say it. It makes people feel better about themselves to say, "I'm fat, look at me, I'm fat," because they really want other people to say, "No you're not." I think a lot of girls in the teenage years eat a crummy breakfast and then don't eat lunch and then go all day without eating. They eat at night. And then they go to sleep. Which is the wrong method. If you're only going to eat one meal a day, you should eat breakfast.

INTERVIEWER: Why is that?

JASON: Because you need the nutrition more during the day when you are active. At night you don't really need that much.

INTERVIEWER: Do you think that it's because girls are into being thin?

JASON: No, to some extent they're just not as hungry any more. And they don't know how do deal with that.

INTERVIEWER: Guys your age are probably always hungry.

JASON: Right. I stuff myself and then fifteen minutes later I'm not full any more.

INTERVIEWER: How do fourteen-year-olds handle drugs and drinking?

JASON: There is some pressure to do drugs and drink, but it comes from within. A lot of people are torn about it. And it's easy for them to blame it on peer pressure when it's really just people offering them some.

INTERVIEWER: Has use of drugs and alcohol changed since junior high?

JASON: Oh, yeah. It increased 100 percent or more than that. Compared to junior high it's phenomenal. But compared to other high schools, at my school alcohol use is not as high but drug use might be higher. I think that people have a certain knowledge and awareness about drugs and alcohol and that a lot of people try to balance off a little bit of drugs with a little bit of alcohol. They realize that drugs like pot hurt your lungs and that alcohol hurts your liver. And if you do all alcohol you're going to hurt your liver a lot, and if you do all pot you're going to hurt your lungs a lot. If you do a little bit of each, it can heal itself over.

Follow-up Questions

1. How does Jason feel about the effects of physical maturation? How consistent are his views with those presented in the chapter?

2. How do hormonal changes influence the changes in height, weight, muscle, and body fat that Jason describes?

3. What nutritional problems might be related to the eating habits of Jason's peer group?

4. To what extent does Jason appreciate the importance of multiple causes of health and health problems? How typical of adolescents his age are his views about health?

They are exposed to situations that are both physically and psychologically violent; and the time and energy needed to support a habit often forces them to abandon normal social, emotional, and intellectual endeavors, and threatens to halt their identity development prematurely.

Alcohol abuse   Alcohol is the most widely advertised and heavily used drug in the United States today, and one of the most physically and psychologically damaging. Its association with serious automobile injuries (more than 40,000 each year) and fatalities among adolescents has led many states to prohibit its sale to teenagers.

Other results of teenage alcoholism are staggering. Chronic alcohol abuse can lead to severe health problems, including destruction of the liver and damage to the central nervous system. It also seriously disrupts the drinker's ability to function effectively in school, at work, at home, and in other areas of social activity. Because alcohol is heavily advertised and socially valued as a sign of adulthood and independence, is readily available at low cost, and is a potent short-term reducer of anxiety, it continues to be very popular among adolescents.

Tobacco   The use of tobacco products has also been widely advertised as a sign of adulthood. Early adolescents are particularly susceptible to adopting this "ready-made" symbol of maturity. Most adolescents are aware of the fact that smoking causes cancer and heart disease; overall smoking rates for teenagers dropped from 16 percent in 1974 to 12 percent in 1979. Smoking among females is increasing, however, at least in part because advertisers have targeted them as a highly lucrative market (USDHEW, 1980; McAlister et al., 1979).

Family influence   Patterns of both drinking and smoking, which are closely associated, are strongly influenced by the lifestyles of family members and peers. Minimal, moderate, and heavy levels of drinking, smoking, and use of drugs, including tranquilizers and other legal medications, among family members are strongly associated with very similar patterns of use among adolescents. A second major factor in adolescent drug use is peer pressure, which can strongly influence which drugs a teenager uses, in what circumstances, and how much and how often.

In conclusion, we should note that at least in modern times, adolescence has always been a period of dramatic physical change and experimentation. As we will see in Chapter 16, the potential conflicts and dangers of adolescence are largely determined by the values and opportunities that a society provides to its youth. If most adults choose to rely on drugs in dealing with the problems of everyday life, it is almost certain that drug use will be an issue for adolescents in our society. Similarly, if people have limited access to adequate health care and health education, not to mention healthy living conditions and lifestyles, it is likely that these limitations will be painfully obvious in the health and lifestyles of adolescents.

Nutritional Problems   The eating habits of adolescents are often disturbing to parents and other adults, although adolescents' nutritional problems are in a sense exaggerations of how adults approach this issue. Meals on the run and highly advertised junk foods dovetail nicely with the active lives of teenagers and of the successful young adults they aspire to be. In the extreme, inadequate nutrition can prevent full physical development and increase susceptibility to illness by lowering the body's resistance to bacteria and viruses. Inadequate nutrition can also inter-

Anorexia Nervosa: the Golden Cage

As a child Irene had not been preoccupied with her weight. When she was eleven years old several girls in her class talked about dieting, and she found this peculiar because they looked all right to her; she felt lucky to like her own figure. However, a year later, when she showed early pubertal development, her pediatrician made some remark about her getting too plump. Irene began a rigorous weight-watching program, not permitting her weight to rise above ninety-five pounds; though she kept on growing, she did not menstruate. At age fifteen, a time of emotional upheaval between her parents and with her one remaining friend, she began to starve herself and lost a dramatic amount of weight, striving to be as thin as possible and hating herself for gaining even as little as an ounce. (Bruch, 1979, p. 67).

Anorexia nervosa is a complex emotional disorder characterized by an obsession with food and weight and the "relentless pursuit of excessive thinness" (Bruch, 1979). Its major symptoms include excessive weight loss (approximately 25 percent of body weight); amenorrhea, the cessation of menstruation; hyperactivity, perhaps including excessive exercise; social isolation; and feelings of insecurity, loneliness, inadequacy, and helplessness. Affecting 1 percent of all twelve- to twenty-five-year-old females in the United States, anorexia often involves a pattern of behavior combining a rigid diet with strenuous exercise to lose weight. When weight loss is maintained for a long period, a number of physical symptoms occur, including lack of energy, paleness of skin, brittle nails, constipation, difficulty urinating, numbness or tingling sensations in arms and legs, fine hairs appearing all over the body, thinning and loss of hair, and extreme sensitivity to cold (Gilbert and DeBlasie, 1984).

Based on observation of seventy anorexic pa-

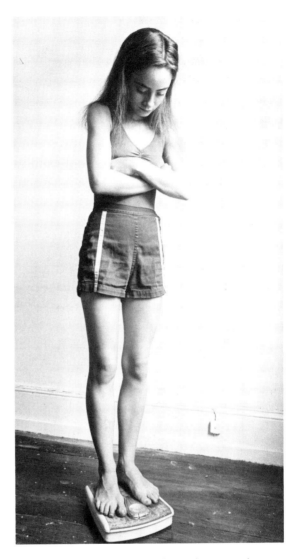

Anorexics, like this teenage girl, use dieting partly as a way of gaining control over their lives. No matter how thin they become, they are likely to view themselves as "too fat." (Susan Rosenberg/Photo Researchers)

fere with a teenager's ability to concentrate at school and work and to actively engage in activities with peers. Poor nutritional habits established during adolescence can have more serious health consequences if continued on a long-term basis.

Obesity As with dependence on drugs, food dependence and the obesity that frequently results are problems that affect a significant portion of the teenage population; it is currently estimated that between 16 and 20 percent of today's teenagers are significantly overweight (Hammar, 1980). Major causes of obesity include a biologically inherited tendency to be overweight, childhood diet and family attitudes and habits about food, and lack of exercise.

---

tients, ten of them males, and psychotherapeutic treatment of about twenty of these cases, Hilde Bruch wrote about the causes, experience, and treatment of this illness (Bruch, 1979). She believes that anorexic youngsters experience severe disturbances in three areas of psychological functioning. The first is a disturbance in body image — the way they see themselves. Although an anorexic adolescent who is five foot six and weighs only eighty-seven pounds looks like a walking skeleton, when she views herself in the mirror she sees someone who is too fat and needs to continue dieting. The second disturbance involves misinterpretations of internal and external stimuli, especially with regard to the way anorexics experience hunger. Although they are literally starving, many strongly state that they enjoy the feeling of hunger, that it makes them feel good to have a flat, empty stomach, and that feeling hungry makes them feel thinner. The third area of disturbance involves a paralyzing sense of ineffectiveness and helplessness in their ability to change anything about their lives. Although self-starvation and physical exhaustion play a major role in these disturbances, they do not fully explain the development of the illness.

Most anorexics are girls from financially and socially successful upper-middle-class and upper-class families. A much smaller number come from upwardly mobile, success-oriented lower-middle-

class or lower-class families. The fathers of the girls in Bruch's study valued them highly for their intellectual and athletic achievements, and paid little attention to their physical changes during puberty — although they did criticize them for becoming plump. Many of the children believed that they had to prove something to their parents, and that it was their responsibility to make their parents feel good, successful, and superior. Curiously, however, they saw their parents' privileged lifestyle achievements as an excessive burden and obligation, feeling somehow condemned to be at least as special and successful as their parents were (Bruch, 1979).

For many of these girls during their childhood, their otherwise successful and well-functioning families somehow failed to help them develop an adequate sense of confidence and self-value, a clear sense of their body and its functions, or an adequate sense of identity, autonomy, and control. As children, the anorexics lacked a conviction of their own inner substance and value and were overly submissive and abnormally considerate, preoccupied with satisfying their parents' expectations of them and trying to outguess others in order to do what they expected. Even in their friendships, rarely if ever were they able to know or express what they wanted. Unsure of their own individuality, they tended to be chameleon-like, developing different

Being obese is particularly difficult for an adolescent who is already struggling to develop a comfortable and realistic view of his changing body. Obesity can therefore have a significant impact on a teenager's sense of himself as a physically attractive person and on his overall identity development. In some cases it can severely limit social opportunities through both exclusion by peers and self-isolation.

Despite a growing appreciation of physical strength and fitness in women, a lean body is still the dominant cultural standard for feminine beauty. As a consequence, many adolescent girls try to lose weight in an effort to achieve a slenderness that may not be possible for them. Inadequate knowledge about dietary requirements and poor judgment lead to inadequate nutrition for many teenage girls.

---

interests and a different personality with each new friend (Bruch, 1979).

For many anorexics, their symptoms serve two important functions: as a means of forestalling and avoiding the physical, sexual, and psychosocial changes and challenges of puberty and adolescence, which they do not feel ready to face; and as a means of asserting control over their own bodies and daily activities and of resisting the intense pressure to conform to the parental expectations they experienced throughout their childhoods (Bruch, 1979; Romeo, 1984).

Although anorexic adolescents are typically high academic achievers, their thinking, problem solving, and moral judgment are only at Piaget's concrete operational stage. Their thinking tends to be egocentric, rigid, and magical, and their capacity for formal operations, abstract thinking, and independent evaluation may be deficient or completely absent, especially when solving personal problems. When their illness becomes apparent, they find themselves out of step with their peers and socially isolated from friends, family, and schoolmates. They feel dominated and directed by some outside, mysterious force beyond their control and maintain their starvation diet and grueling physical activity in the belief that it will somehow make them as "good" as they should be.

The serious health risks of prolonged malnutri-

tion make early diagnosis and treatment very important. Also, electrolyte imbalance may result from the use of diet pills and from compulsive overeating followed by self-induced vomiting. Finally, prolonged isolation from the important social and emotional experiences of adolescence is unhealthy for the anorexic's psychological state.

Bruch suggests that successful treatment must involve a multiple focus. First, it must address the starvation problem in a way that appreciates the anorexic's need for control but makes clear that the resulting malnutrition and distortions in thinking must be addressed for fuller treatment to be possible. The treatment must also address the underlying family problems and abnormal interactions between family members that are invariably related to anorexia. Frequently parents tend to portray their family life as being more harmonious than it really is, and the perfection that the anorexic adolescent seeks to attain is a response to serious but unspoken inadequacies and unhappiness the parents feel. Lastly, individual therapy with the anorexic adolescent must focus on helping her to uncover her own abilities and resources for independent thinking, judging, and feeling. It must help her to achieve autonomy and self-directed identity by helping her to become aware of, express, and act upon her own impulses, feelings, and needs.

Whereas most teens suffer no shortage of calories, their diets often lack balance. This adolescent's meal consists entirely of refined sugar (in the drink and candy) and of fat and starch (in the potato chips). (Carol Palmer)

Obsession with thinness   An extreme form of this quest for thinness is **anorexia nervosa,** a physical and psychological disturbance in which the afflicted teenager starves herself, exercises compulsively, and develops an increasingly unrealistic view of her body. Ninety-five percent of anorexics are females. Many anorexics also suffer from **bulimia,** a disorder in which they eat huge amounts of food and then vomit so that they do not gain weight. The causes and treatment of these disorders are complex, and between 10 and 20 percent of those who do not receive professional treatment die of starvation and its complications.

What seems clear is that the most significant factor in adolescents' taking responsibility for their own health is whether they have a clear perception that they really *are* in fact responsible for it. The achievement of a sense of responsibility for this and other aspects of one's life signals progress in the adolescent transition to young adulthood.

Checkpoint   *Patterns of health and illness established in childhood often continue during adolescence. Individual and family attitudes and expectations, family resources, and the "myth of invulnerability" all influence patterns of health. High-*

risk lifestyles, particularly of male and minority adolescents, contribute to the very high death rate of this age group. Inadequate nutrition is also a major problem.

Finally Young Adults?

After all the bodily changes an adolescent experiences, he certainly looks like an adult. But as we have pointed out, he does not consistently *feel* like an adult yet. Especially early in adolescence, individuals are uncomfortable with their new physical features, which take up the foreground of teenagers' thinking, feeling, and acting. Young people are often self-conscious, meaning (among other things) that they are conscious of their bodies. The nature and strength of that self-consciousness depend in part on the nature, strength, and timing of puberty in all its facets.

It is not surprising, given the newness of their physical changes, that adolescents lack awareness of or concern for their health; so far in life, they have not had much reason to be aware or concerned. Soon, though, this changes. Just as their bodies develop during the teen years, so do their thoughts, feelings, and social relationships. These developments eventually help them to become truly adult, in the physical sense as well as in others.

Summary of Major Ideas

The Concept of Adolescence

1. Adolescence, which begins around the age of twelve and lasts until about age twenty, is a developmental period of transition between childhood and adulthood.

2. Adolescence was "discovered" in the early part of this century as a way of prolonging childhood in a period of rapid social and economic change.

3. Child labor laws, compulsory education, and special laws to combat "juvenile delinquency" helped to solidify the idea of adolescence.

4. Some theories of adolescence emphasize the "storm and stress" of this period, while others find it no more conflict-ridden than earlier periods of development; for most youngsters it is mixed.

Growth in Height and Weight

5. While the amount of increase in height and weight are significant, the unevenness of the adolescent "growth spurt" is even more striking.

6. Increases in height can be predicted fairly accurately, but predicting weight increases is more difficult, in part because they are influenced by differences in living conditions and lifestyle.

7. During the last century, children have tended to begin to mature earlier and to grow taller and heavier than their parents.

Puberty

8. In addition to increases in height and weight, a larger pattern of changes occurs, which leads to full physical and sexual maturity, or puberty.

9. Primary sexual maturation among boys includes rapid growth of the penis and scrotum, and the production of fertile semen.

10. Menarche, or the beginning of menstrual cycles, is a complex biological process that signals the beginning of sexual maturity for girls.

11. In many cultures, including our own, the onset of menarche can be stressful, in part because of the strong personal and cultural expectations that are associated with it.

12. Maturation of secondary sex characteristics includes enlargement and development of the breasts, the growth of body hair, deepening of the voice, and increased production of sex-related hormones.

13. Male and female hormones affect both sexes, though in differing degrees and with differing effects.

14. Although girls and boys are equally muscular prior to adolescence, during puberty boys experience significantly greater increases in muscle tissue than girls do.

15. Girls experience a somewhat greater increase in body fat than boys do.

16. Differences in how muscle and body fat are distributed rather than in their absolute amounts account for much of the differences in the physical appearances of male and female adolescents.

Psychological Effects of Physical Growth in Adolescence

17. Most adolescents are preoccupied with their physical appearance; a teenager's body image is influenced by conventional standards of attractiveness.

18. An adolescent's feelings of attractiveness depend upon the evaluation of peers, parents, and self and affect self-esteem.

19. For boys, the effects of early maturation are positive in the short run but somewhat negative in the long run, while late maturation appears to have the reverse effects.

20. For girls, early maturation is more stressful in the short term but positive in the long run; late maturers tend to experience benefits during adolescence and no serious long-run negative effects.

Health in Adolescence

21. There is considerable continuity between childhood and adolescent patterns of illness and health care; both are influenced by individual and family attitudes and resources.

22. Adolescents are a high-risk group for injury and death due to risky lifestyles and their "myth of invulnerability."

23. Growth in a child's ability to understand concepts of illness and health appears to follow stages of cognitive development.

24. Major health problems during adolescence include sexually transmitted diseases, alcohol and drug abuse, and inadequate diet.

Key Terms

adolescence *(591)*
growth spurt *(594)*
adolescent
  egocentrism *(597)*
secular trend *(597)*
puberty *(598)*
primary sex
  characteristics *(598)*
secondary sex
  characteristics *(598)*
semen *(598)*
nocturnal emissions *(598)*
menarche *(599)*
ovulation *(599)*

pubic hair *(600)*
axillary hair *(600)*
hormones *(602)*
ovaries *(602)*
testes *(602)*
testosterone *(603)*
estrogen *(603)*
sexual dimorphism *(604)*
mesomorphic *(607)*
endomorphic *(607)*
ectomorphic *(607)*
anorexia nervosa *(628)*
bulimia *(628)*

What Do You Think?

1. In what ways has the invention of adolescence as a developmental stage been helpful for teenagers and their families? In what ways has it been a problem?

2. What pattern (timing, rate) did your physical growth follow during adolescence?

3. What do you remember most about how you felt during puberty and how it influenced you socially?

4. In what ways is puberty easier for the opposite sex? In what ways might it be more difficult?

5. Why do you think adolescence is such a risky period for injury, death, and health-care problems? What recommendations might you make to a group of high school students and their parents?

6. What is your philosophy of sickness and health, and how did you come to think this way?

For Further Reading

Bell, R. *Changing Bodies, Changing Lives: A Book for Teens on Sex and Relationships.* New York: Random House, 1980.

This unusual book is based on interviews with hundreds of teenagers throughout the country, as well as parents, sex educators, and junior and senior high school teachers. Relying on direct quotes from the teenagers themselves for much of its material, it provides thorough, practical, and readable information about the physical, sexual, and emotional changes of puberty and adolescence.

Bruch, H. *The Golden Cage: The Enigma of Anorexia Nervosa.* New York: Vintage Books, 1979.

A very readable book about the causes, effects, and treatment of this life-threatening eating disorder, based upon seventy case studies from the author's own clinical practice.

Elkind, D. *All Grown up and No Place to Go: Teenagers in Crisis.* Reading, Mass.: Addison-Wesley, 1984.

An intense and stimulating book about the pressures toward premature adulthood experienced by teenagers in a rapidly changing society. It is based on case studies, research, and clinical experiences of one of the best-known experts on adolescence.

Salinger, J. D. *Catcher in the Rye.* New York: Bantam, 1977.

A humorous and touching novel about Holden Caulfield, a young man who encounters his share of excitement and upset during adolescence.

Chapter

15

Adolescence: Cognitive Development

Focusing Questions

- To what extent, and in what situations, are teenagers capable of abstract reasoning?
- How do adolescents show their improved information-processing skills in everyday activities?
- How, if at all, does the general nature of intelligence change from childhood to adolescence?
- What effects does cognitive development have on adolescents' knowledge and beliefs about ethics, political processes, and religion?

By ABOUT AGE THIRTEEN, children have begun to think in ways that resemble adult thinking much more than before. Now they can consider possibilities and not just actualities; they can ask themselves, "What if the world were flat?" even though it is not really flat. And they can often use their time more efficiently than before; if a teacher assigns a book to read, a teenager is more likely than a younger child to know how to find its main ideas, focus his study on them, and skim the details relatively quickly. All in all, adolescents' cognitive talents tend to be more diverse than those of younger children, and perhaps equally important, they know when and how to apply those talents to particular problems.

This chapter looks at these new skills from three general viewpoints. The first of these is the so-called *cognitive developmental viewpoint,* which is often associated with the work of Piaget. The second is the more recent approach of *information-processing theory,* which uses the workings of a computer as a model for human thinking. And the third is the theory implicit in the long-standing *psychometric tradition* of psychology — the branch that uses standardized ability tests to highlight differences among individuals. Since each of these theories is discussed elsewhere in this textbook, we focus attention here on their applicability to adolescence.

In real life, of course, thinking is always "about" something in particular; in recognition of that fact, this chapter ends with a section that discusses adolescents' ideas about themselves, about morality, about politics, and about religion. The three general theories about adolescent cognition help in understanding how teenagers (and others) make decisions about right and wrong, about the consequences of political actions, and about the nature of God. As it turns out, though, the theories do not deal with several aspects of such thinking. For one thing, they tend to ignore the emotions involved in daily thinking and problem solving. For another thing, they gloss over the difference between knowing and doing; they focus on a question like "Should I pay him back the money I owe?" rather than on an action like "Here, take the money." Since emotions and actions affect cognitive development significantly, we discuss them in some detail, even though they may not be strictly cognitive in nature — another demonstration that cognition, emotions, and behavior are often separated in textbooks but hardly ever in life.

The Cognitive Developmental Viewpoint

Jacob and Maria, both twelfth-graders, were discussing abortion.

"What's the big deal about abortion, anyway?" said Jacob. "Why not just let anybody get one who wants one? It's just a personal choice, like deciding which college to go to."

"You sound like you don't care about the people involved," said Maria. "How would you feel if *you* needed an abortion?"

"But I won't ever need one," said Jacob smugly. "Only girls get pregnant, you know."

"That's why you don't understand," said Maria. "What if it's *your* body that can grow babies, and everybody expects *you* to grow one at the right time — like when you get married. And everybody expects you *not* to grow one at the wrong time — like during high school. How do you deal with all those people — your parents and friends, and the baby's father too?"

Jacob looked thoughtful at this comment. Then he said, "You're getting bogged down in what other people think. Try to imagine what you yourself would want to do with your life if you found out that you were pregnant."

"I do that," said Maria, "and I also try to think about what the baby would want to do with *his or her* life if I allowed it to live."

This example reveals a number of new cognitive competencies acquired by adolescents and described in the cognitive developmental theory represented by Piaget (Inhelder and Piaget, 1958). Jacob and Maria reason about possibilities rather than about actual events; neither of them has ever experienced an abortion. And they use generalizations to draw specific conclusions (for Jacob, abortion is "a personal choice" and should always be treated as such). These are cognitive abilities that middle-years children usually lack.

General Features of Adolescent Thought

What are the practical effects of these new cognitive competencies? For one thing, attention to hypothetical ideas or "mere" possibilities broadens the horizons of adolescents' thinking substantially (Keating, 1980). The question "What if there were a nuclear war?", for example, is relatively more meaningful to an adolescent than to a child, even though both are equally inexperienced with actual nuclear war. So is a question like "What if I had been born poor, or rich, or black?" Adolescents can imagine what these situations might be like even though they have not experienced them in a concrete way. In general, thinking about the possible

Compared to children, teenagers think more often about possibilities and about the future; they also daydream and fantasize more. What do you suppose this adolescent is thinking about? (Victoria Arlak)

Increased use of imagination creates a new talent for speculating about important events and for guessing about daily experiences. It also stimulates adolescents to daydream or fantasize about their actions and feelings. And it helps them to make much more astute inferences about human motivations ("Perhaps she did that because . . .").

Tied to this ability is a greater capacity to plan ahead. Contrary to what frustrated parents sometimes claim, adolescents can set and plan goals for themselves, and they can do so much more competently than children can. Sometimes such goals are socially approved ones, like making sure to take the best courses to get into a desirable college. Just as often, though, they seem to lack redeeming value by conventional adult standards, as when an adolescent carefully plans and finances an expensive trip to a concert in a far-away city.

Another way of stating these competencies is to say that during adolescence, young people develop an ability to think about thoughts, and to do so in a logical way. Most of the time, such thinking serves some purpose, such as developing a **Thinking about thinking** better understanding of human nature or figuring out the best way to have fun. Sometimes, though, thinking about thoughts has no concrete content at all. Many adolescents are quite capable of thinking simply about the form of statements or propositions, even when the statements lack content entirely:

- All wugs are glibs.
- Some glibs are bots.

From these two statements, some adolescents can decide — and even enjoy deciding! — whether or not any "wugs" are in fact "bots."

Formal Operational Thinking

Because these cognitive skills attend to the logic or form of thinking, adolescent thought is sometimes referred to as **formal thought**, or **formal operational thought.** It differs from the style of thinking of middle-years children (concrete operational thought) in three important ways: in emphasizing the real versus the possible, in using scientific reason, and in skillfully coordinating ideas among themselves (Flavell, 1977).

Possibilities Versus Realities   First of all, formal thought involves attention to possibilities and not just actual realities. A parent discovered this feature when he tried to get his two children to make suggestions as to how to improve the humdrum weekly chicken dinner. "Fried is fine," said his nine-year-old, who preferred fried chicken to any other form of cooked chicken. But the fourteen-year-old insisted on a more complicated response: "Let me think about that," he said; then, later, "Can we make some brand-new sauce for it? Maybe one of the cookbooks has some ideas for a sauce which we could modify." Even though the older child had never eaten chicken cooked this way, he thought about trying it.

Scientific Reasoning   Formal thought also involves scientific reasoning — the same kind that psychologists use in designing many of their studies of human development. This quality reveals itself when adolescent students must solve some problem systematically. For example, how do youngsters in an art class figure out methods for mixing basic colors of paint to produce various intermediate shades and other colors? Those capable of formal operations in effect design an experiment to test all the available combinations of colors. They form hypotheses or hunches about how certain colors affect each other when mixed, then they try out their hypotheses by mixing each basic color with every other basic color, being careful to try every possibility. By observing the results of this procedure carefully, they can draw logical conclusions about how to mix colors. This procedure in effect uses the scientific method.

In contrast, concrete operational children would rarely act so systematically. Like the formal operational thinkers, they would probably mix colors, but they would do so haphazardly, and they might not take note of the results of their experiences carefully. As a result, they might not learn to mix colors as rapidly as older, formal operational thinkers do. When confronted with this problem, of course, some younger children might draw on previous experience with art materials in order to solve it; but then their performance would reflect memory about how to mix colors rather than true scientific reasoning.

> Experimentation versus trial and error

Logical Combination of Ideas   The third feature of formal thought involves combining ideas logically. Compared to less cognitively mature children, formal thinkers can hold several ideas in mind at once and combine or integrate them in logical ways. When asked to explain why some students perform better in school than others, concrete operational thinkers are likely to latch onto one reason or

Many teenagers become able to solve problems scientifically. But like these two girls, they usually still rely on ample concrete experience to assist their thinking. (Rosemary Ranck/Black Star)

another — "Some kids are smarter," or "Some kids work harder." In contrast, formal thinkers often give combinations of reasons, as this first-year university student did:

> Well, I think it depends. Sometimes it pays just to be smart. But it also helps to work hard — except when the teacher doesn't notice your effort. Some kids do better, too, because they have taken courses before in the same area. Your first class in literature is likely to be harder than your fifth class in that subject.

As this example shows, the ability to combine ideas can sometimes make formal thinkers seem less definite about their opinions than younger children are.

Concrete Versus Formal Thought: Reasoning about Bending Rods

To understand the features of formal thought, consider how children at different stages of cognitive maturity approach a problem that Piaget designed (Inhelder and Piaget, 1958). A set of flexible rods are attached to the side of a basin of water. The rods differ in length, thickness, and material (metal or wood). In addition, a number of small weights are attached to the ends of the rods. A friendly experimenter — perhaps a teacher — asks the child to determine what factor or factors control how far the rods bend toward the water. Does the amount of bending depend on the rods' length, on their thickness, on what they are made of, or on the weight attached to them?

Imagine that you are a child asked to solve this problem. As a middle-years child, your attention would be captured primarily by the apparatus itself. You would enjoy varying anything that seemed to vary — in this case, the length of the rods and the weights attached to them. You would also enjoy comparing one rod with another — wooden ones with metal ones, and thick ones with thin ones. But your observations and comparisons would lack a system. You might vary more Random comparison than one factor at a time (like length *and* thickness), or forget to vary one of the factors at all. This haphazardness would be likely to prevent you from solving the problem fully, although you might nevertheless make a number of useful observations about the apparatus. The haphazard quality would also mark your efforts as concrete operational. At this age and stage, you are still tied closely to the real or concrete.

As an adolescent, however, you would approach the problem much more systematically. First you would make some good guesses (or hypotheses) about the solution to the problem. You would take mental note of several factors that look like they might affect how far the rods bend: length, thickness, and weight, as well as whether the rods are made of wood or metal. Having noticed these possibilities, you would go on to the next step: devising and carrying out an informal experiment for testing each hypothesis in turn while holding all of the other factors con- Methodical manipulation stant. If you began by varying the weights on the rods, for example, you would make sure that you used only rods of the same thickness, length, and material. Otherwise you could not be sure whether any variations in bending came from differences in weight or from differences in one of the other factors. Having checked for the effects of weight in this way, you could go on to test the effects of each of the other factors, keeping the other three factors constant in every case.

Such a formal operational approach contrasts sharply with the less systematic efforts of younger children. It guarantees that, given enough time, you will find a solution to the problem — assuming, of course, that a solution actually exists. It also makes more cognitive demands: you must devise hypotheses, plan a way to test them, and draw reasonable conclusions from your observations. Using concrete operations, in contrast, simply requires careful observation of events as they unfold; in thinking concretely, the child in essence asks from moment to moment, "Is what I am looking at a solution?"

Evaluation of the Cognitive Developmental Viewpoint

According to Piaget, formal operations begin developing early in adolescence and are fully formed by the end of the high school years. All teenagers supposedly evolve wide-ranging thinking abilities that have a formal, abstract nature and that apply to many specific experiences and daily problems. In reality, however, the actual cognitive performance of adolescents fails to conform with this picture in several ways. Many adolescents (and even adults) use formal thinking inconsistently, or even fail to use it at all. In explaining why a car is not working properly, for example, many adolescents and adults merely describe the car's symptoms: "It's got a bad noise in the brakes," or "It can't shift into third gear." Such comments are in effect concrete operational; even a young child could make them. They cast doubt on whether formal thinking really develops as universally as concrete operational thinking does.

Another difficulty arises in determining when a person has truly attained formal operational thought. The answer depends to a large extent on the criteria or standards adopted to define attainment. The traditional Piagetian *méthode clinique,* or clinical method, adopts rather strict standards. This method involves questioning individuals about their beliefs in some detail, and even cross-examines children with countersuggestions ("Another child said just the opposite from you; what do you think of that?"). As a result, children have to give relatively elaborate explanations of their responses. In the bending-rods problem, for example, adolescents not only have to identify the true influences on the rods but also have to resist challenges to their answers ("Are you *sure* that the weight really matters?"). And they have to explain their reasons ("How do you know that the weight matters? Can you prove it to me?").

Most adolescents and adults cannot meet all of these standards equally well, and in fact might consider it artificial for someone to expect them to do so (Neimark, 1982a, 1982b). In real life, most problems are considered "solved" when much less demanding standards have been met — when a person gives either an explanation or an answer, for example, but not both. In real life, furthermore, hints and prompts are widespread and generally acceptable. Two people might try to figure out the bending-rods problem together, and in doing so they would freely offer each other ideas for solving it.

Even controlled studies of formal operational thinking have confirmed the importance of variations in standards for evaluating performance. One study evaluated how adolescents figured out how fast or slow a pendulum would swing back and forth (Pulos and Linn, 1978). Was it affected by the length of the cord holding it, by the amount of weight on the end, or by the angle from which it started? The adolescents' responses were evaluated in three different ways: (a) by their ability to describe correctly the relative influences of each variable on the swing; (b) by their ability to construct an experiment that tested their ideas; and (c) by the quality of their interpretations of their experiment.

As it turned out, the three standards did not correlate with one another very closely; that is, a student who could meet one standard could not necessarily meet the others. In general, the adolescents did best at constructing visual proofs of their solution and worst at constructing verbal proofs. Over half of them could demonstrate that only length mattered, by actually displaying the period of swing to the experimenter. Only about one quarter could (or at least chose to) explain the same information in words.

Note that most of the tasks that psychologists have used to assess formal thought, like the experiments described in Figure 15-1, have resembled lab experiments in a high school science course (Neimark, 1982a). As shown in the figure,

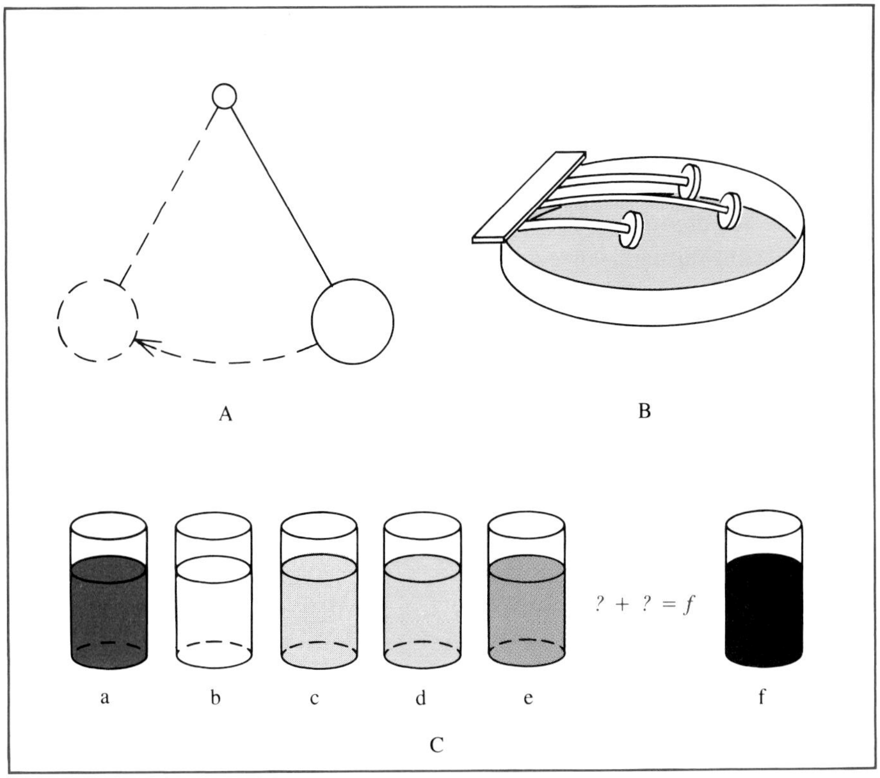

Figure 15–1 Problem-solving Tasks

all of the tasks isolate natural processes for observation and invite comment about these processes. Using a simple, nonsocial task helps psychologists to standardize the experiments and the interviews. The scientific nature of these tasks, though, may limit the number of skilled formal thinkers they reveal. Completing a formal operational task inevitably feels like performing for a high school science teacher, and as science teachers often point out, only a relatively small fraction of all students carry out this role consistently and well. Not surprisingly, then, many researchers have found that large numbers of adolescents show little or no evidence of formal operational thinking (Shayer, 1979). In some studies and some situations, in fact, a large majority of individuals "fail" such tasks, even as adults (Martorano, 1977; Neimark, 1982b).

Studies like these are sometimes mistakenly taken as proof that Piagetian theory is wrong, and that formal operations do not in fact constitute a universal stage of cognitive development. In fact, though, such studies may only show the importance of so-called *performance factors* — influences having to do with human motivation or momentary variations in the situation. These, it seems, probably matter more than Piaget and his followers originally expected. The underlying competence — in this case, formal operational thought — may indeed exist more or less as Piaget has proposed. Strong support for this idea comes from efforts to teach or train youngsters the skills of formal thought.

Influence of
experimental situation

Such efforts have differed widely in their details, but all of them have tried to tell about or demonstrate thinking that has the systematic, abstract quality characteristic of formal operations (Stone and Day, 1978, 1980). They resemble the

Training in formal thinking

methods used for training children in conservation skills and other concrete operations described in Chapter 12; but unlike training for concrete operations, training for formal thought produces dramatic, sudden, and consistent results. The improvements depend very little on exactly how the training is conducted — on whether it consists mainly of telling or showing, for example, or whether it uses one phraseology for instructions or another. These facts suggest that such training actually just evokes pre-existing capacities in adolescents, and does not really teach these abilities for the first time. Apparently it sends a message to the learner, but not the message that the trainer intends; instead of showing *how* to think abstractly, the training shows that the learner *should* do so. This in turn implies that more adolescents can use formal thought than actually choose to do so when evaluated by Piaget's traditional and relatively strict tasks and standards.

Perspectives on Issues

Cognitive Development Beyond Formal Thought

Piaget and other psychologists have identified formal or abstract thought as a major achievement of the adolescent years. But for most human beings, it may not be the final or "highest" cognitive achievement. One clue to this possibility comes from adolescents themselves: teenagers often overrate the importance of logical thinking, at least when they first achieve facility with it (Elkind and Bowen, 1979). They may believe that all problems, including difficult ones like achieving world peace, can be solved by the proper application of rational principles and careful reasoning. Teenagers may fail to notice the limits of logic: that many problems by nature resist the application of general principles, and may lend themselves instead to specific solutions, case by case.

Consider, for example, the case of Anne, a twelfth-grader who has recently begun sleeping with her boyfriend. Anne also gets along well with her parents, and she knows that they will worry and feel hurt if they learn of her sexual involvement. She also believes, in general, that friends and family should have no secrets. By continuing her sexual

activities, she seems to be violating this principle. On the other hand, she (and her boyfriend) regard their intimacy as a private matter, and she worries that telling her parents would violate this privacy, which she also considers her right. Telling her parents might also create a lot of bad feelings among Anne, her boyfriend, and her parents. Her principles, in this case, do not seem to point her toward a good solution: no matter what she does, Anne feels that somebody will get hurt, or some ethical principle will be violated, or both.

Anne's situation suggests the importance of nonrational choices or judgments in solving real-life problems. Like Anne, many people may wish to be "reasonable." They may wish, that is, to rely on formal logic and may even believe that they use it a lot. But in practice most people use formal logic consistently only when solving academic problems posed by teachers (Labouvie-Vief, 1982). The rest of the time, formal reasoning either does not help or actually interferes with effective solutions to daily problems.

Even in approaching formal, academic problems

The Information-Processing Viewpoint

As explained in Chapter 12, information-processing theories describe development as if it worked like a computer. According to one prominent view, a **short-term sensory store (STSS)** receives sensory information and holds it for a brief time — only seconds. If any of that information is processed, it is transferred to

— such as the "bending rods" problem posed in this chapter — most of us do not confine ourselves to logical procedures like those described by Piaget. More often, judgment and wisdom play a large role: instead of setting up a miniature scientific experiment, we recall any previous experiences with rods of different lengths, and with problems of this particular type. If possible, we use these memories to "tell" us the solution, rather than going to all the trouble of "figuring out" a solution systematically. The more experience we accumulate, the better this informal approach works. So it should be no surprise that as we get older, we often use abstract reasoning *less* (Neimark, 1982b).

For older adolescents, the cognitive challenge consists of converting formal reasoning from a goal in itself, to a *tool* used for other, broader purposes (Gilligan and Murphy, 1979). Anne cannot reach a good decision about informing her parents, for example, if she focuses on formal abstractions about truthfulness and privacy to the exclusion of more personal facts — which in this case include her knowledge of her boyfriend's and her parents' prob-

able responses and feelings. Taking these circumstances into account leads to the "best" or most mature solution — but it may not lead to a solution that is fully logical in Piaget's sense.

Likewise, even the less emotional problem of the bending rods requires treating formal reasoning as a tool, rather than a goal in itself. The haphazard methods of an adult thinker really deserve to be called "mature" only if they supplement formal thinking, rather than replace it. Unlike a child, an adult must know when and how to return to the more laborious, systematic methods of abstract thinking described by Piaget. Adults must know, for example, whether they already know the answers to the bending-rods problem; if they do not have the answers, they must know how to do more than guess at them. Adults cannot confine themselves to haphazard methods when such methods do not work: if they do, their thinking will not differ from the concrete reasoning of schoolchildren.

short-term memory (STM). It then may be further processed in **working memory (WM)** into a form where it can be stored indefinitely in **long-term memory (LTM).**

For adolescents, the most important part of this model concerns WM and LTM, both of which alter or process information in important ways. Suppose, for example, that a teenager hears the sentence "Cats like to purr." If he decides to respond to or remember this information permanently, he must relate it to related information already in LTM: that cats also sleep a lot, that they also purr when they are hungry, that purring shows affection, and the like. This activation of prior knowledge orients him to the information and prepares him to respond to it.

Actual responses to new information are organized by instructions contained in the LTM designated for this purpose, and carried out in the WM. In the information-processing model, these instructions operate much like computer programs: they consist of sequenced instructions for modifying, classifying, and transferring information bit by bit. Because of their "supervisory" purpose, the instructions are sometimes called **executive programs.** In processing the sentence "Cats like to purr," for example, a simple executive program might consist of the following instructions:

1. Save sentence ("Cats like to purr") in WM.
2. Recall all "cats" from LTM. Save in WM.
3. Consider the first of these "cats."
4. Did it ever purr?
5. If yes, then save this information in WM.
6. Consider the next "cat" from LTM.
7. Go to instruction no. 4.
8. Continue until all "cats" have been considered in WM.
9. Add up the number of "yes" responses saved in WM.
10. Are the "yeses" more than half the number of "cats"?
11. If more than half, then speak these words: "That's true; cats do purr a lot."
12. If less than half, then speak these words: "I have not found that to be true in my experience."

Although this executive program is less detailed than the ones usually proposed by information-processing psychologists, it conveys the spirit of the approach — namely, to analyze seemingly instantaneous thoughts into their components.

An Example of Information Processing: Studying for a Test

To see how the information-processing viewpoint helps to explain a more everyday example of problem solving, imagine how high school students might study for a midterm test in, say, history. Many aspects of their behavior illustrate facets of information-processing theory, although not always in precise form. Suppose that the test is multiple-choice; that it covers a text that the students read just before the test; and that they have taken one previous test, which was also multiple-choice, from this history teacher. In these conditions, how are they likely to differ from elementary school children in preparing for the test?

Applying Expert Skills   First, adolescents have probably had more time to become experts in taking multiple-choice tests. They therefore already know, without even asking, the approximate form of the questions, as well as the instructions that the teacher will probably provide. They know these features so well, in fact, that they hardly think about them; instead they devote their short preparation time to more difficult matters. Younger children, in contrast, cannot afford to do this; for them, the format of the test itself might be part of the problem they are trying to solve. In information-processing terms, test taking requires use of working memory, and because working memory can handle test taking more automatically for older students, more memory capacity is available for analyzing the actual content of the test questions.

Selective Allocation of Attention   Second, adolescents have probably read enough textbooks to know that authors of such books usually organize material around headings, topic sentences, key terms, and summary paragraphs. They probably also know that the test questions will emphasize these points. So they read these sections of the assigned text carefully, skimming the intervening paragraphs and pages as rapidly as possible. In contrast, middle-years children are more likely to read all the material with equal attention, and consequently to get bogged down in it. In information-processing terms, older children more often possess long-term memories about how to study, and this knowledge directs their attention more efficiently.

Use of Domain-Specific Knowledge   Older students have usually taken more courses in history and in subjects related to history, so they know more than younger children do. Older students use their richer prior knowledge to help remember the new material that they have to learn. Certain familiar historical themes might crop up in the text — ideas like "wars often begin in small, out-of-the-way places" or "economic booms and busts come in cycles." Older students note that they have heard these ideas before, although not necessarily in these same words. Their memories help them to retain these main points better, and to respond to test items about them more appropriately.

Information-Processing Features of Adolescent Thought

Obviously, information-processing theories tend not to emphasize qualitative changes or transformations between major stages or periods of life. Instead, they treat each major stage as a continuation or extension of processes begun earlier in childhood. We discussed some of these extensions in Chapter 12, in our description of childhood cognition. As we pointed out in that chapter, older children organize information more consistently and effectively than younger children do. Even though it seems obvious to say so, older children "know more" than younger children do.

Improved Capacity to Process Information   Typically, an adolescent can deal with, or process, more information than a child can. A first-grader may remember three or four random digits (like 3 9 5 1), but a teenager can usually remember six or seven. And when a first-grader asks an adult how to spell a word, she can hold just two or three letters in her mind at a time; the adult has to dole them out singly or in very small groups (LO . . . CO . . . MO . . . TI . . . VE). A teenager can more often receive much longer groupings of letters and still reconstruct the word accurately.

These differences may result from either of two sources. The first is what information-processing psychologists sometimes call **structural capacity,** a person's basic "mental power" or cognitive ability (Case, 1978, 1985). Differences in structural capacity are like the differences in physical strength between adolescents and children; since teenagers have bigger and more powerful muscles, they naturally

Growth in basic ability

A Talk with Brian

Thinking in Adolescence

Brian, age fifteen, was interviewed on a Saturday afternoon in the backyard of the apartment in which he and his family live. He is a solidly built youngster with red hair, freckles, and a ready smile.

INTERVIEWER: How has your thinking and intellectual activity changed since you were younger?

BRIAN: Well, actually, the difference is that now I like to do everything. I like to think about everything. I really like sciences, but that's not to say that if the history department at school was better I wouldn't have liked history better.

INTERVIEWER: What interests you about science?

BRIAN: You could work with people *and* do research. It's not solely a research-type job or solely a humanities, people-type field. So it sort of gets the best of both worlds. . . .

INTERVIEWER: When you get into science itself, are there questions

that break your head in trying to figure them out?

BRIAN: Yeah, well, they try and keep those away from us so far. I'm taking biology and basically they let you discover things for yourself. For example, if it is a fact that a debt of enzymes in the liver of a chicken causes it to break down, how does it work? Well, you take water and oxygen and then you take the chicken livers and you mix them with hydrogen peroxide and you catch the acid that comes off. And then you do certain variations on that so you can see what else you can get off it.

INTERVIEWER: How do you figure that out?

BRIAN: We just did things to it . . . tried out all the combinations. We heated the liver, cooked the liver, chopped the liver. Like I was afraid we were gonna eat paté for a year! We also used a catalyst in place of an enzyme, which got a little bit more intellectual considering you had to figure why the catalyst did that to the enzyme.

INTERVIEWER: Do you enjoy figuring out things like that?

BRIAN: Yeah, and I enjoy it in math, figuring out how to do a math problem. I like problems that involve less written work and more mental work. So I prefer not to have a problem with great big numbers, but maybe one with more variables or some type of numerical sequence that I haven't figured out yet.

INTERVIEWER: Has this changed in the last few years?

BRIAN: Yes. It's on a higher level now because I see problems that I couldn't figure out two years ago that are easy for me now. Well, it's basically a change in my now being able to think about abstractions and stuff so that I can solve a problem with negative square roots that I could never have done before.

INTERVIEWER: Because it was too hard for you before.

BRIAN: Right, it was too hard to conceptualize. It's still hard to conceptualize. But I can do it now. And I enjoy it more.

can accomplish more physically. Likewise for performance on cognitive tasks: adolescents may remember more digits or letters, for example, partly because their brains can handle more information at any one time.

The second source of differences between children and adolescents is sometimes called **functional capacity,** the ability to make efficient use of existing mental abilities. Differences in functional capacity are more like the improvements in physical performance that come to a gymnast who is already perfectly conditioned: at a certain point in his training, his performance improves mainly because he learns to coordinate his movements more precisely, to rest his muscles when he does not really need them, and to take into account the unique features of the gymnasium in which he is performing. Similarly, functional capacity on cognitive tasks

More skill in using abilities

INTERVIEWER: Have other kids changed in the same way?

BRIAN: I hate to classify people, but there are certain differences in conceptual levels in class. There are people who are at a high conceptual level. There are also people who are at a real high level of knowing the procedures, so they can do a problem and get it right, but they don't necessarily know why they're getting it right. And then there's people who don't do either of them. What I don't like about the class is that people who know the procedure but don't know the concept can do better than people who know the concept but don't know the procedure as well.

INTERVIEWER: You value the conceptual stuff more.

BRIAN: Well, yeah, ... when we started biology it took me a while to get the concept while other people were grasping the procedure. So the first week I did badly. As soon as I got the concept, I got every question right.

INTERVIEWER: How did you figure it out?

BRIAN: I don't exactly know. I read what it said about it in the book and that was inconclusive. And I did what it said on the board, and that was inconclusive. So I just thought about what other people were doing, and I looked at how it was being done and how they were transferring it, and I sort of tried to figure out what it could be if you were doing those things to it. Sort of trial and error. . . . Systematically eliminating the possibilities.

INTERVIEWER: Is there the same kind of challenge in learning a foreign language?

BRIAN: Yeah. It's when you're listening to someone speak a foreign language and you know every word except for one. You realize that language is just abstractions like numbers are just abstractions.

INTERVIEWER: What do you mean?

BRIAN: Like when you say a word over and over again to yourself, any word becomes meaningless. Lan-

guage develops as abstract sounds come to be associated with certain ideas or things or experiences and have certain meanings to people. As soon as you learn the meaning of the abstract word in a different language that you at first couldn't understand and go back and translate something you were trying to read, you realize that it has shifted from being just an abstract word which has no real meaning to something which does. You're on the inside now. It's like an inside joke.

Follow-up Questions

1. Which of Piaget's cognitive stages is Brian probably describing when he distinguishes between people who understand scientific *procedures* and those who understand scientific *concepts*?

2. Which of Piaget's stages of cognitive development best describes Brian's thinking? Why?

3. In what domains of knowledge does Brian seem to have particular expertise?

---

requires coordinating existing skills to best advantage: recalling random digits by using mental tricks or devices for remembering them, for instance.

When it comes to cognitive development, it is usually hard to discriminate between the relative influences of structural and functional capacity — between how much of an adolescent's improved thinking comes from more sheer ability to handle information and how much comes from greater efficiency in using existing talents (Siegler, 1983). Almost any cognitive task allows an individual the freedom to perform it more efficiently with practice, yet the person herself may not be aware that she is trying to do so. For example, many adolescents can write term papers much more easily than they could when they attended elementary school, but try as they may, they might not be able to explain *why* they can do so. Did their extra years of practice make them smarter than before? Or simply more efficient with skills that they have always had? Research on information processing suggests that cognitive development consists of a bit of both.

Expertise in Specific Domains of Knowledge By adolescence, many individuals have become comparative experts in specific domains of knowledge or skill. These may or may not have much to do with school learning. One teenager might excel in knowledge of mathematics, whereas another excels in knowledge of baseball and still another excels in getting along with people.

Much of such expertise may depend not on generalized development of cognitive structures, as the Piagetians would claim, but on the long, slow acquisition of large amounts of specific knowledge. Studies of experts and novices among adults suggest this possibility. Experts in physics, for example, know many more concepts about physics than beginners do, but they do not necessarily know more about foreign policy, English grammar, or other areas of knowledge (Chi and Glaser, 1980; Chi et al., 1982). Experts also know more about problem solving in their particular field of expertise. A mathematician remembers countless formulas and equations, thanks to years of experience in memorizing them, and his memories naturally help him to solve new problems as they come up; he may realize that a new equation is similar to one he has worked with before, and simply recall how he responded to the earlier one (Anderson, 1980).

Remembering details

Ironically, then, expertise may often make creative problem solving unnecessary. Instead of using valuable energy in thinking through a solution, the expert can simply remember what to do; this fact, as much as any other, makes her performance seem fast and effortless. But since this advantage is confined to specific domains or types of problems, an expert's performance contradicts Piaget's assertion that powerful abstract thought develops across many domains at once. Outside of her field, an expert must struggle for solutions just like the rest of us. Within her field, on the other hand, she may often only *look* like she is reasoning at a high level, when in reality much of her performance amounts to a simple recall — the kind we all engage in when we remember the letters of the alphabet or a phone number.

This conclusion does not mean, however, that experts work only by simple recall. On the contrary, their larger number of memories may free them to focus on more difficult aspects of a problem, or on aspects that they have never encoun-

A great deal of cognitive development consists of acquiring specific expertise rather than general knowledge. These girls have learned to raise chickens; their skill at doing so may exceed that of most adults. (Bob Daemmrich/TexaStock)

tered before. Students who are good writers, for instance, tend to spend comparatively more time than others at planning an essay — making notes and outlines — and less time at actually putting words to paper (Applebee et al., 1981). To a large extent, the task of composing sentences takes care of itself for good writers, probably because they can draw on a rich memory of sentence constructions, terms, and phrases, and therefore devote less attention to creating them.

Evaluation of the Information-Processing Viewpoint

By focusing on the detailed features of problem solving, the information-processing viewpoint provides a valuable complement to the broader approach of cognitive developmental theory. Piaget and psychologists with a similar outlook have relatively little to say about these details, and partly as a result, they also have relatively little to say about why individual performance usually varies from one occasion to the next. Information-processing theory answers this question, but at some theoretical cost. Its very strength — fine-grained analysis — prevents it from providing an explanation for any general differences between the major age periods of life. Information-processing theorists see the trees, as the saying goes, rather than the forest. As a result, their descriptions tend to make a child's learning sound similar to that of an adolescent and even to that of an adult.

Age differences   In fairness, most information-processing researchers do acknowledge that cognition is not the same at very different ages (Sternberg, 1984b). Consider two people who set out to learn a foreign language. Both of them read books about the language, use the language with whoever will listen, and study and think about the

---

Perspectives on Research

Cognitive Skills Used in Writing

Researchers have learned much about the process of writing by asking writers, both beginners and experts, to describe their activities while they actually produce written text, such as an academic essay. This technique, called protocol analysis, shows clearly that writing involves combinations of cognitive skills, each of which affects the progress of the others (Hayes and Flower, 1980). For convenience, the cognitive skills of writing can be grouped into three activities traditionally highlighted by teachers of English composition: planning, translating plans into ideas and written expressions, and reviewing the results. Expert writers, whether in high school or elsewhere, handle each of these activities differently than beginners or novices do.

Planning consists primarily of generating ideas to express in an essay, but it also includes some unseen (and possibly unconscious) decisions about framing and organizing a piece of writing. Expert writers usually plan at several levels of generality at the same time: they deliberately translate general goals (like "Make this piece interesting") into subgoals ("I'll start by describing a real child's behavior"). The selection of subgoals proceeds rather opportunistically: selecting one particular subgoal may suggest a modification needed in another subgoal, or even in the main purpose of a piece itself (Matsuhashi, 1982). As a result, experts' compositions often end up different from the writers' first expec-

tations. "I don't know what I'll say until after I write it," said one skillful high school writer. This comment does not show aimlessness so much as dynamic planning during the process of writing.

Beginning-level writers also plan their work, but analysis of their protocols shows fewer subgoals; often their planning simply resembles rehearsals of the final product (Burtis et al., 1983). Instead of truly mulling over the purposes of a piece of writing before putting pen to paper, beginners act as if they are already running through the finished product, much the way a musician or a dancer might prepare for a performance. True analysis is prevented, in part, by the speed with which novices begin actual writing: on the average, high school students wait only three minutes before beginning the first (and usually final) version of an assigned essay (Applebee, 1981). But even this waiting time represents a developmental advance in thoughtfulness; observations of fifth-graders show that they wait an average of only three seconds before beginning similar essays!

For all writers, the greatest time and effort goes into *translating plans* into specific content or ideas for actual expression on paper. Here, too, experts and novices differ: experts typically generate far more ideas than they can use, and face problems of pruning and selecting content. Their advantage probably comes partly from greater knowledge of a

---

language as much as they can. Suppose that one of these people is eight years old and the other is eighteen. After a year of study, who will know the language better?

A common impression is that the younger child will learn a foreign language more quickly, but research actually suggests that the adolescent will learn it faster (Grosjean, 1982). Information-processing theorists claim that this happens for at least three reasons. First, older individuals can draw upon a wider range of strategies for learning. In learning vocabulary, for example, not only can they memorize new words by rote, but they also can categorize them more easily into meaningful

---

topic; after all, that is why they are called "experts."

But experts also make better use of their existing knowledge. Compared to beginners, they know better *what* they know — a form of metacognition (Bereiter and Scardamalia, 1982). As one expert put it, "I steer away from subtopics where I think I'll have to do more research first," implying an awareness of his own levels of knowledge. Partly as a result of sensitivity to their own knowledge, experts can more often make use of partial knowledge, as shown by comments such as "I seem to remember that the topic has something to do with X." Partial knowledge helps experts in searching for more information, whether from books or from their own memories.

Because novices tend to lack these skills, they have trouble using whatever knowledge they already do have about a topic. Analysis of their protocols and essays shows that they tend to stay closer to assigned topics than do experts who work on the same topics. And novices' essays more often use a "follow-your-nose" method of organization: each point may relate to the one immediately before it, but not necessarily to the overall goals of the essay (Flower and Hayes, 1981).

Throughout the process of writing, experts consistently engage in more elaborate and sophisticated *reviewing* of their work. This activity consists of more than the actual redrafting of a manuscript

that composition teachers traditionally assign. As expert writers put sentences on paper, they make thoughtful changes; they also continually evaluate their ideas and overall plans, both before and after they actually produce a draft. Novices do review their work, but they tend to confine themselves to relatively simple revisions, such as choosing new words and resequencing existing sentences (Sommers, 1980).

Psychologists and educators have devised a variety of strategies for helping novice writers to function more like experts (Scardamalia and Bereiter, 1986). In one strategy, novices continually review cue cards that prompt them with various planning suggestions ("Do you need an example now?"). In another, teachers listen attentively to beginners' reflections about their own writing, and offer occasional well-chosen comments to stimulate better planning, content generation, and review. Many of these techniques show promise in helping students learn to write, and show educational value because they also improve students' memories for the topics about which they write. But no interventions turn novice writers instantly into expert authors: that seems to come only with considerable practice, sustained literally for years.

groups. Second, older individuals have a richer knowledge of language in general, to which they can relate their newly learned language. Translations of difficult terms or sentences will puzzle adolescents less often, simply because their command of English is better developed. Third, older individuals can use their learning time more effectively — for example, by giving less study time to words that are similar in both languages and more time to truly unfamiliar words.

These developmental differences in processing are wide-ranging. They are so wide, in fact, that they may amount virtually to a "stage" difference, such as those proposed by cognitive developmental theorists. Viewed broadly, information processing in adolescence may differ qualitatively from information processing in childhood (Markham, 1979). Viewed in fine detail, though, specific processes may be identical during both periods of development.

Checkpoint *Information-processing skills continue to improve during adolescence. Compared to children, teenagers show an improved capacity to allocate attention selectively, and they are more likely to have acquired specific domains of expert knowledge. Because of these qualities, they can often acquire new knowledge more efficiently and thoroughly.*

The Psychometric Viewpoint

Psychometrics refers to the measurement of human abilities, usually with specially constructed tests. Psychometric theorists traditionally conceive of cognitive ability as a set of factors or abilities, such as verbal comprehension or numerical skill, which combine into a hierarchy of more general factors. At the top of the hierarchy is "general intelligence," sometimes abbreviated as *g,* which consists of a mixture of academic skills — usually language, logic, and arithmetic. Psychometrically oriented psychologists disagree about the importance of *g* compared to more specific abilities, but most agree that some form of general intelligence guides a wide variety of human activities, or even all of them (Gottfredson, 1985).

Testing for comparative intelligence

The psychometric viewpoint is concerned more with differences among individuals than with development within individuals (McCall, 1979). Considerable effort has gone to devising standardized tests that measure individual differences, such as those measuring general cognitive ability or "intelligence." A person's answers to questions on these tests yield a score, or sometimes a set of scores, that supposedly indicates something about his intelligence. In fact, though, what it really indicates is usually only comparative intelligence — how much better or worse a person has performed on the test than other individuals who are similar to him in age and general circumstances.

Features of Adolescent Thought: Factors and Individual Differences

Given its emphasis on identifying individual differences, the psychometric tradition has paid relatively little attention to formulating theories about how cognition develops during the human lifespan. Some psychometricians have tried to do so, though (for example, Sternberg and Powell, 1983). They have chiefly asserted two ideas: first, that intelligence tends to differentiate into a larger number of factors or elements as a child becomes an adolescent, and second, that the relative importance of these factors often shifts over time.

Increasing Numbers of Intellectual Factors   In the psychometric tradition, a **factor** is a group of cognitive skills that tend to occur together and that therefore form a more general (or superordinate) ability or type of intelligence (Sternberg, 1980). Typically, factors are identified by statistical analysis of the results of large numbers of ability tests. A verbal factor, for example, might emerge from analysis of a dozen or so tests that all relate to language, such as one that reflects skill with analogies, another that measures skill with reading comprehension, another that measures skill with vocabulary, and so on. Psychometrically minded psychologists have never fully agreed on just how many factors underlie normal human intelligence; serious proposals range from just one (Terman and Merrill, 1973) through half a dozen or so (Thurstone, 1938) to many dozens (Guilford, 1967).

How many factors?

For developmental psychologists, however, settling this question is not as important as knowing how, and whether, cognitive factors change as children grow up. In more everyday terms, this is equivalent to asking whether "being intelligent" means something different at different ages (Siegler, 1976). Is an intelligent child one thing at age four, something else at age eight, and something else again at age sixteen?

In general, the answer seems to be yes. Psychometric studies of the nature of intelligence have tended not to focus on developmental changes in the structure of intellect, but when they have, they have generally found that adolescents and adults have more diverse abilities — that is, more sharply defined factors — than middle-years children and preschoolers do (Sternberg and Powell, 1983; Bayley, 1955, 1970). In other words, a young child is intelligent in a relatively general or global way, whereas an older child or an adolescent tends to possess intelligence in the form of more specific cognitive skills such as good memory, verbal ability, or numerical ability. Among adolescents, these more specific cognitive factors do not correlate (occur together) as strongly as they do among children. Even if a teenager possesses a high degree of one factor, he likely will have only more modest amounts of the others; but a six-year-old is more likely to have relatively equal amounts of all three. In this sense, a term such as *general intelligence* becomes less meaningful with increasing age, and several *intelligences* seems more meaningful (Gardner, 1983).

Increasing diversity of abilities

Stability and Change among Cognitive Factors   Most psychometrically minded psychologists argue that intellectual factors or abilities that emerge during childhood remain essentially constant in nature and in relative importance as a child grows up. Cognitive development, from this viewpoint, is simply a matter of acquiring more of the same. An adolescent is "more intelligent" than a child because she has more of the same skills the child has: more memory, more verbal ability, more whatever.

This idea is supported by the repeated finding that an individual child's scores on ability tests tend to be more similar if the child takes the tests at relatively close intervals in time — if he takes them every year, for instance, rather than at five- or ten-year intervals (Bayley, 1968). The simplest explanation for this pattern is that the child gradually accumulates small bits of some constant ability. Testings close together in time therefore share more of the accumulated ability, compared to testings further apart in time, so the scores correlate relatively closely.

Of course, correlated scores may simply reflect changes in patterns of abilities rather than changes in overall amounts of abilities. Suppose that a general ability test really measures two underlying factors, one of which increases with age and the other of which decreases with age. In this case, cognitive development really consists of a change in the pattern of abilities — but the test might miss this fact, by averaging the two kinds of change.

A number of psychometric studies have indeed found changes in patterns of intelligence during development. For example, one series identified two distinct kinds of intelligence, fluid intelligence and crystallized intelligence (Cattell, 1971). **Fluid intelligence** refers mainly to quickness at handling abstract symbols, such as problems in logical reasoning or in understanding abstract diagrams. **Crystallized intelligence** refers to knowledge gained from living in society, such as vocabulary and general information. Both kinds of ability are stronger in adolescents than in children. Compared to older adults, however, adolescents and young adults show higher average levels of fluid intelligence and lower levels of crystallized intelligence. On the face of it, this suggests that adolescents may be more agile at reasoning, but that older adults may be more "knowing" or wiser. This conclusion has been criticized, though, because it is based on cross-sectional rather than longitudinal information. For example, the older adults on which this research was based were born at a time when people generally received less education than they do now. For this, and other reasons, it may not be accurate to conclude that older people have less fluid intelligence (Baltes and Shaie, 1976; Horn and Donaldson, 1976).

Examples of Psychometric Ability and Performance

Consider and compare four sixteen-year-olds, who attend the same tenth-grade class in the same school. Suppose that they happen to be taking a standardized test of intelligence, and that each has just encountered the following question:

> Water lilies double in area every twenty-four hours. At the beginning of the summer, there is one water lily on a lake. The lake covers exactly 10,000 square feet. It takes sixty days for the lake to become covered with water lilies completely. On what day is the lake half covered?

The simplest way to solve this problem is to reason backward from day 60: since the lake was full on the last day, it must have been half full on the day before.

How, though, will each of the teenagers solve this problem? The first, Yolanda, has taken advanced mathematics courses in high school, and she recognizes the problem as concerning exponential growth — *it's something to do with logarithms and exponents,* she says to herself. She sets about trying to determine the logarithmic formula for this problem, hoping that she can calculate how many days from the beginning are needed to cover the lake halfway. Finding this formula proves very difficult, however. Eventually Yolanda simply guesses at the formula, but she has the distinct impression that her guess is wrong, and that she has spent too much time on the problem.

Paul, the second teenager, has never seen a water lily in his life, so he spends valuable time trying to imagine what one of them looks like. He has the idea that if he can understand something about lilies, it might help him to solve the problem. *Maybe,* he thinks, *the problem on the test is not really as mathematical as it appears; maybe lilies grow in a special way or at some special fixed rate, and if I could just figure these out, then I could solve the problem quickly.*

The third student, Morris, is a cynic about tests: *Surely,* he says to himself, *this question is a trick.* He believes that test-makers would not put a real problem about exponents on a test of general ability. What, then, is the trick? He agonizes over this question for a long time without achieving any insight. Finally, at the last minute, he has an idea. If the lake is full on day 60, then the terms of the problem imply that it must have been exactly half full on the day before — that is, on day 59. He writes down "day 59" as his answer, though with some feeling of guilt. *I have not really solved this problem properly,* he thinks, *although perhaps I have not really cheated.*

Angela, the fourth student, ponders the question for a while, but she has trouble caring about whether or not she finds the answer. It's not that she lacks ability; on the contrary, she has taken a lot of standardized tests in her time, and when she has felt motivated, she has often done fairly well on them. This time, she looks at the question repeatedly but casually; she suspects that solving it may be deceptively easy, but she cannot immediately put her finger on any shortcuts. Instead her mind wanders. She remembers seeing lilies in a pond at her grandmother's farm two summers ago, and wonders at the way they float so perfectly and produce bright, showy flowers. After a while, she goes on to the next question on the test, without ever answering this one.

These four individuals illustrate some of the reasons why psychometric approaches to cognitive development do not always work (Sternberg, 1984b). Two of the adolescents, Yolanda and Morris, show the sort of focused, logical reasoning usually considered appropriate for a test of general cognitive ability. The other two, Paul and Angela, reasoned, or at least thought about, the problem as well, but in more divergent or wide-ranging ways. Only Morris reasoned in a way that actually yielded credit for this particular question on this test. Paul was handicapped by a lack of appropriate experience — he was sidetracked by mulling over the nature of water lilies rather than focusing on their rate of growth. Angela was

Psychometric tests of intelligence estimate students' cognitive performance, but they often show little about the cognitive processes underlying performance. The way this student solves a problem, for example, may differ from the way other test-takers solve it. (Arthur Grace/Stock, Boston)

handicapped by a lack of test-taking motivation; she was filled with interesting ideas and memories, but she did not apply herself, as teachers sometimes say.

Judging by this question, then, the test does reflect cognitive abilities, but it does so only imperfectly. Other, more diverse questions might improve the test somewhat. Genuine computational problems, for example, might reveal Yolanda's greater computational skill, and problems that emphasize verbal skills might help Paul and Angela, although it is hard to know for sure, given the limited information. All in all, the students' variation in performance suggests that for these adolescents, cognition may consist of more than one factor. Some may think in words; others, in formulas; others, with insights. Of course, the four teenagers' responses also suggest that performance can be heavily obscured by noncognitive factors such as lack of motivation or fear of standardized tests.

Evaluation of the Psychometric Viewpoint

As we have already implied in the preceding sections, the psychometric view of cognition has both strengths and limitations. Here is a more explicit list of these.

Empirical Bias Psychometric studies have a strong empirical bias, which means that they have clear, well-developed methods for identifying and measuring intelligence, or at least what psychometricians mean by *intelligence.* As we have noted, these methods rely primarily on standardized tests of ability. Literally hundreds of research projects have documented relationships among the cognitive skills shown on these tests, both for children and for adults. Standardized intelligence tests have proved especially convenient in professional fields such as education, which sometimes need to identify a few students with unusually high or low academic potential from among a very large number of relatively average individuals.

In spite of this advantage, psychometric researchers have not given equal attention to devising theories of cognitive development or to defining precisely the factors that constitute intelligence. The meaning of "psychometric abilities" seems to shift somewhat, depending on which investigator is studying them, and because definitions of these factors are often revised *after* various cognitive tests have been designed and administered. This is a problem even when psychologists study only the most general ability, *g*. In contrast, Piagetian and information-processing theorists go to some length to define and describe the nature of intelligence in detail, sometimes at the risk of not basing their concepts of intelligence on observations of enough individuals.

Lack of consistent definitions

Focus on Individual Differences   As we have noted, the psychometric viewpoint focuses on differences between individuals more than on cognitive growth within individuals. Scores on ability tests often — or even usually — refer to a person's relative standing compared with his peers. A high score therefore means only that the individual performed better than other comparable individuals, and in itself says nothing about the actual content of that person's cognitive skills. Focusing on individual differences in development is like looking at a forest and noticing that some trees are taller than others, but ignoring the fact that all the trees grew from tiny seeds.

This emphasis on differences has practical advantages when professionals must make comparisons among children or adolescents. For example, when educators are awarding one special scholarship to a high school student, it helps to know something of the candidates' relative academic standing. Standardized ability tests give this sort of information, although they are not the only source of it.

Unfortunately, standardized tests really only succeed well at predicting academic success, and contribute rather little to identifying other sorts of talent. They do not predict athletic success very well, or social popularity, or success in business later on in life. To measure these skills, we need tests that simulate them more closely. Administrative success in business, for example, correlates closely with performance on a simulated "in-basket" test in which a person must respond wisely to a set of imaginary correspondence that comes across her desk (Frederiksen, 1986). Since the in-basket task resembles real-life business tasks in both form and content, it is not surprising that it predicts administrative success in business better than psychometric tests of general intelligence do.

Failure to predict abilities

Emphasis on Cognitive Constancy   Relative cognitive standing, it turns out, often remains very constant for most of the lifespan. Given this fact, it is tempting, but not accurate, to conclude that nothing develops in cognition from, say, age four to age seventy-five or so. This fact also may encourage psychologists to theorize only about the nature of cognition in general and to neglect developmental issues. Thus, because it focuses on individual differences, the psychometric viewpoint tends to emphasize the stability rather than the change of cognitive skills during development (Wohlwill, 1980; Horn and Donaldson, 1980).

There is much truth to this bias. As we point out in the section about information-processing theory, for example, young children often solve problems in much

De-emphasis of cognitive changes

the same way that adolescents and adults do. But dramatic changes *do* occur in cognitive skills over the lifespan; adolescents are not merely older versions of schoolchildren or preschoolers.

Cultural Bias As we noted in Chapter 12, most psychometric tests favor white, middle-class children and adolescents in at least two ways. First, the questions on the tests often demand knowledge of middle-class life; a question might ask what a "flight attendant" is, thus assuming that the test-taker has flown in an airplane. Second, the format of standardized tests is often more familiar to middle-class individuals, whose families and teachers often give them better practice at answering testlike questions, even during informal daily conversations. Partly for these reasons, children and youths from the mainstream of society tend to perform better than others on standardized tests of ability. When such tests are used for educational screening, therefore, they pose problems for nonwhite ethnic groups, such as blacks and Hispanics, who seek equality of opportunity from the schools and from society.

Difficulties for minority groups

In fairness to the psychometric tradition, though, note that cognitive developmental theory contains cultural biases as well. Studies of formal operational thinking have repeatedly found that adolescents and adults in many non-Western societies do not use formal thinking nearly as much as those in North American society do. And studies within North American society find that teenagers from higher-income families tend to use formal thinking more consistently and skillfully than those from lower-income families (Munroe and Munroe, 1982). Such research findings emphasize that no single psychological theory provides a valid description of every individual's development; instead, we must take into account as many different ideas and viewpoints as possible in order to understand the developmental changes of adolescence (or any other period of life).

Checkpoint   *The psychometric viewpoint of intelligence has not focused primarily on long-run changes or developments in cognition. Nonetheless, it has pointed out that the number of factors or dimensions of intelligence may change as children and adolescents grow up. These factors may also change character over the years, as Piaget and other cognitive developmental psychologists have argued.*

The Development of Social Cognition

No matter which approach they take, most developmental psychologists agree that the new cognitive skills of adolescents have important effects on their **social cognition** — their knowledge and beliefs about interpersonal and social matters. In this section we look at the most important forms of social cognition, beginning with a description of the special form of self-centeredness, or **adolescent egocentrism,** that affects teenagers' reactions to others and their beliefs about themselves. We consider what causes this form of egocentrism and how these causes affect three other important kinds of social cognition, namely moral beliefs, political attitudes, and religious orientation.

Egocentrism During Adolescence

When adolescents like Neira first begin reasoning abstractly, they often become overly impressed with this skill: it seems to them that anything can be solved "if only people would be reasonable" (that is, logical). This attitude can make teenagers idealistic and keep them from appreciating the practical limits of logic (Piaget, 1967). They may wonder why no one has ever "realized" that world war might be abolished simply by explaining to all the world powers the obvious dangers of war. Or they may wonder why their parents have not noticed the many "errors" they've made in raising children.

The development of formal thought also leads to a new kind of confusion, one between an adolescent's own thoughts and those of others. This confusion of viewpoints amounts to a form of egocentrism. Unlike the egocentrism of preschoolers, which is based on concrete problems, adolescent egocentrism concerns more abstract thoughts and problems. Consider, for example, what happened to Neira. When she was fourteen, she had to perform at a figure-skating recital. For weeks beforehand, she practiced daily to prepare; as the performance date drew near, she naturally began to worry about how well she would do. In fact, she became convinced that "everyone" was talking about her particular performance, and wondering how good it would be. Her parents encouraged her not to worry and said that "people always like what you do on your skates." To Neira these comments just sounded like her parents did not appreciate the unique importance of *her* performance. Even after the recital actually occurred, Neira fretted about others' reactions to it: Had they liked it? What were they saying about it?

To some extent, Neira was egocentric in her thinking about the recital. Some "stage fright" was probably inevitable and natural; it occurs even among seasoned, adult performers. But Neira went beyond this reaction. She assumed that others were thinking about her performance just as hard, and in as much detail, as she did. But she did not have any real evidence that this was so.

The Imaginary Audience Adolescent egocentrism like Neira's primarily shows itself in teenagers' preoccupation with the reactions of others. Thirteen-year-olds, for instance, often fail to differentiate between how they feel about themselves and how others feel about them (Elkind, 1978). Instead, they act as if they are performing for an **imaginary audience,** one that is as concerned with their appearance and behavior as they are themselves. This preoccupation creates extremes of behavior and self-esteem. If a teenage girl believes that she looks attractive, she may not only feel elated when she goes to a party but may also be a bit conceited about her looks. On the other hand, if she doubts her attractiveness, she may not only feel dejected about herself but may also be convinced that others feel equally negative about her appearance.

Preoccupation with
reactions of others

Adolescent Conversational Skills

Informal conversations among peers become more coherent as children develop into adolescents, but they also retain many features of the conversation that occurs among young children (Dorval and Eckerman, 1984). Coherence increases largely because of new cognitive skills: adolescents develop increasing sensitivity to the psychological importance of what others say during conversations, as well as to the unwritten rules about how to participate in a conversation. Certain constant qualities remain, however, because of the intrinsic nature of informal conversation, no matter what the age of the participants.

Even in the middle years, for example, children seem to know that contributions to conversations are supposed to stay on a topic, rather than change topics abruptly as each child takes a turn speaking. Consider this conversation among fifth-graders:

CHILD 1: Did ya see the new Baskin-Robbins *[ice cream store]* yet?

CHILD 2: No, but we're going to McDonald's tomorrow.

CHILD 3: I'm going to my grandparents' on Saturday.

CHILD 4: Dad said we might go to Disneyworld.

CHILD 5: Maybe. Don't know yet. It costs a lot.

Although this conversation may seem a bit disjointed, it does have a topic, namely, "places where I have been or plan to go." Each child reflects an awareness of that topic, although contributions remain confined to "facts" and actions, with little reference to anyone's feelings or evaluations about the facts.

Young adolescents — age fourteen or so — have many factual conversations as well, but their comments more frequently imply evaluations of the facts. Several ninth-graders had the following conversation:

YOUTH 1: Where did you streak *[run naked outdoors]*?

YOUTH 2: From Loyola Street down to the corner.

YOUTH 3: Cool! Must have been funny.

YOUTH 4: Those other kids *[from another neighborhood]* are always doing things like that.

YOUTH 5: Yep; but they do it dumb and get in trouble for it.

This conversation shows more psychological awareness than the first one: it discusses people (the streaker, the "other kids") and implies feelings and motives about what they do. But the conversation remains rather "cold-blooded" and factual. The participants imply feelings and motives, such as approval of streaking and anxiety over being caught for misbehaving, but these feelings and motives never become the explicit topic of conversation.

Late in adolescence — age eighteen or even beyond — young adults begin expressing psychological awareness more explicitly. These twelfth-graders express this kind of awareness:

YOUTH 1: Sarah is so self-righteous; it's sickening.

YOUTH 2: I know how you feel. Her mother can't stand it either — feels ashamed of her. No wonder they argue.

YOUTH 3: Is that why she made Sarah quit the

club? Still, Sarah must be awfully unsure of herself to act that way.

YOUTH 4: Her attitude is the problem. You can see it all over her.

In this conversation, feelings and motives are not just implied, but stated and discussed openly. Comments refer both to the perspectives of the people being discussed ("Her mother ... feels ashamed"), and of the participants in the conversation ("I know how you feel").

In considering these developmental changes, though, note also that important features of informal conversations remain constant across the years; put differently, even the most mature conversations strongly resemble the least mature ones. For one thing, all the speakers take turns talking. Even very young children follow this rule, almost as soon as they can talk (Eisenberg and Garvey, 1981).

For another thing, informal conversations at all ages show a paradoxical combination of coherence and flexibility. Conversations are coherent because most turns at speaking relate directly to the content of the preceding turn. Adults honor this principle in about 95 percent of speaking turns; even preschool children stay on the topic about four turns out of every five (Dorval and Eckerman, 1984).

But two factors make even the most coherent conversation flexible and unpredictable, no matter what the ages of the participants. First, speakers rarely take account of *more* about the preceding conversation than the immediately preceding comment in selecting what they say. Second, even in responding to the previous comment, they do so poorly. About 25 percent of the time, for example, even adults make comments that are only minimally related to the content of previous comment (Tannen, 1984). Both of these facts contribute to the frequent experience, even among adults, of a conversation "veering off" in a new, unexpected direction, as in this exchange among twelfth-graders:

YOUTH 1: We went to California last month.

YOUTH 2: That's nice.

YOUTH 3: I've been there already.

YOUTH 4: *I've* been to Oregon and Washington, too.

In this conversation, the point of the original comment (the trip to California) has nearly become lost, though it was not ignored completely.

The fact that informal group conversations often unfold quickly and unpredictably may explain why adolescents do not really bring up psychological topics in them until rather late in their development. As pointed out in Chapter 10, people do acquire concepts of psychological traits in childhood, and they begin acquiring empathy or understanding about the needs of others even earlier. Expressing these new cognitive skills in informal conversations, though, may require quick thinking and thorough learning — and perhaps also years of practice in talking with peers. Meanwhile, adolescents may be plagued by the sense that they know more about other people than they can easily say (Dorval and Smith, 1984). And ironically, since their peers usually face the same conversational handicap, many adolescents may also get the impression that their peers are comparatively immature and insensitive individuals.

The teenagers shown here illustrate two aspects of adolescent egocentrism: a preoccupation with the reactions of others and a belief that serious catastrophes may happen to others but never to them. (Left, Alan Carey/The Image Works; right, Robert V. Eckert, Jr./EKM-Nepenthe)

Teenagers also reveal concern with an imaginary audience through **strategic interactions** with their peers — encounters that aim either to reveal or to conceal personal information indirectly (Elkind, 1980). Telephoning often serves as a strategic interaction, especially for younger teenagers. Frequent phone calls help to sustain a belief in personal popularity with an imaginary audience, so a teenager may subtly encourage others to phone by casually promising to share special gossip or secrets "if you phone me tonight." An individual can also create the appearance of popularity by talking on the phone for very long periods of time, which means that potential callers get the "busy signal" — an implied message that the youngster is too popular to reach easily by telephone. This message can also be conveyed to the person on the line with an offhand comment like "Gotta go; I'm expecting some other calls."

The Personal Fable As a result of their egocentrism, teenagers often believe in a **personal fable,** or the notion that their own lives embody a special story that is heroic and completely unique. For example, one high school student may be convinced that no love affair has ever reached the heights of romance of his involvement with a classmate; another may believe that she is destined for great fame and fortune by virtue of (what she considers to be) her unparalleled combination of charm and academic talent; still another may "know" that even though serious catastrophes happen to others, they will never happen to him — he will never get seriously ill, or have trouble finding a job, or die.

In experiencing these feelings and ideas, adolescents fail to realize how frequently other individuals feel them as well. Their budding ability to think abstractly leads to excessive awareness of their own social and cognitive abstractions. Early in adolescence, they still have only limited **empathy,** or the ability to understand reliably the abstract thoughts and feelings of others and to compare these thoughts and feelings with their own. Much of adolescence, in fact, consists of developing these social skills. So does most of adulthood, for that matter; we never really finish learning how to understand others, or ever really finish comparing our own experiences with those of others (Labouvie-Vief, 1982). But adolescence serves as the time when most people begin learning to consider other viewpoints in relation to their own and developing complex ideas about moral, political, and religious questions, among others, in response.

Over-awareness of personal ideas and emotions

Moral Judgment

As adolescents gradually overcome egocentrism in their personal relationships, they improve significantly in their **moral judgment,** or understanding of the actions that promote human welfare in a variety of situations. This knowledge does not always translate into actual behavior, but at least it sets the stage for it (Rest, 1983; Carroll and Rest, 1982).

During adolescence, most teenagers begin making ethical judgments according to principles of some sort; compared to children, they are less opportunistic, or inclined to make judgments according to immediate rewards or punishments that they may experience personally. But for most young people, the principles remain rather conventional for most of this period of life (Colby et al., 1983). This means that adolescents base their evaluations of situations either on principles expressed by their immediate peers and relatives (Kohlberg's Stage 3) or on principles widely believed in society as a whole (Kohlberg's Stage 4). (See Chapter 12 for an overview of Kohlberg's six-stage theory of moral development.) If friends argue, for example, that premarital sex is permissible, then many teenagers are likely to adopt this idea as their own. On the other hand, if friends, family, and even an entire community believe that premarital sex is morally wrong, then teenagers may just as easily adopt this belief. Note, though, that whether they actually act according to these beliefs is another matter: some youths are less sexually active than they seem, and others may be more so.

A few teenagers develop **postconventional moral judgment,** which means that for the first time, ethical reasoning goes beyond the judgments that society conventionally makes about right and wrong (Kohlberg, 1976). Adolescents' growing ability to use abstract formal thought makes this possible; unlike schoolchildren, they can evaluate ethical ideas that *might* be right or wrong, given certain circumstances that can only be imagined.

Influence of abstract thought

For example, consider how teenagers respond to hypothetical moral dilemmas, or fictional anecdotes that pose ethical problems, like this one:

A doctor had a patient who was pregnant, but who also had a disease that would probably kill her if she actually delivered the baby when it reached term. The baby, however, would probably survive childbirth. Unfortunately, medical science had no solutions to offer the doctor or the mother for this dilemma. The doctor could either save the mother, by performing an abortion, or save the child, by allowing childbirth to occur. What should the doctor do?

Using principles to solve moral dilemmas

Teenagers respond to this story differently than children do. In spite of variations in their final conclusions, they are more likely than children to recommend solutions that refer to fairly general, if not fully universal, principles. One adolescent might oppose abortion because "babies represent our future, so they are more important." Another might support abortion because "even though this baby will die, the mother might be able to get pregnant again." Still another might point out that "human beings cannot begin judging whether one person's life is more important than another's; all lives are important."

Research suggests that such principles largely represent true convictions and are not simply unthinking statements of conventional moral ideas. One study presented moral dilemmas like the one above, but also asked individuals to "fake" solutions that were not truly their own (Rest, 1979, 1980). In these conditions, adolescents found it very hard to fake solutions higher than their normal moral stage, but very easy to fake solutions lower than their normal stage.

Recognizing moral possibilities

Another aspect of moral development, guilt, changes in both nature and focus as well. Compared with children, adolescents are more likely to feel guilty about taking no action ("sins of omission") as well as about actually doing something wrong ("sins of commission"). The shift occurs whether a teenager is evaluating a hypothetical story that portrays wrongdoing (Hoffman, 1975) or is describing a situation in his own life (Hoffman, 1980). In the story about pregnancy, for example, teenagers are likely to view "doing nothing" as a moral problem for the doctor, whereas children are somewhat more likely to view this option as morally acceptable. Likewise, teenagers are more likely than children to see the problems with inaction in their own lives — that never bothering to invite a friend over to your home, for example, can sometimes hurt that friend as much as openly and actively criticizing her. These insights require formal thought: concern about something that might happen, not only about something that actually does.

Overall, then, moral judgment in adolescence begins taking into account a broader array of circumstances and principles than it did during the school years. Teenagers more often refer to principles in evaluating actions, although they still do not always do so. And they recognize that ethical errors can be caused by actions left undone and unseen, and not only by overtly performed actions. Like a lot of other cognitive developments, these changes result from adolescents' growing capacities to reason abstractly.

The Development of Political Ideas

Political thinking develops in ways similar to moral judgment — perhaps not surprisingly, since politics involves many ethical problems, and vice versa. As with

A Talk with Joan

Thinking in Adolescence

Joan is a slender, poised young woman of fifteen with a friendly but serious manner. She was interviewed on the back porch of her home after school.

INTERVIEWER: How has your thinking and intellectual activity changed over the past several years?

JOAN: For some kids it looks like they haven't changed very much, but for me they have. You read and think about different things — like *1984* — than you did before, and the discussions you have are a lot different . . . about bigger things.

INTERVIEWER: Why does a book like that appeal to you now?

JOAN: Well, you can understand it now. I mean, you can start thinking about all the different . . . the big questions. . . .

INTERVIEWER: What would be an example?

JOAN: Like, . . . the type of government. Serious things. Now if I read a fairy tale it's fun but I'm not so into it. It's not quite as interesting, while before that was exciting.

INTERVIEWER: Have there been changes in the way you use your mind to figure out problems at school?

JOAN: I don't think so. I mean, it's like I do more advanced math and stuff, but it doesn't seem to me that I couldn't have understood it before if someone had taught it to me. Of course, now you don't just deal with facts. You sort of write essays and things and read. You have to think about the connections. Which I'm not sure I couldn't have done before.

INTERVIEWER: How has your thinking about problems changed?

JOAN: It's hard to remember. I mean, I talked about problems before, but I suppose that I didn't think about so many realistic things. I remember thinking about "what if" after I read something or saw something, but it was generally about fantasy rather than something like world war or the nuclear threat. I think that I could have learned what I am learning now in sixth grade. When we get into more interesting things like in history and English, I end up talking about it out of school more. Like with my parents and with some friends. When it's not just facts. I mean, you never talk about math and French out of school, but you may talk about a book you read in history or something connected with other things.

INTERVIEWER: Do you feel more like an intellectual equal with adults?

JOAN: I don't ever remember feeling like I was not an equal. I always thought that if I didn't know it now, I'd learn it in a few months and then I would definitely be as smart or smarter.

INTERVIEWER: Are all kids able to think the same way that you do?

JOAN: Well, it sort of divides up more. I mean, before there were lots of different levels and it was basically who could learn faster. And now it's like, some kids just never get that far and some kids, even if they don't get that far fast, are able to think about things. . . .

So I think it does divide up more into two separate groups instead of many levels.

INTERVIEWER: Have you thought about the reasons for this?

JOAN: Well, sometimes I think it might be just like who spends time thinking about things. And sometimes I think the upper group are just extremely smart. I mean, I think a lot of it's how much energy you're putting into it, and how much interest you have in thinking about it.

INTERVIEWER: So the lower group may spend less time thinking . . .

JOAN: Or at that time in their lives, they're not bothering to think so much about these things; they're worrying about other things. And some people look like they're thinking about things, and when you talk to them, . . . they're not really.

INTERVIEWER: Do you get fooled the other way too?

JOAN: Yes. And then you talk to them and they say something really smart that they thought of, and you say, "Humm!"

Follow-up Questions

1. What signs of adolescent egocentrism do you see in Joan?

2. Which of Piaget's stages of cognitive development best describes Joan's thinking? How typical do you think she is of children her age?

3. Joan mentions her increasing interest in what she calls the "big questions." What might this interest signify about her cognitive approach to moral and political issues?

Participation in political events both reflects and builds adolescents' involvement in society and is an indication of their more sophisticated political thinking. Chances are, though, that these three girls also find political activity gratifying socially — a good way to make and be friends. (Steven Baratz/ The Picture Cube)

Limits on more sophisticated thought

moral development, adolescents show both progress and its limitations. Teenagers often do hold more sophisticated political ideas than children do; they handle political ideas and opinions more abstractly, and they see more relationships among them. They view the formation of laws and legal regulations more democratically, seeing these as something that applies equally to everybody in society rather than to isolated individuals or selected groups. In these ways, adolescent political thinking draws upon elements of formal operational thought and the more advanced forms of moral thinking described by Piaget and Kohlberg (see Chapter 12). At the same time, though, adolescents reveal serious gaps and inconsistencies in their political thinking. These suggest that political thinking is not acquired in an all-or-nothing, stagelike way, but that it involves learning large amounts of specific political knowledge — an idea essential to the information-processing viewpoint.

To understand these developments, consider a common political issue, poverty. What must be done to eliminate it? Can it in fact ever be really eliminated? The answers given by two children, one in the sixth grade and one in the twelfth, differ in significant ways that reflect the children's cognitive development. The answers also share some common limitations, in spite of the six years of living and learning that separate the two individuals. First the sixth-grader:

INTERVIEWER: Do you know what I mean by poverty?

SIXTH-GRADER: No.

INTERVIEWER: That means poorness, not having any money. So . . . would it ever be possible to make it so that nobody was poor?

SIXTH-GRADER: I don't, well, if they got the person to really work hard that there might not be anyone that would, uh, be poor and that, but if there was someone that would just uh would uh be retired, he could just lay around the house because he's already put in his years of work and that.

INTERVIEWER: Do you think it would ever be that there wouldn't be any poor people?

SIXTH-GRADER: Maybe, in the future, if they could enforce the law that all lazy people should work.

The twelfth-grader answered in this way:

INTERVIEWER: Do you think it would ever be possible to eliminate poverty?

TWELFTH-GRADER: Yes, because this is the most highly advanced, richest country in the world. And the world knows because we're putting money over here, overseas there, or we're putting money over there. Money in Africa, putting a hell of a lot of money in Asia, the Southeast. I don't see why we should be putting money there while we still have poor here. I'd say we could put in a little money but why do we have to buy airplanes . . . (Gallatin, 1980, pp. 350–351)

Aside from obvious differences in content, how do these two responses differ in cognitive form? First, the adolescent seems to understand better that a political problem may concern many aspects of society at once. Unlike the younger child, he points out how poverty may be related to or aggravated by activities beyond the borders of his own particular country, the United States, by implying that poverty abroad may worsen poverty at home by stimulating foreign aid and thereby draining away dollars. In contrast, the younger child implies that poverty is simply the fault of the individuals who experience it. If only they would work harder, they might escape their problem with little or no help from the rest of society and with little impact on society either.

Relationships among problems

The two children also have different views of how governments can help ordinary people. The sixth-grader implies that the most helpful thing government can do about poverty is to act like the police: the government, he says, should make poor people work harder ("enforce the law that all lazy people should work"). The twelfth-grader, on the other hand, suggests that government and citizens can genuinely cooperate with each other: in his view, the government should identify the people or groups who need money the most and give it to them. In his opinion, these are the domestic poor, not the foreign poor.

Sense of community

Although the twelfth-grader's ideas are more abstract and less personal than those of the sixth-grader, neither really expresses a true **ideology,** or coherent philosophy, about poverty. Admittedly, neither has a chance to do so in the short interviews quoted above; longer talks might allow them to show their political knowledge and sensitivities more completely. Probably not, though; studies show that most adolescents lack any sort of consistent, conscious system of beliefs about politics (Adelson, 1971; Patrick, 1977; Torney-Purta, 1984). Instead, they tend only to approximate consistency, frequently contradict themselves, and often base political ideas on values that are rather unconscious. The twelfth-grader in this

Lack of political ideology

example may freely contradict himself when the topic shifts to the problems of strategic planning for national defense, by deciding that foreign economic aid does serve a useful if indirect purpose by gaining allies abroad.

In a highly individualistic society like that of the United States, of course, lack of a coherent ideology may also represent a final or true maturity rather than a failure to attain one. Like most adolescents, very few adults really have explicit, complex political philosophies (Bellah et al., 1985), and many adults tend toward rather personalized beliefs on specific issues. The attitudes of the sixth-grader, for example, have been stated publicly in the United States Congress, as well as in many other adult forums. Furthermore, surveys of political knowledge generally suggest surprisingly sketchy knowledge of many basic political facts among both adolescents and adults. Many people do not know how many senators represent each American state in Congress (there are two), or how long members of Congress serve in either the House of Representatives (two years) or the Senate (six) (Jennings and Niemi, 1981). By supporting indifference to knowledge like this, North American society may actually discourage full development of political thinking among its adolescents.

Religious Beliefs and Orientation

During adolescence, cognitive development affects both specific religious beliefs and overall religious orientation. In general, specific beliefs become more sophisticated or complex than they were during childhood. The concept of religious denomination, for example, evolves from comparatively superficial notions to more accurate and abstract ones. In one study that used Piagetian-style interviews, middle-years children tended to identify denominations by easily observed behaviors (Elkind, 1979):

Increased sophistication in defining beliefs

INTERVIEWER: What is a Catholic?

EIGHT-YEAR-OLD: He goes to Mass every Sunday.

or

INTERVIEWER: Can someone be a Catholic and a Protestant at the same time?

SEVEN-YEAR-OLD: No, because you couldn't go to two churches.

By early adolescence, however, the concept of religious denomination begins to depend significantly on the beliefs of adherents rather than on their outward behaviors. Teenagers in this study replied with relatively sophisticated concepts:

INTERVIEWER: What is a Jew?

TWELVE-YEAR-OLD: A person who believes in one God and doesn't believe in the New Testament.

or

INTERVIEWER: What is a Catholic?

TWELVE-YEAR-OLD: Someone who believes in the truths of the Roman Catholic Church.

INTERVIEWER: Can a dog or a cat be a Catholic?

TWELVE-YEAR-OLD: No, because it cannot think.

In these responses, abstract qualities have replaced the more concrete observations of the younger children. As with political ideas, though, these abstractions are not necessarily very profound, nor do they relate consistently to each other yet.

For those involved in religious education and development, children's acquisition of specific beliefs like these often matters less than their development of an overall view of the world, or of a **faith** — a coherent orientation to religious experiences that guides their responses to life. Faith is much more general than "mere" beliefs, and it usually involves feelings as well as thoughts (Smith, 1979). Because of its breadth, faith often touches on topics and problems that are not explicitly religious in content, such as the meaning of birth and death or the best ways of handling personal relationships (Cohen and Lukinsky, 1985).

The development of faith

In childhood, religious orientation amounts largely to loose groupings of concrete religious beliefs and images, often with relatively little coordination and with seemingly little relevance to daily experiences (Fowler, 1981; Cully, 1979). Consider this explanation of the nature of God, by a ten-year-old:

INTERVIEWER: Can you tell me what God is?

MILLIE: God is a like a saint. He's good and he like — he like rules the world, but in a good way. And . . .

INTERVIEWER: How does he rule the world?

MILLIE: Well, he — not really rule the world, but um — let's see, he like — he lives on top of the world and he's always watching over everybody. At least he tries to. And he does what he thinks is right. He does what he thinks is right and tries to do the best and — he lives up in heaven and . . .

What is God?

INTERVIEWER: What does God look like?

MILLIE: I imagine that he's an old man with a white beard and white hair wearing a long robe and that the clouds are his floor and he has a throne. And he has all these people and there's angels around him. (Fowler, 1981, pp. 138–140)

Millie describes God in concrete terms that have little relevance to daily life. In contrast, a fifteen-year-old offers fewer visual images; for her, God is more of a universal presence that she feels permeates her life and helps her:

INTERVIEWER: What do you think God is?

LINDA: God is different to a lot of people . . . I just feel . . . he's there. There might not be any material proof but I *know.* I can bet my life on it. Really. I know because he *has* talked to me . . . [Once when I had trouble with my friends,] I remembered that, you know, there was *God* and I just asked him to tell me something, tell me what I could do, because why can't I be good friends with everybody? Go places with her one time, and then with her and him, and you know, with everybody? (Fowler, 1981, pp. 155–156)

For this adolescent, God is not so much a person living in a specific place as an abstraction. He is a relationship that transcends specific situations and experiences, and that helps to give those specifics fuller meaning.

Religious orientation need not come out of an organized religion, of course, and for many adolescents and adults it does not. Many teenagers prefer to develop a personal faith without reference to other groups' or individuals' beliefs (Bellah et al., 1985). Take this sixteen-year-old, who grew up attending an unusually liberal Protestant church and whose ideas resemble those of many people who never attend church at all:

INTERVIEWER: What means the most to you?

BRIAN: Just life. It fascinates me. I don't know what goes on before or after birth or death. And some things scare me. The unknown is really a factor in my life because I like to think about it a lot and the reason why everything got here. It really bothers me a lot because I don't know the answers and no one knows the answers, and I can't turn to anyone to get the answers — except to God, if there is a God. Maybe someday I'll get a vision from the Almighty! *(spoken sarcastically)* (Fowler, 1981, p. 159)

These ideas have much of the scope of Linda's comments. In spite of appearances, though, they may partially reflect social conformity rather than true, spontaneous conviction. Paradoxically, Brian may be conforming to an ideal of nonconformity or independent thinking. He implies this possibility elsewhere in the interview, by stating that the worst thing that could happen to him would be to agree with conventional, majority opinions. But although Brian and Linda differ dramatically in the source of their religious orientation — Brian comes from a relatively secular, humanist social environment, whereas Linda comes from a more traditional Christian denomination — they are not entirely opposites. Compared to Millie, they share a quality of comprehensiveness; their specific beliefs range relatively widely over life's issues, and fit together at least some of the time.

These developments may result from changes both in general cognitive structures and in knowledge and information-processing strategies. As predicted by Piaget for other realms of knowledge, Brian and Linda have developed the capacity to think abstractly, and as a result, they may have reconstructed their childhood beliefs and faith to use their new abilities. At the same time, they have had several years in which to acquire new knowledge about religion and about the meaning of life. Along with this knowledge may have come broad new strategies for dealing with and organizing this knowledge — strategies similar in scope to Piaget's formal operations, but with more application to religious problems. In their own ways, they may therefore have become modest experts about faith, though not about the same kind of faith.

Adolescents' cognitive development influences many aspects of their knowledge about interpersonal and social matters. Early in this period, they often overrate the powers of formal thinking; they also become confused about whether others are paying as much attention to their thoughts and feelings as they are themselves. Late in this period, some adolescents apply formal thought to moral problems, as well as to political and religious ideas and orientations.

Cognitive Development Versus Social Development

As these sections show, cognition has significant influences on many areas of adolescent life that most of us would consider essentially social in nature. These influences can work in the other direction as well. A motivation to have many friends, for example, can foster the strong development of empathy, which is in part a cognitive skill. Similarly, deep involvement with a church can promote relatively sophisticated knowledge and thinking about religious beliefs, at least as they exist in that particular church.

In real life, then, cognitive and social development do not divide up neatly, as they are made to do in textbooks like this one. Their blending will show up again in the next chapter, which discusses psychosocial development. As is evident there, most psychosocial developments assume the sorts of cognitive accomplishments discussed in this chapter. Some, such as identity development, do so rather explicitly, but all at least imply an awareness of the cognitive abilities described here.

Summary of Major Ideas

The Cognitive Developmental Viewpoint

1. During adolescence, teenagers become capable of formal thought, which is an ability to think about ideas.

2. Formal thought is characterized by an ability to think about possibilities, by scientific reasoning, and by an ability to combine ideas logically.

3. In general, formal thought fosters systematic solutions to many cognitive problems.

4. In daily life, however, adolescents (and adults) often do not use formal thinking, even when it might be appropriate to do so.

The Information-Processing Viewpoint

5. During adolescence, information-processing skills continue to improve.

6. Teenagers acquire more expertise in particular areas of knowledge or skill, and they become more efficient at allocating their attention to tasks.

7. Both structural and functional capacities improve as a result of development, and both probably contribute to improved cognitive performance.

8. Information-processing theory helps the specific mechanisms of cognitive performance.

The Psychometric Viewpoint

9. Psychometric ideas about intellectual development emphasize changes that may occur in the factors or dimensions of cognitive activity.

10. Factors may change either in number (usually getting more numerous) or in nature.

11. Two well-identified factors of cognition are crystallized intelligence and fluid intelligence, both of which first emerge in adolescence, and which become more distinct during adulthood.

12. Because of its history in the standardized testing movement, psychometric views of intellectual development emphasize individual differences in cognitive performance, the stability of intellectual factors, and cognitive skills valued especially in mainstream white culture.

The Development of Social Cognition

13. In spite of their improved cognitive skills, adolescents still sometimes show egocentrism by believing in an "imaginary audience," and by believing in a "personal fable" or biography of their lives.

14. Adolescents begin judging ethical problems according to principles, but most of these principles are still based on conventional attitudes and beliefs.

15. Teenagers also begin thinking about political processes in more sophisticated ways, by seeing more relationships among political problems and by developing more of a sense of society as a community.

16. Even older teenagers, however, usually lack any sort of conscious political ideology or philosophy — just as many adults do.

17. By adolescence, teenagers have already acquired relatively accurate notions of religious denominations; by the end of adolescence, they often show abstract understandings of the concept of God.

Key Terms

formal thought *(637)*
formal operational
  thought *(637)*
executive
  programs *(644)*
structural capacity *(646)*
functional capacity *(647)*
psychometrics *(652)*
g *(652)*
factor *(653)*
fluid intelligence *(654)*
crystallized
  intelligence *(654)*
social cognition *(658)*

adolescent
  egocentrism *(658)*
imaginary
  audience *(659)*
strategic
  interactions *(662)*
personal fable *(662)*
empathy *(663)*
moral judgment *(663)*
postconventional moral
  judgment *(663)*
ideology *(667)*
faith *(669)*

What Do You Think?

1. All things considered, do you think that Piaget overrated the importance of formal operational thought in the development of adolescents? Explain.

2. Think of an activity or area of knowledge where you consider yourself a relative expert. How much of your expertise seems to result from having an unusually large amount of knowledge or practice? How much seems to result from applying "merely" good knowledge in unusually skillful ways?

3. A teenager once said, "My parents get smarter every year." In what sense, if any, do you think this statement is true? What might cause a teenager to make the statement?

4. Why do you suppose that social cognition seems less definitely stagelike than the scientific thinking that Piaget described? Speculate about some of the possible reasons.

For Further Reading

Aero, Rita, and Weiner, Elliot. *The Mind Test: 37 Classic Psychological Tests You Can Score and Analyze Yourself.* New York: Morrow, 1981.

This volume reproduces numerous "classic" psychometric tests, along with instructions for scoring and interpreting your own results. The topics range widely, from your self-image to how sexually satisfied you are. By taking a few of these tests, you can experience, first-hand, the flavor of the psychometric approach to assessing human traits and behaviors. Note that the book does *not* include the major tests of general intelligence.

Loftus, Elizabeth. *Memory: Surprising New Insights into How We Remember and How We Forget.* Reading, Mass.: Addison-Wesley, 1980.

This book is a very readable account of major trends and findings in research on memory. It does not include much information about memory development during childhood; rather, it focuses on adolescents and adults. The author uses an information-processing model to explain many of her main ideas.

Tipton, Steven. *Getting Saved from the Sixties.* Berkeley: University of California Press, 1982.

This book gives an intimate look at adolescents and young adults who joined alternative religious communities, such as a Zen commune or a fundamentalist Christian group that lived apart from society. The individuals describe much of their social cognition: their religious and political thinking, for example, and their impressions about their roles in society.

Chapter

16

Adolescence: Psychosocial Development

Focusing Questions

- What typical conflicts about identity do adolescents have, and what factors influence how they resolve them?
- What conflicts of their own do parents of teenagers face?
- How do differences in parenting style affect parent-teenager relationships?
- Why do adolescents join peer groups?
- What changes in sexual activities and attitudes occur among adolescents?
- To what extent do adolescents encounter special problems such as pregnancy, abuse, delinquency, and suicide?

Separation and independence

As we have discovered, a number of dramatic physical and cognitive changes occur during puberty and adolescence. Although there is a great deal of variation in how fast these changes happen, by the end of this period, adolescents look like adults and are physically and intellectually capable of most adult activities. But as important as these changes are, the most significant accomplishment for an adolescent is the achievement of a full-fledged, independent, psychological identity: one that is mature and adult, and that is unique and separate from parents, friends, and other important childhood figures. An identity provides the teenager with a fuller and more permanent sense of who she really is, what she really needs, what she believes in, and what she is and is not capable of doing. One high school senior put it this way:

> It's not just that I'm all grown up now — physically, I mean. It's that I have grown up inside too. I feel different, more like a grownup than a child. Although there still are many things that I am unsure of, I finally have a much clearer sense of who I am and what is important to me and what I believe in. In a way, it feels like I am at the end of a long journey . . . and ready to start off on a new one.

In this chapter, we look at the process of identity development during adolescence, including the factors that influence identity and some of the possible outcomes. Then we explore several important aspects of the social world of the teenager, including relationships with parents and peers, the development of friendships, and the impact of school. We also look at adolescent sexuality and how it is influenced by current social trends and by personal beliefs. Last, we explore the special problems faced by adolescents today, including teenage pregnancy, physical abuse, depression and suicide, and delinquency, and some strategies for preventing them.

Unconventional hairstyles achieve two things at once: they establish an identity distinct from parents and other adults, and they help to delay fully adult commitments until teenagers feel truly ready for them. (Michael Siluk)

Individuation and Identity Development

The idea that each of us has our own **identity** — a unique and relatively stable set of personal characteristics — does not surprise anyone, but despite our familiarity with this concept, identity is not easy to define. This is because each person's identity is a complicated affair involving many different qualities and dimensions, and it depends on subjective rather than objective experiences.

The process by which an adolescent develops a unique and separate personal identity or sense of self, distinct and separate from all others, is called **individuation.** This process has four distinct but overlapping subphases: differentiation, practice and experimentation, rapprochement, and consolidation (Josselson, 1980).

Four subphases of individuation

During the **differentiation** subphase, which occurs early in adolescence, the adolescent recognizes that he is psychologically different from his parents. This discovery often leads him to question and reject his parents' values and advice, even if the advice is reasonable. For instance, a thirteen-year-old who enjoys and is doing well at music lessons may refuse to continue them because they were his parents' idea and not his own. In addition, sometimes the realization that his parents are not as wise, powerful, and all-knowing as he earlier thought they were leads him to overreact and reject *all* their advice (Josselson, 1980). After attempting, on his parents' advice, to talk with his history teacher about a classroom problem, and failing miserably, the adolescent may go through a period where he refuses to listen to anything his parents have to say about school or, for that matter, social relationships in general.

In the **practicing** subphase, the fourteen- or fifteen-year-old feels that he knows it all and can do no wrong. He denies any need for caution or advice and actively challenges his parents whenever the opportunity presents itself. He also increases his commitment to friends, who provide him with the support and approval that he previously sought from adults. In a discussion of plans to go to a rock concert, for example, he will completely dismiss his parents' concerns about the dangers involved in attending, asserting that his friends went to one last year and told him it was perfectly safe.

The third or **rapprochement** subphase occurs toward the middle of adolescence, when the teenager has achieved a fair degree of separateness from his parents. The pain and fear of being totally separate lead him to return to home base, and he conditionally and partially reaccepts his parents' authority. Often adolescents alternate between practicing and rapprochement, at times challenging their parents and at other times being conciliatory and cooperative. Frequently, a teenager at this subphase will go to great lengths to accept responsibility around the house, yet be indignant when his parents still insist on establishing a curfew and being informed about where he is going when he leaves the house in the evening.

The fourth and final subphase, which lasts until the end of adolescence, is the **consolidation of self.** During this phase, the adolescent develops a sense of personal identity, which continues to be the basis for understanding himself and others and for maintaining a sense of autonomy, independence, and individuality. Parents are often surprised at how much careful thought an eighteen- or nineteen-year-old has given to who he is and how strong a sense of personal direction he can have. For example, in a two-hour discussion with his mother that occurred quite by chance, Jorge, a high school senior, revealed that first and foremost, he thought of himself as an artist and worked very hard to develop a special way of seeing and translating what he saw into creative works; he also considered himself a person who was good at helping others. He said that he planned on first attending art school and becoming an artist, but thought that he would eventually earn his living as a social worker or some other type of mental health professional.

The process of individuation continues through the teenage years and often into young adulthood. As we shall see shortly, it dovetails with Erikson's theory, which holds that the major task of adolescence is to resolve the crisis of identity successfully.

Theories of Identity Development

The Crisis of Identity versus Identity Confusion   Erik Erikson has contributed more than any other theorist to our understanding of identity development during adolescence. As you may recall from Chapter 2, Erikson believes that the psychosocial **crisis of identity versus identity confusion** occurs during this stage of development. To resolve this crisis successfully and achieve a final identity, a person must integrate her many childhood **identifications,** or the conscious and unconscious ways in which she has come to experience herself as being like her parents and other important people in her life.

Teenagers both attempt to and succeed in integrating more knowledge about themselves than younger children do. A middle-years child may simply form disconnected, relatively separate impressions about himself: on one occasion he notices that he excels at hockey, and on another that he excels at baseball or swimming. In adolescence, though, he mulls over the significance of all these impressions taken together: do they mean that I am generally athletic? that I am popular? or that I am just a conformist, just devoting myself to whatever others value — in this case, sports?

In fact, all through childhood, individuals make tentative crystallizations of identity that change as they grow. For example, the identity of a "little girl" gives way to one of a "big girl." Similarly, the cute, ferocious, or good "little girl" later becomes a studious, kind, or tough "big girl" who must combine all these attributes in an identity that permits her to be a combination of "big girl" and "little girl."

Integrating various attributes

In forming an identity during adolescence, a youngster must selectively accept or reject the many different aspects of herself that she acquired as a child, and society (or parts of society) must give her recognition and appreciation for her uniqueness. The ways in which a child's family, community, and society respond can be more or less in tune with her own feelings about herself. The identity that is achieved at the end of adolescence, according to Erikson, includes all significant identifications with individuals of the past, which are altered to form a unique and reasonably integrated whole.

During the final stage of her identity formation, the adolescent may suffer more deeply than she ever did before or ever will again from a confusion of roles. The adolescent personality is likely to be vulnerable, aloof, and lacking in commitment, as well as demanding and opinionated. However, Erikson believes that these traits are all important elements of normal "I dare you" and "I dare myself" role experimentation. He also warns that conflicts about identity are normal and never completely resolved, and that the risk taking and psychological instability of adolescence should not be too quickly interpreted as signs of serious problems (Erikson, 1975). Erikson also believes that in addition to fairly successful identity formation, a number of other possible identity outcomes exist along a scale of completion or resolution.

Identity conflicts are normal

Identity formation during adolescence is more complicated and demanding than in earlier childhood in purely practical terms as well. This is because it involves choices and decisions that must be made about such things as education, career, family, and personal beliefs — all of which are likely to have life-long implications.

According to Erikson, just as the latency period that precedes puberty provides a temporary suspension or moratorium of psychosexual development, adolescence provides a **psychosocial moratorium,** during which the young adult can delay tak-

A time for experimentation

ing on adult commitments. Ideally, adolescence is when a person can be relatively free to experiment with different social roles in order to find a place or niche that is clearly defined and yet seems to be uniquely made for him. He may devote this time to academic life, to trying different jobs, to travel, to social activism, or even to delinquency (a role that has been very attractive for some time), depending on prevailing social, cultural, and economic conditions as well as on his individual capacities and needs. Each society makes certain experiences available to its

---

Perspectives on Research

Vanishing Markers of Adolescence

Developmental psychologist David Elkind has written extensively about the increasing pressures placed on teenagers in the United States to achieve adulthood prematurely, and to forgo the special, protected period of time within which adolescents have traditionally constructed their personal identities. He believes that the absence of this moratorium period and the increasing stresses that the current generation of adolescents is experiencing are major contributors to the growing problems of substance abuse, pregnancy, suicide, and crime among teenagers (Elkind, 1984).

According to Elkind, the absence of a special place for teenagers in our society is evidenced by the progressive erosion of what he calls *markers* of their transition status. Markers are external signs indicating where people stand in their development.

> Markers can be as simple as the pencil lines on the kitchen wall that mark a child's progress in height from birthday to birthday, or as complex as a well-deserved promotion after years of hard work and dedication. Markers are signs of progress to others as well as to ourselves. . . . Confirmation, bar or bas mitzvah, graduation exercises, and the like provide a public acknowledgment that young people have attained new levels of maturity. (Elkind, 1984, p. 93)

Markers tell us about our past, present, and fu-ture and give us a sense of our own developmental progress. Giving up old markers that have been outgrown, such as the belief in Santa Claus or the need for training wheels, helps a youngster assess where she has been. Markers not yet attained serve as goals and guidelines for future development. For the college-bound high school student, attending college is a marker to be achieved; for the college senior, the immediate markers are likely to be graduation and getting a good job, while marriage, having children, and owning a house may serve as markers for the more distant future. In Elkind's words, "Markers protect teenagers against stress by helping them attain a clear self-definition, and they reduce stress by supplying rules, limits, taboos, and prohibitions that liberate teenagers from the need to make age-inappropriate decisions and choices" (p. 94).

Elkind discusses how the loss of five types of markers — clothing markers, activity markers, innocence markers, image markers, and authority markers — has influenced teenage development. In the last few decades, the clothing markers that distinguished teenagers from children and adults have disappeared. Thus, the bobby-sox of the 1950s and the blue jeans and work shirts of the 1960s — both of which typified adolescents of these periods — have given way in the 1980s to a style of dress shared by individuals of all ages. In many ways, the clothing of today's teenagers is no longer distinguishable from that of younger children and

young people, who are also influenced by important historical changes and events such as the Great Depression and the Vietnam War. Children growing up during periods of war, poverty, and social upheaval are generally unlikely to experience the period of moratorium between childhood and adulthood. As a consequence, they may prematurely take on the work and family roles of adults, and ultimately assume adult identities that are more limited than would have been the case had there been opportunities to explore alternative possibilities. On the other hand, an

---

adults. Because special teenage dress provided a firm, positive, secure, and automatic counterpoint to the anxiety and worry about height, weight, complexion, and facial features experienced during that period, its loss is significant.

Certain activities, such as organized team sports, were once the sole domain of adolescents, and thus served as markers of their status. But now Little League baseball and Pee Wee hockey and soccer make these same activities and their trappings — uniforms, formal league schedules, and so forth — available to middle-years and even preschool children. The increasing degree of adult involvement and control in these activities has led to a decrease in the players' spontaneity and independence, and to an overall decline in participation in high school athletics.

Elkind suggests that contemporary society no longer believes in childhood innocence or values it as a characteristic, and thus innocence markers have vanished as well. Young children are readily exposed through television, films, and advertising to all aspects of human life, including sexuality, aggression, and misery. Whereas such exposure is not likely in itself to destroy children's innocence, it does frighten them to see adults so out of control. More important, by making such information available to children whether they understand it or not, we destroy its value as a marker for those who are ready for it — in this case, older teenagers.

Image markers, the unique ways in which teen-agers as a group are portrayed, have also disappeared. Teenagers were once pictured as flighty, impulsive, rash, overambitious, and in need of the restraint, common sense, and good judgment associated with adulthood. Television and films have now reversed these roles and created a new teenage image — the adultified child. This adultified child is portrayed as being sensitive, intelligent, knowledgeable, mature, and worldly, and frequently assumes leadership and parental responsibility in solving family problems. While a view of teenagers that sees them as being less competent and mature than they actually are is problematic, so too is a view that pressures them prematurely to act as adults, thereby depriving them of appropriate image markers.

The final type of marker that has been undermined is the authority marker. The authority of parents and teachers, which is based primarily on superior competence, wisdom, and experience, has been weakened by increasing pressures on families and schools and decreasing economic and social support for the adults who rear and educate children. Media images reinforce a picture of children and teenagers who assume authoritative adult roles that have been abdicated by parents and teachers who are unable to fulfill their traditional roles of leadership and authority.

expansive economic and social climate such as that of the late 1950s and early 1960s provides adolescents with the opportunity to experiment and develop identities that are less restricted.

Setbacks in identity formation **Identity diffusion,** or a failure to achieve a relatively integrated and stable identity, takes a number of different forms. The first is avoidance of intimacy and closeness with others. The second is a diffusion of time perspective. In this case, there is a sense that one is out of step with others and that important opportunities may be lost forever. There are also feelings of depression and a sense of despair about whether the pain and confusion about identity will ever end and a comfortable sense of identity finally be realized. A third form is a diffusion of industry, which is reflected either in an inability to concentrate on required or suggested tasks such as school or work or in a self-destructive preoccupation with some one-sided activity such as reading.

A fourth and final form of identity diffusion is the choice of a **negative identity,** which involves rejection and disparagement of the roles offered by one's family or community as proper and desirable, and an acceptance of socially undesirable roles such as that of the delinquent. Erikson suggests that widespread negative adult attitudes toward teenagers serve to convince many troubled teenagers who are struggling with negative identities that the role of delinquent is best (Erikson and Erikson, 1957). Problems of identity confusion are more likely to occur and more difficult to resolve in families that are experiencing serious problems such as alcoholism and other drug abuse, physical and sexual abuse, marital conflict, and parental separation and divorce.

Various historical, cultural, and personal events and experiences may affect how one's identity is resolved. For example, many people who grew up during the Great Depression developed identities that were preoccupied with work, economic survival, and self-sacrifice, whereas some people who grew up in the 1960s, when traditional social roles were being rejected, developed identities based on alternative roles.

The Relationship Between Identity and Intimacy For Erikson, successful resolution during adolescence of the crisis of identity versus identity confusion prepares the individual to move on to confront the central crisis of early adulthood: intimacy versus isolation. A fairly clear and coherent sense of identity is needed to tolerate the loss of self that intense relationships often threaten and the loneliness and isolation that the end of such relationships bring. It is not unusual for teenage couples to break up suddenly and then unexpectedly reconcile; this behavior may in part reflect a level of identity resolution that is not yet adequate to the task of sustained intimacy. Thus, the development of identity provides the necessary basis for intimacy.

A somewhat different view of the relationship between identity and intimacy is proposed by Harry Stack Sullivan in his interpersonal theory of development (Sullivan, 1953). According to Sullivan, the achievement of intimacy is the central task of adolescence. Intimacy develops first through same-sex friendships or "chumships" during early adolescence and then heterosexual relationships in the middle stages of adolescence. Thus a youngster's sense of identity develops from her intimate experiences, first with members of the same sex and then with members of the opposite sex.

Identity Status Guided by Erikson's ideas, researchers have been able to study identity development during adolescence. Marcia, for instance, interviewed eighteen- to twenty-two-year-old students about their occupational choice and religious and political beliefs and values (Marcia, 1967, 1980). He classified them into four categories of **identity status,** based on two judgments: whether or not they had gone through an "identity crisis" as described by Erikson, and the degree to which they were now committed to an occupational choice and to a set of religious and political values and beliefs. The four categories are:

1. *Identity achievement* Individuals in this group had experienced a crisis and were now committed to an occupation and to a religious and political ideology. Both their occupational choices and religious and political beliefs were based on serious consideration of alternatives and were relatively independent of those of their parents.
2. *Identity diffusion* These students may or may not have experienced a crisis, but showed little commitment to or concern about occupational choice and religious and political beliefs.
3. *Moratorium* Individuals in this category were presently *in* crisis, actively struggling to make commitments and preoccupied with achieving successful compromises between their parents' wishes, the demands of society, and their own capabilities.
4. *Foreclosure* These students had not had a crisis but expressed commitment. Interestingly, it was difficult to tell where their parents' goals for them ended and where their own goals began. Their college experiences served only to confirm their childhood beliefs, which they held to rather rigidly.

In general, adolescents seem to progress in status toward identity achievement. Researchers using Marcia's categories have found that identity achievement is rarest among early adolescents and most likely among the oldest high school students, whereas foreclosure is the most common identity status among adolescents of junior and senior high school age (Meilman, 1979; Pomerantz, 1979). During the college years, individuals who previously experienced foreclosure or identity diffusion generally shifted to identity achievement. Crises were most likely to occur during the freshman year and to be resolved in a positive way. In the area of vocational choice, foreclosure and identity achievement were the most stable ways of resolving identity, whereas questions of religion and political ideology were more likely to involve identity diffusion (Offer, Marcus, and Offer, 1970; Waterman, 1982). When men who were first interviewed during college were studied six years later, it was found that 84 percent who had been identity-diffused or foreclosed during college had not changed their identity statuses (Marcia, 1976).

Researchers have found few differences on measures of identity between males and females, who are equally represented among the four identity statuses and who seem to develop in similar ways. However, there is some indication that the sta-

Identity development over time

tuses have different psychological meanings for males and females. While both sexes adjust equally well to identity achievement, and do poorly with identity diffusion, there is some indication that a foreclosed status may better protect women from conflict with their families and provide them with greater social support than foreclosed men receive (Waterman, 1982; Marcia, 1980). This may be due in part to the "double standard." Foreclosure for a young woman often means getting married and becoming a mother and housewife rather than pursuing other possible career identities. It may thus fit traditional stereotypes and result in less conflict than, say, pursuing a nontraditional career as an engineer or accountant and achieving an identity that combines work, marriage, and parenthood. A foreclosed male, however, who starts a family and settles into a limited, dead-end job is more likely to find himself in conflict with others' expectations of success as well as with his own.

There is also some indication that more fundamental differences may exist between identity formation for females and that for males, based upon their different roles and experiences in society (Gilligan, 1982). Erikson's view is that male identity develops in relationship to the world of work and female identity in a relationship of intimacy to others. Gilligan suggests that women's development of morality, which is an important aspect of identity, focuses not only on rights and rules as it does for men, but also on responsibility and relationships with others (Gilligan, 1982).

Marcia's work has been criticized for several reasons (Skolnick, 1986). First, it assumes that adolescents must experience a crisis to achieve an identity and must be consciously aware of that crisis. Thus, individuals in the foreclosure group were rated low on identity because they didn't report a crisis, even though they seemed to be committed and clear about who they were, while individuals in the diffusion group were rated higher on identity, even though they were unclear about who they were and what their commitments were.

A second criticism is that Marcia's judgments about identity are based solely on the issues of occupation and ideology. For Erikson, identity includes a much broader range of issues, which may differ from person to person. A person can be more committed to his occupation and religion than to his sexual identity and political values. Also, Erikson believes that identity conflicts are never fully resolved, in the sense that conflicts about career, intimacy, and beliefs will continue to arise during a person's life. For example, the psychosocial crisis of generativity versus stagnation that most adults confront during midlife is likely to raise anew adolescent conflicts about intimacy and the range of personal beliefs and values that were largely but not fully resolved during adolescence.

Finally, while Erikson conceives of identity and identity confusion as a continuum from mental health to pathology, Marcia does not. His categories actually describe different identity styles, each of which may have a healthy or a pathological outcome.

Thus, certain important ambiguities still remain about identity development. For one thing, it is as yet unclear whether identity formation means the same thing for boys and girls; for another, the relative stability of the identity status is still, at most, only relative. Some adolescent boys express an achieved identity compara-

Gender affects a child's identity profoundly, by influencing not only choices of toys, activities, and friends but also the child's perception of society's expectations about sex roles. Even young children are aware of these stereotypes and often act in ways that reflect them.

A key accomplishment of adolescence is the development of a distinct and separate personal identity or sense of self. Ideally, adolescence is a time when a person can be relatively free to try out and experiment with a variety of different social roles. And, in fact, despite their reputations as conformists, teenagers actually engage in a wide range of activities, which helps them to develop their own unique identities.

Friendships during adolescence help teenagers learn to appreciate each other's uniqueness as people and can assist in the process of identity formation. At the same time, achieving a clear identity as an individual enables teenagers to develop more intimate relationships with friends, both of their own sex and of the opposite sex.

tively early in their lives — around age eighteen, say — but then later revert to another identity status. Similarly, a girl who may have settled on an identity that emphasized marriage and children over career may find these questions reopened at a later period and at least temporarily find herself confused about who she really is.

Although such backtracking makes little theoretical sense, in reality adolescents who regress often have good reason. A job or career that looked well in hand, for example, may fall through at the last minute; or a person's need for emotional support — from a new spouse, for instance — may not be fulfilled as was originally expected. Identity, by nature, is achieved through the joint action of both the person and his circumstances. And circumstances, as everyone knows, can sometimes change unexpectedly and dramatically.

Checkpoint *According to Erikson, resolving the crisis of identity versus identity confusion is the key psychosocial task of adolescence. This process involves selectively choosing and integrating aspects of one's childhood identity. Successful resolution of normal identity conflicts is influenced by what kind of psychological moratorium a teenager experiences. Research confirms the existence of different styles of identity.*

Social Relationships During Adolescence

The search for identity affects all of an adolescent's relationships. Ties with parents must make room for increasing interest in peers, and a new commitment to the life among comparative equals that peers provide. A young teenager's efforts to become more physically and emotionally separate from her parents and closer to her friends may be stressful, but more often than not, the problems and conflicts of this period are relatively minor. Full-blown upheavals happen to only a minority of families of adolescents, in spite of popular stereotypes to the contrary (Rutter et al., 1976).

Relationships with Parents

It is a widely held belief in our culture that leaving home, at least in a psychological sense, is an important part of the process of becoming a self-reliant individual and achieving an identity. Much of this process occurs during adolescence, and the differences in experiences and understandings between parents and their leave-taking children account for what is sometimes referred to as the **generation gap.** Leaving home is a powerful metaphor for finishing the developmental tasks of adolescence and symbolizes the end of childhood (Coleman, 1980). Many of the conflicts between adolescents and their parents over chores, curfews, school, and

A generation gap?

Most parents and teenagers have plenty of disagreements and conflicts, particularly, over matters related to the teenagers' current social life and behavior, but they tend to share long-run interests, goals, attitudes, and values. (Top, Carol Palmer; right, Billy E. Barnes/Stock, Boston)

social activities reflect mutual ambivalence about the imminent separation. For example, consider an eighteen-year-old about to leave for college. His blatant disregard of household responsibilities and violations of clearly agreed-upon rules leads his father to angrily say, "As long as you are living in my house, you had better abide by the rules; otherwise, you can move out tomorrow." In a sense both teenager and parent probably desire and dread the separation; their fights reflect their struggles to resolve their conflicting feelings.

Interestingly, the overall quality of adolescent-parent relationships may improve after teenagers have left home. For example, in one study, two hundred adolescent males starting college and their parents were asked to describe their relationships with one another at two points in time: at the end of the men's senior year in high school, when they were all still living at home, and during the first months of their freshman year. Half of the students were commuters who continued to live at home, and half lived in a dormitory or apartment. Those students who no longer lived at home showed greater affection toward their parents, improved communication, and a greater sense of independence (Sullivan and Sullivan, 1980).

The identity confusions that teenagers experience may restimulate similar unresolved feelings in their parents. For many parents, adolescent changes create or magnify conflicts in their own lives. As one parent put it, "Sometimes I'm not sure which is more upsetting to me, my teenage daughter's pain and confusion about who she is or similar feelings which are stirred up from my own difficult adolescence."

Parental empathy and envy

Parents may be threatened by their teenager's experimentation with sex, or may be jealous of him, particularly if he has economic privileges, social opportunities, and freedom from responsibility that they themselves did not have in adolescence. And even if they are well established in their careers, family life, and personal identity, middle-aged parents often feel caught between the conflicting demands and needs of their adolescent children, their own aging parents, and of course their own lives (Rapoport et al., 1980).

Their children's seemingly unlimited opportunities for career and happiness sometimes confront parents with the limitations of their own work and emotional lives. Thus, their dissatisfaction and upset can make them difficult people for adolescents to live with. As one twenty-year-old girl who was about to leave for an exciting summer job in another country put it,

> Mom has been absolutely impossible for this last month, and Dad hasn't been much better. They can be so rigid and unreasonable, and even the smallest thing can set them off. Sometimes I think that Mom thinks that *she* is the one who is actually going and that Dad criticizes whatever I do because he is afraid that I will be more successful than he. I get angry and tell him to find someone else to help solve his midlife crisis. Sometimes raising middle-aged parents can be an absolute drag!

On the positive side, however, we should note that although teenagers and their parents at times feel overwhelmed by the challenges of adolescence, on the whole it is the exciting and rewarding culmination of a long process of developmental change in the parent-child relationship. In fact, the majority of adolescents and parents continue to share important values and to get along rather well together (Csikszentmihalyi and Larson, 1984).

Agreement on basic values

Parents and children share similar attitudes about important issues and decisions: about ideas of right and wrong, for example, or what makes a marriage good, or what the long-run value of education is (Coleman, 1980). Where they differ is more in the emphasis or strength of those attitudes. One teenager and her parent may agree that premarital intercourse is not by nature wrong but may disagree about the specific conditions under which it is all right. A second teenager and his parent may argue about the comparative importance of a career in engineering versus one in law, but both will agree that getting some sort of education is important.

Adolescents and parents most often disagree about matters affecting the teenager's current social life and behavior, such as styles of dress, hair length, choices of friends, social activities, participation in household chores and family activities, and choice of music. For preferences like these, teenagers agree more with their peers than with their parents. Yet no one — not even the teenager herself — considers such personal preferences as important as the more basic attitudes or values, since the latter usually guide many life choices over long periods. When asked how much they value various people's opinions, for example, adolescents consistently rated their parents' advice more highly than their friends' advice (Curtis, 1975).

How large a gap is there between generations? It depends on the age of the adolescent and who is making the evaluation. It is likely that early adolescents who are in the differentiation and practicing subphases of identity formation will report greater differences with their parents than older adolescents in the rapprochement and consolidation subphases. Overall, adolescents tend to underestimate and parents to overestimate both the extent of parental influence and the size of the generation gap (Bengston and Troll, 1978; Lerner and Shea, 1982). When asked what attitudes they think the other generation holds about global issues such as disarmament, the real differences that emerge are smaller than what teenagers guess and larger than what parents guess they are (Lerner and Knapp, 1975).

Parenting Styles Four aspects of parent-adolescent relationships appear to be involved in the adolescent's development of identity: (a) parental interest and involvement; (b) the emotional intensity of family interaction; (c) the degree and nature of family conduct; and (d) the nature of parental authority. The most successful adolescent experiences seem to occur in families in which interest, involvement, and intensity of interaction are at moderate levels — families in which teenagers are able to express their own viewpoints freely, even if those viewpoints conflict with those of their parents; and where they can actively participate in family decision making (Douvan and Adelson, 1966).

Benefits of democratic style

In a study involving more than seven thousand adolescents, researchers found that teenagers felt most positively about two parental styles, **democratic parenting** and **equalitarian parenting.** Democratic parents generally encouraged their children to participate in discussions and consulted them about decisions, but reserved the right to make the final decisions; equalitarian parents tried to give adolescents equal say in decisions. Teenagers gave their lowest ratings to parents who were **autocratic** and did not consult with their children in making family decisions (Elder, 1980). These results are consistent with other research, discussed in Chapter 10, which has found that parents who use democratic styles of child-rearing (as contrasted with authoritative, authoritarian, and permissive child-rearing styles) provide children with both the opportunity to gain experience in decision making and an adequate degree of adult guidance and control (Baumrind, 1971).

There is some indication, however, that a fine line exists between sensitive, respectful involvement and the type of intrusive overinvolvement that does not adequately respect adolescents' need for separateness and independence. Here is what Allen, who is almost sixteen, has to say:

> I really appreciate that my parents are interested in what I am doing and what I am feeling — in whether I am happy or unhappy — but sometimes it's just too much. Like, I don't always know just how I am feeling, or maybe I don't feel like talking to them about things. It sometimes makes me guilty to keep things from them, but I think that I have a right to. I sometimes get angry that they can't respect me as being a separate person from them.

In summary, it is not surprising that parents and children get along best in families who make and carry out decisions consistently and jointly, who perceive those decisions as being fair and reasonable rather than arbitrary, and who respect the developmental needs and sensitivities of all family members — both parents and children.

The quality of the relationship between a teenager and her parents may strongly influence the course of her identity development. To the extent that parents encourage her to see herself as a unique, worthwhile, competent, and independent person who is capable of entering the adult world — and also give her the opportunity to explore and integrate the different and sometimes conflicting aspects of her identity — their contribution will be highly positive. To the extent that circumstances and the parents' own personal limitations prevent them from doing this, the teenager will have a more difficult time achieving an integrated and resilient adult identity. For example, if parents are upset with their daughter's "punk" life-style and sexual experimentation because of their own conflicts in these areas and if they therefore belittle her, it may pressure her to foreclose her identity prematurely. As we shall see shortly, teenage pregnancy is frequently associated with this type of foreclosure.

Social-Class Differences   As we note earlier in the chapter, adolescents are significantly influenced by the type of family in which they grow up. One useful way of describing families is by social class, which is determined by parents' level of education, income, and type of work, as well as by their life-style and cultural values. A major series of studies of families in the United States, Great Britain, and Italy reveals some important social-class differences that affect adolescents' development (Kohn, 1977).

In general, differences between the values, child-rearing practices, and expectations of middle-class parents and working- and lower-class parents closely parallel differences in the nature of their day-to-day work experiences. For example, parents who work as professionals (doctors, lawyers), who are upper-level executives, or who own their own businesses generally experience a high degree of autonomy

---

A Talk with Carla

Leaving Home

Carla, age eighteen, was interviewed in the TV room of the apartment in which she and her family live. A high school senior, she had recently returned from spending a year in Italy as an exchange student.

INTERVIEWER: What is it like to be eighteen as compared with when you were a younger teenager?

CARLA: It's much better than being fourteen.

INTERVIEWER: Why is that?

CARLA: I don't really know. But, I think, fourteen was a really bad year and I remember everyone saying that thirteen is supposed to be your worst year because that is when you become a teenager. But fourteen was really bad and it gets better each year since. There was definitely a lot more pressure then than there is now. I don't know. I feel more like just my own person now.

INTERVIEWER: You feel more like your own person?

CARLA: Yes. Maybe it is because now I have to be choosing colleges and stuff like that, and with school, I've been mostly able to make up my program myself and choose what I'm doing. At this age you have more responsibility and more things you decide for yourself. It just comes, like, without even wanting it, really.

INTERVIEWER: Is that sometimes a problem?

CARLA: No. I love it! I think it's great! I think a lot of people, when they're younger, really want to be independent. But, at least for me, now that I'm eighteen, I don't want it so much, but I do like it. I'm not striving towards it, it's just happening and it's just my life.

INTERVIEWER: What makes someone a friend for a person your age?

CARLA: Well, I'm not sure right now. It's kind of weird just getting back from spending a year in Italy because it's like seeing everybody again after a year.

INTERVIEWER: How about before Italy?

CARLA: Well, I guess in a general way, friendships are more important now. Not that I really feel I need to have lots of friends, but I think that having real friendship is more important now . . . you know, not just someone to go hang out with. I think I make more distinctions now about my friendships. Like casual friendship is great, but it's nothing like friendship where we can sit down and really talk to each other and things like that.

INTERVIEWER: Would that be an important sign of a really strong friendship?

CARLA: Oh, yes. I just decided this recently, that being with this person but *not* talking to them is also the biggest sign of friendship. Just being able to be with someone and not doing anything. Like just sitting down together and not having to talk. That is really important, too.

INTERVIEWER: What do people your age do with your peers, with people the same age?

CARLA: I don't even know anymore. Everything. I mean everything! People just hang out. I guess that is the major thing that teenagers do. People also seem to be into sports a lot. Almost all the girls I know are on the soccer team now. . . .

INTERVIEWER: What about parents? What are things like with parents for an eighteen-year-old?

CARLA: Well, right now I'm still adjusting to parents again. It's weird, because I think I really went through a big jump about my parents while I was away.

INTERVIEWER: What was that about?

CARLA: I think a lot of people really feel when they're younger, you know, the whole thing about rebelling and really wanting to get out of the house and not be with their parents. Well, it didn't happen. Going

and independence in deciding how they will spend their time at work. Although they often work quite hard and earn high salaries, much of their sense of satisfaction comes from internal or intrinsic sources, which they control, rather than from extrinsic sources, which are controlled by others. Their values and expectations for their children are consistent with these experiences. Adolescents in middle-

---

to Italy wasn't that sort of decision. It sort of happened after I was in Italy. I'm not sure of why, but I just decided that I didn't want to spend time with my host parents. So I got a little rebellious with them, and they dealt with it really well. They basically let me do what I wanted to do, so I feel like my own parents sort of missed my rebellion.

INTERVIEWER: They were off the hook?

CARLA: Yes, they were off the hook. It's funny, because I didn't get in trouble. It was more like something happened to me, and they didn't realize it until it was almost over. So now it's sort of strange, because in a way I feel closer to my own parents. Now when I talk to them it doesn't feel like parents. Of course they do sometimes feel like parents when they nag and say, "You can't do this, you have to do that."

INTERVIEWER: How do you feel about the nagging part now?

CARLA: Well, in one way I can relate to them better now . . . more like just people. But, on the other hand, now I'm seeing more clearly how they nag me. I guess I'm feeling like I need to leave soon. Being away from home was really important.

INTERVIEWER: In what ways?

CARLA: It gave me a chance to see what would happen in a situation where no one knew me. It was like starting all over again. So this was really interesting because I found out that I did a couple of things differently. But I also found out really that the way I acted is the way I act pretty much at home, too.

INTERVIEWER: So you really had a chance to test out who you were in a totally new situation.

CARLA: Exactly!

INTERVIEWER: Did you like the way it turned out?

CARLA: Yeah . . . it was neat. At the beginning I remember writing a lot about who am I and trying to find myself and all that stuff. I'm just remembering that now because near the end or even in the middle I sort of just forgot about that question.

INTERVIEWER: Do you think that some of these changes might have happened had you not gone away?

CARLA: I don't know. I'm wondering about a lot of things like that. Like how I would have changed over the year. I think I probably would have gone in the same direction. It just might have taken me longer. Or it might not have even happened until I went to college.

INTERVIEWER: What are your thoughts about going off to college?

CARLA: I don't know. You just go out and live happily ever after or something. I just feel like it's time. I feel like I'm going to die being here for this year. It's just time to go do something else without my parents and without my friends and without my sister and all that.

INTERVIEWER: It's a pressure inside of you?

CARLA: Yes, sort of. It's just like in your senior year you don't really have much to look forward to, like what I'm going to do next year in high school and what sports I'm going to play and what club I'll join or whatever. It's like you come to an end. I just have this feeling right now, like it's time to leave.

Follow-up Questions

1. Does Carla show any signs of Erikson's crisis of identity versus role confusion?

2. Which of Marcia's four identity statuses might best apply to Carla at this point in her development? Why?

3. How typical of other teenagers her age are the friendship qualities that Carla values?

---

class families are encouraged to be independent and to learn to regulate or control their own behavior, rather than to rely upon the rewards or punishments of others to determine how they will act. The parents' child-rearing styles tend to be democratic or authoritative rather than authoritarian.

Lower-middle-class families: jobs

Although lower-middle-class adolescents share such influences, they are oriented more toward jobs than careers. A study that compared the work expectations of students at an elite, a mid-range, and a working-class university revealed that working-class students are much less likely to aspire to professional careers, and anticipate having lower levels of leadership and control over their day-to-day work, than children of middle- and upper-middle-class families. In addition, differences in student perceptions of the degree to which their schoolwork was internally motivated (intrinsically controlled) or extrinsically motivated (behaviorally controlled through grades and other tangible rewards) paralleled the social-class makeup of the colleges (Hoffnung and Sack, 1981).

Working-class families: extrinsic motivation

Compared with middle-class families, working-class parents are much more authoritarian in their child-rearing patterns, and until their children are ready to leave home, are less likely to support their children's attempts to be independent and to participate in family decision making (Kohn, 1979). Both their work experience and their family life are more likely to emphasize conformity to extrinsic expectations. For instance, the amount of punishment that a working-class teenager receives for unacceptable behavior is apt to be based on the amount of damage he did rather than on his motivation; the opposite is more likely to be true in middle-class families.

Lower-class families: low expectations

Lower-class families, which include a disproportionate number of blacks, Hispanics, and recent immigrant minorities, must contend with high rates of unemployment and with poverty, discrimination, and limited access to needed opportunities. Consequently, child-rearing and family life are likely to reflect the unpredictability of the future and the "long shot" quality of holding very ambitious long-range expectations. At the same time, lower-class parents are also likely to encourage their children to "be all that they can," and to emphasize the importance of exceptionally hard work and outstanding achievement in overcoming the roadblocks between children's aspirations and their fulfillment.

Divorce, Remarriage, and Single Parenthood It is common knowledge that divorce rates have increased dramatically during the past twenty-five years, and that almost half of marriages of young people will end in divorce. It is estimated that one third of all eighteen-year-olds in 1990 will have lived with a divorced parent, and of the children born in the past ten years, almost half will spend an average of six years in a one-parent household (Glick, 1979).

The impact of separation and divorce on adolescent development is influenced by a variety of factors, including when the divorce occurs, the nature and length of the family conflicts that lead up to and follow the divorce, the quality of the child's relationship with both the absent parent (usually the father) and the parent who has primary custody, and the economic circumstances of the family after the divorce. Separation from the father early in life seems to have a greater effect on both girls and boys than later separation (Levitin, 1979; Wallerstein, 1984; Hetherington et al., 1982).

As we have pointed out, adjusting to divorce is a long-term process that in some ways resembles mourning the death of a loved one. Divorce and its aftermath are particularly hard for teenagers, who are so sensitive about being "normal" and insecure about their identities. Follow-up studies of divorcing families reveal that even ten years afterward, many adolescent children are still struggling to resolve their anger and self-blame and to accept the permanence of the divorce. Barbara, a seventeen-year-old whose parents separated when she was ten, reported that

A lengthy mourning period

> my mom and I are real close now. I stopped being angry at her when I was fifteen, when I suddenly realized that all of the kids who lived in tract houses with picket fences were not any happier than I was. It took me a long, long time to stop blaming her for not being in one of those houses. (Wallerstein, 1983, p. 239)

It can also be difficult for an adolescent in a divorced family to achieve realistic hopes about his own love relationships. Jay, who is fourteen, said, "Dad left because Mom bored him. I do that all the time." And Pamela, also fourteen, "I'm afraid to use the word *love*. I tell my boyfriend that I love him, but I can't really think about it without fear" (Wallerstein, 1983, p. 241). Perhaps the most important factor in an adolescent's adjustment to divorce is his *parents'* ability to resolve their own angry feelings and to allow their child the space to do the same.

Divorce's effect on intimacy

Although a single-parent family is the most likely outcome of divorce, there are several other possibilities: the single parent might remarry, bringing a stepparent into the family; or she may not remarry but bring an informal stepparent into the family. In some cases, divorced parents continue to share parenting, with or without sharing legal custody. Whatever the arrangement, the family's economic situation and the social and emotional resources and support available to its members are key factors (Blechman, 1982).

For single parents, support is often hard to find, and sometimes hard to accept when it is offered. Said one single parent, "Help from my old married friends was a mixed blessing — they cared for me and their help was invaluable. Yet my dependence on them kept me tied in with part of my life that I was moving away from" (Boston Women's Health Book Collective, 1978, p. 146).

Single parents lack social support

On the other hand, the addition of a stepparent can be particularly difficult for an adolescent, because of the extensive family history that the new spouse has not shared, the lack of commonly accepted roles for stepparents and stepchildren, and the teenager's intense need to be independent of adult control and authority. Sometimes children adjust by enlarging their view of the family to make room for three parents — mother, father, and stepfather. For example, when Jerry, who is fifteen, was asked how often he saw his father, he asked, "Which dad do you mean?" But at other times, acceptance of a stepfather can be a problem (Parke, 1981). Phillip, a sixteen-year-old whose parents separated almost four years ago, describes it this way:

Stepparents may seem intrusive

At first I was very upset about my mom and dad breaking up. Like, I knew that they weren't getting along for quite a while, but I never thought that they would really split up. It's all right now and I get to see my dad pretty regularly. But the biggest problem is my mom's new husband. He thinks that he's my father or step-father or something, and tries to boss me around. No way! Things were better when it was just me and my mom.

As we have already briefly noted, although relationships with their parents are very important, adolescent identity is shaped by other social influences as well. One of the most important are a teenager's friendships with peers.

Friendship

Friends matter a lot during adolescence. Friends offer easier and more immediate acceptance than do most adults, who often are trying to "improve" many of a teenager's behaviors and skills, and so friends ease the uncertainty and insecurity of the adolescent years. They offer reassurance, understanding and advice, and a person to talk with when necessary.

Sam is thirteen. Here is how he describes what a best friend is:

A best friend to me is someone you can have fun with and you can also be serious with about personal things, about girls or what you're going to do with your life or whatever. My best friend, Jeff, and I can talk about things. His parents are divorced too, and he understands when I feel bummed out about the fights between my mom and dad. A best friend is someone who's not going to make fun of you just because you do something stupid or put you down if you make a mis-take. If you're afraid of something or someone, they'll give you confidence. (Bell, 1980, p. 62)

An unquestioning appreciation of friends helps adolescents to become more independent of parents and other symbols of authority, and to resist the seemingly arbitrary demands of family living. Friends also promote independence simply by providing knowledge of a world beyond the family. Teenagers learn through their friends that not every young person is required to be home by the same hour every night, that some parents expect their children to do more household chores than other parents do, and that other families hold different religious or political views.

Qualities of Adolescent Friendships Studies of adolescent peer relations reveal a trend toward greater **mutuality** in friendship through increased loyalty and inti-macy over the teen years (Douvan and Adelson, 1966; Douvan and Gold, 1966).

Researchers conducting one large-scale study asked children and adolescents to define friendship, to describe how two people initiate, maintain, and end a friend-ship, and to explain how people become close or best friends. Adolescents indi-cated that mutual understanding and intimacy were most important, whereas children emphasized shared activities.

Sharing interests with friends is important to teenagers, as it is to children. At the same time, though, less tangible qualities such as loyalty, mutual respect, and intimacy become increasingly important in friends — especially among older adolescents. (Paul Conklin)

Mutual understanding involves an appreciation of how different people can interact in ways that are mutually beneficial. Unlike younger children's cooperation, adolescent mutuality depends on the understanding that other people share some of one's own abilities, interests, and inner experiences, and an appreciation of each person's uniqueness. In fact, a characteristic of early adolescence is a fascination with the particular interests, life histories, and personalities of one's friends. Teenagers want to understand friends as unique individuals and to be understood by them in the same way. The ability of adolescents to recognize the advantages of complementary relationships — that is, relationships in which two people with different strengths and abilities cooperate for mutual benefit — makes possible friendships involving greater commitment, permanence, and loyalty (Youniss, 1980; Damon, 1983).

Appreciating others

The other main dimension of friendship for teenagers is **intimacy** — feelings of closeness. Intimacy comprises three different aspects: self-revelation, confidence, and exclusivity, which teenagers describe in the following ways:

> A friend is a person you can talk to, you know, show your feelings and she'll talk to you. You can talk more freely to a friend. Someone you can tell your problems to and she'll tell you her problems. They are open . . . A friend is a person you can really tell your feelings to . . . you can be yourself with them.

> Friends can keep secrets together. They can trust that you won't tell anybody. You won't expect them to tell anybody else. You know she won't tell anybody anything. If you tell somebody something, they won't use it to get revenge on you when you get into a fight. You talk about things you wouldn't tell other people. (Youniss, 1980, p. 181)

Now that we have described the importance of mutuality, loyalty, and intimacy in adolescent friendships and how these features differ from friendships in childhood, let's take a brief look at differences between male and female friendships.

Male–Female Differences   Intimacy as reflected in a friend's willingness to disclose things about herself and to be empathetic to another person's feelings is a key aspect of friendship. In a study of changes in intimacy among fifth, seventh, ninth, and eleventh graders, researchers found that friendships formed by boys had lower levels of intimacy than those of girls (Sharabany et al., 1981). Girls appeared to be better able to express feelings and to be more comfortable with giving emotional support than boys were.

Girls show greater intimacy

Girls also develop more intimacy with the opposite sex than boys do. Although fifth-grade boys and girls showed little intimacy with the opposite sex, seventh- and ninth-grade girls reported much more intimacy with boys than boys did with girls. Toward the end of the eleventh grade, however, differences in reported intimacy between same-sex and opposite-sex friends decreased.

How might these differences in intimacy be explained? Perhaps the most likely explanation is that they are products of traditional sex-role stereotyping, which defines and values intimacy much more as a feminine quality than as a masculine one. Adolescent girls tend to have one or two close friends, whereas adolescent boys tend to have many friends with whom they are less intimate. It is also likely that adolescent males equate intense intimacy exclusively with heterosexual friendships, while females at this age are more comfortable in being close with both male and female friends. These and related issues are explored more fully later in this chapter.

Peer Groups

For most adolescents, social relationships extend beyond family and individual friends to include **peer groups,** or agemates who know each other, sometimes quite well. Adolescent peer groups share many of the characteristics of those in middle childhood (see Chapter 13): they involve social equals who are of roughly the same age, maturity, and background, and who enjoy spending time together pursuing shared activities and goals. However, peer groups play an even greater role in the everyday life of adolescents than the peer groups of younger children do, and they are much less likely to be all male or all female.

A basis for self-evaluation

For a teenager, peers are a central source of information about himself and others. They provide him with critical information about who he is, how he should act, what he is like, and so forth. They serve as a basis for making comparisons between his own actions, attitudes, and feelings and those of others.

One major study used participant observation, interviews, questionnaires, and journals to learn about the social interactions of 303 boys and girls aged from thirteen to twenty-one. The participants were studied at beaches, social clubs, parties, on street corners, and inside their homes, and were asked about their friendships and other peer relationships (Dunphy, 1963). The researchers discovered two types of peer groups. The first, **cliques,** were close-knit groups of two or more people who were intimately involved in a number of shared purposes and activities, and who excluded those who were not. The second, the **crowd,** was a larger, less cohesive group of between fifteen and thirty people. Adolescent crowds were generally informal associations of two to four cliques.

Membership in a clique allows a teenager to have a few select friends whom she knows well and who share important interests and activities, whereas membership in a crowd provides contact with a much broader group of peers on a more casual and informal basis. The small size and the intimacy of a clique make it like a family in which the adolescent can feel comfortable and secure; the major clique activity seems to be talking, and cliques generally meet during the school week. Crowds usually gather at parties and other organized social functions, which typically take place on weekends.

How Do Peer Groups Develop? As adolescents grow older, their cliques and crowds change in important ways. Early in this period, teenagers usually form same-sex cliques which have little to do with each other. Clique members are still very much like schoolchildren; family activities compete heavily with peers for recreational time, and children's general inexperience outside their families tends to prevent the development of true crowds.

With time, though, boys' and girls' cliques initiate contact with each other through activities such as meeting at a shopping mall and watching a video cassette together. These activities still offer the comparative safety of numbers; no one really has to interact intensely with a member of the opposite sex if she does not want to (although complete avoidance is no longer possible, either). The first heterosexual contacts tend to be initiated by the leaders of associated cliques, and when (and if) these contacts become frequent enough, they help create a new, heterosexual clique. This change in turn helps to bring about a general shift toward heterosexual memberships in all cliques. Dual-sex cliques and crowds, however, contain the seeds of their own destruction, in the sense that serious dating results in involvements that eventually reduce the importance of the clique or crowd to the participants.

Parents, teachers, and adolescents all encourage membership in peer groups (Newman, 1982). For example, parents usually discover that children in their teens have less time than ever before for family activities and are thus less subject to influence than ever before. Parents may try to make up for this by encouraging certain friendships and discouraging others. Whether or not they succeed, their efforts become a force to be reckoned with in the social life of an adolescent.

Teachers and other authorities tend to reinforce most peer groups that develop in their schools. They usually tolerate existing cliques and crowds, thereby implying approval of them; in addition, they sometimes actively encourage particular groupings of students, by choosing members of one crowd to monitor the halls, or members of another to organize a school dance. School authorities also rely on the leaders of cliques to help enforce school rules; when vandalism occurs, for instance, leaders are sometimes called in to identify the culprits or to help restore order.

And of course teenagers themselves encourage membership in peer groups.

Roles of cliques and crowds

Gradual inclusion of the opposite sex

Influences favoring peer group membership

They do so partly for the reason we have already mentioned: to give themselves a socially secure base for developing a sense of personal identity and for becoming more independent of parents and other adult authorities. The support and protection of peer groups also provides a relatively safe environment in which to test out ideas and behaviors that individuals might not be secure enough to try alone, such as signing up for a drama class, dressing in a certain way, or trying drugs.

Breaking into a group can sometimes be difficult, given some adolescents' possessiveness about their relationships. Because joining a new clique or crowd is usually harder than staying in one, peer groups tend to maintain themselves, at least for a while.

Popularity and Social Acceptance   Peer groups are central to adolescent experience and provide the adolescent with a basis for evaluation of who she is and how well she is doing. Clearly, then, peer groups are extremely hard to live without. Being popular is very important to teenagers, and popularity is often linked with a particular clique or crowd. But personal qualities are also important.

Bases of popularity   In general, both boys and girls who are popular are perceived as liking other people; they are tolerant, flexible, and sympathetic, and help others by making them feel accepted and involved and by planning and initiating interesting and enjoyable group activities. Popular teenagers are also described as being lively, cheerful, and good-natured, and as having a good sense of humor; they possess initiative, enthusiasm, drive, and good ideas (Conger, 1977).

Teenagers who are not admired and who are most likely to be neglected or rejected outright in many ways have the opposite characteristics of those who are popular. Adolescents who are ill at ease and lacking in self-confidence and who respond to uncomfortable situations by acting timid, nervous, or withdrawn are more likely to be neglected and socially isolated by peers. In contrast, teens who handle their discomfort in an aggressive, conceited, or demanding way are apt to be actively disliked and rejected (Conger, 1977). Finally, physical attractiveness, socially visible talents, and achievements in athletics, the performing arts, and (in some environments) intellectual activity are positively related to popularity.

Conformity   Adolescents do pressure each other to conform, although probably not as much as the popular stereotype decrees. In one classic study of conformity, **Conformity experiments**   adolescent boys were shown simple sets of lines which differed in length in various ways (Constanzo, 1970). Each boy was asked to judge the comparative length of one particular line. He was also told how three other boys had judged the length, but he was *not* told that the other boys were actually fictitious. The judgments of the "other boys" were rigged so as to contradict obvious differences in the lengths of the lines. This put the real boy under pressure in making his judgments: should he go by the evidence of his own eyes, or should he conform to the obviously wrong judgments of the group? In these conditions, somewhere between one third and one half of all boys conformed to the imaginary group judgments. The proportion of conformers was highest among those around age twelve or thirteen, and somewhat lower at older and younger ages.

Whether this finding really represents a high degree of conformity, though,

It is probably no coincidence that all these girls have similar sunglasses and even wear them in similar ways. Adolescent peer groups do encourage conformity, although they also allow for a certain amount of diversity and role distinctions among their members. (Paul Conklin)

depends on how we interpret it. Fifty percent conformity may sound like a lot, but in fairness to the adolescents, note that many adults conform in situations like this one. The same study found that about one third of college-age students, around twenty years old, conformed in the same situation. To this extent, the young adolescents were not unique. Furthermore, note that the "peer groups" in this experiment were actually total strangers to the children who served as subjects. This could encourage more conformity than would be found among friends, because the subjects may have been trying to be courteous and not to ruin the experiment.

Real peer groups, be they cliques or crowds, have a history of relationships that evolve over time, and the overall vitality of the group depends to some extent on its tolerance of differences in these relationships. For example, one person in a clique may slowly become its social center, because she has good social skills and a great sense of humor. An articulate person may become the group's spokesperson to other cliques, and in this sense become its most visible member. Still another teenager may become the group's "keeper of transportation," by virtue of owning a car or having ready access to his parents' wheels. The group derives vigor from such differences, and cannot afford to demand complete conformity if it wishes to survive. At the same time, group survival is endangered by total diversity among its members; if friends feel completely free to go their own way, they may end up spending little time together, and may not develop many common interests or much loyalty to one another. To avoid disintegrating, therefore, the group does need some discipline and conformity, though only in moderation.

Role variety moderates conformity

As we have seen, peer groups contribute in important ways to adolescents' overall social development and particularly to their achievement of identity. Groups are a central source of information for the adolescent about herself and others. Through both observation and direct interaction with peers, a teenager acquires essential social and leadership skills and an increased ability to evaluate herself and others accurately.

Most important, adolescent groups provide a support base outside of the family, from which the teenager can more freely try on and experiment with the different identity roles that will ultimately contribute to her adult personality: good girl, bad girl, jock, greaser, punk, grind, clown, hippie, druggie, lover, and so forth. Groups

---

A Talk with Don

Social Relationships Among Adolescents

Don took time out between homework and football practice to be interviewed. He is athletically built and of average height.

INTERVIEWER: In general, what do kids your age look for in friends?

DON: Right now, a friend to me can be anybody. I don't care if they have a drinking problem. That's up to them, although I wouldn't like a person to drink too much. I have a lot of friends who are college freshmen already, I have friends who are my own age, and I have friends who are sophomores and juniors in high school.

INTERVIEWER: Are there differences in the friendships with guys and girls?

DON: Yes. Guys tend to be more open about everything. They'll tell you what happened on a date. And if they feel they can trust you and believe in you, they'll tell you what this person's like. Whereas with a girl, you can do almost the same thing, but you have to tend to watch your language. You have to deal more with how they think and how they feel and you're not supposed to be cussing around a girl as much. With a girl you tend to try to find out exactly what she wants to know

instead of just telling her the entire story.

INTERVIEWER: You have to be more careful.

DON: Yes, you have to be a lot more careful.

INTERVIEWER: Do you think that this is true for all girls?

DON: Um, yeah. There's an old saying, "You can't live with them, and you can't live without them." And there's also another one: "You really never truly know what a girl's thinking about." I'm not a girl, so I wouldn't know. Why should I tell her everything about what's happened? So, you tend to go on and say, yeah, well that's nice, yeah, yeah. So, what are you exactly getting at? You keep it kind of very focused to find out exactly what she wants to know. And if that's it, then tell her that and then go on to something else.

INTERVIEWER: And with guys, it's easier to know what they want to know.

DON: Yeah, with a guy you just tend to say, "Oh, wow, that's great," and you start from page one. With a girl you might go to the explanation on the back of the book or the middle.

INTERVIEWER: What do you think girls expect of friendship?

DON: I think girls expect a chance to grow and a chance to have a good relationship develop slowly. And I feel that they like to meet people they can confide in, and possibly to be able to tell someone how they feel and not have that person go, "Really," and laugh in their face. They tend to move a lot slower than a guy and to really, really believe they have to trust in that person before they really open up. And that's one thing I've seen in people that I've dated. Girls that are in my group of friends tend not to take that many chances and basically are . . . more serious.

INTERVIEWER: How does that work?

DON: Like you could be playing tennis with a girl and say, "Yeah, but now you have glasses and look at you . . . you look like Martina Navratilova." And she might take that as a serious offense and say, "Well!" and leave you saying, "What? . . . what did I say? Nothing!" They tend to keep a lot of their emotions inside of them, and let them out slowly over a long period of time.

INTERVIEWER: What are relationships like with parents for kids your age?

can also exert powerful pressures to conform. Especially when the family fails to serve as a constructive corrective, such pressures may contribute to a prolonged period of identity diffusion or to premature identity foreclosure — for example, as a gang member, drug addict, or teenage parent.

In the following section we briefly explore how school — a situation where groups are very much in evidence — influences adolescent identity development.

DON: I think they give you a lot more freedom when you're a freshman or sophomore and come down on you when you're a junior or senior. They tell you that once you get your license, you can drive me around and you can do this or that once you start dating; they won't be as strict. But it tends to be somewhat the opposite. Like I didn't get my license until I was almost eighteen years old.

INTERVIEWER: How come?

DON: My father, who I am living with right now, my only parent, kind of uses a two-way street. He tends to say, "Don't bring up the past when you're trying to prove your point," but when he's trying to prove his point, he always brings up the past. He'll say something like, "You're almost grown, but while you're living under my roof, you'll play by my rules." So you're in a no-win situation. It's plain and simple.

INTERVIEWER: How did this affect your getting a license?

DON: My father would not let me go for my license test until he thought that I drove at a level that he was proud of. He said, "I don't want you to be like all those other kids who can barely drive." I wouldn't say I'm a pro or specialist, but I was at a higher level and my skills were more refined when I got my license. That's how my father wanted it to be, and I'm happy now because of it. And I say, "Hey, well, he was right." I can drive better. I can drive on the highway and in the city, and take control of certain situations when another person might freeze.

INTERVIEWER: What other hassles do older teenagers have with their parents?

DON: Being a senior now I find that I never really know what my parent is going to say. I mean, I'll come in and he'll say, "Ah, it's one-thirty" and you start to say, "The movie didn't get out until this time, we had a flat tire, we ran out of gas . . ." and he goes, "It's okay, just be in a little bit earlier next time." And you go upstairs and you sit there and go, "Huh?" And then another time, you come in and he says, "It's two-thirty, where have you been," and you're saying, "We were just all over Freddie's house, we rented a couple of movies and we watched them on the VCR, and after that we sat and talked about our teachers. Nothing really big; it was a boring night." And he says, "It's two-thirty, you should have been in here a long time ago," and this time he really gets on me. So you say, "I really don't understand this." And it gets a lot trickier, too. They start saying things like, "You're going to be in college next year. You should work on this because when you go to college, your roommate won't want you to have a messy room."

INTERVIEWER: Are your parents worried about your leaving?

DON: Maybe not worried too much, but worried to a point of thinking, "Have I taught him the right way, or have I taught him enough to make his own way?"

Follow-up Questions

1. Which parenting style best characterizes the relationship between Don and his father?

2. What indications do you see of a generation gap between Don and his father?

3. How typical for his age group are Don's thinking and experiences regarding male-female relationships?

4. Which of Josselson's four subphases of individuation are reflected in Don's description of his social relationships?

The Influence of School

School plays a central role in the development of adolescents in the United States, who spend most of their days in school, in extracurricular activities, and doing homework. In addition to laws that require them to attend school until they are sixteen, social expectations, parental pressures, and vocational requirements help to keep most adolescents in high school through graduation and, increasingly, in post–high school education of some kind.

Positive contributions to socialization

Schools influence identity development both through the academic demands of formal curricula and through exposure to teachers who emphasize not only academic achievement, motivation to learn, skill mastery, and self-improvement, but also attitudes toward responsibility, leadership, and authority. For example, one study of junior high school boys found that strong patterns of identification with their fathers, teachers, school values, and peer groups appeared to be related to academic achievement. High achievers perceived the school as helping them to develop their talents while average and low achievers saw the school as preparing them for a vocation (Ringness, 1967).

School peer groups also contribute to socialization, by rewarding such attributes as athletic ability, courage, leadership, popularity, and physical attractiveness. Conflicts between the demands of peer groups and those of the curriculum are frequently related to underachievement (Braham, 1965).

An adolescent is most likely to do well in school if he feels that he can meet his teachers' expectations, that his studies are relevant to his long-range objectives, and that required skills fit in with his lifestyle, his emerging sense of identity, and his feelings of self-esteem. Congruence between school values and values of peers, family, and community help to foster social and academic success at school (Muuss, 1975).

The dropout population

Nationally, junior and senior high schools have failed to achieve such a scenario. School attendance drops significantly for teenagers who are sixteen and older. The number of ungraduated sixteen- and seventeen-year-olds in school is about 80 percent for males and females (Conger, 1977). Dropout rates for poor, black or Hispanic teenagers are significantly higher (Young, 1973).

In a study of why capable students drop out of high school, it was found that lower-class adolescents are more likely to do so because they do not conform as readily to the school's expectations and teachers' demands and are less likely to be academically successful; they are also less successful in meeting the demands of peer groups regarding clothing, participation in extracurricular activities, and the like. They receive little encouragement and support from their families, and they drop out of school as a means of avoiding frustration and deprivation from lack of conformity to the school's and peer group's definition of success (Elliot et al., 1966).

Negative contributions to socialization

School dropouts exhibit lower self-esteem and greater alienation than do students who complete high school. Dropping out is correlated with various forms of deviant behavior, including delinquency, drug and alcohol addiction, and teenage pregnancy, all of which are more often than not related to unsuccessful identity resolutions. School failure among adolescents is related to family problems, poverty, and minority status, and failure to complete high school further compounds such problems (Fitzsimmons et al., 1969).

Checkpoint   *The process by which teenagers separate from their families is often stressful, as are the crises that many parents face during this period. During adolescence, friendships become increasingly stable, intimate, and mutual. They are a major source of social acceptance and a base for achieving greater independence from parents. One researcher found that teenage peer groups typically consist of small, cohesive cliques and larger, less cohesive crowds. Encouragement by parents and other adults, as well as popularity, social acceptance, and pressures to conform, play an important role in peer group participation.*

Sexuality During Adolescence

Not surprisingly, developmental changes in sexuality during adolescence are closely tied to the achievement of physical maturity during puberty. The popular idea that adolescence is a very sexual period of life is in fact correct, but people tend to focus on sexual intercourse and the risks of pregnancy rather than consider the broader pattern of interrelated changes that are involved.

During adolescence, the expression of sexual urges interacts closely with two other needs: the need for security, or freedom from anxiety, and the need for intimacy, or close, collaborative relationships with others. Teenagers are intensely and passionately engaged in establishing intimate relationships that are independent of their families, developing social skills, experimenting with new social roles, and establishing a unique personal identity. Sexual maturity is a central aspect of acting and feeling like a mature adult person, and of being recognized as one (Sullivan, 1953; Erikson, 1982).

Over the course of adolescence, teenagers move from the indirect, relatively nonthreatening sexuality of childhood to the more intense, complex, and socially "loaded" sexual feelings and activities of adulthood. Both teenagers and their parents devote a considerable amount of time and emotional energy to these issues, which we examine in this section.

Dating   In the United States, dating is the major way in which adolescents begin their sexual activity. Dating serves a wide variety of purposes for teenagers. It can be a form of recreation involving both entertainment and sexual stimulation; it can be a way to gain status by increasing a teenager's reputation and popularity; it can be a means of asserting independence and separating from one's family. Teen-

Reasons for dating vary widely, from intrinsic interest in a particular member of the opposite sex to a desire to "be seen" and thus gain status or simply to have a good time. (Sybil Shelton/Peter Arnold)

agers also date to learn social skills and thus increase their interpersonal competence, and to experiment with sexual activity. Courtship, or searching for a husband or wife, is another reason to date (Damon and Hart, 1982).

Levels of involvement in dating

Studies reveal that most teenagers hesitantly begin sexual activity in mid-adolescence, around fourteen or fifteen, with casual experimentation in the protective context of the peer group (Miller and Simon, 1980). Delora (1963) has developed a model to describe a five-level pattern of dating among adolescents: casual, steadily, going steady, engaged to be engaged, and engaged. The goal of casual dating is to get acquainted. It tends to be impersonal, uninvolved, and rational, and is more frequently initiated by the male than the female. Teenagers date steadily for entertainment and enjoyment. It is individualistic and free, with no strings attached, and still most frequently initiated and directed by the male.

For couples who are going steady, companionship is an important goal. The relationship is more personal, intimate, and emotional, and it is generally monogamous. Going steady is jointly initiated and directed by both partners. Engaged to be engaged is more or less a trial engagement; it adds a future orientation to "going steady" dating. Engagement, the last type of dating, is preparation for marriage. Rational plans are made, and both members of the couple assume specific responsibilities for the relationship.

Masturbation Masturbation has become more acceptable in recent years. Approximately 75 percent of teenage boys and 50 percent of teenage girls report masturbating at least once a week or more (Hass, 1979). Although exact percentages vary depending on the particular survey, the number has increased over the past several decades (Dreyer, 1982). Feelings of discomfort and guilt because of cultural and religious beliefs about masturbation have decreased in recent years, but many teenagers still find the subject embarrassing. When boys and girls from ages thirteen to nineteen who had masturbated in the past month were asked how often they felt guilty, anxious, or concerned about it, 49 percent replied "sometimes" or "often." In contrast, only one third of those who had experienced premarital intercourse admitted to these same feelings (Sorensen, 1973).

Sexual Fantasies Sexual fantasies about real or imaginary situations often accompany masturbation, although adolescents of all ages report having sexual fantasies throughout their waking hours. Both sexes report that they most commonly imagine or fantasize about "petting or having intercourse with someone [they] are fond of or in love with." In one study, well over 80 percent of all college students reported this sort of theme (Komarovsky, 1976; Miller and Simon, 1980). For their second most common fantasy, however, males reported imagining anonymous sex ("petting or having intercourse with someone you don't know"), whereas women reported imagining intimate but not explicitly sexual activity ("doing nonsexual things with someone you are fond of or in love with.")

Heterosexuality

Most adolescents follow a fairly predictable pattern in the development of heterosexual activity. As shown in Table 16-1, sexual contact typically begins with holding hands and proceeds through progressively more intimate steps, ending eventually in intercourse (Vener and Stewart, 1974). Holding hands is followed by holding or being held, and then by kissing; then come necking (prolonged hugging and kissing), light petting (above the waist), heavy petting (below the waist), "going all the way" (coitus), and lastly, coitus with additional partners.

Progression of sexual experiences

Not every teenager engages in all of the activities listed in the table, of course, but those at the more advanced levels are more likely to have spent time acquiring experience at the lower levels than the other way around. At every age boys have, or at least report, more sexual experience than girls do, and not surprisingly, older adolescents report more experience than younger ones do. By the end of high school, depending on the particular research study, about 20 to 35 percent of young people have experienced full intercourse at least once. Over the past three decades, the frequency of premarital intercourse has increased somewhat for adolescent males and very substantially for adolescent females. For example, in the late 1950s only 20 to 30 percent of college-age females reported premarital intercourse, compared with 60 percent of college males; by the early 1970s however, roughly 61 percent of college females reported premarital intercourse, compared with 83 percent of college males (Elkind and Weiner, 1978).

Although sexual activity may now be fairly similar for boys and girls, differences in attitudes and expectations continue to exist. On the whole, girls still tend to be more conservative than boys in their sexual attitudes, values, and actions. Boys

Male-female differences

Level of Sexual Activity	Percentage of High School Youngsters Who Have Participated at Least Once									
	Age 13 and Younger		Age 14		Age 15		Age 16		Age 17 and Older	
	Boys	Girls	Boys	Girls	Boys	Girls	Boys	Girls	Boys	Girls
Held hands	80	84	87	87	93	89	90	91	92	97
Held arm around or been held	67	72	78	81	87	87	87	90	90	96
Kissed or been kissed	65	68	78	75	84	82	85	89	87	96
Necked (prolonged hugging and kissing)	48	43	56	56	70	65	69	77	78	84
Light petting (feeling above the waist)	40	31	55	40	66	55	65	65	71	71
Heavy petting (feeling below the waist)	34	17	42	28	56	40	55	49	62	59
Going all the way (coitus)	28	10	32	17	38	24	38	31	34	35
Coitus with two or more partners	17	4	15	5	21	10	23	13	23	14

Source: Vener and Stewart, 1974, p. 732.

Table 16-1 *Levels of Adolescent Heterosexual Activity*

tend to be more sexually active in all areas and to have many more sexual encounters. Girls are more likely to emphasize intimacy and love as a necessary part of sexual activity than boys and are less likely to experience sex merely as a physically pleasurable activity.

Consistent with these differences, girls are more likely to be serial monogamists, having only one relationship involving sexual intercourse at a time; boys are more likely to be sexual adventurers, feeling less of a commitment and romantic involvement with only one sexual partner (Sorensen, 1973). It is likely that concerns about pregnancy reinforce other feelings and attitudes that girls have regarding sexual behavior. Boys' behavior is consistent with the "macho" male image that is a strong force in advertising and other media and a strong aspect of identity achievement among adolescent males.

Intimate, loving, and at times sexual feelings for friends of the same sex are experienced by most adolescents, and they play a central role in social development (Sullivan, 1954). Homosexuality, in contrast, is a specifically sexual orientation involving erotic feelings and behavior toward people of the same sex. Some individuals are neither exclusively homosexual nor exclusively heterosexual.

Homosexuality

Largely due to the political and educational efforts of the women's liberation and gay rights movements, public acceptance of homosexuality has increased significantly during the past several decades. This acceptance acknowledges the right of individuals to freely choose their own sexual orientations and lifestyles and to be protected from discrimination. Approximately two thirds of adolescents interviewed approve in principle of homosexual contacts, whether between boys or between girls (Hass, 1979). In this context, a "contact" is defined as petting: touching and fondling the genitals and kissing in its various forms.

Sometime during adolescence, teenagers begin to experiment with sexual activities. But teenagers may worry so much about when, how, and with whom to be sexual that they do not really get much pleasure from early sexual attempts. (Werner H. Muller/Peter Arnold)

There is, however, no indication that homosexual activity has also increased. Very few boys (just 25 percent) and even fewer girls (10 percent) report ever participating in an ongoing homosexual relationship; these rates are about the same as or lower than they were thirty or forty years ago (Chilman, 1979).

Although early homosexual play and adolescent experiences with homosexual partners typically precede "coming out" — publicly acknowledging one's homosexuality — as yet there is little agreement about what specific pattern of factors leads to the development of a homosexual rather than heterosexual sex-role identity. In fact, the American Psychiatric Association no longer officially considers homosexuality a mental disorder, although it does consider it a disturbance in sexual orientation if the individual involved experiences undue conflict and psychological distress because of it.

Achieving a secure sexual identity is a challenging task for most adolescents. It is considerably more difficult for many gay adolescents, who may be rejected by their parents, peer groups, and schools, churches, and other community institutions — the very groups that adolescents depend on for support during this period of development. A seventeen-year-old girl reports:

> When I told my folks that I was a lesbian, they totally freaked out. It was so against their religion, their life style and friends, that they just couldn't deal with it. I'm not living at home anymore and I hardly ever talk with them. (Bell, 1980, p. 115)

Sex and Everyday Life

Although sex plays an important role in adolescents' feelings, fantasies, and social relationships, it does not necessarily dominate their lives. Even a single sexual experience involving intercourse is the rare exception for most junior high school students, and although sexual activity increases during high school, most adolescents have intercourse on a rather sporadic, unpredictable basis, if at all. Masturbation and various forms of petting appear to be the mainstay of adolescent sexual activity.

Does this fact bother teenagers? To some degree it depends on their age. Among college students, for example, a majority of both sexes say that they are content with their comparative lack of sexual experience (Offer and Offer, 1975b). Younger adolescents, however, may feel more strongly. For some, sexual experience confers status with their friends, but it may also lose them the respect of their parents and others. Sexual experience can also "prove" that a teenager is attractive, but it can label the same teenager as "fast."

Whatever their feelings, all adolescents must somehow navigate among the various emotions, meanings, and expectations that their parents, their peers, the media, and they themselves attach to sexuality. As we note at the beginning of this section, changes in sexuality during adolescence are tied not only to the achievement of physical maturity and the development of new social skills and social roles; they are aspects of the most important development: the emergence of a person's identity as a man or woman. Sometimes that identity is complicated by sexual issues; it can also be affected by social problems specific to teenagers, as we see in the next section.

Checkpoint *Developmental changes in sexual activities and attitudes are closely tied to needs for security, intimacy, and independence during adolescence. For both girls and boys, these activities include masturbation, sexual fantasies, dating, petting, and, less often, sexual intercourse. Closeness with friends of the same sex and concerns about homosexuality are common.*

Special Problems of Adolescence

In Chapter 14 we discussed the special physical and health risks faced by adolescents as a group. Their lack of experience, their egocentrism, and their need to experiment with new and sometimes risky social roles in order to establish a unique identity also place them at high risk for developing certain psychosocial problems. In the following section we discuss four such special problems of adolescence: pregnancy and parenthood, physical and sexual abuse, depression and suicide, and juvenile delinquency.

Pregnancy and Parenthood

Childbirth among adolescents continues to be a major problem, despite widespread and longstanding concern. Approximately 3 percent of all girls between fifteen and nineteen become pregnant, which means that there are approximately 780,000 pregnancies in this age group. More than 75 percent of these are carried to term, but only about 30 percent are planned. In 1960, over 80 percent of adolescent mothers gave up their babies for adoption, but by 1980 only about 10 percent of them did so. During this same period, the number of marriages among teenagers declined (National Center for Health Statistics, 1980).

The great majority of teenage pregnancies are the result of inadequate contraception or none at all. A recent review of the research on adolescent contraceptive behavior found that many teenagers are startlingly uninformed about the basics of reproduction, and believe that they are "immune" to pregnancy, or at least at very low risk. While birth control pills are popular, they are not reliable during the first month of use. Only foam and condoms or a diaphragm and contraceptive jelly are really effective for first intercourse, and adolescents do not like to use these contraceptives because they imply a readiness for or premeditation of sex, they are expensive or unavailable when needed, they are messy, and they reduce pleasure.

Inadequate use of contraception

Although teenagers do use contraceptives more as they get older and have intercourse more frequently (Morrison, 1985), only half of adolescents who are sexually active report that they used any form of contraception when they had their first sexual intercourse, and only one fifth of experienced high school students use contraception consistently (Hornick et al., 1979; Chilman, 1982). Often boys do not use contraception because boys assume that their girlfriends are on the pill. In one study, 60 percent of boys who reported having had intercourse during the past month took no precautions themselves (Sorensen, 1973).

Changing attitudes toward pregnancy have also contributed to the increase in teenage pregnancies. Over the past twenty years or so, adolescent girls have grown more permissive about becoming pregnant. A growing percentage choose to keep their baby, and they seem to feel an increasing sense of responsibility for pregnancy: a study of pregnant girls revealed that in 1979, 81 percent felt responsible for their pregnancies, while only 26 percent felt responsible in 1963. Girls are also less worried than they used to be about how their pregnancies will affect their friendships and marriage plans (Patten, 1981).

Attitudes toward pregnancy

One of the most helpful ways of understanding teenage pregnancy is in terms of its role in resolving the psychosocial crisis of identity during adolescence. Many teenage mothers may see having a baby as a way of prematurely crystallizing their identity, in that motherhood and marriage promise to establish them in a secure adult role and to help them escape role confusion. Some boys and girls tend to believe that teenage parenthood and marriage also promise an intense, intimate, and lasting relationship with another human being, a relationship that they may have been deprived of and that figures heavily in a teenager's search for identity.

As we shall soon see, it is generally the exception rather than the rule that such fantasies are actually realized. The consequences of teenage parenthood and the identity foreclosure that it frequently entails are generally negative, not only for the

Consequences of teenage parenthood

A teenage mother's fantasies about motherhood are often dashed once her baby is born and she realizes how much time and energy mothering requires. In addition, teenage parents face a multitude of problems created by the social, economic, and emotional burdens of early parenthood.

teenage mother and father and their infant, but for their parents, friends, teachers, and health-care providers as well. For one thing, teenage mothers are more likely than older women to experience complications such as anemia and toxemia during pregnancy, as well as a prolonged labor. Their babies are more likely to be premature, to have low birth weight, and to have neurological defects. Their infants are also more likely to die during the first year than infants born to adult parents.

One study found that teenage mothers were five times as likely to drop out of school as girls who had no children; and while two thirds of these mothers married within five years of their baby's birth, three out of five of the marriages broke up within six years, a rate that was twice as high as that for their classmates. In addition, only 43 percent were holding jobs after five years, compared with 63 percent of their classmates (Furstenberg, 1976).

Many of the problems of teenage parents appear to be closely tied to the social, economic, and emotional burdens of premature parenthood, as well as single parenthood, which is most often the outcome. We should keep in mind that even for the majority of adult single mothers, surviving economically and emotionally while singlehandedly raising a young child is a very difficult struggle. Thus, although many adolescent mothers are strongly committed to their children, they tend to be limited by their circumstances. Teenage fathers often have positive attitudes toward their children, but generally they lack the material and emotional resources needed to carry out the considerable responsibilities of parenthood.

Abuse of Adolescents

Although public attention has recently focused on abuse of young children, violent encounters between adults and adolescents are quite common. Reliable figures are difficult to obtain, but national surveys of family violence indicate that approximately 66 percent of children aged ten to fourteen and 34 percent of those aged fifteen to seventeen have been hit by their parents. They also indicate that 12 percent of adolescent girls have been beaten and 9 percent raped (Libbey and Bybee, 1979).

Extent of abuse

Abuse tends to be highest for children between three and four and for fifteen- to seventeen-year-olds. However, it is more likely to go unnoticed in the case of adolescents, because their injuries tend to be less severe than those of younger children. This is particularly the case in communities where physical punishment such as hitting, slapping, and whipping with a belt is thought to be acceptable and in the twenty states where child abuse laws specify that only "serious injuries" must be reported (Libbey and Bybee, 1979). When a teenager has broken a rule or law and is perceived by others as intentionally contributing to the situation and therefore deserving of punishment, some people find it difficult to distinguish between discipline and abuse. And of course a teenager sometimes treats his parent in a physically abusive way.

Three sets of explanations have been offered for abuse of adolescents. (See Chapter 10 for a discussion of the causes, treatment, and prevention of child abuse.) The first suggests that the developmental tasks of adolescence, and particularly conflicts regarding separation and control, interact with the normal stresses of middle age and with socioeconomic difficulties to create a situation in which a parent "goes too far." The second proposes that parents who are immature, isolated, and irrational in their behavior respond abusively to their adolescent children who display these same characteristics. The third emphasizes the importance of poverty, job loss, and social isolation as stressful conditions which increase the likelihood of abusive behavior (Libbey and Bybee, 1979). No one explanation appears to be sufficient to explain abuse, and all three probably highlight factors that contribute in varying degrees to the likelihood of abuse.

Explanations for abuse

Since a parent or stepparent is generally responsible for abuse, teenagers often find it hard to know whom to turn to for help. Particularly in the case of sexual abuse, the nonabusing parent may find the reality so difficult to accept that she denies that it has happened, leaving her child with a sense of betrayal and abandonment.

Sexual abuse

Estimates of the incidence of sexual abuse vary depending upon who was surveyed, how the survey was conducted, and how abuse is defined. In one retrospective study of college students, 19.2 percent of the women and 8.6 percent of the men reported some type of sexual exploitation or abuse before age seventeen (Finkelhor, 1979). Because the victim's fears of further harm, of not being believed, and of the stigma that will result are often warranted, there is widespread underreporting of sexual abuse of children and adolescents (Kempe and Kempe, 1984).

Sexual abuse is more likely to occur under circumstances which encourage adults to have sexual feelings toward children, which reduce or overcome both internal and external factors that inhibit abuse, and which lower a child's resistance to the abusive actions (Finkelhor, 1984). For example, a lack of physical and personal privacy in a family and the encouragement of nudity and physical contact that is not clearly affectionate rather than sexual may contribute to sexual abuse. Portrayal in the media of adolescents and younger children in adult situations and roles and in sexual relationships with adults may also be a contributing factor in that it suggests that such roles and behaviors are acceptable.

Ways to decrease sexual abuse

How can sexual abuse of adolescents and children be prevented? Increasing public awareness of how frequently abuse actually occurs, of both the direct and more subtle forms that it often takes, and of the family situations and patterns of interacting that increase the risk of abuse could help to reduce its incidence. Greater awareness on the part of teachers, clergy, doctors, and other professionals of their legal responsibility to report abuse, stricter sanctions for failure to report abuse, and greater protection and support for the victims are also needed. Teenagers who report abuse must be taken seriously and not dismissed, even in the face of denial and countercharges that they are lying or that they are responsible for what happened. Of additional help would be more shelters, halfway houses, and foster homes to provide abused teenagers with a temporary or even permanent place to stay and more programs to help their families resolve the destructive patterns that have allowed the abuse to occur.

Recently, a model has been proposed to help conceptualize and evaluate the degree of trauma that results from sexual abuse. It involves four trauma-causing, or *traumagenic*, dynamics: traumagenic sexualization, betrayal, powerlessness, and stigmatization (Finkelhor and Browne, 1985). *Traumagenic sexualization* refers to the destructive ways in which a child's sexual feelings and attitudes are shaped in a developmentally inappropriate and interpersonally destructive way as a result of abuse. *Betrayal* refers to the process by which children discover that someone upon whom they were vitally dependent has caused them harm. *Powerlessness* refers to the process in which the child is bullied in a way that undermines his ability to protect himself and assert his needs. Lastly, *stigmatization* refers to the negative connotations — including badness, shame, and guilt — that are communicated to the child and become part of his self-image and sexual identity.

This model can help to guide treatment of the adolescent victims of abuse, their families, and the abuser (who is more often than not a family member). In addition, steps should be taken to prevent a recurrence, which generally means that contact between the abuser and victim (and perhaps potential victims) must be eliminated or controlled in a way that reasonably assures all concerned parties that abuse will not happen again.

Schools can take an active role in identifying and reporting abusive situations, and in helping adolescents to take active roles in learning to avoid potentially abusive situations, and in seeking help from peers and professionals. The victim must overcome both the shame, guilt, and stigma involved in admitting to others that he has been abused and the fear that he will not be believed. Ultimately, community-wide changes in how people think and feel about physical and sexual violence, particularly with regard to children and adolescents, must be achieved through new laws, through education, and through economic policies that place a high value on protecting and fostering the growth and development of children and their families.

Juvenile Delinquency

Juvenile delinquency refers both to antisocial and law-breaking activities that are reported to authorities and to antisocial behavior that does not get reported. Minority and lower-class teenagers are much more likely to be labeled as delinquents than suburban, middle-class youngsters, who often commit the very same acts but do not get caught or are not reported (Empey, 1975). A large-scale interview study of almost 1,400 male and female teenagers found that 80 percent or more had committed delinquent acts, including drinking, theft, truancy, destruction of property, assault, gang fighting, carrying a concealed weapon, and using false identification (Haney and Gold, 1973; Williams and Gold, 1972).

As discussed earlier, experimentation with socially deviant roles and countercultural values and activities is a normal part of adolescent development in our society. In many ways delinquency is a distortion and exaggeration of that experimentation. The particular limitations of the teenager, his family, and his general life circumstances interact with the particular moratorium opportunities that are culturally available to prematurely solidify and make permanent roles and activities that might under other conditions be passing experiments.

Reviews of the research on delinquency reveal that family situation, friendships, and personality are associated with a teenager's delinquency. More specific factors associated with delinquency include a broken home; a poor parent-child relationship characterized by hostility, lack of affection, and underinvolvement; overly harsh and authoritarian methods of discipline; a high degree of family conflict and disorganization; and the presence of a parent with a personality disturbance and a delinquent history of her own (Sarafino and Armstrong, 1986).

Factors associated with delinquency

The majority of delinquents belong to gangs, which are similar to crowds in that they include cliques, but differ in that they are more highly structured and focus most of their energies on antisocial activities (Sarafino and Armstrong, 1986). Gangs provide the kind of acceptance and social support that members do not get from their families or at school. Delinquents have consistently been found to be more impulsive, more resentful of authority, less self-confident, lower in self-esteem, less happy, and less popular than nondelinquents (Sarafino and Armstrong, 1986). The gang peer group protects each member from his failures and from the maturity demands from parents, teachers, and more mainstream teenagers that he is unwilling or unable to fulfill. Long-term participation in the antisocial activities and roles that are typical of gangs creates a risk of identity foreclosure and the establishment of a negative identity pattern — that lacks positive identifications with many of the important values and goals of society that contribute to adult happiness.

The problem of juvenile delinquency is difficult to solve because its underlying source may be a basic disturbance in the relationship of society to its adolescent members. As Erikson has pointed out, successful resolution of the identity crisis of

Society and delinquency

adolescence requires adequate opportunities and support for the sometimes deviant and antisocial role experimentations of that period. It also requires not only that society promise teenagers the possibility of productive lives but also that it keep that promise by providing educational, vocational, and career opportunities and support.

Nevertheless, adolescents who are in danger of being confirmed in their delinquent roles can be helped by programs that work to prevent such identity foreclosure by making available the necessary support and opportunities that will allow successful experimentation with other roles and identities. Community houses, YMCAs, police athletic leagues, summer camps, crisis drop-in centers and telephone hotlines, as well as out-patient and residential treatment programs that help more disturbed teenagers and their families, can contribute to helping teenagers already in trouble.

Teenage Suicide

As we note in Chapter 14, suicide is the third leading cause of death among adolescents. Teenage suicide rates have continued to increase over the past twenty years. In 1960, there were 8.2 male and 2.2 female suicides per 100,000 individuals between the ages of fifteen and twenty-four in the United States. By 1980, the rate had climbed to 20.2 male suicides and 4.3 female suicides per 100,000, representing a 146 percent increase for males and a 95 percent increase for females (Klagsbrun, 1981). While most suicide attempts are made by girls, boys succeed three times as often, in part because they use more effective methods, such as knives, guns, or other lethal weapons.

Background for suicide   Studies of the backgrounds of teenagers who attempt suicide suggest that they often experience serious family difficulties, personal turmoil, and intense loneliness and isolation, and that suicide attempts are almost always cries for help (Shaffer, 1974).

Quite frequently symptoms of depression precede a suicide attempt. These symptoms may include feelings of despair, worthlessness, and hopelessness, loss of interest and motivation in usual activities, decreased ability to concentrate and to think clearly, suicidal thoughts, and loss of appetite, weight loss, and difficulty in sleeping. Approximately 10 percent of teenagers admitted to psychiatric hospitals and clinics receive a primary diagnosis of depression, although it is likely that some symptoms of depression are present in many other cases (Albert and Beck, 1975; Murray, 1973).

Being taken seriously by others, particularly when feeling upset or depressed, is a central issue in adolescents' search for recognition and identity. And yet a teenager's concerns and upsets can be too easily overlooked or dismissed by parents whose own guilt or unhappiness makes it difficult to acknowledge their children's feelings. According to Beth, who is sixteen,

> Problems that teenagers have are real. They aren't phony or unimportant.
> Your first crush, the first time you fall in love, deciding whether to go to college,

Teenage Suicide Prevention

Because teenagers as a group have one of the highest suicide rates, many cities have instituted educational programs, twenty-four-hour suicide hotlines, crisis intervention, and counseling services for teenagers who are threatening suicide. The following information taken from Bell is typical of that provided by suicide prevention programs (Bell, 1980, p. 141).

Warning Signs
1. A big change in eating or sleeping habits.
2. Suddenly not caring for prized possessions — giving away favorite records, a pet, clothing.
3. A loss of interest in friends.
4. A long and deep depression over a breakup or the death of a beloved person.
5. A great change in school grades.
6. Feeling hopeless or full of self-hate.
7. Feeling constantly restless or hyperactive.
8. Actually making a suicide attempt.

Danger Signs
1. They say they intend to hurt themselves.
2. They have a plan for how to do it.
3. They have in their possession pills or a weapon of some kind.
4. There is evidence they have already hurt themselves.
5. The person is dazed or unconscious.

In an Emergency, Contact Any of the Following:
1. Your local police.
2. An adult you trust.
3. An ambulance service in your town.
4. The emergency room of a local hospital.
DO NOT LEAVE THE PERSON ALONE!

Myths and Facts about Suicide
   In the next column are a number of myths about suicide and the facts that correct them:

Myth: People who talk about suicide don't kill themselves.

Fact: Eight out of ten people who commit suicide tell someone that they're thinking about hurting themselves before they actually do it.

Myth: Only certain types of people commit suicide.

Fact: All types of people commit suicide — male and female, young and old, rich and poor, country people and city people. It happens in every racial, ethnic, and religious group.

Myth: Suicide among kids is decreasing.

Fact: The suicide rate for young people has [increased by 137% between 1960 and 1980].

Myth: When a person talks about suicide, change the subject to get his or her mind off it.

Fact: Take them seriously. Listen carefully to what they are saying. Give them a chance to express their feelings. Let them know you are concerned. And help them get help.

Myth: Most people who kill themselves really want to die.

Fact: Most people who kill themselves are confused about whether they want to die. Suicide is often intended as a cry for help. (Bell, 1980, p. 142)

   Although there is no way to guarantee that the signs and danger signals of suicide will be apparent or that the response will successfully prevent suicide from occurring, the above information and suggestions are likely to be helpful.

looking for a job — hey, that's real stuff and parents should take it seriously. I know some parents say, "Oh, that's nothing. At least you don't have to worry about putting food on the table." But when you're going through a problem, I don't care who you are, it's real to you. It hurts you, and if parents make us feel like our problems aren't worth anything, then we grow up thinking our feelings don't matter. It's like *you* don't matter. (Bell, 1980, p. 134)

Most teenagers who are not depressed experience moments of unhappiness, and most who are depressed do not attempt suicide. Nonetheless, signs of unhappiness and depression should not be dismissed, particularly if they persist. And since a large percentage of those who attempt suicide have threatened or attempted it before, such threats should be taken very seriously.

Checkpoint *Pregnancy and parenthood pose major social, economic, and psychological problems for both adolescents and their parents. Other special problems faced by adolescents include high rates of physical and sexual abuse, depression, and suicide. Juvenile delinquency, which continues to be a significant problem, appears to have more negative consequences for minority and lower-class teenagers than for those from middle-class families.*

The Emerging Adult

We have now come to the end of our discussion of adolescence. We have seen how relationships with parents, friendships, and activities with groups of peers contribute to the development of identity during this stage. We have also discussed the important contribution of sexuality and sexual experiences to identity formation and explored several of the special problems that can interfere with identity achievement.

Just as the growth spurt and physical changes of puberty and the development of formal cognitive thinking at the beginning of adolescence were a culmination of the long series of maturational and cognitive changes that began with conception and birth, the achievement of identity culminates the psychosocial developments that preceded it.

Although adolescence marks both the end of childhood and the last developmental stage covered in this book, it by no means marks the end of development. As we noted at the beginning of this section, adolescence is a period of transition to adulthood, and many other important developmental changes are yet to come.

The social changes of adolescence make a good place to end this book, because they show vividly one of its major themes: that individuals change dramatically as

By the end of adolescence, most young people have achieved a fairly coherent sense of who they are and are ready to face the challenges of early adulthood. (Jean-Claude Lejeune)

they grow up. As we have seen, in a matter of months, an infant who smiles at everyone becomes devoted to particular adults and siblings; and in just a few years more, persons well outside the family compete seriously with these attachments. The other domains of development show equally dramatic changes. In just a few years, a child grows physically from diapers to climbing trees and riding a bicycle; in just a few years more, he or she starts looking (almost) like an adult. Cognitive changes are equally sweeping: individuals change from infants who think by looking and touching to children who can reason out concrete problems to teenagers who can imagine possibilities they have never personally experienced.

Yet no matter how dramatic they are, developmental changes remain whole, continuous, and human. For convenience, this book has divided human change into topics and discussed the topics one at a time. But real children and youth do not come divided. As this book has tried to show, children and adolescents not only grow, think, and feel; they also do all of these things at once, in a pattern that makes each person truly unique.

Summary of Major Ideas

Individuation and Identity Development

1. A key task of adolescence is successful resolution of the psychosocial crisis of identity versus identity confusion.

2. The process of individuation, or becoming a separate and independent person, appears to follow a fairly predictable pattern: differentiation, practicing, rapprochement, and consolidation of self.

3. Identity formation involves selectively keeping and integrating certain aspects of one's earlier childhood identity while discarding others.

4. Successful resolution of the identity conflicts that are typical of adolescence depends in part on having adequate opportunities to experiment with different identities and roles.

5. Erikson calls the period of experimentation and uncertainty that precedes the achievement of a firm adult identity the psychosocial moratorium.

6. Marcia has identified four identity statuses among older adolescents: identity achievement, identity diffusion, moratorium, and foreclosure.

Social Relationships During Adolescence

7. Struggles over separation and the growing independence of teenagers create the generation gap.

8. The middle-aged parents of adolescents face their own developmental crises, which are caused in part by the conflicting demands they experience.

9. Teenagers appear to feel most positive about democratic and equalitarian parenting styles and more negative about parents who are autocratic.

10. Social-class differences influence the educational and career expectations that parents have for their adolescent children.

11. Adolescents from minority and lower-class families encounter limited developmental opportunities and are more likely than others to develop problematic identity resolutions.

12. In recent years, an increasing number of adolescents have encountered the stresses of growing up in a family that has experienced divorce, remarriage, or single parenthood.

13. During adolescence, friendships become increasingly stable, intimate, and mutual.

14. Male friendships appear to involve lower levels of intimacy than friendships between females.

15. Both small, cohesive cliques, and larger, less intimate crowds appear to be important in peer-group participation.

16. Teenagers participate in peer groups to please parents and teachers, to gain peer acceptance and popularity, and to conform.

17. Many of the social experiences of adolescence take place in school.

18. The quality of both a school's curriculum and its social relationships within and outside the classroom affect students' academic performance, personal development, and likelihood of dropping out.

Sexuality During Adolescence

19. Adolescents' sexual needs are closely tied to their need to establish a secure identity and to achieve both intimacy and independence.

20. Most adolescents follow a fairly predictable pattern in the development of heterosexual activity.

21. In the United States, dating is the major way in which adolescents begin their sexual activity.

22. Acceptance of homosexuality has increased, although its prevalence has remained fairly constant.

Special Problems of Adolescence

23. Pregnancy and parenthood continue to be a major problem faced by a growing number of adolescents.

24. Other problems that are common during adolescence are physical and sexual abuse, juvenile delinquency, depression and suicide.

What Do You Think?

1. To what degree are you aware of having experienced the developmental crisis of identity versus identity confusion proposed by Erikson? Which of Marcia's identity styles best describes you at the present time?

2. In what ways have the parental role conflicts of midlife influenced relationships in your own family?

3. What are your opinions about the positive and negative effects of divorce, remarriage, and single parenthood on a teenager's development?

4. In what ways do your own experiences confirm this chapter's description of the development of friendship and peer groups, and in what ways do they differ?

5. As someone who has experienced adolescent changes in sexuality, what questions would you ask the authors about the information they have presented and the conclusions they have drawn?

6. Why do you think that so little progress has been made in the past twenty-five years in solving the problems of adolescent pregnancy and parenthood, abuse, depression and suicide, and delinquency?

Key Terms

identity *(677)*	identity status *(683)*
individuation *(677)*	generation gap *(685)*
differentiation *(677)*	democratic parenting *(688)*
consolidation of self *(678)*	equalitarian parenting *(688)*
identity versus identity confusion *(679)*	autocratic parenting *(689)*
	mutuality *(694)*
identifications *(679)*	intimacy *(695)*
psychosocial moratorium *(679)*	peer groups *(696)*
	cliques *(696)*
identity diffusion *(682)*	crowds *(697)*
negative identity *(682)*	juvenile delinquency *(713)*

For Further Reading

Adelson, J. (ed.). *Handbook of Adolescent Psychology.* New York: Wiley, 1980.

An excellent collection of original articles that review recent theory and research on various aspects of adolescent development. A high-level reference source.

Freidenberg, E. *Coming of Age in America: Growth and Acquiescence.* New York: Vintage, 1965.

This is a classic, thought-provoking book about the conflicts and confusions in our high schools and in our mass culture, and how they influence and are influenced by the lives of adolescents.

Grinder, R. *Studies in Adolescence: A Book of Readings in Adolescent Development.* New York: Macmillan, 1975.

This collection of readings includes more than forty interesting articles from various books and professional journals. Among the topics covered are the history of the concept of adolescence, schooling, socialization, youth culture, and drugs, deviance, and delinquency. It is an excellent resource.

Potok, C. *The Chosen.* Greenwich, Conn.: Fawcett, 1967.

The Chosen is a best-selling novel set in New York City in the late 1940s. It tells the story of the struggles of two teenagers from very different Jewish immigrant families to develop a friendship and to establish their identities.

Rutter, M. *Changing Growth in a Changing Society: Patterns of Adolescent Development and Disorder.* Cambridge, Mass.: Harvard University Press, 1980.

This book presents clear, well-documented coverage of the problems and disorders of adolescents with an emphasis on the important contributions of social factors.

Bobby's Case

When Bobby was ten, his parents divorced. At first he lived equal amounts of time with his mother and father, but when his mother became seriously involved with another man and the two of them decided to move to a distant city, Bobby moved in permanently with his father. These were not easy adjustments to make; but all things considered, Bobby managed remarkably well. It helped that he was a self-reliant child, with a strong interest in sports. Bobby found that when he played basketball or baseball, he felt really good about himself and didn't think about his parents so much. Bobby began to spend hours each day playing ball with his friends.

It also helped Bobby's adjustment to his parents' divorce that he had a pretty good relationship with his father and that his father's job as a college professor enabled him to work at home a good deal. In the evenings, Bobby often asked his father for help with his homework and then they'd watch a game on television together. Bobby hardly ever spoke about his mother, but sometimes he fantasized that his parents would get back together again.

Camp
Sunnybrook

Dear Mom,

Got your letter and candy and swim fins. Thanks for the stuff. I was telling the guys in my bunk about your chocolate cookies--how about sending some next time?

There's a kid named Kenny in the next bunk. He's a real good ping pong player, but I beat him more than he beats me. His parents are also divorced, but he lives with his mom and visits his dad every other weekend. I still don't see why you needed to move so far away just because things were so bad between you and Dad. It's stupid. I know George works out there, but what's so great about him anyway? If you lived nearby, I could see you a lot more. Oh well, I guess you have your reasons.

Tomorrow we go on a hike to the spillway and then the reservoir. And there's a Baseball World Series--my bunk has a good chance of winning.

The food is awful and the water stinks (even the horses have better water--it's true). So send FOOD and SODA soon. And especially those chocolate cookies.

Bobby

When Bobby was fourteen, it seemed that he was always hungry. He knew he was not supposed to eat junk food and soft drinks so much, but he felt that somehow his teeth and his health would not suffer. Anyway, junk foods saved time when he was alone for meals, although his father tried to have a real sit-down dinner with Bobby at least every two days.

Bobby's grades took a serious slump right after the divorce. But by the time he started high school his grades were better than ever, so his father did not nag him much about studying. His history teacher was impressed with his growing ability to imagine alternative outcomes in social studies — to write essays about "what if history had turned out differently."

Getting housework done without Mom had been hard at first, but after a while Bobby and his father figured out ways of dividing it up. Bobby was in charge of doing the laundry and taking out the trash, his father did the vacuuming, and both shared the shopping.

By the time Bobby was sixteen, he was spending more time than ever before with friends — many of whom his mother had never even met, since she now lived so far away. He had also started dating, but he still felt kind of awkward around girls. He kept thinking that they noticed every little thing that he did wrong and every little blemish on his face.

Most of the time Bobby was on the go, but sometimes he just liked to be alone in his room — to daydream or to think about all the changes he was experiencing in his life. He and his father often got into arguments now when they were together, and Bobby began to spend many evenings in his room.

His mother came back for his high school graduation, and someone took this picture of Bobby and his parents. He had mixed feelings about his mother's visit: he was happy to see her but it reminded him of the old days and he was sad for weeks after his mother went back.

June 29: I can't believe I'm done with school! This term's been a drag, but at least things worked out (sort of) between me and Dad's girlfriend. I kept worrying that Mom would ask me stuff about her and then argue with Dad about what I told her. Actually, Sue isn't all that bad—although she still acts kind of like a "visitor."

July 16: Sue and I had a talk—about how hard it's been for both of us. Funny that I never really thought about how *she* felt all this time. Just felt that she came between me and Dad. I still get mad at Dad for treating me like a kid sometimes. At least Sue doesn't do that, maybe because she's not really my parent.

August 27: Mom called and was really upset about my plans to travel out west. Maybe she's feeling guilty about not seeing me enough to talk about the trip sooner. Or something—I don't know. It's harder to figure her out when we're apart so much. She seemed happier after I told her that me and my friends would definitely stay at her house on the way out to the coast.

When Bobby was eighteen, he looked forward to going away to college. He still sometimes resented his parents' divorce, but increasingly, he regarded it as their problem, not his. He felt a bit uncertain about the future, but he liked the idea of being on his own and he was confident that he would be able to manage.

Glossary

accommodation According to Piaget, the process of modifying existing ideas or action-skills to fit new experiences.

achievement motivation Behavior that enhances competence or that enhances judgments of competence.

achievement test A test that measures skills or knowledge that an individual has learned.

adaptation Piaget's term for the process by which development occurs; concepts are deepened or broadened by assimilation and stretched or modified by accommodation.

adolescence The stage of development between childhood and adulthood, around ages twelve to twenty.

adolescent egocentrism The tendency of adolescents to perceive the world (and themselves) from their own perspective. See also *egocentrism.*

aggression A bold, assertive action that is intended to hurt another person or to procure an object.

allele One of several alternate forms of a gene.

amniocentesis A prenatal diagnostic method in which a sample of amniotic fluid is withdrawn and tested to detect chromosomal abnormalities.

amniotic sac A tough, spongy bag filled with salty fluid that surrounds the embryo, protects it from sudden jolts, and helps to maintain a fairly stable temperature.

anal stage According to Freud, the second stage in psychosexual development, in which the physical center of pleasure shifts to the anus and to activities related to elimination; occurs during toddlerhood.

androgyny A tendency to integrate both masculine and feminine behaviors into the personality.

animism A belief that nonliving objects are alive and human.

anorexia nervosa A physical and psychological disturbance causing a person to refuse to eat sufficient food and to develop an increasingly unrealis-tic view of his or her body; most anorexics are teenage girls.

anxious-avoidant attachment An insecure bond between infant and care-giver, in which the child rarely cries when separated from the care-giver and tends to avoid or ignore the care-giver when reunited.

anxious-resistant attachment An insecure bond between infant and care-giver, in which the child shows signs of anxiety preceding separation, is intensely upset by separation, and seeks close con-tact when reunited while at the same time resisting the care-giver's efforts to comfort.

Apgar score A rating of newborns' health imme-diately following birth, based on heart rate, strength of breathing, muscle tone, color, and reflex responsiveness.

approach behaviors Infant behaviors that estab-lish and maintain physical closeness with care-givers, such as smiling, clinging, non-nutritional sucking, and following.

aptitude test Measurement of ability that esti-mates future performance in some realm of behavior.

artificial insemination Alternative method to nor-mal conception, in which sperm is inserted with a syringe into a woman's vagina, either on or near the cervix.

artificialism A belief that all objects, whether liv-ing or not, are made in the same way, usually by human beings.

assimilation According to Piaget, a method by which a child responds to new experiences by using existing concepts to interpret new ideas and experiences.

associative play A form of social play in which children play together or with the same materials, but each from a separate frame of reference or with separate goals.

attachment An intimate and enduring emotional relationship between two people, such as infant and parent, characterized by reciprocal affection and a periodic desire to maintain physical closeness.

attention deficit disorder   See *hyperactivity*.

auditory cortex   Area of the brain, located near the left side of the cerebral cortex, where the sounds of speech produce their primary response.

authoritarian parenting   A style of child rearing characterized by a high degree of control and demands on children's maturity and a low degree of clarity of communication and nurturance.

authoritative parenting   A style of child rearing characterized by a high degree of control, clarity of communication, maturity demands, and nurturance.

autonomous morality   According to Piaget, a "morality of cooperation" used by children aged nine to twelve. Children begin to take their peers' intentions into account when evaluating their actions.

autonomy   The ability to govern and regulate one's own thoughts, feelings, and actions freely and responsibly.

autonomy versus shame and doubt   According to Erikson, the psychosocial crisis of children aged one to three involving the struggle to control their own thoughts, feelings, and actions; the second of Erikson's developmental stages.

babbling   The combination, repetition, and elaboration of verbal sounds; a normal step in language acquisition.

baby biography   A detailed diary recording a child's development, popular in the nineteenth century; one basis of modern observational studies of children.

basic trust versus mistrust   According to Erikson, the psychosocial crisis of children from birth to twelve months, involving the infant's development of a sense of trust in his or her care-givers; the first of Erikson's developmental stages.

battered-child syndrome   A clinical condition in young children who have received serious physical abuse, generally from a parent or foster parent.

behavior genetics   The scientific study of the relationship between genotype and phenotype, especially with regard to intelligence, personality, and mental health.

behaviorism   A learning theory that focuses on changes in specific observable behaviors and their causes.

behavior modification   A body of techniques based on behaviorism for changing or eliminating specific behaviors.

Black English   A dialect or version of English spoken by many black people in the United States.

blastocyst   The tiny sphere formed from the original cells of the zygote, after dividing and redividing several times. About one week after conception, the blastocyst adheres to the wall of the uterus and becomes the embryo.

blended family   A family created from a combination of stepchildren, stepparents, and stepsiblings.

body image   An individual's concept and evaluation of his or her own physical build.

brain stem   Relatively primitive, or "lower," area of the brain. Along with the midbrain, this area regulates relatively automatic functions such as breathing, digestion, and conciousness.

Brazelton Neonatal Behavior Assessment Scale A detailed assessment of newborns' neurological development and responsiveness; usually given a few days after birth.

breech presentation   The position or orientation, of a fetus in which the feet and rump are pointing downward and emerge first during labor and delivery.

Broca's area   Area of the brain located on the left side of the cerebral cortex, vital to the production of language. See also *Wernicke's area*.

bulimia   A disorder in which a person, usually a teenage girl, eats huge amounts of food and then vomits it up to avoid gaining weight.

caesarean section   A childbirth procedure in which the baby is removed surgically from the mother's abdomen.

canalization   The tendency of many developmental processes to unfold in highly predictable ways under a wide range of conditions.

catch-up growth   Process by which children recover from slow growth by growing faster than usual until they reach the normal size for their age.

central nervous system   The brain and nerve cells of the spinal cord.

centration Perceptual dominance; the tendency (common among preschoolers) to focus on only one aspect of an object or situation and to ignore other relevant aspects.

cephalic presentation The position, or orientation, of the fetus in which the head is pointing downward; the most common and most medically desirable orientation during labor and delivery.

cephalocaudal development The tendency for organs, reflexes, and skills to develop sooner at the top (or head) of the body, and later in areas farther down the body.

cerebral cortex "Higher" part of the brain. With the cerebrum, it controls vision, hearing, and touch, as well as motor actions such as lifting the arm.

cerebrum See *cerebral cortex.*

child abuse Violent mistreatment or neglect of children. See also *battered-child syndrome.*

chromosome Threadlike, rod-shaped structure containing genetic information transmitted from parents to their children; each human sperm or egg cell contains twenty-three and these determine a person's inherited characteristics.

circular reaction Piaget's term for an action often repeated, apparently because it is self-reinforcing.

classical conditioning According to Pavlov, learning in which a neutral stimulus gains the power to bring about a certain response by repeated association with another stimulus that already elicits that same response.

classification Putting objects in groups or categories according to some sort of standards or criteria.

class inclusion The ability to compare a subset of objects with some larger, more inclusive set of objects to which it belongs.

cognition All processes by which humans acquire knowledge; methods for thinking or gaining knowledge about the world.

cognitive domain The area of human development concerned with cognition; concerns all psychological processes by which individuals learn and think about their environment.

cognitive flexibility Skills at detecting multiple meanings of words, alternative orientations of objects, and alternative strategies for solving problems.

cognitive style The forms or manner of thinking.

communicative competence How one adjusts one's utterances to the needs and expectations of different situations and speakers.

conception The moment at which the male's sperm cell penetrates the female's egg cell (ovum), forming a zygote.

concrete operational period According to Piaget, the period (from about age seven to age eleven) when children can see logical relationships among concepts or schemes but are still unable to think abstractly.

conditioned response According to Pavlov, a learned behavior that is elicited by a conditioned stimulus through association with an unconditioned stimulus.

conditioned stimulus According to Pavlov, a neutral sight, sound, or other stimulus that has acquired the power to elicit a certain response.

conservation A belief that certain properties (such as quantity) remain constant in spite of changes in perceived features such as dimensions, position, and shape.

consolidation of self The final subphase of individuation in which the adolescent develops a sense of personal identity.

constructive play A type of play that involves manipulation of physical objects in order to build or construct something.

conventional stages of moral development According to Kohlberg, the third and fourth stages of moral development; characterized by an emphasis on accepted social rules and standards.

convergent thinking Focused, deductive reasoning that leads to a particular solution to a problem.

cooperative play A form of social play in which children carry out roles or informally delegate tasks to each other.

critical period Any period during which one is particularly susceptible to an event or influence, either negative or positive.

cross-sectional study Study that compares individuals of different ages at the same point in time.

crystallized intelligence In psychometrics, knowledge gained from aspects of society, such as formal education and cultural influences.

décallage "Gap"; Piaget's term for the differences in when a child acquires the skills of a particular cognitive stage.

decentration Attending to more than one feature or dimension of a problem or situation at a time.

defense mechanism According to Freud, an unconscious way of reducing anxiety by distorting or repressing reality.

deferred imitation Piaget's term for the ability of preoperational children (ages two to seven) to imitate behavior at a significantly later time than when they first witness it.

democratic parenting A style of parenting in which parents generally encourage their children to participate in discussions and decisions, but reserve the right to make final decisions.

deoxyribonucleic acid (DNA) Molecules containing hereditary information; consist of large conglomerations of amino acids arranged in precise sequences.

dependent variable A factor that is measured in an experiment and that *depends* on, or is controlled by, one or more independent variables. See also *independent variable.*

depth perception A sense of how far away objects are or appear to be.

development Long-term changes in a person's growth, feelings, patterns of thinking, social relationships, and motor skills.

developmental psychology The scientific study of how thoughts, feelings, personality, social relationships, and body and motor skills evolve as an individual grows older.

developmental quotient (DQ) A measure of an infant's performance on activities that assess how quickly the infant is developing motor skills, compared to other infants of the same age.

developmental stages Stages that mark the process of change of an individual, all sharing certain features: (1) all intact organisms follow the same sequence of stages in their development, (2) each stage is qualitatively different from all other stages, (3) stages represent a logical progression in development.

dichotic listening A task in which an individual is fed information or sounds to each ear separately; demonstrates hemispheric lateralization.

differentiation The subphase of individuation in which one recognizes that one is psychologically different from one's parents.

disequilibrium In Piaget's theory, the cognitive state, usually temporary, in which new information cannot be integrated or reconciled with pre-existing information or experiences.

divergent thinking The production of a wide variety of ideas even though they are associated in unusual or indirect ways.

dizygotic twins Twins that develop from two different fertilized ova; fraternal twins.

dominance hierarchy The pattern of status and influence within a group, such as a classroom or a clique of peers.

dominant trait A trait that tends to dominate or be expressed in the phenotype even when present in just one of a pair of matched chromosomes. See also *recessive trait.*

Down syndrome A genetic abnormality in which an individual has an extra twenty-first chromosome; accompanied by some degree of mental retardation and characteristic physical features.

dramatic play Cognitive level of play involving pretense; begins as soon as a child can symbolize or mentally represent objects. Also called *make-believe play.*

dramatization "As if" performance in which a child tries out the role of or plays at being someone else, such as parents or teachers.

duo A two-word utterance.

dyad A two-person relationship, such as between parent and infant, or a mutual friendship between two pairs.

dyslexia A common learning disability involving significant difficulties in reading.

eclampsia A disease related to hypertension that can occur toward the end of pregnancy; involves a build-up of fetal waste materials in the mother's bloodstream.

ecological view The view that developmental changes and problems such as child abuse result not from any single cause but from multiple and overlapping levels of influence that include an individual's history, family situation, work and neighborhood experiences, and prevailing cultural values.

ecosystem The somewhat broader influences outside of the family that directly contribute to the quality of life.

ectoderm The upper layer of the blastocyst, which later develops into the epidermis, nails, teeth, hair, and sensory organs and nervous system.

ectomorph A person with a slender build. See also *endomorph*.

ego According to Freud, the rational, realistic part of the personality, which coordinates impulses from the id with demands imposed by the superego and by society.

ego integrity versus despair According to Erikson, the final psychosocial crisis, reached during late adulthood and old age. In this stage, one looks back on one's life with dignity, optimism, and wisdom while faced with the despair resulting from the negative aspects of old age.

egocentric escape The concept that people distance themselves from unpleasant and overwhelming experiences by acting as if they are unaffected by them or by quickly forgetting them.

egocentrism The inability to distinguish between one's own point of view and that of another person; behavior and thoughts centered only on one's own body, needs, and opinions. See also *adolescent egocentrism.*

ejaculation The sudden discharge or ejection of semen; can happen during intercourse, masturbation, or (less frequently) sleep.

embryo The fully implanted blastocyst; refers specifically to the developing human from the second to eighth week after conception.

embryonic disc A structure along one side of the blastocyst out of which the baby will eventually develop.

embryonic stage Stage in prenatal development that lasts from week 2 through week 8.

endocrine glands Glands that produce growth hormones.

endoderm The lower layer of the blastocyst, which becomes the digestive system, liver, pancreas, salivary glands, and respiratory system.

endomorph A person with a round, padded build. See also *ectomorph.*

equalitarian parenting A style of parenting in which parents try to give their children an equal say in decisions.

equilibration According to Piaget, a stage of cognitive equilibrium in which an individual's thinking becomes increasingly stable, general, and in harmony with the environment.

estrogen A sex hormone, sometimes called the female sex hormone, since its high concentration in girls stimulates the growth of the ovaries and vagina during puberty.

executive programs Sequenced instructions for modifying and classifying information in working memory, and for transferring it to long-term memory.

experimental study Study in which circumstances are arranged so that just one or two factors or influences vary at a time.

expressive language Language that a child can actually use appropriately in conversation.

extinction According to Skinner, the disappearance of response resulting from the removal of the reinforcer that was maintaining it.

factor In the psychometric tradition, a group of cognitive skills that tend to occur together and that therefore form a superordinate ability or more general type of intelligence.

failure-to-thrive syndrome A condition in which an infant seems seriously delayed in physical growth and is noticeably apathetic in behavior; tangible evidence of neglect.

fetal alcohol syndrome A congenital condition exhibited by babies born to mothers who consumed too much alcohol during pregnancy. They do not arouse easily and tend to behave sluggishly in general; they also have distinctive facial characteristics.

fetal stage Stage in prenatal development that lasts from the eighth week of pregnancy until birth.

fetus An embryo that has developed its first bone cells, after about eight weeks of gestation.

field dependence The ability to see things in relatively large, connected patterns, such as overall shape and large patches of color.

field independence The ability to view things as discrete, independent parts—such as noticing individual trees in a forest, or particular colors of flowers in a garden.

fine motor skills Voluntary movements of the body that involve the small muscles located throughout the body.

first stage of labor In childbirth, the stage that begins with relatively mild and irregular contractions of the uterus. As contractions grow stronger, the cervix dilates enough for the baby's head to begin fitting through. May take from eight to twenty-four hours for a first-time mother.

fluid intelligence In psychometrics, quickness at handling abstract symbols, such as problems in logical reasoning.

fontanelle A "soft spot" on an infant's skull; actually a gap in bones covered with tough membrane that grows over with bone by eighteen months.

formal operational period According to Piaget, the period characterized by hypothetical, logical, abstract, and scientific thinking. This stage is generally not reached until adolescence, if at all.

functional play Cognitive level of play that involves simple, repeated movements and a focus on one's own body.

functional relationships Variations in an environment that normally occur together.

g In psychometrics, "general intelligence," consisting of a mixture of academic skills, usually language, logic, and arithmetic.

games with rules Cognitive level of play involving relatively formal activities with fixed rules.

gamete Reproductive cell (sperm or ovum).

gender constancy A belief that a person's sex is biologically determined, permanent, and unchanging, no matter what else about that person may change.

gender identity One's beliefs about what sex one is.

gender preference Attitudes about the sex one prefers to be.

gene Molecular structure, carried on chromosomes, containing genetic information. A gene is the basic unit of heredity.

generation gap Differences in experiences and attitudes between parents and their children.

generative rules Syntactic rules that allow speakers to generate new sentences almost infinitely by applying them to new morphemes.

generativity versus stagnation The seventh of Erikson's psychosocial crises, reached in middle adulthood. One must balance the feeling that one's life is personally satisfying and socially meaningful with feelings of purposelessness.

genetic counseling Assessment of and consultation with a couple about their genetic background and risks for bearing a genetically abnormal child.

genital stage According to Freud, the final stage of psychosexual development. As adolescents undergo the major physical changes associated with puberty, their libidinal energy resurfaces.

genotype The set of genetic traits inherited by an individual. See also *phenotype.*

germinal stage Stage in prenatal development that occurs during the first two weeks of pregnancy; characterized by rapid cell division. Also called the period of the ovum.

glia Brain cells that emit a sheathing that encases neurons and their fibers; helps to transmit impulses more quickly and reliably.

gross motor skills Voluntary movements of the body that involve the large muscles of the arms, legs, and torso.

growth spurt Rapid change in height and weight preceded and followed by years of comparatively little increase, which occurs during puberty.

habituation The tendency to attend to novel stimuli and to ignore familiar ones.

hemispheric lateralization A tendency for the left and right halves of the brain to perform separate functions.

hemophilia A disease in which the blood will not clot properly and therefore characterized by excessive bleeding; example of a sex-linked recessive trait.

heteronomous morality According to Piaget, a "morality of constraint" used in play by children ages six to nine. Children regard the rules of the game as sacred and unchangeable, yet are lax about following them.

heterozygous Describes a genotype consisting of distinct forms of chromosomes for the same gene.

holophrases One-word utterances, or "whole phrases," that express a complete thought; early communication typical of eighteen-month-olds.

hormones Chemicals produced by the endocrine glands and secreted directly into the bloodstream.

hostile aggression Aggressive behavior in which harm is an important intent.

hybrid vigor The tendency of genetically dissimilar individuals to produce comparatively larger and more vigorous offspring.

hyperactivity Attention deficit disorder (ADD); excessive levels of activity and the inability to concentrate for normal periods of time.

hypothesis A precise prediction based on a scientific theory; often capable of being tested in a scientific research study.

id According to Freud, the part of an individual's personality that contains basic, unprocessed sexual energy. The id motivates behavior by demanding reduction of the tension that builds up around a person's physical and emotional needs.

identification According to Freud, the process by which an individual wants to become like a model, usually a parent or another attachment figure.

identity (1) Piagetian term for the constancy of an object. (2) A unique and relatively stable set of personal characteristics.

identity diffusion A failure to achieve a relatively integrated and stable identity.

identity status Marcia's four categories of identity development: identity achievement, identity diffusion, moratorium, and foreclosure.

identity versus identity confusion The fifth of Erikson's psychosocial crises in which one must integrate one's many childhood skills and beliefs, and gain recognition for them from society.

imaginary audience A characteristic of young adolescents in which they act as if they are performing for an audience and believe that others are as concerned with their appearance and behavior as they themselves are.

implantation The attachment of the blastocyst to the wall of the uterus.

impulsivity A style of thinking characterized by rapid tempo and relative inattention to errors. See also *reflectivity*.

inclusive fitness The tendency of genotypes to persist, which encourages the survival of an entire genetic lineage, regardless of the effects on particular individuals.

independent variable A factor that an experimenter manipulates (varies) to determine its influence on the population being studied. See also *dependent variable*.

individuation The process by which an adolescent develops a unique and separate personal identity; consists of four subphases: differentiation, practice and experimentation, rapprochement, and consolidation.

induced labor Artificial contractions that result from the injection of the hormone oxytocin.

industry versus inferiority Erikson's fourth crisis during which children concern themselves with their capacity to do good work and thereby develop confident, positive self-concepts or else be faced with feelings of inferiority.

information-processing theories Theories that focus on the precise, detailed features or steps of mental activities. These theories often use computers as a model for human thinking.

initiative versus guilt Erikson's third crisis, during which a child's increasing ability to initiate verbal and physical activity and expanding imaginative powers lead to fantasies of large and sometimes frightening proportions.

inner speech Toddlers' "mental shorthand"; thinking that occurs without much help from language.

insecure attachment A relationship between parent and child marked by the child's overdependence on the parents, or else by the child's indifference to them. See also *anxious-resistant attachment* and *anxious-avoidant attachment*.

instrumental aggression Assertive behavior with a goal in mind; the action ends when the goal is achieved and sometimes may unintentionally hurt others.

integrity vs. despair The eighth crisis of development in Erikson's theory, in which older adults assess the value of their life's work and fight the tendency to lose hope about life in general.

intelligence A general ability to learn from experience; also refers to ability to reason abstractly.

intelligence quotient (IQ) Score on an intelligence test that supposedly reflects overall intelligence.

internalization (1) According to Freud, the process of taking into one's own personality many of the important qualities of the same-sex parent; operates as the child struggles to resolve oedipal conflict. (2) The process of holding in feelings.

intimacy Feelings of closeness comprised of self-revelation, confidence, and exclusivity.

intimacy versus isolation The sixth of Erikson's psychosocial crises, in which young adults must be able to develop intimate relationships with others while dealing with the fear of loss of identity that such intimacy entails.

intrinsic motivation Interest in an activity because it is enjoyable and rewarding for its own sake rather than because it is useful in achieving something else.

intuitive phase According to Piaget, the second phase of the preoperational period (ages four to seven). Children begin to cease confusing their own thoughts with those of other people and also stop thinking that objects and events are constructed primarily for their own benefit.

in vitro fertilization Alternative method to normal conception in which one or more ova are removed from the mother surgically and mixed in a petri dish with sperm from the father. The zygote is then reinserted surgically into the mother's womb.

joint custody Arrangement in which divorced parents share legal child-rearing responsibility for their children.

Klinefelter's syndrome A genetic abnormality in which a person has at least one extra sex chromosome, usually an X. Such a person is phenotypically male but tends to have small testes and to remain sterile throughout life.

kwashiorkor A condition resulting from protein-calorie deficiency in children. Symptoms are an enlarged abdomen, a tendency to lose hair, and lesions that don't heal.

labor The physical activity involved in giving birth, including periodic contractions of the uterus, delivery of the baby, and expulsion of the placenta. See also specific stages of labor.

language acquisition devise (LAD) The inborn skills through which infants may acquire language.

lanugo Fine, downy hair on the fetus and neonate; especially visible on preterm infants.

latency According to Freud, the stage of development between the phallic and genital stages. Sexual feelings and activities are on hold as the child struggles to resolve the oedipal conflict.

lateralized behaviors Actions that individuals prefer to perform with one side of their body more than the other.

learning Changes that result from relatively specific experiences or events. Learning contributes to development but usually encompasses shorter periods of time and more specific experiences.

learning disabilities Difficulties in learning specific academic skills such as reading and arithmetic.

learning orientation Achievement motivation that comes from the learner and the task.

learning strategies General methods or techniques that help to solve a variety of problems.

learning theory A theory that focuses on explaining changes in specific behavior or thinking, and that identifies specific, observable causes of behavior or thinking.

libido According to Freud, all of the ways in which human beings seek to increase pleasure and avoid discomfort by fulfilling their physical and emotional needs.

localization The ability to identify where a sensation (sight, sound, or touch) is coming from.

logical construction Refers to children's active efforts to understand the world; includes a mixture of assimilation and accommodation.

longitudinal study A study of the same subjects over a relatively long period, often months or years.

long-term memory (LTM) Type of memory that saves information permanently.

low birth weight A birth weight of less than 2,500 grams (about $5\frac{1}{2}$ pounds).

mainstreaming Integrating children with handicaps into regular classrooms to as great a degree as is possible.

make-believe play See *dramatic play.*

malnutrition Chronically insufficient food or

nutrients. Deficiencies can occur in protein, calories, and/or specific vitamins and minerals.

malevolent transformation The development of a sense that the world is a harmful and evil place in which it is difficult to achieve closeness with others; may occur if a child's attempts to initiate social contacts with others are undermined.

marasmus A disease that affects infants who have suffered from prolonged periods of protein and calorie deficiency. They may have delays in motor development and perform lower than healthy infants on intelligence tests.

maturation Physical growth and other developmental changes that occur primarily as a result of growing older.

meiosis A complex process by which gametes form involving duplication and division of reproductive cells and their chromosomes.

menarche The first menstrual period.

mesoderm The middle layer of the blastocyst, which becomes the dermis, muscles, skeleton, and circulatory and excretory systems.

mesomorph A person with a muscular build.

metacognition Knowledge and thinking about cognition, about how learning and memory operate in everyday situations, and about how a person can improve cognitive performance.

metalinguistic awareness The ability to attend to language as an object of thought rather than attending only to the content or ideas of a language.

midbrain Area of the brain that, with the brain stem, regulates relatively automatic functions such as breathing, digestion, and consciousness.

mitosis The creation of new cells through duplication of chromosomes and division of cells.

modeling An approximate copy or imitation of another's behavior.

monozygotic twins Twins that result from a single fertilized ovum that divided into two zygotes; identical twins.

moral judgment Understandings of the actions that promote human welfare in a variety of situations.

Moro reflex The reflexive startle response of newborns. Healthy infants will fling their arms out suddenly and sometimes shake all over or cry in response to sudden loud noise or sudden loss of support.

morphemes The smallest meaningful units of language; includes words as well as a number of prefixes and suffixes that carry meaning.

motherese The simplified language characteristically used by mothers and others to talk with babies and toddlers; tends to emphasize key words and rely on repetitions and questions.

motor cortex Area of the brain located just forward of the top of the head where simple voluntary movements produce their largest neural activity.

motor skills Physical skills using the body or limbs, such as walking and drawing.

myelin The sheathing, emitted by glia, that encases neurons and their fibers.

naturalistic research A study in which the researcher purposely observes behavior as it normally occurs in its natural setting.

nature (1) The essence or basic character of a person or thing. (2) The inborn qualities of a person.

negative identity A form of identity diffusion involving rejection of the roles preferred by one's family or community in favor of socially undesirable roles.

negative reinforcer According to Skinner, a stimulus that increases the frequency or rate of an operant or learned behavior by reducing a person's pain or discomfort.

neonate A newborn infant.

neurons Nerve cell bodies and their extensions or fibers.

nocturnal emissions Ejaculation of semen during sleep.

non-REM sleep A relatively quiet, deep period of sleep. See also *REM sleep.*

norms Behaviors typical at certain ages and of certain groups; standards of normal development.

nurture Environmental influences and experiences that affect a person's development.

obesity The state of being extremely overweight, specifically more than 130 percent of normal weight for height and bone size; affects one American child in ten.

object constancy The perception that an object remains the same in size or shape in spite of continual changes in the sensations it sends to the eye.

object permanence According to Piaget, the belief that people and things continue to exist even when one cannot experience them directly; emerges around age two.

oedipal conflict In Freudian theory, a child's desire for the opposite-sex parent and disappointment that follows the realization that the same-sex parent will always win the sexual competition for this parent; emerges in the phallic stage.

onlooker play A precursor to more truly social forms of play, in which one child observes another child playing.

operant conditioning According to Skinner, a process of learning in which a person or animal increases the frequency of a behavior in response to repeated reinforcement of that behavior.

oral stage Freud's term for the psychosexual stage of development in which the id is dominant and the infant seeks physical and emotional pleasure through the mouth; lasts from birth to one year.

ovaries The female reproductive glands, which produce ova (egg cells).

overgeneralizations Utterances in which a child shifts from using correct but irregular forms to using wrong but more regular forms; represents efforts to try out newly noticed rules of syntax.

ovulation The release of a fully matured egg from the ovary.

ovum Reproductive cell, or gamete, of the female; the egg cell.

parallel play An early form of social play, in which children play near each other but with separate materials and without significant interaction.

parent-infant synchrony Patterns of closely coordinated social and emotional interaction between parent and infant.

peer group A group of age-mates who know and interact with one another.

penis envy According to Freud, a four- or five-year-old girl's desire for a penis and resultant jealousy of boys.

perception The neural activity of combining sensations into meaningful patterns.

perceptual dominance See *centration*.

perceptual masking A phenomenon in which some letters are hard to read because of the presence of other letters nearby.

performance orientation Achievement motivation stimulated by other individuals who may see and evaluate the learner, rather than by the intrinsic nature of the task itself.

permissive parenting Style of child rearing characterized by a high degree of clarity of communication and nurturance and a low degree of demands on children's maturity and control.

permissive-indifferent parenting A type of parenting in which parents' permissiveness reflects an avoidance of child-rearing responsibilities, sometimes with detrimental results.

permissive-indulgent parenting A type of parenting in which parents make relatively few demands on their children but clearly communicate their warmth and interest and provide considerable care and nurturance.

personal fable Adolescents' belief that their own lives embody a special story that is heroic and completely unique.

personality A person's unique pattern of physical, emotional, social, and intellectual characteristics.

phallic stage According to Freud, the stage of psychosexual development (around age four or five) in which a child shifts libidinal interest to the genitals.

phenotype The set of traits an individual actually displays during development; reflects the evolving product of genotype and experience. See also *genotype*.

phenylketonuria (PKU) A disorder that severely diminishes an individual's ability to utilize a particular amino acid—phenylalanine—which is found in milk and milk products and which is essential to normal nutrition and growth.

phoneme A sound, which combines with other sounds to form words.

phonology The individual vocal sounds of a language.

physical domain The area of human development concerned primarily with physical changes, such as growth, motor skill development, and basic aspects of perception.

placenta An organ that delivers oxygen and nutrients from the mother to the fetus and carries away the fetus's waste products, which the mother will excrete.

play therapy A therapeutic technique in which child and therapist communicate through make-believe play, using dolls and other props.

pleasure principle According to Freud, the motivation of the id; focuses on the immediate satisfaction of physical and emotional needs.

polygenic traits Traits resulting from the combined influence of many genes.

population In experimental research, the group being studied.

positive reinforcer Skinner's term for a stimulus that increases the frequency of a response by rewarding the person for making it.

postconventional stages of moral development According to Kohlberg, the fifth and sixth stages of moral development characterized by universal moral principles.

preconceptual phase According to Piaget, the first stage of the preoperational period (ages two to four), in which children begin to use symbolic thinking widely, though without the organized properties characteristic of later thought.

preconventional stages of moral development According to Kohlberg, the first two stages of moral development, which emphasize avoiding punishments, getting rewards, and exchanging favors.

premature baby A baby born prior to the thirty-seventh week of pregnancy; also called *preterm baby.*

preoperational period According to Piaget, the second stage of development (around age two to seven), during which there is a major shift from the action-oriented schemes of the sensorimotor period to schemes based on symbolic representation, such as language and dramatic play.

prepared childbirth A method of childbirth in which parents have rehearsed or simulated the actual sensations of labor and delivery well before the actual delivery date.

preterm baby See *premature baby.*

primary circular reaction According to Piaget, a behavior that is repeated and that focuses on the baby's own body and movements; occurs during the second stage of infant cognition (usually at about one to four months of age).

primary sex characteristics Characteristics that make sexual reproduction possible—for girls, the vagina, uterus, fallopian tubes, and ovaries; for boys, the penis, scrotum, testes, prostate gland, and seminal vesicles.

prosocial behavior Positive social contacts: actions that benefit others.

proximodistal development Growth that exhibits a near-to-far pattern of development, that is, from the center of the body outward.

psychoanalytic theory A group of theories of psychology concerned primarily with the dynamics of emotions and of unconscious drives and motivations. Freud's and Erikson's theories are prominent examples.

psychometrics The measurement of human abilities, usually with specially constructed tests.

psychosocial domain The area of human development concerned primarily with personality, social knowledge and skills, and emotions.

psychosocial moratorium According to Erikson, the latency period that precedes puberty and provides a temporary suspension of psychosexual development.

puberty The period of early adolescence characterized by the development of full physical and sexual maturity.

punishment According to Skinner, any stimulus that temporarily suppresses the response that it follows.

quasi-experimental research Studies that combine elements of both experimental and naturalistic studies.

quickening A mother's sensations of the fetus's simple and reflexive actions in the womb; usually felt by the fourth or fifth month of pregnancy.

random sample In research studies, a group of subjects from a population chosen so that each member of the population has an equal chance of being selected.

reactive attachment disorder Psychosocial dwarfism; a slowing of growth due to family stress.

reality principle According to Freud, the motivation of the ego; the tendency to express physical and emotional needs in socially acceptable ways, delaying immediate gratification.

recall memory Retrieval of information by using relatively few external cues.

receptive language Language that is understood or comprehended when used by others.

recessive trait A genetic trait that is expressed in the phenotype only when carried by both chromosomes of a matched pair in the genotype. See also *dominant trait*.

recognition memory Retrieval of information by comparing an external stimulus or cue with pre-existing experiences or knowledge.

reflectivity A cognitive style characterized by slow tempo and careful avoidance of errors. See also *impulsivity*.

reflex An involuntary, automatic response to a stimulus. The very first movements or motions of an infant are reflexes.

regression In Freudian theory, a defense mechanism in which a person returns to earlier and less mature ways of handling conflicts.

reinforcer According to Skinner, any stimulus that increases the likelihood that a behavior will be repeated in similar circumstances.

REM sleep A relatively active period of sleep, named after the rapid eye movements that usually accompany it. See also *non-REM sleep*.

repetition compulsion The repetition of an experience—usually a painful one—in symbolic play, which helps the child to resolve feelings about it.

repression According to Freud, a defense mechanism in which a person forces thoughts and feelings out of consciousness by forgetting a significant experience.

respiratory distress syndrome (RSD) Irregular breathing, a leading cause of death among preterm infants. One cause is a lack of surfactin, a substance that prevents the lungs from sticking together.

reversibility Piaget's term for the ability to undo a problem mentally and go back to its beginning.

Rh factor A substance in the mother's blood which in certain forms causes antibodies to develop, and which attack the red corpuscles of the fetus's blood, weakening or killing the fetus before it is born.

Rhogam blood Rh negative blood that contains antibodies. Rh negative mothers are inoculated with rhogam blood to prevent them from developing further antibodies that might jeopardize future pregnancies.

rooting A reflexive searching behavior that orients an infant to the mother's breast or a bottle.

rubella German measles; a virus that can cause blindness, deafness, damage to the central nervous system, and other handicaps in a child if the mother contracts it during early pregnancy.

scheme According to Piaget, a behavior or thought that represents a group of ideas and events in a child's experience.

scientific method General procedures of study involving (1) formulating research questions, (2) stating questions as a hypothesis, (3) testing the hypothesis, and (4) interpreting and publicizing the results.

second stage of labor The period of labor that starts with "crowning"—the first moment that the baby's head can be seen—and ends with the baby's birth. Usually lasts between one and one and one half hours.

secondary circular reaction According to Piaget, the third stage of infant cognition that occurs at the age of four to eight months; repeated behaviors that are motivated by external objects and events.

secondary sex characteristics Sex characteristics other than the sex organs themselves, such as extra layers of fat and pubic hair.

secretory IgA One of the proteins of human milk that binds to viruses and bacteria in the infant's intestine; acts as an intestinal "paint," preventing gastrointestinal disorders.

secular trend (1) In general, any long-term historical trend. (2) In human development, the tendency of each new generation in industrialized countries to grow larger and heavier and to experience puberty earlier than their parents.

secure attachment A healthy bond between infant and care-giver. The child is happy when the care-giver is present, somewhat upset during the care-giver's absence, and easily comforted upon the care-giver's return.

self-concept A sense of self or idea about oneself.

self-constancy The belief that identity remains permanently fixed; established sometime after age six.

self-esteem An individual's feeling that he or she is an important, competent, powerful, and worthwhile person who is valued and appreciated.

semantics The purposes and meanings of a language.

semen A sticky fluid produced by the prostate gland; carries sperm to the penis and provides it with a medium in which to live after ejaculation.

sensorimotor period Paiget's term for the period from birth to age two, when thinking is limited to sensing and manipulating.

separation anxiety A child's discomfort at being separated from his or her care-giver.

separation-individuation According to Margaret Mahler, the process by which a child achieves increasingly greater autonomy and independence from the care-giver and develops a distinct and separate identity; occurs about halfway through the infant's first year and continues through the second.

seriation The ability to put objects or quantities into a logical series or sequence.

sex-linked recessive traits Recessive traits resulting from genes on the X chromosome. Because women must inherit two of the recessive genes in order to have the trait, they experience these much less than men do.

sex-role stereotypes General knowledge of a society's expectations about sex roles.

sexual dimorphism The physical differences between males and females.

shape constancy The perception that an object remains the same even though its shape seems to change when it is viewed from different angles.

short-term memory (STM) "Momentary awareness"; type of memory that retains information for a very short time—no more than a few seconds.

short-term sensory store (SSTS) Area in the brain that receives information exactly as the senses provide it, and that saves the information only briefly (usually one second or less).

sickle-cell anemia A genetically transmitted condition in which a person's red blood cells intermittently acquire a curved, sickle shape. The condition can sometimes clog circulation in the small blood vessels.

signaling behaviors Infant behaviors that establish and maintain physical closeness with care-givers, such as crying, smiling, and babbling.

sleep apnea Temporary stoppage of breathing during sleep.

small-for-date infant An infant who develops more slowly than normal during pregnancy; could be born full-term or preterm.

social cognition Knowledge and beliefs about interpersonal and social matters.

social conventions Arbitrary customs and agreements about behavior that members of a society use.

social learning theory The theory that learning results from observing and imitating others.

social transmission According to Piaget, the process by which people are influenced by, and to some extent adopt, the information and ideas of their culture and society.

sociobiology The study of the biological and genetic basis of social behavior, including human social behavior.

solitary play Play that occurs alone, either by choice or by accident.

spermatozoa Male gametes, or reproductive cells; produced in the testicles. (Also know as *sperm.*)

stage theory A theory that proposes steps of development that occur in a fixed sequence, and that often form a logical hierarchy with one another.

stimulus Any event that causes a physical or mental response, such as a sight, sound, taste, or smell; in some usages, mental activity itself can also serve as a stimulus to physical or mental responses.

"strange situation" A widely used method for studying attachment; confronts the infant with a series of controlled separations and reunions with a parent and stranger.

stranger anxiety An infant's wariness and avoidance of unfamiliar people and places.

sublimation Freud's term for a defense mechanism in which sexual and aggressive energies are channeled into socially acceptable outlets, such as school, sports, hobbies, and friendships.

sucking reflex   One of the neonate's first and most powerful reflexes, triggered by any object intruding into the mouth.

sudden infant death syndrome (SIDS)   "Crib death" syndrome in which apparently healthy infants stop breathing unaccountably and die in their sleep; most frequently strikes infants between the ages of two and four months.

superego   According to Freud, the portion of one's personality that acts like an all-knowing, internalized parent and enforces morality and social conventions; the conscience.

symbiotic mother-child relationship   According to Margaret Mahler, a characteristic of the infant's first year in which the mother psychologically experiences the child as an extension of herself rather than as an independent person, and vice versa.

symbolic thought   Cognition that makes one object or action stand for another.

symbol   A word, object, or behavior that stands for something else.

tactile perception   The ability to recognize an object or discriminate among objects by touching them.

Tay-Sachs disease   A genetically transmitted disorder of the nervous system that occurs mainly among infants of Jewish people of Eastern European descent.

telegraphic speech   Early utterances that leave out most articles, prepositions, and conjunctions.

temperament   Characteristic patterns or styles of physical and emotional activity and responsiveness.

teratogen   Any substance ingested by a pregnant woman that can harm the developing embryo or fetus.

tertiary circular reaction   According to Piaget, repeated variations of action schemes, organized by trial and error; the fifth stage in infant cognition, occurring between twelve and eighteen months of age.

testes   Male sex glands, responsible for producing sperm, or male gametes.

testosterone   Sex hormone sometimes called the male sex hormone since its high concentration in boys stimulates the growth of the penis and related male reproductive organs.

third stage of labor   Final stage, in which the afterbirth (placenta and umbilical cord) is expelled; normally lasts only a few minutes.

toxoplasmosis   A disease caused by a parasite present in uncooked meat and the feces of infected cats; can lead to fetal brain damage, blindness, and death.

transition   Follows the first stage of labor; the cervix nears full dilation, contractions become rapid and irregular and the baby's head begins to move into the birth canal.

trimester   One of the three-month stages in the nine months of pregnancy.

trophoblast   The outer layer of blastocyst cells; produces villi, which attach to the placenta.

ultrasound   A prenatal diagnostic method that allows medical personnel and others to view the fetus by projecting high-frequency sound waves through the mother's womb.

umbilical cord   Three large blood vessels that connect the embryo to the placenta, one to provide nutrients and two to remove waste products.

unconditioned response   According to Pavlov, an involuntary response that is elicited by an unconditioned stimulus; a reflex.

unconditioned stimulus   Pavlov's term for a stimulus that elicits an involuntary reaction.

undergeneralizations   Early utterances in which children tend to define grammatical categories more narrowly than adults do.

unoccupied play   A precursor to true play, in which a child's activities seem to have no clear purpose or goals.

vernix   A white, waxy substance on the skin of neonates, especially those born preterm.

villi   Threads produced by the outer layer of blastocyst cells that enable it to attach to the uterine wall.

visual cliff   Classic laboratory setup of a ledge covered by a sheet of glass, used to test the acquisition of depth perception. Young babies crawling on the glass discriminate between the two sides of the "cliff."

visual cortex Area of the brain located near the back of the head in the cerebral cortex, where visual images produce the strongest activity.

visual integration The ability to coordinate particular sights with each other, as well as with appropriate physical actions.

visual memory The ability to recall or recognize simple sights.

Wernicke's area Part of the auditory cortex where the sounds of speech produce their primary response.

working memory (WM) Memory that is concerned with information currently being processed.

zygote The single new cell formed when a sperm cell attaches itself to the surface of an ovum (egg).

Bibliography

Abramovitch, R., and Strayer, F. (1978). Preschool social organization: Agonistic, spacing and attentional behaviors. In P. Pliner, T. Kramer, and T. Alloway (eds.), *Recent advances in the study of communication and affect* (vol. 6). New York: Plenum Press.

Acredolo, L. (1979). Laboratory versus home: The effect of environment on the 9-month-old infant's choice of spatial reference system. *Developmental Psychology, 15,* 666–667.

Acredolo, L., and Evans, D. (1980). Developmental changes in the effects of landmarks on infant spatial behavior. *Developmental Psychology, 16,* 312–318.

Acredolo, L., and Hake, J. (1983). Infant perception. In B. Wolman, G. Stricker, S. Ellman, P. Keith-Spiegel, and D. Palermo (eds.), *Handbook of developmental psychology.* Englewood Cliffs, N.J.: Prentice-Hall.

Adams, G., and Fitch, S. (1982). Ego stage and identity status development: A cross-sequential analysis. *Journal of Personality and Social Psychology, 43,* 574–583.

Adcock, D., and Segal, M. (1983). *Making friends: Ways of encouraging social development in young children.* Englewood Cliffs, N.J.: Prentice-Hall.

Adelson, J. (1971). The political imagination of the young adolescent. In J. Kagan and R. Coles (eds.), *Twelve to sixteen: Early adolescence.* New York: Norton.

Ainslie, R. (1985). *The psychology of twinship.* Lincoln: University of Nebraska Press.

Ainsworth, M. (1973). The development of infant-mother attachment. In B. M. Caldwell and H. N. Ricciuti (eds.), *Review of child development research* (vol. 3). Chicago: University of Chicago Press.

Ainsworth, M. (1978). Infant-mother attachment. In M. Richards (ed.), *The child's integration into the social world.* New York: Cambridge University Press.

Ainsworth, M. (1979). Infant-mother attachment. *American Psychologist, 34,* 932–937.

Ainsworth, M., Blehar, M., Waters, E., and Wall, S. (1978). *Strange-situation behavior of one-year-olds: Its relation to mother-infant interaction in the first year and to qualitative differences in the infant-mother attachment relationship.* Hillsdale, N.J.: Erlbaum.

Albert, N., and Beck, A. (1975). Incidence of depression in early adolescence: A preliminary study. *Journal of Youth and Adolescence, 4,* 301–308.

Aldis, O. (1975). *Play fighting.* New York: Academic Press.

Alexander, J., and Alexander, C. (1983). Parental investment: The hominid adaptation. In D. Ortner (ed.), *How humans adapt.* Washington, D.C.: Smithsonian Institution Press.

Alexander, J., and Noonan, K. (1979). Concealment of ovulation, parental care, and human social evolution. In N. Chagnon and W. Irons (eds.), *Evolutionary biology and human social behavior.* North Scituate, Mass.: Duxbury Press.

Allen, V. (1976). *Children as teachers: Theory and research on tutoring.* New York: Academic Press.

Ambrus, C., Ambrus, J., and Horvath, E. (1978). Phenylalanine depletion for the management of phenylketonuria: Use of enzyme reactors with immobilized enzymes. *Science, 201,* 837–839.

American Humane Association (1983). *Annual statistical report: National analysis of official child neglect and abuse reporting, 1982.* Englewood, Colo.: American Humane Association.

American Medical Association (1980). *Handbook of first aid and emergency care.* New York: Random House.

American Psychiatric Association (1980). *Diagnostic and statistical manual of mental disorders* (3rd ed.). Washington, D.C.: American Psychiatric Press.

American Psychological Association (1981). Ethical principles of psychologists. *American Psychologist, 36,* 633–638.

Ames, L., Gillespie, C., Haines, J., and Ilg, F. (1979). *The Gesell Institute's child from one to six.* New York: Harper and Row.

Anastasi, A. (1985). Psychological testing: Basic concepts and common misconceptions. In A. Rogers and C. J. Scheirer (ed.), *The G. Stanley Hall lecture series* (vol. 5). Washington, D.C.: American Psychological Association.

Anders, T., and Chalemian, R. (1974). The effect of circumcision on sleep-wake states in human neonates. *Psychosomatic Medicine, 36,* 174–179.

Anderson, C., and Creswell, W. (1980). *School health practice* (7th ed.). St. Louis: Mosby.

Anderson, E. (1978). Will you don't snore please? Directives in young children's role-play speech. *Papers and Reports on Child Language Development, 15,* 140–150.

Anderson, J. (1980). *Cognitive Psychology and its implications.* San Francisco: Freeman.

Andre-Thomas, C., and Autgaurden, R. (1953). Les deux marches. *La Presse Medicale, 61,* 582–584.

Annis, L. (1978). *The child before birth.* Ithaca, N.Y.: Cornell University Press.

Antenatal diagnosis (1979). Report of a conference sponsored by the National Institute of Child Health and Human Development. Bethesda, Md.: NIH Publication No. 79–1973.

Apgar, V. (1953). A proposal for a new method of evaluation in the newborn infant. *Current Research in Anesthesia and Analgesia, 32,* 260.

Apgar, V., and Beck, J. (1973). *Is my baby all right?* New York: Trident.

Applebee, A. (1981). *Writing in the secondary school.* Urbana, Ill.: National Council of Teachers of English.

Applebee, A., Lehr, F., and Auten, A. (1981). Learning to write in the secondary school. *English Journal, 70,* 78–82.

Arehart-Treichel, J. (1981). Down's syndrome: The father's role. *Science News, 116* (22), 381–382.

Arend, R., Gove, F., and Sroufe, L. (1979). Continuity of individual adaptation from infancy to kindergarten: A predictive study of ego-resiliency and curiosity in preschoolers. *Child Development, 50,* 950–959.

Ariès, P. (1962). *Centuries of childhood: A social history of family life.* (R. Baldick, trans.). New York: Vintage.

Aronson, S. (1984). Injuries in child care. In J. Brown (ed.), *Administering programs for young children.* Washington, D.C.: National Association for the Education of Young Children.

Asher, S., and Renshaw, P. (1981). Social skills and social knowledge of high and low status kindergarten children. In S. Asher and J. M. Gottman (eds.), *The development of children's friendships.* Cambridge, England: Cambridge University Press.

Asher, S., Renshaw, P., and Hymel, S. (1982). Peer relations and the development of social skills. In S. Moore and C. Cooper (eds.), *The young child: Reviews of research* (vol. 3). Washington, D.C.: National Association for the Education of Young Children.

Asher, S., Singleton, L., and Taylor, A. (1982). *Acceptance versus friendship: A longitudinal study of racial integration.* Paper presented at the meeting of the American Educational Research Association, New York.

Aslin, R., Pisoni, D., and Jusczyk, P. (1983). Auditory development and speech perception in infancy. In P. Mussen (ed.), *Handbook of child psychology* (vol. 2). New York: Wiley.

Atkinson, J., and Feather, N. (eds.) (1966). *A theory of achievement motivation.* New York: Wiley.

Atwood, G., and Tomkins, S. (1976). On the subjectivity of personality theory. *Journal of the History of the Behavioral Sciences, 12,* 166–177.

Au, K., and Mason, J. (1981). Social organizational factors in learning to read: The balance of rights hypothesis. *Reading Research Quarterly, 17,* 115–152.

Ault, R. (1983). *Children's cognitive development* (2nd ed.). New York: Oxford University Press.

Axelrod, S. (1977). *Behavior modification for the classroom teacher.* New York: McGraw-Hill.

Ayers, A. J. (1978). *California sensory-motor integration test manual.* Los Angeles: Western Psychological Corporation.

Baggett, P. (1979). Structurally equivalent stories in movie and text and the effect of the medium on recall. *Journal of Verbal Learning and Verbal Behavior, 18,* 333–356.

Bailey, D. (1982). Sport and the child: Physiological considerations. In R. Magill, M. Ash, and F. Smoll (eds.), *Children in sport.* Champaign, Ill.: Human Kinetics Publishers.

Bailey, D., Malina, R., and Rasmussen, R. (1978). The influence of exercise, physical activity, and athletic performance on the dynamics of human growth. In F. Faulkner and J. Tanner (eds.), *Human growth* (vol. 2). New York: Plenum.

Bakeman, R., and Brownlee, J. (1980). The strategic use of parallel play: A sequential analysis. *Child Development, 51,* 873–878.

Bakan, D. (1975). Adolescence in America: From idea to social fact. In R. E. Grinder (ed.), *Studies in adolescence* (3rd ed.). New York: Macmillan.

Baker, L., and Brown, A. (1983). Metacognitive skills of reading. In D. Pearson (ed.), *Handbook of reading research.* New York: Wiley.

Baldwin, W., and Cain, V. (1980). The children of teenage parents. *Family Planning Perspectives, 12,* 34–43.

Baltes, P. (1982). Life-span developmental psychology. In P. Baltes and O. Brim (eds.), *Life-span development and behavior* (vol. 4). New York: Academic Press.

Baltes, P., Cornelius, S., and Neselroade, J. (1978). Cohort effects in behavioral development: Theoretical and methodological perspectives. In W. Collins (ed.), *Minnesota Symposium on Child Psychology* (vol. 11). Hillsdale, N.J.: Erlbaum.

Baltes, P., and Shaie, K. (1976). On the plasticity of intelligence in adulthood and old age. *American Psychologist, 31,* 720–725.

Bandura, A. (1977). *Social learning theory.* Englewood Cliffs, N.J.: Prentice-Hall.

Bandura, A. (1978). The self system in reciprocal determinism. *American Psychologist, 33,* 344–358.

Bandura, A. (1982). The psychology of chance encounters and life paths. *American Psychologist, 37,* 747–756.

Bandura, A. (1986). *Social foundations of thought and action: A social-cognitive theory.* Englewood Cliffs, N.J.: Prentice-Hall.

Bank, S., and Kahn, M. (1982). *The sibling bond.* New York: Basic Books.

Banks, M. (1983). Infant visual perception. In P. Mussen (ed.), *Handbook of child psychology* (vol. 2). New York: Wiley.

Bannister, D., and Agnew, J. (1971). The child's construing of self. In J. Cole (ed.), *Nebraska symposium on motivation.* Lincoln: University of Nebraska Press.

Bard, B., and Sachs, J. (1977). *Language acquisition patterns in two normal children of deaf parents.* Paper presented to the second annual Boston University Conference on Language Acquisition.

Barenbaum, C. (1981). The development of person perception in childhood and adolescence: From behavioral comparisons to psychological comparisons. *Child Development, 52,* 129–144.

Barker, G. (1975). Social functions of language in a Mexican-American community. In E. Hernandez-Chavez, A. Cohen, and A. Beltramo (eds.), *El lenguaje do los Chicanos.* Arlington, Va.: Center for Applied Linguistics.

Barker, R., and Wright, H. (1955). *Midwest and its children.* New York: Harper and Row.

Barnard, K. (1981). A program of temporally patterned movement and sound stimulation for premature infants. In V. Smeriglio (ed.), *Newborns and parents.* Hillsdale, N.J.: Erlbaum.

Barnes, A., Colton, T., Gundersen, J., Noller, K., Tilley, B., Strama, T., Townsend, D., Hatab, P., and O'Brien, P. (1980). Letter. *New England Journal of Medicine, 303* (5), 281.

Barnes, G. M. (1977). The development of adolescent drinking behavior: An evaluative review of the impact of the socialization process within the family. *Adolescence, 12,* 571–591.

Barnett, M., Howard, J., King, L., and Dino, G. (1980). Antecedents of empathy: Retrospective accounts of early socialization. *Personality and Social Psychology Bulletin, 6,* 361–365.

Barnhardt, C. (ed.) (1982). *Cross-cultural issues in Alaskan education* (vol. 2). Fairbanks: University of Alaska Center for Cross-Cultural Studies.

Bates, J. (1979). A naturalistic study of sex differences in children's aggression. *Merrill-Palmer Quarterly, 25,* 193–203.

Battaglia, F., and Simmons, M. (1979). The low-birth-weight infant. In F. Falkner and J. Tanner (eds.), *Human growth* (vol. 2). New York: Plenum.

Baumeister, A., and Maisto, A. (1977). Memory scanning by children: Meaningfulness and mediation. *Journal of Experimental Child Psychology, 24,* 97–107.

Baumrind, D. (1967). Child care practices anteceding three patterns of preschool behavior. *Genetic Psychology Monographs, 75,* 43–88.

Baumrind, D. (1971). Current patterns of parental authority. *Developmental Psychology, 4,* 1–103.

Baumrind, D. (1973). The development of instrumental competence through socialization. In A. Pick (ed.), *Minnesota symposium on child psychology* (vol. 7). Minneapolis: University of Minnesota Press.

Bayley, N. (1955). On the growth of intelligence. *American Psychologist, 10,* 805–818.

Bayley, N. (1968). Behavioral correlates of mental growth: Birth to thirty-six years. *American Psychologist, 23,* 1–17.

Bayley, N. (1969). *Bayley scales of infant development.* New York: The Psychological Corporation.

Bayley, N. (1970). Development of mental abilities. In P. Mussen (ed.), *Carmichael's manual of child psychology* (vol. 1, 3rd ed.). New York: Wiley.

Beal, C., and Flavell, J. (1983). Young speakers' evaluations of their listener's comprehension in a referential communication task. *Child Development, 54,* 149–153.

Beard, R. (1969). *An outline of Piaget's developmental psychology.* London: Routledge & Kegan Paul.

Beck, R., (1978). *Motivation: Theories and principles.* Englewood Cliffs, N.J.: Prentice-Hall.

Becker, E. (1973). *The denial of death.* New York: Free Press.

Becker, W., Peterson, D., Lurie, A., Schoemaker, D., and Hellmer, K. (1962). Relations of factors derived from parent interviews to ratings of behavior problems of five-year-olds. *Child Development, 33,* 509–535.

Beeson, P., and McDermott, W. (eds.) (1971). *Cecil-Loeb textbook of medicine* (13th ed.). Philadelphia: Saunders.

Beilin, H. (1981). Language and thought. In I. Sigel, D. Brodzinsky, and R. Golinkoff (eds.), *New directions in Piagetian research.* Hillsdale, N.J.: Erlbaum.

Bell, N., Grossen, M., and Perret-Clermont, A.-N. (1985). Sociocognitive conflict and intellectual growth. In M. Berkowitz (ed.), *Peer conflict and psychological growth.* New Directions for Child Development, No. 29. San Francisco: Jossey-Bass.

Bell, R. (1980). *Changing bodies, changing lives, : A book for teens on sex and relationships.* New York: Random House.

Bellah, R., Madsen, R., Sullivan, W., Swidler, A., and Tipton, S. (1985). *Habits of the heart: Individualism and commitment in American life.* Berkeley: University of California Press.

Bellugi, V. (1970). Learning the language. *Psychology Today, 4,* 32–35 ff.

Belsky, J. (1980). Child maltreatment: An ecological integration. *American Psychologist, 35,* 320–335.

Belsky, J., Gilstrap, B., and Rovine, M. (1984). Stability and change in mother-infant and father-infant interaction in a family setting: One-to-three-to-nine months. *Child Development, 55,* 706–717.

Belsky, J., Lerner, R., and Spanier, G. (1984). *The child in the family.* Reading, Mass.: Addison-Wesley.

Belsky, J., and Steinberg, L. (1978). The effects of day care: A critical review. *Child Development, 49,* 920–949.

Bem, S. (1974). The measurement of psychological androgyny. *Journal of Consulting and Clinical Psychology, 42,* 155–162.

Bem, S. (1976). Probing the promise of androgyny. In A. Kaplan and J. Bean (eds.), *Beyond sex-role stereotypes: Readings toward a psychology of androgyny.* Boston: Little, Brown.

Bem, S. (1981). Gender scheme theory: A cognitive account of sex typing. *Psychological Review, 88,* 354–364.

Benawra, R., Mangurten, H., and Duffell, D. (1980). Cyclopia and other anomalies following maternal ingestion of salicylates. *Journal of Pediatrics, 96,* 1069–1071.

Benbow, C., and Stanley, J. (1982). Intellectually talented boys and girls: More facts. *Gifted Child Quarterly, 28,* 82–88.

Bench, J. (1978). The auditory response. In V. Stave (ed.), *Perinatal physiology.* New York: Plenum.

Bench, J., Collyer, Y., Langford, C., and Toms, R. (1976). A comparison between the neonatal sound-evoked startle response and the head-drop (Moro) reflex. *Developmental Medicine and Child Neurology, 14,* 308–317.

Bengston, V., and Troll, L. (1978). Youth and their parents: Feedback and intergenerational influence in socialization. In R. Lerner and G. Spanier (eds.), *Child influences on marital and family interaction.* New York: Academic Press.

Ben-Zeev, S. (1977). The influence of bilingualism on cognitive strategy and cognitive development. *Child Development, 48,* 1009–1018.

Bereiter, C., and Scardamalia, M. (1982). From conversation to composition: The role of instruction in a developmental process. In R. Glaser (ed.), *Advances in instructional psychology* (vol. 2). Hillsdale, N.J.: Erlbaum.

Berezin, N. (1982). *After a loss in pregnancy.* New York: Simon and Schuster.

Berg, K., and Berg, K. (1979). Psychophysiological development in infancy: Stat, sensory function, and attention. In J. Osofsky (ed.), *Handbook of infant development.* New York: Wiley.

Bergman, C. (1976). Interference vs. independent development in infant bilingualism. In G. Kellar, R. Teschnes, and S. Viera (eds.), *Bilingualism in the bicentennial and beyond.* New York: Bilingual Press.

Berk, L. (1985). Why children talk to themselves. *Young Children, 40,* 46–52.

Berko, J. (1958). The child's learning of English morphology. *Word, 14,* 150–177.

Berlinsky, E., and Biller, H. (1982). *Parental death and psychological development.* Lexington, Mass.: Lexington Books.

Berman, P. (1980). Are women more responsive than men to the young? A review of developmental and situational variables. *Psychological Bulletin, 88,* 668–695.

Berndt, T. (1979). Developmental changes in conformity to peers and parents. *Developmental Psychology, 15,* 608–616.

Bernstein, R. (1980). The development of self-esteem during adolescence. *Journal of Genetic Psychology, 136,* 231–245.

Berreuta-Clement, J., Schweinhart, L., Barnett, W. S., Epstein, A., and Weikart, D. (1984). *Changed lives: The effects of the Perry preschool program through age 19.* Ypsilanti, Mich.: High/Scope Press.

Bertenthal, B., and Fischer, K. (1978). The development of self-recognition in the infant. *Developmental Psychology, 14,* 44–50.

Bibace, R., and Walsh, M. E. (1979). Developmental stages in children's conceptions of illness. In G. C. Stone, F. Cohen, and N. E. Adler (eds.), *Health psychology.* San Francisco: Jossey-Bass.

Bibbo, M., Gill, W., and Azizi, F. (1977). Follow-up study of male and female offspring of DES-exposed mothers. *Obstetrics and Gynecology, 49,* 1.

Bigelow, B., and La Gaipa, J. (1975). Children's written descriptions of friendship: A multidimensional analysis. *Developmental Psychology, 4,* 178–181.

Binet, A., and Simon, T. (1905/1916). *The development of intelligence in children.* Baltimore: Williams and Wilkins.

Birch, L. (1976). Age trends in children's time-sharing performance. *Journal of Experimental Child Psychology, 22,* 331–345.

Bizzi, E. (1974). Coordination of eye-head movements. *Scientific American, 231,* 100–106.

Blau, A. S. (1972). Maternal aspirations, socialization, and achievement of boys and girls in the white working class. *Journal of Youth and Adolescence, 1* (1), 35–37.

Blechman, E. (1982). Are children with one parent at psychological risk? A methodological review. *Journal of Marriage and the Family, 44,* 179–195.

Block, J. (1973). Conceptions of sex role: Some cross-cultural and longitudinal perspectives. *American Psychologist, 28,* 516–526.

Block, J. (1978). Another look at sex differentiation in the socialization behaviors of mothers and fathers. *Merrill-Palmer Quarterly, 22,* 285–308.

Block, J. H., Block, J., and Morrison, A. (1981). Parental agreement-disagreement on child-rearing orientations and gender-related personality correlates in children. *Child Development, 52,* 965–974.

Bloom, B. (1985). Generalizations about talent development. In B. Bloom (ed.), *Developing talent in young people.* New York: Ballantine.

Bloom, L., Hood, L., and Lightbown, P. (1974). Imitation in language development: If, when and why. *Cognitive Psychology, 6,* 380–428.

Blum, B. (ed.) (1980). *Psychological aspects of pregnancy, birthing, and bonding.* New York: Wiley.

Bogart, K. (1985). Improving sex equity in postsecondary education. In S. Klein (ed.), *Handbook of achieving sex equity in education.* Baltimore: Johns Hopkins University Press.

Boismier, J. (1977). Visual stimulation and the wake-sleep behavior in human neonates. *Developmental Psychology, 10,* 219–227.

Bonvillian, J., Orlansky, M., and Novack, L. (1983). Developmental milestones: Sign language acquisition and motor development. *Child Development, 54,* 1435–1445.

Borg, S., and Lasker, J. (1981). *When pregnancy fails.* Boston: Beacon Press.

Boston Women's Health Book Collective (1978). *Ourselves and Our Children.* New York: Random House.

Bouchard, T. (1981). The Minnesota study of twins reared apart. Paper presented at the annual meeting of the American Psychological Association, Los Angeles, August.

Bouchard, T., and McGue, M. (1981). Familial studies of intelligence: A review. *Science, 212,* 1055–1059.

Bourne, E. (1978). The state of research on ego identity: A review and appraisal. *Journal of Youth and Adolescence, 7,* 223–251, 371–392.

Bower, T. G. R. (1966). The visual world of infants. *Scientific American, 215,* 80–92.

Bower, T. G. R. (1972). Object perception in infants. *Perception, 1,* 15–30.

Bower, T. G. R. (1977). Comment on Yonas et al., Development of sensitivity to information for impending collision. *Perception and Psychophysics, 21,* 281–282.

Bower, T. G. R. (1977). *The perceptual world of the infant.* Cambridge, Mass.: Harvard University Press.

Bower, T. G. R. (1981). *Development in infancy* (2nd ed.). San Francisco: Freeman.

Bower, T. G. R., Broughton, J., and Moore, M. (1970a). The coordination of vision and touch in infancy. *Perception and Psychophysics, 8,* 51–53.

Bower, T. G. R., Broughton, J., and Moore, M. (1970b). Infant response to approaching objects: An indication of response to distal variables. *Perception and Psychophysics, 9,* 193–196.

Bower, T. G. R., and Paterson, J. (1973). The separation of place, movement, and object in the world of the infant. *Journal of Experimental Child Psychology, 15,* 161–168.

Bowerman, M. (1976). Semantic factors in the acquisition of rules for word use and sentence construction. In D. M. Morehead and A. E. Morehead (eds.), *Normal and deficient child language.* Baltimore: University Park Press.

Bowerman, M. (1982). Starting to talk worse: Clues to language acquisition from children's late speech errors. In S. Strauss and R. Stavey (eds.), *U-shaped behavioral growth.* New York: Academic Press.

Bowlby, J. (1980). *Attachment and loss* (vol. 1–3). New York: Basic Books.

Braham, M. (1965). Peer group deterrents to intellectual development during adolescence. *Educational Theory, 15,* 251–258.

Braine, M. (1976). Children's first word combinations. *Monographs of the Society for Research on Child Development, 41.*

Brainerd, C. (1978). The stage question in cognitive-developmental theory. *The Behavioral and Brain Sciences, 2,* 173–213.

Brandt, I. (1979). Growth dynamics of low-birth-weight infants with emphasis on the perinatal period. In F. Falkner and J. Tanner (eds.), *Human growth* (vol. 2). New York: Plenum.

Bray, G. (1976). The obese patient. In *Major problems in internal medicine* (vol. 9). Philadelphia: Saunders.

Brazelton, T. B. (1973). *The Infant Neonatal Assessment Scale.* Philadelphia: Lippincott.

Brazelton, T. (1974). *Toddlers and parents: A declaration of independence.* New York: Delta.

Brazelton, T. B. (1979). Behavioral competence of the newborn infant. *Seminars in Perinatology, 3,* 35–44.

Brazelton, T. B. (1980). *On becoming a family.* New York: Delacorte.

Brazelton, T. B. (1982). Early parent-infant reciprocity. In V. C. Vaughn and T. B. Brazelton (eds.), *The family: Can it be spared?* Chicago: Yearbook Medical Publishers.

Brazelton, T. (1983). *Infants and mothers: Differences in development* (rev. ed.). New York: Delacorte.

Bremner, J., and Bryant, P. (1977). Place versus response as the basis of spatial errors made by young infants. *Journal of Experimental Child Psychology, 23,* 162–171.

Brenner, D., and Hinsdale, G. (1978). Body build stereotypes and self-identification in three age groups of females. *Adolescence, 13,* 551–561.

Bretherton, I. (1985). Attachment theory: Retrospect and prospect. In I. Bretherton and E. Waters (eds.), *Growing points of attachment theory and research. Monographs of the Society for Research on Child Development, 50,* (1–2, Serial No. 200).

Bretherton, I., McNew, S., and Beeghly-Smith, M. (1981). Early person knowledge as expressed in gestural and verbal communications. In M. Lamb and L. Sherrod (eds.), *Infant social cognition.* Hillsdale, N.J.: Erlbaum.

Bridges, K. (1933). A study of social development in early infancy. *Child Development, 4,* 36–49.

Brierley, J. (1976). *The growing brain.* London: NFER Publishers.

Brody, J. (1982). *Jane Brody's New York Times guide to personal health.* New York: Avon.

Bronfenbrenner, U. (1979a). Contexts of child rearing: Problems and prospects. *American Psychologist, 34,* 844–850.

Bronfenbrenner, U. (1979b). *The ecology of human development.* Cambridge, Mass.: Harvard University Press.

Bronfenbrenner, U., and Crouter, A. (1982). Work and family through time and space. In S. Kamerman and C. Hayes (eds.), *Families that work: Children in a changing world.* Washington, D.C.: National Academy Press.

Brooks, C. (ed.) (1985). *Tapping potential: English and language arts for the black learner.* Urbana, Ill.: National Council of Teachers of English.

Brown, A., Bransford, J., Ferrara, R., and Campione, J. (1983). Learning, remembering, and understanding. In P. Mussen (ed.), *Handbook of child psychology* (vol. 3). New York: Wiley.

Brown, A., Campione, J., and Day, J. (1981). Learning to learn: On training students to learn from texts. *Educational Researcher, 10,* 14–21.

Brown, R. (1973). *A first language: The early stages.* Cambridge, Mass.: Harvard University Press.

Brown, S. (1982). Early childbearing and poverty: Implications for social services. *Adolescence, 17,* 397–408.

Bruch, H. (1979). *The golden cage: The enigma of anorexia nervosa.* New York: Vintage.

Bruner, J. (1978, September). Learning the mother tongue. *Human Nature,* pp. 42–49.

Bruner, J., Oliver, R., and Greenfield, P. (1966). *Studies in cognitive growth.* New York: Wiley.

Bryant, B. (1985). The neighborhood walk: Sources of support in middle childhood. *Monographs of the Society for Research on Child Development, 50* (3, #210).

Buckley, K., and Kulb, N. (eds.) (1983). *Handbook of maternal-newborn nursing.* New York: Wiley.

Burgess, R., and Conger, R. (1978). Family interaction in abusive, neglectful, and normal families. *Child Development, 49,* 1163–1173.

Burtis, P., Bereiter, C., Scardamalia, M., and Tetroe, J. (1983). The development of planning in writing. In G. Wells and B. Kroll (eds.), *Explorations in the development of writing.* New York: Wiley.

Buscaglia, L. (ed.). (1983). *The disabled and their parents* (rev. ed.). New York: Holt, Rinehart, and Winston.

Butler, J., Starfield, B., and Stenmark, S. (1984). Child health policy. In H. Stevenson and A. Siegel (eds.), *Child development research and social policy.* Chicago: University of Chicago Press.

Butler, J., Vudetti, P., McManus, P., Stenmark, S., and Newacheck, P. (1984). Health care expenditures for children with chronic disabilities. In N. Hobbs, H. Ireys, and J. Perrin (eds.), *Public policies affecting chronically ill children and their families.* San Francisco: Jossey-Bass.

Butnarescu, G. F., and Tillotson, D. M. (1983). *Maternity nursing.* New York: Wiley Medical.

Butterworth, G. (1977). Object disappearance and error in Piaget's Stage 4 task. *Journal of Experimental Child Psychology, 23,* 391–401.

Bybee, R. (1979). Violence toward youth: A new perspective. *The Journal of Social Issues, 35,* 1–14.

Cahill, G., and Rossini, A. (1978). Obesity. In G. Faulkner and J. Tanner (eds.), *Human growth* (vol. 2). New York: Plenum.

Calfee, R., and Drum, P. (1986). Research on teaching reading. In M. Wittrock (ed.), *Handbook of research on teaching* (3rd ed.). New York: Macmillan.

Camaras, L. (1980). Children's understanding of facial expressions used during conflict encounters. *Child Development, 51,* 879–885.

Campione, J. (in press). The logic of training studies: Application to reading comprehension interventions. In

H. Madnl, N. Stein, and T. Trabasso (eds.), *Learning from texts.* Hillsdale, N.J.: Erlbaum.

Campos, J., Hiatt, S., Ramsay, D., Henderson, C., and Svejda, M. (1978). The emergence of fear on the visual cliff. In M. Lewis and L. Rosenblum (eds.), *The origins of affect.* New York: Plenum.

Campos, J., and Stenberg, C. (1981). Perception, appraisal, and emotion: The onset of social referencing. In M. Lamb and L. Sherrod (eds.), *Infant social cognition.* Hillsdale, N.J.: Erlbaum.

Canada Safety Council (1983). *Accident fatalities: 1983.* Ottawa: Canada Safety Council.

Card, J. (1978). *Long-term consequences for children born to adolescent parents.* Palo Alto, Calif.: American Institutes of Research.

Carns, D. (1973). Talking about sex: Notes on first coitus and the double standard. *Journal of Marriage and the Family, 35,* 677–688.

Caron, A., Caron, R., and Carlson, V. (1979). Infant perception of the invariant shape of objects varying in slant. *Child Development, 50,* 716–721.

Caron, R., Caron, A., Carlson, V., and Cobb, L. (1979). Perception of shape-at-a-slant in the young infant. *Bulletin of the Psychonomic Society, 1,* 229–243.

Carroll, J., and Rest, J. (1982). Moral development. In B. Wolman (ed.), *Handbook of developmental psychology.* Englewood Cliffs, N.J.: Prentice-Hall.

Case, R. (1978). Intellectual development from birth to adulthood: A neo-Piagetian interpretation. In R. Siegler (ed.), *Children's thinking: What develops?* (1982). Hillsdale, N.J.: Erlbaum.

Case, R. (1980). The underlying mechanism of intellectual development. In J. Kirby and J. Biggs (eds.), *Cognition, development, and instruction.* New York: Academic Press.

Case, R. (1982). *Intellectual development: A systematic reinterpretation.* New York: Academic Press.

Case, R. (1984). The process of stage transition: A neo-Piagetian view. In R. Sternberg (ed.), *Mechanisms of cognitive development.* San Francisco: Freeman.

Cassill, K. (1982). *Twins reared apart.* New York: Atheneum.

Cataldo, C. (1983). *Infant and toddler programs.* Reading, Mass.: Addison-Wesley.

Cater, J. (1980). Correlates of low birth weight. *Child: Care, Health, and Development, 6,* 267–277.

Cattell, R. (1971). *Abilities: Their structure, growth, and action.* Boston: Houghton Mifflin.

Cavior, N., and Dokecki, P. (1973). Physical attractiveness, perceived attitude similarity, and popularity in adolescents. *Developmental Psychology, 9,* 44–54.

Cazden, C., and Leggett, E. (1981). Culturally responsible education: Recommendations for achieving *Lau* remedies. In H. Trueba (ed.), *Culture and the bilingual classroom.* Rowley, Mass.: Newbury House.

Chandler, M., and Boyes, M. (1982). Social-cognitive development. In B. Wolman (ed.), *Handbook of developmental psychology.* Englewood Cliffs, N.J.: Prentice-Hall.

Chang, H., and Trehub, S. (1977). Infants' perception of temporal grouping in auditor patterns. *Child Development, 48,* 1666–1670.

Chapman, A., and Chapman, M. (1980). *Harry Stack Sullivan's concepts of personality development and psychiatric illness.* New York: Brunner/Mazel.

Chavez, C., Ostrea, E., Stryker, J., and Smialek, Z. (1979). Sudden infant death syndrome among infants of drug-dependent mothers. *Journal of Pediatrics, 95,* 407–409.

Chi, M., and Glaser, R. (1980). The measurement of expertise: Analysis of the development of knowledge and skill as a basis for assessing achievement. In E. Baker and E. Quellmalz (eds.), *Educational testing and evaluation.* Beverly Hills: Sage.

Chi, M., Glaser, R., and Rees, E. (1982). Expertise in problem solving. In R. Sternberg (ed.), *Advances in the psychology of human intelligence* (vol. 1). Hillsdale, N.J.: Erlbaum.

Chi, M., and Koeske, R. (1983). Network representations of knowledge base: Exploring a child's knowledge and memory performance of dinosaurs. *Developmental Psychology, 19,* 29–39.

Chilman, C. (1968). Families in development in mid-stage of the family life cycle. *Family Coordinator, 17* (4), 306.

Chilman, C. (1979). *Adolescent sexuality in a changing American society.* Washington, D.C.: U.S. Government Printing Office.

Chilman, C. (1982). Adolescent childbearing in the United States. In T. Field et al. (eds.), *Review of human development.* New York: Wiley.

Chomsky, C. (1969). *The acquisition of syntax in children from five to ten.* Cambridge, Mass.: MIT Press.

Chomsky, N. (1965). *Aspects of a theory of syntax.* Cambridge, Mass.: MIT Press.

Chomsky, N. (1976). *Reflections on language.* New York: Pantheon.

Cicchetti, D., and Rizley, R. (1981). Developmental perspectives on the etiology, intergenerational transmission, and sequelae of child maltreatment. In R. Rizley and D. Cicchetti (eds.), *Developmental perspectives on child maltreatment.* San Francisco: Jossey-Bass.

Claeys, W., and DeBoeck, P. (1976). The influence of

some parental characteristics on children's primary abilities and field independence. *Child Development, 46,* 842–845.

Clark, R. (1977). What is the use of imitation? *Child Language, 3,* 341–358.

Clarke-Stewart, A. (1973). Interactions between mothers and their young children: Characteristics and consequences. *Monographs of the Society for Research on Child Development, 38.*

Clarke-Stewart, A. (1978). The father's impact on the mother and young child. *Child Development, 49,* 466–478.

Clarke-Stewart, A. (1983). *Day care.* Cambridge, Mass.: Harvard University Press.

Clarren, S., and Smith, D. (1978). The fetal alcohol syndrome. *New England Journal of Medicine, 298,* 1063–1067.

Claridge, G., and Margan, G. (1983). Genetics of human nervous system functioning. In J. Fuller and E. Simmel (eds.), *Behavior genetics.* Hillsdale, N.J.: Erlbaum.

Cleveland, D., and Miller, N. (1977). Attitudes and life commitments of older siblings of mentally retarded adults. *Mental Retardation, 15,* 38–41.

Clifford, E. (1971). Body satisfaction in adolescence. *Perceptual and Motor Skills, 33,* 119–125.

Clifton, R. (1978). The relation of infant cardiac responding to behavioral state and motor activity. In A. Collins (ed.), *Minnesota symposium on child psychology* (vol. 2). Hillsdale, N.J.: Erlbaum.

Clifton, R., Morrongiello, B., Kulig, J., and Dowd, J. (1981a). Developmental changes in auditory localization in infancy. In R. Aslin, J. Alberts, and M. Petersen (eds.), *Development of perception: Psychobiological perspectives* (vol. 1). New York: Academic Press.

Clifton, R., Morrongiello, B., Kulig, J., and Dowd, J. (1981b). Newborns' orientation toward sound: Possible implications for cortical development. *Child Development, 53,* 833–838.

Cobb, S., and Kasl, S. (1977). *Termination: The consequences of job loss.* Department of Health, Education and Welfare Publication No. 77–224. Washington, D.C.: U.S. Government Printing Office.

Cohen, B., and Lukinsky, J. (1985). Religious institutions as educators. In M. Fantini and R. Sinclair (eds.), *Education in school and non-school settings.* 84th Yearbook of the National Society for the Study of Education, Part 1. Chicago: University of Chicago Press.

Cohen, J., and Parmalee, A. (1983). Prediction of five-year Stanford Binet scores in preterm infants. *Child Development, 54,* 1242–1253.

Cohen, L., DeLoache, J., and Strauss, M. (1979). Infant visual perception. In J. Osofsky (ed.), *Handbook of infant development.* New York: Wiley.

Cohen, L., and Strauss, M. (1979). Concept acquisition in the human infant. *Developmental Psychology, 50,* 410–424.

Cohen, S. (1982). *Healthy babies, happy kids.* New York: Putnam's.

Coie, J., Dodge, K., and Coppotelli, H. (1982). Dimensions and types of social status: A cross-age perspective. *Developmental Psychology, 18,* 557–570.

Colby, A., Kohlberg, L., Gibbs, J., and Lieberman, M. (1983). A longitudinal study of moral judgment. *Monographs of the Society for Research on Child Development, 48,* (200).

Cole, J., Dodge, K., and Coppotelli, H. (1982). Dimensions and types of social status: A cross-age perspective. *Developmental Psychology, 18,* 557–570.

Coleman, J. (1961). *The adolescent society.* New York: Free Press.

Coleman, J. (ed.) (1978). Current contradictions in adolescent theory. *Journal of Youth and Adolescence, 7,* 1–11.

Coleman, J. (1980). Friendship and the peer group in adolescence. In J. Adelson (ed.), *Handbook of adolescent psychology.* New York: Wiley.

Collins, W., Sobol, B., and Westby, S. (1981). Effects of adult commentary on children's comprehension and inferences about a televised aggressive portrayal. *Child Development, 52,* 158–163.

Condon, W. S., and Sandor, L. (1974). Neonate movement is synchronized with adult speech: Interactional participation and language acquisition. *Science, 183,* 99–101.

Condon-Paolini, D., Johnston, F., Cravioto, J., DeLicardie, E., and Scholl, T. (1977). Morbidity and growth of infants and young children in a rural Mexican village. *American Journal of Public Health, 67,* 651–656.

Conger, J. (1977). *Adolescence and youth: Psychological development in a changing world* (2nd ed.). New York: Harper and Row.

Consortium for Longitudinal Studies. (1983). *As the twig is bent.* Hillsdale, N.J.: Erlbaum.

Constanzo, P. (1970). Conformity development as a function of self-blame. *Journal of Personality and Social Psychology, 14,* 366–374.

Coopersmith, S. (1967). *The antecedents of self-esteem.* San Francisco: Freeman.

Coren, S., Porac, C., and Duncan, P. (1981). Lateral preference behaviors in preschool children and young adults. *Child Development, 52,* 443–450.

Cornell, E., and Gottfried, A. (1976). Intervention with premature human infants. *Child Development, 47,* 32–39.

Corno, L., and Snow, R. (1986). Adapting teaching to individual differences. In M. Wittrock (ed.), *Handbook of research on teaching* (3rd ed.). New York: Macmillan.

Corsaro, W. (1981). Friendship in the nursery school: Social organization in a peer environment. In S. Asher and J. Gottman (eds.), *The development of children's friendships.* Cambridge, England: Cambridge University Press.

Cowan, C., and Cowan, P. (1985). *Parents' work patterns, couple and parent-child relationships.* Paper presented at the biennial meeting of the Society for Research on Child Development, Toronto, April.

Cowan, W. (1979). The development of the brain. *Scientific American, 241,* 112 ff.

Cox, C. (1926). *The early mental traits of 300 geniuses.* Stanford, Calif.: Stanford University Press.

Cratty, B. (1973). *Dynamic visual acuity: A developmental study.* Los Angeles: University of California at Los Angeles, School of Education.

Cratty, B. (1979). *Perceptual and motor development in infants and preschool children* (2nd ed.). Englewood Cliffs, N.J.: Prentice-Hall.

Cravioto, J., and Delicardie, E. (1982). Nutrition, mental development, and learning. In D. Falkner and J. Tanner (eds.), *Physical growth.* New York: Wiley.

Crnic, K., Ragozin, A., Greenberg, M., Robinson, N., and Basham, R. (1983). Social interaction and developmental competence of preterm and full-term infants in the first year of life. *Child Development, 54,* 1199–1210.

Crockenberg, S. (1981). Infant irritability, mother responsiveness, and social support influences on the security of infant-mother attachment. *Child Development, 52,* 857–865.

Crook, C. (1978). Taste perception in the newborn infant. *Infant Behavior and Development, 1,* 52–69.

Crook, C. (1979). The organization and control of infant sucking. *Advances in Child Development and Behavior, 14,* 209–252.

Csikszentmihalyi, M., Larson, R., and Prescott, S. (1977). The ecology of adolescent activity and experience. *Journal of Youth and Adolescence, 6,* 281–294.

Csikszentmihalyi, M., and Larson, R. (1984). *Being adolescent: Conflict and growth during the teenage years.* New York: Basic Books.

Cully, I. (1979). *Christian child development.* San Francisco: Harper and Row.

Cummins, J. (1977). Cognitive factors associated with intermediate levels of bilingual skill. *Modern Language Journal, 61,* 3–12.

Cummins, J. (1978). The cognitive development of children in immersion programs. *Canadian Modern Language Review, 34,* 855–883.

Cunningham, A. (1979). Morbidity in breastfed and artificially fed infants. *Journal of Pediatrics, 95,* 685–689.

Curtis, R. (1975). Adolescent orientations toward parents and peers: Variations by sex, age, and socioeconomic status. *Adolescence, 10,* 483–494.

Dale, P. (1976). *Language development.* New York: Holt, Rinehart, and Winston.

Damon, W. (1977). *The social world of the child.* San Francisco: Jossey-Bass.

Damon, W. (1980). Patterns of change in children's social reasoning: A two-year longitudinal study. *Child Development, 51,* 1010–1017.

Damon, W., and Hart, D. (1982). The development of self-understanding from infancy through adolescence. *Child Development, 53,* 831–857.

Darvill, D., and Cheyne, J. (1981). *Sequential analysis of responses to aggression.* Paper presented at the meeting of the Society for Research on Child Development, Boston.

Darwin, C. (1877). A biographical sketch of an infant. *Mind, 2,* 286–294.

Day, R. H., and McKenzie, B. E. (1977). Constancies in the perceptual world of the infant. In W. Epstein (ed.), *Stability and constancy in visual perception.* New York: Wiley.

DeCastro, F., Rolfe, U., and Heppe, M. (1978). Child abuse: An operational longitudinal study. *Child Abuse and Neglect: The International Journal, 2,* 51–55.

Delia, J., and Clark, R. (1977). Cognitive complexity, social perception, and the development of listener-adapted communication in six-, eight-, ten-, and twelve-year-old boys. *Communication Monographs, 44,* 326–345.

Delora, J. (1963). Social systems of dating on a college campus. *Marriage and Family Living, 25,* 81–84.

Dement, W. (1976). *Some must watch while others must sleep.* New York: Norton.

Denny, F., and Clyde, W. (1983). Acute respiratory tract infections: An overview. *Pediatric Research, 17,* 1026–1029.

DeOreo, K. (1974). The performance and development of fundamental motor skills in preschool children. In M. Wade and R. Martens (eds.), *Psychology of motor behavior and sport.* Urbana, Ill.: Human Kinetics Press.

Derlega, J., and Chaiken, A. (1977). *Privacy and self-disclosure in social relationships.* Paper presented to the American Psychological Association, San Francisco.

DeVilliers, J. (1980). The process of rule learning in child speech. In K. Nelson (ed.), *Children's language* (vol. 2). New York: Gardner Press.

DeVilliers, J., and DeVilliers, P. (1977). *Early language.* Cambridge, Mass.: Harvard University Press.

DeVilliers, P., and DeVilliers, J. (1978). *Language development.* Cambridge, Mass.: Harvard University Press.

DeVries, D., and Slavin, R. (1978). Teams-games-tournaments: Review of ten classroom experiments. *Journal of Research and Development in Education, 12,* 28–38.

Diaz, R. (1983). Thought and two languages: The impact of bilingualism on cognitive development. In E. Gordon (ed.), *Review of research in education* (vol. 10). Washington, D.C.: American Educational Research Association.

Diederen, I. (1983). Genetics of schizophrenia. In J. Fuller and E. Simmel (eds.), *Behavior genetics.* Hillsdale, N.J.: Erlbaum.

Diers, D. (1981). Nurse-midwifery as a system of care. In L. Aiken (ed.), *Health policy and nursing practice.* New York: McGraw-Hill.

DiPietro, J. (1981). Rough-and-tumble play: A function of gender. *Developmental Psychology, 17,* 50–58.

DiSimoni, F. (1975). Perceptual and perceptual-motor characteristics of phonemic development. *Child Development, 46,* 243–246.

DiStefano, V. (1982). Athletic injuries. In R. Magill, M. Ash, and F. Smoll (eds.), *Children in sport.* Champaign, Ill.: Human Kinetics Publishers.

Dodd, B. (1972). Effects of social and vocal stimulation of infant babbling. *Developmental Psychology, 7,* 80–83.

Donaldson, M. (1978). *Children's minds.* New York: Norton.

Donaldson, M. (1979). The mismatch between school and children's minds. *Human Nature, 2,* 60–67.

Dorval, B., and Eckerman, C. (1984). Developmental trends in the quality of conversation achieved by small groups of acquainted peers. *Monographs of the Society for Research in Child Development, 49* (206).

Dorval, B., and Smith, P. (1984). Developmental trends in descriptions of videotaped conversation. Paper presented at the annual meeting of the American Psychological Association, Toronto, Canada, August.

Douglas, V., and Peters, K. (1979). Toward a clearer definition of the attentional deficit of hyperactive children. In G. Hale and M. Lewis (eds.), *Attention and cognitive development.* New York: Plenum.

Douvan, E., and Adelson, J. (1966). *The adolescent experience.* New York: Wiley.

Douvan, E., and Gold, H. (1966). Modal patterns in American adolescence. In M. L. Hoffman and L. W. Hoffman (eds.), *Review of developmental research* (vol. 2). New York: Russell Sage.

Dreyer, P. (1982). Sexuality during adolescence. In B. Wolman (ed.), *Handbook of developmental psychology.* Englewood Cliffs, N.J.: Prentice-Hall.

Dubnowitz, L., Dubnowitz, V., and Goldberg, C. (1970). Clinical assessment of gestational age in the newborn infant. *Journal of Pediatrics, 77,* 1–10.

Dubois, S., Hill, D., and Beaton, G. (1979). An examination of factors believed to be associated with infantile obesity. *American Journal of Clinical Nutrition, 32,* 1997–2004.

Duncan, S., and DeAvila, E. (1979). Bilingualism and cognition: Some recent findings. *NABE Journal, 4,* 15–50.

Dunn, J. (1983). Sibling relationships in early childhood. *Child Development, 54,* 787–811.

Dunn, J. (1985). *Sisters and brothers.* Cambridge, Mass.: Harvard University Press.

Dunn, L., and Dunn, L. (1981). *Peabody picture vocabulary test* (rev. ed.). Circle Pines, Minn.: American Guidance Services.

Dunphy, D. C. (1963). The social structure of urban adolescent peer groups. *Sociometry, 26,* 230–246.

Dweck, C., and Elliott, E. (1983). Achievement motivation. In P. Mussen (ed.), *Handbook of child psychology* (vol. 4). New York: Wiley.

Dweck, C., and Wortman, C. (1982). Learned helplessness, anxiety, and achievement motivation: Neglected parallels in cognitive, affective, and coping responses. In H. Krohne and L. Laux (eds.), *Achievement, stress, and anxiety.* Washington, D.C.: Hemisphere.

Eaves, L., and Eysenck, H. J. (1976). A genotype-environment model for psychoticism. *Advances in Behavioral Research Therapy, 1,* 5–26.

Edelsky, C. (1977). Acquisition of an aspect of communicative competence: Learning what it means to talk like a lady. In S. Ervin-Tripp and C. Mitchell-Kernan (eds.), *Child discourse.* New York: Academic Press.

Eder, D., and Hallinan, M. (1978). Sex differences in children's friendships. *American Sociological Review, 43,* 237–250.

Edwards, C., and Lewis, M. (1979). Young children's concepts of social relations. In M. Lewis and L. Rosenblum (eds.), *The child and its family: Genesis of behavior* (vol. 2). New York: Plenum.

Edwards, L., Alton, I., Barrada, M., and Hakanson, E. (1979). Pregnancy in the underweight woman: Course, outcome, and growth patterns of the infant. *American Journal of Obstetrics and Gynecology, 135,* 297–302.

Eichorn, D. (1979). Physical development: Current foci of research. In J. Osofsky (ed.), *Handbook of infant development.* New York: Wiley.

Eifermann, R. (1971). Social play in childhood. In R. Herron and B. Sutton-Smith (eds.), *Child's play.* New York: Wiley.

Eimas, P., and Miller, J. (1980). Discrimination of information for manner of articulation. *Infant Behavior and Development, 3,* 367–375.

Eimas, P., and Miller, J. (1981). Organization in the perception of segmental and suprasegmental information by infants. *Infant Behavior and Development, 4,* 395–399.

Eisenberg, A., and Garvey, C. (1981). Children's use of verbal strategies in resolving conflicts. *Discourse Processes, 4,* 161–180.

Eisenberg, R. (1976). *Auditory competence in early life: The roots of communicative behavior.* Baltimore: University Park Press.

Eisenberg-Berg, N. (1979). Development of children's prosocial moral judgment. *Developmental Psychology, 15,* 128–137.

Eisenberg-Berg, N., and Neal, C. (1979). Children's moral reasoning about their own spontaneous prosocial behavior. *Developmental Psychology, 15,* 228–229.

Eisenberg-Berg, N., and Roth, K. (1980). The development of young children's prosocial moral judgment: A longitudinal follow-up. *Developmental Psychology, 16,* 375–376.

Eitzen, D. (1975). Athletics in the status system of male adolescents. *Adolescence, 10,* 267–276.

Elbers, L. (1982). Operating principles in repetitive babbling: A cognitive continuity approach. *Cognition, 12,* 45–63.

Elder, G. (1978). Approaches to social change and the family. *American Journal of Sociology, 84,* 1–38.

Elder, G., Jr. (1980). Adolescence in historical perspective. In J. Adelson (ed.), *Handbook of adolescent psychology.* New York: Wiley.

Elder, G. (1981). History and life course. In D. Bertaux (ed.), *Biography and society: The life history approach in the social sciences.* Beverly Hills, Calif.: Sage.

Elkind, D. (1976). *Child development and education.* New York: Oxford University Press.

Elkind, D. (1978). *Children and adolescents: Interpretative essays on Jean Piaget* (3rd ed.). New York: Oxford University Press.

Elkind, D. (1979). The study of spontaneous religion in the child. In D. Elkind, *The child and society.* New York: Oxford University Press.

Elkind, D. (1980a). Egocentrism in children and adolescents. In D. Elkind (ed.), *Childhood and adolescents: Interpretive essays on Jean Piaget* (3rd ed.). New York: Oxford University Press.

Elkind, D. (1980b). Strategic interactions. In J. Adelson (ed.), *Handbook of adolescent psychology.* New York: Wiley.

Elkind, D. (1983). *The hurried child.* New York: Oxford University Press.

Elkind, D. (1984). *All grown up and no place to go: Teenager in crisis.* Reading, Mass.: Addison-Wesley.

Elkind, D., and Bowen, R. (1979). Imaginary audience behavior in children and adolescence. *Developmental Psychology, 15,* 38–44.

Elkind, D., and Weiner, I. (1978). *Development of the child.* New York: Wiley.

Elliot, D., Voss, H., and Aubarey, W. (1966). Capable dropouts and the social milieu of the high school. *Journal of Educational Research, 60,* 180–186.

Ellis, S., Rogoff, B., and Cromer, C. (1981). Age segregation in children's social interactions. *Developmental Psychology, 17,* 399–407.

Elms, A. (1981). Skinner's dark year and Walden Two. *American Psychologist, 36,* 470–479.

Emde, R., Gaensbauer, T., and Harmon, R. (1976). Emotional expression in infancy: A biobehavioral study. *Psychological Issues Monograph Series, 10,* 37.

Emde, R., and Robinson, J. (1979). The first two months: Recent research in developmental psychobiology and the changing view of the newborn. In J. Noshpiz and J. Call (eds.), *Basic handbook of child psychiatry.* New York: Basic Books.

Emery, R. (1982). Interparental conflict and the children of discord and divorce. *Psychological Bulletin, 92,* 310–330.

Emery, R., Hetherington, M., and DiLalla, L. (1984). Divorce, children, and social policy. In H. Stevenson and A. Siegel (eds.), *Child development research and social policy.* Chicago: University of Chicago Press.

Emmerich, W., and Sheppard, K. (1982). Development of sex-differentiated preferences during late childhood and adolescence. *Developmental Psychology, 18,* 406–417.

Empey, L. (1975). Delinquency theory and recent research. In R. E. Grinder (ed.), *Studies in adolescence.* New York: Macmillan.

Engelmann, S. (1980). *DISTAR* (3rd ed.). Chicago: Science Research Associates.

Erikson, E. (1963). *Childhood and society* (2nd ed.). New York: Norton.

Erikson, E. (1968). *Identity: Youth and crisis.* New York: W.W. Norton.

Erikson, E. (1975). 'Identity Crisis' in autobiographic perspective. In E. Erikson, *Life history and the historical moment.* New York: Norton.

Erikson, E. (1982). *The life cycle completed: A review.* New York: Norton.

Erikson, E., and Erikson, K. (1957). The confirmation of the delinquent. *Chicago Review, 10,* 15–23.

Erikson, F. (1986). Qualitative methods in research on teaching. In M. Wittrock (ed.), *Handbook of research on teaching* (3rd ed.). New York: Macmillan.

Erikson, F., and Mohatt, G. (1982). The cultural organization of participation structures in two classrooms of Indian students. In G. Spindler (ed.), *Doing the ethnography of schooling.* New York: Holt, Rinehart, and Winston.

Espenschade, A., and Eckert, H. (1980). *Motor development* (2nd ed.). Columbus, Ohio: Merrill.

Etaugh, C. (1974). Effects of maternal employment on children: A review of recent research. *Merrill-Palmer Quarterly, 20,* 71–98.

Evans, D., Newcombe, R., and Campbell, H. (1979). Maternal smoking habits and congenital malformations: A population study. *British Medical Journal, 2,* 171–173.

Eveleth, P. (1979). Population differences in growth: Environmental and genetic factors. In F. Falkner and J. Tanner (eds.), *Human growth* (vol. 2). New York: Plenum.

Eveleth, P., and Tanner, J. (1976). *Worldwide variation in human growth.* Cambridge, England: Cambridge University Press.

Eysenck, H. (1979). *The structure and measurement of intelligence.* New York: Springer-Verlag.

Fafouti-Milenkovic, M., and Uzgiris, I. (1979). The mother-infant communication system. In I. Uzgiris (ed.), *Social interaction and communication during infancy.* San Francisco: Jossey-Bass.

Fagan, J. (1973). Infants' delayed recognition memory and forgetting. *Journal of Experimental Child Psychology, 16,* 425–450.

Fagan, J. (1977). Infant recognition memory: Studies in forgetting. *Child Development, 48,* 68–78.

Fagot, B. (1977). Consequences of moderate cross-gender behavior in preschool children. *Child Development, 48,* 902–907.

Fagot, B. (1982). Adults as socializing agents. In T. Field, A. Huston, H. Quay, L. Troll, and G. Finley (eds.), *Review of human development.* New York: Wiley.

Fagot, B., and Kronsberg, S. (1982). Sex differences: Biological and social factors influencing the behavior of young boys and girls. In S. Moore and C. Cooper (eds.),

The young child: Reviews of research (vol. 3). Washington, D.C.: National Association for the Education of Young Children.

Falek, A. (1975). Ethical issues in human behavior genetics. In K. W. Schaie, V. E. Anderson, G. McClearn, and J. Money (eds.), *Developmental human behavior genetics.* Lexington, Mass.: Heath.

Fantz, R. (1963). Pattern vision in newborn infants. *Science, 140,* 296–297.

Farber, S. (1981). The telltale behavior of twins. *Psychology Today, 15* (1), 58–62 ff.

Farnham-Diggory, S. (1977). The cognitive point of view. In D. J. Treffinger, J. Davis, and R. E. Ripple (eds.), *Handbook on teaching educational psychology.* New York: Academic Press.

Farnham-Diggory, S. (1978). *Learning disabilities.* Cambridge, Mass.: Harvard University Press.

Farnham-Diggory, S., and Gregg, L. (1975). Color, form and function as dimensions of natural classification. *Child Development, 46,* 101–114.

Fein, G. (1981a). The physical environment: Stimulation or evocation? In R. Lerner and N. Busch (eds.), *Individuals as producers of their development* (vol. 1). New York: Academic Press.

Fein, G. (1981b). Pretend play: An integrative view. *Child Development, 52,* 1095–1118.

Fein, G., Schwartz, P., Jacobson, S., and Jacobson, J. (1983). Environmental toxins and behavioral development: A new role for psychological research. *American Psychologist, 38* (11), 1188–1197.

Feingold, B. (1974). *Why your child is hyperactive.* New York: Random House.

Feiring, C., and Lewis, M. (1980). Temperament: Sex differences and stability in vigor, activity, and persistence in the first three years of life. *Journal of Genetic Psychology, 136,* 65–75.

Feld, S., Ruhland, D., and Gold, M. (1979). Developmental changes in achievement motivation. *Merrill-Palmer Quarterly, 25,* 43–60.

Feldman, D. (1980). *Beyond universals in cognitive development.* Norwood, N.J.: Ablex.

Field, T. (1978). Interaction behaviors of primary versus secondary caretaker fathers. *Developmental Psychology, 14,* 183–185.

Field, T. (1979). Visual and cardiac responses to animate and inanimate faces by young term and preterm infants. *Child Development, 83,* 353–375.

Field, T. (1980). Interactions of high risk infants: Quantitative and qualitative differences. In D. Sawin, R. Hawkins, L. Walker, and J. Penticuff (eds.), *Exceptional infants.* Vol. 4: Psychosocial risks in infant environmental transactions. New York: Brunner/Mazel.

Field, T., Muir, D., Pilon, R., Sinclair, M., and Dodwell, P. (1980). Infants' orientation to lateral sounds from birth to three months. *Child Development, 50,* 295–298.

Field, T., and Roopnarine, J. (1982). Infant-peer interactions. In T. Field (ed.), *Review of human development.* New York: Wiley.

Fincher, J. (1977). *Sinister people: The looking-glass world of left-handed people.* New York: Putnam.

Fincher, J. (1982). Before their time. *Science, 82,* 68–78.

Fine, G. (1982). Friends, impression management, and preadolescent behavior. In S. Asher and J. Gottman (eds.), *The development of children's friendships.* New York: Cambridge University Press.

Finkelhor, D. (1979). *Sexually victimized children.* New York: Free Press.

Finkelhor, D. (1984). *Child sexual abuse: New theory and practice.* New York: Free Press.

Finkelhor, D., and Browne, A. (1985). The traumatic impact of child sexual abuse: A conceptualization. *American Journal of Orthopsychiatry, 55,* 530–541.

Fischer, K. W. (1980). A theory of cognitive development: Control of hierarchies of skill. *Psychological Review, 87,* 477–531.

Fitzsimmons, S., Cheever, J., Leonard, E., and Macunovica, D. (1969). School failures: Now and tomorrow. *Developmental Psychology, 1,* 134–146.

Flavell, J. (1977). *Cognitive development.* Englewood Cliffs, N.J.: Prentice-Hall.

Flavell, J. (1978). Metacognitive development. In J. Scandura and C. Brainerd (eds.), *Structural/process theories of complex human behavior.* The Hague: Sijthoff and Noordoff.

Flavell, J., Speer, J., Green, F., and August, D. (1981). The development of comprehension monitoring and knowledge about communication. *Monographs of the Society for Research on Child Development, 46* (5).

Flavell, J., and Wellman, H. (1977). Metamemory. In R. Kail, and J. Hagen (eds.), *Perspectives on the development of memory and cognition.* Hillsdale, N.J.: Erlbaum.

Flower, L., and Hayes, J. (1981). The pregnant pause: An inquiry into the nature of planning. *Research in the Teaching of English, 15,* 229–244.

Foot, H., Chapman, J., and Smith, J. (eds.) (1980). *Friendship and social relations in children.* New York: Wiley.

Forbes, D., and Yablick, G. (1984). The organization of dramatic content in children's fantasy play. In F. Kessel and A. Goncu (eds.), *Analyzing children's play dialogues.* New Directions in Child Development, No. 25. San Francisco: Jossey-Bass.

Forer, L. (1976). *The birth order factor.* New York: Mckay.

Forrest, D., and Waller, T. (1979). *Cognitive and meta-cognitive aspects of reading.* Paper presented at the biennial meeting of the Society for Research on Child Development, San Francisco.

Forrest, J., Tietze, C., and Sullivan, E. (1978). Abortion in the United States, 1966–1977. *Family Planning Perspectives, 10,* 271–280.

Foulkes, D. (1982). *Children's dreams: Longitudinal studies.* New York: Wiley.

Fowler, J. (1981). *Stages of faith: The psychology of human development and the quest for meaning.* San Francisco: Harper and Row.

Fowler, W. (1985). *Infant and child care* (2nd ed.). Reading, Mass.: Addison-Wesley.

Fowler, W., and Swenson, A. (1979). Influence of early language stimulation on development. *Genetic Psychology Monographs, 100,* 73–109.

Fox, H., Steinbrecher, M., Pessel, D., Inglis, J., Medvid, L., and Angel, E. (1978). Maternal ethanol ingestion and the occurrence of human fetal breathing movements. *American Journal of Obstetrics and Gynecology, 132,* 354–358.

Franciosi, R. (1983). Perspectives on sudden infant death syndrome. In J. Schowalter (ed.), *The child and death.* New York: Columbia University Press.

Frank, R., and Cohen, D. (1979). Psychosocial concomitants of biological maturation in preadolescence. *American Journal of Psychiatry, 136,* 1518–1524.

Frankenburg, W., and Dodds, J. (1967). The Denver Developmental Screening Test. *Journal of Pediatrics, 71,* 181–191.

Frederiksen, N. (1986). Toward a broader conception of human intelligence. *American Psychologist, 41,* 445–452.

Freedman, D. (1976). Infancy, biology, and culture. In L. Lipsitt (ed.), *Developmental psychobiology: The significance of infancy.* New York: Wiley.

Freeman, N. (1980). *Strategies of representation in young children.* London: Academic Press.

French, M. (1983). Stepping stones. In L. Buscaglia (ed.), *The disabled and their parents* (rev. ed.). New York: Holt, Rinehart, and Winston.

Freud, A. (1937). *The ego and the mechanisms of defense.* New York: International Universities Press.

Freud, A. (1946). *The ego and the mechanisms of defense.* New York: International Universities Press.

Freud, A. (1958). Adolescence. In R. S. Eissler, A. Freud, M. Kris, and H. Hartmann (eds.), *Psychoanalytic study of the child* (vol. 13). New York: International Universities Press.

Freud, S. (1938). The transformations of puberty. In A. A. Brill (ed. and trans.), *The basic writings of Sigmund Freud*. New York: Random House.

Freud, S. (1953). Three essays on sexuality. In J. Strachey (ed. and trans.), *The standard edition of the complete works of Sigmund Freud* (vol. 7). London: Hogarth.

Freud, S. (1955). *Beyond the pleasure principle*. In J. Strachey (ed. and trans.), *The standard edition of the complete works of Sigmund Freud* (vol. 18). London: Hogarth.

Freud, S. (1965). *New introductory lectures in psychoanalysis*. New York: Norton.

Freud, S. (1983). *A general introduction to psychoanalysis*. (rev. ed.) New York: Washington Square Press.

Frieze, I., Francis, W., and Hanusa, B. (1981). Defining success in classroom settings. In J. Levine and M. Wang (eds.), *Teacher and student perceptions*. Hillsdale, N.J.: Erlbaum.

Frisancho, A., Cole, P., and Klayman, J. (1977). Greater contribution to secular trend among offspring of short parents. *Human Biology, 49,* 51–60.

Frostig, M., Lefever, W., and Whittesley, J. (1966). *Administration and scoring of the developmental test of visual perception*. Palo Alto, Calif.: Consulting Psychologists Press.

Fucigna, C., and Wolf, D. (1981). *The earliest two-dimensional symbols: The onset of graphic representation*. Unpublished manuscript.

Furman, W. (1982). Children's friendships. In T. Field (ed.), *Review of human development*. New York: Wiley.

Furman, W., and Bierman, K. (1983). Developmental changes in young children's conceptions of friendship. *Child Development, 54,* 549–556.

Furrow, D., Nelson, K., and Benedict, H. (1979). Mothers' speech to children and syntactic development. *Journal of Child Language, 6,* 423–442.

Furstenberg, F. (1976). *Unplanned parenthood: The social consequences of teenage childbearing*. New York: Free Press.

Furstenberg, F., Spanier, G., and Rothschild, N. (1982). Patterns of parenting in the transition from divorce to remarriage. In P. Berman and E. Ramey (eds.), *Women: A developmental perspective*. Washington, D.C.: National Institutes of Health.

Furth, H. (1973). *Deafness and learning*. Boston: Little, Brown.

Gal, S. (1979). *Language shift*. New York: Academic Press.

Gallagher, J., and Gallagher, R. (1985). Family adaptation to a handicapped child and assorted professionals. In A. Turnbull and H. Turnbull (eds.), *Parents speak out: Then and now*. Columbus, Ohio: Merrill.

Gallatin, J. (1980). Political thinking in adolescence. In J. Adelson (ed.), *Handbook of adolescent development*. New York: Wiley.

Garbarino, J., and Sherman, D. (1980). High-risk neighborhoods and high-risk families: The human ecology of child maltreatment. *Child Development, 51,* 188–198.

Gardner, E. (1983). *Human genetics*. New York: Wiley.

Gardner, H. (1980). *Artful scribbles: The significance of children's drawings*. New York: Basic Books.

Gardner, H. (1983). *Frames of mind: The theory of multiple intelligences*. New York: Basic Books.

Garvey, C. (1977). *Play*. Cambridge, Mass.: Harvard University Press.

Garvey, C. (1984). *Children's talk*. Cambridge, Mass.: Harvard University Press.

Gazzaniga, M., and LeDoux, J. (1978). *The integrated mind*. New York: Plenum.

Gelfand, D., and Hartmann, D. (1982). Some detrimental effects of competitive sports on children's behavior. In R. Magill, M. Ash, and F. Smoll (eds.), *Children in sport*. Champaign, Ill.: Human Kinetics Publishers.

Gelles, R. (1978). Violence toward children in the United States. *American Journal of Orthopsychiatry, 48,* 580–592.

Gelles, R., and Straus, M. (1979). Determinants of violence in the family: Toward a theoretical integration. In W. Burr, R. Hill, F. Nye, and I. Reiss (eds.), *Contemporary theories about the family*. New York: Free Press.

Gelman, R. (1969). Conservation acquisition: A problem of learning to attend to relevant attributes. *Journal of Experimental Child Psychology, 7,* 176–187.

Gelman, R. (1978). Cognitive development. *Annual Review of Psychology, 29,* 297–332.

Gelman, R., and Shatz, M. (1977). Appropriate speech adjustments: The operation of conversational constraints on talk to two-year-olds. In M. Lewis and L. Rosenblum (eds.), *Interaction, conversation, and the development of language*. New York: Wiley.

George, C., and Main, M. (1979). Social interactions of young abused children: Approach, avoidance, and aggression. *Child Development, 50,* 306–318.

Geschwind, P. (1985). *Selected papers on language and the brain*. New York: Reidel.

Gesell, A. (1926). *The mental growth of the preschool child* (2nd ed.). New York: Macmillan.

Gesell, A. (1943). *Infant and child in the culture of today*. New York: Harper.

Gesell, A., Ames, L., and Ilg, F. (1977). *The child from five to ten*, (rev. ed.). New York: Harper and Row.

Gesell, A., and Thompson, H. (1929). Learning and growth in identical infant twins. *Genetic Psychology Monographs, 6,* 1–125.

Gibson, E. (1969). *Principles of perceptual learning and development.* New York: Appleton-Century-Crofts.

Gibson, E., and Walk, R. (1960). The visual cliff. *Scientific American, 202,* 64–71.

Gibson, J., and Yonas, P. (1968). A new theory of scribbling and drawing in children. In H. Levin, E. Gibson, and J. Gibson (eds.), *The analysis of reading skill.* Washington, D.C.: U.S. Office of Education.

Gil, D. (1973). *Violence against children.* Cambridge, Mass.: Harvard University Press.

Gilbert, E., and DeBlassie, R. (1984). Anorexia nervosa: Adolescent starvation by choice. *Adolescence, 19,* 839–846.

Giles, H., Bourhis, R., and Taylor, D. (1977). Towards a theory of language in ethnic group relations. In H. Giles (ed.), *Language, ethnicity, and intergroup relations.* New York: Academic Press.

Gilligan, C. (1982). *In a different voice: Psychological theory and women's development.* Cambridge, Mass.: Harvard University Press.

Gilligan, C., and Murphy, J. (1979). Development from adolescence to adulthood: The philosopher and the dilemma of the fact. *New Directions for Child Development, 5,* 85–99.

Glick, P. (1979). Children of divorced parents in demographic perspective. *Journal of Social Issues, 35,* (4), 170–182.

Glover, J., and Gary, A. (1976). Procedures to increase some aspects of creativity. *Journal of Applied Behavioral Analysis, 9,* 79–84.

Gold, D., and Andres, D. (1978). Developmental comparisons between ten-year-old children with employed and non-employed mothers. *Child Development, 49,* 75–84.

Gold, D., and Andres, D. (1979). Relations between maternal employment and development of nursery school children. *Canadian Journal of Behavioral Science, 11,* 169–173.

Gold, M., and Petronio, R. J. (1980). Delinquent behavior in adolescence. In J. Adelson (ed.), *Handbook of adolescent psychology.* New York: Wiley.

Goldman, A., and Goldblum, R. (1982). Anti-infective properties of human milk. *Pediatric Update, 2,* 359–363.

Goldsmith, H., Bradshaw, D., and Riesser-Danner, L. (1986). Temperament as a potential developmental influence on attachment. In J. Lerner and R. Lerner (eds.), *Temperament and social interaction in infants and children.* New Directions for Child Development, No. 31. San Francisco: Jossey-Bass.

Goldsmith, H. H., and Campos, J. (1982). Toward a theory of infant temperament. In R. Emde and R. Harmon (eds.), *The development of attachment and affiliative systems.* New York: Plenum.

Goleman, D. (1980). Leaving home: Is there a right time to go? *Psychology Today, 14,* 52–61.

Gollin, E. (1981). Development and plasticity. In E. Gollin, *Developmental plasticity: Behavioral and biological aspects of variations in development.* New York: Academic Press.

Golomb, C. (1981). Representation and reality: The origins and determinants of young children's drawings. *Review of Research in Visual Arts Education, 14,* 36–48.

Good, T. (1981). Teacher expectations and student perceptions: A decade of research. *Educational Leadership, 38,* 415–422.

Goode, W. (1975). *World revolution and family patterns.* New York: Free Press.

Goodenough, F. (1931). *Anger in young children.* Minneapolis: University of Minnesota Press.

Goodnow, J. (1977). *Children's drawing.* Cambridge, Mass.: Harvard University Press.

Gordon, I., Guinagh, B., and Jestor, E. (1977). The Florida infant and toddler programs. In M. Day (ed.), *The preschool in action.* Boston: Allyn and Bacon.

Gottesman, I. (1978). Schizophrenia and genetics. In L. Wynne (ed.), *The nature of schizophrenia.* New York: Wiley.

Gottfredson, L. (1985). *Some misconceptions about the link between education and work.* Paper presented at the annual meeting of the American Educational Research Association, Chicago, April.

Gottfried, A., Wallace-Lande, P., Sherman-Brown, S., King, J., and Coen, C. (1981). Physical and social environment of newborn infants in special care units. *Science, 214,* 673–675.

Gottlieb, J., Semmel, M., and Veldman, D. (1978). Correlates of social status among mainstreamed mentally retarded children. *Journal of Educational Psychology, 70,* 396–405.

Gottman, J., and Parkhurst, J. (1980). A developmental theory of friendship and acquaintanceship. In A. Collins (ed.), *Minnesota symposia on child psychology* (vol. 13). Hillsdale, N.J.: Erlbaum.

Grant, J. (1982). *The state of the world's children.* New York: Oxford University Press.

Grant, W. V., and Snyder, T. (1984). *Digest of educational statistics, 1983–84.* Washington: National Center for Educational Statistics.

Gratch, G. (1977). Review of Piagetian infancy research: Object concept development. In W. Overton and J. Gallagher (eds.), *Knowledge and development.* New York: Plenum.

Gray, S., Ramsey, B., and Klaus, R. (1983). The early training project: 1962–1980. In Consortium for Longitudinal Studies, *As the twig is bent.* Hillsdale, N.J.: Erlbaum.

Greenberg, S. (1984). Early education for educational equity. In S. Klein (ed.), *Handbook of educational equity.* Baltimore: Johns Hopkins University Press.

Greenberg, S. (1985). Educational equity in early education environments. In S. Klein (ed.), *Handbook for achieving sex equity through education.* Baltimore: Johns Hopkins University Press.

Greenfield, P. (1982). The role of perceived variability in the transition to language. *Journal of Child Language, 9,* 1–12.

Greenfield, P. (1984). *Mind and media: The effects of television, video games, and computers.* Cambridge, Mass.: Harvard University Press.

Greenfield, P., Geber, B., Beagles-Roos, J., Farrar, D., and Gat, I. (1981). *Television and radio experimentally compared: Effects of the medium on imagination and transmission of content.* Paper presented at the biennial meeting of the Society for Research in Child Development, Boston, April.

Greenfield, P., and Tronick, E. (1980). *Infant curriculum.* Palo Alto: Goodyear.

Greenwood, S. G. (1979). Warning: Cigarette smoking is dangerous to reproductive health. *Family Planning Perspectives, 11,* 196.

Greulich, W. (1976). Some secular changes in the growth of American-born and native-born Japanese children. *American Journal of Physical Anthropology, 45,* 553–558.

Grieve, R. (1981). Observations on communication problems in normal children. In W. Fraser (ed.), *Communicating with normal and retarded children.* Bristol, England: Wright.

Grinder, R. (1966). Relations of social dating attractions to academic orientation and peer relations. *Journal of Educational Psychology, 57,* 27–34.

Grosjean, F. (1982). *Living with two languages.* Cambridge, Mass.: Harvard University Press.

Gross, L. (ed.) (1981). *The parents' guide to teenagers.* New York: Macmillan.

Grossman, K., Grossman, K., Spangler, G., Suess, G., and Unzner, L. (1985). Maternal sensitivity and newborns' orientation responses as related to quality of attachment in northern Germany. In I. Bretherton and E. Waters (eds.), Growing points of attachment theory and research. *Monographs of the Society for Research on Child Development, 50,* 209.

Grotevant, H., and Thorbecke, W. (1982). Sex differences in styles of occupational identity formation in late adolescence. *Developmental Psychology, 18* (3), 396–405.

Gruber, H. (1985). Giftedness and moral responsibility. In F. Horowitz and M. O'Brien (eds.), *The gifted and talented: Developmental perspectives.* Washington, D.C.: American Psychological Association.

Grusec, J., and Kuczynski, L. (1980). Direction of effect in socialization: A comparison of the parent's versus the child's behavior as determinants of disciplinary technique. *Developmental Psychology, 16,* 1–9.

Guardo, C., and Bohan, J. (1971). Development of a sense of self-identity in children. *Child Development, 42,* 1909–1921.

Guilford, J. (1967). *The nature of human intelligence.* New York: McGraw-Hill.

Guralnik, M. (1981). The efficacy of integrating handicapped children in early education settings: Research implications. *Journal of Early Childhood Special Education, 1,* 57–81.

Guthrie, L., and Hall, W. (1983). Continuity/discontinuity in the function and use of language. In E. Gordon (ed.), *Review of research in education* (vol. 10). Washington, D.C.: American Educational Research Association.

Guttmacher, A., and Kaiser, I. (1984). *Pregnancy, birth, and family planning.* New York: Signet.

Haan, N., Smith, B., and Block, J. (1968). Moral reasoning of young adults. *Journal of Personality and Social Psychology, 10,* 183–201.

Hagen, M., and Jones, R. (1978). Cultural effects on pictorial perception: How many words is one picture really worth? In R. Walk and H. Pick (eds.), *Perception and experience.* New York: Plenum.

Haggerty, R., Roghmann, K., and Pless, I. (1975). *Child health and the community.* New York: Wiley.

Haith, M. (1980). Visual competence in early infancy. In R. Held, H. Liebowitz, and H. Teube (eds.), *Handbook of sensory physiology* (vol. 8). Berlin: Springer-Verlag.

Hale, G. (1979). Development of children's attention to stimulus components. In G. Hale and M. Lewis (eds.), *Attention and cognitive development.* New York: Plenum.

Halliday, M. A. K. (1979). One child's protolanguage. In M. Bullowa (ed.), *Before speech: The beginning of interpersonal communication.* Cambridge, England: Cambridge University Press.

Hallinan, M. (1981). Recent advances in sociometry. In S. Asher and J. Gottman (eds.), *The development of children's friendships.* New York: Cambridge University Press.

Halpern, W. (1983). Parental mortification and restitutional efforts upon the sudden loss of a child. In J. Schowalter (ed.), *The child and death.* New York: Columbia University Press.

Hamill, P., Drizd, T., Johnson, C., Reed, R., Roche, A., and Moore, W. (1979). Physical growth: National Center for Health Statistics percentiles. *Clinical Nutrition, 32,* 607–629.

Hamill, P., Johnston, F., and Grams, W. (1970). *Height and weight of children: United States.* Vital Health Statistics Series II, No. 104. Washington, D.C.: U.S. Government Printing Office.

Hamilton, P. M. (1984). *Basic maternity nursing* (5th ed.). St. Louis: Mosby.

Hammar, S. L. (1978). Adolescence. In D. W. Smith, E. L. Bierman, and N. M. Robinson (eds.), *The biologic ages of man: From conception through old age.* Philadelphia: Saunders.

Haney, B., and Gold, M. (1973). The juvenile delinquent nobody knows. *Psychology Today* (September), 49–55.

Hareven, T. (1986). Historical changes in the family and the life course: Implications for child development. In A. Smuts and H. Hagen (eds.), *History and research in child development.* Monographs of the Society for Research on Child Development, 50 (4–5), Serial No. 211.

Harlap, S., and Shiono, P. (1980). Alcohol, smoking, and incidence of spontaneous abortions in the first and second trimester. *The Lancet* (July 26), 173–176.

Harlow, H. (1959). Love in infant monkeys. *Scientific American, 200,* 68–74.

Harlow, H., and Harlow, M. (1962). Social deprivation in monkeys. *Scientific American, 207,* 136–144.

Harper's Index. (1986). *Harper's, 272* (1629), 13 ff.

Harris, D. (1963). *Children's drawings as a measure of intellectual maturity.* New York: Harcourt, Brace, and World.

Harris, J. (1983). Pregnancy: The fetal perspective. In G. F. Butnarescu and D. M. Tillotson (eds.), *Maternity Nursing.* New York: Wiley.

Harris, P. (1983). Infant cognition. In Paul Mussen (ed.), *Handbook of child psychology* (vol. 4). New York: Wiley.

Harter, S. (1977). A cognitive-developmental approach to children's expression of conflicting feelings and a technique to facilitate such expression in play therapy. *Journal of Consulting and Clinical Psychology, 45,* 417–432.

Harter, S. (1981). A model of intrinsic mastery motivation in children: Individual differences and developmental change. In *Minnesota Symposium on Child Psychology* (vol. 14). Hillsdale, N.J.: Erlbaum.

Harter, S. (1982a). Children's understanding of multiple emotions: A cognitive-developmental approach. In W.

Overton (ed.), *The relationship between social and cognitive development.* Hillsdale, N.J.: Erlbaum.

Harter, S. (1982b). A cognitive-developmental approach to children's use of affect and trait labels. In F. Serafica (ed.), *Social cognition and social relations in context.* New York: Guilford.

Harter, S., and Barnes, R. (1983). *Children's understanding of parental emotions: A developmental study.* Unpublished paper, 1981. Cited in S. Harter, Developmental perspectives on the self-system. In P. Mussen (ed.), *Handbook of child psychology* (vol. 4). New York: Wiley.

Hartford, T. C. (1975). Patterns of alcohol use among adolescents. *Psychiatric Opinion, 12,* 17–21.

Harth, E. (1983). *Windows on the mind.* New York: Quill.

Hartshorne, H., and May, M. (1928). *Studies in deceit.* New York: Macmillan.

Hartup, W. (1974). Aggression in childhood: Developmental perspectives. *American Psychologist, 29,* 336–341.

Hartup, W. (1983). Peer relations. In P. Mussen (ed.), *Handbook of child psychology,* (vol. 4). New York: Wiley.

Hass, A. (1979). *Teenage sexuality: A survey of teenage sexual behavior.* New York: Macmillan.

Hattie, J. (1980). Should creativity tests be administered under testlike conditions? An empirical study of three alternative conditions. *Journal of Educational Psychology, 72,* 87–98.

Hausknecht, R., and Heilman, J. (1978). *Having a caesarean baby.* New York: Dutton.

Hayes, J., and Flower, L. (1980). Identifying the organization of writing processes. In L. Gregg and E. Steinberg (eds.), *Cognitive processes in writing.* Hillsdale, N.J.: Erlbaum.

Hays, J., and Siegel, A. (1981). *Way finding and spatial representation: A test of a developmental model of cognitive mapping of large-scale environments.* Paper presented to the Society for Research on Child Development, Boston, April.

Heckhausen, H. (1981). The development of achievement motivation. In W. Hartup (ed.), *Review of child development research* (vol. 6). Chicago: University of Chicago Press.

Heinonen, O., Slone, D., Shapiro, S., Gaetana, L. Hartz, S., Mitchell, A., Monson, R., Rosenberg, L., Siskind, V., and Kaufman, D. (1977). *Birth defects and drugs in pregnancy.* Littleton, Mass.: PSG.

Herrenkohl, R., and Herrenkohl, E. (1981). Some antecedents and developmental consequences of child maltreatment. In R. Rizley and D. Cicchetti (eds.), *Developmental perspectives on child maltreatment.* San Francisco: Jossey-Bass.

Hetherington, E., Cox, M., and Cox, R. (1971). Play and social interaction in children following divorce. *Journal of Social Issues, 35,* 26–49.

Hetherington, E. M., Cox, M., and Cox, R. (1982). Effects of divorce on parents and children. In M. Lamb (ed.), *Nontraditional families: Parenting and child development.* Hillsdale, N.J.: Erlbaum.

Hinde, R., and Stevenson-Hinde, J. (eds.) (1973). *Constraints on learning.* New York: Academic Press.

Hirschman, R., Melamed, L., and Oliver, C. (1982). The psychophysiology of infancy. In B. Wolman (ed.), *Handbook of developmental psychology.* Englewood Cliffs, N.J.: Prentice-Hall.

Hiscock, M., and Kinsbourne, M. (1980). Asymmetries of selective listening and attention switching in children. *Developmental Psychology, 16,* 70–82.

Hodapp, R., and Mueller, E. (1982). Early social development. In B. Wolman (ed.), *Handbook of developmental psychology.* New York: Wiley.

Hoffman, J. (1975). Developmental synthesis of affect and cognition and its implications for altruistic motivation. *Developmental Psychology, 11,* 607–622.

Hoffman, L. (1961). Effects of maternal employment on the child. *Child Development, 32,* 187–197.

Hoffman, L. (1983). Increased fathering: Effects on the mother. In M. Lamb and A. Sagi (eds.), *Fatherhood and family policy.* Hillsdale, N.J.: Erlbaum.

Hoffman, L. (1984). Work, family, and the socialization of the child. In R. Parke (ed.), *Review of child development research.* (vol. 7). Chicago: University of Chicago Press.

Hoffman, M. (1970). Moral development. In P. H. Mussen (ed.), *Carmichael's manual of child psychology* (vol. 2, 3rd ed.). New York: Wiley.

Hoffman, M. (1980). Moral development in adolescence. In J. Adelson (ed.), *Handbook of adolescent development.* New York: Wiley.

Hoffman, W. (1974). The effects of maternal employment on the child—a review of the research. *Developmental Psychology, 10,* 204–228.

Hoffnung, R. (1983). *Parent run day care cooperatives and the development of community child rearing networks.* Paper presented to the American Orthopsychiatric Association, Boston.

Hoffnung, R., and Sack, A. (1981). *Does higher education reduce or reproduce social class differences? The impact of Yale University, University of Connecticut, and University of New Haven on student attitudes and expectations regarding future work.* Paper presented at the annual meeting of the Eastern Psychological Association, New York.

Hogan, R., and Emler, N. (1978). Moral development. In M. Lamb (ed.), *Social and personality development.* New York: Holt, Rinehart, and Winston.

Holland, B. (1982). Among pros, more go Suzuki. *The New York Times,* 11 July, p. E9.

Honeck, R., and Hoffman, R. (eds.) (1980). *Cognition and figurative language.* Hillsdale, N.J.: Erlbaum.

Honzik, M. P. (1957). Developmental studies of parent-child resemblance in intelligence. *Child Development, 28,* 215–228.

Hopmann, M., and Maratosos, M. (1978). A developmental study of factivity and negation in complex syntax. *Journal of Child Syntax, 5,* 295–309.

Hoppe, C., Kagan, S., and Zahn, G. (1977). Conflict resolution among field-independent Anglo-American and Mexican-American children and their mothers. *Developmental Psychology, 13,* 591–598.

Hopson, J. (1984). A love affair with the brain. *Psychology Today, 18* (11), 62–73.

Horn, J., and Donaldson, G. (1976). On the myth of intellectual decline in adulthood. *American Psychologist, 31,* 701–719.

Horn, J., and Donaldson, G. (1980). Cognitive development in adulthood. In O. Brim and J. Kagan (eds.), *Constancy and change in human development.* Cambridge, Mass.: Harvard University Press.

Hornick, J., Doran, L., and Crawford, S. (1979). Premarital contraceptive usage among male and female adolescents. *Family Coordinator, 28,* 181–190.

Howard, J., and Barnett, M. (1981). Arousal of empathy and subsequent generosity in young children. *Journal of Genetic Psychology, 138,* 307–308.

Howes, C., and Mueller, E. (1984). Early peer friendships: Their significance for development. In W. Spiel (ed.), *The psychology of the twentieth century.* Zurich: Kindler.

Huba, G. J., and Bentler, P. M. (1980). The role of peer and adult models for drug taking at different stages in adolescence. *Journal of Youth and Adolescence, 9,* 449–465.

Huba, G. J., and Bentler, P. M. (1982). A developmental theory of drug use: Derivation and assessment of a causal modeling approach. In P. B. Baltes and O. G. Brim, Jr. (eds.), *Life-span development and behavior* (vol. 4). New York: Academic Press.

Hubley, P., and Trevarthen, C. (1979). Sharing a task in infancy. In I. Uzgiris (ed.), *Social interaction and communication during infancy.* San Francisco: Jossey-Bass.

Huff, R., and Pauerstein, C. (1979). *Human reproduction: Physiology and pathophysiology.* New York: Wiley.

Humphreys, L. (1979). The construct of general intelligence. *Intelligence, 3,* 105–120.

Hurley, L. (1977). Nutritional deficiencies and excesses. In J. Wilson and F. Fraser (eds.), *Handbook of teratology* (vol. 1). New York: Plenum.

Hurley, L. (1980). *Developmental nutrition.* Englewood Cliffs, N.J.: Prentice-Hall.

Huston, A. (1983). Sex-typing. In P. Mussen (ed.), *Handbook of Child Psychology* (vol. 4). New York: Wiley.

Hutt, C. (1979). Exploration and play. In B. Sutton-Smith (ed.), *Play and learning.* New York: Gardner.

Ilg, F., Ames, L., and Baker, S. (1981). *Child behavior* (rev. ed.). New York: Harper and Row.

Imedadze, N., and Uznadze, D. (1978). On the psychological nature of child speech formation under conditions of exposure to two languages. In E. Hatch (ed.), *Second language acquisition.* Rowley, Mass.: Newbury House.

Inhelder, B. (1976) The sensorimotor origins of knowledge. In B. Inhelder and H. Chipman (eds.), *Piaget and his school.* New York: Springer-Verlag.

Inhelder, B., and Piaget, J. (1958). *The growth of logical thinking from birth to adolescence.* New York: Basic Books.

Istomina, Z. (1975). The development of voluntary memory in preschool-age children. *Soviet Psychology, 13,* 5–64.

Itard, J. (1806/1962). *The wild boy of Aveyron.* New York: Appleton-Century-Crofts.

Jacklin, C., and Maccoby, E. (1978). Social behavior at 33 months in same-sex and mixed-sex dyads. *Child Development, 49,* 557–569.

Janoff-Bulman, R., and Brickman, P. (1981). Expectations and what people learn from failure. In N. Feather (ed.), *Expectancy, incentive, and action.* Hillsdale, N.J.: Erlbaum.

Janos, P., and Robinson, N. (1985). Psychosocial development in intellectually gifted children. In F. Horowitz and M. O'Brien (eds.), *The gifted and talented: Developmental perspectives.* Washington, D.C.: American Psychological Association.

Jennings, M., and Niemi, R. (1981). *Generations and politics.* Princeton, N.J.: Princeton University Press.

Jensen, A. (1969). How much can we boost IQ and scholastic achievement? *Harvard Educational Review, 39,* 1–123.

Jensen, A. (1978). The current status of the IQ controversy. *Australian Psychologist, 13,* 7–27.

Jensen, L. C. (1985). *Adolescence: Theories, research and applications.* New York: West.

Jessor, S., and Jessor, R. (1975). Transition from virginity to nonvirginity among youth: A social-psychological study over time. *Developmental Psychology, 11,* 473–484.

Jester, R. E., and Guinagh, B. (1983). The Gordon parent education infant and toddler program. In Consortium for Longitudinal Studies, *As the twig is bent.* Hillsdale, N.J.: Erlbaum.

Joffe, L., and Vaughn, B. (1982). Infant-mother attachment. In B. Wolman (ed.), *Handbook of human development.* New York: Wiley.

Johnson, L., Driscoll, S., Hertig, A., Cole, P., and Nickerson, R. (1979). Vaginal adenosis in stillborns and neonates exposed to DES and steroidal estrogens and progestins. *Obstetrics and Gynecology, 53,* 671–679.

Johnson, L., Townsend, R., and Wilson, M. (1975). Habituation during sleeping and waking. *Psychophysiology, 3,* 8–17.

Johnston, F. (1979). Somatic growth of the infant and preschool child. In F. Falkner and J. Tanner (eds.), *Human growth* (vol. 2). New York: Plenum.

Johnston, J., and Slobin, D. (1979). The development of locative expressions in English, Italian, Serbo-Croatian, and Turkish. *Journal of Child Language, 6,* 529–545.

Johnston, L. D. (1974). Drug use during and after high school: Results of a national longitudinal study. *American Journal of Public Health, 64,* 29–37.

Jorgenson, H. (1983). Anti-school parodies. In F. Manning (ed.), *The world of play.* West Point, N.Y.: Leisure Press.

Josselson, R. (1980). Ego development in adolescence. In J. Adelson (ed.), *Handbook of adolescent psychology.* New York: Wiley.

Josselson, R. (1982). Personality structure and identity status in women as viewed through early memories. *Journal of Youth and Adolescence, 11,* 11–23.

Juel-Nielson, N. (1980). *Individual and environment: Monozygotic twins reared apart.* New York: International Universities Press.

Justice, B., and Duncan, D. (1977). Child abuse as a work-related problem. *Journal of Behavior Technology, Methods and Therapy, 23,* 53–55.

Kadushin, A., and Martin, J. (1981). *Child Abuse: An interactional event.* New York: Columbia University Press.

Kagan, J. (1973). Meaning and memory in two cultures. *Child Development, 44,* 221–223.

Kagan, J. (1978). The baby's elastic mind. *Human Nature, 1*, 66–73.

Kagan, J. (1979). Structure and process in the human infant: The otogeny of mental representation. In M. Bornstein and W. Kessen (eds.), *Psychological development from infancy: Image to intention.* Hillsdale, N.J.: Elbaum.

Kagan, J. (1981). *The second year.* Cambridge, Mass.: Harvard University Press.

Kagan, J. (1984). *The nature of the child.* New York: Basic Books.

Kagan, J., Rosman, B., Day, D., Albert, J., and Phillips, W. (1964). Information processing in the child: Significance of analytic and reflective attitudes. *Psychological Monographs, 78* (578).

Kalinowski, A. (1985a). The development of Olympic swimmers. In B. Bloom (ed.), *Developing talent in young people.* New York: Ballantine.

Kalinowski, A. (1985b). One Olympic swimmer. In B. Bloom (ed.), *Developing talent in young people.* New York: Ballantine.

Kamii, C., and DeVries, R. (1977). Piaget for early education. In M. Day and R. Parker (eds.), *The preschool in action.* (2nd ed.). Boston: Allyn and Bacon.

Kandel, D. B., and Faust, R. (1975). Sequence and stages in patterns of adolescent drug use. *Archives of General Psychiatry, 32*, 923–932.

Kane, B. (1977). Children's concepts of death. *Journal of Genetic Psychology, 24*, 315–320.

Kaplan, A. (ed.) (1976). *Human behavior genetics.* Springfield, Ill.: Thomas.

Kaplan, A., and Bean, J. (eds.) (1976). *Beyond sex-role stereotypes: Readings toward a psychology of androgyny.* Boston: Little, Brown.

Karniol, R. (1978). Children's use of intention cues in evaluating behavior. *Psychological Bulletin, 85*, 76–86.

Karniol, R. (1980). A conceptual analysis of imminent justice responses in children. *Child Development, 51*, 118–130.

Katz, L. (1984). Ethical issues in working with young children. In L. Katz (ed.), *More talks with teachers.* Urbana, Ill.: ERIC Clearinghouse.

Katz, P. (1976). The acquisition of racial attitudes in children. In P. Katz (ed.), *Towards the elimination of racism.* New York: Pergamon.

Kavale, K., and Schreiner, R. (1979). The reading processes of above average and average readers: A comparison of the use and reasoning strategies in responding to standardized comprehension measures. *Reading Research Quarterly, 15*, 102–118.

Kaye, K. (1976). Infants' effects upon their mothers' teaching strategies. In J. Glidewell (ed.), *The social context of learning and development.* New York: Gardner.

Kaye, K. (1979). The maternal role in developing communication and language. In M. Bullowa (ed.), *Before speech.* Cambridge, England: Cambridge University Press.

Keating, D. P. (1980). Thinking processes in adolescence. In J. Adelson (ed.), *Handbook of adolescent development.* New York: Wiley.

Kegan, R. (1982). *The evolving self.* Cambridge, Mass.: Harvard University Press.

Kellogg, R. (1969). *Analyzing children's art.* Palo Alto, Calif.: National Press Books.

Kempe, C. H., Silverman, E., Steele, B., Droegemueller, W., and Silver, H. (1962). The battered-child syndrome. *Journal of the American medical Association, 181*, 17.

Kempe, R., and Kempe, C. H. (1978). *Child abuse.* Cambridge, Mass.: Harvard University Press.

Kempe, R., and Kempe, C. H. (1984). *The common secret: Sexual abuse of children and adolescents.* New York: Greeman.

Kendel, D. B., and Lesser, G. (1969). Parental and peer influence on educational plans of adolescents. *American Sociological Review, 34*, 213–223.

Keniston, K. (1970). Youth: A 'new' stage of life. *The American Scholar, 39*, 631–641.

Kennell, J., Voos, D., and Klaus, M. (1979). Parent-infant bonding. In J. Osofsky (ed.), *Handbook of infant development.* New York: Wiley.

Kessen, W. (ed.) (1965). *The child.* New York: Wiley.

Kimmel, D. (1979). *Adulthood and aging* (2nd ed.). New York: Wiley.

Kinsbourne, M. (1982). Hemispheric specialization and the growth of human understanding. *American Psychologist, 37* (4), 411–420.

Kinsey, A., Pomeroy, W., and Martin, C. (1948). *Sexual behavior in the human male.* Philadelphia: Saunders.

Kinsey, A., Pomeroy, W., Martin, C., and Gebhard, P. (1953). *Sexual behavior in the human female.* Philadelphia: Saunders.

Kisilevsky, B., and Muir, D. (1984). Neonatal habituation and dishabituation to tactile stimulation during sleep. *Developmental Psychology, 20* (3), 367–373.

Kitson, G., and Raschke, H. (1981). Divorce research: What we know; what we need to know. *Journal of Divorce, 4*, 1–37.

Klagsbrun, F. (1981). *Too young to die: Youth and suicide.* New York: Pocket Books.

Klaus, M., and Kennell, J. (1976). *Maternal-infant bonding.* St. Louis: Mosby.

Kliot, D., and Silverstein, L. (1980). The Leboyer approach: A new concern for psychological aspects of childbirth experience. In B. Blum (ed.), *Psychological aspects of pregnancy, birthing, and bonding*. New York: Human Sciences Press.

Knittle, J., Tiommer, K., Ginsberg-Fellner, F., Brown, R., and Katz, D. (1979). The growth of adipose tissue in children and adolescents. *Journal of Clinical Investigation, 63*, 239–246.

Kogan, N. (1973). Creativity and cognitive style: A lifespan perspective. In P. Baltes and K. Schaie (eds.), *Lifespan developmental psychology: Personality and socialization*. New York: Academic Press.

Kogan, N. (1982). Cognitive styles in older adults. In T. Field (ed.), *Review of human development*. New York: Wiley.

Kogan, N., Connor, K., Gross, A., and Fava, D. (1980). Understanding visual metaphor: Developmental and individual differences. *Monographs of the Society for Research on Child Development, 45* (183).

Kohlberg, L. (1964). Development of moral character and moral ideology. In M. L. Hoffman and L. W. Hoffman (eds.), *Review of child development research* (vol. 1). New York: Russell Sage.

Kohlberg, L. (1966). A cognitive-developmental view of sex-role development. In E. Maccoby (ed.), *The development of sex differences*. Stanford, Calif.: Stanford University Press.

Kohlberg, L. (1976). Moral stages and moralization: The cognitive-developmental approach. In T. Lickona (ed.), *Moral development and behavior*. New York: Holt, Rinehart, and Winston.

Kohlberg, L. (1984). *Essays on moral development: The psychology of moral development*. New York: Harper and Row.

Kohn, M. (1970). *Class and conformity: A study in values* (2nd ed.). Chicago: University of Chicago Press.

Komarovsky, M. (1976). *Dilemmas of masculinity: A study of college youth*. New York: Norton.

Kopp, C., and Parmalee, A. (1979). Prenatal and perinatal influences on infant behavior. In J. Osofsky (ed.), *Handbook of infant development*. New York: Wiley.

Korner, A. (1981). Intervention with preterm infants: Rationale, aims, and means. In V. Smeriglio (ed.), *Newborns and parents*. Hillsdale, N.J.: Erlbaum.

Kotelchuck, M. (1976). The infant's relationship to the father: Experimental evidence. In M. E. Lamb (ed.), *The role of the father in child development*. New York: Wiley.

Kovar, M. (1982). Health status of U.S. children and use of medical care. *Public Health Reports, 97*, 3–15.

Kovar, M., and Meny, D. (1981). A statistical profile. In the Report of the Select Panel for the Promotion of Child Health, *Better health for our children* (vol. 3). Washington, D.C.: U.S. Government Printing Office.

Kramer, M. W., and Rifkin, A. H. (1969). The early development of homosexuality: A study of adolescent lesbianism. *American Journal of Psychiatry, 116*, 91–96.

Krasnor, L., and Rubin, K. (1983). Preschool social problem solving: Attempts and outcomes in naturalistic interaction. *Child Development, 54*, 1545–1558.

Krech, D., Rosenzweig, M., and Bennett, E. (1962). Relations between brain chemistry and problem-solving among rats in enriched and impoverished environments. *Journal of Comparative and Physiological Psychology, 55*, 801–807.

Krech, D., Rosenzweig, M., and Bennett, E. (1966). Environmental impoverishment, social isolation, and changes in brain chemistry and anatomy. *Physiology and Behavior, 1*, 99–104.

Kubler-Ross, E. (1983). *On children and death*. New York: Macmillan.

Kuhl, P. (1976). Speech perception by the chinchilla. *Journal of the Acoustical Society of America, 60*, #S81.

Laboratory of Comparative Human Cognition. (1982). Culture and intelligence. In R. Sternberg (ed.), *Handbook of human intelligence*. New York: Cambridge University Press.

Labouvie-Vief, G. (1982). Discontinuities in development from childhood to adulthood: A cognitive-developmental view. In T. Field (ed.), *Review of human development*. New York: Wiley.

Labov, W., Robins, C., Cohen, P., and Lewis, J. (1977). Classroom correction tests. In J. Dillard (ed.), *Perspectives on black English*. The Hague: Mouton.

Lacey, B., and Lacey, J. (1978). Two-way communication between the heart and the brain. *American Psychologist, 33*, 99–113.

Lakoff, R. (1975). *Language and woman's place*. New York: Harper and Row.

Lamaze, F. (1958). *Painless childbirth*. London: Burke.

Lamb, M. (1977a). The development of mother-infant and father-infant attachments in the second year of life. *Developmental Psychology, 13*, 637–648.

Lamb, M. (1977b). *The role of the father in child development*. Hillsdale, N.J.: Erlbaum.

Lamb, M. (1977c). Father-infant and mother-infant interactions in the first year of life. *Child Development, 48*, 167–181.

Lamb, M. (1982). Maternal employment and child development: A review. In M. E. Lamb (ed.), *Nontraditional families: Parenting and childrearing.* Hillsdale, N.J.: Erlbaum.

Lamb, M., and Hwang, C. (1982). Maternal attachment and mother-neonate bonding: A critical review. In M. Lamb and A. Brown (eds.), *Advances in developmental psychology* (vol. 2). Hillsdale, N.J.: Erlbaum.

Lamb, M., and Roopnarine, J. (1979). Peer influences on sex-role development in preschoolers. *Child Development, 50,* 1219–1222.

Lamb, M., and Sagi, A. (eds.) (1983). *Fatherhood and family policy.* Hillsdale, N.J.: Erlbaum.

Lambert, N., and Hartsough, C. (1984). Contribution of predispositional factors to the diagnosis of hyperactivity. *American Journal of Orthopsychiatry, 54,* 97–109.

Lambert, W., and Tucker, G. R. (1977). White and Negro listeners' reactions to various American-English dialects. In J. Dillard (ed.), *Perspectives on black English.* The Hague: Mouton.

Langer, W. (1972). Checks on population growth: 1750–1850. *Scientific American, 226,* 93–100.

Langlois, J., and Downs, A. (1980). Mothers, fathers and peers as socialization agents of sex-typed play behaviors in young children. *Child Development, 48,* 1694–1698.

Langlois, J., and Stephan, C. (1981). Beauty and the beast: The role of physical attractiveness in the development of peer relations and social behavior. In S. Brehm, S. Kassin, and F. Gibbons (eds.), *Violence and the mass media.* New York: Harper and Row.

Laosa, L. (1980). Maternal teaching strategies and cognitive styles in Chicano families. *Journal of Educational Psychology, 72,* 45–54.

Larson, L. (1972). Influence of parents and peers during adolescence: The situation hypothesis revisited. *Journal of Marriage and the Family, 34,* 67–74.

Larson, R. (1973). Physical activity and the growth and development of bone and joint structures. In G. Rarick (ed.), *Physical activity: Human growth and development.* New York: Academic Press.

Larson, R. (1983). Adolescents' daily experience with family and friends: Differing opportunity systems. *Journal of Marriage and Family, 45,* 739–750.

Larson, R., and Csikszentmihalyi, M. (1983). The experience sampling method. In H. Reis (ed.), *New directions for naturalistic methods in the behavioral sciences.* San Francisco: Jossey-Bass.

Lasch, C. (1975–1976). The family and history. *New York Review of Books,* November-January.

Lasch, C. (1979). *The culture of narcissism.* New York: Norton.

Laslett, P. (1975). *The world we have lost.* New York: Scribner's.

Laslett, P., and Wall, R. (eds.) (1975). *Household and family in past time.* Cambridge, England: Cambridge University Press.

Lassen, N., Ingvar, D., and Skinhoj, E. (1978). Brain function and blood flow. *Scientific American, 227,* 62–71.

Laurendeau, M., and Pinard, A. (1972). *Causal thinking in the child.* New York: International Universities Press.

Leavitt, J. (ed.). (1983). *Child abuse and neglect.* The Hague: Martinus Nijhoff.

Leavitt, L., Brown, J., Morse, P., and Graham, F. (1976). Cardiac orienting and auditory discrimination in six-week-old infants. *Developmental Psychology, 12,* 514–523.

Lebel, R. (1978). Ethical issues arising in the genetic counseling relationship. In D. Bergsma (ed.), *Birth defects.* Washington, D.C.: March of Dimes.

LeBow, M. (1984). *Childhood obesity.* New York: Springer.

LeBow, M. (1986). Child obesity: Dangers. *Canadian Psychology, 27,* 275–285.

Leboyer, F. (1975). *Birth without violence.* New York: Knopf.

Lemon, J. (1977). Women and blacks on prime-time television. *Journal of Communication, 27,* 70–79.

Lenneberg, E. (1967). *Biological foundations of language.* New York: Wiley.

Lerner, R., and Knapp, J. (1975). Actual and perceived intrafamilial attitudes of late adolescents and their parents. *Journal of Youth and Adolescence, 4,* 17–36.

Lerner, R., and Shea, J. (1982). Social behavior in adolescence. In B. Wolman (ed.), *Handbook of developmental psychology.* Englewood Cliffs, N.J.: Prentice-Hall.

Lever, J. (1976). Sex differences in the games children play. *Social Problems, 23,* 479–487.

Levinson, D. (1978). *The seasons of a man's life.* New York: Ballantine.

Levinson, D. (1986). A conception of adult development. *American Psychologist, 41,* 3–13.

Levinson, D., Darrow, C., Klein, E., Levinson, M., and McKee, B. (1978). *The seasons of a man's life.* New York: Ballantine.

Levitin, T. (1979). Children of divorce. *Journal of Social Issues, 35,* 1–25.

Lewis, C., and Lewis, M. (1983). Improving the health of children: Must the children be involved? *Annual Review of Public Health, 4,* 259–283.

Lewis, M. (1976). *Origins of intelligence.* New York: Plenum.

Lewis, M., and Brooks-Gunn, J. (1979a). *Social cognition and the acquisition of self.* New York: Plenum.

Lewis, M., and Brooks-Gunn, J. (1979b). Toward a theory of social cognition: The development of the self. In I. Uzgiris (ed.), *Social interaction and communication during infancy*. San Francisco: Jossey-Bass.

Lewis, M., Feiring, C., and McGuffog, C. (1986). Profiles of young gifted and normal children. *Topics in Early Childhood and Special Education, 6*, 9–23.

Lewis, M., and Lewis, D. (1983). Dying children and their families. In J. Schowalter, M. Tallmer, A. Kutscher, S. Gullo, and D. Peretz (eds.), *The child and death*. New York: Columbia University Press.

Libbey, P., and Bybee, R. (1979). The physical abuse of adolescents. *The Journal of Social Issues, 35*, 101–116.

Liben, L. (1982). The developmental study of children's memory. In T. Field (ed.), *Review of human development*. New York: Wiley.

Liben, L., and Posnansky, C. (1977). Inferences on inference: The effects of age, transitive ability, memory load, and lexical factors. *Child Development, 48*, 1490–1497.

Lickona, T. (1976). Research on Piaget's theory of moral development. In T. Lickona (ed.), *Moral development and behavior*. New York: Holt, Rinehart, and Winston.

Lieberman, J. (1977). *Playfulness: Its relationship to creativity*. New York: Academic Press.

Lifton, R., and Falk, R. (1982). *Indefensible weapons: The political and psychological case against nuclearism*. New York: Basic Books.

Lindzey, G., and Thiessen, D. (eds.) (1970). *Contributions to behavior genetic analysis: The mouse as a prototype*. New York: Appleton.

Lipsitt, L. (1977). Taste in human infants: Its effects on sucking and heart rate. In J. Weiffenbach (ed.), *Taste and development*. Washington, D.C.: U.S. Government Printing Office.

Lipsitt, L. (1979). Critical conditions in infancy. *American Psychology, 34*, 973–980.

Lipsitt, L. (1982). Infant learning. In T. Field (ed.), *Review of human development*. New York: Wiley.

Lipsitt, L., and Kaye, H. (1964). Conditioned sucking in the newborn. *Psychonomic Science, 1*, 29–30.

Lipsitt, L., and Levy, N. (1959). Electrotactual threshold in the neonate. *Child Development, 30*, 547–554.

Livson, N., and Peskin, H. (1981a). Perspectives on adolescence from longitudinal research. In J. Adelson (ed.), *Handbook of adolescent psychology*. New York: Wiley.

Livson, N., and Peskin, H. (1981b). Psychological health at 40: Predictions from adolescent personality. In D. Eichorn, J. Clausen, N. Haan, M. Honzik, and P. Mussen (eds.), *Present and past in middle life*. New York: Academic Press.

Ljung, B., Bergsten-Brucefors, A., and Lindgren, G.

(1974). The secular trend in physical growth in Sweden. *Annals of Human Biology, 1*, 245–266.

Locke, J. (1693/1699). *Some thoughts concerning education*. London: Churchill.

Logan, D. D. (1980). The menarche experience in twenty-three foreign countries. *Adolescence, 58*, 247–257.

Londerville, S., and Main, M. (1981). Security of attachment, compliance and maternal training methods in the second year of life. *Developmental Psychology, 17*, 289–299.

Lopata, L. (1981). *Interweave of social roles* (vol. 1). Greenwich, Conn.: JAI Press.

Lord, C. (1982). Psychopathology in early development. In S. Moore and C. Cooper (eds.), *The young child: Reviews of research* (vol. 3). Washington, D.C.: National Association for the Education of Young Children.

Lorenz, K. (1960). *On aggression*. New York: Harcourt, Brace, and World.

Lorenz, K. (ed.). (1970). *Studies in animal and human behavior* (vol. 1). Cambridge, Mass.: Harvard University Press.

Lubic, R. (1981). Evaluation of an out-of-hospital maternity center for low-risk patients. In L. Aiken (ed.), *Health policy and nursing practice*. New York: McGraw-Hill.

Lynch, G., and Gall, C. (1979). Organization and reorganization in the central nervous system. In F. Falkner and J. Tanner (eds.), *Human Growth*. New York: Plenum.

McAlister, A., Perry, C., and Maccoby, N. (1979). Adolescent smoking: Onset and prevention. *Pediatrics, 4*, 650–658.

McArthur, L., and Eisen, S. (1976). Television and sex-role stereotyping. *Journal of Applied Social Psychology, 6*, 329–351.

McCall, R. (1979). The development of intellectual functioning in infancy and the prediction of later IQ. In J. Osofsky (ed.), *Handbook of infant development*. New York: Wiley.

McCall, R. (1981). Nature-nurture and the two realms of development: A proposed integration with respect to mental development. *Child Development, 52*, 1–12.

McCall, R., and Kagan, J. (1967). Stimulus schema discrepancy and attention in the infant. *Journal of Experimental Child Psychology, 5*, 381–390.

McCall, R., and Kennedy, C. (1980). Attention to babyishness in babies. *Journal of Experimental Child Psychology, 29*, 189–201.

McCall, R., Parke, R., and Kavanaugh, R. (1977). Imitation of live and televised models by children one to three years of age. *Monographs of the Society for Research on Child Development, 42,* 173.

McClelland, D. (1973). Testing for competence rather than for "intelligence." *American Psychologist, 28,* 1–14.

Maccoby, E. (1980). *Social development, psychological growth, and parent-child relations.* New York: Harcourt Brace Jovanovich.

Maccoby, E. (1984). Socialization and developmental change. *Child Development, 55* (2), 317–328.

Maccoby, E., and Jacklin, C. (1974). *The psychology of sex differences.* Stanford, Calif.: Stanford University Press.

Maccoby, E., and Jacklin, C. (1980). Sex differences in aggression: A rejoinder and reprise. *Child Development, 48,* 964–980.

Maccoby, E., and Martin, J. (1983). Socialization in the context of the family: Parent-child interaction. In P. Mussen (ed.), *Handbook of child psychology* (vol. 4). New York: Wiley.

MacFarlane, A. (1975). Olfaction in the development of social preferences in the human neonate. *In Parent-child interaction.* Amsterdam: CIBA Foundation Symposium No. 33.

MacFarlane, A. (1977). *The psychology of childbirth.* Cambridge, Mass.: Harvard University Press.

McGarrigle, J., and Donaldson, M. (1974). *Conservation accidents.* Cognition, 3, 341–350.

McGarrigle, J., Grieve, R., and Hughes, M. (1978). Interpreting inclusion. *Journal of Experimental Child Psychology, 26,* 528–550.

McGraw, M. B. (1935). *Growth: A study of Johnny and Jimmy.* New York: Appleton-Century.

McGraw, M. B. (1939). Later development of children specially trained during infancy. *Child Development, 10,* 1–19.

McKay, H., Sinisterra, L., McKay, A., Gomez, H., and Lloreda, P. (1978). Improving cognitive ability in chronically deprived children. *Science, 200,* 270–278.

McKenry, P., Walters, L., and Johnson, C. (1979). Adolescent pregnancy: A review of the literature. *The Family Coordinator, 23,* 17–28.

McKenzie, C. (1983). Risk factors in perinatology. In C. McKenzie and K. Vestal (eds.), *High-risk perinatal nursing.* Philadelphia: Saunders.

MacWhinney, B. (1978). The acquisition of morphophonology. *Monographs of the Society for Research on Child Development, 43,* 174.

Madsen, M. (1971). Developmental and cross-cultural differences in the cooperative and competitive behavior of young children. *Journal of Cross-Cultural Psychology, 2,* 365–371.

Mahler, M. (1974). Symbiosis and individuation. *Psychoanalytic Study of the Child, 29,* 89–106.

Mahler, M., Pine, F., and Bergman, A. (1975). *The psychological birth of the human infant: Symbiosis and individuation.* New York: Basic Books.

Main, M., Kaplan, N., and Cassidy, J. (1985). Security in infancy, childhood, and adulthood: A move to the level of representation. In I. Bretherton and E. Waters (eds.), Growing points of attachment theory and research. *Monographs of the Society for Research on Child Development, 50* (209).

Malina, R. (1982). Motor development in the early years. In S. Moore and C. Cooper (eds.), *The young child: Reviews of research* (vol. 3). Washington, D.C.: National Association for the Education of Young Children.

Maltz, D., and Borker, R. (1982). A cultural approach to male-female miscommunication. In J. Gumperz (ed.), *Language and social identity.* New York: Cambridge University Press.

Manicas, P., and Secord, P. (1983). Implications for psychology of the new philosophy of science. *American Psychologist, 38,* 399–413.

Manning, F. (ed.) (1983). *The world of play.* West Point, N.Y.: Leisure Press.

Maratsos, M. (1973). Non-egocentric communication abilities in preschool children. *Child Development, 44,* 697–700.

Marcia, J. (1967). Ego identity status: Relationship to change in self-esteem, 'general maladjustment,' and authoritarianism. *Journal of Personality, 35* (11), 119–133.

Marcia, J. (1976). Identity six years after: A follow-up study. *Journal of Youth and Adolescence, 5,* 145–160.

Marcia, J. (1980). Identity in adolescence. In J. Adelson (ed.), *Handbook of adolescent psychology.* New York: Wiley.

Marcus, D., and Overton, W. (1978). The development of cognitive gender constancy and sex role preferences. *Child Development, 49,* 434–444.

Markham, E. (1979). Review of Siegler's *Children's thinking. Contemporary Psychology, 24,* 963–964.

Marshall, W., and Swan, A. (1971). Seasonal variation in growth rates of normal and blind children. *Human Biology, 43,* 502–516.

Marsland, D., Wood, M., and Mayo, F. (1976). A data bank for patient care, curriculum, and research in family practice: 526,196 patient problems. *Journal of Family Practice, 3,* 24.

Martin, B. (1975). Parent-child relations. In F. Horowitz (ed.), *Review of child development research* (vol. 4). Chicago: University of Chicago Press.

Martin, G. (1978). *Behavior modification: What it is and how to do it.* Englewood Cliffs, N.J.: Prentice-Hall.

Martin, G. (1980). *Helping the community: Behavioral applications.* Englewood Cliffs, N.J.: Prentice-Hall.

Martinez, G., and Nalezienski, J. (1981). 1980 update: The recent trend in breastfeeding. *Pediatrics, 67,* 260.

Martorano, C. S. (1977). A developmental analysis of performance on Piaget's formal operations tasks. *Developmental Psychology, 13,* 666–672.

Maslow, A. (1962). *Toward a psychology of being.* Princeton, N.J.: Van Nostrand.

Masnick, G., and Bane, M. J. (1980). *The nation's families: 1960–80.* Cambridge, Mass.: Joint Center for Urban Studies of MIT and Harvard University.

Masters, J., and Furman, W. (1981). Popularity, individual friendship selection, and specific peer interactions among children. *Developmental Psychology, 17,* 344–350.

Matas, L., Arend, R., and Sroufe, L. (1978). Continuity and adaptation in the second year: The relationship between quality of attachment and later competence. *Child Development, 49,* 547–556.

Mather, K., and Jinks, J. (1977). *Introduction to biometrical genetics.* London: Chapman and Hall.

Matsuhashi, A. (1982). Explorations in the real-time production of written discourse. In M. Nystrand (ed.), *What writers know: The language, process, and structure of written English.* New York: Academic Press.

Matsunaga, E., and Shiota, K. (1980). Search for maternal factors associated with malformed human embryos: A prospective study. *Teratology, 21,* 323–331.

Mattsson, A. (1983). Death in a family of hemophiliacs. In J. Schowalter, M. Tallmer, A. Kutscher, S. Gullo, and D. Peretz (eds.), *The child and death.* New York: Columbia University Press.

Maurer, D., Siegel, L., Lewis, T., Kristofferson, M., Barnes, R., and Levy, B. (1979). Long-term memory improvement? *Child Development, 50,* 106–118.

Mayer, J. (1975). Obesity during childhood. In M. Winick (ed.), *Childhood obesity.* New York: Wiley.

Medrich, E. (1981). *The serious business of growing up: A study of children's lives outside of school.* Berkeley: University of California Press.

Meichenbaum, D. (1977). *Cognitive behavior modification.* New York: Plenum.

Meichenbaum, D., and Goodman, J. (1971). Training impulsive children to talk to themselves. *Journal of Abnormal Psychology, 77,* 115–126.

Meilman, P. (1979). Cross-sectional age changes in ego identity status during adolescence. *Developmental Psychology, 15,* 230–231.

Melamed, B., Hawes, R., Heiby, E., and Glick, J. (1975). Use of filmed modeling to reduce uncooperative behavior of children during dental treatment. *Journal of Dental Research, 54,* 797–801.

Mellen, S. (1981). *The evolution of love.* San Francisco: Freeman.

Meltzoff, A., and Moore, M. (1977). Imitation of facial and manual gestures by human neonates. *Science, 198,* 75–78.

Menning, B. (1980). The emotional needs of infertile couples. *Fertility Sterility, 34* (4), 313 ff.

Merck Laboratories. (1985). *The Merck manual of diagnosis and therapy* (10th ed.). Rahway, N.J.: Merck, Sharp, and Dohme.

Meredith, H. (1967). A synopsis of pubertal changes in youth. *Journal of School Health, 37,* 171–176.

Meredith, H. (1981). Body size and form among ethnic groups of infants, children, youth, and adults. In R. Munroe, R. Munroe, and B. Whiting (eds.), *Handbook of cross-cultural human development.* New York: Garland STPM Press.

Meringoff, L., Vibbert, M., Kelly, H., and Char, C. (1981). *How shall you take your story: With or without pictures?* Paper presented at the biennial meeting of the Society for Research on Child Development, Boston, April.

Messer, S. (1976). Reflection-impulsivity: A review. *Psychological Bulletin, 83,* 1026–1053.

Michaels, R., and Mellin, G. (1960). Prospective experience with maternal rubella and the associated congenital malformations. *Pediatrics, 26,* 200–209.

Miesels, S. (1984). Prediction, prevention, and developmental screening in the EPSDT Program. In H. Stevenson and A. Siegel (eds.), *Child development and social policy.* Chicago: University of Chicago Press.

Mikaye, K., Chen, S., and Campos, J. (1985). Infant temperament, mother's mode of interaction, and attachment in Japan. In I. Bretherton and E. Waters (eds.), Growing points of attachment theory and research. *Monographs of the Society for Research on Child Development, 50* (209).

Milgram, R., and Feingold, S. (1977). Concrete and verbal reinforcement in creative thinking of disadvantaged children. *Perceptual and Motor Skills, 45,* 675–678.

Miller, P., and Simon, W. (1980). The development of sexuality in adolescence. In J. Adelson (ed.), *Handbook of adolescent psychology.* New York: Wiley.

Mischel, W. (1984). Convergences, challenges, and the search for consistency. *American Psychologist, 39,* 351–364.

Mitchell, J. (1974). *Psychoanalysis and feminism.* New York: Pantheon.

Mittwoch, U. (1973). *Genetics and sex differentiation.* New York: Academic Press.

Moen, P., Kain, E., and Elder, G. (1981). *Economic conditions and family life.* Washington, D.C.: National Academy of Sciences, Committee on Child Development and Public Policy.

Molfese, D., Molfese, V., and Carrell, P. (1982). Early language development. In B. Wolman (ed.), *Handbook of developmental psychology.* New York: Wiley.

Money, J. (1975). Counseling in genetics and applied behavior genetics. In K. W. Schaie, V. E. Anderson, G. McClearn, and J. Money (eds.), *Developmental human behavior genetics.* Lexington, Mass.: Heath.

Money, J., and Ehrhardt, A. (1972). Man and woman, boy and girl: The differentiation and dimorphism of gender identity from conception to maturity. Baltimore: Johns Hopkins University Press.

Montemayor, R., and Eisen, M. (1977). The development of self-conceptions from childhood to adolescence. *Developmental Psychology, 13,* 314–319.

Montessori, M. (1964). *The Montessori method.* New York: Schocken Books.

Morrison, D. (1985). Adolescent contraceptive behavior: A review. *Psychological Bulletin, 98,* 538–568.

Morrongiello, B., Clifton, R., and Kulig, J. (1982). Newborn cardiac and behavioral orienting responses to sound under varying precedence-effect conditions. *Infant Behavior and Development, 5,* 249–260.

Morse, P., and Snowdon, C. (1975). An investigation of categorical speech discrimination by rhesus monkeys. *Perception and Psychophysics, 17,* 9–16.

Moskowitz, B. A. (1978). The acquisition of language. *Scientific American, 239,* 92–108.

Mowrer, A. H. (1960). *Learning theory and the symbolic process.* New York: Wiley.

Mueller, E., and Vandell, D. (1978). Infant-infant interaction. In J. Osofsky (ed.), *Handbook of infancy.* New York: Wiley.

Muir, B. (1983). *Essentials of genetics for nurses.* New York: Wiley.

Muir, D., and Field, J. (1979). Newborn infants' orientation to sound. *Child Development, 50,* 431–436.

Munroe, R., Munroe, R., and Whiting, J. (1981). Male sex-role resolutions. In *Handbook of cross-cultural human development.* New York: Garland.

Murphy, L. (1937). *Social behavior and child personality.* New York: Columbia University Press.

Murray, D. (1973). Suicidal and depressive feelings among college students. *Psychological Reports, 33,* 175–181.

Murray, F. (1981). The conservation paradigm: The conservation of conservation research. In I. Sigel, D. Bradzinsky, and R. Galinkoff (eds.), *New directions in Piagetian research.* Hillsdale, N.J.: Erlbaum.

Muuss, R., (ed.) (1975). *Adolescent behavior and society: A book of readings* (2nd ed.). New York: Random House.

Nadeau, W., Haaliwell, K., Newell, G., and Roberts, C. (1980). *Psychology of motor behavior and sport.* Champaign, Ill.: Human Kinetics Press.

Naeye, R. (1979). Causes of fetal and neonatal mortality by race in a selected U.S. population. *American Journal of Public Health, 69,* 857.

Naeye, R. (1981). Teen-aged and pre-teen-aged pregnancies: Consequences of fetal maternal competition for nutrients. *Pediatrics, 67,* 146–150.

Naeye, R., Blanc, W., and Paul, C. (1973). Effects of maternal nutrition on the human fetus. *Pediatrics, 52,* 494.

National Academy of Sciences/National Research Council (1980). Food and Nutrition Board. *Toward healthful diets.* Washington, D.C.

National Center for Education Statistics (1978). Geographic distribution, nativity and age distribution of language minorities in the United States. Publication no. 78 B-5. Washington, D.C.: U.S. Department of Health, Education and Welfare.

National Center for Health Statistics (1980). *Monthly vital statistics report, 29* (1). Hyattsville, Md.

National Institute of Mental Health (1982). *Television and behavior: Ten years of scientific progress and implications for the eighties.* Washington, D.C.: U.S. Department of Health and Human Services.

National Institute on Drug Abuse (1979). *National survey on drug abuse: Main findings 1979.* Washington, D.C.: U.S. Department of Health and Human Services.

National Safety Council (1985). Accidental deaths and injuries in 1984. In *Accident facts, 1985.* Chicago.

Neimark, E. (1975). Longitudinal development of formal operational thought. *Genetic Psychology Monographs, 91,* 171–225.

Neimark, E. (1982a). Adolescent thought: Transition to formal operations. In B. Wolman (ed.), *Handbook of developmental psychology.* Englewood Cliffs, N.J.: Prentice-Hall.

Neimark, E. (1982b). Cognitive development in adulthood: Using what you've got. In T. Field (ed.), *Review of human development.* New York: Wiley.

Neisser, U. (1979). The concept of intelligence. *Intelligence, 3,* 217–227.

Nelms, B., and Mullins, R. (1982). *Growth and development: Primary health care approach.* Englewood Cliffs, N.J.: Prentice-Hall.

Nelson, K. (1973). Structure and strategy in learning to talk. *Monographs of the Society for Research on Child Development, 38,* 149.

Nelson, K. (1981). Individual differences in language development. *Developmental Psychology, 17,* 170–187.

Newell, A., and Simon, H. (1972). *Human problem solving.* Englewood Cliffs, N.J.: Prentice-Hall.

Newman, P. (1982). The peer group. In B. Wolman (ed.), *Handbook of developmental psychology.* Englewood Cliffs, N.J.: Prentice-Hall.

Nichol, T., and Bryson, J. (1977). *Intersex and intrasex stereotyping on the Bem sex-role inventory.* Paper presented to the American Psychological Association, San Francisco.

Nichols, R. C. (1978). Twin studies of ability, personality, and interests. *Homo, 29,* 158–173.

Norman, J., and Harris, M. (1981). *The private life of the American teenager.* New York: Rawson-Wade.

Nucci, L. (1981). Conceptions of personal issues: A domain distinct from moral or social concepts. *Child Development, 52,* 114–121.

Nucci, L. (1982). Conceptual development in the moral and conventional domains. *Review of Educational Research, 52,* 92–122.

Nyhan, W. (1976). *The heredity factor.* New York: Grosset and Dunlop.

O'Brien, M., Huston, A., and Risley, T. (1981). Emergence and stability of sex-typed toy preferences in toddlers. Paper presented at the meeting of the Association for Behavior Analysis, Milwaukee, May.

O'Connor, D. (1983). The teacher-counselor in the classroom. In L. Buscaglia (ed.), *The disabled and their parents.* New York: Holt, Rinehart, and Winston.

O'Donnell, W. (1976). Adolescent self-esteem related to feelings toward parents and friends. *Journal of Youth and Adolescence, 5,* 179–185.

Offer, D. (1969). *The psychological world of the teenager: A study of normal adolescent boys.* New York: Basic Books.

Offer, D., Marcus, D., and Offer, J. (1970). A longitudinal study of normal adolescent boys. *American Journal of Psychiatry, 126,* 917–924.

Offer, D., and Offer, J. (1975a). *From teenage to manhood.* New York: Basic Books.

Offer, D., and Offer, J. (1975b). *The sexual behavior and attitudes of one group of normal males, ages 13–22.* Paper

presented at the annual meeting of the American Sociological Association, San Francisco.

Offer, D., Ostrov, E., and Howard, K. (1977). The self-image of adolescents: A study of four cultures. *Journal of Youth and Adolescence, 6,* 265–280.

O'Leary, K., and O'Leary, S. (eds.). (1977). *Classroom management: The successful use of behavior modification* (2nd ed.). New York: Pergamon.

Oliver, J. (1977). Some studies of families in which children suffer maltreatment. In A. Franklin (ed.), *The challenge of child abuse* (pp. 16–37). New York: Grune and Stratton.

Olson, G., and Sherman, T. (1983). Attention, learning, and memory in infants. In P. Mussen (ed.), *Handbook of child psychology* (vol. 2). New York: Wiley.

Omenn, G. (1978). Prenatal diagnosis of genetic disorders. *Science, 200,* 952–958.

Omenn, G. (1983). Medical genetics, genetic counseling, and behavior genetics. In J. Fuller and E. Simmel (eds.), *Behavior genetics.* Hillsdale, N.J.: Erlbaum.

Opie, I., and Opie, P. (1969). *Children's games in streets and playgrounds.* London: Clarendon Press.

Orlick, T., and Botterill, C. (1975). *Every kid can win.* Chicago: Nelson-Hall.

Orlofsky, J., Marcia, J., and Lesser, I. (1973). Ego identity status and the intimacy versus isolation crisis of young adulthood. *Journal of Personality and Social Psychology, 27,* 211–219.

Ornstein, P., and Naus, M. (1978). Rehearsal processes in children's memory. In P. Ornstein (ed.), *Memory development in children.* Hillsdale, N.J.: Erlbaum

Ortner, D. (1983). Biocultural interaction in human adaptation. In D. Ortner (ed.), *How humans adapt.* Washington, D.C.: Smithsonian Institution Press.

Owings, R., Peterson, G., Bransford, J., Morris, C., and Stein, B. (1980). Spontaneous monitoring and regulation of learning: A comparison of successful and less successful fifth graders. *Journal of Educational Psychology, 72,* 250–256.

Palmer, R., Ouellette, M., Warner, L., and Leichtman, S. (1974). Congenital malformations in offspring of a chronic alcoholic mother. *Pediatrics, 53,* 490–494.

Paneth, N., Kiely, J., and Walenstein, S. (1982). Newborn intensive care and neonatal mortality in low-birthweight infants. *New England Journal of Medicine, 307,* 149–155.

Papert, S. (1980). *Mindstorms.* New York: Basic Books.

Paris, S., Lindauer, B., and Cox, G. (1977). The development of inferential comprehension. *Child Development, 48,* 1728–1733.

Paris, S., and Myers, M. (1981). Comprehension monitoring in good and poor readers. *Journal of Reading Behavior, 13* (1), 5–22.

Paris, S., Newman, R., and McVey, K. (in press). From tricks to strategies: Learning the functional significance of mnemonic actions. *Journal of Experimental Child Psychology.*

Parke, R. (1977). Some effects of punishment on children's behavior—revisited. In P. Cantor (ed.), *Understanding a child's world.* New York: McGraw-Hill.

Parke, R. (1981). *Fathers.* Cambridge, Mass.: Harvard University Press.

Parke, R., and O'Leary, S. (1976). Father-mother-infant interaction in the newborn period: Some feelings, some observations, and some unresolved issues. In K. Riegel and J. Meacham (eds.), *The developing individual in a changing world: Vol. 2. Social and environmental issues.* The Hague: Mouton.

Parke, R., and Sawin, D. (1976). The father's role in infancy: A re-evaluation. *The Family Coordinator, 25,* 365–371.

Parker, W. (1980). Designing an environment for childbirth: An architect's approach. In B. Blum (ed.), *Psychological aspects of pregnancy, birthing, and bonding.* New York: Human Sciences Press.

Parmalee, A. (1975). Neurophysiological and behavioral organization of premature infants in the first months of life. *Biological Psychiatry, 10,* 501–512.

Parmalee, A. (1986). Children's illnesses: Their beneficial effects on behavioral development. *Child Development, 57,* 1–10.

Parmalee, A., and Sigman, M. (1983). Perinatal brain development and behavior. In P. Mussen (ed.), *Handbook of child psychology* (vol. 2). New York: Wiley.

Parmalee, A., and Stern, E. (1972). The development of states in infants. In C. Clemente, D. Purpura, and F. Mayer (eds.), *Sleep and the maturing nervous system.* New York: Academic Press.

Parten, M. (1932). Social play among preschool children. *Journal of Abnormal and Social Psychology, 27,* 243–269.

Pascual-Leone, J., Goodman, D., Ammon, P., and Subelman, I. (1978). Piagetian theory and neo-Piagetian analysis as psychological guides in education. In J. McCarthy Gallagher and J. Easley (eds.), *Knowledge and development* (vol. 2). New York: Plenum.

Passer, M. (1982). Psychological stress in youth sports. In R. Magill, M. Ash, and F. Smoll (eds.), *Children in sport.* Champaign, Ill.: Human Kinetics Publishers.

Passman, R. H. (1977). Providing attachment objects to reduce distress. *Developmental Psychology, 13,* 25–28.

Patrick, J. (1977). Political socialization and political education in the schools. In S. Renshon (ed.), *Handbook of political socialization.* New York: Free Press.

Patten, M. (1981). Self-concept and self-esteem: Factors in adolescent pregnancy. *Adolescence, 16,* 765–778.

Patterson, G. (1982). *Coercive family processes.* Eugene, Ore.: Castilia Press.

Pavlov, I. (1927/1980). *Conditioned reflexes.* London: Oxford University Press.; New York: Dover.

Pedzek, K., and Stevens, E. (1985). Children's memory for auditory and visual information on television. *Developmental Psychology, 21,* 400–415.

Peery, J. C. (1980). Neonate-adult head movement: No and yes revisited. *Developmental Psychology, 16,* 245–250.

Peller, L. (1954). Libidinal phases, ego development, and play. *Psychoanalytic Study of the Child, 9,* 178–198.

Pelton, L. (1978). Child abuse and neglect: The myth of classlessness. *American Journal of Orthopsychiatry, 48,* 608–616.

Pepler, D., and Ross, H. (1981). The effects of play on convergent and divergent problem solving. *Child Development, 52,* 1202–1210.

Peretti, P. (1976). Closet friendships of black college students: Social intimacy. *Adolescence, 11,* 395–403.

Perfetti, C. (1986). Reading acquisition and beyond: Decoding includes cognition. In N. Stein (ed.), *Literacy in American schools.* Chicago: University of Chicago Press.

Perkins, D. (1981). *The mind's best work.* Cambridge, Mass.: Harvard University Press.

Perrin, E., and Gerrity, P. (1981). There's a demon in your belly: Children's understanding of illness. *Pediatrics, 67,* 841–849.

Petersen, A., and Taylor, B. (1980). The biological approach to adolescence: Biological change and psychological adaptation. In J. Adelson (ed.), *Handbook of adolescent psychology.* New York: Wiley.

Phillips, J. (1969). *The origins of intellect: Piaget's theory.* San Francisco: Freeman.

Phillips, S. (1982). *The invisible culture: Communication in classroom and community.* New York: Longmans.

Piaget, J. (1959). *The language and thought of the child* (M. Gabain, trans.). London: Routledge & Kegan Paul.

Piaget, J. (1962). *Play, dreams, and imitation in childhood.* New York: Norton.

Piaget, J. (1963). *The origins of intelligence in children.* New York: Norton.

Piaget, J. (1964). *The moral judgment of the child.* New York: Free Press.

Piaget, J. (1965). *The child's conception of the world.* Totowa, N.J.: Littlefield, Adams.

Piaget, J. (1970). Piaget's theory. In P. Mussen (ed.), *Carmichael's manual of child psychology* (3rd ed., vol. 1). New York: Wiley.

Piaget, J. (1976). *The psychology of intelligence.* Totowa, N.J.: Littlefield, Adams.

Piaget, J. (1983). Piaget's theory. In P. Mussen (ed.), *Handbook of child psychology* (vol. 1). New York: Wiley.

Piaget, J., and Inhelder, B. (1967). *The child's conception of space.* New York: Norton.

Piaget, J., and Inhelder, B. (1969). *The psychology of the child.* New York: Basic Books.

Piaget, J., and Inhelder, B. (1971). *Science of education and the psychology of the child.* New York: Viking.

Piaget, J., and Inhelder, B. (1973). *Memory and intelligence.* New York: Basic Books.

Piaget, J., Sinclair, H., and Bang, V. (1968). *Knowledge and the psychology of identity.* Paris: Presses Universitaires de France.

Piaget, J., and Szeminska, A. (1952). *The child's conception of number* (C. Gattegno and F. M. Hodgson, trans.). New York: Humanities Press.

Pipes, P. (1981). Infant feeding and nutrition. In P. Pipes (ed.), *Nutrition in infancy and childhood* (2nd ed.). St. Louis: Mosby.

Pissanos, B., Moore, J., and Reeve, T. (1983). Age, sex, and body composition as predictors of children's performance on basic motor abilities and health-related fitness items. *Perceptual and Motor Skills, 56,* 71–77.

Pleck, J. (1982). Husbands' paid work and family roles. In L. Lopata (ed.), Interweave of social roles (vol. 3). Greenwich, Conn.: JAI Press.

Pleck, J. (1983). Husbands' paid work and family roles. In L. Lopata, (ed.), *Research on the interweave of family and work* (vol. 3). Greenwich, Conn.: JAI Press.

Pless, I., and Satterwhite, B. (1975). Chronic Illness. In R. Haggerty, K. Roghmann, and I. Pless (eds.), *Child health and the community.* New York: Wiley.

Plomin, R., and Rowe, D. (1979). Genetic and environmental etiology of social behavior in infancy. *Developmental Psychology, 15,* 62–72.

Podd, M. (1972). Ego identity status and morality: The relationship between two developmental constructs. *Developmental Psychology, 6,* 497–507.

Pollitt, E., Eichler, A., and Chan, C. (1975). Psychosocial development and behavior of mothers of failure-to-thrive children. *American Journal of Orthopsychiatry, 45,* 527–537.

Pollitt, E., Garza, C., and Leibel, R. (1984). Nutrition and public policy. In H. Stevenson and A. Siegel (eds.), *Child development research and social policy.* Chicago: University of Chicago Press.

Poskitt, E., and Cole, T. (1977). Do fat babies stay fat? *British Medical Journal, 1,* 7–9.

Powell, D. (1986). Parent education and support programs. *Young Children, 41* (3), 47–52.

Powell, T., and Ogle, P. (1985). *Brothers and sisters—A special part of exceptional families.* Baltimore: Brookes.

Premack, D. (1965). Reinforcement theory. In M. R. Jones (ed.), *Nebraska Symposium on Motivation: 1965.* Lincoln: University of Nebraska Press.

Presson, C. (1981). *The development of map-reading skills.* Paper presented to the Society for Research on Child Development, Boston, April.

Preston, S. (1976). *Mortality patterns in national populations.* New York: Academic Press.

Pringle, S., and Ramsey, B. (1982). *Promoting the health of children.* St. Louis: Mosby.

Prinz, P., and Prinz, E. (1979). Simultaneous acquisition of ASL and spoken English. *Sign Language Studies, 25,* 283–296.

Pulos, S., and Linn, M. (1978). Pitfalls and pendulums. *Formal Operator, 1* (2), 9–11.

Quigley, M., Sheehan, K., Wilkes, M., and Yen, S. (1979). Effects of maternal smoking on circulating catecholamine levels and fetal heart rates. *American Journal of Obstetrics and Gynecology, 133,* 685–690.

Rader, N., Bausano, M., and Richards, J. (1981). On the nature of the visual-cliff avoidance response. *Child Development, 51,* 61–68.

Radin, N. (1982). The unique contribution of parents to early childrearing: The preschool years. In S. Moore and C. Cooper (eds.), *The young child: Reviews of research* (vol. 3). Washington, D.C.: National Association for the Education of Young Children.

Radke-Yarrow, M., and Zahn-Waxler, C. (in press). Roots, motives, and patterns in children's prosocial behavior. In J. Reykowski, J. Karylowski, D. Bar-Tal, and E. Staub (eds.), *Origins and maintenance of prosocial behaviors.* New York: Plenum.

Rapoport, R., Rapoport, R., and Strelitz, A. (1980). *Father, mothers, and society: Perspectives on parenting.* New York: Vintage.

Raven, J. (1962). *Progressive matrices,* Form 1962. New York: The Psychological Corporation.

Re:act (1984). Viewing goes up. *Action for Children's Television Magazine, 13,* 4.

Reaves, J., and Roberts, A. (1983). The effect of type of information on children's attraction to peers. *Child Development, 54,* 1024–1031.

Rebelsky, F., and Hanks, C. (1971). Fathers' vocal interactions with infants in the first three months of life. *Child Development, 42,* 63–68.

Reiss, I. (1967). *The social context of sexual permissiveness.* New York: Holt, Rinehart, and Winston.

Rest, J. (1979). *Development in judging moral issues.* Minneapolis: University of Minnesota Press.

Rest, J. (1980). Development in moral judgment research. *Developmental Psychology, 16,* 251–256.

Rest, J. (1983). Morality. In P. Mussen (ed.), *Handbook of child psychology* (vol. 4). New York: Wiley.

Rheingold, H., and Cook, K. (1975). The content of boys' and girls' rooms as an index of parents' behavior. *Child Development, 46,* 459–463.

Rice, M. (1982). Child language: What children know and how. In T. Field (ed.), *Review of human development.* New York: Wiley.

Rierdan, J., and Koff, E. (1980). The psychological impact of menarche: Integrative versus disruptive changes. *Journal of Youth and Adolescence, 9,* 49–54.

Rieser, J., Yonas, A., and Wikner, K. (1976). Radial localization of odors by human neonates. *Child Development, 47,* 856–859.

Ringness, T. (1967). Identification patterns, motivation, and school achievement of bright junior high school boys. *Journal of Educational Psychology, 58,* 93–102.

Rinkoff, R. F., and Carter, C. M. (1980). Effects of setting and maternal accessibility on infants' response to brief separation. *Child Development, 51,* 603–606.

Robert, M., and Charbonneau, C. (1978). Extinction of liquid conservation by modeling: Three indicators of its artificiality. *Child Development, 49,* 19–200.

Roberton, M. (1977). Stability of stage categorizations across trials: Implications for the "stage theory." *Journal of Human Movement Studies, 3,* 49–59.

Roberton, M. (1978). Stages in motor development. In M. Ridenour (ed.), *Motor development: Issues and applications.* Princeton, N.J.: Princeton Book Company.

Robinson, J. (1980). Housework technology and household work. In S. Bern (ed.), *Women and household labor.* Beverly Hills: Sage.

Roche, A., and Malina, R. (1983). *Manual of physical status and performance in childhood* (vol. 1–2). New York: Plenum.

Rode, S., Chang, P., Fisch, R., and Sroufe, L. (1981). Attachment patterns of infants separated at birth. *Developmental Psychology, 17,* 188–191.

Rodin, J. (1977). Bidirectional influences in emotionality, stimulus responsivity, and metabolic events in obesity. In J. Maser and M. Seligman (eds.), *Psychopathology: Experimental models.* San Francisco: Freeman.

Rodnick, R., and Wood, B. (1973). The communication strategies of children. *Speech Teacher, 22,* 114–124.

Roesler, T., and Deisher, R. (1972). Youthful male homosexuality. *Journal of the American Medical Association, 21,* 1018–1023.

Rogers, C. (1984). *Freedom to learn* (2nd ed.). Columbus, Ohio: Merrill.

Roghmann, K. (1975). The use of medications: A neglected aspect of health and illness behavior. In R. Haggerty, K. Roghmann, and I. Pless (eds.), *Child health and the community.* New York: Wiley.

Roghmann, K., and Pless, I. (1975). Acute illness. In R. Haggerty, K. Roghmann, and I. Pless (eds.), *Child health and the community.* New York: Wiley.

Romeo, F. (1984). Adolescence, sexual conflict, and anorexia nervosa. *Adolescence, 19,* 551–555.

Roopnarine, J., and Field, T. (1982). Peer-directed behaviors of infants and toddlers during nursery school play. In T. Field (ed.), *Review of human development.* New York: Wiley.

Root, A. L. (1983). Respiratory crises. In K. Vestal and C. McKenzie (eds.), *High-risk perinatal nursing.* Philadelphia: Saunders.

Rose, S., and Blank, M. (1974). The potency of context in children's cognition. *Child Development, 45,* 499–502.

Rosenberg, M. (1979). *Conceiving the self.* New York: Basic Books.

Rosenthal, D., Gurney, R., and Moore, S. (1982). From trust to intimacy: A new inventory for examining Erikson's stages of psychological development. *Journal of Youth and Adolescence, 11,* 411–419.

Rosett, H., Weiner, L., Zuckerman, B., McKinlay, S., and Edelin, K. (1980). Reduction of alcohol consumption during pregnancy with benefits to the newborn. *Alcoholism: Clinical and Experimental Research, 4,* 178–184.

Ross, D., and Ross, S. (1976). *Hyperactivity: Research, theory, action.* New York: Wiley.

Ross, D., and Ross, S. (1982). *Hyperactivity: Current issues, research, and theory* (2nd ed.). New York: Wiley.

Rotenberg, K. (1980). Children's use of intentionality in judgments of character and disposition. *Child Development, 51,* 282–284.

Rothbart, M. K. (1981). Measurement of temperament in infancy. *Child Development, 52,* 569–578.

Rousseau, J. (1763/1911). *Emile, or on education*. London: Dent.

Rousso, H. (1984). Fostering healthy self-esteem. *The Exceptional Parent, 8,* 9–14.

Rubenstein, J., and Howes, C. (1976). The effects of peers on toddler interaction with mother and toys. *Child Development, 47,* 597–605.

Rubin, K., Fein, G., and Vandenberg, B. (1984). Play. In P. Mussen (ed.), *Handbook of child psychology* (vol. 4). New York: Wiley.

Rubin, K., and Krasnor, L. (1980). Changes in the play behaviors of preschoolers: A short-term longitudinal investigation. *Canadian Journal of Behavioral Science, 12,* 278–282.

Rubin, K., Maioni, T., and Hornung, M. (1976). Free play behaviors in middle and lower class preschools: Parten and Piaget revisited. *Child Development, 47,* 414–419.

Rubin, K., Watson, K., and Jambor, T. (1978). Free play behaviors in preschool and kindergarten children. *Child Development, 49,* 534–536.

Ruble, D., and Ruble, T. (1980). Sex stereotypes. In A. G. Miller (ed.), *In the eye of the beholder: Contemporary issues in stereotyping*. New York: Holt, Rinehart, and Winston.

Ruff, H. (1980). Infant recognition of the invariant form of objects. *Child Development, 49,* 293–306.

Ruhland, D., and Feld, S. (1977). The development of achievement motivation in black and white children. *Child Development, 48,* 1362–1368.

Rule, B., Nesdale, A., and McAra, M. (1974). Children's reactions to information about the intentions underlying an aggressive act. *Child Development, 45,* 794–798.

Russell, D. (1983). The incidence and prevalence of intrafamilial and extrafamilial sexual abuse of female children. *Child Abuse and Neglect, 7,* 133–146.

Rutter, M. (1980). *Changing youth in a changing society: Patterns of adolescent development and disorder.* Cambridge, Mass.: Harvard University Press.

Rutter, M. (1983). Developmental psychopathology. In P. Mussen (ed.), *Handbook of child psychology* (vol. 4). New York: Wiley.

Rutter, M., Chadwick, O., and Shaffer, D. (1984). Head injury. In M. Rutter (ed.), *Developmental neuropsychiatry*. New York: Guilford.

Rutter, M., and Garmezy, N. (1983). Developmental psychopathology. In P. Mussen (ed.), *Handbook of child psychology* (vol. 4). New York: Wiley.

Rutter, M., Graham, P., Chadwick, O., and Yule, W. (1976). Adolescent turmoil: Fact or fiction? *Journal of Child Psychology and Psychiatry, 17,* 35–36.

Rutter, M., Graham, P., and Yule, W. (1970). *A neuropsychiatric study in childhood*. London: Heinemann Medical.

Rutter, M., Maughan, B., Mortimore, P., and Ouston, J. (1979). *Fifteen thousand hours: Secondary schools and their effects on children*. Cambridge, Mass.: Harvard University Press.

Ryan, E. B. (1979). Identifying and remediating failures in reading comprehension: Toward an instructional approach for poor comprehenders. In T. Waller and G. MacKinnon (eds.), *Advances in reading research*. New York: Academic Press.

Salkind, N., and Nelson, C. (1980). A note on the developmental nature of reflection-impulsivity. *Developmental Psychology, 3,* 237–238.

Saltz, E., and Brodie, J. (1982). Pretend-play training in childhood: A review and critique. In D. Pepler and K. Rubin (ed.), *The play of children: Current theory and research*. Basel, Switzerland: Karger.

Sameroff, A. (1978). Organization and stability of newborn behavior: A commentary on the Brazelton Neonatal Behavior Assessment Scale. *Monographs of the Society for Research on Child Development, 43* (177).

Sameroff, A. (1979). *The organization and stability of newborn behavior*. Chicago: University of Chicago Press.

Sameroff, A., and Cavanaugh, P. (1979). Learning in infancy: A developmental perspective. In J. Osofsky (ed.), *Handbook of infant development*. New York: Wiley.

Sandis, S. E. (1975). The transmission of mothers' educational ambitions, as related to specific socialization techniques. *Journal of Marriage and the Family, 32,* 204–211.

Santrock, J., and Warshak, R. (1979). Father custody and social development in boys and girls. *Journal of Social Issues, 35,* 112–125.

Sarafino, E., and Armstrong, J. (1986). *Child and adolescent development,* New York: West.

Savic, S. (1980). *How twins learn to talk*. London: Academic Press.

Savin-Williams, R. C., and Demo, D. H. (1984). Developmental change and stability in adolescent self-concept. *Developmental Psychology, 20,* 1100–1110.

Sawin, D. (1979). Assessing empathy in children: A search for an elusive construct. Paper presented at the meeting of the Society for Research on Child Development, San Francisco.

Scardamalia, M., and Bereiter, C. (1986). Research on written composition. In M. Wittrock (ed.), *Handbook of research on teaching* (3rd ed.). New York: Macmillan.

Scarr, S. (1984). Intelligence: What the introductory psychology student might want to know. In A. Rogers and C. J. Scheirer (eds.), *The G. Stanley Hall lecture series* (vol. 4). Washington, D.C.: American Psychological Association.

Scarr, S. (1984). *Mother care, other care.* New York: Basic Books.

Scarr, S. (1985). Constructing psychology: Making facts and fables for our times. *American Psychologist, 40,* 499–512.

Scarr, S., and Carter-Saltzman, L. (1983). Genetics and intelligence. In J. Fuller and E. Simmel (eds.), *Behavior genetics.* Hillsdale, N.J.: Erlbaum.

Scarr, S., and Salapatek, P. (1970). Patterns of fear development during infancy. *Merrill-Palmer Quarterly, 16,* 53–90.

Scarr-Salapatek, S. (1976). An evolutionary perspective on infant intelligence: Species patterns and individual variations. In M. Lewis (ed.), *Origins of intelligence.* New York: Plenum.

Schaffer, H. (1978). Acquiring the concept of the dialogue. In M. Bornstein and W. Kessen (eds.), *Psychological development from infancy: Image to intention.* Hillsdale, N.J.: Erlbaum.

Schaffer, H. (1984). *The child's entry into the social world.* New York: Academic Press.

Schaffer, H., and Emerson, P. (1964). Patterns of response to physical contact in early human development. *Journal of Child Psychology and Psychiatry, 5,* 1–13.

Schiff, H. (1977). *The bereaved parent.* London: Penguin.

Schinke, S., and Gilchrist, L. (1977). Adolescent pregnancy: An interpersonal skills training approach to prevention. *Social Work in Health Care, 3,* 158–167.

Schleifer, M., Weiss, G., Cohen, N., Elman, M., Cvejic, H., and Kruger, E. (1975). Hyperactivity in preschoolers and the effect of methylphenedate. *American Journal of Orthopsychiatry, 21,* 77–88.

Schlesinger, I. M. (1977). The role of cognitive development and linguistic input in language acquisition. *Journal of Child Language, 4,* 153–169.

Schofield, J. (1981). Complementary and conflicting identities: Images and interactions in an interracial school. In S. Asher and J. Gottman (eds.), *The development of children's friendships.* New York: Cambridge University Press.

Schofield, J., and Sugar, H. (1977). Peer interaction patterns in an integrated middle school. *Sociometry, 40,* 130–138.

Schowalter, J., Patterson, P., Tallmer, M., Kutscher, A.,

Gullo, S., and Peretz, D. (eds.) (1983). *The child and death.* New York: Columbia University Press.

Schulman-Galambos, C., and Galambos, R. (1979). Brain stem evoked response audiometry in newborn hearing screening. *Archives of Otolaryngology, 105,* 86–90.

Schwartz, J., Strickland, R., and Krolick, G. (1974). Infant day care: Behavioral effect at preschool age. *Developmental Psychology, 10,* 502–506.

Schwartz, R., and Leonard, L. (1982). Do children pick and choose? An examination of phonological selection and avoidance. *Journal of Child Language, 9,* 319–336.

Schwartzman, H. B. (1978). *Transformations: The anthropology of children's play.* New York: Plenum.

Schweinhart, L., and Weikart, D. (1980). *Young children grow up: The effects of the Perry Preschool Program on youths through age 15.* Ypsilanti, Mich.: High/Scope Press.

Schweinhart, L., and Weikart, D. (1983). The effects of the Perry Preschool Program on youths through age 15: A summary. In Consortium for Longitudinal Studies, *As the twig is bent.* Hillsdale, N.J.: Erlbaum.

Scott, P., Cross, D., and Lipson, M. (1984). Informed strategies for learning: A program to improve children's reading awareness and comprehension. *Journal of Educational Psychology, 76,* 1239–1252.

Searle, L. V. (1949). The organization of hereditary maze-brightness and maze-dullness. *Genetic Psychology Monographs, 39,* 279–325.

Sears, R., Maccoby, E., and Levin, H. (1957). *Patterns of childrearing.* Evanston, Ill.: Row Peterson.

Secord, P., and Peevers, B. (1974). The development and attribution of person concepts. In T. Mischel (ed.), *Understanding other persons.* Totowa, N.J.: Rowman & Littlefield.

Segalowitz, S. (1983). *Two sides of the brain.* Englewood Cliffs, N.J.: Prentice-Hall.

Seidel, U., Chadwick, O., and Rutter, M. (1975). Psychological disorders in crippled children: A comparative study of children with and without brain damage. *Developmental Medicine and Child Neurology, 17,* 563–573.

Seifert, K. (1973). *The development of qualitative identity.* Unpublished doctoral dissertation, University of Michigan.

Select Committee on Children, Youth, and Families (1983). *U.S. children and their families: Current conditions and recent trends.* Washington, D.C.: U.S. Government Printing Office.

Select Panel for the Promotion of Child Health (1981a). *Better health for our children* (vol. 1). Washington, D.C.: U.S. Government Printing Office.

Select Panel for the Promotion of Child Health (1981b). *Better health for our children* (vol. 3). Washington, D.C.: U.S. Government Printing Office.

Selman, R. (1980). *The growth of interpersonal understanding.* New York: Academic Press.

Selman, R. (1981a). The child as friendship philosopher. In S. Asher and J. Gottman (eds.), *The development of children's friendships.* New York: Cambridge University Press.

Selman, R. (1981b). The development of interpersonal competence: The role of understanding in conduct. *Developmental Review, 1,* 401–422.

Serbin, L., Tonick, I., and Sternglanz, S. (1977). Shaping cooperative cross-sex play. *Child Development, 48,* 924–929.

Serbin, L., Connor, J., and Iler, I. (1979). Sex-stereotyped and nonstereotyped introductions of new toys in the preschool classroom. *Psychology of Women Quarterly, 4,* 261–265.

Shaffer, D. (1974). Suicide in childhood and adolescence. *Journal of Child Psychiatry, 15,* 275–291.

Shaffer, D., Chadwick, O., and Rutter, M. (1975). Psychiatric outcome of localized head injury in children. In R. Porter and D. FitzSimons (eds.), *Outcome of severe damage to the central nervous system.* Amsterdam: Excerpta Medica.

Shaftesbury, Earl of (A. A. Cooper) (1868). *Speeches of the Earl of Shaftesbury.* London: Chapman and Hall.

Shanan, J., Brzezinski, H., Shilman, F., and Saron, M. (1965). Active coping behavior, anxiety, and cortical steroid excretion in the prediction of transient amenorrhea. *Behavioral Science, 10,* 461–465.

Shannon, D. (1980). Sudden infant death syndrome and near miss infants. In S. Gellis and B. Kagan (eds.), *Current pediatric therapy.* Philadelphia: Saunders.

Shantz, C., and Shantz, D. (1985). Conflict between children: Social-cognitive and sociometric correlates. In M. Berkowitz (ed.), *Peer conflict and psychological growth.* New Directions for Child Development, No. 29. San Francisco: Jossey-Bass.

Shapiro, E., and Weber, E. (eds.) (1982). *Cognitive and affective growth: Developmental interaction.* New York: Erlbaum.

Sharabany, R., Gershoni, R., and Hoffman, J. (1981). Girlfriend, boyfriend: Age and sex differences in intimate friendship. *Developmental Psychology, 17,* 800–809.

Shatz, M. (1983). Communication. In P. Mussen (ed.), *Handbook of child psychology* (vol. 4). New York: Wiley.

Shayer, M. (1979). Has Piaget's construct of formal operational thinking any utility? *British Journal of Educational Psychology, 49* (3), 265–276.

Shepherd-Look, D. (1982). Sex differentiation and the development of sex roles. In B. Wolman (ed.), *Handbook of developmental psychology.* Englewood Cliffs, N.J.: Prentice-Hall.

Shultz, T., Dover, A., and Amsel, E. (1979). The logical and empirical bases of conservation judgments. *Cognition, 7,* 99–123.

Sidell, R. (1972). *Women and child care in China.* New York: Hill and Wang.

Siegel, A., Herman, J., Allen, G., and Kirasic, K. (1979). The development of cognitive maps of large- and small-scale spaces. *Child Development, 50,* 582–585.

Siegel, L. (1982). Reproductive, perinatal, and environmental factors as predictors of the cognitive and language development of preterm and full-term infants. *Child Development, 53,* 963–973.

Siegel, O. (1982). Personality development in adolescence. In B. Wolman (ed.), *Handbook of developmental psychology.* Englewood Cliffs, N.J.: Prentice-Hall.

Siegler, R. (1976). Three aspects of cognitive development. *Cognitive Psychology, 4,* 481–520.

Siegler, R. (1978). The origins of scientific reasoning. In R. Siegler (ed.), *Children's thinking: What develops?* Hillsdale, N.J.: Erlbaum.

Siegler, R. (1983). Information processing approaches to cognitive development. In P. Mussen (ed.), *Manual of child psychology* (4th ed., vol. 1). New York: Wiley.

Sigel, I., and Cocking, R. (1977). *Cognitive development from childhood to adolescence: A constructivist perspective.* New York: Holt, Rinehart, and Winston.

Sigel, I., Dreyer, A., and McGillicuddy-DeLisi, A. (1984). Psychological perspectives of the family. In R. Parke (ed.), *Review of child development research* (vol. 7). Chicago: University of Chicago Press.

Silber, S. J. (1980). *How to get pregnant.* New York: Warner.

Sillanpaa, M. (1973). Medico-social prognosis of children with epilepsy. *Acta Paediatrica Scandinavica, 237.*

Silvern, S., Williamson, P., and Countermine, T. (1983). Video game playing and aggression in young children. Paper presented at the annual meeting of the American Educational Research Association, Montreal.

Simmel, E. C. (ed.) (1980). *Early experiences and early behavior.* New York: Academic Press.

Simmel, E. C., and Bagwell, M. (1983). Genetics of exploratory behavior and activity. In J. Fuller and E. Simmel (eds.), *Behavior genetics.* Hillsdale, N.J.: Erlbaum.

Simms, M., and Smith, C. (1981). Young fathers: Attitudes to marriage and family life. In L. McKee and M. O'Brien (eds.), *The father figure.* London: Tavistock.

Simon, W., Berger, A., and Gagnon, J. (1972). Beyond anxiety and fantasy: The coital experiences of college youth. *Journal of Youth and Adolescence, 1,* 203–222.

Sinclair, D. (1978). *Human growth after birth.* New York: Oxford University Press

Sinclair, H. (1969). Developmental psycholinguistics. In D. Elkind and J. Flavell (eds.), *Studies in cognitive development.* New York: Oxford University Press.

Sinclair, H. (1976). Epistemology and the study of language. In B. Inhelder and H. Chipman (eds.), *Piaget and his school.* New York: Springer-Verlag.

Singleton, L., and Asher, S. (1979). Racial integration and children's peer preferences: An investigation of developmental and cohort differences. *Child Development, 50,* 936–941.

Skinner, B. F. (1957). *Verbal behavior.* New York: Appleton-Century-Crofts.

Skinner, B. F. (1967). Autobiography. In E. Boring and G. Lindzey (eds.), *A history of psychology in autobiography* (vol. 3). New York: Appleton-Century-Crofts.

Skinner, B. F. (1972). *Beyond freedom and dignity.* New York: Knopf.

Skinner, B. F. (1974). *About behaviorism.* Chicago: Rand.

Skinner, B. F. (1976). *Particulars of my life.* New York: Knopf.

Skinner, B. F. (1979). *The shaping of a behaviorist.* New York: Knopf.

Skipper, J., and Nass, G. (1966). Dating behavior: A framework for analysis and an illustration. *Journal of Marriage and the Family, 28,* 412–420.

Skodak, M., and Skeels, H. M. (1949). A final follow-up study of one hundred adopted children. *Journal of Genetic Psychology, 75,* 85–125.

Skolnick, A. (1986). *The psychology of human development.* New York: Harcourt Brace Jovanovich.

Slaughter, D. (1983). Early intervention and its effects on maternal and child development. *Monographs of the Society for Research on Child Development 48,* 202.

Slavin, R. (1983). *Cooperative learning.* New York: Longman.

Slavin, R. (1984). Students motivating students to excel: Cooperative incentives, cooperative tasks and student achievement. *Elementary School Journal, 85,* 53–64.

Sloane, K. (1985). Home influences on talent development. In B. Bloom (ed.), *Developing talent in young people.* New York: Ballantine.

Slobin, D. (1973). Cognitive prerequisites for the development of grammar. In C. Ferguson and D. Slobin (eds.), *Studies of child language development.* New York: Holt, Rinehart, and Winston.

Smeriglio, V. (ed.) (1981). *Newborns and parents.* Hillsdale, N.J.: Erlbaum.

Smilansky, S. (1968). *The effects of sociodramatic play on disadvantaged preschool children.* New York: Wiley.

Smith, C. (1968). *Adolescence.* London: Longmans.

Smith, D. (1977). *Growth and its disorders.* Philadelphia: Saunders.

Smith, D. W., Bierman, E. L., and Robinson, N. M. (eds.) (1978). *The biologic ages of man: From conception through old age.* Philadelphia: Saunders.

Smith, J. (1981). *Philosophical considerations of mastery learning theory: An empirical study.* Paper presented at the annual meeting of the American Educational Research Association.

Smith, M. E. (1926). An investigation of the development of the sentence and the extent of vocabulary development in young children. *University of Iowa Studies in Child Welfare, 3,* 5.

Smith, R., and Smoll, F. (1982). Psychological stress: A conceptual model and some intervention strategies in youth sports. In R. Magill, M. Ash, and F. Smoll (eds.), *Children in sport.* Champaign, Ill.: Human Kinetics Publishers.

Smith, W. (1979). *Faith and belief.* Princeton, N.J.: Princeton University Press.

Smitherman, G. (1977). *Talkin and testifyin.* Boston: Houghton Mifflin.

Smolak, L. (1982). Cognitive precursors of receptive vs. expressive language. *Journal of Child Language, 9,* 13–22.

Snow, C., and Ferguson, C. (eds.) (1977). *Talking to children.* Cambridge, England: Cambridge University Press.

Sommers, N. (1980). Revision strategies of student writers and experienced adult writers. *College Composition and Communication, 31,* 378–388.

Sorensen, R. (1973). *Adolescent sexuality in contemporary America: Personal values and sexual behavior ages 13–19.* New York: Abrams.

Sosniak, L. (1985). Phases of learning. In B. Bloom (ed.), *Developing talent in young people.* New York: Ballantine.

Speizer, J. (1978). The teenage years. In Boston Women's Health Book Collective (eds.), *Ourselves and our children: A book by and for parents.* New York: Random House.

Spelke, E. (1979). Perceiving bimodally specified events in infancy. *Developmental Psychology, 15,* 626–636.

Spelke, E., and Owsley, C. (1979). Intermodal exploration and knowledge in infancy. *Infant Behavior and Development, 2,* 13–27.

Spitz, R. (1965). *The first year of life.* New York: International Universities Press.

Spock, B. (1976). *Baby and child care* (rev. ed.). New York: Bantam.

Spodek, B., Saracho, O., and Lee, R. (1984). *Mainstreaming young children.* Belmont, Calif.: Wadsworth.

Sponseller, D., and Jaworski, A. (1979). Social and cognitive complexity in young children's play. Paper presented at the annual meeting of the American Educational Research Association, San Francisco.

Sprague, R., and Ullman, R. (1981). Psychoactive drugs and child management. In J. Kaufman and D. Hallahan (eds.), *Handbook of special education.* Englewood Cliffs, N.J.: Prentice-Hall.

Sroufe, L. A. (1975). Drug treatment of children with behavior problems. In E. Horowitz (ed.), *Review of child development research* (vol. 4). Chicago: University of Chicago Press.

Sroufe, L. A. (1979). Socioemotional development. In J. Osofsky (ed.), *Handbook of infant development.* New York: Wiley.

Sroufe, L. A. (1979). The coherence of individual development: Early care, attachment, and subsequent developmental issues. *American Psychologist, 34,* 834–841.

Sroufe, L. A., Fox, N., and Pancake, V. (1983). Attachment and dependency in developmental perspective. *Child Development, 54,* 1615–1627.

Sroufe, L. A., and Waters, E. (1976). The onogenesis of smiling and laughter: A perspective on the organization of development in infancy. *Psychological Review, 83,* 173–189.

Sroufe, L. A., and Wunsch, J. (1972). The development of laughter in the first year of life. *Child Development, 43,* 1326–1344.

Staffieri, J. (1972). A study of social stereotypes of body image in children. *Journal of Personality and Social Psychology, 7,* 101–104.

Stallings, J., and Stipek, D. (1986). Research on early childhood and elementary school teaching programs. In M. Wittrock (ed.), *Handbook of research on teaching* (3rd ed.). New York: Macmillan.

Standfast, S., Kuter, B., Jereb, S., and Janerich, D. (1983). Predicting the risk of sudden infant death: Dilemmas for the practitioner. In J. Schowalter (ed.), *The child and death.* New York: Columbia University Press.

Stark, P., and Traxler, A. (1974). Empirical validation of Erikson's theory of identity crises in late adolescence. *The Journal of Psychology, 86,* 25–33.

Starr, R. (1979). Child abuse. *American Psychologist, 34,* 872–878.

Staub, E. (1979). *Positive social behavior and morality* (vol. 2). New York: Academic Press.

Staurovsky, L. (1983). Reproductive related health care problems of women. In G. Butnarescu and D. Tillotson (eds.), *Maternity nursing.* New York: Wiley.

Stechler, G., and Halton, A. (1983). Prenatal influences on human development. In B. Wolman, G. Stricker, S. Ellman, P. Keith-Spiegel, and D. Palermo (eds.), *Handbook of developmental psychology.* Englewood Cliffs, N.J.: Prentice-Hall.

Steffenson, M., and Guthrie, L. (1980). *Effect of situation on the verbalization of black inner-city children* (Report No. 180). Urbana, Ill.: University of Illinois, Center for the Study of Reading.

Stein, Z., Susser, M., Saenger, G., and Marolla, F. (1975). *Famine and human development.* New York: Oxford University Press.

Steinmetz, S. (1977). The use of force for resolving family conflict: The training ground for abuse. *Family Coordinator, 26,* 19–26.

Stern, D. (1974). Mother and infant at play: The dyadic interaction involving facial, vocal and gaze behaviors. In M. Lewis and L. Rosenblum (eds.), *The effect of the infant on its caretaker.* New York: Wiley.

Stern, D. (1977). *The first relationship: Infant and mother.* Cambridge, Mass.: Harvard University Press.

Sternberg, R. (1980). Factor theories of intelligence are all right almost. *Educational Researcher, 9,* 6–13 ff.

Sternberg, R. (1981). Intelligence and nonentrenchment. *Journal of Educational Psychology, 73,* 1–16.

Sternberg, R. (1983). The development of intelligence. In P. Mussen (ed.), *Handbook of child psychology* (vol. 4). New York: Wiley.

Sternberg, R. (1984a). *Beyond IQ: A triarchic theory of human intelligence.* New York: Cambridge University Press.

Sternberg, R. (ed.) (1984b). *Mechanisms of cognitive development.* San Francisco: Freeman.

Sternberg, R. (1984c). What should intelligence tests test? Implications of a triarchic theory of intelligence for intelligence testing. *Educational Researcher, 13* (1), 5–15.

Sternberg, R., and Davidson, R. (1985). Cognitive development in the gifted and talented. In F. Horowitz and M. O'Brien (eds.), *The gifted and talented: Developmental perspectives.* Washington, D.C.: American Psychological Association.

Sternberg, R., and Powell, J. (1983). The development of intelligence. In P. Mussen (ed.), *Handbook of child psychology* (3rd. ed., vol. 3). New York: Wiley.

Stevenson, J., and Richman, N. (1978). Behavior, language and development in three-year-old children. *Journal of Autism and Childhood Schizophrenia, 8,* 299–314.

Stewart, M., and Olds, I. (1973). *Raising a hyperactive child.* New York: Harper and Row.

Stini, W. (1972). Malnutrition, body size and proportion. *Ecology of Food and Nutrition, 1,* 121 ff.

Stipek, D., and Hoffman, J. (1980). Children's achievement related expectancies as a function of academic performance histories and sex. *Journal of Educational Psychology, 72,* 861–865.

Stone, C., and Day, M. (1978). Levels of availability of a formal operational strategy. *Child Development, 49,* 1054–1065.

Stone, C., and Day, M. (1980). Competence and performance models and the characterization of formal operational skills. *Human Development, 23,* 323–353.

Stores, G. (1978). School children with epilepsy at risk for learning and behavior problems. *Developmental Medicine and Child Neurology, 20,* 502–508.

Strauss, M., Starr, R., Ostrea, E., Chavez, C., and Stryker, J. (1976). Behavioral concomitants of prenatal addiction to narcotics. *Journal of Pediatrics, 89,* 842–846.

Strauss, S., Danziger, J., and Ramati, T. (1977). University students' understanding of nonconservation: Implications for structural reversions. *Developmental Psychology, 13,* 359–363.

Streissguth, A., Herman, C., and Smith, D. (1978). Intelligence, behavior, and dysmorphogenesis in the fetal alcohol syndrome: A report on 20 patients. *Journal of Pediatrics, 92,* 363–367.

Stuckey, M., McGhee, P., and Bell, N. (1982). Parent-child interaction: The influence of maternal employment. *Developmental Psychology, 4,* 635–644.

Sullivan, H. (1953). *The interpersonal theory of psychiatry.* New York: Norton.

Sullivan, K., and Sullivan, A. (1980). Adolescent-parent separation. *Developmental Psychology, 16,* 93–99.

Super, C. (1981). Behavioral development in infancy. In R. Munroe, R. Munroe, and B. Whiting (eds.), *Handbook of cross-cultural human development.* New York: Garland STPM Press.

Super, C. (1982). Unpacking African infant precocity. In N. Warren (ed.), *Studies in cross-cultural psychology* (vol. 3). London: Academic Press.

Susman, E., Huston-Stein, A., and Friedrich-Coffer, L. (1980). Relation of conceptual tempo to social behaviors of Head Start children. *Journal of Genetic Psychology, 137,* 17–20.

Sutton-Smith, B. (1981). *A history of children's play.* Philadelphia: University of Pennsylvania Press.

Sutton-Smith, B. (1984). Text and context in imaginative play and the social sciences. In A. Kessel and A. Goncu (eds.), *Analyzing children's play dialogues.* New Directions For Child Development, No. 25. San Francisco: Jossey-Bass.

Sutton-Smith, B., and Kelly-Byrne, D. (1984a). The idealization of play. In D. Smith (ed.), *Play in animals and humans.* London: Van Nostrand.

Sutton-Smith, B., and Kelly-Byrne, D. (1984b). *The masks of play.* West Point, N.Y.: Leisure Press.

Suzuki, S. (1969). *Nurtured by love.* New York: Exposition Press.

Svejda, M., Campos, J., and Emde, R. (1980). Mother-infant "bonding": Failure to generalize. *Child Development, 51,* 775–779.

Swain, H. (1979). Childhood views of death. *Death Education, 2,* 341–358.

Tannen, D. (1984). *Conversational style.* Norwood, N.J.: Ablex.

Tanner, J. (1972). Sequence, tempo and individual variation in growth and development of boys and girls aged twelve to sixteen. In J. Kagan and R. Coles (eds.), *Twelve to sixteen: Early adolescence.* New York: Norton.

Tanner, J. (1973). Trend towards earlier menarche in London, Oslo, Copenhagen, the Netherlands and Hungary. *Nature, 243,* 95–96.

Tanner, J. (1978a). *Education and physical growth* (2nd ed.). London: Hodder and Stoughton.

Tanner, J. (1978b). *Fetus into man: Physical growth from conception to maturity.* Cambridge, Mass.: Harvard University Press.

Taub, H., Goldstein, K., and Caputo, D. (1977). Indices of neonatal prematurity as discriminators of development in middle childhood. *Child Development, 48,* 797–805.

Teitelbaum, M. (ed.) (1976). *Sex differences: Social and biological perspectives.* Garden City, N.Y.: Doubleday.

Terman, L., and Merrill, M. (1973). *Stanford-Binet intelligence scale: Manual for the third revision.* Boston: Houghton Mifflin.

Terman, L., and Merrill, M. (1974). *Stanford-Binet intelligence scale* (rev. ed.). Iowa City, Iowa: Riverside.

Thomas, A., and Chess, S. (1977). *Temperament and development.* New York: Brunner/Mazel.

Thomas, A., and Chess, S. (1981). The role of temperament in the contributions of individuals to their development. In R. Lerner and N. Busch-Rossnagle (eds.), *Individuals as producers of their development: A life-span perspective.* New York: Academic Press.

Thomas, J., Gallagher, J., and Thomas, K. (1982). Developmental memory factors in children's perception of sport. In R. Magill, M. Ash, and F. Smoll (eds.), *Children in sport.* Champaign, Ill.: Human Kinetics Publishers.

Thornburg, H. (1975). Adolescent sources of initial sex information. In R. Grinder (ed.), *Studies in adolescence:*

A book of readings on adolescent development (3rd ed.). New York: Macmillan.

Thurstone, L. (1938). *Primary mental abilities.* Chicago: University of Chicago Press.

Tobach, E., and Rosoff, B. (eds.) (1978). *Genes and gender.* New York: Gordian Press.

Torney-Purta, J. (1984). Political socialization and policy: The United States in a cross-national context. In H. Stevenson and A. Siegel (eds.), *Child development research and social policy.* Chicago: University of Chicago Press.

Tough, J. (1977). *Talking and learning.* London: Ward Lock Educational.

Tryon, R. C. (1940). Individual differences. In F. A. Moss (ed.), *Comparative psychology.* Englewood Cliffs, N.J.: Prentice-Hall.

Turiel, E. (1978). Distinct conceptual and developmental domains: Social-convention and morality. In C. Keasey (ed.), *Nebraska symposium on motivation* (vol. 25). Lincoln: University of Nebraska Press.

Turiel, E. (1982). Domains and categories in social cognitive development. In W. Overton (ed.), *The relationship between social and cognitive development.* Hillsdale, N.J.: Erlbaum.

Turiel, E., and Smetana, J. (1984). Social knowledge and action: The coordination of domains. In W. Kurtines, and J. Gewirtz (eds.), *Morality, moral behavior, and moral development.* New York: Wiley.

Turnbull, A., and Turnbull, H. (1986). *Families, professionals, and exceptionality: A special partnership.* Columbus, Ohio: Merrill.

Turrini, P. (1980). Psychological crises in normal pregnancy. In B. Blum (ed.), *Psychological aspects of pregnancy, birthing, and bonding.* New York: Human Sciences Press.

Umiker-Sebeok, D. J. (1980). Silence is golden? The changing role of non-talk in preschool conversations. In M. Key (ed.), *The relationship of verbal and non-verbal communication.* New York: Mouton.

U.S. Bureau of the Census (1985). *Statistical abstract of the United States.* Washington, D.C.: U.S. Government Printing Office.

U.S. Commission on Civil Rights (1977). *Window dressing on the set: Women and minorities in television.* Washington, D.C.: Government Printing Office.

U.S. Department of Commerce, Bureau of the Census (1976). *Historical statistics of the United States, colonial times to 1970.* Washington, D.C.: U.S. Government Printing Office.

U.S. Department of Commerce, Bureau of the Census (1978). *Statistical portrait of women in the United States.* Washington, D.C.: U.S. Government Printing Office.

U.S. Department of Commerce, Bureau of the Census (1985). *Statistical abstract of the United States.* Washington, D.C.: U.S. Government Printing Office.

U.S. Department of Health, Education and Welfare (1980). Publication No. (PHS) 80-1232. Hyattsville, Md.

U.S. Department of Labor, Bureau of Labor Statistics (1981). *Marital and family characteristics of labor force* (Report No. 237). Washington, D.C.: Department of Labor.

U.S. Department of Labor, Bureau of Labor Statistics (1984). *Marital and family characteristics of workers.* Washington, D.C.

U.S. Department of Labor, Bureau of Labor Statistics (1986). *Employment and earnings, 1985.* Washington, D.C.: U.S. Government Printing Office.

Uzgiris, I., and Hunt, J. (1975). *Assessment in infancy.* Chicago: University of Illinois Press.

Vadasy, P., Fewell, R., Meyer, D., and Schell, G. (1984). Siblings of handicapped children: A developmental perspective on family interactions. *Family Relations, 33,* 155–167.

Vandell, D. (1980). Sociability with peers and mothers in the first year. *Developmental Psychology, 16,* 355–361.

Vandell, D., and Powers, C. (1983). Day care quality and children's free play activities. *American Journal of Orthopsychiatry, 53,* 493–500.

Vandenberg, B. (1978). Play and development from an ethological perspective. *American Psychologist, 33,* 724–738.

Vandenberg, S. (1979). Twin studies. In A. Kaplan (ed.), *Human behavior genetics.* Springfield, Ill.: Thomas.

Van Duyne, H. (1973). Foundations of tactile perception in three- to seven-year-olds. *Journal of the Association for the Study of Perception, 8,* 1–9.

Van Wieringen, J. (1979). Secular growth changes. In F. Falkner and J. Tanner (eds.), *Human growth* (vol. 2). New York: Plenum.

Varenne, H. (1977). *Americans together: Structured diversity in a midwestern town.* New York: Teachers' College Press.

Vaughn, B., Gove, F., and Egeland, B. (1980). The relationship between out-of-home care and the quality of infant-mother attachment in an economically disadvantaged population. *Child Development, 51,* 1203–1204.

Vener, A., and Stewart, C. (1974). Adolescent sexual

behavior in middle America revisited: 1970–1973. *Journal of Marriage and the Family, 36,* 728–735.

Vener, A., Stewart, C., and Hager, D. (1972). The sexual behavior of adolescents in middle America: Generational and American-British comparisons. *Journal of Marriage and the Family, 34,* 696–705.

Vermeersch, J. (1981). The physiological basis of nutritional needs. In B. Worthington-Roberts, J. Vermeersch, and S. R. Williams (eds.), *Nutrition in pregnancy and lactation.* St. Louis: Mosby.

Vital Statistics of the United States, 1985. Washington, D.C.: Mortality Statistics Branch, Division of Vital Statistics, National Center for Health Statistics.

Volterra, V., and Teaschner, R. (1978). The acquisition and development of language by bilingual children. *Journal of Child Language, 5,* 311–326.

Vygotsky, L. (1962). *Thought and language.* Cambridge, Mass.: M.I.T. Press.

Vygotsky, L. (1967). Play and its role in the mental development of the child. *Soviet Psychology, 12,* 62–76.

Vygotsky, L. (1978). *Mind in society.* Cambridge, Mass.: Harvard University Press.

Wallace, D. (1985). Giftedness and the construction of a creative life. In F. Horowitz and M. O'Brien (eds.), *The gifted and talented: Developmental perspectives.* Washington, D.C.: American Psychological Association.

Wallach, M. (1985). Creativity testing and giftedness. In F. Horowitz and M. O'Brien (eds.), *The gifted and talented: Developmental perspectives.* Washington, D.C.: American Psychological Association.

Wallerstein, J. (1983). Children of divorce: The psychological tasks of the child. *American Journal of Orthopsychiatry, 53,* 230–243.

Wallerstein, J. (1984). Children of divorce: Preliminary report of a ten-year follow-up of young children. *American Journal of Orthopsychiatry, 54,* 444–458.

Wallerstein, J., and Kelly, J. (1980). *Surviving the breakup: How children actually cope with divorce.* New York: Basic Books.

Wallisch, S. (1983). Stress: The infant, family, and nurser. In K. Vestal and C. McKenzie (eds.), *High-risk perinatal nursing.* Philadelphia: Saunders.

Walters, G., and Grusec, J. (1977). *Punishment.* San Francisco: Freeman.

Wanamaker, N., Hearn, K., and Richarz, S. (1979). *More than graham crackers: Nutrition education and food preparation with young children.* Washington, D.C.: National Association for the Education of Young Children.

Wass, H., and Corr, C. (1984). *Helping children cope with death: Guidelines and resources.* Washington, D.C.: Hemisphere.

Waterman, A. (1982). Identity development from adolescence to adulthood: An extension of theory and a review of research. *Developmental Psychology, 18,* 341–358.

Waterman, A., and Goldman, J. (1976). A longitudinal study of ego identity development at a liberal arts college. *Journal of Youth and Adolescence, 5,* 361–370.

Waterman, A., Kohutis, E., and Pulone, J. (1977). The role of expressive writing in ego identity formation. *Developmental Psychology, 13,* 286–287.

Waters, E., and Deane, K. (1985). Defining and assessing individual differences in attachment relationships: Q-methodology and the organization of behavior in infancy and early childhood. In I. Bretherton and E. Waters (eds.), Growing points of attachment theory and research. *Monographs of the Society for Research on Child Development, 50,* 209.

Waters, E., Vaughn, B., and Egeland, B. (1980). Individual differences in infant-mother attachment relationships at age one: Antecedents in neonatal behavior in an urban, economically disadvantaged sample. *Child Development, 51,* 208–216.

Webb, N. (1982). Peer interaction and learning in cooperative small groups. *Journal of Educational Psychology, 74,* 642–655.

Webster's New World Dictionary (2nd ed.) (1984). New York: Simon and Schuster.

Wechsler, D. (1974). *Manual for the Wechsler intelligence scale for children* (rev. ed.). New York: The Psychological Corporation.

Weinberger, N., Gold, P., and Sternberg, D. (1984). Epenephrine enables Pavlovian fear conditioning under anesthesia. *Science, 223,* 605–607.

Weiss, J. S. (1981). *Your second child.* New York: Summit Books.

Weiss, L., and Lowenthal, M. (1975). Life-course perspectives on friendship. In M. F. Lowenthal, M. Thurner, and D. Chiriboga (eds.), *Four stages of life.* San Francisco: Jossey-Bass.

Weisz, J. (1980). Autonomy, control, and other reasons why "Mom is the greatest": A content analysis of children's Mother's Day letters. *Child Development, 51,* 801–807.

Welch, R., Huston-Stein, A., Wright, J., and Plehal, R. (1979). Subtle sex-role cues in children's commercials. *Journal of Communication, 29,* 202–209.

Wenegrat, B. (1984). *Sociobiology and mental disorder.* Boston: Allyn and Bacon.

Whitbourne, S., and Waterman, A. (1979). Psychosocial

development during the adult years: Age and cohort comparisons. *Psychological Bulletin, 15,* 373–378.

White, B. (1959). Motivation reconsidered: The concept of competence. *Psychological Review, 66,* 297–333.

White, B. (1975a). Critical influences in the origins of competence. *Merrill-Palmer Quarterly, 21,* 243–266.

White, B. (1975b). *The first three years of life.* New York: Avon.

White, B., Kaban, B., and Attanucci, J. (1979). *The origins of human competence.* Lexington, Mass.: Lexington Books.

White, D. (1986). Treatment of mild, moderate, and severe obesity in children. *Canadian Psychology, 27,* 262–274.

White, E., Elsom, B., and Prawat, R. (1978). Children's conceptions of death. *Child Development, 49,* 307–310.

Whitehurst, G. (1982). Language development. In B. Wolman (ed.), *Handbook of developmental psychology.* New York: Wiley.

Whiting, B. (1978). The dependency hand-up and experiments in alternative life-styles. In S. Cutler and M. Yinger (eds.), *Major social issues: A multidisciplinary view.* New York: Free Press.

Whiting, B., and Whiting, J. (1975). *Children of six cultures: A psychocultural analysis.* Cambridge, Mass.: Harvard University Press.

Whiting, J. (1981). Environmental constraints on infant care practices. In R. Munroe, R. Munroe, and J. Whiting (eds.), *Handbook of cross-cultural human development.* New York: Garland.

Wickstrom, R. (1977). *Fundamental Motor Patterns* (2nd ed.). Philadelphia: Lea and Febiger.

Wilkinson, D. (1980). *Information processing in reading.* New York: Wiley.

Williams, H. (1983). *Perceptual and motor development.* Englewood Cliffs, N.J.: Prentice-Hall.

Williams, H., Temple, I., and Bateman, J. (1978). Perceptual-motor and cognitive learning in young children. In H. Williams (ed.), *Psychology of motor behavior and sport.* Champaign, Ill.: Human Kinetics Press.

Williams, H., Temple, I., and Bateman, J. (1979). A test battery to assess intrasensory and intersensory development of young children. *Perceptual and Motor Skills, 48,* 643–659.

Williams, J. (1977). *Psychology of women: Behavior in a biosocial context.* New York: Norton.

Williams, J. R., and Gold, M. (1972). From delinquent behavior to official delinquency. *Social Problems, 20,* 209–229.

Wilmore, J. (1982). The female athlete. In R. Magill, M. Ash, and F. Smoll (eds.), *Children in sport.* Champaign, Ill.: Human Kinetics Publishers.

Wilson, E. (1975). *Sociobiology: The new synthesis.* Cambridge, Mass.: Belknap Press.

Wilson, R. (1972). Twins: Early mental development. *Science, 175,* 915–917.

Wilson, R. (1976). Concordance in physical growth for monozygotic and dizygotic twins. *Annals of Human Biology, 3,* 1–10.

Winick, M. (ed.). (1975). *Childhood obesity.* New York: Wiley.

Winner, E. (1982). *Invented worlds: The psychology of the arts.* Cambridge, Mass.: Harvard University Press.

Winnicott, D. (1977). *The piggle.* New York: International Universities Press.

Winnicott, D. (1979). *The child, the family, and the outside world.* New York: Penguin.

Winship, E. (1981). *Reaching your teenager.* Boston: Houghton Mifflin.

Witkin, H. (1978). *Cognitive styles in personal and cultural adaptation.* Worcester, Mass.: Clark University Press.

Witkin, H., and Goodenough, D. (1977). Field dependence and interpersonal behavior. *Psychological Bulletin, 84,* 661–689.

Wohlwill, J. (1980). Cognitive development in childhood. In O. Brim and J. Kagan (eds.), *Constancy and change in human development.* Cambridge, Mass.: Harvard University Press.

Wolff, P. (1966). The causes, controls, and organization of behavior in the neonate. *Psychological Issues, 5,* 1–105.

Wood, B. (1981). *Children and communication: Verbal and nonverbal language development* (2nd ed.). Englewood Cliffs, N.J.: Prentice-Hall.

Wylie, R. (1974/1979). *The self-concept* (vols. 1 and 2). Lincoln: University of Nebraska Press.

Yancy, W. S., Nader, P. R., and Burnham, K. L. (1972). Drug use and attitudes of high school students. *Pediatrics, 50,* 739–745.

Yarrow, L. (1979). Emotional development. *American Psychologist, 34,* 951–957.

Yarrow, M., and Waxler, C. (1978). The emergence and functions of prosocial behavior in young children. In M. Smart and R. Smart (eds.), *Infants, development and relationships.* New York: Macmillan.

Yogman, M., Dixon, S., Tronick, E., Als, H., and Brazelton, T. B. (1977). *The goals and structure of face-to-face interaction between infants and fathers.* Paper presented at the biennial meeting of the Society for Research in Child Development, New Orleans.

Yonas, A. (1979). Studies of spatial perception in infants. In A. D. Pick (ed.), *Perception and its development.* Hillsdale, N.J.: Erlbaum.

Yonas, A., and Pettersen, L. (1979). *Responsiveness of newborns to optical information for collision.* Paper presented at the biennial meeting of the Society for Research in Child Development, San Francisco.

Young, A. (1973). The high school class of 1972: More at work, fewer in college. *Monthly Labor Review, 96,* 26–32.

Youniss, J. (1980). *Parents and peers in social development: A Sullivan-Piaget perspective.* Chicago: University of Chicago Press.

Youniss, J., and Volpe, J. (1978). A relationship analysis of children's friendships. In W. Damon (ed.), *Social cognition* (New Directions for Child Development, No. 1). San Francisco: Jossey-Bass.

Zack, P. M., Harlan, W. R., Leaverton, P. E., and Coroni-Huntley, J. (1979). A longitudinal study of body fatness in childhood and adolescence. *Journal of Pediatrics, 95,* 126–130.

Zahn-Waxler, C., and Chapman, M. (1982). Immediate antecedents of caretakers' methods of discipline. *Child Psychiatry and Human Development, 12,* 179–192.

Zahn-Waxler, C., and Radke-Yarrow, M. (1982). The development of altruism. In N. Eisenberg-Berg (ed.), *The development of prosocial behavior.* New York: Academic Press.

Zaichowsky, L., Zaichowsky, L., and Martinek, T. (1980). *Growth and development: The child and physical activity.* St. Louis: Mosby.

Zaslow, M., Pederson, F., Suwalsky, J., and Cain, R. (1985). *Fathering during the infancy period: Implications of the mother's role.* Paper presented at the biennial meeting of the Society for Research on Child Development, Toronto.

Zelazo, P., Zelazo, N., and Kalb, S. (1972). "Walking" in the newborn. *Science, 176,* 314–315.

Zelnik, M., and Kantner, J. (1977). Sexual and contraceptive experience of young unmarried women in the United States. *Family Planning Perspectives, 9,* 55–73.

Zelnik, M., and Kantner, J. (1979). Reasons for non-use of contraceptives by sexually active women, ages 15–19. *Family Planning Perspectives, 11,* 289–294.

Zelnik, M., and Kantner, J. (1980). Sexual activity, contraceptive use and pregnancy among metropolitan-area teenagers. 1971–1979. *Family Planning Perspectives, 12,* 230–237.

Zelson, C. (1973). The infant of the addicted mother. *New England Journal of Medicine, 288,* 1393–1395.

Zey-Ferell, M., Tolone, W., and Walsh, R. (1978). The intergenerational socialization of sex-role attitudes: A gender or generation gap? *Adolescence, 13,* 95–108.

Ziajka, A. (1981). *Prelinguistic communication in infancy.* New York: Praeger.

Zill, N. (1982). Development of childhood social indicators. In E. Zigler, S. Kogan, and E. Klugman (eds.), *America's unfinished business: Childhood and family policy.* New York: Cambridge University Press.

Zill, N. (1983). *Healthy, happy, and insecure.* New York: Doubleday.

Ziller, R. (1973). *The social self.* New York: Pergamon.

Zimbardo, P. (1977). *Shyness.* Reading, Mass.: Addison-Wesley.

Acknowledgments

Part and Chapter Openers
Part 1: Jean-Claude Lejeune
Chapter 1: Fred Ward/Black Star
Chapter 2: Michael D. Sullivan/TexaStock
Part 2: Judith Black/Lightwave
Chapter 3: Martin M. Rotker/Taurus Photos
Chapter 4: H. Armstrong Roberts
Part 3: Andrew Brillant
Chapter 5: H. Armstrong Roberts
Chapter 6: David Phillips
Chapter 7: Erika Stone
Part 4: J. Berndt/The Picture Cube
Chapter 8: Rohn Engh
Chapter 9: Erika Stone
Chapter 10: David Mansell
Part 5: Andrew Brillant
Chapter 11: David Mansell
Chapter 12: Ulrike Welsch
Chapter 13: Jean-Claude Lejeune
Part 6: Susan Lapides
Chapter 14: Jean-Claude Lejeune
Chapter 15: Jean-Claude Lejeune
Chapter 16: Jean-Claude Lejeune

Case-Study Photo Essays
David's Case: All photographs (except page 2, *top left*) by Alan Carey/Image Works; page 2, *top left,* Mark Antman/Image Works
Jennifer's Case: All photographs by Erika Stone
Johanna's Case: All photographs by Joel Gordon
Bobby's Case: All photographs by Erika Stone

Color Inserts
The Concept of Childhood in History
Page 1: *top left, Portrait of a Family,* Jacob Maentel, courtesy, The Henry Francis du Pont Winterthur Museum; *top right, Daughters of Edward D. Boit,* 1882, John Singer Sargent. Gift to Mary Louisa Boit, Florence D. Boit, Jane Hubbard Boit, and Julia Overing Boit in memory of their father Edward Darley Boit. Courtesy, Museum of Fine Arts, Boston; *bottom left, Mrs. Elizabeth Freake and Baby Mary,* unknown artist, Worcester Art Museum, Worcester, Massachusetts; *bottom right, Mother and Child,* Mary Cassatt, courtesy Wichita Art Museum, the Roland P. Murdock Collection.

Page 2: *Las Meninas* (The Maids of Honor), 1656, by Diego Rodriguez de Silva y Velasquez, Museo deo Prado/Scala/Art Resource.
Page 3: *top, Snap the Whip,* 1872, Winslow Homer, The Metropolitan Museum of Art, Gift of Christian A. Zabriskie, 1950; *bottom left, Children Playing on the Beach,* 1884, Mary Cassatt, National Gallery of Art, Washington; Ailsa Mellon Bruce Collection; *bottom right, The Fairy Tale,* Walter Firle (1859–1929), courtesy New York Graphic Society Ltd.
Page 4: *top left,* Photograph by Lewis Hine, courtesy International Museum of Photography at George Eastman House; *top right, Freedom from Fear,* 1943, Norman Rockwell. Printed by permission of the Estate of Norman Rockwell, copyright © 1943 Estate of Norman Rockwell. Courtesy of the Norman Rockwell Museum at Stockbridge, Stockbridge, MA; *bottom, Girl Before the Mirror,* 1954, Norman Rockwell. Printed by permission of the Estate of Norman Rockwell, copyright © 1954 Estate of Norman Rockwell. Courtesy of the Norman Rockwell Museum at Stockbridge, Stockbridge, MA.

Prenatal Development and the Neonate
Page 1: *both,* Science Source/Photo Researchers
Page 2: *all,* Science Source/Photo Researchers
Page 3: *top,* Science Source/Photo Researchers; *bottom left,* Paolo Koch/Photo Researchers; *bottom right,* Suzanne Szasz/Photo Researchers
Page 4: *top,* Glauberman/Photo Researchers; *middle,* Anne Purcell; *bottom,* Carl Purcell

Aspects of Family Life
Page 1: *top,* Sybil Shelton/Peter Arnold; *middle,* Elisabeth Crews; *bottom left,* Victoria Arlak; *bottom right,* Erika Stone/Peter Arnold
Page 2: *top,* Elizabeth Crews; *middle,* Stephen Feld/The Stock Solution; *bottom,* Susan Lapides
Page 3: *top,* Erika Stone/Peter Arnold; *middle,* Robert Frerck/Odyssey Productions; *bottom,* Victoria Arlak
Page 4: *top,* Victoria Arlak; *bottom left,* Victoria Arlak; *bottom right,* Nancy Sheehan

Identity Formation
Page 1: *top,* Susan Lapides; *bottom left,* Elizabeth Crews; *bottom right,* Victoria Arlak

Page 2: *top,* James H. Karales/Peter Arnold; *bottom right,* Susan Lapides; *bottom left,* Susan Lapides

Page 3: *top,* Elizabeth Crews; *bottom,* Robert Frerck/Odyssey Productions

Page 4: *top,* Nancy Sheehan; *middle,* Susan Lapides; *bottom right,* Sybil Shelton/Peter Arnold; *bottom left,* Joel Gordon

Text, Tables, and Line Art

Pages 48–49: Excerpts from *Life History and the Historical Moment* by Erik H. Erikson, by permission of W. W. Norton & Company, Inc. Copyright © 1975 by Rikan Enterprises, Ltd.

Page 183: Table 5–4 adapted from W. Frankenburg and J. Dodds, "The Denver Developmental Screening Test," *Journal of Pediatrics, 71* (1967), 181, by permission of The C. V. Mosby Company.

Page 491: Figure 12–3 from N. L. Gage and David C. Berliner, *Educational Psychology* (3rd ed.), p. 301. Copyright © 1984 by Houghton Mifflin Company. Used by permission.

Page 557: Figure 13–2 from U.S. Department of Commerce, Bureau of the Census, 1978; U.S. Department of Labor, Bureau of Labor Statistics, 1986. Figure 13–3 from U.S. Public Health Service.

Pages 666–667: Excerpts from "Political Thinking in Adolescence," by J. Gallatin, in J. Adelson (ed.), *Handbook of Adolescent Development,* copyright © 1980 by John Wiley & Sons, Inc. Reprinted by permission of John Wiley & Sons, Inc.

Pages 669–670: Excerpts from *Stages of Faith* by James Fowler, copyright © 1981 by James W. Fowler. Reprinted by permission of Harper & Row, Publishers, Inc.

Page 706: Table 16–1 adapted from "Adolescent Sexual Behavior in Middle America Revisited: 1970–1973," by A. Vener and C. Stewart, *Journal of Marriage and the Family, 36* (1974), 732. Copyrighted 1974 by the National Council on Family Relations, 1910 West County Road B, Suite 147, St. Paul, Minnesota 55113. Reprinted by permission.

Page 715: Excerpts from *Changing Bodies, Changing Lives,* by Ruth Bell et al. Copyright © 1980 by Ruth Bell. Reprinted by permission of Random House, Inc.

Author/Name Index

Subject Index

Domain-specific knowledge, 645, 648
Dominance hierarchy, 422
Dominant genes, 85, 86(tab)
Down syndrome, 91–92, 107, 113
Dramatic play, *see* Make-believe or dramatic play
Dramatization, in Sullivan's theory, 392
Draw-a-Man Test, 518
Drawing, representational and prerepresentational, 330–333
Drawing skills, 330–335
Dreams, and symbolic thinking, 376
Dropouts, school, 702–703
Drug abuse, 620–624
   and adolescence, 616, 620–622, 623–624, 626
   and hepatitis, 619
Drugs, and unborn baby, 122, 127, 131–132, 146, 189
Dual-career (two-job) families, 260–261, 563–564
Duos (two-word sentences), 188, 362–364, 371
Dyads (friendship), 545
Dyslexia, 470, 471–472

Early childhood, *see* Preschoolers
Early (first) grammars, 362, 370
Early medical treatments, for genetic disorder, 112–113
Early school years, cognitive development in, *see* Cognitive development in middle years
Early school years, physical development in, *see* Physical development in middle years
Early school years, psychosocial development in, *see* Psychosocial development in middle years
Eclampsia, 138
Ecosystem, for child abuse, 292
Ectoderm, 121
Ectomorphic builds, 607
Education
   and children of earlier times, 11
   developmental psychology used in, 26
   and Piaget's (cognitive) theory, 68, 70, 485–486
   preschool, 378–379, 425
   Rousseau on, 12
   training in formal thinking, 642
   see also Schools; Teachers
Education-for-parenthood programs
   and child abuse, 294
   PEP in Florida, 232–233

Ego, in Freudian theory, 40, 43
Egocentric escape, 391
Egocentrism, 60, 220, 349
   adolescent, 597, 658–663
   animism and artificialism as, 353
   and grammatical organization, 508
   and illness, 465
   and peers, 541
   in preschool years, 349–352
   and self-guiding speech, 377
Ego integrity, in Erikson's theory, 46(tab), 48–49
Electra conflict, 42
Embryo, 121
Embryonic disk, 121
Embryonic stage, 118, 122–123
Emotions, in infancy, 264–265
Empathy
   in adolescence, 663, 671
   among preschoolers, 413–417
   see also Moral development
Empirical bias, in psychometric studies, 656
Endocrine glands, 313, 602–603
Endoderm, 121
Endomorphic builds, 607
Environment, first attention to, 12
Environmental hazards, and prenatal development, 138
Environment vs. heredity, *see* Heredity-environment relationship
Equalitarian parenting, 688–689
Equilibration, in Piaget's theory, 63
Erikson's theory, 45–51, 70(tab)
   change as active in, 37
   on identity development, 46(tab), 47, 678–682, 683, 684 (*see also* Identity)
   and infancy, 46–47, 69, 270
   on middle years, 535
   and other theories, 69
   and Piaget, 68
   on play, 395
   on preschool years, 390–391
   use of, 70
Estrogen, 603
Ethics
   and diet-during-pregnancy testing, 135
   and genetic counseling, 111
   and heredity-environment study, 96, 98
   and infant-pain experiments, 175
   and judgments from genetic information, 107–108
   and mass screening, 110–111
   sociobiology on, 105
   and study methods, 22–23

see also Morality
Executive programs (information processing), 644
Expectations
   and adolescent sense of self, 615
   of experimenter, 358
   toward infant's temperament, 267
   and twins' personalities, 101
   see also Standards; Stereotypes
Experience
   in Locke's theory, 11–12
   and stage theories, 37
Experience vs. nature, *see* Heredity-environment relationship
Experimental studies, 21
   anthropomorphism in, 98
   and Piaget's clinical method, 60–61
   preschoolers' responding to experimenter in, 355, 358
   see also Research
Experimental thought, in Piaget's formal operational stage, 67–68
Expert skills, 645, 648–649, 650–651
Exploration
   by infants, 182, 274, 338–339
   vs. play, 393
Expressive language, 244, 245(tab)
Extinction, of reinforcement, 56
Extroversion, 106
Eye contact, gender difference in, 372, 374

Factor (cognitive), 653
Failure to thrive, 289, 308–309
Faith, 669
False labor, 144
Family
   of anorexics, 626, 627
   blended, 556, 562
   changing nature of, 556
   and divorce, 556–562, 614, 692–693
   and drinking/smoking/drugs, 626
   dual-career, 260–261, 563–564
   effect of pregnancy on, 140–141, 143
   effects of new baby on, 260–261
   effects of work on, 562–566
   in failed pregnancies, 129
   and handicapped children, 576–577
   and identity confusion, 682
   and infant temperament, 102–104
   and mental illness, 106–107
   in middle years, 533, 553–556
   and newborn, 142, 196–197
   single-parent, 557, 693, 710

and twins' development, 98–102
and use of developmental psychology, 27
see also Fathers; Mothers; Parents; Siblings
Family background
  and adolescent delinquency, 713
  and middle-years health, 460, 463, 465
  and preterm-birth effects, 190, 191
  and school achievement, 538
  and sexual abuse, 711–712
  and test-taking, 374
  see also Cultural differences; Minority children; Socioeconomic differences
Fantasies
  about new sibling, 143
  from parents' divorce, 560, 561
  in play, 395 (*see also* Make-believe or dramatic play)
  of preschooler, 391
  sexual, 705
Father-infant interactions, 259–260
Fathers
  an attachment formation, 279
  after divorce, 559–560
  in older age group, 91–92, 120
  during pregnancy, 141, 143
  and pregnancy failure, 128–129
  and SIDS, 171
  teenage, 710
  in two-job families, 260–261, 563–564
  unemployed, 280, 566
  see also Family; Parents
Fear responses, of infant, 264–265
Feeding
  at eight months, 186–187
  of newborn, 196–197
  see also Nutrition
Fertilization process, 81–82. *See also* Conception
Fetal alcohol syndrome, 132
Fetal stage, 118, 123–126
Fetus, 118, 123
Field dependence and independence, 502–503, 510–511
Figurative language, 353, 500, 502
Fine motor coordination, 330–335
Fine motor skills, 179
First two years, *see* Infancy
First words, 244–246
Florida Parent Education Infant and Toddler Program (PEP), 232–233
Fluid intelligence, 654
Fontanelles, 163
Forceps, 152

Foreclosure, identity, 683, 684, 689, 709–710
Formal operational period of Piaget, 64(tab), 67–68
Formal operational thinking by adolescents, 637–640
  and cultural bias, 658
  and political thought, 666
  and religious belief, 670
Fraternal twins, 102, 142, 310–311
Free will, and sociobiology, 105–106
Freudian theory, 38–45, 70(tab)
  and breast feeding, 198
  defense mechanisms in, 43, 535
  developmental stages in, 39–43
  on gender development, 427, 428
  and infancy, 39–40, 69, 268–270
  latency period in, 40(tab), 42, 534–535
  and other theories, 69, 270–271
  and Piaget, 68
  on play, 395
  popularly held notions from, 38
  on preschool years, 391
  as qualitative, 18
  strengths and weaknesses of, 43–44
  and unconscious, 37, 38
Friendships
  in adolescence, 690, 694–696, 700
  in early childhood, 403, 411–413, 426
  in middle years, 550–552
  see also Peers
Functional capacity of thought, 647–648
Functional play, 396
Functional relationships, 347

g (general intelligence), 652, 653, 657
Games
  of girls, 546–547
  in middle years, 453
  vs. pretend play, 394
  with rules, 394, 399–401, 454–455
  see also Athletics
Gametes, 80–83, 120
Gaps
  in conservation acquisition, 483
  in conversation, 360–361
  generation gap, 685
Gender (sex), 423. *See also* Sexuality
Gender constancy, 423
Gender determination at conception, 87–89
Gender development, 423–432
Gender (sex) differences

and accidental death, 619
in aggressiveness, 421, 424
and athletics, 458–459
in body satisfaction, 610
in childhood-disease deaths, 321
in childhood illness, 463
in friendship, 696
genetic influence on, 89
and identity status, 683–684
in infancy, 191–192
in jumping rope, 326
in language, 372, 374
in muscle development and fat tissue, 603–604
through observational learning, 495
in peer groups, 545, 546–547
in preschool physical development, 336–337
in reaction to divorce, 559
in sex learning, 605
and sexual differences extent, 604, 606
in sexual experience, 705–706, 707
and sexual maturation, 598–604
and timing of puberty, 610–615
Gender (sexual) identity, 423
  in adolescence, 707
  in Freudian theory, 42, 44
  in sense of self, 569
  and social learning, 59
Gender preferences, 423
Gender prejudice, vs. racial prejudice, 548
Generation gap, 685
Generative rules, 361
Generativity, in Erikson's theory, 46(tab), 48
Genes, 80
  abnormal, 93–95
  dominant and recessive, 85, 86(tab), 95
  and multiple variations, 85–86
Genetic abnormalities, 89(tab), 91–95
  early medical treatment for, 112–113
  fear over, 138
  and genetic counseling, 108–113
  hemophilia, 89, 89(tab), 90
  hyperactivity/ADD, 468
  prenatal diagnosis for, 108, 110
  sex difference in, 89
Genetically transmitted response strategies, 104–106
Genetic counseling, 108–113
Genetics
  and developmental psychology, 114
  growth influenced by, 310–311
  and hemophilia, 89, 89(tab), 90

Language
    black English, 510–511
    syntax of, 359–362
    and thought, 375–380
Language acquisition and development, 239–240
    and bilingualism, 370, 509–512
    and brain development, 169
    concrete vs. conceptual, 356
    duos and telegraphic speech in, 362–365
    first words, 244–246
    gender differences in, 372, 374
    genetic programming of, 97
    and hearing loss, 249
    in infancy, 239–250, 287–288
    as inference vs. imitation, 364–365, 367, 369–371
    measurement of, 17
    mechanisms of, 365, 367, 369–371
    in middle years, 507–512
    nature and nurture in, 14
    parent-child interaction in, 240, 246–250, 259, 367, 371–372
    phonology in, 240, 241–243
    in preoperational period, 65
    in preschool years, 356, 358–375
    prestarts in, 360–361
    semantics in, 240, 243–244
    through sign language, 373
    socioeconomic differences in, 374
    theories of, 240–241
Language acquisition device (LAD), 241, 369–371
Lanugo, 163, 189
Latency stage, in Freudian theory, 40(tab), 42, 534–535
Lateralized behaviors, 319–320
Learning, 51–52
    as cognitive development, 5
    experiment on, 97
    of foreign language at different ages, 650–652
    vs. maturation, 186
    and stage theories, 37
    see also Behavioral learning theory; Observational learning
Learning disabilities, 470–472
Learning orientation, 538–540
Learning strategies, 492–497
Learning theory, see Behavioral learning theory
Leaving home, 685, 687, 690–691, 701
Lexicon, 370
Libido, in Freudian theory, 39
Liquor, see Alcohol
Localization

of sensation, 384
of sound, 218–219
Locomotion, by infants, 180
Logical combination of ideas, in formal operational thought, 637–638
Logical construction, as learning strategy, 494–495
Logical reasoning, see Reasoning
Longitudinal study, 23, 24–25
Long-term memory, 487–488, 489–490, 644
Loom-zoom procedure, 216
Low-birth-weight infants, 189–191, 315, 710

Macrosystem, for child abuse, 292–293
Mahler's theory of symbiosis and individuation, 270–271
Mainstreaming, 575, 576
Make-believe or dramatic play, 346, 394, 396, 397–399
    as communication, 349
    and divergent thinking, 499
    and language, 376
    Piaget on, 65
    as symbolic, 348, 349
Malevolent transformation, 392
Malnutrition, 199–201
    in infants, 194
    from nutritional disorder, 313
Manic-depressive, 106
Marasmus, 200
Markers, of adolescence, 680–681
Mastery
    play as, 395, 399
    see also Control
Masturbation, 704–705, 708
"Math anxiety," 53
Maturation, 37
    vs. learning, 186
    in Piaget's theory, 63
    and stage theories, 37
    see also Physical development
Meal planning, for preschool children, 314–315
Meal times, for preschool children, 315
Mean (of test scores), 515
Means-end connections, in Piaget's theory, 223, 224
Measurement, usefulness of, 17–18
Media
    and adolescent physical standards, 606
    developmental psychology used in, 27

and gender development, 431–432
and sexual abuse, 712
and "social puberty," 605
violence in, 293, 422–423
see also Television
Median, 515
Medical science, vs. acceptance of death, 129
Medical services, see Health care
Medication
    for childbirth pain, 146–147
    teratogens among, 131–132
Medicine, developmental psychology used by, 26
Meiosis, 82–83
Memory
    activity of, 491
    capacity of, 488–490
    development of, 490–492
    long-term (LTM), 487–488, 489–490, 644
    and Piaget's analysis, 222, 232–234
    short-term (STM), 487, 488–489, 643–644
    visual, 380, 383
    working (WM), 487, 644
Menarche, 599
Menstrual cycle, 599
Mental illnesses and disturbances, 106–107
Mentally retarded, 57, 91–92
Mesoderm, 121
Mesomorphic build, 607, 611
Metacognition, 492–497, 651
Metalinguistic awareness, 510
Metaphor, 500, 502
Méthode clinique (clinical method) of Piaget, 60–61, 640
Microsystem, for child abuse, 291–292
Midbrain, 169
Middle years, cognitive development in, see Cognitive development in middle years
Middle years, physical development in, see Physical development in middle years
Middle years, psychosocial development in, see Psychosocial development in middle years
Midlife, in Erikson's theory, 48
Midwives, 149, 150, 152
Minimal brain damage, 471
Minority children, 692
    and school achievement, 538
    test bias against, 658
    see also Family background; Socioeconomic differences

Racial prejudice
vs. gender prejudice, 548
in middle years, 547–548
RAD (reactive attachment disorder), 308–309
Radiation, and prenatal development, 138
Radio
and developmental psychology, 27
vs. television, 504–505
Random sample, 21
Rapprochement subphase of individuation, 678
Raven's Progressive Matrices Test, 518
Reaching, by infants, 181–182
Reactive attachment disorder (RAD), 308–309
Reading, learning of, 496–497
Reality principle, in Freudian theory, 40
Reasoning
in formal operational thinking, 67–68, 637–639
about form of argument, 636
limits of, 642–643
and memory, 490–491
parental use of, 407, 410, 554
see also Thinking
Reasoning skills, and IQ test, 13
Recall memory, 489
Recasting, of child's utterances, 372
Receptive language, 244
Recessive genes, 85, 86(tab)
Reciprocal determinism, 59
Recognition, by infants, 210
Recognition memory, 488–489
Recreation, see Athletics; Games; Play
Recreation programs, developmental psychology used in, 27
Reductionism, of Skinner, 53
Reflective thinking, and television, 505
Reflectivity and impulsivity, in thinking, 504–506
Reflexes, 163, 176
and Brazelton Scale, 165
breathing, 170, 176, 179(tab)
of fetus, 124
grasping, 178, 179, 179(tab)
Moro, 174, 178, 179(tab)
of newborn, 176–179
Piaget's view of, 221(tab), 221–222, 228
of preterm infants, 189
rooting, 176, 179(tab)
and sensitivity to touch, 175

stepping, 178, 179(tab)
sucking, 176, 177(illus), 179(tab), 197 (see also Sucking reflex and behavior)
unconditioned, 52
Regression, in Freudian theory, 43
Reinforcement
in language acquisition, 240, 243, 367
negative, 54
in operant conditioning, 54–56 (see also Operant conditioning)
positive, 54, 409
see also Behavioral learning theory
Reinforcer, 54
appropriate choice of, 57
Relationships, and psychosocial development, 5
Reliability, of tests, 516
Religious beliefs and orientations, in adolescence, 668–670
Remarriage, and adolescents' development, 693–694
REM sleep, 170–171, 173(tab), 266
Repetition compulsion, 395
Replication of experimental results, 19
and Piaget's method, 61
Reporting, of study results, 19
Representational drawing, 330, 333
Representations, in Piaget's theory, 228, 230
Repression, 43, 535
Research
experimental method in, 21 (see also Experimental studies)
on genetic determination, 97–98
on heredity and environment (twins), 98–102, 185
naturalistic method in, 20–21 (see also Naturalistic studies)
and Piaget's theory, 68
vs. practical priorities, 27–29
quasi-experimental, 21–23
questions in, 19
see also Developmental study
Research bias, see Bias; Cultural bias
Respiratory distress syndrome (RSD), 152
Response
in classical conditioning, 52
in operant conditioning, 54, 56
Response strategies, genetically transmitted, 104–106
Retarded children, 57, 91–92
Reversibility of thought, 355–358, 479

Rh disease, 93, 108, 112–113
Rhogam blood, 93
Risk factors
for child abuse, 291—292
for low birth weight, 189
in pregnancy, 127, 128–139
for SIDS, 171
Rites of passage, 591
Role confusion, in Erikson's theory, 46(tab), 47
Role models
and cultural stereotypes, 608–609
of empathy/prosocial behavior, 417
older siblings as, 410
see also Modeling
Role reversal, parent-child, 292
Roles, and infant's language, 288
Rooting reflex, 176, 179(tab)
RSD (respiratory distress syndrome), 152
Rubella, 130, 131
Rules
games with, 394, 399–401, 454–455
parental influence through, 554
of peers, 532
in play, 394
in preoperational thinking, 65
preschool shift toward, 339
syntactic, 359–362, 364–365 (see also Syntax)
Running, preschoolers' development of, 324–325

Safety, in infant toys, 218–219
Sample, random, 21
Schemes, in Piaget's theory, 63, 64, 64(tab), 220–221, 222–226, 231
Schizophrenia, 107
Schools
and adolescent-child abuse, 712
and adolescent social development, 702–703
and adolescent thinking, 646–647, 665
cultural attitudes toward achievement in, 538–539
dropouts from, 702–703
experience of (fifth grade), 501
health self-care programs in, 618
mainstreaming of handicapped in, 575, 576
and peers, 543, 547, 697–698, 702
and teenage mothers, 710
see also Education; Teachers
Scientific experimentation, emergence of, 12

Wernicke's area, 317
Wife beating, 566
"Wilde boy," Itard's rehabilitation of,
  12
Women
  and Freudian theory, 43, 44
  see also Gender differences
Word meanings, definition of, 507–
  508
Working memory (WM), 487, 644
Writing, cognitive skills in, 650–651

Zygote, 81, 118, 119

Reader Response Form

We would like to find out what your reactions are to *Child and Adolescent Development.* Your evaluation of the book will help us respond to the interests and needs of the readers of future editions. Please complete the questionnaire below and mail it to College Marketing, Houghton Mifflin Company, One Beacon Street, Boston, MA 02108.

1. We would like to know how you rate our textbook in each of the following areas:

		Excellent	Good	Adequate	Poor
a.	Selection of topics	———	———	———	———
b.	Writing style/readability	———	———	———	———
c.	Explanation of concepts	———	———	———	———
d.	Interviews	———	———	———	———
e.	Case-study photo essays	———	———	———	———
f.	Study aids (e.g., marginal glosses, focusing questions, checkpoints, end-of-chapter summaries and key terms lists, glossary)	———	———	———	———
g.	Attractiveness of design	———	———	———	———
h.	Illustrations and four-color inserts	———	———	———	———

2. Please cite specific examples that illustrate any of the above ratings.

_____

_____

_____

3. Describe the strongest feature(s) of the book.

_____

_____

_____

4. Describe the weakest feature(s) of the book.

_____

_____

_____

5. What other topics should be included in this text?

_____

_____

_____

6. What recommendations can you make for improving this book?

_____

7. We would appreciate any other comments or reactions you are willing to share with us: